Michael J. Young
Professional software developer and award-winning computer book author

Michael Halvorson
Microsoft Office and Microsoft Visual Basic® expert

Microsoft®
Office System
2003 EDITION

INSIDE
OUT

Microsoft®
Office

PUBLISHED BY
Microsoft Press
A Division of Microsoft Corporation
One Microsoft Way
Redmond, Washington 98052-6399

Library of Congress Cataloging-in-Publication Data
Young, Michael J.
    Microsoft® Office System Inside Out — 2003 Edition / Michael J. Young, Michael Halvorson.
       p. cm.
    Includes index.
    ISBN 0-7356-1512-8
    1. Microsoft Office. 2. Business--Computer programs. I. Halvorson, Michael. II. Title.

HF5548.4.M525M5253 2003
005.369--dc21   2003052693

Printed and bound in the United States of America.

2 3 4 5 6 7 8 9   QWT   8 7 6 5 4 3

Distributed in Canada by H.B. Fenn and Company Ltd.

A CIP catalogue record for this book is available from the British Library.

Microsoft Press books are available through booksellers and distributors worldwide. For further information about international editions, contact your local Microsoft Corporation office or contact Microsoft Press International directly at fax (425) 936-7329. Visit our Web site at www.microsoft.com/mspress. Send comments to *mspinput@microsoft.com*.

Encarta, FrontPage, Hotmail, InfoPath, Microsoft, Microsoft Press, MSN, NetMeeting, OneNote, Outlook, PivotChart, PivotTable, PowerPoint, SharePoint, Visio, Visual Basic, Visual FoxPro, Windows, Windows Media, and Windows NT are either registered trademarks or trademarks of Microsoft Corporation in the United States and/or other countries. Other product and company names mentioned herein may be the trademarks of their respective owners.

The example companies, organizations, products, domain names, e-mail addresses, logos, people, places, and events depicted herein are fictitious. No association with any real company, organization, product, domain name, e-mail address, logo, person, place, or event is intended or should be inferred.

Acquisitions Editor: Alex Blanton
Project Editor: Sandra Haynes
Series Editor: Sandra Haynes
Technical Editors: Mannie White and Don Lessor, Pioneer Training

Body Part No. X09-70558

Contents at a Glance

Part 1
Getting Going with Office 2003

Chapter 1
An Office 2003 Overview 3

Chapter 2
Installing and Configuring Office 2003 17

Chapter 3
Getting Expert Help on Office 2003 25

Part 2
Using Shared Office 2003 Application Features

Chapter 4
Working with Office 2003 Applications, Documents, and Program Windows 39

Chapter 5
Using Speech and Handwriting in Office 2003 83

Chapter 6
Adding Professional Graphics and Special Effects to Office 2003 Documents 107

Chapter 7
Exchanging Data in Office 2003 153

Chapter 8
Using Windows SharePoint Services in Professional Workgroups 177

Chapter 9
Customizing the Office 2003 Application Interface 209

Part 3
Word

Chapter 10
Word Fundamentals 241

Chapter 11
Efficient Editing in Word 259

Chapter 12
Effective Formatting in Word 307

Chapter 13
Arranging Text Using Tables, Columns, and Lists 345

Chapter 14
Advanced Word Formatting Techniques 389

Chapter 15
Managing Large or Complex Documents 419

Chapter 16
Using Word in Workgroups 447

Chapter 17
Proofing Word Documents 479

Chapter 18
Designing and Printing Professional-Looking Pages 509

Chapter 19
Using Word to Automate Mailings 549

Chapter 20
Creating Web Pages and Working with XML in Word 569

Contents At A Glance

Part 4
Excel

Chapter 21
Excel Fundamentals 605

Chapter 22
Advanced Worksheet Editing 627

Chapter 23
Expert Formatting Techniques . . .647

Chapter 24
**Power Organizing
with Workbooks** 679

Chapter 25
**Customizing Excel to Work
the Way You Do** 705

Chapter 26
**Crunching Numbers with
Formulas and Functions** 727

Chapter 27
Advanced Worksheet Charts 747

Chapter 28
**Power Database Techniques:
Lists, Filters, and PivotTables** . . .771

Chapter 29
Advanced Business Analysis 805

Chapter 30
**Publishing on the Web and
Working with XML in Excel** 823

Part 5
PowerPoint

Chapter 31
PowerPoint Fundamentals 849

Chapter 32
**Advanced Presentation
Formatting** 877

Chapter 33
**Mastering Tables, Graphics,
Video, and Sound.** 895

Chapter 34
**Adding Special Effects to a
Presentation** 909

Chapter 35
**Setting Up and Presenting
the Slide Show** 923

Part 6
Outlook

Chapter 36
Outlook Fundamentals 945

Chapter 37
**Working with Outlook Items and
Folders.** 955

Chapter 38
**Managing Messages and
Appointments.** 999

Chapter 39
**Managing Contacts, Tasks, and
Other Types of Information** 1047

Chapter 40
Customizing Outlook. 1077

Part 7
Access

Chapter 41
Access Fundamentals. 1097

Chapter 42
**Setting Up Tables
and Relationships.** 1113

Chapter 43
**Using Queries to Select and
Combine Information** 1149

Chapter 44
**Creating Forms and Data Access
Pages for Working with Data.** . . . 1171

Chapter 45
**Generating Reports to Present
Information** 1199

Contents At A Glance

Part 8
FrontPage Fundamentals

Chapter 46
FrontPage Fundamentals **1219**

Chapter 47
Managing Your Web Site with FrontPage **1239**

Chapter 48
Creating and Editing Web Pages **1279**

Chapter 49
Formatting Your Web Pages **1321**

Chapter 50
Adding Advanced Features to Your Web Pages and Working with Source Code **1363**

Part 9
InfoPath

Chapter 51
InfoPath Fundamentals **1393**

Chapter 52
Designing Forms in InfoPath . . .**1399**

Chapter 53
Filling Out and Delivering Forms in InfoPath **1417**

Part 10
Customizing Office 2003 Using VBA

Chapter 54
VBA Fundamentals **1427**

Chapter 55
Using Variables, Operators, and Functions to Manage Information **1439**

Chapter 56
Adding Logic and Computing Power with Control Structures **1461**

Chapter 57
Using Toolbox Controls to Create a User Interface **1477**

v

Table of Contents

We'd Like to Hear from You . . . . **xxix**
About the CD . . . . **xxxi**
  What's on the CD xxxi
  Using the CD xxxii
  System Requirements xxxii
  Support Information xxxii
Conventions and Features Used in This Book . . . . **xxxiii**
  Text Conventions xxxiii
  Design Conventions xxxiii
Introduction . . . .**xxxv**
  Who This Book Is For xxxv
  How This Book Is Organized xxxv
  Contacting the Author. xxxvi

Part 1
Getting Going with Office 2003

Chapter 1
An Office 2003 Overview   3

A Rundown on Office 2003 3
  Advantages of the New Microsoft Office System 4
An Office 2003 Map 7
  What's New in Office 2003 10
  New Shared Office 2003 Features 11
  New Word Features 13
  New Excel Features 13
  New PowerPoint Features 13
  New Outlook Features. 14
  New Access Features 15
  New FrontPage Features 15
  New Application: InfoPath 16

Chapter 2
Installing and Configuring Office 2003   17

Installing Office 2003 from the CD 17
Activating Office 2003 20
Revisiting Office Setup 22

Chapter 3
Getting Expert Help on Office 2003   25

Getting Help with the Assistant 25
Getting Help with the Ask A Question List. 29
Getting Help Using the Help Task Pane 30
Finding Resources on Office Online 33

Part 2
Using Shared Office 2003 Application Features

Chapter 4
Working with Office 2003 Applications, Documents, and Program Windows   39

Running the Office Applications 39
Using the Task Panes in Office Applications 42
     Going to the Getting Started Task Pane 44
     Using the Research Task Pane 44
     Using Smart Documents. 47
Creating New Office Documents 47
     Creating a Document Using the New Office Document Dialog Box . . . 47
     Creating an Empty Office Document in a Folder. 52
     Creating a Document Using the New Document Task Pane 53
     Downloading and Using Templates from Office Online 55
Opening Existing Office Documents 56
     Opening an Existing Document Using the Open Office Document
     Dialog Box. 57
     Opening Documents Within Office Applications. 62
     Finding Office Files or Outlook Items Using the File Search Feature . . 63
Saving Office Documents 69
     Saving a Document as a Web Page 73
Working with Multiple Documents 74
     Comparing Two Documents Side by Side 75
Using Office Document Properties. 76
Using Information Rights Management to Restrict Document
Permissions. 80

Chapter 5
Using Speech and Handwriting in Office 2003   83

Using Speech in Office 83
     Training Speech Recognition 84
     Using Speech Recognition 86
     Using Speech Recognition Dictation Mode 89
     Using Speech Recognition Voice Command Mode. 93
     Customizing Speech Recognition. 94
     Customizing the Language Bar 96

Using Handwriting in Office 96
    Accessing the Handwriting Interface 97
    Entering Handwriting. 97
    Inserting Sketches 103
    Using the On-Screen Keyboards. 105

Chapter 6
Adding Professional Graphics and Special Effects to Office 2003 Documents   107

Inserting Pictures into Office Documents 107
    Inserting Pictures with the Clip Organizer 107
    Importing Pictures 117
    Modifying Pictures 119
Using AutoShapes to Create Drawings 123
Generating Conceptual Drawings Using Office Diagrams 127
    Creating an Organization Chart 128
    Creating Other Types of Diagrams 130
Using WordArt to Produce Special Text Effects 133
Constructing Charts Using Microsoft Graph 136
Building Equations with Microsoft Equation 139
Modifying Graphic Objects. 142
    Using the Mouse to Resize, Reshape, Rotate, or Move
    Graphic Objects 142
    Using the Drawing Toolbar to Modify Graphic Objects 144
    Using the Format *Object* Dialog Box to Format Graphic Objects 149

Chapter 7
Exchanging Data in Office 2003   153

Different Ways to Exchange Data. 153
Copying and Moving Data Statically 155
    Using the Office Clipboard. 158
Linking Data 162
    A Linking Example 168
Embedding Data. 170
    An Embedding Example 174

Chapter 8
Using Windows SharePoint Services in Professional Workgroups   177

Windows SharePoint Services Essentials 177
Connecting to a SharePoint Team Web Site in Your Browser. 179
Sharing Office Documents and Graphics on a SharePoint Site 183
    Accessing SharePoint Document Libraries Using Your Browser. 183
    Accessing SharePoint Document Libraries from Office
    Applications. 187
    Using SharePoint Picture Libraries 189
    Sharing Documents Using a Document Workspace 190

Using SharePoint Discussions. 193
    Participating in a Discussion Board 193
    Discussing an Online Document 195
Exchanging Information on a SharePoint Site 198
Customizing a SharePoint Site 201
    Creating New Site Components. 201
    Customizing a Free-Form Web Page or the Home Page. 203
    Customizing an Information Page. 204
    Modifying a Team Web Site 206

Chapter 9

Customizing the Office 2003 Application Interface   209

Customizing Toolbars, Menus, and Shortcut Keys. 209
Creating and Managing Custom Toolbars 210
Modifying Toolbars and Menus 213
    Using the Rearrange Commands Dialog Box. 220
Defining Shortcut Keys (Word Only) 222
Recording and Running Macros 224
    Knowing When to Build a Macro 224
    Recording a Macro. 225
    Running a Macro 227
    Setting Macro Security 229
Setting Office Interface Options. 232
Saving and Restoring Your Office Settings 235

Part 3
Word

Chapter 10
Word Fundamentals   241

A Rundown on Word 241
Using the Word Workplace 243
Setting Up the Word Interface 248
    Changing the View 249
    Modifying the Way Documents Are Displayed 251
Creating, Opening, and Saving Word Documents. 255
    Converting Groups of Files 256
    Storing Different Document Versions 257

Chapter 11
Efficient Editing in Word   259

Adding Text 259
    Inserting Symbols and Foreign Characters 260
    Inserting the Date and Time 264
    Replaying Your Editing Actions with the Repeat Command 265
    Reusing Text with the AutoText Feature. 266

Automatically Fixing Your Text with AutoCorrect 271
Using Smart Tags in Word 276
Positioning the Insertion Point 280
Editing Document Text 281
Selecting the Text 282
Editing the Selection 287
Finding and Replacing Text and Formatting 293
Replacing Text and Formatting 298
Moving Quickly Through a Document 300
Using Bookmarks to Label and Locate Text 300
Moving the Insertion Point with the Go To Command 302
Navigating with the Browse Buttons 304

Chapter 12
Effective Formatting in Word   307

Directly Formatting a Word Document 307
Formatting Characters Directly 308
Formatting Paragraphs Directly 318
Applying Styles and Reusing Formats 327
Checking the Consistency of Your Formatting 330
Assigning Paragraph Styles, Character Styles, and Saved Formats . . 330
Removing All Formatting 333
Selecting All Text with the Same Style or Formatting 335
Working with Paragraph Styles 336
Assigning Styles and Saved Formats Using the
Formatting Toolbar 337
Assigning Styles Using Shortcut Keys 337
Using the Reveal Formatting Task Pane to View or Modify
Formatting Features 338
Formatting Your Documents Automatically 340

Chapter 13
Arranging Text Using Tables, Columns, and Lists   345

Arranging Text with Tables 345
Creating a Table 346
Adding Content to a Table 347
Adding and Removing Table Cells, Rows, and Columns 347
Resizing Table Cells 350
Moving and Copying Table Cells, Rows, and Columns 353
Creating Tables with the Table Drawing Tools 355
Formatting Tables by Applying Table Styles 357
Using Other Methods for Creating and Modifying Tables 359
Adding Borders and Shading 361
Applying Borders and Shading with the Tables And
Borders Toolbar 363
Applying Borders and Shading with the Borders And Shading
Dialog Box 366

Applying Borders to Pages. 370
Arranging Text in Newspaper-Style Columns 371
Applying Columns with the Columns Button 372
Applying Columns with the Columns Dialog Box 373
Fine Tuning Columns 374
Ordering Text in Bulleted and Numbered Lists. 377
Creating Lists with the Formatting Toolbar 377
Creating Lists with the Bullets And Numbering Dialog Box
and List Styles. 379
Sorting Lists and Tables 384

Chapter 14
Advanced Word Formatting Techniques   389

Customizing Styles. 389
Customizing Paragraph and Character Styles by Example 393
Customizing Styles Using the Modify Style Dialog Box. 394
Deleting a Style 402
Creating New Styles 403
Creating Paragraph Styles by Example 404
Creating Styles with the New Style Dialog Box 404
Reusing Your Styles by Making Copies. 406
Copying Styles from a Template to a Document 406
Copying Styles from a Document to a Template 407
Copying Styles from a Document or Template to Another
Document or Template 408
Customizing and Creating Document Templates 408
Customizing Templates. 411
Creating New Templates 414
Attaching a Template to a Document 415
Loading Global Templates and Word Add-Ins. 416

Chapter 15
Managing Large or Complex Documents   419

Working with Documents in Outline View 419
Switching to Outline View 420
Changing Outline Levels 422
Moving Blocks of Text. 425
Collapsing and Expanding Outline Text 426
Navigating Through an Outline. 429
Printing an Outline 432
Inserting Footnotes and Endnotes 434
Generating Indexes and Tables of Contents 438
Generating an Index 438
Generating a Table of Contents 443

Chapter 16
Using Word in Workgroups   447

Tracking and Reviewing Document Changes 447
　　Tracking Your Document Changes 447
　　Reviewing Tracked Document Changes. 452
Merging and Comparing Documents 458
Inserting Comments in Documents 459
　　Inserting Comments. 459
　　Viewing, Editing, and Deleting Comments 462
　　Working with Ink Annotations 466
Highlighting Text. 466
Sharing Word Documents 468
　　Sharing Word Documents on a Network 469
　　Sharing Word Documents Using E-Mail. 470
　　Protecting Shared Documents. 472
　　Sharing Fonts. 477

Chapter 17
Proofing Word Documents   479

Using the Word Proofing Tools 479
Checking Spelling. 479
　　Checking Your Spelling as You Type 479
　　Checking the Spelling of Existing Text 482
　　Customizing the Spelling Checker 485
　　Using Custom Dictionaries 487
Checking Your Grammar 490
　　Checking Your Grammar as You Type 490
　　Checking the Grammar of Existing Text. 493
　　Customizing the Grammar Checker 496
Finding Synonyms with the Thesaurus 497
Translating Text 499
Hyphenating Your Documents 500
　　Automatically Hyphenating a Document 501
　　Manually Hyphenating a Document 503
　　Inserting Hyphen Characters. 504
Marking the Language 505
　　Taking Advantage of Automatic Language Detection 507

Chapter 18
Designing and Printing Professional-Looking Pages   509

Designing Pages 509
Using Text Boxes to Create Precise Page Layouts 510
Combining Text with Graphic Objects and Text Boxes. 514
Displaying Watermarks 517
Adding Page Numbering, Headers, and Footers 519
　　Adding Automatic Page Numbering 519
　　Adding Headers and Footers. 524

Modifying the Page Setup 532
    Setting the Margins and Page Orientation 533
    Adjusting the Paper Size and Source 540
    Adjusting the Page Layout 541
Previewing and Printing Documents 543

Chapter 19
Using Word to Automate Mailings   549

Using the Mail Merge Wizard to Automate Large Mailings 549
Generating Individual Envelopes and Labels 559
    Generating Individual Envelopes 560
    Generating Individual Labels 563

Chapter 20
Creating Web Pages and Working with XML in Word   569

Online Documents 569
    Using Reading Layout View 571
Creating and Publishing Web Pages 573
    Adding Web Page Elements 580
    Formatting Web Pages 591
    Publishing Your Page 593
Creating, Editing, and Viewing XML Documents 594
    Creating XML Documents in Word 596

Part 4
Excel

Chapter 21
Excel Fundamentals   605

Starting Excel and Getting Comfortable 605
    Navigating a Worksheet 608
Entering Information 611
    Entering Numeric Values 611
    Entering Text Values 613
    Entering Dates and Times 614
    Entering Comments 616
    Entering Formulas 618
    Adding Artwork 621
Inserting Hyperlinks 622
    Creating a Hyperlink in Your Worksheet 622
    Activating a Hyperlink 625
    Editing and Removing Hyperlinks 626
Saving the Workbook 626

Chapter 22
Advanced Worksheet Editing   627

Essential Editing Techniques. 627
    Selecting Cells and Ranges. 627
    Clearing Cells and Deleting Cells. 630
    Finding and Replacing Data. 632
    Undoing Commands 633
    Using Cut and Paste to Move Data 635
    Using Copy and Paste to Duplicate Data 637
    Moving Cells by Dragging 638
    Adding Rows and Columns to the Worksheet 639
    Using Smart Tags in Excel. 640
Entering a Series of Labels, Numbers, and Dates. 641
    Using AutoFill to Create a Series. 641
Checking for Errors. 644
    Correcting Your Spelling 644
    Checking for Common Errors. 645

Chapter 23
Expert Formatting Techniques   647

Formatting Cells. 647
    Changing Alignment 648
    Changing Number Formats 651
    Changing the Text Font and Text Color 656
    Adding Borders to Cells 658
    Adding Shading to Cells 660
    Copying Formatting Using the Format Painter Button 662
Changing Column Widths and Row Heights. 662
    Adjusting the Height or Width Manually 662
    Using the AutoFit Command 665
    Applying a Combination of Effects Using AutoFormat. 665
Creating Conditional Formatting. 666
Using Styles 668
    Creating Your Own Styles 669
    Applying Existing Styles 671
    Merging Styles from Other Workbooks 671
Creating and Modifying Templates 672
    Creating a New Template File 673
    Opening and Modifying an Existing Template File 674
Changing Page Breaks 675
    Using Page Break Preview. 676

Chapter 24
Power Organizing with Workbooks   679

Managing Worksheets 679
    Switching Between Worksheets. 680

Naming Worksheets 681
Changing Tab Color. 681
Deleting Worksheets 681
Inserting Worksheets 682
Moving or Copying Worksheets 683
Referencing Cells in Other Worksheets 685
Using More Than One Workbook 687
Linking Information Between Workbooks 688
Consolidating Worksheets with Identical Formats 689
Managing Shared Workbooks 693
Creating a Shared Workbook. 693
Monitoring a Shared Workbook 695
Accepting or Rejecting Revisions 696
Protecting Worksheets and Workbooks 698
Protecting Worksheets 699
Protecting Workbook Structure 701
Requiring a Password for File Access. 702

Chapter 25
Customizing Excel to Work the Way You Do   705

Adjusting Views 705
Using the Zoom Command 706
Saving Views Using the Custom Views Command 707
Setting Printing Options 708
Controlling Page Orientation 709
Adjusting the Margins. 710
Adding Headers and Footers 710
Adding Gridlines and Other Options 716
Using Multiple Panes 718
Splitting a Worksheet into Panes. 719
Freezing Panes in a Worksheet 719
Customizing Excel Using the Options Dialog Box. 720
Controlling Calculation 721
Customizing Worksheet Appearance 722
Customizing Editing Options 723
Installing Add-In Commands and Wizards 725

Chapter 26
Crunching Numbers with Formulas and Functions   727

Building a Formula 727
Multiplying Numbers. 728
Replicating a Formula 729
Combining Arithmetic Operators 732
Parentheses and Order of Evaluation 733
Using Built-In Functions 733
The Versatile SUM Function 735
The Insert Function Command. 736

Using Functions to Analyze Finances 737
  Using PMT to Determine Loan Payments 738
  Using FV to Compute Future Value. 739
  Using the RATE Function to Evaluate Rate of Return 740
  Using Function Error Values. 741
Using Names in Functions 742
  Creating Cell and Range Names 742
  Putting Names to Work. 744
  Deleting and Modifying Names 745

Chapter 27
Advanced Worksheet Charts   747

Planning a Chart 747
  Choosing a Chart Type 748
  Understanding Chart Elements, Excel-Style 750
Creating a Chart. 751
  Creating an Embedded Chart 754
Formatting a Chart 758
  Exploring the Chart Menu 758
  Using the Chart Toolbar 759
  Changing the Chart Type. 759
  Changing Titles and Data Labels 760
  Adjusting Gridlines 763
  Modifying the Chart Legend. 764
  Copying Chart Formats 765
Adding Labels and Arrows. 766
Printing a Chart 768

Chapter 28
Power Database Techniques: Lists, Filters, and PivotTables   771

Using a List as a Database. 771
  Using a Form for Data Entry 773
  Validating Data as You Enter It 775
Sorting Rows and Columns. 778
  Sorting on More than One Column. 779
  Creating Your Own Custom Sort Order 781
  Using a Custom Sort Order 782
Using AutoFilter to Find Records 783
  Creating a Custom AutoFilter. 784
Analyzing a List with the Subtotals Command. 785
  Working in Outline View 788
Converting an Excel List into an Access Database 788
Creating PivotTables and PivotCharts. 789
  Using the PivotTable And PivotChart Wizard 790
  Evaluating a PivotTable 793

Rearranging Fields in a PivotTable 794
Using the Page Area 794
Changing the Function in a PivotTable 796
Adjusting the Formatting in a PivotTable 797
Displaying PivotCharts 798
Using External Data Sources in PivotTables 799
Using the New Excel List Commands 800

Chapter 29
Advanced Business Analysis   805

Using the Goal Seek Command to Forecast 805
Using the Solver to Set Quantity and Pricing 808
Setting Up the Problem 808
Running the Solver 810
Editing Your Solver Forecast 813
Using the Scenario Manager to Evaluate What-If Questions 815
Creating a Scenario 816
Viewing a Scenario 818
Creating Scenario Reports 819

Chapter 30
Publishing on the Web and Working with XML in Excel   823

Designing an Excel Web Page 824
Static Pages vs. Interactive Pages 824
Publishing an Excel Web Page 825
Running an Excel Web Page on the Internet 830
Working with an Interactive Web Page in Your Browser 830
Using Web Queries 832
Importing Data from the Web 833
Revising Web Queries 835
Working with XML Data in a Worksheet 838
Customizing an XML List 844

Part 5
PowerPoint

Chapter 31
PowerPoint Fundamentals   849

Exploring the PowerPoint Window 849
Elements of a Slide 851
Understanding PowerPoint Views 852
Using a Web Browser to View a Presentation 855
Using Print Preview to View a Presentation 855

Creating a Presentation 856
   Using the AutoContent Wizard 857
   Starting a Blank Presentation 859
   Using a Design Template 861
   Using an Existing Presentation as a Model 863
   Other Ways to Start a Presentation from a Template 863
   Creating a Custom PowerPoint Template 865
Entering and Editing Text 866
   Entering Text in Placeholders 866
   Working with Automatic Text Formatting 867
   Using Smart Tag Recognizers 868
   Editing Text 869
Using Outlines 870
   Entering an Outline from Scratch 871
   Modifying an Outline 871
   Rearranging Slides on the Outline Tab 872
   Expanding and Duplicating Slides 872
   Creating a Summary Slide 873
Adding Comments 873
Checking Spelling and Style 874
Saving a Presentation 876

Chapter 32
Advanced Presentation Formatting   877

Formatting Text 878
   Formatting Text Using the Formatting Toolbar 878
   Text Formatting Using the Font Dialog Box 880
   Replacing Fonts 880
   Copying Formatting 881
   Working with Bullets and Numbering 881
   Formatting Indents and Tab Settings 883
Working with Color and Color Schemes 886
   Creating a Custom Scheme 887
Changing the Background 888
Working with Presentation Masters 890

Chapter 33
Mastering Tables, Graphics, Video, and Sound   895

Creating Tables 896
   Formatting a Table 897
Adding Graphics 898
   Saving PowerPoint Elements as Pictures 900
   Using Grids and Drawing Guides 900
   Creating a Photo Album 902

Adding Video Clips and Sound. 902
Inserting Video Clips 903
Inserting Sound Clips 905
Playing CD Audio Tracks 907

Chapter 34
Adding Special Effects to a Presentation   **909**

Applying Animation. 910
Customizing Animation 911
Animating Diagrams and Charts 914
Creating Motion Paths 914
Applying Transitions 917
Creating Hyperlinks 918
Assigning Actions to Objects 920

Chapter 35
Setting Up and Presenting the Slide Show   **923**

Picking a Presentation Medium 923
Using Overheads 925
Ordering 35-mm Slides. 926
Preparing an Electronic Presentation 926
Rehearsing the Show 926
Recording Narration 929
Creating a Custom Show. 930
Hiding Slides 931
Using the Package for CD Feature 932
Giving an Electronic Presentation. 933
Annotating Slides. 935
Printing Slides, Notes Pages, and Handouts. 936
Creating Handouts 937
Publishing Your Presentation on the Web 938
Previewing Your Presentation in a Browser 938
Saving Your Presentation as a Web Page 939

Part 6
Outlook

Chapter 36
Outlook Fundamentals   **945**

A Rundown on Outlook 945
Setting Up Outlook. 946
Viewing Information in Outlook 947
Using Other Methods to Open Folders 951

Chapter 37
Working with Outlook Items and Folders   955

Working with Outlook Items. 955
   Creating New Items 955
   Editing Items 961
   Moving and Copying Items 966
   Removing and Archiving Items. 969
   Changing the Way You View Items 973
   Switching and Customizing Views 973
   Sorting, Filtering, and Grouping Items in Folders. 979
   Quickly Arranging Folder Items. 983
   Using the Reading Pane 984
   Finding Outlook Items. 986
   Organizing Items Using the Organize Pane 990
Working with Outlook Folders 991
Printing Outlook Information 994
Using Outlook Today to Get an Overview. 995

Chapter 38
Managing Messages and Appointments   999

Receiving and Sending E-Mail Messages Using the E-Mail Folders 999
   Receiving and Viewing E-Mail Messages. 1001
   Reading HTML Messages Privately and Safely 1005
   Using Quick Flags. 1007
   Using Groups to Manage Several E-Mail Accounts. 1008
   Composing and Sending E-Mail Messages 1014
   Sending Shared Attachments 1018
   Using Search Folders to Categorize Your Messages 1019
   Organizing Your E-Mail Messages. 1021
   Handling Junk E-Mail 1022
   Using an Internet Fax Service 1025
Maintaining Your Schedule with the Calendar Folder 1026
   Scheduling Appointments 1027
   Setting Up Events. 1032
   Scheduling Meetings 1033
   Creating and Linking to a SharePoint Meeting Workspace 1039
   Working with Your Calendar Folder 1043
   Opening a SharePoint Calendar in Outlook 1045

Chapter 39
Managing Contacts, Tasks, and Other Types of Information   1047

Maintaining Your Address List with the Contacts Folder. 1047
   Defining Contacts and Distribution Lists. 1047
   Using Your Contacts Folder 1055
   Opening a SharePoint Contacts List in Outlook 1058

Managing Tasks and Projects with the Tasks Folder 1060
    Defining Tasks 1061
    Working with Your Tasks Folder 1066
Recording Events with the Journal Folder 1068
    Recording Entries in Your Journal Folder 1068
Storing Miscellaneous Information in the Notes Folder 1074

Chapter 40
Customizing Outlook   1077

Customizing the Navigation Pane 1077
    Configuring the Navigation Pane Buttons 1077
    Customizing the My Folders Lists 1078
    Customizing the Favorite Folders List 1078
    Customizing the Shortcuts List 1079
Adding, Modifying, and Removing Outlook Accounts 1080
Managing Outlook Data Files 1088
    Creating and Modifying Outlook Data Files 1091
    Opening, Closing, and Working with Outlook Data Files 1092

Part 7
Access

Chapter 41
Access Fundamentals   1097

A Rundown on Access 1097
Designing and Planning an Access Database 1100
Creating a New Database 1104
Using the Database Window and Object Views 1107
Saving, Closing, and Opening Databases in Access 1110
    Opening a Database 1111
    Backing Up Your Database 1112

Chapter 42
Setting Up Tables and Relationships   1113

Creating a Table 1113
    Importing and Exporting XML Documents 1116
Customizing a Table in Design View 1118
    Adding, Removing, and Rearranging Fields 1119
    Setting the Field Properties 1122
    Designating a Primary Key 1127
Setting Up Table Relationships 1128
Working in Datasheet View 1134
    Entering and Editing Data in Datasheet View 1134
    Customizing Datasheet View 1137
    Adding and Using Subdatasheets 1139
    Sorting and Filtering in Datasheet View 1141

Chapter 43
Using Queries to Select and Combine Information   **1149**

Creating a Query 1149
   Creating a Basic Query with the Simple Query Wizard 1150
   Creating a Maintenance Query 1154
Modifying a Query 1154
   Using Top-Value Queries 1158
   Summarizing Your Information. 1160
   Adding Calculated Fields. 1163
Creating a Crosstab Query 1166
Creating and Running Queries to Modify Data. 1168
   Make-Table Query. 1170
   Append Query 1170
   Delete Query 1170
   Update Query. 1170

Chapter 44
Creating Forms and Data Access Pages for Working with Data   **1171**

Creating a Form 1171
   Creating a Form Using the Form Wizard 1173
Customizing a Form 1178
   Formatting a Form 1183
Viewing and Modifying Data in a Form 1189
Publishing Data on an Intranet Using a Data Access Page. 1193
   Creating a Data Access Page 1195
   Modifying a Data Access Page. 1197
   Publishing a Data Access Page 1197

Chapter 45
Generating Reports to Present Information   **1199**

Creating a Report. 1199
   Using the Report Wizard 1201
Modifying a Report. 1210
   Understanding Report Sections. 1211
   Controlling the Groupings 1213
Previewing and Printing a Report 1215

Part 8
FrontPage Fundamentals

Chapter 46
FrontPage Fundamentals   **1219**

A Rundown on FrontPage 1219

Creating and Opening Web Sites 1221
    Customizing and Creating SharePoint Team Web Sites 1231
Navigating in FrontPage. 1233

Chapter 47
Managing Your Web Site with FrontPage   1239

Working with Your Web Site's Folders and Files. 1239
    Working with Folders. 1242
    Adding Document Libraries, Lists, and Other Information
    Components to a SharePoint Team Web Site 1243
    Working with Files 1247
    Importing Web Site Files and Folders 1250
Setting Up Your Web Site's Navigation Structure 1254
    Using Navigation View. 1255
    Using Hyperlinks View 1260
Managing Your Web Site Projects. 1262
Viewing Web Site Reports. 1265
    Viewing, Verifying, and Repairing Hyperlinks 1270
Publishing Your Web Site 1273

Chapter 48
Creating and Editing Web Pages   1279

Creating a New Web Page 1279
    Creating Your Own FrontPage Templates. 1283
    Working with Dynamic Templates. 1284
    Creating a Web Part Page on a SharePoint Team Web Site. 1286
Opening an Existing Web Page. 1288
Common Editing Tasks 1289
    Selecting. 1289
    Moving, Copying, and Deleting 1289
    Undoing and Redoing Editing Actions 1291
Adding the Text Content 1291
    Finding and Replacing Text in Your Web Pages 1293
    Proofing Text in Your Web Pages 1297
Inserting Images 1300
    Creating a Thumbnail Image 1303
    Adding a Photo Gallery 1304
    Inserting a Video Clip 1305
Separating Content with Horizontal Dividing Lines. 1305
Including Internal and External Hyperlinks 1306
Using Tables Effectively 1308
    Using Layout Tables and Cells 1311
Working with Shared Borders 1313
Previewing and Printing Your Page 1317

Chapter 49
Formatting Your Web Pages 1321

A Page Formatting Overview 1321
Formatting Paragraphs 1322
    Applying Borders and Shading 1329
    Creating Dynamic HTML Effects 1331
Formatting Characters 1332
Formatting Images 1336
    Modifying Image Properties 1337
    Enhancing Images Using the Pictures Toolbar 1340
    Modifying a Video Clip 1344
Positioning Paragraphs, Images, Tables, and Other Elements 1346
Formatting Other Page Elements 1349
Formatting the Whole Page 1350
    Modifying Page Properties 1350
    Using Themes to Quickly Change the Overall Page Format 1353
    Applying Dynamic Page Transition Effects 1356
Modifying, Creating, and Using Cascading Style Sheet Styles 1358

Chapter 50
Adding Advanced Features to Your Web Pages and Working with Source Code 1363

Creating Interactive Forms to Collect Information 1363
Using Frames to Display Multiple Pages 1367
    Adding Inline Frames 1372
Adding Dynamic Content with Web Components 1374
    Inserting Advanced Controls 1379
Working Directly with Source Code 1382
    Working with HTML Source Code in Design View 1383
    Directly Editing Source Code Files 1384
    Finding and Replacing HTML Elements 1389

Part 9
InfoPath

Chapter 51
InforPath Fundamentals 1399

A Rundown on InfoPath 1393
Opening a Form Template in Design Mode 1394
    1. Design the Form 1394
    2. Fill Out the Form 1397
    3. Deliver the Form 1398

Chapter 52
Designing Forms in InfoPath   **1399**

Opening a Form Template in Design Mode 1399
Customizing a Form Template 1403
Adding a Layout to a Form. 1404
Inserting Controls in a Form 1406
Working with a Form's Data Source 1408
Managing Form Views. 1410
Using Other Form Design Tools 1411
Saving a Form Template 1412

Chapter 53
Filling Out and Delivering Forms in InfoPath   **1417**

Opening a New Form in Edit Mode 1417
Filling Out a Form 1419
Saving and Delivering a Form 1423

Part 10
Customizing Office 2003 Using VBA

Chapter 54
VBA Fundamentals   **1427**

Using the Visual Basic Development Environment to Edit a Macro 1427
Learning the Visual Basic Programming Tools. 1431
Using the Menu Bar 1432
Using the Visual Basic Toolbars. 1433
Using Project Explorer. 1434
Using the Properties Window. 1436
Exiting Visual Basic 1438

Chapter 55
Using Variables, Operators, and Functions
to Manage Information   **1439**

Reading a Visual Basic Program Statement 1439
What Is an Object?. 1440
What Are Properties and Methods? 1440
Learning More About the Office Object Model 1441
Using Office Constants 1442
Using Constants to Create Custom Formatting 1443
Declaring Variables. 1447
Making Reservations for Variables: The Dim Statement. 1447
Putting Variables to Work 1448
Using Visual Basic Functions 1448
Using a Variable to Store Input 1448

Using a Variable for Output 1452
Using Object Variables to Process Text. 1454
Using an Object Variable to Copy Text 1454
Building Formulas. 1456
Computing Formulas in Your Documents 1456

Chapter 56
Adding Logic and Computing Power with Control Structures   1461

Writing Conditional Expressions. 1461
Writing If...Then Decision Structures 1462
Testing Several Conditions in an If...Then Decision Structure. . . . 1462
Writing Select Case Decision Structures 1466
Using Select Case to Determine a Document's Paper Size. 1467
Writing For...Next Loops 1469
Using a Loop to Manage Tables. 1470
Using For...Each Loops. 1472

Chapter 57
Using Toolbox Controls to Create a User Interface   1477

Getting Started with UserForms. 1477
Designing the User Interface. 1477
Setting Properties 1481
Writing Event Procedures 1484
Using the TextBox Control to Process Paragraphs 1487
Processing Text in a Word Document 1487
Reviewing the ParaScan Macro Code 1489

Index of Troubleshooting Topics **1493**
Index **1499**

We'd Like to Hear from You

Our goal at Microsoft Press is to create books that help you find the information you need to get the most out of your software.

The *Inside Out* series was created with you in mind. As part of our ongoing effort to ensure that we're creating the books that meet your learning needs, we'd like to hear from you. Let us know what you think. Tell us what you like about this book and what we can do to make it better. When you write, please include the title and author of this book in your e-mail message, as well as your name and contact information. We look forward to hearing from you!

How to Reach Us

E-Mail: nsideout@microsoft.com
Mail: Inside Out Series Editor
          Microsoft Press
          One Microsoft Way
          Redmond, WA 98052

Note: Unfortunately, we can't provide support for any software problems you might experience. Please go to http://support.microsoft.com *for help with any software issues.*

About the CD

The companion CD that ships with this book contains many tools and resources to help you get the most out of your Inside Out book.

What's On the CD

Your INSIDE OUT CD includes the following:

- **Complete eBook.**   In this section you'll find the an electronic version of *Microsoft Office System Inside Out—2003 Edition*. The eBook is in PDF format.

- **Insider Extras.**   This section includes sample files referenced in the book. Copy these files to your hard disk, and use them to follow along with the books examples or as a starting point for your own work.

- **Microsoft Resources.**   In this section you'll find information about additional resources from Microsoft that will help you get the most out of the Microsoft Office System. Building on the familiar tools that many people already know, the Microsoft Office System includes servers, services, and desktop programs to help address a broad array of business needs.

- **Extending Office.**   In this section, you'll find great information about third-party utilities and tools you use to further enhance your experience with Office 2003.

- *Microsoft Computer Dictionary, Fifth Edition*, **eBook.**   Here you'll find the full electronic version of the *Microsoft Computer Dictionary, Fifth Edition*. Suitable for home and office, the dictionary contains more than 10,000 entries.

- *Microsoft Networking Encylopedia, Second Edition*, **eBook.**   Here you'll find the full electronic version of the *Microsoft Encyclopedia of Networking, Second Edition*. This encyclopedia contains thousands of entries detailing the latest technologies, standards, products, and services.

The companion CD provides detailed information about the files on this CD, and links to Microsoft and third-party sites on the Internet.

> **Note**   Please note that the links to third-party sites are not under the control of Microsoft Corporation, and Microsoft is therefore not responsible for their content, nor should their inclusion on this CD be construed as an endorsement of the product or the site.

Using the CD

To use this companion CD, insert it into your CD-ROM drive. If AutoRun is not enabled on your computer, run the StartCD.exe in the root of the CD.

System Requirements

Following are the minimum system requirements necessary to run the CD:

- Microsoft Windows XP or later or Windows 2000 Professional with Service Pack 3 or later
- 266-MHz or higher Pentium-compatible CPU
- 64 megabytes (MB) RAM
- 8X CD-ROM drive or faster
- Microsoft Windows–compatible sound card and speakers
- Microsoft Internet Explorer 5.01 or higher
- Microsoft Mouse or compatible pointing device

> **Note** An Internet connection is necessary to access the some of the hyperlinks. Connect time charges may apply.

Support Information

Every effort has been made to ensure the accuracy of the book and the contents of this companion CD. For feedback on the book content or this companion CD, please contact us by using any of the addresses listed in the "We'd Like to Hear from You" section.

Microsoft Press provides corrections for books through the World Wide Web at *http://www.microsoft.com/mspress/support/*. To connect directly to the Microsoft Press Knowledge Base and enter a query regarding a question or issue that you may have, go to *http://www.microsoft.com/mspress/support/search.htm*.

For support information regarding Windows XP, you can connect to Microsoft Technical Support on the Web at *http://support.microsoft.com/*.

Conventions and Features Used in This Book

This book uses special text and design conventions to make it easier for you to find the information you need.

Text Convention

Convention	Meaning
Abbreviated menu commands	For your convenience, this book uses abbreviated menu commands. For example, "Click Tools, Track Changes, Highlight Changes" means that you should click the Tools menu, point to Track Changes, and click the Highlight Changes command.
Boldface type	**Boldface** type is used to indicate text that you enter or type.
Initial Capital Letters	The first letters of the names of menus, dialog boxes, dialog box elements, and commands are capitalized. Example: the Save As dialog box.
Italicized type	*Italicized* type is used to indicate new terms.
Plus sign (+) in text	Keyboard shortcuts are indicated by a plus sign (+) separating two key names. For example, Ctrl+Alt+Delete means that you press the Ctrl, Alt, and Delete keys at the same time.

Design Conventions

 This icon identifies a new or significantly updated feature in this version of the software.

 Inside Out

This statement illustrates an example of an "Inside Out" problem statement.

These are the book's signature tips. In these tips, you'll get the straight scoop on what's going on with the software—inside information about why a feature works the way it does. You'll also find handy workarounds to deal with software problems.

Tip Tips provide helpful hints, timesaving tricks, or alternative procedures related to the task being discussed.

Troubleshooting

This statement illustrates an example of a "Troubleshooting" problem statement.

Look for these sidebars to find solutions to common problems you might encounter. Troubleshooting sidebars appear next to related information in the chapters. You can also use the Troubleshooting Topics index at the back of the book to look up problems by topic.

Cross-references point you to other locations in the book that offer additional information about the topic being discussed.

 This icon indicates information or text found on the companion CD.

Caution Cautions identify potential problems that you should look out for when you're completing a task or problems that you must address before you can complete a task.

Note Notes offer additional information related to the task being discussed.

Sidebars

The sidebars sprinkled throughout these chapters provide ancillary information on the topic being discussed. Go to sidebars to learn more about the technology or a feature.

Introduction

Microsoft Office 2003 Edition has more power, more application integration, and greater sharing of features than any previous version of Office. Microsoft has worked hard to make the Office applications easy to use, but the new Office System's sheer size and complexity can make it challenging to find your way around the software, to learn the applications and the ways they work together, and to solve the problems that result from the software's intricacy. *Microsoft Office System Inside Out—2003 Edition* is designed to help you meet this challenge.

Who This Book Is For

This book is written for the power user, the software enthusiast, the consultant, the solutions developer, or the company guru—the one others come to for help. It's designed for the person who wants to learn the essentials quickly and then go on to more interesting topics— advanced timesaving techniques, bug workarounds, troubleshooting advice, and insights into Office's inner workings. It's written for the computer user who needs to solve the problems that will inevitably occur with software as complex as Office. And it's targeted to the reader who wants an honest, objective evaluation of the different Office components, clarifying which features to use and which to avoid.

Rest assured that the book also covers the essentials. Contrary to the typical media depiction of a computer genius, even the savviest computer expert needs to learn the basics of a new program. In this book, however, the essentials are taught as they would be in a graduate seminar rather than in a freshman 101 course—quickly and concisely, relying on your general computer understanding and your ability to translate your current insights and skills to the topic at hand.

Consequently, to get the most out of this book, you should know the basics of computer hardware and software. You should know Microsoft Windows. You should know how to use the file system, how to access the Internet, and how to manage your e-mail. You should have used a word processor and spreadsheet program before, so that the essential concepts are familiar to you. But most important, you should be excited about exploring the fascinating territory that lies just beyond the surface of Office 2003.

How This Book Is Organized

Part 1, "Getting Going with Office 2003," is designed to get you started with Office in as few pages as possible. Chapter 1, "An Office 2003 Overview," includes a concise Office road map to help you quickly choose the Office application or applications you need to accomplish your intended tasks, plus a comprehensive summary of the new Office features, which will be especially valuable if you've used previous Office versions. Chapter 2, "Installing and Configuring Office 2003," provides succinct instructions to help you install Office and maintain your Office installation. And Chapter 3, "Getting Expert Help on Office 2003," shows you how to make the most of the online help provided with Office and how to access the online resources available on the Microsoft Office Online Web site.

Part 2, "Using Shared Office 2003 Application Features," focuses on the common features of the Office applications and on the ways to take advantage of Office application integration. For instance, this part explains how to use the Office task panes, the search feature, the speech recognition and handwriting interfaces, the enhanced Office Clipboard, and the many commands for adding graphics to documents, including the Clip Organizer and diagram features. It also shows how to create compound documents that combine data from several applications; how to use Office applications to share documents and information on a team Web site on a server running the new Microsoft Windows SharePoint Services; and how to record macros and customize the menus, toolbars, and other features of the common Office application interface.

Parts 3 through 9 provide in-depth coverage of each of the major Office applications: Microsoft Word, Excel, PowerPoint, Outlook, Access, FrontPage, and InfoPath. For a brief rundown on each of these applications, see "An Office 2003 Map" on page 6, as well as the first chapter of each application part.

Finally, Part 10, "Customizing Office 2003 Using VBA," covers the common macro and development language of the Office applications: Visual Basic for Applications (VBA). These chapters explain how to use Office's Visual Basic Editor to enhance macros that you've recorded in Office applications, as well as to develop more sophisticated macros from scratch.

Keep in mind that *Microsoft Office System Inside Out—2003 Edition* isn't the type of book you need to read through from the beginning. Nor must you read an individual chapter in its entirety. Rather, the book has been designed so that you need to consult only the specific section or sections that are relevant to completing your pending Office task or to solving your current Office problem. The sections in this book are concise, down-to-business, and are largely self-sufficient. If a section does depend on material found elsewhere, you'll find a cross-reference to the chapter, section, or page containing that information.

In addition to cross-references, you'll find many notes and sidebars that provide supplemental and in-depth insights and techniques, as well as tips presenting advanced tricks and workarounds. You'll also discover candid Inside Out elements in each chapter, which often point out flaws and shortcomings in the Office software and suggest ways to deal with them. And finally, the chapters include special troubleshooting sidebars to help you solve specific problems that you're likely to encounter.

To quickly find the section or sections you need to read, be sure to take advantage of the book's comprehensive table of contents and indexes, including a separate index of troubleshooting sidebars, which should be the first resource you consult when Office trouble strikes.

Contacting the Author

The author welcomes your feedback and comments and will try to help you with problems you encounter in using the techniques covered in this book. You can contact Michael J. Young through his Web site at *http://www.mjyOnline.com*.

> **Note** If you wish to send general comments or suggestions about this book specifically or about the Inside Out series in general, please see page xxix.

Part 1

Getting Going with Office 2003

1 An Office 2003 Overview   3

2 Installing and Configuring Office 2003   17

3 Getting Expert Help on Office 2003   25

1

An Office 2003 Overview

A Rundown on Office 2003 3   An Office 2003 Map. 7

A Rundown on Office 2003

The Microsoft Office 2003 Editions provide more applications and utility programs than ever before. Which ones you have depends on which edition of Office 2003 you own or which individual Office applications you've obtained. This book covers the following major Office 2003 applications:

- Microsoft Word (Part 3)
- Microsoft Excel (Part 4)
- Microsoft PowerPoint (Part 5)
- Microsoft Outlook (Part 6)
- Microsoft Access (Part 7)
- Microsoft FrontPage (Part 8)
- Microsoft InfoPath (Part 9)

The book also covers many of the valuable utility programs, add-ons, and Web server extensions that help you work with the major Office applications:

- Microsoft Office Application Recovery (Chapter 4).
- Microsoft Clip Organizer (Chapter 6).
- Microsoft Graph (Chapter 6).
- Microsoft Equation (Chapter 6).
- Microsoft Windows SharePoint Services (Chapter 8). See Figure 1-1.
- Save My Settings Wizard (Chapter 9).
- Microsoft Visual Basic development environment (Part 10).

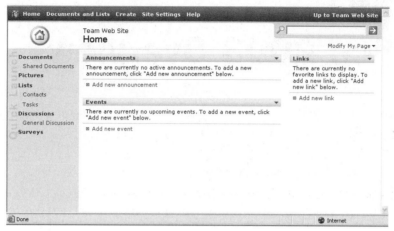

Figure 1-1. This figure shows the home page of a team Web site on a server running the new version of SharePoint, known as Windows SharePoint Services.

Even if you don't have one or more of the applications covered in this book, you might want to read some of the information about these applications to help you decide whether to add an Office program to your software collection or whether you're better off using the applications you already have.

Advantages of the New Microsoft Office System

Obtaining and installing the new Microsoft Office System, rather than acquiring individual applications here and there, isn't just a way to economize by buying programs "cheaper by the dozen." The real advantages of a software suite such as Office 2003 lie in the common user interface and the application integration features.

In Office 2003, the individual applications share more common features than in any previous version of Office. An obvious advantage of a common user interface is that once you learn one application, it's much easier to learn another. Also, as you switch between applications, you won't have to switch working modes quite so radically. And, perhaps most important, a common user interface frees your focus from the individual applications and their idiosyncrasies and lets you concentrate on the documents you're creating. The following are examples of important common features in Office 2003:

- The menus, toolbars, shortcut keys, and the methods for customizing these features.
- The common dialog boxes (notably, the Open and Save As dialog boxes), with shared features such as the Search command (in the Open dialog box) that lets you find Office files, Outlook items, or Web pages.

● The task panes, such as the new Getting Started task pane, which is shown in Figure 1-2.

Figure 1-2. Each application's Getting Started task pane, a new feature in Office 2003, contains a basic collection of commands and features that are useful in that application.

● The speech and handwriting interfaces.

● The drawing features (the Drawing toolbar, AutoShapes, Diagrams, WordArt, and others).

● The methods for displaying and setting document properties.

● The ability to store and share documents and picture files on a SharePoint team Web site.

● The ability to fax documents using an Internet fax service. See Figure 1-3.

● The proofing tools (Spelling, Thesaurus, AutoCorrect, and others).

● Integrated access to the resources provided on the enhanced Office Web site, now known as Microsoft Office Online. These resources include help information, training, templates, clip art, and Web services.

● The help interface, including the new Help and Research task panes.

● The Check For Updates, Detect And Repair, and Activate Product commands, all found on the Help menu.

● The ability to record macros, or to write macros using the Visual Basic for Applications (VBA) language.

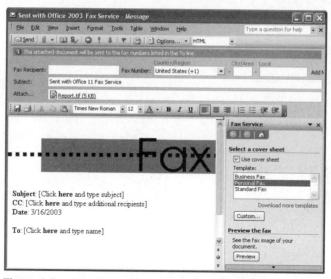

Figure 1-3. This figure shows the Message form that appears when you send a fax from an Office application using an Internet fax service.

The Office 2003 applications are also more tightly integrated than ever. Application integration extends the usefulness of the individual applications. It lets you combine applications in a synergistic way to solve more complex problems and to easily accomplish otherwise difficult tasks. The following are examples of application integration features available in Office 2003:

- Commands for linking and embedding data from several Office applications in a single compound document.

- Features for inserting hyperlinks into Office documents, which allow you to link together different types of documents, files, or Web pages.

- The ability of Office applications to import and export each other's documents (using the Open and Save As dialog boxes, as well as special-purpose commands for importing and exporting documents or data).

- Enhanced support for XML (Extensible Markup Language), which allows you to exchange data among different Office applications using XML as a common data format.

- Integrated access to a SharePoint team Web site, which allows you to store different document types, as well as information derived from various Office applications, in a single shared work environment.

- The New Office Document and Open Office Document dialog boxes, which let you create or open any type of Office document.

- The capability of using data stored in Outlook or Access when creating mail-merge documents in Word.
- VBA, the common programming language of the Office applications and the most powerful way to create solutions using multiple Office applications.

An Office 2003 Map

If you're not sure where to start with Office 2003, you can use Table 1-1 to select the best Office application to use for creating the type of document you want or for performing the task you need to complete.

> **Note**   For a more detailed rundown on an Office 2003 application, see the first chapter in the part of the book that covers that application.

Table 1-1. The Best Office 2003 Application to Use for Performing Specific Tasks

Task	Office 2003 Application to Use
Create general printed or online documents of all kinds—for example, memos, letters, faxes, reports, contracts, résumés, manuals, theses, and books.	Word
Enter and organize research notes, outlines, and other types of free-form text information.	
Generate form letters, envelopes, labels, and other mail-merge documents.	
Print individual labels and envelopes.	
Create general-purpose, relatively simple Web pages, which can include almost any Word document element, plus movies, sounds, forms, frames, visual themes, navigation bars, and components for accessing information on a SharePoint team Web site. Use templates to create personal Web pages and other types of pages.	
Create, edit, or view an XML document that conforms to any XML schema that you supply.	
Read documents using a clear, book-like interface (the new Reading Layout view). See Figure 1-4 on page 10.	
Translate words, phrases, or sentences into a different language.	

Table 1-1. **The Best Office 2003 Application to Use for Performing Specific Tasks**

Task	Office 2003 Application to Use
● Organize, calculate, analyze, chart, and save numeric business or personal data in a spreadsheet (row and column) format; for example, balance checking accounts, prepare invoices, plan budgets, track orders, or maintain general accounting ledgers.	Excel
● Store relatively simple text or numeric data in lists that organize the information into records (rows) and fields (columns)—for example, a product inventory or descriptions of members of your rowing club. Sort, find, filter, automatically fill, summarize, group, outline, or subtotal data. Display data in varying combinations using pivot tables or pivot charts. Publish lists of data on a SharePoint team Web site.	
● Publish static or interactive spreadsheets, charts, or pivot tables, for displaying numeric, text, or graphic information on the Web. Publish forms on the Web for collecting data in lists or other databases.	
● Import, view, analyze, modify, or export XML data that conforms to any specified schema.	
● Create multimedia presentations consisting of sets of slides to teach, sell, communicate, or persuade. Include text, graphics, animations, sound, and video in your presentations. Present multimedia information using 35-mm slides, transparencies for overhead projectors, speaker notes, printed handouts, or live slide shows on a computer or computer projector.	PowerPoint
● Publish presentations on the Web that consist of a series of multimedia slides displaying text, graphics, animations, sounds, or videos.	
● Send, receive, and organize e-mail messages. Exchange instant Internet messages.	Outlook
● Send and receive faxes using an Internet fax service.	
● Store and manage personal information (appointments, names and addresses, to-do lists, journal entries, or free-form notes).	
● Communicate and coordinate with members of your workgroup (schedule meetings, create meeting workspaces on a SharePoint team Web site, manage group projects, or view shared calendars (events lists) or contacts stored on a SharePoint team Web site).	

Table 1-1. The Best Office 2003 Application to Use for Performing Specific Tasks

Task	Office 2003 Application to Use
● Store, organize, select, and present data in a relational database, which allows you to easily manage large amounts of complex or interrelated data and to divide data into separate, related tables to maximize storage efficiency and simplify data maintenance.	Access
● Publish an interactive form on an intranet that allows users to view or update information from a database.	
● Store XML data in a database table, or export data to an XML document.	
● Create entire Web sites using templates or wizards—such as a site for establishing a corporate presence, displaying personal information, conducting an online discussion, managing a project, or accessing shared information stored on a SharePoint team Web site (see Figure 1-5). Use visual themes to apply consistent formatting to all pages in your site.	FrontPage
● Create special-purpose team Web sites on a server running Windows SharePoint Services—for example, an issue tracking site for a workgroup, a news and review site for an organization, or a Web log.	
● Manage your Web site (maintain files and folders, display reports, create and update hyperlinks, track tasks, copy files between a local and remote Web site or synchronize files, or control the source files in workgroups).	
● Create a Web page quickly using a template or wizard (for example, a page containing a bibliography, a feedback form, or a table of contents).	
● Create Web part pages on a SharePoint team Web site. A *Web part page* is a free-form Web page that you can quickly build by adding and customizing predefined components known as *Web parts*.	
● Create or edit a Web page using a full-featured HTML (Hypertext Markup Language) editor, which supports all standard Web page elements and provides ready-to-use Web-page components (date and time stamps, comments, interactive buttons and other dynamic effects, forms for searching the site, spreadsheets and charts, hit counters, galleries of photos, included files, link bars, tables of contents, site usage statistics, views of information stored on a SharePoint team Web site, and controls that display information from Web sites such as MSN).	
● Create or edit any type of plain text source file, such as a cascading style sheet (CSS) file, an XML document, or a C++ source file.	
● Design, fill out, and deliver electronic business forms that are stored in the industry-standard XML format and are structured using any standard XML schema that you supply.	InfoPath

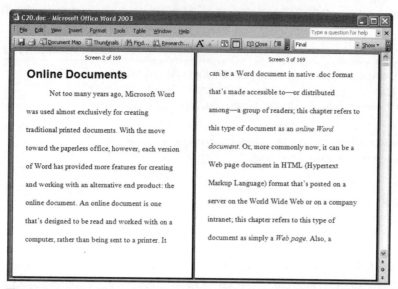

Figure 1-4. Word's new Reading Layout view is optimized for reading an online document.

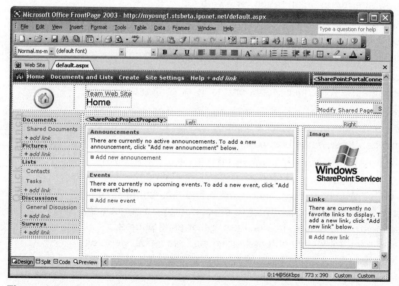

Figure 1-5. In FrontPage you can create a new SharePoint team Web site. This figure shows the home page of a newly created team site opened for editing in FrontPage.

 ## What's New in Office 2003

The following sections briefly describe many of the new features and enhancements found in Office 2003. (Office 2003 has so many new features and enhancements that it would be difficult to list them all!)

New Shared Office 2003 Features

Each of the following new features is available in most—or many—of the major Office 2003 applications.

Getting Started task pane   Most of the major Office applications now have a Getting Started task pane, which contains a basic collection of commands and features that are useful in each application. For example, the Getting Started task pane in Word lets you open an existing document, create a new document, or access Word information and resources (such as templates) on the Microsoft Office Online Web site (see Figure 1-2).

Help task pane   The Help command in Office applications now opens the new Help task pane, which you can use to search for help information in local help files as well as from the Microsoft Office Online Web site.

Research task pane   In Word, Excel, PowerPoint, and Outlook you can use the new Research task pane to look up information from local and Internet information sources.

Office Online   Office applications now provide more integrated tools for locating and using resources on the Office Web site, known as Office Online. These resources include assistance (help information), Office training, templates for Office applications, clip art and other media clips, Office updates, and services from the Office Marketplace site. Most of the tools for accessing these resources are located in Office task panes.

Enhanced thesaurus   An enhanced online thesaurus available in Word, Excel, PowerPoint, and Outlook uses the new Research task pane.

Templates from Office Online   Office 2003 provides a larger collection of downloadable online templates and wizards for creating new Office documents—through the Office Online Web site—and it makes it easier to find, download, and use these templates.

Information Rights Management   Word, Excel, PowerPoint, and the Outlook Message form now allow you to use Information Rights Management to restrict access to a sensitive document that you distribute or a sensitive message that you send. You do this by using the new File, Permission menu command or the Permission toolbar button.

My Recent Documents   The Open and Open Office Document dialog boxes now include a My Recent Documents folder that lets you quickly reopen recently opened folders or Office documents.

Side by side document viewing   Word and Excel now let you quickly display two documents side by side and synchronize scrolling in the two documents, making it easy to scan and visually compare the documents' contents.

Smart documents   Word and Excel now allow Office solutions developers to create documents that display custom, context-sensitive task panes. These documents are known as smart documents.

Internet faxing You can now send faxes from an Office application using an Outlook e-mail message and an Internet fax service.

Simplified customization You can use the new Rearrange Commands dialog box to customize toolbars and menus, all by issuing commands within a single dialog box.

Windows SharePoint Services A new SharePoint version, now known as Windows Share-Point Services (WSS), provides enhanced features that can be accessed through a browser or from Office 2003 applications, including the following:

- *Document workspaces*, which are special-purpose SharePoint Web sites designed for a group of colleagues to work together on a set of documents. You can create a document workspace within a SharePoint team Web site using your browser or through an Office application.

- *Meeting workspaces*, which are special-purpose SharePoint Web sites designed for a group of colleagues to plan a meeting. You can create a meeting workspace within a SharePoint team Web site using your browser or through a Meeting form in Outlook.

- *Picture libraries* for sharing collections of graphics files.

- *Form libraries* for creating, storing, and sharing XML-based business forms managed by InfoPath or another Windows SharePoint Services-compatible XML editor.

- Issue tracking lists for working with issues or problems that need to be resolved.

- Custom free-form Web pages known as *Web part pages*, which are built from predefined components known as *Web parts*.

- Customizing a team Web site's home page using your browser.

- Viewing the contents of a document library, list, or other information component in a datasheet format.

- Creating subfolders within a document library, picture library, or form library.

- Checking out a file in a document library, picture library, or form library so that only you can make changes to it.

- Working with file versions in a document library, picture library, or form library.

- Linking an events list to Outlook so that you can view your SharePoint events in an Outlook calendar folder.

- Linking a contacts list to Outlook so that you can view your SharePoint contacts in an Outlook contacts folder. Also, importing contacts from Outlook to a SharePoint contacts list.

- Exporting the list of items contained in a document library, list, or other information component to Excel.

New Word Features

Reading Layout view   Word's new Reading Layout view displays a document in a format that's optimized for online reading. It divides the document into small pages that fit completely within the screen, and features a large, smoothed font and a simpler application interface.

Formatting and editing restrictions   When you protect a shared Word document, you can now restrict the types of formatting and editing actions that other users can perform in the document. You can also exempt specific regions of a document from editing restrictions.

Enhanced translation feature   Word's enhanced translation feature lets you translate a word, phrase, or sentence into a different language, using the new Research task pane together with bilingual dictionaries on your computer or on the Internet.

General XML document editing   Word now lets you create, edit, view, or validate a custom XML document that conforms to any schema that you supply. Word also allows you to apply a custom transform to an XML document so that it can be displayed in Word using any Word formatting, text, or graphics.

New Excel Features

Enhanced List commands   Excel 2003 provides a set of new commands for working with a List, most notably the ability to publish a List on a SharePoint team Web site.

Enhanced XML support   You can now import, view, analyze, modify, and export XML data that conforms to any XML schema that you provide. You can import XML data from a variety of sources, including XML documents, Web services, or databases that can return data in XML format. You can now also work directly with the XML elements within the worksheet.

New PowerPoint Features

Smart tag recognizers   PowerPoint now lets you use smart tag recognizers to convert specific types of data in your presentations—such as dates, financial symbols, and names—to smart tags that you can use to perform useful actions on the data—such as looking up a stock quote for a financial symbol.

Package for CD   The new Package for CD feature replaces the Pack and Go feature in previous versions of PowerPoint and lets you copy your presentation to a CD or other portable medium. You can have Package for CD copy all linked files and include a complete PowerPoint viewer program that you can use to run a slide show on a computer that doesn't have PowerPoint itself installed.

New Outlook Features

Navigation pane   The new Navigation pane replaces the former Outlook Bar. The lower portion of the Navigation pane contains a set of buttons you can click to select a particular type of information (e-mail messages, calendar items, contacts, and so on), and the upper portion of the Navigation pane displays folder lists and tools for working with the selected information type.

Search folders   You can use Outlook's new search folders to selectively view e-mail messages or other items that meet specified criteria—for example, to view unread e-mail messages, large messages, or messages flagged for follow-up.

Reading pane   You can display the new Reading pane, which replaces the former Preview pane, either at the right of the Outlook window or at the bottom of the window.

Arranging items   You can use the commands on the new View, Arrange By submenu to quickly sort or group Outlook items that are displayed in a table view. The commands on this submenu sort or group the items using a set of 13 standard categories, such as Date, Conversation, From, and To.

Enhanced junk e-mail filter   Outlook now includes an enhanced filter that gives you more control over the management of unwanted e-mail messages.

HTML message security   You can now have Outlook block all external content contained in incoming HTML messages to avoid signaling junk e-mailers that you have received their messages. Also, you can now opt to view all HTML messages in plain text to prevent scripts from running.

Shared Attachments   You can now send an Office document in an e-mail message as a *shared attachment*. Sending a shared attachment creates a shared copy of the document in a SharePoint document workspace, which provides an environment where the message recipients can collaborate on developing the document.

Faxing   You can now send and receive faxes in Outlook using an Internet fax service.

Side-by-side calendars   If you have more than one calendar folder available in Outlook 2003, you can now open several of these folders at the same time and view them side by side in the Outlook window.

Viewing SharePoint events lists   You can now open and view a SharePoint events list in Outlook as a calendar folder. This feature allows you to view and work with a shared calendar belonging to your SharePoint team within the Outlook environment.

SharePoint meeting workspaces   In Outlook you can now create a meeting workspace on a SharePoint team Web site and link it to an Outlook Meeting form to help organize the meeting that you're planning.

Viewing SharePoint contacts lists   You can now open and view a SharePoint contacts list in Outlook as a contacts folder. This feature allows you to view and work with a shared list of contacts belonging to your SharePoint team within the Outlook environment.

Name smart tag button   When you view an incoming or outgoing message in the Preview pane or open it in a Message form, Outlook now displays a smart tag button next to any name or e-mail address that appears in the message header. You can click this button to schedule a meeting with the person, contact the person using instant messaging, add the person to your Contacts folder, or perform other tasks.

Quick flags   You can now quickly add a flag to an e-mail message displayed in the Outlook window by simply clicking the Flag Status button at the right end of the message.

New Access Features

Database backups   Access provides a new command for backing up a database to a series of backup files.

Enhanced XML support   You can now create a table by importing any XML document or schema, optionally converting the format of the data according to a transform file that you supply. You can also export a table to an XML document or schema, optionally generating a Web page, and transform for viewing the table data in a browser.

Smart Tags property   You can use the new Smart Tags property to add a smart tag recognizer to a field, which displays a button and allows you to perform actions on recognized data (such as looking up a stock quote for a financial symbol).

New FrontPage Features

Revamped interface   The FrontPage Views bar has been replaced by the new Web Site tab. You now access the specific tools you want by first clicking a tab—the Web Site tab to access the Web site management tools or a file tab to edit an open Web page or source code file. You then select a view for that tab by clicking a view button at the bottom of the window. The new Split view of a Web page displays two panes—you can work on the page's design in one and on its HTML source code in the other.

Dynamic templates   You can now attach to a Web page a *dynamic template*, which provides content and formatting, restricts the areas where the page can be modified, and keeps the page up-to-date with template modifications.

Layout tables and cells   You can use FrontPage's new layout tables and cells to quickly arrange and format the content on your pages. You can choose from a variety of pre-defined layout tables or draw your own.

Enhanced find and replace   You can now search for and replace specific HTML elements, you can save and reuse your search criteria, and you can employ several new search options (such as using regular expressions in your search text).

Enhanced preview   You can now preview your Web pages in several browsers simultaneously, and you can simulate different browser resolutions when designing or previewing a page.

Enhanced publishing   The new Remote Web Site view has replaced the former Publish Web dialog box, and allows you to exchange and synchronize files between the opened FrontPage Web site and a remote Web site. You can now publish to FTP (File Transfer Protocol) servers and DAV (Distributed Authoring and Versioning) servers, as well as to servers with Microsoft extensions or to disk locations.

New reports   Reports view now includes a set of reports that show the status of shared Web site content—dynamic templates, shared borders, style sheet links, or themes.

Quick Tag Selector   You can use the new Quick Tag Selector to work directly with a page's HTML tags while you work in Design view.

Enhanced source code editor   You can now use FrontPage's source code editor to edit any type of source code file or other plain text file. The editor also provides new tools for working with code—for example, an IntelliSense feature that assists you in inserting HTML tags, code snippet commands for storing and inserting frequently used blocks of code, and an XML View toolbar for working on XML documents.

Packages   You can now create specialized SharePoint Web sites using Web site templates known as *packages*—for example, an issue tracking site for a workgroup, a news and review site for an organization, or a Web log.

Web part pages   If you are creating or customizing a SharePoint team Web site in FrontPage, you can now use FrontPage to create a *Web part page*, which is a free-form Web page that you can quickly build by adding and customizing predefined components known *Web parts*.

New Application: InfoPath

Design   Create or customize flexible and dynamic electronic forms based on XML.

Fill out   Complete forms using editing tools similar to those provided by other Office applications.

Deliver   Send forms to the next destination in your organization's workflow by printing them, forwarding them using e-mail, saving them on a shared network or Internet location, or submitting them directly to a data source.

Installing and Configuring Office 2003

Installing Office 2003 from the CD......17   Revisiting Office Setup...............22
Activating Office 2003 20

Installing Office 2003 from the CD

To install the Microsoft Office System on your computer from the product CD, perform the following steps:

1 Insert the first Office CD into your CD-ROM drive. If AutoPlay is enabled on your computer, the Office Setup program will run automatically. If for some reason Setup doesn't start, you'll need to manually run the Setup.exe program in the root folder of the Office CD.

Using the Windows Installer program, Setup will now guide you through the process of installing Office 2003.

2 Complete the first three Setup dialog boxes. In the Product Key dialog box, you need to enter the product key displayed on the label on the Office CD container. In the User Information dialog box, you need to enter your name, your initials, and (optionally) the name of your organization. In the End-User License Agreement dialog box, you need to accept the Office 2003 license agreement.

> **Note** To see an explanation of the options in the currently displayed Setup dialog box, click the Help button in the lower-left corner.

3 In the Type Of Installation dialog box (the fourth Setup dialog box), shown in Figure 2-1, choose the type of installation you want.

The exact options you'll see depend on whether a previous version of Office was installed on your computer. To obtain an explanation of a particular option, select it and you'll see a description in the Description area of the dialog box.

With any of the installation options, you can change the default installation location by typing a new folder path into the Install To text box or by clicking the Browse button to select an installation folder.

> **Note** Keep in mind that the set of Office 2003 components you choose to install isn't final. You can later rerun Office Setup to add or remove components, as explained in "Revisiting Office Setup," on page 22. Setup will remember and display the exact set of applications, tools, and features you previously installed. You can then adjust that set, adding or removing specific features.

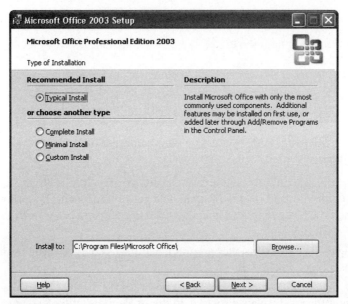

Figure 2-1. The installation type you select in the fourth Setup dialog box determines the basic set of components that are installed. Here, a previous version of Office wasn't installed.

> **Note** Steps 4 through 6 in this procedure apply only if you selected the Custom Install option (whether or not you had a previous Office version installed).

4 In the Custom Setup dialog box (the fifth Setup dialog box), shown in Figure 2-2, check the major Office 2003 applications you want to install. To choose the specific application features and Office tools that will be installed, check the Choose Advanced Customization Of Applications option.

Figure 2-2. In the fifth Office Setup dialog box, you can select the main Office applications that will be installed.

5 If, in the fifth Setup dialog box, you checked the Choose Advanced Customization Of Applications option, Setup will now display the Advanced Customization dialog box, shown in Figure 2-3, where you can select the specific application features and Office tools that you want to install.

Figure 2-3. In this Setup dialog box, you can select the specific application features and Office 2003 tools you want to install.

To control the installation of a particular application, tool, or feature, expand the hierarchy if necessary to reveal the component and click the down arrow to open the menu of choices, as shown below:

Then, choose Run From My Computer to install the component, choose Run All From My Computer to install the component plus all components underlying it in the hierarchy, choose Installed On First Use to have Office prompt you to install the component the first time you attempt to use it, or choose Not Available to omit installing the component.

Note If you choose Run From My Computer for a component, you won't be able to choose Not Available for an underlying component that's required. If you choose Installed On First Use for a component, all underlying components will also be installed on first use, except a component that was tagged as Not Available. If you choose Not Available for a component, all underlying components will also be tagged as Not Available.

6   If you had a previous version of Office installed on your computer when you ran Setup, you'll now see the Previous Version Of Office dialog box. In this dialog box, choose whether to have Setup remove your complete previous Office version, preserve your complete previous Office version, or remove one or more specific applications from your previous version.

Note You *must* remove any previous version of Microsoft Outlook that you have installed on your computer.

7   Setup will now display the Summary dialog box, which will show a list of the applications that will be installed. Click the Install button to complete the installation.

Activating Office 2003

After you install Office 2003 on your computer, you're required to *activate* it. If you don't activate Office, you'll be able to start an Office application only 50 times, and then you'll be required to activate it. Activation involves connecting with Microsoft on the Internet or by telephone.

> **Note** If you haven't activated Office 2003 after running Office applications 50 times, you'll still be able to start an application, but it will run in Reduced Functionality Mode, which will prevent you from saving or creating new documents and possibly from using certain other features. You can activate Office 2003 at any time before or after reaching the Reduced Functionality Mode, and you'll then have unlimited use of Office.

The first time you run an Office application, it displays the Microsoft Office 2003 Activation Wizard, shown in Figure 2-4, which allows you to activate Office 2003. You can now do one of the following:

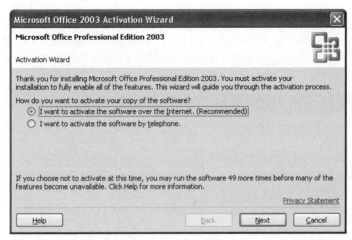

Figure 2-4. The Activation Wizard allows you to activate Office 2003 through the Internet or by telephone.

- To activate Office 2003 through the Internet, select the I Want To Activate The Software Over The Internet option and then click the Next button. The wizard will then automatically activate your Office 2003 installation.

> **Note** After the activation of Office is complete, you can click the Register Now button in the final Activation Wizard dialog box to register your copy of Office, although doing so is optional.

- To activate the product by telephoning the Microsoft Product Activation Center, select the I Want To Activate The Software By Telephone option and then click the Next button to see complete instructions for calling the Product Activation Center and completing the activation process.
- To skip the activation and immediately run the application, click the Cancel button. Keep in mind, however, that you'll be able to run the product with full functionality a total of only 50 times before activating, and in the meantime the Activation Wizard will keep coming up every time you start an Office 2003 application.

You can run the Activation Wizard at any time by choosing Activate Product from the Help menu of an Office 2003 application.

Revisiting Office Setup

You can rerun Office Setup in *maintenance mode* at any time to add or remove specific features, to repair or reinstall Office 2003 if you've been having serious problems with one or more programs or features and you suspect that program files or registry settings may have become corrupted, or to remove Office 2003 from your computer. To use Setup in maintenance mode, complete the following steps:

> **Note** The specific instructions given here are for Microsoft Windows XP. The procedure for other Windows versions is similar.

1   Run the Add Or Remove Programs utility in the Windows Control Panel, select the Microsoft Office 2003 item in the list, and click the Change button. The first Setup maintenance-mode dialog box will appear, which is titled Maintenance Mode Options and is shown in Figure 2-5.

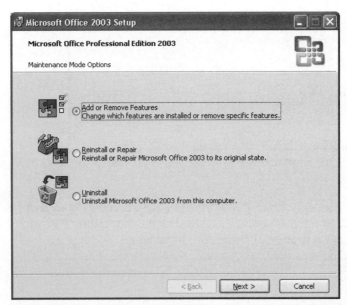

Figure 2-5.   When you run the Office Setup program after installing Office 2003, it begins by displaying the Maintenance Mode Options dialog box.

2   In the Maintenance Mode Options dialog box, select an option (as explained in the following list), click the Next button, and fill in any additional dialog boxes or message boxes that are displayed.

■   To add or remove one or more Office applications or features, select Add Or Remove Features. Setup will display the same installation options you selected when you most recently ran Setup. You need to change only the installation options for features you want to add or remove; the rest of your installation won't be disturbed.

- To repair your Office installation or, if necessary, to completely reinstall the Office applications and features that have already been installed, select the Reinstall Or Repair option. In the next dialog box you can then select one of the following options:

  - To force Setup to reinstall all Office 2003 files and redo all registry settings, whether or not they appear to be defective, select Reinstall Office.

  - To have Setup detect defective files or settings and make just the repairs that are necessary, select Detect And Repair Errors In My Office Installation. If you're in doubt about which option to select, you might choose this simpler option first and select the more radical Reinstall Office option only if your problem persists. If you've changed or deleted any of the default shortcuts that Office Setup adds to your Windows Start menu and you want to restore the original shortcuts, check the Restore My Start Menu Shortcuts option.

- To completely remove Office 2003 from your computer, select Uninstall.

> **Note** Another way to have Office 2003 detect and repair errors in your Office 2003 installation is to choose the Detect And Repair command from the Help menu of any of the major Office applications. This command provides an additional option that discards your customized settings and restores all defaults.

> **Tip** **Avoid problems by updating Office**
>
> A good way to avoid having problems with Office applications is to frequently check for new Office service packs or application patches (also known as *hotfixes*). One of the most important reasons for regularly updating Office is that updating will remove the security vulnerabilities that Microsoft has identified and has provided fixes for. To check for updates, choose the Help, Check For Updates command in any of the major Office applications.
>
> Note that the Check For Updates command will be nonfunctional if the Show Content And Links From Microsoft Office Online option is cleared. This is one of the online content options you can set by choosing Help, Customer Feedback Options and displaying the Online Content category in the Service Options dialog box.

Getting Expert Help on Office 2003

Getting Help with the Assistant 25

Getting Help with the Ask
A Question List .29

NEW FEATURE! Getting Help Using the Help
Task Pane. 30

NEW FEATURE! Finding Resources on Office Online. 33

Getting Help with the Assistant

In Office 2003 you can use the Assistant, shown below, to get help quickly by typing plain English questions or phrases.

To use the Assistant, complete the following steps:

1 If the Assistant isn't visible, choose Help, Show The Office Assistant.

> **Note** When you choose the Help, Show The Office Assistant command, the Assistant is *turned on*—if it hasn't already been turned on—and it will remain turned on until you explicitly turn it off, as described later in this section. When the Assistant is turned on, it will automatically display help in various situations that are described later in this section.

2 If the Assistant balloon isn't visible, click the Assistant to display it:

(To hide the balloon, click the Assistant again.)

> **Note** When the Assistant is displayed on the screen, Office shows messages using the Assistant balloon rather than the usual message box. For example, if you close a document containing unsaved changes, Office will display the "Do you want to save the changes to the document?" message in the Assistant balloon rather than in a standard message box.
>
> Messages appear in the Assistant, however, only if the Display Alerts option is checked in the Options tab in the Office Assistant dialog box, described later in this section.

3 Type a question or phrase, in ordinary English, into the Assistant balloon—for example, "How do I use Help?"—and click the Search button. The Office application will then open the Search Results task pane, a new feature in Office 2003, which will display a list of help topics matching your question, as shown in Figure 3-1.

> **Note** The Search Results task pane will show help topics from help files that are installed on your computer. It will also show help topics downloaded from the Office Online Web site provided that the following two online content options are checked: Show Content And Links From Microsoft Office Online and Search Online Content When Connected. For information on these options, see the tip "Setting online content options," on page 32.

Figure 3-1. The Search Results task pane shows the topics that were found for the question "How do I use Help?"

4 Scroll through the topics, if necessary, by using the scroll bars. Then click the topic you want to view. The help text will appear in a separate Help window, as shown in Figure 3-2.

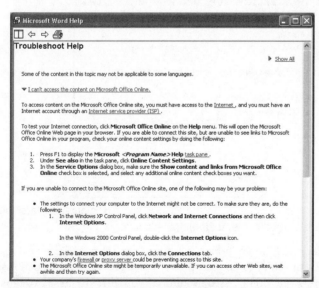

Figure 3-2. This help information appears if you click the Troubleshoot Help topic in the Search Results task pane.

> For more information on using the Search Results task pane, see "Getting Help Using the Help Task Pane," later in the chapter.

You can work with the Assistant in the following ways:

- To hide the Assistant, choose Help, Hide The Office Assistant. Or right-click the Assistant and choose Hide from the shortcut menu.

> **Note** Don't confuse merely *hiding* the Assistant with *turning off* the Assistant. When you hide the Assistant, it's removed from the screen but it will still automatically appear in various situations (described later).

- To turn off or to customize the Assistant, click the Options button in the Assistant balloon, or right-click the Assistant itself and choose Options from the shortcut menu. This will display the Office Assistant dialog box.

In the Options tab of the Office Assistant dialog box, shown in Figure 3-3, you can turn off the Assistant by clearing the Use The Office Assistant check box and you can modify the way the Assistant works by checking or clearing other options. If one or more of the options in the Show Tips About area are checked, the Assistant periodically displays a light bulb to indicate that it has a tip relevant to your current actions. To read the tip, click the bulb. (If the Assistant is turned on but hidden, the light bulb appears on the Help toolbar button, which you can click to read the tip.)

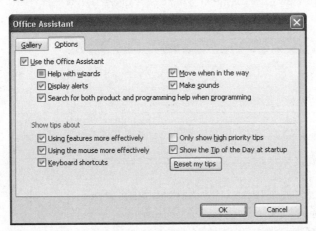

Figure 3-3. The Options tab in the Office Assistant dialog box lets you turn off the Assistant or modify the Assistant's behavior.

In the Gallery tab, shown in Figure 3-4, you can select a different Assistant, such as The Dot, F1, or Office Logo (Clippit is the default Assistant, which is shown in the figures in this chapter). The Assistant options you select in these two tabs affect all Office applications.

Chapter 3

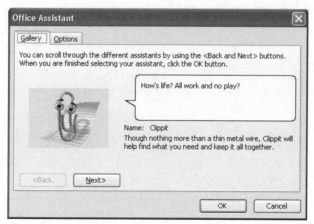

Figure 3-4. The Gallery tab in the Office Assistant dialog box lets you view different Assistants and select the one you want.

Getting Help with the Ask A Question List

Office 2003 provides a convenient alternative to using the Assistant: the Ask A Question list. You can now get help by typing a question or phrase, in plain English, into the Ask A Question drop-down list that you'll find in the upper right corner of every major Office application, and then pressing Enter.

If you want to repeat a question you've already typed into the Ask A Question list during the current application session, you can simply select the question from the drop-down list.The Ask A Question list works just like the Assistant, and it will find and display the identical list of topics in the Search Results task pane, as shown in Figure 3-1. Scroll through the topics, if necessary, by using the scroll bars. Then click the topic you want to view. The help text will be displayed in a separate Help window, as shown in Figure 3-2.

> **Note** The Search Results task pane will show help topics from help files that are installed on your computer. It will also show help topics downloaded from the Office Online Web site provided that the following two online content options are checked: Show Content And Links From Office Online and Search Office Online Content Automatically When Connected. For information on this option, see the tip "Setting online content options," on page 32.

> For more information on using the Search Results task pane, see the next section, "Getting Help Using the Help Task Pane."

Getting Help Using the Help Task Pane

A third way to obtain Office help information is to use the new Help task pane, shown in Figure 3-5. The Help task pane not only lets you ask a help question, like the Assistant and the Ask A Question list, but also lets you browse through the contents of the help information for the current application and to access resources on the Office Online Web site. To use the Help task pane, perform the following steps:

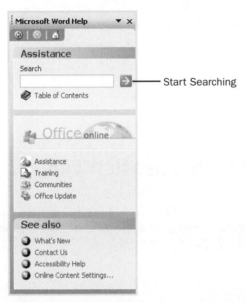

Figure 3-5. This Help task pane appears in Microsoft Word.

 1 Display the Help task pane by clicking the Help button on the Standard toolbar; by choosing Help, *Application* Help (where *Application* is the name of the current application, such as Microsoft Word); or by pressing F1.

2 To ask a help question—such as "How do I use Help?"—type your question in the Search For text box and then click the Start Searching button or press Enter.

As with the Assistant and the Ask A Question list, the topics matching your question will appear in the Search Results task pane, as shown in Figure 3-1. Scroll through the topics, if necessary, by using the scroll bars. When you find the topic you want, you can click the topic title to view the help text for that specific topic in a separate Help window, as shown in Figure 3-2. Or, if a description of the help information section that contains the topic appears in light type below the topic title, you can click that description to browse through the entire section of the help information.

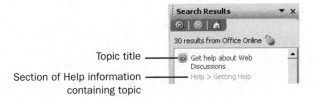

Topic title ——————— Get help about Web
Discussions

Section of Help information ——————— Help > Getting Help
containing topic

If you don't find an appropriate help topic, scroll to the bottom of the topic list to see a
list of links to other places to look, as shown in Figure 3-6. You can also use the Search
area at the bottom of the Search Results task pane to search for other Office resources
that might help, as explained in the following section.

Figure 3-6.   When the topic list in the Search Results task pane has been
scrolled to the end, it provides a list of links to other places you can look for help.

Microsoft Office System Inside Out—2003 Edition

Tip Setting online content options

The Search Results task pane will show help topics from help files that are installed on your computer. It will also show help topics downloaded from the Office Online Web site provided that the following two online content options are checked: Show Content And Links From Microsoft Office Online and Search Online Content When Connected.

You can access the online content options by choosing Help, Customer Feedback Options and selecting the Online Content category in the Service Options dialog box, as shown in Figure 3-7. Alternatively, you can click the Online Content Settings command at the bottom of the Help task pane. The settings you select in the Online Content category will be applied to every Office application (not just the current one) as soon as you restart the application.

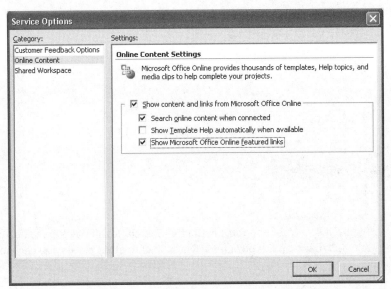

Figure 3-7.   You can control the display of online content in Office applications using the Online Content category in the Service Options dialog box.

3 To browse through the contents of the help information for the current Office applica-tion, click the Table Of Contents command in the Assistance area of the Help task pane. An expandable/collapsible table of contents will replace the original contents of the Help task pane (see Figure 3-8). To view a topic, click it. To return to the original Help task pane, click the Back button in the upper-left corner of the task pane.

Back

Forward

Figure 3-8. Here, the Help task pane displays the table of contents for the help information on Word.

4 To access helpful pages on the Microsoft Office Online Web site, you can click the links in the Microsoft Office Online area of the Help task pane.

5 To read useful general help topics, you can use the commands in the See Also area at the bottom of the Help task pane.

Finding Resources on Office Online

You can use the search tools provided in the Getting Started task pane or the Search Results task pane to locate relevant resources available from the Microsoft Office Online Web site. The resources include assistance (help information), Office training, templates for Office applications, clip art and other media clips, services from the Office Marketplace site, and research information.

> **Note** An alternative way to locate resources on the Office Online Web site is to open the site in your browser and browse through the pages or use the site's search tools. You can have an Office application run your browser and open the home page of the Office Online site by choosing Microsoft Office Online from the Office application's Help menu.
>
> Note, however, that *neither the Microsoft Office Online command nor the Office Online search tools described in this section will be available if the Show Content And Links From Microsoft Office Online option is currently cleared.* For information on this option, see the tip "Setting online content options," on page 32.

Chapter 3

To use the Office Online search tools, perform the following steps:

1 Open the Getting Started task pane by pressing Ctrl+F1 to open the most recently displayed task pane, and then, if necessary, clicking the Home button at the top of the task pane to switch to the Getting Started task pane (see Figure 3-9). Alternatively, if you've already performed a search using either the search tools described in this section or the Office Help feature described previously in the chapter, Office will display your results in the Search Results task pane, and you can use the search tools found at the bottom of this pane (see Figure 3-6). The advantage of using the search tools in the Search Results task pane is that you can select a particular area of Office Online to search.

Figure 3-9. This figure shows the Getting Started task pane that appears in Word.

2 If you are using the search tools at the bottom of the Search Results task pane, in the Search drop-down list, select the area on Office Online where you want to look for resources.

> **Note** If you select Research in the Search drop-down list, after you enter your search text and click the Start Searching button, Office will open the Research task pane and enter your search text in the Search For text box. You can then carry out your search using the instructions given in "Using the Research Task Pane," on page 44.

3 In the text box, enter a brief description of the resources you're trying to locate—for example, *Excel PivotTables* or *document translation*—and then press Enter or click the

Start Searching button. Office will then search the Microsoft Office Online site and display a list of matching resources in the Search Results task pane (shown in Figure 3-6). To access a resource, click it in the list.

To refine your search or to perform a different search, you can use the search tools found at the bottom of the Search Results task pane.

Tip **Connect to the author's Web site**

For additional help on Office, you can connect to Michael J. Young's Web site at *www.mjy-Online.com*. This site provides a companion Web page for *Microsoft Office System Inside Out—2003 Edition* (including book information, error reports, and links to related sites), an Office Tips page (including a list of current links to Office help resources and reader questions and answers), recommendations for books about Office, and information on contacting the author.

Part 2
Using Shared Office 2003 Application Features

4   Working with Office 2003 Applications,
    Documents, and Program Windows   39

5   Using Speech and Handwriting
    in Office 2003   83

6   Adding Professional Graphics and Special
    Effects to Office 2003 Documents   107

7   Exchanging Data in Office 2003   153

NEW FEATURE! 8   Using Windows SharePoint Services
    in Professional Workgroups   177

9   Customizing the Office 2003 Application
    Interface   209

Working with Office 2003 Applications, Documents, and Program Windows

Running the Office Applications 39

Using the Task Panes in Office Applications 42

Creating New Office Documents. 47

Opening Existing Office Documents 56

Saving Office Documents. 69

Working with Multiple Documents. 74

Using Office Document Properties. 76

NEW FEATURE! Using Information Rights Management to Restrict Document Permissions 80

Running the Office Applications

When the Setup program finishes installing Microsoft Office 2003 Edition on your computer, you won't be at a loss for ways to run the Office programs. Office provides many ways for you to run its applications and utilities. Here's a summary of these techniques to help you find the easiest method to use in various situations.

> **Note** If you have a version of Microsoft Windows prior to Windows XP, or if you've chosen the "Classic" Start menu in Windows XP, the All Programs submenu will be labeled Programs.

Microsoft Office submenu You can run any of the major Office applications you've installed by choosing the application from the Start menu in Windows; click Start, All Programs (or Programs), Microsoft Office, and then choose the application. In Microsoft Office Word, Microsoft Office Excel, Microsoft Office PowerPoint, and Microsoft Office FrontPage the application will open with a new, blank document.

> **Note** In this book, the expression "major Office applications" refers to the main Office applications that are covered in the book—namely Word, Excel, PowerPoint, Microsoft Office Outlook, Microsoft Office Access, FrontPage, and Microsoft Office InfoPath.

New Office Document command You can create a new Office document based on a template and run the corresponding Office application by clicking the Start button in Windows and choosing All Programs (or Programs), New Office Document. This will display the New Office Document dialog box.

> The New Office Document dialog box is explained in "Creating New Office Documents," on page 47.

Open Office Document command   You can open an existing Office document and run the appropriate Office application by clicking the Start button in Windows and choosing All Programs (or Programs), Open Office Document. This will display the Open Office Document dialog box.

The **Open Office Document** dialog box is explained in "Opening Existing Office Documents," on page 56.

Quick Launch toolbar   You can run Outlook by clicking the Launch Microsoft Outlook button on the Quick Launch toolbar displayed on the Windows taskbar. Note that the icon for Outlook doesn't appear on the Quick Launch toolbar until after the first time you run Outlook.

You can easily install additional buttons on the Quick Launch toolbar for running other Office applications, opening documents, or displaying folders (see Figure 4-1).

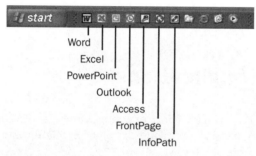

Word
Excel
PowerPoint
Outlook
Access
FrontPage
InfoPath

Figure 4-1.   You can set up the Quick Launch toolbar so that it allows you to quickly open any of the major Office applications.

The fastest way to add a button to the Quick Launch toolbar is to *right-drag*—drag using the right mouse button—the appropriate object (file, shortcut, or folder) from a folder (displayed in Windows Explorer, a folder window, or the desktop), drop it on the Quick Launch toolbar, and then choose Create Shortcuts Here from the shortcut menu, as shown here:

(If the Create Shortcuts Here command isn't available, choose Copy Here instead.)

You can also drag a command from the Start menu using this same method. This is a good way to quickly add buttons to the Quick Launch toolbar for running Office applications and other programs.

Folder   You can run an Office application and open an existing Office document by double-clicking the document—or a shortcut to the document—in a folder displayed in

Chapter 4

Windows Explorer, a folder window, or the Windows desktop. You can run an Office application by double-clicking a shortcut to that program.

Note If you've enabled Web-style single-clicking in Windows, substitute "single-click" for "double-click" in these instructions.

You can easily include shortcuts on the Windows desktop—or in any other folder—for running Office applications, opening documents, or displaying folders. To do this, right-drag as discussed under the previous item in this list, but drop the object on the desktop (or in the folder) rather than on the Quick Launch toolbar.

Tip Double-clicking an Office template or a wizard file creates a new document based on that template. For information on templates and wizards, see "Creating New Office Documents," on page 47.

Microsoft Office Tools submenu You can run the tools or utilities provided with Office from the Microsoft Office Tools submenu, which you open by choosing All Programs (or Programs), Microsoft Office, Microsoft Office Tools from the Start menu in Windows. The Microsoft Office Tools submenu is shown here:

Inside Out

No Office Shortcut Bar

As of the 2003 Editions, Office no longer includes the Office Shortcut Bar. However, you can set up the Quick Launch toolbar, using the methods just explained, to obtain much of the same utility.

Note Some of the Office tools run only when you embed an object in an Office document and can't be run as freestanding programs. These applications, which include Microsoft Graph and Microsoft Equation, are known as OLE (object linking and embedding) servers. They're discussed in Chapter 6, "Adding Professional Graphics and Special Effects to Office 2003 Documents."

41

Using the Task Panes in Office Applications

The new Office application *task panes* can—or must—be used to execute many of the commands discussed in this book. You'll find them in all the major Office applications. A task pane is a Web-style area that you can either dock along one of the four edges of the window or float anywhere on the screen. It displays information, commands, and controls for choosing options (check boxes, buttons, lists, and so on). Like links on a Web page, the commands on a task pane are highlighted in blue text, they're underlined when you move the mouse pointer over them, and you run them with a single click (see Figure 4-2).

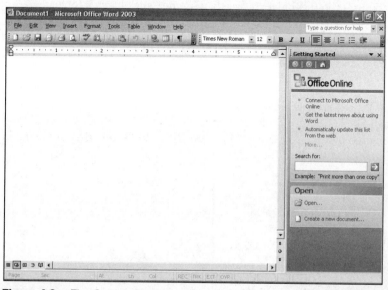

Figure 4-2. The Getting Started task pane is shown here displayed on the right side of the Word window.

Although a task pane takes up a lot of space on the screen and adds to the many ways to perform tasks, it has some unique advantages over a dialog box—primarily that you can easily work with a task pane and with your document at the same time. A task pane doesn't cover your work, nor does it require that you close it before resuming other tasks. It's especially valuable for performing fairly complex jobs, such as creating form letters in Word or searching for files using multiple criteria.

A task pane pops up automatically when you perform certain tasks—for example, when you choose File, New to create a new document.

To display a task pane at any time, choose View, Task Pane. Or, use any of the standard methods for displaying a toolbar, namely:

- Choose View, Toolbars, Task Pane.
- Right-click the menu bar or any toolbar and choose Task Pane from the shortcut menu.

> **Note** These methods for displaying the task pane aren't all available in every Office application. In Outlook (in the main window or in a form), if a task pane hasn't yet been displayed, the only way to get the task pane to appear is to choose Help, Microsoft Outlook Help or press F1. Either of these commands will display the Help task pane, from which you can navigate to the other panes.

Each of these methods opens the task pane that was most recently displayed. You then need to navigate to the particular task pane you want to work with. You can go to any of the main application task panes by clicking the title bar at the top of the initial pane (but don't click the Close button, which is marked with an X at the right end of the title bar!). Then, choose the name of the pane you want to open from the drop-down menu, as shown here:

Title bar

Note, however, that you can initially display some less frequently used or subsidiary task panes only by issuing an application command or by clicking a command in another pane. For example, you can initially display the Basic File Search task pane only by choosing File, File Search. And you can initially display the Advanced File Search task pane only by clicking the Advanced File Search command in the Basic File Search pane.

You can navigate among the task panes you've recently displayed by clicking the Back and Forward Web-style buttons, as shown here:

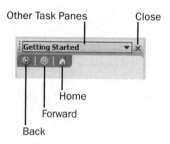

Each task pane contains a set of related commands. The particular task panes that are available depend on the Office application you're running. They're described throughout this book.

 ## Going to the Getting Started Task Pane

Each of the major applications in the Office System except Outlook and InfoPath has a Getting Started task pane. You can navigate to the Getting Started pane by clicking the Home button near the top of any other task pane. Each application's Getting Started task pane contains a basic collection of commands and features that are useful in that application. For example, the Getting Started task pane in Word lets you open an existing document, create a new document, or access Word information and resources (such as templates) on the Microsoft Office Online Web site (see Figure 4-2 on page 42).

 ## Using the Research Task Pane

In Word, Excel, PowerPoint, and Outlook you can use the new Research task pane to look up information from local information sources, as well as from information sources on the Internet. The Research task pane is initially configured to provide access to local information sources provided with Office 2003 (for example, thesauruses for various languages), research sources on the Microsoft Web sites (for example, the Encarta Encyclopedia), and several third-party Internet information sources (such as Factiva for news searches). You can configure the Research task pane to access additional local information sources provided by your company and third-party information sources on the Internet. Whether local or on the Internet, these information sources are known in the Research task pane as *services*.

The following is the procedure for using the Research task pane:

Research

1 Open the Research task pane by using the general method described in the previous section or by using one of the following shortcuts:

   ■ Click the Research button on the Standard toolbar.

   ■ Choose Research from the Tools menu.

Chapter 4

The Office application will display the Research task pane, which is shown in Figure 4-3.

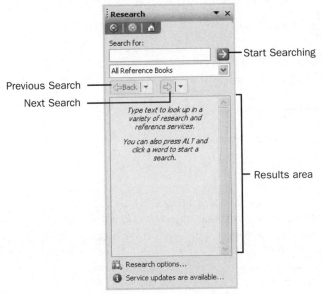

Figure 4-3. You can use the new Research task pane to look up information on local or Internet information services.

Note After you've installed Office 2003, the Research pane is also available in Microsoft Internet Explorer. To display it, click the Research button on Internet Explorer's Standard Buttons toolbar.

2 In the drop-down list below the Search For text box, select the information service you want to search. For example, to look up synonyms you could select a thesaurus for your language, such as Thesaurus: English (U.S.). The list contains several items that you can select to search an entire group of similar services; for instance, selecting All Reference Books searches all reference-book type services appearing in the list.

3 Type the search text you want to look for in the Search For text box; for example, to find synonyms for the word *lucid*, you'd type in that word. Then click the Start Searching button or press Enter. (During a lengthy search, the button will turn red and display an X, and you can click the button to halt the search.)

The search results will appear in the Results area. The way the information is displayed and used depends on the service(s) you searched, as well as on the particular Office application that you're running when you use the Research task pane (Word, Excel, or PowerPoint). For instance, if you're running Word and look up *lucid* in one of the thesauruses supplied with Office, the Results area will display a list of synonyms for each

Chapter 4

meaning of the word and also allow you to move the pointer over a synonym and click the down arrow to choose an action, as shown here:

> **Tip** **Quickly look up a word or phrase in your document**
>
> You can quickly look up a single word that appears in a document (that is, you can perform steps 1 through 3 of these instructions) by simply clicking the word while holding down the Alt key. You can look up a word or an entire phrase by selecting the text, clicking it with the right mouse button, and choosing Look Up from the shortcut menu.
>
> The Research feature will display the Research task pane and will search for the word or phrase using the information service that was most recently selected in the drop-down list. For example, if you had previously selected a thesaurus in the drop-down list, you could look up synonyms by simply clicking a word while pressing Alt. Or, if you had previously selected the Encarta Encyclopedia in the drop-down list, you could look up a phrase such as *Magna Carta* in this encyclopedia by selecting the phrase, right-clicking it, and choosing Look Up.

4 To view previous searches, use the Previous Search (Back) and Next Search buttons to navigate through the task panes for the searches.

5 To modify the Research task pane, click Research Options at the bottom of the pane. This will display the Research Options dialog box, which displays a list of your currently installed information services and allows you to perform one or more of the following modifications:

- ▪ Select the installed services that you want to appear in the drop-down list in the Research task pane. To select a service, check the box next to it.

- ▪ View or—in some cases—modify the properties of the selected service by clicking the Properties button.

- ▪ Install additional services by clicking the Add Services button. You can add any local or Internet information service that's compatible with Office's Research task pane.

- ▪ Update or remove the services that are currently installed by clicking the Update/Remove button.

Chapter 4

■ Make information services block potentially offensive results by clicking the Parental Control button. Note that not all services provide blocking, but you can limit your information searches to those that do.

Using Smart Documents

Microsoft Office Word 2003 and Microsoft Office Excel 2003 now allow Office solutions developers to create documents that display custom, context-sensitive task panes. These documents are known as *smart documents*. When you edit a smart document, or create a new document based on a smart document, the task pane will display relevant help information and useful tools that change according to the part of the document you are working on. The available content and actions can also vary according to your identity or other factors.

For example, if you were working on a Word smart document designed for creating an academic paper, the task pane could display information on the style rules for the particular part of the paper you are currently writing (the title page, abstract, introduction, footnotes, reference list, and so on). It might also provide boilerplate text you could insert in or formatting features you could apply to the current section of the paper (for example, a model reference that you could insert while working on the reference list or formatting features that you could apply while writing the title page). And, finally, it could allow you to perform actions that are relevant to various stages of writing the paper (for instance, it could connect you with journal databases or order copies of journals while you are working on the outline, or it could submit the paper to your instructor when you have completed it).

Creating New Office Documents

The methods for creating new Office documents are quite uniform among most of the major applications in the Office System—namely, Word, Excel, PowerPoint, Access, and FrontPage. The three basic methods for creating new Office documents are the following:

● Using the New Office Document dialog box
● Creating an empty Office document in a folder
● Using the New Document task pane

You can use the first two methods from Windows without first starting an Office program. With the third method you have to first decide which application you want to use to create the document and then run that application.

Creating a Document Using the New Office Document Dialog Box

The New Office Document dialog box (shown in Figure 4-4) lets you create almost any type of Office document. To use this dialog box, complete the following steps:

1 Open the dialog box by clicking the Start menu in Windows and choosing All Programs (or Programs), New Office Document.

Chapter 4

2 Click the tab corresponding to the general category of document you want to create (General, Letters & Faxes, Presentations, Spreadsheet Solutions, and so on).

3 Double-click the icon for the specific type of document you want to create. This will run the appropriate application and create the document. When you select a particular icon, the Preview area shows a preview image of the document, if one is available.

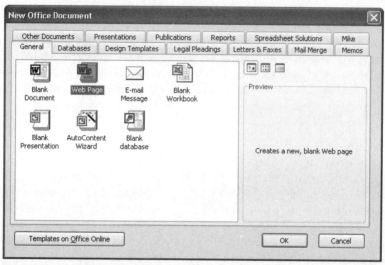

Figure 4-4. The New Office Document dialog box lets you create an Office document from Windows.

For information on the new Templates On Office Online button in the New Office Document dialog box, see "Downloading and Using Templates from Office Online," on page 55.

Almost all the icons in the New Office Document dialog box create a document by using a template or by running a wizard, giving you a head start in putting together a particular type of document. A *template* contains a blueprint for a specific document type and immediately creates the document, usually adding initial content to get you started. A *wizard* first displays a series of pages that let you customize the new document's content. An icon that runs a wizard is marked with a magic wand and usually has "wizard" in its name.

> **Note** FrontPage provides a large internal set of templates and wizards that you can use to create Web sites or Web pages. These templates and wizards, however, aren't available through the New Office Document dialog box. To use them, you need to run the application and create a new Web site or Web page using the program's commands, as explained in the part of this book covering FrontPage.

In the New Office Document dialog box, it might not be obvious which application will be used to create the document type you've selected. This dialog box conforms to the document-centric philosophy, according to which the type of document you're creating is more important than the particular application that you use to create it. In the real world, however, you'll probably want to know which application is used (maybe you're a whiz at Word, but a klutz with PowerPoint). The image in the icon indicates the application, but not always obviously (yes, the big W stands for Word and the big X for Excel, but the others aren't so apparent). To be certain, click the Details button to switch into the Details view. This view also clearly indicates whether the icon uses a template or runs a wizard (see Figure 4-5). You'll learn about the templates provided by specific applications—and how to work with them—in the parts of the book that cover the individual Office applications.

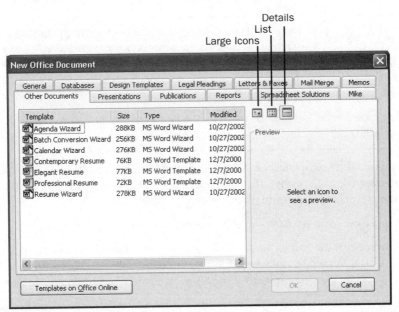

Figure 4-5. Viewing document types in Details view indicates which application is used to create a document.

Table 4-1 shows the extensions used for files that store Office templates and wizards.

Table 4-1. **Extensions Used for Template and Wizard Files**

Type of Template or Wizard	Extension of Template or Wizard File
Access database wizard	.mdz
Excel template	.xlt
FrontPage standard Web-page template	.tem (extension of the folder that contains the template files)
FrontPage dynamic Web-page template	.dwt
Outlook item template	.oft
PowerPoint template	.pot
Word template	.dot
Word wizard	.wiz

NEW FEATURE!

Word, Excel, and PowerPoint let you modify the standard templates that come with Office and create new custom templates. You'll learn the details in the chapters on these individual applications.

> **Note** When you create custom standard Web-page templates in FrontPage, the locations where these templates are stored, as well as the procedures for working with them, are different from the locations and procedures described here for Word, Excel, and PowerPoint. For information on FrontPage standard Web-page templates, see "Creating Your Own FrontPage Templates," on page 1283.
>
> For information on working with the new FrontPage dynamic Web-page templates, see "Working with Dynamic Templates," on page 1284.

The standard Office templates for Word, Excel, and PowerPoint are stored in subfolders of your Program Files\Microsoft Office\Templates folder. However, you should normally store any custom templates you create in the following folder:

Documents And Settings*UserName*\Application Data\Microsoft\Templates

where *UserName* is the name you use for logging on to Windows. (Application Data is a hidden folder. To make hidden folders visible in Windows Explorer, choose Tools, Folder Options, click the View tab, and select the Show Hidden Files And Folders option.)

If you store a custom template directly within the Templates folder (the one in Documents And Settings) it will appear in the General tab of the New Office Document dialog box (or in the Templates dialog box displayed by Word or Excel, or in the New Presentation dialog box displayed by PowerPoint). If you place it in a subfolder that you create within this Templates folder, the template will appear in a tab of the New Office Document (or Templates or New Presentation) dialog box that has the same name as the subfolder. For instance, if you create a subfolder within Templates named My Templates, all templates you put in that folder will appear in the My Templates tab.

Be aware, however, that you can use Word to change the location where you store templates, and the settings you make in Word affect all Office applications.

For more information, see "Customizing and Creating Document Templates," on page 408.

Inside Out

Take note where you save templates

The New Office Document (or Templates or New Presentation) dialog box displays the standard templates supplied with Office that are stored within subfolders of Program Files\Microsoft Office\Templates. However, for some reason it won't display any new custom templates that you create and store in this area. Therefore, be sure to follow the guidelines given in this section for storing your templates, and don't attempt to save them in the same location as the standard templates.

To make sure that you save a custom template in the right place, follow these steps:

1   After you've completed the Word document, Excel workbook, or PowerPoint presentation that you want to use as a template, choose File, Save As.

2   In the Save As dialog box, select the Template item in the Save As Type drop-down list. This item will be labeled Document Template in Word, Template in Excel, and Design Template in PowerPoint. The Save As dialog box will automatically switch to the proper folder for storing custom templates.

3   Enter a name for your template and save it in the current folder—in this case the template will appear in the General tab of the New Office Document (or Templates or New Presentation) dialog box. Or, save it in a subfolder of the current folder—in this case, the template will appear in a tab that's labeled with the name of the subfolder. You can quickly create a subfolder by clicking the Create New Folder button near the top of the Save As dialog box or by pressing Alt+5.

Inside Out

Templates are now less essential

As explained in "Creating a Document Using the New Document Task Pane," on page 53, you can use an existing standard document as if it were a template. This feature makes modifying templates and creating custom templates less important.

Creating an Empty Office Document in a Folder

You can use the New command in Windows to quickly create and save a new Word, Excel, or PowerPoint document or Access database—ready for later editing—without even running an Office application. To do so, perform the following steps:

1   In Windows Explorer or in a folder window, open the folder in which you want to store the document.

2   Choose File, New. Or, right-click on a blank area within the folder and choose New from the shortcut menu.

3   Choose the appropriate command from the New submenu, as shown here:

Windows and Office will then create and save a new document, giving it a default name and highlighting the name so that you can change it if you wish. You can open the document later for editing.

Normally, the New command creates a blank document. However, you can customize the content of the documents that New creates for a particular application by editing the appropriate file in the Windows\ShellNew (or WINNT\ShellNew) folder, as shown in Table 4-2.

Table 4-2. The Applications and Files Used by the New Command

Office Application Used by New Command	File Used for New Documents
Word	Winword8.doc
Excel	Excel9.xls
PowerPoint	Pwrpnt10.pot
Access	Access9.mdb

For example, if you frequently write memos in Word, you could edit the Windows\ShellNew\Winword8.doc file so that it contains the basic content—text, formatting, graphics, and so on—for a memo. Whenever you subsequently use the New command, the new document created will already contain the basic memo content. All you'd then need to do is to open the document and type in the message. (To modify a file in the ShellNew folder in Windows 2000 or Windows XP, you must have computer administrator rights.)

Creating a Document Using the New Document Task Pane

The third main way to create a new Office document is to open the application you want to use and then click the New toolbar button (labeled New Blank Document in Word); or choose File, New. Details vary among applications, but typically, clicking the New button immediately creates a new blank document and choosing the New menu command opens the New Document task pane, as shown in Figure 4-6. You'll find this pane in all the major Office applications except Outlook and InfoPath. The actual label of this pane varies by application—for example, in Word it's labeled New Document, and in Excel it's labeled New Workbook.

 Tip You'll find some of the most commonly used features of the New Document task pane within the new Getting Started task pane of the application you're using.

For general information on using task panes, see "Using the Task Panes in Office Applications," on page 42.

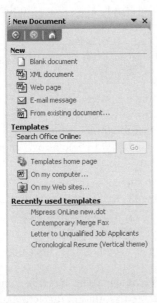

Figure 4-6. This is the New Document task pane that's displayed in Word.

Chapter 4

53

To create a new document in the task pane, use one of the following methods:

- To create a new blank document, click one of the commands in the New group, except the From Existing command. Most Office applications provide several commands in this group to let you create various types of documents. For example, in Word you can click Blank Document to create an empty Word document based on the Normal template, XML Document to create a new XML document, Web Page to create a blank document in HTML (Hypertext Markup Language) format, or E-Mail Message to create a new e-mail message that you can send using Outlook.

- To create a new document based on an existing one, click the From Existing Document command in the New group. This will open the New From Existing Document dialog box, which lets you select an existing document. The new document created will contain all of the content from the existing document, just as if the existing document were a template. (The labels of the command and dialog box vary by application; for example, in Excel the command is From Existing Workbook and the dialog box is New From Existing Workbook.) The New From Existing Document dialog box lets you select a file from a local, network, or Internet location. It's similar to the Open dialog box, which is explained in the next section.

  The "new from existing" feature provides a safe alternative to the somewhat precarious practice of opening a boilerplate document, choosing the Save As command to create a new copy of that document, and then customizing the document (precarious because it's too easy to forget to use the Save As command *before* you edit and save the document, thus overwriting your boilerplate).

- To create a document based on one of the templates that are available for the current application, choose a command in the Templates group. Most Office applications let you select a template from one of four different sources:

> Templates and wizards are discussed in "Creating a Document Using the New Office Document Dialog Box," on page 47.

- To use one of the templates stored on your computer, click the On My Computer command to open the Templates (or New Presentation) dialog box. This dialog box is similar to the New Office Document dialog box discussed in "Creating a Document Using the New Office Document Dialog Box," on page 47, except that it shows only those templates used by the current application.

- To open a template that's stored on a Web site belonging to you or your company, click On My Web Sites (not available in Access). This will display the New From Templates On My Web Sites dialog box, which lets you view or open a Web site that has been set up in your My Network Places folder.

- To use one of the online Office templates provided on the Office Online Web site, use the Search Office Online text box to search for a template, or click Templates Home page to open the Templates Home page of the Office Online site and browse for a template. These tools are both found in the Templates area of the task pane.

■ To quickly reuse a template you've employed recently, click the template name in the Recently Used Templates area.

Using My Network Places is discussed in "Accessing SharePoint Document Libraries from Office Applications," on page 187.

Using online templates from Office Online is explained in the next section, "Downloading and Using Templates from Office Online" on this page.

Tip   **Use the drag-and-drop feature to open a document**
Another way to open an existing document in an Office application is to drag the document file from Windows Explorer, or from a folder window, and drop it on the window of the application in which you want to open it. The surest way to simply open the document is to drop it on the application window's title bar. The effect of dropping it within a document window varies with the application and the type of file you've dragged.

Downloading and Using Templates from Office Online

Office 2003 provides a larger collection of downloadable online templates and wizards for creating new Office documents—through the Microsoft Office Online Web site—and it makes it easier to find, download, and use these templates.

You can locate and download an online template by running your browser and opening the Templates home page of the Microsoft Office Online site. An easy way to do this is to click the new Templates On Office Online button at the bottom of the New Office Document dialog box (shown in Figure 4-4) or the Templates dialog box (the New Presentation dialog box in PowerPoint). Or, you can click the Templates On Office Online command in the New Document task pane (shown in Figure 4-6).

You can also search for an online template by entering one or more keywords (such as *resume* or *amortization*) into the Search Online For text box in the New Document task pane and clicking the Go button. A list of all matching online templates will then be displayed in the Search Results task pane. Click the name of the most suitable template to display a preview. If you decide you want to use that template, click the Download button at the bottom of the Template Preview window to download the template and create a new document based on that template.

Tip   Once you've opened the Template Preview window to see a preview of a particular template, you can see previews of the other templates currently listed in the Search Results task pane by clicking the Next and Previous commands at the bottom of the Template Preview window.

When a new document based on an online template is first opened, and whenever you later reopen that document, the new Template Help task pane will be displayed (see Figure 4-7). (You might first be prompted to display this task pane.) If help information is available for the particular template you downloaded, you can access that information through the

Template Help task pane. The task pane might also provide links to related topics and allow you to rate the current template (from one to five stars).

> **Note** The Template Help task pane will appear automatically (without prompting) whenever you create a new document based on an online template or open an existing document based on an online template, provided that the Show Template Help Automatically When Available option is checked. You can access this option by choosing Help, Customer Feedback Options and clicking the Online Content category.

Figure 4-7. The new Template Help task pane displays information on working with an online template that you downloaded from Office Online.

Opening Existing Office Documents

The basic methods for opening existing Office documents are the same across most of the major Office applications—namely, Word, Excel, PowerPoint, FrontPage, and Access. (In FrontPage, the procedures differ somewhat because you can open either a file or a Web site. InfoPath is based on a different model because you can open either a form template in design mode or a form in edit mode.)

> The FrontPage-specific techniques are described in Part 8 of this book. The InfoPath specifics are given in Part 9.

The following are the two basic methods for opening Office documents:

- Using the Open Office Document dialog box to open any Office document
- Running an Office application and opening a document specific to that application

Chapter 4

Keep in mind that you can also open an Office document by double-clicking (or single-clicking if single-clicking is enabled in Windows Explorer) a document file or a shortcut to that file in a folder, as discussed in "Running the Office Applications," on page 39.

Opening an Existing Document Using the Open Office Document Dialog Box

You can use the Open Office Document dialog box (shown in Figure 4-8) to open any kind of Office document without having to first start an application. The document will be opened in the particular Office application that's registered to open that document type, as determined by the document's file extension. For example, Word is registered by default to open files with the .doc extension, Excel files with the .xls extension, and Notepad files with the .txt extension.

> **Note** In Office 2003 you can adjust the size of the Open Office Document dialog box. You can't, however, make the box smaller than its original size.

To display the Open Office Document dialog box, click the Start menu in Windows and choose All Programs (or Programs), Open Office Document. To use this dialog box, complete the following steps:

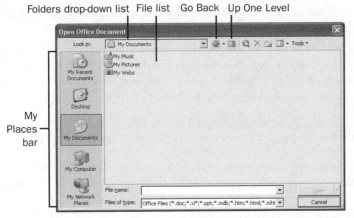

Figure 4-8. The Open Office Document dialog box lets you open any type of Office document.

1 In the Files Of Type drop-down list, select the type of the document you want to open. This will narrow the number of files you'll have to look at. The default selection, Office Files, shows all the standard Office document types, which is quite a large collection of file types.

2 In the My Places bar, select a folder to look in. Alternately, use the file list, together with the Folders drop-down list, Go Back button, and Up One Level button at the top of the dialog box to navigate to the folder that contains the document.

Tip To quickly reopen a recently opened Office document, click My Recent Documents in the My Places bar to open the Recent folder. This folder (which is maintained by Office) contains a list of shortcuts to recently opened Office documents, as well as to recently accessed file folders. When the Recent folder is displayed in the Open Office Document (or Open) dialog box, you can empty it by choosing Clear Document History from the Tools drop-down menu.

3 Type the filename into the File Name text box or click the filename in the file list.

4 Click the Open button. As an alternative to steps 3 and 4, you can just double-click the filename in the file list.

Tip   Convert a document

If you want to open a document that's in a nonnative format (for example, you want to open a WordPerfect 5.*x* document in Word), you have to first run the application in which you want to open the document, and then use the Open dialog box, as discussed in the next section. The Files Of Type list in the Open Office Document dialog box does *not* list the nonnative formats.

To open an Office document stored in a location other than on a local disk, use one of the following techniques in the Open Office Document dialog box:

- To open a document on a shared drive on your network, click My Network Places in the My Places bar to view or open your network drives. You can also get to a network location through a mapped network drive if you've created one.

- To open a document on a Web site that has SharePoint Team Services or other Microsoft server extensions, click My Network Places in the My Places bar. You can then use a shortcut to a particular Web site to display the documents stored on that site. You can also save the document back to the site when you've finished editing it.

For information on using My Network Places and for setting up shortcuts to Web sites, see "Accessing SharePoint Document Libraries from Office Applications," on page 187.

- To open a document on a Web site that does *not* have Microsoft server extensions (which allow you to save documents), type the file's URL directly into the File Name box. The file will be opened in read-only mode. You can edit it and save a local copy by using the File menu's Save As command.

- To open a document on a File Transfer Protocol (FTP) Internet site, type the *full* URL into the File Name text box (for example, *ftp://ftp.microsoft.com*). Or, navigate to the site using the FTP Locations folder in the Folders drop-down list of the Open Office Document dialog box. FTP Locations lists the FTP sites you've previously accessed. To

Chapter 4

add a new site to FTP Locations, double-click Add/Modify FTP Locations in the FTP Locations folder, as shown here:

You can save the document back to the FTP site (or save any document to the site through the Save As dialog box), provided that you have the required permissions.

You can select multiple files in the file list of the Open Office Document dialog box to open them all at once. To select an adjoining set of files, click the first one and then click the last one while pressing the Shift key. To select nonadjoining files, click the first one and then click each additional one while pressing the Ctrl key.

For tips on managing several open documents, see "Working with Multiple Documents," on page 74.

To open a file in alternative ways, click the down arrow on the Open button and choose a command from the drop-down list shown here:

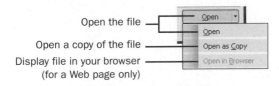

Open the file

Open a copy of the file

Display file in your browser
(for a Web page only)

Inside Out

Use the "new from existing" feature

The Open As Copy command creates a copy of the selected document and saves it in the same folder as the original. The name of the copy is based on the original filename (for instance, if you select Memo.doc, the copy will be called Copy(1) of Memo.doc). Usually, however, a better way to create a new document based on an existing one is to use the "new from existing" feature of the New Document task pane, described in "Creating a Document Using the New Document Task Pane," on page 53." The "new from existing" feature is preferable because it lets you name the new document yourself, and it doesn't automatically save a document to disk (which would leave clutter on your disk if you decide to abandon the new document).

You can perform many file and folder management tasks right within the Open Office Document dialog box by using the controls at the top right of the dialog box, as shown here:

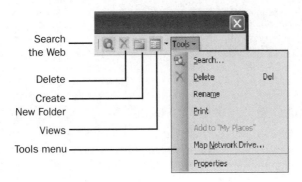

Search the Web

Delete

Create New Folder

Views

Tools menu

You can also perform many management tasks by right-clicking on a blank area in the current folder:

or on a file or folder:

and choosing a command from the shortcut menu. (The commands on the shortcut menu that appear when you right-click a file vary according to the type of file.)

In Office 2003 you can easily customize the My Places bar in the Open Office Document dialog box (without editing the Windows Registry, which was required in Office 2000 and earlier versions). Here's how:

- To add a folder to the bar, select it in the file list, click the Tools button, and choose Add To "My Places" from the drop-down menu.

- To remove, rename, or change the position of a folder in the bar, right-click it and choose the appropriate command from the shortcut menu, as shown here:

You can remove or rename only folders you've added, not the standard ones that are originally displayed in the bar.

Once you've added one or more folders, you might need to scroll through the My Places bar to get to a particular folder. To scroll, just click the small arrow at the top or bottom of the bar. To avoid having to scroll, you can reduce the size of the icons by choosing Small Icons from the shortcut menu that appears when you right-click anywhere in the bar. You can later restore the icons to their original size by choosing Large Icons.

The following are some general methods that will make it easier to locate the documents you want to open:

- To make it easier to identify documents, click the Views button and choose the Details, Properties, or Preview view, as shown here:

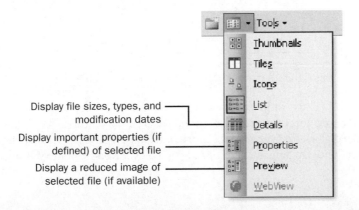

Display file sizes, types, and modification dates

Display important properties (if defined) of selected file

Display a reduced image of selected file (if available)

- To view *all* properties of the selected file—and to be able to set many of them—choose Properties from the Tools drop-down menu.

- To find documents based on a wide variety of criteria, use the Office File Search feature.

You can learn more about the File Search feature in "Finding Office Files or Outlook Items Using the File Search Feature," on page 63.

- To make it easier to identify documents, assign distinguishing properties to documents before you save them.

Assigning properties is explained in "Using Office Document Properties," on page 76.

Opening Documents Within Office Applications

Rather than displaying the Open Office Document dialog box, you can run the particular Office application in which you want to open the document and then display the Open dialog box (shown in Figure 4-9), using one of the following methods:

Open

- Click the Open toolbar button.

- Choose File, Open.

- Press Ctrl+O.

- In the application's Getting Started task pane, click the More command in the Open group. The Open group also displays a list of recently opened documents. You can click one of them to quickly reopen the document, bypassing the Open dialog box.

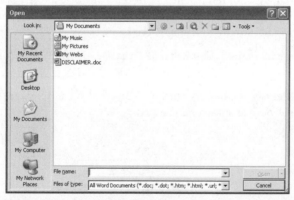

Figure 4-9. This figure shows the Open dialog box displayed in Word.

The Open dialog box works just like the Open Office Document dialog box described in the previous section. One important exception, however, is that the Files Of Type drop-down list in the Open dialog box displays *all* the different file types that the current application can open. (The Open Office Document dialog box displays only the native Office document types.)

To open a file with a nonnative format in a particular Office application (for example, to open a Lotus 1-2-3 file in Excel), run the application, display the Open dialog box, and select the file's format in the Files Of Type drop-down list, which will display all formats that the application can open and convert to its native format.

> **Tip**   **Convert more file formats**
>
> If, in the Files Of Type drop-down list, you don't find a description of the format of the file you want to import, make sure that you've installed all the text converters supplied with Office. (You should also do this if you're saving a document to a nonnative format and don't see the desired format in the Files Of Type list.) To install all converters, rerun Office Setup, as explained in "Revisiting Office Setup" on page 22, and select the Run From My Computer option for the entire Text Converters group of features. You'll find this feature in the Converters And Filters section, under the Office Shared Features group. Because the converters don't take up a lot of disk space, it's a good idea to install all of them, rather than just the one you currently need.

Another way to quickly reopen a recently opened document is to choose it from the recently used file list at the bottom of the application's File menu. Also, Windows lets you reopen a document that was recently opened in any program by choosing it from the Start menu's My Recent Documents (or Documents) submenu. (This list is distinct from the ones maintained by Office applications.)

> **Tip**   **Adjust the length of the recently used file list**
>
> In Word, Excel, PowerPoint, and Access, you can modify the number of documents displayed in the recently used file list—on the File menu and in the Open group of the Getting Started task pane—by choosing Tools, Options, clicking the General tab, and changing the number in the Recently Used File List text box. The maximum number you can set is nine. Clearing the Recently Used File List check box completely removes the recently used file list from the File menu and from the Getting Started task pane.

Finding Office Files or Outlook Items Using the File Search Feature

You can quickly locate Office document files, as well as Outlook items, using the File Search feature in Office 2003. The File Search feature is a completely revamped version of the Find command that you could run through the Open Office Document and Open dialog boxes in Office 2000. An important improvement of the File Search feature is that it makes it easy to search for Office files containing specified text, a common task that was quite cumbersome with the Office 2000 Find command.

> The more common way of finding Outlook items is using Outlook's Find command or Advanced Find command, discussed in "Finding Outlook Items," on page 986.

In Office 2003 you can access the File Search feature from the File Search task panes in all the major applications except Outlook and InfoPath. You can also access it through the File Search dialog box, which you open by choosing Search from the Tools drop-down menu in the Open Office Document dialog box, as shown here, or in the Open dialog box in all major Office applications.

The File Search task panes and the File Search dialog box work in basically the same way, although the File Search task panes offer several additional features (for example, a command for setting search options and a command for searching within the current document). This section, therefore, describes just the File Search task panes.

To display the File Search task panes, choose File, File Search. The File Search task panes comprise a basic pane (Basic File Search), an advanced pane (Advanced File Search), and a results pane that shows the files found through the search (Search Results). To quickly search for files or Outlook items containing specified text, use the Basic File Search task pane (shown in Figure 4-10) as follows:

1 If the Advanced File Search pane is currently displayed, switch to the basic pane by clicking the Basic File Search command near the bottom of the pane.

2 In the Search Text box, enter the text you want to find.

3 In the Search In drop-down list, select the specific file folders (local or network) or Outlook folders you want to search or select Everywhere to search all of them.

4 In the Results Should Be drop-down list, select the specific types of files or Outlook items you want to search for or select Anything to search for any type of file or item.

5 Click the Go button to start the search.

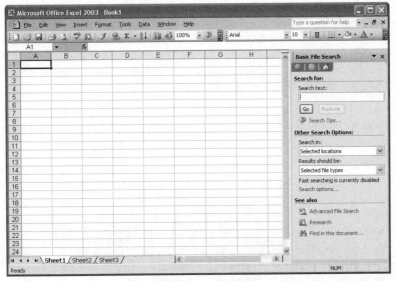

Figure 4-10. This figure shows the Basic File Search task pane displayed in Excel.

In the Basic File Search task pane, you can also perform the following tasks:

- To recall your previous search (after you've entered options for a new search), click the Restore button.

- To open the Advanced File Search task pane, described later in this section, click the Advanced File Search command.

- To search for or replace text in the currently opened document, click the Find In This Document command (not available in Access).

> To learn more about the Find In This Document command, see "Finding and Replacing Text and Formatting," on page 293.

- To modify the Office Indexing Service, click the Search Options command to open the Indexing Service Settings dialog box, shown here:

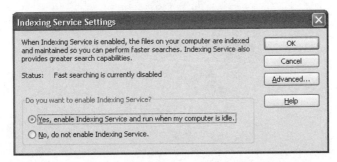

When enabled, the Office Indexing Service runs in the background and maintains an index of the contents of your Office files. This index allows the File Search feature to work more quickly. However, if you discover that the Indexing Service slows down applications you're running, or if you find the periodic disk activity that it generates annoying, consider modifying the service's behavior by clicking the Advanced button, or turning it off completely by selecting No, Do Not Enable Indexing Service.

The Advanced File Search task pane (shown in Figure 4-11) lets you search for files or Outlook items based on the values of one or more properties of the file or item. In this task pane you can perform a simple property search by using the following steps:

1 In the Property drop-down list, select the property you want to use as a search criterion—for example, Author or Last Modified. Choosing the Contents item lets you search for specific text in the content of the document file, as you do in the Basic File Search task pane. Choosing Text Or Property lets you search for all Office files that contain specific text in either the document content or in the value of a document property.

2 In the Condition drop-down list, select the search condition. The available options depend on the property you selected in step 1. For instance, with the Author property, you can select Is (Exactly) or Includes. With the Last Modified property, you can select On, On Or After, On Or Before, Today, and so on. With the Contents or Text Or Property properties, you can select only Includes.

3 In the Value text box, enter the property value you want to search for.

4 In the Search In drop-down list, indicate *where* you want to search; that is, select the file folders or Outlook folders you want to search, or select Everywhere to search them all.

5 In the Results Should Be drop-down list, indicate *what* you want to search for. That is, select the types of files you want to search for: Office files (Word files, Excel files, and so on), Outlook items (e-mail messages, appointments, and so on), or Web pages. Or, select Anything to search for any type of file or Outlook item.

6 Click the Go button to start the search.

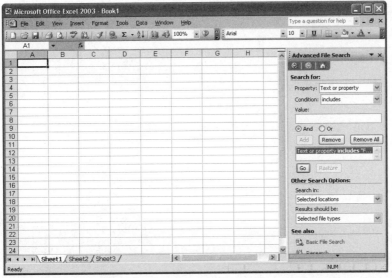

Figure 4-11.   This figure shows the Advanced File Search task pane displayed in Excel.

You can perform a more precise search by combining criteria, as follows:

1   Define the first criterion by specifying the property, search condition, and value as explained in steps 1 through 3 in the preceding instruction list.

2   Click the Add button to add the criterion to the list near the center of the task pane.

3   Define another criterion and select either the And or the Or option to specify the way you want to combine this criterion with the previously defined one.

4   Click Add to add the new criterion to the list.

5   Repeat steps 3 and 4 for any additional criteria you'd like to use in your search.

6   Complete the search by following steps 4 through 6 in the preceding instruction list.

You can perform the following additional tasks in the Advanced File Search task pane:

● To remove the selected criterion from the list, click the Remove button.

● To remove all criteria from the list, click the Remove All button.

● To return to the Basic File Search task pane, click the Basic File Search command.

When you click the Go button in either the Basic or the Advanced File Search task pane, Office will display the Search Results task pane, which will list any files or Outlook items it found (see Figure 4-12).

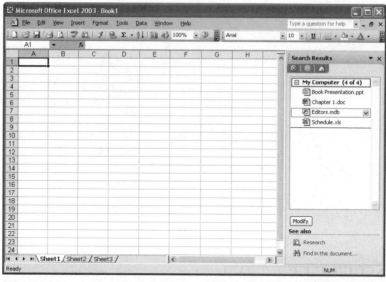

Figure 4-12. This figure shows the Search Results task pane displayed in Excel.

When you hold the pointer over a particular file or item listed in the Search Results task pane, detailed information on the file or item will appear in a ScreenTip. To open a file or item, click it. To perform other actions on the file or item, click the down arrow that appears when you move the pointer over the name and choose a command from the drop-down menu, as shown here:

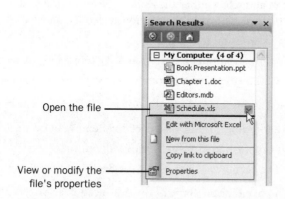

For information on document properties, see "Using Office Document Properties," on page 76.

To create a new document using the found document as if it were a template, choose New From This File. (This command works just like the New From Existing Document feature of the New Document task pane.)

> The New From Existing Document feature is described in "Creating a Document Using the New Document Task Pane," on page 53.

To create a hyperlink in an Office document to the found file or item, rather than opening the file or item now, choose the Copy Link To Clipboard command, and then paste the link into a document.

> For information on using hyperlinks, see "Adding and Using Hyperlinks," on page 580.

To return to the Basic File Search or Advanced File Search task pane in which you defined the search, so that you can modify the search or define another one, click the Modify button.

Saving Office Documents

Like the methods for creating and opening Office documents, the methods for saving documents are fairly similar across most of the major Office applications—namely, Word, Excel, PowerPoint, FrontPage, and InfoPath.

Save

To save a document that you've created or edited in an Office application, click the Save button on the application's Standard toolbar button; choose File, Save; or press Ctrl+S.

Preserving Your Data

When an application in the Office System encounters a fatal error and terminates—that is, when it *crashes*—the application attempts to save any unsaved data that you've entered into an open document. However, the application might not be able to save all or any of your data. Also, the application doesn't have the opportunity to save data following a power outage, and possibly following a computer failure. Therefore, in Word, Excel, and PowerPoint you should use the AutoRecover feature to have the application automatically save a temporary backup copy of your document at regular intervals so that you can recover your work in the event of an unexpected program termination. To enable AutoRecover, choose Tools, Options, click the Save tab, check the Save AutoRecover Info Every option, and enter the desired frequency of automatic saves (in minutes) into the adjoining text box (the default is 10 minutes).

When you restart an application after a crash, power outage, or computer failure, the application will display the Document Recovery pane, which lists all saved versions of the documents you had open when the program terminated. (Note that after a crash the application will attempt to restart automatically.) In the Document Recovery pane, a file marked [Original] is the version of the file that was saved on disk by your last manual save operation; one marked [Recovered] is a copy of the document that was saved either by AutoRecover or during a crash. With the help of the Document Recovery pane, you can open, examine, save, or delete any document version. You can save just the best document version and delete all the others; however, a safer option is to save all document versions on disk until you're certain that you've recovered as much data as possible.

Chapter 4

Keep in mind that during an AutoRecover save or crash the application saves a copy of your document in a special temporary backup file; it does *not* save the data in your original permanent document file on disk. Thus, an AutoRecover save doesn't do the same thing as clicking the Save button, and the AutoRecover feature *should not be used as a substitute for performing regular document saves.*

Note that if a document file somehow becomes corrupted, the Office application will attempt to repair the file when you open it. In this event, the application will also show the Document Recovery task pane, which will let you view the repairs that have been made and to work with the document versions as just described.

Finally, if a program stops responding but doesn't actually terminate—that is, it *hangs*—it doesn't normally have an opportunity for a last-minute attempt to save your data. To remedy this situation, you can use the Microsoft Office Application Recovery utility that's included with Office. To run the utility, click the Start button in Windows and then choose All Programs (or Programs), Microsoft Office Tools, Microsoft Office Application Recovery. In the utility's window, select the name of the hung application and click the Recover Application button. This will terminate the hung application and cause it to attempt to save any unsaved changes (just as if the application had crashed). Caution: If you click the End Application button in Office Application Recovery, the program will terminate *without* attempting to save your data.

The first time you save a new document, the application will display the Save As dialog box, where you can specify a name and location for the file (see Figure 4-13). If you want to create a copy of a document under a new filename or in a new location, you can open the Save As dialog box at any time by choosing File, Save As.

To save a document using the Save As dialog box, complete the following steps:

1 In the My Places bar, click the folder in which you want to save the document or use the file list, together with the Folders drop-down list, Go Back button, and Up One Level button at the top of the dialog box to navigate to the desired folder.

2 Type a name for your document into the File Name text box, or accept the default name.

3 Click the Save button.

Note You can adjust the size of the Save As dialog box. You can't, however, make the box smaller than its original size.

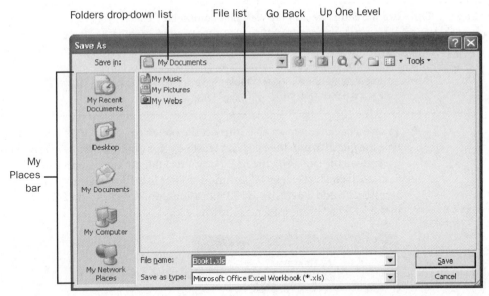

Figure 4-13. This figure shows the Save As dialog box displayed in PowerPoint.

If you want to convert the saved copy of the file to a different format (for example, you want to convert a Word 2003 document to a WordPerfect 5.0 document), choose the desired format in the Save As Type drop-down list before you type in the document name and click the Save button. Note that if the filename entered into the File Name text box doesn't include the file extension, Office will save it with the standard extension for the selected format. In Word, for example, if you type the filename **Bonzo** into the File Name text box and select the Document Template format in the Save As Type drop-down list, the document will be saved as Bonzo.dot.

> If you don't find the format you want in the Save As Type list, see the tip **"Convert More File Formats,"** on page 63.

To save an Office document to a location that's not on a local disk, use one of the following techniques in the Save As dialog box:

- To save a document to a shared drive on your network, click My Network Places in the My Places bar to access your network drives. You can also access a network location through a mapped network drive if you've created one.

- To save a document to a Web site that has SharePoint Team Services or other Microsoft server extensions, click My Network Places in the My Places bar. You can then use a shortcut to a particular Web site to open a folder on that site so you can save your document there.

> For information on using My Network Places and on setting up shortcuts to Web sites, see "Accessing SharePoint Document Libraries from Office Applications," on page 187.

Chapter 4

Tip Use the Templates On My Web Site command

If you store a custom document template that you've created on a Web site that has Microsoft server extensions, you or any member of your workgroup can subsequently use that template to create new documents by means of the On My Web Sites command in the New Document task pane (not available in Access). See "Sharing Office Documents and Graphics on a SharePoint Site," on page 183.

- To save a document to an FTP Internet site on which you have the required permissions, type the *full* URL into the File Name text box (for example, *ftp://ftp.microsoft.com*). Or, navigate to the site using the FTP Locations folder in the Folders drop-down list of the Save As dialog box. The FTP Locations folder lists the FTP sites you've previously accessed. To add a new site to FTP Locations, double-click Add/Modify FTP Locations in the FTP Locations folder, as shown here:

As with the Open Office Document and Open dialog boxes, you can perform many file and folder management tasks in the Save As dialog box. You can also customize the My Places bar. In fact, the Open Office Document, Open, and Save As dialog boxes all share the same My Places bar: changes you make to the bar in one dialog box will affect the bar in the other dialog boxes in all Office applications.

For information on these topics, see "Opening an Existing Document Using the Open Office Document Dialog Box," on page 57.

Keep in mind, however, that in the Save As dialog box, the Tools drop-down menu has a slightly different set of commands. Here's the Tools menu in PowerPoint's Save As dialog box:

The commands on the Tools menu below Properties vary among the different Office applications.

Tip **Guard your privacy**

You can have Word, Excel, PowerPoint, or Access remove personal information from a document when you save it. The information removed includes any text assigned to the Author, Manager, and Company document properties. Also, the author's actual name is removed from all comments, tracked changes (in Word), and macros, and is replaced with the word *Author*. To enable this feature, choose Tools, Options, click the Security tab, and check the Remove Personal Information From File Properties On Save option. (In Access, click the General tab and check Remove Personal Information From This File.)

Saving a Document as a Web Page

One of the most important features of Word, Excel, PowerPoint, FrontPage, and Access is the ability to save a document as a Web page—that is, in HTML format—so that you can publish it on the World Wide Web or on a company intranet.

For information on choosing the best Office application for creating the particular type of Web page you want to publish, see "An Office 2003 Map," on page 7.

In each application's part of the book, you'll learn how to use that application to publish effectively on the Web. When you create a Web page in a particular Office application,the page will contain the identity of the creating application. You can determine which application was used to create a particular Web page by looking at the page's icon in the folder where it is stored, as shown here:

Data Access Page Created in Access.htm
Page Created in Excel.htm
Page Created in FrontPage.htm
Page Created in PowerPoint.htm
Page Created in Word.htm

If you double-click the icon for a Web page in a folder, it will be displayed in your browser, rather than being opened for editing. To edit the page, you can right-click the icon and choose Edit from the shortcut menu. Of course, you can also open the page for editing through the Open Office Document dialog box (which will open the page in the creating Office application) or you can run the creating application and use its Open dialog box.

Office normally opens a page for editing in the application that created it. For example, if you use the Open dialog box in Word to open a Web page created in PowerPoint, the page will be opened in PowerPoint, not in Word. This design helps to prevent loss of features; for example,

Chapter 4

Word might not be able to view or edit a feature in a Web page that was created by Power-Point. To circumvent this limitation and edit a page in an application other than the one that created it, follow these steps:

1 Open the page in Microsoft Internet Explorer, for example, by double-clicking the page's icon in the folder where it is stored.

2 In Internet Explorer, click the down arrow on the Edit button on the Standard Buttons toolbar and choose the name of the application you want to use to edit the page, as shown here:

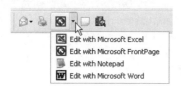

Working with Multiple Documents

In Word, Excel, and PowerPoint you can have several documents open at the same time. In other words, if you have a document open in one of these applications, you can use the program's commands to open another document, and both documents will be open at the same time within a single running copy of the application.

> **Note** In contrast, a single running copy of either Access or FrontPage allows you to have open only a *single* database or Web site at a given time.
>
> If you have a database open in Access and you use the Open command in Access to open another one, the first database will be closed. To have an additional database open at the same time, you must run another copy of Access by choosing it from the Windows Start menu or by using a comparable technique.
>
> If you have a Web site open in FrontPage and you use FrontPage's Open command to open another one, FrontPage will automatically run a second copy of the program and display the second Web site in that copy. (FrontPage does allow you to have several Web *files* open at the same time.)
>
> You can run only one copy of Outlook and open only one Outlook personal folders file at a given time.

Table 4-3 describes a set of procedures that are useful for managing multiple open documents in Word, Excel, or PowerPoint.

Table 4-3. Procedures for Managing Multiple Open Documents in Word, Excel, and PowerPoint

Window Management Task	Procedure
Display a separate button in the Windows task bar for each open document.	Choose Tools, Options, click the View tab, and check the Windows In Taskbar option. If you clear this option, only a single button will appear in the Windows taskbar for all open documents.
Switch to another document window	Press Ctrl+F6, or choose document name from Window menu. If Windows In Taskbar is enabled, you can also click the Taskbar button for that document window.
Open the active document in an additional window	Choose Window, New Window.
Tile (display side-by-side) all document windows	Choose Arrange All (Arrange in Excel) from Window menu.
Display two documents side-by-side for easy document comparison	Choose Compare Side By Side With from Window menu. (In Word and Excel only.) See the next section for details.
Split the active document window into two views	Choose Split from Window menu or drag the split box toward bottom of window. (The split box is the horizontal bar immediately above the vertical scrollbar.) (In Word and Excel only.)
Close all windows displaying the active document	Choose File, Close.
Close all windows for all open documents	Press the Shift key while opening the File menu and then choose Close All. (In Word and Excel only.)
Save all open documents (saves only documents with unsaved changes)	Press the Shift key while opening the File menu and then choose Save All. (In Word only.)

Comparing Two Documents Side by Side

If you have two or more documents open in Word or Excel, you can use the new Compare Side By Side mode to quickly arrange the document windows side by side and (optionally) to synchronize scrolling of the two documents, making it easy to scan and visually compare the documents' contents. The following is the procedure:

1 Choose Compare Side By Side With from the Window menu. If only two documents are open, the command will include the name of the inactive document (for example, Compare Side By Side With Bozo.doc) and will immediately activate the Compare Side

By Side mode. If more than two documents are open, the command will read Compare Side By Side With and will display a dialog box that lets you choose the other open document that you want to display alongside the active document. In either case, Word or Excel will then tile the two document windows (vertically or horizontally) on the screen and will display the Compare Side By Side toolbar, shown here:

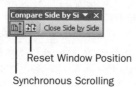

Reset Window Position

Synchronous Scrolling

2 Use the methods given in Table 4-4 to work in the Compare Side By Side mode.

Table 4-4. Working in Compare Side By Side Mode

To Do This	Perform This Action
Synchronize scrolling, so that when you scroll one of the documents (using the scroll bar or shortcut keys), the other document automatically scrolls the same amount.	Select the Synchronous Scrolling button on the Compare Side By Side toolbar. (It's selected by default when you first switch on the mode.)
Restore the document windows to their original side-by-side arrangement if you've moved or resized a window while in Compare Side By Side mode.	Click the Reset Window Position button on the Compare Side By Side toolbar.
End Compare Side By Side mode and restore the document windows to their original configuration before you switched on this mode.	Click the Close Side By Side button on the Compare Side By Side toolbar or choose Close Side By Side from the Window menu.

Using Office Document Properties

A Word, Excel, or PowerPoint document—as well as an Access database—has a set of properties that are saved in the document file together with the document content. Assigning meaningful values to various document properties—such as the Subject, Category, or Keywords properties—can make it easier to organize, identify, and find your documents.

To give you an idea how useful and ubiquitous document properties are, the following is a list of ways properties are used or displayed in Office and Windows.

- The Office File Search feature can find documents on local or network drives using property values or combinations of property values as search criteria.

For more information about the Office File Search feature, see "Finding Office Files or Outlook Items Using the File Search Feature," on page 63.

- In the Open Office Document and Open dialog boxes, you can display a brief summary of the properties of the selected document by switching to the Properties view. You can see all properties of the selected document—and set many of them—by choosing Properties from the Tools drop-down menu.
- For Word, Excel, and PowerPoint documents, Windows Explorer—as well as a folder window or the Windows desktop—will display the Author, Title, Subject, and Comments properties in a ScreenTip when you hold the mouse pointer over the document. It will display and let you set many of a document's properties if you right-click the document and choose Properties from the shortcut menu.
- A Visual Basic for Applications (VBA) program can read or set a document's properties. You can thus use properties as a part of a custom Office application.

VBA is covered in Part 10 of this book, "Customizing Office 2003 Using VBA."

If you want to make use of properties, you should set them before you first save a document. To set properties, choose File, Properties (Database Properties in Access), and then enter the desired property values into the tabs of the Properties dialog box (see Figure 4-14).

Tip Preview your documents

In the Properties dialog box Summary tab, if you check the Save Preview Picture option, Windows Explorer or a folder window will show a preview image of the selected document in the Thumbnails view. Also, the Open Office Document, Open, and Save As dialog boxes will show a preview image if the Preview view is active.

Chapter 4

Information on the document,
such as the number of words
(can't be set)

Summary of
document contents
(can't be set)

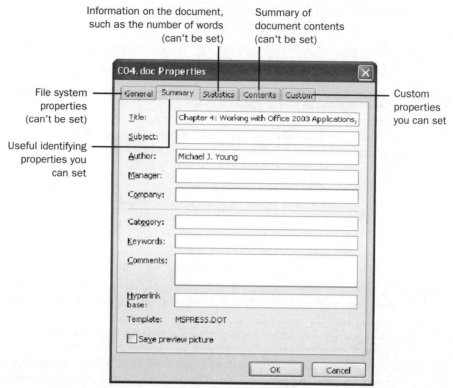

File system
properties
(can't be set)

Useful identifying
properties you
can set

Custom
properties
you can set

Figure 4-14. This is the Properties dialog box that's displayed for a new Word document.

When you create a new document, the Office application you use will automatically assign values to the Author and Company properties using the information you supplied when you installed Office. (If you've changed your user name within an Office application, the Author property will be set to the new name you specified rather than to the one you originally gave during installation.) Once you've saved the document, Word, PowerPoint, and Access also assign a tentative value to the Title property. When you first save a document, Windows automatically stores the file system properties that are displayed on the General tab (this tab doesn't display information before the first save).

Tip Have Office remind you to set properties

You can have Word, Excel, or PowerPoint automatically display the Properties dialog box the first time you save a document. To do this, choose Tools, Options, click the Save tab (the General tab in Excel), and check the Prompt For Document Properties option (the option is worded slightly differently in Excel and PowerPoint).

In the Properties dialog box, the Custom tab allows you to add custom properties to a document, such as Date Completed, Department, Editor, Group, and Status (see Figure 4-15). You can choose a predefined property or create a new property with any name you want.

Chapter 4

Custom properties can be especially useful for organizing, tracking, and locating documents shared by a workgroup, provided that members of the workgroup use the properties consistently. To set a custom property, complete the following steps (repeat this procedure for each additional custom property you want to define):

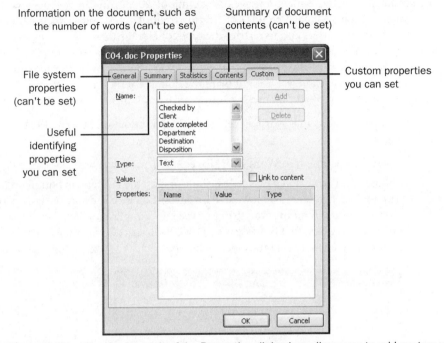

Figure 4-15. The Custom tab of the Properties dialog box allows you to add custom properties.

1 Select a predefined property in the Name list, or type a new property into the Name text box at the top of the list.

2 In the Type drop-down list, choose the type of data you want the property to contain.

3 Enter a property value into the Value text box. (The value you enter must conform to the type you chose in step 2.)

> **Note**   Rather than assigning a fixed value to a property, you can derive its value from a named block of text in the document (a Word bookmark, an Excel named range, or Power-Point selected text). To do this, check the Link To Content option and then select the specific named block of text in the Source drop-down list, which will replace the Value text box. The property's value will then be derived from the named text, and therefore its value will change whenever that text changes.

4 Click the Add button to save the property in the document. The new property will be displayed in the Properties list at the bottom of the Custom tab.

5 To remove a custom property, select it in the Properties list and click the Delete button.

Using Information Rights Management to Restrict Document Permissions

If you are distributing a sensitive Word 2003, Excel 2003, or PowerPoint 2003 document, or are sending a sensitive e-mail message using Outlook 2003, you can use the new Office 2003 Information Rights Management (IRM) feature to limit access to the document or message to a specified set of users and to restrict the types of actions these users can perform on the document or message. For instance, you might allow a particular user to read a document but not change, print, or copy the document. Or you might allow a user to read or change a document (and save changes) but not print the document. For an e-mail message, you can allow the recipient to read that message but not forward, print, or copy the message.

To restrict permissions in a Word, Excel, or PowerPoint document using IRM, perform the following steps:

1 Open the document in Word 2003, Excel 2003, or PowerPoint 2003.

2 Choose File, Permission, Do Not Distribute or click the Permission button on the Standard toolbar. If you need to download updated IRM client software or sign up for the IRM service, Office will prompt you to do so. The Office application will then display the Permission dialog box. In this dialog box, check the Restrict Permission To This *Document* option (where *Document* is the document type, such as a Workbook), as shown here:

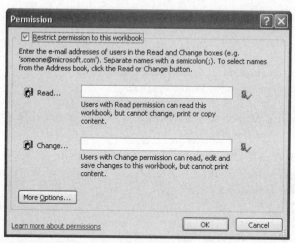

3 In the Read text box, enter the e-mail address of each user you want to grant read-only access, and in the Change text box, enter the e-mail address of each user you want to grant read and change permission. Separate e-mail addresses using semicolons. You can click the Read or the Change button to select users from your Outlook address book rather than typing the addresses.

4 To fine-tune the document's permissions and to set advanced permission options, click the More Options button in the Permission dialog box.

5 Click the OK button to apply the restrictions to the document. You can now save and distribute the document.

Chapter 4

A user whose e-mail address you added to the Permission dialog box can open the document using the corresponding Office 2003 application and can work with the document within the constraints you specified for that user. If the user *doesn't* have the corresponding Office 2003 application and if you checked the Allow Users With Earlier Versions Of Office To Read With Browsers Supporting Information Rights Management option (one of the options that's available if you click the More Options button in the Permission dialog box, as mentioned in step 4), the user can view the document in a browser that supports IRM. Specifically, the user can work with the document within an Internet Explorer 6 window, provided the user downloads and installs the Rights Management Add-On For Internet Explorer product from Microsoft.

Note that as the author of the document, you retain full control over the document, including the ability to remove document restrictions (by clearing the Restrict Permission To This *Document* option in the Permission dialog box).

If you are using Outlook 2003 to send a sensitive e-mail message, you can use IRM to permit the recipient to read the message but not to forward, print, or copy the message. To do this, simply click the Permission toolbar button in the Message form. (You might be prompted to select your IRM user account.)

> For more information on using Information Rights Management in Office 2003, see the topic "Information Rights Management" in the Office 2003 online Help.

Chapter 4

Using Speech and Handwriting in Office 2003

Using Speech in Office 83   NEW FEATURE! Using Handwriting in Office 96

Using Speech in Office

The Microsoft Office System has a major new capability in its interface: speech recognition, a long-anticipated feature that is finally becoming a practical reality. (Speech recognition was first introduced with Office XP.) With speech recognition you can dictate text rather than type it, and you can issue basic commands by speaking them rather than by using a mouse or keyboard. You can use speech recognition in Microsoft Office Word, Excel, PowerPoint, Outlook, Access, and FrontPage.

Speech recognition technology is still in its relative infancy. It's not perfect, and it certainly won't free you completely from the keyboard. It's good enough, however, to make working with Office more efficient and enjoyable and to provide a welcome break from incessant typing and the strained posture that usually accompanies it.

To use speech recognition, first make sure that your microphone is attached to the correct output jack on your computer and—if the microphone has a switch—that it's turned on. If you're using a headset with both a microphone and earphones, you'll also need to plug the earphone jack into the correct output jack on your computer.

Then, turn on speech recognition by choosing Tools, Speech in the Office application you're using (in Excel, choose Tools, Speech, Speech Recognition). You'll then be able to use speech recognition in any of the Office applications that support it. (To turn speech recognition off, choose Tools, Speech again.)

(Speech recognition is an operating system resource. It works basically the same way in all Office applications, and settings that you make in one application affect the way it works in all applications.)

> **Tip**   Install Speech Recognition
>
> If the Speech command isn't on the Tools menu of your Office applications, then speech recognition hasn't been installed. To install it, rerun Office Setup, and select the Run From My Computer option for the Speech feature. You can find this feature in the Office Shared Features section, under the Alternative User Input group (see Figure 5-1).

Rerunning Office Setup is explained in "Revisiting Office Setup," on page 22.

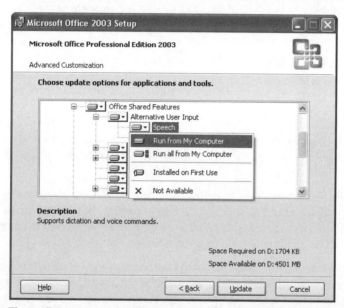

Figure 5-1.   Choose the Run From My Computer option to install Office speech recognition.

Training Speech Recognition

To enhance the reliability and accuracy of speech recognition, you need to adjust your microphone and train Office to recognize your personal speech patterns. When you first turn on speech recognition by choosing Tools, Speech, Office runs two wizards to accomplish these tasks.

First, Office runs the Microphone Wizard (shown in Figure 5-2).

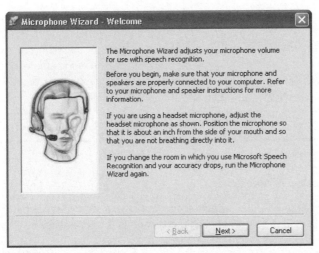

Figure 5-2. The Microphone Wizard displays an introductory page upon opening.

Click the Next button and follow the instructions in the remaining Microphone Wizard pages. These pages do the following:

- They test and adjust the volume of your microphone.
- They help you to position the microphone properly.

Next, Office runs the Speech Recognition Training Wizard (the pages of this wizard are labeled Voice Training). Make sure that the room is quiet, and keep the microphone in the position you used when you worked with the Microphone Wizard. The training process should take about 10 minutes. In the first Training Wizard dialog box, click the Next button and follow the instructions on the remaining pages. The Speech Recognition Training Wizard does the following:

- It lets you speak a series of sentences so it can analyze your speech patterns.
- It saves the data it has collected on your personal speech patterns.

The introductory training session will probably be enough to get you started using speech recognition. To enhance the accuracy of speech recognition, however, you should complete two or more training sessions. You can run additional sessions later, at any time.

For information on adjusting your microphone settings and running additional Speech Recognition Training Wizard sessions, see "Customizing Speech Recognition," on page 94.

When you've finished running the Speech Recognition Training Wizard, Office will attempt to run the Microsoft Voice Training video in your browser. You may need to download the Macromedia Flash Player in order to use this video. The video will explain the basics of using voice recognition in Office 2003.

Chapter 5

> **Tip** **Speak naturally**
>
> When you use the Speech Recognition Training Wizard, be sure to speak in your natural tone of voice, pronouncing words the way you normally do, so that you can speak that way when you use speech recognition to dictate text and issue commands. You might, however, need to speak a little more slowly and distinctly than you normally do.

Troubleshooting

Speech recognition is slow or unreliable

Speech recognition seems to be working, but recognition of your words lags behind your speech, even when you speak slowly. Or speech recognition fails to understand many of your words.

The *minimum* requirements for speech recognition are a 400-MHz computer with 128 MB of RAM. However, if you use speech recognition regularly, you'll probably want an even faster computer and more RAM.

In addition, you need a good microphone that connects either to a high-quality sound card or to a universal serial bus (USB) port. The best kind is a close-talk headset microphone with noise cancellation. With this type of microphone, you should adjust the microphone so that it's about a thumb's width to one side of your mouth to avoid breathing directly into it. The primary advantage of a headset microphone is that the relative position of the microphone with respect to your mouth can easily be kept constant. If you use a microphone on your desktop or computer, you'll tend to get inconsistent results as you move closer to or further away from the microphone.

Once you position your microphone, always use it in that same position. Also, the room where you work with your computer should be relatively quiet so that the microphone doesn't pick up background sounds.

Finally, if you meet the hardware requirements but speech recognition fails to understand quite a few of your words, try running additional training sessions.

Using Speech Recognition

The Language Bar, shown here, is your primary tool for using speech recognition. It automatically appears on the screen when you turn on speech recognition.

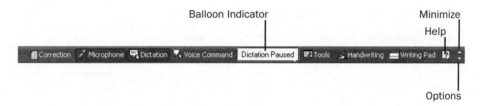

You can move the Language Bar onto the Windows Taskbar by clicking the small Minimize button. To move the Language Bar back to the main part of the screen, click this button again (when the bar is minimized, the button will be labeled Restore).

When the Language Bar is displayed on the main part of the screen, you can move it anywhere on the screen by dragging its left border, shown here:

Unlike the standard Office application toolbars, the Language Bar and its settings are shared by all Office applications. For example, if you display and position the Language Bar when Word is active, it will remain displayed in the same position if you then switch to Excel, PowerPoint, or another application.

Table 5-1 contains brief descriptions of the Language Bar buttons.

> **Note** As you switch among different Microsoft Windows applications, you'll notice that the set of buttons displayed on the Language Bar changes. That's because the Language Bar displays only those buttons that are supported by the current active application. Also, the full set of speech buttons described in Table 5-1 is displayed only if speech recognition is currently turned on.
>
> All the buttons in Table 5-1 will appear when any of the Office applications that support speech recognition is active, except the Correction button, which is available only when Word is active. If speech recognition is on and one of the available buttons isn't visible, you can display it by clicking the Options button on the Language Bar and choosing the description of the button on the menu that pops up. On this menu, a button that is displayed has a check mark next to it. You can remove the check mark and hide the button by choosing the button name again. There isn't a menu command for the Microphone button because when speech recognition is installed, that button is always displayed.

Chapter 5

Table 5-1. The Buttons on the Language Bar

Language Bar Button	Purpose/Effect
Correction (Word only)	Displays a menu of alternative words for the word under the insertion point (or the selected word), provided that speech recognition inserted this word. Choose an alternative to replace the word in your document. Choose Replay Dictation to hear how you spoke the word. Or click Delete to erase the word so you can start over.
Microphone	Turns speech recognition off or on. Clicking this button has basically the same effect as choosing Tools, Speech in an Office application. When speech recognition is on, the Microphone button is selected and the Tools, Speech menu command is checked.
Dictation	Turns on *dictation mode*, in which your spoken words are inserted into text as if you had typed them. This mode is discussed in the next section, "Using Speech Recognition Dictation Mode," on page 89.
Voice Command	Turns on *voice command mode*, in which a spoken command is executed as if you had used the mouse or keyboard to issue the command. This mode is covered in the section "Using Speech Recognition Voice Command Mode," on page 93.
Balloon Indicator	Displays messages. For example, in voice command mode, it displays the names of the commands you speak or execute using the mouse. And in dictation mode, it displays the message "Dictating…" when speech recognition is processing dictated text and the message "What was that?" if it fails to understand something you said.
Speak	Causes the Office speech tools to dictate the currently selected text in the active document. (If no text is selected, this command reads the text from the insertion point to the end of the text that's visible in the window.) You will hear the text spoken over your computer's speakers. You can stop the dictation by clicking this button again (it's labeled Stop during the dictation).
Pause	Causes a temporary pause in speech dictation (started by the Speak button). To continue the dictation, click this button again (during a pause, the button is labeled Resume).

Table 5-1. The Buttons on the Language Bar

Language Bar Button	Purpose/Effect
Tools	Displays a menu that lets you modify different speech recognition settings. These commands are explained in "Customizing Speech Recognition" and Table 5-4, later in the chapter.
Handwriting	Displays a menu of commands for accessing the Office 2003 handwriting interface, described in "Using Handwriting in Office," on page 96.
Writing Pad, Drawing Pad, and so on	Displays or hides the handwriting tool that's currently selected on the Handwriting menu. The button name indicates the currently selected tool.
Help	Displays a menu of Language Bar help resources. Normally, this menu contains only a single command, Language Bar Help, which displays online help explaining how to use the Language Bar and speech recognition.
Minimize	Moves the Language Bar onto the Windows Taskbar. When the Language Bar is on the Windows Taskbar, this button is labeled Restore and clicking it moves the Language Bar back to the main part of the screen.
Options	Displays a menu that lets you modify the Language Bar or change the text input language settings. The commands on this menu are explained in "Customizing the Language Bar," on page 96.

To use speech recognition successfully, place the microphone in the same position you used with the Microphone Wizard and speak in the same natural tone of voice you employed when using the Speech Recognition Training Wizard.

To begin using speech recognition, make sure that the Microphone button is selected (highlighted), indicating that speech recognition is turned on. When speech recognition is off, the Dictation and Voice Command buttons and the Balloon Indicator are hidden. You can also choose Tools, Speech in an Office application to turn speech recognition on or off (the command will be checked when speech recognition is on). The Microphone button and the Tools, Speech menu command are tied together—turning one on or off turns the other on or off.

Using Speech Recognition Dictation Mode

You can use speech recognition's *dictation mode* to enter text into an Office application by speaking. For example, you can enter text into the body of a Word document, into an Excel worksheet, into a PowerPoint slide, or into a text box in a dialog box. To dictate text, click the Dictation button—if it's not already selected—to switch on dictation mode, and then begin speaking the words you want to enter (see Figure 5-3).

Figure 5-3. In this figure, text has been dictated into a Web page in FrontPage.

To insert a punctuation character, say the name of the character as given in Table 5-2. In dictation mode you can also speak commands to select text, to correct text (for example, to delete recently recognized text), to change the capitalization of text, or to perform other tasks (for example, to turn the microphone off or delete the selected word). For an up-to-date list of these commands, see the topic "Commands You Can Use In Dictation Mode" in the Language Bar help file. (To open this file, click the Help button on the Language Bar and choose Language Bar Help.)

> **Note** The voice commands that are available in dictation mode depend upon the current settings in the Speech Input Settings dialog box, which is explained in Table 5-4 in the section, "Customizing Speech Recognition."

Table 5-2. Phrases for Dictating Punctuation Characters

To Insert This Punctuation Character	Say This
&	"Ampersand"
*	"Asterisk"
@	"At sign"
\	"Backslash"
{	"Open brace" or "Left brace"
}	"Close brace" or "Right brace"
[	"Open bracket" or "Left bracket"
]	"Close bracket" or "Right bracket"
^	"Caret"
:	"Colon"
,	"Comma"
–	"Double dash" or "Dash"
$	"Dollar sign"
…	"Ellipsis"
Enter	"New line" or "Enter"
Enter twice	"New paragraph"
=	"Equals"
!	"Exclamation" or "Exclamation point"
>	"Greater than"

Table 5-2. Phrases for Dictating Punctuation Characters

To Insert This Punctuation Character	Say This
-	"Hyphen"
<	"Less than"
(	"Open paren" or "Left Paren" or "Paren"
)	"Close paren" or "Right paren"
%	"Percent" or "Percent sign"
.	"Period" or "Dot"
+	"Plus sign"
#	"Pound sign"
?	"Question mark"
"	"Quote" or "Open quote"
;	"Semicolon"
'	"Single quote"
/	"Slash"
Space character	"Space"
Tab	"Tab"
~	"Tilde"
_	"Underscore"
		"Vertical bar"

Troubleshooting

Speech recognition inserts extra spaces

Speech recognition dictation mode inserts a space character between a word and the following punctuation character.

To make a punctuation character come immediately after a word without an intervening space, say the name of the punctuation character immediately after saying the word. For example, say "QUOTEhelloQUOTE" rather than "QUOTE hello QUOTE." If either you or speech recognition makes a mistake while you're dictating text, you can make a correction by right-clicking a recently dictated word to display the shortcut menu (see Figure 5-4).

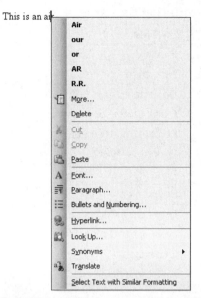

Figure 5-4. This shortcut menu is displayed in Word when you right-click an erroneous word that speech recognition has inserted.

Then choose an item from the shortcut menu as follows:

- If the correct word is among the alternatives displayed in bold type at the top of the shortcut menu, click the word to insert it and replace the original word you right-clicked.

- If you don't see the correct word, choose the More command to display a longer list of alternatives, as shown in this example:

If you find the correct word on the expanded list, click it to make the replacement. Another way to display the expanded list of alternatives is to place the insertion point on the erroneous word and click the Correction button on the Language Bar. (If you don't see this button, click the down arrow at the right end of the Language bar and choose Correction from the drop-down menu.)

Also, at the bottom of the expanded list you can choose Replay Dictation to hear how you spoke the word, or you can click Delete to erase the word so you can start over.

- If you don't find the right word among the alternatives, you can choose Delete on the shortcut menu—or erase the word using any editing method—and then either dictate it again (if you're stubborn) or just type it in.

Tip **Replace a misspelled word**

If the application's while-you-type spelling checker has underlined a word that speech recognition has inserted, the shortcut menu won't display the alternative words or commands described here. However, you can choose the Speech Alternatives command at the bottom of the shortcut menu to display speech recognition's expanded list of alternatives.

Using Speech Recognition Voice Command Mode

You can use speech recognition's *voice command mode* to issue basic program commands by voice—for example, to save a file, to change the document view, to apply bold formatting, or to undo the previous command. To issue a verbal command, click the Voice Command button on the Language Bar—if this button isn't already selected—to switch into voice command mode and then speak the command.

How do you know which words to say to issue a specific command? The available commands are specific to the particular application that you're using. However, some general principles and common commands are shared by most Office applications. For example, to issue a menu command, first say the name of the menu (for example, "file," "edit," or "view") to open the menu. Then say the name of the specific command on the menu you want to execute (for example, "close," "find," or "ruler"). In Word, for example, saying "file close" would choose the Close command on the File menu, closing the current document. If the command is on a submenu, first say the name of the main menu, then the name of the submenu, and then the name of the specific command. In Word, for example, saying "view toolbars formatting" would display (or hide) the Formatting toolbar.

To issue a toolbar button command, make sure that toolbar is displayed and then say the button name (the one that appears in the ScreenTip when you hold the mouse pointer over the button). For example, saying "bold" when the Word Formatting toolbar is displayed applies bold formatting to the currently selected text, just as it would if you clicked the Bold button.

In voice command mode you can also issue a keyboard command by saying the name of the command key, as shown in Table 5-3.

To reverse your previous editing or formatting action, just say "undo."

For a description of additional voice commands that are common to most Office applications, see the topic "Commands You Can Use In Voice Command Mode" in the Language Bar help file. (To open this file, click the Help button on the Language Bar and choose Language Bar Help.)

Chapter 5

Table 5-3. **Spoken Commands for Issuing Keyboard Commands**

To Issue This Keyboard Command	Say This
Left arrow key	"Left"
Right arrow key	"Right"
Up arrow key	"Up"
Down arrow key	"Down"
Home key	"Home"
End key	"End"
Enter key	"Enter"
Esc key	"Escape"

Notice that whenever you issue a menu or toolbar command—verbally or by using the mouse—the Balloon Indicator on the Language Bar displays a description of the command. For example, if you open the Edit menu, the Balloon Indicator displays the word *Edit*, as shown here:

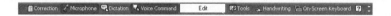

Customizing Speech Recognition

You can extensively modify the way speech recognition works. For instance, you can create and train additional speech recognition *profiles*. A speech recognition profile (also known as a *user*) contains a set of speech recognition settings as well as speech recognition training data. When you first turn on speech recognition, it automatically creates a profile named Default Speech Profile. Each person who uses speech recognition should have a unique profile that matches the person's voice and preferences. If you use your computer in different rooms or attach different microphones, you might also want to create a separate profile for each environment.

> **Note** There is a separate Default Speech Profile for each user that is set up in Windows (just as there is a separate Favorites folder and Start menu configuration for each Windows user). Therefore, if each speech recognition user logs on to Windows as a separate user, it isn't necessary for them to create additional speech recognition profiles.

To modify the way speech recognition works, click the Tools button on the Language Bar to open the Tools drop-down menu shown here:

Then, choose the appropriate command, as shown in Table 5-4.

Note When you open the Tools drop-down menu from the Language Bar, some of the commands described in Table 5-4 might not be available. That's because the menu lets you choose only those commands that are supported by the currently active application, and all other commands are either hidden or disabled. For example, if Windows Explorer is currently active, you can choose only the Options command (and this command has limited functionality).

Table 5-4. Using the Tools Menu Commands on the Language Bar

To Do This	Choose This Command
Scan the document for new words to add to the speech recognition dictionary. When a word is added to this dictionary, Office speech recognition is then able to recognize that word. You can add individual words using the Add/Delete Word(s) command, described later in this table. It's a good idea to add to the dictionary the specialized words you use that aren't found in speech recognition's standard dictionary (business names, technical terms, and so on).	Learn From Document (Word only)
Open the Speech Input Settings dialog box, which allows you to change a large number of speech recognition features. For instance, you can control the display of speech messages, select the commands available in dictation mode, adjust your microphone settings, train and configure speech recognition profiles, and create new profiles.	Options
Run one or more speech recognition training sessions using the Speech Recognition Training Wizard, as discussed in "Training Speech Recognition," earlier in the chapter.	Training
Add or remove individual words from the speech recognition dictionary (see the first item in this table).	Add/Delete Word(s)
Activate a different speech recognition profile, if you have more than one.	Current User

Customizing the Language Bar

To modify the Language Bar itself or to change the input language settings, click the Options button on the bar (the small down arrow at the right end) to open the menu shown here:

To hide or display one of the Language Bar buttons, choose the corresponding command from this menu. (On this menu, a button that is displayed has a check mark next to it.) To return to the set of buttons shown by default, choose Restore Defaults. Choosing the Settings command opens the Text Services And Input Languages dialog box, which lets you do the following:

- Select an alternative default input language.
- Add, remove, or set the properties of a text service, such as a keyboard layout, speech recognition, or handwriting recognition.
- Change other input settings, such as modifying the Language Bar and changing the behavior of Caps Lock.

> **Tip** Another way to access commonly used Language Bar settings is to right-click the Language Bar and choose a command from the shortcut menu that appears. The specific commands that appear depend upon whether the Language Bar is displayed in the main part of the screen or has been minimized to the Windows taskbar.

NEW FEATURE! Using Handwriting in Office

The new handwriting interface in Office 2003 lets you enter text into a document using an electronic tablet and pen or (with some difficulty) an ordinary mouse. Specifically, the handwriting feature lets you do any of the following:

- Insert handwritten characters into a document. For example, you could insert your signature at the end of a letter or an e-mail message.
- Convert handwritten characters to regular document text.

- Quickly insert a freehand sketch.

- Issue a keyboard command (Enter, Backspace, Up arrow, Down arrow, Left arrow, Right arrow, or Tab) using an electronic pen or a mouse.

- Type a keyboard character, insert a symbol, or issue a keyboard command using an onscreen keyboard and an electronic pen or mouse, without using an actual keyboard. (Not every keyboard shortcut works, but most do.)

Accessing the Handwriting Interface

To access the handwriting interface, you begin by clicking the Handwriting button on the Language Bar and choosing a writing option from the drop-down menu, displayed here. These options are explained in the following sections.

General instructions on working with the Language Bar were given previously in the chapter (in the section "Using Speech in Office"). If the Language Bar isn't present, or if either the Handwriting button or its drop-down menu is missing from the Language Bar, you need to rerun Office Setup and install the Handwriting component. (That is, you must select Run From My Computer for this component.) You can find the Handwriting component in the Office Shared Features section, under the Alternative User Input group.

For information on rerunning Setup, see the tip "Install Speech Recognition," on page 84.

Entering Handwriting

To enter handwriting into an Office document, click the Handwriting button on the Language Bar and choose the Writing Pad option from the drop-down menu. This will open the Writing Pad window, shown in Figure 5-5. When the Writing Pad option is selected on the Handwriting drop-down menu, the button to the right is labeled Writing Pad, and you can click it to hide or redisplay the Writing Pad window.

Chapter 5

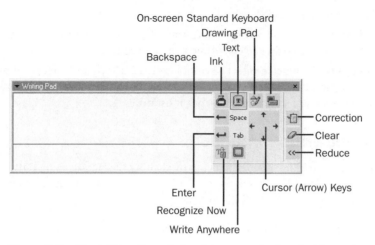

Figure 5-5. The Writing Pad window lets you enter handwriting using a separate program window. Here, all the buttons are shown; to hide some of the buttons, you would click the Reduce button.

> **Tip** Move the writing pad window to a convenient place
> You can drag the Writing Pad window to any convenient position on the screen. For example, you might want to drag it almost completely off the screen to temporarily make room for other work.

To enter handwritten characters directly into the document, so that the characters appear just as you sketch them, click the Ink button in the Writing Pad window to turn on the *ink mode*. You could use this mode, for example, to enter a signature. After switching on ink mode, use the pen with your electronic tablet (or use your mouse) to write in the Writing Pad window. To write, just press the main pen or mouse button and drag. Here's an example of a handwritten signature produced using this method:

Chapter 5

If you pause writing for a second or longer, the text you've written will be inserted into the document as an embedded Ink object, which displays the characters (or anything else you've scrawled) exactly as you sketched them, as shown in this example:

Until then, I remain

Yours Very Truly,

Mike

(Later in this section you'll learn how to change the length of the pause before the Ink object is inserted.)

> For more information on embedded objects, see "Embedding Data," on page 170.

An Ink object is a graphic object, not text, so you can't edit it in the document using text editing techniques. You can, however, format the text of an Ink object using standard character formatting methods. For example, you can change the characters' point size, make them bold or italic, change their color, and so on. To apply character formatting to an Ink object, complete the following steps:

1 Click the Ink object to select it. (All characters in an Ink object will be formatted the same way—you can't select or format individual characters.)

2 Apply the desired character formatting features using the controls on the Formatting toolbar (such as the Bold button), keyboard commands (such as Ctrl+I for italic), or the Font dialog box (to open it, choose Format, Font).

> Character formatting techniques for Word are described in "Formatting Characters Directly," on page 308.

Some character formats have no effect—or a very minimal effect—on an Ink object, for example, All Caps or changing the font.

To have the Handwriting interface *recognize* your handwritten letters and insert them into the document as regular text, click the Text button in the Writing Pad window to turn on text mode. Then use the pen with your electronic tablet (or use your mouse) to write the characters

Chapter 5

into the Writing Pad window. To write, just press the main pen or mouse button and drag. Here's an example:

If you pause writing for a second or longer, the letters entered into the window will be recognized and inserted as regular text into the document. (Later in this section, you'll learn how to change the length of this pause.)

Like speech recognition, handwriting recognition can make mistakes. If it inserts the wrong word, you can right-click the word and use the shortcut menu, shown here, to make a correction:

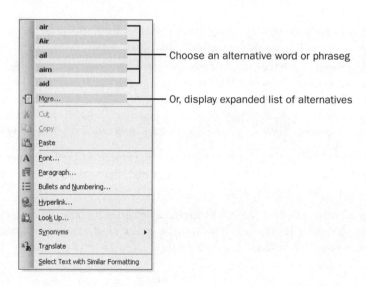

Chapter 5

The expanded list of alternatives looks like the one shown here:

Ink Object command

Another way to display the expanded list is to place the insertion point on the erroneous word and click the Correction button on the Language Bar or in the Writing Pad window. To insert the characters you've written as an Ink object rather than as text, so that they appear exactly as you wrote them, choose the Ink Object command below the expanded list.

If you don't find the right word among the alternatives, you can delete the erroneous letters and rewrite them in the Writing Pad window or just type them in. Unlike an Ink object, recognized text is regular text so you can fully edit or format it in the document.

Tip　**Replace a misspelled word**

If the application's while-you-type spelling checker has underlined a mistakenly inserted word, the shortcut menu won't display the alternative words or the More command. However, you can choose the Handwriting Alternatives command at the bottom of the shortcut menu to display handwriting recognition's expanded list of alternatives.

In either ink mode or text mode, you can click the buttons displayed along the side of the Handwriting window to issue common keyboard commands: Backspace, Space, Enter, or Tab. (See Figure 5-5.) Using these buttons might free you from the need to use a keyboard to navigate, edit text, or add space between words.

In either ink mode or text mode, you can use your electronic pen or mouse to write text within the document window itself, rather than within the Handwriting window, by clicking the Write Anywhere button in the Writing Pad window to enable write anywhere mode, as shown here:

Notice that in write anywhere mode, the Writing Pad window is converted to a toolbar containing the same buttons that were displayed at the right end of the Writing Pad window.

Note Another way to activate the write anywhere mode is to click the Handwriting button on the Language Bar and then choose Write Anywhere from the drop-down menu.

Finally, to change the way the handwriting interface works, click the Options button in the upper-left corner of the Writing Pad window and choose Options from the menu, as shown here:

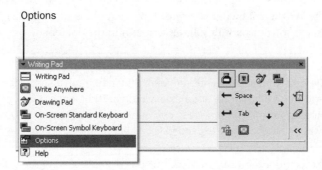

Then, select the options you want in the tabs of the Handwriting Options dialog box, shown in Figure 5-6.

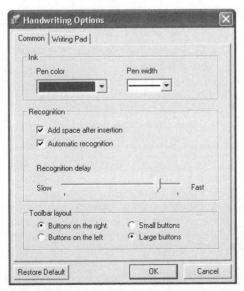

Figure 5-6. You use the Handwriting Options dialog box to modify the features of handwriting recognition.

Inserting Sketches

To insert freehand sketches into your documents, click the Handwriting button on the Language Bar and then choose the Drawing Pad option from the drop-down menu, if it's not already selected, as shown here:

The Drawing Pad window, shown in Figure 5-7, will then appear. If the Drawing Pad option is already selected on the Handwriting drop-down menu, you can display the Drawing Pad window by clicking the Drawing Pad button on the Language Bar.

Then, create your sketch in the Drawing Pad window as follows:

- To draw, press the main pen or mouse button and drag in the window.
- To insert your sketch into the document, click the Insert Drawing button.

Chapter 5

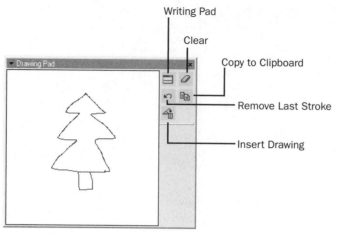

Writing Pad

Clear

Copy to Clipboard

Remove Last Stroke

Insert Drawing

Figure 5-7. You can create a freehand sketch in the Sketch window.

The sketch will be inserted into your document at the current position of the insertion point as an embedded graphic object known as a *drawing object.* Unlike an Ink object, a sketch isn't inserted automatically after you pause in drawing. Rather, you need to click the Insert Drawing button.

For more information on embedded objects, see "Embedding Data," on page 170.

Table 5-5 provides a summary of the tasks you can perform in the Drawing Pad window.

Table 5-5. Using the Drawing Pad Window

To Perform This Task in the Drawing Pad Window	Do This
Close the Drawing Pad window and open the Writing Pad instead	Click the Writing Pad button, or click the Options button (the down arrow in the upper left corner of the Drawing Pad window) and choose Writing Pad from the menu.
Erase the entire contents of the Drawing Pad window	Click the Clear button.
Erase the most recent sketch element drawn	Click the Remove Last Stroke button.
Copy the current contents of the Drawing Pad window to the Clipboard, so that you can paste the sketch anywhere in a document	Click the Copy To Clipboard button.
Insert the current contents of the Drawing Pad window into the document	Click the Insert Drawing button.

Table 5-5. Using the Drawing Pad Window

To Perform This Task in the Drawing Pad Window	Do This
Modify the color or thickness of the lines in the sketch or the size or the position of the buttons (on left or right)	Click the Options button (the down-arrow in the upper-left corner of the Drawing Pad window) and choose Options from the menu.
Close the Drawing Pad window	Click the Close button (the x in the upper right corner of the Drawing Pad window).

Using the On-Screen Keyboards

To use the pen with an electronic tablet or a mouse, to enter any keyboard character or to issue any keyboard command, click the Handwriting button on the Language Bar and then choose On-Screen Standard Keyboard from the drop-down menu. Then, use your pen or mouse to click buttons on the standard keyboard image displayed on your screen.

Clicking a button has the same effect as pressing the corresponding key on a keyboard. To "press" a key combination, such as Shift+A for a capital A or Ctrl+F6 to issue a command, first click the Shift, Ctrl, or Alt key (or several of these keys) and then click the letter or command key.

To use a pen or mouse to insert symbols, as well as to issue keyboard commands, click the Handwriting button on the Language Bar and then choose On-Screen Symbol Keyboard from the drop-down menu. Then, use your pen or mouse to click buttons on the symbol keyboard image displayed on your screen.

Note When either On-Screen Standard Keyboard or On-Screen Symbol Keyboard is selected on the Handwriting drop-down menu, you can hide or redisplay the on-screen keyboard by clicking the On-Screen Keyboard button on the Language Bar.

Adding Professional Graphics and Special Effects to Office 2003 Documents

Inserting Pictures into Office
Documents 107

Using AutoShapes to Create
Drawings 123

Generating Conceptual Drawings Using
Office Diagrams 127

Using WordArt to Produce Special
Text Effects 133

Constructing Charts Using Microsoft
Graph 136

Building Equations with Microsoft
Equation 139

Modifying Graphic Objects 142

Inserting Pictures into Office Documents

This section explains how to insert pictures into a Microsoft Office document. In Office, the term *picture* refers to a graphic object that's derived from outside the Office application. Specifically, you'll learn how to:

- Insert a picture from the Clip Organizer program
- Import a picture from a graphics file or from another Microsoft Windows program

Inserting Pictures with the Clip Organizer

You can use the Office Clip Organizer program to organize, find, preview, and insert into your documents the contents of media files (picture, movie, or sound) that are stored on your computer. The Clip Organizer, introduced with Office XP, replaces the Microsoft Clip Gallery program that was included with Microsoft Office 2000.

The Clip Organizer provides access only to those media files that have been imported into the program. In the Clip Organizer, these imported files are known as *media clips*. The Office Setup program automatically imports a set of media files that are provided with Office. If you wish, you can import additional media files that are stored on your local or network drives.

For each imported media file, the Clip Organizer stores the file's location and description, as well as a list of keywords (to help you find an appropriate clip) and a thumbnail image of the file's contents (to let you preview the clip). The file itself remains in its original location.

> Some of the Clip Organizer clips provided with Office insert AutoShapes, not pictures. For information on AutoShapes, see "Using AutoShapes to Create Drawings," on page 123.

Insert Clip
Art

In Microsoft Office Word, Excel, PowerPoint, or FrontPage, the fastest way to use the Clip Organizer to insert a graphic clip into a document is to place the insertion point at the position in your document where you want to display the picture and then either choose Insert, Picture, Clip Art or click the Insert Clip Art button on the Drawing toolbar (if it's displayed). This will display the Clip Art task pane within the Office application you're using (see Figure 6-1).

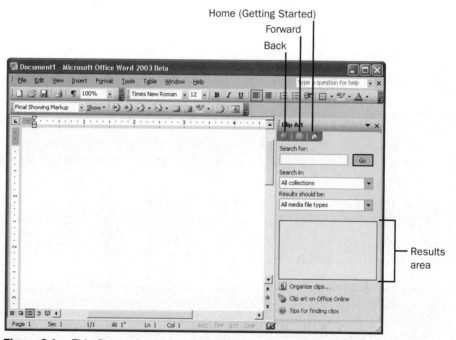

Figure 6-1. This figure shows the Clip Art task pane displayed in Word.

When you first display the Clip Art task pane (or run the freestanding Clip Organizer program, as explained later), you'll see the following dialog box:

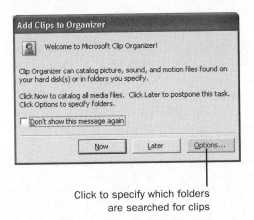

Click to specify which folders
are searched for clips

If you click the Now button, the Clip Organizer will find and import media files that are currently located on your computer. (These are imported in addition to the previously imported clips provided with Office.) The Clip Organizer will categorize the imported clips (that is, add each one to a particular collection that's named according to the folder where the clip is stored) and assign keywords to each clip. If you let the Clip Organizer perform this search, you might discover clips you didn't know you had stored on your computer. If you want to start using the Clip Organizer without importing additional clips, click the Later button.

> For information on other ways to import clips into the Clip Organizer, see "Importing Clips into the Clip Organizer," on page 116.

To search for clips using keywords in the Clip Art task pane, perform the following steps:

1 Enter a keyword in the Search For text box. For example:
   - To find all pictures of leaves, enter **leaves**.
   - To find all pictures that depict seasons, enter **seasons**.

2 In the Search In drop-down list, select the collection or collections you want to search, or select Everywhere to search all your collections.

   The Clip Organizer stores your clips within different named collections, such as Academic, Fantasy, or Nature. Like file folders, collections are arranged in a hierarchical treelike structure, with collections stored within other collections. That is, a given collection may contain one or more subcollections as well as media clips.

> **Note**   There's a subtlety in selecting collections in the Search In list. If a collection has subcollections within it and if it is expanded to show all subcollections, then the first time you click the collection's checkbox, that collection alone is selected. The second time you click the checkbox, that collection plus all its subcollections are selected. The third time you click, that collection alone is deselected. And the fourth time you click, that collection plus all its subcollections are deselected.

Tip Browse a collection

If you want to view all clips in a particular collection, select that collection in the Search In drop-down list and leave the Search For box empty.

3 In the Results Should Be drop-down list, select the specific types of clips you want to find—Clip Art, Photographs, Movies, or Sounds—or select All Media Types to find all types. To insert a picture into your document, select Clip Art, Photographs, or both types. (Graphics of the Photographs type typically have a large number of colors and are in Joint Photographic Experts Group [JPEG] format.)

4 Click the Go button to begin the search.

If you're creating a document meant to be viewed online (rather than printed) or if you're designing a Web page, you might want to insert movie or sound clips as well as pictures. For information on inserting movie and sound clips in Word documents, see "Adding Movies and Sounds," on page 585.

When you click the Go button, the results area of the Clip Art task pane will display all matching clips (see Figure 6-2).

Figure 6-2. This figure shows the results of searching for "leaves" in the Clip Art task pane.

> **Tip** You can widen the results area of the Clip Art task pane, so that you can view more clips at once, by clicking the Expand Results button.

The fastest way to insert a particular clip is to just click on it, as shown here:

You can also insert a clip, or manage it in other ways, by clicking the down arrow that appears when you move the pointer over the clip and choosing a command from the drop-down menu shown here:

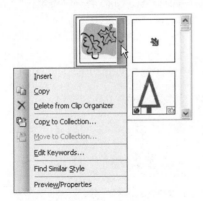

Tip **Access online clips**

The Clip Organizer includes a collection named Web Collections, which is displayed within the Search In drop-down list on the Clip Art task pane as well as in the freestanding Clip Organizer program, discussed later. This collection is intended for media clip collections that are located on the Web. Office provides a subcollection within Web Collections named Microsoft Office Online, which lets you directly access the media clips provided on the Office Online Web site (when an Internet connection is available). When a clip is located on the Web, a small globe icon appears in the lower left corner of the clip's thumbnail image, and the Copy To Collection command on the menu shown above is replaced with the Make Available Offline command, which lets you download the clip and store a permanent copy in one of your local collections.

If you want to view and download clips from Microsoft's site in your browser rather than from the Clip Art task pane, click the Clip Art On Office Online command at the bottom of the Clip Art task pane.

Note, however, that neither the Web Collections clip art collection nor the Clip Art On Office Online command will be available if the Show Content And Links From Microsoft Office Online option is cleared. To access this option, choose Help, Customer Feedback Options, and then select the Online Content category in the Service Options dialog box.

When you insert a clip, it will appear as a picture in your document, as shown in this example:

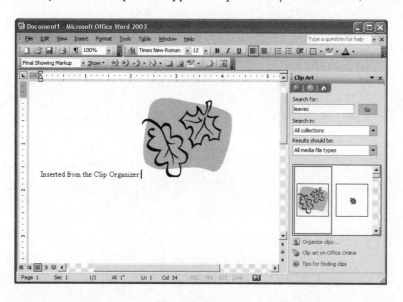

For instructions on modifying the picture once you've inserted it into the document, see "Modifying Pictures," on page 119, and "Modifying Graphic Objects," on page 142.

Running the Clip Organizer in Freestanding Mode

Rather than working with the Clip Organizer through an application task pane, you can run it as a freestanding program. When you run the Clip Organizer in freestanding mode, you can't paste a clip directly into a document. Rather, you have to copy the clip into the Clipboard and then insert it into your document using the Paste command. However, the freestanding program lets you view and work with your clips in ways that aren't possible in the task pane. It also lets you add clips to a Microsoft Outlook item or a Microsoft Access database object (these applications don't display the Clip Art task pane).

If you're currently displaying the Clip Art task pane in an Office application, the fastest way to run Clip Organizer in freestanding mode is to click the Organize Clips command in the task pane.

You can also run the freestanding program by choosing the Start, All Programs (or Programs), Microsoft Office Tools, Microsoft Clip Organizer command in Windows.

To use the freestanding Clip Organizer, first select one of its two main views: Search or Collection List. To perform a keyword search for a clip, click the Search button to open the Search view, shown in Figure 6-3. Then, perform your search using the Search task pane in the Clip Organizer window, which works just like the Clip Art task pane that appears in other Office applications, as explained in the previous section. The search results will appear in the main part of the program window.

Activate Search or Collection List view

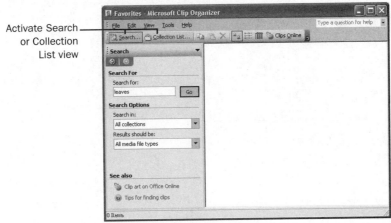

Figure 6-3. This figure shows the freestanding Clip Organizer program in Search view.

> **Tip** You can modify the way the Clip Organizer program displays clips by choosing the Thumbnails, List, or Details option on the View menu (the figures in this chapter show the Thumbnails view).

To work with a particular clip, click the down arrow that appears when you move the pointer over the clip in Thumbnails view and choose a command from the drop-down menu (see Figure 6-4).

Chapter 6

113

Figure 6-4. To work with one of the clips that has been found, open the drop-down menu.

Notice that this drop-down menu is similar to that shown in the Clip Art task pane of other Office applications. To insert a clip into a document, you need to choose the Copy command. Then, switch to the document, place the insertion point where you want to insert the clip, and use the application's Paste command to insert it. You can also perform several operations on a clip (such as copying it to a different collection) by clicking the clip to select it and then choosing a command from the Edit menu, as shown here:

Tip   **Insert a clip using drag-and-drop**

An alternative way to insert a Clip Organizer clip into any type of Office document is to drag the clip and drop it at the position in your document where you want to display it. You can use this technique with either the freestanding Clip Organizer program or with the Clip Art task pane displayed in another Office application.

To browse the available clips or to organize your clips, click the Collection List button to display the Collection List view, shown in Figure 6-5. To open a particular collection, expand the hierarchy (if necessary) in the Collection List task pane and then click on the collection. Its contents will then appear in the main part of the window.

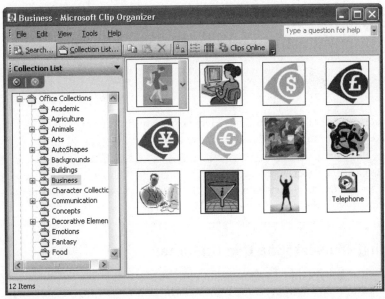

Figure 6-5.   This figure shows the freestanding Clip Organizer program in Collection List view, displaying the clips in the Business collection.

In the Collection List view you can also manage your collections by right-clicking a particular collection in the Collection List task pane and then choosing a command from the shortcut menu, shown here:

You can add a new collection or a new media clip only within My Collections, and you can modify a collection only if it's one that you've added.

> **Note** Clicking the Clips Online toolbar button in the freestanding Clip Organizer program has the same effect as clicking Clip Art On Office Online in the Clip Art task pane—running your browser and opening the Clip Art And Media home page on the Office Online site.

Importing Clips into the Clip Organizer

The fastest way to have the Clip Organizer import all the media files stored on your computer is to run the automatic import feature through the Add Clips To Organizer dialog box that's displayed when you start Clip Organizer. After you use the automatic import feature, the dialog box will no longer appear automatically. However, you can display it and use the automatic import feature at any time in the freestanding Clip Organizer program by choosing File, Add Clips To Organizer, Automatically.

You can also import an individual clip into the Clip Organizer using any of the following methods. (You can import the clip to any collection *except* one of the collections in the predefined Office Collections or Web Collections group.)

- To import a clip from a media file, in the freestanding Clip Organizer program choose File, Add Clips To Organizer, On My Own.

- To import a graphic object that's displayed in a document (such as a Word document), drag the object and, in the freestanding Clip Organizer program, drop it on the collection in which you want to store it. You can drop it either on the name of the destination collection in the Collection List view, or if the collection is currently displayed, you can drop it in the main part of the window (which shows the collection's contents).

- Another way to import a graphic object displayed in a document is to copy the graphic to the Clipboard, switch to the freestanding Clip Organizer program, open the collection where you want to store the clip, and choose Edit, Paste or press Ctrl+V.

Inside Out

Add meaningful keywords for imported clips

The Clip Organizer automatically assigns keywords to a clip that you import. However, it derives these keywords not from the actual content of the clip but rather from fairly irrelevant information, such as the folder where the media file is stored, the format of the clip, and even the name of the current Windows user. To make it easier to find the clip when you need it, you should add meaningful keywords based on the actual content of the clip. To do this, select the clip in the main window of the freestanding Clip Organizer program. Then choose Edit, Keywords. To assign the same keywords to an entire set of clips, select them all prior to choosing the Keywords command. You can select several clips by pressing Ctrl while clicking each one (to select adjoining clips, click the first one in the range and then press Shift and click the last one).

Importing Pictures

You can import a picture into a Word, Excel, PowerPoint, or FrontPage document either by inserting the contents of an entire graphics file or by copying a block of graphics from another program and pasting it into the document.

To import a picture from a graphics file, do the following:

1. Place the insertion point at the position in your document where you want to insert the picture.
2. Choose Insert, Picture, From File. This will open the Insert Picture dialog box, which is similar to the Open Office Document (or Open) dialog box for opening documents (see Figure 6-6).

Using the Open Office Document dialog box is explained in "Opening Existing Office Documents," on page 56.

3. In the Insert Picture dialog box, locate and select the graphics file you want to import. You can import graphics files in a wide variety of formats—for example, files with the extensions .bmp, .wmf, .gif, and .jpg. To see preview images of your graphics files, click the Views button and choose the Preview or Thumbnails view from the drop-down menu.
4. Click the Insert button.

Chapter 6

117

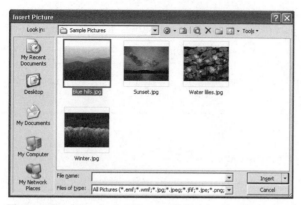

Figure 6-6. The Insert Picture dialog box is shown in the Thumbnails view.

Tip **Import more graphics formats**

To maximize the number of graphics formats that you can import into an Office document, make sure that all the Office graphics filters are installed. To do this, rerun Office Setup and select the Run From My Computer option for the Graphics Filters feature, which will install all the individual graphics filters. You'll find this feature in the Converters And Filters section, under the Office Shared Features group (see Figure 6-7). Because the filters don't take up a lot of disk space, it's a good idea to install all of them, rather than just the one you currently need.

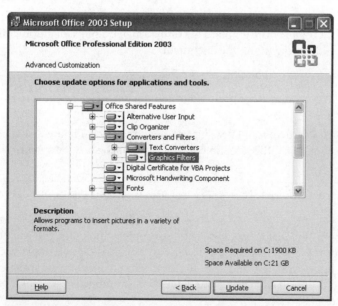

Figure 6-7. Installing all Office graphics filters is recommended.

Rerunning Office Setup is explained in "Revisiting Office Setup," on page 22.

To insert a picture into an Office document by copying graphics from another program (such as the Paint program that comes with Windows), perform the following steps:

1 Select the graphics in the other program, and from that program's Edit menu, choose Copy.

2 Place the insertion point at the approximate position in the Office document where you want to insert the picture.

3 From the Office application's Edit menu, choose Paste or press Ctrl+V.

For instructions on modifying the picture once you've inserted it into the document, see the next section.

Modifying Pictures

This section explains how to modify pictures using the commands and options provided by the Picture toolbar and the Picture tab of the Format Picture dialog box that apply specifically to pictures.

To learn about the common techniques, commands, and options for modifying pictures and other types of graphic objects, see "Modifying Graphic Objects," on page 142.

The fastest way to modify a picture is to use the Picture toolbar, shown below. Unless you previously hid the Picture toolbar, it appears whenever you click a picture to select it. (If the Picture toolbar doesn't appear when you select a picture, choose View, Toolbars, Picture.)

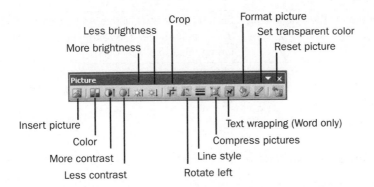

To modify the selected picture use the Picture toolbar as shown in Table 6-1.

Table 6-1. Methods for Modifying the Selected Picture Using the Picture Toolbar

To Modify the Selected Picture Like This	Do This with the Picture Toolbar
Add a new picture from a graphics file.	Click the Insert Picture From File button. (Clicking this button is equivalent to choosing Insert, Picture, From File.)
Set the picture colors to Grayscale (shades of gray), Black & White, Wash-out (faded tones), or Automatic (the original color values).	Click the Color button and choose an option from the drop-down menu.
Make light colors lighter and dark colors darker.	Click the More Contrast button, repeatedly if necessary, to achieve the result you want.
Make light colors darker and dark colors lighter.	Click the Less Contrast button, repeatedly if necessary, to achieve the result you want.
Make all colors lighter.	Click the More Brightness button, repeatedly if necessary, to achieve the result you want.
Make all colors darker.	Click the Less Brightness button, repeatedly if necessary, to achieve the result you want.
Crop the picture. (For more information on cropping, see "Cropping a Picture," on page 122.)	Click the Crop button and then drag one of the sizing handles displayed around the picture.
Rotate the picture image 90 degrees counterclockwise.	Click the Rotate Left 90° button.
Draw a border around the selected picture.	Click the Line Style button and choose a style from the drop-down menu. See the InsideOut element following this table.
Modify either the selected picture or all pictures in the document in one or more of the following ways: ● Optimize the picture resolution for either the Web or for printing. ● Compress the graphic data for the pictures. ● Delete cropped areas of pictures (if you do this, you won't be able to restore cropped areas).	Click the Compress Pictures button and select the desired options in the Compress Pictures dialog box.

Table 6-1. **Methods for Modifying the Selected Picture Using the Picture Toolbar**

To Modify the Selected Picture Like This	Do This with the Picture Toolbar
Change a picture's text wrapping style (available in Word only). (For information on wrapping styles, see "Combining Text with Graphic Objects and Text Boxes," on page 514.)	Click the Text Wrapping button (displayed in Word only) and choose a wrapping style from the drop-down menu.
Open the Format Picture dialog box. (For more information, see "Using the Format *Object* Dialog Box to Format Graphic Objects," on page 149.)	Click the Format Picture button (or choose Format, Picture).
Make a particular color in a picture transparent.	Click the Set Transparent Color button and then click an area in the picture with the color you want to make transparent. (This command isn't available for pictures in certain formats, such as a picture in .wmf format inserted from the Clip Organizer.)
Restore the size, cropping, and colors of the picture to their original values, and remove the border if you applied one.	Click the Reset Picture button.

Inside Out

Apply a border to an inline object

If a picture or other graphic object in a Word document has the In Line With Text wrapping style, Word won't let you use the Line Style button on the Picture toolbar to apply a border. A workaround is to assign a different wrapping style, apply the border, and then switch back to the In Line With Text style.

Note FrontPage displays an extended version of the Picture toolbar known as the Pictures toolbar. You can display it by choosing View, Toolbars, Pictures.

The Picture tab of the Format Picture dialog box provides an alternative way to crop a picture, to change the color (to Grayscale, Black & White, Washout, or Automatic), to adjust the contrast or brightness, to compress a picture, or to reset a picture. Although less convenient

Chapter 6

than the Picture toolbar, it lets you crop by entering precise measurements. You can also adjust the brightness and contrast by entering exact percentages. To do that, follow these steps:

1 Click the picture to select it.

2 Choose Format, Picture. Or, click the Format Picture button on the Picture toolbar.

3 Set options in the Picture tab of the Format Picture dialog box (see Figure 6-8).

Format Picture

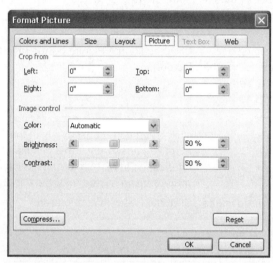

Figure 6-8. The Picture tab of the Format Picture dialog box is shown.

> **Tip** **Compress pictures when saving a document**
> You can also display the Compress Pictures dialog box when you save a Word, Excel, or PowerPoint document. In the Save As dialog box, choose Compress Pictures from the Tools drop-down menu.

Cropping a Picture

Changing the size of a picture by dragging a sizing handle or by using the Size tab of the Format Picture dialog box *scales* the picture—that is, it compresses or expands the graphics contained in the picture.

> The techniques for scaling pictures are covered in "Modifying Graphic Objects," on page 142.

Chapter 6

Alternatively, with a picture you can use the Picture toolbar's Crop button or the Picture tab in the Format Picture dialog box (shown in Figure 6-8) to *crop* a picture. Cropping a picture changes the size or proportions of the picture itself without changing the size or proportions of the graphics it contains. Cropping results in either cutting off some of the graphics or adding white space around them. Figure 6-9 shows the difference.

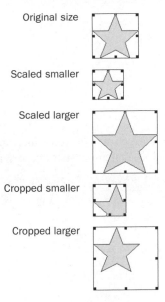

Original size

Scaled smaller

Scaled larger

Cropped smaller

Cropped larger

Figure 6-9. Scaling a picture is not the same as cropping it.

To crop using the Picture toolbar's Crop button, select the picture, click the button, and then drag any sizing handle on the picture. To use the Picture tab of the Format Picture dialog box, enter the amount that you want to crop each side of the picture—as a positive or negative number—into the Left, Right, Top, or Bottom box.

Using AutoShapes to Create Drawings

As an alternative to importing graphics, you can create drawings within Word, Excel, PowerPoint, or FrontPage by using AutoShapes. An AutoShape is a predefined or free-form figure—such as a line, oval, cube, flowchart symbol, banner, or free-form scribble—that you can quickly insert into a document and then customize.

To insert an AutoShape, perform the following steps:

1 Choose Insert, Picture, AutoShapes to display the AutoShapes toolbar shown here:

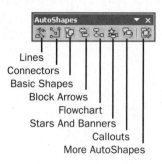

On the AutoShapes toolbar, click the button for the type of shape you want to insert. This will open a drop-down menu of AutoShapes belonging to that category, as shown in this example:

2 Click the button for the particular shape you want to insert. Notice that when you hold the mouse pointer over a button, a ToolTip displays a description of the shape, as shown here:

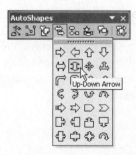

3 To insert a standard-sized AutoShape, click the position in your document where you want to display the figure, as shown here. (You can later change its size, shape, or position.)

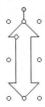

To give the AutoShape a specific initial size and shape, press the mouse button and drag to create the figure, as in this example:

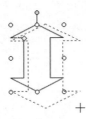

Inside Out

More AutoShapes command inserts clips as well as AutoShapes

Don't be misled by the label of the More AutoShapes button. It doesn't insert just AutoShapes. Rather, it displays the Clip Art task pane so you can insert pictures or other media clips, in addition to the AutoShapes contained in the Clip Organizer.

Drawing Canvases

In a Word document, when you click a button to insert an AutoShape, Word automatically inserts a graphic object known as a *drawing canvas*. A drawing canvas is a rectangular area that can contain one or more AutoShapes. The automatically inserted drawing canvas initially contains the message "Create Your Drawing Here." However, you can insert the AutoShape anywhere in the document—you don't need to put it within the drawing canvas. (Word removes the drawing canvas if you place the AutoShape outside of it.) You can also remove the drawing canvas by pressing the Esc key after you select a drawing tool but before you begin drawing.

A drawing canvas is primarily useful for creating a drawing consisting of two or more separate AutoShapes. The drawing canvas preserves the relative positions of these AutoShapes and prevents them from getting separated by page breaks or intervening text. The drawing canvas also makes it easy to move the entire set of AutoShapes in the drawing as a unit.

You can insert a blank drawing canvas in a Word document by choosing Insert, Picture, New Drawing.

Drawing

You might find it more convenient to use the Drawing toolbar to insert an AutoShape rather than the AutoShape toolbar. (When you display the AutoShapes toolbar, the application usually displays the Drawing toolbar at the same time. If the Drawing toolbar isn't present, you can display by choosing View, Toolbars, Drawing or by clicking the Drawing toolbar button if it's displayed in the application you're using.) The Drawing toolbar lets you insert any type of AutoShape; you can insert some of the more common ones with a single button click. The buttons for inserting AutoShapes are labeled here:

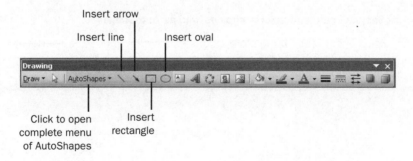

> For information on changing the size, shape, position, and other features of an AutoShape, see "Modifying Graphic Objects," on page 142.

Troubleshooting

AutoShapes disappear in Word

You inserted one or more AutoShapes, diagrams, or organization charts into a Word document. However, you no longer see them in the document.

The following are two situations in which AutoShapes, diagrams, or organization charts are hidden from view:

- You're viewing the document in Normal or Outline view. To insert or view AutoShapes, diagrams, or organization charts, however, you must be in Web Layout, Print Layout, Print Preview, or Reading Layout view. If you aren't in one of these views when you insert one of these objects, Word automatically switches to Print Layout view. However, if you later change to Normal or Outline view, the objects disappear.

- The Drawings view option is turned off. Word won't display these graphic objects— even in Web Layout or Print Layout view—if this option is off. (Print Preview and Reading Layout views always display graphic objects.) To turn on the option, choose Tools, Options, click the View tab, and check the Drawings option in the Print And Web Layout Options area.

Generating Conceptual Drawings Using Office Diagrams

You can create almost any type of conceptual drawing by using one or more individual AutoShapes, as described in the previous section. However, in Word, Excel, or PowerPoint you can get a head start in building a conceptual drawing—such as an organization chart or a Venn diagram—by inserting a ready-made Office *diagram*. When you insert a diagram, Office instantly adds all the necessary AutoShapes and places them within a rectangular drawing area (which is similar to a Word drawing canvas, described in the previous section). Office also provides tools that make it easy to customize the drawing and add text to it.

Creating an Organization Chart

You can insert an organization chart into a document to illustrate an organization's structure or to depict other hierarchical relationships—for example, the families, genera, and species of a particular order of biological organisms. To add an organization chart, perform the following steps:

1 Choose Insert, Picture, Organization Chart.

Office will then insert an organization chart with a single top-level box and three subordinate boxes, and it will display the Organization Chart toolbar, shown in Figure 6-10. (This toolbar appears automatically whenever you select an organization chart.)

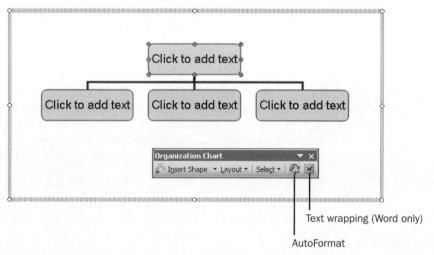

Figure 6-10. This figure shows an organization chart inserted into a Word document.

For information on text wrapping in Word, see "Combining Text with Graphic Objects and Text Boxes," on page 514.

2 To add text to a box, click in it and type the desired text.

3 To add a new box, click an existing box to select it, click the down arrow on the Insert Shape button on the Organization Chart toolbar, and from the drop-down menu choose the desired relationship of the new box to the selected box, as shown here:

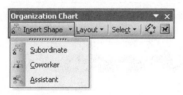

Or, to insert a new box with the Subordinate relationship, simply click the Insert Shape button (but not on the down arrow).

To delete a box, click on one of the box's borders to select the box (so that eight moving handles appear around the box) and then press Delete.

4 To modify the overall structure of the organization chart, click the Layout button on the Organization Chart toolbar and choose the structure you want from the drop-down menu, as shown here:

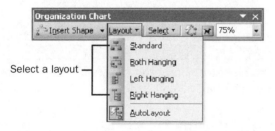

You can move a particular box within the chart by dragging one of the box's borders and dropping the box on another box.

Tip   **Control automatic layout**

The AutoLayout option on the Layout drop-down menu (which is on by default) causes Office to automatically maintain the positions and sizes of the individual AutoShape objects that make up an organization chart (or one of the other types of diagrams you'll see later). This option restricts the ways you can modify the AutoShapes—for example, you might not be able to drag an AutoShape to a particular position if this option is on. If you're customizing a diagram and can't modify an AutoShape the way you want, try turning this option off. Otherwise, you should leave it on.

Chapter 6

5 To modify the organization chart's overall style, click the AutoFormat button on the Organization Chart toolbar and choose a style in the Organization Chart Style Gallery dialog box (shown in Figure 6-11).

> To learn how to modify the individual AutoShapes in an organization chart, see "Modifying Graphic Objects," on page 142.

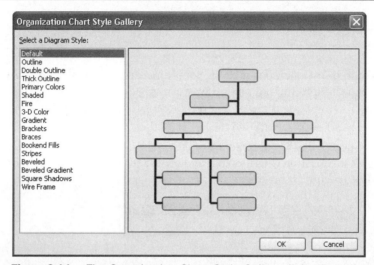

Figure 6-11. The Organization Chart Style Gallery dialog box allows you to customize an organization chart's overall style.

Creating Other Types of Diagrams

To insert a cycle, radial, pyramid, Venn, or target diagram, perform the following steps:

1 Choose Insert, Diagram.

2 In the Diagram Gallery dialog box, click the particular type of diagram you want to create and then click the OK button. Or, just double-click the diagram type, as shown here:

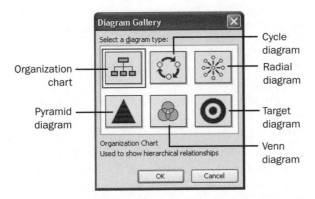

Selecting the Organization Chart diagram type has the same effect as choosing Insert, Picture, Organization Chart. The procedure for creating an organization chart is different from that for creating the other diagram types. If you want an organization chart, follow the instructions given in the previous section.

Office will insert the basic diagram and will display the Diagram toolbar. (This toolbar appears automatically whenever you select a diagram other than an organization chart.) The diagram will consist of a collection of AutoShapes, all inside a rectangular drawing area (see Figure 6-12).

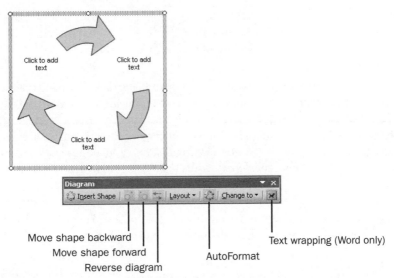

Figure 6-12. This is a cycle diagram inserted into a Word document, showing the Diagram toolbar, which appears when the diagram is selected.

For information on text wrapping in Word, see "Combining Text with Graphic Objects and Text Boxes," on page 514.

3   To add text to the diagram, click in any of the AutoShapes that are labeled "Click to add text" and type in your text.

4   To add a new shape to the diagram (for example, a new sector to a cycle diagram or a new level to a pyramid diagram), click the Insert Shape button on the Diagram toolbar. To delete a shape, click on one of its borders and press Delete.

5   To rearrange your text labels within the diagram, select the AutoShape containing the particular label you want to move, and then on the Diagram toolbar, click the Move Shape Backward button to move the label within the diagram in one direction or the Move Shape Forward button to move it in the other direction.

6   To reverse the order of the labels in the diagram, click the Reverse Diagram button on the Diagram toolbar.

7   To adjust the size of the drawing area containing the diagram, click the Layout button on the Diagram toolbar and choose an option from the drop-down menu, shown here:

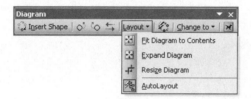

The Fit Diagram To Contents and Expand Diagram commands change the overall size of the drawing area that contains the diagram without scaling the diagram itself.

Note   The Resize Diagram and AutoLayout commands on the Layout drop-down menu work the same way as the Resize Organization Chart and AutoLayout commands on the Layout menu for an organization chart, as described in "Creating an Organization Chart," earlier in this chapter.

8   To modify the diagram's overall style, click the AutoFormat button and select a style in the Diagram Style Gallery dialog box, shown in Figure 6-13.

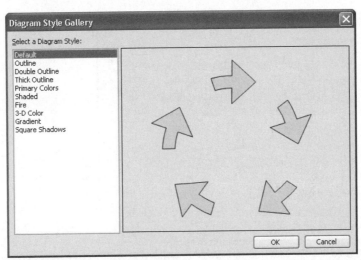

Figure 6-13. You use the Diagram Style Gallery dialog box to customize the overall style of an Office diagram.

9 To convert the diagram to another type (for example, to change a cycle diagram to a Venn diagram) while preserving your text labels, click the Change To button on the Diagram toolbar and choose the drawing type you want from the drop-down menu, shown here:

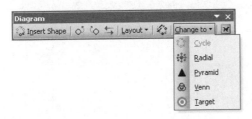

> To learn how to modify the AutoShapes in a diagram, see "Modifying Graphic Objects," on page 142.

Using WordArt to Produce Special Text Effects

In a Word, Excel, PowerPoint, or FrontPage document you can add unusually formatted text—for example, curved, slanted, or three-dimensional text—by inserting a WordArt object. To do this, perform the following steps:

1 Choose Insert, Picture, WordArt. Or, if the Drawing toolbar is displayed, you can click the WordArt button.

2 In the WordArt Gallery dialog box (shown in Figure 6-14), double-click the style you want.

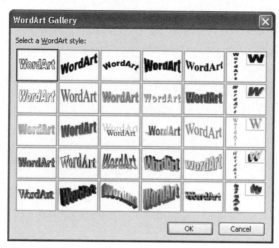

Figure 6-14. You use the WordArt Gallery dialog box to insert special text effects.

3 In the Edit WordArt Text dialog box (shown in Figure 6-15), type your text and select the desired font and size.

Bold   Italic

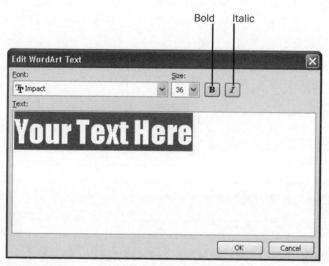

Figure 6-15. In the Edit WordArt Text dialog box, you enter the text and select the desired font, size, and style.

Click the Bold or Italic button to make *all* text bold or italic. (You can't apply bold or italic to a selected portion of the text.)

4 In the Edit WordArt Text dialog box, click the OK button. Office will insert your text into the document.

Whenever the WordArt object is selected, Office displays the WordArt toolbar (shown in Figure 6-16). If this toolbar isn't visible when you've selected a WordArt object, choose View, Toolbars, WordArt to display it.

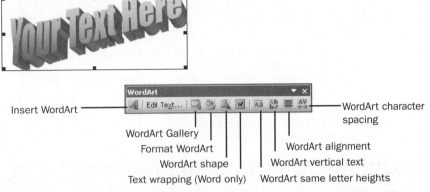

Figure 6-16. The WordArt toolbar lets you insert and work with WordArt objects.

> For information on text wrapping in Word, see "Combining Text with Graphic Objects and Text Boxes," on page 514.

5 If you want to modify the WordArt object, use the WordArt toolbar, as shown in Table 6-2.

Table 6-2. Using the WordArt Toolbar

To Modify a WordArt Object Like This	Click This WordArt Toolbar Button
Add a new WordArt object.	Insert WordArt
Open the Edit WordArt Text dialog box, where you can edit the text, change the text font or size, or apply bold or italic.	Edit Text
Open the WordArt Gallery dialog box, where you can select a different text style.	WordArt Gallery
Open the Format WordArt dialog box, where you can change many features of the WordArt object. (For general instructions on using this dialog box, see "Using the Format *Object* Dialog Box to Format Graphic Objects," on page 149.)	Format WordArt
Display a drop-down menu from which you can choose a different text pattern (for example, various types of curved or slanted text).	WordArt Shape
Toggle between text with same-height letters and text in which the first letter of each word is higher.	WordArt Same Letter Heights

Table 6-2. Using the WordArt Toolbar

To Modify a WordArt Object Like This	Click This WordArt Toolbar Button
Toggle between vertical and horizontal text.	WordArt Vertical Text
Display a drop-down menu from which you can choose a text alignment style.	WordArt Alignment
Display a drop-down menu from which you can choose a character spacing style.	WordArt Character Spacing

> For information on common formatting techniques that you can use to modify a WordArt object, see "Modifying Graphic Objects," on page 142.

Constructing Charts Using Microsoft Graph

Using the Microsoft Graph program, you can insert charts into your Office documents. Graph supports a wide variety of chart types and provides a handy alternative to using Excel charts.

The fastest way to create a chart with the Graph program is to use a Word table (you can later move the chart to a different Office application). To do that, complete the following steps:

1 Insert a table into a Word document, enter into this table the data that you want to graph, and then select the entire table. (An easy way to select an entire table is to place the insertion point within the table and choose Table, Select, Table.) An example is shown in Figure 6-17.

Contract	Gross Profit
Corn	6,392.00
Oats	3,920.00
Soybean Meal	-1,560.00
Soybean Oil	1,598.00
Soybeans	-2,598.00
Wheat	9,403.00

Figure 6-17. Select the Word table containing the data that you want to graph.

> For information on Word tables, see "Arranging Text with Tables," on page 345. For details on creating charts in Excel, see Chapter 27, "Advanced Worksheet Charts."

2 Choose Insert, Picture, Chart.

Graph will immediately embed a chart into the document that depicts the data contained in the Word table. Graph will also display a datasheet containing the chart data (see Figure 6-18).

> For more information on embedded objects, see "Embedding Data," on page 170.

Chapter 6

Table entered in the
Word document in step 1

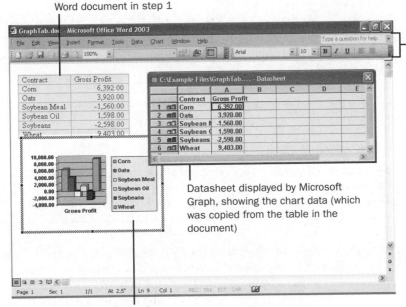

Menu commands
and toolbar buttons
provided by
Microsoft Graph

Datasheet displayed by Microsoft
Graph, showing the chart data (which
was copied from the table in the
document)

Chart that Microsoft Graph inserted into
the document as an embedded object

Figure 6-18. This figure shows a Chart object, based on the Word table shown
in Figure 6-17, embedded in a Word document.

3   The datasheet contains a copy of the data from the original Word table that you
    selected. If you want to change the values plotted on the chart, you must edit the num-
    bers within the datasheet, not within the original table.

4   If you want, you can now make modifications to the chart using the menu commands
    and toolbar buttons provided by the Graph program. You can access detailed online
    information on using the Graph commands by choosing Microsoft Graph Help from
    the Help menu or by pressing F1.

Note   The Graph program toolbar buttons and menu commands are available (interspersed with Word commands) whenever the Graph chart is opened in *editing mode* (it's
opened in this mode when you first insert it). If you click outside the chart, it will no longer
be in editing mode—to reopen the chart in editing mode, double-click it.

Chapter 6

5 To change the chart's size or proportions, drag the sizing handles displayed around the embedded object.

6 When you've finished modifying the chart, click in the Word document outside the chart and the datasheet. The datasheet and the menu commands and toolbar buttons provided by the Graph program will disappear, leaving the chart embedded in your document.

Inside Out

The table and chart aren't linked

Once the chart is inserted, a copy of the data from the table in the Word document is stored independently within the embedded chart object. Changing the table data won't affect the chart; in fact, you can delete the Word table if you want to.

View
Datasheet

If you want to modify the chart later, simply double-click the embedded chart object. The commands provided by Graph will return, and you can change the features of the chart. If the datasheet isn't visible and you need to change the numbers shown on the chart, you can display it by choosing View, Datasheet or by clicking the View Datasheet button on the Graph toolbar. If you want to display the chart within another Office document (for example, in a PowerPoint presentation), select the Chart object, cut or copy it, and then paste it into the other document.

You can modify a chart's appearance using the Picture toolbar or the Picture tab of the Format Object dialog box, which were explained in "Modifying Pictures," on page 119.

Inside Out

It's easiest to create a chart from a Word table

If you embed a new Graph chart within a program other than Word (by choosing the Object command from the program's Insert menu and selecting the Microsoft Graph Chart object type), or if you embed a new Graph chart in a Word document without first selecting a table containing valid chart data, Graph will create an example chart displaying example data. You then need to manually enter the actual data, as well as the row and column headings, cell by cell, into the Graph datasheet. (You can also import data into the datasheet from an Excel workbook or other file. To import data, make sure that the Graph object is active, choose Edit, Import File, and select the file in the Import Data dialog box.)

For information on common formatting techniques that you can use to modify a chart, see "Modifying Graphic Objects," on page 142.

Building Equations with Microsoft Equation

If you create Office documents that involve mathematics, you'll find the little-publicized Microsoft Equation program useful for accurately formatting equations in your documents. You can insert an equation into Word, Excel, PowerPoint, Outlook (in the large text box of an item opened in a form), or Access (in an OLE Object type field). To enter an equation, perform the following steps:

1   Choose Insert, Object.

2   In the Object dialog box, click the Create New tab, choose the Microsoft Equation 3.0 object type, and click OK. Equation will insert a blank working area into your document, and the Equation toolbar and menus will appear within the Office application's window (see Figure 6-19).

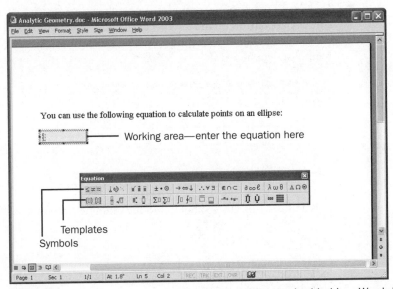

Figure 6-19.   This figure shows an Equation object embedded in a Word document.

> The equation you insert is an embedded object created by the Equation program. For more information on embedded objects, see "Embedding Data," on page 170.

3 Use the following instructions to create a mathematical expression:

■ To enter numbers or variables, simply type them using the keyboard, such as the y typed to begin the following example equation:

■ To enter a mathematical operator that appears on the keyboard, such as the plus sign (+), the minus sign (−), or the equals sign (=), you can simply type it. For instance, you could add an equals sign to the example equation, as shown here:

■ To enter an operator or symbol that doesn't appear on the keyboard, click the appropriate button on the top row of the Equation toolbar and then click the desired symbol on the drop-down palette of symbols. For example, clicking the symbol shown here:

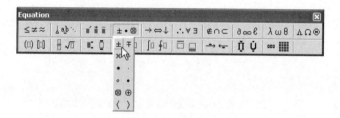

adds a plus-or-minus symbol (±) to the example equation, as shown here:

■ To enter an expression such as a fraction, a square root, an exponent, or an integral, click the appropriate button on the bottom row of the Equation toolbar, and then choose one of the templates on the drop-down palette. For example, you would click the following template:

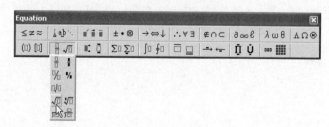

to add a square-root expression to the example equation, as shown here:

Then enter the desired numbers and variables into the area marked by dotted lines within the template. For example, you could type the following into the radical expression in the example equation:

$$y = \pm\sqrt{1+a}$$

You can insert templates within other templates to create nested operator expressions, such as a fraction within a square-root operator.

You can modify the font, font size, position (for example, subscript or superscript), or format (that is, normal, bold, or italic) of characters or symbols by selecting them and choosing commands from the Style and Size menus.

Note   When you hold the mouse pointer over a button on the Equation toolbar, a description of the button will be displayed in the Office application's status bar and sometimes also in a ScreenTip next to the button.

Troubleshooting

Can't enter spaces into an equation

The Equation Editor won't let you enter space characters when you're typing an expression. (It beeps when you make the attempt.)

To create consistent spacing, Equation Editor automatically sets the spacing between the numbers and symbols that you enter and won't let you type in space characters manually. You can adjust the spacing or alignment of symbols, however, by selecting symbols from the Spaces And Ellipses palette, as shown in the following figure, or by choosing commands from the Format menu.

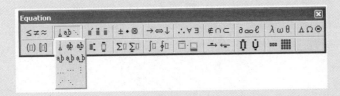

Tip Format an equation

You can display an equation in faded letters by means of the Picture toolbar by clicking the Color button and choosing Washout from the drop-down menu. You can also crop (rather than scale) an equation by means of the Picture toolbar by clicking the Crop button or by using the Picture tab of the Format Object dialog box.

The Picture toolbar techniques are explained in "Modifying Pictures," on page 119. For a description of common formatting methods you can use with an equation, see the next section, "Modifying Graphic Objects."

Modifying Graphic Objects

This section summarizes the general methods that you can use to modify any of the types of graphic objects described previously in this chapter: pictures, AutoShapes, organization charts and other types of diagrams, WordArt objects, Graph charts, and equations (as well as text boxes, described in Chapter 18, "Designing and Printing Professional-Looking Pages"). Keep in mind that the particular commands and features that are available for working with a given graphic object depend on the Office application you're using, the type of object, and the formatting features currently assigned to the object. The best way to work with a particular type of graphic object is to explore the three general approaches introduced in the following sections—using the mouse, using the Drawing toolbar, and using the Format *Object* dialog box—and discover exactly which commands are available for the object you're working with.

Using the Mouse to Resize, Reshape, Rotate, or Move Graphic Objects

To change the dimensions of a graphic object, click it to select it and then drag one of the uncolored, round sizing handles that appear around the object, as shown here:

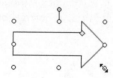

To maintain the object's original proportions as you change its size, press Shift while dragging one of the corner sizing handles. To resize the object symmetrically about its center (that is, to change the object's size without moving the position of its center), hold down the Ctrl key while dragging a sizing handle.

Changing the size of a picture using the technique given here *scales* the picture. To learn about *cropping* a picture instead of scaling, see "Cropping a Picture," on page 122.

With WordArt objects, as well as some AutoShapes, Office displays a yellow, diamond-shaped reshaping handle. Dragging this handle lets you change some aspect of the object's shape, such as the angle of the sides of a trapezoid or the thickness of the shaft or the length of the head of an arrow, as shown here:

Reshaping handle

The effect of dragging a reshaping handle varies widely among different types of AutoShape and WordArt objects.

To rotate a graphic object, drag the green, round rotation handle, shown in this example:

Rotation handle

To move a graphic object to a different position in your document, place the mouse pointer over the object (but not over a handle if the object is selected) and when the pointer displays cross-arrows, drag the object to the desired location, as shown here:

143

To copy rather than move the object, hold down the Ctrl key while you drag. Alternatively, when an object is selected, you can use the keyboard to move it by pressing the appropriate arrow key: Up, Down, Left, or Right. (You can't copy the object using the keyboard method. However, the advantage of the keyboard method is that you can precisely control the direction and amount of movement.)

Inside Out

Working with an inline graphic object in Word

When you select a graphic object in Word that's assigned the In Line With Text wrapping style, Word sometimes displays rectangular sizing handles only, and you can't reshape or rotate the object using the methods described here. (See "Combining Text with Graphic Objects and Text Boxes," on page 514.) A workaround is to assign a different wrapping style, reshape or rotate the object as desired, and then switch back to the In Line With Text style.

Also, because an object with the In Line With Text wrapping style is an integral part of the text and is treated like a single text character, you must move or copy it to a different position in the text using the standard methods for moving and copying text, which are discussed in "Editing the Selection," on page 287.

Using the Drawing Toolbar to Modify Graphic Objects

Drawing

The Drawing toolbar in Word, Excel, PowerPoint, and FrontPage provides a large, heterogeneous set of commands for creating and modifying graphic objects. To display this toolbar, choose View, Toolbars, Drawing or click the Drawing toolbar button (if available). The Drawing toolbar is shown here:

The Drawing toolbar contains three groups of buttons. To select and modify graphic objects, use the first group, as shown here:

Select Objects

As when you work with document text, the general procedure for working with a graphic object is to first select the object and then perform an action on it. You can often select a graphic object by simply clicking it when you're in the normal text editing mode. Alternatively, you can click the Select Objects button to switch into selection mode, which lets you easily select several objects at once.

Selection mode also lets you select a Word object that's contained in the layer underneath text. Layers are explained in "Combining Text with Graphic Objects and Text Boxes," on page 514.

When you click the Select Objects button to switch into selection mode, the pointer turns into an arrow slanting up and to the left. While in this mode, click the object you want to select. To select several objects so that you can perform some action on them simultaneously, drag a selection rectangle around all of them, as shown here:

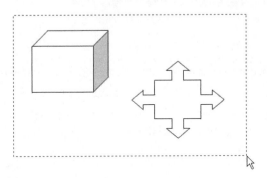

Chapter 6

The selection rectangle must completely surround each object you want to include in the selection.

Alternatively, you can select several objects at once by pressing Shift while you click each one. This method allows you to select several objects in an area without selecting all the objects in this area. (To remove the selection from one of the objects, press Shift and click it again.) To switch off selection mode so that you can work with text, click the Select Objects button again (this button toggles selection mode on and off) or press Esc.

To delete the selected graphic object or objects, press the Delete key.

To modify the selected graphic object or objects, you can click the Draw button and choose a command from the menu shown here:

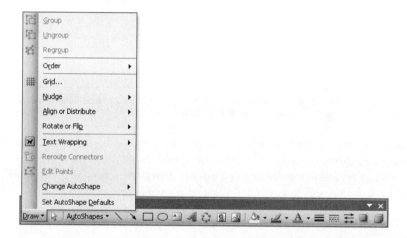

The Draw menu in Word also has a Text Wrapping submenu, which allows you to change the wrapping style of the selected object, as explained in "Combining Text with Graphic Objects and Text Boxes," on page 514.

If you have selected several graphic objects, you can combine them into a single object so that you can work with them as a unit. To do this, choose the Group command from the Draw menu. You can later break apart the group into its constituent objects by selecting the group and choosing Ungroup from this same menu. (You can later choose Regroup to reestablish this same group without first selecting the individual objects that belonged to the group.)

To control the overlapping order of different drawing objects that intersect on the page, select an object, click the Draw button on the Drawing toolbar, point to Order on the menu, and choose the appropriate command from the submenu, as shown here:

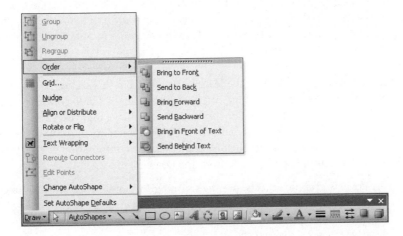

You can also use commands on the Draw menu to align, move, rotate, or flip the selected object or objects, as shown here:

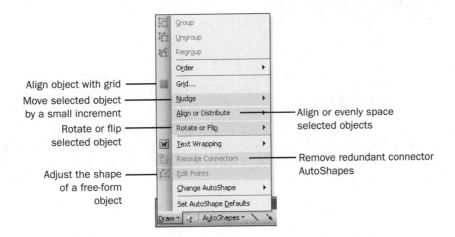

Tip Transform an AutoShape

If you've spent some time inserting, sizing, and formatting a particular AutoShape and then realize that you'd rather be working with a different type of AutoShape, you don't need to delete the object and start over. Rather, you can simply convert it to the AutoShape object you want. To do this, select the object and choose the new type of AutoShape object you want from the Change AutoShape submenu of the Draw menu on the Drawing toolbar.

You can experiment freely with all of the features discussed in this section. If you don't like the result of applying a particular feature or effect, just issue the Undo command to remove it. If you do like the result of a particular combination of effects that you've applied to an AutoShape, you can make them the default effects to be applied to all AutoShapes that you subsequently draw. To do this, select the object that has the combination of effects you want and then choose Set AutoShape Defaults from the Draw menu.

To quickly insert new graphic objects, use the second group of buttons on the Drawing toolbar, shown here:

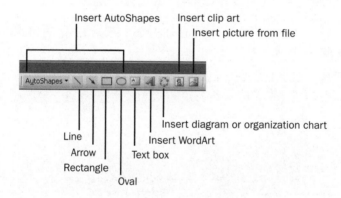

To change the selected object's fill color or pattern, line color or style, or font color, or to add shadow or three-dimensional effects to the object, use the buttons in the third group on the Drawing toolbar, shown here:

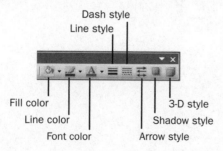

Table 6-3 shows how to modify the selected graphic object(s) with these buttons.

Table 6-3. Modifying Graphic Objects Using the Drawing Toolbar

To Modify the Selected Graphic Object(s) Like This	Click This Drawing Toolbar Button
Select a fill color or effect	Fill Color
Select a line color or line pattern	Line Color
Select a color for text in a text box or in an AutoShape	Font Color
Select a solid line style	Line Style
Select a dotted or dashed line style	Dash Style
Add (or change) an arrow on an AutoShape line	Arrow Style
Add a shadow effect to the drawing object	Shadow Style
Add a three-dimensional effect to the drawing object	3-D Style

The following example shows an AutoShape rectangle as it appeared when it was first inserted and then as it appears after a fill color and a three-dimensional effect are applied.

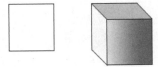

Using the Format *Object* Dialog Box to Format Graphic Objects

The Format *Object* dialog box provides the largest set of formatting options. The actual title of the dialog box depends on the type of the selected graphic object—for example, Format Picture, Format AutoShape, or Format Diagram. To format an object using this dialog box, perform the following steps:

1 Click the object to select it. (To select an object that's behind text in Word, you must first click the Select Objects button on the Drawing toolbar.)

2 From the Format menu, choose the Picture, AutoShape, Organization Chart, Diagram, WordArt, or Object command. The command name depends on the type of object you've selected. (The command will be Format Object if you've selected a Graph or Equation object.) The command will open the Format *Object* dialog box.

3 Select formatting options in the tabs of the Format *Object* dialog box. The specific tabs and options that are available depend on the type of graphic object you've selected and the application you're using. Figure 6-20 shows the Format Picture dialog box that would be displayed if you selected a picture in Word.

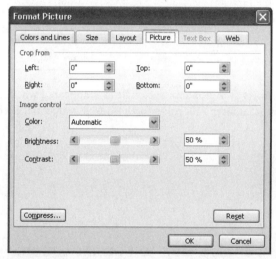

Figure 6-20. This is the Format Picture dialog box shown in Word.

Table 6-4 shows what you can do in the six tabs of the Format *Object* dialog box.

Note Some Office applications include additional tabs in the Format *Object* dialog box that aren't listed in Table 6-4. These tabs have uses specific to the application. For example, Excel includes a Protection tab for locking objects in a protected worksheet and a Properties tab for controlling the positioning and printing of the object.

Table 6-4. **Modifying Graphic Objects Using the Format *Object* Dialog Box**

To Modify the Selected Graphic Object(s) Like This	Use This Tab in the Format *Object* Dialog Box
● Select a background fill color *or* ● Set the color, style, and thickness of the lines used for drawing an AutoShape; or draw a border around other kinds of objects *or* ● Add arrows at the ends of an AutoShape line (or modify existing arrows)	Colors And Lines
Resize or rotate the object or restore its original size	Size
Select the object's wrapping style and horizontal alignment (Word only)	Layout (Word only)
For a picture, crop the picture, convert the picture colors (to Grayscale, Black & White, or Washout), or set the brightness and contrast of the picture colors	Picture
For a text box, modify the margins between the text and the edges of the text box	Text Box
Assign alternative text that a Web browser will display while the object is downloading if the object's file is missing or if graphics are disabled in the browser	Web

Wrapping styles are explained in "Combining Text with Graphic Objects and Text Boxes," on page 514. Text boxes are discussed in "Using Text Boxes to Create Precise Page Layouts," on page 510. Creating Web pages in Word is covered in Chapter 20, "Creating Web Pages and Working with XML in Word."

Chapter 6

Modifying a Graphic Object Using the Shortcut Menu

You can perform several of the operations discussed in this section by right-clicking a drawing object and choosing the command that accomplishes what you want from the shortcut menu that appears. The commands provided on this menu depend on the application you're using, the type of the drawing object, and the features you've applied to it. Here's the shortcut menu shown for an AutoShape in Word:

If you right-click a closed AutoShape figure, such as an oval or star, the shortcut menu provides an interesting command that isn't available elsewhere: Add Text. This command lets you add text to the AutoShape object so that it functions just like a text box, but with an interesting shape, as in the following example:

Exchanging Data in Office 2003

Different Ways to Exchange Data 153
Copying and Moving Data Statically . . . 155

Linking Data 162
Embedding Data 170

Different Ways to Exchange Data

In the parts of this book covering the individual applications in the Microsoft Office System, you'll learn the basic, traditional methods for copying and moving data within a single document or among separate documents within a single program. In this chapter you'll learn the different ways of exchanging data among separate Office applications. You'll also learn how to use the enhanced Clipboard features provided by Office, which allow you to store and exchange multiple blocks of data. (Although you can use the Office Clipboard for exchanging data within an application as well as among separate applications, it's covered here because it's a shared Office facility.)

This section provides a general overview of the three basic ways to exchange data among separate Office applications:

- Static copying or moving of data
- Linking of data
- Embedding of data

This discussion will help you choose the most appropriate method. The following sections discuss the specific techniques for performing each method.

With *static copying* or *static moving*, the data that you insert becomes an integral part of the receiving document and retains no link or connection with the document or program from which it was obtained. This is the type of copying or moving that you normally use when you work within a single document or application, using the techniques discussed in the later parts of the book. When you statically copy or move data from one application to another, you might or might not be able to edit the data within the receiving document. If the data can be converted to a format that the receiving program understands, you'll be able to edit it—for example, when you copy text from a Microsoft Excel worksheet and paste it into a Microsoft Word document. If, however, the data can't be converted into a format native to the receiving program, the data can be displayed and printed but not edited in the receiving program—for example, when you copy a bitmapped graphic from a drawing program such as Microsoft Paint and paste it as static data into a Word document.

With *linking*, the data that you insert retains its connection with the document and the program from which it was obtained. In fact, a complete copy of the data is stored only within the source document; the receiving document stores only the linking information and the information required to display the data. When the data in the source document is edited (by you or by someone else), the linked data in the receiving document can be updated automatically or manually to reflect the changes.

With *embedding*, the inserted data retains its connection with the source program but not with the source document. In fact, there might not even be a source document, because you can create new embedded data contained only in the receiving document. The receiving document stores a complete copy of the information, just as it does with statically copied data. However, because of the connection between this data and the source program, you can use the source program's tools to edit the data.

A document that contains linked or embedded data from other programs is known as a *compound document*.

You should use linking rather than embedding when you want to store and maintain data within a single document and merely display an up-to-date copy of the data in one or more other documents. Linking would be especially useful in the following situations:

- You want to display only part of the source document within the receiving document. For example, in a Word document you want to display only a totals line from a large Excel worksheet. (If you embedded the data, the entire workbook would be copied into the receiving document.)

- You maintain a single master document that you want to display in several other documents. For example, you have a Word document containing instructions that you want to display within several other Word documents and Microsoft Power-Point presentations. By using linking, you need to update the data in only one place—the source Word document—to ensure that all copies of the information displayed in other documents are identical.

- You want to minimize the size of the receiving document. (In linking, the receiving document stores only the linking information plus the data required to display the object.)

You should use embedding rather than linking when you want to store an independent block of data as an integral part of the document in which it's displayed. Maintaining documents that contain embedded data is simpler than maintaining documents that contain linked data, because you don't have to keep track of source documents. (To update linked data, the source document must be present in its original location under its original filename.) And you can easily share with other users a document containing only embedded data, without having to provide linked source documents along with it.

In later parts of the book, you'll learn how to copy or move data within an Office application using the drag-and-drop technique, as well as by using the Copy or Cut command followed by the Paste command. You'll also learn how to use the Office Paste Options button that usually appears after you paste data. You can use any of these techniques to copy or move data among separate Office applications, as well as within a single application. When you use these general-purpose methods, however, you have less control over how the data is transferred (even with the Paste Options button). The data might be copied or moved statically, or it might be embedded in the receiving document, depending on the nature of the data and the specific applications involved. Because of the importance of the way the data is copied or moved, in the following sections you'll learn how to use the Copy or Cut command followed by the Paste Special command to precisely control the format and the manner in which the data is transferred.

Note Although you generally use the linking and embedding methods discussed in this chapter to exchange data among separate Office applications, you can sometimes use them to exchange data among separate documents in a single application or even within a single document.

You can use many of the techniques given in Chapter 6, "Adding Professional Graphics and Special Effects to Office 2003 Documents," to modify the appearance of embedded data, as well as linked data in certain formats. In particular, see "Modifying Pictures," on page 119, and "Modifying Graphic Objects," on page 142.

Copying and Moving Data Statically

To copy or move data statically from one Office application to another, as explained in the previous section, perform the following steps:

1 Select the data in the source program and choose Cut or Copy from the source program's Edit menu.

2 Switch to the receiving program and place the insertion point at the position in the receiving document where you want to insert the data.

3 Choose Paste Special from the receiving program's Edit menu to open the Paste Special dialog box.

Note When you choose the Paste Special command in Microsoft FrontPage, rather than displaying the standard Paste Special dialog box, the program displays the Convert Text dialog box, shown here, which has fewer options.

4 In the Paste Special dialog box, select the Paste option, and in the As list select the desired format. Select any format except one containing the word *object*. (Selecting an object format would embed the data rather than copy it statically.)

The formats listed depend on the source program and the nature of the data. Notice that when you select a format in the As list, a description of that format appears in the Result area near the bottom of the dialog box (shown in Figure 7-1).

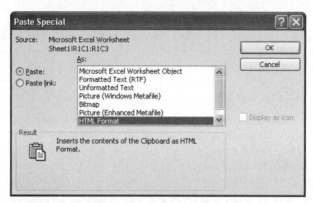

Figure 7-1. You can paste data statically between applications using the Paste Special dialog box.

5 Click the OK button to paste the data.

> **Tip** **Drop the formatting of pasted data**
> One very useful format is Unformatted Text, which lets you paste only the text you copied without including the formatting that was assigned to the text in the source program. The text is inserted just as if you typed it on the keyboard in the receiving program.

A faster, although less reliable, alternative to steps 3, 4, and 5, is to press Ctrl+V or choose Edit, Paste. The data will then be pasted in a default format and, in most cases, the receiving application will display a temporary Paste Options button, shown here, following the data:

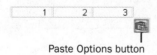

Paste Options button

Click this button and choose the desired format from the drop-down menu, as shown here:

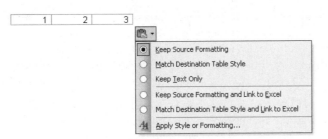

Choose any format except one containing the word *link* (which would link the data) or the name of the source application, such as "Excel Table (entire workbook)," which appears when you paste Excel data into a PowerPoint presentation and would embed the data. (That format doesn't appear in the above example.)

> **Note**   The Paste Options button will appear only if the Show Paste Options Buttons option is selected. To access this option in Word, Excel, or PowerPoint, choose Tools, Options and then click the Edit tab. In Microsoft Outlook, choose Tools, Options, click the Other tab, and click the Advanced Options button. In FrontPage, choose Tools, Page Options, and then click the General tab.

When you copy or move data statically, you use a feature known as the *Clipboard*. In the next section you'll learn how to use the enhanced Clipboard features provided by Office for statically copying or moving data among Office applications, as well as within Office applications.

Inside Out

Use the Paste Special dialog box for greater control

Although pasting and using the Paste Options button is faster than employing the Paste Special dialog box, the Paste Options button offers fewer alternative formats, and the somewhat vague wording of the options makes it difficult to determine whether you're pasting statically, linking, or embedding. Also, the options it provides differ wildly from one situation to another. In general, it's safer to use the Paste Special dialog box when copying data across applications and to limit your use of the Paste Options button to data transfers within a single application.

> **Tip**   You can also use the Paste Special dialog box when copying or moving data within a single Office application to gain more control over the format of the pasted data.

Using the Office Clipboard

The Clipboard is a Windows system feature that allows you to copy or move text or graphics within a document, between two documents in the same application, or between separate Windows applications. Traditionally, when you issue the Copy or Cut command to copy content to the Clipboard, any previous content in the Clipboard is lost. Consequently, the Paste command inserts only the content that was most recently copied to the Clipboard.

Office provides enhanced Clipboard features that allow you to copy or cut several blocks of text or graphics and store them all in the Clipboard so that you can later paste any or all of these blocks into an Office document. This book uses the term *Office Clipboard* to refer to the enhanced Clipboard facilities that are available to Office applications and the term *Windows Clipboard* to refer to the traditional Clipboard facilities that are available to non-Office applications.

The Office Clipboard even collects multiple blocks copied from non-Office applications. However, in a non-Office application, you can paste only the most recently copied block, as usual.

To work with the Office Clipboard, you use the Clipboard task pane and (optionally) the Clipboard icon in the system tray at the right (or bottom) of the Windows taskbar. These elements have replaced the Clipboard toolbar found in Office 2000.

The Clipboard stores multiple blocks of text or graphics only when the Office Clipboard is active. If the Office Clipboard isn't active, only the most recently copied or cut block is retained, as with the Windows Clipboard. To activate the Office Clipboard, use any of the following four methods:

- Display the Clipboard task pane in the Office application by choosing Edit, Office Clipboard or by using any of the other available methods for displaying a particular task pane. See Figure 7-2 for an example of the Clipboard task pane in Excel. *The Office Clipboard is always active when the Clipboard pane is displayed in at least one Office application.*

The general methods for displaying task panes are described in "Using the Task Panes in Office Applications," on page 42.

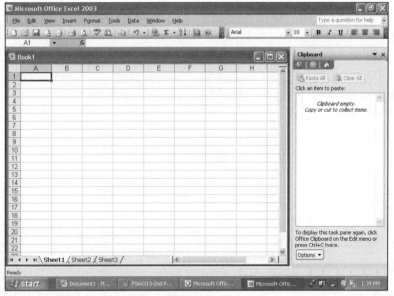

Figure 7-2. This figure shows the Clipboard task pane displayed in Excel.

- If the Show Office Clipboard Automatically option is selected, the Clipboard task pane opens automatically (thereby activating the Office Clipboard) if you copy a block of text or graphics to the Clipboard using the Cut or Copy command and then copy another block *without* issuing an intervening command (such as editing, formatting, or saving the document). When the Clipboard task pane appears, it will display items for both of the blocks you copied (plus any previously copied blocks).

To turn the Show Office Clipboard Automatically option—or another Clipboard option—on or off, click the Options button near the bottom of the Clipboard task pane and choose the option from the menu, shown here:

- If the Show Office Clipboard When Ctrl+C Pressed Twice option is selected, the Clipboard task pane will open automatically (thereby activating the Office Clipboard) if you hold down the Ctrl key and press C twice in rapid succession. If you selected text prior to pressing the keys, you'll see that text in the Clipboard (plus any previously copied blocks).

- If you turn on the Collect Without Showing Office Clipboard option, the Office Clipboard will always be active, even when the Clipboard task pane isn't displayed in any application.

While the Office Clipboard is active, each block of text or graphics that you copy or cut to the Clipboard will be stored, up to a maximum of 24 blocks. If you copy a twenty-fifth block, the Office Clipboard will discard the first one.

To paste one or more blocks into a document, open the Clipboard task pane if it isn't already visible. The pane will display a preview of each stored block, together with an icon indicating the block's source program. The blocks will be listed in order from the most recently copied one to the least recently copied one (see Figure 7-3).

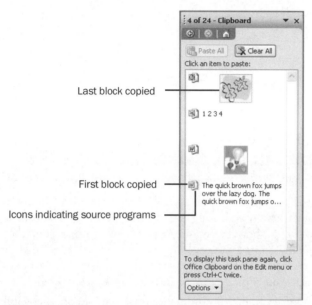

Figure 7-3.   Here, the Clipboard task pane lists four blocks of text or graphics that have been copied to the Clipboard.

To paste a particular block into your document at the position of the insertion point, simply click the description of the block in the list, as shown in this example:

You can also paste a block—or delete it from the Clipboard—by clicking the down arrow that appears to the right of the description when you move the pointer over it and choosing a command from the drop-down menu, shown here:

To paste all blocks stored in the Clipboard, click the Paste All button. The blocks will be inserted into the document in the order in which they were copied to the Clipboard (that is, the bottom item will be pasted first and the top item last). To remove all blocks from the Clipboard, click the Clear All button near the top of the Clipboard task pane.

If the Show Office Clipboard Icon On Taskbar option is on, the Clipboard icon will appear in the system tray at the right (or bottom) of the Windows taskbar whenever the Office Clipboard is active, as shown here:

Clipboard icon

If the Show Status Near Taskbar When Copying option is on, each time you copy a block to the Clipboard (even from a non-Office program), a small ScreenTip will appear above the Clipboard icon indicating that the block was added to the Clipboard, as in this example:

To display the Clipboard task pane if it's hidden, you can double-click the Clipboard icon. To customize the Office Clipboard, right-click the Clipboard icon to display the shortcut menu shown here:

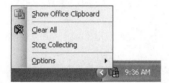

Chapter 7

Then choose a command from the shortcut menu. Table 7-1 provides a summary of these commands.

Table 7-1. Using the Clipboard Icon Shortcut Menu

To Do This	Choose This Command from the Clipboard Icon Shortcut Menu
Display the Clipboard task pane.	Show Office Clipboard
Remove all blocks currently stored in the Office Clipboard.	Clear All
Close the Clipboard task pane and turn off the Always Copy To Office Clipboard option, thereby deactivating the Office Clipboard. Subsequently, only one block will be stored in the Clipboard at a time.	Stop Collecting
Set Office Clipboard options.	Options, which opens a submenu containing the same five options you can set through the Options button at the bottom of the Clipboard task pane (as explained earlier in this section)

Troubleshooting

Copied text missing from the Office Clipboard

You copied several blocks of text to the Clipboard but don't find them in the Clipboard task pane when you open it.

The Clipboard doesn't store multiple blocks of text or graphics unless the Office Clipboard is active. The Office Clipboard isn't active unless the Clipboard task pane is displayed in at least one Office application or the Collect Without Showing Office Clipboard option is on.

Linking Data

You can transfer and link many kinds of data among Office applications. The following are a few examples:

- You can insert and link part or all of an Excel worksheet or an Excel chart into a Word document or a PowerPoint slide.
- You can insert and link part or all of a Word document into an Excel worksheet or a PowerPoint slide.
- You can insert and link a PowerPoint slide into a Word document or an Excel worksheet.

Note   In an Access database, you can insert linked or embedded data into a field in a table, provided that the field has been assigned the OLE Object data type (OLE stands for *object linking and embedding*).

You can't link data from the Microsoft Graph or Microsoft Equation programs provided with Office, which were discussed in Chapter 6, "Adding Professional Graphics and Special Effects to Office 2003 Documents." These programs can be used only to embed data.

You can transfer and link either a selected part of a document or an entire document. To transfer and link part of a document, do the following:

1 Select the data in the source document, and from the source program's Edit menu, choose Copy (don't choose Cut!) to copy the data to the Clipboard.

2 Place the insertion point at the position in the receiving document where you want to insert the data, and from the receiving program's Edit menu, choose Paste Special.

3 In the Paste Special dialog box, select the Paste Link option, select the desired data format in the As list, and click the OK button (shown in Figure 7-4).

Select Paste link to link data

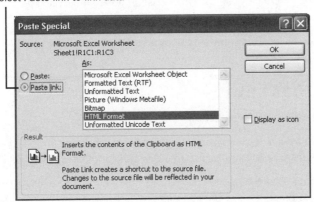

Figure 7-4.   You can use the Paste Special dialog box to link data.

Note   If the Paste Link option isn't available, this means that the data in the Clipboard can't be linked or that the source program doesn't support linking.

To link an entire document, use the following method:

1 Place the insertion point at the position in the receiving document where you want to insert the data.

2 From the receiving program's Insert menu, choose Object. In the Object dialog box, click the Create From File tab. (In PowerPoint and Access, the dialog box is titled Insert Object, and Create From File is an option button that you select, rather than a tab.)

3 Select the Link To File option, and in the File Name box, enter the filename of the document you want to insert. (In PowerPoint and Access, the option is called Link and the text box is called File.) Click the Browse button if you need help locating the file. (See Figure 7-5.)

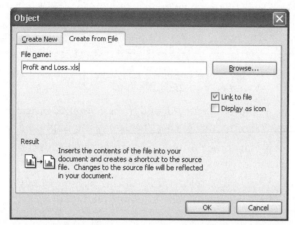

Figure 7-5. You can use the Object dialog box to insert and link an entire document.

4 Click the OK button to link the document.

Troubleshooting

You can't link data from PowerPoint

You copied data from a PowerPoint slide or you copied several slides, but in other Office applications, in the Paste Special dialog box, the Paste Link option is disabled.

To link data from a PowerPoint presentation, you must either link a single slide in its entirety or link the whole presentation. You can't link part of a slide, nor can you link two or more slides out of a presentation without linking the entire presentation.

To link a single slide, switch to Slide Sorter view in PowerPoint (by choosing View, Slide Sorter), select a single slide by clicking on it, and then choose Edit, Copy or press Ctrl+C. You can then switch to the receiving document and link the slide using the Paste Special dialog box as described in the three-step procedure for linking part of a document, given earlier in this section.

To link an entire PowerPoint presentation, you must use the Object dialog box as described in the four-step procedure for linking an entire document, given previously in this section.

Tip Display your data as an icon

If you select the Display As Icon option in either the Paste Special or the Object dialog box (the Insert Object dialog box in PowerPoint and Access), the receiving program will display an icon representing the linked data rather than displaying the data itself. Also, when you print the document, only the icon will be printed. After you select Display As Icon, you can click the Change Icon button—which will appear in the Paste Special, Object, or Insert Object dialog box—to change the icon and the caption that are displayed in the document. To view the linked data within the source program, use one of the methods for editing linked data described next. Using icons to display linked data is a convenient way to present various types of information in a compact format within a document intended to be viewed on the screen.

To edit linked data you must make the changes within the source document. To do this, you can use one of the following methods:

- Run the source program and open the source document.
- Select the block of linked data in the receiving document (or the icon that represents it) or simply place the insertion point anywhere within the data. Then, on the Edit menu, point to Linked *Item* (where *Item* is a description of the selected data, such as Worksheet Object), and choose either Edit Link or Open Link from the submenu that appears, which is shown here:

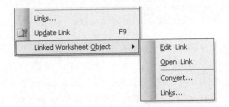

(The specific commands that appear on this submenu depend on the source program and the nature of the data.) The source document is then opened in the source program, and you can edit the data.

- For some types of linked data, you can open the source document in the source program by simply double-clicking the linked data in the receiving document.

Caution Although you might be able to edit certain types of linked data directly within the receiving document (for example, unformatted text in a Word document), your changes will be overwritten the next time the data is updated! However, formatting changes (such as applying bold or italic to text) will be preserved when the data is updated, provided that the Preserve Formatting After Update option is selected in the Links dialog box, as described later in this section.

You can modify one or more links within a document by choosing Edit, Links to open the Links dialog box, which lists all the links contained in the active document. The options available in the dialog box vary among Office applications; Figure 7-6 shows the Links dialog box displayed in Word. To modify a link, select it in the list. To simultaneously modify several links, select them by clicking the first one and then pressing the Ctrl key while clicking each additional link. You can now modify the link or links you have selected. Note that although all of these actions are available in Word, some of them aren't available in other Office applications.

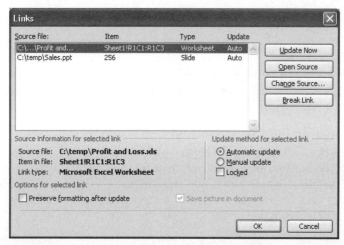

Figure 7-6. You can modify links in the active document using the Links dialog box.

- To make a link either automatic or manual, select the Automatic Update or Manual Update option in the Update Method For Selected Link area of the Links dialog box. By default, a link is automatic, which means that the data is automatically updated whenever the receiving document is opened and whenever the data is modified in the source document while the receiving document is open. If you make a link manual, it won't be updated until you explicitly issue a command (described next). You might want to make links manual to avoid slowdowns while working with a document that contains many links or contains linked data with a source that is modified frequently.

- To update a manual link, click the Update Now button. (You can also manually update a link without opening the Links dialog box by selecting it—or just placing the insertion point within it—and choosing Edit, Update Link or pressing F9.)

- To modify the link so that updating the link will update the data but will leave unchanged any formatting you've applied to the linked data in the receiving document, check the Preserve Formatting After Update option.

- To change the name or location of the source document for the linked data, click the Change Source button to open the Change Source dialog box, which is similar to the Open dialog box (shown in Figure 7-7). (You might also be able to change the description of the data location within the source document—for example, the range of cells in a spreadsheet.) You would need to do this to repair a link after the source document has been moved or renamed.

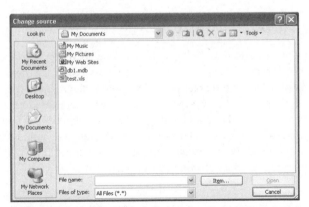

Figure 7-7. Use the Change Source dialog box to change the document that is the source of linked data.

To specify a new source document, in the Change Source dialog box, open the folder that contains that document and enter its filename into the File Name box. To select a new data location within the source document, click the Item button and enter a description of the location into the Set Item dialog box. For a Word document, you'd enter a bookmark name. For an Excel workbook, you'd enter the name of the worksheet and the row and column range within this worksheet, as in the following example:

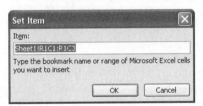

- To open the source document within the source program, click the Open Source button. This action has the same effect as using one of the techniques for editing linked data, which were described previously.

- To remove the link, click the Break Link button. The data will become an integral part of the receiving document, just as if you had copied it statically. After doing this, you won't be able to restore the link.

- In Word, to prevent the link from being updated, select the Locked option.

Tip A good way to help ensure that the source document is always available to maintain the link is to store both the source document and the receiving document together in the same folder.

Using Hyperlinks to Link Data

Instead of inserting a block of data that's linked to a source document, as described in this section, in Word, Excel, PowerPoint, or Access you can insert a simple *hyperlink* to the data in the source document. Clicking the link opens the source document and scrolls to the specific data that's the target of the hyperlink. Using this method, the data won't be displayed or printed in the document containing the hyperlink, which can be a disadvantage. However, using a hyperlink is simpler and less error-prone than conventional linking, it consumes less space in the document containing the hyperlink, and it's more in keeping with the increasingly popular Web model of working with documents.

To create the hyperlink in Word, Excel, or PowerPoint, select the data in the source document and drag it to the destination document using the right mouse button. When you release the mouse button to drop the data, choose Create Hyperlink Here from the shortcut menu that appears, as shown here:

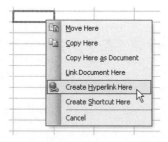

Alternatively, in Office 2003 you can now insert a hyperlink in a Word, Excel, or PowerPoint document by using the Paste Special dialog box, selecting the Paste Link option (as described earlier in this section), and selecting the item containing the word "Hyperlink" in the As list (the exact wording of this item varies by application—in Word, for example, it's Word Hyperlink).

You can also create a hyperlink in Word, Excel, PowerPoint, or Access by first copying the text from the source document into the Clipboard and then pasting it into the destination document choosing Edit, Paste As Hyperlink (this command, however, isn't available in Outlook or FrontPage). With either method, the text you copy must be from a file that has been saved on disk. Otherwise the command for creating the hyperlink won't be available.

A Linking Example

Imagine that you've created an Excel worksheet containing the daily prices of a commodity—wheat—for an historical period, together with a chart illustrating those prices for 25 days within that period. Figure 7-8 presents such a spreadsheet. (A copy of this workbook is provided on the book's companion CD under the filename Futures.xls.) You now want to write an article in Word that describes the price action over that period. To link a copy of the Excel chart to your report, you would perform the steps on the next page.

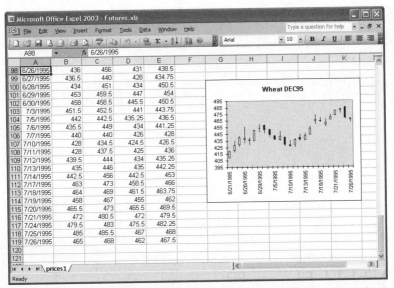

Figure 7-8. This figure shows an Excel worksheet together with a chart.

1 In the Excel worksheet, click the chart to select it. From Excel's Edit menu, choose Copy.

2 In the Word document containing your report, place the insertion point at the position where you want the chart. Choose Paste Special from Word's Edit menu. Complete the dialog box as shown in Figure 7-9 and then click the OK button. The resulting report is shown in Figure 7-10. (A copy of this document is provided on the book's companion CD under the filename Futures.xls.)

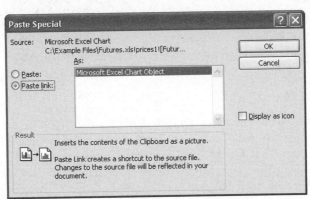

Figure 7-9. Here, the Paste Special dialog box is used to link the Excel chart to a Word document.

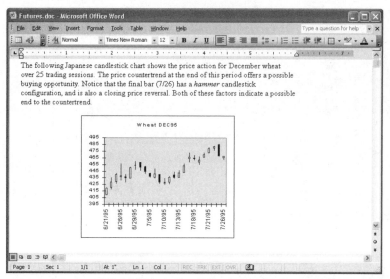

Figure 7-10. This figure shows the Excel chart seen in Figure 7-8, linked to a Word document.

The following are some advantages of linking this chart rather than embedding it:

● Only the linking information and the data required to draw the chart are copied into the receiving document. If you embedded the chart, the entire workbook, including all the price data, would be copied into the receiving document, significantly increasing its size. (Although you would normally see only the chart, the workbook data is also stored in the document so that you can edit both the chart and the data on which the chart depends.)

● The same chart could be linked to additional Word documents, PowerPoint presentations, or other documents. The chart would then be updated within all receiving documents whenever you changed the price data in the Excel worksheet.

Embedding Data

A block of embedded data is known as an *embedded object*. In an Office document, you can embed data that you've created in another Office application, including the Graph and Equation programs discussed in Chapter 6, "Adding Professional Graphics and Special Effects to Office 2003 Documents," or in any other Windows–based program that's designed to be a source of embedded data, such as Microsoft Visio. You can create an embedded object in three ways, which differ in how you obtain the data for the object.

First, you can obtain the data for an embedded object from a portion of an existing document by doing the following:

1 Select the data in the source document and then, from the source program's Edit menu, choose Copy or Cut.

2 Place the insertion point at the position in the receiving document where you want to add the embedded object. From the receiving application's Edit menu, choose Paste Special.

3 In the Paste Special dialog box, select the Paste option, and in the As list, choose the first format description that contains the word *object* (see Figure 7-11). Click the OK button.

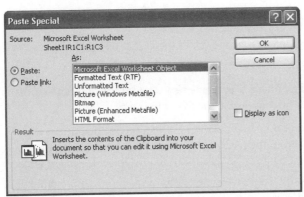

Figure 7-11. In this figure, the Paste Special dialog box is used to embed an Excel worksheet object.

The second way to create an embedded object is to use an entire existing document that is saved on disk as the source of the data, as follows:

1 Place the insertion point at the position in the receiving document where you want to embed the object. From the receiving program's Insert menu, choose Object and then click the Create From File tab (or option button) in the Object (or Insert Object) dialog box.

2 Make sure that the Link To File (or Link) option is not selected and either type the filename of the source document into the File Name (or File) text box or click the Browse button to locate the file (see Figure 7-12). Click the OK button.

Chapter 7

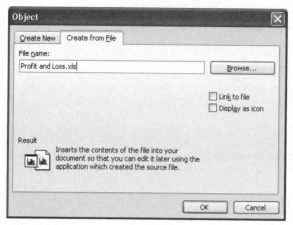

Figure 7-12. Here, the Create From File tab of the Object dialog box is used to embed an entire document.

The third way to embed an object is to create new data for the object using the source program's tools. You do that by completing the following steps:

1. Place the insertion point at the position in the receiving document where you want to embed the object. From the receiving program's Insert menu, choose Object and then click the Create New tab (or option button) in the Object (or Insert Object) dialog box.

2. In the Object Type list, select the type of object that you want to embed. This list contains one or more items for every installed Windows program that can be the source of an embedded object. Click the OK button, and one of two things will happen, depending on the source application:

   - A blank working area will appear within the receiving document, and the source program's menus and buttons will be displayed within the receiving program's window (interspersed with the receiving program's commands) . The source program's keyboard commands will also become available.

     or

   - The source program's window will open and display a blank working area (for example, blank worksheet cells) or other tools (for example, a set of commands for working with a media clip).

3. In either case, use the source program's commands to enter the data for the embedded object into the working area.

4. When you've finished entering the data, exit the editing mode. If you're working in the receiving program's window, simply click in the receiving document outside the object.

   If you're working in the source program's window, exit the editing mode by choosing File, Exit. (The command might have a label such as Exit And Return To My Document.) You can also use any other method to quit the source program. Click Yes if the source program displays a message box asking whether you want to update the object in the receiving document (some programs update the object automatically).

> **Note** In an Access database, you can insert linked or embedded data into a field in a table, provided that the field has been assigned the OLE Object data type.

> With the Graph and Equation programs discussed in Chapter 6, "Adding Professional Graphics and Special Effects to Office 2003 Documents," you must use this third method for creating an embedded object, because these programs can't create independent documents.

> When you use any of these three methods for embedding an object, you might be able to select the Display As Icon option in the Object dialog box. For an explanation of this option, be sure to see the tip "Display your data as an icon," on page 165.

To edit an embedded object, simply double-click it. The object will then be opened for editing either within the source program or, more commonly, within the receiving program. (The action that occurs depends on how the source application is designed.)

> **Note** For some types of embedded objects, double-clicking the object doesn't open it for editing. For example, if you double-click an object containing a sound or video clip, the clip is played. To edit the object, you must use the alternative method, given below.

An alternative way to edit an embedded object is to select the object by clicking it, and then, on the receiving program's Edit menu, point to *Item* Object (where *Item* is a description of the selected object, such as Worksheet) to display the submenu shown here:

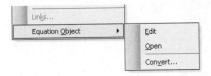

Choose one of the following commands from this submenu:

- To edit the object within the receiving program's window using the source program's menus, toolbars, and keyboard commands, choose the Edit command, if it's present.
- To edit the object within a separate window provided by the source program, choose the Open command, if it's present.

These are the typical commands and their actions. The actual commands that appear on the submenu—and their actions—depend on the source program and the nature of the embedded data.

When you've finished editing the object, exit the editing mode. If you're editing in the source program, do this by exiting from the source program and clicking the Yes button in the message box if the source program asks whether you want to update the object in the receiving document. If you're editing in the receiving program, click in the receiving document outside the object.

Tip Convert objects to the format you prefer

If the Object submenu includes a Convert command, you can choose it to change the embedded object to a different object type. The available object types depend on the object you've selected. For example, if you select a PowerPoint Slide object, you can convert it to a PowerPoint Presentation object. Changing a Slide object to a Presentation object would allow you to add additional slides to the object (a presentation is composed of a group of slides) or to display the presentation in a slide show by double-clicking the object. (You can also convert a Presentation object to a Slide object, which will consist of the first slide in the presentation—the other slides will be discarded.)

An Embedding Example

Imagine that you're preparing a PowerPoint presentation and you want to include a table of numeric values in a slide. By embedding an Excel Worksheet object, you can use all the features provided by Excel for creating the table. (A copy of this workbook is provided on the book's companion CD under the filename Profit.xls.) You could do this as follows:

1 Run Excel, open a new workbook, and enter the data into a worksheet.

2 Select the worksheet cells that you want to display in the PowerPoint slide, as shown in Figure 7-13, and choose Copy from Excel's Edit menu.

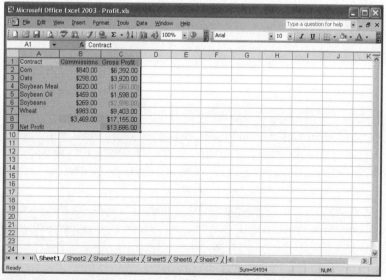

Figure 7-13. Here, cells are selected in an Excel worksheet prior to embedding the data in a PowerPoint slide.

3 Open the slide in the PowerPoint presentation in which you want to display the worksheet cells. (You must be in PowerPoint's Normal view; to switch to this view, from PowerPoint's View menu, choose Normal.)

4 From PowerPoint's Edit menu, choose Paste Special. In the Paste Special dialog box, select the Paste option and select the Microsoft Excel Worksheet Object item in the list, as shown in Figure 7-14. Click the OK button.

5 To adjust the size of the embedded object, drag one of the uncolored, round sizing handles that appear around the object when it's selected.

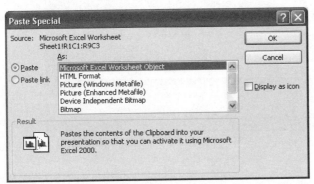

Figure 7-14. Here, the Paste Special dialog box is used to embed the Excel worksheet cells shown in Figure 7-13 into a PowerPoint slide.

Note After you've pasted the worksheet cells into the slide, you can either save or discard the original Excel document. In the example, we created the embedded object by copying cells from an Excel document—rather than choosing Object from PowerPoint's Insert menu to create new data—because the copying method lets you specify the exact number of cells to display in the slide and makes it easier to scale the worksheet within the PowerPoint slide.

The resulting PowerPoint slide is shown in Figure 7-15. (A copy of this presentation is provided on the book's companion CD under the filename Profit.ppt.)

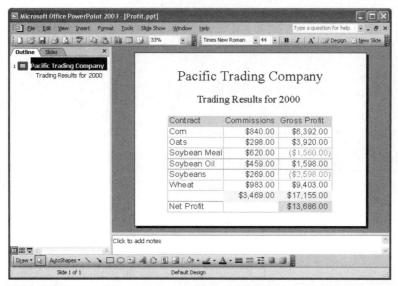

Figure 7-15. This figure shows the Excel worksheet cells embedded in a PowerPoint slide.

After embedding the worksheet in the slide, you can edit it within PowerPoint by double-clicking the worksheet. The Excel menu and toolbar will then be displayed within the Power-Point window to let you edit the object (see Figure 7-16).

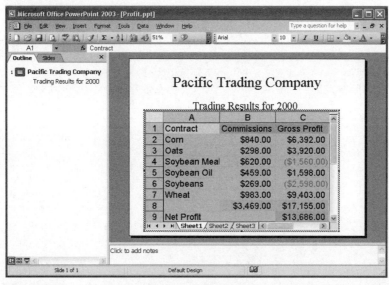

Figure 7-16. You can edit Excel worksheet cells embedded in a PowerPoint slide.

Chapter 8

Using Windows SharePoint Services in Professional Workgroups

Windows SharePoint Services
Essentials 177

Connecting to a SharePoint Team Web
Site in Your Browser 179

Sharing Office Documents and Graphics
on a SharePoint Site 183

Using SharePoint Discussions 193

Exchanging Information on a
SharePoint Site 198

NEW FEATURE! Customizing a SharePoint Site 201

Windows SharePoint Services Essentials

Microsoft Windows SharePoint Services is a set of program extensions that can be installed on a Web server—the software that manages a site on the World Wide Web or on a company intranet—to add features that a Web server normally doesn't provide.

SharePoint was introduced with Microsoft Office XP (it was then known as SharePoint Team Services from Microsoft). The concept of Web server extensions, however, goes back further. For example, the Microsoft FrontPage Server Extensions have been used for years to make it easy to publish Web sites from Microsoft FrontPage and to add dynamic features, such as hit counters and search forms, to FrontPage Web sites. Also, the Microsoft Office 2000 Server Extensions allowed users of Office 2000 to save and share files on a Web site, to conduct newsgroup-like discussions about any online document, and to subscribe to online documents or folders in order to be notified by e-mail whenever the document or folder changed.

Windows SharePoint Services includes all the features offered by its Office 2000 Server Extensions ancestor. However, rather than simply providing an empty folder for storing documents, plus support for discussions and alerts (e-mail messages sent when a specified object changes, formerly known as *subscriptions*), it provides an entire customizable Web site. This site is known as a *team Web site*, and it offers extensive collaboration features that allow workgroups to share documents, exchange information, and work together on projects. Here are some of the main features of a SharePoint team Web site:

- Customizable *document libraries* for storing and sharing Office documents. Each document library can be assigned a default template for quickly creating a particular type of Office document.

- *Picture libraries* for sharing collections of graphics files.
- *Form libraries* for creating, storing, and sharing XML-based business forms managed by Microsoft Office InfoPath or another Windows Sharepoint Services–compatible XML editor.

> **InfoPath is covered in Part 9 of this book.**

- Standard *lists* that allow team members to post announcements, contact descriptions, event notices, favorite Internet links, summaries of tasks that need to be performed, and issue-tracking information.
- *Custom lists* for sharing any type of information.
- *Discussion boards* that allow members to conduct online discussions.
- *Surveys* for collecting information from members.

- Custom free-form Web pages.
- Extensive browser-based customization tools that allow members to create or customize pages on a team Web site. Members can also customize the entire site or create additional Web sites nested within the main site (including newly available specialized sites known as *document workspaces* and *meeting workspaces*, which are explained later in the chapter).

As with the Office 2000 Server Extensions, you can access a team Web site through the My Network Places folder in Microsoft Windows. This folder appears in Windows Explorer, as well as in the Open and Save As dialog boxes in Office applications. Also, like the Office 2000 Server Extensions, SharePoint lets you conduct document discussions and sign up for alerts using the Web Discussions toolbar in Office applications. However, because SharePoint provides a complete Web site, the main new way for Office users to access its features is through their browsers. Microsoft Office 2003 Edition also includes new features for accessing information on a SharePoint Web site from within Office applications—for example, the Shared Workspace task pane in Office 2003 applications and the Meeting Workspace task pane in Microsoft Office Outlook 2003.

Connecting to a SharePoint Team Web Site in Your Browser

To access a team Web site, enter the site's URL (Uniform Resource Locator) into your browser. This will open the site's Home page. Figure 8-1 shows the Home page of a newly created team Web site, before documents have been stored, information has been entered, or customizations have been performed.

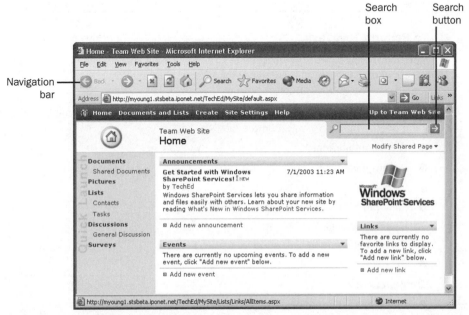

Figure 8-1. Here, the Home page of a newly created SharePoint team Web site is opened in Microsoft Internet Explorer.

From the Home page, you can perform four main tasks:

- To navigate to one of the main site pages, click a link on the navigation bar at the top of the Home page. See Table 8-1 for instructions on which page you should visit to perform various tasks.

- To quickly go to a particular page, you can click one of the links displayed on the Home page below the navigation bar. For example, to go to the page where you can view the announcements that have been posted, click the Announcements link in the main part of the Home page. To view a particular announcement (if any are listed on the Home page), click the announcement's title. To post a new event notice, click the Add New Event link. And to work with the contents of the Shared Documents document library, click the Shared Documents link in the Quick Launch area.

● To locate list items (announcements, for example) or Office documents (stored on the team Web site) that contain specific text, enter that text into the Search box in the upper-right corner of the page and press Enter or click the Go button.

● To customize the Home page, click Modify My Page or Modify Shared Page in the upper-right corner and choose a command from the drop-down menu. (Customization of a SharePoint site is discussed later in the chapter.)

Table 8-1. **Tasks You Can Perform in the Main Pages of a SharePoint Team Web Site**

To Perform This Task	Go to This Page Using the Navigation Bar
Get an overview of the site, navigate to commonly used pages or to selected list items, or search for list items or Office documents stored on the site.	Home
Access any of the following types of SharePoint information components that are located on the site: ● Document libraries ● Picture libraries ● Form libraries ● Lists (links, announcements, contacts, events, tasks, issues, or custom lists) ● Discussion boards ● Surveys	Documents And Lists
Create a new: ● SharePoint information page (document library, picture library, form library, list, discussion board, or survey) ● Free-form Web page ● Web site nested within the current SharePoint site (a team Web site, document workspace, or meeting workspace)	Create

Table 8-1. **Tasks You Can Perform in the Main Pages of a SharePoint Team Web Site**

To Perform This Task	Go to This Page Using the Navigation Bar
Perform team Web site administration:	Site Settings
● Manage site users and their permissions.	
● Manage Web sites (including workspaces) nested within the current SharePoint site.	
● Allow users belonging to various permission groups to create new Web sites (including workspaces) nested within the current SharePoint site.	
● Access the main Site Administration page, where you can perform other types of management tasks.	
or	
Customize the team Web site:	
● Edit the title and description of the site.	
● Assign a default theme to the site. A theme is a visual scheme that sets the colors and fonts.	
● Modify site content. That is, change the design of a document library, picture library, form library, list, discussion board, or survey.	
● Customize the site's Home page.	
or	
Manage your personal information on the site.	
Read online help explaining how to use a SharePoint Team Web site.	Help

A SharePoint team Web site contains a set of information components, each of which stores either files (Office documents, graphics files, or form templates) or information items (links, announcements, contacts, events, tasks, and so on). A SharePoint information component is thus a repository for documents or information items of a particular type, and is analogous to a *folder* in Outlook. Some types of information components are known as *lists*. A list can contain links, announcements, contacts, events, tasks, issues, or custom information items. Table 8-2 gives the type of information component that you use to manage each type of file or information item on a SharePoint site.

Note Each information component in a SharePoint site has an associated file folder on the Web server that runs SharePoint. For a document library, picture library, or form library, the folder contains the actual files stored by the information component, as well as the files for the Web pages that are used to access the files. For all other types of information components, the folder contains just the files for the Web pages; the actual data is stored in a Microsoft SQL Server database on the Web server. You can view these file folders in Windows Explorer if you create a shortcut to your SharePoint site in your My Network Places folder, as discussed later in the chapter.

Table 8-2. The Uses for SharePoint Information Pages

To Manage This Type of File or Information	Use This Type of Information Component	Default Information Component Set Up by SharePoint
Office documents that are to be shared by site members	Document library	Shared Documents
Graphics files that are to be shared by site members	Picture library	(None)
Shared XML-based business forms created in InfoPath or another Windows Sharepoint Services-compatible XML editor	Form library	(None)
Bulletins and news items relevant to your Share-Point team	Announce-ments list	Announcements
Names, addresses, and other information on people that team members work with	Contacts list	Contacts
Descriptions of upcoming events, such as meetings, due dates, and social occasions	Events list	Events
A set of issues or problems that need to be resolved	Issues list	(None)
A collection of useful Web links	Links list	Links
Summaries of jobs that need to be completed by you or other members of your team	Tasks list	Tasks
Any type of information that doesn't fit into one of the standard list types, such as an inventory, a membership roster, or a bibliography	Custom list *or* Custom list in datasheet view *or* Custom list based on an imported spreadsheet	(None)

NEW FEATURE! — Picture library

NEW FEATURE! — Form library

NEW FEATURE! — Issues list

Table 8-2. The Uses for SharePoint Information Pages

To Manage This Type of File or Information	Use This Type of Information Component	Default Information Component Set Up by SharePoint
A newsgroup-style online discussion	Discussion board	General Discussion
A survey (a question and list of possible answers) for polling site members, and the results of that survey	Survey	(None)

Sharing Office Documents and Graphics on a SharePoint Site

The members of a SharePoint team Web site can share Office documents that are stored in a document library, as well as graphics files that are stored in a picture library. You can access the document libraries and picture libraries on a team Web site either using your browser or through the My Network Places folder in Office applications or Windows Explorer.

> The latest version of SharePoint lets you create form libraries as well as document libraries and picture libraries. A form library is designed for filling out and storing a particular type of XML-based business form, such as an expense report or purchase order. For general information on InfoPath, see Part 9 of this book, "InfoPath." For details on using SharePoint form libraries, see the sidebar "Working with Form Libraries on a SharePoint Team Web site," on page 1415.

Accessing SharePoint Document Libraries Using Your Browser

To access SharePoint document libraries using your browser, perform the following steps:

1 Connect to your team Web site (as explained earlier in the chapter) and click the Documents And Lists item on the navigation bar at the top of the Home page to open the Documents And Lists page. All the document libraries on your site will be listed in the Document Libraries section near the top of this page (see Figure 8-2). (A new SharePoint site has only the Shared Documents document library. Later in this chapter you'll learn how to create new document libraries.) Figure 8-2 shows the Documents And Lists page for a site in which two additional document libraries have been created: Chapters and Research Notes.

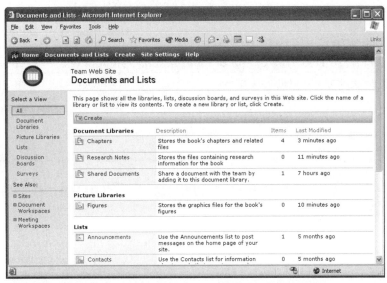

Figure 8-2. The Document Libraries section of the SharePoint Documents And Lists page displays the document libraries contained on the site.

2   Click the name of the particular document library you want to access. This will open the page for that document library (see Figure 8-3).

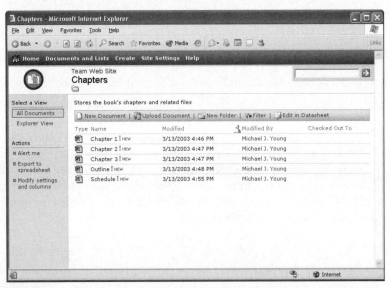

Figure 8-3. Shown here is the SharePoint Web page for the Chapters document library.

3 In the document library's information page, you can do any of the following:

- To create a new document, click New Document on the toolbar near the top of the page. The new document will be based on the template assigned to the library. The type of the document (Microsoft Word, Microsoft Excel, and so on) depends upon the type of the template. The default template provided in a new document library creates a blank Word document.

- To copy an Office document from your computer to the document library on the Web site, click Upload Document on the toolbar near the top of the page.

- To create a subfolder within the document library's folder, click New Folder on the toolbar near the top of the page. Creating subfolders allows you to group and organize your documents. A subfolder is listed along with the documents in the page that displays the document library. To open a subfolder, click the subfolder name or the icon displayed to its left; its contents will then be displayed in a separate page. To modify a subfolder's properties, to remove a subfolder, or to have SharePoint send you an alert e-mail message whenever the folder's contents change, hold the mouse pointer over the subfolder name, click the down arrow that appears, and choose a command from the drop-down menu:

- To control which documents are shown, click Filter on the toolbar near the top of the page.

- To view the contents of the document library's page in a spreadsheet-like grid of rows and columns, click Edit In Datasheet on the toolbar near the top of the page.

- To change the way the documents are displayed, click a view in the Select A View area at the left of the page.

- To have SharePoint send you an e-mail message whenever a change occurs within the document library, click Alert Me in the Actions area at the left of the page.

- To run Excel on your computer and download a copy of the document listing to a worksheet—so you can edit and save a local copy of the listing—click Export To Spreadsheet in the Actions area at the left of the page.

- To customize the current document library, click Modify Settings And Columns in the Actions area at the left of the page. This will open the Customize page for that document library.

- To open a document in the application on your computer that's registered to open the document's type, click the name of the document or the icon to the left of the name. A document with the .doc file extension will be opened in Word, a

Chapter 8

document with the .xls extension will be opened in Excel, a document with the .htm extension will be opened in your browser, and so on.

■ To work with a specific document that's stored in the document library, hold the pointer over the document name, click the down arrow that appears, and choose a command from the drop-down menu:

■ To see the properties of the document, choose View Properties.

■ To modify the properties of the document—the filename or title—choose Edit Properties.

■ To open the document in the application on your computer that's registered to *edit* the document's type, choose Edit In *Application* (where *Application* is Word, Excel, and so on). For example, a document with the .doc file extension will be opened for editing in Word, and a document with the.htm extension that was created in Word will also be opened in Word. (Notice that this action isn't the same as clicking the document name in the document library, which opens the document in the application that's registered to open the document's type, as described above.)

■ To remove the document from the document library, choose Delete.

■ To reserve a document in your name so that only you can make changes to it, choose Check Out. After you have checked out a document, you can end its checked-out status by choosing Check In.

■ To work with all versions (backup copies) of the document, choose Version History. You can view, restore, or delete any version. (To "restore" a selected version means to substitute the selected version for the current version.) Through the document library's Customize page you can have SharePoint automatically create a version—that is, a backup copy—of the document each time the document is saved.

■ To have SharePoint send you an e-mail message whenever the document is changed, choose Alert Me.

■ To open the document for an online discussion in your browser, choose Discuss. Discussions are described in "Discussing an Online Document," later in the chapter.

■ To create a document workspace and copy the document into this workspace, choose Create Document Workspace. Document workspaces are discussed in "Sharing Documents Using a Document Workspace," later in the chapter.

Accessing SharePoint Document Libraries from Office Applications

To open a document stored in a SharePoint document library from within an Office application, perform the following steps:

1 In Windows Explorer, open the My Network Places folder. If this folder doesn't already contain a shortcut to your SharePoint team Web site, click the Add A Network Place button in the command pane at the left of the Windows Explorer window (if this pane isn't displayed, click the Folders toolbar button in Windows Explorer to hide the folder list). Then, enter the URL and other settings for your team Web site into the Add Network Place Wizard.

Once you've created the shortcut, you can skip step 1.

> **Tip** After you've created a shortcut to a team Web site within the My Network Places folder, an alternative way to open an Office document (or other type of file) on that site is to open the file's document library (or picture or form library) directly in Windows Explorer and double-click the filename.

2 In the Office application, choose File, Open.

3 Click My Network Places in the My Places bar at the left of the Open dialog box to open the My Network Places folder.

4 Double-click the shortcut to your team Web site (see Figure 8-4). If you're prompted to establish a dial-up connection, click the OK button. The Open dialog box will then display a listing of all the document, picture, and form libraries on your site (see Figure 8-5).

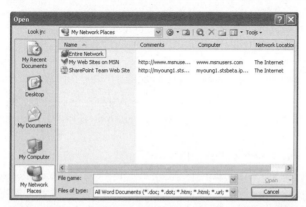

Figure 8-4. Here, the My Network Places folder is opened in the Open dialog box.

Chapter 8

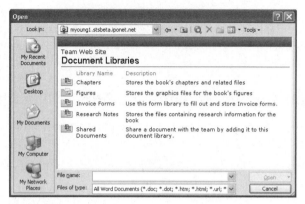

Figure 8-5.   In this figure, a team Web site is opened and is displayed in the WebView view.

5   Double-click the name of the document library that contains the document you want to open. This will display the contents of that document library and allow you to open any document or subfolder that it contains.

Note   When a SharePoint team Web site is opened in the Open dialog box, it's initially displayed in the WebView view, which lists all the document, picture, and form libraries on the site and lets you open any of them. (A document or form library that you subsequently open will also be shown in WebView.) If you want to see the actual files and folders contained in each folder on the site—perhaps so that you can access a nested site—you'll need to open the Views drop-down menu at the top of the Open dialog box and select another view (such as List or Details).

For information on working with the Open dialog box, see "Opening an Existing Document Using the Open Office Document Dialog Box," on page 57.

Note   You can also use this technique to open a document on a Web site that has one of the earlier types of Microsoft server extensions, such as the FrontPage Server Extensions or the Office 2000 Server Extensions.

To save a document in a SharePoint document library, follow these steps:

1   If you haven't created a shortcut to your team Web site in your My Network Places folder, create one following the directions given in Step 1 of the previous instruction list.

2   In the Office application, choose File, Save As.

3   Access your team Web site using the My Network Places folder, open the document library where you want to store your document, and save the document. See the more detailed directions given in the previous instruction list.

Using SharePoint Picture Libraries

SharePoint picture libraries are similar to document libraries, although they're designed specifically for storing, displaying, and working with shared graphics files. To access a team Web site's picture libraries, do the following:

1   Click the Documents And Lists item on the navigation bar at the top of any page to open the Documents And Lists page. All of the site's picture libraries will be listed in the Picture Libraries section near the top of this page. (There are no picture libraries in a newly created SharePoint site; you'll learn how to create them later in the chapter. Figure 8-2 shows the Documents And Lists page for a site in which a picture library titled Figures has been created.)

2   In the Picture Libraries section of the Documents And Lists page, click the name of the picture library you want to access in the Picture Libraries section. This will open the page for that picture library (see Figure 8-6).

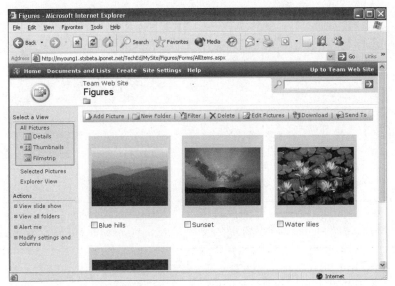

Figure 8-6.   Shown here is the SharePoint Web page for the Figures picture library, with the Thumbnails view activated.

You work with a picture library through your browser or through an Office application using the same basic techniques that were explained for document libraries in the previous two sections ("Accessing SharePoint Document Libraries Using Your Browser" and "Accessing SharePoint Document Libraries from Office Applications"). The Web page for a picture library, however, includes some unique features designed specifically for working with graphics files, including the following:

- You can apply any of the following commands—found on the toolbar near the top of the page—to an entire group of files by checking the box next to each file you want to include, and then clicking a command:

  - To remove the selected files from the picture library, click Delete.

■ To modify the selected files in the new Microsoft Office Picture Manager utility that's included with Office 2003, click Edit Pictures (see Figure 8-7).

■ To download the selected files to your computer (full size, preview, or thumbnail images), click Download.

■ To export the selected files to a Word document, Excel spreadsheet, Microsoft PowerPoint presentation, or Outlook message, click Send To.

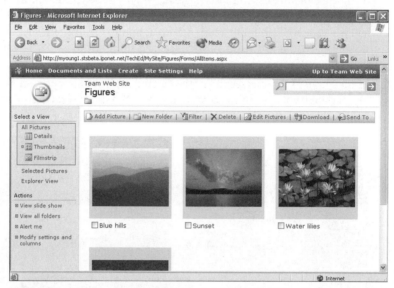

Figure 8-7. You can use Office's new Microsoft Office Picture Manager program to work with graphics files.

> **Note** You can also edit or download an individual file by activating the Details view and choosing Edit Picture or Download Picture from a graphic file's drop-down menu.

● To see all the graphics files in a full-screen slide show presentation, click View Slide Show in the Actions area at the left of the page.

● To view all the folders in the picture library (allowing you to open any of them), click View All Folders in the Actions area at the left of the page.

Sharing Documents Using a Document Workspace

A SharePoint *document workspace* is type of nested Web site (an entire SharePoint site nested within another team Web site) that's designed specifically for a group of colleagues to work together on a set of documents—usually a primary document plus one or more supporting files. An important unique feature of a document workspace is that it can be accessed through a task pane in Office applications (Shared Workspace), as well as through a Web browser.

If you have a document open in Word, Excel, or PowerPoint, you can use the new Shared Workspace task pane (see Figure 8-8) to create a document workspace and make a copy of the current document within a document library in the new document workspace. To display the Shared Workspace task pane, choose Tools, Shared Workspace; or use any of the general methods for opening a task pane described in "Using the Task Panes in Office Applications" on page 42. To create the workspace, in the Members tab of the Shared Workspace task pane (shown in Figure 8-8) fill in a workspace name (or accept the default name, based on the name of the document), provide the workspace location, and then click the Create button.

Tasks

Member

Status

Documents

Links

Document information

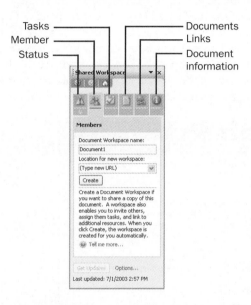

Figure 8-8. You can create a document workspace and access its features through the new Shared Workspace task pane in Word, Excel, and PowerPoint.

As mentioned earlier in the chapter (in the section "Accessing SharePoint Document Libraries Using Your Browser" on page 183), if a document is stored in a SharePoint document library, you can create a document workspace and copy that document to the workspace by opening the document library's page in your browser and choosing the Create Document Workspace command from the document's drop-down menu. And as explained later in the chapter, you can also create an empty document workspace (that is, one that doesn't initially contain a document) by opening a SharePoint team Web site's Create page in your browser, clicking the Sites And Workspaces command at the bottom of the page, and choosing the Document Workspace Template for creating the new site.

> Yet another way to create a document workspace is to include a *shared attachment* in an e-mail message that you send from Outlook, as explained in "Sending Shared Attachments," on page 1018.

Like a general-purpose team Web site, a Document Workspace provides document libraries, picture libraries, form libraries, lists (links, announcements, contacts, events, tasks, issues, or custom lists), discussion boards, surveys, and free-form Web pages. You would normally store the primary document in a document library, perhaps store one or more supplemental graphics files in a picture library, and use the other types of information components to exchange ideas and data that are relevant to working on the primary document.

When you open a document that you've added to a document workspace, you can access most of the features of the workspace through the Shared Workspace task pane, which was shown in Figure 8-8. To customize the way the Shared Workspace task pane works and the way that documents contained in a document workspace are updated, choose Help, Customer Feedback Options and open the Shared Workspace category in the Service Options dialog box (see Figure 8-9). Alternative ways to open the Service Options dialog box are to click the Options command at the bottom of the Shared Workspace task pane, or to choose Tools, Options, click the General tab, and then click the Service Options button.

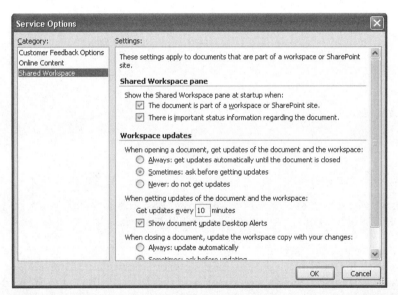

Figure 8-9. The Shared Workspace category of the new Service Options dialog box lets you modify the Shared Workspace task pane and the way workspace documents are updated.

To gain full access to a document workspace, you need to open it in your browser. If a document belonging to a workspace is opened in an Office application, you can open the corresponding workspace in your browser by clicking Open Site In Browser near the top of the Shared Workspace task pane (this command appears only if the active document is part of a document workspace or SharePoint site). If you're not currently working with a workspace document, you can open the workspace using a shortcut—if you've created one—in your My Network Places folder or your Favorites folder in Windows. You can also open a document workspace in your browser by first opening the SharePoint team Web site that contains the workspace, and then navigating to the Site Settings page, clicking the Manage Sites And Workspaces command, and clicking the name of the document workspace. Figure 8-10 shows the Home page of a newly created document workspace within a SharePoint site. The features contained in the pages of a document workspace work like the features of a regular SharePoint team Web site that are described in this chapter.

> For information on creating shortcuts in your My Network Folders folder, see "Accessing SharePoint Document Libraries from Office Applications," on page 187.

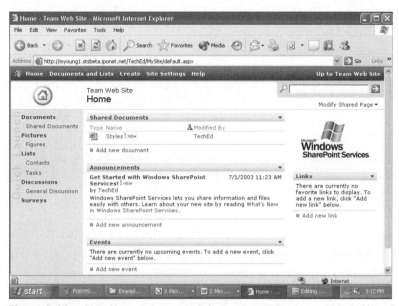

Figure 8-10. Here's a newly created document workspace within a SharePoint team Web site.

Using SharePoint Discussions

Using a team Web site, you can communicate with your fellow team members by participating in a discussion board or by joining an online discussion about a shared document.

Participating in a Discussion Board

Your team Web site might have one or more active discussion boards set up for conferring about various topics. (A newly created site has a discussion board named General Discussion. Later in this chapter you'll learn how to create others.) To participate in a discussion board, do the following:

1 In your browser, connect to the Home page of the team Web site, and then click the Documents And Lists link on the navigation bar at the top of the page to open the Documents And Lists page. All the site's discussion boards will be listed in the Discussion Boards section near the bottom of this page.

2 Click the name of the particular discussion board you want to access. This will open the page for that discussion board, which will display all the discussion items that members have posted, organized by subject (see Figure 8-11).

193

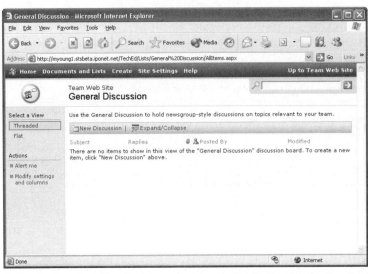

Figure 8-11. This figure shows the SharePoint Web page for the Book Content example discussion board.

3 In the discussion board's page, you can do any of the following:

- To view the text and all replies to a particular discussion item, click the box with the + sign to the item's left to expand the information.

- To expand or collapse all items, click Expand/Collapse on the toolbar near the top of the page.

- To reply to a particular discussion item, to view the item in a full window, to edit or delete the item, or to have SharePoint send you an alert e-mail message whenever the item is modified, hold the mouse over the item's subject, click the down arrow that appears, and choose a command from the drop-down menu:

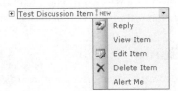

You can also view the item in a full window by simply clicking the item's subject.

- To create a discussion item on a new topic, click New Discussion on the toolbar near the top of the page.

- To change the way the documents are displayed, click a view—Threaded or Flat—in the Select A View area at the left of the page.

■ To have SharePoint send you an e-mail message whenever any change occurs in the discussion board, click Alert Me in the Actions area at the left of the page.

■ To customize the current discussion board, click Modify Settings And Columns in the Actions area at the left of the page. This will open the Customize page for that discussion board.

Discussing an Online Document

You and your fellow team Web site members can conduct a discussion about an Office document located on a SharePoint team Web site. A member of the team Web site can add discussion remarks about the document and can view remarks added by other members.

> **Note** If you use a Windows SharePoint Services server as the discussion server, the document you discuss must be located on the same server.

All the discussion remarks on each document are stored in a database on the team Web site. Because the remarks aren't stored in the document itself, using a SharePoint discussion is a good way for a workgroup to comment on a document without altering the document's content.

You can participate in a document discussion within Word, Excel, or PowerPoint using the following procedure:

1 Open the document in the application by opening the SharePoint document library in your browser and choosing the Edit In *Application* command (where *Application* is Word, Excel, or PowerPoint) from the document's drop-down menu, as explained in "Accessing SharePoint Document Libraries Using Your Browser," earlier in the chapter. Or, run the appropriate Office application and use the Open command to navigate to the SharePoint site (through your My Network Folders folder) and open the document, as discussed in "Accessing SharePoint Document Libraries from Office Applications," also earlier in the chapter.

2 From the application's Tools menu, choose Online Collaboration, Web Discussions. This will display the Web Discussions toolbar, shown here:

Chapter 8

Note The figure above shows the Web Discussions toolbar as it appears in Excel and PowerPoint. The toolbar displayed in Word has all these buttons, plus several more. One of the additional buttons, Insert Discussion In The Document, is explained in the following note.

3 The first time you use the discussion feature for a document on a particular Share-Point site, you'll need to specify the site's URL. To do this, click the Discussions button on the Web Discussions toolbar and choose Discussion Options from the drop-down menu, as shown here:

Then, in the Discussion Options dialog box, click the Add button and enter the URL, as well as a friendly name, for the team Web site that contains the document you want to discuss. Alternatively, if the document is located on the same server used as the discussion server, you can simply select Active Document's Server in the Select A Discussion Server drop-down list.

4 To add a new discussion remark, click the Insert Discussion About The *Document* button on the Web Discussions toolbar and enter the subject and your remark into the Enter Discussion Text dialog box. (The button's actual ScreenTip text depends on the application you're using. In Excel, for example, it's Insert Discussion About The Workbook.)

Note The Web Discussions toolbar in Word also has an Insert Discussion In The Document button that inserts an *inline* discussion, which is a discussion remark attached to specific document text, like a Word comment. Keep in mind, though, that unlike a Word comment, the remark text isn't actually inserted into the document content.

5 In the Discussion Pane at the bottom of the Office application window, you can view any discussion remarks that you or other team Web site members have added (see Figure 8-12). If this pane isn't visible, click the Show/Hide Discussion Pane button on the Web Discussions toolbar. Note that you won't be able to open this window until at least one discussion remark has been added.

Chapter 8

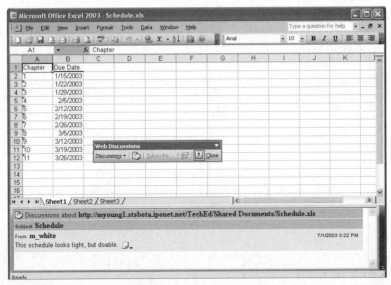

Figure 8-12. Conducting a discussion on an Excel workbook is shown in this example.

6   To reply to an existing discussion remark, click the button at the end of the remark in the Discussion pane and choose Reply from the shortcut menu that appears, shown here:

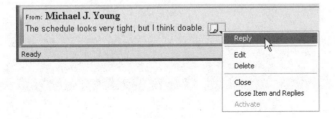

Then, in the Enter Discussion Text dialog box, enter your reply in the Discussion Text box. (Don't modify the subject; otherwise, your reply won't be listed under the remark you're replying to.)

7   To terminate the discussion, click the Close button on the Web Discussions toolbar. Both the Web Discussions toolbar and the Discussion pane will be removed.

Tip **Join a document discussion through the SharePoint team Web site**

Another way to participate in a discussion about a file that's stored in a document library or picture library on your team Web site is to connect to the site in Microsoft Internet Explorer and open the Web page for the document or picture library that contains the file. Then, choose Discuss from the file's drop-down menu (for a picture library, you must be in Details view). (All these techniques are explained in "Accessing SharePoint Document Libraries Using Your Browser," on page 183.) Internet Explorer might then display the File Download dialog box; if it does, be sure to click the Open button. Internet Explorer will then open the file in the Internet Explorer window and displays the Discussion pane and Discuss bar, which you can use to view and add discussion remarks. (If the Discuss bar isn't visible, click the Discuss button on Internet Explorer's Standard Buttons toolbar. If the Discussion Pane isn't visible, click the Show/Hide Discussion Pane button on the Discuss bar.) Use the same techniques employed in an Office application, described earlier in this section.

Exchanging Information on a SharePoint Site

To view or add items to a SharePoint list (links, announcements, contacts, events, tasks, issues, or custom lists) or survey, perform the following steps:

1 In your browser, connect to the Home page of the team Web site.

2 Click the Documents And Lists link on the navigation bar at the top of the page to open the Documents And Lists page, which will display all the lists (links, announcements, contacts, events, tasks, issues, or custom lists) and surveys stored on the team Web site (see Figure 8-13).

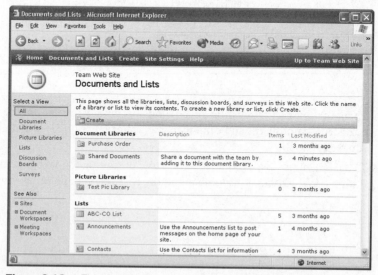

Figure 8-13. This figure shows the Documents And Lists page of a SharePoint team Web site.

3 Click the name of the particular list or survey you want to access. This will open the Web page for that list or survey, which displays all the list items or survey responses that members have posted. For example, Figure 8-14 shows the page for an announcements list named Announcements.

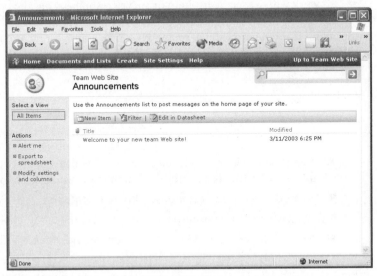

Figure 8-14. This page displays the Announcements list.

4 The following is the basic set of tasks that you can perform in the Web page for any type of list or (where indicated) a survey:

- To create a new list item (link, announcement, contact, event, and so on), click New Item on the toolbar near the top of the page. To create a new survey response, click Respond To This Survey.

- To control which list items are shown, click Filter on the toolbar near the top of the page.

- To view the contents of a list in a spreadsheet-like grid of rows and columns, choose Edit In Datasheet on the toolbar near the top of the page.

- To change the way the list items or survey results are displayed, click a view in the Select A View area at the left of the page.

- To have SharePoint send you an e-mail message whenever the list or survey is changed, click Alert Me in the Actions area at the left of the page.

- To run Excel on your computer and download a copy of the listing of list items to a worksheet—so you can analyze, edit, and save a local copy of the listing—click Export To Spreadsheet in the Actions area at the left of the page. To download a copy of the results of a survey, click Export Results To A Spreadsheet on the toolbar near the top of the page.

■ To customize a list, click Modify Settings And Columns. To customize a survey, click Modify Survey And Questions. These commands are in the Actions area at the left of the page. SharePoint will open the Customize page for that list or survey.

■ To work with a specific list item or survey response, hold the pointer over the item or response name, click the down arrow that appears, and choose a command from the drop-down menu. Here's the menu for an announcement:

■ To display the item or response in a separate page, so that you can see all its information and work with just that item or response, choose View Item.

■ To modify the item or response, choose Edit Item.

■ To remove the item or response from the list or survey, choose Delete Item.

■ To have SharePoint send you an e-mail message whenever the item or response is changed, choose Alert Me.

In addition to the basic set of commands described under step 4 in the instructions above, some types of lists provide additional features and tasks you can perform. The following are some of the useful and interesting ones:

 ● In the page for a contacts list, you can link the contact items to Outlook by clicking Link To Outlook. This will let you view and work with your SharePoint contacts in Outlook. Also, you can import contacts from Outlook into your SharePoint contacts list by clicking Import Contacts. Both commands are on the toolbar near the top of the page.

> For information on viewing a SharePoint contacts list in Outlook, or importing contacts from Outlook to a SharePoint contacts list, see "Opening a SharePoint Contacts List in Outlook," on page 1058.

 ● In the page for an events list, you can link the event items to Outlook by clicking Link To Outlook in the toolbar near the top of the page. This will let you view and work with your SharePoint events list in Outlook, along with your other Outlook calendar folder or folders. Also, you can copy an individual SharePoint event item to an Outlook Appointment form by choosing View Item from the item's drop-down menu and then, in the item's page, clicking Export Event in the toolbar near the top of the page. You'll then be able to save the appointment in your default Outlook Calendar folder.

> For information on viewing a SharePoint events list in Outlook, or exporting an individual event, see "Opening a SharePoint Calendar in Outlook," on page 1045.

- When you create or edit an item in an events list, you can add a *meeting workspace* to your SharePoint site and copy the event to it by checking the Use a Meeting Workspace option in the page where you create or edit a events item. A meeting workspace is a highly specialized type of SharePoint Web site that you can create within a SharePoint team Web site. It is designed for organizing a meeting. SharePoint meeting workspaces are discussed in "Creating and Linking to a SharePoint Meeting Workspace," on page 1039.

Customizing a SharePoint Site

You can use your browser to customize a team Web site. The site provides pages that allow you to do any of the following:

- Create a new site component—that is, a new document library, picture library, form library, list (links, announcements, contacts, events, tasks, issues, or custom), discussion board, survey, free-form Web page, or nested Web site (including a workspace).

- Customize the Home page or a free-form Web page that you've created.
- Customize the Web page for a document library, picture library, form library, list, discussion board, or survey.
- Modify the site's overall look and behavior.

Creating New Site Components

To create a new document library, picture library, form library, list, discussion board, survey, free-form Web page, or nested Web site, perform the following steps:

1 In your browser, connect to the Home page of the team Web site.

2 Click Create on the navigation bar at the top of the Home page to open the Create page (see Figure 8-15).

3 Click the name of the particular type of entity you want to create—Document Library, Picture Library, Announcements, Discussion Board, and so on. SharePoint will open a page containing a form that lets you specify the features for the component you're creating.

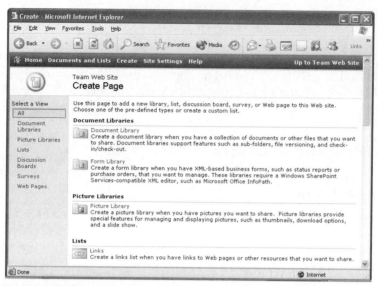

Figure 8-15. In the Create page, you can create any of the types of components that can be part of a SharePoint team Web site.

To create a custom list, click one of the commands in the Custom area, as follows:

- To create a custom list with a Web page that has the traditional format you've seen in the figures of standard lists in this chapter, click Custom List.

- To create a custom list with a Web page that automatically displays the list items in a spreadsheet-like grid of rows and columns, click Custom List In Datasheet View.

  (For a Web page that has the traditional format, created through the Custom List command, you can click Edit In Datasheet on the toolbar near the top of the page to display the items in a datasheet view.)

- To create a custom list based on a spreadsheet you have that contains the columns and information you want in your list, click Import Spreadsheet.

To add a free-form Web page to your site, click either Basic Page or Web Part Page in the Web Pages area of the Create page. Clicking Basic Page will create a simple Web page that contains a single working area. After you click this command, you'll need to specify a filename for the page and the name of the document library in which you want to store the page. SharePoint will then display a simple rich text editor that allows you to create the page's content by inserting and formatting text, graphics, tables, hyperlinks, and so on.

Clicking Web Part Page will create a more complex page, known as a *Web part page*. A Web part page consists of multiple *zones*, which are separate areas in which you can add content by inserting and customizing predefined components known as *Web parts*. After you click this command, you'll need to specify a filename for the page, the name of the document library in which you want to store the page, and a layout template that defines the number and arrangement of the page's zones. SharePoint will then display a set of interactive tools that you can use to design the Web page within your browser, using basic Windows techniques (see Figure 8-16). You create the page content by adding and customizing one or more Web parts to each zone. Some types of Web parts display data from an external source (for example, a Web part might display the items belonging to the Announcements list on the site, or stock quotes from a Web service). Other types of Web parts allow you to add fixed content (for example, formatted text or an image file).

The page you create will be stored in a document library on the site. You can later display the page by opening the page's document library and clicking the page's icon or title. Also, you could add a Content Web Part (a type of Web part that lets you add formatted text or HTML elements) to the Home page (or to another free-form Web page you've created) and insert a hyperlink to the new page into the Component Web part.

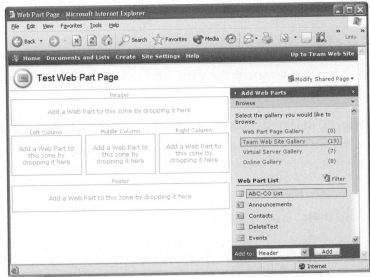

Figure 8-16. This figure shows the SharePoint design tools for creating a new SmartPage.

To create a new Web site that's nested within the current SharePoint team Web site, click Sites And Workspaces near the bottom of the Create page. You can create another team Web site, a document workspace site, or a meeting workspace site.

Customizing a Free-Form Web Page or the Home Page

You can modify a free-form Web page that you've created or the team Web site's Home page at any time. To do that, follow these steps:

1 Open the page in your browser.

2 If the Web page is a basic page that you've created as explained in the previous section, click the Edit Content button in the page's upper-right corner to open the Rich Text Editor dialog box, where you can edit the page's content. If the page is a Web part

Chapter 8

page, such as the site's Home page or a Web part page that you've created as explained in the previous section, click Modify My Page or Modify Shared Page, found in the page's upper-right corner, and choose commands from the drop-down menu, as follows:

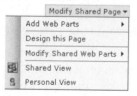

> **Note** You can select the Personal View option on the drop-down menu to view or modify the personal view of the page that's available only to you. In this case, the drop-down menu will be labeled Modify My Page. Or, you can select the Shared View option to view or modify the shared view of the page that's available to all site users. In this case, the drop-down menu will be labeled Modify Shared Page.

- To add one or more new Web parts to the page, choose a command from the Add Web Parts submenu.

- To customize an existing Web part on the page, choose the name of the Web part from the Modify My Web Parts or Modify Shared Web Parts submenu.

- If you just want to rearrange the Web parts (by dragging-and-dropping them), select the Design This Page menu option. This will activate the design mode without displaying the tools for adding or customizing Web parts.

Customizing an Information Page

Use the following procedure to customize the Web page that's used to display one of the information components in the current SharePoint team Web site—a document library, picture library, form library, list, discussion board, or survey.

1 On the team Web site, open the information page that you want to customize.

2 Click Modify Settings And Columns (for a survey, Modify Survey And Questions) in the Actions area at the left of the page, which will open the Customize page for the current information page (see Figure 8-17).

3 Make the changes you want in the Customize page.

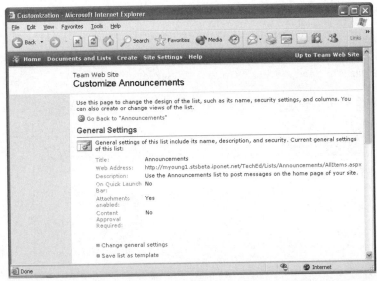

Figure 8-17. Here, the Customize page is used to modify the Announcements list.

An alternative way to customize the page for an information component is to click the Site Settings link in the navigation bar at the top of any of the main SharePoint pages to open the Site Settings page. Then, in the Customization area near the center of this page, click Modify Site Content to open the Modify Site Content page, which will display a Customize command for each of the site's current information pages (see Figure 8-18). Click the command for the page you want to customize.

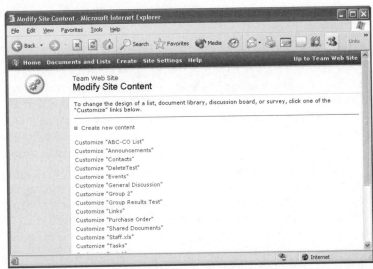

Figure 8-18. The Modify Site Content page provides a command to modify each of the pages used to access one of the site's current information components.

Modifying a Team Web Site

To modify features of the overall team Web site, perform the following steps:

1 Click the Site Settings link in the navigation bar at the top of any of the main Share-Point pages to open the Site Settings page (see Figure 8-19).

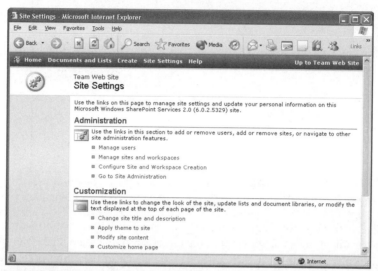

Figure 8-19. The Site Settings page allows you to modify features of the overall team Web site.

2 To perform site administration tasks, click Go To Site Administration in the Administration area of the Site Settings page. This will open the Site Administration page, where you can:

- Manage users and permissions.

- Perform other management tasks and view site usage statistics

- If the site you're modifying is nested within another SharePoint site, you can click Go To Top-Level Site Administration to open the Administration page for the root SharePoint Web site—that is, the site at the top of the hierarchy of nested sites—provided that you are a member of that site and have the required permissions. This page will be labeled Top-Level Site Administration.

- A top-level site administration page will contain two additional groups of links. The first group, labeled Site Collection Catalogs, lets you manage the site's catalogs of Web parts and templates. The second group, labeled Site Collection Administration, lets you perform management tasks that affect the entire collection of sites—that is, top-level site plus all sites nested directly or indirectly within it.

> **Note** You can go directly to the page for managing users and permissions, for managing sites and workspaces, or for controlling the creation of nested sites and workspaces by clicking the corresponding link in the Administration area of the Site Settings page. (These pages are also accessible through the Site Administration page.)

3 To customize the site's design, click a command in the Customization area of the Site Settings page, as follows:

- To change the site title that appears on every page or the site description that appears on the Home page, click Change Site Title And Description.

- To assign a default theme to the site, click Apply Theme To Site. A theme is a visual scheme that sets the colors and fonts on the site's pages.

- To customize one or more of the site's information pages, as explained in the previous section, click Modify Site Content.

- To display the site's Home page in design mode, click Customize Home Page. Customizing the Home page was discussed in "Customizing a Free-Form Web Page or the Home Page," earlier in this chapter.

4 To modify the information that the SharePoint site stores for you, click a command in the Manage My Information area of the Site Settings page, as follows:

- To change your display name, e-mail address, password, and other information, click Update My Information.

- To add or remove alerts that are set up for you, click My Alerts On This Site. Recall that setting up an alert causes the SharePoint server to send you an e-mail message whenever an information component (document library, list, and so on) or an item within an information component (document, event, and so on) changes.

- To view information about you and all other members of the team Web site, click View Information About Site Users.

> You can use FrontPage to customize a team Web site more extensively than you can by working with the site in your browser. For information, see "Customizing a SharePoint Site," on page 201.

Customizing the Office 2003 Application Interface

Customizing Toolbars, Menus,
and Shortcut Keys. 209

Creating and Managing
Custom Toolbars 210

Modifying Toolbars and Menus 213

Defining Shortcut Keys (Word Only) . . . 222

Recording and Running Macros 224

Setting Office Interface Options 232

Saving and Restoring Your
Office Settings 235

Customizing Toolbars, Menus, and Shortcut Keys

You can extensively modify the interface of any of the major Microsoft Office 2003 Edition applications—Microsoft Word, Excel, PowerPoint, Outlook, Access, FrontPage, and Info-Path—to suit your working style. You can create new custom toolbars and you can modify existing toolbars and menus. In Word, you can define new shortcut keys for quickly executing commands or running macros. In Word, Excel, and PowerPoint, you can record macros to automate tasks—usually relatively complex tasks or those that you perform frequently. You can also set a variety of other options that affect the application interface. And finally, you can run a utility to save your Office settings so that you can restore them on another computer where you use Office. This section discusses several general principles that apply to all ways of customizing the Office application interface. The following sections then present the specific techniques for making each type of modification.

In Word, when you create a toolbar, modify a toolbar or menu, or define a shortcut key, you can choose where to save your modification by selecting an item in the Make Toolbar Available To, Save In, or Save Changes In drop-down list, which is displayed at the bottom of the dialog box in which you make the modification. In most cases you must select the item in this list *before* you make the modification in the dialog box. (If you select a new item in the list *after* you've made a modification in the dialog box, your modification might not be stored in the selected location.) If you choose the Normal.dot (or Normal) item, the modification will be stored in the Normal template and will be in effect while you work on any document. This choice is best for designing a general-purpose toolbar or menu or for defining a shortcut key that you'll use frequently.

Alternatively, you can choose the name of the current document's template (assuming that the document is based on a template other than Normal). In this case the modification will be in effect only while you work on a document based on the same template. This choice is best when you make changes that are useful for a specific type of document. For example, if you want to create a menu with commands for writing faxes, you could save your modifications in the Word template you use for creating faxes.

For information on Word templates, see "Creating New Office Documents," on page 47, and "Customizing and Creating Document Templates," on page 408.

Finally, you can choose the name of the document itself. In this case the modification will be in effect only when you work on that particular document. This choice is best for highly specific modifications.

Note that while you use the Customize dialog box to make modifications, you can get help from the Office Assistant. If the Office Assistant isn't visible, click the question-mark button in the lower-left corner of the Customize dialog box.

The Office Assistant is described in Chapter 3, "Getting Expert Help on Office 2003."

Caution Making extensive modifications to the toolbars, menus, or shortcut keys in one or more Office applications may make it difficult to learn tasks from this book or from the Office online Help, because these sources refer to the standard configurations. You might therefore want to wait until you're familiar with the Office skills involved before making extensive customizations.

Creating and Managing Custom Toolbars

You can create new custom toolbars that you can display in addition to the toolbars that are supplied with the Office application. To create a custom toolbar, perform the following steps:

1   Choose Tools, Customize. In the Customize dialog box, click the Toolbars tab. The particular toolbars you'll see listed depend on the Office application you're using (see Figure 9-1 for an example of the Toolbars tab in Word).

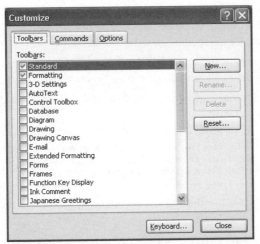

Figure 9-1. This is the Toolbars tab of the Customize dialog box that's displayed in Word.

There are several other ways to open the Customize dialog box. Choose View, Toolbars, Customize. Or, right-click a toolbar or the menu bar and choose Customize from the drop-down menu. Or, click the down arrow on the right end of a toolbar and choose Add Or Remove Buttons, Customize from the shortcut menu, shown here:

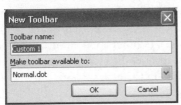

2 Click the New button to open the New Toolbar dialog box (shown in Figure 9-2).

Figure 9-2. This is the New Toolbar dialog box that's displayed in Word.

3 Type a name for your toolbar in the Toolbar Name text box.

4 If you're customizing Word, select an item in the Make Toolbar Available To drop-down list. If you choose Normal.dot (or Normal), the toolbar can be displayed when you work on any document; if you choose the name of the document template, it can be displayed only when you work on a document based on this same template; and if you choose the name of the current document, it can be displayed only when you work on that document. These choices were explained in greater detail in the previous section.

5 Click OK. The Office application will display your new toolbar (which initially won't contain any buttons), and will return you to the Toolbars tab.

6 Add buttons to your toolbar using the Customize dialog box Commands tab, as explained in the next section.

Although Task Pane is listed in the Toolbars tab, as well as on the Toolbars submenu of the View menu, a task pane isn't an actual toolbar and you can't modify it using the techniques given in this chapter. For more information, see "Using the Task Panes in Office Applications," on page 42.

In the Toolbars tab of the Customize dialog box, you can also show, hide, rename, delete, or reset a toolbar, as follows:

- To show a toolbar that isn't currently visible (a custom or built-in toolbar), select the check box to the left of the toolbar name in the Toolbars list. To hide the toolbar, clear the check box.

Tip **Display toolbars more quickly**

To quickly show or hide a commonly used toolbar, on the View menu, click Toolbars or click any toolbar or the menu bar with the right mouse button, and then choose the name of the toolbar from the menu. If the toolbar you want to show or hide doesn't appear on the menu, open the Toolbars tab of the Customize dialog box, which shows all toolbars available in the application.

- To rename or delete a custom toolbar you've created (not a built-in one), select the toolbar in the Toolbars list and click the Rename or Delete button.

- To remove any modifications that you've made to one of the built-in toolbars supplied with Office (not a custom toolbar), select the toolbar in the Toolbars list and click the Reset button. In Word, you'll see the Reset Toolbar dialog box, in which you need to select the template or document for which you want to reset the toolbar (the choices were explained in the previous section). In other applications, you'll see a message box asking you to confirm that you want to reset the toolbar. The methods for making modifications to toolbars are discussed in the next section.

For instructions on using the Word Organizer to copy, delete, or rename a custom toolbar you've created in Word, see "Using the Organizer," on page 412.

Modifying Toolbars and Menus

Office applications let you extensively modify menus and both custom and built-in toolbars. The different objects you can work with are so interchangeable that the terminology becomes a bit confusing. The following terms are used in this chapter to describe three of the basic objects you work with when you customize toolbars and menus:

- A *menu* is one of the drop-down lists of items that appear on the application's menu bar, such as the File menu or the Edit menu. A menu can also be displayed as an item on another menu, where it's known as a *submenu*. In addition, a menu can be displayed as a button on a toolbar, where you can open it by clicking a down arrow. A menu label consists of text only—it can't include an icon.

- A *menu item* is one of the objects listed on a menu. A menu item can be a *command*, which immediately performs an action, sets an option, or opens a dialog box. It can also be another menu, which in this context is known as a submenu. The label for a command on a menu can consist of both text and an icon or text only.

- A *toolbar button* is one of the objects that appear on a toolbar, such as the Standard or Formatting toolbar. It can be a command or it can be a menu. The label for a command on a toolbar can consist of an icon only, text only, or both an icon and text.

Note A command can be either a simple object that you click to execute the command or a drop-down list control from which you select an item or type in a value (such as the Style, Font, and Font Size drop-down lists on the Formatting toolbar in Word).

You can add, remove, or rearrange toolbar buttons, menu items, or menus. You can also change the text or the icon that's associated with a command on a toolbar or menu, and you can change the name of a menu. And you can specify whether a toolbar or menu command displays text only, an icon only (on a toolbar), or both text and an icon.

To make any of these modifications, the first step is to choose Tools, Customize, which displays the Customize dialog box. If you want to modify a toolbar that isn't visible, you must first display it by clicking the Toolbars tab of the Customize dialog box and checking the box next to the toolbar name. Then, click the Commands tab (shown in Figure 9-3).

Chapter 9

Figure 9-3. This is the Commands tab of the Customize dialog box that's displayed in Word.

Tip Customize a shortcut menu

In Word, PowerPoint, and Access, you can modify the shortcut menus the program displays when you right-click various items. To modify a shortcut menu, click the Toolbars tab in the Customize dialog box and then check the Shortcut Menus item. This will temporarily display a special floating toolbar—labeled Shortcut Menus—on which you'll find copies of the application's shortcut menus, arranged by category. (This toolbar will be hidden when you close the Customize dialog box.) Then, to modify a particular shortcut menu, use the techniques given in this section to modify the copy of the shortcut menu found on the Shortcut Menus toolbar.

If you're working in Word, before you make any of the modifications described in this section, choose the appropriate item in the Save In drop-down list at the bottom of the Customize dialog box. If you choose Normal.dot (or Normal), the modifications will be in effect when you work on any document; if you choose the name of the document template, they will be in effect only when you work on a document based on this same template; and if you choose the name of the current document, they will be in effect only when you work on this document.

These three choices were explained in greater detail at the beginning of "Customizing Toolbars, Menus, and Shortcut Keys," on page 209.

To add a new toolbar button, menu item, or menu, perform the following steps:

1   Select an item in the Categories list, as follows:

■   If you want to add a command that executes a built-in application command or a menu that contains a set of related commands (for example, a menu with both

Print Preview and Web Page Preview), select a command category (File, Edit, View, and so on).

- If you want to add a command that runs a macro, assigns a font, inserts an AutoText entry, or applies a style, select the Macros (in Access, All Macros), Fonts, AutoText, or Styles item (Fonts, AutoText, and Styles are available in Word only).

- If you want to add a menu to the menu bar, to a toolbar, or to another menu, select Built-In Menus (in Outlook, Menu Bar) to add a copy of one of the application's standard menus (File, Edit, View, and so on). Or, select New Menu to add an empty menu (you can then add items to it using this numbered procedure).

> **For information on Office macros, see "Recording and Running Macros," on page 224. Fonts are discussed in "Formatting Characters Directly," on page 308; AutoText in "Reusing Text with the AutoText Feature," on page 266; and styles in "Applying Styles and Reusing Formats," on page 327.**

2   In the Commands list, select the specific application command, other command (macro, font, AutoText entry, or style), or menu that you want to add. (Word shows a description or preview—if available—of a selected macro, font, AutoText entry, or style.) Then use the mouse to drag the command or menu directly to the position on the toolbar, menu bar, or menu where you want to insert it. Note that when you drag an object to a menu, Office automatically opens the menu when the mouse pointer moves over the menu label.

While the Customize dialog box is displayed, you can *move* a toolbar button, menu item, or menu to any position on a toolbar, menu, or the menu bar by simply dragging the object to the new location. To make a *copy*, press the Ctrl key while you drag. When you've dragged an object to a position where you can insert it, the mouse pointer will display an I-beam symbol at the point of insertion and also—if you're copying—a + symbol, as shown here:

To *remove* a toolbar button, menu item, or menu, drag it away from its current position and drop it anywhere except on a toolbar, a menu, or the menu bar. When you've dragged the object to a position where dropping it will remove the object, the mouse pointer will display an X, as seen here:

While the Customize dialog box is open, you can also modify a specific toolbar button, menu item, or menu by clicking the button, the menu item, or the menu label (Office will draw a selection border around the object you click). In the Commands tab, click the Modify Selection button and choose the appropriate command from the menu that pops up, which is shown here:

This menu is referred to as the Modify Selection menu throughout the remainder of this discussion. Table 9-1 lists what you can do using the commands on the Modify Selection menu.

Table 9-1. Modifying a Toolbar Button, Menu Item, or Menu Using the Modify Selection Menu

To Do This	Perform This Action on the Modify Selection Menu
Undo any changes you've made to the selected toolbar button, menu item, or menu.	Choose Reset.
Remove the selected toolbar button, menu item, or menu.	Choose Delete.
Change the label text for the selected toolbar button, menu item, or menu. (This command also changes the text of the ScreenTip for a toolbar button.)	Type the new text into the Name text box. You can specify a shortcut key by inserting an & in front of one of the characters in the label (that character will be underlined in the label, indicating that it's a shortcut key).
Copy the selected toolbar or menu command's icon (if any) into the Clipboard.	Choose Copy Button Image.
Assign the previously copied icon to the currently selected command on a toolbar or menu.	Choose Paste Button Image.

Table 9-1. Modifying a Toolbar Button, Menu Item, or Menu Using the Modify Selection Menu

To Do This	Perform This Action on the Modify Selection Menu
Restore the selected toolbar or menu command's default icon. (If the command doesn't have a default icon—like the Save As command on the File menu—the icon will simply be removed.)	Choose Reset Button Image.
Open the Button Editor, in which you can modify the toolbar or menu command's icon or design a new, custom icon.	Choose Edit Button Image.
Assign a stock icon to a toolbar command or menu command.	Choose the icon from the Change Button Image submenu.
● Display the icon only on a toolbar command. *or* ● Display the text label plus the icon on a menu command.	Choose Default Style.
Display the text label only on either a toolbar command or menu command	Choose Text Only (Always).
● Display the icon only on a toolbar command. *or* ● Display the text label only on a menu command.	Choose Text Only (In Menus).
Display both the text label and the icon (if there is one) on either a toolbar command or a menu command.	Choose Image And Text.
Display a dividing line before the selected toolbar button, menu item, or menu.	Choose Begin a Group.
Assign or remove a hyperlink from a toolbar command or menu command.	Choose one of the following commands from the Assign Hyperlink submenu (not available in FrontPage or InfoPath): ● Open: To assign to the command a hyperlink that opens a document ● Insert Picture: To assign to the command a hyperlink that inserts a picture into the active document ● Remove Link: To remove a previously assigned hyperlink from the command

Chapter 9

Note In all the major Office applications covered in this book except Excel, FrontPage, and InfoPath you add a command that runs a macro by selecting Macros (or All Macros) in the Categories list and then dragging a specific macro from the Commands list to the target location. In Excel and FrontPage, however, after choosing Macros in the Categories list, you drag either Custom Menu Item (for a text label only) or Custom Button (for an icon only) from the Commands list to the target location. To specify *which* macro the command runs, you must then click the command and choose Assign Macro from the Modify Selection menu. (Alternatively, you can close the Customize dialog box and click the new command. You'll then be prompted to select the specific macro.) InfoPath doesn't support macros.

Note that while the Customize dialog box is open, you can select an object and open the Modify Selection menu (as a shortcut menu) by simply clicking a toolbar button, a menu item, or a menu label using the right mouse button.

If you selected a menu prior to opening the Modify Selection menu, the command you choose will affect the entire menu. However, only the Reset, Delete, Name, and Begin A Group commands will be available; that is, you can only reset the menu, delete the menu, change the menu label, or insert a dividing line before the menu.

Most of the commands that you can add to a toolbar or menu have a default icon. For example, the Open command in the File category has a default icon that depicts an opened file folder, as shown here:

If you don't like the default icon for the selected toolbar or menu command (or if there is no icon), you can replace the icon (or add an icon) in one of three ways. First, you can choose Change Button Image from the Modify Selection menu and choose an icon from the palette of images that Office displays, shown here:

Second, you can modify the icon or draw a new one by choosing the Edit Button Image command and designing the image you want in the Button Editor dialog box.

Finally, if you've spotted an attractive icon on another toolbar or menu command, you can copy that icon to your command, as follows:

1 Right-click on the command that has the icon you want to copy.

2 Choose Copy Button Image from the shortcut menu.

Chapter 9

3 Right-click the button or menu item you want to modify.

4 Choose Paste Button Image from the shortcut menu.

You can restore the default icon for the selected toolbar or menu command by choosing the Reset Button Image command from the Modify Selection menu.

If you choose the Reset command with a toolbar or menu command selected, any change that you've made to the command will be removed. If you choose Reset with a menu selected, the menu will be restored to its default configuration—that is, any item you've added to the menu will be removed, any item you've removed will be restored, and any item you've modified will be returned to its default state.

You can also reset the entire menu bar by opening the Toolbars tab of the Customize dialog box, selecting the Menu Bar item in the list (in Excel select Chart Menu Bar or Worksheet Menu Bar), and clicking the Reset button. This will remove any menus you've added, restore any menus you've removed, and reset individual menus to their default configurations.

Finally, to restore a built-in toolbar to its default configuration, select the name of the toolbar in the Toolbars tab and click Reset. Note, however, that you can't use this method for a custom toolbar. (The Reset command was explained more thoroughly at the end of "Creating and Managing Custom Toolbars," earlier in this chapter.)

A Quick Way to Add or Remove Toolbar Buttons

You can quickly add or remove a button from a built-in toolbar by clicking the down arrow at the right end of the toolbar (or the arrow at the bottom of a vertically positioned toolbar), clicking the Add Or Remove Buttons command, clicking the command that has the same name as the toolbar, and then choosing the button you want to add or remove, as shown here (the command for a button that's currently displayed has a check mark next to it):

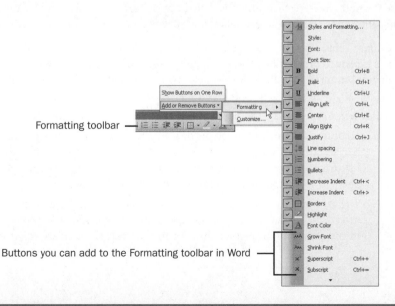

Although this is a fast way to add a button, the menu typically includes only a few buttons—if any—that aren't already displayed on the default toolbar. The technique is useful mainly for reducing a toolbar's size by hiding buttons that you seldom use. Note that you can't use this technique with a custom toolbar you've created.

Choosing the Reset Toolbar command on the bottom of the menu has the same effect as clicking the Reset button in the Toolbars tab of the Customize dialog box.

Inside Out

Customizing image menus

Office toolbars include a number of menus that have images instead of, or in addition to, text labels—for example, the Highlight and Font Color menus on the Formatting toolbar in Word and the New menu on the Standard toolbar in Outlook. The customization features of these menus are limited and differ from those described in this chapter in several ways. For example, you can't modify, remove, or copy the image. If the button doesn't have a text label, you can't add one (with this type of menu, the value entered into the Name item on the Modify Selection menu specifies only the ScreenTip and not the menu label). And even if you've radically modified the items on the menu, you can't reset the menu with the Reset command on the Modify Selection menu. A workaround to this last limitation is to use the new Rearrange Commands dialog box to reset the menu, as explained in the next section.

 ## Using the Rearrange Commands Dialog Box

As an alternative to using the drag-and-drop methods discussed in the previous section, you can use the new Rearrange Commands dialog box to customize toolbars and menus, all by issuing commands within a single dialog box. The following is the procedure:

1   Choose Tools, Customize to open the Customize dialog box (or use one of the other methods explained previously). Then click the Commands tab and click the Rearrange Commands button. This will display the Rearrange Commands dialog box (see Figure 9-4).

2   Use the controls in the Choose A Menu Or Toolbar To Rearrange area at the top of the dialog box to specify the toolbar or menu that you want to customize, as follows:

  ■   To customize one of the menus or submenus located on the application's menu bar, select the Menu Bar option and select an item in the adjoining drop-down list (for example, select File to customize the entire File menu or select File | Send To to customize the Send To submenu of the File menu).

  ■   To customize one of the application's toolbars or one of the menus located on a toolbar, select the Toolbar option and select the specific toolbar or toolbar menu in the adjoining drop-down list (for instance, select Standard to customize the

Standard toolbar or select Standard | Paste to customize the Paste menu located on the Standard toolbar). To modify the entire menu bar (for example, to add a new menu to it), select Menu Bar (in Excel, select Worksheet Menu Bar or Chart Menu Bar) in the drop-down list.

3 To add a new toolbar button, menu item, or menu to the selected toolbar or menu, click the Add button.

4 To modify a command or menu on the selected toolbar or menu, select the command or menu in the Controls list and do one of the following:

- To remove the command or menu, click the Delete button.

- To change the relative position of the command or menu, click the Move Up or Move Down button.

- To customize the command or menu, click the Modify Selection button and choose a command from the Modify Selection menu, which was explained in Table 9-1 in the previous section.

5 To restore the original configuration of the toolbar or menu that's selected in the Choose A Menu Or Toolbar To Rearrange area at the top of the Rearrange Commands dialog box, click the Reset button. (In contrast, choosing Reset on the Modify Selection menu restores only the specific command or menu that's selected in the Controls list.)

Figure 9-4. You can use the new Rearrange Commands dialog box to fully customize any toolbar or menu.

Chapter 9

Defining Shortcut Keys (Word Only)

In Word, you can assign a shortcut key to a built-in application command, a macro, a font, an AutoText entry, a style, or a symbol. Pressing the shortcut key will immediately execute the command, run the macro, apply the font, insert the AutoText entry, assign the style, or insert the symbol.

To assign a shortcut key to one of these items, perform the following steps:

1 Choose Tools, Customize. At the bottom of the Customize dialog box, click the Keyboard button. (You can be in any tab of the Customize dialog box when you do this.) Word will open the Customize Keyboard dialog box, shown here.

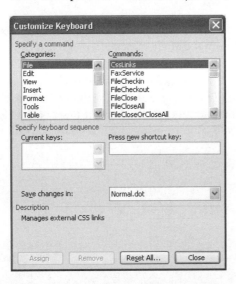

2 Select an item displayed in the Save Changes In drop-down list. If you choose Normal.dot (or Normal), the shortcut key will be available when you work on any document; if you choose the name of the document template, it will be available only when you work on a document based on this same template; and if you choose the name of the current document, it will be available only when you work on this document.

> These three choices were explained in greater detail at the beginning of "Customizing Toolbars, Menus, and Shortcut Keys," on page 209.

3 Select a category in the Categories list. Notice that in addition to the categories available for adding commands to toolbars or menus (described previously in the chapter), you can select the Common Symbols category to assign a key combination to a symbol so that you can quickly insert a symbol that doesn't appear on the keyboard.

4 In the list to the right of the Categories list, select the specific command to which you want to assign the shortcut key. (This list is named Commands, Macros, Fonts, AutoText, Styles, or Common Symbols, according to the current selection in the Categories

Chapter 9

list. To simplify the remainder of the discussion, the term *command* will be used to refer to a built-in Word command, macro, font, AutoText entry, style, or symbol that you select in the list.) You'll see a description of the selected command in the Description area at the bottom of the dialog box.

If you've chosen the Common Symbols category but don't see the character you want in the Common Symbols list, select the Insert category and the Symbol command, click the Symbol button that Word displays, and choose the character you want in the Symbol dialog box.

Note If the name of a command in the Commands list ends with a colon (such as the Symbol command in the Insert category), you'll need to supply additional information using the control or controls that appear in the Customize Keyboard dialog box when you select the command.

For information on using the Symbol dialog box, see "Inserting Symbols and Foreign Characters," on page 260.

If one or more shortcut keys have already been assigned to the selected command, these keys will be shown in the Current Keys list. Note that you can assign several shortcut keys to a command; each shortcut key will provide an alternate way to carry out the command.

5 Click in the Press New Shortcut Key text box and press the key combination you want to assign to the selected command. Word will then display a message below the box indicating whether the shortcut key is already assigned to another command. If the shortcut key is already assigned, the assignment you make will replace the former one. In general, you should try to find a key combination that isn't already assigned to a command, so that you don't lose keyboard functionality in Word.

6 Click the Assign button. The key combination will then be added to the Current Keys list.

Tip Assign a shortcut key to any style

If you've selected the Styles category in the Customize Keyboard dialog box but don't see the style you want in the Styles list, you can assign a shortcut key to *any* paragraph, character, or list style by opening that style in the Modify Style dialog box, clicking the Format button at the bottom of the dialog box, and choosing Shortcut Key from the shortcut menu. See "Customizing Styles Using the Modify Style Dialog Box," on page 394.

7 To make additional shortcut key assignments, repeat steps 3 through 6 for each one. Click the Close button when you're done.

You can remove a specific shortcut key assignment by selecting the key combination in the Current Keys list and clicking the Remove button. You can remove all shortcut key assignments you've made for all commands by clicking the Reset All button. (Note that this action will remove the assignments only from the template or document currently selected in the Save Changes In list.)

Chapter 9

Recording and Running Macros

If you're like most Microsoft Office 2003 users, much of the work that you do in Office applications can be repetitive. For example, you might always enter a series of headings in Word 2003 documents or routinely increase the width of the first few columns in your Excel worksheets. If these actions take up much of your time, you might consider recording your commands as a macro and then running the macro whenever you need to do the work. A *macro* is a named set of instructions that tells Office 2003 to perform a series of actions for you. In the following sections you'll learn how to record and run macros to increase your productivity. The last section on macros provides important information about configuring Office to minimize the threat posed by macro viruses.

> For information on using the Visual Basic Editor to edit existing macros or to write new ones from scratch with the Visual Basic for Applications programming language (VBA), see Part 10 of this book, "Customizing Office 2003 Using VBA."

Knowing When to Build a Macro

Office's macro recording capabilities are impressive, but before you forge ahead, you should make sure that Office doesn't already provide a built-in solution for your repetitive task. For example, you could record a macro in Word to assign appropriate formatting to a document heading. However, if one of Word's built-in heading styles applies acceptible formatting, it would be faster to just assign that style rather than recording and using a macro. (Styles also have other advantages. For instance, you can instantly change the formatting of all text that is assigned a particular style by simply modifying that style.) In other words, don't use macros unless the commands that you want to record are involved enough to require a macro.

This certainly doesn't mean that you shouldn't use macros to automate your Office documents. Actually, we're arguing just the opposite. Before you get started, though, it makes sense to take the time to become familiar with the majority of each Office application's features so that you know when Office offers a built-in solution and when to use macros to their greatest effect. The Visual Basic macro language in each Office application is sophisticated enough for many advanced tasks, such as communicating with other Microsoft Windows–based applications or controlling an entire inventory management system. However, the most useful macros are often the ones that automate just four or five simple commands.

In Office 2003 you can record and run macros in three applications: Word, Excel, and PowerPoint. You can also create macros in Access, but the process is quite different, and we won't cover it in this book. (Rather than recording a macro in Access, you build one by selecting the Macros object type and clicking the New button in the Database window, and then specifying actions and action arguments in a macro design grid.)

In Word, Excel, and PowerPoint, you follow the same basic process to record a new macro: Choose Tools, Macro, Record New Macro. Run the commands you want to record. Then click the Stop Recording button.

Recording a Macro

Let's start with a simple example. Imagine that you want to insert a standard mailing address for your company into a variety of Word documents. Rather than type the text from scratch each time or use AutoText, you decide to create a macro that inserts the text automatically when you press the key combination Alt+A. Complete the following steps to record the macro:

1 Open the Word, Excel, or PowerPoint document in which you want to record the macro. If you want to follow these instructions exactly, open a blank Word document now.

2 Choose Tools, Macro, Record New Macro to open the Record Macro dialog box. This dialog box, as it appears in Word, is shown here:

Notice the Store Macro In drop-down list, which prompts you for a place to save the macro. Your choices vary by application:

■ In Word, you can store your macro in the Normal.dot (or Normal) template so that you can run the macro while working on any Word document. You can store it in the document's template (if other than Normal) so that you can run the macro while working on any document based on the same template. Or you can store it in the current document so that you can run the macro only while working on that document.

■ In Excel, you can store the macro in the Personal Macro Workbook so that it's always available. You can store it in This Workbook so that it's available only when the current workbook is open. Or you can store it in New Workbook so that Excel will create a new workbook and store the macro in it, and the macro will be available only when the new workbook is open.

■ In PowerPoint, you can store the macro in any open presentation. You'll be able to run the macro only while working on the presentation in which the macro is stored.

3 In the Macro Name text box, type **InsertAddress**, the name of your macro. (Be sure not to include spaces within the name you type.)

4 Click the Keyboard button in the Record Macro dialog box to display the Customize Keyboard dialog box, where you can specify the shortcut key that runs your macro. (In Excel you just specify the shortcut key in the Record Macro dialog box. The Record Macro dialog box in PowerPoint doesn't let you assign a shortcut key.)

> **Note** In Word, you can also create a toolbar button or menu command for the macro at this time. To do so, click the Toolbars button in the Record Macro dialog box and specify a custom menu command or toolbar button that will run the macro.

5 Press Alt+A to assign the shortcut key Alt+A to your macro and then verify that the Save Changes In drop-down list is set to Normal.dot (or Normal). Your dialog box should look similar to the one shown here:

6 In the Customize Keyboard dialog box, click the Assign button and then click the Close button to accept your keyboard shortcut and start recording the macro. Office will display the Stop Recording toolbar, shown here, and will change the mouse pointer to a recording icon:

From this point on, the macro recorder records any key you press or any command that you execute in Word.

7 Type the following address (or one of your own) in the active Word document, and then press Enter:

Adventure Works

1234 Hill Garden Drive

San Francisco, CA 55555

(555) 555-0100

8 Click the Stop Recording button on the Stop Recording toolbar to end your macro.

That's all there is to it! Now that you've recorded your first macro, run it in your Word document, using the instructions given in the next section, to verify that it displays the address as you specified.

Inside Out

Options for macro recording

The Stop Recording toolbar in Word contains two useful toolbar buttons: Stop Recording and Pause/Resume Recording. When you've finished recording your macro, click Stop Recording, and Word will stop saving your commands and store the completed macro. If you want to pause the recording temporarily, click the Pause Recording button, modify your document as needed, and then click Resume Recording when you're ready to continue.

Running a Macro

To give you flexibility in automating your work, Office 2003 provides four ways to run your macros:

- Choose Tools, Macro, Macros, and then double-click the macro name in the Macros dialog box.
- Press the macro shortcut key (if you assigned one).
- Choose the macro from a menu (if you added a menu command for running the macro).
- Click the custom macro button on a toolbar (if you created a custom toolbar button for running the macro).

Note If a macro is stored in a document or in a document's template (other than the Normal template), macros must be enabled before you can run that macro in the document. To enable them, select the Medium macro security level, as explained in "Setting Macro Security," on page 229. With this setting, you'll be able to enable macros in a document that you know to be safe when you first open the document.

Using the Macros Dialog Box to Run Macros

To run a macro using the Macros dialog box, follow these steps:

1 Press Enter to add a blank line to your document.

2 Choose Tools, Macro, Macros. You'll see the following dialog box:

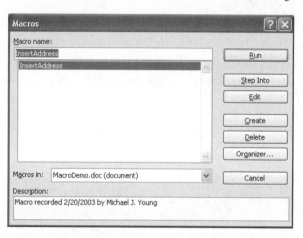

The Macros dialog box is a comprehensive tool for managing macros. Using this dialog box, you can run, step into (debug), edit, create, delete, or (in Word) organize macros. Debugging, editing, or creating a macro uses the Microsoft Visual Basic editor program.

> **Tip** Because the Macros dialog box is so useful, you might want to memorize the keyboard shortcut for opening it (Alt+F8).

3 In the Macros In drop-down list, specify the location of the macro you want to run.

4 Finally, in the Macro Name list, double-click the macro you want to run. If you double-click the InsertAddress macro (or select the macro and click the Run button), your company address text will be inserted into the current document.

Using a Shortcut Key to Run Macros

If you assigned a shortcut key to your macro when you created it, you can also run the macro in Word by pressing the designated shortcut key. To run the InsertAddress macro using the Alt+A shortcut key, follow these steps:

1 Press Enter to add a blank line to your document.

2 Press Alt+A to run the InsertAddress macro.

Word will run the macro and insert your company address in the current document. That's all there is to it!

Troubleshooting

Reversing the effects of an Office macro

You've run a macro in an Office application, but now you want to undo it.

When you run standard menu commands in Office applications, you can reverse them with the Edit menu's Undo command. But when you run an Office macro, you can't use Undo to reverse its effects in just one step. This creates a potential problem—how do you undo a macro that has produced unwanted results?

The solution is to use the Undo drop-down list on the Standard toolbar, which lets you undo more than one Office command at once. Office records each action that a macro completes individually and displays it in the Undo drop-down list. You can reverse the effects of a macro by clicking the Undo drop-down list on the Standard toolbar and then selecting all the commands in the macro you want to undo. If you didn't create the macro yourself, you may need to study the commands in the Undo drop-down list carefully—sometimes it can be difficult to determine which command was the first one in the macro.

Setting Macro Security

If you've been using computers for a while, you've probably heard about the threat created by computer viruses. A *virus* is a hidden macro or software program that works behind the scenes to annoy computer users and (in the most extreme circumstances) to destroy important data files and application software. Viruses don't just appear on computers—they're transmitted from one machine to another through computer networks, the Internet, disks, or other media. The transmission or infection process is usually silent and painless (at first): The nasty software developers who create viruses build the programs so that they attach themselves in hidden ways to files, folders, and application documents.

Because most of the applications in the Microsoft Office System have the ability to run macros, it's possible that a rogue software developer will try to pass along a hidden macro virus to you in an Office document such as an innocent-looking Word document or Excel workbook. Although you shouldn't lose sleep over this potential danger, you should be aware of the threat that viruses pose and practice safe computing by using only documents that come from authorized or known sources and that you expected to receive. (Because certain viruses can cause e-mail messages to be unknowingly sent to addresses stored in an innocent party's address book, it's wise to be cautious even of documents arriving from known sources.) To help simplify the process, Office 2003 provides a special Security command on the Macro submenu that works to detect macros originating from unsafe (or at least unrecognized) sources. If you're concerned about the threat posed to your data by computer viruses, you might want to use this command to further protect your system.

Chapter 9

To use the Security command to seek protection from unsafe macros in Word, Excel, or PowerPoint, follow these steps:

1 Choose Tools, Macro, Security to open the Security dialog box, which contains two tabs—Security Level and Trusted Publishers:

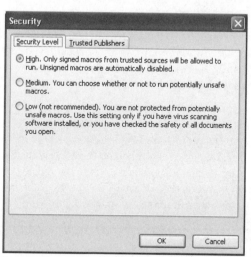

The Security Level tab is pretty self-explanatory. You're given three security options against macro viruses in documents you open in this application: High, Medium, and Low. The High option allows the application to run only a macro that carries a valid digital signature from a trusted source (that is, a source on your list of trusted publishers). If a macro has a valid digital signature from an unknown source, you're given the option to add that source to your list of trusted publishers so that macros with valid signatures from that source will then be automatically enabled.

Note that the presence of a valid digital signature indicates that the macro did in fact come from the signer and that it hasn't been altered. It doesn't guarantee that the macro is actually safe to run. However, unless your trust in a trusted source is misplaced, it's unlikely that the macro from that source will contain intentionally harmful instructions.

The Medium option asks this Office application to display a dialog box each time a document that contains a potentially unsafe macro is opened. (As with the High option, the application will automatically enable a macro that carries a valid digital signature from a trusted source, without showing the dialog box.) The dialog box, shown below, gives you the choice to enable those macros or not.

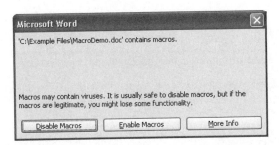

Finally, the Low option directs your application to enable all macros in documents without warning you in any way. This option is acceptable only if you know for certain that all the documents you open will be okay, or if you're developing several Visual Basic macros and don't want to be bothered with warning messages from your own macro routines. However, be aware that some rogue macros have the ability to start themselves automatically, so don't think that you can safely open any document just because you don't run the macros. In a worst-case scenario, these macros could delete files on your hard disk, send out e-mail messages from your account, or subtly corrupt important business documents.

Tip A message at the bottom of the Security dialog box indicates whether or not you've installed virus scanning software. If you haven't, it's a very good idea to install a well-rated and up-to-date virus scanner.

2 Click the Security Level option that you feel comfortable with. We recommend that you choose the High option or possibly the Medium option but *never* the Low option.

3 Click the Trusted Publishers tab to learn more about the trusted sources (if any) that have been accepted on your system. This tab comes with a handy Remove button, so you can remove any source from the list that you no longer trust.

In the Trusted Sources dialog box, you'll also see a check box that's been designed to disable most of the dangerous macros that were written before June 2000. The feature is named Trust Access To Visual Basic Project, and except under very unusual configurations, *this check box should be left empty at all times*. Do not place a check mark in the Trust Access To Visual Basic Project dialog box unless you're instructed to do so by your system administrator or by a trusted software publisher. This feature attempts to break the replication method of most Visual Basic macro viruses by limiting access to the VBProject and VBE objects—internal libraries in Office 2003 that rogue macros have used to corrupt system files in the past. In rare situations (for example, if an add-in you're using depends on VBProject or VBE), you may need to check this box, but don't do so unless you're told to by a "trusted" person. This feature alone prevents many rogue macros from damaging your system, and you want to make sure that the default setting (no check mark) is selected.

4 When you're finished setting macro security, click OK to close the Security dialog box. Office 2003 enforces your security wishes in this application until you update this dialog box.

231

Troubleshooting

You want to enable macro security in all Office applications, not just one

When you choose Tools, Macro, Security, the macro security settings you select take effect only in the Office application you're currently using, but you want them to apply to all your applications.

To make all your applications safe from rogue viruses, configure macro security settings individually in Word, Excel, and PowerPoint. This will enforce security measures consistently across all three applications. If you like, you can set different security options for each application, too—you don't need just one setting. In addition, you'll find a more comprehensive database security system in Access, with several commands and options that you can set through commands on the Tools, Security submenu. The design of Office 2003 gives you the flexibility to set macro security differently for each application, but you need to remember to configure each one individually if you don't want to use the default security level.

Setting Office Interface Options

To set options that affect toolbars, menus, and other interface elements, click the Options tab in the Customize dialog box, as shown here:

Then, proceed as explained in Table 9-2.

Table 9-2. **Modifying the Application Interface Using the Options Tab of the Customize Dialog Box**

To Do This	Perform This Action in the Options Tab
Dock the Standard and Formatting toolbars on separate rows.	Check the Show Standard And Formatting Toolbars On Two Rows option. When this option isn't selected, these two toolbars share a single row, which conserves screen space but usually hides some of the buttons. You can also turn this option on (or off) by clicking the down arrow on the right end of either toolbar and choosing Show Buttons On One Row (Two Rows) from the shortcut menu.
Enable personalized menus, which display only the most basic commands plus the commands you use most frequently.	Clear the Always Show Full Menus option. When this option is cleared, you can still display all commands by double-clicking the menu label or by clicking the double down arrow displayed at the bottom of a partially displayed menu, shown here:

Make all menu commands belonging to a personalized menu appear if, after you open the menu, you hold the pointer over the menu label for about six seconds.	Check the Show Full Menus After A Short Delay option. This option is available only if you've cleared the Always Show Full Menus option.
Remove the information that Office stores on the menu and toolbar commands you use most frequently.	Click the Reset Menu And Toolbar Usage Data button.
Display big toolbar buttons, making it easier to see the buttons but also consuming a large amount of screen space. (This option doesn't affect menu items.)	Check the Large Icons option.

Chapter 9

233

Table 9-2. **Modifying the Application Interface Using the Options Tab of the Customize Dialog Box**

To Do This	Perform This Action in the Options Tab
Display each font name in a drop-down toolbar list (such as the Style or Font list) using the named font, providing a sample of how the font looks.	Check the List Font Names In Their Font option. Turning this option off results in a faster display of font lists. This option doesn't affect the way font names are displayed in the Font dialog box or the way styles and formats are displayed in Word's Styles And Formatting task pane.
Display a description—that is, a ScreenTip—when you hold the mouse pointer over a toolbar button, a view or browse button (adjoining a scrollbar), or an indicator on the status bar. (A ScreenTip for a toolbar button displays the text that's set through the Name item on the Modify Selection menu, described in "Modifying Toolbars and Menus," on page 213.)	Check the Show ScreenTips On Toolbars option.
Include a description of the shortcut key for the command (if it has one) in the text of a toolbar button's ScreenTip.	Check the Show Shortcut Keys In ScreenTips option. This option is available only if you've checked the Show ScreenTips On Toolbars option.
Add an animation effect to the opening of menus.	Select an animation from the Menu Animations drop-down list or select (System Default) to eliminate special Office menu animation effects.

You can change settings in the Options tab of any one of the major Office applications—Word, Excel, PowerPoint, Outlook, Access, FrontPage, or InfoPath—and your settings will affect all these applications. An exception is the Show Standard And Formatting Toolbars On Two Rows option, which you can set individually for each application.

If you position two or more toolbars on the same row (or even if you place only one toolbar on a row but have a small window size or a low screen resolution), there might not be enough room to display all the toolbar buttons. In this case, with a built-in toolbar, Office shows the buttons you use most frequently based on data it collects as you work. To click a button that's been hidden, click the chevron (») on the right end of the toolbar. This displays a palette of all the buttons that have been hidden from toolbars on the current row, as shown on the next page.

If you click one of the buttons on the palette, the corresponding command will be carried out and the button will be displayed on the visible part of the toolbar so you can click it more easily the next time.

Office also selects the items it shows on personalized menus based on the data it collects about your usage. (Office displays personalized menus if the Always Show Full Menus option isn't checked.) If you click the Reset Menu And Toolbar Usage Data button, Office discards the usage data it has collected and begins showing the toolbar commands and menu items that it considers most important, without regard to your personal usage habits. (This method is also how Office selects the buttons to display on a custom toolbar.) Office then starts collecting usage data again and gradually adjusts the set of buttons it displays on built-in toolbars and the set of items it displays on personalized menus based on which buttons you use most frequently.

Saving and Restoring Your Office Settings

You can use the Save My Settings Wizard to save the customizations and other settings you've made in Office applications and then later restore these settings on the same computer or on a different one. For example, if you've been using Office on one computer and now want to start using it on a second computer, you could use the Save My Settings Wizard to transfer your Office settings to the second computer, eliminating the need to re-create them one at a time. The settings that the wizard saves and restores include the following:

- Customizations you've made through the Customize dialog box, as discussed in this chapter
- Options you've selected through the Options command on the Tools menu
- Settings you've made through common menu options, such as the Ruler option on the View menu
- Your arrangements of the application toolbars

To save or restore your Office settings, perform the following steps:

1 Quit all Office applications.

2 From the Start menu in Windows, choose All Programs (or Programs), Microsoft Office, Microsoft Office Tools, Microsoft Office 2003 Save My Settings Wizard. This displays the first page of the Save My Settings Wizard, shown here:

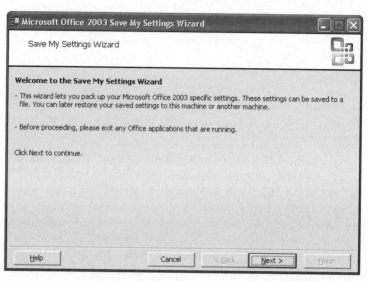

3 Click the Next button, and in the second wizard page, shown below, select the Save The Settings From This Machine option to save your settings or select Restore Previously Saved Settings To This Machine to restore them.

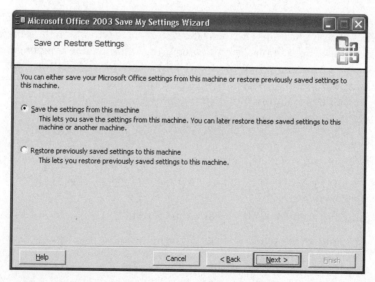

4 Click the Next button, and in the final wizard page, shown below, enter the file path and filename of the file to which or from which you want to save or restore your settings. Or, click the Browse button to locate the file. The file that stores your settings has the .ops filename extension (for Office Profile Settings). You should include this extension in the filename you enter or omit the extension and let Office supply it. Then click the Finish button.

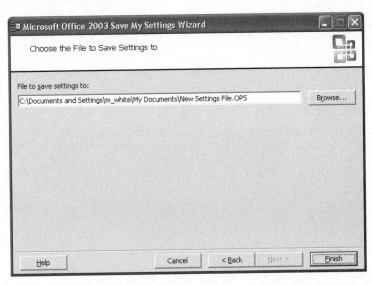

Tip To learn about ways to customize the Save My Settings Wizard, about exactly what's stored in an Office Profile Settings file, and about how to migrate settings from one version of Office to another version, click the Help button in any of the wizard pages.

Part 3

Word

10	Word Fundamentals	241
11	Efficient Editing in Word	259
12	Effective Formatting in Word	307
13	Arranging Text Using Tables, Columns, and Lists	345
14	Advanced Word Formatting Techniques	389
15	Managing Large or Complex Documents	419
16	Using Word in Workgroups	447
17	Proofing Word Documents	479
18	Designing and Printing Professional-Looking Pages	509
19	Using Word to Automate Mailings	549
20	Creating Web Pages and Working with XML in Word	569

Chapter 10

Word Fundamentals

A Rundown on Word 241

Using the Word Workplace 243

Setting Up the Word Interface 248

Creating, Opening, and Saving
Word Documents 255

A Rundown on Word

Microsoft Office Word 2003 is an incredibly powerful, general-purpose, word-processing program that you can use to create basic documents of all kinds—memos, letters, faxes, reports, contracts, resumes, manuals, theses, and books—to mention only some of the possibilities. Word is also surprisingly good at creating complex or specialized documents that are normally the province of more specialized software applications—for example:

- **Web pages**   Although it's not as good at creating Web pages and managing Web sites as Microsoft FrontPage (see Part 8 of this book), Word now has more Web publishing features than ever, and it lets you easily create attractive and dynamic Web pages.

> For more information on creating Web pages with Word, see Chapter 20, "Creating Web Pages and Working with XML in Word."

- **Brochures, newsletters, and other documents with complex page layouts**   You might be able to do a better job at creating short, layout-intensive documents using a program such as Microsoft Publisher. However, Word's improved drawing and layout features make it a highly viable tool for creating these kinds of documents.

> For more information on creating complex layouts using Word, see Chapter 18, "Designing and Printing Professional-Looking Pages."

- **Printer-ready publications**   Dedicated desktop publishing packages (such as Adobe PageMaker, Corel Ventura, or QuarkXPress) do a superb job of creating printer-ready publications with precise page layouts, cross-references, indexes, tables of contents, and so on. Word is ideal for the initial organizing, writing, editing, and proofing of a publication. However, you can also do quite a good job in Word of preparing the final printer-ready publication. (Many books and other manuscripts have gone directly from Word to the printer.) If your page layout needs are a bit demanding for Word's tools, you can always transfer your Word document to a dedicated desktop publishing program to create the final layout.

> For more information on desktop publishing techniques in Word, see Chapter 15, "Managing Large or Complex Documents," and Chapter 18, "Designing and Printing Professional-Looking Pages."

- **Tables of numbers or other data**   Clearly, Microsoft Excel is the tool of choice for working with numbers and Microsoft Access for working with databases (for more information on those applications, see Parts 4 and 7 of this book). However, you can use Word tables to store and display reasonable amounts of numeric or textual data. Word even provides mathematical functions for working with numbers in tables, as well as database tools for working with data fields and records in tables.

- **XML (Extensible Markup Language) documents**   A custom XML editor or a full-featured text editor might be your tool of choice for creating XML documents. However, Word now lets you create, edit, and check the validity of any XML document using convenient interactive tools. It also allows you to apply a custom transform to an XML document so that it can be displayed in Word using any Word formatting, text, or graphics.

For information on working with XML documents in Word, see "Creating, Editing, and Viewing XML Documents," on page 594.

Why use Word for a task that can be performed with a more specialized software program, perhaps one already installed on your computer? The main reason is that you probably already know how to use Word, and the extra features of a more specialized program might not be worth the time required to learn a new software package, especially if you create only an occasional Web page, brochure, or other specialized document. You might also have existing Word documents that you can quickly convert to Web pages or other specialized formats. You can thus use Word to leverage not only your current skills but also your existing collection of documents.

For a description of the new features included in Word 2003, see "New Word Features," on page 13.

The first eight chapters in this part of the book are basically about laying down the content of a Word document—organizing, editing, formatting, arranging, footnoting, indexing, annotating, and proofing the document text. These chapters present techniques for creating simple documents yourself, as well as methods for generating complex publications in a workgroup.

The last three chapters in this part deal with producing the final end product. Chapter 18 covers the methods for laying out and printing a traditional hard copy document. Chapter 19, "Using Word to Automate Mailings," explains the techniques for producing multiple, customized copies of a document—form letters, labels, envelopes, faxes, or e-mail messages. And Chapter 20 presents the methods for creating an increasingly important end product: the online document, which is intended to be read on a computer. Online documents not only save trees, but also—unlike printed documents—they can include background colors and patterns, interactive forms, hyperlinks, and other dynamic elements. An online document can be a Word file stored on a network disk or on a SharePoint team Web site; or, it can be a Hypertext Markup Language (HTML) page on the Web or on a company intranet.

Word Fundamentals

 Chapter 20 also explains how to use Word to create XML documents. You can use an XML
document to store and deliver the data that's shown in an HTML Web page, or you can display it directly in Word or in a browser like other types of online documents.

This chapter summarizes the unique features and tools you'll find in the Word workplace and
shows you how to set up the Word interface—the windows, task panes, document view,
zoom factor, rulers, and other elements—to suit your working style before you begin creating
and editing documents.

Using the Word Workplace

If you run Word without opening an existing document—for example, you choose the All
Programs (or Programs), Microsoft Office, Microsoft Office Word 2003 command from the
Start menu in Windows—Word will automatically create a new, blank document. Figure 10-
1 shows the Word window as it might appear when you first start Word. Because Word is so
highly customizable, your window might look quite different. In "Setting Up the Word Interface," on page 248, you'll learn the basic techniques for adding and removing interface elements and for modifying the interface in other ways.

For information on the ways to start Word and other Microsoft Office 2003 applications, see "Running
the Office Applications," on page 39.

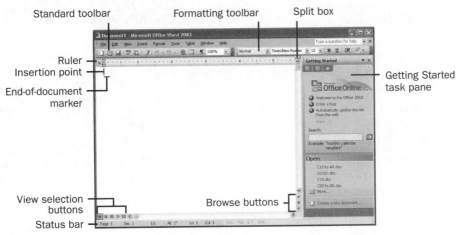

Figure 10-1. When you start Word, this window appears.

Table 10-1 explains what you can do using Word's main task panes. These are the task panes
you can display by clicking the down arrow near the upper right corner of the pane and
choosing the name of a pane from the drop-down menu, shown on next page.

Getting Started	▼	×
✓ Getting Started		
Help		
Search Results		
Clip Art		
Research		
Clipboard		
New Document		
Shared Workspace		
Document Updates		
Protect Document		
Styles and Formatting		
Reveal Formatting		
Mail Merge		
XML Structure		

☐ Create a new document…

> For general information on working with application task panes, such as the Getting Started task pane shown in Figure 10-1, see "Using the Task Panes in Office Applications," on page 42.

Table 10-1. Tasks You Can Perform in Word's Main Task Panes

To Do This	Use This Word Task Pane
Open existing documents, create new documents, or access Word information and resources (such as templates) on the Office Online Web site.	Getting Started (see "Going to the Getting Started Task Pane," on page 44)
Search for help information, browse help topics, or connect to help resources on the Office Online Web site.	Help (see Chapter 3, "Getting Expert Help on Office 2003")
Create a new Word document, Web page, XML document, or e-mail message. You can base the new document on an existing document or on a template located on your computer, on the Office Online Web site, or on another Web site.	New Document (see "Creating a Document Using the New Document Task Pane," on page 53)
View the results of a search you initiated in the Getting Started, Help, or New Document task pane. Also, search for Word information or resources (such as templates) on the Office Online Web site.	Search Results (this task pane is opened automatically when you perform a search in one of the other task panes mentioned)
Insert clip art, photographs, movies, or sounds into a Word document.	Clip Art (see "Inserting Pictures with the Clip Organizer," on page 107)

Chapter 10

Table 10-1. Tasks You Can Perform in Word's Main Task Panes

To Do This	Use This Word Task Pane
Look up information from local information sources, as well as from information sources on the Internet.	Research (see "Using the Research Task Pane," on page 44)
Work with the Office Clipboard.	Clipboard (see "Using the Office Clipboard," on page 158)
Create or work with a document workspace. (A document workspace is a SharePoint Web site designed for a workgroup to collaborate on creating a document.)	Shared Workspace (see "Sharing Documents Using a Document Workspace," on page 190)
Synchronize the current document with a linked copy of that document in a document workspace.	Document Updates (see "Sharing Documents Using a Document Workspace," on page 190)
Protect a document that you share with others in your workgroup.	Protect Document (see "Protecting Shared Documents," on page 472)
Apply or customize Word styles or reuse document formats.	Styles And Formatting (see "Applying Styles and Reusing Formats," on page 327)
View, modify, or clear any formatting feature.	Reveal Formatting (see "Using the Reveal Formatting Task Pane to View or Modify Formatting Features," on page 338)
Create form letters or multiple labels, envelopes, or e-mail messages.	Mail Merge (see Chapter 19)
Create or edit an XML document.	XML Structure (see "Creating, Editing, and Viewing XML Documents" on page 594)

Chapter 10

The Word status bar (shown in Figure 10-2) provides information about the program's operation. To display or hide the status bar, choose Tools, Options. In the Options dialog box, click the View tab and check or clear the Status Bar option in the Show group. Each piece of information in the status bar is displayed in a separate indicator, as shown in Figure 10-2.

Note The status bar will also include a Language indicator, displaying the current default language, if you've enabled one or more languages in addition to the default Office language using the Microsoft Office Language Settings program. You run this program in Windows by choosing Start, All Programs (or Programs), Microsoft Office, Microsoft Office Tools, Microsoft Office 2003 Language Settings. The Language indicator will appear between the OVR indicator and the indicator used for the spelling and grammar checker and background printing.

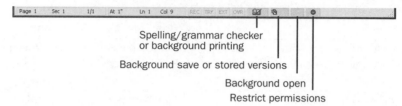

| Page 1 | Sec 1 | 1/1 | At 1" | Ln 1 | Col 9 | REC | TRK | EXT | OVR | | | | |

Spelling/grammar checker
or background printing

Background save or stored versions

Background open

Restrict permissions

Figure 10-2. The Word status bar provides information about the program's operation.

You can double-click indicators in the status bar to quickly issue certain Word commands, as shown in Table 10-2.

Table 10-2. Performing Actions by Double-Clicking Status Bar Indicators

To Do This	Double-Click This Status Bar Indicator
Issue the Go To command (see "Moving the Insertion Point with the Go To Command," on page 302)	Any of the first six indicators (which give the position of the insertion point)
Start recording a macro—by opening the Record Macro dialog box—or stop recording a macro (see "Recording and Running Macros," on page 224)	REC
Start tracking document changes and display the Reviewing toolbar or stop tracking document changes (see "Tracking and Reviewing Document Changes," on page 447)	TRK
Switch the Extend selecting mode on or off (see "Selecting by Using the Keyboard," on page 283)	EXT
Turn Overtype mode on or off (see "Adding Text," on page 259)	OVR
Mark the language of the selected text (see "Marking the Language," on page 506)	Language (if present)

Table 10-2. **Performing Actions by Double-Clicking Status Bar Indicators**

To Do This	Double-Click This Status Bar Indicator
Display suggested spellings for the next spelling or grammar error in the document that has been marked by the as-you-type spelling or grammar checker (see "Checking Your Spelling as You Type," on page 479 and "Checking Your Grammar as You Type," on page 490)	Spelling And Grammar Status (You can perform this action only when you see the Spelling And Grammar Status icon, which is displayed after the as-you-type spelling or grammar checker has examined text in the document.)
Open the Versions dialog box (see "Storing Different Document Versions," on page 257)	Versions (You can perform this action only when you see the Versions icon, which is displayed only if you've stored one or more document versions in the current file.)

If you have enabled toolbar ScreenTips, placing the mouse pointer over an indicator on the status bar displays a ScreenTip describing the effect of double-clicking that indicator, as shown in this example:

Toolbar ScreenTips are also displayed when you place the pointer over a toolbar button or other type of button on the Word interface (such as a browse button or view selection button). To enable toolbar ScreenTips, choose Tools, Customize, click the Options tab in the Customize dialog box, and check the Show ScreenTips On Toolbars option. Changing this option affects other Office applications as well. If you want the toolbar ScreenTips to display the key combination for executing each command, also check Show Shortcut Keys In Screen-Tips.

> **Tip**   As explained in Chapter 16, "Using Word in Workgroups," Word also displays Screen-Tips when you hold the mouse pointer over a marked change or comment in a document. To turn these ScreenTips on or off, choose Tools, Options, click the View tab, and check or clear the ScreenTips option.

Table 10-3 shows what you can do with some of the other visible interface elements that are unique to Word (see Figure 10-1 for the locations of these elements).

Table 10-3. Using Word Interface Elements

To Do This	Use This Interface Element
Change the document margins and set the indents and tab stops for individual paragraphs, using the mouse	**Rulers.** To display or hide the rulers, choose View, Ruler. You can display the horizontal or vertical ruler temporarily by moving the pointer over the colored band at the top or left of the document area of the window. The vertical ruler appears only in Print Layout view. (For information on the horizontal ruler, see "Formatting Paragraphs with the Horizontal Ruler," on page 326. For information on the vertical ruler, see Chapter 18.)
Divide the document window into two panes	**Split box.** (See the next section, "Setting Up the Word Interface.")
Navigate quickly through the document by going to the next or previous browse object (page, section, target of Find command, and so on)	**Browse buttons.** (See "Navigating with the Browse Buttons," on page 304.)
Select a document view	**View selection buttons.** (See the next section, "Setting Up the Word Interface.")
Identify the end of the document in Normal or Outline view	**End-of-document marker**.
Open, save, or print a document; copy text or formats; obtain help; or perform other basic tasks	**Standard toolbar.** To display a particular toolbar, choose View, Toolbars or right-click any toolbar or the menu bar and then choose the name of the toolbar from the submenu or shortcut menu.
Modify the format of characters or paragraphs	**Formatting toolbar.** The Formatting toolbar is typical of a special-purpose Word toolbar. (See Chapter 12, "Effective Formatting in Word.")

> **For general information on displaying and customizing toolbars, see Chapter 9, "Customizing the Office 2003 Application Interface."**

Setting Up the Word Interface

Chapter 9 explained how to make serious modifications to the toolbar, menu, and keyboard interface of Word or other Office applications. This section focuses on quick ways to set up the Word interface and arrange the Word tools to suit your working style, using menu commands and dialog box options. This discussion focuses on Word-specific techniques (although some of them are available in Excel or other applications).

Changing the View

You can modify the basic way that Word displays a document—as well as the way you work with it—by changing the document *view*. Table 10-4 lists the different document views, briefly describes each, and identifies the chapters in which you can find fuller discussions on each one.

Table 10-4. Word Document Views

View	Description	For More Information
Normal	Shows the document in a general-purpose format for efficient editing and formatting. Doesn't display margins, headers, or footers.	See Chapter 11, "Efficient Editing in Word."
Web Layout	Displays the document in a format that's easy to read on the screen. Ideal for previewing Web pages or for reading regular Word documents online. The text is shown without page breaks and with only minimal margins. Lines of text are wrapped to fit within the window, and any background color or image assigned to the document is visible.	See Chapter 20.
Print Layout	Displays text and graphics exactly as they'll appear on the printed page, showing all margins, headers, and footers. All editing and formatting commands are available, but Word runs somewhat more slowly than in Normal view and scrolling is not as smooth.	See Chapter 18.
Outline	Shows the organization of the document. Lets you view various levels of detail and rapidly rearrange document text.	See Chapter 15.
Reading Layout	Displays the document in a format that's optimized for online reading. Divides the document into small pages that fit completely within the screen, simulating a book. Features a large, smoothed font and a simpler application interface.	See "Using Reading Layout View," on page 571.
Print Preview	Displays an image of one or more entire printed pages and lets you adjust the page setup.	See Chapter 18.

To switch the view of a document to any view except Print Preview, choose the appropriate option from the View menu, as shown here:

You can also switch to Normal, Web Layout, Print Layout, Outline, or Reading Layout view by clicking a button at the left end of the horizontal scroll bar, as seen here:

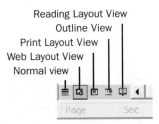

If the horizontal scroll bar isn't visible, choose Tools, Options and in the Options dialog box, click the View tab (shown in Figure 10-3) and check the Horizontal Scroll Bar option.

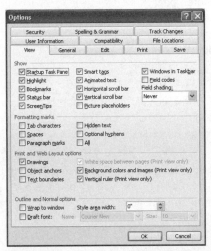

Figure 10-3. The View tab of the Options dialog box lets you set many options that affect the Word interface. Some options affect only certain views.

Print
Preview

An alternative way to switch on Reading Layout view is to click the Read button on the Standard toolbar. To return to your previous view, click the Close button on the Reading Layout toolbar that's displayed in Reading Layout view. To switch to Print Preview view, choose File, Print Preview, or click the Print Preview button on the Standard toolbar.

Changing the view affects only the document in the active document window; you can set the view of each open document independently. Also, if you have split a document window into two panes (as described in the next section), you can assign a different view—Normal, Web Layout, Print Layout, or Outline—to each pane. (Switching to the Reading Layout or Print Preview view, however, removes the division and displays the document in a single pane.)

Modifying the Way Documents Are Displayed

In addition to changing the basic view, you can also set a variety of options that affect the way a document is displayed in the current view.

To divide the document window into two panes, click the split box and drag the pane divider to the desired position, as shown here:

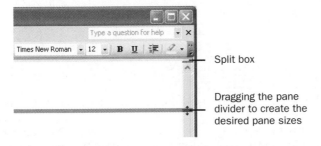

Split box

Dragging the pane
divider to create the
desired pane sizes

You can then scroll each pane independently, so that you can view and work with two portions of the document at the same time.

Troubleshooting

The split box isn't visible

You want to divide the document window into two panes but the split box isn't present.

The following are two possible reasons for the absence of the split box:

- The Document Map is displayed. You can hide (or show) the document map by choosing View, Document Map.

For an explanation of the Document Map, see "Navigating Through an Outline," on page 429.

- The vertical scroll bar isn't visible. The split box is an integral part of this scroll bar. Display the vertical scroll by choosing Tools, Options and in the Options dialog box clicking the View tab and checking the Vertical Scroll Bar option.

Chapter 10

To scale the characters and graphics on the screen choose View, Zoom and enter a scaling factor into the Zoom dialog box (shown in Figure 10-4). You can specify the scaling factor by typing or selecting a percentage of the normal size of the text and graphics or by selecting the Page Width, Text Width, or Whole Page zooming option. In Print Layout view, you can select the Many Pages option to display several full pages on the screen at once (as you can in Print Preview view). Click the button immediately below the Many Pages option to select the number of pages you want to display (from 1 to 24) and their arrangement. Displaying multiple pages might make it impossible to read the text, but it can be useful for examining the overall layout of a group of adjoining pages.

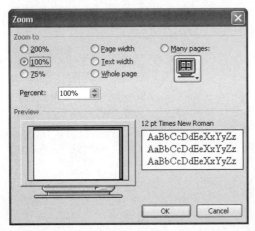

Figure 10-4. This figure shows the Zoom dialog box as it's displayed in Print Layout view.

An alternative way to change the zooming factor is by using the Zoom drop-down list on the Standard toolbar (or on the Print Preview toolbar if you're in Print Preview view). Here's how the Zoom drop-down list appears in Print Layout view:

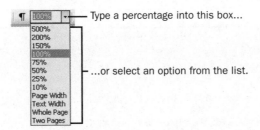

Zooming is available in all views. However, the particular zooming options that are available vary by view (the Print Layout and Print Preview views support them all). Zooming affects only the view in which you set it, so you need to set it separately for each view you work with. Rest assured that zooming does *not* change the actual size of the text or graphics that are printed and stored in the document; rather, it affects only the level of magnification at which you view the document in the window.

Chapter 10

To expand the Word workspace to fill the entire screen—hiding all menus, toolbars, other tools, and even the Windows taskbar—choose View, Full Screen. You can use this command in any view. To restore the normal Word window, press the Esc key or click the Close Full Screen button that Word displays on the Full Screen toolbar, as shown here:

> **Tip** Access menus and toolbars in full-screen mode
>
> In full-screen mode, you can temporarily display the menu bar by simply moving the mouse pointer to the top of the window. After you choose a menu command, the menu bar will disappear again.
>
> You can also display any Word toolbar while you're in full-screen mode by right- clicking the Full Screen toolbar (or the menu bar while it's displayed) and choosing the name of the toolbar from the shortcut menu. The toolbar will remain displayed whenever you use full-screen mode.
>
> Alternatively, to avoid cluttering up the full-screen window with additional toolbars, you can add buttons for your favorite commands directly to the Full Screen toolbar, using the methods explained in "Modifying Toolbars and Menus," on page 213.

To display all characters in the document using the same font and size, regardless of the applied formatting, you can turn on the *draft font* option. This option affects only the way the document is displayed on the screen in Normal or Outline view. It doesn't change the formatting information stored in the document, nor does it affect the way the document is printed. As soon as you turn the option off, the document goes back to its original appearance. In the days of slow computer displays, the draft font option was useful for speeding up scrolling. But even with fast displays, it has two possible uses:

- You might find it easier to type in document text if you select an easy-to-read, mono-space draft font (such as Courier New) that clearly shows the number of spaces between individual characters. You can turn off the draft font before formatting the document.

- If you have trouble reading characters on the screen, you can select a large, easy-to-read draft font to facilitate typing in text. (Although you can use zooming to increase the character size, you can't use it to switch to an easier-to-read font.)

To switch on the draft font option, choose Tools, Options and in the Options dialog box, click the View tab, check the Draft Font option, and select a character font and size for the draft font in the Name and Size drop-down lists, as shown here:

Troubleshooting

Document is too wide to view

The lines in your Word document are too wide to view within the Word window, so you have to scroll horizontally to read each line.

This problem might crop up if you've formatted your document with wide lines or if you're using a low graphics resolution (typical with a notebook computer or a computer with a small monitor). The following are several ways to alleviate or remove the problem:

● First, be sure to maximize the Word program window and hide any task pane that's currently displayed.

● You can gain a little more window width by choosing View, Full Screen to work in full-screen mode.

● If you're using Normal or Outline view, you can have Word wrap all lines so that they fit within the current window width. To do this, choose Tools, Options, click the View tab, and check the Wrap To Window option in the Outline And Normal Options area near the bottom of the dialog box.

● You can switch to the Web Layout or Reading Layout view. Both of these views always wrap lines so they fit within the window.

● In any view, you can scale the size of the text on the screen so that the lines just fit within the width of the window. You do this by selecting the appropriate option in the Zoom drop-down list on the Standard toolbar or in the Zoom dialog box (opened by choosing View, Zoom). In Normal or Outline view, the appropriate option is Page Width. In Print Layout view, the appropriate option is Text Width. The Web Layout and Reading Layout views don't have an option for fitting the lines to the screen, but zooming isn't necessary because these views always wrap lines to fit.

Word Fundamentals

Creating, Opening, and Saving Word Documents

Chapter 4, "Working with Office 2003 Applications, Documents, and Program Windows," discussed the different ways to create, open, and save documents in Word and other Office applications. The remainder of this chapter explains some of the techniques and options that are specific to Word.

When you first display the Open or Save As dialog box to open or save a Word document, it normally displays the contents of your My Documents folder. However, you can change the folder that's initially displayed in these dialog boxes by choosing Tools, Options, clicking the File Locations tab, selecting the Documents item in the list, and clicking the Modify button (see Figure 10-5).

Figure 10-5. The File Locations tab of the Options dialog box allows you to change the default folder displayed in the Open and Save As dialog boxes.

You can change the way Word saves documents by selecting options in the Save tab of the Options dialog box (shown in Figure 10-6). For example, to change the default format that Word displays in the Save As Type drop-down list in the Save As dialog box, select a format in the Save Word Files As drop-down list in the Save tab.

Microsoft Office System Inside Out—2003 Edition

Figure 10-6.   The Save tab of the Options dialog box allows you to change the way Word saves documents.

Troubleshooting

Watch out for fast saves

The Allow Fast Saves option causes Word to use a faster—although less safe—method for saving your documents to disk. This option may have been useful in the days of slow disk drives, but now it's best to disable it. If a fast save operation is interrupted (by a power outage, for example), your document can become severely corrupted. With a reasonably fast computer, fast saves aren't needed—especially if you enable background saves (by checking the Allow Background Saves option). You can access the Allow Fast Saves and Allow Background Saves options in the Save tab of the Options dialog box.

Converting Groups of Files

Chapter 4 explained how to convert files in various formats to Office 2003 documents and how to convert Office 2003 documents to other formats.

In Word, you can use the Conversion Wizard to efficiently convert an entire group of files to Word 2003 format or to convert a group of Word 2003 files to another format. The Conversion Wizard eliminates the need to separately open and convert each file. The files that you convert must all be contained in the same folder.

To convert files, choose File, New, click the On My Computer command in the Templates area of the New Document task pane, click the Other Documents tab in the Templates dialog box, and double-click the Batch Conversion Wizard item. Then, complete the pages displayed by the Conversion Wizard (shown in Figure 10-7). You'll need to specify the format you want to covert to or from, the source and destination folders, and the specific files to be converted.

Figure 10-7. This is the opening dialog box displayed by Word's Conversion Wizard.

Storing Different Document Versions

You can use Word's Versions command to store several separate versions of a document, all within a single document file. Say, for example, that you have written Chapter 1 for your latest novel and you saved the current version in a file named *Chapter1*. You now want to revise the chapter, but you also want to keep the original version intact so that you can refer back to it if necessary. Without the Versions command, you would have to save the current version in a separate file. Using the Versions command, however, you can save a copy of the current document version right within the Chapter1.doc file so that you can easily refer back to it later and avoid having to keep track of separate files.

To do this, choose File, Versions (or double-click the Versions indicator in the status bar if it's present) and in the Versions dialog box, click the Save Now button. Word will prompt you to add a descriptive comment for the version. You can then proceed to revise your chapter and save your work in the usual way. Now, both versions of the document will be stored within the Chapter1.doc file. However, when you open the document you won't see the original version unless you again choose File, Versions and use the Versions dialog box to open the original version in a separate window, as shown in Figure 10-8. You can use this technique to store additional document versions within the same document file.

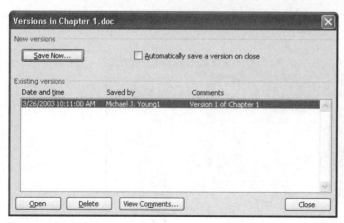

Figure 10-8. You can use the Versions dialog box to work with separate document versions stored in a single document file.

Chapter 11

Efficient Editing in Word

Adding Text 259
Positioning the Insertion Point 280
Editing Document Text 281

Finding and Replacing Text and
Formatting 293
Moving Quickly Through a Document . . 300

Adding Text

This chapter focuses on the *content* of a Microsoft Office Word 2003 document—that is, the characters, words, sentences, and paragraphs that compose a document. You'll learn about the many ways to add, edit, find, and navigate through document text. The next chapter focuses on the *format* of a Word document—that is, the appearance of the characters and paragraphs. These two topics are treated separately to make your learning task easier, not to imply that you must finish editing the entire document before you begin formatting it. Typically, you'll use formatting techniques as you are entering and editing the text.

To enter text, simply move the insertion point to the desired location in the document and type the text. Word provides two editing modes: *Insert* and *Overtype*. In Insert mode (the most common mode), any existing characters beyond the insertion point are moved ahead in the document as you type. In Overtype mode, the new characters you type replace any existing characters. When Overtype mode is active, the OVR indicator on the status bar is darkened. To switch between the two modes, double-click the OVR indicator. You can also use the Insert key to do this, provided that the Use The INS Key For Paste option isn't checked (to access this option, choose Tools, Options, and then click the Edit tab).

> **Note** Overtype mode isn't available while you are tracking changes in a document. For information on tracking changes, see "Tracking and Reviewing Document Changes," on page 447.

> For a description of the techniques for moving the insertion point, see "Positioning the Insertion Point," on page 280.

> **Tip** Create a new line within a paragraph
> To create a new line within a paragraph, press Shift+Enter. Why not just press Enter and create a new paragraph? Some paragraph formatting affects only the first or last line of the paragraph, such as an initial indent or additional space above or below the paragraph. By pressing Shift+Enter, you can create a new line without introducing this formatting. The section "Combining Text with Graphic Objects and Text Boxes," on page 514, explains how to add a *text wrapping* line break, which causes the following line to be moved below an adjoining text box or graphic object.

Show/Hide

Pressing Enter creates a new paragraph. Word marks the end of each paragraph by inserting a *paragraph mark*. A paragraph mark (¶) is one of the nonprinting characters that can be contained in a Word document. Nonprinting characters never appear on the final printed copy of the document. Normally, they are also invisible on the screen. You can, however, make them visible on the screen by clicking the Show/Hide ¶ button on the Standard toolbar or by checking the Show All Formatting Marks option in the Reveal Formatting task pane. (These commands also reveal hidden text.) The following is an example of some document text on the screen after nonprinting characters have been made visible:

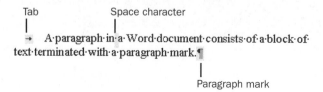

> **Caution** Avoid deleting a paragraph mark unintentionally. (It can be deleted whether or not it's visible.) Deleting this mark will merge the paragraphs on either side of the mark, and any paragraph formatting assigned to the second paragraph will be lost. (Paragraph formatting is discussed in Chapter 12, "Effective Formatting in Word.")

You can also display or hide specific nonprinting characters by choosing Tools, Options, clicking the View tab, and selecting the appropriate options in the Formatting Marks area.

Inserting Symbols and Foreign Characters

You can use the Symbol dialog box to insert into your text a variety of symbols and foreign characters that you won't find on your keyboard. To insert a symbol or foreign character at the current position of the insertion point, perform the following steps:

1 Choose Insert, Symbol to open the Symbol dialog box.

2 Click the Symbols tab (shown in Figure 11-1) if it isn't already displayed.

Chapter 11

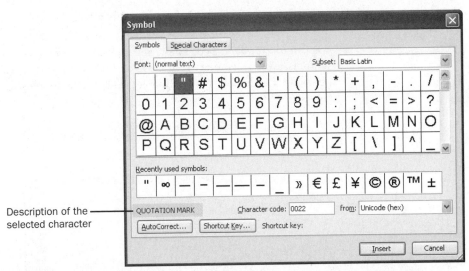

Description of the selected character

Figure 11-1. The Symbols tab of the Symbol dialog box lets you find and insert any of the characters belonging to your installed fonts.

3 In the character list, double-click the character you want to insert. Or, select the character by clicking it and then click the Insert button. The symbol will appear in your document at the position of the insertion point, just as if you had typed it. The following tips will help you find the character you want:

- If you don't find the character you want in the list, or if you'd prefer to enter a character using a different font, select a different font name in the Font drop-down list. This will display all the characters belonging to that font. The (normal text) item at the beginning of the list of fonts displays the set of characters belonging to the font at the current position of the insertion point in your document. You might see some fonts for languages that don't use the Roman alphabet, for instance, the Gautami, Latha, and Mangal fonts. The following are examples of special *symbol fonts* that contain only symbols and not the ordinary keyboard characters (such as a, A, 1, !, and so on): Marlett, MS Outlook, MS Reference Specialty, MT Extra, Symbol, Webdings, Wingdings, Wingdings 2, and Wingdings 3.

- You can scroll through the character list to view additional characters, or—for a font that isn't a symbol font—you can go immediately to a particular character group by choosing an item (such as Basic Greek, General Punctuation, or Mathematical Operators) in the Subset drop-down list box.

- If you've selected a font that isn't a symbol font and want to see the full set of characters belonging to that font, make sure that the Unicode (Hex) item is selected in the From drop-down list in the lower right corner of the Symbols tab. Selecting the ASCII (Decimal) or the ASCII (Hex) item will display only the first part of the character set (namely, the font's ASCII character set, which consists of fewer than 255 visible characters).

Chapter 11

- You can reuse a character that you recently inserted by double-clicking an item in the Recently Used Symbols area.

- You can insert one of a collection of commonly used punctuation characters, symbols, and special space characters by clicking the Special Characters tab of the Symbol dialog box (shown in Figure 11-2) and double-clicking an item in the list.

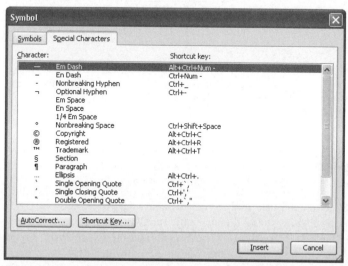

Figure 11-2. The Special Characters tab of the Symbol dialog box allows you to insert commonly used special characters in a document.

4 After you've inserted the symbols you need, click the Close button to close the Symbol dialog box.

Note You can enlarge the Symbol dialog box by dragging an edge or corner.

You can also use the keyboard to insert any of the characters displayed in the Symbol dialog box's Symbols tab. For a character belonging to a symbol font, you'll have to define your own shortcut key as explained in the tip "Set Up Shortcut Keys for Symbols You Frequently Use," on page 264. Word provides built-in shortcut keys for all characters belonging to the regular character fonts. When you select a character from one of these fonts that can't be directly typed on the keyboard, the shortcut key for inserting the character is displayed following the Shortcut Key label near the bottom of the dialog box on the next page.

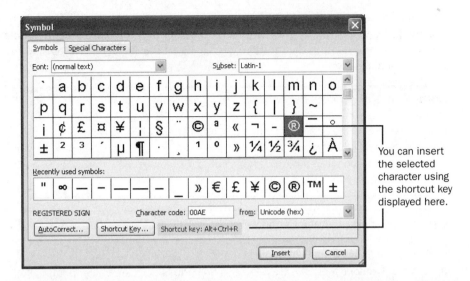

You can insert the selected character using the shortcut key displayed here.

Table 11-1 gives examples of the different kinds of shortcut keys displayed following the Shortcut Key label and how you'd type each one. Make sure that Num Lock is on before you try to use the Keypad numbers.

Table 11-1. Examples of Shortcut Key Descriptions and How You Type Them

Shortcut Key Description Displayed After the Shortcut Key Label	Character Inserted	How to Type the Shortcut Key
Alt+Ctrl+C	©	Press Alt, Ctrl, and C simultaneously.
Alt+Ctrl+!	¡	Press Alt, Ctrl, Shift, and 1 simultaneously (you need to press Shift to type ! rather than 1).
Alt+0163	£	Hold down Alt and type **0163** on the numeric keypad with Num Lock on. The character will be inserted when you release the Alt key.
Ctrl+/, C	¢	Press Ctrl and / simultaneously. Release both keys. Then, press C.
03A3, Alt+X	?	Type **03A3** or **03a3**. Then, press Alt and X simultaneously. (The number you type is the Unicode value for the character in hexadecimal. This type of shortcut key lets you insert a character that isn't included in the standard ASCII set.)

Chapter 11

Of course, once the Symbol dialog box is open you could just insert the character by double-clicking it. However, for a symbol or foreign character that you use frequently, you can learn the keystroke and use it in the future to quickly insert the character without having to open the Symbol dialog box.

Note The Symbol dialog box's Symbols tab displays the character code for the selected character in the Character Code text box. The code is displayed in decimal if ASCII (Decimal) is selected in the adjoining From drop-down list. It's displayed in hexadecimal if either Unicode (Hex) or ASCII (Hex) is selected in the From list. To select a particular character, you can type its code into the Character Code box (use decimal or hexadecimal according to the current selection in the From list).

Tip   Set up shortcut keys for symbols you frequently use

You can define your own shortcut key for a character in a symbol font (such as Symbol or Wingdings) or an alternative shortcut key for a character in a regular character font. To do this, in the Symbol dialog box, click the Symbols tab, select the character in the list, and click the Shortcut Key button. This will display the Customize Keyboard dialog box, which is explained in "Defining Shortcut Keys (Word Only)," on page 222.

You can also define a character or group of characters—such as "(ae)"—that Word will automatically replace with a specified symbol—such as æ. To do this, in the Symbols tab, select the symbol you want to use as the replacement and click the AutoCorrect button. The AutoCorrect feature is explained in "Automatically Fixing Your Text with AutoCorrect," on page 271.

For information on entering symbols using an on-screen symbol keyboard, together with a pen and electronic tablet or a mouse, see "Using the On-Screen Keyboards," on page 105.

Inserting the Date and Time

To insert the current date, the current time, or both, into your document, perform the following steps:

1   Choose Insert, Date And Time to open the Date And Time dialog box (shown in Figure 11-3).

2   Select the desired date or time format in the Available Formats list.

3   To have the date or time automatically updated whenever you print the document, check Update Automatically. If this option isn't checked, the date or time remains the same as it was when you inserted it.

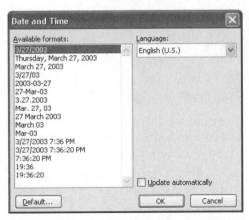

Figure 11-3. You can insert the current date or time using the Date And Time dialog box.

4   To have your current settings in the Date And Time dialog box displayed by default the next time you open the dialog box, click the Default button.

5   Click the OK button.

Replaying Your Editing Actions with the Repeat Command

If you've just typed a block of text, you can have Word insert that same text at any location in a document. Perform the following steps:

1   Type the original text.

2   Move the insertion point to the location where you want to repeat the text (in the same Word document or in a different Word document).

3   Choose Edit, Repeat Typing, or press Ctrl+Y or F4. Word will automatically insert the text you originally typed. You can do this repeatedly to insert multiple copies of this same text.

Undo

If you don't like the result, you can reverse it by immediately choosing Edit, Undo Typing, pressing Ctrl+Z, or clicking the Undo button on the Standard toolbar. (The Undo command is described later in the chapter.)

> **Note**   Repeat Typing is only one example of how you can use the Repeat command. The Repeat command repeats any editing or formatting action, not simply text that you've typed. As explained later in the chapter, this command will also redo an action that you've just reversed by using the Undo command.

Chapter 11

Reusing Text with the AutoText Feature

A second way to automate the insertion of text is to use the AutoText feature, which allows you to save commonly used blocks of text or graphics as *AutoText entries* and lets you quickly insert one of these blocks wherever you need it.

To create an AutoText entry, perform the following steps:

1 Type into a document the block of text that you want to save. (Typing the text into a paragraph that has the same style as the paragraphs in which you'll later use the text can make it easier to insert the entry from the AutoText submenu, as you'll see later.)

2 Select the block of text. One way to select text is to hold down the Shift key while pressing the appropriate arrow key. Selection methods are discussed later in the chapter.

3 Choose Insert, AutoText, New. Alternatively, you can press Alt+F3. Word will display the Create AutoText dialog box.

4 Type a name for your AutoText entry into the text box and click the OK button. Word proposes a name based on the selected text, but you'll probably want to invent a name of your own. If you type the name of an existing entry, Word will ask whether you want to redefine that entry; click Yes to replace the original text for the entry or No to choose a new name.

To make it faster to insert your entry, you might want to use one of these two approaches:

■ Enter a short name so you can type it in quickly when you want to insert the text (for example, **w** for an entry containing the text "World Wide Web").

or

■ Enter a fully descriptive name, but make sure that the first four letters are different from the first four letters of any of your other AutoText entries. (To see a list of all your AutoText entries, including those defined by Word, choose Insert, AutoText, AutoText and look in the AutoText tab.) Then, the AutoComplete feature (explained later) will let you quickly insert the entry after typing just the first four letters of the name. For example, if you assigned the name "hypertext" to an entry containing the text "Hypertext Markup Language," you could insert the entry by typing **hype**, provided that no other AutoText entry begins with those letters.

Figure 11-4 shows an example.

Efficient Editing in Word

Figure 11-4. In this example a standard letter closing is stored as an AutoText entry named "closing."

After you create an AutoText entry, it's stored permanently. You can insert an AutoText entry into a document by performing the following steps:

1 Place the insertion point at the position in your document where you want to insert the text.

2 Type the name of the AutoText entry as a separate word. This means that you must type the name at the beginning of a line or following a space, tab, or punctuation symbol. The case of the letters you type doesn't matter. You need type only a sufficient number of characters to distinguish the name from the names of all other AutoText entries.

3 Press F3 or Ctrl+Alt+V. Word will immediately replace the entry name with the entry text. For example, if you had defined the AutoText entry shown in Figure 11-4, at the end of a letter you could simply press Enter, type **closing** (or perhaps just **cl** if none of the names of your other entries begins with those letters), and then press F3 or Ctrl+Alt+V, as seen here:

I am looking forward to hearing from you soon.

closing

Press F3 or Ctrl+Alt+V here.

Word would replace the word "closing" with your standard letter closing, as shown here:

I am looking forward to hearing from you soon.

Yours very truly,

Michael J. Young

Chapter 11

> **Tip** Use AutoComplete to insert AutoText entries and dates more quickly
>
> If the Show AutoComplete Suggestions option is checked, as you begin typing an AutoText entry name into a document, Word will display the entry text (or at least part of the text) in a box near the insertion point. The box will appear as soon as you've typed at least four characters and enough of the name to identify the entry. You can then insert the entry text by simply pressing Enter (or the usual F3 or Ctrl+Alt+V shortcut key) without typing the complete entry name. If Show AutoComplete Suggestions is on, you can also have Word complete partially typed dates using the same method. To turn this option on or off, choose Insert, AutoText, AutoText. In the AutoText tab, check or clear the Show AutoComplete Suggestions check box. (The AutoText tab is located within the AutoCorrect dialog box, discussed in the following section.)

As an alternative to steps 2 and 3, you can insert an AutoText entry by choosing it from the Insert menu's AutoText submenu, seen here:

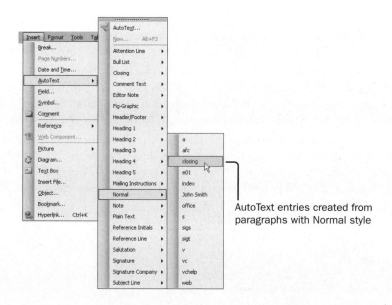

AutoText entries created from paragraphs with Normal style

The AutoText submenu lists all AutoText entries you've defined. Each entry is placed on a submenu labeled according to the style of the paragraph from which the entry was originally obtained; for example, if you created an entry by selecting text in a paragraph with the Normal style, the entry is placed on a submenu labeled Normal. (This arrangement helps you locate entries that are relevant to the type of paragraph you're currently working on.)

The AutoText submenu also displays a large collection of entries defined by Word, grouped on submenus named according to their functions (for example, Attention Line, Salutation, and Signature). To get the most use out of the predefined AutoText entries, be sure to check the Show AutoComplete Suggestions option, described in the tip "Use AutoComplete to

Insert AutoText Entries and Dates More Quickly," on page 268. Then, as you type documents, an AutoComplete suggestion will occasionally pop up for one of these entries, as shown here, allowing you to save a little typing.

```
Yours truly, (Press ENTER to Insert)
        Your
```

Note, however, that if the insertion point is currently in a paragraph with a style other than Normal, and if you created one or more AutoText entries from paragraphs having that style, the AutoText submenu will list only entries created from paragraphs with the same style. In this case, if you want to see all AutoText entries, hold down the Shift key when you open the AutoText submenu.

Tip   **Change the text for an AutoText entry**

To modify the contents of an AutoText entry without having to delete it and reenter it, insert the entry text into the document (using one of the methods just described), make the changes you want, and then use the procedure given at the beginning of this section to save the text again as an AutoText entry, using its original name. You must answer Yes when Word asks whether you want to redefine the entry.

Using the AutoText Tab of the AutoCorrect Dialog Box

You can use the AutoText tab of the AutoCorrect dialog box to create AutoText entries, to view their contents, or to delete them. You can open this tab using either of the following methods:

- Choose Insert, AutoText, AutoText.

  or

- Choose Tools, AutoCorrect Options. In the AutoCorrect dialog box click the AutoText tab. (The other tabs in the AutoCorrect dialog box are discussed later in the book.)

To create an AutoText entry using the AutoText tab, perform the following steps:

1. Select the document text you want to save.
2. Display the AutoText tab using one of the methods just given.
3. Type a name for the AutoText entry into the Enter AutoText Entries Here text box. Note that if you type the same name as an existing entry, the existing entry will be overwritten.
4. In the Look In drop-down list, select the template in which you want to store the AutoText entry. If you select All Active Templates or Normal.dot (Global Template), the Normal template will store the entry and all Word documents will have access to it. If the current document is attached to a template other than Normal, and if you select the name of that template in the Look In drop-down list, then the attached template

will store the entry and it will be available only to documents attached to this same template.

> Chapter 14, "Advanced Word Formatting Techniques," explains how templates are attached to documents and shows how to copy AutoText entries from one template to another, as well as how to rename entries.

Note that your selection in this list also affects the location where AutoText entries are subsequently stored when you create entries using the Insert, AutoText, New command, as described in the previous section.

5 Click the Add button.

Figure 11-5 shows a completed AutoText tab just before the Add button is clicked.

Figure 11-5. You can create an AutoText entry using the AutoText tab of the AutoCorrect dialog box.

To view the contents of an AutoText entry or to delete or insert an entry, perform the following steps:

1 Display the AutoText tab using one of the methods given previously.

2 Select a template in the Look In drop-down list. Word will list only the AutoText entries stored in the template you select. Note that if you choose All Active Templates, Word will list all entries stored in the Normal template, in the template attached to the document (if other than Normal), and in any other loaded templates.

Your selection in the Look In drop-down list will also affect the AutoText entries that are subsequently displayed on the Insert menu's AutoText submenu, as well as those that are displayed by the AutoText toolbar, which is described in the next section.

3 Select the name of an AutoText entry in the Enter AutoText Entries Here list. You can now do one of the following:

- ■ You can view the current contents of the entry in the Preview area.
- ■ You can delete the entry by clicking the Delete button.
- ■ You can insert the entry into your document by clicking the Insert button. (The advantage of inserting an entry from the AutoCorrect dialog box is that it allows you to preview the contents of any entry immediately before you insert it.)

Displaying the AutoText Toolbar

If you use AutoText frequently, you can save time by displaying the AutoText toolbar, shown in Figure 11-6. To display it, choose View, Toolbars, AutoText. You can also display the toolbar by clicking the Show Toolbar button in the AutoText tab, described in the previous section.

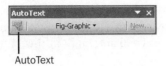

AutoText

Figure 11-6. The AutoText toolbar can save you time in working with AutoText.

You can work with the AutoText toolbar as follows:

- ● To display the AutoText tab of the AutoCorrect dialog box, click the AutoText button.
- ● To insert an AutoText entry, click the All Entries button and choose an entry from the menu.

> **Note**   If the insertion point is currently in a paragraph with a style other than Normal, and if you created one or more AutoText entries from paragraphs having that style, the middle button on the AutoText toolbar will be labeled with the name of the paragraph style rather than All Entries, and it will list only entries created from paragraphs with the same style. If you want to see all AutoText entries, hold down the Shift key while clicking the middle button.

- ● To create a new AutoText entry, select the text or graphics in your document and click the New button. This will display the Create AutoText dialog box, shown in Figure 11-4.

Automatically Fixing Your Text with AutoCorrect

A final way to automate text insertion is to use the AutoCorrect feature, which is similar to the AutoText feature. The primary difference between the two is that after you've typed the name of an AutoCorrect entry followed by a space or a punctuation symbol, Word automatically

Chapter 11

replaces the name with the entry text; you don't need to press a special key or issue a command. Thus, you might want to use AutoCorrect rather than AutoText for text that you insert frequently. You can also have AutoCorrect perform certain general text replacements; for example, you can have it automatically capitalize the first letter of a sentence if you fail to do so.

To enable AutoCorrect text replacements and define one or more AutoCorrect entries, perform the following steps:

1 If the text or graphics you want to save in the AutoCorrect entry has already been entered in a document, select it. (If the content you want to save consists of text only, this step is optional because you can type in the text later.)

2 Choose Tools, AutoCorrect Options to open the AutoCorrect dialog box. Click the AutoCorrect tab if it isn't already displayed.

3 Make sure the Replace Text As You Type option is checked to activate the AutoCorrect entries.

4 In the Replace text box, type a name for the AutoCorrect entry you want to define. Keep in mind that whenever you subsequently type this name into a document, followed by a space or a punctuation symbol, Word will automatically insert the Auto-Correct entry content.

> **Caution** Make sure that the name you choose for an AutoCorrect entry isn't a word that you might need to type into a document. For example, if you assigned the name *a*, each time you tried to enter the word *a* into a document, Word would insert the associated Auto-Correct entry. Also, if you type the name in capital letters, you'll always have to type it in capital letters for Word to insert the AutoCorrect entry.

5 If you selected text or graphics prior to opening the AutoCorrect dialog box, that content will already be contained in the With text box. To save your selected content without including its formatting, select the Plain Text option above the With box. To save the selected content together with its formatting, select the Formatted Text option.

6 If you didn't select content, type the text for the entry into the With box.

7 Click the Add button (or the Replace button if the entry name has already been used) to define the new entry and to add it to the list. Figure 11-7 shows the AutoCorrect dialog box after a new entry has been defined.

The list in the AutoCorrect tab displays the AutoCorrect entries that have already been defined. Notice that the list initially contains a collection of useful predefined entries for inserting frequently used symbols (for example, *(c)* will be replaced with ©) and correcting common spelling errors and typos (for example, *acheive* will be replaced with *achieve*, and *hte* with *the*).

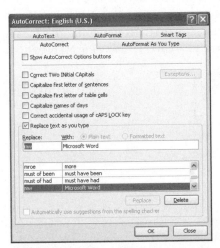

Figure 11-7. This figure shows the AutoCorrect tab after a new entry named *mw* has been added.

8 To remove an AutoText entry, click on it in the list and then click the Delete button.

9 To define an additional entry, repeat steps 4 through 7. When you're finished adding AutoCorrect entries, click the OK button to save your entries and close the dialog box.

Tip **Create an AutoCorrect entry for a symbol**

As mentioned in the tip "Set Up Shortcut Keys for Symbols You Frequently Use," on page 264, in the Symbol dialog box (which you can open by choosing Insert, Symbol), you can select a symbol and then click the AutoCorrect button to quickly create an AutoCorrect entry for that symbol.

After you've performed these steps, Word will immediately replace the name of the AutoCorrect entry you defined with the entry text whenever you type the name followed by a space, tab, punctuation character, or line break (inserted by pressing Enter or Shift+Enter). Note that you must type the entry name as a separate word; that is, the word must immediately follow a space, tab, or punctuation character, or be typed at the beginning of a line. For example, if you had defined the entry shown in Figure 11-7, typing **mw** followed by a space would cause Word to erase the "mw" and insert "Microsoft Word" in its place.

You can also have Word perform several kinds of general text replacements by checking one or more of the options in the upper part of the AutoCorrect dialog box. For example, if you check the Correct TWo INitial CApitals option, whenever you type a word beginning with two capital letters (with the rest of the characters lowercase), Word will automatically correct the error by converting the second letter to lowercase. If you select the second option (Capitalize First Letter Of Sentences), Word will automatically capitalize the first letter of a sentence if you fail to do so.

Chapter 11

To add or delete exceptions to corrections made by the Capitalize First Letter Of Sentences or Correct TWo INitial CApitals options, click the Exceptions button in the AutoCorrect dialog box. Word will display the AutoCorrect Exceptions dialog box, shown here:

In the AutoCorrect Exceptions dialog box, you can do the following:

- The Capitalize First Letter Of Sentences option normally capitalizes a word that comes after an abbreviation ending in a period, because a period usually ends a sentence. To prevent Word from capitalizing a word that comes after a specific abbreviation ending in a period, click the First Letter tab, type the abbreviation—including the period—into the Don't Capitalize After text box, and click the Add button. (Notice that the list initially includes quite a few predefined exceptions.) To remove an exception, click on it and then click the Delete button.

- To specify a word containing two initial capital letters (such as *POs* for *purchase orders*) that you don't want the Correct TWo INitial CApitals option to correct, click the INitial CAps tab, type the word into the Don't Correct text box, and click the Add button. To remove an exception, click on it and then click the Delete button.

- To add a word to your default custom spelling dictionary, so that the spelling checker will no longer flag the word, click the Other Corrections tab, type the word into the Don't Correct text box, and click the Add button.

For information on custom spelling dictionaries, see "Using Custom Dictionaries," on page 487.

- To have Word automatically add words to the First Letter or the INitial CAps exceptions list, check the Automatically Add Words To List option in any of the tabs. Then, if the Capitalize First Letter Of Sentences or the Correct TWo INitial CApitals option makes a correction, and you reverse that correction by issuing the Undo command or by backspacing and retyping, Word will automatically add the word to the corresponding exceptions list.

Efficient Editing in Word

Inside Out

Making sense of the Other Corrections tab

The Other Corrections tab, which affects the spelling checker and not AutoCorrect, is rather misplaced and confusing. In fact, if your Replace Text As You Type list in the AutoCorrect tab contains an entry for correcting a misspelling (for example, replacing *colour* with *color*), entering *colour* into the Other Corrections tab will stop the spelling checker from flagging that word, but it *won't* prevent AutoCorrect from making the replacement. To stop the Auto-Correct replacements, you'll have to delete the AutoCorrect entry.

If the Show AutoCorrect Options Buttons option is checked in the AutoCorrect tab, Word lets you modify an AutoCorrect correction using the AutoCorrect Options button. After AutoCorrect has made a correction, use this button as follows:

1 Move the mouse pointer (or the insertion point) to the text that AutoCorrect has inserted. A bar will appear below the left end of the text indicating that an options button is available, as shown here:

Please send in your Pos

2 Move the pointer over the bar. The AutoCorrect Options button then appears, as seen here:

3 Click the button and choose a command from the drop-down menu shown here:

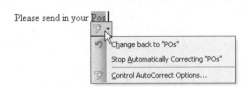

■ To reverse the correction, choose the Change Back or Undo command. (The wording of the command depends on the correction AutoCorrect made.)

■ To prevent AutoCorrect from making similar corrections in the future, choose the Stop… command. (The full wording of the command depends on the particular type of correction AutoCorrect made. Choosing the command turns off the corresponding AutoCorrect option, adds an exception to the appropriate

Chapter 11

exception list, or removes the corresponding entry from the Replace Text As You Type list.)

■ To open the AutoCorrect tab of the AutoCorrect dialog box, choose Control AutoCorrect Options.

4 If you later change your mind about reversing an AutoCorrect correction, you can reopen the drop-down menu and choose the Redo command. (The full wording of the command depends on the type of correction AutoCorrect reversed.)

Tip Use AutoCorrect to correct your spelling

The collection of predefined AutoCorrect entries in the Replace Text As You Type list includes many that correct common misspellings (such as *accomodate*, *acheive*, and *embarass*). The AutoCorrect replacements take place before the as-you-type spelling checker checks the word.

When you use Word's spelling checker and encounter a misspelling that isn't in the Auto-Correct list, you can quickly add a spelling correction to this list so that AutoCorrect will automatically fix the spelling error in the future. The two techniques for adding AutoCorrect entries while checking spelling are covered in "Checking Spelling," on page 479.

Also, if you check the Automatically Use Suggestions From The Spelling Checker option in the AutoCorrect tab (shown in Figure 11-7), whenever you misspell a word, AutoCorrect will immediately replace it with a word from the spelling checker's suggestion list, before the as-you-type spelling checker has a chance to underline the word. This feature works, however, only if there's a *single* word on the suggestion list. Also, the as-you-type spelling checker must be turned on (choose Tools, Options; click the Spelling & Grammar tab; and check the Check Spelling As You Type option).

Using Smart Tags in Word

Versions of Word prior to version 2002 (in Office XP) were able to recognize hyperlinks and e-mail addresses contained in a Microsoft Office document and have performed an appropriate action when you click on the data (namely, opening the target document of a hyperlink or sending an e-mail message). Beginning with version 2002, Word greatly extended this type of capability with the introduction of *smart tags*. Word can now recognize a wide range of different data types entered into a document, such as names, dates, addresses, and financial (stock ticker) symbols. It converts each recognized piece of data into a smart tag, and you can then use a menu attached to the smart tag to perform useful actions on that data, automatically invoking the required Microsoft Windows program or Internet site. For instance, for a smart tag containing the name of a person in your Outlook Contacts folder, you could send that person an e-mail message, schedule a meeting with the person, or insert the person's address into the document. For a financial symbol marked as a smart tag, you could connect to the Web and obtain a stock quote, read a company report, or browse recent company news.

The particular types of data that Word can convert to smart tags depend on the specific smart tag *recognizers* installed on your computer and activated in Word. Smart tag recognizers are included with Office, and you can obtain additional recognizers from various third-party companies or developers.

To enable smart tags in Word and to activate one or more specific smart tag recognizers, perform the following steps:

1   Choose Tools, AutoCorrect Options.

2   In the AutoCorrect dialog box, click the Smart Tags tab (shown in Figure 11-8).

Figure 11-8.   The settings in the AutoCorrect tab shown in this figure enable smart tag recognition, activate all available smart tag recognizers, and display smart tag actions buttons.

3   Check the Label Text With Smart Tags option to have Word recognize smart tags contained in a document.

4   Check Show Smart Tag Actions Buttons to have Word display smart tag buttons so that you can perform actions on smart tag data in your documents.

5   Activate the specific smart tag recognizers you want to use by checking them in the list.

6   To download additional smart tag recognizers from Microsoft, click the More Smart Tags button.

7   To change the way smart tags are saved, click the Save Options button. This will open the Save dialog box, which is the same as the Save tab of the Options dialog box. It includes two options that affect the saving of smart tags: Embed Smart Tags (saves all smart tags so they don't have to be recognized again when you reopen the document) and Save Smart Tags As XML Properties In Web Pages (in HTML [Hypertext Markup Language] documents, saves all smart tags in one place).

8   Click the OK button.

Assuming that you've activated the Person Name recognizer shown in Figure 11-8, whenever you type a proper name into a document, Word will convert the name to a smart tag as soon as you press Enter at the end of the paragraph containing the name. If the Smart Tags option is checked in the View tab of the Options dialog box (opened by choosing Tools, Options), Word will mark the smart tag with a dotted underline like this:

Mike Halvorson

If the Smart Tags option isn't checked, the smart tag will look like ordinary text.

To work with the smart tag, do the following:

1 Move the mouse pointer (or insertion point) over the smart tag text. Word will display an "information" icon above and to the left of the text, shown here, to indicate that it's a smart tag.

2 Move the pointer over the icon. The smart tag button will now appear, as seen here:

3 Click the button and choose a command from the drop-down menu shown here:

The particular items you see on the menu depend entirely on the type of data contained in the smart tag and the recognizer that's used to convert the text to a smart tag. In the preceding example shown, you could perform any of the following actions:

● To send an e-mail message to the person, choose Send Mail.

● To send that person a meeting invitation using Outlook, choose Schedule A Meeting.

● To search for an Outlook Contacts item for the person and open the item if found, choose Open Contact.

- To create a new item in your Outlook Contacts folder for that person, choose Add To Contacts.

- To search for an Outlook Contacts item for that person and insert the person's address if the item is found, choose Insert Address.

- To remove the smart tag, converting the data to ordinary document text, choose Remove This Smart Tag.

- To remove the smart tag and to stop recognizing the text found in that smart tag, click Stop Recognizing "*Text*" (where *Text* is the smart tag's text) and choose an item from the submenu.

- To open the Smart Tags tab, shown in Figure 11-8, choose Smart Tag Options.

Tip   **Remove or add smart tags**

To remove all smart tags in the document, converting the smart tag data to ordinary text, open the Smart Tags tab and click the Remove Smart Tags button. To have Word scan the whole document, converting all recognized blocks of text to smart tags, click the Recheck Document button.

For information on scheduling Outlook e-mail and meetings, see Chapter 38, "Managing Messages and Appointments." For information on the Outlook Contacts folder, see Chapter 39, "Managing Contacts, Tasks, and Other Types of Information."

Troubleshooting

You'd rather do it yourself

Word keeps making automatic changes to your documents as you work on them, even after you turn off all AutoCorrect options. You'd really like to turn off all automatic editing and formatting changes so that you have complete control over editing and formatting your document.

Word's automatic editing and formatting features become more pervasive with every version, so it's difficult to know where to turn them all off. To turn off every automatic editing or formatting feature that we could think of, go through the following list. (To open the Auto-Correct dialog box, choose Tools, AutoCorrect Options.)

- To turn off AutoCorrect, click the AutoCorrect tab in the AutoCorrect dialog box and clear every check box. (Unfortunately, there isn't a master option that turns off Auto-Correct. Instead, you have to turn off each option and then try to remember which options you had used if you decide to enable AutoCorrect again.)

- To turn off automatic formatting as you type, click the AutoFormat As You Type tab in the AutoCorrect dialog box and clear every check box. (Don't worry about the options in the AutoFormat tab of the AutoCorrect dialog box, because they aren't applied unless you explicitly choose AutoFormat from the Format menu.)

- To turn off automatic completion of AutoText entries, click the AutoText tab in the AutoCorrect dialog box and clear the Show AutoComplete Suggestions check box. If this option is enabled, Word sometimes automatically inserts an AutoText entry if you type the first part of the entry name and press Enter. For example, if you type your first name and press Enter, Word might insert your full name, even though your intention may have been to simply insert your first name and then start a new paragraph.

- To turn off automatic conversion of text to smart tags, click the Smart Tags tab in the AutoCorrect dialog box and clear the Label Text With Smart Tags option.

- To turn off automatic updating of a particular style, open the Modify Style dialog box for that style and clear the Automatically Update check box. If the Automatically Update option is turned on for a style, when you manually reformat one paragraph with that style, Word automatically redefines the style and reformats all other paragraphs in the document that have the same style. This option can have surprising results!

For information on using the Modify Style dialog box, see "Customizing Styles Using the Modify Style Dialog Box," on page 394.

- To stop Word from modifying styles in your document whenever you or someone else modifies the corresponding style in the document's template, choose Tools, Templates And Add-Ins. In the Templates And Add-Ins dialog box, click the Templates tab and clear the Automatically Update Document Styles option.

For information on the Automatically Update Document Styles option, see "Copying Styles from a Template to a Document," on page 406.

Positioning the Insertion Point

After you've created a document, the first step in editing it is to move the insertion point to the position where you want to make the change. Word provides many ways to move quickly through your documents. This section describes some of the essential ones.

To learn advanced methods for navigating through a document, see "Moving Quickly Through a Document," on page 300.

The easiest way to move the insertion point to a document position that's currently visible in the window is to simply click the position using the left (primary) mouse button. You can use the shortcut keys listed in Table 11-2 to move the insertion point to any position in a document.

Table 11-2. **Shortcut Keys for Moving the Insertion Point**

To Move	Use This Shortcut Key
To previous character	
To next character	
One line up	
One line down	
Backward through the document one word at a time	Ctrl+
Forward through the document one word at a time	Ctrl+
Backward through the document one paragraph at a time	Ctrl+
Forward through the document one paragraph at a time	Ctrl+
To the beginning of the line	Home
To the end of the line	End
To the beginning of the document	Ctrl+Home
To the end of the document	Ctrl+End
One window up (that is, up a distance equal to the height of the window)	Page Up
One window down	Page Down

For information on searching for text, see "Finding and Replacing Text and Formatting," on page 293.

You can also use the horizontal and vertical scroll bars to bring text into view in a document window. If either scroll bar is currently hidden, you can display it by choosing Tools, Options, clicking the View tab, and checking the Horizontal Scroll Bar or the Vertical Scroll Bar option. Note that when you navigate using a scroll bar, the insertion point isn't moved relative to the document; in fact, after you scroll, the insertion point is often not even visible in the window. To move the insertion point, scroll and then click the position in the document where you want the insertion point to appear.

Editing Document Text

Once you've moved the insertion point to the position in your document where you want to make a change, the next step is to apply a Word editing command. Word provides an assortment of editing commands for deleting, replacing, copying, moving, or capitalizing text.

Chapter 11

You can delete a limited number of characters by simply positioning the insertion point and pressing one of the shortcut keys shown in Table 11-3.

Table 11-3. Shortcut Keys for Deleting Text

To Delete	Press This Shortcut Key
The character after the insertion point	Delete
Through the end of the word containing (or following) the insertion point	Ctrl+Delete
The character before the insertion point	Backspace
Through the beginning of the word containing (or preceding) the insertion point	Ctrl+Backspace

Undo

You can hold down any of these shortcut keys to delete several characters or words. Remember that you can choose Undo from the Edit menu, click the Undo button on the Standard toolbar, or press Ctrl+Z to restore text that you've deleted by mistake. If you held down the Backspace key to delete a group of characters, the Undo command restores all of them. If you used any of the other deletion shortcut keys, Undo restores only the most recently deleted character or word. (You can then repeat the Undo command to restore additional characters or words.)

> For more information on using the Undo button, see the sidebar "Undoing and Redoing Editing and Formatting Actions," on page 285.

Selecting the Text

Most of the Word editing techniques—as well as the formatting techniques discussed in the next chapter—require that you first *select* (that is, highlight) one or more blocks of text, and then issue a command that affects that text. The highlighted block or blocks of text constitute the current *selection*. Selecting lets you precisely control the part or parts of your document that are affected by a Word command, from one or more single characters or graphic objects to the entire document. This example shows two blocks of selected text.

This text is selected. In Word, you first select text and then act on the selection. This text is also selected.

For example, you could first select one or more blocks of text, and then press the Delete key. Having a selection changes the usual effect of the Delete command—it erases one or more entire blocks of characters rather than erasing a single space or character. Selecting text removes the normal insertion point; that is, at a given time a document has either a selection or an insertion point, but never both. You can select text or graphics using either the keyboard or the mouse.

Selecting by Using the Keyboard

The basic method for using the keyboard to select a single block of text or graphics is to hold down the Shift key, and then press any of the shortcut keys for moving the insertion point that were described in Table 11-2 on page 281. With the Shift key pressed, the keyboard command selects text rather than merely moving the insertion point. For example, you can hold down Shift and an arrow key to extend the selection character by character or line by line in the direction you want.

Using the keyboard method alone, you can select only a single block of text. To select an additional block, you have to use the mouse as described in the next section.

Table 11-4 summarizes the shortcut keys for selecting text. Keep in mind that these shortcut keys simply combine the Shift key with the shortcut keys used to move the insertion point, which were described in Table 11-2.

Table 11-4. Shortcut Keys for Extending a Selection

To Extend the Selection	Press This Shortcut Key
Through the previous character	Shift+
Through the next character	Shift+
One line up	Shift+
One line down	Shift+
Through the beginning of the current word (or previous word if already at the beginning of a word)	Shift+Ctrl+
Through the beginning of the next word	Shift+Ctrl+
Through the beginning of the current paragraph (or previous paragraph if already at the beginning of a paragraph)	Shift+Ctrl+
Through the end of the current paragraph	Shift+Ctrl+
Through the beginning of the line	Shift+Home
Through the end of the line	Shift+End
Through the beginning of the document	Shift+Ctrl+Home
Through the end of the document	Shift+Ctrl+End
One window up (that is, extend the selection up a distance equal to the height of the window)	Shift+Page Up
One window down	Shift+Page Down

An alternative way to use the keyboard to select a single block of text is to press the F8 key or double-click the EXT indicator on the status bar to activate the *Extend mode*. (When the Extend mode is active, the EXT indicator is displayed in darker characters.) While working in Extend mode, you can make selections by pressing any of the shortcut keys given in Table 11-4 *without* pressing the Shift key. For example, you can select all characters through the end of the line by pressing F8 and then pressing End. To turn off Extend mode, either press the Esc key or double-click the EXT status bar indicator again. (This won't remove the selection but will merely end Extend mode.) Also, Extend mode will be canceled automatically if you perform any editing or formatting action on the selected text.

Tip   Use F8 to select parts of a document

You can press F8 repeatedly to select increasingly larger portions of your document. The first press activates the Extend mode, the second press selects the current word, the third press selects the current sentence, the fourth press selects the current paragraph, and the fifth press selects the entire document.

You can also extend the selection through the next occurrence of a character by pressing F8 and then typing the character.

Finally you can select the entire document by choosing Edit, Select All or by pressing Ctrl+A.

To cancel a selection—and display the insertion point instead—simply press an arrow key or click at any position in the document. (If you're in Extend mode, you must first press Esc or double-click the EXT indicator on the status bar.)

Selecting by Using the Mouse

The basic technique for using the mouse to select a block of text or graphics is to move the pointer to the beginning of the desired selection, press the left mouse button, and then drag over the text or graphics you want to select. If you reach a window border while dragging, Word will scroll the document so that you can keep extending the selection. If one or more blocks of text are already selected, you can select an additional block of text by pressing the Ctrl key while you drag. If you don't press Ctrl while dragging, the selection will be removed from any previously selected blocks.

Note   If the When Selecting, Automatically Select Entire Word option is checked, dragging selects text word by word rather than character by character. That is, as the selection is extended, entire words are added to the selection rather than individual characters. If you prefer to select text character by character, clear this option. To access the option, choose Tools, Options and click the Edit tab.

You can also select a single block of text or graphics by performing the following steps (using this method removes the selection from any previously selected block or blocks):

1 Click the position where you want to start the selection.
2 Hold down the Shift key while you click the position where you want to end the selection.

Note   If you activate Extend mode, as explained in the previous section, you can extend the selection to any point in the document by simply clicking *without* holding down Shift.

Undoing and Redoing Editing and Formatting Actions

You can reverse the effect of your most recent editing or formatting action by choosing Edit, Undo or by pressing Ctrl+Z. Clicking the Undo button on the Standard toolbar has the same effect.

If you repeat the Undo command, Word will undo your next most recent action. Suppose, for example, that you type a word, format a paragraph, and then delete a character. If you subsequently issue the Undo command three times, Word will replace the character, restore the paragraph to its original format, and then erase the word.

Also, as a shortcut for undoing multiple actions, you can click the down arrow next to the Undo button, drag the pointer down to highlight all the actions you want to undo, and then release the button, as shown in this example:

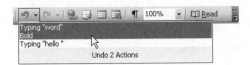

The actions are listed in order from the most recent to the least recent, and you can select them for undoing only in this order.

As explained in "Replaying Your Editing Actions with the Repeat Command," on page 265, you can issue the Repeat command (by choosing Edit, Repeat, or by pressing Ctrl+Y or F4) to perform again your most recent editing or formatting operation. If, however, your most recent operation was to undo an action using any of the methods just described, the Repeat command will redo the action. (In this case, the command on the Edit menu will be labeled Redo rather than Repeat.) For example, if you delete a word and then press Ctrl+Z, the word will be restored; if you then press Ctrl+Y, the word will again be removed. (It makes sense for the Repeat command to perform this action, because repeating an undo action "undoes the undo"; that is, it reverses the effect of the Undo command.)

You can also redo an action by clicking the Redo button on the Standard toolbar.

Like the Undo button, the Redo button has an adjoining down arrow you can click to select the exact actions you want to redo.

When you redo an action, the action reappears at the top of the undo list. So you can toggle back and forth between undoing and redoing an action by alternately clicking the Undo and Redo buttons. You might use this technique to compare two versions of a block of text—for example, text with and without italics.

(Unlike the Ctrl+Y and F4 shortcut keys and the Repeat [Redo] Edit menu command, you can use the Redo button only to redo an action. You can't use it to repeat an action.)

Table 11-5 lists some mouse shortcuts you can use to select various amounts of text. Perform the action in the third column—in addition to the action in the second column—to preserve any current selection; if you don't, the current selection will be canceled. The *selection bar* referenced in this table is the area within the document window to the immediate left of the text. It's easy to tell when the mouse pointer is within the selection bar because the pointer changes to an arrow pointing up and to the right, as seen here:

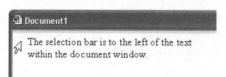

Table 11-5. Mouse Shortcuts for Selecting Text

To Select	Do This	To Add to a Current Selection, Also Do This
A word	Double-click the word.	Press Ctrl while clicking.
A sentence	Hold down the Ctrl key while clicking within the sentence.	This technique works only if there's no current selection.
A line	Click in the selection bar next to the line.	Press Ctrl while clicking.
Several lines	Drag down or up in the selection bar.	Press Ctrl while dragging.
A paragraph	Double-click in the selection bar next to the paragraph.	This technique won't work if you press Ctrl while clicking, so it always removes any current selection.
Several paragraphs	Double-click in the selection bar, and then drag down or up.	This technique won't work if you press Ctrl while clicking, so it always removes any current selection.
The entire document	Hold down the Ctrl key while clicking in the selection bar.	This technique works only if there's no current selection.

You can select a column of text by holding down the Alt key and dragging over the area you want to select (this technique always removes any current selection), as shown in the example:

> To select a column of text, hold
> down the Alt key while
> dragging over the desired block
> of text.

Pressing the Delete key after selecting as shown above would erase the first character of each line. Note that an editing or formatting action won't affect a character unless it's *entirely* selected. (In the preceding example, even though parts of the *r* and *f* in the last two lines are selected, these characters aren't deleted.)

To cancel the selection, either click any place in the document or press an arrow key. If more than one block of text is selected, you can cancel the selection from a single block by clicking it while holding down Ctrl.

Editing the Selection

Once you've selected one or more blocks of text, you're ready to apply an editing or formatting command to the selection. This section describes the essential editing commands you can apply to selections.

> As you use these techniques, keep in mind that you can reverse your editing action by issuing the Undo command, as described in the sidebar "Undoing and Redoing Editing and Formatting Actions," on page 285, even if the amount of text deleted or altered is large.

If the Typing Replaces Selection option is checked, you can replace the selection by simply typing the new text. When you type the first letter, the entire selection is automatically deleted, and the new text you type is inserted in its place. If Typing Replaces Selection isn't checked, the selected text is left in place, the selection is canceled, and the new text is inserted in front of the formerly selected text. To access the Typing Replaces Selection option, choose Tools, Options and click the Edit tab in the Options dialog box.

To erase the selected text, press the Delete key or the Backspace key, or choose Edit, Clear, Contents.

To change the case of the letters in the selection (to sentence case, lowercase, uppercase, or title case), or to toggle all letters between uppercase and lowercase, choose format, change case and select the desired capitalization option in the change case dialog box (Figure 11-9). Alternatively, you can press Shift+F3—repeatedly if necessary—to switch among various capitalization styles.

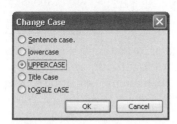

Figure 11-9. The Change Case dialog box allows you to change the capitalization style of the selected text.

Moving and Copying Text Using the Mouse

To use the mouse to quickly move or copy text, perform the following steps:

1 Select the text.

> **Note** If several blocks of text are selected, using drag-and-drop to move or copy one of them will move or copy them all. When you drop the text, Word will insert a paragraph break following each moved or copied block.

2 Place the mouse pointer over the selection (the pointer will change from an I-beam to an arrow), and hold down the left mouse button, as seen here.

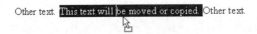

3 To move the text, simply drag it to its new location. To copy the text, hold down the Ctrl key while you drag. If the target location isn't visible, just drag the text to the edge of the window, and the document will automatically be scrolled in the corresponding direction. The target location can be within the same Word document, within a different Word document, or even within a document in another Office application (such as a Microsoft Excel worksheet). If a target location in a different document isn't currently visible, drag the text to the target document's button on the Windows taskbar and hold the pointer there for a few seconds. The target document's window will then be activated, and you can complete the drag operation (keep the left mouse button pressed the whole time).

When the text is inserted in its new location, Word will display the Paste Options button, as seen here, at the end of the moved or copied text.

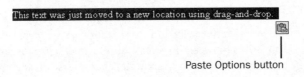

Paste Options button

> **Note** To use the Paste Options button, the Show Paste Options Buttons option must be enabled. To access this option, choose Tools, Options and click the Edit tab.

4 Normally, when you copy or move text, the text's formatting is copied or moved along with it. If you want to copy or move the text without transferring its formatting, click the Paste Options button and choose Match Destination Formatting or Keep Text Only from the drop-down menu, shown here:

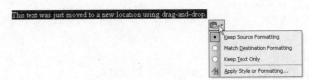

> **Tip** Use shortcut keys to move a paragraph up or down
> You can select and move an entire paragraph by pressing a single key combination. First place the insertion point anywhere within the paragraph. Then, to move the paragraph up (that is, before the previous paragraph), press Shift+Alt+Up arrow. To move it down (that is, after the next paragraph), press Shift+Alt+Down arrow.

 Troubleshooting

Drag-and-drop editing doesn't work

When you try to drag a block of selected text, the selection changes rather than the text moving.

To drag selected text, make sure that when you press the mouse button to start dragging, the tip of the arrow pointer is within the selected area. Otherwise, you'll merely change the selection.

Also, to move or copy text using the drag-and-drop method, the Drag-And-Drop Text Editing option must be checked. To access this option, choose Tools, Options and then click the Edit tab.

For information on moving blocks of text in Outline view, see "Working with Documents in Outline View," on page 419.

Moving and Copying Text Using the Clipboard

You can also move or copy text using the Clipboard, by performing the following steps:

1. Select the text.

> **Note** If several blocks of text are selected when you issue the Cut or Copy command, the Clipboard will store them all. When you paste the text, Word will insert a paragraph break following each moved or copied block.

2. To move the text, choose Edit, Cut or press Ctrl+X. This will *cut* the text; that is, it will remove it from the document and place it in the Clipboard.

   To copy the text, choose Edit, Copy or press Ctrl+C. This will *copy* the text; that is, it will leave the text in the document and place a copy of it in the Clipboard.

3. Place the insertion point at the position where you want to insert the text that has been cut or copied to the Clipboard. The target location can be within the original document or within a different document.

4. Choose Edit, Paste or press Ctrl+V. This will *paste* the text; that is, it will insert it into the document.

Word will display the Paste Options button at the end of the moved or copied text, as seen here:

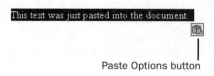

Paste Options button

5 Normally, when you copy or move text, the text's formatting is copied or moved along with it. If you want to copy or move the text without transferring its formatting, click the Paste Options button and choose Match Destination Formatting or Keep Text Only from the drop-down menu, shown here:

> **Note** To use the Paste Options button, the Show Paste Options Buttons option must be checked. You'll find this option by choosing Tools, Options and then clicking the Edit tab.

Word provides two additional ways to cut, copy, or paste text with the Clipboard. One method is to click the appropriate buttons on the Standard toolbar, shown here:

Paste

Copy

Cut

Another way to cut or copy a block of selected text is to right-click it and then choose Cut or Copy from the shortcut menu that's displayed, as seen on the next page.

Efficient Editing in Word

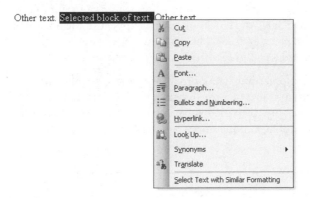

Likewise, to paste the text, you can right-click the target location and then choose Paste from the shortcut menu. To remove the shortcut menu without choosing a command, press the Esc key or click anywhere within the document.

An advantage of using the Clipboard is that you can move or copy text or graphics between separate Windows-based programs. (The Clipboard is a shared Windows facility.) Another advantage is that the text is retained in the Clipboard after you paste, allowing you to insert several copies of the text by pasting repeatedly.

> For information on different ways to use the Clipboard to transfer data between Office applications, see Chapter 7, "Exchanging Data in Office 2003."

This section has explained the techniques for cutting or copying a single block of data into the Clipboard and then pasting that block. Alternatively, you can use the enhanced Office Clipboard to store multiple blocks of text or graphics and then paste any of them into a document.

> For information on activating and using the Office Clipboard, see "Using the Office Clipboard," on page 158.

To transfer multiple blocks of text or data, you can also use the Spike, described in the next section.

Using the Spike

You can use the *Spike* to remove several blocks of text from a document and then insert all these blocks together at a single document location. The Spike is based on a special-purpose AutoText entry that's assigned the name "Spike." (This name derives from the old days when newspaper editors would cut out blocks of lines from typed copy and impale them on a metal spike for possible later use.) The following is the usual procedure for using the Spike:

1   Select a block of text.
2   Press Ctrl+F3 to remove the block from the document and store it in the Spike.
3   Repeat steps 1 and 2 for each additional block of text you'd like to add to the Spike.

4 Place the insertion point at the document position where you want to insert the text, and press Ctrl+Shift+F3. All the blocks of text will appear in the document and the Spike will be emptied. The blocks will be inserted in the order in which they were stored in the Spike, and a paragraph break will be added after each block.

In the first three steps of the preceding list, Word adds text to the Spike AutoText entry. In step 4, Word inserts all the entry text into the document and deletes the entry. You can insert the text without deleting the entry by typing **Spike** and then pressing F3. You can also use any of the other AutoText insertion techniques discussed in "Reusing Text with the AutoText Feature," on page 266.

Setting Clipboard Options

Word provides several options that affect moving and copying text with the Clipboard. To set these options, choose Tools, Options and click the Edit tab.

If you want to be able to paste by pressing the Insert key (in addition to the other methods), check the Use The INS Key For Paste option. (If the Use The INS Key For Paste option is checked, you can double-click the OVR indicator in the Word status bar to toggle between Insert and Overtype editing modes, which is the function of the Insert key when this option is off.)

To have Word display the Paste Options button whenever you move or copy text using drag-and-drop or the Clipboard, check the Show Paste Options Buttons option.

To have Word remove extraneous spaces that remain after you cut text (or after you delete it by choosing Edit, Clear, Contents or by pressing the Delete or Backspace key), check the Smart Cut And Paste option. For example, if this option is enabled and you cut only the word "expression," without removing any spaces, from the text "(a parenthetical expression)," Word would automatically remove the space following "parenthetical."

To set a variety of additional options that affect pasting and other editing functions in Word, click the Settings button to open the Settings dialog box, shown here:

In the Settings dialog box, you can select a version of Word (Word 2002 to 2003 or Word 97 through 2000) to use the default editing settings for that version, or you can check or clear individual options to create custom settings.

Finding and Replacing Text and Formatting

You can easily search for text, formats, or special items such as paragraph marks and graphics using the Find command. The following is the essential procedure for using this command to conduct a search in Word:

1   If you want to limit the search to one or more specific blocks of text, select that text.

2   Choose Edit, Find or press Ctrl+F to display the Find tab of the Find And Replace dialog box (shown in Figure 11-10).

Figure 11-10.   The Find tab of the Find And Replace dialog box is shown without the search options displayed.

3   To perform a search using the options you set the previous time you used the Find command, skip to step 6 now. Otherwise, complete steps 4 and 5 to select the search options you want.

4   To have the Search command immediately select all matching blocks of text it finds, check Highlight All Items Found In. In the drop-down list, select the part of the document that you want Word to search; you can select Main Document, Current Selection (if you've selected text), or—for documents that contain these items—Headers And Footers, Footnotes, or Comments. For instance, if you've added comments to a document, you could have Word search and highlight in either the main document or in your comment text, by selecting one of the items shown here:

To have the Search command select matching blocks one at a time so that you can view or work with each one separately, clear the Highlight All Items Found In check box.

5   To set one or more additional search options, click the More button to display the options, if they aren't already shown, and select the ones you want (see Figure 11-11). The search options are summarized in Table 11-6. (If you selected text in step 1 and

Chapter 11

want Word to search only within the selection, you must choose Down or Up in the Search drop-down list. If the All option is selected, Word will search the entire document.)

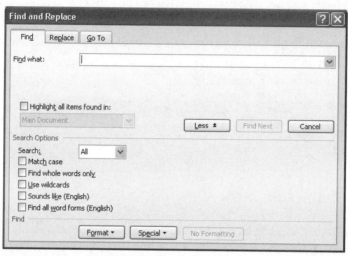

Figure 11-11. The Find tab of the Find And Replace dialog box is shown displaying all options.

6 If you want to search for text (that is, specific words or phrases), enter that text into the Find What box. (You can click the down arrow to select previous search text from the drop-down list.)

To include a nonprinting character or other document element in your search text (for example, a tab character or a graphic object), click the Special button and choose the appropriate item from the menu. (If the Special button or other button mentioned in these instructions isn't visible, click the More button to reveal it.) This will insert into your search text a code for finding the item (for example, ^t to find a tab character or ^g to find a graphic object). If you've checked the Use Wildcards option, the Special menu also lets you insert wildcard expressions (as explained in the sidebar "Using Wildcards in Your Search Text," on page 296). However, when Use Wildcards is checked, the Special menu doesn't offer as many options for finding nonprinting characters and document elements.

7 If you want to search for a particular format or combination of formats, click the Format button, choose a formatting type, and specify the format in the dialog box that's displayed. Alternatively, if Word provides a shortcut key for applying a specific format (such as Ctrl+B for bold text or Ctrl+E for centered paragraph alignment), you can specify that format by pressing the shortcut key when the insertion point is within the Find What text box.

Formatting and the shortcut keys you can use for formatting are described in Chapter 12.

When searching for certain formats (such as bold or superscript text), you can search either for text that has the format or for text that doesn't have the format. For example, you can select Bold (to search for text that's bold and meets other criteria) or Not Bold (to search for text that isn't bold and meets other criteria), or you can select neither option (to search for text that meets other criteria whether it's bold or not). The formatting that you choose is displayed below the Find What box.

> **Note** If you specify a search format in a dialog box, a check box that has just a check mark means to find text that has the format, an empty check box means to find text that doesn't have the format, and a check box with a square means the format isn't part of your search criteria. If you specify a search format using a shortcut key (for example, Ctrl+B for bold text), repeatedly pressing the key toggles between these three states (for example, Bold, Not Bold, and either Bold or Not Bold).

You can enter search text into the Find What text box *and* choose formatting. In this case, Word will search for text that matches your search text and has the specified formatting. To remove all your formatting specifications, click the No Formatting button.

8 If you checked the Highlight All Items Found In option, click the Find All button to have Word select all instances of the search text or formatting all at once.

If you *didn't* check Highlight All Items Found In, click the Find Next button to have Word find and select each occurrence of the search text or formatting one at a time. You can edit your document while the Find And Replace dialog box is open; simply click the document when you want to edit it, and then click in the Find And Replace dialog box to continue searching. (If the Find And Replace dialog box covers the text you want to edit, point to the title bar of the dialog box and drag the box out of the way.)

9 To close the Find And Replace dialog box, click the Cancel button.

Table 11-6. Search Options on the Find Tab of the Find And Replace Dialog Box

To Search Like This	Select This Option
To search the entire document from the insertion point (or start of the selection) to the end of the document, and then from the beginning of the document down to the insertion point (or start of the selection), including headers, footers, comments, and footnotes	Select All in the Search drop-down list.
To search from the insertion point (or start of the selection) to the end of the document (or selection), excluding headers, footers, comments, and footnotes	Select Down in the Search drop-down list.
To search from the insertion point (or end of the selection) to the beginning of the document (or selection), excluding headers, footers, comments, and footnotes	Select Up in the Search drop-down list.

Chapter 11

Table 11-6. **Search Options on the Find Tab of the Find And Replace Dialog Box**

To Search Like This	Select This Option
To search only for text that matches the case of each letter in the search text you enter	Check the Match option.
To exclude matching text that's part of another word (for example, if searching for *cat*, don't match *catatonic*)	Check the Find Whole Words Only option.
To include wildcards in your search text (for an explanation of this option, see the sidebar "Using Wildcards in Your Search Text," later on this page)	Check the Use Wildcards option.
To search for all text that sounds like the search text you enter into the Find What text box (for example, if the search text is *there*, this option would find *their* as well as *there*)	Check the Sounds Like (English) option.
To find all forms of the search text (for example, if the search text is *go*, this option finds *go*, *goes*, *gone*, and *went*)	Check the Find All Word Forms (English) option.

Using Wildcards in Your Search Text

If you check the Use Wildcards option in the Find tab or in the Replace tab of the Find And Replace dialog box, you can include wildcards in the search text you enter into the Find What text box. A *wildcard* is a special character that matches a particular class of characters or text strings. For example, the ? wildcard matches any character (hence, c?t matches cat, cot, cut, and so on). The * wildcard matches any string of characters (hence, b*d matches bad, bard, board, and so on). To search for an actual wildcard character, precede it with a backslash (\)—for example, \? to find "?" and * to find "*."

The fastest way to insert wildcards into your search text is to click the Special button and, from the menu, choose the type of character or string you want to find. Be sure that you check the Use Wildcards option *before* choosing an item from the Special menu. (Otherwise, the Special menu lists standard Word search codes rather than wildcards, and also allows you to insert several codes that aren't compatible with the wildcard option.)

Wildcards are often combined in fairly complex expressions, known as *regular expressions*. After inserting an item from the Special menu, you might therefore need to manually complete the wildcard expression in the Find What text box, as well as type in the rest of your search text. You can also manually type wildcards into the Find What box rather than using the Special menu. For details on the specific wildcards and wildcard expressions you can use, look up *wildcards* in the Word online Help.

The primary advantage of using wildcards is that they give you greater control in searching for text. When you use wildcards, however, you might need to look up the syntax and manually type in (or complete) fairly complex expressions. We recommend using them only if you're comfortable with regular expressions, or if you're unable to find the text you want without using wildcards.

After the dialog box is closed, you can continue to search for the same text or formatting using the keyboard. Each time you press Shift+F4, Word searches for the next occurrence of the text or formatting, moving in the direction you specified in the Find And Replace dialog box. Each time you press Ctrl+Page Down, Word searches for the next occurrence moving down in the document, and each time you press Ctrl+Page Up, Word searches for the next occurrence moving up in the document. You can also have Word search for the next occurrence by clicking the Next browse button, or search for the previous occurrence by clicking the Previous browse button. These buttons are described in "Navigating with the Browse Buttons," on page 304.

Tip If you're searching for multiple occurrences of text or formatting, you'll probably find it most convenient to use the Find And Replace dialog box to locate the first occurrence and then close the dialog box to get it out of your way and use the keystrokes described here to find additional occurrences.

Inside Out

Be careful of using other browse commands while searching

Keep in mind that the Ctrl+Page Up, Ctrl+Page Down, and Shift+F4 keystrokes, as well as the Previous and Next browse buttons, are multipurpose commands that browse through instances of whatever *browse object* you last specified. The browse object can be the search text of the Find command, a target set up in the Go To tab, or a target selected through the Select Browse Object browse button. (The Go To tab is covered in "Moving the Insertion Point with the Go To Command," on page 302.)

Consider, for example, that you just closed the Find tab and are now navigating through instances of your search text using the Ctrl+Page Up and Ctrl+Page Down keystrokes or the Previous and Next browse buttons. However, you now use the Go To command to locate a comment. You'll then discover that these keystrokes and buttons no longer locate instances of your search text, but rather move through comments. To resume browsing through instances of your search text using the keystrokes or browse buttons, you'll need to reopen the Find tab and use it to find at least one instance of the search text.

For information on using Word's new Styles And Formatting task pane to find or reformat all text throughout the document that has a particular style or formatting, see "Selecting All Text with the Same Style or Formatting," on page 335.

Chapter 11

Replacing Text and Formatting

You can find and replace text or formatting using the Replace command. Like the Find command, Replace allows you to search for text, formatting, or a combination of text and formatting. You can replace the text that's found, change its formatting, or both replace the text and change its formatting. The following are the essential steps. (See the instructions in the previous section for more information on the steps that are common to both finding and replacing text.)

1   If you want to replace only within one or more specific blocks of text, select the text.

2   Choose Edit, Replace or press Ctrl+H to display the Replace tab of the Find And Replace dialog box.

3   If you want to perform a replace operation using the options you set the previous time you used the Replace command, proceed now to step 4. If, however, you want to set one or more search options, click the More button to display the options—if they aren't already shown—and select the ones you want (see Figure 11-12). These options are the same as those available in the Find tab, as summarized in Table 11-6. (If you selected text in step 1 and want Word to search only within the selection, you must choose Down or Up in the Search drop-down list. If the All option is selected, Word will search the entire document.)

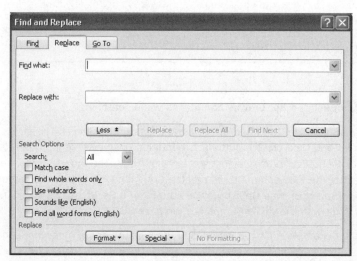

Figure 11-12.   The Replace tab of the Find And Replace dialog box is shown displaying all options.

4   If you want to search for text, type it into the Find What box. (You can click the down arrow to select previous search text from the drop-down list.) To include a nonprinting character or other document element in your search text (for example, a tab character or a graphic object), click the Special button and choose the appropriate item from the menu.

5   If you want to search for a particular format or combination of formats, make sure that the insertion point is within the Find What box. Then, click the Format button, choose a formatting type, and specify the format you want in the dialog box that's displayed. Alternatively, if Word provides a shortcut key for applying a specific format (such as Ctrl+B for bold text), you can specify that format by pressing the shortcut key when the insertion point is within the Find What text box.

> For information on choosing formatting, see Chapter 12.

6   If you want to replace the text that's found, type the replacement text into the Replace With box. To include a special character in the replacement text (such as a paragraph mark), click the Special button. Word will display only those special characters that are appropriate for replacement text.

> **Tip**   Replace text with graphics
> You might want to replace text with graphics throughout your document. (Perhaps, for example, you've inserted placeholder text in your document for a particular icon and now want to replace each placeholder with the actual graphic object.) Although you can't insert a graphic object directly into the Replace With text box, you can copy the graphic object into the Clipboard prior to opening the Find And Replace dialog box, and then type ^c into the Replace With text box, causing Word to use the current contents of the Clipboard (that is, your graphic object) as the replacement text.

7   If you want to change the formatting of the text that's found, make sure that the insertion point is within the Replace With box, and choose the formatting you want, as described previously. Word will display the replacement format you've chosen below the Replace With box. Note that if you leave the Replace With box empty and don't choose replacement formatting, each block of text that's found will be deleted.

8   Either click the Replace All button to replace all occurrences of the text or formatting, without confirmation, or click the Find Next button to view and verify the first replacement.

9   If you clicked Find Next, Word will highlight the first matching text. You can then click Replace to replace the text or formatting and find the next occurrence, or you can click Find Next to leave the text unaltered and continue to the next occurrence. You can repeat this step until all text has been replaced. Or, at any time, you can click Close to close the dialog box and stop the process or Replace All to replace all remaining occurrences without confirmation. (The Cancel button is labeled Close after the first replacement, reminding you that you can't cancel replacements you've already made.) Recall that you can leave the Find And Replace dialog box displayed while you manually edit the document. (You might have to move the dialog box out of the way by dragging its title bar.)

Chapter 11

> **Tip   Reverse your replacements**
>
> If you replaced all occurrences of text in your document by clicking the Replace All button in the Replace tab, issuing the Undo command immediately afterward reverses all these replacements at once. If you replaced occurrences one at a time by clicking the Replace button, the Undo command reverses only your most recent replacement. (You can then repeat the Undo command to reverse previous replacements.)

For information on searching for specified text or properties in multiple Office documents or in Outlook items, see "Finding Office Files or Outlook Items Using the File Search Feature," on page 63.

Moving Quickly Through a Document

"Positioning the Insertion Point," on page 280, summarized the keystrokes you can use to move the insertion point through a document. The following sections explain how to move through a document using some quick ways that are especially useful for larger documents.

Using Bookmarks to Label and Locate Text

You can use Word's bookmarks to mark and then quickly return to specific positions in a document.

To mark a position in a document, you need to define a bookmark using the following steps:

1   Place the insertion point at the position you want to mark or select a single block of text to mark. (You can't assign a bookmark if you've selected more than one block of text.)

2   Choose Insert, Bookmark, or press Ctrl+Shift+F5. Word will open the Bookmark dialog box.

3   Type an identifying name into the Bookmark Name box and then click the Add button (shown in Figure 11-13).

Figure 11-13.   This example shows how to define a bookmark named start in the Bookmark dialog box.

Chapter 11

You can use this technique to mark any number of positions in a document. Note that you can make bookmarks visible by choosing Tools, Options, clicking the View tab in the Options dialog box, and checking the Bookmarks option (in the Show area). Word will then display an I-beam symbol at the location of each bookmark, or, if you marked a block of text, Word will place bracket markers around the bookmark text.

> **Note** You can use bookmarks for a variety of other purposes, some of which are discussed later in the book—for example, for specifying the target of a hyperlink (discussed in "Adding and Using Hyperlinks," on page 580), for defining cross-references, and for creating index entries that refer to a range of pages. Indexes are discussed in "Generating Indexes and Tables of Contents," on page 438.

To move the insertion point to a position marked with a bookmark, open the Bookmark dialog box (choose Insert, Bookmark, or press Ctrl+Shift+F5), select the name that you assigned when you defined the bookmark (in step 3 above), and click the Go To button. Word will immediately move the insertion point to the marked position. You can also use the Go To command, discussed in the next section, to move to a particular bookmark.

> **Note** If you select a block of text prior to defining a bookmark, the bookmark will be assigned to the entire selection. In this case, when you go to the bookmark, Word will select the text.

Writing Macros for Saving and Restoring Your Place in a Document

This sidebar presents an invaluable pair of macros that use bookmarks for saving your place in a document and rapidly returning to that place. (It's surprising that Word doesn't provide build-in commands for doing this!) You can enter these macros yourself using the Visual Basic for Applications (VBA) Editor, following the brief instructions given here. (For complete information on macros and using the VBA Editor, see Part 10 of this book.) Alternatively, you can use the Organizer to copy the macros from the WordInsideOut module in the WordInsideOut.dot file provided on the book's companion CD into your own Normal template. For instructions on using the Organizer, see "Using the Organizer," on page 412.

To enter these macros, perform the following steps:

1 From the Tools menu in Word, choose Macro, Visual Basic Editor. This will run the Microsoft Visual Basic Editor.

2 In the Project Explorer pane at the upper left of the Visual Basic Editor window, double-click the Normal/Microsoft Word Objects/This Document item. (Expand the tree, if necessary, to access this item. If the Project Explorer pane isn't displayed, choose View, Project Explorer.) This will open a code window labeled Normal - This Document, where you can enter code that's stored in your Normal template.

3 Type the following macro code into the code window:

```
Sub SavePlace()
`SavePlace Macro
   With ActiveDocument.Bookmarks
      .Add Range:=Selection.Range, Name:="MarkedLocation"
   End With
End Sub

Sub ReturnToPlace()
`ReturnToPlace Macro
   Selection.GoTo What:=wdGoToBookmark, Name:="MarkedLocation"
End Sub
```

4 In the Visual Basic editor, choose File, Close And Return To Microsoft Word.

5 Use the procedures described in "Defining Shortcut Keys (Word Only)" on page 222 to define a shortcut key for the SavePlace macro and a shortcut key for the Return-ToPlace macro.

You can now test these macros as follows: place the insertion point anywhere in a document (or select a single block of text), and then press the shortcut key you defined for the SavePlace macro. This will save your position (or selection).

Then move the insertion point anywhere else within the same document and perform any editing or formatting actions you want. When you're ready to go back to your original location in the document, press the shortcut key you defined for the ReturnToPlace macro. Word will immediately move the insertion point back to its original position (or restore the original selection).

Moving the Insertion Point with the Go To Command

You can use the Go To command to move the insertion point (or the selection highlight) to a position marked by a bookmark (described in the previous section) or to one of a variety of other locations in a document, as follows:

1 Choose Edit, Go To, press Ctrl+G or F5, or double-click anywhere on the left half of the status bar (to the left of the REC indicator). Word will display the Go To tab of the Find And Replace dialog box (shown in Figure 11-14).

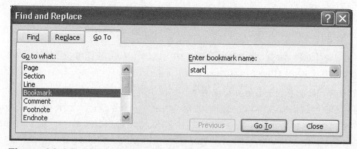

Figure 11-14. The Go To tab of the Find And Replace dialog box is shown as you'd fill it out to go to a bookmark named start.

2 In the Go To What list, select the type of target you want to navigate to. For example, to go to a particular bookmark, select Bookmark in the list; or, to go to a particular page, select Page.

3 Enter the name or number for the specific target into the text box on the right side of the dialog box and click the Go To button. The text box will be labeled according to the type of target you selected in step 1. For instance, if you selected Bookmark it will be labeled Enter Bookmark Name, or if you selected Page it will be labeled Enter Page Number. For certain types of targets, such as bookmarks or comments, you can select the name of the target from a drop-down list.

> **Note** To go to a particular document line, select Line in the Go To What list and type the line number into the Enter Line Number box. For the Go To command, line numbering begins at 1 with the first line in the document and is incremented throughout the rest of the document. In contrast, the line number displayed on the status bar refers to the number of the line within the current page.

For any type of target except a bookmark, if you don't enter a specific target into the text box, the dialog box will display buttons labeled Next and Previous. You can use these buttons to browse through the different instances of the target item. For example, if you select Section in the Go To What list and leave the Enter Section Number text box blank, clicking Next will take you to the beginning of the next document section and clicking Previous will take you to the beginning of the previous one. (Document sections are discussed in Chapter 13, "Arranging Text Using Tables, Columns, and Lists," and Chapter 18, "Designing and Printing Professional-Looking Pages.")

You can also enter into the text box a plus (+) or minus (–) sign followed by a number to move forward or back by a certain number of objects. For example, if you've selected Page in the Go To What list, you can enter +4 in the Enter Page Number box to move forward by four pages.

You can leave the Go To tab of the Find And Replace dialog box displayed while you work in your document. Whether or not the dialog box is displayed, you can navigate to the next instance of the type of target you specified in the Go To tab (for example, the next page, section, or bookmark) by pressing Ctrl+Page Down or by clicking the Next browse button. You can navigate to the previous instance of your Go To target by pressing Ctrl+Page Up or by clicking the Previous browse button. (The browse buttons are discussed in the next section.) If you entered a specific target in the Go To tab (such as a specific page number or a particular named bookmark), you can press Shift+F4 to go back to that target (if you didn't enter a specific target, Shift+F4 works just like Ctrl+Page Down).

Another way to move through a document is to press Shift+F5, the Go Back key. Pressing Shift+F5 moves you back through the locations where you most recently performed editing or formatting actions or moved to using a navigation command (Find, Go To, or browse button). You can move to three prior positions, at most. If you press the key a fourth time, the insertion point will cycle back to its original position.

Chapter 11

Inside Out

Be careful of using other browse commands while browsing Go To targets

Keep in mind that the Ctrl+Page Up, Ctrl+Page Down, and Shift+F4 keystrokes, as well as the Previous and Next browse buttons, are multipurpose commands that browse through instances of whatever *browse object* you last specified. The browse object can be the search text of the Find command, a target set up in the Go To tab, or a target selected through the Select Browse Object browse button.

Consider, for example, that you selected the Comment target in the Go To tab and are now happily navigating through your document's comments using the Ctrl+Page Up and Ctrl+Page Down keystrokes or the Previous and Next browse buttons. However, you now use the Find command to locate a text item. You'll then discover that these keystrokes and buttons no longer navigate through comments but rather move though instances of your search text. To resume browsing through comments using the keystrokes or browse buttons, you'll need to reopen the Go To tab and use it to go to at least one comment (or, you could use the Select Browse Object button described in the next section to reselect the comment browse object).

Navigating with the Browse Buttons

To use the browse buttons to quickly locate various types of objects within your documents, perform the following steps:

1   If the vertical scroll bar isn't displayed, choose Tools, Options, click the View tab, and check the Vertical Scroll Bar option. You'll find the three browse buttons at the bottom of the vertical scroll bar, as shown here:

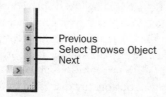

Previous
Select Browse Object
Next

2   If you've previously selected a browse object—search text in the Find tab, a target in the Go To tab, or an object in the Select Browse Object menu (described in the next step)—you can click the Next button to go to the next instance of this object in your document or click the Previous button to go to the Previous instance of the object. The ScreenTips displayed on the Next and Previous buttons indicate your most recently selected browse object. For example, if your most recent browsing action was to use the Find command to search for text, the buttons will be labeled Next Find/Go To and Previous Find/Go To, and they will cause Word to locate the next or previous instance of your search text.

Note that pressing Ctrl+Page Down is equivalent to clicking the Next button, and pressing Ctrl+Page Up is equivalent to clicking the Previous button.

3 If you haven't selected a browse object, or if you want to select a new one, click the Select Browse Object button and choose a target from the menu, shown here:

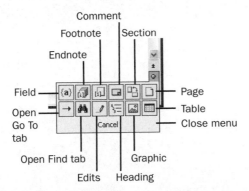

When you choose an object type from the menu (field, endnote, footnote, comment, section, page, edits, heading, graphic, or table) Word will move the insertion point to the next object of that type (the next field, endnote, comment, and so on). You can subsequently use the Next and Previous buttons to navigate to additional objects of the same type.

> **Note** Choosing the Edits browse object moves you through the locations where you've performed your most recent editing or formatting actions, just like the Go Back key (Shift+F5) described in the previous section.

Should you use the browse buttons rather than the Go To command? On the negative side, the browse buttons don't provide some of the targets that the Go To command offers (such as Line and Bookmark). Also, you can't specify a particular item number (for example, you can't go directly to page 25); you can only browse forward or back through the objects. However, the browse buttons are quicker to use. Also, if you've previously used the Find command or the Go To command, you can just click the Next or Previous browse button to instantly go to the next or previous Find or Go To target, without the need to first select a browse object on the menu.

> You can also use hyperlinks as a navigation tool in a document. For information, see "Adding and Using Hyperlinks," on page 580.

Effective Formatting in Word

Directly Formatting a Word
Document 307

Applying Styles and Reusing
Formats. 327

Using the Reveal Formatting Task
Pane to View or Modify Formatting
Features 338

Formatting Your Documents
Automatically 340

Directly Formatting a Word Document

You can directly format a Microsoft Office Word 2003 document at four main levels:

- You can format individual characters—for example, changing the font or making the characters bold or italic. This level of formatting is covered primarily in this chapter.

- You can format individual paragraphs—for example, changing the alignment, indentation, or line spacing. This level of formatting is also covered primarily in this chapter.

- You can format document sections. A *section* is a division of a document that you create specifically for applying unique formatting to that part of the document. The types of formatting that you can apply to document sections include newspaper-style columns, page borders, page numbering, headers and footers, margins, and the page layout. This level of formatting is covered in Chapter 13, "Arranging Text Using Tables, Columns, and Lists," and Chapter 18, "Designing and Printing Professional-Looking Pages."

- You can format the entire document. The types of formatting you can apply to an entire document are the same as those you can apply to individual document sections.

For information on finding and replacing formatting or formatting styles within a document, using the Find command or the Find And Replace command, see "Finding and Replacing Text and Formatting," on page 293.

Tip   Remember the Undo command

As you learn the techniques presented in this chapter, keep in mind that you can reverse the effect of any formatting command by issuing the Undo command using any of the methods discussed in the sidebar "Undoing and Redoing Editing and Formatting Actions," on page 285.

Formatting Characters Directly

Directly applying individual formatting features to characters within your document gives you the finest level of control over character formatting. The paragraph style specifies the predominant character formatting of the paragraph text. You typically apply direct character formatting to one or more characters within a paragraph to emphasize or modify them in some way. For example, you might italicize a word or convert a character to superscript. The character formatting that you directly apply overrides the character formatting that's specified by the paragraph style or by any character style assigned to the text.

Styles are discussed in "Applying Styles and Reusing Formats," on page 327.

Tip Don't overuse direct character formatting

Avoid directly applying character formatting to entire paragraphs or groups of paragraphs. It's better to assign each paragraph a paragraph style that includes the basic character formatting that you want and to use direct character formatting only to modify smaller blocks of text within paragraphs. This approach makes it easier to change the basic character formatting of your text and tends to make your character formatting more consistent throughout the document.

To directly apply character formatting, perform the following steps:

1 Select one or more blocks of text or, to apply the formatting to the text you're about to type, place the insertion point at the position where you want your new text to appear.

For a description of text selection methods, see "Selecting the Text," on page 282.

Tip Format a word without selecting it

To apply character formatting to a word, you can simply place the insertion point anywhere within the word rather than selecting the word. This technique works, however, only if the When Selecting Automatically Select Entire Word option is checked. To access this option, choose Tools, Options and click the Edit tab.

2 Apply the character formatting. Table 12-1 summarizes the different types of character formatting you can apply. For each type, it indicates which of the three basic methods you can use to apply the formatting:

- The Font dialog box, which you open by choosing Format, Font (for details, see "Formatting Characters with the Font Dialog Box," on page 313)

- The Formatting toolbar, which you can display by choosing View, Toolbars, Formatting (for details, see "Formatting Characters with the Formatting Toolbar," on page 317)

- Shortcut keys (for details, see "Formatting Characters with Shortcut Keys," on page 318)

3 If you didn't select characters in step 1, begin typing. The character formatting will be applied to all characters you type until you move the insertion point or press Ctrl+Spacebar or Ctrl+Shift+Z.

> **Note** A newly inserted character normally acquires any directly applied character formatting assigned to the previous character. Or if you type the character at the beginning of a new paragraph, it acquires any directly applied character formatting assigned to the *following* character. However, in either case, this formatting will be removed if you press Ctrl+Spacebar or Crtl+Shift+Z immediately before typing, and it will be overridden by any character formatting you select immediately before typing.

> For information on applying character formatting to handwriting you've inserted into a Word document, see "Entering Handwriting," on page 97.

To remove directly applied character formatting and restore the character format- ting specified by the paragraph's style, select the text and press Ctrl+Spacebar or Ctrl+ Shift+Z. Also, if you're inserting new text, you can press one of these key combinations to discard any directly applied character formatting acquired from the adjoining text. For example, if you're inserting text following an italicized phrase, you can press Ctrl+Spacebar to begin inserting nonitalicized text—assuming the italics were directly applied and aren't part of the paragraph style.

> For information on using Word's Clear Formatting command to remove formatting, see "Removing All Formatting," on page 333.

Table 12-1. Types of Character Formatting You Can Apply to Text

Character Formatting Type	Description	Methods You Can Use to Apply the Formatting
Font		
Font	The general type of the characters: Times New Roman, Arial, Courier New, and so on.	• Font dialog box (Font tab) • Formatting toolbar (Font drop-down list)
Font style	The basic look of the characters: regular, italic, bold, or bold italic.	• Font dialog box (Font tab) • Formatting toolbar • Shortcut keys
Size	The height of the characters, measured in points (1 point = 1/72 inch).	• Font dialog box (Font tab) • Formatting toolbar (Font Size drop-down list) • Shortcut keys (to increase or decrease size)

Chapter 12

309

Table 12-1. Types of Character Formatting You Can Apply to Text

Character Formatting Type	Description	Methods You Can Use to Apply the Formatting
Underline	Character underlining, which can be single, double, thick, dashed, dotted, or in one of many other styles. You can also select Words Only underlining to apply single underlining that skips spaces.	● Font dialog box (Font tab) ● Formatting toolbar (single underline only) ● Shortcut keys (single, double, or Words Only underlining)
Underline color	The color of the underlining. You can select a standard color, create a custom color, or choose Automatic (which uses the Window Font color selected in the Display program of the Windows Control Panel).	● Font dialog box (Font tab)
Color	The color of the characters. You can select a standard color, create a custom color, or choose Automatic (which uses the Window Font color selected in the Display program of the Windows Control Panel).	● Font dialog box (Font tab) ● Formatting toolbar (Font Color drop-down palette)
Effects	Character enhancements: strikethrough, double strikethrough, superscript, subscript, shadow, outline, emboss, engrave, small caps, all caps, and hidden.	● Font dialog box (Font tab) ● Shortcut keys (superscript, subscript, hidden, small caps, or all caps)
Character Spacing		
Scale	The amount by which the characters are increased or decreased in width, expressed as a percentage of the normal character width.	● Font dialog box (Character Spacing tab)
Spacing	The amount added to or subtracted from the intercharacter spacing to produce expanded or condensed text.	● Font dialog box (Character Spacing tab)
Position	Amount by which the characters are raised or lowered from the baseline. (Unlike the subscript or superscript effects, the character size isn't reduced.)	● Font dialog box (Character Spacing tab)

Chapter 12

Table 12-1. Types of Character Formatting You Can Apply to Text

Character Formatting Type	Description	Methods You Can Use to Apply the Formatting
Kerning for fonts	Moving certain character pairs (for example, A and W) closer together.	● Font dialog box (Character Spacing tab)
Other Character Formatting Types		
Animations	Visual special effects displayed by text, such as blinking, shimmering, sparkling, and so on. Intended primarily for regular Word documents that will be read online. Text animation, of course, won't print. If it's applied to a Web page document, it won't be displayed by popular browsers (such as Microsoft Internet Explorer).	● Font dialog box (Text Effects tab) ● To view animated text, the Animated Text option must be checked in the View tab of the Options dialog box (opened by choosing Tools, Options, View)
Language	Controls which dictionary (English, French, or German, for example) the Word proofing tools (such as the spelling and grammar checkers) use to correct the text. Can also be used to exclude text from proofing. The proofing tools are discussed in Chapter 17, "Proofing Word Documents."	● Language dialog box, described in "Marking the Language," on page 505
Borders and shading	Borders around the text and background shading. (Borders and shading can be applied either as a character format to one or more characters or as a paragraph format to one or more entire paragraphs.)	● Borders And Shading dialog box and Tables And Borders toolbar, both discussed in "Adding Borders and Shading," on page 361

To find out what formatting and style (or styles) have been applied to characters in your document, you can use the Reveal Formatting task pane.

> The Reveal Formatting task pane is described in "Using the Reveal Formatting Task Pane to View or Modify Formatting Features," on page 338.

Chapter 12

Tip Control font substitution

If you open a document that contains text in a font that isn't installed on your machine, Word will choose one of your installed fonts and use it to display the text. If you'd rather substitute a different font, choose Tools, Options, click the Compatibility tab in the Options dialog box, and click the Font Substitution button. Then, in the Font Substitution dialog box (shown in Figure 12-1), select the missing font in the Font Substitutions list and select the substitute font that you want to use to display the text in the Substituted Font drop-down list. (The Default choice in the Substituted Font list causes Word to choose the substitute font. When this item is selected, a message near the bottom of the dialog box indicates the particular font that Word chooses.)

Selecting a substitute font doesn't normally change the actual font formatting assigned to text that's formatted with the missing font. Rather, it merely specifies the font that Word uses to display and print that text (in any Word document in the current and in future Word sessions). The original font will still be used if the document is opened on a computer where that font is installed.

If, however, you want to change the actual font formatting assigned to the text, click the Convert Permanently button. In this case, the text will always be displayed and printed using the substitute font, even if the document is later opened on a computer that has the missing font. Note that this will permanently convert *all* missing fonts in the document to their current substitute fonts.

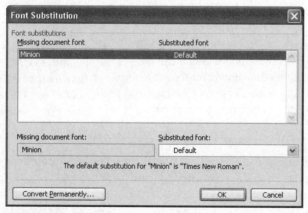

Figure 12-1. The Font Substitution dialog box allows you to temporarily or permanently assign substitute fonts.

Formatting Characters with the Font Dialog Box

To open the Font dialog box, choose Format, Font, or right-click the selected text and choose Font from the shortcut menu. To apply character formatting, click the appropriate tab—Font, Character Spacing, or Text Effects—and select the features you want. The three tabs are shown in Figures 12-2, 12-3, and 12-4. Selecting the formatting you want is easy because the Preview area in all tabs of the Font dialog box shows a text example formatted with the formatting selected in all the tabs.

For tips on entering measurement values into the text boxes of the Font dialog box, see the sidebar "Entering Measurements into Dialog Boxes," on page 316.

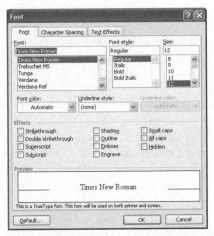

Figure 12-2. The Font tab of the Font dialog box allows you to change many character formatting features.

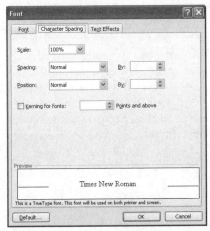

Figure 12-3. The Character Spacing tab of the Font dialog box lets you adjust the spacing and positioning of the selected characters.

Chapter 12

313

Figure 12-4. The Text Effects tab of the Font dialog box allows you to apply text animations to the selected characters.

When the Font dialog box is first displayed, it shows the current formatting of the selected text. If a particular formatting feature varies within the selected text (for example, part of the text is bold and part isn't bold), a text box indicating the formatting will be left blank. Or, if the formatting is selected by checking an option, the check box will contain a square. If you select a formatting option, it will be applied to *all* text in the selection.

> **Note** With a formatting option that you select using a check box in the Font dialog box, a check mark in the box applies the feature to all the selected text, an empty check box removes the feature (if it was originally applied) from all the selected text, and a square in the box leaves the selected text as it was (a square appears only if part of the selected text was originally assigned the formatting feature). Clicking the check box repeatedly cycles through these three states (the third state is available only if the selected text was partially formatted with the feature before you opened the Font dialog box).

Notice that Word displays information on the font that's currently selected in the Font list box on the Font tab. This information is shown at the bottom of the tab and indicates, for example, whether the font is a *TrueType* font. A TrueType font is a scalable font (one that you can make any size) that's installed in Windows. A TrueType font produces high-quality characters on almost any screen or printer and is a good choice if you want to be able to display the characters in a range of sizes or if you want to be able to print your document on a variety of printers.

Clicking the Superscript or Subscript box (also on the Font tab) raises or lowers the text by a standard amount and reduces the character size. To raise or lower the text by any amount without changing its size, click the Character Spacing tab and select either Raised or Lowered in the Position drop-down list (see Figure 12-3). Then enter into the By box the exact amount that the text should be moved, in points (1 point = 1/72 inch).

If you check the Hidden option on the Font tab, you can make the text invisible on the screen or on a printed copy of the document. To control the visibility of hidden text, choose Tools, Options. Hidden text will be visible on the screen only if the Hidden Text or All option is checked on the View tab (or if the Show/Hide ¶ button is selected on the Standard toolbar), and it will be visible on a printed copy of the document only if the Hidden Text option is checked on the Print tab.

Note that the Small Caps and All Caps effects on the Font tab change only the way the text is displayed and printed; they don't change the actual characters stored in the document. Therefore, if you remove the effect, the original capitalization of the text will reappear.

When you specify a value other than 100% in the Scale drop-down list on the Character Spacing tab, you change the width of each character. In contrast, when you select Expanded or Condensed in the Spacing drop-down list, you affect the spaces between the characters, but you leave the widths of the characters themselves unchanged, as shown here:

200% Scale

Expanded Spacing

Checking the Kerning For Fonts option on the Character Spacing tab reduces the spacing between certain character pairs—such as A and W—to give the text a more compact appearance. (In contrast, selecting the Condensed option in the Spacing drop-down list reduces the spacing between all characters in the selected text.) Word performs kerning only on characters that have a size equal to or greater than the size you enter into the Points And Above text box. Also, the selected font must be a TrueType or Adobe Type 1 font.

You can click the Default button, displayed on all tabs of the Font dialog box, to change the default character formatting so that it conforms to the styles that you have selected in the Font, Character Spacing, and Text Effects tabs. Clicking Default (and responding Yes when prompted) assigns the selected formatting to the Normal style of the document and to the Normal style of the template that was used to create the document. (As explained in Chapter 14, "Advanced Word Formatting Techniques," modifying Normal affects all the other styles that are based on Normal.) As a result, whenever you create a new document using this template, the document text will display the new formatting. (Clicking Default will not, however, affect other documents that have already been created using the template.)

Entering Measurements into Dialog Boxes

Some of the text boxes in Word dialog boxes require you to enter measurements (for example, the By boxes following the Spacing and Position drop-down lists on the Character Spacing tab of the Font dialog box). Word displays the current value as a number followed by an abbreviation for the units. If you enter a new value, you should generally use the same units.

For example, consider a box in which Word displays the value 3 pt, meaning 3 points. If you type either **5** or **5 pt** into this box, the value will be changed to 5 points. You can use another unit of measurement, provided that you specify the units. For example, you could type **.05 in** into this box, and the value would be changed to .05 inches. The next time you opened the dialog box, Word would display this value in points—that is, 3.6 pt. (In some cases, Word will adjust the measurement to match its internal rules. For example, text can be raised or lowered only in half-point increments; therefore, in the By box following the Position drop-down list, Word would change .05 in to 3.5 pt.)

Note that you can change the standard units that Word uses for many of the values entered into dialog boxes. To do this, choose Tools, Options. Then click the General tab and select the units you want in the Measurement Units drop-down list.

The following table will help you work with the different units of measurement that Word recognizes:

Units	Abbre-viation	Points	Picas	Lines	Centi-meters	Milli-meters	Inches
Points	pt	1	1/12	1/12	.035	.35	1/72
Picas	pi	12	1	1	.42	4.2	1/6
Lines	li	12	1	1	.42	4.2	1/6
Centimeters	cm	28.35	2.36	2.36	1	10	.39
Millimeters	mm	2.83	.24	.24	.10	1	.04
Inches	in or "	72	6	6	2.54	25.4	1

Troubleshooting

Cannot underline trailing spaces

You want to use one of Word's fancy underlining styles (double, thick, dotted, dashed, wavy, or one of the others) to underline spaces at the end of a line, but Word won't display the underlining.

Word underlines spaces between two characters on a line, but it doesn't underline spaces that occur between the last nonspace character on a line and the end of the line. In the following example, Word underlines the spaces between the e and the x:

Sign here〰〰〰〰〰〰〰〰〰〰〰〰〰〰x

However, if you delete the x, the underlining disappears. To get around this limitation, you can replace the x with a nonbreaking space, which you insert by pressing Ctrl+Shift+Spacebar. Although a nonbreaking space is normally invisible, it's treated as a text character and preserves the underlining, as shown here:

Sign here〰〰〰〰〰〰〰〰〰〰〰〰〰〰

Formatting Characters with the Formatting Toolbar

You can use the buttons on the Formatting toolbar, shown here, to apply character formatting features to the current selection (or to the position of the insertion point).

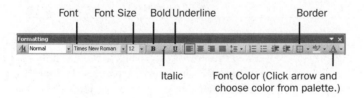

If the formatting applied by a button is currently assigned to all characters in the selection, the button is selected (that is, displayed with a box around it and with a contrasting background color). The Bold, Italic, and Underline buttons *toggle* the formatting, as follows: if the first character of the selection doesn't have the formatting, clicking the button applies the format to all characters. If the first character of the selection already has the formatting, clicking the button removes the formatting from all characters. For example, if you select text in which the first character isn't bold and click the Bold button, all the text will become bold; if you click Bold again, all the text will become nonbold.

Formatting Characters with Shortcut Keys

You can also use the shortcut keys listed in Table 12-2 to apply character formatting to the selected text (or to the position of the insertion point).

Table 12-2. Character Formatting Shortcut Keys

Character Formatting Option	Shortcut Key	Toggles?
Bold	Ctrl+B	Yes
Italic	Ctrl+I	Yes
<u>Underline</u>	Ctrl+U	Yes
<u>Double Underline</u>	Ctrl+Shift+D	Yes
<u>Words</u> <u>Only</u> <u>Underline</u>	Ctrl+Shift+W	Yes
Subscript (P_1)	Ctrl+=	Yes
Superscript (1st)	Ctrl+Shift+=	Yes
Hidden	Ctrl+Shift+H	Yes
SMALL CAPS	Ctrl+Shift+K	Yes
ALL CAPS	Ctrl+Shift+A	Yes
Increase font size to next size in Font Size list	Ctrl+> (that is, Ctrl+Shift+period)	No
Decrease font size to previous size in Font Size list	Ctrl+< (that is, Ctrl+Shift+comma)	No
Increase font size by exactly 1 point	Ctrl+]	No
Decrease font size by exactly 1 point	Ctrl+[	No
Assign Symbol font	Ctrl+Shift+Q	No

The shortcut keys that toggle work as follows: if the first character of the selection doesn't have the formatting, pressing the key applies the format to all characters. If the first character of the selection already has the formatting, pressing the key removes the formatting from all characters. For example, if you select text in which the first character isn't bold and press Ctrl+B, all the text will become bold. If you press Ctrl+B again, all the text will become nonbold.

Formatting Paragraphs Directly

Paragraph formatting affects the appearance of entire paragraphs. In general, the best way to format your paragraphs is by applying appropriate styles. Doing so will make your formatting easier to modify and help enhance its uniformity. (If you don't have a suitable style for a particular type of paragraph, you can modify an existing style or define a new one, as explained in Chapter 14.) However, you might want to directly apply paragraph formatting to make an occasional adjustment to the appearance of a paragraph. For example, you might want to center a specific paragraph or increase its left indent. (Directly applied paragraph formatting overrides the formatting specified by the paragraph's style.) Also, even if you use only styles for formatting your paragraphs, you'll need to know the techniques presented here to be able to customize or create styles.

Styles are discussed in "Applying Styles and Reusing Formats," on page 327.

To directly apply paragraph formatting, perform the following steps:

1 To format a single paragraph, place the insertion point anywhere within the paragraph, or select all or part of the paragraph. To format several paragraphs, select at least a portion of each one.

For a description of text selection methods, see "Selecting the Text," on page 282.

2 Apply the paragraph formatting. Table 12-3 summarizes the different types of paragraph formatting you can apply, and for each type it indicates which of the four basic methods you can use to apply the formatting:

- The Paragraph dialog box, which you open by choosing Format, Paragraph (for details, see "Formatting Paragraphs with the Paragraph Dialog Box," on page 323)

- The Formatting toolbar, which you can display by choosing View, Toolbars, Formatting (for details, see "Formatting Paragraphs with the Formatting Toolbar," on page 325)

- The rulers, which you can display by choosing View, Ruler (for details, see "Formatting Paragraphs with the Rulers," on page 326)

- Shortcut keys (for details, see "Formatting Paragraphs with Shortcut Keys," on page 326)

Note When you press Enter within an existing paragraph to create a new paragraph, the new paragraph automatically acquires the paragraph formatting you assigned to the existing paragraph.

Table 12-3. Types of Paragraph Formatting

Paragraph Formatting Type	Description	Methods You Can Use to Apply the Formatting
Indents and Spacing		
Alignment	Justification of the paragraph text: left (text aligned with left indent), right (aligned with right indent), centered (centered between left and right indents), or justified (aligned with both indents).	● Paragraph dialog box (Indents And Spacing tab) ● Formatting toolbar ● Shortcut keys

Chapter 12

Table 12-3. **Types of Paragraph Formatting**

Paragraph Formatting Type	Description	Methods You Can Use to Apply the Formatting
Indentation	Horizontal position of the paragraph text relative to document margins: left indent, right indent, first line indent, or hanging indent. If you're creating a Web page, keep in mind that a negative left or right indent may cause text to be cut off in the browser (because a browser doesn't show the full margin areas).	● Paragraph dialog box (Indents And Spacing tab) ● Formatting toolbar (left indent only) ● Ruler ● Shortcut keys (left or hanging indent only)
Spacing before	Additional space inserted above the paragraph.	● Paragraph dialog box (Indents And Spacing tab) ● Shortcut keys (only to add or remove 12 points of spacing before the paragraph)
Spacing after	Additional space inserted below the paragraph.	● Paragraph dialog box (Indents And Spacing tab)
Line spacing	Height of each line of text in the paragraph—for example, single or double spacing, or an exact line height.	● Paragraph dialog box (Indents And Spacing tab) ● Formatting toolbar ● Shortcut keys (single, 1.5, and double spacing only)
Line and Page Breaks		
Widow/orphan control	Prevents printing the last line of the paragraph by itself at the top of a new page (a *widow*) or printing the first line by itself at the bottom of a page (an *orphan*).	● Paragraph dialog box (Line And Page Breaks tab)
Keep lines together	All lines in the paragraph are printed on the same page—that is, Word does not insert a page break within the paragraph.	● Paragraph dialog box (Line And Page Breaks)

Table 12-3. Types of Paragraph Formatting

Paragraph Formatting Type	Description	Methods You Can Use to Apply the Formatting
Keep with next	Prevents Word from inserting a page break between the paragraph and the next paragraph.	● Paragraph dialog box (Line And Page Breaks)
Page break before	The paragraph is printed at the top of a new page.	● Paragraph dialog box (Line And Page Breaks)
Suppress line numbers	If you apply line numbering to the document, the paragraph is excluded from numbering. (See "Adjusting the Page Layout," on page 541.)	● Paragraph dialog box (Line And Page Breaks)
Don't hyphenate	If you hyphenate the document, the paragraph is excluded from hyphenation. (See "Hyphenating Your Documents," on page 500.)	● Paragraph dialog box (Line And Page Breaks)
Other Character Formatting Types		
Outline level	Converts the paragraph to a heading that you can work with in Outline view.	● Paragraph dialog box (Indents And Spacing tab) Outline level paragraph formatting is discussed in "Changing Outline Levels," on page 422.
Tabs	Position and type of tab stops in effect within a paragraph.	● Ruler ● Tabs dialog box You can set tab stops in the selected paragraph by using the ruler, or by choosing Format, Tabs to open the Tabs dialog box.

Chapter 12

Table 12-3. Types of Paragraph Formatting

Paragraph Formatting Type	Description	Methods You Can Use to Apply the Formatting
Borders and shading	Borders around the text and background shading. Borders and shading can be applied either as a character format to one or more characters or as a paragraph format to one or more entire paragraphs.	● Borders And Shading dialog box ● Tables And Borders toolbar Using the Borders And Shading dialog box or the Tables And Borders toolbar to apply borders or background shading to paragraphs is covered in "Adding Borders and Shading," on page 361.
Bullets and numbering	Automatic display of a bullet character or number for a paragraph in a list.	● Formatting toolbar ● Bullets And Numbering dialog box Using the Formatting toolbar or the Bullets And Numbering dialog box to apply bullets or numbering to paragraphs is covered in "Ordering Text in Bulleted and Numbered Lists," on page 377.

To remove directly applied paragraph formatting and restore the paragraph formatting that's specified by the paragraph's style, select the paragraph or paragraphs as described in step 1, and then press Ctrl+Q. Also, if you press Enter within an existing paragraph to create a new paragraph, you can press Ctrl+Q before typing in the new paragraph to discard any directly applied paragraph formatting acquired from the existing paragraph. For example, if you typed in a heading and assigned it centered alignment, when you press Enter to begin typing in the body text following the heading, you can press Ctrl+Q to discard the centered alignment format (and, as explained earlier in the chapter, you can press Ctrl+Spacebar or Ctrl+Shift+Z to discard any character formatting you directly applied to the heading).

> For information on using Word's Clear Formatting command to remove formatting, see "Removing All Formatting," on page 333.

To find out what formatting and style (or styles) have been applied to characters in your document, you can use the new Reveal Formatting task pane.

The Reveal Formatting task pane is described in "Using the Reveal Formatting Task Pane to View or Modify Formatting Features," on page 338.

Formatting Paragraphs with the Paragraph Dialog Box

To open the Paragraph dialog box, choose Format, Paragraph, or right-click within the selected text, and then choose Paragraph from the shortcut menu. To apply paragraph formatting, click either the Indents And Spacing tab (shown in Figure 12-5) or the Line And Page Breaks tab (shown in Figure 12-6), and then select the features you want. As with the Font dialog box, choosing formatting features in the Paragraph dialog box is easy because Word displays a text example formatted with the selected features in the Preview area of both tabs.

For tips on entering measurement values into the text boxes of the Paragraph dialog box, see the sidebar "Entering Measurements into Dialog Boxes," on page 316.

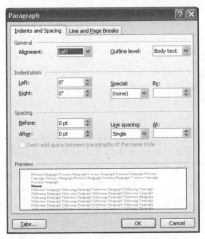

Figure 12-5.   The Indents And Spacing tab of the Paragraph dialog box lets you adjust the alignment, indentation, and spacing of paragraphs.

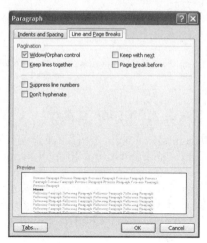

Figure 12-6.   The Line And Page Breaks tab of the Paragraph dialog box allows you to control pagination, line numbering, and hyphenation of paragraphs.

The *left paragraph indent* is the distance that the left edge of the paragraph text is moved in from the left margin area (a positive indent) or out into the left margin area (a negative indent). Likewise, the *right paragraph indent* is the distance the right edge of the text is moved in from the right margin area (a positive indent) or out into the right margin area (a negative indent). The *margins* are the distances between the text and the edges of the page when the indents are set to 0. You set the margins when you adjust the page setup. The easiest way to learn how to use the various indentation settings is to change the values and observe the effects on the preview text.

> Adjusting the page setup is described in Chapter 18. For instructions on setting the document margins and a description of the difference between margins and indents, see "Setting the Margins and Page Orientation," on page 533.

If you select First Line in the Special drop-down list on the Indents and Spacing tab, the first line of the paragraph will be moved to the right of the other paragraph lines (by the amount you enter into the following By text box). If you select the Hanging option in the Special list, all lines except the first will be moved to the right (by the amount you enter into the following By text box).

Line spacing is the total height of each line of text in a paragraph. Table 12-4 shows how to use the options in the Line Spacing drop-down list to achieve various line spacing effects.

Table 12-4. Creating Different Types of Paragraph Line Spacing

To Produce This Line Spacing Effect	Do This Using the Line Spacing Drop-Down List and the At Text Box
Make each line just high enough to accommodate the characters in the line. (If a particular line contains an unusually tall character, that line will be made higher than the others.)	In the Line Spacing drop-down list, select Single.
Make the height of each line 1.5 times its height with Single spacing. (If a particular line contains an unusually tall character, that line will be made higher than the others.)	In the Line Spacing drop-down list, select 1.5 Lines.
Make the height of each line two times its height with Single spacing. (If a particular line contains an unusually tall character, that line will be made higher than the others.)	In the Line Spacing drop-down list, select Double.
Set the *minimum* height of a line. (If a character in a line is taller than this value, the height of that line will be increased.)	In the Line Spacing drop-down list, select At Least and enter the desired line height into the At text box.
Set the *exact* height of each line. (This option makes all lines evenly spaced. However, if a character in a line is taller than the line height specified, it will be cut off.)	In the Line Spacing drop-down list, select Exactly and enter the desired line height into the At text box.
Make the height of each line any multiple of its height with Single spacing. (If a particular line contains an unusually tall character, that line will be made higher than the others.)	In the Line Spacing drop-down select Multiple and enter the desired multiple into the At text box.

Formatting Paragraphs with the Formatting Toolbar

You can use the buttons on the Formatting toolbar, shown here, to apply paragraph formatting features to the currently selected paragraph or paragraphs.

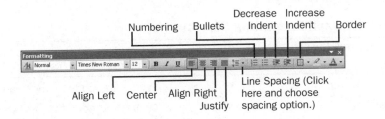

Note   The Decrease Indent and Increase Indent buttons affect the *left* paragraph indent.

Formatting Paragraphs with the Horizontal Ruler

You can also use the horizontal ruler to apply paragraph formatting. If the horizontal ruler isn't displayed, choose View, Ruler. You can also display it temporarily by placing the mouse pointer over the colored band at the top of the document area of the window, as shown here:

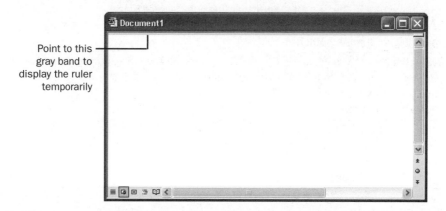

Point to this gray band to display the ruler temporarily

You can use the horizontal ruler to set paragraph indents, as shown here:

Drag to set left indent of first line only.

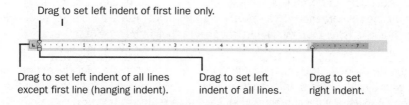

Drag to set left indent of all lines except first line (hanging indent).

Drag to set left indent of all lines.

Drag to set right indent.

The use of the vertical ruler is explained in Chapter 18.

Formatting Paragraphs with Shortcut Keys

You can use the shortcut keys listed in Table 12-5 to quickly apply paragraph formatting to the selected paragraph or paragraphs.

Table 12-5. Paragraph Formatting Shortcut Keys

Paragraph Formatting Action	Shortcut Key	Comment
Increase left paragraph indent	Ctrl+M	Indent is moved to the next tab stop.
Decrease left paragraph indent	Ctrl+Shift+M	Indent is moved to the previous tab stop. You can't use this key to create a negative left indent.

Table 12-5. Paragraph Formatting Shortcut Keys

Paragraph Formatting Action	Shortcut Key	Comment
Increase hanging indent	Ctrl+T	All paragraph lines are indented except the first line. Each time you press the shortcut key, the hanging indent is moved right to the next tab stop.
Decrease hanging indent	Ctrl+Shift+T	Hanging indent is moved left to the previous tab stop.
Add or remove 12 points of extra space above the paragraph	Ctrl+0 (zero at top of keyboard, *not* on numeric keypad)	Toggles feature on or off.
Create single spacing	Ctrl+1 (1 at top of keyboard, *not* on numeric keypad)	Same as Single option in the Paragraph dialog box.
Create 1.5 spacing	Ctrl+5 (5 at top of keyboard, *not* on numeric keypad)	Same as 1.5 Lines option in the Paragraph dialog box.
Create double spacing	Ctrl+2 (2 at top of keyboard, *not* on numeric keypad)	Same as Double option in the Paragraph dialog box.
Left-align paragraph	Ctrl+L	Text is aligned with left indent.
Right-align paragraph	Ctrl+R	Text is aligned with right indent.
Center paragraph	Ctrl+E	Text is centered between left and right indents.
Justify paragraph	Ctrl+J	Text is aligned with both left and right indents. (Word adjusts the character spacing as necessary.)

Applying Styles and Reusing Formats

A style is a named collection of formatting features that you can apply to text in your document. For example, the built-in Normal style supplied with Word consists of the Times New Roman font, a 12-point font size, left paragraph alignment, single line spacing, and widow and orphan control. If you assign the Normal style to a paragraph of text, the text instantly acquires this entire set of formatting features. The advantages of applying a style, rather than assigning individual character and formatting features as described earlier in the chapter, include the following:

- If you want to assign an entire set of formatting features, applying a style can be faster than assigning the individual formatting features one at a time. And you can easily

Chapter 12

assign the style to a toolbar button or shortcut key to make it even faster to apply the features.

- Using styles helps you maintain consistent formatting within a document. For example, to maintain uniform-looking top-level headings in a document, it would be much easier to simply assign all those headings the Heading 1 built-in style, rather than to try to remember the individual formatting features you use for headings and assign them directly. And because a style can be stored in a document template, copied between templates and documents, and shared by members of your workgroup, you can easily maintain consistent formatting within *all* your documents.

- If you use styles, it's much easier to globally modify the format of a particular element. For example, if all the top-level headings in a document have the Heading 1 style, you can quickly reformat all of them by modifying the Heading 1 style, rather than having to find and change each heading separately. You can even apply your modifications to existing or new documents by using the modified Heading 1 style in those documents.

> For information on creating and modifying styles and on copying styles between documents and templates, see Chapter 14.

Word uses four different types of styles:

- **Paragraph styles**   A paragraph style includes both paragraph and character formatting features and applies to one or more entire paragraphs. It fully specifies the format of the paragraph—the font, font size, alignment, and line spacing, plus optional features such as italic characters, an indentation, or widow and orphan control. Every paragraph in a Word document has a paragraph style. The paragraphs in a new document usually have the Normal paragraph style unless you explicitly assign a different one. (Certain templates, however, might create paragraphs assigned other styles, such as Body Text.)

> The methods for applying paragraph styles are covered in "Assigning Paragraph Styles, Character Styles, and Saved Formats," later in this chapter.

- **Character styles**   A character style includes one or more character formatting features and can be assigned to any block of characters. Unlike a paragraph style, a character style doesn't need to fully specify the character format. For example, a particular character style might specify only bold and italic formatting. If you assigned this style to a block of text, Word would remove any directly applied character formatting, apply the bold and italic formats to the text, and preserve all the other character formatting specified by the paragraph style, such as the character font, size, and effects.

> The methods for applying character styles are covered in "Assigning Paragraph Styles, Character Styles, and Saved Formats," later in this chapter. Because Word provides relatively few built-in character styles, the techniques you learn in this chapter won't be truly useful until you learn how to create custom character styles in Chapter 14.

> **Note** If a character style includes formatting that's also part of the paragraph's style, applying the character style can result in turning off the formatting. This happens with optional formatting features that can be turned on or off, such as bold, italic, all caps, and strikethrough. For example, if a character style includes italic, applying the character style to text within a paragraph whose style also includes italic removes the italics. This is in accord with common writing practices; for example, a typical way to emphasize a word within an all-italic heading is to remove the italics from that word.

- **Table styles** A table style includes a set of formatting features and table properties. You can apply a table style to a Word table to quickly change the overall look of the table.

> Table styles are discussed in "Formatting Tables by Applying Table Styles," on page 357.

- **List styles** A list style includes a set of formatting features that create a particular type of outline numbered list (that is, a multilevel numbered or bulleted list).

> List styles are discussed in "Ordering Text in Bulleted and Numbered Lists," on page 377.

Word provides an alternative to defining and using styles: *automatically saved formats*. Whenever you apply a unique set of formatting features to a block of text in a document, Word automatically saves a description of that format combination and lists it along with your available styles (in the Styles And Formatting task pane and in the Style drop-down list on the Formatting toolbar, which is described in the following sections). You can later apply one of these saved formats to additional text in the document in the same way you would apply a style.

> **Note** Word saves and displays saved formats only if the Keep Track Of Formatting option is checked. To access this option, choose Tools, Options and click the Edit tab.

Saved formats offer some of the advantages of styles. Primarily, you can use them to maintain consistent document formatting. Consider, for example, that you type the first top-level heading into a new document and then directly apply a bold, 16-point font to the whole paragraph, together with centered alignment. Word will automatically save the format and list its description ("16 pt, Bold, Centered") together with your styles. When you type another top-level heading later in the document, you can simply apply this saved format rather than trying to remember the different formatting features you used previously and apply them individually.

> The methods for applying your saved formats are discussed in the "Assigning Paragraph Styles, Character Styles, and Saved Formats," later in this chapter.

Chapter 12

Inside Out

The limitations of saved styles

Although saved formats eliminate the need to define styles and are thus somewhat more convenient, they aren't as easy to use as styles (once the styles are defined), nor are they as effective as styles at maintaining formatting consistency. First, because saved formats don't have names that indicate their purposes as styles do (such as Heading 1, Body Text, and List Bullet), it can be difficult to pick the appropriate one; and the more saved formats you accumulate, the harder it becomes. Also, because you can't store saved formats in templates or copy them between documents and templates (as you can with styles), they don't help you maintain formatting consistency among the separate documents that you or your workgroup create. So if you find yourself repeatedly reusing the same set of formatting features, it's best to define a new style, as explained in Chapter 14.

Checking the Consistency of Your Formatting

If the Keep Track Of Formatting option is checked (enabling saved formats, as discussed in the previous section), you can also check the Mark Formatting Inconsistencies option, which turns on Word's *formatting consistency checker*. (You access both options by choosing Tools, Options and clicking the Edit tab.) If the formatting consistency checker is on, as you type in and format your document, Word will display a wavy, blue underline under any text it considers inconsistently formatted with the rest of the document. To change the formatting—or to have Word ignore the inconsistency—right-click the underlined text and choose a command from the top of the shortcut menu shown here:

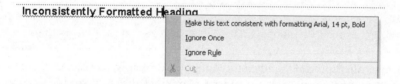

Assigning Paragraph Styles, Character Styles, and Saved Formats

To apply paragraph or character style, or a saved format, to text in your document, perform the following steps:

1   Select the text as follows:

- To apply a paragraph style (or a saved format containing paragraph formatting) to a single paragraph, place the insertion point anywhere within the paragraph. To apply the style or saved format to several paragraphs, select at least a portion of all of the paragraphs. To apply the style or saved format to a new paragraph that doesn't yet contain text, place the insertion point before the paragraph mark for that paragraph (you can do this whether or not the paragraph mark is visible).

■ To apply a character style (or a saved format containing only character formatting), select the text. Or, to apply the style or saved format to the text you're about to type, place the insertion point at the position where you want to insert the text.

Tip **Apply a style to a word without selecting it**

To apply a character style (or a saved format containing only character formatting) to a single word, you can place the insertion point anywhere within the word rather than selecting the word. This technique works, however, only if the When Selecting Automatically Select Entire Word option is checked. To access this option, choose Tools, Options and click the Edit tab.

Styles And
Formatting

2 Choose Format, Styles And Formatting, or click the Styles And Formatting button on the Formatting toolbar. This will open the Styles And Formatting task pane (shown in Figure 12-7).

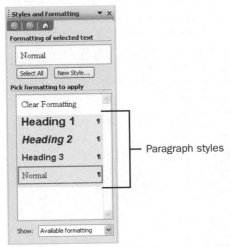

Paragraph styles

Figure 12-7. This figure shows the Styles And Formatting task pane with Available Formatting selected in the Show drop-down list.

3 In the Show drop-down list near the bottom of the task pane, select a category to control the styles that are displayed, as shown here:

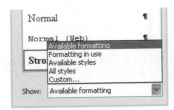

Chapter 12

- To show all styles and saved formats currently used in the document, styles stored in the document, and frequently used heading styles (Heading 1, Heading 2, and Heading 3), select Available Formatting.

- To show all styles and saved formats currently used in the document, select Formatting In Use.

- To show all styles currently used in the document, and frequently used heading styles (Heading 1, Heading 2, and Heading 3), select Available Styles.

- To show all user-defined styles and most built-in styles that are available to the document, but not saved formats, select All Styles.

Note Word displays saved formats only if the Keep Track Of Formatting option is checked. To access this option, choose Tools, Options and click the Edit tab. If the Keep Track Of Formatting option is cleared, the Show drop-down list will omit the Available Formatting option and will replace the Formatting In Use option with the Styles In Use option.

Tip Control which styles are displayed

To specify exactly which styles and saved formats Word displays in the Styles And Formatting task pane, at the bottom of the Show drop-down list, click the Custom item, which opens the Format Settings dialog box (shown in Figure 12-8). Using this dialog box, you'll be able to display some built-in styles that aren't normally shown even if you select the All Styles option in the Show list (such as Caption and Comment Text).

Figure 12-8. The Format Settings dialog box allows you to specify exactly which styles and saved formats Word displays in the Styles And Formatting task pane.

4   To apply a particular style or saved format to the selected text, click the item name in the Pick Formatting To Apply list in the Styles And Formatting task pane. Paragraph and character styles each have a name (such as Heading 2 or Strong). A paragraph style is marked with ¶ and a character style is marked with a. A saved format has a format description (such as "16 pt, Bold, Centered") rather than a name and isn't marked with a symbol. To help you select the appropriate style or saved format, Word displays each item using the item's formatting.

Note Some of the built-in styles are used for standard Word elements. For example, Word automatically assigns the Comment Text style to comment text and the Header style to page headers. You can, however, assign these styles to any paragraphs in your document.

Notice that at the top of the Styles And Formatting task pane, the Formatting Of Selected Text box displays the style or saved format currently assigned to the selected text (or the text containing the insertion point). You can click the down arrow to work with the selection or with other styles, as seen here:

The first two commands on this menu are discussed in the following sections. The New Style and the Modify Style commands, which create a new style or modify an existing one, are discussed in Chapter 14. The Reveal Formatting command displays the Reveal Formatting task pane, explained in "Using the Reveal Formatting Task Pane to View or Modify Formatting Features," on page 338.

Removing All Formatting

To use the Clear Formatting command to remove all formatting from text, perform the following steps:

1   Select the text like this:

- To remove directly applied character formatting or a character style, select the characters with the formatting or style you want to remove, but be sure *not* to select all the text in a paragraph. The Clear Formatting command will then remove all character formatting or a character style and restore the character formatting specified by the paragraph style of the paragraph containing the text.

Chapter 12

Microsoft Office System Inside Out—2003 Edition

That is, Clear Formatting will have the same effect as the Ctrl+Spacebar or Ctrl+Shift+Z shortcut keys.

■ To remove directly applied paragraph formatting plus the paragraph style, place the insertion point within the paragraph or select all text in the paragraph (you don't need to include the paragraph mark). Clear Formatting will then remove all directly applied paragraph formatting, and—if the paragraph has a style other than Normal—it will convert the paragraph's style to Normal. (Also, if you selected all text in the paragraph, any directly applied character format or style will be removed. If you didn't select all text, any directly applied character format or style will be removed from the word containing the insertion point.) Note that Clear Formatting does *not* have the same effect as the Ctrl+Q shortcut key, which removes directly applied paragraph formatting but doesn't remove the style (or directly applied character formats and styles).

> The Ctrl+Spacebar and Ctrl+Shift+Z shortcut keys are described in "Formatting Characters Directly," on page 308.

> The Ctrl+Q shortcut key was explained in "Formatting Paragraphs Directly," on page 318.

2 Issue the Clear Formatting command in one of the following ways:

■ From the Formatting Of Selected Text drop-down menu at the top of the Styles And Formatting task pane (shown in Figure 12-7), choose Clear Formatting.

■ Choose Edit, Clear, Formats.

■ In the Pick Formatting To Apply list in the Styles And Formatting task pane, click the Clear Formatting item, as shown here:

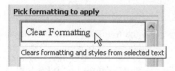

(This item doesn't appear if you selected All Styles in the Show drop-down list.)

■ In the Style drop-down list on the Formatting toolbar, select the Clear Formatting item. (This item doesn't appear if you selected All Styles in the Show drop-down list in the Styles And Formatting task pane.)

> **Note** The Clear Formatting command preserves all hyperlinks in the text, as well as the formatting of the hyperlinks (usually a blue font color with underlining).

Selecting All Text with the Same Style or Formatting

You can instantly select all text throughout the document that has a particular style or saved format. Once you do this, you can apply a new style or saved format to the text, directly apply new formatting, use the Clear Formatting command to remove all formatting from the text, or work with the text in other ways.

To select all text that has the same style or saved format as the current selection, click the Select All button near the top of the Styles And Formatting task pane, or choose Select All *Count* Instances (where *Count* is the number of instances) from the Formatting Of Selected Text drop-down menu shown here:

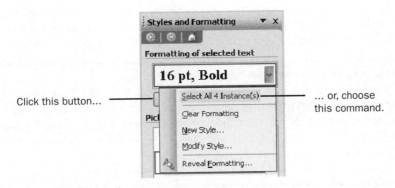

Click this button...   ... or, choose this command.

To select all text that has one of the styles or saved formats listed in the Pick Formatting To Apply list in the Styles And Formatting task pane, click the down arrow next to the style or saved format and choose the Select All *Count* Instances command, as seen here:

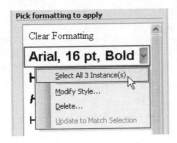

(If no instances of the style or saved format are in the document, the command will be disabled.)

For example, if you've been using a particular saved format (for instance, "16 pt, Bold, Centered") to consistently format your top-level headings throughout a document, but then decide you'd like to globally change the font size to 18 points, you could select all text that has this saved format and then directly apply an 18-point font size (using the Font dialog box or the Font Size drop-down list on the Formatting toolbar). This would reformat all your headings and also update the saved format description in the Styles And Formatting task pane.

> For information on using Word's Find or Replace command to globally select or reformat all text with a particular format or style, see "Finding and Replacing Text and Formatting" on page 293. For a description of the commands in the Styles And Formatting task pane that are used to create, modify, or delete styles, see Chapter 14.

Working with Paragraph Styles

When you press Enter at the end of a paragraph, the new paragraph that's inserted generally has the same style as the previous paragraph. Some styles, however, are defined so that the new paragraph has a different style. For example, if you press Enter while in a paragraph with the default Heading 1 style, the new paragraph will be assigned the Normal style.

> **Tip**   Use the body text style for more formatting control
>
> If you use the Body Text style—rather than Normal—for the body text in your document, you'll be able to easily modify the formatting of the body text without altering other text in your document. Changing Normal alters most other paragraph styles as well, because these styles are *based on* Normal. In contrast, other styles aren't commonly based on Body Text. This topic is discussed fully in Chapter 14.

> **Tip**   Take advantage of the predefined heading styles
>
> Use the predefined styles Heading 1 through Heading 9 for the headings in your document whenever possible. Not only do these styles provide appropriate and consistent formatting for various levels of headings, but also using them allows you to view the organization of your document in Outline view, to navigate quickly through your document with the Document Map, and to generate tables of contents easily.
>
> Additionally, when you drag the scroll box on the vertical scroll bar, Word will display the text of each heading to make it simpler to find the desired location in your document. (Headings, outlines, the Document Map, and tables of contents are covered in Chapter 15, "Managing Large or Complex Documents.")

Assigning Styles and Saved Formats Using the Formatting Toolbar

An alternative way to apply a style or saved format is to select it from the Style drop-down list on the Formatting toolbar (or by typing the style name or the saved format description into the box at the top of the list), as shown here:

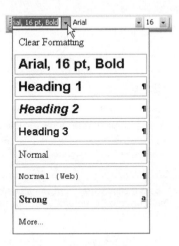

The drop-down list displays the same set of styles and saved formats that are currently displayed in the Styles And Formatting task pane. If this task pane isn't currently displayed, you can select the More item at the bottom of the Styles list to display the task pane, thereby accessing additional styles and saved formats. Also, if you press Shift when you open the Style drop-down list, the list will show all styles (although not saved formats).

Assigning Styles Using Shortcut Keys

Word provides the shortcut keys shown in Table 12-6 for applying several of the built-in paragraph styles.

Table 12-6. Shortcut Keys for Applying Common Paragraph Styles

To Apply This Style	Press This Shortcut Key
Normal	Ctrl+Shift+N
List Bullet	Ctrl+Shift+L
Heading 1	Alt+Ctrl+1
Heading 2	Alt+Ctrl+2
Heading 3	Alt+Ctrl+3

For details on defining your own shortcut keys for quickly applying any styles, see "Defining Shortcut Keys (Word Only)," on page 222, and "Inserting Symbols and Foreign Characters," on page 260.

Chapter 12

Troubleshooting

Formatting changes mysteriously

You have your document formatted the way you want it. However, as you work on the document, you notice certain formatting features changing by themselves.

The following Word options can cause automatic formatting changes in a document:

- If the Automatically Update feature is enabled for a particular paragraph style, when you make changes to text that's assigned that style, Word will automatically update the style and all text throughout the document that's assigned that style.

- If the Automatically Update Document Styles option is enabled for the document, whenever you or a co-worker updates a style within your document's template, the next time you open the document Word will update the style in the document to match.

For information on the Automatically Update feature, see "Customizing Styles Using the Modify Style Dialog Box," on page 394. For information on the Automatically Update Document Styles option, see "Copying Styles from a Template to a Document," on page 406.

Using the Reveal Formatting Task Pane to View or Modify Formatting Features

Word's Reveal Formatting task pane lets you view a detailed description of the formatting of any text in your document. It describes directly applied character and paragraph formatting features, as well as formatting features defined by the paragraph style or by the character style (if any) that's assigned to the text. You can also use this task pane to modify or clear formatting, to compare the formatting of different selections, or to find blocks of text with similar formatting.

To use the Reveal Formatting task pane, perform the following steps:

1. Select the text you want to examine or reformat. To examine the formatting of a single word, you can just place the insertion point within that word.

2. Choose Format, Reveal Formatting or press Shift+F1 to display the Reveal Formatting task pane (shown in Figure 12-9).

Figure 12-9. Here, the Reveal Formatting task pane shows the formatting features of a paragraph that's been assigned the built-in Heading 1 style.

3 To work with the formatting of the selection, do one or more of the following:

- To modify the formatting of the selection, click one of the underlined commands in the format description, as shown here:

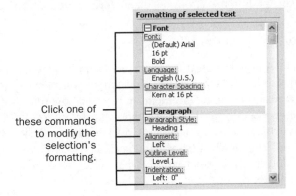

For example, clicking Font opens the Font dialog box for changing the character formatting; clicking Language opens the Language dialog box for setting the text's language; clicking Alignment, Outline Level, Indentation, or Spacing opens the Paragraph dialog box for setting the paragraph formatting; and clicking Character Style or Paragraph Style opens the Style dialog box, where you can apply a character style or change the paragraph style.

- To view a feature-by-feature comparison of the selection's formatting with the formatting of another block of text, check the Compare To Another Selection option and then select the other block of text.

- To work with the selected text in other ways, click the down arrow in the Selected Text box and choose a command from the drop-down menu shown here:

Chapter 12

339

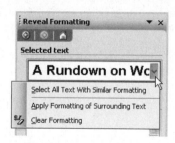

Formatting Your Documents Automatically

Word provides a number of tools that automatically format documents in various ways. Although you will probably discover a few useful automatic formatting features, in general, these tools are not for the Microsoft Office 2003 Edition expert. The automatic formatting features can help an Office beginner get started. However, once you learn the manual formatting skills explained earlier in this chapter (and in Chapter 14), you'll probably find the manual formatting methods easier to use, less frustrating, and much more precise than the automatic formatting tools. Also, some of the automatic tools can literally wreak havoc on formatting that you've already carefully applied using the more exacting manual methods. If you're creating Office documents in a workgroup, you'll probably also need to rely mainly on the manual formatting methods to make your document formatting conform to the workgroup's standards.

Here's a summary of Word's automatic formatting tools:

- **AutoFormat** The AutoFormat feature uses a set of simple rules to apply appropriate, built-in paragraph styles to the paragraphs throughout your document. You can also have AutoFormat make certain replacements in your document text—for example, it can replace straight quotes (" ") with smart (that is, curly) quotes (" "). To control the way AutoFormat works, choose Tools, AutoCorrect Options and click the AutoFormat tab in the AutoCorrect dialog box (shown in Figure 12-10). To have AutoFormat format your document, choose Format, AutoFormat, select the desired options in the AutoFormat dialog box (shown in Figure 12-11), and click OK.

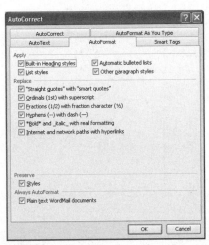

Figure 12-10. The AutoFormat tab of the AutoCorrect dialog box allows you to select options that affect the way AutoFormat works.

Figure 12-11. You use the AutoFormat dialog box to run the AutoFormat feature.

● **AutoFormat As You Type** The AutoFormat As You Type feature automatically makes formatting changes as you type in your document text. You can have it make text replacements (for example, change fractions like 1/2 to single-character fractions like ½), apply paragraph styles (for instance, apply built-in heading styles to document headings), and perform other automatic changes. To control the specific changes this feature makes, choose Tools, AutoCorrect Options and click the AutoFormat As You Type tab (shown in Figure 12-12). To turn AutoFormat As You Type completely off, you need to clear all check boxes on this tab.

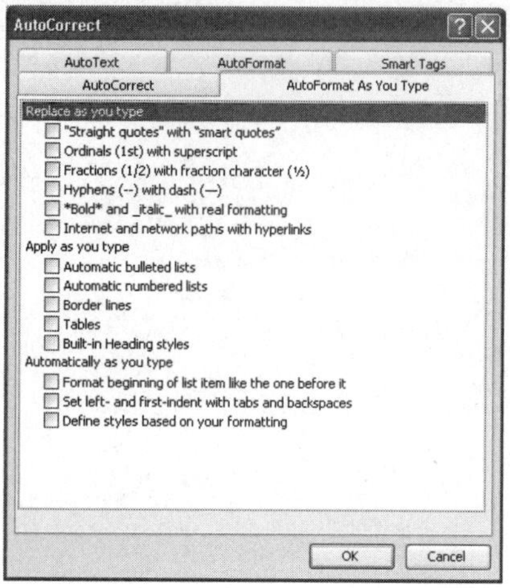

Figure 12-12. The AutoFormat As You Type tab of the AutoCorrect dialog box allows you to control the changes made by the AutoFormat As You Type feature.

● **Themes**   A theme is a predesigned visual scheme that applies consistent formatting to elements throughout a document. You use a theme by choosing Formatting, Theme. Themes are primarily useful for formatting Web pages.

Themes are covered in "Applying a Web Page Theme," on page 592.

● **Style Gallery**   The Style Gallery lets you copy the styles from any document template into your current document, instantly changing the overall document formatting. You should use the Style Gallery only after you have already applied appropriate styles to various document elements, such as headings, lists, and body text. The Style Gallery will then replace each of these styles with the same-named style from a different template, quickly (but somewhat dangerously) altering your document's overall appearance. To use the Style Gallery, choose Format, Theme and click the Style Gallery button at the bottom of the Theme dialog box. Then, in the Style Gallery dialog box (shown in Figure 12-13), select a template and click OK.

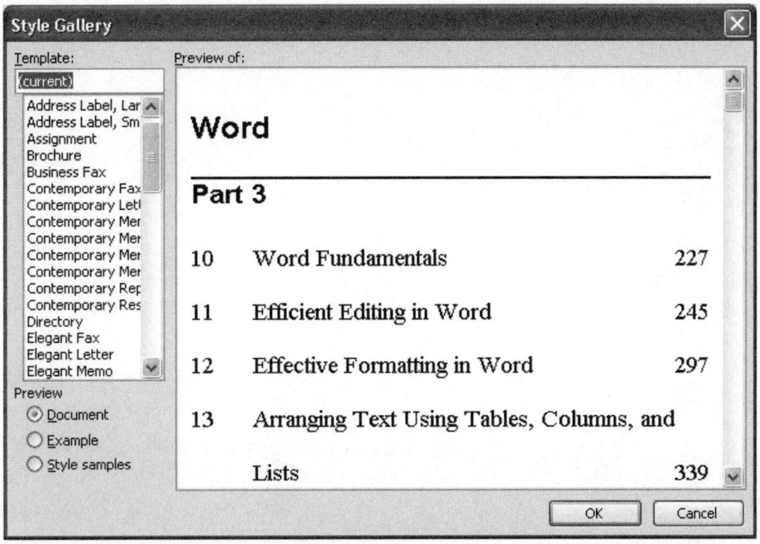

Figure 12-13. The Style Gallery dialog box lets you change a document's overall formatting by copying styles from a template.

Arranging Text Using Tables, Columns, and Lists

Arranging Text with Tables 345
Adding Borders and Shading 361
Arranging Text in Newspaper-Style
Columns 371

Ordering Text in Bulleted and
Numbered Lists 377
Sorting Lists and Tables 384

Arranging Text with Tables

A Microsoft Office Word 2003 *table* is a highly versatile tool for arranging text in rows and columns. Figure 13-1 shows a Word table as it appears on the screen. Using a table offers many advantages over arranging text using tab characters or other methods. For example, if a particular text item doesn't fit on a single line, Word automatically creates a new line and increases the height of the row. (The table shown in Figure 13-1, for instance, would be difficult to create using tabs.) Also, when you use tables, you can easily rearrange and adjust the size of the rows and columns, and you can emphasize table items by using borders and background shading.

Paragraph formatting action	Shortcut key	Comment
To increase left paragraph indent	Ctrl+M	Indent is moved to the next tab stop.
To decrease left paragraph indent	Ctrl+Shift+M	Indent is moved to the previous tab stop. This key cannot be used to create a negative left indent.
To increase hanging indent	Ctrl+T	All paragraph lines are indented except the first line. Each time you press the shortcut key, the hanging indent is moved right to the next tab stop.
To decrease hanging indent	Ctrl+Shift+T	Hanging indent is moved left to the previous tab stop.
To add or remove 12 points of extra space above the paragraph	Ctrl+0 (zero at top of keyboard, *not* on numeric key pad)	Toggles feature on or off.

Figure 13-1. This figure shows a Word table as it appears on the screen.

Creating a Table

To construct a table at the position of the insertion point, perform the following steps:

1 Point to the Insert Table button on the Standard toolbar, shown here:

2 Press the left mouse button and drag down and to the right to select the number and arrangement of table cells that you want, as seen here:

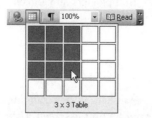

The new table will consist of rows and columns of empty *cells*. The lines defining these cells are known as *gridlines* and they can be shown in a variety of ways. The gridlines in a newly created table are usually marked with thin, solid *borders*. A border is a line that's visible on the screen in Word, on a printed copy of the document, and on a Web page document viewed in a browser. (You can also add borders to paragraphs and other objects.) As explained later in this chapter, you can modify or remove one or more borders from a table. If you remove a border, the gridline will be marked with a light gray line that appears on the screen in Word, but it won't be printed or show in a browser. This line will appear on the screen, however, only if the Show Gridlines option is selected on the Table menu.

> For information on adding or modifying borders in tables and applying background shading to tables, see "Adding Borders and Shading," on page 361.

Tip   Don't worry about the number of rows

If you don't know how many rows you'll need when you insert a table, just choose a single row. It's easy to add new rows to the end of a table as you enter the table text by pressing Tab in the last cell. You should, however, try to choose the actual number of columns, because inserting additional columns is not as easy.

Tip   Insert text above a table

If you add a table at the very beginning of a document and then want to insert text above the table, you won't be able to move the insertion point to the necessary position above the table to type the text. To get around this, place the insertion point anywhere in the first row of the table and press Ctrl+Shift+Enter. This will insert a new paragraph above the table. You can then move the insertion point to that paragraph and type text.

Adding Content to a Table

To add text or graphics to a cell in a table, click in the cell and type the text or insert the graphics in the same way that you would in an ordinary paragraph. Notice that if you reach the right border of the cell, Word will wrap the text down to the next line and increase the height of the entire row, if necessary, to accommodate the new text. If you press Enter while typing in a cell, Word will insert a new paragraph *within* the cell. (Each cell contains one or more entire paragraphs.) You can edit and format text within a cell using the standard Word editing and formatting techniques given in the previous chapters.

> **Tip**   **Nest tables for complex layouts**
> You can insert a table within a cell of another table, creating a nested table. To do this, place the insertion point at the position in the cell where you want the nested table and use any of the methods given in this chapter for inserting a table.

To move the insertion point to another cell, click in the cell or use the arrow keys to move the insertion point. To move to the next cell (in row-by-row order) and select any text it contains, press Tab. To move to the previous cell and select any text it contains, press Shift+Tab. When you're in the last cell of the table, pressing Tab adds a new row to the end of the table.

> **Tip**   **Insert tabs in tables**
> To insert a tab character into a table cell, press Ctrl+Tab. You can set the position of tab stops as in a paragraph outside of a table. Watch for one oddity, though—if you set a decimal tab, the text in the cell is moved to that tab stop without you manually inserting a tab character in front of it.

Adding and Removing Table Cells, Rows, and Columns

To insert or delete rows, columns, or groups of cells, you must first select the appropriate portion of the table. You can easily select a cell, row, or column as shown here:

Click here to select a single cell.

Units	Abbreviation	Points	Picas	Centimeters	Inches
Points	pt	1	1/12	.035	1/72
Picas	pi	12	1	.42	1/6
Centimeters	cm	28.35	2.38	1	.39
Inches	in *or* "	72	6	2.54	1

Click here to select a row.

Units	Abbreviation	Points	Picas	Centimeters	Inches
Points	pt	1	1/12	.035	1/72
Picas	pi	12	1	.42	1/6
Centimeters	cm	28.35	2.38	1	.39
Inches	in *or* "	72	6	2.54	1

Click here to select a column ————

Units	Abbreviation	Points	Picas	Centimeters	Inches
Points	pt	1	1/12	.035	1/72
Picas	pi	12	1	.42	1/6
Centimeters	cm	28.35	2.38	1	.39
Inches	in or "	72	6	2.54	1

After you have selected a single cell, row, or column, you can drag to select additional cells, rows, or columns. Alternatively, you can select any block of cells by placing the insertion point within a cell and then pressing an arrow key while holding down Shift. You can select the entire table by placing the insertion point anywhere within it and pressing Alt+5 (the 5 on the numeric keypad with Num Lock off).

To add entire rows or columns to an existing table, perform the following steps:

1 To insert rows at a particular position in a table, select existing rows just below that position; select the same number of rows as the number you want to add, as in this example:

Row 1		
Row 2		
Row 3		
Row 4		

To insert two rows above row 2, select two rows as shown here.

2 Likewise, to insert columns, select an equal number of columns to the right of the position where you want to add the new ones.

Insert Rows

3 To insert one or more new rows at the bottom of a table, you can place the insertion point immediately below the table without selecting text. (You can also insert a single row at the end of a table by pressing Tab when the insertion point is in the last cell, rather than using this two-step procedure.)

Insert Columns

4 If you're inserting rows, click the Insert Rows button on the Standard toolbar. If you're inserting columns, click the Insert Columns button. If you placed the insertion point immediately below the table, Word will ask how many rows you want to add to the end of the table.

> **Note** The Standard toolbar actually has only one button for table insertion. When one or more entire table rows are selected or the insertion point is immediately below a table, the button's ScreenTip reads Insert Rows. When one or more entire columns are selected, it reads Insert Columns. When one or more entire cells are selected or one or more characters within a cell are selected, it reads Insert Cells. In all other cases, the ScreenTip reads Insert Table and the button inserts a new table (outside of or within an existing table). As the selection changes, the image on the button changes to indicate its function.

Alternatively, you can right-click the selection and choose Insert Rows or Insert Columns from the shortcut menu. (The command on the shortcut menu changes depending on whether you have selected rows or columns.)

After you click the Insert Rows button or choose Insert Rows from the shortcut menu, the example table shown earlier (under step 1) would look like this:

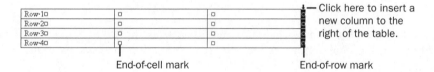

Two new rows have been inserted above row 2.

¶

Show/Hide

Word marks the end of each table cell with an end-of-cell mark and it marks the end of each table row with an end-of-row mark to the right of the row, outside of the table. You can make these marks visible by clicking the Show/Hide ¶ button on the Standard toolbar or check the Show All Formatting Marks option in the Reveal Formatting task pane. In step 1, if you want to insert rows, you must include the end-of-row marks in your selection whether or not they're visible. (Selecting a row by clicking to the left of the row, outside the table, automatically includes the end-of-row mark.) To insert a column at the right end of a table, select the entire column of end-of-row marks, as shown here, before clicking the Insert Columns button. (You can select these marks whether or not they're visible.)

Click here to insert a new column to the right of the table.

End-of-cell mark   End-of-row mark

To insert a block of one or more cells without inserting entire rows or columns, perform the following steps:

1 Select a block of existing cells that has the number and arrangement of the cells you want to insert.

Insert Cells

2 Click the Insert Cells button on the Standard toolbar. Word will display the Insert Cells dialog box, shown in Figure 13-2.

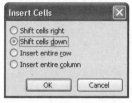

Figure 13-2. The Insert Cells dialog box gives you options for including new cells in a table.

3 Select Shift Cells Right to have Word move the existing cells to the right when it inserts the new cells, or select Shift Cells Down to have it move the cells down. You can also select Insert Entire Row or Insert Entire Column to insert complete rows or columns even though you didn't select complete rows or columns.

349

> **Note** When you have Word move cells down, Word adds extra cells, if necessary, at the bottom of the table to complete the rows.

To delete table rows, columns, or cells, simply select them, right-click the selection, and choose Delete Rows, Delete Columns, or Delete Cells from the shortcut menu. (The command will be labeled according to the current selection.) Alternatively, you can choose Table, Delete, and then choose Rows, Columns, or Cells from the submenu. (You can also choose Table from this submenu to remove the entire table.) If you selected a block that doesn't include complete rows or columns and you choose to delete cells, Word will display the Delete Cells dialog box (shown in Figure 13-3), which lets you specify how the remaining cells are rearranged after the deletion.

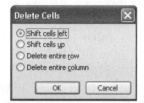

Figure 13-3. The Delete Cells dialog box gives you options when removing cells from a table.

To delete the *contents* of rows, columns, or cells—that is, the text or graphics contained within them—without removing the cells themselves, select the rows, columns, or cells and press Delete.

Resizing Table Cells

You can adjust the width of a table column by dragging its right vertical gridline, as shown here:

To change the
width of this column...   ...drag this vertical gridline.

Units	Abbreviation	Points	Picas	Centimeters	Inches
Points	pt	1	1/12	.035	1/72
Picas	pi	12	1	.42	1/6
Centimeters	cm	28.35	2.38	1	.39
Inches	in *or* "	72	6	2.54	1

To adjust the width of one or more specific cells in a column (rather than the entire column), select the cells before dragging. The cells in a single column can vary in width.

When adjusting the width of a column, you can modify the way Word changes the widths of the cells to the right of the column, if any exist, by pressing additional keys while dragging (see Table 13-1). Of course, if you drag the rightmost vertical gridline in a table, you'll always change the overall table width. (Pressing Ctrl or Shift will have no effect.) Note that if you drag the leftmost vertical gridline in the table, you'll change the indent of the selected rows (or of the entire table if no rows are selected) from the left document margin.

Table 13-1. **Different Ways to Modify Table Column Widths**

To Modify Column Widths Like This	Press This Key While Dragging the Vertical Gridline
Change the width of only the column to the immediate right of the gridline, without changing the overall table width	No key
Display the width of each column in the horizontal ruler while you drag the gridline (has the same effect on column widths as pressing no key)	Alt
Change the width of all cells to the right proportionately, without changing the overall table width (for example, if the cells to the right have equal widths, they will remain equal in width after you drag)	Ctrl
Change the overall table width, rather than changing the widths of the columns to the right	Shift

You can also rapidly adjust the width of one or more cells to accommodate the current contents of the cells. To do this, select the cell or cells and double-click the rightmost vertical gridline of the selection. To adjust one entire column of cells, you can simply double-click the right gridline without selecting cells. Here's an example:

Units	Abbreviation	Points	Picas	Centimeters	Inches
Points	pt	1	1/12	.035	1/72
Picas	pi	12	1	.42	1/6
Centimeters	cm	28.35	2.38	1	.39
Inches	in *or* "	72	6	2.54	1

To have Word adjust the width of this column to accommodate the widest cell entry...

...double-click anywhere on this vertical gridline.

Here's how the example looks after double-clicking:

Units	Abbreviation	Points	Picas	Centimeters	Inches
Points	pt	1	1/12	.035	1/72
Picas	pi	12	1	.42	1/6
Centimeters	cm	28.35	2.38	1	.39
Inches	in *or* "	72	6	2.54	1

(If Word adjusts more than one cell in a particular column, it resizes them equally to accommodate the widest block of text in a cell.) If you later change the contents of a cell, you'll have to readjust the cell or column width.

Alternatively, you can apply the AutoFit command to a table to have Word adjust the widths of all columns to fit the cell contents or the window width and to dynamically maintain the adjustment as you change the contents or window width. To do this, right-click anywhere in the table and choose AutoFit from the shortcut menu to open the submenu shown here:

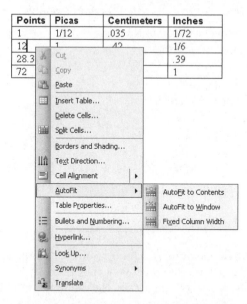

Points	Picas	Centimeters	Inches
1	1/12	.035	1/72
12	1	.42	1/6
28.3			.39
72			1

Then choose one of the three commands, as in Table 13-2.

Table 13-2. Using the Commands on the AutoFit Submenu

To Apply AutoFit Like This	Choose This AutoFit Submenu Command
Have Word immediately adjust the width of each column in the table to accommodate the widest block of text in that column, and then dynamically adjust the column widths to maintain the fit as you add or delete text	AutoFit To Contents
Have Word expand the overall table width, if necessary, so the table fills the entire width of the window, and then dynamically adjust the width to maintain this fit if the window is resized (this command works only when you view the document in the Web Layout view of Word or when you view a Web page document in a browser)	AutoFit To Window
Keep the column widths constant unless you manually adjust them using one of the techniques described previously in this section	Fixed Column Width

Alternatively, you can place the insertion point within the table and choose one of these three commands from the AutoFit submenu on the Table menu.

Word automatically adjusts the height of a table row to accommodate the text contained in the row. You can also manually adjust the height of a row by dragging the horizontal gridline at the bottom of the row. To do this, you must be in Web Layout or Print Layout view. Note that you can't adjust the height of selected cells within a row—you always have to change the height of all the cells in the row.

You can give two or more rows the same height by selecting them, right-clicking the selection, and choosing Distribute Rows Evenly from the shortcut menu. Likewise, you can give two or more columns the same width by selecting them, right-clicking the selection, and choosing Distribute Columns Evenly from the shortcut menu. Note that to use this method, you must select entire rows (including the end-of-row markers) or entire columns.

Alternatively, after you make the selection, you can choose either of these commands from the AutoFit submenu on the Table menu. To make all rows or all columns in the table the same height or width, you can simply place the insertion point within the table and then choose one of these two menu commands.

Move or Resize a Table Quickly

In Web Layout or Print Layout view, you can easily move or resize an entire table by performing the following steps:

1 Hold the mouse pointer over the table until the Move and Resize handles appear, as seen here:

Move handle

Units	Abbreviation	Points	Picas	Centimeters	Inches
Points	pt	1	1/12	.035	1/72
Picas	pi	12	1	.42	1/6
Centimeters	cm	28.35	2.38	1	.39
Inches	in or "	72	6	2.54	1

Handles appear when you point to the table.

Resize handle

2 To move the table to a new position in your document, drag the Move handle.

3 To change the table's overall size and proportions, drag the Resize handle. Word will change the sizes of all the cells in the table proportionately.

Moving and Copying Table Cells, Rows, and Columns

To move rows or columns within a table, select entire rows or entire columns, and then use the mouse to drag them to a new location. The rows or columns will be removed from their current location and inserted into the table at the new location. To copy rows or columns, press the Ctrl key while you drag. When you select rows, you must include the end-of-row marks; otherwise, you'll merely move or copy the contents of the cells.

Changing the Text Orientation and Alignment in a Table Cell

You can modify the orientation of the text in a table cell so that rather than the text reading from left to right, it reads from bottom to top or top to bottom. You might want to do this to make information fit into a particular table or to improve a table's appearance or readability. If you're creating a Web page, however, keep in mind that a browser will ignore vertical text and will display the text in the conventional left-to-right orientation.

To change the text orientation within a table, select one or more cells, right-click within the selection, and choose Text Direction from the shortcut menu. (To change a single cell, you can right-click within the cell without selecting it.) Then select the desired orientation by clicking one of the three options in the Orientation area of the Text Direction dialog box, shown here:

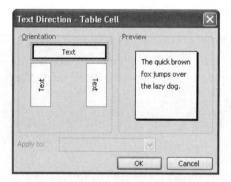

To change the alignment of the text within one or more cells, select them and right-click the selection. (To change a single cell, you can just right-click it.) Then choose Cell Alignment from the shortcut menu and choose an alignment style from the submenu shown here:

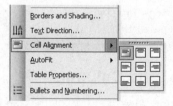

Note that Word creates the horizontal component of the alignment by assigning the Left, Center, or Right paragraph formatting features to the paragraphs in the cell.

Note To use the techniques discussed in this section, the Drag-And-Drop Text Editing option must be checked. To locate this option, choose Tools, Options, and click the Edit tab.

To move the contents of table cells, select the cells and drag them to a new location in the table. Word will delete the contents of the cells you selected (leaving empty cells behind) and it will insert these contents into the cells at the target location, overwriting the current contents of the target cells. To copy the contents of table cells, press the Ctrl key while you drag. To move or copy cell contents, you must not select entire columns. You can select entire rows as long as you don't include the end-of-row marks.

You can also move or copy text from one cell to another without overwriting the contents of the second cell. To move text this way, select only the text within the first cell (rather than selecting the entire cell), and then drag the selection to the new location. Press Ctrl while you drag to copy. The moved or copied text will be added to the contents of the second cell.

Creating Tables with the Table Drawing Tools

Tables And Borders

Another way to insert a table is to interactively draw it, in much the same way that you would draw lines or rectangles in a drawing program. To draw a table, choose Table, Draw Table, or click the Tables And Borders button on the Standard toolbar. When you choose Draw Table or click the Tables And Borders button, Word does the following:

- If you're in Normal view, Word switches to Print Layout view. (You must be in either Print Layout or Web Layout view to draw a table. If you're currently in Outline view, you must manually switch to one of these views.)

- Word displays the Tables And Borders toolbar, which provides buttons for working with tables, borders, and shading. This toolbar is shown in Figure 13-4.

- Word selects the Draw Table button on the Tables And Borders toolbar, which converts the mouse pointer into a pencil and switches to table-drawing mode. (Clicking the Draw Table button toggles this mode on or off.)

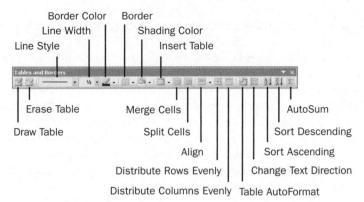

Figure 13-4. The Tables And Borders toolbar provides buttons for working with tables, borders, and shading.

To create a table, perform the following steps:

1 Place the pencil-shaped pointer at one corner of the position in your document where you want to insert the table, press the mouse button, and drag the pointer to the opposite corner. (If you don't have the pencil pointer, click the Draw Table button on the Tables And Borders toolbar.) The rectangle you draw defines the outside gridlines of the table, which will initially consist of a single cell, as seen here:

Click here to start drawing the table

Then, drag to draw the outside gridlines of the table

If you draw the gridlines around an existing paragraph of text, that paragraph will be included within the table cell.

2 You can divide the table into any number of cells by using the mouse to draw internal cell gridlines. Drag the pencil-shaped pointer to draw each gridline, as shown here:

Table drawn in step 1

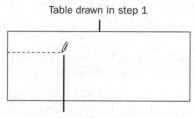

Dragging to add a gridline that divides the table into separate cells

3 To remove a table gridline, click the Eraser button on the Tables And Borders toolbar, which changes the mouse pointer to an eraser. Then click the gridline. When you press the mouse button, the gridline will be highlighted, and when you release the mouse button, the gridline will be removed. To erase several gridlines at once, you can use the eraser-shaped pointer to drag a selection rectangle around the gridlines. As you drag, all gridlines that will be removed (those that are partially or completely within the selection rectangle) will be highlighted; when you release the button, they will be removed. Note that if you attempt to remove a gridline that can't be removed (for example, one of the gridlines on the outside of the table), Word will only remove the border, if any, that's assigned to the gridline. When you're finished removing gridlines, click the Eraser button again to deselect it.

Tip Remove a gridline while drawing

When the Draw Table button is selected and you have the pencil-shaped pointer, you can press Shift to temporarily convert the pointer to an eraser for conveniently removing one or more gridlines. When you release Shift, the pointer will change back to a pencil and you can continue drawing gridlines.

When you draw a table, the way the gridlines are marked depends on the current selections in the Line Style, Line Weight, and Border Color buttons on the Tables And Borders toolbar. If you choose No Border in the Line Style drop-down list, the gridlines will be marked with light gray lines, provided that the Show Gridlines option on the Table menu is selected. These lines will appear on the screen in Word but won't be printed and won't be visible in a browser. If you choose a border style in the Line Style list (such as a single, double, or dotted line), the gridlines will be marked with borders that appear on the screen in Word, on a printed copy, and in a Web browser. The appearance of these borders will be affected by the current settings in the Line Weight and Border Color buttons.

In "Adding Borders and Shading," on page 361, you'll learn how to add, modify, or remove borders in a table you have already drawn and also how to apply shading to table cells. Borders and shading are discussed in a separate section because you can apply them to text outside of tables, as well as to tables.

Inside Out

Set the properties *before* applying borders

Changing a setting in the Line Style, Line Weight, or Border Color button affects only the table gridlines that you subsequently draw or redraw with the mouse (or borders that you subsequently apply using the Border button). It *doesn't* affect table gridlines that you have already drawn even if the cells are selected.

As you can see in Figure 13-4, the Tables And Borders toolbar provides a number of buttons that you can use for modifying existing tables. You might therefore want to display this toolbar whenever you work with tables, even if you don't use the mouse to draw the table.

Formatting Tables by Applying Table Styles

You can instantly change a table's overall appearance by applying one of the built-in table styles provided with Word. Applying an appropriate style can make your table stand out on the page, rendering it both more attractive and easier to read. A table style can apply borders and background shading to the table itself and character formatting features to the text within the table. Figures 13-5 and 13-6 show a table (one used in previous examples in this chapter) formatted with two of the built-in styles, giving you an idea of the range of effects you can achieve.

Units	Abbreviation	Points	Picas	Centimeters	Inches
Points	pt	1	1/12	.035	1/72
Picas	pi	12	1	.42	1/6
Centimeters	cm	28.35	2.38	1	.39
Inches	in *or* "	72	6	2.54	1

Figure 13-5. This table was formatted with the Table 3D Effects 2 built-in table style.

Units	Abbreviation	Points	Picas	Centimeters	Inches
Points	pt	1	1/12	.035	1/72
Picas	pi	12	1	.42	1/6
Centimeters	cm	28.35	2.38	1	.39
Inches	in *or* "	72	6	2.54	1

Figure 13-6. This table was formatted with the Table Columns 3 built-in table style.

The following procedure is the fastest way to apply a table style to a table:

1 Place the insertion point within the table.

2 Choose Table, Table AutoFormat.

3 Select a style in the Table Styles list in the Table AutoFormat dialog box (shown in Figure 13-7).

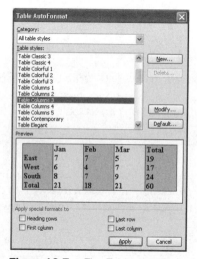

Figure 13-7. The Table AutoFormat dialog box allows you to apply a style to a table.

4 Select any other options you want in the Table AutoFormat dialog box and click the Apply button. To help you make your choices, the dialog box displays a table in the Preview area that shows the effect of the currently selected style and options.

> You can create, remove, or customize a table style by clicking the New, Delete, or Modify button in the Table AutoFormat dialog box, or by using the Styles And Formatting task pane. These techniques are discussed in Chapter 14, "Advanced Word Formatting Techniques."

If you want to reuse a particular style, click the Default button in the Table AutoFormat dialog box to make that style the default (either for the current document or for all documents you create based on the document's template). Word will then automatically apply that style whenever you create a new table using the Insert Table button on the Standard toolbar or the

Insert Table dialog box (opened by choosing Table, Insert, Table). The style won't be applied to tables that you draw using the Tables And Borders toolbar.

> **Note** Because table styles are standard Word styles, you can also apply them using the Styles And Formatting task pane or the Style drop-down list on the Formatting toolbar. In these places, a table style is marked with this icon:
>
> ⊞

> For information on applying and modifying individual table borders, as well as background shading, see "Adding Borders and Shading," on page 361.

Using Other Methods for Creating and Modifying Tables

The previous sections have focused on working with tables using the Standard toolbar, mouse, and shortcut menus. In general, these interactive methods are the fastest and most convenient. The Table menu provides alternative methods for inserting and modifying tables; it also allows you to perform some additional table operations not possible using the interactive techniques. Table 13-3 summarizes the ways you can work with tables using these commands. Keep in mind that for many of these commands, merely placing the insertion point within a table, row, column, or cell is equivalent to selecting that element.

> **Note** You can perform some of the commands listed in Table 13-3 by right-clicking a table—or a selection within a table—and choosing the command from the shortcut menu.

Table 13-3. Tasks You Can Perform Using the Table Menu

To Perform This Task	Do This on the Table Menu
Draw a table using the mouse, as explained in "Creating Tables with the Table Drawing Tools," on page 355.	Choose the Draw Table command.
Insert a new table into a document or into a table cell, insert columns (to the left or right of the selection), insert rows (above or below the selection), or insert cells (specifying the direction in which the existing cells will be shifted). The effects of these commands depend on the current selection or position of the insertion point.	Choose the appropriate command from the Insert submenu.
Delete the selected cells, columns, rows, or the entire table.	Choose the appropriate command from the Delete submenu.
Select the column(s), row(s), cell(s), or the entire table containing the insertion point or selection.	Choose the appropriate command from the Select submenu.
Combine selected adjacent cells into a single cell.	Choose the Merge Cells command.
Divide the selected cell (or each cell in a group of selected cells) into two or more cells. You can specify the resulting number of rows and columns of cells.	Choose the Split Cells command.

Table 13-3. Tasks You Can Perform Using the Table Menu

To Perform This Task	Do This on the Table Menu
Divide a table into two separate tables and insert a regular (Normal style) paragraph between the two tables. The division occurs above the selected row.	Choose the Split Table command (or press Ctrl+Shift+Enter).
Instantly modify the selected table's overall look by applying a table style, as explained in the previous section.	Choose the Table AutoFormat command.
Apply the AutoFit command to the selected table or distribute rows or columns evenly. (These features were described in "Resizing Table Cells," on page 350.)	Choose the appropriate command from the AutoFit submenu.
Mark the selected row or rows at the top of a table as a heading. If a page break occurs within a table, Word repeats the heading row(s) at the top of the next page.	Choose the Heading Rows Repeat command.
Convert the selected table to text (removes the table and converts the text it contains to ordinary paragraphs) or convert selected text outside a table to a table (creates a new table and inserts the selected text into the table).	Choose Text To Table or Table To Text from the Convert submenu.
Sort the contents of the selected rows and columns within a table. If the selection is outside a table, the command sorts paragraphs of text. For information on this command, see "Sorting Lists and Tables," on page 384.	Choose the Sort command.
Insert a formula into a table cell. A formula displays the result of a mathematical computation on numbers within table cells. This command lets you create a Word table that functions as a simple spreadsheet.	Choose the Formula command and type or select the formula you want in the Formula dialog box (shown in Figure 13-8).
Mark the gridlines around cells in all tables using light gray lines. These lines are visible in the Word window only where borders haven't been applied. Unlike borders, they don't print or show in a Web browser. Note that when the option is selected, it's labeled Hide Gridlines; when it isn't selected, it's labeled Show Gridlines.	Choose the Show Gridlines option.
Display the Table Properties dialog box, which allows you to modify the size, alignment, indent, and text-wrapping style of the selected table; the height and page-breaking style of rows; the width of columns; and the width and vertical text alignment style (top, center, or bottom) of the selected cell or cells. By modifying the text-wrapping style, you can have adjoining text outside the table wrap around the table rather than staying above and below it.	Choose the Table Properties command.

Figure 13-8. You use the Formula dialog box to insert a formula that performs a calculation on numbers in a table.

Troubleshooting

Table text is cut off

The text in a table cell is cut off horizontally (that is, you can't see the beginnings or you can't see the endings of the lines). Or it's cut off vertically (that is, you can't see the bottom part of the text).

You won't be able to see the left ends of the lines if the paragraph in a table cell has a negative left indent. You won't be able to see the right ends of the lines if it has a negative right indent. The hidden text will be inaccessible—you won't even be able to scroll to it.

You can remove the negative indents using the techniques discussed in "Formatting Paragraphs Directly," on page 318.

The bottom part of the text in a table row might be cut off (even in the middle of a line of text) if it's assigned an exact height. To remove the exact height setting, right-click in the row, choose Table Properties from the shortcut menu, click the Row tab in the Table Properties dialog box, and select the At Least item in the Row Height Is drop-down list.

Adding Borders and Shading

You can emphasize, organize, or set apart portions of your document by adding borders or background shading to entire tables, to cells within tables, or to blocks of characters or paragraphs outside of tables (see Figure 13-9). You can also have Word print borders around entire pages in your document (see Figure 13-10).

You can apply borders and shading to blocks of characters *within* a paragraph.

You can apply borders and shading to entire paragraphs.

You can apply borders and shading to tables:

Units	Points	Picas	Centimeters	Inches
Points	1	1/12	.035	1/72
Picas	12	1	.42	1/6
Centimeters	28.35	2.38	1	.39
Inches	72	6	2.54	1

Figure 13-9. You can apply borders and shading to a block of characters, a paragraph, or a table.

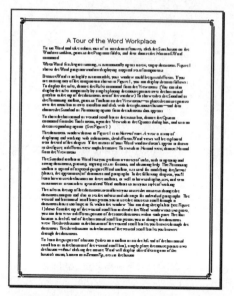

Figure 13-10. You can have Word include borders around a document page.

Note If you create a table using the Insert Table toolbar button or the Table, Insert, Table menu command, it will initially be assigned the borders (and other formatting features) specified by the default table style. If you create a table using the Draw Table button on the Tables And Borders toolbar, you can use any style of borders (or no borders). In the following sections you'll learn how to modify, remove, or add borders to a table that has already been created. Recall also that if you remove a border, Word will mark the cell gridline with a light gray line (which appears on the screen in Word but doesn't print or show in a browser), provided that the Show Gridlines option on the Table menu is selected.

For information on adding borders, background shading, and character formatting to a table by applying a table style, see "Formatting Tables by Applying Table Styles," on page 357.

To apply borders and shading to characters, paragraphs, or tables, you can use either the Tables And Borders toolbar or the Borders And Shading dialog box. To apply borders to pages, you must use the Borders And Shading dialog box.

Note If you're creating a Web page, remember that a browser won't display a border applied to a block of characters (you'll need to apply the border to the entire paragraph). Also, regardless of the line style you assign to a border, a browser will display either single or double solid lines.

Applying Borders and Shading with the Tables And Borders Toolbar

This section explains how to use the Tables And Borders toolbar to apply (or modify) borders or shading around characters, paragraphs, cells within tables, or entire tables. Figure 13-11 shows the Tables And Borders toolbar, labeling each of the buttons that you use for applying borders and shading. Table 13-4 briefly explains the tasks you can perform with these buttons (the following discussion provides more details on using the buttons). If the toolbar isn't visible, you can display it by choosing View, Toolbars, or by right-clicking the menu bar or another toolbar and then choosing Tables And Borders.

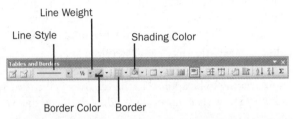

Figure 13-11. You can use these buttons on the Tables And Borders toolbar to apply borders and shading.

Table 13-4. Using the Tables And Borders Toolbar to Apply Borders and Shading

To Do This	Perform This Action on the Tables And Borders Toolbar
Select the style of the borders that you subsequently apply.	Select a style from the Line Style drop-down list or select No Border to remove borders.
Select the thickness of the borders that you subsequently apply.	Select a thickness in points from the Line Weight drop-down list.
Set the color of the borders that you subsequently apply.	Choose a color from the Border Color drop-down palette. Or, to make the border color the same as your current Window Font color (set in the Windows Control Panel), choose Automatic.
Apply or remove border(s). The border(s) will have the features that are currently selected in the Line Style, Line Weight, and Border Color controls.	Click the down arrow on the Border button and choose a border arrangement from the drop-down palette.
Apply or remove background shading.	Click the down arrow on the Shading Color button and choose a color from the drop-down palette, or choose No Fill to remove background shading.

The first step in adding borders or shading is to make an appropriate selection in one of the following ways:

- To add borders or shading to a block of characters, select the characters *without* including the paragraph mark at the end of the paragraph.

- To add borders or shading to one or more entire paragraphs, select the paragraphs. To add borders or shading to a single paragraph, include the paragraph mark in your selection, or place the insertion point anywhere within the paragraph without selecting text.

- To add borders or shading to table cells, select one or more cells. To add borders or shading to the whole table, you must select all cells in the table. To format a single cell, you can just place the insertion point within the cell without selecting any text.

- To add borders or shading to text within a table cell, without assigning borders or shading to the cell itself, select just that text. Note, however, that selecting *all* the text in the cell causes the borders or shading to be applied to the cell, not to the text. To apply a border or shading to all the text, you can temporarily add a character that you leave out of your selection.

Applying Borders

To apply borders to your selection, perform the following steps:

1 From the Line Style, Line Weight, and Border Color drop-down lists or palettes on the Tables And Borders toolbar, select the desired style, thickness, and color of the border or borders you want to apply.

> **Note** Choosing Automatic from the Border Color drop-down palette applies the current Window Font color, which is usually black. You set the Window Font color by running the Display program in the Windows Control Panel, clicking the Appearance tab in the Display Properties dialog box, clicking the Advanced button, selecting Window in the Item drop-down list, and then choosing the color you want from the Color drop-down palette (*not* from the Color 1 drop-down palette).

2 Click the down arrow on the Border button, and on the drop-down palette click the button for the specific border or combination of borders that you want to apply to the selection. As you position the pointer over each button on the palette, Word will display a ScreenTip describing the border—or combination of borders—that will be applied (Outside Border, Top Border, Left Border, Bottom Border, and so on), as shown in this example:

Borders labeled *Inside* are applicable only if you have selected more than one paragraph or table cell. (They will be added between the paragraphs or cells.) Diagonal borders can be applied only to table cells. (If you're creating a Web page, note that a browser won't display diagonal borders.) Clicking the Horizontal Line button inserts a horizontal dividing line, not a border. When you click a button on the palette, Word will immediately apply the border or borders to the selection in your document.

Horizontal dividing lines are described in "Inserting Horizontal Dividing Lines," on page 583.

Note   If ScreenTips don't appear, you can enable them by choosing Tools, Customize, clicking the Options tab in the Customize dialog box, and checking the Show ScreenTips On Toolbars option.

If the Border drop-down palette doesn't have a button for the particular combination of borders you want to add, you can apply the borders one at a time. For example, to apply borders to the left and right of a paragraph, you could first click the Left Border button and then click the Right Border button.

If you want the borders you apply to have varying properties (for example, you want each border to have a different color), return to step 1 before applying each border.

Note   The Border button also appears on the Formatting toolbar. On either the Formatting toolbar or the Tables And Borders toolbar, you can simply click the Border button (rather than opening and using the palette) to apply the border style you most recently applied. The button's icon and ScreenTip indicate the type of border that will be applied (Outside Border, All Borders, Top Border, and so on).

To remove a border from the selection, you can click the same button on the Border drop-down palette that's used to apply that border. Repeatedly clicking the button will toggle the border off and on. If you've changed the style, weight, or color settings on the Tables And Borders toolbar since you originally applied a border, clicking the button when the border is present will apply the new border type rather than removing the border; to remove the border, just click again.

You can remove all borders from the selection by clicking the No Border button on the Border palette. Note, however, that clicking this button again won't restore the borders.

Tip   **Change an existing border**
To modify the properties of a border that has already been applied, select the new properties using the Line Style, Line Weight, and Border Color buttons on the Tables And Borders toolbar (as described in step 1, given earlier). Then, use the Border button to reapply the border (as described in step 2).

Applying Shading

To apply shading to the selected paragraph or table cells, click the down arrow on the Shading Color button on the Tables And Borders toolbar to display the palette of color choices, shown here:

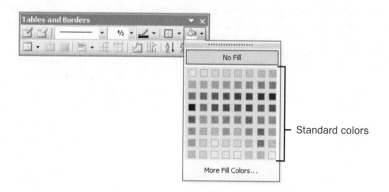

Standard colors

Then choose one of the following options:

- To apply a standard shading color, click one of the standard colors on the palette.
- To select from a larger collection of standard colors or to create a custom color, click More Fill Colors.
- To remove background shading from the selection, click No Fill.

Applying Borders and Shading with the Borders And Shading Dialog Box

The Borders And Shading dialog box is not quite as easy to use as the Tables And Borders toolbar, but it provides the following additional options:

- You can create borders that have a shadow or 3-D effect.
- You can specify the distance between the borders and the text.
- You can apply a background shading pattern as well as a solid shading color. (The Tables And Borders toolbar lets you apply only a solid background shading color.) If you're creating a Web page, keep in mind that a browser will display a patterned background as a solid color.
- You can place a border around entire document pages (explained in the next section).

To apply one or more borders to your document, perform the following steps:

1 Select the character(s), paragraph(s), table cell(s), or table to which you want to apply borders. To apply a border to a single paragraph, to a single table cell, or to a table, you can just place the insertion point within the paragraph, cell, or table without making a selection.

Note   When you use the Borders And Shading dialog box, you don't need to be as precise in your selection as you do when you use the Tables And Borders toolbar, because the dialog box gives you the opportunity to specify the exact part of the document that will be affected. For instance, if you place the insertion point within a table cell, the Borders And Shading dialog box will let you choose whether to apply the borders to the entire table, to the cell, or to the paragraph inside the cell.

2   Choose Format, Borders And Shading. In the Borders And Shading dialog box, click the Borders tab, as shown here:

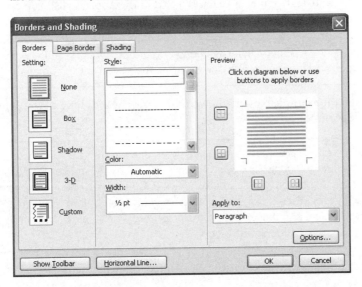

3   From the Style, Color, and Width lists, choose the properties of the border or borders you want to apply.

4   Click one of the items in the Setting area to specify the basic look and arrangement of the border or borders. Pick the one that's closest to what you want—you can customize it later.

The specific choices in the Setting area depend on what you selected prior to opening the Borders And Shading dialog box. (If you begin customizing borders, as explained in the next step, the Custom item will be automatically selected so you don't need to click it yourself.) If you want to remove all borders, click None, and then click OK to close the dialog box. In this case, you can skip the remaining steps.

5   To add or remove specific borders, click the appropriate buttons in the Preview area (each button toggles between applying and removing the corresponding border). If you want to modify the properties of a specific border, make the desired selections in the Style, Color, and Width lists just before clicking the button to add the border. (You can thus assign different properties to each border.)

6 To specify the portion of your document that receives borders, choose an item in the Apply To drop-down list. For example, if you selected one or more paragraphs prior to opening the Borders And Shading dialog box, the Paragraph item will initially be selected in the list, causing Word to apply borders to the entire paragraph or paragraphs. If you choose the Text item, however, Word will place the borders around each line of characters rather than around the entire paragraph(s).

7 If the Paragraph item is selected in the Apply To drop-down list, you can modify the clearance between the borders and the text by clicking the Options button. Then, in the Border And Shading Options dialog box, adjust the measurements in the From Text area. If Text, Table, or Cell is selected in the Apply To list, you can't adjust the text clearance.

> **Tip**   After you have applied borders to one or more paragraphs, you can adjust the clearance between a border and the text by dragging the border with the mouse.

8 When the example borders shown in the Preview area have the look you want, click the OK button.

> **Note**   When applying borders or shading, keep in mind that the Automatic color choice applies the current Window Font color, which is usually black. You set the Window Font color by running the Display program in the Windows Control Panel, opening the Appearance tab in the Display Properties dialog box, clicking the Advanced button, selecting Window in the Item drop-down list, and then choosing the color you want from the Color drop-down palette (*not* from the Color 1 drop-down palette).

To apply shading to your document, perform the following steps.

1 Select the character(s), paragraph(s), table cell(s), or table to which you want to apply shading. To apply shading to a single paragraph, to a single table cell, or to a table, you can just place the insertion point within the paragraph, cell, or table without making a selection.

2 Choose Format, Borders And Shading and click the Shading tab of the Borders And Shading dialog box, as shown here:

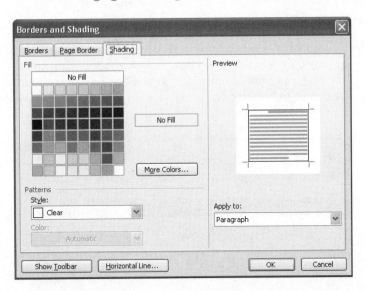

3   To apply a solid shading color, select a color in the Fill area. To pick a standard color, click one of the colors in the palette. To choose from a larger set of standard colors or to create a custom color, click the More Colors button and make your choice in the Colors dialog box. If you don't want a solid shading color, select No Fill at the top of the palette.

4   To apply a shading pattern, select a pattern from the Style drop-down list in the Patterns area. Then select a color for the pattern in the Color drop-down palette. If you don't want a pattern, choose Clear in the Style list.

Note   You can apply both a solid shading color and a shading pattern to your selection.

5   If you want to change the portion of your document that's to be shaded, select an item in the Apply To list box as explained in step 5 of the previous procedure for applying borders.

6   When the example shading shown in the Preview area has the look you want, click the OK button.

You can also apply background shading to an entire Word document. You can view this shading in Web Layout view, or, if you've saved the document as a Web page, in a browser. For information, see "Applying a Background Color or Pattern," on page 591.

Applying Borders to Pages

To give your document a polished or decorative look, you can have Word draw borders around entire pages. You can add page borders to the entire document or to just part of it. Borders will be visible in Print Layout view, in Print Preview, and of course, on the printed page. If you're creating a Web page, however, page borders aren't for you—they won't be displayed in a browser.

To add page borders, perform the following steps:

1 Choose Format, Borders And Shading to open the Borders And Shading dialog box and then click the Page Border tab, as shown here:

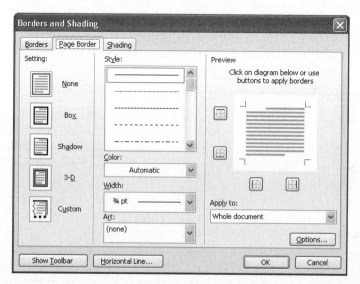

2 Using the techniques described in the previous section for applying borders to characters, paragraphs, or tables, choose options until the example borders shown in the Preview area have the look you want.

When you apply a page border, however, as an alternative to selecting a particular style of line from the Style list, you can select an "artwork" border from the Art drop-down list to create a highly decorative border, consisting of apples, ice cream cones, stars, or one of many other patterns. Choose (None) to remove an artwork border and restore whatever border type is currently selected in the Style list. (Figure 13-10 shows one of the artwork borders.)

3 In the Apply To list box, select one of the following options to specify which part of the document is to be given page borders.

- To apply borders to the entire document, select Whole Document.
- If you have divided your document into sections, to apply borders to the current section only, select This Section.

- To apply borders to the first page of the document or to the first page of the current section if you've created sections, select This Section-First Page Only.

- To apply borders to all the pages except the first page of the document or to all pages except the first page of the current section if you've created sections, select This Section - All Except First Page.

4   To modify the clearance between the page border and either the edge of the page or the text or to set other page border options, click the Options button, select the settings you want in the Border And Shading Options dialog box, shown here, and click OK.

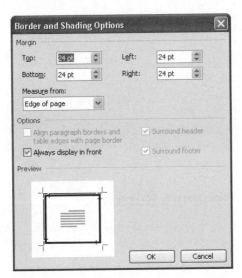

5   When the example border in the Preview area of the Page Border tab has the look you want, click OK.

Arranging Text in Newspaper-Style Columns

Unlike the columns created with tables, newspaper-style columns aren't divided into rows of side-by-side items. Rather, the text flows from the bottom of one column to the top of the next column, just like it does in the familiar columns of newspapers and magazines (see Figure 13-12). Newspaper-style columns are intended for regular Word documents that you're going to print or view online in Word. If you're creating a Web page document, forget about newspaper-style columns—they won't display in a browser; rather, the text will be displayed in a single column.

If you want to view newspaper-style columns on the screen, you must switch to Print Layout view or to Print Preview. In the other Word views, text is always displayed in a single column.

You can create newspaper-style columns using either the Columns button on the Standard toolbar or the Columns dialog box.

Figure 13-12. In this Word document page, the text following the heading is divided into two newspaper-style columns.

Applying Columns with the Columns Button

To set up equal-width newspaper-style columns throughout your entire document or in a part of the document, perform the following steps:

1. To create columns in a part of your document, select that part. To create columns throughout your entire document, place the insertion point anywhere in the document.

2. Click the Columns button and drag to indicate the number of columns you want (from 1 to 6), as in this example:

Word will divide the selected text or the entire document into the specified number of columns. The columns will be equal in width and will be separated by 0.5 inches.

If you selected part of the document in step 1, Word will insert *section breaks* before and after your selection; that is, the selected text will be placed in a separate document section, and newspaper-style columns will be applied to that section. In general, a Word document can be divided into separate sections, and each section can be assigned different page setup features, such as margins, headers, footers, and newspaper-style columns. Sections allow you to vary page setup features within a document. You can manually divide a document into sections using the Insert, Break menu command. The steps given in this part of the chapter work somewhat differently if you have previously divided your document into sections.

> For more information on sections, as well as on the formatting features that can be applied to sections, see Chapter 18, "Designing and Printing Professional-Looking Pages."

Applying Columns with the Columns Dialog Box

Although using the Columns dialog box isn't as quick as creating columns with the Columns button, it provides the following additional options:

- You can create columns of unequal widths.
- For each column, you can specify the exact column width and the amount of space between that column and the next.
- You can force the columns and column spacings to remain equal in width, even if you later adjust the width of a particular column.
- You can add vertical lines between the columns.

To set up newspaper-style columns with the Columns dialog box, perform the following steps:

1 To create columns in a part of your document, select that part. To create columns from a specific position in the document through the end of the document, place the insertion point at that position. To create columns throughout the entire document, place the insertion point anywhere within the document.

2 Choose Format, Columns to open the Columns dialog box, shown in Figure 13-13.

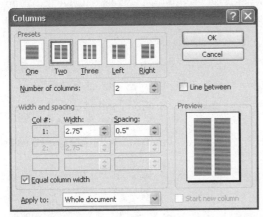

Figure 13-13. You can use the Columns dialog box to apply newspaper-style columns.

3 Choose an option in the Apply To list box to tell Word which portion of your document to modify. If you selected text prior to opening the Columns dialog box, choose Selected Text to add columns to the selection only or Whole Document to add columns to the entire document. If you didn't select text, choose Whole Document to add columns to the entire document or This Point Forward to add columns from the position of the insertion point through the end of the document.

4 Choose a column arrangement as follows:

- To use a standard column arrangement, choose one of the items in the Presets area.

- To create a custom column arrangement, enter the number of columns you want into the Number Of Columns text box. Then, for each column, specify the column width in the Width box and enter the space you want between that column and the next column in the Spacing box. (To enter separate widths and spacings, the Equal Column Width option, discussed next, must not be checked.)

5 To force Word to keep the column widths and spacings equal, check the Equal Column Width option. If this option is checked, adjusting the column width—using the procedures described in the next section—will affect all columns simultaneously. If this option isn't checked, you can adjust the width of each column individually. Note that if you choose the One, Two, or Three option in the Presets area, Equal Column Width will be checked automatically.

6 To add a vertical line between each column, check the Line Between option.

7 Click the OK button to apply the columns. Word might insert one or more section breaks, as discussed under the previous heading.

Fine Tuning Columns

Once you have applied newspaper-style columns, you can change the column widths, insert breaks within columns, and adjust other features.

The easiest way to change column widths is as follows:

1 If you're not in Print Layout view, activate it by choosing View, Print Layout.

2 If the horizontal ruler isn't visible, display it by choosing View, Ruler.

3 If the columns you want to adjust are contained within a particular document section, click in that section.

4 Drag the appropriate "Move Column" marker on the horizontal ruler, as shown on the next page.

Center Move Column marker

Left Move Column marker | Right Move Column marker

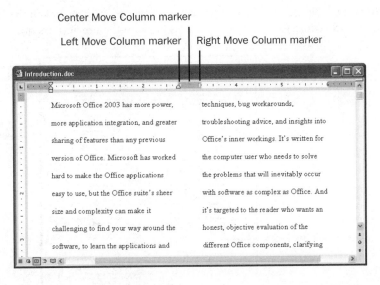

- ■ To change the width of the column on the left, drag the left Move Column marker. (This will alter the column spacing.)
- ■ To change the width of the column on the right, drag the right Move Column marker. (This will also alter the column spacing.)
- ■ To change the width of both columns simultaneously, drag the center Move Column marker. (This will increase the width of one column and decrease the width of the other without altering the column spacing.)

> **Note** The instructions here assume that you haven't checked the Equal Column Width option in the Columns dialog box. If this option is checked, dragging the left or right Move Column marker adjusts the widths of all columns simultaneously, keeping their widths equal, and the ruler won't display a center Move Column marker.

When the pointer is over one of the Move Column markers, it changes to a two-headed arrow and you'll see "Move Column" in a ScreenTip, as seen here:

You can force Word to move text into the next column by inserting a *column break* anywhere within a column (as shown in Figure 13-14). To do this, place the insertion point where you want to break the column. Then choose Insert, Break and select the Column Break option; or just press Ctrl+Shift+Enter.

You can prevent Word from inserting a column break within a particular paragraph by selecting that paragraph, choosing Format, Paragraph, clicking the Line And Page Breaks tab, and checking the Keep Lines Together option. Then, if the paragraph won't fit at the end of a column, Word will move the entire paragraph to the beginning of the next column rather than breaking the paragraph across columns.

If you want to change any of the other column features, such as the number of columns, just repeat the procedure for setting up columns given in the previous section.

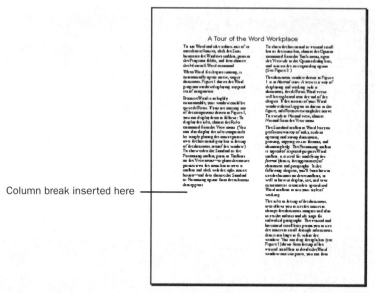

Column break inserted here ——

Figure 13-14. This figure shows a column break inserted within a newspaper-style column.

Tip Do you know where your columns are?

To see the exact boundaries of your columns in Print Layout view, you can have Word draw dotted lines around them. Choose Tools, Options, click the View tab, and check the Text Boundaries option (see Figure 13-15).

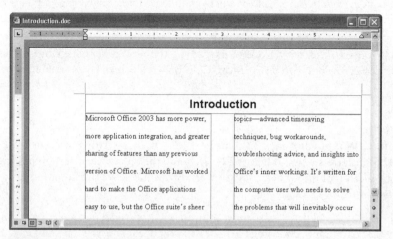

Figure 13-15. This figure shows a document in Print Layout view with boundary lines drawn around paragraphs and columns.

Ordering Text in Bulleted and Numbered Lists

You can create lists in your document by having Word add bullet characters or automatic numbering, together with hanging indents. These bullets and numbering are part of the paragraph formatting. Unlike any bullet characters or numbers you might type in manually, you can't select or perform normal editing on automatic bullets or numbers. Also, if you rearrange the paragraphs in a numbered list, Word will renumber the list for you. Figure 13-16 shows examples of the three kinds of lists you can create by adding automatic bullets or numbers.

You can apply bullets and numbers using the Formatting toolbar or using the Bullets And Numbering dialog box.

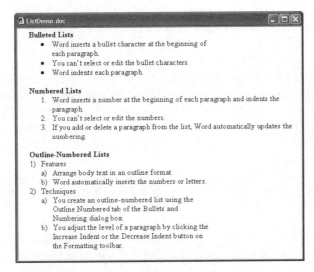

Figure 13-16. These are examples of bulleted, numbered, and outline-numbered lists.

> **Note** Because bullets and numbering are considered to be paragraph formatting, you can use most of the techniques for paragraph formatting that are covered in Chapter 12, "Effective Formatting in Word," and Chapter 14. For example, you can apply bullets or numbering by using a saved format in the Styles And Formatting task pane, or you can assign bullet or numbering formatting to a paragraph style.

Creating Lists with the Formatting Toolbar

The fastest way to have Word apply bullets or numbering to a list is to use the Bullets button or the Numbering button on the Formatting toolbar, using the following steps:

1 Type the list. Press Enter at the end of each list item so that each is contained in a separate paragraph.

2 Select all the paragraphs in the list.

3 Click the Bullets button to apply bullets, or click the Numbering button to apply numbering, as shown here:

Numbering   Bullets

Decrease
Indent

Tip **Remove the initial indent**

When you create a bulleted or numbered list by clicking the Bullets or the Numbering button or by using a standard format in the Bullets And Numbering dialog box, Word indents the entire list by .25 inch. If you'd rather have the list flush with the left margin, simply click the Decrease Indent button on the Formatting toolbar while the list paragraphs are still selected.

If you apply numbering to a series of paragraphs and then delete or rearrange one or more of them, Word will update the numbering. If you place the insertion point at the end of a bulleted or numbered paragraph and press Enter, the new paragraph will also be bulleted or numbered. If, however, you press Enter twice without typing text, the new paragraphs won't be bulleted or numbered; this is a convenient way to stop adding bullets or numbering when you reach the end of your list.

For instructions on numbering the lines in a document, see "Adjusting the Page Layout," on page 541.

You can remove bullets or numbering by selecting one or more paragraphs and clicking the Bullets button or Numbering button again. You can also remove the bullet or number from a single paragraph by placing the insertion point immediately following the bullet or number and pressing Backspace.

To control the starting number for a list of automatically numbered paragraphs, use the Bullets And Numbering dialog box, described in the next section.

Tip **Number cells in tables**

You can number the cells in a Word table by selecting the cells and clicking the Numbering button. Word will number the cells beginning with the upper-left cell and progressing through each row from left to right. The cells you number don't have to be adjoining, as shown in this example.

To select nonadjacent cells, click at the left of the first one and then click at the left of each additional cell while pressing Ctrl.

Creating Lists with the Bullets And Numbering Dialog Box and List Styles

If you apply bullets or numbering using the Bullets And Numbering dialog box rather than using the Formatting toolbar, you have the following additional options:

- You can choose any character or graphic image for the bullets in a bulleted list.
- You can specify the starting number for a numbered list.
- You can modify the appearance and position of the bullet characters or images or the numbers.
- You can create and customize an outline numbered list. An outline numbered list displays text in an attractive outline format, without using the Heading styles or Outline view. The list items can be automatically numbered in various ways or marked with bullet characters. You can create an outline numbered list by directly applying the features you want, or by assigning a list style (a feature introduced with Microsoft Office XP) to the selected paragraphs.
- You can automatically number your document's headings.

To apply or modify any kind of list formatting, perform the following steps:

1 Select all the paragraphs in the list.
2 Open the Bullets And Numbering dialog box by choosing Format, Bullets And Numbering or by right-clicking the selection and choosing Bullets And Numbering from the shortcut menu.
3 Follow the instructions given in the following sections to apply a specific type of list formatting.

Creating a Bulleted List Using the Bulleted Tab

To create a bulleted list, click the Bulleted tab of the Bullets And Numbering dialog box (shown in Figure 13-17) and do one or more of the following:

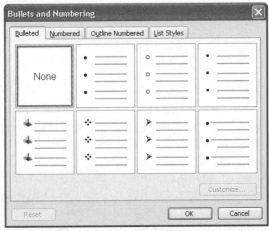

Figure 13-17. You can apply one of a variety of bullet types by using the Bulleted tab of the Bullets And Numbering dialog box.

- To apply one of the standard bullet types, double-click one of the seven types displayed in the "gallery" of bullet types in the dialog box.

- To customize one of the standard bullet types, click it to select it and then click the Customize button. This will display the Customize Bulleted List dialog box, in which you can select a different bullet character or graphic, modify the indent of the bullet or the text, and adjust the size of the tab space between the bullet and the first line of text. Use the preview image to guide your selections.

- To restore a bullet type that you've customized, select it and click the Reset button.

- To remove bullets that were previously applied, double-click the None option at the upper left of the tab.

> **Note** Applying a theme to your document modifies the bullets in bulleted lists throughout the document. Themes are discussed in "Applying a Web Page Theme," on page 592.

Creating a Numbered List Using the Numbered Tab

To create a numbered list, click the Numbered tab of the Bullets And Numbering dialog box (shown in Figure 13-18) and do one or more of the following:

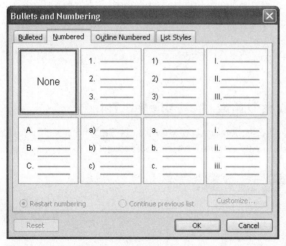

Figure 13-18. You can apply any one of several numbering types using the Numbered tab of the Bullets And Numbering dialog box.

- To apply one of the standard numbering types, double-click one of the seven types displayed in the "gallery" of numbering types in the dialog box.

- To customize one of the standard numbering types, click it to select it and then click the Customize button. This will display the Customize Numbered List dialog box, in which you can modify the number format, style, starting number, and position, as well as the position of the text. Use the preview image to guide your selections.

- To restore a numbering type that you've customized, select it and click the Reset button.

- To continue the numbering sequence from the previous numbered list in the document, select the Continue Previous List option. To start numbering with 1 (or with a custom starting number you select through the Customize Numbered List dialog box), select Restart Numbering. These options are available only if the document contains a numbered list prior to the paragraphs you selected.

- To remove numbering that was previously applied, double-click the None option at the upper left of the tab.

Creating an Outline Numbered List Using the Outline Numbered Tab

To create an outline numbered list by directly applying the formatting features you want, click the Outline Numbered tab of the Bullets And Numbering dialog box (shown in Figure 13-19) and do one or more of the following:

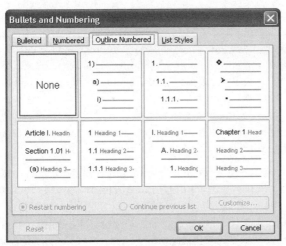

Figure 13-19. You can create an outline numbered list using the Outline Numbered tab of the Bullets And Numbering dialog box.

- To apply one of the standard types of outline numbering, double-click one of the three outline numbering types displayed on the *first row* of types in the Outline Numbered tab. (The types in the second row are explained later in this section.)

- To customize one of the standard outline numbering types, click it to select it and then click the Customize button. This will display the Customize Outline Numbered List dialog box, in which you can modify the number format, style, starting number, font, and position—as well as the text position and other features—for any of the levels of the outline numbered list. Use the preview image to guide your selections.

- To restore an outline numbering type that you've customized, select it and click the Reset button.

- To continue the numbering sequence from the previous numbered list in the document, select the Continue Previous List option. To start numbering with 1 (or with a custom starting number you select through the Customize Outline Numbered List dialog box), select Restart Numbering. These options are available only if the document contains a numbered list prior to the paragraphs you select.

● To remove outline numbering that was previously applied, double-click the None option at the upper left of the tab.

Inside Out

Remove unwanted indentation

Decrease Indent

Double-clicking the None option might leave the paragraphs with various levels of indentation. You can remove an indentation by clicking the Decrease Indent button on the Formatting toolbar, repeatedly if necessary.

Note The Outline Numbered List feature is convenient for permanently formatting any amount of document text as an attractive outline. In contrast, the Outline view allows you to temporarily view an entire document in outline form so that you can quickly organize the text. (Outline view is covered in "Working with Documents in Outline View," on page 419.)

Once you've applied an outline numbered list format to a series of paragraphs using this procedure, you can adjust the level of each paragraph as follows:

Increase Indent

● To demote a paragraph (that is, convert it to a lower level list item), place the insertion point in the paragraph and press Alt+Shift+Right Arrow or click the Increase Indent button on the Formatting toolbar.

● To promote a paragraph (that is, convert it to a higher level list item), place the insertion point in the paragraph and press Alt+Shift+Left Arrow or click the Decrease Indent button on the Formatting toolbar.

Tip   Convert a simple bulleted or numbered list to an outline

You can convert a simple bulleted or numbered list (created using the Bulleted or Numbered tab or the Bullets or Numbering toolbar button) to an outline numbered list by demoting some of the paragraphs in the list. When you do this, Word will apply default bullet characters or numbering to the lower outline levels. If you want to choose the style of all levels, you must create or modify the outline numbered list using the Outline Numbered tab of the Bullets And Numbering dialog box, as explained previously in this section, or by applying a list style, as covered in the next section.

You can also use the Outline Numbered tab of the Bullets And Numbering dialog box to apply automatic outline numbering to all the headings throughout your document, even though they aren't contained in a list of adjoining paragraphs, provided that you have assigned all your heading paragraphs the standard Heading styles, Heading 1 through Heading 9. To do this, place the insertion point within any heading in the document, click the Outline Numbered tab of the Bullets And Numbering dialog box, and select one of the four outline numbering types in the bottom row, shown in Figure 13-19. Notice that the sample in the Outline Numbered tab for each of these types contains the names of Heading styles.

Creating an Outline Numbered List by Applying a List Style

An alternative way to create an outline numbered list is to apply a *list style* to the selected paragraphs. A list style is one of the four types of Word styles (the other three are paragraph, character, and table). Using a style to create your outline numbered lists gives you the following advantages:

- Because a style can be stored in a template, copied between templates and documents, and shared by members of your workgroup, you can easily maintain consistent formatting of your outline numbered lists within all your documents.

- You can quickly update all your outline numbered lists by modifying the style, rather than changing each list.

- You can easily assign a list style to a toolbar button or shortcut key for quick application.

The fastest way to assign a list style to the selected paragraphs is to click the List Styles tab of the Bullets And Numbering dialog box (shown in Figure 13-20) and do one or more of the following:

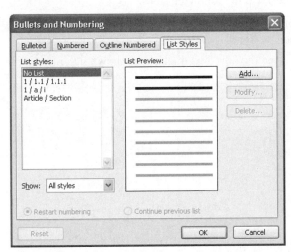

Figure 13-20. You can assign list styles using the List Styles tab of the Bullets And Numbering dialog box.

- To apply one of the built-in styles, double-click one of the styles (other than No List) in the List Styles list. To control which styles are shown, select an item in the Show drop-down list.

- To customize a list style, select it in the List Styles list and click the Modify button. This will display the Modify Style dialog box, in which you can change any formatting feature of the style.

- To create a new list style, click the Add button and define the formatting features in the New Style dialog box.

- To remove a style in the List Styles list, select it and click the Delete button.

- To continue the numbering sequence from the previous numbered list in the document, select the Continue Previous List option. To start numbering with 1 (or with a custom starting number you select through the Modify Style dialog box), select Restart Numbering. These options are available only if the document contains a numbered list prior to the paragraphs you selected.

- To remove a list style that was applied previously, double-click the No List item in the list.

> For information on creating, modifying, removing, or copying list styles (as well as other types of Word styles), see Chapter 14. For information on adjusting the level of a paragraph in an outline numbered list, see the previous section. You can also apply, modify, or delete a list style using the Styles And Formatting task pane, as discussed in Chapter 12 and Chapter 14.

Sorting Lists and Tables

You can have Word sort the items in a list consisting of a series of paragraphs. You can also have it sort rows within a table.

To sort a list of paragraphs, perform the following steps:

1 Select all the paragraphs that make up the list. (Recall that a paragraph consists of any amount of text followed by a paragraph mark.)

2 Choose Table, Sort to open the Sort Text dialog box, shown here:

3 In the Sort By drop-down list, choose the part of the text that is to be used as the sort criterion. To sort a list of paragraphs, you normally choose Paragraphs to base the sort on all text in each paragraph. If, however, each paragraph is divided into *fields* (entries within the paragraphs separated with tabs, commas, or another character), you can

base the sort on a specific field by choosing Field 1, Field 2, and so on. For instance, if you wanted to sort the following list by birth date, you would select Field 2:

John, December 18

Sue, April 25

Pete, April 25

Joan, June 10

You can also choose a second and a third sort field in the Then By controls, which Word will use if the previous sort fields are identical. In this example, if you chose Field 1 in the second Then By box, Word would use the names to sort the paragraphs for Sue and Pete, who have identical birthdays—that is, it would place Pete before Sue in an ascending sort.

4   Select an item in the Type drop-down list to indicate the way the text should be sorted. You can choose Text to sort alphabetically. If the information you're sorting by consists of numbers, you can choose Number to sort it numerically. If it consists of dates, you can choose Date to sort it chronologically. (In the previous example, you would choose Date for the first sort field and Text for the second.)

5   Select Ascending to sort text from the beginning to the end of the alphabet, numbers from smaller to larger, and dates from earlier to later. Select Descending to sort in the opposite order.

6   Select Header Row to eliminate the first paragraph from the sort or No Header Row to sort all selected paragraphs. When Header Row is selected, the items in the first row are used to name the fields; in this case you can select a name from the Sort By or Then By list (rather than selecting Field 1, Field 2, and so on).

7   If you want to modify the way Word sorts text, click the Options button to open the Sort Options dialog box (see Figure 13-21). This dialog box lets you specify the character used to separate fields. (The example in step 3 uses commas.) Also, if you check the Case Sensitive option, Word will consider a lowercase letter to come before the same letter in uppercase (if you sort text in ascending order). If Case Sensitive isn't checked, Word will ignore the case of letters. You can select a specific language in the Sorting Language drop-down list to cause Word to use the sorting rules defined by that language.

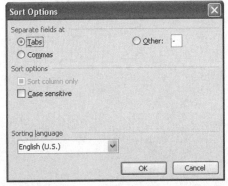

Figure 13-21.   You can define sorting criteria in the Sort Options dialog box.

Note If you sort a list of paragraphs to which you have applied automatic numbering, Word will renumber it properly.

You can also use the steps listed previously to sort rows within a Word table, with the following provisos:

- The dialog box is titled Sort and has several additional controls (Using drop-down lists), as shown in Figure 13-22.

Figure 13-22. This figure shows the Sort dialog box as it's displayed when you have selected text in a table.

- In step 1, select the rows and columns you want to sort. To sort the entire table, place the insertion point anywhere within the table. Note that Word sorts only vertically; you can't, for example, select a single row and have Word sort the cells in that row.

- In the Sort By and Then By lists, choose the table columns that you want to use as sort criteria (assuming that you have selected more than one column in the table).

- If the text in one of the columns you're sorting by is divided into fields (using tabs, commas, or another character), in the Using drop-down list you can select a particular field to sort by (just as you do in the Sort By drop-down list when you sort paragraphs outside of a table, as explained in step 3).

● If your selection doesn't span all the table's columns, in the Sort Options dialog box, you can select the Sort Column Only option to have Word sort only the selected column or columns. Otherwise, Word will sort entire rows even though you haven't selected all the columns.

After you have sorted a list of paragraphs or the contents of a table, you can unsort it by immediately issuing the Undo command.

For information on using the Undo command, see the sidebar "Undoing and Redoing Editing and Formatting Actions," on page 285.

Tip Arrange text using dividing lines

Another way to arrange or organize the text in your document is to insert horizontal dividing lines, which commonly appear in Web pages but can be added to any type of document. For information, see "Inserting Horizontal Dividing Lines," on page 583.

Advanced Word Formatting Techniques

Customizing Styles 389
Creating New Styles 403
Reusing Your Styles by Making Copies . 406

Customizing and Creating
Document Templates 408

Customizing Styles

All documents have access to the general-purpose, built-in styles that are provided by Microsoft Office Word 2003—for example, Normal, Body Text, Heading 1 through Heading 9, and List. Also, when you first create a document, the document obtains a copy of any user-defined styles or customized versions of built-in styles that are stored within the template on which the document is based. Many of the special-purpose templates supplied with Word store user-defined or customized versions of built-in styles that are useful for formatting the types of documents these templates are designed to create. An example is the Professional Report template, which stores many user-defined styles (for example, the Company Name, Title Cover, and Subtitle Cover styles that are used for formatting elements on the report's title page), as well as versions of built-in styles that have been customized for creating professional reports. When you create a document based on the Professional Report template, all the user-defined and customized styles it contains are copied into your document and are stored in the document file.

If you later create a user-defined style or customize a built-in style within your document, the new or modified style definition is also stored in the document file. When you format text in the document, you can use any of the styles stored in the document file in addition to any of the original built-in Word styles.

Built-In vs. User-Defined Styles

A *built-in* style is one that is hard-coded into Word and is available to every document. Examples are Normal, Block Text, Body Text (and the Body Text variations such as Body Text 2 and Body Text Indent), Emphasis, Footer, Header, Heading 1 through Heading 9, List and the many List variations such as List 2 and List Bullet, Plain Text, and Strong. (There are many others.) If a built-in style is modified, the modified version of the style is stored in the document or template where the modification was made. The modified style can later be copied to another document or template. (When you create a new document, any modified built-in styles in the template are automatically copied into the document.) If a modified version of a built-in style is stored in a document, it takes precedence over the unmodified version of the style.

A *user-defined* style is a new style that has been created in a document or template. You or a coworker can create user-defined styles. User-defined styles are also included in some of the templates shipped with Word (in this case, the *user* would be the Microsoft developer who defined the style). User-defined styles are stored in a document or template and may be copied to another document or template. (When you create a new document, any user-defined styles in the template are automatically copied into the document.) In a document, you can use only those user-defined styles stored within the document's file.

Creating user-defined styles is explained in "Creating New Styles," on page 403.

You can determine which of the styles available to your document are user-defined—as opposed to original or modified built-in styles—as follows:

1 If the Styles And Formatting task pane isn't visible, choose Format, Styles And Formatting.

2 Near the bottom of the Styles And Formatting task pane, select Custom in the Show drop-down list.

3 At the bottom of the Format Settings dialog box, click the Styles button.

4 In the Style dialog box, select User-Defined Styles in the Category drop-down list. The Styles list will then display all user-defined styles stored in the document. Figure 14-1 shows the list of user-defined styles that you would find in a new document created by using the Professional Report template.

You can modify any of the styles to which your document has access—those stored in the document, plus the built-in Word styles. When you modify a style, all text in your document that is assigned that style automatically acquires the style's new format—an important advantage of using styles rather than directly formatting text. Modifying a style initially affects only the document itself; it doesn't affect the document's template or other documents based on that template. (When you modify a built-in style in a document, the modified version of that style is stored only within the document.) As explained later in the chapter, however, you can easily copy styles between documents and templates to make any of the style definitions stored in a document available to other documents.

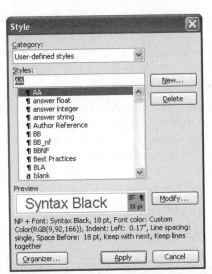

Figure 14-1. You can view all the document's user-defined styles in the Style dialog box.

Applying a theme to a document, as described in "Applying a Web Page Theme," on page 592, modifies the document's Normal style as well as its Heading styles (Heading 1 through Heading 9). These styles are given a look that's consistent with the theme.

When you modify or create a paragraph or character style, keep in mind that one style can be based on another style. The Normal paragraph style is the base style for most of the other built-in paragraph styles. For example, Body Text is defined as "Normal plus 6 points of space following the paragraph." This definition means that Body Text has all the formatting stored in Normal except the amount of space after the paragraph—Normal has 0 points of space after the paragraph, whereas Body Text has 6 points of space. (Normal itself isn't based on any other style.) Any formatting specifically assigned to a style supersedes the formatting of the base style.

If you change a style such as Normal, all styles based on it instantly change. For example, if you assigned the Courier New font and "10 points of space following the paragraph" to the Normal style, Body Text would acquire the Courier New font. Body Text would not, however, acquire "10 points of space following the paragraph" because it contains an explicit "space following" value (that is, it doesn't derive this formatting from Normal).

Tip   Use built-in styles to change the appearance of standard document elements
Word assigns certain built-in styles to standard elements in your document. For example, it assigns the Comment Text style to comment text, the Footer style to page footers, and the Page Number style to page numbers. You can therefore change the appearance of one of these standard elements by changing the corresponding style. For example, if you change the Header style, you'll modify the appearance of the headers on all pages of your document. (Assigning headers, footers, and page numbers is discussed in Chapter 18, "Designing and Printing Professional-Looking Pages." Comments are discussed in "Inserting Comments in Documents," on page 459.)

Basing one style on another fosters formatting consistency. For example, if you assign a new font to the Normal style, derived styles will automatically acquire the new font, and you'll avoid having dissimilar fonts throughout your document. (The only derived styles that won't acquire the new font are any that include a font specification.)

Chapter 12, "Effective Formatting in Word," described one way to modify the Normal style: When you click the Default button in the Font dialog box, you change the character formatting stored in Normal to the features selected in the dialog box. You can also modify the Normal style by clicking the Default button in the Language dialog box, which is discussed in "Marking the Language," on page 505. The next two sections of this chapter explain the two basic ways to modify any feature of any style:

- Modifying styles using example text
- Modifying styles using the Modify Style dialog box

Tip Display style names

You can have Word display the name of each paragraph's style in a separate *style area* at the left of the document window—in Normal or Outline view only—by choosing Tools, Options, clicking the View tab, and entering a nonzero measurement into the Style Area Width box. If the width value is 0, Word doesn't display the style area. Don't worry about the exact value you enter; once the style area is displayed, you can easily change its width by dragging the right border, as seen here:

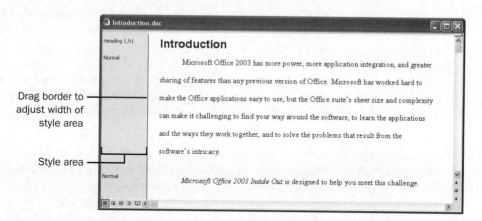

You can quickly remove the style area by dragging the border all the way to the left of the window.

Also, you can print a description of the document styles by choosing File, Print and selecting Styles in the Print What drop-down list.

Customizing Paragraph and Character Styles by Example

The fastest way to modify a paragraph or character style is to use example text. This method instantly updates the style definition to match the formatting of example text you have selected in your document. You can use this technique to modify any style except Normal by performing the following steps:

1   Select the example text you want to use to update the style. To save time, select text with formatting that's as close as possible to the formatting you want to assign to the style. You can select text that has been assigned the same style that you want to modify, or text with a different style.

2   If necessary, modify the formatting of the selected text so that it has the exact formatting you want to assign to the style you're customizing. Apply the new formatting directly to the text. You can use any of the methods for directly formatting text that were described in Chapter 12. Be sure to leave the text you modified selected.

3   If the Styles And Formatting task pane isn't currently shown, display it by choosing Format, Styles And Formatting.

4   Locate the name of the style you're modifying in the Pick Formatting To Apply list in the Styles And Formatting task pane, click the down arrow that appears when you move the pointer over the style name and choose Update To Match Selection from the drop-down menu. The following example shows how you would modify the Heading 1 style with the formatting features of the selected paragraph:

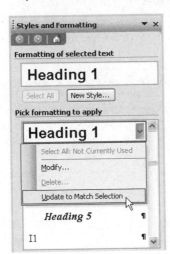

Word will now assign the formatting of the selected text to the style.

> **Caution**   When you display the style's drop-down menu in the Pick Formatting To Apply list of the Styles And Formatting task pane, be sure to click the down arrow. Don't accidentally click the style name itself, which would immediately remove any formatting you applied in step 2 and would apply the unmodified style to the text.

Chapter 14

> For information on directly formatting text, see "Formatting Characters Directly," on page 308, and "Formatting Paragraphs Directly," on page 318.

Customizing Styles Using the Modify Style Dialog Box

Modifying a style by using the Modify Style dialog box is not as fast as modifying the style by example, but it provides the following additional options:

- You can modify any type of style: paragraph, character, table, or list.
- You can rename the style or assign it one or more aliases (explained later).
- You can change the style on which a paragraph, character, or table style is based.
- For a paragraph style, you can change the style that Word automatically assigns to a paragraph that follows a paragraph that's assigned the modified style.
- You can define a shortcut key for quickly applying a paragraph, character, or list style.
- You can copy the modified style to the document's template.
- You can have Word automatically update a paragraph style. With automatic updating, whenever you apply direct formatting to a paragraph that's assigned the style, Word will update the style to match the new format.

To modify a style using the Modify Style dialog box, perform the following steps:

1 If the Styles And Formatting task pane isn't currently shown, display it by choosing Format, Styles And Formatting.

2 Locate the style you want to modify in the Pick Formatting To Apply list in the Styles And Formatting task pane.

> If you don't see the style you want, see "Assigning Paragraph Styles, Character Styles, and Saved Formats," on page 330, for information on controlling the styles that are displayed.

3 Click the down arrow that appears when you move the pointer over the style name, and choose Modify from the drop-down menu, as shown on the next page (for modifying the Heading 1 style).

Advanced Word Formatting Techniques

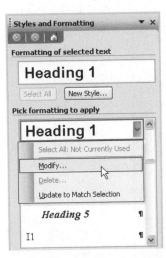

Word will display the Modify Style dialog box. Figures 14-2 through 14-5 show the Modify Style dialog box as it appears for each of the four types of Word styles.

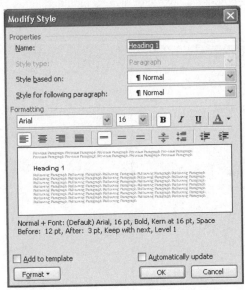

Figure 14-2. In this figure the Heading 1 paragraph style is modified in the Modify Style dialog box.

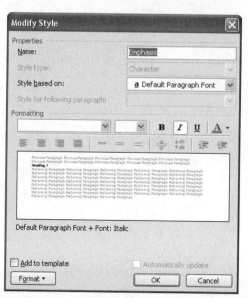

Figure 14-3. Here, the Emphasis character style is modified in the Modify Style dialog box.

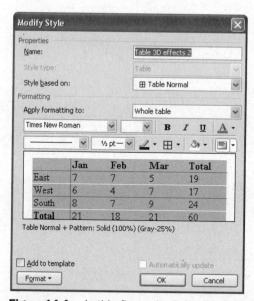

Figure 14-4. In this figure the Table 3D Effects 2 table style is modified in the Modify Style dialog box.

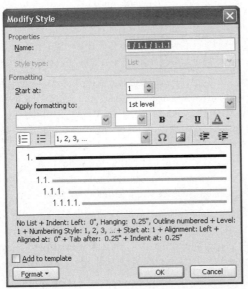

Figure 14-5. Here, the "1/1.1/1.1.1" list style is modified in the Modify Style dialog box.

4 In the Modify Style dialog box, perform one or more of the following actions:

- To change the name of a user-defined style, type a new name into the Name text box.

  Each style must have a unique name, and style names are case-sensitive—for example, *List* and *list* are considered different styles. You can include spaces in the name. Also, for a user-defined or built-in style, you can define one or more *aliases*, or alternative names for a style, by typing them after the style name in the Name box, separating the names with commas. (If you attempt to rename a built-in style, Word will add the new name you type as an alias for the style. See the sidebar "Style aliases and AutoComplete" for more information.)

- To change the base style (for a paragraph, character, or table style), select a style name from the Style Based On drop-down list.

  For a paragraph style, if you choose the (No Style) option, the style will not be based on another style, and it will contain its own complete set of paragraph and character formatting features. (The Normal style can't be based on another style.)

  For a character style, if you choose the Default Paragraph Font or (Underlying Properties) option, the style will not be based on another character style. Rather, it will store only the character formatting features that are explicitly assigned to the style.

Chapter 14

A table style must always be based on another table style (usually, Table Normal, which has minimal formatting features).

- For a paragraph style, to change the style for the following paragraph, choose a style name in the Style For Following Paragraph drop-down list.

  For example, if you were modifying the Heading 1 style, you might choose Body Text in the Style For Following Paragraph list. As a result, if you pressed Enter after typing a paragraph with the Heading 1 style, Word would assign the Body Text style to the newly inserted paragraph. (For most styles, you typically choose the same style in the Style For Following Paragraph list so that the style doesn't change when you press Enter.) The result of basing one style on another was discussed in "Customizing Styles," on page 389; for more information on the limitations of Style For Following Paragraph, see the Inside Out sidebar later in this section.

- To copy the modified style to the document's template, check the Add To Template option. In this case, the modified style will be available to any new documents you subsequently create using that template (but not to existing documents). If you don't check this option, modifying the style will affect only the current document.

- To have Word automatically modify a paragraph style (and instantly apply the new formatting to all other paragraphs in the document that have this style) whenever you directly apply formatting to a paragraph that has been assigned the style, check the Automatically Update option.

  The Automatically Update option helps ensure that all text throughout the document that has a particular style will remain consistent in formatting. However, this feature can easily cause unexpected results. If you aren't fond of Word making automatic changes to your documents, you'll probably want to turn it off. (See the tip "Reverse automatic style updating" later in the section.)

- To change the formatting stored in the style, use the Font, Font Size, Bold, Italic, Underline, or Font Color controls displayed in the Modify Style dialog box, shown here:

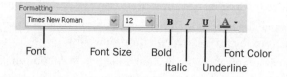

You can also use any of the other controls that appear in the Modify Style dialog box. The particular controls you'll see depend on which type of style you're modifying (see Figures 14-2 through 14-5).

Alternatively, you can select the formatting features for the style by using one of the standard dialog boxes used for directly applying formatting. This approach provides you with more formatting options and gives you a finer level of control over the formatting. To open a formatting dialog box, click the Format button at the bottom of the Modify Style dialog box and choose the appropriate command from the menu, as shown here:

Table 14-1 shows which command to use to open a particular dialog box and provides additional information on the commands. When you have made the changes you want in each of the dialog boxes, click the OK button in the dialog box to return to the Modify Style dialog box.

■ To assign a shortcut key to a paragraph, character, or list style so that you can quickly apply the style to selected text, choose Shortcut Key from the Format menu, as shown here:

Then, define the shortcut key in the Customize Keyboard dialog box.

Defining shortcut keys is explained in "Defining Shortcut Keys (Word Only)," on page 222.

Tip   **Reverse automatic style updating**
If you've assigned the Automatically Update option to a style, you can reverse the effect of this option by issuing the Undo command immediately after you directly apply paragraph formatting to a paragraph that has the style. The first Undo reverses the automatic style update and the second Undo removes the paragraph formatting you just applied.

For more information on the Undo command, see the sidebar "Undoing and Redoing Editing and Formatting Actions," on page 285.

5   When you have finished making changes to the style, click OK in the Modify Style dialog box to save your modifications.

Inside Out

Style aliases and AutoComplete

Before you spend a lot of time creating aliases, keep in mind that in Word 2003 they aren't nearly as useful for applying styles as they used to be. With versions of Word prior to version 2002, you could quickly apply a style by typing a short alias into the box at the top of the Style drop-down list on the Formatting toolbar and immediately pressing Enter. Word 2003, however, attempts to autocomplete an alias, often coming up with a different style.

Consider, for example, that b is an alias for the Body Text style. As soon as you type **b** into the Style box, however, Word might fill in the style name Block Text. Pressing Enter would then apply the Block Text style rather than the Body Text style.

To get rid of any autocompleted text in the style drop-down list, press the Delete key right after you type the name of the alias but before you press Enter. You don't have to select the autocompleted text because Word selects it automatically.

Inside Out

Limitations of the Style For Following Paragraph option

Keep in mind that the Style For Following Paragraph option doesn't work in the following two situations:

1. If there are one or more characters, even a single space character, between the insertion point and the paragraph mark at the end of the paragraph.
2. If you're working in Outline view.

In both these cases, the following paragraph is assigned the *same* style as the current paragraph, regardless of the style assigned to the Style For Following Paragraph option.

Table 14-1. Using the Format Menu in the Modify Style Dialog Box

To Open This Formatting Dialog Box	Choose This Command	For These Style Types	Comments
Font	Font	● Paragraph ● Character ● Table ● List	See "Formatting Characters with the Font Dialog Box," on page 313.
Paragraph	Paragraph	● Paragraph ● Table	See "Formatting Paragraphs with the Paragraph Dialog Box," on page 323.

Table 14-1. **Using the Format Menu in the Modify Style Dialog Box**

To Open This Formatting Dialog Box	Choose This Command	For These Style Types	Comments
Tabs	Tabs	● Paragraph ● Table	This dialog box lets you assign the positions and the types of tab stops that are used in the paragraph.
Borders And Shading	Border	● Paragraph ● Character	See "Applying Borders and Shading with the Borders And Shading Dialog Box," on page 366.
Language	Language	● Paragraph ● Character	See "Marking the Language," on page 505.
Frame	Frame	● Paragraph	A *frame* is an obsolete element for positioning a block of text on the page. (In this context, *frame* doesn't refer to one of the panes used to view multiple documents in a Web browser.) Rather than using frames, you should use *text boxes* (which are handled as graphic objects rather than as paragraph formatting), as explained in "Using Text Boxes to Create Precise Page Layouts," on page 510.
Bullets And Numbering	Numbering	● Paragraph ● List	See "Creating Lists with the Bullets And Numbering Dialog Box and List Styles," on page 379.
Table Properties	Table Properties	● Table	See "Using Other Methods for Creating and Modifying Tables," on page 359.
Borders And Shading	Borders And Shading	● Table	See "Applying Borders and Shading with the Borders And Shading Dialog Box," on page 366.
Stripes	Stripes	● Table	Applies shading to alternate rows or columns to make the table easier to read. Techniques for manually applying table shading are covered in "Adding Borders and Shading," on page 361.

If you modified a style that was stored in your document, the modified version of the style will replace it. If you modified the original version of a built-in style, Word will save the modified style definition in your document.

Word will also copy the modified style definition to the template attached to the document if you checked the Add To Template option in the Modify Style dialog box.

For information on ways to copy the modified style to other templates or documents, see "Reusing Your Styles by Making Copies," on page 406.

Deleting a Style

To delete any user-defined style stored in the current document, perform the following steps:

1 If the Styles And Formatting task pane isn't visible, choose Format, Styles And Formatting.

2 Locate the style you want to delete in the list, click the down arrow next to the style name, and choose Delete, as shown here:

3 Click the Yes button when Word asks whether you want to delete the style. Word will then remove the style definition from the document. Word will also remove the style from any text that it was assigned to. A paragraph that was assigned a deleted paragraph style will be converted to Normal. Text that was assigned a deleted character, table, or list style will simply be left without a character, table, or list style.

You can use this same procedure to delete any built-in style that's stored in the document, *except* the Normal paragraph style or the Heading paragraph styles (Heading 1 through Heading 9). This method works as follows:

● Deleting a *modified* built-in style erases the modified style definition from the document and removes the style from all text to which it was assigned. A paragraph assigned a deleted paragraph style will be converted to Normal. Text assigned a deleted character, table, or list style will be left without a character, table, or list style. Although the modified style definition will no longer be available, you can still apply the original built-in style to text. Deleting a modified built-in style is a convenient way to reset the style to its "factory settings."

For example, if you've modified the built-in paragraph style Body Text, you can delete it. This will remove the modified Body Text definition from the document and will convert all Body Text paragraphs to Normal. Although the modified Body Text style definition will no longer be available, you can still assign Body Text to paragraphs; doing so will format them with the original, built-in Body Text features.

- Deleting an *unmodified* built-in style removes the copy of the style from the document and removes the style from all text to which it was assigned. (The only unmodified built-in styles that are stored in the document and that you can therefore delete are ones that have been assigned to text within the document.) A paragraph assigned a deleted paragraph style will be converted to Normal. Text assigned a deleted character, table, or list style will be left without a character, table, or list style. The built-in style will still be available for applying to text. This is a convenient way to globally remove a style from text in a document.

For a description of the different types of styles that can be stored in a document file, see the sidebar "Types of Styles Stored in a Document or Template," on page 410.

Tip Delete a Group of Styles Quickly
To delete multiple styles quickly and efficiently, you can use the Organizer, as explained in "Using the Organizer," on page 412.

Creating New Styles

If you find yourself frequently applying the same set of formatting features to characters, paragraphs, tables, or lists it's probably time to define a new user-defined style. Doing so will save you time and help improve the consistency of your formatting. For example, if you routinely format figure captions by applying an italic, 12-point Arial font, double line spacing, and 6 points of space following the paragraph, you could define a paragraph style—perhaps named Label—that has all these features. Likewise, if you frequently emphasize words by assigning a 14-point font and a red font color, you could define a character style—named, say, Big Red—that has these two features. And if you normally display numbers in a table with a particular design, you could define a table style—maybe called Number Table—that stores the table design.

You can quickly create a user-defined paragraph style by example and you can create any kind of style using the New Style dialog box.

Creating Paragraph Styles by Example

The fastest way to create a user-defined paragraph style is by example. (You can't use this method to create a character, table, or list style, though.) To do so, perform the following steps:

1   Select or place the insertion point within a paragraph in a document. You can save time if you choose a paragraph that already has formatting close to the formatting you want to assign to the user-defined style.

2   Directly apply any additional character or paragraph formatting that you want to assign to the style, using the methods given in Chapter 12. When you're done applying formatting, be sure to leave the text selected.

3   Type a unique name for the new style into the box at the top of the Style drop-down list on the Formatting toolbar, and press Enter.

As you type in a style name, Word's Autocomplete feature might attempt to fill in the name of an existing style. If this happens, be sure to edit the entry so that the Style box contains the name you want to assign to your new style before you press Enter. (Otherwise, the existing style will be applied to the text and your directly applied formatting will be lost!)

Word will add the new user-defined paragraph style to the styles stored in the document and it will apply the style to the example paragraph. The new style will be based on the style that was originally assigned to the example paragraph, and it will store all the paragraph and character formatting you directly applied to the example paragraph.

> For information on formatting text directly, see "Formatting Characters Directly," on page 308, and "Formatting Paragraphs Directly," on page 318.

Creating Styles with the New Style Dialog Box

Although using the New Style dialog box to create a user-defined style is a little less convenient than using the Style control on the Formatting toolbar, it provides the following additional options:

●   You can create any type of user-defined style: paragraph, character, table, or list.

●   You can choose the style on which a new paragraph, character, or table style is based.

●   For a user-defined paragraph style, you can change the style that Word automatically assigns to a paragraph that follows a paragraph that's assigned the new style.

●   You can define a shortcut key for quickly applying a paragraph, character, or list style.

●   You can copy the new style to the document's template.

●   You can have Word automatically update a new paragraph style. With automatic updating, whenever you apply direct formatting to a paragraph that's assigned the style, Word will update the style to match the new format.

To define a new style using the New Style dialog box, follow this basic procedure:

1 To save time, select—or just place the insertion point within—text that has formatting similar to the formatting you want to assign to the new style. (This step is optional because you can select all the formatting features you want later in the procedure.)

2 If the Styles And Formatting task pane isn't currently shown, display it by choosing Format, Styles And Formatting.

3 Click the New Style button near the top of the Styles And Formatting task pane, as shown here:

Word will display the New Style dialog box. Word will initially assign the new style a tentative name, such as Style1, which you can easily change. The formatting features of the text that is selected in the document already will be entered into the New Style dialog box, saving you time in defining a style with similar formatting. Except for the dialog title (and the availability of the Style Type drop-down list) this dialog box is the same as the Modify Style dialog box. Figures 14-2 through 14-5 earlier in this chapter show the Modify Style dialog box as it appears for each of the four types of Word styles.

4 In the Style Type drop-down list, select Paragraph, Character, Table, or List to specify the type of style you want to create.

5 Select the formatting and other features you want for your new user-defined style, following the instructions that were given under step 4 of the procedure for modifying an existing style (see page 397). As you apply those instructions, note the following:

- Word initially sets the base style to the style that's assigned to the selected text in the document (for any type of style except a List type). To base the new style on a different style—or on no style—choose the appropriate option in the Style Based On drop-down list.

- For a paragraph style, Word initially makes the style for the following paragraph the same as the new style. To have Word assign a different style to a paragraph that follows a paragraph with the new style, choose a style in the Style For Following Paragraph drop-down list.

6 When you've finished making changes to the style, click OK in the New Style dialog box to save your new user-defined style.

Word will save the new style definition within the current document. It will also copy the new style to the template attached to the document if you checked the Add To Template option in the New Style dialog box. For information on ways to copy the new style to other templates or documents, see the next section.

> **Tip**   **Work with table and list styles in other ways**
> An alternative way to modify, create, or delete Table styles is to choose Table, Table Auto-Format, and use the Modify, New, or Delete button in the Table AutoFormat dialog box, discussed in "Formatting Tables by Applying Table Styles," on page 357.
>
> Another way to modify, create, or delete List Styles is to choose Format, Bullets And Numbering, and use the Modify, Add, or Delete button in the List Styles tab of the Bullets And Numbering dialog box, described in "Creating an Outline Numbered List by Applying a List Style," on page 383.

Reusing Your Styles by Making Copies

Each document and each template stores its own private set of user-defined styles and modified built-in styles. Therefore, adding or modifying a style in a document doesn't normally affect the template, and adding or modifying a style in a template doesn't normally affect documents that were already created using the template. You can, however, use several Word options and commands to copy these types of styles from a document or template to another document or template. Copying styles allows you to take advantage of any style that's contained in any document or template and to share styles with other members of your workgroup. The next three sections describe various ways to copy styles between documents and templates.

Copying Styles from a Template to a Document

To take advantage of a style that is stored in a template, you must copy it into a document. Styles can be copied from a template to a document in the following ways:

- When you create a new document, it automatically acquires a copy of all the user-defined styles and modified built-in styles that are stored in the template that the document is based on.

- To have Word automatically copy all styles from a document's template into the document each time you open the document, choose Tools, Templates And Add-Ins, click the Templates tab, and check the Automatically Update Document Styles option (shown in Figure 14-6). This option is useful if you periodically update the styles stored in the template and want a particular document to always have the latest style versions.

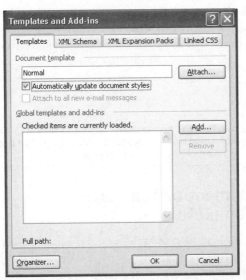

Figure 14-6. Check the Automatically Update Document Styles option to have Word copy styles from a document's template into the document each time you open the document.

- You can use the Style Gallery to copy entire sets of styles from any template into your current document, thereby rapidly changing the overall look of the document.

Using the Style Gallery is explained in "Formatting Your Documents Automatically," on page 340.

- You can use the Organizer to copy as many or as few styles as you want from a template to a document.

For information on the Organizer, see "Using the Organizer," on page 412.

Copying Styles from a Document to a Template

When you create or modify a style in a document, you might want to copy the style into a template so that it will be stored there and will be available in any document you subsequently create using that template (and in any document that's updated from that template through the Automatically Update Document Styles option, discussed in the previous section). You can do this several different ways.

- When you modify or create a style in the Modify Style or the New Style dialog box, you can check the Add To Template option. Word will then copy the modified or new style to the document template, as explained earlier in the chapter. (If you want to copy a style without changing it, you can open the Modify Style dialog box for that style, click the Add To Template option, and click OK without altering any of the formatting settings.)

● When you select character formatting in the Font or Language dialog boxes, you can click the Default button and respond Yes when prompted. Word will assign the selected formatting to the document's Normal style and it will copy the updated Normal style to the document template.

● You can use the Organizer to copy as many or as few styles as you want from a document to a template.

> For a description of the Font dialog box, see "Formatting Characters with the Font Dialog Box," on page 313. For a description of the Language dialog box, see "Marking the Language," on page 505. For information on the Organizer, see "Using the Organizer," on page 412.

Copying Styles from a Document or Template to Another Document or Template

The Organizer has already been mentioned several times in the previous sections. The Organizer is the ultimate tool for copying styles. It lets you copy individual styles or groups of styles from any document or template to any other document or template. It also lets you delete or rename one or more styles. To run the Organizer, choose Tools, Templates And Add-Ins and click the Organizer button in the Templates And Add-Ins dialog box.

> The Organizer is discussed in "Using the Organizer," on page 412.

Customizing and Creating Document Templates

A template stores a variety of items that form the basis of a Word document. When you create a new document, some of the items, such as text and styles, are copied into the document from the template that you select. Other items, such as AutoText entries and macros, are kept in the template; the template, however, remains attached to the document so that the document can access these items.

> **Note** Every Word document is based on a template. If you create a document using the File, New command (together with the New Document task pane) or if you create it using the Start, All Programs (or Programs), Microsoft Office Tools, New Office Document command in Microsoft Windows, you can choose the template. If you create a new document by clicking the New button on the Standard toolbar, the document will be based on the Normal template. Note that the template that the document is based on is also called the *document template* or the *template attached to the document*. As explained later in this chapter, you can change the document template after you have created the document.

Table 14-2 lists the template items that are copied into a new document. Once you have created a new document, the document and the template have separate copies of these items. Normally, changing one of these items in the document won't affect the template, and changing an item in the template won't affect the document. (An exception is that Word will copy style changes between documents and templates—*after* the document has been created—in the situations that were described in "Reusing Your Styles by Making Copies," on page 406.)

Table 14-2. Template Items That Are Copied to a New Document

Template Item	Comments
Text and graphics, together with the formatting assigned to them	Includes headers, footers, footnotes, and comments.
Page setup	Includes the margins, paper size and source, page layout, and other features (explained in Chapter 18). Also includes the default tab stop setting (which you define by choosing Format, Tabs and entering a value into the Default Tab Stops text box).
Styles	All the styles stored in the template are copied to the document. See the sidebar "Types of Styles Stored in a Document or Template," on page 410.

For information on choosing a template when you create a new document, see "Creating a Document Using the New Office Document Dialog Box," on page 47.

Table 14-3 lists the items that are kept in the template when a new document is created. A document can access any item stored in the document template. It can also access any item stored in the Normal template. (Of course, if the document is based on Normal, the document template and Normal are the same.) In addition, a document can access any item that is stored in a template that has been explicitly loaded as a *global template.*

Loading global templates is discussed in "Loading Global Templates and Word Add-Ins," on page 416.

For example, if an AutoText entry named Close is defined in either the document template or the Normal template, you can insert it into your document using any of the methods discussed in "Reusing Text with the AutoText Feature," on page 266. If an AutoText entry named Close is defined in both the document template and the Normal template, Word will insert the text defined in the document template. (That is, an item defined in the document template overrides a similarly named item in the Normal template or in a global template that has been loaded as described later in the chapter.)

Table 14-3. Template Items Kept Within the Document Template

Template Item	Comments
AutoText entries	An AutoText entry is a stored block of text or graphics that you can insert anywhere into a document, as explained in "Reusing Text with the AutoText Feature," on page 266.
Macros	A macro is a script for automating a Word task, as discussed in "Recording and Running Macros," on page 224.

Table 14-3. Template Items Kept Within the Document Template

Template Item	Comments
Custom toolbars, as well as modifications to toolbars, menus, or shortcut keys	Creating custom toolbars and modifying toolbars and menus is discussed in Chapter 9, "Customizing the Office 2003 Application Interface."
Shortcut key definitions	Defining shortcut keys to run commands, apply styles, or perform other tasks is covered in "Defining Shortcut Keys (Word Only)," on page 222.

Note When you create a macro, a custom toolbar or menu, or a shortcut key definition, you have the option of storing it within the document rather than within a template so that the item will be private to that document. AutoText entries, however, can be stored only in a template.

Types of Styles Stored in a Document or Template

The following types of styles can be stored directly within a document or template file:

- All documents and templates store five basic "default" built-in styles (whether or not these styles have been used in the document or have been modified): Normal, Normal (Web), Default Paragraph Font, No List, and Table Normal.

  Default Paragraph Font, No List, and Table Normal are atypical styles that are applied to text to remove character, list, or table styles or formatting. They can't be modified.

- Any built-in style that was used in the document, even if it is no longer applied to document text and even if it hasn't been modified.

- Modified versions of built-in styles.

- User-defined styles.

You can view a complete list of the styles currently stored in a document or template by using the Styles tab of the Organizer, discussed later in this chapter.

Keep in mind that when you apply styles to text in a document or template, you can use any of the styles that are actually stored in the document or template, *plus* any of the built-in styles stored in Word.

Customizing Templates

You can modify Word templates in a variety of ways. First, performing any of the following common Word actions can automatically modify a template.

- Creating any of the items listed in Table 14-3: an AutoText entry, a macro, a custom toolbar or menu, or a shortcut key. When you create any of these items, you can save it in the Normal template or in the document template if it's other than Normal. (You also have the option of saving any of these items, except an AutoText entry, right within the document.)

- Clicking the Default button in the Font, Language, or Page Setup dialog box and responding Yes when prompted. Clicking Default saves the character formatting, language, or page setup in the document template. The character formatting and language are stored within the Normal style of the document template.

- Selecting the Add To Template option when modifying or creating a style (in the Modify Style or New Style dialog box) will copy the modified or new style to the document template.

Another way to modify a template is to open the template file and edit it in the same way you edit a document. To do so, perform the following general steps:

1 Choose File, Open.

2 In the Open dialog box, select Document Templates (*.dot) in the Files Of Type drop-down list and then select the template file you want to modify.

The templates supplied with Word (except Normal) are stored in subfolders of C:\Program Files\Microsoft Office\Templates. The Normal template, plus any templates you create, are usually stored within the following folder, or subfolders of this folder: C:\Documents And Settings*User Name*\Application Data\Microsoft\Templates, where *UserName* is the name you use for logging on to Windows.

> You can change the locations where Normal and user-created templates are stored, as explained in the tip "Choose locations for your templates," on page 415.

3 Edit and format the template using the same techniques used for documents. You can add or modify any of the template items listed in Table 14-2 or Table 14-3. For the items listed in Table 14-3, be sure to save your changes in the template itself rather than in the Normal template.

4 Choose File, Save, or click the Save button to save your changes.

Tip   Open a template file for editing

In Microsoft Windows Explorer or in a folder window, double-clicking a Word template file (such as Elegant Fax.dot) will create a Word document based on that template. To open the template file itself, right-click the file and choose Open from the shortcut menu, as shown here:

(Choosing New would have the same effect as double-clicking the file.)

Using the Organizer

You can also directly change the contents of one or more templates by using the Organizer. With the Organizer you can delete, rename, or copy styles, AutoText entries, custom toolbars, or macro project items (macro modules or forms). You can copy styles, custom toolbars, or macro project items from a template or document to another template or document. You can copy AutoText entries only from one template to another.

To use the Organizer, perform the following steps:

1   Choose Tools, Templates And Add-Ins, and then click the Organizer button in the Templates And Add-Ins dialog box. This will open the Organizer log box (shown in Figure 14-7).

2   In the Organizer dialog box, click the tab corresponding to the type of template item you want to manage: styles, AutoText entries, custom toolbars, or macro project items.

A tab in the Organizer displays two lists, each of which displays the items belonging to a particular template or document. (In this discussion, *item* is used to refer to a style, AutoText entry, custom toolbar, or macro project item.)

> The lists in the Styles tab itemize all the styles currently stored within the template or document file. For details, see the sidebar "Types of Styles Stored in a Document or Template," on page 410.

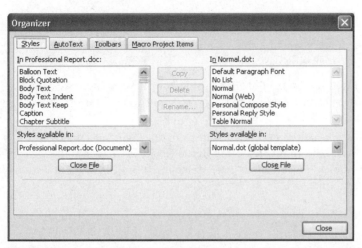

Figure 14-7. This figure shows the Styles tab of the Organizer dialog box.

3   If you want to work with the items in a different document or template (that is, one whose items aren't currently displayed in the tab), select the file from either of the *Items* Available In drop-down lists. (In the actual list labels, *Items* will be Styles, Auto-Text, Toolbars, or Macro Project Items, according to the tab you have opened. In this discussion, *file* refers to either a document or a template.) If you don't find the file in either list, click one of the Close File buttons to close the currently displayed file, and then click the button again (it will then be labeled Open File) and select the file in the Open dialog box.

4   In the appropriate list, select the item or items you want to work with. To select a single item, click it. To select a range of items in a list, click the first one and then press Shift and click the last one. To select several items that are not adjoining, click the first one and then press Ctrl and click each additional item.

5   Perform one of the following actions:

-   To copy the selected item or items into the file whose items are shown in the other list, click the Copy button.

-   To rename the selected item, click the Rename button. (Only a single item can be selected.)

-   To delete the selected item or items, click the Delete button.

Note   You can delete, copy, or rename styles, custom toolbars, or macros stored in either a document or a template. AutoText entries, however, are stored only in templates.

Tip   Don't forget to copy macros
If you copy a custom toolbar that contains buttons to which you've assigned macros, be sure to also copy the macro project item or items containing those macros!

Creating New Templates

The procedure for creating a new template is similar to that for creating a new document. Perform the following basic steps:

1 Create a new Word document using any of the methods discussed in "Creating New Office Documents," on page 47. To save time, base the document on a template that's similar to the new template you want to create.

If you create the new document using the Templates dialog box in Word, be sure to select the Template option in the Create New area in the lower-right corner of the dialog box, as shown here (selecting this option will make it a bit easier to save the template):

2 Enter text and graphics, edit, and format the new template using the same techniques used for documents. You can add any of the items listed in Table 14-2 and Table 14-3. For the items listed in Table 14-3, be sure to save your changes in the document itself (which will already be designated as a template if you selected the Template option in Step 1), rather than in another template.

3 Choose File, Save, or click the Save button to open the Save As dialog box. Unless you created the document using the Templates dialog box in Word and selected the Template option as described in step 1, you'll need to select Document Template (*.dot) in the Save As Type drop-down list.

When Document Template (*.dot) is selected in the Save As Type list, the Save As dialog box automatically opens your current User Templates folder. If you want the Templates dialog box to display the new template you're creating, you must save it in the file folder designated as your User Templates folder or in one of its subfolders. The default User Templates folder is C:\Documents and Settings*User Name*\ Application Data\Microsoft\Templates, where *UserName* is the name you use for logging on to Windows. You can save the template directly within your User Templates folder; in this case, the template will be displayed in the General tab of the Templates (or New Office Document) dialog box. Alternatively, you can place it within a subfolder of your User Templates folder (an existing subfolder or a new one that you create); in this case, the template will be displayed in the Templates (or New Office Document) dialog box in a tab that's labeled with the name of the subfolder.

4 In the Save As dialog box, enter a name for your new template in the File Name box and click the Save button.

You must name the template file with the .dot extension or omit the extension. (If you omit it, Word will add the .dot.) Note that file extensions might not be displayed when you list files, depending on the options you have chosen in Windows.

Tip Choose locations for your templates

You can designate a different folder as your User Templates folder, causing the Templates (or New Office Document) dialog box to display the templates stored in the new folder you specify, rather than in the original User Templates folder. To do this, choose Tools, Options, click the File Locations tab, click User Templates in the list, click the Modify button, and enter the new folder path. This change will affect all Office applications that use templates, not just Word.

Notice that in the File Locations tab, you can also designate a Workgroup Templates folder. (Initially, no folder is designated for this item.) If you do so, the Templates (or New Office Document) dialog box will display the templates in the Workgroup Templates folder in addition to those in your User Templates folder. Typically, the Workgroup Templates folder is located on a network and contains a set of templates that you share with coworkers.

In addition to the new and customized templates stored in the User Templates and Workgroup Templates folders, the Templates (or New Office Document) dialog box displays the templates that are supplied with Word, such as Contemporary Letter and Professional Memo.

Note also that when Word creates a Normal.dot template file (when you first start using Word or if Normal.dot has been deleted) it stores it in the current User Templates folder.

Tip Base a new template on an existing document

If an existing document already contains many of the features you want to add to a new template, you can save time by basing the new template on that document. To do this, choose File, New, and then click the From Existing Document command in the New area of the New Document task pane. In the New From Existing Document dialog box, select the document you want to use as a basis for your template and then click the Create New button. When you first save the new document after editing it, be sure to select the Document Template (*.dot) item in the Save As Type drop-down list of the Save As dialog box.

Attaching a Template to a Document

You can change the template that's attached to a document. When you do this, all the Auto-Text entries, custom toolbars, interface modifications (toolbar, menu, and shortcut key), and macros that are stored in the newly attached template become available to the document in place of the items stored in the previously attached template. To change the document template for the current document, perform the following steps:

1   Choose Tools, Templates And Add-Ins and click the Templates tab in the Templates And Add-Ins dialog box (shown in Figure 14-6).

2   Click the Attach button.

Chapter 14

3   Select the desired template in the Attach Template dialog box, which works just like the standard Open dialog box for opening a Word document. Make sure that Document Templates (*.dot) is selected in the Files Of Type drop-down list. Then click the Open button.

Loading Global Templates and Word Add-Ins

Word allows you to load one or more templates *in addition* to the Normal template and (if separate from Normal) the document template. An additional template that you have loaded is known as a *global template*. All the AutoText entries, custom toolbars, interface modifications (toolbar, menu, and shortcut key), and macros that are stored in a global template become available to *any* document currently open in Word. (An item defined in a document template, however, overrides a similarly named item in any of the global templates you load.) To load a global template, choose Tools, Templates And Add-Ins, click the Templates tab in the Templates And Add-Ins dialog box, and perform one of the following actions:

- If the template is listed within the Global Templates And Add-Ins list, simply check the adjoining check box.

- If the template isn't in the list, click the Add button to open the Add Template dialog box. In this dialog box, make sure that the Document Templates (*.dot) item is selected in the Files Of Type drop-down list, select the template you want, and click OK. The template will be added to the Global Templates And Add-Ins list and will be checked.

> **Note**   You can also load a Word add-in, which is a utility program that supplies enhancement features to Word. (You can obtain Word add-ins from various software vendors.) To do this, follow the procedure for opening an additional template, except that in the Add Template dialog box you must choose the Word Add-Ins (*.wll) item in the Files Of Type drop-down list.

A global template or add-in will remain loaded only for the remainder of your current Word session. When you exit and restart Word, you'll need to reload it by checking it in the Global Templates And Add-Ins list. (The template or add-in will still be in the list, although it won't be checked.)

Troubleshooting

Missing AutoText, macros, or customizations

You moved or copied a document to a different computer or network location (perhaps you sent the file to a co-worker), and now you or your coworker can no longer access the AutoText entries, the macros, or the menu, toolbar, and keyboard customizations that you previously used with that document.

The most likely reason that the items are missing is that they're stored in the document's template (or in the Normal template) and Word can't access that template from the document's new location. Here are two possible solutions to this problem:

- Before you move or copy the document, use the Organizer to copy all macros and custom toolbars from the document template directly into the document. This method won't work, however, for AutoText entries (which can be stored only in a template) or for other customizations (that is, modifications to toolbars, menus, or shortcut keys, which you can't copy using the Organizer).

- Create a new template located in the same folder as the document on your computer, attach the template to your document, and use the Organizer to copy all needed items into the new template. (Be sure *not* to name the new template Normal.dot.) Then, copy or move both the document and its new template to the new location.

The techniques mentioned have all been discussed in this chapter.

Managing Large or Complex Documents

Working with Documents in
Outline View 419

Inserting Footnotes and Endnotes 434

Generating Indexes and
Tables of Contents 438

Working with Documents in Outline View

Outline view can be a great help while you're planning or organizing a document and even while you're entering the bulk of the document text. The following are among the important features and advantages of Outline view:

- The outline headings in the document—and the text that follows them—are indented by various amounts, so that you can immediately see your document's hierarchical structure.

- You can control the level of detail that is visible in the outline. For example, you can hide all body text and view only the headings to see your document's overall organization. Or, you can hide the content under all top-level headings except the one you're working on to help you focus on that part of the document.

- You can quickly move an individual paragraph or an entire heading together with all text and subheadings that follow it.

- You can usually see more text on the screen in Outline view than in other views because all text is single spaced and extra space before or after a paragraph isn't shown, regardless of the paragraph formatting.

 Inside Out

Modifying paragraph formatting in Outline view

In Outline view, paragraph formatting isn't displayed and you can't open the Paragraph dialog box to apply paragraph formatting. (You can control whether or not character formatting is displayed, as explained later.) Therefore, to modify the formatting of your paragraphs, you should switch out of Outline view.

> **Note** This chapter explains how to organize, footnote, index, and add tables of contents to your Word 2003 documents. Although these techniques are especially useful for developing long or complex documents, such as books, manuals, and academic papers, you can use them when writing any type of document.

Switching to Outline View

To activate Outline view, choose View, Outline, or click the Outline View button on the left end of the horizontal scroll bar shown here:

Word will display the document as an outline, and it will show the Outlining toolbar, shown in Figure 15-1. In Outline view, *heading* refers to any paragraph that has been assigned one of the built-in Heading styles, Heading 1 through Heading 9. A heading assigned the Heading 1 style is at the highest level and is not indented. A heading assigned Heading 2 is at a lower level and is indented a small amount when displayed in Outline view. A heading assigned Heading 3 is at an even lower level and is indented more in Outline view, and so on. *Body text* refers to all paragraphs displayed in Outline view that have not been assigned a Heading style.

> **Note** Switching to Outline view doesn't change the content or format of your document. It merely displays the document in a different way and allows you to work with it differently.

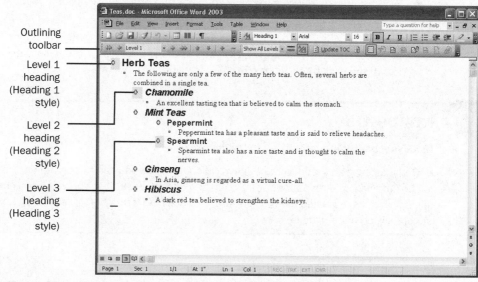

Figure 15-1. This figure shows a Word document in Outline view.

In Outline view, Word displays one of the symbols shown in Table 15-1 in front of each paragraph. *Subtext* refers to all subheadings and body text that come under a heading.

Table 15-1. **Symbols Used in Outline View**

Symbol	Type of Paragraph
✛	Heading with subtext
▭	Heading without subtext
▫	Body text

If you have already assigned the Heading 1 through Heading 9 styles to your document headings (as recommended in Chapter 12, "Effective Formatting in Word"), Word will indent the headings appropriately in Outline view and the document will look like an outline, as shown in Figure 15-1. If, however, you haven't already assigned the built-in Heading styles to your heading paragraphs, the document will consist of a simple list of body text paragraphs, as shown in Figure 15-2, and it won't look much like an outline. Don't worry—by using the buttons on the Outlining toolbar, you can easily apply Heading styles and convert the document into outline form.

> **Note** Because each level of heading is assigned a different Heading style, each generally has different formatting. Higher-level headings are typically formatted with larger, bold fonts to convey their relative importance; lower-level headings are typically formatted with smaller, nonbold fonts.

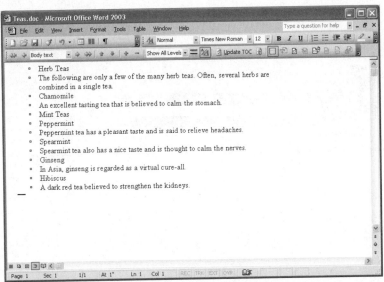

Figure 15-2. A document containing headings that haven't been assigned the built-in Heading styles looks like a simple list of paragraphs in Outline view.

To quickly change the appearance of a particular level of heading throughout your document, you can modify the corresponding built-in Heading style, as explained in "Customizing Styles," on page 389.

Changing Outline Levels

You can use the first five controls on the Outlining toolbar, shown below, to change the level of a heading, to convert a paragraph of body text to a heading, or to convert a heading to a paragraph of body text:

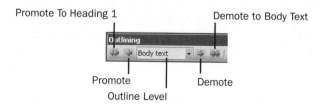

Promote To Heading 1

Demote to Body Text

Promote

Demote

Outline Level

In general, you can perform outlining operations on more than one paragraph (headings or body text) by selecting several paragraphs prior to issuing the command. For simplicity, however, the discussions on outlining use the singular terms *heading* or *paragraph*.

Tip   Select a heading and its contents quickly

To select a heading together with all its subtext, just click the symbol in front of the heading, as shown here:

Click here

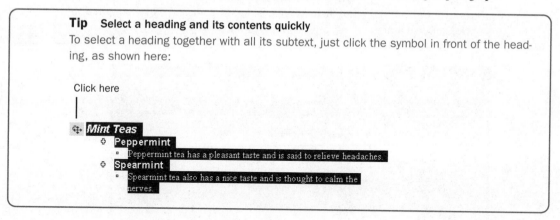

Chapter 15

To change the level of a heading, perform the following steps:

1   Place the insertion point in the heading you want to change (or select several headings).

2   Do one of the following:

   ■   To promote the heading to the next higher level, click the Promote button, or press Alt+Shift+Left Arrow or Shift+Tab.

   ■   To demote the heading to the next lower level, click the Demote button, or press Alt+Shift+Right Arrow or Tab.

   ■   To promote the heading to a level 1 heading in a single step, assigning it the Heading 1 style, click the Promote To Heading 1 button.

   ■   To promote or demote the heading directly to any level—or to convert it to body text—select an outline level from the Outline Level drop-down list on the Outlining toolbar, shown here:

Tip   To enter a tab character while you're in Outline view, press Ctrl+Tab.

You can also change the level of a heading, as well as any subheadings that follow it, by dragging the heading symbol to the left to promote it or to the right to demote it, as seen here:

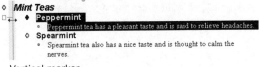

Vertical marker

423

The vertical marker that temporarily appears when you drag a heading horizontally indicates the new level that would be assigned to the highest-level heading in the selection if you released the mouse button at the current position.

When Word changes the level of a heading, it assigns it a new Heading style. For example, if you demote a top-level heading, Word changes the style from Heading 1 to Heading 2.

You can convert a paragraph of body text (that is, a paragraph that isn't assigned one of the built-in Heading styles) to an outline heading by either promoting it or demoting it, using any of the methods just described. You can select more than one paragraph of body text, but don't include a heading in the selection. If you promote a paragraph of body text by one level, it's converted into a heading at the same level as the preceding heading. If you demote it by one level, it's converted into a heading one level lower than the preceding heading. If you click the Promote To Heading 1 button on the Outlining toolbar, it becomes a top-level (Heading 1) heading. And if you promote or demote it by selecting a level in the Outline Level drop-down list on the Outlining toolbar, it's converted directly to the heading level you select.

> **Tip** Use styles to change outline levels
>
> You can also change the level of a heading, convert body text to a heading, or convert a heading to body text by directly assigning the paragraph the appropriate style (Heading 1 through Heading 9 for a heading, or a style such as Normal or Body Text for body text). You can quickly apply the Heading 1, Heading 2, or Heading 3 style by pressing Alt+Ctrl+1, Alt+Ctrl+2, or Alt+Ctrl+3, respectively, and you can apply the Normal paragraph style by pressing Ctrl+Shift+N.

To convert a heading to body text, place the insertion point within the heading (or select several headings), and click the Demote To Body Text button or press Alt+Shift+5 (5 on the numeric keypad with Num Lock off). Word will assign the paragraph the Normal style.

> **Tip** Number your outline headings automatically
>
> You can apply automatic outline numbering to all the outline headings throughout your document (that is, to all paragraphs assigned the built-in Heading styles, Heading 1 through Heading 9). To do this, place the insertion point within any heading, choose Format, Bullets And Numbering, click the Outline Numbered tab in the Bullets And Numbering dialog box, select one of the four outline numbering styles on the bottom row, and click OK. (Notice that the sample in the Outline Numbered tab for each of these styles contains the names of Heading styles.) For more information, see "Creating an Outline Numbered List Using the Outline Numbered Tab," on page 381.

Creating Headings Using Outline-Level Formatting

The discussions in this chapter assume that your outline headings are assigned the built-in Heading styles (Heading 1 through Heading 9). However, you can also create an outline heading by assigning outline-level formatting to a paragraph that hasn't been assigned a Heading style. To do this, switch out of Outline view, select the paragraph, choose Format, Paragraph, click the Indents And Spacing tab, and choose the desired heading level (Level 1 through Level 9) in the Outline Level drop-down list. (You can choose the Body Text item in this list to convert an outline heading to outline body text.)

In general, however, it's easier to create outline headings by assigning the Heading 1 through Heading 9 built-in styles for several reasons:

● In Outline view, you can rapidly and easily assign a Heading style using the Outlining toolbar or the shortcut keys that were described. (In contrast, to assign outline-level formatting, you have to switch out of Outline view and perform the time-consuming procedure just described.)

● If you're not using the Heading styles, when you work in Outline view it's likely that you'll lose the style (and the style's formatting) that you've applied to a paragraph. Some of the controls on the Outlining toolbar (such as the Promote To Heading 1 button) will apply a Heading style, overwriting the paragraph's original style.

● Assigning a Heading style will apply appropriate formatting for a heading (such as a larger font, bold type, and so on). Using the Heading styles will also make it easier to maintain consistent formatting of your headings and to quickly modify this formatting throughout the document.

● You can have Word number Heading styles, as explained in the tip "Number your outline headings automatically," on page 424. (You can also do this with non-Heading styles, but only by defining a custom outline numbering type.)

Moving Blocks of Text

You can quickly move one or more paragraphs by using the two buttons shown here on the Outlining toolbar:

Move up ———  ——— Move down

The paragraphs can be either headings or body text. To move these paragraphs, perform the following steps:

1 Place the insertion point within the paragraph you want to move (or select several paragraphs).

2 Do one of the following:

- To move the paragraph above the previous paragraph, click the Move Up button or press Alt+Shift+Up Arrow.

- To move the paragraph below the following paragraph, click the Move Down button or press Alt+Shift+Down Arrow.

3 Repeat step 2 as necessary to move the paragraph to the desired final position.

You can also quickly move a paragraph by dragging the paragraph symbol up or down in the document, as shown here:

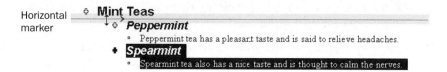

The horizontal marker that temporarily appears when you drag a heading vertically indicates the new position the paragraph would occupy if you released the mouse button at the current position. If you use this method to move a heading, it moves all the heading's subtext as well, because both the heading and its subtext are selected when you begin dragging the symbol.

Collapsing and Expanding Outline Text

You can use the buttons on the Outlining toolbar shown here to change the level of detail that's visible in the outline:

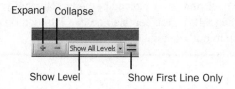

To hide the subtext—subheadings or body text—that follows a particular heading, perform these steps:

1 Place the insertion point within the heading (or select several headings).

2 Click the Collapse button, press Alt+Shift+- (the hyphen key on the top row of the keyboard), or press – (the minus key on the numeric keypad). Word will hide the lowest level of subtext that is currently visible.

For example, if your cursor is in a level 1 heading and the level 1 heading is followed by level 2 headings, level 3 headings, and body text, the first time you click the Collapse button, the body text will be hidden. (Body text is considered to be at the lowest level.) The next time you click Collapse, the level 3 headings will be hidden, and the third time you click Collapse, the level 2 headings will be hidden.

3 Repeat step 2 as necessary to hide the desired amount of subtext.

To redisplay collapsed subtext, use this same procedure, but in step 2, click the Expand button, press Alt+Shift+=, or press + (plus key) on the numeric keypad.

You can also fully collapse a heading (that is, hide all its subtext) by double-clicking the paragraph symbol, as shown here:

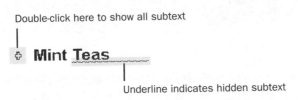

Double-click to hide all subtext

To fully expand the heading, double-click again. Notice that when a heading contains collapsed subtext, Word marks it with thick underlining, as seen here:

Double-click here to show all subtext

Mint Teas

Underline indicates hidden subtext

To change the levels of headings displayed throughout the entire document, open the Show Level drop-down list on the Outlining toolbar, shown here:

Then, select an item in the list, as follows:

- To display all headings through a particular heading level, hiding body text, select an item in the range from Show Level 1 through Show Level 9. For example, selecting Show Level 3 would show all level 1, level 2, and level 3 headings. Selecting Show Level 9 would show all headings in the document. Rather than selecting a specific level in the Show Level list, you can press the equivalent shortcut key, Alt+Shift+1, Alt+Shift+2, Alt+Shift+3, and so on (press the number on the top row of the keyboard, *not* on the numeric keypad).

- To show all headings in the document, plus all body text, select Show All Levels. Rather than using the Show Level list, you can press the equivalent shortcut key, Alt+Shift+A, or

* (asterisk) on the numeric keypad. Pressing the shortcut key repeatedly toggles between Show All Levels and Show Level 9.

If body text is shown, you can have Word display only the first line of each paragraph of body text by turning on the Show First Line Only mode. You can turn this mode on or off by clicking the Show First Line Only button on the Outlining toolbar or by pressing the Alt+Shift+L shortcut key. Word will indicate the presence of hidden body text by displaying an ellipsis (…) at the end of the first line of each body text paragraph.

To display all text in the outline (including headings) using the character formatting currently assigned to the Normal style, rather than the actual formatting assigned to each paragraph, turn off the Show Formatting mode. You can turn this mode off or on by clicking the Show Formatting button on the Outlining toolbar, shown here, or by pressing the / (slash) key on the numeric keypad. The Show Formatting mode doesn't remove character formatting but merely suppresses its display.

Show Formatting   Master Document View

Master Document View is a special mode of Outline view that allows you to divide a long Word document into separate subdocuments, all of which belong to a single *master document*. If you're creating a very large manuscript (such as a book) and want to be able to format, print, and work with the entire manuscript as a unit, creating a master document—together with subdocuments—might be a more manageable solution than attempting to store the entire manuscript in a single document file.

You can turn the Master Document View mode on or off by clicking the Master Document View button on the Outlining toolbar. The buttons on the Outlining toolbar to the right of the Master Document View button are displayed only when the Master Document View mode is active, and are provided for working with master documents. For information on creating and using master documents, look up the topic "master documents" in the Word online Help.

> The Update TOC and Go To TOC buttons on the Outlining toolbar are explained in "Generating a Table of Contents," later in the chapter.

Tip   Include documents using an alternative method

You can also tie together separate documents so that you can print them in series and work with them as a unit by creating a single overview document (analogous to a master document created in Master Document View). In the overview document, include each of the separate Word documents that make up your manuscript by inserting an IncludeText field. To insert this field, choose Insert, Field, select IncludeText in the Field Names list, fill in the other options in the Field dialog box, and click the OK button (see Figure 15-3). Note that in Word 2003, the IncludeText field can also be used to embed XML (Extensible Markup Language) data in the document.

Chapter 15

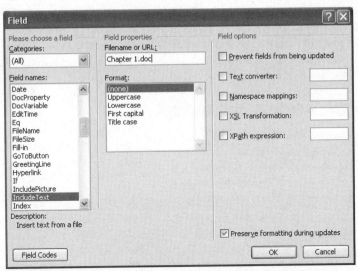

Figure 15-3. You can include a document in another Word document using the IncludeText field.

Troubleshooting

Your document is too big to save

You issue the Save command but you get a message indicating that your document is too large to save.

Don't panic. Nothing has been lost yet. Word is just unable to put all the pieces of your document together in a single disk file. What you should do first is cut part of the document's text into the Clipboard, paste it into a new document, and then save both documents on disk. Once you've safely saved all your text on disk, you can think about how to organize the text contained in the separate document files.

One way to organize a collection of separate document files that make up a single, large manuscript is to create a Master Document and include each of the separate document files within it as subdocuments, as discussed in "Collapsing and Expanding Outline Text," on page 426. Alternatively, you can tie together separate documents in a single overview document by using IncludeText fields, as explained in the tip "Include documents using an alternative method," on page 428.

Navigating Through an Outline

Word provides two features that let you quickly scroll to a particular document heading that is formatted with one of the built-in Heading styles. These features offer additional reasons to use the built-in Heading styles.

When you drag the scroll box on the vertical scroll bar, Word displays the page number of the current position as well as the text of the preceding outline heading (or at least the first part of the text), as shown in Figure 15-4. This feature works only if the Show ScreenTips On Toolbars option is selected. To set this option, choose Tools, Customize, and click the Options tab. Note also that this feature isn't available in Web Layout view.

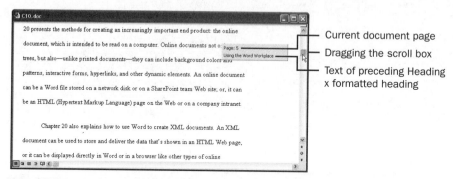

Current document page

Dragging the scroll box

Text of preceding Heading x formatted heading

Figure 15-4. The ScreenTip shown here displays your current document position as you scroll.

To locate a particular outline heading, simply drag the scroll box until you see the heading displayed and then release the mouse button. Note that you don't need to be in Outline view to use this feature.

Document Map

A second feature that makes it easy to scroll to a particular heading is the Document Map, which is available in all views except Print Preview and is displayed in a separate pane at the left of the Word window (see Figure 15-5). To display the Document Map, choose View, Document Map, or click the Document Map button on the Standard toolbar.

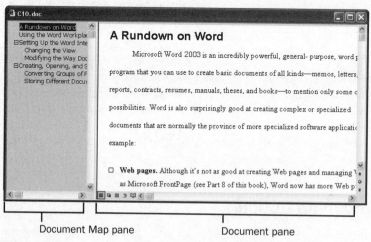

Document Map pane

Document pane

Figure 15-5. The Document Map makes it easy to display and scroll to headings in a document.

Chapter 15

The Document Map lets you see all your document headings even if you're not in Outline view. Notice that if the full text of a heading isn't visible, you can display a ScreenTip showing the full heading text by placing the pointer over the heading, as shown in this example:

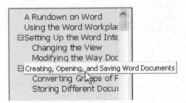

Inside Out

Using heading styles for displaying the Document Map

The Document Map works well if you've consistently formatted your document headings using the built-in Heading styles. If you've formatted some or all of your headings by directly applying formatting features (such as a large font size, bold, and so on) rather than using a built-in Heading style, the Document Map attempts to identify document headings by their formatting. However, it often mistakenly identifies document elements such as figure captions, notes, sidebar titles, and so on, as headings, and displays them in the Document Map. It displays suspected headings in the Document Map by permanently changing their paragraph formatting to include outline-level formatting (discussed in the sidebar "Creating Headings Using Outline-Level Formatting," on page 425). The next time you view the document in Outline view, you might be quite surprised to see many of your document elements (such as figure captions) appearing as outline headings.

To avoid this problem, use the built-in Heading styles to format *all* your document headings!

To have Word scroll your document to a particular heading, just click that heading within the Document Map. If not all headings fit in the Document Map, you can use the vertical scroll bar within the Document Map pane to see additional headings.

Notice that if a heading is followed by one or more subheadings, Word displays a square box containing either a + or – symbol to the left of the heading in the Document Map. You can hide the subheadings in the Document Map by clicking the box with the – symbol, as shown here:

Click here to hide subheadings

This symbol means subheadings are currently visible

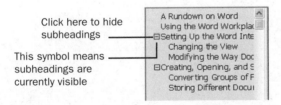

Chapter 15

You can show the subheadings by clicking the box with the + symbol, as seen here:

This symbol means subheadings
are currently hidden ————————

Click here to show subheadings ————————

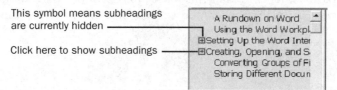

You can also collapse or expand the selected heading in the Document Map or change the level of headings shown throughout the Document Map by right-clicking in the Document Map pane and choosing the appropriate command from the shortcut menu.

If you're in Outline view, hiding or showing headings in the Document Map also hides or shows them in the document pane. In Normal, Web Layout, Print Layout, and Reading Layout views, hiding or showing headings in the Document Map doesn't affect the document pane.

Inside Out

Disappearing document panes

You can't display the Document Map when an additional pane is opened in the document window (such as the Reviewing pane, the Footnotes pane, or a second document pane opened by choosing Window, Split). If you open the document pane when an additional pane is open, Word will close the additional pane before displaying the Document Map.

Also, if you change the Word view, Word will hide the Document Map unless the Document Map was previously displayed in that view. You need to control whether or not it's displayed separately in each view.

Printing an Outline

When you print a document while in Outline view, Word prints only the headings and body text that are currently visible. To print the whole document, select Show All Levels in the Show drop-down list on the Outlining toolbar or switch out of Outline view before printing.

Inside Out

Create a better looking printed outline

The appearance of a document printed in Outline view is often disappointing. Paragraph formatting features don't show, lines are always single spaced, and you can't add extra space between paragraphs. Also, the small box symbols that visually separate paragraphs of body text on the screen don't print, so the paragraphs of body text all run together. To print an attractively formatted outline, consider switching out of Outline view and formatting the text in the document as an outline numbered list, as explained in "Creating Lists with the Bullets And Numbering Dialog Box and List Styles," on page 379.

For information on printing documents, see "Previewing and Printing Documents," on page 543.

Troubleshooting

You have trouble copying outline headings

Your editor has asked you to submit a Word document containing an outline of the chapter you're writing. You open the chapter, switch into Outline view, and display the levels of headings you want to include. However, when you try to copy those headings to a different document, all body text and subheadings are included with it. The only solution seems to be to manually copy all the headings one at a time.

To solve this problem, try the following method:

1. Insert a table of contents anywhere in the document. In the Table Of Contents tab, clear the Show Page Numbers and the Use Hyperlinks Instead Of Page Numbers options to eliminate page numbers and hyperlinks from the table of contents.

   For details on inserting a table of contents, see "Generating a Table of Contents," on page 443.

2. Select the entire table of contents, press Ctrl+Shift+F9 to convert the table of contents from a Word field to regular document text, and press Ctrl+X to move the text into the Clipboard.

3. Open the document that you want to contain the outline and press Ctrl+V to paste the outline headings.

4. Format the outline as desired.

Inserting Footnotes and Endnotes

Word makes it easy to add footnotes or endnotes to your document. The text for a *footnote* is placed (or at least starts) at the bottom of the page that contains the reference mark (or you can choose to place a footnote just beneath the text on the page that contains the reference mark). The text for an *endnote* is placed at the end of the document (or you can choose to place an endnote at the end of the document section that contains the reference mark). Figure 15-6 shows a footnote.

To add a footnote or endnote to your document, perform the following steps:

1   Place the insertion point where you want to insert the footnote or endnote reference mark.

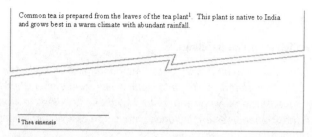

Common tea is prepared from the leaves of the tea plant[1]. This plant is native to India and grows best in a warm climate with abundant rainfall.

[1] Thea sinensis

Figure 15-6.   This figure shows a footnote in a Word document.

2   Choose Insert, Reference, Footnote. This will open the Footnote And Endnote dialog box, shown here:

3 In the Footnote And Endnote dialog box, do one of the following:

- To insert a footnote, select the Footnotes option and specify where you want the footnote positioned by selecting Bottom Of Page or Below Text from the adjoining drop-down list.

- To insert an endnote, select the Endnotes option and specify where you want the endnote positioned by selecting End Of Document or End Of Section from the adjoining drop-down list.

> **Tip** **Move endnotes**
>
> If you have displayed endnotes at the end of a particular document section, you can move those endnotes to the end of the *next* document section (if any), where they will be displayed before the endnotes belonging to the next section. To do this, place the insertion point in the section containing the endnotes you want to move, choose File, Page Setup, click the Layout tab in the Page Setup dialog box, select This Section in the Apply To drop-down list, and check the Suppress Endnotes option.

4 Specify the numbering format of the footnote or endnote reference marks in one of the following two ways:

- To use automatically incremented numbers or symbols (*, †, ‡, §, ...), select the type of number you want (or the symbol set) from the Number Format drop-down list, specify the starting number (or symbol) in the Start At text box, and select the way you want the numbering to restart from the Numbering drop-down list. Also, if you've divided your document into sections, select This Section or Whole Document to specify the part of the document where you want to use the numbering format you specified. (If you select the "i, ii, iii, ..." format, keep in mind that lowercase roman numerals can be difficult for many readers to comprehend after about xv, or 15.)

- To use a custom reference mark (such as *), type the symbol into the Custom Mark text box or click the Symbol button to select the symbol from the Symbol dialog box.

> For information on using the Symbol dialog box, see "Inserting Symbols and Foreign Characters," on page 260.

> **Note** If you select an automatically incremented number or symbol for your reference marks, the format you specify will be applied to all automatic reference marks in the document (or in the current document section if the document is divided into sections and you selected This Section in the Apply Changes To list).
>
> If you want to change the format of the automatic reference marks without inserting a mark, you can open the Footnote And Endnote dialog box, specify the format, and click the Apply button rather than the Insert button.
>
> If you specify a custom reference mark, your selection will apply only to the mark you insert, not to other reference marks in the document.

5 Click the Insert button.

Word will insert the reference mark into the body text. Also, in Normal, Web Layout, or Outline view, it will open a separate footnote pane and position the insertion point in this pane, as shown in Figure 15-7. (In this discussion, *footnote pane* refers to the pane that you use to enter or view either footnotes or endnotes.)

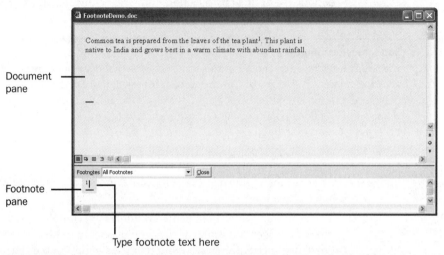

Figure 15-7. In Normal view, you enter footnote text in the footnote pane.

In Print Layout, Reading Layout, or Print Preview view, Word will place the insertion point at the actual position of the footnote or endnote on the page.

6 Type the footnote or endnote text.

7 In Normal, Web Layout, or Outline view, if you want to close the footnote pane when you've finished typing the footnote or endnote text, click the Close button at the top of the pane or double-click the copy of the footnote or endnote reference within the footnote pane. The insertion point will be moved back to the position where you inserted the footnote or endnote reference in the document text. If you want to leave the footnote pane open, you can switch back and forth between that pane and your current position in the document pane by pressing F6.

In Print Layout, Reading Layout, or Print Preview view, after you finish typing the footnote or endnote text, you can move the insertion point back to the position in the document text where you inserted the footnote or endnote reference by double-clicking the copy of the reference in the footnote or endnote area, by pressing Shift+F5, or by using any other navigation method.

> **Tip** **Insert a note with a shortcut key**
>
> To quickly add a footnote or endnote using the options you previously chose in the Footnote And Endnote dialog box (or using default options if you didn't choose any), place the insertion point where you want the reference mark, and press Alt+Ctrl+F for a footnote or Alt+Ctrl+D for an endnote.

Tip   Convert note types
You can click the Convert button in the Footnote And Endnote dialog box to convert all footnotes in your document to endnotes, to convert all endnotes to footnotes, or to swap footnotes and endnotes.

If you later want to view or edit your footnote or endnote text, choose View, Footnotes. If you have both footnotes and endnotes, Word will ask which you want to view. You can also simply double-click a footnote or endnote reference mark. In Normal, Web Layout, or Outline view, Word will open the footnote pane. In Print Layout, Reading Layout, or Print Preview view, Word will move the insertion point to the footnote or endnote area of the page. You can also view the text of your footnote or endnote in a ScreenTip by holding the mouse pointer over the reference mark, as shown in the following example. (This feature works only if the ScreenTips option is turned on. You set this option by choosing Tools, Options and clicking the View tab.)

Thea sinensis

Common tea is prepared from the leaves of the tea plant[1] This plant is native to India and grows best in a warm climate with abundant rainfall.

To move or copy a footnote or endnote, move or copy the reference mark to the desired document location using any of the editing methods explained in Chapter 11, "Efficient Editing in Word." If you used automatically incremented reference marks, Word will automatically renumber your reference marks if necessary. If you copy the reference mark, Word will make a copy of the footnote or endnote text.

For techniques on moving or copying text, see "Editing the Selection," on page 287.

Tip   Reformat footnotes or endnotes globally
To change the formatting of footnote or endnote reference marks or text throughout your document, you can modify the built-in character style Footnote Reference or Endnote Reference or the built-in paragraph style Footnote Text or Endnote Text. These styles, however, aren't normally displayed in the Styles And Formatting task pane or in the Style drop-down list on the Formatting toolbar. To list them, select Custom in the Show drop-down list near the bottom of the Styles And Formatting task pane, and in the Format Settings dialog box, select All Styles in the Category drop-down list and then check the style or styles you want to modify. The style(s) will then appear in the Styles And Formatting task pane and in the Styles drop-down list, and you'll be able to modify them as explained in "Customizing Styles," on page 389.

To delete a footnote or endnote, select the reference mark and press Delete. Word will delete both the reference mark and all the footnote or endnote text.

Generating Indexes and Tables of Contents

You can have Word generate an index or a table of contents for your document. A comprehensive index and an accurate table of contents are important assets for a document, especially a lengthy or technical one.

Tip   Use a table of contents for a Web page

If you're creating a Web page document, you should use a table of contents rather than an index. The page numbers given in an index are meaningless in a Web page displayed in a browser, because the browser doesn't divide the document into separate pages. However, a table of contents displayed in a browser normally consists of a list of hyperlinks that a visitor can click to navigate to different parts of the document, making it quite useful.

Note   If you have inserted captions using the Insert, Reference, Caption command, you can have Word generate a table of figures. You can also have it generate a table of authorities for a legal brief. These sorts of tables aren't as common as indexes and tables of contents and aren't discussed in this book. For information, look up the following topics in the Word online Help: "captions," "tables of figures," and "tables of authorities."

Generating an Index

Preparing an index in Word is a two-step process: First, you mark a series of index entries and then you compile and insert the index itself, based on these entries.

A typical index entry consists of the name of a topic followed by the number of the page on which the topic is discussed, as seen here:

oolong tea, 1

When you mark an index entry, you specify the topic name and you tag the location of the topic in the document so that Word can determine its page number when you compile the index. To mark an index entry, perform the following steps:

1   If all or part of the word or phrase that you want to appear in the index entry (such as *oolong tea* in the preceding example) is contained in the document text to be indexed, select this word or phrase, as shown here:

Select the text you want to
appear in the index entry

There are three types of tea: green, black, and oolong. The leaves for black and oolong teas are first fermented and are then dried and heated. The leaves for green tea are dried and heated without fermentation.

Otherwise, simply place the insertion point at the beginning of the document text you want to index.

2   Choose Insert, Reference, Index And Tables. Then click the Mark Entry button on the Index tab of the Index And Tables dialog box to open the Mark Index Entry dialog box, shown here. An alternative way to open this dialog box is to press the Alt+Shift+X key combination.

3   If you selected text in step 1, it will appear in the Main Entry text box; otherwise, the box will be empty. If necessary, edit the contents of this box so that it contains the exact text you want to appear in the index, as shown here:

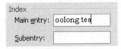

4   If you want to create an index subentry, enter the subentry text in the Subentry text box. For example, typing the following into the Main Entry and Subentry text boxes

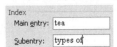

would create the following index entry and subentry:

tea
    types of, 1

5   Make sure the Current Page option is selected so that the index entry will display the number of the page that contains the indexed topic.

> **Note** Rather than selecting the Current Page option, you can select the Cross-Reference option or the Page Range option. If you select Cross-Reference, the index entry will display the cross-reference that you type into the adjoining text box—for example, "*See herb teas,*" rather than a page number. If you select Page Range, the index entry will display the range of pages that are marked with the bookmark that you select in the Bookmark list. Bookmarks are discussed in "Using Bookmarks to Label and Locate Text," on page 300.

6 To modify the format of the page number in the index entry, check Bold, Italic, or both.

7 Click the Mark button.

> **Tip   Mark the selected text globally**
> If you selected text in step 1, you can have Word globally mark as index entries all occurrences of that text within your document. To do this, click the Mark All button rather than the Mark button. Word will apply the entry, subentry, and other settings that you've entered in the Mark Index Entry dialog box to all marked occurrences.

8 If you want to mark additional index entries, you can leave the Mark Index Entry dialog box open while you move the insertion point to additional locations in your document. When you have finished marking entries, click Close to remove the dialog box.

Show/Hide

> **Note** Word marks an index entry by inserting a block of instructions known as a *field* into the document. The field contains the XE field name (for *index entry*) and is formatted as hidden text. When you mark an index entry, Word automatically shows hidden text (as well as nonprinting characters, such as paragraph marks) so that you can see the XE fields. If at any time you can't see the XE fields in your document, you can make them appear by clicking the Show/Hide ¶ button on the Standard toolbar or by checking the Show All Formatting Marks option in the Reveal Formatting task pane. (To view just the XE fields and other hidden text, without showing the nonprinting characters, you can choose Tools, Options, click the View tab, and check the Hidden Text option.)

When you have marked all the index entries, the next step is to compile and insert the index itself. To do this, perform the following steps:

1 Place the insertion point at the position in your document where you want to display the index.

Chapter 15

2 Choose Insert, Reference, Index And Tables to display the Index And Tables dialog box and then click the Index tab, shown here:

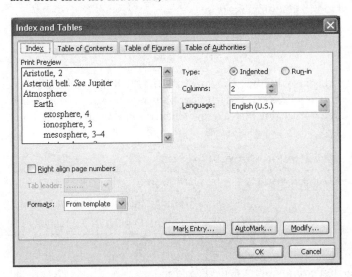

3 If you want to modify the appearance of the index, choose options in the Index tab until the model index in the Print Preview area has the look you want for your index. You can set the index type, the number of columns, the language, the alignment of page numbers, the tab leader character, and the overall format of the index.

4 Click the OK button. Word will compile the index and insert it into the document. Word will also add section breaks before and after the index so that it's contained in its own document section.

Tip Customize your index entries

When you generate an index using the Index tab of the Index And Tables dialog box, you can create custom formatting for your index entries. To do this, select the From Template item in the Formats drop-down list. Then, click the Modify button to open the Style dialog box, which lets you modify the built-in styles that Word assigns to index entries: Index 1 for main entries and Index 2 through Index 9 for subentries. To customize a style, select it in the Styles list and click the Modify button.

You can also change the formatting of index headings (that is, the A, B, and C headings, and so on, that precede each index section) by using the Styles And Formatting task pane to modify the Index Heading built-in style. (This style isn't normally displayed in the Styles And Formatting task pane. To list it, select Custom in the Show drop-down list near the bottom of the task pane. In the Format Settings dialog box, select All Styles in the Category drop-down list and check the Index Heading item in the Styles To Be Visible list.)

For instructions on modifying styles, see "Customizing Styles," on page 389.

Chapter 15

Word creates the index by inserting an INDEX field into the document. Under certain circumstances, rather than seeing the index itself, you might see the field code for the index, which would look something like this:

{ INDEX \c "2" \z "1033" }

The field code begins with the field name, INDEX. Following that are one or more *switches*. Each switch begins with the \ character and indicates one of the options that you selected in the Index And Tables dialog box. The switches in this example have the meanings given in Table 15-2.

Table 15-2. INDEX Field Code Switches

INDEX Field Code Switch	Meaning
\c "2"	Arrange the index in two columns
\z "1033"	Use the English (U.S.) language

If you see the field code rather than the actual index, you can make the index appear by placing the insertion point within the field code and pressing Shift+F9. (Pressing Shift+F9 again would redisplay the field code. This key toggles back and forth between displaying the field contents and displaying the field code.)

If your document changes after you insert an index, you can update the index by placing the insertion point anywhere within the index and pressing F9. To have Word automatically update the index when you print the document, choose Tools, Options, click the Print tab, and make sure that the Update Fields option is checked.

Troubleshooting

Spelling errors in index

You notice outrageous spelling errors in your index and you're wondering why Word didn't catch them.

Word formats the XE fields that mark your index entries as hidden text. If hidden text isn't visible, neither the as-you-type spelling checker nor the spelling checker you run by choosing Tools, Spelling And Grammar, checks the spelling of the words contained in the text. Also, because the index itself is generated from a field, neither spelling checker checks its contents.

To check the spelling of your index entries, make hidden text visible by clicking the Show/Hide ¶ button on the Standard toolbar, or by choosing Tools, Options, clicking the View tab, and checking the Hidden Text option. You can then use either spelling checker to check the spelling of the text directly within the XE fields, which will be used to build the index entries the next time you insert or update the index.

Chapter 15

Generating a Table of Contents

You can also use Word to compile and insert a table of contents, which lists the document headings, in your document. When you view a table of contents in any Word view except Web Layout or Reading Layout, each entry typically includes the page number of the heading and functions as a hyperlink that you can click to navigate to that heading. When you view a table of contents in Web Layout or Reading Layout view or when you view a Web page document in a browser, each entry usually consists of only a hyperlink without a page number. (Page numbers would be meaningless in a browser, which doesn't divide a document into separate pages. The page numbers, which refer to the printed document pages, would be erroneous in Reading Layout view, which divides the document into screen-sized pages rather than showing the printed pages.) When you generate the table of contents, however, you can choose whether or not to include page numbers or hyperlinks.

The following is the fastest way to create a table of contents:

1 Make sure that every heading you want to include in the table of contents has been assigned one of the built-in Heading styles, Heading 1 through Heading 9. You can assign these styles using Outline view, as explained earlier in this chapter.

You can also assign styles using the methods given in "Assigning Paragraph Styles, Character Styles, and Saved Formats," on page 330.

2 Place the insertion point at the position in your document where you want to display the table of contents.

3 Choose Insert, Reference, Index And Tables. Then click the Table Of Contents tab, shown here:

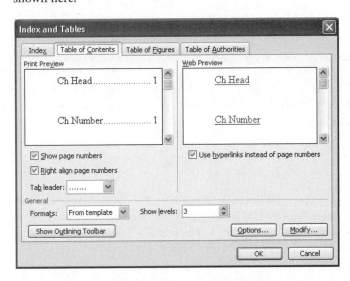

4 If you want to modify the appearance of the table of contents, choose options in the Table Of Contents tab until the model table of contents in the Print Preview or Web Preview area has the look you want.

The Print Preview area shows how the table of contents will appear in any Word view except Web Layout and Reading Layout, and the Web Preview area shows how it will look in Web Layout view or when a Web page document is viewed in a browser. You can specify the alignment of page numbers, the tab leader character, the overall format of the table of contents, and the number of heading levels that should be included in the table of contents.

Checking both the Show Page Numbers option and the Use Hyperlinks Instead Of Page Numbers option includes page numbers in Normal, Print Layout, Outline, and Print Preview views and includes hyperlinks in all views (including the view of a Web page document in a browser). Clearing Show Page Numbers removes page numbers from all views. Clearing Use Hyperlinks Instead Of Page Numbers removes hyperlinks from all views, and—provided that Show Page Numbers is checked—causes page numbers to appear in Web Layout and Reading Layout views (and in a browser).

5   Click the OK button.

Tip   Customize your table of contents

When you generate a table of contents using the Table Of Contents tab of the Index And Tables dialog box, you can create custom formatting for the table of contents. To do this, select From Template in the Formats drop-down list. Then click the Modify button to open the Style dialog box, which lets you modify the built-in styles that Word assigns to table of contents entries: TOC 1 through TOC 9 for each of the different heading levels shown in the table of contents. To customize a style, select it in the Styles list and click the Modify button. Also, you can click the Options button in the Table Of Contents tab to have Word build the table of contents using paragraphs with styles other than the built-in Heading styles, instead of—or in addition to—using paragraphs with the built-in Heading styles.

For instructions on modifying styles, see "Customizing Styles," on page 389.

Word creates a table of contents by inserting a TOC field. Under certain circumstances, rather than seeing the table of contents itself, you might see the field code for the table of contents, which would look something like this:

{ TOC \o "1-3" \h \z \u }

The field code begins with the field name, TOC. Following that are one or more *switches*. Each switch begins with the \ character and indicates one of the options you selected in the Index And Tables dialog box. The switches in this example have the meanings shown in Table 15-3.

Table 15-3. **TOC Field Code Switches**

TOC Field Code Switch	Meaning
\o "1-3"	Build the table of contents from document paragraphs that are assigned the built-in Heading styles Heading 1 through Heading 3.
\h	Assign a hyperlink to each table of contents entry.
\z	In Web Layout and Reading Layout views (and for a Web page document, in a browser), hide the page numbers as well as the tab leader (the dots, dashes, or underlining between the end of the entry text and the page number).
\u	In addition to using the headings with the built-in heading styles to build the table of contents, use paragraphs that have been assigned outline-level formatting. (You assign outline-level formatting to a paragraph by choosing Format, Paragraph, clicking the Indents And Spacing tab, and selecting a level in the Outline Level drop-down list.)

If you see the field code for the table of contents rather than the table of contents itself, you can make the table of contents appear by selecting the *entire* field code and pressing Shift+F9. Note that a table of contents usually includes nested HYPERLINK and PAGEREF fields; if you see any of these field codes rather than the field contents, you can likewise select the entire field code and press Shift+F9 to show the contents. (The Shift+F9 keystroke toggles back and forth between displaying the field contents and displaying the field code.)

If you chose to include hyperlinks in your table of contents, when you view the document in Word or in a browser, you can click a table of contents entry to navigate to the referenced heading. In Word, if the Use Ctrl + Click To Follow Hyperlink option is checked, you'll have to press Ctrl when you click a hyperlink. (You access this option by choosing Tools, Options and clicking the Edit tab.)

If the content or page locations of your outline headings change—or if you added or removed headings—after you insert a table of contents, you can update the table of contents by clicking the Update TOC button on the Outlining toolbar.

Go To TOC
(Click to select the TOC)

Tip A quick way to navigate to the table of contents and to select all of it (whether the content or the field code is displayed) is to click the Go To TOC button on the Outlining toolbar.

445

You can also select or place the insertion point within the table of contents and press F9. Word will ask whether you want to update the page numbers only or update the entire table of contents. To have Word automatically update the table of contents when you print the document, choose Tools, Options, click the Print tab, and make sure that the Update Fields option is checked.

Tip   **Change a table of contents to regular text**

As explained in this section, a table of contents consists of a dynamic Word field so that it can be automatically updated to reflect changes in the document headings. If you want to convert it to regular, static text, select the entire table of contents and press Ctrl+Shift+F9. You can then edit, format, or copy the table of contents like any other regular document text.

Troubleshooting

Edits to index or table of contents are lost

You edited text within an index or a table of contents. However, when you updated the index or table of contents or when you printed the document, your edits disappeared.

Remember that an index or a table of contents is a dynamic *field*, not regular text. Any edits you make directly to an index or table of contents will be overwritten when Word updates the field. Therefore, to edit index entries, you should edit the contents of the XE fields in the document that are used to build the index (if you don't see them, click the Show/Hide ¶ button on the Standard toolbar). Likewise, to edit the entries in a table of contents, you should edit the document headings that are used to build the table of contents.

Chapter 16

Using Word in Workgroups

Tracking and Reviewing Document
Changes 447
Merging and Comparing Documents . . 458

Inserting Comments in Documents 459
Highlighting Text 466
Sharing Word Documents 468

Tracking and Reviewing Document Changes

You can have Microsoft Office Word 2003 track and mark all changes you make to a document so that you or a coworker can later review these changes and either accept them to make them permanent or reject them to restore the original text. When Word tracks changes, it always stores the details on every change made to the document—the exact modification that was made, the name of the person making the change, and the date and the time of the change. (The name used to indicate the author of a change is the name that was contained in the Name box on the User Information tab of the Options dialog box at the time the revision was made.) You can display this information when you review the changes. You can also have Word mark the changes on the screen in various ways so you can see at a glance the proposed corrections and changes to the document. Or you can temporarily hide the markings, letting Word store the change information internally only.

Word 2003 has enhanced the change-tracking feature of previous versions of Word, offering new ways to display and work with tracked changes. Working with tracked changes can be divided into two phases:

- Tracking and marking your changes as you edit a document
- Reviewing tracked document changes made by you or a coworker

> **Note** The Word document merging and comparing feature also generates tracked changes—automatically—to mark merged text or to indicate differences between two document versions. See "Merging and Comparing Documents," on page 458.

Tracking Your Document Changes

You can turn on change tracking whenever you want to start saving a record of all modifications you make to a document so that the modifications can be viewed and later either accepted or rejected. For example, you could turn on change tracking before making tentative document alterations that you might want to reverse later. You could also turn on change tracking in order to communicate to a coworker the exact ways that you edit a document.

To track your document changes, perform the following steps:

1 To take advantage of Word's most advanced ways of showing changes, switch to either Print Layout or Web Layout view. In these views—as well as in Reading Layout and Print Preview view and on the printed document—you can have Word display all deletions and indicate all formatting changes within margin "balloons." Displaying deleted text in the margins makes it easier to read your modified paragraphs and avoids throwing off the positions of line and page breaks (see Figure 16-1). Although you *can* track and view changes in Normal or Outline view, in these views Word will always use its old method for marking tracked changes, in which deleted text is left in place, making it more difficult to read the document and visualize the way the final text will actually appear on the page (see Figure 16-2). The discussions in this section assume that you're in Print Layout or Web Layout view.

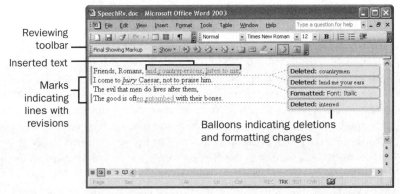

Figure 16-1. When you display a Word document in Print Layout view or (shown here) Web Layout view, you can have tracked changes shown in margin balloons.

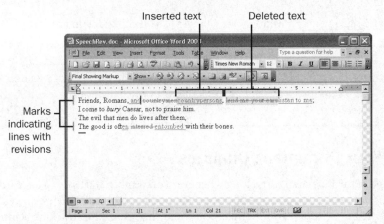

Figure 16-2. A Word document containing tracked changes displayed in Normal view always shows the changes within the text itself.

2 Turn on change tracking by double-clicking the TRK indicator in the status bar, by choosing Tools, Track Changes or by pressing the Ctrl+Shift+E shortcut key. Word will now start tracking all insertions, deletions, and formatting changes you make to the document. When change tracking is turned on, the TRK indicator in the status bar is displayed in darker type.

To turn change tracking off, repeat any of these three commands. When you turn off change tracking, Word will retain its record of all changes that have already been tracked, but it won't track changes that you subsequently make.

> **Note** If the Reviewing toolbar is currently displayed, you can turn change tracking on or off by clicking the Track Changes button.

When you turn on change tracking, Word will automatically display the Reviewing toolbar (shown in Figure 16-3).

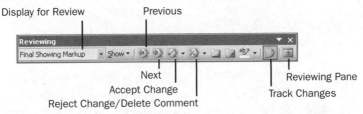

Figure 16-3. This figure labels the controls on the Reviewing toolbar that are used for tracking document changes.

3 To adjust the change marking mode, open the Display For Review drop-down list on the Reviewing toolbar, shown here:

Then, select one of the following two change marking options from the list (the other two options are more suitable for reviewing changes and are discussed in the next section):

- To have Word mark all your changes as you edit the document, choose Final Showing Markup. Use this option if you want to monitor your changes as you make them.

- To turn off all marking of changes, choose Final. Word will continue to track changes and store the change information internally, and you can have Word show the changes later if you want. (The only way to permanently remove a tracked change is to accept or reject it, as described in the next section.) Use this option if you want to record your changes but don't want the window to be cluttered with markings while you edit. In this mode Word works *almost* as it does

Chapter 16

when change tracking is off. However, you'll occasionally notice minor quirks. For example, once in a while you might have to press Backspace several times before it erases the preceding character. (If pressing Backspace repeatedly doesn't work, you'll have to use another method to delete the text.)

4 To filter the particular changes that Word shows, click the Show button on the Reviewing toolbar, shown here:

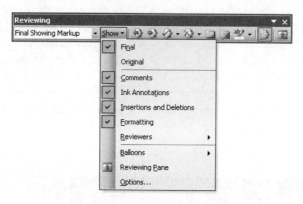

Then, choose an option from the drop-down menu, as follows:

- To show or hide markings for all insertions and deletions, choose Insertions And Deletions. The markings are shown when the menu item is checked.

- To show or hide markings for all formatting changes, choose Formatting.

- To show or hide markings for changes made by a particular Word user, click Reviewers and choose a user name from the submenu seen here. To show or hide markings made by all users, choose All Reviewers.

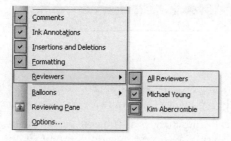

Note that your choice affects only the items that are *shown*. As long as change tracking is on, Word will continue to record all changes to the document, and you can later show any changes that aren't currently marked.

5 To modify the way Word marks changes, choose Options from the Show drop-down menu on the Reviewing toolbar, and select the desired options in the Track Changes tab (see Figure 16-4). Another way to display this tab is to choose Tools, Options in

Word and click the Track Changes tab in the Options dialog box. In the Track Changes tab you can do any of the following:

- Modify the types of markings and colors that Word uses to mark insertions, deletions, formatting changes, and changed lines. (You can also change the colors used for comments, which are discussed later in the chapter.)

- Control the display of balloons. By selecting an item in the Use Balloons drop-down list, you can show all balloons, turn off all balloons, or show just the balloons that display formatting changes and comments. When balloons are turned off, Word displays items as it does in Normal and Outline view—insertions, deletions, and formatting changes are displayed in the body of the text and comments are displayed in the Reviewing pane. Note that as a shortcut, you can also choose one of the three balloon display modes from the Balloons submenu on the Show drop-down menu, as seen here:

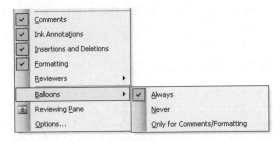

- Set the orientation of the paper that Word uses when it prints the document with balloons showing. To do this, select an option in the Paper Orientation drop-down list. The Preserve option prints the document with the orientation—either portrait or landscape—that's currently set in the Margins tab of the Page Setup dialog (displayed by choosing File, Page Setup). The Force Landscape option always prints in landscape orientation, providing the most room for displaying balloons. With Auto, Word selects the page orientation that provides the best layout for the document.

> **Note** When selecting a color for change markings in the Track Changes tab, keep in mind that the Auto item refers to your normal Window Font color, which is usually black. (The Window Font color is selected in the Display program of the Windows Control Panel.)

Chapter 16

Figure 16-4. The Track Changes tab lets you modify the way Word marks tracked changes.

Reviewing Tracked Document Changes

To remove tracked changes from a document—converting the document permanently to its final form—you'll need to review the tracked changes, accepting or rejecting each one. The document might be one that you or a coworker has edited with change tracking turned on, or a document generated by the Word document merging or comparing feature. Keep in mind that the following sections assume that you are viewing the document in Print Layout or Web Layout view.

> The merging and comparing features are discussed in "Merging and Comparing Documents," on page 458.

Adjusting the Way Changes Are Shown

While reviewing tracked changes, you might want to modify the way Word displays the changes, as follows:

● To view the modified version of the document with changes marked, select the Final Showing Markup option in the Display For Review drop-down list on the Reviewing toolbar, as shown here:

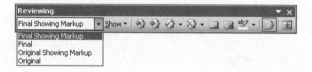

Figure 16-1, on page 448, shows the result of selecting this change marking option.

● To view the modified version of the document without changes marked, select Final. This option shows the document as it would appear if you accepted all changes (see Figure 16-5).

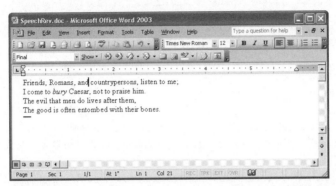

Figure 16-5. The example document is displayed with the Final change marking option.

● To view the unmodified version of the document (that is, the version before you made any tracked changes) with changes marked, choose Original Showing Markup. With this option, you'll notice that deletions are left in the body of the text and insertions are displayed in margin balloons (the opposite of the way changes are shown with the Final Showing Markup option; see Figure 16-6).

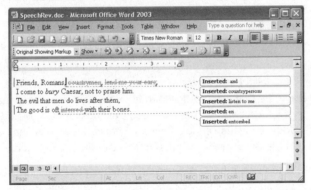

Figure 16-6. The example document is displayed with the Original Showing Markup change marking option.

● To view the unmodified version of the document without changes marked, choose Original. This option shows the document as it would appear if you rejected all changes (see Figure 16-7).

Chapter 16

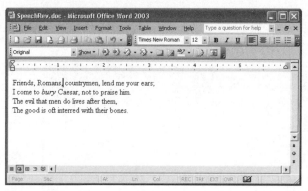

Figure 16-7. The example document is displayed with the Original change marking option.

Note In Outline or Normal view, the Final Showing Markup option and the Original Showing Markup option have the same effect.

● If changes are shown, you can filter the specific changes that are marked by choosing options from the Show drop-down menu on the Reviewing toolbar, as explained in the previous section.

Toggling Change Marking Modes

Word 2003 now provides two ways to quickly toggle between change marking modes.

First, if you've selected either the Final Showing Markup or the Final change marking mode, you can toggle back and forth between these modes by choosing View, Markup. Likewise, if you've selected either the Original Showing Markup or the Original change marking mode, you can toggle back and forth between these modes by choosing View, Markup. When this command toggles markup on, it also enables the Comments, Insertions And Deletions, and Formatting options on the Show drop-down menu (if any of these options are disabled).

Second, if you've selected either the Final Showing Markup or the Original Showing Markup change marking mode, you can toggle back and forth between these modes by selecting either the Original or the Final option on the Show drop-down menu on the Reviewing toolbar. Likewise, if you've selected either the Final or the Original change marking mode, you can toggle back and forth between these modes by selecting either the Original or the Final option on the Show drop-down menu.

Chapter 16

> **Tip** **Track a change balloon to its source**
> If more than one tracked change occurs on the same line (as in the first line of the example document shown in Figure 16-6), it can be hard to determine which part of a sentence a change balloon refers to. However, if you click a particular balloon, it will display a thick line that points more clearly to the location of the change.

Viewing Change Details

You can view the details of each change, using one of the following methods:

- Hold the mouse pointer over either the marked change itself or over its balloon in the margin to see details about the change in a ScreenTip, as seen here:

```
Friends, Roman:  Michael Young, 4/24/1996 7:14:00 PM
I come to bury    inserted:
The evil that mer  en
The good is often entombed with their bones.
```

> **Note** If you don't see the ScreenTips, choose Tools, Options, click the View tab, and check the ScreenTips option.

- Click the Reviewing Pane button on the Reviewing toolbar (shown in Figure 16-3, on page 449) to display the Reviewing pane at the bottom of the document window. This pane always lists details about all tracked changes (as well as comments, discussed later in the chapter), plus the complete text content of changes and comments, regardless of the current change marking mode in effect in the document window. The tracked changes are grouped according to the part of the document that contains them (main document, header and footer, text box, header and footer text box, footnote, and endnote; see Figure 16-8). To close the Reviewing pane, click the Reviewing Pane button again. To switch the insertion point back and forth between the Reviewing pane and the document pane, press F6. Note that if Word is unable to fit all the text belonging to a change or comment within a balloon, it will display as much text as will fit and it will show an ellipsis (…) at the end. Click the ellipsis to open the Reviewing pane, which will display the complete text.

Chapter 16

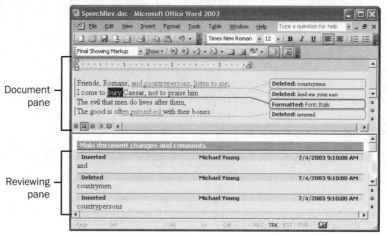

Figure 16-8. The Reviewing pane shows details on all tracked changes and comments in a document.

Note If several Word users have created tracked changes in a single document, each user's changes are usually marked in a distinct color, helping you to identify the author of each change. However, in the Track Changes tab, shown in Figure 16-4 on page 452, you can choose to use a single color for all authors, for each type of tracked change (and for comments).

Accepting or Rejecting Changes

When you accept a tracked change, Word discards the information it has stored on that change, removes the change marking, and permanently incorporates the change into the document. When you reject a change, Word discards the change information, removes the change marking, and permanently reverses the change in the document.

To accept or reject changes, use the following techniques:

- Whether or not changes are marked on the screen, you can accept or reverse all changes in a particular portion of the document by selecting the affected text and clicking the Accept Change or the Reject Change/Delete Comment button on the Reviewing toolbar (shown in Figure 16-3).

- If changes are currently marked on the screen, you can accept or reject a particular marked change by right-clicking the changed text and choosing the Accept or Reject command from the shortcut menu. (The command label will indicate the type of the change—for example, Accept Insertion.)

- If changes are currently marked on the screen, you can have Word select the next or the previous change by clicking the Next or the Previous button on the Reviewing toolbar.

> **Note** If the document contains visible comments, the Next and Previous buttons will navigate through comments as well as marked changes.

- You can globally accept all tracked changes that are currently marked on the screen or all tracked changes in the document (whether or not they're marked) by choosing the Accept All Changes Shown command or the Accept All Changes In Document command from the Accept Change drop-down menu on the Reviewing toolbar, shown here:

- You can globally reject all tracked changes that are currently marked on the screen or all tracked changes in the document (whether or not they're marked) by choosing the Reject All Changes Shown command or the Reject All Changes In Document command from the Reject Change/Delete Comment drop-down menu on the Reviewing toolbar, as seen here:

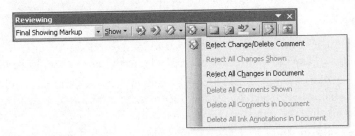

> **Note** The Accept All Changes Shown and Reject All Changes Shown commands are enabled only if you've filtered out some of the change markings (using the Show drop-down menu on the Reviewing toolbar).

> **Tip** **Process tracked changes in batches**
> To accept or reject an entire batch of tracked changes, first use the commands on the Show drop-down menu to display the set of tracked changes you want to modify. Then choose the Accept All Changes Shown or the Reject All Changes Shown command on the Accept Change or the Reject Change/Delete Comment drop-down menu.

Merging and Comparing Documents

If you have two different versions of a document, you can have Word merge or compare the two versions. Word uses change marking to indicate the merged text resulting from merging documents or the differences between two documents that you're comparing. This is the same type of change marking that Word employs when you turn on change tracking, as described in the previous sections.

Merging would be useful, for example, if you and a coworker have been editing separate copies of the same document, and you now want to create a single document that includes both your edits. The merged document will contain all the text from both documents, and any text that's contained in one document but not in the other will be included in the merged document but will be marked with change marking (either as an insertion or a deletion). You can then accept or reject each marked change to control exactly what text is kept in the final merged document.

If formatting differs between two merged documents (for example, the headings have been italicized in only one of the two documents), and if you choose to have Word find formatting, Word will prompt you to decide which document's formatting to display. Although the formatting from only one document will be displayed, all formatting differences will be indicated with change marking. By accepting or rejecting these tracked changes, you can decide which version of the formatting to use for each instance.

To merge two documents, perform the following steps:

1 Open either of the documents you want to merge; it doesn't matter which one you open first. (The remaining instructions refer to this as the *first* document.)

2 Choose Tools, Compare And Merge Documents. In the Compare And Merge Documents dialog box, select the second document you want to merge. (This dialog box works just like the standard Open dialog box.)

3 In the Compare And Merge Documents dialog box, clear the Legal Blackline check box.

4 If you want Word to mark formatting differences so you can later choose which formatting to use wherever there's a difference, check the Find Formatting option.

5 In the Compare And Merge Documents dialog box, do one of the following:

- To overwrite the second document with the resulting merged document, click the Merge button. This will preserve the current contents of the first document.

- To overwrite the first document with the resulting merged document, click the down arrow on the Merge button and choose Merge Into Current Document. This will preserve the current contents of the second document.

- To store the merged document in a new file, choose Merge Into New Document from the Merge drop-down menu. This will preserve the current contents of both the first and the second document.

> **Note**   If you choose the name of an existing document when you save a document using the Save As dialog box, Word will display a message box giving you the opportunity to merge the two documents into the existing document, rather than simply overwriting it. Also, if you attempt to open a shared network document that's currently locked by another user, Word will display a message box; one of the options in this message box lets you create a local copy of the document and then later merge that copy with the original document.

Whenever you simply want to determine the differences between two documents, you can compare rather than merge them, by performing the following steps:

1 Open one of the documents you want to compare. (In the remaining instructions, this is referred to as the *first* document.)

2 Choose Tools, Compare And Merge Documents. In the Compare And Merge Documents dialog box, select the second document for the comparison. (This dialog box works just like the standard Open dialog box.)

3 Check the Legal Blackline option.

4 If you want Word to mark formatting differences, check the Find Formatting option.

5 Click the Compare button.

Word will then create a new document that contains the text from the second document, *plus* all the marked changes that would be required to produce the first document—just as if you had opened the second document, turned on change tracking, and then edited the text so that it matched the first document. If you rejected all marked changes in the new document, you would end up with the second document, but if you accepted all marked changes, you would end up with the first document. (That sentence might take a moment's thought to understand!)

Inserting Comments in Documents

You can add comments that refer to specific blocks of text within a Word document without altering the main document text. You can use comments to store alternative text, criticisms, ideas for other topics, research notes, and other information useful in developing a document. Or you can use them for communicating ideas, corrections, requests, or other information to others who are working on the document.

> You can exchange comments about a shared online document using the Web Discussions feature in Word or through a SharePoint team Web site. For more information, see "Discussing an Online Document," on page 195.

Inserting Comments

You can insert comments while you are in Web Layout, Reading Layout, or Print Layout view or in Normal or Outline view. (You can't insert a comment while you're in Print Preview view.) In the former three views, a comment's text is normally displayed in a balloon in the margin (just like a tracked change), which makes it easy to insert, view, or edit the text (see Figure 16-9). In the latter two views, you must enter or edit the comment text in a separate Reviewing pane at the bottom of the document window, making it less convenient to insert, view, or edit comment text (see Figure 16-10).

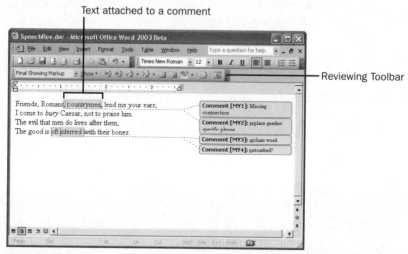

Figure 16-9. A document with comments is displayed in Web Layout view.

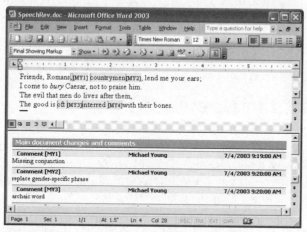

Figure 16-10. A document with comments is displayed in Normal view, showing the text of the first two comments in the Reviewing pane.

To insert a comment, perform the following steps:

1 Select the text in your document that's associated with the comment. The comment will be attached to that text, meaning that comment-marking brackets will surround the text, the text will be highlighted, and you'll be able to work with the comment by placing the insertion point anywhere within the text. If you don't select text prior to inserting a comment, Word will automatically attach the comment to the nearest word.

2 Choose Insert, Comment. In Web Layout, Reading Layout, or Print Layout view, this will open a new comment balloon and place the insertion point within it, as shown here:

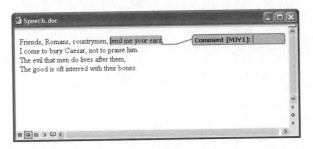

In Normal or Outline view, this will open the Reviewing pane and place the insertion point within a new, blank comment, as shown here:

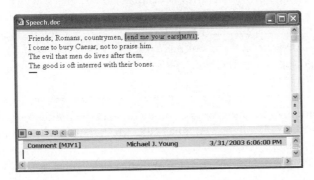

When you insert a comment, Word will automatically display the Reviewing toolbar (see Figure 16-11). Once it's displayed, you can quickly insert a comment by clicking the Insert Comment button.

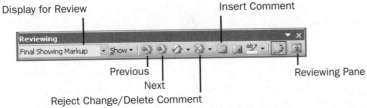

Figure 16-11. The controls on the Reviewing toolbar that are labeled in this figure are used for working with comments.

3 Type the comment text into the balloon or into the Reviewing pane. When you're done, click back in the document. You can move the insertion point back and forth between the Reviewing pane and the document pane by pressing F6. You can close the Reviewing pane by clicking the Reviewing Pane button on the Reviewing toolbar or by dragging the top border of the Reviewing pane down to the bottom of the window.

Chapter 16

> **Note** You can turn off the comment balloons (as well as all change tracking balloons) in Web Layout, Reading Layout, and Print Layout views by selecting the Balloons, Never option on the Show drop-down menu on the Reviewing toolbar. You'll then need to enter or edit comment text in the Reviewing pane, as you do in Normal or Outline view.

Viewing, Editing, and Deleting Comments

In Web Layout, Reading Layout, or Print Layout view, you can view or edit comments by following these guidelines:

- You can easily read the comment text in the balloons. However, if more than one comment (or tracked change) occurs on the same line (as in the first and last lines of the example document shown in Figure 16-9), it can be hard to determine which block of text a particular comment balloon is associated with. In this case you can click the balloon, and it will display a thick line that points more clearly to the attached text.

> **Note** The name and initials used to indicate the author of a comment are the name and initials that were specified in the User Information tab of the Options dialog box at the time the comment was inserted.

- To see the author, date, and time of a comment, hold the pointer over the comment balloon or over the document text attached to the comment. The comment information will be displayed in a ScreenTip. If you hold the pointer over the document text, the ScreenTip will also display the full text of the comment, as shown here:

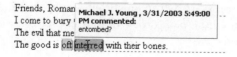

> **Note** If you don't see the ScreenTips, choose Tools, Options, click the View tab, and check the ScreenTips option.

- If the text for a comment is long, it might not all be displayed in the balloon. In this case, or if you simply prefer to read the comment in a separate pane, open the Reviewing pane (if it's not already shown) by clicking the Reviewing Pane button on the Reviewing toolbar (see Figure 16-11). Once the Reviewing pane is open, you can navigate to any comment's information and full text by clicking the corresponding balloon.
- You can edit the comment text either in the balloon or in the Reviewing pane.

In Normal or Outline view, you can view or edit comments by following these guidelines:

- You can view the author, date, time, and content of a comment in a ScreenTip by holding the pointer over the attached document text, as shown here:

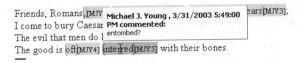

Friends, Romans, [MJY **Michael J. Young , 3/31/2003 5:49:00** ears[MJY3],
I come to bury Caesar **PM commented:**
The evil that men do 1 entombed?
The good is oft[MJY4] interred[MJY5] with their bones.

> **Note** In Normal or Outline view Word 2003 now displays the author's initials and a comment number in bracket characters immediately following the text that's attached to the comment.

- If a comment's text is too long to fit in a ScreenTip, or if you want to edit a comment, click the Reviewing Pane button on the Reviewing toolbar to open the Reviewing pane. Then click the document text that's attached to the comment to have Word scroll to the entry for that comment in the Reviewing pane, where you can view the comment information and full text or edit the text.

> **Tip** There's a convenient alternative method for editing a comment, which you can use in any view, provided that the document text attached to the comment isn't within a block of inserted or deleted text with change marking: click the document text that's attached with the comment using the right mouse button and choose Edit Comment from the shortcut menu. Word will display either the balloon containing the comment text or the entry containing the comment text in the Reviewing pane, and it will place the insertion point within the text.

If you have a microphone connected to your computer, you can add a voice comment, which is a comment containing an embedded sound object. The sound object contains a sound clip that you record and that any user can play back. The sound clip would usually be a verbal comment about some part of the document. You can insert a voice comment in any view except Print Preview, by performing the following steps:

1. Select the text that's associated with the voice comment.
2. Click the Insert Voice button on the Reviewing toolbar. Word will insert a new comment, embed a sound object in the comment text, and open the Sound Object dialog box.
3. Record your comment using the Sound Object dialog box, seen here:

When you're done, choose File, Exit & Return in the Sound Object dialog box.

4 To play back the sound clip, double-click the sound object.

You can delete a single comment in any view by performing the following steps:

1 Place the insertion point anywhere within the comment text in a balloon or in the Reviewing pane.

2 Click the Reject Change/Delete Comment button on the Reviewing toolbar.

> **Tip** There's a convenient alternative method for deleting a single comment, which you can use in any view: right-click the document text that's attached to the comment or right-click the comment text in a balloon or in the Reviewing pane and choose Delete Comment from the shortcut menu. Note, however, that if you right-click the document text attached to the comment, this text must not be within a block of inserted or deleted text with change marking.

> **Caution** You can also delete a comment by placing the insertion point within the text that's attached to the comment in the body of the document and then clicking the Reject Change/Delete Comment button on the Reviewing toolbar. However, if the attached document text is inside of a block of text that was inserted with change tracking on, clicking Reject Change/Delete Comment will delete the entire block rather than simply removing the comment.

To delete a group of comments or all comments, in any view, perform the following steps:

1 If you want to delete only the comments created by one or more particular authors who have added comments to the document, check just those authors on the Reviewers submenu of the Show drop-down menu on the Reviewing toolbar. Word will then display only the comments created by the selected authors.

2 Click the down arrow on the Reject Change/Delete Comment button on the Review toolbar to open the drop-down menu shown here:

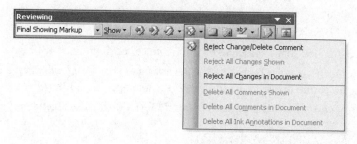

Then, choose a command as follows:

- If you displayed only the comments created by selected authors in step 1, you can remove just those comments by choosing Delete All Comments Shown.

- To remove *all* comments, whether or not they are currently displayed, choose Delete All Comments In Document.

> **Note** The Delete All Comments Shown command is enabled only if you filtered out comments for one or more of the document's authors in step 1.

Troubleshooting

You need to scroll to see change or comment balloons

You're working in Print Layout view, but you can't see both the document text and all the change or comment balloons in the margin, which forces you to scroll back and forth.

If you don't need the features of Print Layout view (such as the display of page breaks, margins, and headers and footers), switch to Web Layout view, which automatically wraps the text so that you can see both the text and the change and comment balloons at once. If you do require Print Layout, reduce the zooming factor as explained in "Modifying the Way Documents Are Displayed," on page 251.

To navigate through the comments in the document in any view, perform the following steps:

1. Hide change marking by deselecting the Insertions And Deletions option and the Formatting option on the Show drop-down menu on the Reviewing toolbar. (If change marking is visible, the technique given here will navigate through both comments and marked changes.)

2. Navigate through the comments as follows:

   - To select the next comment following the insertion point, the text selection, or the selected comment, click the Next button on the Reviewing toolbar. Word will select the next comment balloon (in Web Layout, Reading Layout, or Print Layout view) or the next comment entry in the Reviewing pane (in Normal or Outline view).

   - To select the previous comment, click the Previous button.

> **Note** If there isn't a next or a previous comment in the document, Word—after prompting you—will wrap around and start searching from the beginning or from the end of the document.

Troubleshooting

Comments have disappeared!

When you entered comments into the document, you could see the comment marking brackets in the main text, and in Print Layout, Web Layout, and Reading Layout views you could see the comment balloons in the margin. Later, however, both disappeared, and you're wondering what happened to your comments.

To see comment markings in the body text, the Final Showing Markup or the Original Showing Markup mode must be selected in the Display For Review drop-down list on the Reviewing toolbar, *and* the Comments item must be checked on the Show drop-down menu.

> **Tip**   To switch both these options on at once, you can choose View, Markup.

If comment markings still don't show up, make sure that the comment author or authors are checked on the Reviewers submenu of the Show drop-down menu on the Reviewing toolbar.

If the comment markers are shown in Web Layout, Print Layout, Reading Layout, or Print Preview view, but not the comment balloons, choose Balloons, Always from the Show drop-down menu on the Reviewing toolbar. (Or choose Balloons, Only For Comments/Formatting if you want to see balloons containing comments and formatting changes, but not balloons containing inserted or deleted text.)

 ## Working with Ink Annotations

If you are using a Tablet PC computer, you can add ink annotations to a Word 2003 document. Although without a Tablet PC, you won't be able to add or edit ink annotations, you'll be able to view or remove ink annotations that you or a co-worker previously added to the document using a Tablet PC.

To show or hide ink annotations in the document, choose Ink Annotations from the Show drop-down menu on the Reviewing toolbar.

To remove all ink annotations from the document, choose Delete All Ink Annotations In Document from the Reject Change/Delete Comment drop-down menu on the Reviewing toolbar.

Highlighting Text

You can use the Highlight button in Word to permanently mark blocks of text in a document, much the same way you use a colored marker to highlight text on a printed page. The text you mark is highlighted both on the screen and on the printed copy of the document. Highlighting is useful for drawing attention to specific blocks of text, either for your own benefit or to communicate with other members of your workgroup. Word provides a variety of highlighting colors, so you can color-code your highlighted text (for example, you could highlight important text in yellow, potential deletions in green, and so on).

To highlight a block of text, perform the following steps:

1 Select the text you want to highlight.

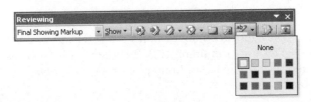
Highlight

2 Use the Highlight button, which can be found on the Formatting and Reviewing toolbars. To highlight using the color currently shown on the Highlight button (which is the most recently selected color), just click the Highlight button. To highlight using a different color, click the down arrow on the right side of this button, and then click the color you want on the drop-down palette shown here:

You can rapidly highlight several blocks of text as follows:

1 Without selecting text beforehand, click the Highlight button or click a color on its drop-down palette, as described previously.

2 Using the mouse, drag over each block of text that you want to highlight.

3 When you have finished highlighting text, click the Highlight button again or press Esc to return to normal editing mode.

Tip **Find highlighted text**
You can easily locate blocks of highlighted text in your document by using the Find command. Choose Edit, Find, and in the Find tab, click the More button (if the Search Options are not displayed), click the Format button, and choose Highlight from the menu shown here:

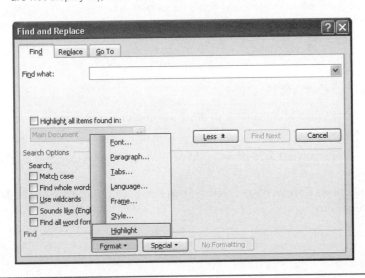

Chapter 16

You can remove highlighting by doing the following:

1 Select the text from which you want to remove the highlighting.

2 Click the down arrow on the right side of the Highlight button and click None on the drop-down palette, as shown here:

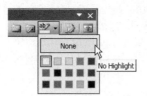

Alternatively, if the Highlight button currently shows the same color as the highlighting applied to the text, you can simply click the button. (You could also remove highlighting by choosing the same color from the drop-down palette, but it's probably easier to choose None.)

> **Tip** **Hide highlighting**
>
> You can temporarily hide all highlighting on the screen by choosing Tools, Options, clicking the View tab, and clearing the Highlight option in the Show area. You can make highlighting reappear by checking this same option. Also, highlighting will automatically become visible if you add new highlighting to a document. If highlighting is hidden on the screen, it will also be hidden on printed copies of the document.

You can quickly remove highlighting from several blocks of text using the same technique described for highlighting several blocks. In Step 1, simply click the None item on the palette.

> **Tip** **Print highlighting effectively**
>
> If you print a document containing highlighting on a monochrome printer, the highlight color will be converted to a shade of gray. For best results on a monochrome printer, choose a light highlighting color, such as yellow, bright green, or turquoise.

Sharing Word Documents

You can easily share Word documents with other members of your workgroup, using any of the following methods:

- Store documents on a shared network drive to which members of your workgroup have access

- Store documents on a Web site running SharePoint Team Services or other Microsoft server extensions

- Store documents on an FTP (File Transfer Protocol) site on the Internet or on a company intranet
- Store documents in shared Exchange Server folders
- Exchange documents using e-mail
- Exchange documents using floppy disks or other portable media

For information on saving or opening documents on a network drive, an FTP site, or a Web site, see Chapter 4, "Working with Office 2003 Applications, Documents, and Program Windows."

The remaining sections in this chapter discuss the following topics related to sharing Word documents:

- Sharing documents on a network
- Sharing documents using e-mail
- Protecting your shared documents
- Sharing fonts

Sharing Word Documents on a Network

Chapter 4 discussed the general methods for saving and opening Office documents on shared network drives to which you have access. When a network user has a document open in Word, the document is locked to prevent other network users from opening and editing the document in a way that would cause conflicts or loss of edits. If you attempt to open a locked document, Word will display this message box:

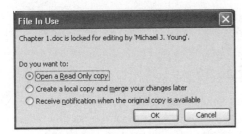

Choose an option as follows:

- To open the document in read-only mode, select Open A Read Only Copy. You'll actually be able to freely edit the document. However, when you issue the Save command, Word will display the Save As dialog box and you'll have to select a new filename or location, saving a separate copy of the document rather than overwriting the original copy. If you wish, you can later merge the two document versions.

To merge document versions, use the techniques discussed in "Merging and Comparing Documents," on page 458.

Chapter 16

● To open the document in read-only mode and later merge your copy of the document with the original, select Create A Local Copy And Merge Your Changes Later. This option is almost the same as Open A Read Only Copy, except that if you still have the document open when the first user closes the original copy of the document, Word will display a message box that lets you merge your copy of the document with the original, as shown here:

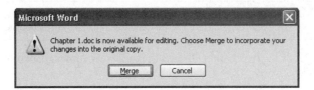

If you choose to merge, your read-only copy of the document will be replaced with the version of the document that resulted from merging your read-only copy with the copy of the document that was formerly opened by the other user. The merged document will be opened in read-write mode, and you can accept or reject any of the merged text or formatting and then save the document on disk under the original filename.

Merging documents is discussed in "Merging and Comparing Documents," on page 458.

● To open the document in read-only mode but have Word notify you when the original copy is closed, select Receive Notification When The Original Copy Is Available. This option is the same as Open A Read Only Copy, except that when the first user closes the original copy, Word will display the File Now Available message box, shown here, which lets you open the original copy in normal read-write mode:

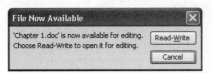

If you made changes to the document while you had it open in read-only mode, the File Now Available message box will let you either discard those changes or save those changes in a separate file, before Word opens the original copy in read-write mode. If you wish, you can later merge any edits you made in the read-only copy with the original copy.

To merge edits, use the techniques discussed in "Merging and Comparing Documents," on page 458.

Sharing Word Documents Using E-Mail

You can easily send a Word document to a coworker by attaching it to an e-mail message in Microsoft Outlook 2003 or another e-mail program. You can also send a Word document to a coworker by e-mail by opening the document in Word and choosing a command from the File, Send To submenu, shown here:

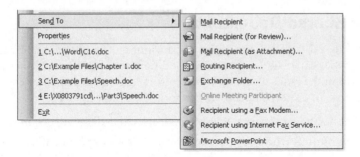

Choose a command as follows:

E-Mail

- To send a copy of the document in the body of an e-mail message, choose Mail Recipient. You can also do this by clicking the E-Mail button on the Standard toolbar.

- To e-mail the document to one or more reviewers, choose Mail Recipient (For Review). This will create an e-mail message that includes the document either as a link (if the document is contained in a shared network or Web location) or as an attachment (if the document isn't contained in a shared location). The document will be specially marked for review. As a result, Word will automatically display the reviewing tools when a recipient opens the document and, when the reviewed copy of the document is returned to you, Word will prompt you to merge the changes back into the original document.

> For information on how to send e-mail message attachments with Microsoft Office Outlook 2003 or how to work with attachments you've received, see "Receiving and Sending E-Mail Messages Using the E-Mail Folders," on page 999.

- To create an e-mail message and send a copy of the document as an attachment to that message, choose Mail Recipient (As Attachment).

- To e-mail the document to a group of coworkers, either sequentially or all at once, choose Routing Recipient. Word will open the Routing Slip dialog box, in which you can enter a list of recipients from your Outlook address book, type a subject and a message, protect the document if you wish (as described in the next section), and set other options. Word will create an e-mail message and include a copy of the document as an attachment to this message. The attached document will internally store a *routing slip* containing the list of recipients and their e-mail addresses. When a recipient has finished reading or editing the document, he or she can choose File, Send To, Other Routing Recipient in Word to send the document to the next recipient on the list. Eventually, the document will come back to you.

- To use Word's Fax Wizard to fax a copy of the document to a coworker using your fax modem, choose Recipient Using A Fax Modem.

- To fax the document using an Internet fax service provider, choose Recipient Using Internet Fax Service.

Chapter 16

For information on working with an Internet fax service, see "Using An Internet Fax Service," on page 1025.

 ## Protecting Shared Documents

Before you distribute a document—or copies of a document—to other members of your workgroup so that they can review, edit, or make additions to the document, you can protect the document to limit the kinds of changes your coworkers can make, thereby ensuring the document's integrity. To protect a document, perform the following steps:

1 Make sure the document you want to protect is displayed in the active document window.

2 Choose Tools, Protect Document to open the new Protect Document task pane, shown here:

3 To restrict the formatting that other users can apply to the document, check the Limit Formatting To A Selection Of Styles option, click the Settings command, and in the Formatting Restrictions dialog box (see Figure 16-12), select the particular styles that other users will be allowed to apply to the document. Checking the Limit Formatting To A Selection Of Styles option has the following effects:

- Other users won't be permitted to directly apply formatting to the document.

- Other users will be able to format the document by applying styles, but they will be permitted to apply only those styles that you select in the Formatting Restrictions dialog box.

- Other users won't be able to modify styles.

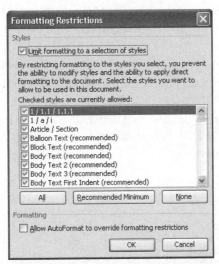

Figure 16-12. In the Formatting Restrictions dialog box, you can select the specific styles that other users will be permitted to apply to the document.

4   To restrict the ways that other users will be able to edit the document, check the Allow Only This Type Of Editing In The Document option and then select an option in the drop-down list, as follows:

- To prevent other users from making any editing changes, select No Changes (Read Only).

- To allow other users to edit the document only with change tracking on, select Tracked Changes. The option permanently turns on change tracking. Other users won't be able to turn change tracking off, nor will they be able to accept or reject tracked changes. They will, however, be able to add comments to the document. (After you remove the document protection, you'll be able to review, accept, or reject any of the changes that reviewers made.)

- To allow other users only to add comments to the document, select Comments.

- If you added a *form* to the document, to allow other users to make changes only within form fields (such as check boxes or text boxes), select Filling In Forms. (A form is a collection of check boxes, text boxes, and other fields that you add to a Word document for collecting information.)

5   If you checked the Allow Only This Type Of Editing In The Document option (step 4), you can set up one or more *exceptions*. Each exception grants full editing permissions (that is, it removes all editing restrictions) for a selected user (or for all users) within one or more regions of the document. To set up an exception, first select the region or regions of the document to which you want a particular user (or all users) to have complete editing permissions. Then, check the user in the Groups list (or check Everyone to grant permissions to all users). You can repeat this process to add regions for a

Chapter 16

particular user. Word will mark the region(s) with light shading and brackets (similar to the brackets used to mark bookmarks). You can work with exceptions in the following additional ways:

- To add more users to the Exceptions list, click the More Users command.

- To remove permissions from a particular region, select it and clear the check mark from the user (or from Everyone) in the Exceptions list.

- To locate the document region or regions in which a user (or Everyone) has permissions, or to remove all permission regions for a user, click the down arrow next to the user's name and choose a command from the drop-down menu, shown here:

6 To apply the document protection you specified in the previous steps, click the Yes Start Enforcing Protection button. Word will then prompt you to enter a password. If you later want to remove or modify the document protection, you'll need to enter this password.

Note that the protection you choose will apply to you as well as to other users. However, because you have the password, you'll be able to remove the protection when necessary.

If you have routed a single copy of the document among the members of your workgroup, when you receive the document back, you'll probably want to remove the protection. You can do so by choosing Tools, Unprotect Document. (When the document is protected, Unprotect Document replaces the Protect Document command.) If you entered a password when you protected the document, Word will prompt you for it.

If you have distributed a separate copy of the document to each member of the workgroup, when these documents are returned to you, you can merge the changes they contain into the original document.

Merging changes is explained in "Merging and Comparing Documents," on page 458.

File-Sharing Protection

You can also protect a document against unauthorized changes by selecting file-sharing options, using the following steps:

1 Open the document you want to protect.

2 Choose Tools, Options, and click the Security tab (see Figure 16-13). If the Save As dialog box is currently displayed, you can open the Security tab by choosing Security Options from the Tools drop-down menu.

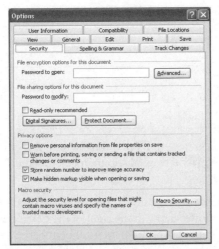

Figure 16-13. This figure shows the Security tab of the Options dialog box.

3 Set one or more of the options in the top portion of the Security tab, as follows:

- To encrypt the document and prevent unauthorized users from opening (and decrypting) the document, type a password into the Password To Open text box. Word will ask you to retype the password when you click OK. No user will be able to open the document in Word without typing this password, and because the document is encrypted, no one will be able to read its contents by using other software. To select the type of encryption that Word uses and to choose whether or not the document's properties will also be encrypted, click the Advanced button.

- To prevent unauthorized users from modifying the document, type a password into the Password To Modify text box. Word will ask you to retype the password when you click OK. Any user will be able to open the document in read-only mode, which will allow the user to modify the document and save the modified document version in a separate file (but not to overwrite the original document file). Only users who know the password will be able to open the document in the normal read-write mode, which allows them to save changes to the original document file.

- To have Word suggest that users open the document in read-only mode, check the Read-Only Recommended option. When any user opens the document, Word will display a message suggesting that the document be opened in read-only mode. The user, however, can choose whether to open the document in read-only or in normal read-write mode.

- If you have obtained a digital certificate from a certification authority (such as Veri-Sign) you can digitally sign the document by clicking the Digital Signatures button and adding the certificate to the Signatures tab in the Digital Signature dialog box. A digital signature attached to a document verifies to all document recipients that you created the document and that it hasn't been modified since you signed it.

- To open the Protect Document dialog box, discussed in the previous section, click the Protect Document button.

Chapter 16

475

> **Note** An open password or a modify password is case-sensitive—that is, you'll always have to type it with the same combination of uppercase and lowercase letters.

> **Caution** If you forget a document-protecting password, you won't be able to open the document (for an open password) or to modify the document (for a modify password), nor will you be able to recover the password.

You can turn off file-sharing protection (assuming that the document is open in the normal read-write mode) by opening the Security tab again and then deleting the password or clearing the Read-Only Recommended option.

Note that you can open any document in read-only mode—even one that's not protected—by choosing File, Open, clicking the down arrow to the right of the Open button, and choosing the Open Read-Only option from the drop-down menu shown here:

When you open a document in read-only mode, you can freely make changes to its contents. You can't, however, save the modified document under the same filename and in the same folder (that is, you can't overwrite the original document file with the changed version), although you can save a copy of the modified document under a different filename or in a different folder by choosing File, Save As.

Inside Out

Protect your privacy and guard against viruses

You can use the settings in the Privacy Options area of the Security tab to avoid unintentionally disseminating private information contained in the current document.

To remove personal information from the document—for example, the author name stored in the document properties or the names of reviewers stored in tracked changes and comments—check the Remove Personal Information From File Properties On Save option. (For slightly more detailed information on this option, see the tip "Guard your privacy," on page 73.)

To avoid inadvertently distributing private information contained in tracked changes or comments, you might want to check the Warn Before Printing Saving Or Sending A File That Contains Tracked Changes Or Comments option.

When you merge or compare documents, Word normally tags related documents by inserting the same randomly generated number in each of the documents. (This somehow improves the accuracy of merge and compare operations.) Although these numbers are hidden, they could potentially be used to prove that the documents are related. If this is a problem, you can turn off the marking of related documents by clearing the Store Random Number To Improve Merge Accuracy option. (To read general information about personal information in documents and Microsoft's privacy policies, you can choose Help, Customer Feedback Options and open the Customer Feedback Options category in the Service Options dialog box.)

If you want to keep tabs on all information contained in your documents, you can have Word automatically show any hidden tracked changes or comments when you first open a document by checking the Make Hidden Markup Visible When Opening Or Saving option.

Also in the Security tab, you can click the Macro Security button to open the Security dialog box, where you can change your macro security options.

> When you share Word documents with others, it's especially important to take precautions against receiving viruses contained in Word macros. For information on macro security, see "Setting Macro Security," on page 229.

Sharing Fonts

One problem that you might encounter when you work in a workgroup is that a coworker might not be able to view or print a particular font that you have assigned to text in a document. To avoid this problem, you should make sure that your document uses only TrueType fonts, which are widely available and don't depend on using a particular printer. Common TrueType fonts (such as Times New Roman, Arial, and Courier New) are installed on virtually every computer that runs Microsoft Windows. If, however, you use one or more TrueType fonts that might not be installed on a coworker's computer, you can embed TrueType fonts in your document so that your coworker can view and print them even on a machine that doesn't have them installed. (Doing so, however, will increase the document's size.)

> For a brief description of TrueType fonts, see "Formatting Characters with the Font Dialog Box," on page 313.

To embed TrueType fonts, perform the following steps:

1. Open the document in which you want to embed fonts.

2. Choose Tools, Options, and click the Save tab.

3. Select the Embed TrueType Fonts option. To reduce the document's size, you can also check the Embed Characters In Use Only option, which causes Word to save font information only for those characters that actually appear in the document. You can also check Do Not Embed Common System Fonts to avoid wasting space by including common fonts—such as Times New Roman, Arial, and Courier New—that the document recipient is sure to have on his or her computer.

Chapter 16

Proofing Word Documents

Using the Word Proofing Tools 479
Checking Spelling 479
Checking Your Grammar. 490
NEW FEATURE! Finding Synonyms with the
Thesaurus 497
NEW FEATURE! Translating Text 499
Hyphenating Your Documents 500
Marking the Language 505

Using the Word Proofing Tools

The proofing tools available in Microsoft Office Word 2003 help you polish your writing and improve the appearance of your documents. Word provides some proofing tools that you can use while you enter the text into a document: namely, the as-you-type spelling and grammar checkers and the thesaurus. It provides other proofing tools—the full-featured spelling and grammar checkers and the hyphenation command—that you generally use after you have finished entering, editing, and formatting the text in your document but before you preview the printed appearance of the document and make the final adjustments to the page setup, as discussed in the next chapter.

For information on using Word's new formatting consistency checker, see "Checking the Consistency of Your Formatting," on page 330.

Checking Spelling

You can use the Word spelling checker to verify and to help you correct the spelling of the text in your document. You can have Word automatically check your spelling as you type, or you can manually run the full-featured version of the spelling checker to check text that you have already entered.

If your document contains text in a foreign language or text that you want to exclude from proofing, you should perform the steps discussed in "Marking the Language," on page 505, before using the Word spelling, grammar, thesaurus, or hyphenation tools.

Checking Your Spelling as You Type

To have Word check your spelling as you type, choose Tools, Options, click the Spelling & Grammar tab, and check the Check Spelling As You Type option in the Spelling section at the top of the tab (see Figure 17-1).

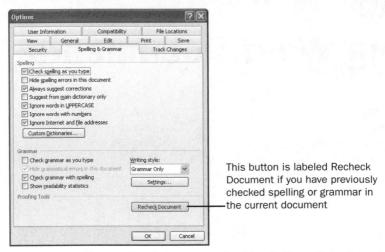

Figure 17-1. The Spelling & Grammar tab of the Options dialog box allows you to select options for the spelling checker.

Word will then check the spelling of any text that has already been entered into your document, and it will check the spelling of each new word immediately after you type it. If the spelling checker encounters a word that it judges to be misspelled (that is, a word that it doesn't find in its dictionary), it marks the word with a wavy red underline. You can ignore the word, correct it manually, or right-click it to display the following shortcut menu:

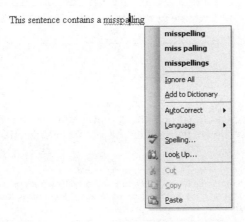

From the shortcut menu, choose one of the following options:

- To correct the word, choose one of the suggested spellings in bold type at the top of the menu (if any are shown).

- To have the spelling checker stop marking the word, choose Ignore All. Word will stop marking the word in all documents until you click the Recheck Document button in the Spelling & Grammar tab.

- To add the word to the default custom dictionary so that Word will permanently stop marking it as misspelled, choose Add To Dictionary.

> Custom dictionaries are discussed in "Using Custom Dictionaries," on page 487.

- To correct the word and add the word to AutoCorrect, choose one of the suggested spellings from the AutoCorrect submenu shown here:

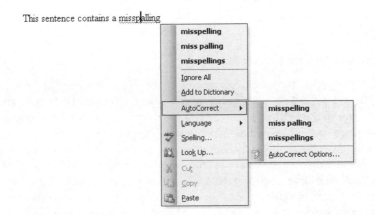

Word will then correct the word in your document and it will add the correction to the Replace Text As You Type list of the AutoCorrect feature. From then on, AutoCorrect will automatically correct the misspelling whenever you type it, before the as-you-type spelling checker has a chance to underline it, provided that you have checked the Replace Text As You Type option. To locate this option, choose Tools, AutoCorrect Options, and click the AutoCorrect tab in the AutoCorrect dialog box.

> **Note** Any spelling corrections you add to the Replace Text As You Type list of the AutoCorrect feature will be used in addition to the many spelling corrections that Word has predefined. For information on the Replace Text As You Type option and on using AutoCorrect, see "Automatically Fixing Your Text with AutoCorrect," on page 271, and see the tip "Use AutoCorrect to correct your spelling," on page 279.

- To change the language formatting of the wavy underlined text, use the Language submenu.

> Language formatting is discussed in "Marking the Language," on page 505.

- To open the Spelling dialog box, choose Spelling. This dialog box provides several additional options for correcting spelling and is described in the next section.

If the as-you-type spelling checker (or the as-you-type grammar checker) has marked one or more words in your document, you can locate (and correct) these words by double-clicking the Spelling And Grammar Status icon on the Word status bar, shown here:

Spelling And Grammar Status

Each time you double-click this icon, Word will select the next marked word or phrase and display the shortcut menu shown earlier so that you can correct the spelling.

Inside Out

Make sure spelling errors aren't hidden

Once you've turned on the as-you-type spelling checker (by checking the Check Spelling As You Type option in the Spelling & Grammar tab, shown in Figure 17-1), the option will stay on as you work with various documents and as you quit and restart Word, until you explicitly turn it off. Once you've turned the option on, can you therefore trust that any word you subsequently type will be correctly spelled unless it has a red underline? Unfortunately, no, because of the Hide Spelling Errors In This Document option, also in the Spelling & Grammar tab. Unlike the Check Spelling As You Type option, Hide Spelling Errors In This Document applies only to the current document. If you or someone else has checked this option for a particular document or for the template used to create that document, even though you've turned on the as-you-type spelling checker and are relying on it to flag your misspellings, misspelled words *won't* be underlined in the document.

So, if you've been using the as-you-type spelling checker but suspect that Word isn't catching misspellings in the document you're currently typing, make sure that the Hide Spelling Errors In This Document option *isn't* checked. And if this option is always checked for the new documents you create based on a particular template, open that template, clear the option, and resave the template file. You might also routinely verify that this option is off before sending out important documents to avoid embarrassing spelling errors.

Checking the Spelling of Existing Text

Another way to check your spelling is to manually run the full-featured, dialog-box version of the spelling checker *after* you've entered a block of text or an entire document. If you're planning to run the full-featured spelling checker, you might want to turn off the as-you-type spelling checker so you won't be bothered with the wavy underlines while you write.

To check the spelling of text you have already entered, perform the following steps:

1 If you want to check the spelling of your entire document, place the insertion point anywhere in the document. (Word will check spelling from the position of the insertion point to the end of the document, and then from the beginning of the document down to the insertion point.) If you want to check the spelling of a portion of your document, select that portion. (Recall that you can quickly select a single word by double-clicking it.)

2 Begin the spelling check by choosing Tools, Spelling And Grammar, by clicking the Spelling And Grammar button on the Standard toolbar, or by pressing F7.

3 Whenever the spelling checker encounters a word that it can't find in its dictionary, it selects the word in the document and displays the Spelling And Grammar dialog box (see Figure 17-2). Within this dialog box, the Not In Dictionary box displays a copy of the sentence containing the questionable word (which is shown in red). The Suggestions list contains one or more possible correct spellings for the word (provided that the spelling checker can derive any, and that the Always Suggest Corrections option is selected, as discussed later).

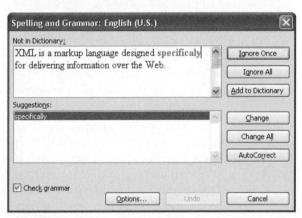

Figure 17-2. The Spelling And Grammar dialog box flags each spelling error.

To deal with this word, you should do one or more of the following:

■ To change the word and then search for the next misspelling, either correct the spelling of the word within the Not In Dictionary box (for your convenience, Word places the insertion point just after the word), or simply select the correct spelling—if present—in the Suggestions list. Then click the Change button or the Change All button. Clicking Change will replace only the current occurrence of the word. Clicking Change All will replace the current occurrence of the word plus all occurrences that the spelling checker subsequently finds in the document. (It won't correct any occurrences that the spelling checker previously

Spelling
And
Grammar

encountered and you chose to ignore. Nor will it correct occurrences in text that you don't check—for example, if you're checking only a selected block of text or if you stop the spelling checker before it has finished checking the whole document, the word won't be corrected in the unchecked portions of the document.)

If you edit the word within the Not In Dictionary box, you can click the Undo Edit button (which replaces the Ignore Once button) before you click another button, to restore the word. Also, if you retype the word in the Not In Dictionary box and Word still doesn't recognize the spelling, it will flag the word again.

- To leave the word unchanged and search for the next misspelling, click the Ignore Once or the Ignore All button. If you click Ignore Once, the spelling checker will continue to flag other occurrences of the word that it subsequently finds. If you click Ignore All, Word won't flag the word again during the remainder of the spelling check or during any future spelling check in any document (even if you quit and restart Word) until you click the Recheck Document button in the Spelling & Grammar tab (as described in Table 17-1 in the next section).

- To leave the word unchanged and add it to your default custom dictionary so that Word will permanently stop flagging it, click the Add To Dictionary button. (Custom dictionaries are discussed in "Using Custom Dictionaries," on page 487.)

- To reverse your previous correction, click the Undo button.

- After you have selected the correct spelling in the Suggestions list or have manually corrected the word in the Not In Dictionary box, to have Word define an AutoCorrect entry that will correct the misspelling whenever you type it in the future, click the AutoCorrect button.

- To check the spelling of the current word using a word list for a different language, choose that language in the Dictionary Language drop-down list. (The Dictionary Language drop-down list will be displayed only if one or more additional languages are enabled in the Microsoft Office Language Settings dialog box. This list contains the languages for which dictionaries have been installed—initially, dialects of English, French, and Spanish.) For example, if the current word is *colour* and you choose English (U.K.) in the Dictionary Language list, the spelling checker would accept the spelling and search for the next misspelling. (However, if the word is *coluor*, it would remain displayed as a misspelling.) (See "Taking Advantage of Automatic Language Detection," on page 507, for information on enabling languages using the Microsoft Office Language Settings dialog box.)

- To have Word start or stop checking your grammar throughout the remainder of the document or selection, check or clear the Check Grammar option (near the bottom of the Spelling And Grammar dialog box).

- To change the way Word checks your spelling, click the Options button. (Spelling options are discussed in the next section.)

Note If the Check Grammar With Spelling option in the Spelling & Grammar tab of the Options dialog box (opened by choosing Tools, Options) was checked before you ran the spelling check, after Word checks the spelling of the words in each sentence, it will check the grammar of the sentence. You can start or stop grammar checking during a spelling check by checking or clearing the Check Grammar option in the Spelling And Grammar dialog box. Checking grammar is discussed in "Checking Your Grammar," on page 490.

4   The spelling checker will also stop at any word that repeats the previous word (except for words that are commonly repeated, such as *that* and *had*). When the spelling checker encounters a repeated word, it replaces the Change button with the Delete button. You can click Ignore Once to leave the repeated word in the document or click Delete to delete the second occurrence of the word.

Tip Edit while you display the Spelling And Grammar dialog box
You can edit your document while the Spelling And Grammar dialog box remains displayed. To edit, click in the document. To start checking spelling again, click the Resume button in the Spelling And Grammar dialog box. Word will start checking from the current position of the insertion point, or within the current selection, not necessarily from the point where it left off.

If the Check Grammar With Spelling and the Show Readability Statistics options were checked before you ran the spelling check, after Word completes the spelling and grammar check, it will display readability statistics. (You access these options by choosing Tools, Options and clicking the Spelling & Grammar tab. You can't check Show Readability Statistics unless Check Grammar With Spelling is also checked.)

These readability statistics are described in "Checking the Grammar of Existing Text," on page 493.

Customizing the Spelling Checker

You can tailor the way Word checks your spelling by clicking the Options button in the Spelling And Grammar dialog box to open the Spelling & Grammar tab, which was shown in Figure 17-1. You can also display the Spelling & Grammar tab by choosing Tools, Options and then clicking this tab in the Options dialog box. Table 17-1 describes the ways you can use the Spelling & Grammar tab to modify the spelling checker. Note that changes you make affect both the as-you-type spelling checker and the full-featured spelling checker unless otherwise noted in the table.

The Check Spelling As You Type and Hide Spelling Errors In This Document options were discussed in the previous section, and the options that affect the grammar checker are covered in "Customizing the Grammar Checker," on page 496.

Table 17-1. Modifying the Word Spelling Checker in the Spelling & Grammar Tab

To Do This	Perform This Action in the Spelling & Grammar Tab
Have Word display, if possible, one or more replacement words in the Suggestions list in the Spelling And Grammar dialog box whenever the spelling checker finds a misspelled word. You can choose an appropriate replacement word from this list to instantly correct your misspelling. This option doesn't affect the as-you-type spelling checker.	Check the Always Suggest Corrections option
Have the spelling checker suggest words only from its main dictionary and not from any custom dictionaries. Word, however, will continue to use both its main dictionaries and all custom dictionaries to check spelling. (Custom dictionaries are discussed in the next section.)	Check the Suggest From Main Dictionary Only option
Have the spelling checker omit checking the spelling of words that are in all capital letters. This option prevents the spelling checker from flagging acronyms.	Check the Ignore Words In UPPERCASE option
Have the spelling checker omit checking the spelling of words that contain one or more numbers, such as *3-D*.	Check the Ignore Words With Numbers option
Have the spelling checker omit checking the spelling of Internet addresses (such as *http: //www.microsoft.com*) or file paths (such as C:\Book\Chapter1.doc).	Check the Ignore Internet And File Addresses option
Display the Custom Dictionaries dialog box, which allows you to create, open, remove, or edit custom dictionaries, as discussed in the next section.	Click the Custom Dictionaries button
Have the spelling checker delete its list of ignored words (that is, words for which you chose the Ignore All option), and begin flagging them again. Also, have the grammar checker delete its list of grammatical errors for which you clicked the Ignore Rule button and start flagging them again, as explained later in this chapter.	Click the Recheck Document button (labeled Check Document if you haven't checked spelling or grammar in the current document)

Using Custom Dictionaries

Both the as-you-type spelling checker and the full-featured spelling checker look up words in the main spelling dictionary and in one or more custom dictionaries. When Word is installed, a single custom dictionary file named Custom.dic is created. Initially, this dictionary file is empty. However, every time you click the Add To Dictionary button in the Spelling And Grammar dialog box, and whenever you choose Add To Dictionary from the shortcut menu while you're correcting a word underlined by the as-you-type spelling checker, the current word is added to Custom.dic so that the word will no longer be flagged as misspelled.

If using a single custom dictionary meets your needs, you don't need to do anything except occasionally add a word to it by using the Add To Dictionary command. You might, however, want to create and use one or more special-purpose custom dictionaries. For example, if you write both computer books and science fiction, you might create one dictionary that contains the technical terms you use when writing computer books (perhaps named Computer.dic) and another dictionary that contains the invented words you use when writing science fiction (perhaps named Fiction.dic).

To create a new custom dictionary, perform the following steps:

1 Choose Tools, Options and click the Spelling & Grammar tab, or click the Options button in the Spelling And Grammar dialog box that appears during a spelling check, to open the Spelling & Grammar tab (see Figure 17-1).

2 Click the Custom Dictionaries button in the Spelling & Grammar tab to open the Custom Dictionaries dialog box, shown here:

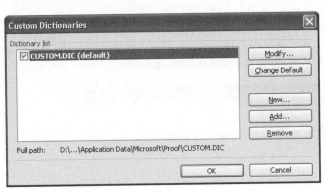

3 Click the New button, and in the Create Custom Dictionary dialog box, type a filename for the dictionary into the File Name text box, shown in the figure on the top of the next page.

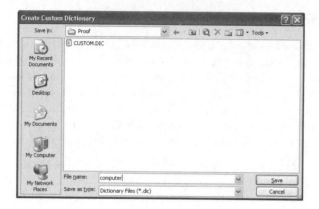

You can either include the .dic extension in the name you type, or omit adding an extension. (In the latter case, Word will add the .dic extension for you.) You can accept the default file location that Word initially selected or you can select a new one. When you click the Save button, Word will create a new, empty custom dictionary. Also, it will add this dictionary to the Dictionary List in the Custom Dictionaries dialog box, and it will check the box next to the dictionary name to indicate that the dictionary has been activated. (Activating custom dictionaries is explained later.)

4 Click the OK button.

To begin using a custom dictionary that you have created or one that you have purchased or obtained from someone else, perform the following steps:

1 *Activate* the dictionary. (If you created a new dictionary using the preceding steps, it should already be activated and you can skip this step.) To activate a dictionary, click the Custom Dictionaries button on the Spelling & Grammar tab (shown in Figure 17-1), and check the box next to the name of the dictionary in the Dictionary List, as shown here:

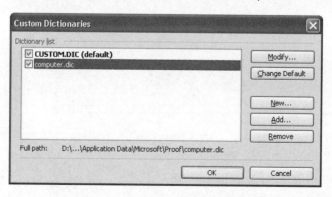

If the dictionary isn't in the list, click the Add button and select the dictionary file. Leave the Custom Dictionaries dialog box open for the next steps.

The spelling checker will look up words in all custom dictionaries that have been activated. To deactivate a dictionary and have Word not use the words it contains, repeat this step but clear the check box next to the dictionary name in the Custom Dictionaries dialog box.

Tip **Remove a dictionary**

While the Custom Dictionaries dialog box is open, you can remove a custom dictionary from the Dictionary List by clicking on it to select it and then clicking the Remove button. This doesn't delete the dictionary file itself, but merely takes it out of the list.

---

2   To manually add words to your new dictionary, select it in the Dictionary List in the Custom Dictionaries dialog box and click the Modify button. Then add new words to the dictionary using the dialog box that appears (the name of the dictionary is displayed as the dialog box title), as shown in this example:

You can use this procedure to add or remove words from any custom dictionary. (For more on custom dictionaries, see the Inside Out sidebar, "Add only single words to a custom dictionary," on the next page.)

Note   If you want a custom dictionary to check text in a specific language, choose that language in the Language drop-down list at the bottom of the dialog box in which you modify the dictionary (described in step 2). The spelling checker will use the dictionary only for text that has been marked for that language or text that Word's automatic language detection has determined to be in that language. (Marking the language of text is described in "Marking the Language," on page 505.) If you select All Languages in the Language list, the dictionary will be used for all text, regardless of its language.

---

3 To have Word automatically add words to your custom dictionary, make it the *default* custom dictionary by selecting it in the Dictionary List in the Custom Dictionaries dialog box and clicking the Change Default button. Whenever you click the Add To Dictionary button in the Spelling And Grammar dialog box or choose Add To Dictionary from the shortcut menu of the as-you-type spelling checker, Word adds the current word to the default custom dictionary.

4 Click the OK button in the Custom Dictionaries dialog box and in the Spelling & Grammar tab.

Inside Out

Add only single words to a custom dictionary

The dialog box for modifying a custom dictionary (described in step 2) misleadingly allows you to enter phrases consisting of more than one word. However, these entries won't work. For example, if you added the phrase *Thea sinensis* to a custom dictionary, Word would continue to flag occurrences of *Thea sinensis* in your documents. To stop the flagging, you would have to add *Thea* as one word and *sinensis* as another word.

Checking Your Grammar

You can use the Word grammar checker to help polish your writing. The grammar checker indicates possible grammatical errors, such as a disagreement between subject and verb, a double negative, or incorrect punctuation (such as extra spaces inserted between words). It also flags expressions that exhibit possible poor writing style, such as clichés, misused words, or long sentences (more than 60 words). You can have Word automatically check your grammar as you type, or you can manually run the full-featured grammar checker (along with the spelling checker) to check text that you've already entered. When you run the grammar checker manually, you can have it display statistics on the general readability of your document after it has completed its check.

> If your document contains text in a foreign language or text that you want to exclude from proofing, you should perform the steps discussed in "Marking the Language," on page 505, before using the Word spelling, grammar, thesaurus, or hyphenation tools.

Checking Your Grammar as You Type

To have Word check your grammar as you type, choose Tools, Options, click the Spelling & Grammar tab, and check the Check Grammar As You Type option (see Figure 17-3).

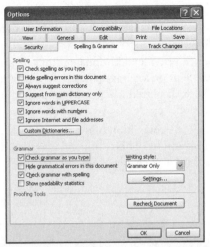

Figure 17-3. You activate the as-you-type grammar checker in the Spelling & Grammar tab of the Options dialog box.

Word will then check the grammar of any text that has already been entered into your document, and it will begin checking the grammar of each new sentence you enter immediately after you finish typing it. If the grammar checker encounters a sentence that violates one of its current grammar or style rules (later you'll see how to modify these rules), it marks the offending portions of the sentence with a wavy green underline. (Recall that Word marks a misspelled word with a wavy *red* underline.) You can then ignore the mark, correct the sentence manually, or right-click the underlined portion to display the following shortcut menu:

On the shortcut menu, choose one of the following options:

- To have Word correct the sentence, choose one of the suggested grammar corrections displayed in bold type at the top of the menu (if any are given). Note that rather than displaying actual substitute text that you can choose, the menu might display a tip for manually correcting the sentence. For example, if the checker encounters a sentence fragment, the menu will display Fragment (Consider Revising).

Chapter 17

● To have the grammar checker ignore the error and remove the wavy underline from the word or words, choose Ignore Once. (Word will, however, continue to search for violations of the same grammar or style rule.)

● To open the Grammar dialog box, which provides additional options for correcting grammatical errors, choose Grammar. This dialog box is the same (except for its title) as the Spelling And Grammar dialog box displayed when you manually run the grammar checker, described in the next section.

● Choose About This Sentence to display an explanation of the grammatical error that was flagged, as shown in the following example. (This command is available only if the Office Assistant is enabled. If the Assistant isn't enabled, you can enable it by choosing Help, Show The Office Assistant.)

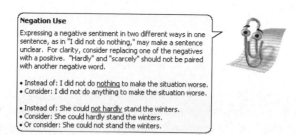

If the as-you-type grammar checker (or the as-you-type spelling checker) has marked one or more errors in your document, you can locate and correct them by double-clicking the Spelling And Grammar Status icon on the Word status bar, shown here:

Spelling And Grammar Status

Each time you double-click this icon, Word will move the insertion point to the next flagged error and display a shortcut menu for correcting the error.

Note If you check the Hide Grammatical Errors In This Document option in the Spelling & Grammar tab of the Options dialog box, Word will remove the wavy lines from all grammar errors in the active document and stop marking them in new text you type into that document. If you rely on Word to flag your grammar errors, see the Inside Out on page 482 regarding the Hide Spelling Errors In This Document option for the as-you-type spelling checker (which works just like Hide Grammatical Errors In This Document).

Checking the Grammar of Existing Text

You might prefer to manually run the full-featured, dialog-box version of the grammar checker to examine the grammar of a block of text—or an entire document—after you have typed it, rather than having to deal with possible grammatical errors while you write. In this case, you can turn off the as-you-type grammar checker or just ignore the wavy underlines. Then, when you're ready to check your grammar, you can run the grammar checker.

To use the full-featured grammar checker, choose Tools, Options, click the Spelling & Grammar tab, and make sure that the Check Grammar With Spelling option is checked. If you want to see readability statistics, make sure that the Show Readability Statistics option is also checked (you can't check this option unless you've also checked the Check Grammar With Spelling option).

When the Check Grammar With Spelling option is checked, Word will run the grammar checker whenever you run the full-featured spelling checker, as described in "Checking the Spelling of Existing Text," on page 482. The specific steps for checking your grammar are as follows:

1   If you want to check your entire document, place the insertion point anywhere in the document. (Word will check grammar from the sentence containing the insertion point to the end of the document, then from the beginning of the document down to the sentence before the one with the insertion point.) If you want to check only a portion of your document, select that portion.

Spelling
And
Grammar

2   Choose Tools, Spelling And Grammar, click the Spelling And Grammar button on the Standard toolbar, or press F7.

3   For each sentence in the document (or selection), Word first checks the spelling of the words it contains. To handle any word that is flagged as a possible misspelling, follow the instructions that were given in step 3 of the process for checking your spelling on page 483.

4   After checking the spelling of a sentence, Word will check the grammar. If the grammar checker finds a violation of one of its grammar or style rules, it opens the Spelling And Grammar dialog box (see Figure 17-4). At the top of this dialog box is a description of the possible grammar or style violation, together with a copy of the sentence showing the offending words in green. Below this, the Suggestions list displays one or more blocks of replacement text (if the grammar checker can generate a replacement) or a general suggestion to help you manually edit the sentence; for example, Negation Use (Consider Revising).

Chapter 17

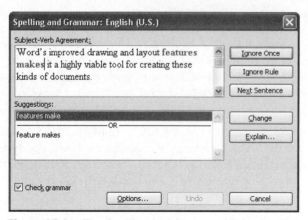

Figure 17-4. The Spelling And Grammar dialog box flags each grammatical error.

To deal with the possible error, do one or more of the following:

- To correct or improve your sentence, either directly edit the copy of the sentence displayed at the top of the Spelling And Grammar dialog box or select a block of replacement text in the Suggestions list (if one is present). Then click the Change button.

- To ignore the suggestions and move on to the next error, click the Ignore Once button. The next error might be in the same sentence.

- To ignore the suggestions for the current sentence and to move on to the next sentence, click the Next Sentence button. If the current sentence has additional errors, the grammar checker will skip them.

- To ignore the suggestions and stop Word from flagging violations of the same grammar or style rule, click the Ignore Rule button. Violations of the rule won't be flagged again during the remainder of the grammar check, or during any future grammar check in any document (even if you quit and restart Word), until you click the Recheck Document button in the Spelling & Grammar tab, as described in Table 17-1. The checker will then move on to the next error.

- To reverse your previous correction, click the Undo button.

- To check the current error using the rules for a different language, choose that language in the Dictionary Language drop-down list. (This list contains the languages for which dictionaries have been installed—initially, dialects of English, French, and Spanish.)

- To stop Word from checking your grammar, clear the Check Grammar option. Word will then check only your spelling until you check the option again.

- To modify the way the grammar checker works, click the Options button. (Setting options is explained in the next section.)

> **Tip** **Edit while you display the Spelling And Grammar dialog box**
>
> You can edit your document while the Spelling And Grammar dialog box remains displayed. To edit, click in the document. To start checking grammar again, click the Resume button in the Spelling And Grammar dialog box. Word will start checking from the current position of the insertion point, or within the current selection, not necessarily from the point where it left off.

If the Show Readability Statistics option was checked in the Spelling & Grammar tab before you started the spelling and grammar check, Word will display the Readability Statistics dialog box after it has finished the check. This dialog box shows statistics about the text that was checked, including several standard indicators of the text's general readability. For an explanation of any of the information in the dialog box, click the question-mark icon at the upper-right corner of the dialog box and then click the part of the dialog box displaying the information. Figure 17-5 shows the statistics that Word displayed for the original draft of the chapter you're reading.

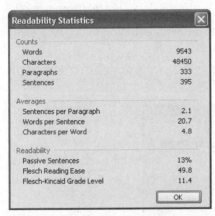

Figure 17-5. This figure shows the Readability Statistics dialog box that was displayed after running a spelling and grammar check on a preliminary draft of this chapter.

> **Tip** **Other ways to display document statistics**
>
> You can display statistics about the number of pages, words, characters, and so on in your document by choosing File, Properties and clicking the Statistics tab or by choosing Tools, Word Count. You can also display the number of words, characters, lines, pages, or paragraphs by choosing View, Toolbars, Word Count to display the Word Count toolbar, shown here:
>
>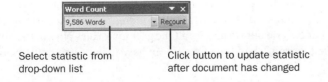
>
> Select statistic from   Click button to update statistic
> drop-down list   after document has changed

Customizing the Grammar Checker

You can modify the way the grammar checker works by choosing Tools, Options and clicking the Spelling & Grammar tab in the Options dialog box, shown in Figure 17-3. You can also display this tab by clicking the Options button in the Spelling And Grammar dialog box. The options discussed in this section affect both the as-you-type grammar checker and the full-featured grammar checker that you run manually through the Spelling And Grammar command.

To have the grammar checker flag grammatical errors only, select Grammar Only in the Writing Style drop-down list. The checker will then apply only its grammar rules. To have it flag both grammatical errors and stylistic weaknesses, applying both its grammar and its style rules, select Grammar & Style. You can also customize either of these options, specifying exactly which rules the grammar checker applies when you select that option. For example, you could change the Grammar Only option so that it would cause Word to apply some of its grammar rules and some of its style rules. (Doing this, however, would make the name of the option, Grammar Only, a misnomer. Unfortunately, Word doesn't let you create new options with appropriate names.) To customize a Writing Style option, perform the following steps:

1 In the Spelling & Grammar tab, click the Settings button to display the Grammar Settings dialog box (shown in Figure 17-6).

2 Select the option that you want to modify in the Writing Style drop-down list at the top of the Grammar Settings dialog box.

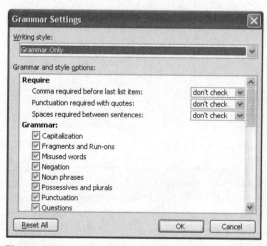

Figure 17-6. The Grammar Settings dialog box allows you to customize the grammar checker's Writing Style options.

3 Check or clear the individual grammar or style rules that you want the modified option to apply. (By default, the Grammar Only option applies all the Grammar rules, while the Grammar & Style option applies all the grammar rules plus all the Style rules except Use Of First Person.) Additionally, you can have the option apply one of the

three Require rules given at the top of the list, by choosing an option in the drop-down list other than Don't Check. For example, to have Word check your use of a comma after the last item in a list, you would select Always (a comma would be required) or Never (a comma wouldn't be allowed) in the Comma Required Before Last List Item drop-down list, shown here:

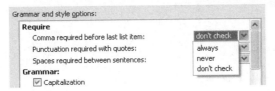

4   To restore the option that's currently selected in the Writing Style drop-down list (Grammar Only or Grammar & Style) to its default set of rules, click the Reset All button.

5   Click the OK button.

Finding Synonyms with the Thesaurus

You can use the Office thesaurus to look up synonyms or antonyms for a word or phrase in your document. You'll probably want to use the thesaurus as you're entering text into your document, in contrast to the other proofing tools, which you often use after you have finished entering text.

> If your document contains text in a foreign language or text that you want to exclude from proofing, you should perform the steps discussed in "Marking the Language," on page 505, before using the Word spelling, grammar, thesaurus, or hyphenation tools.

The thesaurus in Word 2003 and other Office 2003 applications now uses the new Research task pane.

> For details on working with the Research task pane to locate synonyms or other information, see "Using the Research Task Pane," on page 44.

To use the thesaurus, perform the following basic steps:

1   Select the word or phrase for which you want to find synonyms.

2   Choose Tools, Language, Thesaurus, or press Shift+F7. Word will open the Research task pane and will look up the word or phrase in the appropriate thesaurus for the selected text's language—for example, in "Thesaurus: English (U.S.)" or "Thesaurus: French (France)." (Word ascertains the language of the text from the text's language formatting, as explained in "Marking the Language," on page 505.) The synonyms and antonyms that are found for each meaning of the word are displayed in a separate group in the results list. You can expand or collapse a group by clicking the + or –

Chapter 17

symbol. Here's the Research task pane as it would appear if you had looked up synonyms for the word *agreeable*:

Previous Search   Next Search

3 To work with a particular synonym, point to it, click the down arrow that appears, and choose a command from the drop-down menu, shown here. (Throughout the remainder of this discussion, *synonym* refers to either a synonym or an antonym.)

- ■ To insert the synonym into your document, replacing the selected word, choose Insert.

- ■ To copy the synonym into the Clipboard so that you can paste it wherever you want it, choose Copy.

- ■ To look up synonyms for the word, choose Look Up or just click the synonym. Looking up synonyms for a synonym—repeatedly if necessary—can help you find just the right word to use in your document.

Tip **Use the shortcut menu to access the thesaurus**

An alternative way to use the thesaurus is to right-click a word or a selected phrase to display the shortcut menu. Then, from the Synonyms submenu, shown here, either choose a synonym or antonym (if any are displayed), or choose the Thesaurus command to open the Research task pane and look up the word or phrase, as discussed in this procedure.

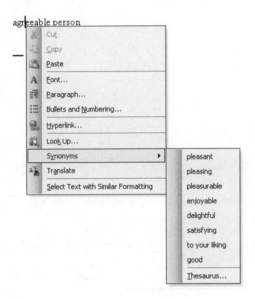

 ## Translating Text

You can use Word's translation feature to translate a word, phrase, or sentence into a different language. In Word 2003 the translation feature uses the new Research task pane and makes use of bilingual dictionaries both on your computer and on the Internet, as well as Internet machine translation services.

For details on working with the Research task pane, see "Using the Research Task Pane," on page 44.

To translate text, perform the following steps:

1. If the word, phrase, or sentence you want to translate is in your document, select it. (This will save you from having to type the text later.)

2. Choose Tools, Language, Translate to display the Research task pane and to select the Translation information service (see Figure 17-7).

Tip As a quick alternative to steps 1 and 2, you can right-click a word or a selected block of text and choose Translate from the shortcut menu.

Chapter 17

499

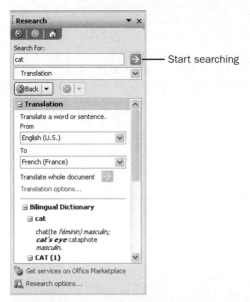

Start searching

Figure 17-7. This figure shows the Research task pane as it might appear after you selected the word cat and chose Tools, Language, Translate.

3   If the "from" and "to" languages displayed in the From and To drop-down lists are not the ones you wish to use, select the languages you want.

Note   To select the language pairs that are available in the From and To drop-down lists or to set other translation options, click the Translation Options command.

4   If you didn't select text in step 1, type the word, phrase, or sentence you want to translate into the Search For box at the top of the Research task pane and press Enter or click the Start Searching button. The translation results will be displayed in the results list, as shown in Figure 17-7. If you selected text in step 1, your results will automatically be displayed in the results list.

Hyphenating Your Documents

You can improve the appearance of a document by hyphenating words at the ends of the lines. Once hyphenated, text that is not justified will be less ragged at the right indent, and justified text will have more uniform spacing between the characters. You can hyphenate your document in one of three ways.

● You can have Word automatically hyphenate your document. The advantage of automatic hyphenation is that it's applied instantly (Word won't ask you to confirm each hyphenation, as it does with manual hyphenation). Also, if you later edit or reformat the document, Word will automatically rehyphenate it as needed. (When you apply automatic hyphenation, Word stores syllable information for all words in the document, so it can immediately hyphenate any word.) If you're creating a Web page, keep in mind that automatic hyphenation will work when you view the page in Word; however, it won't work when you display the page in a browser.

- You can manually hyphenate your document. With manual hyphenation, Word lets you confirm or adjust the placement of each hyphen. If you later edit or reformat the document, however, you'll probably have to rehyphenate the modified text to maintain consistent hyphenation throughout the document. The advantage of manual hyphenation is that it gives you more control over the way words are hyphenated; you can specify the exact location of each hyphen. If you're creating a Web page, keep in mind that manual hyphenation will probably not be very effective when the page is viewed in a browser. (A manually hyphenated word will break properly if it falls at the end of a line. However, because the line lengths are unpredictable in a browser, you would have to hyphenate almost every word to maintain consistent hyphenation.)

- You can insert various types of hyphen characters one at a time.

> If your document contains text in a foreign language or text that you want to exclude from proofing, you should perform the steps discussed in "Marking the Language," on page 505, before using the Word spelling, grammar, thesaurus, or hyphenation tools.

Automatically Hyphenating a Document

To have Word automatically hyphenate the current document, perform the following steps:

1 If you want to exclude one or more paragraphs in your document from hyphenation, select them. Choose Format, Paragraph, click the Line And Page Breaks tab, and check the Don't Hyphenate option.

Automatic hyphenation will affect all paragraphs in the document, except those with Don't Hyphenate paragraph formatting, even if you select only a portion of the document before proceeding. Note that if you later remove the Don't Hyphenate formatting from a paragraph, automatic hyphenation will begin working in that paragraph—you won't have to reapply automatic hyphenation.

> **Note** The Don't Hyphenate paragraph formatting excludes a paragraph only from automatic or manual hyphenation. In contrast, the Do Not Check Spelling Or Grammar character formatting (discussed in "Marking the Language," on page 505) excludes text from *all* proofing (spelling, grammar, and hyphenation).

2 Choose Tools, Language, Hyphenation. This will open the Hyphenation dialog box, shown here:

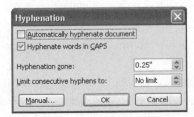

Chapter 17

3 In the Hyphenation dialog box, check the Automatically Hyphenate Document option.

4 Choose any other hyphenation options you want in the Hyphenation dialog box, as follows:

- To have Word hyphenate words in all capital letters, such as acronyms, check the Hyphenate Words In CAPS option.

- To adjust the hyphenation zone, explained later, enter a new value into the Hyphenation Zone text box.

- To limit the number of consecutive lines Word will hyphenate, enter a number into the Limit Consecutive Hyphens To text box. Limiting consecutive hyphenations prevents unsightly "stacking" of hyphen characters along the right margin.

5 Click the OK button.

The *hyphenation zone* affects the particular hyphenations that Word performs. It works as follows: when Word encounters a word that extends beyond the right indent, it must decide whether to simply wrap the word (that is, move the entire word down to the next line) or whether to attempt to hyphenate the word. If wrapping the word would leave space at the end of the line that is narrower than the hyphenation zone (.25 inch wide by default), Word wraps it, as shown here:

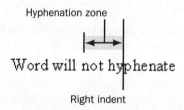

If, however, wrapping the word would leave a space wider than the hyphenation zone, Word attempts to hyphenate it, as seen here:

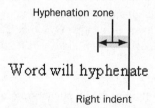

(However, if Word can't hyphenate the word so that it fits within the right indent, it will wrap it.)

Choosing a wide hyphenation zone reduces the number of hyphenations that Word will perform, but it increases the raggedness of the margin (or makes the intercharacter spacing less uniform in justified text).

To remove automatic hyphenation from a document, reopen the Hyphenation dialog box, clear the Automatically Hyphenate Document option, and click the OK button.

Chapter 17

Manually Hyphenating a Document

To manually hyphenate the current document, perform the following steps:

1 If you want to hyphenate your entire document, place the insertion point anywhere in the document. If you want to hyphenate only part of your document, select the block or blocks of text you want to hyphenate.

2 Choose Tools, Language, Hyphenation. This will open the Hyphenation dialog box, as seen here:

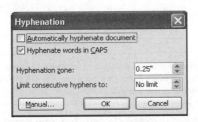

3 In the Hyphenation dialog box, set the hyphenation options you want, but make sure that the Automatically Hyphenate Document option is not checked. These options were explained in the previous section.

4 Click the Manual button. Word will activate Print Layout view and begin looking for possible hyphenations. (When Word is finished hyphenating, it will restore your original document view.)

5 Whenever Word encounters a word that requires hyphenation, it displays the Manual Hyphenation dialog box, which shows the word and the proposed position of the hyphen, together with all other possible hyphen positions in the word, as shown here:

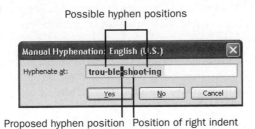

Possible hyphen positions

Proposed hyphen position   Position of right indent

Each possible hyphenation position is marked with a hyphen. The proposed hyphenation position is marked with a blinking highlight in addition to the hyphen. The position of the right indent is marked with a vertical line. Word also carries out the proposed hyphenation in the document and highlights the hyphen character.

You should now do one of the following:

■ To hyphenate the word at the proposed position, just click the Yes button.

Chapter 17

■ To hyphenate the word at a different position (say, to avoid a hyphen after only the first two letters of a long word), use the Left or Right arrow key to move the blinking highlight to that position, and then click Yes.

■ To skip hyphenating the word, click No. The word will be wrapped rather than hyphenated.

Note You can assign a paragraph the Don't Hyphenate paragraph formatting to exclude it from manual or automatic hyphenation. You can also assign a block of text the Do Not Check Spelling Or Grammar character formatting to exclude the text from *all* proofing (spelling, grammar, and hyphenation).

For information on applying the Don't Hyphenate and other paragraph formatting features, see "Formatting Paragraphs Directly," on page 318. For information on applying the Do Not Check Spelling Or Grammar feature to a block of text, see "Marking the Language," on page 505.

When Word manually hyphenates a word, it inserts a special character known as an *optional hyphen*. If a word containing an optional hyphen is shifted so that it no longer falls at the end of a line, the hyphen is hidden and the letters on either side of the hyphen come together. However, the optional hyphen remains within the word, and it will reappear and allow the word to be broken if the word shifts back to the end of a line.

To remove a manually applied hyphenation, you need to delete the optional hyphen character. You can delete one or more of these characters using either of the following methods:

Show/Hide

● Make optional hyphens visible by clicking the Show/Hide ¶ button on the Standard toolbar or checking the Show All Formatting Marks in the Reveal Formatting task pane (which displays all nonprinting characters). Or you can choose Tools, Options, click the View tab, and check the Optional Hyphens option in the Formatting Marks area to make just optional hyphens visible. Then use standard editing methods to delete the optional hyphen characters.

● To quickly delete optional hyphens throughout your document, choose Edit, Replace, enter the code for an optional hyphen into the Find What box by choosing Optional Hyphen from the Special menu, leave the Replace With box empty, and click Replace or Replace All.

For details on using the Replace command, see "Replacing Text and Formatting," on page 298.

Inserting Hyphen Characters

You can manually insert optional hyphens (discussed in the previous section), as well as several other related special characters, as shown in Table 17-2. If you click the Show/Hide ¶ button on the Standard toolbar or check the Show All Formatting Marks in the Reveal Formatting task pane, Word will display on the screen all the characters listed here, using the symbols shown in the second column.

Table 17-2. Manually Inserted Hyphens and Nonbreaking Spaces

Special Character	Symbol Shown on Screen	Shortcut Key for Inserting Character	Character Properties
Optional hyphen	¬	Ctrl+hyphen (the hyphen key on the top row of the keyboard, *not* on the numeric keypad)	When an optional hyphen falls at the end of a line, it's displayed and the word that contains it is broken. When it falls within a line, it's hidden and the characters on either side come together (unless you make it visible on the screen).
Nonbreaking hyphen	-	Ctrl+Shift+hyphen (the hyphen key on the top row of the keyboard, *not* on the numeric keypad)	A nonbreaking hyphen is always displayed. A word is never broken at the position of a nonbreaking hyphen. It can be used to keep a hyphenated word or expression (such as *Stratford-Upon-Avon*) together on a single line.
Normal hyphen	-	Hyphen (the hyphen key on the top row of the keyboard *or* on the numeric keypad)	A normal hyphen is always displayed. Word breaks a word at the position of a normal hyphen if it falls at the end of a line.
Nonbreaking space	°	Ctrl+Shift+Spacebar	A line break can't occur at the position of a nonbreaking space. This character can be used to keep several words together on a single line.

Marking the Language

If your document contains text in a foreign language or text that you want to exclude from proofing, you should perform the steps discussed in this section and in "Taking Advantage of Automatic Language Detection," on page 507, before using the proofing tools; otherwise, you can safely skip these sections.

In the version of Word sold in the United States, all text is initially marked as English (U.S.), meaning English as written in the United States. If all or some of the text in your document is written in a different language or in non-U.S. English and you want to be able to proof this text, you should mark each block of such text by performing the following steps:

1 Select the non-U.S. English text in your document.

2 Choose Tools, Language, Set Language to open the Language dialog box (see Figure 17-8).

Chapter 17

Figure 17-8. The Language dialog box lets you mark the language of the selected text.

3 In the Mark Selected Text As list, click the language you want to use to mark the selected text.

The languages that are available for the proofing tools are marked with an *ABC* spelling check icon, as seen here:

ᴬᴮᶜ✓English (U.S.)

The available languages supplied with the English-language version of Word are the various dialects of English, French, and Spanish. If you choose a different language, you'll need to obtain the Microsoft Office 2003 Proofing Tools. For information about this product, look up *proofing tools* in the Word online help.

4 Click the OK button.

Your document might also contain blocks of text that you want to exclude from proofing. For example, if you're writing a paper on *Beowulf*, you might want to exclude direct quotations that come from the poem so that the spelling checker won't flag all the archaic words and the grammar checker won't attempt to "improve" the writing style. To do this, perform the following steps:

1 Select the text you want to exclude from proofing.

2 Choose Tools, Language, Set Language to open the Language dialog box (see Figure 17-8).

3 In the Language dialog box, check the Do Not Check Spelling Or Grammar option.

> **Note** Applying the Do Not Check Spelling Or Grammar formatting to a block of text won't affect the functioning of the Thesaurus within that text.

> **Tip** Use styles to assign language to text
>
> If you frequently mark blocks of text with a particular language (or to exclude proofing), you can save time by assigning that language (or the Do Not Check Spelling Or Grammar option) to a style that you can apply to all blocks of text written in that language (or that you want to exclude). Language marking is a form of character formatting, which you can apply directly as described in this section or assign to a paragraph or character style. For information on assigning character formatting to a style, see "Customizing Styles," on page 389.

If you click the Default button in the Language dialog box, Word will add the selected language format to the Normal style of the document and to the document's template. As a result, the language (or the Do Not Check Spelling Or Grammar option) will be assigned to all text based on the Normal style in the current document as well as in all new documents you subsequently create using the same template.

Taking Advantage of Automatic Language Detection

Rather than marking each block of foreign language text individually, you can have Word automatically detect the language of text in your document and use the appropriate dictionary (if available) for proofing that text. Word will detect only those languages that you explicitly enable for Office applications. To have Word automatically detect one or more languages, perform the following steps:

1 In Windows, choose Start, All Programs (or Programs), Microsoft Office, Microsoft Office Tools, Microsoft Office 2003 Language Settings. This will open the Microsoft Office 2003 Language Settings dialog box.

2 Click the Enabled Languages tab, shown in Figure 17-9.

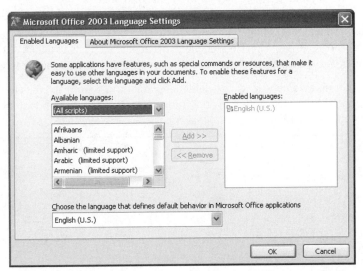

Figure 17-9. Choose languages for automatic detection in the Enabled Languages tab of the Microsoft Office 2003 Language Settings dialog box.

3 For each language you want Word to detect, click the language in the Available Languages list and then click the Add button to move the language name over to the Enabled Languages list. (To narrow down the number of languages displayed in the Available Languages list, select a specific language category—rather than All Scripts—in the drop-down list above the Available Languages list.) Click the OK button when you're done specifying languages to enable.

4 If Word is currently running, you'll have to stop it and then restart it for the changes you made in the Microsoft Office Language Settings dialog box to take effect.

5 In Word, choose Tools, Language, Set Language.

6 In the Language dialog box, make sure that the Detect Language Automatically option is checked and click OK (see Figure 17-8). Word will then begin detecting the language in all open documents and in all documents you subsequently open.

This procedure causes Word to detect each enabled language and to look for the appropriate proofing dictionary. (If Word doesn't find the dictionary for a detected language, it doesn't proof that text.) As noted earlier in this chapter, the languages that are available for the proofing tools are marked with an *ABC* spelling check icon in the Language dialog box, as seen here:

> English (U.S.)

The available languages supplied with the English-language version of Word are the various dialects of English, French, and Spanish. If you've enabled one or more languages other than these, you'll need to obtain the Microsoft Office 2003 Proofing Tools. For information about this product, look up *proofing tools* in the Word online help.

Tip **Use manual formatting if automatic detection fails**

Automatic language detection isn't foolproof. It's especially prone to failure with small blocks of text in a particular language (which don't give Word enough of a sample to work with).

If you've set up automatic language detection properly and Word still fails to detect the language of a particular block of text, apply the appropriate language formatting manually to that text, as described in the previous section.

Designing and Printing Professional-Looking Pages

Designing Pages 509
Using Text Boxes to Create
Precise Page Layouts 510
Combining Text with Graphic
Objects and Text Boxes 514
Displaying Watermarks 517
Adding Page Numbering,
Headers, and Footers 519
Modifying the Page Setup 532
Previewing and Printing Documents . . . 543

Designing Pages

The previous chapters in this part of the book have dealt with entering the content of a Microsoft Office Word 2003 document and adjusting the appearance of individual document elements, such as characters, paragraphs, headings, lists, tables, and graphic objects. This chapter is about the appearance of the document pages, which appear in Print Layout view, Print Preview, and on the printed copy of a document. It focuses on the way document elements—those just listed, as well as headers, footers, and watermarks—are arranged on the individual pages of the document.

This chapter will be of interest primarily if you're creating a traditional hard copy document consisting of a series of pages, such as a memo, letter, résumé, form, report, pamphlet, brochure, newsletter, manual, thesis, or book. However, if you're using Word to create Web pages, other types of online documents, labels, envelopes, e-mail messages, or other end products, you'll still find some of the information in this chapter important. For example, the text-wrapping styles discussed in "Combining Text with Graphic Objects and Text Boxes," on page 514, affect the display of a graphic object in a Web browser or on a mailing label, as well as on a full printed page. And some of the page setup features discussed in "Modifying the Page Setup," on page 532, as well as the printing techniques covered in "Previewing and Printing Documents," on page 543, affect the printing of labels and envelopes. The sections in this chapter indicate the techniques that aren't suitable for creating Web pages.

Creating Web pages and other types of online documents is covered in Chapter 20, "Creating Web Pages and Working with XML in Word." Creating labels, envelopes, or multiple e-mail messages is covered in Chapter 19, "Using Word to Automate Mailings." Creating individual e-mail messages is discussed in "Sharing Word Documents Using E-Mail," on page 470.

Some of the techniques presented in this chapter affect the look of a specific page; namely, adding text boxes and formatting graphic objects. Other techniques affect the general look of pages throughout a document or document section—for example, adding watermarks, headers, or footers, or adjusting the margins or page orientation.

Using newspaper-style columns is another way to arrange text and graphics on the pages throughout a document or document section. For information, see "Arranging Text in Newspaper-Style Columns," on page 371.

Using Text Boxes to Create Precise Page Layouts

The text in the body of a document is contained in a stream of characters that flows from line to line and from page to page. This section describes how to use a *text box* to place a block of text or graphics outside of the normal stream of characters in the body text, at a precise position on the page or at a specific position relative to the adjoining text. You can use text boxes to position margin notes, figures, tables, sidebars, and other elements that you want to set apart from the main text. By adjusting the *wrapping style* of a text box, you can have it overlap the body text (either in front of or behind the text) or you can have the body text wrap around the text box. (You can also place a text box inline with the body text, although you can then no longer freely position it outside of the main flow of text.)

Wrapping styles are discussed in "Combining Text with Graphic Objects and Text Boxes," on page 514.

Figure 18-1 shows a Word document containing a margin note created by inserting text into a text box and an inset table created by inserting a Word table into a text box. (The margin note text box was assigned the In Front Of Text wrapping style. The table text box was assigned the Square wrapping style, which causes the adjoining body text to wrap around the text box.)

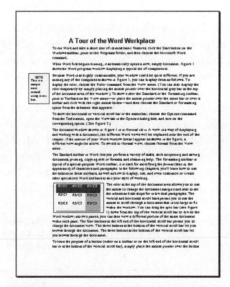

Figure 18-1. This figure shows a margin note and an inset Word table, both created using text boxes.

To place a text box around existing text in your document, perform the following steps:

1 Select the text you want to include in the text box. You can include one or more characters or paragraphs or a Word table.

2 Choose Insert, Text Box, or click the Text Box button on the Drawing toolbar.

Text Box

Word will then create a new text box, and it will move the selected text into the text box. You'll now probably need to adjust the size, position, and format of the text box, as described later in this section.

You can also create an empty text box and then insert text into it, using the following steps:

1 Without selecting text, choose Insert, Text Box or click the Text Box button on the Drawing toolbar. The insertion point can be anywhere within the document.

2 Word will insert a drawing canvas graphic object that will contain the label "Create your drawing here." For best results, press Esc to remove the drawing canvas. (See the Inside Out sidebar, "How to discard a drawing canvas," on the next page.)

3 Drag the mouse pointer to indicate the size and position you want for the text box, as shown here:

Or simply click in the document to insert a default-sized text box.

4 You can now insert text into the text box. If the insertion point isn't already in the text box, click *within* the box (not on one of its borders), so that the insertion point appears in the box. You can then enter, edit, and format text just as you would in the main body of a document. A text box can contain one or more paragraphs.

> **Caution** If you're creating a Web page document, don't place a text box in a margin area, because it will probably be partially or completely cut off when the page is viewed in a browser. Neither Web browsers nor Word's Web Layout view display the full document margins.

Inside Out

How to discard a drawing canvas

Although a drawing canvas is useful for containing a drawing that consists of several AutoShape objects, placing a text box within a drawing canvas only complicates working with the text box. (A text box can be positioned, sized, and formatted by itself—it doesn't need to be inserted within another graphic object.) When you add a text box without selecting text, Word automatically inserts a drawing canvas and invites you to put your text box within it. Fortunately, however, you can easily remove the drawing canvas by pressing Esc before you click or drag to insert the text box. For information on drawing canvases, see the sidebar "Drawing Canvases," on page 126.

As you type text in a text box, Word will wrap the text when you reach the right text box edge. Word *won't*, however, automatically increase the height of the box when you reach the bottom; you'll have to manually increase the height of the box to make the text at the bottom visible. (Or, as you'll see later, you can link the text box to another text box so that excess text automatically flows into the second box.)

To change the height or width of a text box, perform the following steps:

1 Click anywhere on the text box to select it. When a text box is selected, Word displays a thick band around it, which contains eight round sizing handles, as shown here:

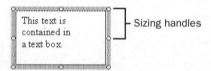

2 Drag any of the sizing handles to resize the box. To maintain the original proportions of the text box as you change its size, press Shift while dragging one of the *corner* sizing handles. To resize the text box symmetrically about its center (that is, to change the box size without moving the center of the box), hold down Ctrl while dragging any sizing handle.

To move or copy a text box, perform the following steps:

1 Place the pointer over one of the edges of the text box (but *not* over a sizing handle if the text box is selected). Cross-arrows will appear at the tip of the mouse pointer, as seen here:

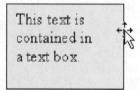

Chapter 18

2 Drag the text box to the position you want on the page. If you want to copy the text box rather than move it, hold down Ctrl while you drag.

If you move or copy a text box onto an area of the page occupied by text, you'll notice one of the following two types of behavior:

● If you selected existing text in the document before inserting the text box (that is, if you used the first method given for creating a text box), the document text will wrap around (that is, move away from) the text box. (The text box has the Square wrapping style.)

● If you didn't select text before inserting the text box (that is, if you used the second method for creating a text box), the text box will overlap the document text. (The text box has the In Front Of Text wrapping style.)

The next section explains how to change the wrapping style of a text box.

When a text box is selected, Word will usually display the Text Box toolbar, shown here. (If it isn't displayed when a text box is selected, choose View, Toolbars, Text Box.)

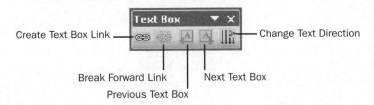

Create Text Box Link — Change Text Direction
Break Forward Link — Next Text Box
Previous Text Box

You can use the Text Box toolbar to create a series of two or more linked text boxes. Text will flow from one text box to the next one in the linked series. That is, any text that doesn't fit in a text box will be moved to the next one, in the same way that document text flows from one page to the next. To create a set of linked text boxes, perform these steps:

1 Add the text boxes to your document. All text boxes except the first one in the series must be empty.

2 Click the first text box in the series to select it, click the Create Text Box Link button on the Text Box toolbar, and then click the second text box. This will create the first link.

3 If you want to add additional text boxes to the linked series, repeat step 2 for each additional text box you want to link.

You can remove the link between a text box and the next one in the series by clicking the first text box and then clicking the Break Forward Link button on the Text Box toolbar.

If one of the text boxes in a linked series is selected, you can move the selection to other boxes in the series by clicking the Next Text Box button to select the next box in the series or by clicking the Previous Text Box button to select the previous one.

To modify the direction of the text in the selected text box and in any text boxes that are linked to it, click the Change Text Direction button. The button will toggle the text direction from left to right, to top to bottom, to bottom to top.

Chapter 18

513

To remove a text box, plus the text it contains, select it by clicking one of its *edges*, and then press Delete. (If you select the text box by clicking inside the edges, Word will place the insertion point within the text, and pressing Delete will delete only a single character.) If you want to move text from a text box into the main part of the document, be sure to copy the text from the text box and paste it into the document *before* you delete the box. Note, however, that if a text box is linked to one or more others, deleting the text box won't erase the text but will merely shift it to the remaining linked text boxes.

> For information on changing the formatting features of text boxes, other than the wrapping style, see the general instructions for modifying graphic objects in "Modifying Graphic Objects," on page 142. Changing the wrapping style is covered in the next section.

Troubleshooting

Text boxes disappeared

You inserted one or more text boxes into your document, but you can no longer see them.

To view text boxes, you must be in Word's Print Layout, Web Layout, Reading Layout, or Print Preview view. If you're in Normal or Outline view when you choose Insert, Text Box or click the Text Box button on the Drawing toolbar, Word will switch automatically into Print Layout view. (You can't insert a text box when you're in Reading Layout view.) However, if you later switch to Normal or Outline view, your text boxes will be hidden.

Text boxes will also be hidden in all views except Reading Layout, if the Drawings view option isn't checked. You'll find this option by choosing Tools, Options, clicking the View tab, and looking in the Print And Web Layout Options area of the tab.

Combining Text with Graphic Objects and Text Boxes

"Modifying Graphic Objects," on page 142, explained the general methods for formatting graphic objects in Office applications. Because a text box is a type of graphic object, you can use these methods to modify text boxes that you've added to a Word document. One type of formatting that is unique to Word is the *wrapping style*, which affects the way a graphic object—such as a picture, AutoShape, diagram, or text box—is positioned on the page and its relation to the text in the body of the document.

To modify the wrapping style of the selected object, choose the name of the object from the Format menu (such as Picture, AutoShape, Diagram, or Text Box) and click the Layout tab of the Format dialog box (as shown in Figure 18-2).

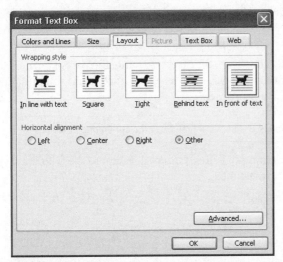

Figure 18-2. This figure shows the Layout tab of the Format dialog box as displayed when a Text Box is selected.

> **Note** You can also change the wrapping style of the selected graphic object by clicking the Text Wrapping button on the Picture toolbar and choosing a wrapping style from the drop-down menu. Or you can click the Draw button on the Drawing toolbar and choose a wrapping style from the Text Wrapping submenu on the pop-up menu. The Picture and Drawing toolbars are discussed in Chapter 6, "Adding Professional Graphics and Special Effects to Office 2003 Documents."

In the Layout tab, you can choose from five different wrapping styles. To choose from a larger selection of wrapping styles and to fine-tune the positioning of the object, click the Advanced button in the Layout tab to open the Advanced Layout dialog box and then use the Text Wrapping Tab in the dialog box. When selecting a wrapping style, keep in mind that the styles can be broken down into three basic groups:

● **Square, Tight, Through, and Top And Bottom** With these styles, you can place the object anywhere on the page. Document text will wrap around the object in various ways.

> **Note** Objects with the Square, Tight, Through, or Top And Bottom wrapping style behave somewhat differently in Web Layout view than they do in Print Layout or Print Preview view. That's because Web Layout view simulates the way objects in a Web page document will be displayed in a browser. Specifically, if the object has the Square, Tight, or Through wrapping style, you'll be able to drag it only to the left or right of the body text (*not* to a point within the body text). And if the object has the Top And Bottom wrapping style, you'll be able to drag it only above or below a paragraph of body text (in Print Layout and Print Preview view you can drag it to a point within a paragraph, causing the paragraph's text to be displayed above and below the object).

- **In Front Of Text and Behind Text**   With these styles, you can also position the object anywhere on the page. However, if the object intersects document text, it will overlap the text and will appear either in front of the text or behind it.

- **In Line With Text**   With this style, the object is an integral part of the body text in the document. It's positioned as if it was a single text character, and you can move or copy it using the standard text editing methods.

> Standard text editing methods are discussed in Chapter 11, "Efficient Editing in Word."

You can change the initial wrapping style that Word will assign to the following types of graphic objects when you first insert them:

- Pictures
- WordArt objects
- Microsoft Graph chart objects
- Equation objects
- Other types of embedded objects

(You can't change the initial wrapping style of newly inserted text boxes.) To change the initial wrapping style for these graphic object types, choose Tools, Options, click the Edit tab, and select the wrapping style you want from the Insert/Paste Pictures As drop-down list, shown here:

> For information on adding pictures, AutoShapes, diagrams, WordArt objects, Microsoft Graph charts, and Equation objects to Word documents (as well as other types of Office documents), see Chapter 6. For information on adding other types of embedded objects, see Chapter 7, "Sharing Data Among Office 2003 Applications."

> **Tip** **Use a text wrapping break**
>
> If an object is assigned the Square, Tight, or Through wrapping style, you can insert a special line break known as a *text wrapping break* into a line of text that's to the right or to the left of the object. The text following this break will be moved down below the object. To insert the break, place the insertion point at the position where you want to break the text, choose Insert, Break, and select the Text Wrapping Break option in the Break dialog box.

Displaying Watermarks

Word makes it easy to add a watermark to a document. A watermark consists of faint text or graphics displayed across every page in the document or in a document section. A text watermark, for example, might consist of the words *Confidential*, *Draft*, *Urgent*, or *Top Secret*, as shown in Figure 18-3.

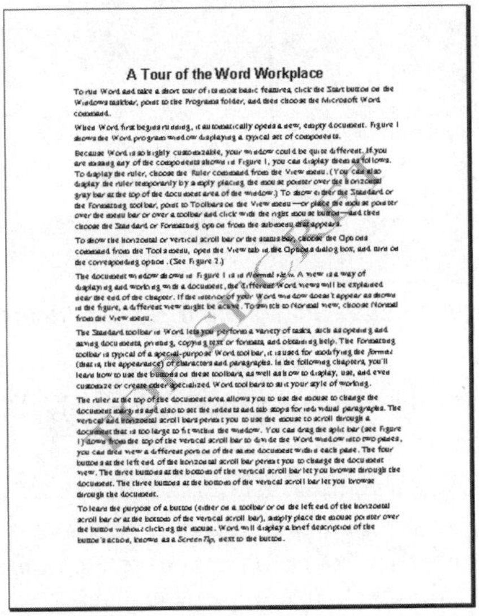

A Tour of the Word Workplace

To run Word and take a short tour of its most basic features, click the Start button on the Windows taskbar, point to the Programs folder, and then choose the Microsoft Word command.

When Word first begins running, it automatically opens a new, empty document. Figure 1 shows the Word program window displaying a typical set of components.

Because Word is so highly customizable, your window could be quite different. If you are missing any of the components shown in Figure 1, you can display them as follows. To display the ruler, choose the Ruler command from the View menu. (You can also display the ruler temporarily by simply placing the mouse pointer over the horizontal gray bar at the top of the document area of the window.) To show either the Standard or the Formatting toolbar, point to Toolbars on the View menu—or place the mouse pointer over the menu bar or over a toolbar and click with the right mouse button—and then choose the Standard or Formatting option from the submenu that appears.

To show the horizontal or vertical scroll bar or the status bar, choose the Options command from the Tools menu, open the View tab in the Options dialog box, and turn on the corresponding option. (See Figure 2.)

The document window shown in Figure 1 is in *Normal view*. A view is a way of displaying and working with a document; the different Word views will be explained near the end of the chapter. If the interior of your Word window doesn't appear as shown in the figure, a different view might be active. To switch to Normal view, choose Normal from the View menu.

The Standard toolbar in Word lets you perform a variety of tasks, such as opening and saving documents, printing, copying text or formats, and obtaining help. The Formatting toolbar is typical of a special-purpose Word toolbar; it is used for modifying the *format* (that is, the appearance) of characters and paragraphs. In the following chapters, you'll learn how to use the buttons on these toolbars, as well as how to display, use, and even customize or create other specialized Word toolbars to suit your style of working.

The ruler at the top of the document area allows you to use the mouse to change the document margins and also to set the indents and tab stops for individual paragraphs. The vertical and horizontal scroll bars permit you to use the mouse to scroll through a document that is too large to fit within the window. You can drag the split bar (see Figure 1) down from the top of the vertical scroll bar to divide the Word window into two panes; you can then view a different portion of the same document within each pane. The four buttons at the left end of the horizontal scroll bar permit you to change the document view. The three buttons at the bottom of the vertical scroll bar let you browse through the document. The three buttons at the bottom of the vertical scroll bar let you browse through the document.

To learn the purpose of a button (either on a toolbar or on the left end of the horizontal scroll bar or at the bottom of the vertical scroll bar), simply place the mouse pointer over the button without clicking the mouse. Word will display a brief description of the button's action, known as a *ScreenTip*, next to the button.

Figure 18-3. This document has a text watermark that displays the message *TOP SECRET* across each page.

To add a watermark, follow these steps:

1. If you're in Web Layout or Reading Layout view, switch to one of the other views.
2. Choose Format, Background, Printed Watermark to open the Printed Watermark dialog box.
3. In the Printed Watermark dialog box, do one of the following:
   - To display the contents of a graphic file as the watermark, select the Picture Watermark option, click the Select Picture button, and select the file in the Insert Picture dialog box, which works just like the standard Open dialog box.

To adjust the scale of the graphic, select a scaling percentage in the Scale drop-down list or select Auto to have Word scale the graphic so that it just fits on the page. The Washout option, which is checked by default, displays the graphic in light tones.

■ To display text as the watermark, select Text Watermark. Then type or select the text in the Text drop-down list and choose the font, font size, and text color in the other drop-down lists. Specify the text direction by selecting Diagonal (selected for the watermark shown in Figure 18-4) or Horizontal. The Semi-transparent option, which is checked by default, lightens the color of the text.

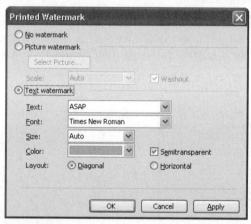

Figure 18-4. Here, a text watermark is defined in the Printed Watermark dialog box.

■ To remove a watermark you added previously, select No Watermark.

4 Click the OK button.

Note To create the watermark, Word adds a picture (for a graphic watermark) or a Word-Art object (for a text watermark) to the document's headers, which causes the watermark to appear on every document page. Headers are described in the next section.

Tip Remove or modify watermarks in document sections

When you create a watermark using the method explained in this section, Word will add the watermark to *all* pages in the document, even if you divided your document into separate sections and selected one or more specific sections before creating the watermark.

However, if you have divided your document into sections, you can remove the watermark from a particular section by deleting the picture or WordArt object from that section's header, using the techniques discussed in the next section for working with headers. (For information on document sections, see the sidebar "Working with Document Sections," on page 522.) You can also directly modify the watermark object in the header, rather than using the Printed Watermark dialog box to change it.

> **Note** Watermarks aren't visible in Web pages displayed in a browser because they're part of the document's headers, which aren't shown in Web pages.

Adding Page Numbering, Headers, and Footers

A *header* is a block of text or graphics that Word displays at the top of every page in your document or every page in a document section. Likewise, a *footer* is text or graphics displayed at the bottom of every page. With the exception of page numbers, the text or graphics that appear in the headers or footers of a document—or of a document section—are generally the same on every page. (Although, as explained later, it's possible to create different headers or footers on odd and even pages or to create a different header or footer on the first page of a document or document section.) You don't see headers and footers in Normal, Web Layout, Reading Layout, or Outline view. They appear, however, in Print Layout view, Print Preview, and on printed document pages.

The following section explains how to create simple headers or footers consisting of just automatic page numbers. The section after that shows how to create headers and footers containing any text, graphics, or formatting you want.

> **Note** If you're creating a Web page in Word, forget about headers and footers because they won't be displayed in a browser.

Adding Automatic Page Numbering

You can use the Page Numbers dialog box to quickly add automatic page numbering to the pages in your document. You can display numbers within headers at the top of each page or within footers at the bottom of each page, and you can choose from a variety of numbering formats. If your document doesn't already have headers or footers when you add page numbers using the Page Numbers dialog box, Word will create simple headers or footers containing only the page number. Keep in mind that you can also add page numbering, as well as other header or footer text or graphics, by working directly with the page header or footer areas, as described in the next section.

To add automatic page numbering to the currently opened document, perform the following steps:

1 Switch into Normal, Print Layout, or Reading Layout view, if necessary, and choose Insert, Page Numbers to open the Page Numbers dialog box, shown here:

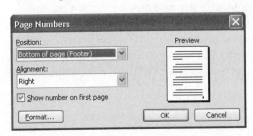

2 In the Position list, select Top Of Page (Header) to place the page numbers at the top of each page (that is, within headers), or Bottom Of Page (Footer) to place the page numbers at the bottom of each page (that is, within footers).

3 In the Alignment list, choose the position of the page numbers within the headers or footers, as follows:

- To place the page numbers at the left margin, centered between the margins, or at the right margin on each page, choose Left, Center, or Right.

- To place the page numbers at the right on even-numbered pages and at the left on odd-numbered pages, choose Inside.

- To place the page numbers at the left on even-numbered pages and at the right on odd-numbered pages (as in this book), choose Outside.

4 If you want to eliminate the page number from the first page of the document, clear the Show Number On First Page check box.

If you clear Show Number On First Page, Word will omit the page number from the first page, although it will count the first page in numbering the pages. For example, if you start numbering at 1, Word won't display a number on the first page, but it will number the second page with 2.

5 If you want to modify the style of the numbering or change the starting number, click the Format button to open the Page Number Format dialog box, shown here:

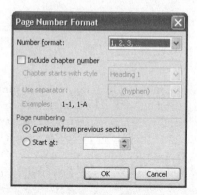

In the Page Number Format dialog box, do one or more of the following:

- To select the type of numbering, choose an item in the Number Format drop-down list. You can select various styles of Arabic numbers, letters of the alphabet, or Roman numerals.

- To add chapter numbers to the page numbering (for example, 1-1 and 1-2 on the first two pages of Chapter 1), check Include Chapter Number, select the style used to format your chapter headings in the Chapter Starts With Style drop-down list, and select the character you want to use between the chapter and page number (such as a hyphen, period, or colon) in the Use Separator drop-down list.

■ To start numbering the pages with 1, select Continue From Previous Section. (If you've divided your document into sections, the Continue From Previous Section option will cause the numbering in the current section to continue the numbering from any previous section. For more information, see the Inside Out sidebar on this page.)

■ To start numbering the pages with a specific number, select the Start At option and enter the desired starting number in the adjoining text box.

> **Note** To add chapter numbers to your page numbering, you must have formatted all your chapter headings using the same built-in Heading style (Heading 1 through Heading 9), and you must have applied automatic outline numbering to these headings, as explained in "Creating an Outline Numbered List Using the Outline Numbered Tab," on page 381.

To modify page numbering that you previously added, you can reopen the Page Numbers or Page Number Format dialog box and change any of the options. You can also edit or delete page numbering by using the View, Header And Footer command, as described in "Adding Headers and Footers," on page 524. (Even though you can see page numbers in Print Layout view, you can't edit them unless you choose the Header And Footer command or double-click the header or footer area.)

Inside Out

Apply page numbering options to the intended sections

If you've divided your document into separate sections, adding page numbering using the Insert, Page Numbers command is a bit confusing. The command will add page numbering to *all* document sections, even if you haven't selected all sections. (An exception: if you've turned off the Same As Previous option in a section following the current one, numbering won't be added to that section or any sections following it. This option is discussed later in this chapter.) However (and here's where it gets confusing), if you change the default setting of the Show Number On First Page option or change any of the settings in the Page Number Format dialog box when you insert the page numbers, your changes will affect the numbering *only within the currently selected section or sections* (even if the Same As Previous option is turned on for all sections, supposedly making all headings identical). For instance, clearing Show Number On First Page will remove the page number from the first page of only the selected section or sections.

If you want to apply your selected options to the entire document, press Ctrl+A to select all document sections before you choose Insert, Page Numbers to create page numbering. After you've added numbering, you can later modify the numbering options (such as the Start At option to vary the starting number) in a specific section by placing the insertion point in that section, reissuing the Page Numbers command, and selecting the new options you want. (Keep in mind that you can "select" a single section by simply placing the insertion point within it.)

For information on document sections, see the sidebar "Working with Document Sections," on page 522.

> **Tip** **Reformat your document's page numbering quickly**
>
> To change the character formatting of page numbering throughout your document, you can modify the Page Number character style, which Word assigns to automatic page numbers. For information on modifying styles, see "Customizing Styles," on page 389.

Working with Document Sections

You can divide a document into separate sections and then assign different formatting features to each section. The following are the features that you can vary from section to section:

- Page borders (discussed in "Applying Borders to Pages," on page 370).

- The number of columns (discussed in "Arranging Text in Newspaper-Style Columns," on page 371).

- Headers and footers, including page numbering (discussed in "Adding Page Numbering, Headers, and Footers," on page 519), as well as watermarks (which are part of headers and are discussed in "Displaying Watermarks," on page 517).

- The features that you set using the Page Setup dialog box, such as the margins and the paper size (discussed in "Modifying the Page Setup," on page 532).

To divide your document into separate sections, perform the following steps:

1 Place the insertion point at the position where you want to insert a section break.

2 Choose Insert, Break to open the Break dialog box, seen here:

3 Select one of the options in the Section Break Types area, as follows:

- To start the following section's text at the beginning of a new page, select Next Page.

- To start the following section's text immediately following the text in the previous section, with no line or page break, select Continuous.

- To start the following section's text at the beginning of the next even-numbered page, select Even Page. (If the next page is odd-numbered, this option will create a blank page. Note that a blank page will be shown in Print Preview, but not in Print Layout view.)

■ To start the following section's text at the beginning of the next odd-numbered page, select Odd Page. (If the next page is even-numbered, this option will create a blank page.)

In Normal view, Word marks a section break as shown here:

> This is the last line of the previous section.
>
> ═══════════════════════════Section Break (Next Page)═══════════════════════════
>
> This is the first line of the next section.

Show/Hide

The text in parentheses varies according to the type of break you insert. In Web Layout, Print Layout, or Outline view, section breaks are marked only if the All viewing mode is on. (You can turn this mode on or off by checking or clearing the All option in the View tab of the Options dialog box, or by clicking the Show/Hide ¶ button on the Standard toolbar.) Here's how a section break is marked in Print Layout view:

> This·is·the·last·line·of·the·previous·section.¶═══════════════Section Break (Next Page)═══════════

Section breaks aren't marked in Reading Layout or Print Preview view.

To remove a section break, follow these steps:

1 Switch into Normal view.

2 Select the section-break mark and press Delete.

Word will merge the sections before and after the break into a single section, which will acquire the section formatting features (those listed at the beginning of this sidebar) of the section that *followed* the mark. Any section formatting features that you assigned to the section preceding the mark will be lost. Conceptually, a section-break mark stores the formatting features of the preceding section, so if you delete the section mark, you delete these features.

To copy section formatting to a different part of the same document or to a different document, go into Normal view, select the section-break mark at the end of the section with the formatting you want to copy, and then copy the mark to the new location using any of the standard techniques for copying text. The text preceding the copied section mark will then acquire the section formatting stored in the section mark.

You can conveniently store an entire collection of section formatting features by selecting the section-break mark at the end of a section that has these features and creating an AutoText entry that contains just that mark. You can then quickly apply all of the section formatting features by simply inserting this AutoText entry at the end of the text you want to format.

Adding Headers and Footers

This section explains how to create full-featured headers and footers containing any text, graphics, or formatting you want. If you used the Page Numbers dialog box to create simple headers or footers consisting of only page numbers, you can use the techniques given here to edit or delete these headers or footers, or to add additional header or footer content. If you're creating a Web page document, keep in mind that headers and footers won't be displayed in a browser.

To create or edit headers or footers throughout the currently opened document, perform the following steps:

1 Choose View, Header And Footer. (If you're in Print Layout view or Print Preview, you can edit existing headers or footers by double-clicking the header area at the top of the page or the footer area at the bottom of the page.) Word will then do the following:

- Switch to Print Layout view, if it's not already active.

- Mark the header and footer areas on the page with dotted lines and activate these areas so that you can work within them.

- Dim all document text outside the header or footer area. (You won't be able to work on this text. You can also have Word completely hide the document text.)

- Display the Header And Footer toolbar, which provides commands for working on the headers and footers.

Figure 18-5 shows the header area in the Word window after the Header And Footer command has been chosen. The footer area at the bottom of the page is similar.

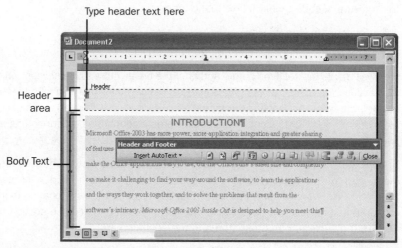

Figure 18-5. This figure shows the header area and the Header And Footer toolbar.

2 If you need to move the insertion point from the header to the footer area or from the footer to the header area, press the Down or Up arrow key or click the Switch Between Header And Footer button on the Header And Footer toolbar (shown in Figure 18-6).

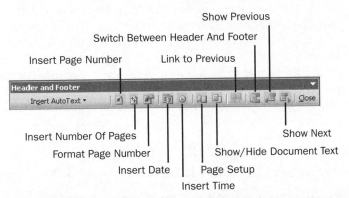

Figure 18-6. The Header And Footer toolbar provides tools for working with headers and footers.

> **Note** Using the arrow keys or other navigation key combinations, you can move to the header or footer area on any page in the document. Usually, it doesn't matter which page you work on because the headers and footers are the same throughout the document. However, as explained in "Varying Headers or Footers Within a Document," on page 529, you can vary the headers or footers within the document (to reflect, for example, different section or chapter names in the document). In this case you must move to the appropriate page before working on the header or footer.

3 Type the text for the header or footer into the header area or the footer area. You can enter one or more paragraphs of text into a header or footer, and you can edit and format the text in the same way that you edit and format text in the body of a document.

> You can also insert graphic objects or text boxes into a header or footer, using the techniques covered in Chapter 6 and "Using Text Boxes to Create Precise Page Layouts," on page 510.

The following are some techniques that will help you build your header or footer content:

- To align your text on one of the two predefined tab stops in the header or footer area, press Tab. The first tab stop aligns text in the center of the header or footer, and the second tab stop right-aligns text at the right edge of the header or footer. (Note that the tabs might be set differently in documents based on certain templates.)

- To remove headers or footers, just delete all the text or graphic objects in the header or footer area.

- To quickly insert the page number, the total number of pages in the document, the date, or the time into your header or footer text, place the insertion point at the position where you want the information, and click the Insert Page Number, Insert Number Of Pages, Insert Date, or Insert Time button on the Header And

Chapter 18

Footer toolbar (shown in Figure 18-6). Note that when you print your document, the number of pages, the date, or the time that you insert will be updated to reflect the current value.

■ To add automatic page numbering to your headers or footers, click the Insert Page Number button. This will insert the same type of automatic page numbering added by the Insert, Page Numbers command (described in the previous section), except that the page number won't be placed inside a frame. You can modify the format of the numbers or the starting number by clicking the Format Page Number button on the Header And Footer toolbar to open the Page Number Format dialog box, also described in the previous section. (For an explanation of frames, see "Adjusting the Size and Position of Headers or Footers," on page 527.)

■ To quickly insert various types of information into your header or footer, click the Insert AutoText button and choose an item from the submenu shown here:

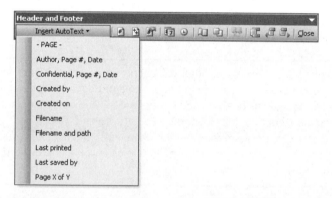

For example, you can choose Filename to insert the name of the current document. Or you can choose "Author, Page #, Date" to insert your name, the page number, and the date. (The items on this menu are predefined AutoText entries provided with Word.)

Tip   **Hide body text**

To reduce distraction while you work on headers or footers, you can completely hide the body text on the page by clicking the Show/Hide Document Text button on the Header And Footer toolbar. (Normally, when you work on headers and footers, document text is shown in a dimmed font.)

---

4 When you have finished creating or modifying the headers or footers, click the Close button on the Header And Footer toolbar, or choose View, Header And Footer to return to the view you were using previously.

Tip   Use styles to format headers, footers, and page numbers

Word assigns the Header paragraph style to header text, the Footer paragraph style to footer text, and the Page Number character style to automatic page numbers within headers or footers. You can therefore uniformly change the formatting of headers, footers, or page numbers throughout your entire document by modifying the corresponding style. Doing this will affect headers or footers in all document sections, even if the headers or footers vary from section to section.

You might, for example, assign to a style borders or shading, distinctive character formatting (such as a font, style, size, color, or enhancement), or other formatting to emphasize your headers or footers and make them stand apart from the text in the body of the document.

For information on modifying styles, see "Customizing Styles," on page 389.

Adjusting the Size and Position of Headers or Footers

The header or footer text you enter is normally confined within the header area or the footer area at the top or bottom of each page. You can change the size or position of these areas, however, or extend the header or footer text outside the header or footer area using one or more of the following techniques:

- To adjust the top or bottom boundary of the header area, double-click in the header area to activate it (or single click if the Header And Footer option on the View menu is already enabled) and then drag the Top Margin marker or the Bottom Margin marker up or down on the vertical ruler, as shown on page 528:

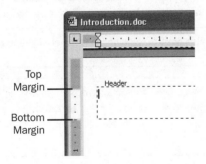

To see the exact measurements, press the Alt key while you drag. If the vertical ruler doesn't appear when the View, Ruler option is selected, choose Tools, Options, click the View tab, and check the Vertical Ruler (Print View Only) option.

- To adjust the top boundary of the footer area, double-click in the footer area to activate it (or single click if the Header And Footer option on the View menu is already enabled) and drag the Top Margin marker up or down on the vertical ruler, as shown here:

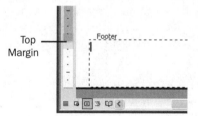

To see the exact measurements, press the Alt key while you drag.

> **Note**   If the text you insert into a header is higher than the current header area, Word will move the bottom boundary of the header area down so that the header content won't over-lap the main document text. Likewise, if the text you insert into a footer is higher than the footer area, Word will move the top boundary of the footer area up.

- To enter precise measurement values to adjust the clearance between the header or footer text and the top or bottom of the page (respectively), click the Page Setup button on the Header And Footer toolbar (shown in Figure 18-6), and enter the measurements you want into the Header box or Footer box in the From Edge area of the Layout tab.

- To move text to the left or to the right of the header or footer area, assign a negative left indent or a negative right indent to one or more paragraphs of header or footer text. To do this, you can use the horizontal ruler or the Paragraph dialog box.

> The horizontal ruler and Paragraph dialog box are explained in "Formatting Paragraphs Directly," on page 318.

> **Note**   A page number inserted by the Page Numbers dialog box is placed within a *frame*, which is an obsolete Word element similar to a text box. Like a text box, it can be dragged to any position on the page. To change a frame's properties, click it to select it and then choose Format, Frame.

- To position header or footer text anywhere on the page, place the insertion point within the header or footer, add a text box as described in "Using Text Boxes to Create Precise Page Layouts," on page 510, and assign the text box a wrapping style *other than* In Line With Text, as explained in "Combining Text with Graphic Objects and Text Boxes," on page 514. You can then drag the text box to any position on the page. Because the header or footer area was active when you inserted the text box, it remains an integral part of the header or footer, and it is therefore displayed on all pages in the document or section. You can modify it only after you activate the header or footer area (by enabling the View, Header And Footer menu option or by double-clicking in the area).

> **Note** If a text box or a graphic object you've added to a header or footer overlaps the document's body text, the text in the text box or the graphic object will be displayed behind the text (even if you've assigned the text box the In Front Of Text wrapping style) and it will be displayed in fainter tones.

- To display a graphic object—such as a picture, AutoShape, or WordArt object—on every page of the document or section, insert it into the header or footer. If the object is assigned a text wrapping style other than In Line With Text, you can drag it to any position on the page. (Note that when you create a watermark by choosing Format, Background, Printed Watermark, Word adds a picture or a WordArt object to the document's header, but positions it in the middle of the page.)

> **Tip** Overlap headings and body text to create special effects
> Normally, if you extend the header or footer area beyond the current top or bottom margin area, Word will automatically adjust the top or bottom margin so that the header or footer content won't overlap the text in the body of the document. However, if you enter a minus sign before the Top or Bottom margin measurement in the Margins tab of the Page Setup dialog box (discussed in "Setting the Margins and Page Orientation," on page 533), Word won't adjust the margins. Rather, Word will extend the header or footer area into the area of the page occupied by the document text, allowing you to freely enter text or graphics into the header or footer that overlaps the document text. When header or footer content overlaps the document text, the header or footer content is displayed behind the document text and in fainter tones. You can use this technique as an alternative way to create watermarks or other special effects.

Varying Headers or Footers Within a Document

Normally, the same header or footer is printed on every page in the document. There are, however, three ways that you can vary headers and footers within your document.

You can create a different header or footer on the first page of the document, or on the first page of a section, if you have divided your document into sections that begin on a new page. (This procedure doesn't work for continuous section breaks.) You might want to do this, for example, to eliminate the header from the title page of a report or to avoid placing a page number on the first page of a letter. To do so, perform the following steps:

1 If you have divided your document into sections, and if you want to create a different first-page header for a specific section or for a specific section plus all following sections, place the insertion point in that section.

2 Choose View, Header And Footer.

3 Click the Page Setup button on the Header And Footer toolbar (shown in Figure 18-6, on page 525) to open the Layout tab of the Page Setup dialog box.

Chapter 18

4 Check the Different First Page option.

5 Select an option in the Apply To drop-down list, as follows:

- To create a different header for the first page of your document, or for the first page in all document sections if you've divided the document into sections, select Whole Document.

- To create a different header on the first page of the section containing the insertion point, select This Section.

- To create a different header on the first page of the section containing the insertion point and on the first page of every section following it, select This Point Forward.

6 Click the OK button.

In addition, you can create different headers and footers on odd and even pages. You might do this, for example, if you're writing a book and want the book title at the top of the left page of facing pages (called the *verso* page by book designers) and the chapter title at the top of the right page (called the *recto* page). To do this, follow these steps:

1 Choose View, Header And Footer. (The insertion point can be anywhere in the document.)

2 Click the Page Setup button on the Header And Footer toolbar to open the Layout tab of the Page Setup dialog box.

3 Check the Different Odd And Even option, and click OK.

Word will always create odd and even headers throughout your entire document, even if it's divided into sections and regardless of your choice in the Apply To drop-down list in the Layout tab.

Finally, if you have divided your document into sections, the headers or footers in separate sections can have different contents. Initially, the headers and footers in every section (except the first) are connected to the headers and footers in the previous section, meaning that they'll be exactly the same as those in the previous section. When headers and footers are all connected this way, making a change (except for reformatting numbering) in a header or footer in any section will change the headers and footers in all sections. To create different headers and footers in different sections, perform the following steps:

1 Place the insertion point within the section where you want the headers and footers to be different from the previous section.

2 Choose View, Header And Footer.

3 Click the Link To Previous button on the Header And Footer toolbar to toggle this setting off. This will remove the connection between the current section and the previous one. You can now modify the headers or footers for the current section without changing those of the previous section. (Your changes will, however, modify any following sections that are still connected to the current section.)

Designing and Printing Professional-Looking Pages

> **Tip** Modify automatic page numbering in a specific section
>
> If you have inserted automatic page numbering into your headers or footers—either by choosing Insert, Page Numbers or by clicking the Insert Page Number button on the Header And Footer toolbar—you can modify the format and starting number of the numbering or add chapter numbers to the numbering within a particular document section.
>
> To do this, place the insertion point in the section you want to modify, choose View, Header And Footer, click the Format Page Number button on the Header And Footer toolbar, and change options as desired in the Page Number Format dialog box, which was explained in "Adding Automatic Page Numbering," on page 519. The options you set in this dialog box will apply only to the current document section (even if the Link To Previous option is turned on for all sections, supposedly making all headings identical).
>
> The most important numbering change you might want to make for a particular section is to select the Continue From Previous Section option to continue the numbering sequence from the previous section or to select the Start At option to restart the numbering of the current section with a specific page number.

Troubleshooting

Headers or footers cut off

When you print a document, part or all of the header or footer text is cut off.

The header or footer text might be too close to the edge of the page. Find out from your printer's documentation how close it can print to the edge of the paper. Then choose File, Page Setup, click the Layout tab of the Page Setup dialog box, and adjust the distances of the headers or footers from the edge of the page in the Header or Footer text boxes (in the From Edge area near the center of the dialog box).

If you have varied the headers and footers using any of the three methods just described, then you must, when you choose the Header And Footer command, move to an appropriate document page to enter or modify each of the different headers or footers. For example, if you have created a different first-page header, you must move to the first page to enter or modify the first-page header or footer. You must then move to any other page to enter or modify the headers or footers for the other pages. The area for each header or footer is labeled to help you find the right one, for example, *Header -Section 2-* or *First Page Footer*, as shown here:

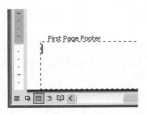

To quickly move to the header or footer on the appropriate page, you can click the Show Previous or Show Next button on the Header And Footer toolbar, seen here:

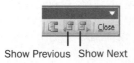

Show Previous   Show Next

Modifying the Page Setup

The Page Setup dialog box allows you to adjust a wide variety of options that affect the general appearance of the pages throughout your entire document or in one or more document sections. These options include the document margins, the paper size, the vertical alignment of text on the page, and line numbering.

> **Note**   If you're creating a Web page document, keep in mind that none of the settings you make in the Page Setup dialog box will affect the way the page appears in a browser.

To set any of these options, follow these steps:

1   Select the portion of your document that you want to modify by doing one of the following:

- If you want to modify the entire document, place the insertion point anywhere within the document.

- If you want to modify the document from a given position through the end of the document, place the insertion point at that position.

- If you want to modify a portion of the document, select that portion.

- If you have divided the document into sections, place the insertion point in the section you want to modify, or select several sections.

2   Choose File, Page Setup to open the Page Setup dialog box, which has three tabs: Margins, Paper, and Layout.

3   In the Apply To drop-down list (which appears in all tabs), choose the part of the document you want to modify, as shown here:

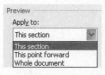

The selection you make in the Apply To drop-down list in one tab will change the selection in this list in all tabs and will control the part of the document that settings in *all* tabs will be applied to. In general, you can modify either the entire document or one or more document sections. The specific choices that appear in the Apply To drop-down list depend on the part of the document that you have selected and whether you have divided your document into sections. Note that if you choose the This Point Forward option (which appears if you didn't select text), Word will insert a section break at the position of the insertion point, and if you choose the Selected Text option (which appears if you selected text), Word will insert a section break at the beginning and at the end of the selected text. Choosing one of these options is a convenient way to divide your document into sections without having to manually insert section breaks.

4   If you want to use the options you select as the default settings, click the Default button (which appears in all tabs) and respond Yes. Word will assign the current settings in each of the three tabs to the document and to the document template so that the settings will apply to any new documents you create based on this template.

5   Select the page setup options you want. The options displayed on each of the three tabs are discussed in the following three sections. Use the document model in the Preview area as an aid in selecting options.

Setting the Margins and Page Orientation

To set the page margins and the orientation of the text on the page, perform the following steps:

1   Click the Margins tab of the Page Setup dialog box (shown in Figure 18-7).

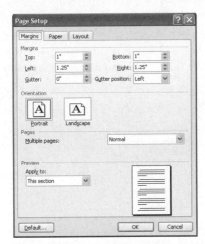

Figure 18-7.   You can set the margins for a document in the Margins tab of the Page Setup dialog box.

2 In the Orientation area of the dialog box, choose Portrait (the usual setting) to print the lines of text at right angles to the direction of the paper feed or choose Landscape to print the lines of text in the direction of the paper feed, as shown here:

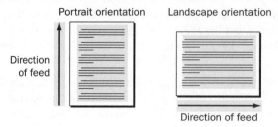

If, for example, your document contains a wide table, you might place the table in its own section and assign the Landscape orientation to that section, leaving the other document sections in Portrait orientation. Word would then print the table sideways so that it would fit on the paper.

> **Note** When you switch paper orientations, Word automatically swaps the current settings of the top and bottom margins for the settings of the left and right margins so that the text occupies the same area on the page.

3 Select an item in the Multiple Pages drop-down list to specify the way you want the text laid out on the sheets of paper, as follows:

- To print a single document page on each sheet of paper (or on each side of a sheet if you're printing on both sides) using the same margins for all pages, select Normal, as shown here. This is the usual printing option.

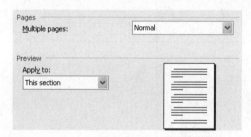

- To print a single document page on each sheet of paper (or on each side of a sheet if you're printing on both sides) with symmetric margins on even and odd pages, select Mirror Margins, as seen in the following example. With this option the left margin on an even-numbered page will match the right margin on an odd-numbered page (this margin is known as the *outside* margin), and the right margin on an even-numbered page will match the left margin on an odd-numbered page (this margin is known as the *inside* margin).

- To print two half-sized document pages on each sheet of paper (or on each side of a sheet if you're printing on both sides) with symmetric margins, select 2 Pages Per Sheet. If you choose the Portrait orientation, the pages will be printed one above the other, as seen here:

If you choose the Landscape orientation, the pages will be printed side by side, as shown here:

With the 2 Pages Per Sheet option, the pages will be printed in the order they occur in the document. If you think about that, you'll realize that you won't be able to create a booklet by simply printing on both sides of the paper and then folding the stack of sheets in half—to do that, you'll want to select the option discussed next.

- To print two pages on each side of a sheet of paper with symmetric margins, so that you can create a booklet or book directly from the printed sheets, select Book Fold, as shown in the following example. This option uses the Landscape orientation only (you won't be able to switch to Portrait), and it can be applied only to the entire document (not to a particular section). To be able to make a booklet directly from the printed sheets, you'll need to print on both sides of each sheet (that is, you must print in duplex mode).

Chapter 18

535

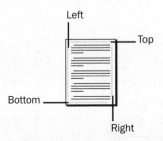

As you can see, the placement of the pages on a sheet with the Book Fold option is the same as that with the 2 Pages Per Sheet option in Landscape orientation. However, rather than printing the pages in the order they occur in the document, the Book Fold option prints the pages in the proper order so that you can quickly create a booklet by folding the stack of sheets in half and stapling in the center. If you've selected this option, you can divide the document into a series of separate booklets by selecting a specific number of sheets in the Sheets Per Booklet drop-down list.

For step-by-step instructions, see the sidebar "Creating a Booklet or Book," on page 539.

4   Set the page margins in the four text boxes in the Margins area at the top of the Margins tab. The labels on the boxes will correspond to the option that's currently selected in the Multiple Pages drop-down list. For example, if the Normal option is selected, the boxes will be labeled Top, Bottom, Left, and Right, and they will set the margins as shown here:

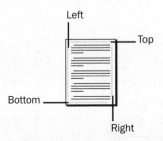

And, if you selected Mirror Margins, the boxes will be labeled Top, Bottom, Inside, and Outside, and they will set the margins as shown here:

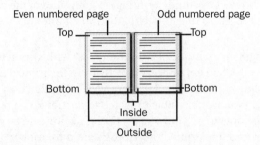

Chapter 18

> **Tip** **Create symmetric headers or footers**
> If you've selected one of the options in the Multiple Pages drop-down list that creates symmetric margins (Mirror Margins, 2 Pages Per Sheet, or Book Fold), you might also want to create symmetric headers or footers. You can do this by checking the Different Odd And Even option in the Layout tab of the Page Setup dialog box and formatting your headers and footers appropriately, as explained in "Adding Headers and Footers," on page 524.

5 You can add extra space to the left, top, or inside margin on each page to make room for the binding. To do this, enter the desired amount of space into the Gutter text box. If you've selected the Normal option in the Multiple Pages drop-down list, you can select either Left or Top in the Gutter Position drop-down list to specify the page margin where you want to add the gutter.

If you've selected Mirror Margins, 2 Pages Per Sheet, or Book Fold in the Multiple Pages list, Word places the gutter on the inside margin and you can't change its position. The position of the gutter with the Mirror Margins option and the Portrait orientation would be as shown here:

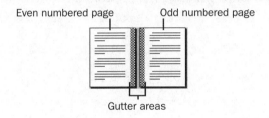

> **Tip** **Mark your margins**
> In Print Layout or Web Layout view, you can have Word mark with dotted lines the inside boundaries of the page margins (as well as the boundaries of multiple columns, if you've applied them to the text). To show these marker lines, choose Tools, Options, click the View tab, and check the Text Boundaries option in the Print And Web Layout Options area.

Setting Margins Using the Rulers

Another way to adjust the page margins is by using the horizontal and vertical rulers, following these steps:

1 If you have divided your document into sections, place the insertion point in the section you want to modify or select several sections to modify all of them.

View Ruler

2 Switch to Print Layout view or Print Preview view and display the horizontal and vertical ruler. To display the rulers in Print Layout view, choose View, Ruler. If the vertical ruler still isn't visible, choose Tools, Options, click the View tab, and check the Vertical Ruler (Print View Only) option. To display both rulers in Print Preview, choose the same menu command or click the View Ruler button on the Print Preview toolbar.

Chapter 18

3 Drag the appropriate marker on the horizontal or vertical ruler. Figure 18-8 shows the markers for adjusting the top, left, and right margins in Print Layout view. (The marker for adjusting the bottom margin is similar to that for adjusting the top margin.) When you're adjusting the left or right margin, make sure the pointer has become a double-headed arrow, and—if you have ScreenTips enabled—that the ScreenTip reads Left Margin or Right Margin, as shown here. You could otherwise inadvertently change the indent for the selected paragraph rather than the margin. (The indents are set using the button-like objects on the ruler.)

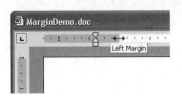

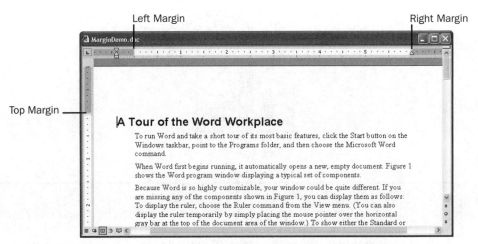

Figure 18-8. This figure shows the markers on the horizontal and vertical rulers for adjusting the top, left, and right margins in Print Layout view.

> **Tip** To see the exact margin measurements, hold down the Alt key while you drag a margin marker on a ruler.

Don't confuse the left and right *margins* with the left and right *indents*. A margin is the normal distance between the text and the edge of the paper, and it applies to an entire document or section. An indent is an adjustment to this distance that applies to one or more individual paragraphs. (An indent is a paragraph formatting feature.) If the left or right indent measurement is 0, the paragraph text is aligned with the left or right margin. If the indent measurement is positive, the paragraph text is moved in from the margin, and if it's negative the text is moved out from the margin (see Figure 18-9).

Left margin ———

——— Right margin

Positive left indent ———

Negative left indent ———

——— Positive right indent

——— Negative right indent

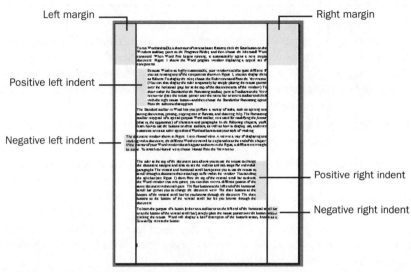

Figure 18-9. This figure shows different types of margins and indents.

Setting indents is discussed in "Formatting Paragraphs Directly," on page 318.

Creating a Booklet or Book

Using Word you can directly print the pages for a booklet, or even a book. Each page will be printed on one half of a side of a sheet of paper. So if you're using 8½-inch by 11-inch paper, each booklet page will measure 5½-inches wide by 8½-inches high. It might take some trial and error to perfect the process for your printer, so *be sure to start by printing a small test booklet.*

To create a booklet from the currently opened document, perform the following steps:

1 Choose File, Page Setup and click the Margins tab in the Page Setup dialog box (see Figure 18-7, on page 533).

2 In the Multiple Pages drop-down list, select Book Fold.

3 Make sure that All is selected in the Sheets For Booklet drop-down list.

4 Set the margins, make any other adjustments to the page setup that you want in the Page Setup dialog box, and click OK.

5 When you print the document, be sure to print on both sides of the paper (that is, print in *duplex* mode). If you have a duplex printer, you should be able to select duplex printing by clicking the Properties button in the Print dialog box.

Details on printing are given in "Previewing and Printing Documents," on page 543.

Chapter 18

If you don't have a duplex printer, you can print on both sides of the paper manually by checking the Manual Duplex option in the Print dialog box. Word will print the first side of each sheet of paper, prompt you to flip the stack of sheets over and reinsert them into your paper tray, and then print the second sides. (Discovering the correct way to flip the sheets over for your printer will probably take a little trial and error. Again, start with a small test booklet!)

6 After the pages are printed, fold the stack of sheets down the center and staple them together in the center using a long-reach stapler.

Rather than printing all of the pages of a large document as a single booklet, you can print them as a series of separate booklets. To do this, follow the same procedure, but in step 3 select the number of pages you want to include in each booklet from the Sheets Per Booklet drop-down list, rather than selecting All (because four pages are printed on each sheet of paper, the numbers you can select are multiples of four). To create a book, you could bind the separate booklets together using appropriate bookbinding methods. (Book designers call each one of these booklets a *signature*.)

Adjusting the Paper Size and Source

Word normally assumes that you're printing on 8½-inch by 11-inch paper. If you're using a different paper size, you must change the paper size setting by following these steps:

1 Click the Paper tab of the Page Setup dialog box (shown in Figure 18-10).

Figure 18-10. The Paper tab of the Page Setup dialog box lets you specify the paper size and source.

2 If you're using a standard paper size, choose that size in the Paper Size drop-down list. (The contents of this list depend on your current default printer.)

3 If you can't find the size of your paper in the Paper Size list, enter the correct size into the Width and Height boxes.

If your printer has more than one paper tray, a manual feed slot, or another paper source, you can print the first page of the document (or of the section) on paper from one source and print all remaining pages on paper from a different source. You could use this technique, for example, to print the first page of a letter on letterhead stock and the remaining pages on blank stock. To set the paper source, perform the following steps:

1 Click the Paper tab of the Page Setup dialog box (see Figure 18-10).

2 Select a paper source for the first page in the document (or document section) from the First Page list.

3 Select a paper source for the remaining document (or section) pages from the Other Pages list.

> **Note** To set printer options, click the Print Options button in the Paper tab to open the Print tab. Another way to access this tab is to choose Tools, Options.

Adjusting the Page Layout

You can adjust a variety of page setup options in the Layout tab of the Page Setup dialog box, shown in Figure 18-11, as follows:

Figure 18-11. You can set several layout options in the Layout tab of the Page Setup dialog box.

● To control the location of the text at the beginning of the selected document section or sections, choose an item in the Section Start drop-down list.

● To affect the way Word arranges paragraphs—in the vertical direction—on pages that are not completely filled with text, choose an option in the Vertical Alignment list. Figure 18-12 shows the effects of the different options. You might, for example, choose the Center option for the title page of a report.

| Top | Center | Bottom | Justified |

Figure 18-12. This figure shows the effect of each of the Vertical Alignment options.

> **Note** The effect of the Vertical Alignment option you've chosen will be visible only in Print Layout and Print Preview views, and on the printed pages.

● To have Word print line numbers in the left margin within one or more document sections, click the Line Numbers button. In the Line Numbers dialog box (see Figure 18-13), check the Add Line Numbering option and select the line numbering options you want. Line numbers are displayed only in Print Layout and Print Preview view and on the printed copy of the document. Lawyers and publishers often use line numbering to facilitate discussion of specific lines among several people. Note that you can block line numbering for a specific paragraph by applying the Suppress Line Numbers paragraph formatting option, which you'll find in the Line And Page Breaks tab of the Paragraph dialog box.

Figure 18-13. The Line Numbers dialog box allows you to add line numbering to a document.

For a description of the Paragraph dialog box, see "Formatting Paragraphs with the Paragraph Dialog Box," on page 323.

> **Tip** **Reformat line numbers**
>
> You can change the character formatting of line numbers throughout your document by modifying the Line Number character style, using the techniques given in Chapter 14, "Advanced Word Formatting Techniques."

● To apply a page border to the pages in your document or in one or more document sections, click the Borders button to open the Page Border tab of the Borders And Shading dialog box.

> The procedure for applying page borders is described in "Applying Borders to Pages," on page 370. For information on the Different Odd And Even and the Different First Page options in the Layout tab, see "Varying Headers or Footers Within a Document," on page 529. For an explanation of the Header and Footer text boxes in the From Edge area of the Layout tab, see "Adjusting the Size and Position of Headers or Footers," on page 527, and the Troubleshooting sidebar "Headers or footers cut off," on page 531. And for instructions on using the Suppress Endnotes option, see "Inserting Footnotes and Endnotes," on page 434.

Previewing and Printing Documents

When you have finally finished entering text and graphics into your document, as well as editing, formatting, proofing, and adjusting the page design, you're ready to print the document. Before doing so, however, you might want to preview the printed appearance of the document on the screen and possibly make a few last-minute adjustments.

Word provides two document views that display the document exactly as it will be printed: Print Layout and Print Preview. These two views have many features in common; in general, however, Print Layout view is best for editing the document and working with text boxes and graphics, and Print Preview is best for viewing the overall appearance of the document pages immediately before printing.

> **Tip** **Compress top and bottom margins in print layout view**
>
> Normally, Print Layout view shows the complete document page, including the top and bottom margin areas, as well as some background between the pages. These areas take up a lot of screen space and also cause the insertion point to jump when you use an arrow key to move it from one page to the next. You can see more of your document in Print Layout view and make scrolling smoother by hiding the top and bottom margin areas. To do this, choose Tools, Options, click the View tab, and clear the White Space Between Pages (Print View Only) option. You can also quickly hide (or show) the top and bottom margin areas in Print Layout view by simply clicking anywhere on the boundary between two pages.

Chapter 18

**Print
Preview**

To switch to Print Preview, choose File, Print Preview or click the Print Preview button on the Standard toolbar. The Print Preview screen is shown in Figure 18-14. To edit your document while in Print Preview, click the Magnifier button on the toolbar to disable the Magnifier. Click the Close button to close Print Preview and return to the view you were working in earlier.

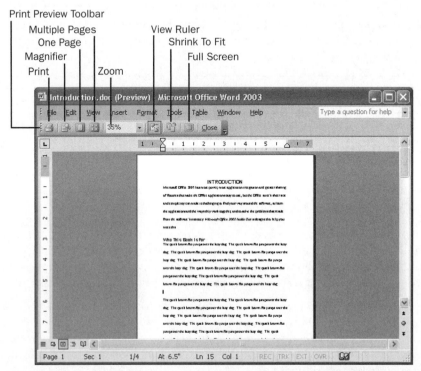

Figure 18-14. This figure shows a document displayed in Print Preview.

When you're ready to print your document, choose File, Print or press Ctrl+P. Word will display the Print dialog box, which is shown in Figure 18-15. Before clicking the OK button to start printing, you can choose the printer, change printer settings, and select printing options.

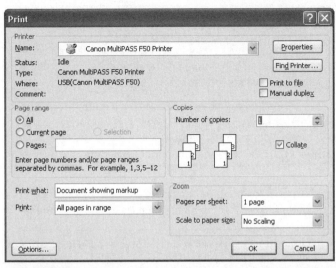

Figure 18-15. The Print dialog box lets you set options before printing a document.

Rather than printing the document itself, you can print various document elements by choosing an item other than Document in the Print What drop-down list of the Print dialog box, as follows:

- To print the information displayed and set by the File, Properties command, select Document Properties.

- To print the document plus all tracked change markings and comments that have been added to it, select Document Showing Markup.

- To print a list of all tracked changes and all comments, including the page, author, date, and time of each, select List Of Markup. Word will print the same information that it displays in the Reviewing pane.

- To print a description of the document styles, select Styles.

- To print the contents of the document's AutoText entries, select AutoText Entries.

- To print a list of the document's current shortcut key assignments, select Key Assignments.

Print

Alternatively, you can quickly print your document using the current default printer and the default print settings by simply clicking the Print button on the Standard toolbar or on the Print Preview toolbar (which is displayed when you switch to Print Preview).

Chapter 18

Adjusting the Pagination

Before printing your document, you might want to view and adjust the positions of the page breaks. You should do this after editing, formatting, and proofing your document because these actions can change the positions of page breaks.

In Print Layout view or in Print Preview, you can easily see the positions of page breaks because each page is displayed exactly as it will print. In Normal view, Word marks the position of each page break with a dotted horizontal line if you have checked the Background Repagination option. (To access this option, choose Tools, Options and click the General tab.)

The following paragraph formatting features can affect the positions of page breaks: Widow/Orphan Control, Keep Lines Together, Keep With Next, and Page Break Before.

These paragraph formatting features are explained in detail in Chapter 12, "Effective Formatting in Word." See Table 12-3 for an explanation of each of them.

Also, the positions of page breaks can be affected by the current settings of the print options that tell Word what to include in the printed copy of the document. These options are contained in the Include With Document area of the Print tab of the Options dialog box, shown in Figure 18-16. To access this tab, choose Tools, Options, or click the Options button in the Print dialog box, shown in Figure 18-15.

Figure 18-16. You can select several printing options in the Print tab of the Options dialog box.

A page break that Word automatically generates when the text reaches the bottom of a page is known as a *soft page break*. You can also force a page break at any position in a document by inserting a *hard page break*. The position of a hard page break is fixed, and it always causes a page break regardless of its location on the page. To insert a hard page break at the insertion point, press Ctrl+Enter, or choose Insert, Break and select the Page Break option. In Normal view, Word marks the position of a hard page break with a horizontal dotted line labeled Page Break, as shown here (in contrast, the horizontal line marking the position of a soft page break is not labeled):

Soft page break mark ....

Hard page break mark ....Page Break..

Show/
Hide

In Print Layout view, the text following a hard page break is forced to a new page, but the mark itself appears only if all nonprinting characters are displayed. (To display all nonprinting characters, select All under Formatting Marks in the View tab of the Options dialog box, or click the Show/Hide ¶ button on the Standard toolbar.)

To remove a hard page break, just select the mark and press Delete.

Writing a Macro for Printing the Current Selection Quickly

This sidebar presents a useful macro for printing the current selection in the document using the default printer settings. You can quickly print bits and pieces of a document by selecting the text or graphics and running this macro, rather than having to open the Print dialog box, select the Selection option, and click OK.

You can enter the macro yourself using the Visual Basic Editor, following the brief instructions given here. (For complete information on using the Visual Basic Editor, see Part 10 of this book.) Or you can use the Organizer to copy the macro from the WordInsideOut module in the WordInsideOut.dot file provided on the book's companion CD into your own Normal template.

For complete information on macros and using the Visual Basic Editor, see Part 10 of this book. For instructions on working with the Organizer, see "Using the Organizer," on page 412.

1 In Word, choose Tools, Macro, Visual Basic Editor. This will run the Microsoft Visual Basic Editor.

2 In the Project Explorer pane at the upper-left of the Visual Basic Editor window, double-click the Normal/Microsoft Word Objects/This Document item. (Expand the tree, if necessary, to access this item. If the Project Explorer pane isn't displayed, choose View, Project Explorer.) This will open a code window labeled Normal - This Document, where you can enter code that will be stored in your Normal template.

Chapter 18

3 Type the following macro code into the code window:

```
Sub PrintSelection()
`PrintSelection macro
    Application.PrintOut Range:=wdPrintSelection
End Sub
```

4 In the Visual Basic Editor, choose File, Close And Return To Microsoft Word.

5 Use the procedures described in "Defining Shortcut Keys (Word Only)," on page 222, to define a shortcut key for the PrintSelection macro. You can also use the techniques given in "Modifying Toolbars and Menus," on page 213, to add a toolbar button for running this macro.

You can now test the macro as follows: select a block of text or graphics in a document and press the shortcut key or click the toolbar button that you defined for the macro. Word should now print just the selected text or graphics using the default printer settings.

Chapter 19

Using Word to Automate Mailings

 Using the Mail Merge Wizard to Automate Large Mailings 549

Generating Individual Envelopes and Labels 559

Using the Mail Merge Wizard to Automate Large Mailings

The Microsoft Office Word 2003 *mail merge* feature merges a main document with a recipient list to generate a set of output documents:

- The *main document* is a specially marked Word document that serves as a blueprint for creating the output documents. It contains the basic text that is the same in every output document—for example, a letterhead, the main body of a letter, and a letter closing—plus instructions (known as *merge fields*) for inserting the text that varies from one output document to another—for example, the recipients' names and addresses.

- The *recipient list* is a database—for example, a Microsoft Office Access 2003 database file or a Microsoft Office Excel 2003 workbook—that contains the data that is to be merged into the output documents. Typically, it stores a list of names, mailing addresses, e-mail addresses, fax numbers, and so on.

- The end product of the mail merge feature is a set of *output documents*. Some of the text is the same in all output documents, while some varies from document to document. You can use mail merge to create any of the following types of output documents:

    - Form letters
    - E-mail messages
    - Faxes
    - Envelopes
    - Labels
    - A directory (a list of names and addresses or other information that is printed or is stored in a single Word document, also known as an *address list*)

Figure 19-1 shows how mail merge works when you create a set of form letters.

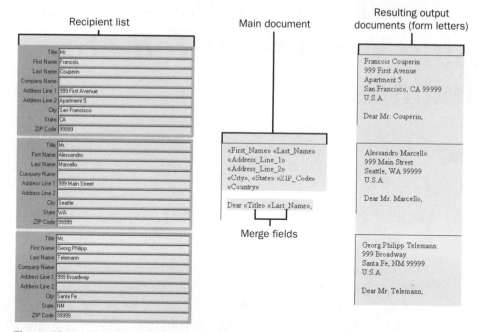

Figure 19-1. This figure shows the process of merging a recipient list with a main mail merge document to generate a set of form letters.

The fastest way to use the mail merge feature is to run the Mail Merge Wizard. The following basic method lets you create any of the types of output documents just listed, except faxes (a method for creating faxes is described later in this section):

1 If you want to use an existing document for your mail merge main document, open it now. Otherwise, just open a blank document.

2 Choose Tools, Letters And Mailings, Mail Merge. This will display the Step 1 Mail Merge task pane, the first of six Mail Merge panes.

3 In the Step 1 Mail Merge task pane, titled Select Document Type, choose one of the five options displayed at the top of the pane to specify the type of output documents you want to create (as shown in Figure 19-2). Then, click the Next command to display the next Mail Merge task pane. (In the wizard panes, the Next command is labeled according to the title of the pane that follows—for example, Next: Starting Document or Next: Select Recipients.)

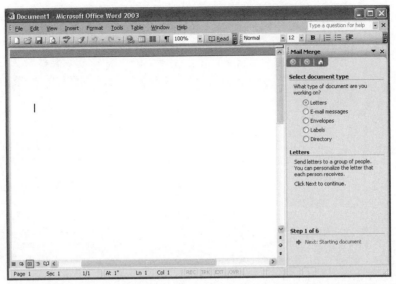

Figure 19-2. Here, the Letters output document type is selected in the Step 1 pane of the Mail Merge Wizard to generate form letters.

4 In the Step 2 Mail Merge task pane, titled Select Starting Document, select an option to tell the wizard how to create your mail merge main document.

 Note When you select a template for a mail merge main document, you can click the Templates On Office Online button at the bottom of the Select Template dialog box to choose a template from a large collection of templates that can be downloaded from the Office Online Web site. For information on working with downloadable templates, see "Downloading and Using Templates from Office Online," on page 55.

- To convert the document in the active document window to a mail merge main document, select Use The Current Document (as shown in Figure 19-3).

- To create a new main document based on a template, select Start From A Template, and then click the Select Templates command to choose the template you want to use (see earlier Note).

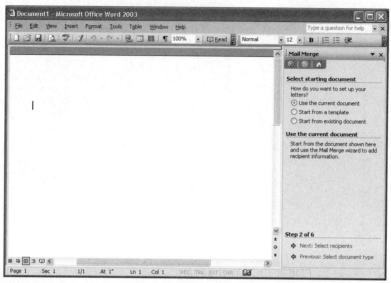

Figure 19-3. In this figure, the current document is chosen as the mail merge main document in the Step 2 task pane of the Mail Merge Wizard.

■ To create a new main document based on an existing document, select Start From Existing Document and then select the document in the list that appears. If the document doesn't appear in the list, select the (More Files…) option. Then click the Open button.

When you're finished, click the Next command to display the next Mail Merge task pane.

Note If you're creating envelopes or labels, the Step 2 task pane provides the following two options, rather than the three just listed:

● To set up a custom layout for your envelopes or labels, select Change Document Layout. Then click the Envelope Options (or Label Options) button that appears and select the layout and printing options you want in the dialog box that's displayed.

● To use an existing mail merge main document that contains an envelope or label layout, select Start From Existing Document, select the document in the list that appears—or select the (More Files) option to choose a document that doesn't appear in the list—and then click the Open button.

Tip In the Mail Merge Step 2 through Step 6 task panes, you can click the Previous command to go back to a previous pane and modify your selections.

5 In the Step 3 Mail Merge task pane, titled Select Recipients, specify what you want to use as your recipient list—that is, as the source of your mail merge data:

■ To use an existing database file that contains the names and addresses or other data you want to merge, select Use An Existing List, and then click the Browse command to select the file.

■ To use a Microsoft Outlook Contacts folder as the source of the mail merge data, select the Select From Outlook Contacts option, and then click the Choose Contacts Folder command to pick the contacts folder you want to use.

■ To create a new recipient list by typing the data, select Type A New list, and then click the Create command and type each entry in the New Address List dialog box (see Figure 19-4 and Figure 19-5). When you close the dialog box, Word will display the Save Address List dialog box (similar to the Save As dialog box), so that you can select a filename and location for your new recipient list. The wizard will save the recipient list as an Access database file (with the .mdb extension). Finally, the wizard will display the Mail Merge Recipients dialog box, in which you can sort or filter the entries in the recipient list, if you like, or work with them in other ways.

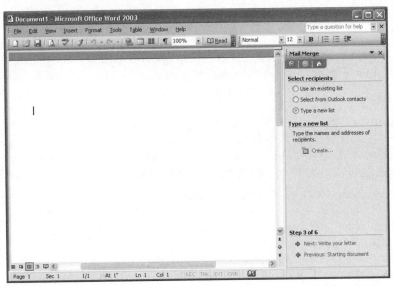

Figure 19-4. Here, a new recipient list is created in the Step 3 task pane of the Mail Merge Wizard.

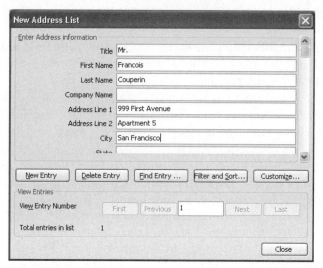

Figure 19-5. In this figure, a new recipient list entry is typed in the New Address List dialog box.

When you've finished, click the Next command to display the next Mail Merge task pane.

6 When the wizard displays the Step 4 Mail Merge task pane, you can enter or edit the mail merge main document that appears in the active document window (which you selected in step 4), as follows:

Note An alternative way to insert merge fields, to work with your mail merge main document, or to run a mail merge, is to use the Mail Merge toolbar that Word displays when you open the Step 4 Mail Merge task pane (see Figure 19-6). You can also display this toolbar at any time by choosing Tools, Letters And Mailings, Show Mail Merge Toolbar.

Although the Mail Merge toolbar isn't as easy to use as the Mail Merge Wizard (especially if you employ mail merge only occasionally), if you become a mail merge expert, you might find it faster to display and use the toolbar rather than running the wizard. The Mail Merge toolbar provides all the commands you need to run a mail merge. In fact, the toolbar provides several commands not included in the Mail Merge Wizard task panes. For example, you can use the Insert Word Field drop-down menu on the Mail Merge toolbar to insert Word fields for controlling the merge process (for instance an IF field that inserts text only if a particular merge field has a specified value). Or, you can click the Check For Errors button to have Word run the mail merge and report any errors contained in the main document.

Using Word to Automate Mailings

- To enter the text that remains the same in all the output documents (such as a letterhead, the main body of a letter, or a letter closing) use standard Word editing and formatting methods.

- To enter the text that varies from one output document to another, insert the appropriate merge fields using the commands in the Step 4 task pane, as shown in Figure 19-6. Table 19-1, on page 558, describes these commands and what they do.

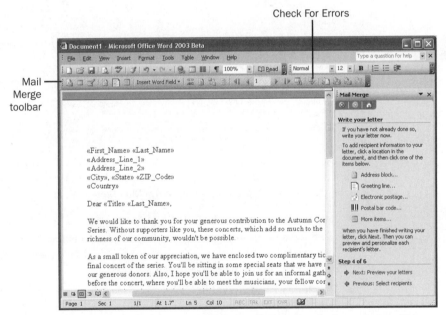

Figure 19-6. This figure shows a completed mail merge main document, written using the commands displayed in the Step 4 pane of the Mail Merge Wizard.

When you've finished writing the main document, save your work and then click the Next command in the Mail Merge task pane to display the next pane.

When the wizard displays the Step 5 Mail Merge task pane, it replaces each of the merge fields in the main document with the actual text from the first entry of the recipient list, so you can see what your first output document will look like (see Figure 19-7). You can now work with your output documents as follows:

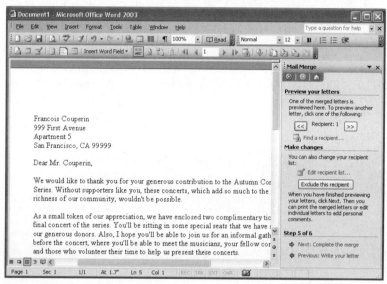

Figure 19-7. You can view and work with output form letters using the commands displayed in the Step 5 pane of the Mail Merge Wizard.

- To view other output documents, click the << and >> buttons.

- To find an entry in your recipient list that contains specific text and to view the output document showing that entry, click the Find A Recipient command and type the text into the Find Entry dialog box.

- To modify the recipient list (which you selected or created in step 5), click the Edit Recipient List command.

- To remove the currently displayed output document from the final output (that is, from the printed copies, Word document, e-mail messages, and so on), click the Exclude This Recipient button.

When you're finished previewing and working with the output documents, click the Next command to display the final Mail Merge task pane.

> **Note** The Step 5 Mail Merge task pane is labeled according to the type of output document you're creating—Preview Your Letters, Preview Your E-Mail Messages, and so on.

7 In the Step 6 (and final) Mail Merge task pane, labeled Complete The Merge, generate your final output documents by clicking the appropriate command (see Figure 19-8).

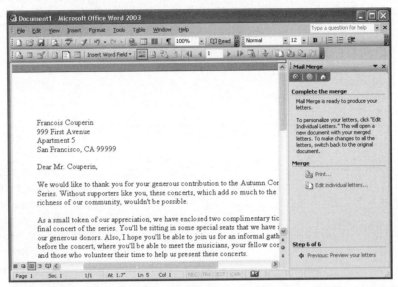

Figure 19-8. The Step 6 Mail Merge task pane lets you print the form letters or output them all to a single Word document.

If you're creating form letters, envelopes, or labels, you can do one of the following:

- To print the letters, envelopes, or labels immediately, click the Print command.

- To store all the letters, envelopes, or labels in a single, new Word document, click the Edit Individual Letters (or Edit Individual Envelopes or Edit Individual Labels) command. The advantage of using this command is that it gives you the chance to double-check the output, touch up its content or formatting, and then print or reprint the items whenever you want. However, if you find that you're making the same change to all letters, envelopes, or labels, you'll probably save time by going back to the Mail Merge Wizard, editing the main document or recipient list, and regenerating the output.

> **Note** If you're creating e-mail messages, click the Electronic Mail command to create the messages. If you're creating a directory, click the To New Document command to store the resulting directory in a Word document. And if you're creating faxes (as explained later), click Print to print the faxes or click Fax to send out the faxes using your fax modem.

Table 19-1. **The Commands in the Step 4 Mail Merge Task Pane**

To Insert These Merge Fields	Click This Command in the Step 4 Task Pane
Name and address fields, in various formats—for example: *Francois Couperin* *999 First Avenue* *Apartment 5* *San Francisco, CA 99999* *U.S.A.*	Address Block
Salutation field, in various formats—for example: *Dear Mr. Couperin,*	Greeting Line
E-postage field. If you have installed electronic postage software, this field prints postage on envelopes or mailing labels.	Electronic Postage If you haven't installed electronic postage software, when you click this command, Word will give you the option to visit a Web site where you can find information on electronic postage software.
Postal bar code field. A postal bar code is a machine-readable representation of the ZIP code, and including it on an envelope or label might expedite mail delivery.	Postal Bar Code
Merge fields for specific fields in your recipient list, such as the Title, First Name, Last Name, Company Name, or Address Line 1 field.	More Items

The following alternative way to use the Mail Merge Wizard lets you create faxes, as well as form letters or a directory:

1 Choose File, New to open the New Document task pane.

2 Click the On My Computer command in the Templates group to open the Templates dialog box.

3 In the Templates dialog box, click the Mail Merge tab (as shown in Figure 19-9) and double-click the template you want to use. Word provides mail merge templates for creating faxes, letters, or an "address list" (another term for a directory).

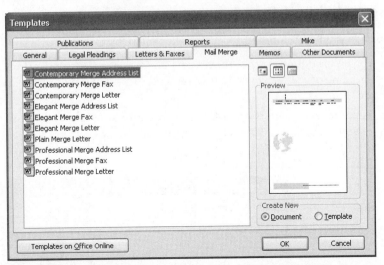

Figure 19-9. The Mail Merge tab of the Templates dialog box allows you to create a mail merge document by using a template.

Word will then create the new document based on the selected template, and will open the Mail Merge task pane. By selecting a specific mail merge template, you have already completed the first two steps of the Mail Merge Wizard. Therefore, the wizard displays the task panes for only the final four steps (although they will be labeled Step 1 through Step 4).

> **Note**   You can also use the New Document task pane to search for a mail merge template on the Office Online Web site, or on a personal or company Web site. Use the same techniques that you employ for other types of templates, which are explained in "Creating a Document Using the New Document Task Pane," on page 53.

   4   Complete the four Mail Merge Wizard task panes as explained in the previous procedure in this section. However, keep in mind that the Step 1 through Step 4 panes are equivalent to the Step 3 through Step 6 panes described in the previous procedure.

Generating Individual Envelopes and Labels

You can print an individual envelope or label using the Envelopes And Labels command. This command is especially useful for addressing an envelope or label for a letter that you have just finished typing.

> For information on using Word's mail merge feature to print envelopes or labels for an entire group of delivery addresses, see "Using the Mail Merge Wizard to Automate Large Mailings," on page 549.

Generating Individual Envelopes

To print a single envelope, perform the following steps:

1 If you have already typed the delivery address into a document (for example, in the heading of a letter), open that document. (This step is optional because you can type the address later.)

2 Choose Tools, Letters And Mailings, Envelopes And Labels. Then, in the Envelopes And Labels dialog box, click the Envelopes tab, shown here:

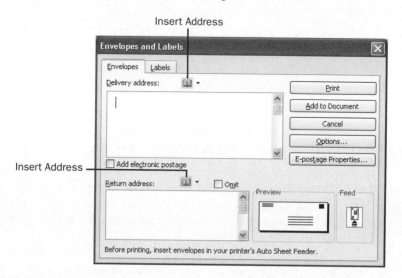

3 Type the delivery address in the Delivery Address text box.

If Word finds an address in the document, this address will already be contained in the Delivery Address box. In this case, you can simply edit the text, if necessary.

4 If you want to print a return address, type it into the Return Address text box.

If you have specified a personal mailing address in Word, this address will automatically appear in the Return Address box. In this case, you can edit the text, if necessary. (To specify a personal mailing address, choose Tools, Options, click the User Information tab, and type the address in the Mailing Address text box. Be sure to include your name at the beginning of the return address if you want your name to be included automatically in the Return Address box in the Envelopes tab.) Note that if you enter or edit text in the Return Address box of the Envelopes tab, when you click the Print or Add To Document button (in step 7), Word will ask whether you want to save the new address as your default return address. If you click Yes, Word will save the text as your personal mailing address.

If you don't want to print a return address (perhaps you're using preprinted envelopes), you can either delete the text in the Return Address box or check the Omit option above the box.

Insert Address

Tip   Save time by getting an address from Outlook
If you have entered names and addresses into your Outlook Contacts folder, you can use the Insert Address button above the Delivery Address box or above the Return Address box to select an address from Outlook rather than typing one.

- To select any of the contact items stored in your Outlook Contacts folder, click the main part of the Insert Address button and choose a name in the Select Name dialog box.
- To quickly select a contact item you've used previously, click the down arrow on the button and choose a name from the drop-down menu.

Tip   Either action will insert both the name and the address of the selected contact. If you've defined more than one address for the contact, the one designated as the mailing address will be inserted.

For information on working with the Contacts folder in Outlook, see "Maintaining Your Address List with the Contacts Folder," on page 1047.

5   If you want to change features of the envelope itself, click the Options button on the Envelopes tab, and select the desired settings in the Envelope Options tab (shown in Figure 19-10). Use the model envelope in the Preview area to guide your selections.

Tip   Print your postage
If you have installed electronic postage add-in software, you can have Word print postage directly on your envelopes (or mailing labels) rather than affixing a postage stamp or using a postage meter. To do this, check the Add Electronic Postage option. If you want to modify e-postage features, click the E-Postage Properties button.

If you haven't installed electronic postage software, when you check the Add Electronic Postage option Word will give you the option to visit a Web site where you can find information on electronic postage software.

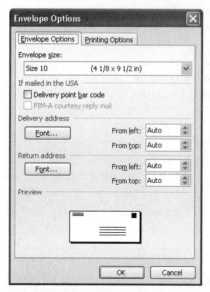

Figure 19-10. You can change features of an envelope in the Envelope Options tab of the Envelope Options dialog box.

6 If you want to modify the way the envelope is printed, click the Options button in the Envelopes tab, and select the desired settings in the Printing Options tab (shown in Figure 19-11). If you've changed any settings in the Printing Options tab, you can click the Reset button to restore Word's default settings.

Figure 19-11. You can modify the way an envelope is printed using the Printing Options tab of the Envelope Options dialog box.

> **Tip** Vary the formatting of your envelope text
>
> The Envelope Options tab lets you select the basic character formatting of all the delivery address and return address text. You can also change the formatting of one or more individual characters within the Delivery Address or Return Address box in the Envelopes tab (overriding the basic formatting). To do this, select the text, and press the shortcut key for applying (or removing) character formatting—for example Ctrl+B, Ctrl+I, or Ctrl+U to apply (or remove) bold, italics, or underlining, respectively. You can use any of the first 10 shortcut keys that are listed in Table 12-2, on page 318.

7 To complete the envelope, do either of the following:

■ To print the envelope immediately, place an envelope in your printer and click the Print button. You should insert the envelope into the printer so that it has the orientation shown in the Feed area in the lower right corner of the Envelopes tab. (You select the orientation in the Printing Options tab of the Envelope Options dialog box, shown in Figure 19-11. You can quickly display this tab by clicking in the Feed area.)

■ To add the text for the envelope to the document in the active window, click the Add To Document button. (If you have already added envelope information to the document, this button will be labeled Change Document, and it will replace the former envelope text with the new text.) Word will insert the envelope text into a separate section at the beginning of the document, and it will assign to this section the correct margins, paper size, printing orientation, and paper source for printing the envelope. If necessary, you can edit the envelope text or add text or graphics to it. Thereafter, the envelope will be printed automatically whenever you print the document. You can use this technique to include the text for both a letter and its envelope within a single document, so that you can print both using only one print command.

> For information on setting the margins, paper size, printing orientation, paper source, and other page setup options for a document section, see "Modifying the Page Setup," on page 532.

Generating Individual Labels

You can print a single label, or you can print the same text on every label on a full sheet of labels, by performing the following steps:

1 If you have already typed the label text into a document (for example, an address in a letter heading), open that document. (This step is optional because you can type the text later.)

2 Choose Tools, Letters And Mailings, Envelopes And Labels. Then click the Labels tab in the Envelopes And Labels dialog box, shown here:

Insert Address

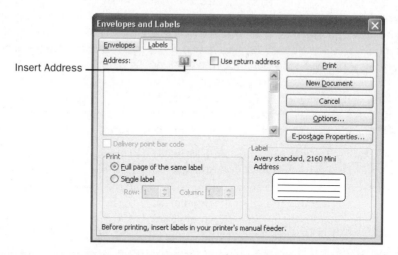

3 Type the label text into the Address box. If Word finds an address in the document, this text will already be contained in the Address box. In this case, you can simply edit the text, if necessary.

Alternatively, you can check the Use Return Address option to have Word copy into the Address box your personal mailing address (the address you set by using the User Information tab of the Options dialog box, as described in the previous section). You could do this to print return address labels for yourself.

Also, if you have entered names and addresses into your Outlook Contacts folder, you can use the Insert Address button above the Address box to select an address.

For more information on using the Insert Address button, see the tip "Save time by getting an address from Outlook," on page 561.

Tip Format your label text

You can change the character formatting of any block of text in the Address box in the Labels tab. To do this, select the text, and press the shortcut key for applying (or removing) character formatting—for example Ctrl+B, Ctrl+I, or Ctrl+U to apply (or remove) bold, italics, or underlining, respectively. You can use any of the first 10 shortcut keys that are listed in Table 12-2, on page 318.

4 To tell Word how many labels to print, do either of the following:

- To print a full page of identical labels, select the Full Page Of The Same Label option. You might select this option, for example, to prepare a full sheet of return address labels.

- To print a single label, select Single Label and enter the row and column position on the label sheet of the label you want to print.

> **Caution** If you print a single label on a label sheet, you will of course later want to put the partially used label sheet back into your printer to print another label. Keep in mind, however, that for some printers attempting to print on a label sheet with one or more labels already removed is likely to cause a paper jam. Your printer's documentation might offer some insight on its ability to print on partially used label sheets.

5 If you need to change any of the label printing options, click the Options button to open the Label Options dialog box (shown in Figure 19-12).

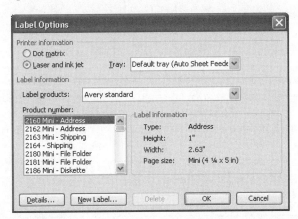

Figure 19-12. You can select options for printing labels in the Label Options dialog box.

If your label sheet doesn't match any of the standard labels listed in the Product Number list of the Label Options dialog box, you can specify custom label measurements by selecting the closest standard label, clicking the New Label button, and modifying the measurements in the New Custom dialog box (shown in Figure 19-13). You must give your custom label a name. You can later delete the custom label by selecting its name in the Product Number list of the Label Options dialog box and clicking the Delete button.

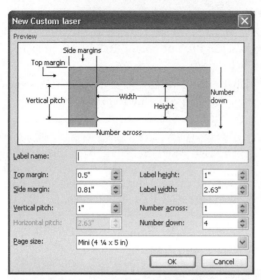

Figure 19-13. The New Custom dialog box allows you to create custom label measurements.

Note You can click the Details button in the Label Options dialog box to see the exact measurements of the selected label in an information dialog box. An alternative way to create a custom label is to modify one or more measurements in this dialog box, enter a new name for your custom label into the Label Name text box, and click OK. (You can't change the measurements of one of the standard labels.)

When you click OK in the Label Options dialog box, you'll return to the Labels tab of the Envelopes And Labels dialog box.

Tip Insert postal bar codes for faster delivery

If you have selected a sufficiently large label and if the label text contains a valid ZIP code, you can print a postal bar code at the top of the label by checking the Delivery Point Barcode option in the Labels tab of the Envelopes And Labels dialog box. (If the Delivery Point Barcode option isn't enabled, the selected label probably isn't large enough to print a bar code.) The bar code is a machine-readable representation of the ZIP code, and including it might expedite mail delivery.

6 To finish the label, do either of the following:

- To print the label immediately, insert a label sheet into your printer, and click the Print button.

- If you're printing a full page of labels (that is, if you chose the Full Page Of The Same Label option), you can click the New Document button to have Word store the label text in a new document. You can then modify the labels if you want (perhaps adding a graphic logo to each label or applying formatting), and you can print the labels by printing this document. You can save the document so that you can print the same labels again in the future. (In this document, you'll notice that Word has created a table and has inserted each label into a separate table cell.)

Tip   Include a picture on an envelope or label

You can include a graphic image in the delivery address (but not the return address) of an envelope or label using the following method: Insert the graphic into a Word document and select it before you open the Envelopes And Labels dialog box. The graphic must have the In Line With Text wrapping style. When you open the dialog box, you will see the graphic in the Delivery Address text box on the Envelopes tab and the Address text box on the Labels tab. You can then type in the address text. (Word doesn't let you copy and paste a picture into a text box in the Envelopes And Labels dialog box.)

Wrapping styles are explained in "Combining Text with Graphic Objects and Text Boxes," on page 514. For information on printing e-postage on your labels, see the tip "Print your postage," on page 561.

Tip   Have Word write your letters

You can have Word automatically insert into a document all the basic elements of a letter (the date line, return and recipient's addresses, salutation, closing, and so on), and format them according to your specifications. To do this, choose Tools, Letters And Mailings, Letter Wizard to open the Letter Wizard dialog box. Then, in the tabs of this dialog box, choose the options you want and supply the required information about the letter sender and recipient. Of course, you'll still have to type in the text for the body of the letter!

Chapter 20

Creating Web Pages and Working with XML in Word

Online Documents. 569

Creating and Publishing Web Pages. . . 573

NEW FEATURE! Creating, Editing, and Viewing XML
Documents. 594

Online Documents

Not too many years ago, Microsoft Word was used almost exclusively for creating traditional printed documents. With the move toward the paperless office, however, each version of Word has provided more features for creating and working with an alternative end product: the online document. An online document is one that's designed to be read and worked with on a computer, rather than being sent to a printer. It can be a Word document in native .doc format that's made accessible to—or distributed among—a group of readers; this chapter refers to this type of document as an *online Word document*. Or, more commonly now, it can be a Web page document in HTML (Hypertext Markup Language) format that's posted on a server on the World Wide Web or on a company intranet; this chapter refers to this type of document simply as a *Web page*. Also, a document in XML (Extensible Markup Language) format can be used to store and deliver the data that's displayed in an HTML Web page, or it can be displayed directly in Word or in a browser like other types of online documents.

For a description of different ways to share native Word documents, as well as a discussion on related techniques, see "Sharing Word Documents," on page 468.

In addition to saving trees, the main advantage offered by an online document is that it can be made dynamic and interactive. For example, an online document can contain hyperlinks for navigating to other locations; interactive forms for collecting information; frames for viewing several documents at once; a background color, pattern, or sound; animated text or graphics; or movie or sound clips. An online document can contain ActiveX controls, Microsoft Visual Basic for Applications (VBA) macros, or scripts for performing a wide variety of tasks. When a smart document is opened in Word 2003, it can provide context-sensitive help and tools in a custom task pane. And, finally, an XML document can deliver up-to-date data from a network or Internet location.

For information on VBA macros, see "Recording and Running Macros," on page 224. For a definition of a smart document, see "Using Smart Documents," on page 47.

When you create a Web page or online Word document, you primarily use the general Word editing and formatting techniques presented in the previous chapters in this part of the book, as well as in Part 2, "Using Shared Office 2003 Application Features." Even when you use Word to create an XML document (which, as you'll learn, is a highly specialized type of document), you can use many of the general Word editing and formatting techniques.

In this chapter, the section "Creating and Publishing Web Pages" describes the specialized tools and techniques that are designed primarily for creating Web pages or online Word documents. When you create Web pages or online Word documents, you'll use both these specialized tools, as well as the general-purpose tools described previously in the book. Keep in mind that although the section "Creating and Publishing a Web Page" focuses on Web pages, almost all of the editing and formatting techniques it presents can also be used for creating and working with online documents in native Word format, although you'll have to view the document in Web Layout view to see Web-style features such as background images. (This section notes any techniques or elements that *aren't* suited for native Word documents. In addition, it points out a few features that work *only* in native-format documents.)

Also in this chapter, the section "Creating, Editing, and Viewing XML Documents" describes XML, explains the new Word 2003 support for XML documents, and shows you how to use the Word tools for creating, editing, and displaying XML documents.

Tip Use linking or embedding in online documents

Using object linking or embedding with the Display As Icon option lets you include a great variety of information in a small amount of space within an online document that's in native Word format. Each block of information is represented by an icon that the reader can click to view the full text or graphics. For instructions, see Chapter 7, "Exchanging Data in Office 2003."

Using Fields in Online Word Documents

Fields are dynamic document elements that you can use to add interactivity to online documents, primarily documents in native Word format. To cite only a few examples, you can add fields for displaying the date and time, going to another document location, running a macro, downloading commands to a printer, displaying the document author or the number of characters, performing calculations, numbering document items, prompting the user for text, or embedding other documents or XML data. The previous chapters in this part of the book have described several common fields—for example merge fields used in mail merge main documents, IncludeText fields for embedding other documents or XML data within the current document, and the fields used to create index entries, indexes, and tables of contents.

To insert a field, perform the following steps:

1 Choose Insert, Field to display the Field dialog box (shown in Figure 20-1).

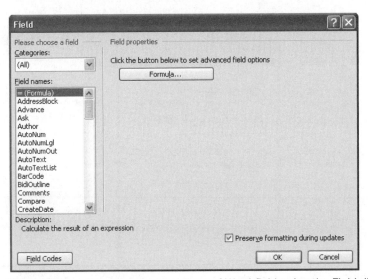

Figure 20-1. You can insert any type of Word field using the Field dialog box.

2 Select the general category of the field you want in the Categories drop-down list.

3 Select the specific field in the Field Names list. Below the list you'll see a description of the currently selected field.

4 Select the desired field properties and options, which vary according to the field you've selected.

For further details, see the Word online help topic "Field Types and Switches."

Using Reading Layout View

Word has now enhanced its support for online documents by providing a new document view that is optimized for reading—rather than creating or editing—documents that are opened in Word. This view, known as Reading Layout view, divides the document into small pages that fit completely within the Word window, simulating a book. (You can display one or two pages at a time.) It displays the document in a large, smoothed font. And it presents a simpler application interface to minimize distractions to reading the document. See Figure 20-2.

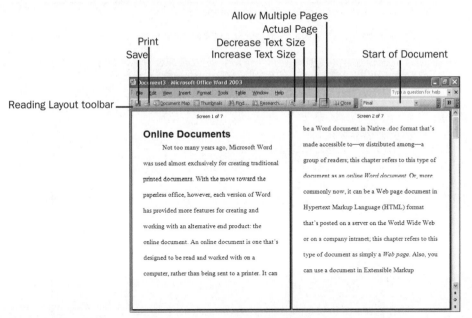

Figure 20-2. The new Reading Layout view is optimized for reading an online document.

The following is the procedure for using Reading Layout view to read the active document:

1 Click the Read button on the Standard toolbar or click the Reading Layout button at the left end of the horizontal scrollbar. Word will switch into Reading Layout view and will display the Reading Layout toolbar, which provides tools for reading the document. It will also display the Reviewing toolbar, which is discussed in Chapter 16, "Using Word in Workgroups."

2 Adjust the view according to your preferences, as follows (all buttons mentioned in these instructions are on the Reading Layout toolbar):

- To display two pages at once (if they fit within the Word window), rather than a single page at a time, select the Allow Multiple Pages button.

- To adjust the text size, use the Increase Text Size and Decrease Text Size buttons.

- To display one or two full pages as they would be printed, rather than displaying small reading-sized pages, select the Actual Page button. (This option displays the pages as they would appear in Print Layout or Print Preview view.)

3 Navigate through the document using the normal Word navigation commands described in Chapter 11, "Efficient Editing in Word," or using any of the following tools provided in Reading Layout view (all buttons mentioned in these instructions are on the Reading Layout toolbar):

- To view a thumbnail image of each of the document's pages, select the Thumbnails button. To view a particular page, you can click its thumbnail image.

- To go to the beginning of the document, click the Start Of Document button.

- To view the Document Map, described in "Navigating Through an Outline," on page 429, click the Document Map button.

4 To turn off Reading Layout view and return to your previous view, click the Close button on the Reading Layout toolbar.

The Research task pane, opened by clicking the Research button on the Reading Layout toolbar, is explained in "Using the Research Task Pane," on page 44. Word's Find And Replace dialog box, opened by clicking the Find button, is described in "Finding and Replacing Text and Formatting," on page 293

Creating and Publishing Web Pages

Since the introduction of Word 2000, creating a Web page has hardly been different from creating a regular Word document. The Word commands, interface, and features are basically the same whether you're creating a regular document in native Word format or a Web page in HTML format (a few exceptions are noted in this chapter).

Because HTML is one of the standard Word formats—like the native .doc format or Rich Text Format (.rtf)—when you save a Word document in HTML, the vast majority of document features are preserved (again, a few exceptions are noted in this chapter). Even if a feature isn't used by a browser (such as the page margins set through the Page Setup dialog box in Word), all of the feature's settings (for example, the margin sizes) are carefully saved in the HTML file or in a supporting file. These features will be used whenever you open the document in Word (for instance, the margins will be shown unless you're in Web Layout view). Because you can save a native Word document in an HTML file and then later reopen the HTML file and convert it back to a native Word document if you wish, with almost no loss of features, Word is said to provide "round-trip" support for HTML.

To create a Web page in Word, follow these three basic steps:

1 Open the document. You can open a document by choosing File, New to display the New Document task pane (shown in Figure 20-3), and then doing one of the following:

- To create a new, blank Web page, click the Web Page command in the New area.

- To look for an online template that you can use as the basis for your new Web page, use the Search Office Online text box and Go button, or click the Templates Home Page command in the Templates area. These controls are explained in "Downloading and Using Templates from Office Online," on page 55.

  To open an existing Web page or native Word document, choose File, Open, and select the file in the Open dialog box.

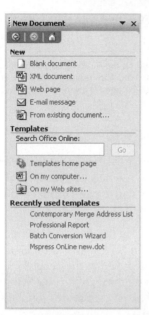

Figure 20-3. The New Document task pane allows you to open a new document.

> For general instructions on using the Open dialog box, see Chapter 4, "Working with Office 2003 Applications, Documents, and Program Windows."

2 Enter or edit the text and graphic content of your page and format the document using the standard Word techniques discussed in the previous chapters in this part of the book, as well as in Part 2, "Using Shared Office 2003 Application Features." But keep in mind the following points:

- Some Word features aren't displayed or supported by common browsers. Examples of these features are negative paragraph indents; diagonal table borders; vertical text in table cells; character, nonsolid, or page borders; newspaper-style columns; automatic hyphenation; watermarks; headers and footers; margins and other settings made in the Page Setup dialog box; and certain character formatting features such as an underline color or style, some of the effects like Shadow, and text animations (for example, Blinking Background). Most of the features that aren't supported in browsers have been noted as such in the previous chapters. Also, some features will look different in a browser from the way they appear in Word; for instance, tabs might not align correctly, patterned shading will become solid, and a text-wrapped graphic object or table will be moved to the left or right of the adjoining paragraph.

- When you edit a Web page, Word generally lets you go ahead and apply most of the features that aren't supported by common browsers. (As mentioned, it will save these features in the HTML file and use them whenever you open the page in Word.) You can, however, have Word block most of the character, paragraph, or table formatting features that are incompatible with specific browsers. To do this, choose Tools, Options, click the General tab, click the

Web Options button, and click the Browsers tab. Then, in the drop-down list, select the browser versions that readers of your Web page will be using, and in the list below, check the Disable Features Not Supported By These Browsers option (as shown in Figure 20-4). Word will then disable the nonsupported features in the dialog boxes you use to apply them (the Font dialog box, the Borders And Shading dialog box, and so on). And, if your document already contained one of these features before you blocked them, when you save the document, Word will first warn you and will then convert the feature, if possible, to a similar supported feature. Note that Word will disable these features only for a Web page. So, if you're working on a native Word document that you're going to later convert to HTML and want to take advantage of the blocking feature, save your document in HTML before formatting it.

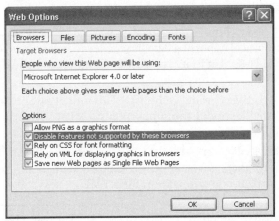

Figure 20-4.   The settings shown here cause Word to disable formatting features not supported in Microsoft Internet Explorer 4.0 or later.

- When you work on a Web page, you'll notice a few changes in the Word interface from the way it appears when you work on a regular Word document. For example, the New Blank Document button becomes the New Web Page button and clicking it creates a blank Web page. The Versions command is disabled on the File menu. And the HTML Source command appears on the View menu to let you work directly with the HTML source for the Web page.

- In addition to the basic Word features discussed in the previous chapters, Word provides elements and formatting features that are especially useful for creating Web pages (as well as online Word documents). The elements include hyperlinks, horizontal dividing lines, movie and sound clips, background sounds, scrolling text, Web forms for collecting information, and frames for viewing several pages or Word documents simultaneously. The formatting features include background colors or patterns and themes.

- It's best to create a Web page using the Web Layout view, which displays the document in much the same way that popular browsers would display it. For a more accurate preview, you can open the document in your browser by choosing File, Web Page Preview.

> The elements used to create Web pages are described in "Adding Web Page Elements," on page 580. Formatting features useful for Web pages are explained in "Formatting Web Pages," on page 591.

3 Save the document. If you created a new Web page or opened an existing Web page in step 1, you can use the usual Save or Save As command to save your work, and your document will be stored by default in the HTML format. If, however, you created or opened a native Word document in step 1, you should choose File, Save As Web Page. This will open the Save As dialog box and will select an HTML format in the Save As Type drop-down list.

Word uses several different HTML formats. You can choose the specific format in which to save the document by selecting one of the following items in the Save As Type drop-down list in the Save As dialog box:

- **Web Page (*.htm; *.html)** This format saves the Web page in an HTML file but saves graphics and other supporting data in separate files. The format provides round-trip support for HTML; that is, it saves all Word features contained in the document, as explained previously in this section.

- **Single File Web Page (*.mht; *.mhtml)** This format saves everything in a single Web file. It also provides round-trip support for HTML. (This format was known as Web Archive in Office XP.)

- **Web Page, Filtered (*.htm; *.html)** This format is like the first one [Web Page (*.htm; *.html)], except that it saves only the essential document information, and therefore does *not* provide round-trip support for HTML.

> **Caution** Although the filtered format generates a smaller and "cleaner" HTML file (one that's perhaps easier to edit in other programs), if you reopen the file in Word, some of the document's original features—such as headers or footers—might no longer be present. Therefore, if you create a filtered HTML file from a document, you might also want to save a copy of the document in one of the other HTML formats [Web Page (*.htm; *.html) or Single File Web Page (*.mht; *.mhtml)] to preserve all the document's features.

Inside Out

No automatic backups of Web pages

If you've checked the Always Create Backup Copy option (in the Save tab of the Options dialog box) and have been relying on Word always making a backup copy of a document when you save it, keep in mind that Word *won't* make a backup copy of a Web page when you save it, even if this option is checked. You'll have to back up the file manually.

> **Note** When an HTML format is selected in the Save As Type list, the Change Title button appears in the Save As dialog box. You can click this button to change the page's title. (The title appears in the browser's title bar when it displays the page.) You can also change the title by choosing File, Properties, opening the Summary tab, and editing the contents of the Title text box.

For general information on saving documents in Office, see "Saving Office Documents," on page 69. For information on choosing the application that a Web page is opened in, see "Saving a Document as a Web Page," on page 73.

Setting Web Page Options

You can set a variety of options that affect the way Word manages the Web pages you create by choosing Tools, Options, clicking the General tab, and clicking the Web Options button to open the Web Options dialog box. You can also open this dialog box by choosing Web Options from the Tools drop-down menu in the Save As dialog box. Then select the settings you want in the tabs of the Web Options dialog box, as follows:

- To have Word disable formatting features that aren't supported by specified browsers (as explained under step 2, on page 574), and to set general Web options, use the Browsers tab (see Figure 20-4, on page 575). Note that when you select a particular browser in the drop-down list at the top, Word automatically checks the general options in the list below that are compatible with that browser.

- To modify the way Word saves your Web pages, use the Files tab (shown in Figure 20-5).

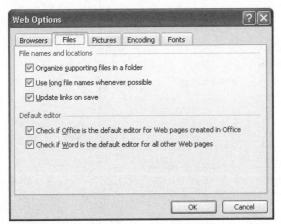

Figure 20-5. You can change the way Word saves your Web pages in the Files tab of the Web Options dialog box.

● To specify the size and resolution of the typical monitor on which your Web pages will be viewed (if you know this information), so that Word can optimize the display of graphics in a page, use the Pictures tab (shown in Figure 20-6).

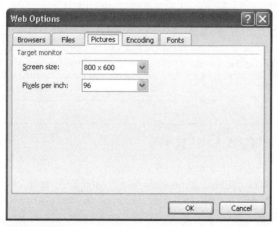

Figure 20-6. You can change the monitor settings in the Pictures tab of the Web Options dialog box.

● To specify the language used for your Web pages, use the Encoding tab (shown in Figure 20-7).

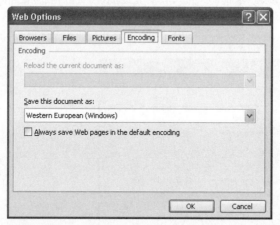

Figure 20-7. The Encoding tab of the Web Options dialog box allows you to specify the language used for your Web pages.

● To select the appropriate character set for the language used in your Web pages, or to choose the default Web page fonts and font sizes, use the Fonts tab (as shown in Figure 20-8).

Figure 20-8. You can choose the character set and default font settings for your Web pages in the Fonts tab of the Web Options dialog box.

Also, you can have Word use pixels as the default unit of measurement in some of the dialog boxes that affect the display of Web pages (such as the Paragraph and Tabs dialog boxes). To do this, check the Show Pixels For HTML Features option in the General tab of the Options dialog box.

Troubleshooting

Lost document versions

You created a document containing several versions and then saved the document as a Web page. However, you now can't access the document versions other than the one that's displayed.

If a document file stores several document versions, when you save the document in HTML format (by choosing File, Save As Web Page, for example), Word will store in the HTML file only the document version that's currently displayed, and any saved document versions will be lost. (You'll notice that the Versions command on the File menu is dimmed for a Web page.) This occurrence is an exception to the general rule that Word saves all your document information—even features not supported by Web browsers—when you convert it to HTML format. Word will warn you about losing saved versions only if you've checked the Disable Features Not Supported By These Browsers option, shown in Figure 20-4 on page 575.

To access your other versions, you'll have to open the original native Word (.doc) document in which you stored these versions. *Be sure to save this file if you want to be able to access the document versions it contains.*

For information on storing multiple versions in a document, see "Storing Different Document Versions," on page 257.

Chapter 20

Adding Web Page Elements

The following Word elements, which are described in the sections that follow, are especially valuable for Web pages, or for native Word documents that are intended to be read online:

- Hyperlinks
- Horizontal dividing lines
- Movie clips, sound clips, and background sounds
- Scrolling text
- Web forms
- Frames

Adding and Using Hyperlinks

You can assign a hyperlink to a block of text or to a picture in a Word document. The hyperlink connects the text or picture to a target location. The target location can be a Web page, an Office document or other file, or a folder. The page, file, or folder can be located on a disk, network drive, or Internet site. The target location can also be a specific place within the current document or within another file. Or it can be an e-mail address. Clicking the hyperlink displays the target location or sends a message to the target e-mail address. You can click a hyperlink when a document is open in Word, or—for a Web page—when it's displayed in a browser. Hyperlinks can be useful in any type of Word document, but they are especially important in Web pages, where you can use them to tie together the pages in your Web site or to connect to other sites.

Note If the Use CTRL + Click To Follow Hyperlink option is checked, clicking a hyperlink in Word while pressing Ctrl displays the target location, and clicking the hyperlink without pressing Ctrl places the insertion point within a text hyperlink (so you can edit the text) or selects a picture hyperlink (so you can modify the picture). If the Use CTRL + Click To Follow Hyperlink option isn't checked, the opposite occurs. That is, clicking a hyperlink while pressing Ctrl places the insertion point within it or selects it, and clicking the hyperlink without pressing Ctrl displays the target location. When you place the pointer over a hyperlink, Word shows a ScreenTip that indicates whether you need to press Ctrl and click or just click the hyperlink to follow the link.

You'll find the Use CTRL + Click To Follow Hyperlink option by choosing Tools, Options, clicking the Edit tab, and looking in the Editing Options area.

To create a hyperlink, perform the following steps:

1 Select the text or picture to which you want to assign the hyperlink or simply place the insertion point at the position in your document where you want Word to insert the hyperlink text that you later specify.

Insert Hyperlink

2 Open the Insert Hyperlink dialog box (shown in Figure 20-9) by choosing Insert, Hyperlink, by clicking the Insert Hyperlink button on the Standard toolbar, or by pressing Ctrl+K.

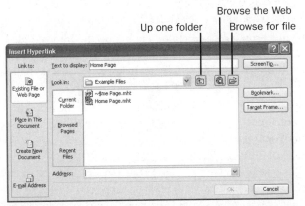

Figure 20-9. You create hyperlinks using the Insert Hyperlink dialog box.

3 Enter or edit the hypertext text in the Text To Display box. Skip this step if you selected the desired text in step 1 or if you are assigning the hyperlink to a picture.

4 In the Link To bar at the left of the Insert Hyperlink dialog box, select the general category of hyperlink you want to create:

- To link to a different existing document or Web page, select Existing File Or Web Page.

- To link to a different location within the current document, select Place In This Document.

- To create a new document or Web page and link to it, select Create New Document.

- To link to an e-mail address, so that clicking the hyperlink sends a message to that address, select E-Mail Address.

The controls that Word displays in the rest of the dialog box depend on which of these options is selected.

5 If you selected Existing File Or Web Page in step 4, select the target document or Web page using one of the following methods (the controls you use are shown in Figure 20-8):

- To specify any target, type the target's file path or URL (Uniform Resource Locator) into the Address text box.

- To select a target file or folder on a local or network disk, click the Current Folder item in the Look In bar, and then select the file in the main list. To navigate to a different folder, use the Look In drop-down list and the Up One Folder button, which work just like they do in the standard Open dialog box. Alternatively, you can click the Browse For File button to select the target file or folder in the Link To File dialog box, which is modeled after the standard Open dialog box.

■ To link to an Internet location or disk file that you've recently browsed, click the Browsed Pages item in the Look In bar and then select the specific browsed target in the main list.

■ To link to a disk file that you've recently opened, click the Recent Files item in the Look In bar and then select the file in the main list.

■ To run your browser to search for a target on the Internet, click the Browse The Web button. Once you have opened the desired target page in your browser, leave the browser running and switch back to the Insert Hyperlink dialog box. You'll then find the page's URL in the Address box.

To link to a specific location within the target file, click the Bookmark button and indicate the target location by selecting a document heading or bookmark in the Select Place In Document dialog box.

Note If in step 4 you selected any of the Link To bar items except E-Mail Address, you can select the specific frame where the target file will be displayed—if you've added frames to your document—or you can have the target file opened in a separate browser window if the link is clicked in a browser. To do this, click the Target Frame button and select the option you want in the Set Target Frame dialog box.

Frames are briefly discussed in "Use Frames to View Several Documents at Once," on page 590.

6 If you selected Place In This Document in step 4, specify the target location by selecting a document heading or bookmark in the main list.

7 If you selected Create New Document in step 4, specify the name and location of the new document or Web page as follows:

■ To create a file in the current directory, just type its name into the Name Of New Document text box.

■ To create a file in a different directory, click the Change button to select the directory.

8 If you selected E-Mail Address in step 4, type the target e-mail address into the E-Mail Address text box and, if you want, type a message subject in the Subject text box.

9 To have Word or the browser (Internet Explorer 4.0 or later) display a specific message when you hold the pointer over the hyperlink, click the ScreenTip button and type the message into the Set Hyperlink ScreenTip dialog box.

10 Click the OK button.

Tip Change hyperlink formatting
By default, hyperlink text is initially blue and underlined. After you have *followed* the hyperlink (that is, clicked it in Word or in a browser to open the target), the color will change to violet. You can change the format of an unfollowed or a followed hyperlink by modifying the Hyperlink or FollowedHyperlink built-in Word style. (For instructions, see "Customizing Styles," on page 389.) The hyperlink colors are also modified when you apply a theme to the document, as discussed later in this chapter.

To modify a hyperlink you have already defined, select the text or picture again, and then use any of the techniques that were given for opening the Insert Hyperlink dialog box. The dialog box will now be labeled Edit Hyperlink. You can use it to modify the hyperlink or you can click the Remove Link button in the lower-right corner of the dialog box to remove the hyperlink from the text or picture in your document.

If you click a hyperlink in Word, and if the target of that hyperlink is a regular Office document (that is, one saved in native format, not HTML), you can use the Web toolbar to navigate back and forth through the document locations you have visited or to open other documents (as shown in Figure 20-10). When you first click the hyperlink, the Web toolbar will be displayed automatically. (You can display it at any time by choosing View, Toolbars, Web, or by right-clicking a toolbar and then choosing Web from the shortcut menu.)

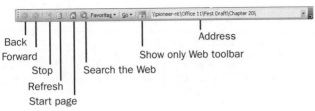

Figure 20-10. You can navigate among document locations you have visited using the Web toolbar.

Inserting Horizontal Dividing Lines

You can use horizontal dividing lines to separate different parts of your document. Although horizontal dividing lines are typically used in Web pages, you can insert them into any type of Word document to help organize the document's contents. Adding a horizontal dividing line provides an alternative to applying a horizontal border above or below a paragraph. Unlike a border, a horizontal dividing line is a separate document element that you can independently select, move, delete, or format. You can insert a plain, standard dividing line; or you can use a graphic image for a dividing line, so it can serve as a decorative element consistent with the overall look of your document.

To insert a horizontal dividing line, perform the following steps:

1 Place the insertion point at the position where you want to divide your document. The horizontal dividing line will be inserted immediately before the insertion point and will be placed on a separate document line (in its own paragraph).

2 Choose Format, Borders And Shading, and click the Horizontal Line button at the bottom of the Borders And Shading dialog box. This will open the Horizontal Line dialog box (shown in Figure 20-11), which will display a gallery of your available dividing lines.

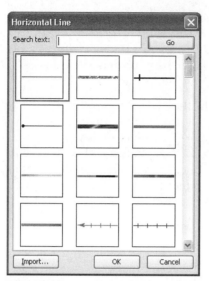

Figure 20-11. The Horizontal Line dialog box displays the available dividing lines you can insert.

3 Select the line style you want.

The first item in the list (at the upper-left corner) inserts a plain, standard dividing line. (Word creates the line by adding an <HR>, horizontal rule, HTML element, which causes a browser to display its standard dividing line.) Each of the other items inserts a dividing line created from a graphics file. (Word generates the line by adding an <IMG>, image, HTML element, which causes a browser to display the specified graphics file.)

To add a new line to the list from a graphics file, click the Import button and select the file in the Add Clips To Organizer dialog box (which works just like the standard Open dialog box).

4 Click the OK button.

Once you've used this procedure to select and insert a horizontal dividing line, you can quickly insert additional dividing lines that have the same style. You do this by clicking the down arrow next to the Border button on the Formatting toolbar or on the Tables And Borders toolbar and then clicking the Horizontal Line item on the palette, shown here:

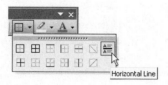

As a further shortcut, once you have clicked the Horizontal Line button on the palette, you can insert additional dividing lines by simply clicking the Border button on the Formatting or Tables And Borders toolbar.

To modify a horizontal dividing line that you've inserted into a document, click it to select it. You can then drag it up or down to move it to a new location in the document, or you can press Delete to remove it.

To format the selected horizontal dividing line, choose Format, Horizontal Line (or just double-click the line) to open the Format Horizontal Line dialog box. In this dialog box, you can adjust the width, height, or alignment of any type of line. You can change the color of a standard line. And you can change the cropping, color control, brightness, or contrast of a graphic line. Note that applying a theme to the document will modify the horizontal dividing lines throughout the document.

Themes are discussed in "Applying a Web Page Theme," on page 592.

Themes are discussed in "Applying a Web Page Theme," on page 592.

Adding Movies and Sounds

You can add a movie clip or a background sound to liven up your Web page or online Word document. These elements function when a document is viewed in Word, as well as when a Web page is displayed in a browser.

You can add a movie clip or background sound using the Web Tools toolbar (shown in Figure 20-12). To display it, choose View, Toolbars, Web Tools, or choose Web Tools from the shortcut menu that appears when you right-click a toolbar.

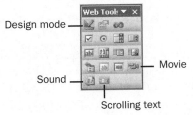

Design mode

Movie

Sound

Scrolling text

Figure 20-12. You can use the Web Tools toolbar to add various items to a Web page or online Word document.

A movie clip displays a video sequence, with sound, in a rectangular area in your page or document. To insert a movie clip, perform the following steps:

1 Click the Movie button on the Web Tools toolbar to open the Movie Clip dialog box (shown in Figure 20-13).

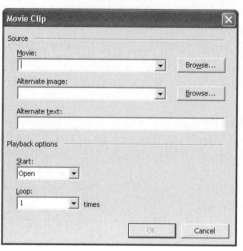

Figure 20-13. Use the Movie Clip dialog box to insert a movie clip into your Web page or online Word document.

2 Type the path of the file containing the movie clip into the Movie text box or click the adjoining Browse button to locate the file in the Open dialog box (which is a compact version of the standard Open dialog box for opening documents).

Note Movie clips are contained in files using a variety of different formats. The following are the standard file extensions for movie files in some of the formats that Word supports: .avi, .mov, .movie, .mp2, .mpeg, .mpg, and .qt.

3 If you wish, you can set or modify any of the following options in the Movie Clip dialog box:

- To have a browser display a static picture if movie clips aren't enabled, type the path of a graphics file into the Alternate Image text box or click the adjoining Browse button to locate the file. You should select a .gif or .jpeg graphic file.

- To have a browser display text if neither movie clips nor pictures are enabled, type the text into the Alternate Text box. Some browsers also display the alternate text while downloading the movie clip or if the clip is missing.

- To control *when* the movie clip is played, select an item in the Start drop-down list.

- To control *how many times* the movie clip is played each time it's started, select an item in the Loop drop-down list. Select Infinite to keep playing the movie clip continuously.

4 Click the OK button.

If you later want to modify a movie clip, right-click the clip in Word and choose Properties from the shortcut menu, or just double-click the clip to reopen the Movie Clip dialog box.

To play the movie clip in Word or in Internet Explorer at any time—in addition to the playing times you specified when you added the clip—right-click the clip and choose Play from the shortcut menu. To stop a movie clip from playing, right-click it and choose Stop.

> **Tip** **Make big movies optional**
> A movie clip in a Web page can take a long time to download over a slow Internet connection. To avoid forcing the reader to wait for a large movie clip to download, you can make viewing the movie optional by inserting a hyperlink to a movie clip file, rather than inserting the movie clip directly into the page as described in this section. Hyperlinks are discussed in "Adding and Using Hyperlinks," on page 580.

If you assign a background sound to a Web page or online Word document, Word or a browser will play that sound when you first open the file. To add a background sound, perform the following steps:

1   Click the Sound button on the Web Tools toolbar to open the Background Sound dialog box (shown in Figure 20-14).

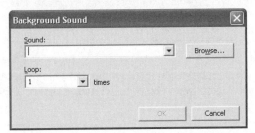

Figure 20-14.   Use the Background Sound dialog box to add a background sound to a Web page or online Word document.

2   Type the path of the file containing the sound you want to use as a background sound into the Sound text box or click the Browse button to locate the file using the Open dialog box.

> **Note**   Sounds are stored in files using a variety of different formats. The following are the standard file extensions for sound files in some of the formats that Word supports: .wav, .mid, .midi, .rmi, .au, .aif, .aiff, and .snd.

3   To control how many times the sound is played, select an item in the Loop drop-down list. Select Infinite to keep playing the sound continuously.

4   Click the OK button.

You can turn off the background sound while you work on a document in Word by switching on design mode. To turn design mode on or off, click the Design Mode button on the Web Tools toolbar.

Tip   **Use the Clip Organizer to add clips**

You can use the Microsoft Clip Organizer—through the Clip Art task pane or by running the freestanding Clip Organizer program—to insert a movie or sound clip. A sound clip is analogous to a movie clip. Adding a sound clip to your document displays a sound object, which you can double-click to play the sound. For instructions on using the Clip Organizer, see "Inserting Pictures with the Clip Organizer," on page 107.

When you add a movie or sound clip, Word inserts an embedded object or a control, which you can format using some of the methods discussed in "Modifying Graphic Objects," on page 142.

Troubleshooting

Can't remove a background sound

You want to remove a background sound from a Web page or online Word document but the Background Sound dialog box doesn't provide a control for removing the sound, and when you delete the contents of the Sound text box, the OK button is disabled.

When you add a background sound, Word inserts a control at the position of the insertion point, but formats it as hidden text so it's not normally visible. To remove the background sound, click the Show/Hide ¶ button on the Standard toolbar to temporarily display hidden text, click the background sound object (which displays a small image of a speaker), and press Delete to remove the object.

Adding Scrolling Text

You can use a *marquee,* a block of scrolling text that travels repeatedly across the width of your Web page or online Word document, to draw attention to a message. To insert scrolling text, click the Scrolling Text button on the Web Tools toolbar (shown in Figure 20-11) and enter the text and display options that you want into the Scrolling Text dialog box (shown in Figure 20-15).

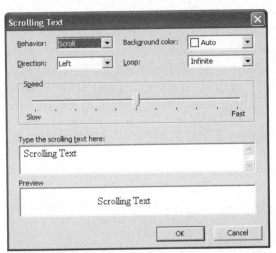

Figure 20-15. Add a marquee to a document using the Scrolling Text dialog box.

Creating Web Forms to Gather Information

A Web form is a collection of controls—such as check boxes, option buttons, lists, text boxes, and buttons—that allow you to collect information from readers of your online Word document or Web page. For example, you could add a form to a Web page that allows visitors to your site to sign up for a newsletter that you send out, to request information, or to enter their names and comments in a guest log.

To add a form to a document or Web page, perform the following steps:

1 Place the insertion point at the position in your document or page where you want to add the first form control.

2 Display the Web Tools toolbar (shown in Figure 20-16) by choosing View, Toolbars, Web Tools.

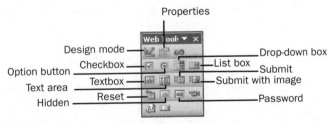

Figure 20-16. This figure labels the buttons on the Web Tools toolbar that are used for creating Web forms.

Chapter 20

3 Add the controls. To add each control, click the appropriate button on the Web Tools toolbar. When you add the first control, Word will do the following:

■ It will insert a top-of-form and a bottom-of-form boundary. Be sure to add all additional controls that belong to the form you're creating within these boundaries, as seen here:

■ It will switch into *design mode*, which lets you add or modify form controls. (When you're out of design mode, the controls will function as intended; for example, you'll be able to check a check box or enter text into a text box.) You can switch design mode off or on by clicking the Design Mode button on the Web Tools toolbar.

Be sure to add either a *submit button* (click the Submit button on the Web Tools toolbar) or a *submit image* (click the Submit With Image button). A submit button or image allows the user to send you the information that they've entered into the form.

In addition to adding controls to the form area, you can type any text you want for labeling the controls, providing instructions, or displaying other information. You can also add spaces and tabs and insert new paragraphs to arrange the controls.

4 Customize the controls as necessary. To customize a control, double-click it while you're in design mode and set the desired properties in the Properties dialog box.

For a submit button or a submit image, you must assign the Action property the URL of the custom program or script on the server that receives and processes the form information (consult your Web hosting service or webmaster about creating this program or script).

> **Note** For a description of each type of control and its properties, see the Word online help topic "Form controls you can use on a Web page."

5 When you're done creating the form, click the Design Mode button (now labeled Exit Design Mode) to return to normal editing mode.

Use Frames to View Several Documents at Once

You can show several documents simultaneously in the Word or Web browser window by displaying each document within a separate *frame*, which is an adjustable pane within the window.

> **Note** In Word, the term *frame* also refers to a seldom-used element for positioning text on a page, which is similar to a text box.

You can use the Frames submenu on the Format menu to create a document that displays frames (known as a *frames document* or *frames page*) or to add individual frames to such a document. And you can use the Frames toolbar to add or remove frames or to modify the properties of the frames document or of one or more frames. Note that you can use either the submenu or the toolbar to add a frame containing a table of contents, which lets the viewer select the document or document section that's displayed in another frame.

For detailed information on using frames in Word, see the Word online help topic "Frames and Frames Pages." For general information on frames and for instructions on creating them in Microsoft FrontPage, see "Using Frames to Display Multiple Pages," on page 1367.

Formatting Web Pages

Word provides the following formatting features that are especially useful for a Web page or an online Word document:

- A background color or pattern
- A theme

For information on general Word formatting techniques, see Chapter 12, "Effective Formatting in Word."

Applying a Background Color or Pattern

You can assign your Web page or online Word document a solid background color, a standard background pattern, or a background picture derived from a graphics file that you select, by choosing an option from the Format, Background submenu, shown here:

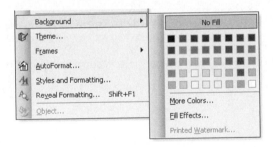

- To apply a standard, solid background color, choose one of the colors directly from the palette on the submenu.
- To select from a larger set of solid colors, or to create a custom solid color, choose More Colors.

- To apply a background pattern or picture, choose Fill Effects, which opens the Fill Effects dialog box. The first three tabs of this dialog box (Gradient, Texture, and Pattern) let you select from a large collection of standard background patterns. The fourth tab (Picture) lets you display a picture in the document background by selecting any graphics file.

- To remove a previously applied background, choose No Fill.

> **Note** A background color or pattern is shown only in Web Layout, Print Layout, or Reading Layout view or when a Web page is displayed in a browser.

Applying a Web Page Theme

You can modify the overall appearance of your Web page or online Word document by applying a *theme*, which is a predesigned visual scheme that applies a consistent look to elements throughout the document. You can choose from a list of almost 80 themes provided with Office 2003.

Applying a theme affects the following document elements:

- The font, size, color, and other features of text throughout the document. (The theme modifies text by changing features of the built-in Normal and Heading styles.)

- The page background. A theme might apply either a solid background color or a background pattern to the document. (Backgrounds are discussed in the previous section.)

- The images used for horizontal dividing lines and for bullets in bulleted lists.

- Hyperlink text colors (for both unfollowed and followed hyperlinks).

- The color of table borders.

To apply a theme to the current Web page or online Word document, perform the following steps:

1 Choose Format, Theme to open the Theme dialog box (shown in Figure 20-17).

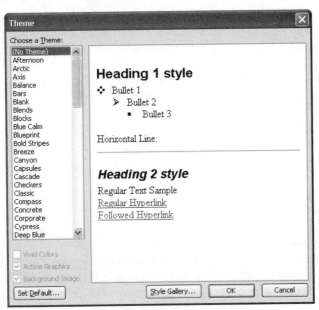

Figure 20-17. The Theme dialog box provides a collection of visual schemes that you can apply to Web pages.

2 Select the theme you want in the Choose A Theme list, or select (No Theme) to remove a previously applied theme.

The Sample area of the dialog box shows the visual effect of the selected theme and theme options.

3 Choose options, as follows:

- To apply bright colors to the document text, table borders, and background, check Vivid Colors.

- To display any animated pictures included with the theme, check Active Graphics.

- To display the background pattern included with the theme, check Background Image. (Clearing this option displays a solid background color rather than a pattern.)

- To use the selected theme as the default for all new Web pages you create in Word, click the Set Default button (this won't affect the new native-format Word documents you create).

Publishing Your Page

When you've finished creating your Web page, you need to *publish* it—that is, copy it to the appropriate folder on the computer on which your Web server is installed, so that the page will be available on the World Wide Web or on your company intranet.

You might be able to save the page in the appropriate Web server folder directly from Word. This may be possible, for instance, if the Web server folder is on your computer, if it's on your network, if it's on an FTP (File Transfer Protocol) site where you have the required permissions, or if it's on a Web site on which Microsoft server extensions (such as SharePoint Team Services) have been installed.

For information on saving files to each of these locations, see "Saving Office Documents," on page 69.

If you can't publish your Web page directly from Word, you'll have to post it to the Web server using an FTP utility or service (such as the FTP service provided by Microsoft Internet Explorer), or by other means. Use the method that your Web hosting service, company webmaster, or network administrator recommends.

Creating, Editing, and Viewing XML Documents

XML (Extensible Markup Language) is currently the most popular emerging format for storing and exchanging structured data, primarily on the Internet. Unlike proprietary data formats, such as the native Word document format or the Access native database format, XML is universal, open, nonproprietary, and uses plain text. Although HTML is a suitable language for representing traditional Web pages (described previously in this chapter), it has a limited capacity for storing structured data. In contrast, an XML document labels each piece of information and clearly shows the data's hierarchical structure. Therefore, a program written to process an XML document can sort, filter, search, and manipulate that information in highly flexible ways.

As an example, the following is a very simple XML document that stores, labels, and shows the structure of the information needed to describe a book:

```xml
<?xml version="1.0"?>
<!-- File Name: Book.xml -->
<BOOK InStock="true" xmlns="urn:schemas-mjyonline-com.book">
    <TITLE>The Marble Faun</TITLE>
    <AUTHOR>Nathaniel Hawthorne</AUTHOR>
    <BINDING>trade paperback</BINDING>
    <PAGES>473</PAGES>
    <PRICE>10.95</PRICE>
</BOOK>
```

 Note You'll find a copy of this XML document on the book's companion CD under the filename Book.xml.

Note that an XML document normally has the .xml filename extension.

An XML document contains a collection of *elements*, which are marked using *tags*. The element at the root of the example document is BOOK, which is marked with the `<BOOK InStock="true">` start-tag and the `</BOOK>` end-tag. The elements storing the individual pieces of information on the book (TITLE, AUTHOR, BINDING, PAGES, and PRICE) are nested inside the BOOK element to indicate that these pieces of information belong to the book. In addition to the element's name, the start-tag of an element may also contain one or more attribute settings, such as `InStock="true"` in the BOOK element's start-tag (this attribute setting indicates that this particular book is in stock). Assigning a value to an attribute is simply another way to attach information to a particular XML element—in addition to placing text and nested elements within the element.

> **Note** The `xmlns="urn:schemas-mjyonline-com.book"` expression in the BOOK start-tag of the example XML document assigns all elements to a default *namespace*. Placing an element within a namespace qualifies the element's name so that it doesn't conflict with identically named elements that are in other namespaces (or in no namespace).

Although the XML standard specifies the overall syntax of a document, it *doesn't* specify the particular element names you may use or the types of information the elements may contain. If you were writing a document to describe a book, you could have chosen entirely different names (for example, ITEM and NAME rather than BOOK and TITLE). Because XML allows you to create your own elements, attributes, and document structure, you can use it to describe virtually any kind of information—from a simple recipe to a complex business database. (In contrast, HTML has a fixed set of available elements, which are suitable only for describing a fairly typical Web page.)

If, however, a group of people are using XML for a specific purpose (perhaps to describe books or auto parts), it can be important for them to all follow the same conventions in naming and structuring their documents. One way to specify a particular set of allowed elements, the required order of the elements, and the types of information that each element may contain, is to write a document known as a *schema* (which is itself a type of XML document and normally has the .xsd filename extension). For example, the following schema specifies a set of rules for creating a document that stores book information:

```
<?xml version="1.0"?>
<!-- File Name: Book.xsd -->
<xsd:schema xmlns:xsd=http://www.w3.org/2001/XMLSchema
            targetNamespace="urn:schemas-mjyonline-com.book"
            elementFormDefault="qualified">
   <xsd:element name="BOOK">
      <xsd:complexType>
         <xsd:sequence>
            <xsd:element name="TITLE" type="xsd:string"/>
            <xsd:element name="AUTHOR" type="xsd:string"/>
            <xsd:element name="BINDING" type="xsd:string"/>
            <xsd:element name="PAGES" type="xsd:positiveInteger"/>
            <xsd:element name="PRICE" type="xsd:decimal"/>
         </xsd:sequence>
         <xsd:attribute name="InStock" type="xsd:boolean"
            use="required"/>
      </xsd:complexType>
   </xsd:element>
</xsd:schema>
```

Note You'll find a copy of this schema on the book's companion CD under the filename Book.xsd.

Explaining the workings of schemas (which can be quite complex) is well beyond the scope of this book. In general terms, however, this particular schema says that a conforming XML document must contain a root element named BOOK. The BOOK element must contain, in the order listed, TITLE, AUTHOR, BINDING, PAGES, and PRICE elements, as well as an attribute named *InStock*. The PAGES element must contain a positive integer, the *InStock* attribute must be assigned a Boolean value (*true* or *false*), and all other nested elements may contain any text. The example XML document given previously conforms to this schema and is therefore known as a *valid* XML document. (A document that conforms to the general syntax rules of the XML specification but doesn't necessarily conform to a schema is termed *well-formed*.)

To display an XML document or to use its data for another purpose, it's often necessary to convert the document into another format. You can specify a blueprint for converting a particular type of XML document by writing a document known as a *transform*. Like a schema, a transform is also written in XML. It conforms to a standard known as Extensible Stylesheet Language Transformations, or XSLT, and is also known as an *XSLT style sheet*. A transform document normally has the .xsl or .xslt filename extension. Often, a Web page script uses a transform to convert an XML document to HTML that's displayed in the browser.

Note For a comprehensive general introduction to XML, see *XML Step by Step, Second Edition* (Michael J. Young, Microsoft Press, 2002). This book explains how to write well-formed and valid XML documents and how to display XML documents on the Web. It includes complete instructions for writing XML schemas and transforms.

Creating XML Documents in Word

Word now allows you to create and edit XML documents. You can do this in two different ways. First, you can save any Word document as an XML document that conforms to Word's built-in schema. Second, you can use Word as a general-purpose XML editor to create a custom XML document that conforms to any schema that you supply. These two approaches are described in the following two sections.

Note that an XML document that you create in Word is not as immediately usable as a Web page that you create according the instructions given previously in this chapter. You can simply copy a Web page to a server, and users can immediately begin viewing it in a browser. In contrast, an XML document is typically part of a more complex solution. For instance, even just displaying an XML document in a browser normally requires writing a style sheet or Web page script. Although developing complete XML solutions in Office is beyond the scope of this book, the Word user or power user may need to create, edit, or display XML documents while working with XML solutions that have already been developed. Therefore, this chapter covers these essential techniques.

Saving a Word Document in XML Format

To save the active Word document as an XML document, perform the following steps:

1 Choose File, Save As to open the Save As dialog box.

2 Select XML Document (*.xml) in the Save As Type drop-down list.

3 Make sure that the Save Data Only option is *not* checked.

4 Enter a document name and click the Save button. Either include the .xml extension in the filename you type or omit the extension (Word will then append this extension).

When you save a document using these instructions, Word converts the active document to an XML document that conforms to Word's built-in schema, which is known as WordML (or Word Markup Language). The XML document stores all document features (such as tracked changes and comments) and formatting. You can later reopen the document and continue editing it, without loss of features or formatting, just as if you had saved the document in native Word .doc format.

> **Note** If you have a transform for converting a particular XML document to a different format, you can have Word apply that transform when you save the document by checking the Apply Transform option in the Save As dialog box, clicking the Transform button, and selecting the transform file in the Choose An XSL Transformation dialog box.

Creating and Editing Custom XML Documents

You can create a custom XML document that conforms to any schema that you have. For example, if you had the example XML schema shown previously, you could use it to create a conforming XML document that describes a book. The following is the basic procedure:

1 Choose File, New to display the New Document task pane.

2 In the New Document task pane, click the XML Document command in the New area. Word will then open a blank XML document and display the XML Structure task pane.

3 In the XML Structure task pane, click the Templates And Add-Ins command. (Initially, that will be the only command in the task pane.) Word will then open the Templates And Add-Ins dialog box.

4 In the XML Schema tab of the Templates And Add-Ins dialog box, click the Add Schema button and select your schema file in the Add Schema dialog box and click the Open button. Word will then display the Schema Settings dialog box, where you can enter an *alias* for your schema (that is, a "friendly" name, such as Book Schema, which will appear in the XML Structure task pane). When you click the OK button in the Schema Settings dialog box, Word will add the schema you select to the Available XML Schemas list in the XML Schema tab.

Note Supplying an alias is optional. If you don't supply one, Word will identify the schema using its *URN* (Uniform Resource Name). A URN is an address that uniquely identifies an Internet resource. To ensure uniqueness, a URN typically includes a value such as a registered domain name or book ISBN.

A schema's URN is the value that is assigned to the targetNamespace attribute of the root schema element. (In the example book schema given previously in this chapter, I assigned a URN based on my domain name, urn:schemas-mjyonline-com.book.)

If the schema you are attempting to add doesn't have a URN (that is, it lacks a target-Namespace attribute setting), you'll need to enter a URN into the URN text box when Word displays the Schema Settings dialog box.

5   In the Available XML Schemas list in the XML Schema tab, make sure that the box next to the name of the schema you just added is checked and click the OK button. Word will then attach the schema to the new document and, within the XML Structure task pane, it will display the tools you need to add elements to the document (see Figure 20-18).

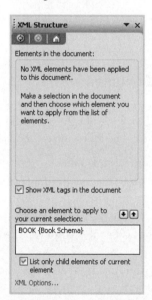

Figure 20-18.   This figure shows the XML Structure task pane as it would initially appear if the example schema given earlier in the chapter were attached to a new XML document.

6   Enter the XML document elements and the data contained in each element as follows. (To see some of these features, you can look ahead at Figure 20-19, which shows a completed XML document).

   ■   To insert the tags for a particular element (such as BOOK in the example XML document given above) at the position of the insertion point, click the element name in the Choose An Element To Apply To Your Current Selection list at the bottom of the XML Structure task pane. Then, between the element's start-tag and end-tag, type the element's text or insert nested elements.

- To insert element tags around text you've already typed into the document, select the text and then click the element name in the Choose An Element To Apply To Your Current Selection list. (For an alternative way to insert element tags, see the Tip later in this section.)

- To make the structure of the XML document easy to see, you can freely insert new paragraphs between elements and indent elements using tabs or spaces.

- To see the XML tags in the document, make sure that the Show XML Tags In The Document option is checked in the XML Structure task pane. The Ctrl+Shift+X keystroke toggles this option off and on. (To see the tags on a printed version of the document, choose Tools, Options, click the Print tab, and make sure the XML Tags option is checked.)

- If you want Word to make available only those elements that are legal (according to the attached schema) at the current position of the insertion point or selection, make sure that the List Only Child Elements Of Current Element option is checked.

- To supply an attribute value for an element, right-click the element's start-tag in the document and choose Attributes from the shortcut menu.

Tip An alternative way to insert element tags is to right-click a position in the document or a block of selected text and choose the element name from the Apply XML Element submenu on the shortcut menu.

Figure 20-19 shows a completed XML document. The example schema given previously is attached to this document, and the document conforms to this schema. Notice that the Elements In The Document list in the XML Structure task pane shows the hierarchical structure of the elements that have been added to the document. If some element doesn't conform to the attached schema (which is known as a *validity error*), Word displays a yellow error symbol to the left of the element's name. To see an error description in a ScreenTip, move the mouse pointer over the error symbol.

Note To have Word flag validity errors, the Validate Document Against Attached Schemas option must be checked. To set this option, as well as other options that affect creating and editing XML documents, choose Tools, Templates And Add-Ins, and click the XML Schema tab. To access additional XML options, you can either click the XML Options button in the XML Schema tab or click the XML Options command at the bottom of the XML Structure task pane.

Chapter 20

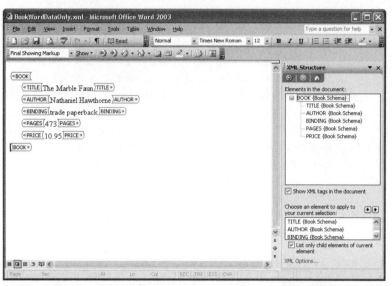

Figure 20-19. This figure shows a completed XML document. The example schema given previously is attached to this document.

7 Save your XML document by choosing File, Save As. Make sure that XML Document (*.xml) is selected in the Save As Type drop-down list. Before clicking the Save button, specify the way the document is to be saved as follows:

■ To save only the XML elements shown on the screen and the text that's contained in these elements, discarding all other content, formatting, and Word features such as change marking, check the Save Data Only option. When this option is checked, Word will generate a "pure" XML document that conforms only to the schema that you attached to the document. You'll need to select this option if the XML document is going to be processed using software that expects the document to conform to the attached schema. You'll find a copy of the example XML document saved as data only on the book's companion CD, under the filename BookWordDataOnly.xml.

■ To save the visible XML elements and the text they contain, as well as all other text, graphics, formatting, and Word features, clear the Save Data Only option. In this case Word will generate a document that conforms to its built-in WordML schema. You'll be able to reopen the document in Word without loss of content, formatting, or features. However, because the document as a whole won't conform to the attached schema (only the text you inserted into visible XML elements will conform to the attached schema), the document might not be suitable for processing with software other than Word. You'll find a copy of the example XML document saved as a WordML XML document on the book's companion CD, under the filename BookWordML.xml.

Chapter 20

You can open any XML document for editing in Word using the File, Open command. The way this works depends on the type of the XML document, as follows:

- If the document was saved from Word using its WordML schema (that is, the Save Data Only option was cleared when the document was saved), Word will reopen the document, displaying all its original content, formatting, and features and reattaching the original schema. You can then edit the document using the XML Structure task pane, as described previously.

- If the document was saved from Word as "pure" XML (that is, the Save Data Only option was checked when the document was saved) or if the document wasn't created in Word, Word will open the document and display the XML Document task pane, which lets you choose the way the document is viewed (but only if one or more transforms were attached to the document's schema, as described in the following sidebar, "Using Transforms to View an XML Document"). To edit the document, open the XML Structure task pane (you can do this by choosing XML Structure from the drop-down menu at the top of any task pane). If possible, Word will attach the appropriate schema to the document. If Word doesn't attach a schema (evidenced by the fact that element names don't appear in the Choose An Element To Apply To Your Current Selection list in the XML Structure task pane), choose Tools, Templates And Add-Ins, click the XML Schema tab, and attach a schema as explained in step 4 of the previous procedure. (If you don't attach a schema, Word will offer little help in editing the document.)

Chapter 20

Using Transforms to View an XML Document

You can assign one or more custom transforms to a schema that's stored in Word's Schema Library. (You work with the Schema Library by clicking the Schema Library button in the XML Schema tab of the Templates And Add-Ins dialog box, described earlier.) A transform is one type of "solution" that you can assign to a schema in the Schema Library. The purpose of such a transform is to convert a "pure" (non-WordML) XML document to a full-featured WordML document, adding the text, graphics, or formatting that's needed to effectively display the document in Word. When you open a "pure" XML document in Word, if one or more custom transforms have been assigned to the document's schema, Word will display these transforms in the XML Document task pane, where they are known as *views*. For instance, an XML document for a résumé might have three transforms available, perhaps named Contemporary, Elegant, and Professional. Selecting one of these transforms would display the document using Word formatting features and perhaps additional text or graphics, each in a different way.

You can also have Word use a transform to convert the format of an XML document when you open it. To do this, rather than clicking the Open button in the Open dialog box, click the down arrow next to the Open button and choose Open With Transform from the drop-down menu.

Part 4

Excel

21 Excel Fundamentals   605

22 Advanced Worksheet Editing   627

23 Expert Formatting Techniques   647

24 Power Organizing with Workbooks   679

25 Customizing Excel to Work
    the Way You Do   705

26 Crunching Numbers with Formulas
    and Functions   727

27 Advanced Worksheet Charts   747

28 Power Database Techniques: Lists,
    Filters, and PivotTables   771

29 Advanced Business Analysis   805

30 Publishing on the Web and Working
    with XML in Excel   823

Chapter 21

Excel Fundamentals

Starting Excel and Getting
Comfortable 605
Entering Information 611

Inserting Hyperlinks 622
Saving the Workbook 626

Microsoft Office Excel 2003 is a general-purpose electronic spreadsheet used to organize, calculate, and analyze data. The tasks you can perform with Excel range from preparing a simple invoice for your house-painting service or planning a budget for a family vacation to creating elaborate 3-D charts or managing a complex accounting ledger for a medium-sized business. This part of the book introduces Excel and teaches you how to accomplish a variety of tasks with the newest version of Microsoft's flagship spreadsheet application. You'll receive training and support for virtually all your Excel needs, from creating a simple worksheet to forecasting expenses, publishing spreadsheets on the Web, and importing or exporting XML data using any schema. Along the way, you'll learn how to use Excel's newest features and how to customize Excel to work the way you do. We'll also share our favorite Excel productivity tips, including several that come directly from the Excel development team.

This introductory chapter gives you a quick tour of the Excel workplace and shows you how to build a simple worksheet from start to finish. A *worksheet* is the main component of an Excel document. (As explained later, an Excel document can contain one or more worksheets and is known as a *workbook*.) A worksheet contains rows and columns of information that can be formatted, sorted, analyzed, and charted. Building a worksheet involves starting Excel, entering information, adding formulas, and saving your data. If you want to get fancy, you can even add hyperlinks to your worksheet to access supporting files on your hard disk or on the Internet.

For a description of the new features included in Excel 2003, see "New Excel Features," on page 13.

Starting Excel and Getting Comfortable

You start Excel like you start most programs in the Microsoft Office System; click the Start button on the taskbar, and then choose All Programs (or Programs), Microsoft Office, Microsoft Office Excel 2003 (the icon is shown here).

Microsoft Office Excel 2003

When Excel first starts, it displays a new, empty workbook (which will be defined shortly) in the application workplace. Figure 21-1 shows the default opening Excel screen, featuring many of the common window elements for Office applications: a standard menu bar, toolbars, a task pane, a formula bar, and a status bar. The application window has been maximized to display all the elements of the Excel user interface. If your application window doesn't appear maximized when you start it, you can click the Maximize sizing button on the Excel title bar to give you more space to work with.

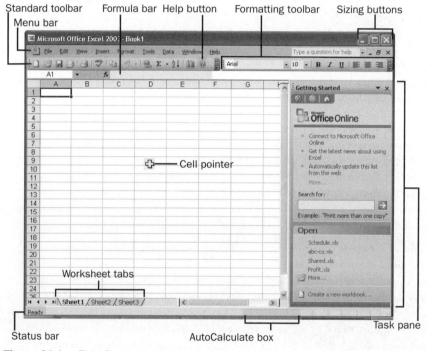

Figure 21-1. This figure labels some of the important features of the Excel user interface.

Tip Display other toolbars

To display other toolbars—or to hide toolbars that appear by default—point to the toolbar region with your mouse and click the right mouse button. The checked items are toolbars that are currently displayed. Select an unchecked item from the list to display the associated toolbar; select a checked item to hide the associated toolbar.

Like most Office applications, the Excel application window also contains *sizing buttons* you can use to minimize, maximize, restore, and close windows, plus a *status bar* that shows the state of various keyboard keys, including Num Lock. A special feature of the Excel status bar is the *AutoCalculate box*, which displays the result of the selected function (Sum by default) using the highlighted cells in the active worksheet. (To use a different function, right-click the AutoCalculate box and choose a function from the shortcut menu.) To get additional help with the Excel interface or with any Excel command, click the Microsoft Excel Help button on the right end of the Standard toolbar. This will display the new Microsoft Excel Help task pane.

Troubleshooting

Installation revisited

When you start Excel, errors surface that point to missing program components.

In this chapter, we assume that Excel is installed and ready to go on your computer. If Excel displays an error message or notes a problem when you start it, try evaluating and repairing your software with the Detect And Repair command on the Help menu. For more information, see "Revisiting Office Setup," on page 22.

For more information about using menus, dialog boxes, toolbars, and application windows, see Chapter 4, "Working with Office 2003 Applications, Documents, and Program Windows." For more details about starting and configuring the Office Assistant, see Chapter 3, "Getting Expert Help on Office 2003."

When you first open Excel, the default workbook (Book1) appears on the screen and displays the first worksheet (Sheet1). A worksheet is divided into a grid of rows and columns, as shown in Figure 21-1. (An Excel worksheet can contain up to 65,536 rows and 256 columns.) A letter is assigned to each column of the worksheet, and a number is assigned to each row. The intersection of each row and column is a worksheet *cell*, which is identified by a *cell reference*. For example, the cell at the intersection of column A and row 1 is known by the cell reference A1.

For information about managing the worksheets in a workbook and opening additional workbooks, see Chapter 24, "Power Organizing with Workbooks."

A *workbook* is an Excel document, which contains a collection of one or more worksheets, plus (optionally) chart sheets containing graphic pictures of your worksheet data. You can also store special macros in Visual Basic modules in the workbook, but they aren't listed among the worksheets.

> For information on working with macros, see "Recording and Running Macros," on page 224. For instructions on writing macros from scratch using the VBA (Visual Basic for Applications) programming language, see Part 10 of this book, "Customizing Office 2003 Using VBA."

At the bottom of the workbook window are tabs that give you instant access to the remaining worksheets in the workbook. Excel allows you to name your worksheets, add new worksheets, or delete blank or obsolete worksheets. Each workbook window contains scroll bars you can use to move from one worksheet to the next or from place to place in the active worksheet.

Navigating a Worksheet

To create a typical Excel worksheet, you'll store information in dozens or even hundreds of cells. Each time you enter information in a cell, you must first move to the cell to make it the *active cell*. Accordingly, you need to be comfortable with several methods for moving around in, or *navigating*, a worksheet.

To activate a cell, you can press the arrow keys (the Up, Down, Left, and Right arrow keys), or you can click the cell you want to activate with the mouse. This is called *selecting* or *highlighting* a cell. The reference of the selected cell appears in the Name box, as shown in Figure 21-2. Also notice that when you first move the mouse pointer onto the worksheet, it changes its shape to the *cell pointer*. You can use the cell pointer to select individual cells or ranges of cells, as you'll learn later in this chapter.

> A cell or range of cells can also be identified using a meaningful *name*, such as GrandTotal or PriceList. Working with names is discussed in "Using Names in Functions," on page 742.)

To view part of a worksheet that isn't currently visible in the workbook window, you can click the vertical or horizontal scroll bar. Each time you click a scroll arrow at the top or bottom of the vertical scroll bar, the active worksheet scrolls vertically one row. Each time you click a scroll arrow at the left or right end of the horizontal scroll bar, the active worksheet scrolls horizontally one column. Note that when you scroll with the scroll bars, you change only your view of the worksheet—scrolling moves the screen but doesn't change the active cell. Your relative position in the worksheet is identified by the size and position of the scroll boxes in each scroll bar. These boxes change size as your worksheet changes size, representing the relative portion of the entire worksheet that's currently visible.

> **Tip** If you scroll far from the active cell so that it's no longer visible, you can redisplay the active cell by pressing Ctrl+Backspace, as noted in Table 21-1.

Chapter 21

Cell pointer
Active cell
Name box showing active cell

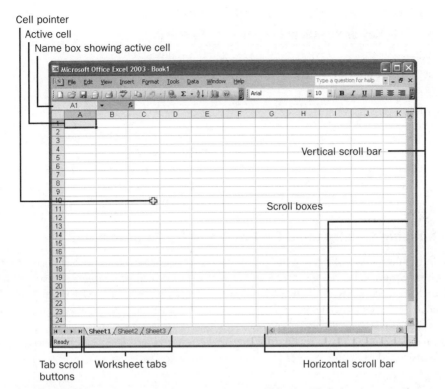

Figure 21-2. Use the cell pointer to select a cell in the worksheet or use the scroll bars to move to cells not currently visible.

To move among the worksheets in your workbook, you can click the worksheet tabs. If necessary, first use the tab scroll buttons to display worksheet tabs that are not visible because of limited space. Be careful not to confuse the tab scroll buttons with the buttons for the horizontal scroll bar.

Using the Keyboard

Several key combinations let you move quickly throughout your worksheet. Unlike scroll bar movements, these key combinations also select a new active cell. Table 21-1 lists the most useful keyboard navigation keys in a worksheet.

Table 21-1. Useful Worksheet Navigation Keys

Use This Key or Key Combination	To Move
↑ ,↓, →←	To the next cell in the direction pressed
Ctrl+↑ , Ctrl+↓, Ctrl+→ Ctrl+←	To the next cell containing data (the next non-blank cell) in the direction pressed
Home	To column A of current row
Page Up	Up one screen

Table 21-1. Useful Worksheet Navigation Keys

Use This Key or Key Combination	To Move
Page Down	Down one screen
Alt+Page Up	One screen to the left
Alt+Page Down	One screen to the right
Ctrl+Home	To cell A1
Ctrl+End	To the cell in the last row and last column that contains data
Ctrl+Backspace	To reposition the visible portion of the worksheet to display the active cell or selected ranges that have scrolled out of view

Jumping to a Specific Cell with the Go To Command

To highlight a specific cell in the active worksheet by reference, you can choose Edit, Go To or press either Ctrl+G or F5. When you choose the Go To command, Excel displays the Go To dialog box, as shown in Figure 21-3. You can jump to a specific cell by typing the cell's reference in the Reference text box and clicking the OK button. You can also double-click the reference of the cell if it appears in the Go To list. (If you have assigned a name to a cell, such as Salary or SalesTax, you can enter or double-click its name. Assigning names to cells or ranges is discussed in "Using Names in Functions," on page 742.)

If you'd like to highlight a range of cells based on a special attribute, such as all the cells containing formulas or comments, click the Special button in the Go To dialog box and specify the cell contents you're interested in.

Figure 21-3. The Go To dialog box lets you jump instantly to the cell you specify.

> **Tip**   Notice that the cell reference of the active cell appears in the Name box, which is located to the left of the formula bar. You can also move to a specific cell by clicking the Name box, typing the cell's reference, and pressing Enter (see Figure 21-2).

Entering Information

Excel lets you enter the following types of information into a worksheet cell:

- Numeric values, such as the numbers 22,000, $29.95, and 33%
- Text values, such as the words *Total*, *1st Quarter*, and *1820 Warren Avenue*
- Dates and times, such as Feb-97, 11/19/63, or 1:00 P.M.
- Comments to yourself or others, such as *This region leads in sales*, or an appropriate recorded sound or voice message
- Formulas, such as =B5*1.081 or =SUM(B3:B7)
- Hyperlinks to Internet sites or other documents
- Electronic artwork, such as clip art, scanned photographs, maps, and illustrations

Each kind of information has its own formatting characteristics, meaning that Excel stores and displays each entry type differently. The following sections show you how to enter these values into a worksheet.

Entering Numeric Values

To enter a number in a cell, select the cell you want by using the mouse or keyboard, type the number, and press Enter. Selecting, or highlighting, a cell makes it the active cell. Then, as you type, the number appears simultaneously in the active cell and on the *formula bar* above the worksheet.

The formula bar serves as an editing scratch pad. If you make a mistake entering a long cell entry, you can click within the formula bar to move the insertion point and then correct the mistake without having to retype the entire entry. Conveniently, you can also double-click the active cell, and then move the insertion point within the cell to edit your entry. To the left of the formula bar is a Cancel button, which you can click to discard an unwanted entry on the formula bar (if you haven't already accepted the entry by pressing Enter). Alongside the Cancel button is an Enter button, which you can click to accept or *lock in* a revised entry. See Figure 21-4.

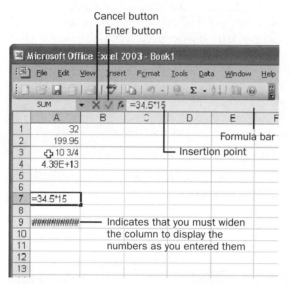

Cancel button
Enter button

Formula bar

Insertion point

9 ########## — Indicates that you must widen the column to display the numbers as you entered them

Figure 21-4. New values appear both on the formula bar and in the cell when you enter them.

A numeric value can be an integer (such as 32), a decimal number (such as 499.95), an integer fraction (such as 10 3/4), or a number in scientific notation (such as 4.09E+13). You can use several mathematical symbols in numbers, including plus (+), minus (–), percent (%), fraction (/), and exponent (E), as well as the dollar sign ($). If you enter a number that's too large to fit into a cell, Excel will automatically widen the cell to accommodate the number or adjust its display of the number by using scientific notation or by showing fewer decimal places. If Excel displays the number in scientific notation or places a row of number signs (#######) in the cell, you'll need to increase the column width manually to see the number in its entirety.

Troubleshooting

Avoid misinterpretation of a fraction

When you enter a fraction, a date appears in the cell.

When you use a slash to create a fraction in a numeric entry, be sure to include a leading zero (0) and a space if the fractional value is less than 1. If you don't, Excel will interpret your fraction as a date. For example, Excel interprets the fraction 3/4 as the date March 4 unless you enter the fraction as 0 3/4. You'll learn more about date and time formatting in Chapter 23, "Expert Formatting Techniques."

Excel always internally stores the actual number you typed, no matter how it appears in the cell, and you can view this *underlying value* on the formula bar whenever the cell is active. By default, numeric values are aligned to the right edge of a cell.

> **Tip** **Use arrow keys to move from cell to cell**
>
> If you plan to enter additional numbers, you can use the arrow keys to enter a number and move to a new cell in one step. For instance, if you type a number and press the Down arrow key, the cell pointer will move down one line. The Left, Up, and Right arrow keys will move the pointer one cell left, up, or right.

Entering Text Values

To enter a text value in a cell, select the cell, type your text, and press Enter. A text value, or *label*, can be any combination of alphanumeric characters, including uppercase and lowercase letters, numbers, and symbols. Excel recognizes text values and aligns them to the left margin of each cell. If no information appears in adjacent cells, Excel allows longer text entries to overlap the cells on the right. If the adjacent cells do contain information, the display of the text is cut off, or truncated; however, just as with a truncated value, Excel correctly stores the full text internally, and you can see it on the formula bar when the cell is active.

> For details about changing column widths to make room for more information in cells, see "Changing Column Widths and Row Heights," on page 662.

If you want Excel to store as text a value such as a numeric address, date, or part number, precede the value with a single quotation mark. For example, if you enter '55 in a cell, the number 55 will appear left-aligned in the cell (without the quotation mark). A quotation mark will appear on the formula bar to identify the number as a text value.

 Numeric values that are inadvertently stored as text can be troublesome, especially if they are expected to behave as numbers in formulas. To flag a cell that contains this type of value, Excel's background error checking feature displays a small triangular error indicator in the cell's upper left corner, and when the cell is activated it shows an error button next to the cell. To see a description of the possible error, activate the cell and place the mouse pointer over the error button, as shown here:

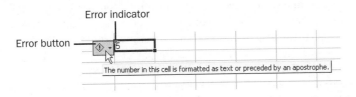

Error indicator

Error button

The number in this cell is formatted as text or preceded by an apostrophe.

To have Excel stop flagging that cell, click the error button and choose Ignore Error from the shortcut menu, as seen on the next page. You can also use this shortcut menu to convert the entry to a number or perform other actions.

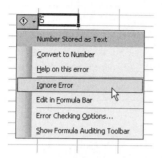

Background error checking is part of Excel's error checking feature, which is described in "Checking for Common Errors," on page 645.

Figure 21-5 shows several examples of text entries: a cell that has overlapping text, a few cells that have truncated text, and several numeric text entries (that is, numbers stored internally as text).

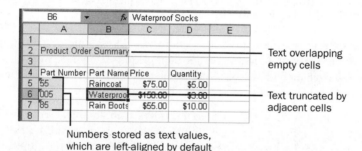

Figure 21-5. Text values are left-aligned and can overlap adjacent empty cells.

Tip   Speed up your work with AutoComplete

If Excel recognizes the pattern you're typing when you enter a sequence of characters, it will attempt to complete the pattern using a feature called *AutoComplete*. AutoComplete can be a major time saver if you manage lists in Excel or find that you're entering the same values or functions over and over again. If you use the AutoComplete feature while entering data, review the characters Excel inserts and if they make sense to you, press Enter and move on.

For information about turning off AutoComplete, see "Customizing Editing Options," on page 723.

Entering Dates and Times

If you want to store a date or a time in a worksheet cell, you should use one of Excel's pre-defined date and time formats to enter the value so that Excel will recognize the number as a chronological entity and apply appropriate formatting. (Internally, Excel stores identifiable dates and times as *serial numbers*, counters that commence with January 1, 1900. In this form the dates and times are easier to use in functions and formulas.) As you'll learn in Chapter 23, "Expert Formatting Techniques," Excel lets you specify the format of times and dates with a few simple commands.

> **Tip**   To enter the current date in the active cell, press Ctrl+; (the semicolon key). Excel will use the format *m/d/yyyy* for the date.

Table 21-2 shows you some of the time and date formats Excel supports. Date formats with a four-digit placeholder for the current year (the patterns *m/d/yyyy* and *d-mmm-yyyy*) are included to help manage the year 2000 problem. This confusion arises in spreadsheets and accounting ledgers when the century portion of a numeric entry is recorded ambiguously. (For example, the date 3/14/02 could be read as March 14, 1902 or March 14, 2002.) As a rule Excel treats a date with a two-digit year as belonging to the twenty-first century if it precedes 1/1/30; subsequent dates entered in this form fall in the twentieth century. To clarify which century you mean, use one of the new four-digit-year date formats.

Table 21-2. Popular Date and Time Formats Supported by Excel

Format	Pattern	Example
Date	m/d/yy	10/1/99
Date	d-mmm-yy	1-Oct-99
Date	d-mmm	1-Oct
Date	mmm-yy	Oct-99
Date (four-digit year)	m/d/yyyy	10/1/1999
Date (four-digit year)	d-mmm-yyyy	1-Oct-2002
Time	h:mm AM/PM	10:22 PM
Time	h:mm:ss AM/PM	10:22:30 PM
Time	h:mm	22:22
Time	h:mm:ss	22:22:30
Time	mm:ss.0	22:30.3
Combined	m/d/yy h:mm	10/1/99 22:22

Figure 21-6 shows working examples of the most popular date and time formats and the procedure to enter them. You can change the format of a date or time in the active cell by choosing Format, Cells, clicking the Number tab, and then choosing a different pattern in the Date or Time category.

	A	B	C	D
1	Entered: 4/1/03	Entered: 10:15 PM	Entered: 4/1/03 10:15 PM	
2				
3	**Date Formats**	**Time Formats**	**Combined**	
4	4/1/2003	10:15 PM	4/1/2003 22:15	
5	1-Apr-03	10:15:00 PM	4/1/03 10:15 PM	
6	1-Apr	22:15		
7	Apr-03	22:15:00		
8	April 1, 2003	15:00.0		
9	1-Apr-2003			
10				

TimeDateDemo.xls

Figure 21-6. You can enter time and date values in one of these popular formats.

 You'll find a copy of this workbook on the book's companion CD, under the filename Time-DateDemo.xls.

> For information about changing the format of date and time values, see "Changing Number Formats," on page 651.

Entering Comments

If you plan to share your Excel worksheets with other users, you might want to annotate a few important cells by using *comments* to provide instructions or to highlight critical information. You can add a pop-up comment to a cell by selecting the cell and choosing Insert, Comment. Excel will open a pop-up text box that contains your name and displays an arrow pointing to the associated cell. Type a short note in the text box, as illustrated in Figure 21-7. When you're finished typing the comment text, click another cell to lock in the comment.

> **Tip** To change the name that appears when you enter a comment, choose Tools, Options, click the General tab, and change the name in the User Name text box.

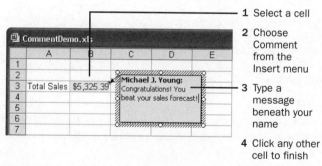

1 Select a cell

2 Choose Comment from the Insert menu

3 Type a message beneath your name

4 Click any other cell to finish

Figure 21-7. The Comment command allows you to add a descriptive note to a cell.

The presence of a comment is indicated by a tiny red triangle in the upper right corner of a cell. To display a comment in a worksheet, hold the mouse pointer over the annotated cell until a pop-up comment box appears. Remember that because comments are cell annotations, they exist in *addition* to the other entries in cells—they don't *replace* them. To delete an existing comment, select the cell containing the comment in the worksheet and choose Edit, Clear, Comments.

Managing Comments

You can view all the comments in your workbook by selecting the Comments option on the View menu. When the Comments option is selected, all the comments in your workbook will appear in pop-up windows; when it's deselected, a comment will appear only when you move the mouse pointer over the cell in which it resides. The Selecting the Comments menu option also displays the Reviewing toolbar, which contains a number of useful command buttons. To edit an existing comment, click the cell containing the comment and then click the Edit Comment button on the Reviewing toolbar, or right-click the cell containing the comment that needs editing and choose Edit Comment from the shortcut menu.

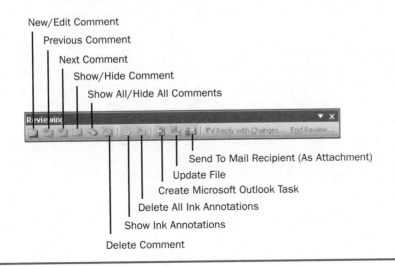

Working with Ink Annotations

If you are using a Tablet PC computer, you can add ink annotations to an Excel 2003 workbook. Although without a Tablet PC, you won't be able to add or edit ink annotations, you'll be able to view or remove ink annotations that you or a co-worker previously added to the document using a Table PC.

To show or hide ink annotations in the workbook, click the Show Ink Annotations or the Hide Ink Annotations button on the Reviewing toolbar, described and shown in the previous sidebar, "Managing Comments."

To remove all ink annotations from the workbook, click the Delete All Ink Annotations button on the Reviewing toolbar.

Entering Formulas

A *formula* is an equation that calculates a new value from existing values. Excel lets you enter a formula in a cell and display the calculated result in your worksheet. For example, a simple formula could calculate the total cost of an item by adding its price, sales tax, and shipping costs.

Formulas can contain numbers, mathematical operators, cell references, and built-in *functions,* which calculate and return values. One of Excel's great strengths is its vast collection of powerful and easy-to-use functions. These functions can help you perform a wide range of tasks, from rounding a number to the nearest integer to determining the one-tailed probability of the chi-squared distribution (yes, statistics).

All formulas in Excel begin with an equal sign (=). The equal sign signals the beginning of a mathematical operation and tells Excel to store the expression that follows as a formula. For example, the following formula calculates the sum of three numbers:

=10+20+30

Excel stores your formulas internally (you can see them on the formula bar), but it displays the result of each calculation in the cell in which you placed the formula. You can use the standard mathematical operators in a formula—addition (+), subtraction (–), multiplication (*), division (/), and exponentiation (^), as well as a few specialty operators described in Chapter 26, "Crunching Numbers with Formulas and Functions." Figure 21-8 lists the steps to follow to enter a simple formula in a worksheet cell.

For detailed information about formula syntax, see "Building a Formula," on page 727. For detailed information about Excel's collection of built-in functions, see "Using Built-In Functions," on page 733.

Troubleshooting

Does not compute

Excel doesn't calculate the result of your formula.

If you don't begin formulas with an equal sign (=), Excel will interpret the equation as a text value and the formula won't be calculated. If you make this common mistake, press F2 to edit the cell, press the Home key to move the insertion point to the beginning of the formula, type an equal sign (=), and then press Enter.

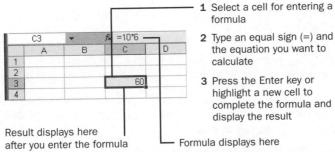

1 Select a cell for entering a formula

2 Type an equal sign (=) and the equation you want to calculate

3 Press the Enter key or highlight a new cell to complete the formula and display the result

Result displays here after you enter the formula

Formula displays here

Figure 21-8. A simple formula might involve only a few numbers and operators.

Using Cell References in Formulas

Formulas can also contain worksheet *cell references*—such as A1 or B5—so that you can include the contents of cells in formulas and combine them in any way you choose. You can use cell references along with numbers, mathematical operators, and built-in functions. To specify a cell reference while you're entering a formula, you can

- Type in the cell reference, such as **B5**
- Highlight the cell using the mouse
- Highlight the cell by moving the selection to that cell using the keyboard (for example, by pressing an arrow key)

For example, to add the contents of cell B5 to the contents of cell C5, you'd create the following formula:

=B5+C5

You can also include groups of cells, such as A3:A9, in formulas. See "Selecting Cells and Ranges," on page 627.

Figure 21-9 shows the results of such a calculation.

D6	▼	f_x =B6+C6		
	A	B	C	D	E

	A	B	C	D	E
1					
2	Global Sales Summary				
3					
4			Fiscal Year		
5	Region	FY 02	FY03	Total	
6	North America	$200,000.00	$260,000.00	$460,000.00	
7	South America	$85,000.00	$110,000.00		
8	Europe	$120,000.00	$75,000.00		
9	Africa	$50,000.00	$50,000.00		
10	Asia	$110,000.00	$230,000.00		
11	Total	$565,000.00	$725,000.00		
12					

Figure 21-9. To use the contents of cells in a formula, include cell references in the equation.

 You'll find a copy of this workbook on the book's companion CD, under the filename Refer-enceDemo.xls.

To create a formula such as the one in Figure 21-9, complete the following steps. This procedure includes cell references you highlight with the mouse, but you could easily substitute other methods for including the cell references.

1 Select the cell—D5, for example—in which you want to place the formula.

2 Type an equal sign (=) to start the formula. Click the first cell you want to place in the formula, and then type a mathematical operator. For example, click cell B5, and then press the plus (+) key to add B5+ to the cell you're editing and to the formula bar. When you click the cell that you are adding to the formula, a flashing border will surround it, and its reference will appear in the cell you're editing and on the formula bar. The flashing border will be replaced with a solid border when you type the operator. Both the solid border and the cell reference will be colored blue.

3 Click the second cell you want to place in the formula. If the cell you want isn't currently visible, use the scroll bars to locate it.

If you want to include additional mathematical operators and cell references, you can add them now. Each additional cell reference will appear in a different color, and the border around the corresponding cell will be given a matching color. (This color coding lets you easily see which cell corresponds to a particular cell reference in the formula. To change a cell reference in the formula, you can drag the corresponding cell's border to a new location.)

4 Press the Enter key to store the formula. Excel will calculate the result and display it in the cell. All colors and borders will disappear when you press Enter.

Chapter 21

Adding Artwork

After you enter your worksheet's basic facts and figures into Excel, you might want to spruce things up a bit by adding some electronic artwork such as clip art, scanned photographs, background images, organization charts, or hand-drawn illustrations. The basic technique for adding these items to worksheet cells is the same in all Office applications: click a command on the Picture submenu of the Insert menu.

Follow these steps to add a piece of electronic artwork to a worksheet:

1   Select the cell in which you want to place the artwork. (Allow some room in neighboring cells to accommodate the image.)

2   Choose Insert, Picture to open the Picture submenu.

3   Choose the artwork type you want to use from the Picture submenu. You will see the following options:

   ■   **Clip Art**   A picture gallery containing thousands of pieces of electronic art for presentations, reports, and brochures

   ■   **From File**   An Open dialog box that lets you locate existing artwork on your system

   ■   **From Scanner Or Camera**   A utility that helps you insert scanned images and digital photographs into worksheet cells

   ■   **Organization Chart**   A utility that helps you build corporate organization charts

   ■   **AutoShapes**   A toolbar that lets you add arrows, lines, and other shapes

   ■   **WordArt**   A wizard and toolbar that helps you build creative banners, headlines, and text elements

4   Move or resize the artwork as desired in the worksheet.

5   If you want to delete the image later, select the artwork object you inserted and press Delete.

> For detailed information on inserting and working with artwork in Office applications, see Chapter 6, "Adding Professional Graphics and Special Effects to Office 2003 Documents."

Inserting a Background Graphic

If the worksheet you're creating will take center stage in a report or presentation, you might want to embellish it further by adding a subtle piece of artwork to the background. When you add background artwork, Excel places the image you specify in a layer that is displayed behind the contents of the current worksheet or chart. (The data in your worksheet cells will appear on top of the image.) If you specify a small pattern rather than a complete image, Excel will automatically repeat, or *tile*, the pattern to fill the entire worksheet or chart.

To add a bitmap, metafile, or other electronic image to the background of your worksheet, follow these steps:

1. Display the worksheet you want to customize by adding background artwork.
2. Choose Format, Sheet, Background. The Sheet Background dialog box will appear.
3. Browse the folders on your hard disk or network to locate the electronic artwork you want to display as a background graphic. When you find and select it, click the Insert button to insert the graphic. (You'll find many graphics files that are provided with Office in subfolders of the following folder on your hard drive: Program Files\Microsoft Office.)

> **Tip** Try to use simple, light-colored background images in your worksheets and charts so that the artwork doesn't overpower the text you're using for labels and numbers. Subtle, light gray images often work best.

If at some point you decide you don't want the background image, choose Format, Sheet, Delete Background to remove it.

Inserting Hyperlinks

Excel allows you to add *hyperlinks* to cells in your workbook, connecting them to other electronic documents on your hard disk, the Internet, or an attached computer network. Hyperlinks in Excel give you a handy way to combine a series of related workbooks or let you provide your users with on-demand access to supporting documents, Web pages, or other reference materials on the Internet. You create a hyperlink using the Hyperlink command on the Insert menu, and the command prompts you for the name of the supporting file or Web page and underlines the text in the worksheet cell that was selected when you chose the command. After a hyperlink to another document has been established, you can activate it by clicking the underlined word in your worksheet.

> **Note** You can specify any supporting document for your hyperlink—provided that you have the application necessary to open the document on your computer. Similarly, if you have Microsoft Internet Explorer or another Internet browser, you can create a hyperlink to any resource on the Internet for which you have a proper address.

Creating a Hyperlink in Your Worksheet

To add to your worksheet a hyperlink that opens a document on your hard disk, the Internet, or a network to which you're attached, complete the following steps:

1. In your worksheet, select the cell with which you want to associate the hyperlink. You can create a hyperlink in an empty cell or in a cell containing information, artwork, or a formula.

Insert Hyperlink

2 Choose Insert, Hyperlink or click the Insert Hyperlink button on the Standard toolbar. The Insert Hyperlink dialog box will appear, as shown in Figure 21-10. Excel will now ask you two fundamental questions about your selection: what type of hyperlink are you creating, and what content should the hyperlink contain? (See Troubleshooting sidebar later in this section for more information on inserting a hyperlink.)

Browse for File
Browse the Web
Up One Folder

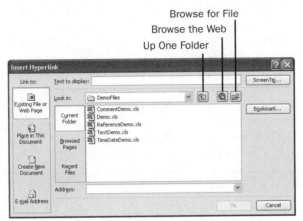

Figure 21-10. The Insert Hyperlink dialog box gives you several options when creating hyperlinks.

3 Answer the first question by clicking one of the four buttons on the left side of the dialog box. The Existing File Or Web Page button creates a link in your worksheet to a file on your hard disk or a page on the Web. On a day-to-day basis, this option will probably cover most of your hyperlink needs because it's the fastest way to create links in your worksheet to useful files and Internet resources.

You have three additional options.

- The second button, Place In This Document, creates a link to a different location in the current workbook. Use this option if you want to jump quickly from one location in a spreadsheet to another. (It works like the Go To command but is more convenient.)

- The third button, Create New Document, allows you to open a new Office document from within your worksheet,; this new document can be another Excel spreadsheet, a Word document, a PowerPoint presentation, and so on. This option gives users a quick way to write notes or jot down estimates while using a worksheet.

Chapter 21

623

■ Finally, E-Mail Address (the fourth button on the left side) allows you to create a link in your worksheet that automatically sends an e-mail message to another user.

4 Fill out the dialog box options corresponding to the type of hyperlink you're creating.

If you're identifying a particular document name or Web page that should be loaded when the user clicks the hyperlink, locate it on your system by using one of the browse buttons (Browse The Web or Browse For File). If you want to customize the hyperlink text that will appear within the cell, edit the contents of the Text To Display text box. (This text box will be available only if the cell is blank or contains a text label.) If you want to customize the ScreenTip that will appear when you hold the mouse pointer over the cell, click the ScreenTip button and enter your text into the Set Hyperlink ScreenTip dialog box. (If you don't customize the ScreenTip, it will display the target location and instructions for using the hyperlink.) You can also use three buttons within the dialog box corresponding to frequently used documents: Current Folder, Browsed Pages, and Recent Files.

Tip **Use a Web page as a hyperlink**

When you browse for a Web page link by clicking the Browse The Web button in the Insert Hyperlink dialog box, Office opens your Internet browser and allows you to locate the Web page you want to use. After you locate the page you want, return to the Insert Hyperlink dialog box (with your Internet browser still running), select any additional options you want, and click the OK button. The trick here is to jump back to the Insert Hyperlink dialog box while your browser is still running, or you won't link to the Web page you opened.

---

5 When you're finished identifying the content of your hyperlink, click the OK button to add the hyperlink to your worksheet. When the Insert Hyperlink dialog box closes, the text in the selected cell will appear underlined, and a ScreenTip will appear when you hold the mouse pointer over the hyperlink.

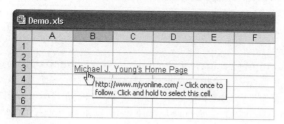

Troubleshooting

Can't insert a hyperlink

The Insert Hyperlink command is unavailable.

Does the Insert Hyperlink command appear dimmed? If so, the command is unavailable, probably because the workbook is being shared. For more information, see "Managing Shared Workbooks," on page 693.

Activating a Hyperlink

To activate a hyperlink in a worksheet, click the underlined cell containing the hyperlink, and Excel will start any necessary applications and load the linked document. If the hyperlink requires an Internet or other network connection, you might be prompted for a member ID and password when your browser activates the link.

The Web Toolbar

When you activate a hyperlink in Excel, a special Web toolbar might appear. This toolbar lets you switch back and forth between open hyperlinks, establish additional Internet connections, or run special network-related commands. If the toolbar doesn't appear, click View, Toolbars, Web. You don't have to use the Web toolbar when using hyperlinks to switch to other Excel workbooks (you can use the Excel Window menu instead), but in many cases you will benefit from doing so.

The Web toolbar is shown here as a freestanding toolbar, which you can duplicate by dragging the toolbar from its default locked position beneath the Formatting toolbar.

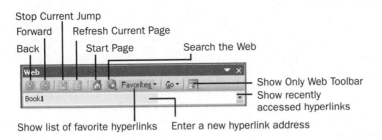

> **Tip** If you're not sure whether an underlined word represents a hyperlink, place the mouse pointer directly over the cell and see if the mouse pointer changes shape. The mouse pointer over a cell containing a hyperlink resembles a hand with a pointing finger and is normally accompanied by a ScreenTip describing the hyperlink, as shown previously (in "Creating a Hyperlink in Your Worksheet").

After a hyperlink has been activated, you can jump back and forth between the home document and any hyperlinks in the same workbook by clicking the Back and Forward buttons, respectively, on the Web toolbar. If the hyperlink launched a separate Microsoft Windows application to load the document—say, the hyperlink started Microsoft Word or Internet Explorer—you can also use the Windows taskbar to move back and forth quickly between the applications. When you're finished viewing a hyperlinked Excel workbook, close it by choosing Close from the Excel File menu. When you're finished using documents associated with other applications, simply close those applications.

Editing and Removing Hyperlinks

To edit or remove a hyperlink from a worksheet cell, follow these steps:

> **Note** Don't left-click the cell containing the hyperlink or you'll activate it.

1 Right-click the cell containing the hyperlink to display a shortcut menu of commands used to manipulate spreadsheet cells.

2 On the shortcut menu that appears, choose Edit Hyperlink if you want to customize or change the hyperlink in the cell you clicked. To remove the hyperlink, choose Remove Hyperlink.

Saving the Workbook

After you enter information into a new workbook, it's a good idea to save the data to disk—before you make some phone calls and get distracted or go to lunch! Each workbook is stored in its own file on disk and is assigned a filename that's unique to the folder in which it's stored. To save the workbook, use the Save command on the File menu. (The first time you save a new document, this command will open the Save As dialog box, which allows you to specify the filename and location. If you later want to save a separate copy of your workbook under a different filename or in a different folder, you can reopen the Save As dialog box by choosing File, Save As.)

> For information about saving workbooks, see "Saving Office Documents," on page 69. For information about including worksheets in document libraries on SharePoint Team Services Web sites, see "Sharing Office Documents and Graphics on a SharePoint Site," on page 183.

Advanced Worksheet Editing

Essential Editing Techniques. 627
Entering a Series of Labels,
Numbers, and Dates. 641

Checking for Errors 644

If you make a mistake while building a worksheet, you're not expected to live with it. Microsoft Office Excel 2003 features a variety of traditional and innovative electronic editing techniques. They enable you to fix your typos, of course, and also to reorganize your data, find and replace data, check for common input errors, fill cells with data, and create room for more information. In this chapter you'll learn the essential editing techniques you'll need when managing worksheet data in Excel. You'll also learn how to use innovative features such as AutoFill and the Office Clipboard to replicate and rearrange vital information.

Essential Editing Techniques

When you need to remember how data is moved from cell to cell in Excel, refer to this part of the book. In this section you'll learn the following editing techniques:

- How to select cells and ranges
- How to clear cells and delete cells
- How to copy data from one cell to another
- How to use the Office Clipboard
- How to move cells by dragging
- How to add new rows and columns to the worksheet
- How to undo and repeat commands

For information about tracking and approving edits in a multiuser environment, see "Accepting or Rejecting Revisions," on page 696.

Selecting Cells and Ranges

Several Excel commands work with individual cells or groups of cells called *ranges*. Selecting a cell means making it the active cell; as a result, its reference appears in the Name box to the left of the formula bar. To select an individual cell or a range of cells, you can use either the mouse or the keyboard.

> **Tip** To make cell ranges easier to work with, you can assign a meaningful *name* to a cell range and then use the name in place of the cell references. See "Using Names in Functions," on page 742.

When you select a range of cells, Excel indicates the range with a bold border (the same border that identifies a single active cell), and the background color within the range changes from the default white to light blue. (If you've used versions of Excel prior to Excel 2000, you'll notice that light blue has replaced black as the default highlight color for a selected range.)

A range of cells in Excel is always a contiguous rectangular block. In expressions—such as formulas—Excel uses a simple notation for a range of cells: the first cell (at the upper left corner of the block), followed by a colon, and then the last cell (at the lower right corner of the block). For example, A1:E1 represents a single row of five cells along the top edge of the worksheet, and E5:F8 represents two adjacent columns of four cells in the worksheet. You'll use cell ranges in many of the formulas and functions you create in Excel worksheets. In this illustration the user has selected a rectangular block of 50 cells (ten rows by five columns) with the reference A1:E10.

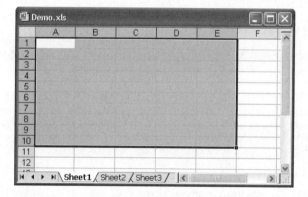

Selecting a Range Using the Mouse

To select a range of cells using the mouse, complete the following steps:

1 Position the cell pointer over the first cell you want to select, which is normally the top left cell in the range.

2 Hold down the mouse button and then drag the mouse over the remaining cells in the selection. Release the mouse button.

3   If you want to select multiple cell ranges simultaneously, drag the mouse over the first range and release the mouse button to highlight the first range; then hold down the Ctrl key, use your mouse to make another selection, and release the Ctrl key. You can continue to add ranges to a selection using the Ctrl key each time. Figure 22-1 shows a multiple-range selection.

Note   In Figure 22-1, two ranges of cells are selected (A6:A10 and C6:C10). Only one of the cells, however, is the active cell—C6—denoted by the Name box and the bar around the cell. Most commands will affect all the selected cells, including the active cell, but there are exceptions. Entering new information, for example, will affect only the active cell and won't change anything in the other selected, or highlighted, cells.

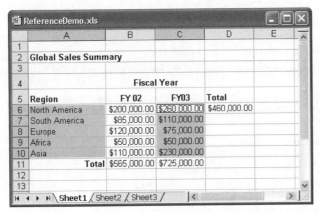

Figure 22-1.   To select noncontiguous ranges using the mouse, hold down the Ctrl key.

Selecting a Range Using the Keyboard

To select a range of cells using the keyboard, complete the following steps:

1   Use the arrow keys to move to the first cell you want to select.

2   Hold down the Shift key and then press the appropriate arrow key to select the remaining cells in the range. Release the Shift key.

3   To select additional, noncontiguous cell ranges, press Shift+F8. The ADD indicator will appear on the status bar, indicating that you can add a range to the selection. Repeat steps 1 and 2 to add another range. You can continue to add ranges to a selection using Shift+F8 each time.

Selecting Rows and Columns Using the Mouse

If you want to quickly select part or all of your worksheet, you can click one of several hot spots on your screen.

To select an entire column with a single mouse click, click the column letter at the top of the column. To select an entire row, click the row number on the left edge of the row. You can also select multiple columns or rows by selecting a row or column head and dragging across the heads of the rows or columns you want to select. Be careful when you select multiple rows or columns: If the row numbers or column letters aren't consecutive, the sheet probably has some hidden rows or columns. If you clear or delete the visible range, you'll do likewise to the hidden data.

> For an explanation of hidden data, see "Hiding Columns and Rows," on page 664.

If you need to select the entire worksheet, you can click the Select All box in the upper-left corner of the worksheet. Here is a worksheet that has two columns selected.

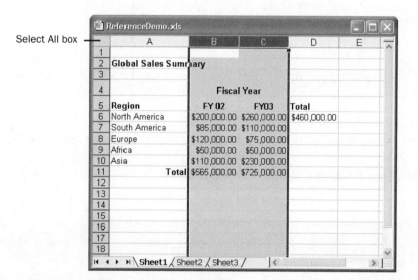

Clearing Cells and Deleting Cells

Now that you know how to select ranges of cells, you can put your new skill to work clearing and deleting cells. If you want to clear the contents from a group of cells, select the cells, right-click within the selection, and choose Clear Contents from the shortcut menu. Excel will remove the content but keep the cell formatting so that you can enter new values in the same format. (For example, if you clear cells formatted for dollar values, the next time you place a number in one of these cells it will be formatted for dollars.) To see the complete range of clear options, choose Clear from the Edit menu, and Excel will display a submenu that contains commands for clearing the formatting, the contents, the comments, or all three items together.

Inside Out

Clear cells using the Delete key

You can also clear the contents of the active cell (or a selection) by pressing the Delete key. It's not the most intuitive way to distinguish between clearing and deleting—to use the Delete key to clear contents—but it's quick if you can keep it straight.

If you'd rather delete a single cell from the worksheet, moving the rows below it up or shifting columns over to the left, display the Edit menu and choose the Delete command rather than the Clear command. In many applications the terms *delete* and *clear* have the same meaning, but in Excel there's a distinct difference between the two commands. Clearing a cell is like using an eraser to remove the contents or the format from a cell, but deleting a cell is like cutting it out with a tiny pocketknife and then moving the remaining cells up or over to fill the gap.

To use the Delete command to delete cell ranges, entire rows, or entire columns from a worksheet, complete the following steps:

1 To delete a cell, select it. To delete a row or column, select any cell in that row or column. To delete a range of cells, select the range.

2 Choose Edit, Delete. The dialog box shown in Figure 22-2 will appear.

3 Click the option button that corresponds to the way you want remaining cells moved after the deletion.

   In Figure 22-2, for example, where B3 is the selected cell, to delete cell B3 and move cells over to fill the gap, click Shift Cells Left. To delete cell B3 and move cells up to fill the gap, click Shift Cells Up. You can also click Entire Row or Entire Column to delete the entire row or column that contains the selected cell (or all rows or columns that are spanned by a multicell selection). In Figure 22-2 you could, for example, remove row 3 or column B.

4 Click the OK button to delete the selected cells and move other cells to fill the gap.

Chapter 22

631

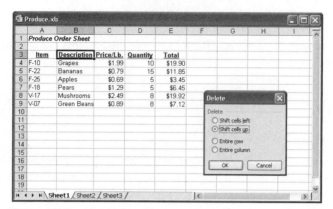

Figure 22-2. The Delete command lets you remove a cell, row, or column from the worksheet and fill the gap with adjacent cells. You'll find a copy of this workbook on the book's companion CD, under the filename Produce.xls.

 Finding and Replacing Data

The Find command on the Edit menu is handy both for navigating and editing worksheets that are extensive or densely packed with data. Find lets you specify a string of characters and move directly to each instance of that string. The string can be any series of characters: a word or part of a word, a numeric value, a cell reference, or the functions and operators in a formula.

After you find a string, Excel can automate the process of revising the string. Allied to the Find command is a Replace command, the second tab shown in Figure 22-3. With Replace you can substitute a replacement string for any or all instances of the target string.

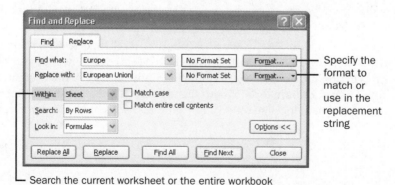

Specify the format to match or use in the replacement string

Search the current worksheet or the entire workbook

Figure 22-3. The Replace command offers flexible options for targeting the replacement.

The options in the Find and Replace tabs help you streamline your search. You can specify that you want to match only strings with the same (upper and lower) case characters as those in the search string. And you can narrow the search with the Match Entire Cell Contents check box so that the search string matches only cells for which the search string represents the entire contents; that is, the cell contains no additional characters. In that case, *Yankees* would match a cell that contains *Yankees* but not a cell that contains *New York Yankees*.

Find and Replace lets you specify a format to match for the search string and—for Replace—a format to use for the replacement string. When you use these options, you can define the formats either by hand or by choosing a cell that already has the desired formatting. Another option lets you search beyond the current worksheet across the entire workbook. Both features are labeled in Figure 22-3.

Find All is a powerful command that generates a list of the matching instances. For each match it shows the worksheet and cell location as well as the value and formula (if any) contained in the cell. You can click any of the matches in the list to select the matching cell and to view the cell contents or make replacements as appropriate.

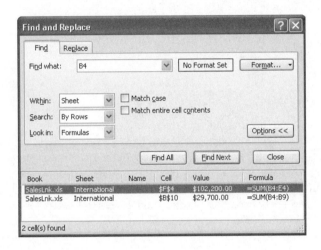

Undoing Commands

If you make a mistake when executing an Excel command, you can undo your mistake by immediately choosing Edit, Undo. For example, if you deleted a range of cells in error, choosing Undo will return the cells to the worksheet as if you had never deleted them.

Undo

You can also click the Undo button on the Standard toolbar or press Ctrl+Z to undo a command.

The Undo button on the Standard toolbar also has multiple levels of undo (like Microsoft Word). This extremely useful feature lets you "go back in time" to fix editing mistakes you made 3, 4, or 10 commands back. Now and then you'll probably think better of a modification you made that took several steps to accomplish. By clicking the small arrow attached to the Undo button, you can scroll through a list of the edits you've made and determine how many actions you want to undo, as shown in Figure 22-4. Excel will then undo each command, from your most recent action back to and including the one you just picked.

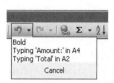

Figure 22-4. Using the Undo button, you can undo one or more of your previous editing mistakes.

Undo has a few limitations. For example, you can't undo the actions of adding a new worksheet to your workbook or deleting an existing worksheet. You also can't undo the actions of saving revisions to a file or customizing the Excel interface. If Undo isn't available for a particular command or action, the Undo command on the Edit menu will be dimmed and read "Can't Undo."

Troubleshooting

Undo unavailable

The Undo command isn't available for the action you want to undo.

Excel is smart about tracking your actions during a given work session. It doesn't create an Undo command when you use the scroll bars, press keyboard navigation keys, run online Help, or look for cell data using the Go To or Find commands. Remember, however, that your ability to undo ends when you save or close your workbook. Saving frequently is encouraged, of course, but if you're editing a workbook in which you have invested a great deal of time and effort, consider saving changes to a new location or keep a backup for recovery until you're confident that you want to retain the new version.

Redoing Commands

Redo

What happens if you decide to, well, undo an Undo command? For example, what do you do if you delete a range of cells, restore them with Undo, and then, on reflection, decide to remove them after all? One option is to select the cells again and choose Delete. But Excel makes it even easier to be fickle. Excel adds the commands you've reversed to the Redo button on the Standard toolbar, letting you redo commands one by one or several commands at once. (This makes the Redo button the functional opposite of the Undo button, allowing you to restore and remove edits you've made.)

Note The Redo and Repeat commands are different, although easy to confuse. Redo reverses one or more actions that you undid, whereas Repeat enables you to reexecute (with a different selection) the command that you last used.

Repeating Commands

Below the Undo command on the Edit menu is the Repeat command, which allows you to repeat the command you just executed—but at a different place in the worksheet. Here's how it works: Let's say you just used the Cells command on the Format menu to place a border around cell B3. Excel then displays a Repeat Format Cells command on the Edit menu, enabling you to add the same border to a new cell by simply highlighting the new cell and clicking Repeat on the Edit menu. An even faster way is to press F4 or the shortcut key combination Ctrl+Y.

> **Tip**   **Think about repetitive actions**
> The Repeat command is a speed feature designed to help you work faster in Excel. But most people forget to use it because they don't anticipate repetitive actions. Think about how you work, and you might discover several clever uses for the Repeat command. (We use Repeat most often for formatting labels and changing number formats.)

Using Cut and Paste to Move Data

At times you'll want to move cell entries from one place to another on your worksheet. To do this, you can use the Cut and the Paste commands on the Edit menu. When you cut a cell or range of cells using the Cut command, Excel places a dotted-line marquee around the selection to indicate which cells will be moved, and then it copies the cell contents (including comments) and formatting to a temporary storage location known as the Clipboard. Excel lets you move a rectangular range of cells only—no noncontiguous blocks.

When you select a new location for the data and choose Paste, the cell contents and formatting are cleared from their former location and are pasted from the Clipboard into their new location, replacing the contents and formatting of the cell or cells at the new location. To cancel the move after the marquee appears, press the Esc key.

> **Note**   In contrast to other Microsoft Windows applications, Excel lets you paste only once after you cut. Use the Copy command to paste multiple times. Using Copy you can also paste the contents of a single cell to all the cells in a selection.

Figure 22-5 shows a group of cells after the Cut command was chosen (notice the marquee), while Figure 22-6 shows the same worksheet after the Paste command was chosen. Note that when you use the Paste command, you might inadvertently copy over cells containing data that you don't want to delete, so be cautious when moving information. As alternatives to using the Edit menu's Cut and Paste commands, you can use the Cut and Paste buttons on the Standard toolbar or the standard Windows key combinations Ctrl+X and Ctrl+V.

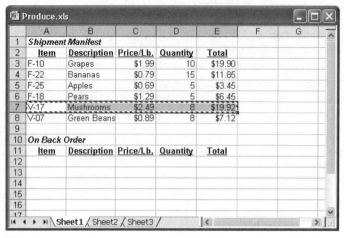

Figure 22-5. The Cut command marks the selected cells with a marquee.

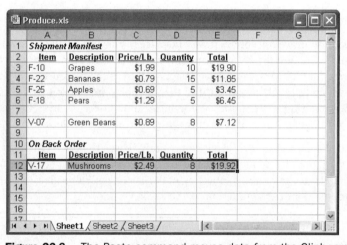

Figure 22-6. The Paste command moves data from the Clipboard to the active cell.

To move a range of cells using the Cut and Paste commands, complete the following steps:

1 Select the group of cells you want to move.

2 Choose Edit, Cut. (You can also click the Cut button on the Standard toolbar or press the Ctrl+X key combination.)

3 Click the cell to which you want to move the data. (If you're moving a group of cells, highlight the cell in the upper left corner of the area you're copying to.)

4 Choose Edit, Paste. (Or click the Paste button on the Standard toolbar or press the Ctrl+V key combination.)

Cut

Paste

Using Copy and Paste to Duplicate Data

If you just want to duplicate the contents and formatting of a range of cells in the worksheet and not clear them from their current location, you can use the Copy command on the Edit menu. This command places a copy of the cells you've selected into the Clipboard, and you can transfer these cells any number of times to your worksheet using the Paste command. The Copy command indicates the cells you're duplicating with a dotted-line marquee so that you can see what you're copying as you do it. As when you use the Cut command, when you use the Copy command you're limited to copying contiguous blocks of cells. If you cut or copy a sequence of data items, you can use the Office Clipboard (discussed in "Using the Office Clipboard," on page 158) to paste an item other than the one most recently copied.

To speed up your copy operations, you can use the Copy button on the Standard toolbar or press the Ctrl+C key combination.

To copy a range of cells using the Copy and Paste commands, complete the following steps:

Copy

1 Select the group of cells you want to copy.

2 Choose Edit, Copy. (You can also click the Copy button on the Standard toolbar or press Ctrl+C.)

3 Click the cell into which you want to copy the data. (If you're duplicating a group of cells, highlight the cell in the upper left corner of the area you're copying to.)

4 Choose Edit, Paste. (Or click the Paste button on the Standard toolbar or press Ctrl+V.)

> **Tip** You can use the *Office Clipboard* to copy or cut several blocks of data—from Excel or another Windows application—and store them all in the Clipboard so that you can later paste any or all of these blocks into Excel or into another Office application. For information, see "Using the Office Clipboard," on page 158.

Inside Out

Use the Office Clipboard when the Excel Paste command isn't available

If you've used versions of Excel prior to Excel 2002, you might recognize this aggravating situation: You copy a range of cells, causing the marquee to appear; then, before you paste the data, you become briefly sidetracked (to edit a cell or the like) only to find that the marquee has disappeared and the Paste command has become unavailable. In Excel 2003 nothing has changed, *but* with the Office Clipboard you're no longer reduced to repeating the select-and-copy procedure. The copied data is there on the Clipboard, so you can highlight the destination and paste the data from the Clipboard—using the Clipboard task pane—even though the Paste command on the Edit menu is dimmed.

Chapter 22

Moving Cells by Dragging

The fastest way to move a group of worksheet cells is by dragging. By using the drag-and-drop technique, you can edit a worksheet in an efficient and visibly uncomplicated way—by dragging a group of cells from one location to another. To enable drag-and-drop editing, you need to select cells (usually with the mouse), release the mouse button, and then move the cell pointer toward an outside edge of the selected cells until the cell pointer changes to a white arrow pointer (with a four-way arrow at its tip). When the pointer changes shape, you can hold down the left mouse button and drag the selection to a new location. As you move the cells, Excel will display both an outline of the range you are dragging and the current range reference, so that you can align the cells properly in your worksheet. See Figure 22-7 for an illustration of the drag-and-drop procedure.

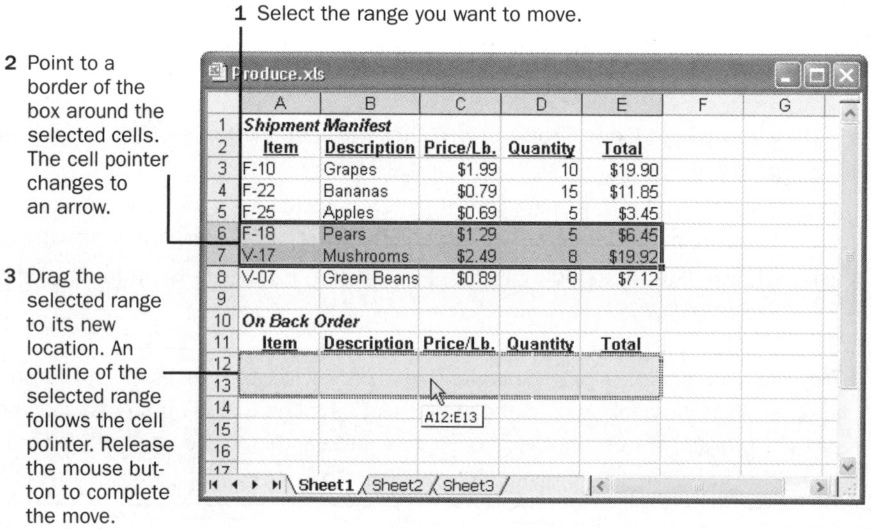

1 Select the range you want to move.

2 Point to a border of the box around the selected cells. The cell pointer changes to an arrow.

3 Drag the selected range to its new location. An outline of the selected range follows the cell pointer. Release the mouse button to complete the move.

Figure 22-7. The quickest way to move cells in the worksheet is by using the drag-and-drop mouse technique.

To copy (rather than move) cells by dragging, hold down the Ctrl key while you drag the selected cells. When you drag with the Crtl key down, a plus (+) sign—rather than the four-way arrow—will appear at the tip of the mouse pointer to let you know that you're copying data.

Note If you drop cells onto existing data when you're moving them (but *not* when you're copying them), Excel will warn you that you're about to replace the contents of your copy destination. Click OK if you want to replace the old cells or click Cancel if you want to choose a new place for the data.

Inside Out

Control your Move or Copy operation by right-dragging

A consistently satisfactory way to copy or move cells is to click and hold the right mouse button on the border of the selected cell or range and then drag the data to the destination. When you release the right button, Excel presents a list of actions, including Move Here and Copy Here and Cancel. Other options let you elect how to deal with any overlapping data in the destination cells. This technique often produces an extra step, but it helps you check yourself to be sure that you are performing the action you intend.

Adding Rows and Columns to the Worksheet

Now and then you'll want to add new rows or columns to your worksheet to create space. You might decide to add cells because your existing data is too crowded, or perhaps you're creating a report that has changed in scope and requires a new layout to communicate effectively. You add new rows and columns to your worksheet by using the Rows and Columns commands on the Insert menu. When you add rows or columns to your worksheet, the existing data shifts down to accommodate new rows or shifts to the right to allow for new columns.

If you're rearranging rows or columns of cells in a worksheet, you can avoid the extra steps involved in creating empty rows or columns to paste data into. Select the row(s) or column(s) you want to relocate, choose the Cut command from the Edit menu or press Ctrl+X. The dotted marquee will appear, indicating the range to be deleted. Then select the row below or the column to the right of the intended destination and choose Insert, Cut Cells. Excel will delete the cells marked for removal and insert the row(s) or column(s) into the intended location.

To add one or more blank rows to your worksheet, complete the following steps:

1 Select one or more rows *below* the place where you want to enter the new row(s). Excel will insert the number of rows that you select. (Rather than selecting entire rows, you can just select a single cell in each row.)

2 Choose Insert, Rows.

To add one or more columns to your worksheet, complete the following steps:

1 Select one or more columns to the *right* of the place where you want to enter the new column(s). Excel will insert the number of columns that you select. (Rather than selecting entire columns, you can just select a single cell in each column.)

2 Choose Insert, Columns.

Chapter 22

Inserting Individual Cells

Excel lets you add individual cells to your worksheet's rows or columns by choosing Insert, Cells. Before you use the Cells command, you should select the worksheet cell below or to the right of the new cell you want. For example, if you want to add a new cell to column B between cells B3 and B4, highlight cell B4 before choosing the Cells command. To insert multiple cells, select the number and the arrangement of cells that you want to insert. For instance, to insert a two-by-two block of cells above cells B4 and C4, you would select the range B4:C5.

When you choose Insert, Cells, the Insert dialog box will appear. Use this dialog box to tell Excel whether to shift the existing cells to the right or down.

Using Smart Tags in Excel

You can have Excel recognize certain types of data in a worksheet cell and add a corresponding *smart tag* to the cell. A smart tag lets you quickly perform useful actions on data—such as a financial (stock ticker) symbol—that would normally require you to run a separate program. Smart tags in Excel work the same basic way they do in Word, so a good starting point is to read the general description of smart tags in "Using Smart Tags in Word," on page 276. The following is a brief summary of the techniques for enabling and using smart tags in Excel:

1   To enable smart tags, choose Tools, AutoCorrect Options and click the Smart Tags tab.

2   When a smart tag recognizer has recognized data that you've typed into a cell and has added a smart tag to that cell, Excel will display a small, triangular indicator in the cell's lower-right corner. To perform an action on the data, place the mouse pointer over the cell, click the smart tag button that appears, and choose a command from the drop-down menu, as shown here:

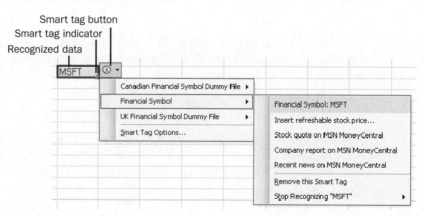

Chapter 22

Entering a Series of Labels, Numbers, and Dates

Excel streamlines the task of entering worksheet data by allowing you to fill a range of cells with one repeating value or a sequence of values, called a *series*. This capability saves you time when you're entering groups of labels, numbers, or dates in a report. For example, you can replicate the same price for many products in a report or create part numbers that increment predictably. To enter a series of values into a range of cells, you use the Fill command on the Insert menu or a mouse technique called *AutoFill*. The following sections show you how you can enter data automatically using these commands.

For information about replicating formulas in a worksheet, see "Replicating a Formula," on page 729.

Using AutoFill to Create a Series

The easiest method for entering repeating or incrementing data is to use Excel's AutoFill feature. To create a series of labels, numbers, or dates, select two or more cells (to establish a pattern for the series) and look for the *fill handle*, a tiny black square located in the lower-right corner of the active cell or of a selected range of cells, as shown in Figure 22-8. When you position the cell pointer over the fill handle, the cell pointer changes to a plus sign (+), indicating that the AutoFill feature is enabled. Click the fill handle and drag it over the cells you want to fill with information. (Notice that Excel shows the next value in the series in a pop-up box.) When you release the mouse button, you have, like magic, a list of new values!

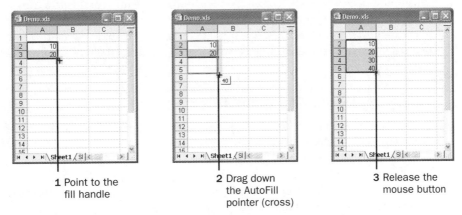

1 Point to the fill handle   **2** Drag down the AutoFill pointer (cross)   **3** Release the mouse button

Figure 22-8.   Follow these steps to AutoFill a series of cells.

The AutoFill feature obeys a clear set of rules when it replicates data in cells, as shown in Table 22-1. When you drag the fill handle down or to the right, AutoFill creates values that increase based on the pattern in the range of cells you first select. When you drag the fill handle up or to the left, AutoFill creates values that decrease based on the pattern. If AutoFill doesn't recognize the pattern, it simply duplicates the selected cells.

Chapter 22

> **Tip** To suppress the AutoFill feature (and just duplicate the selected cells), hold down the Ctrl key while you drag the fill handle. Another technique is to click and hold the right mouse button when you drag, release the button, and then choose Copy Cells from the shortcut menu.

Table 22-1. AutoFill Insertion Patterns

Pattern Type	Series	Example
Label (Text)	No pattern, text is duplicated	Units, Units, Units
Number	Values increase based on pattern	10, 20, 30
Text with number	Series created by changing number based on pattern	Unit 1, Unit 2, Unit 3
Day	Series created to match day format	Mon, Tues, Wed
Month	Series created to match month format	Jan, Feb, Mar
Year	Series created to match year format based on pattern	1998, 1999, 2000
Time	Series created to match time interval	1:30 PM, 2:00 PM, 2:30 PM

Using the Fill Commands

The mouse-driven AutoFill feature is designed to handle most of the data copying and replication in a worksheet, but you can also use a collection of Fill commands on the Edit menu to accomplish simple copying tasks. You'll find these commands useful if you want to copy one cell into many adjacent cells or if you want to fine-tune the way patterns in an AutoFill series are created.

Filling Up, Down, Right, and Left

When you choose Fill from the Edit menu, a submenu appears that contains several replication commands, including Up, Down, Right, and Left. These commands let you copy information from a cell (or series of cells) to a group of selected, adjacent cells. Figure 22-9 shows how to use the Fill Down command to copy the contents of cell A2 to cells A3 through A5. Note that cell comments aren't copied when you use the Fill commands (because comments aren't considered essential to the calculation process).

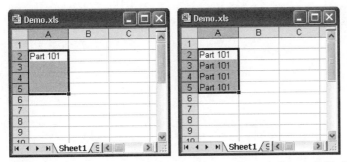

Figure 22-9. Select the range you want to fill and choose Edit, Fill, Down.

> **Note** The Excel key combination for the Copy Down command is Ctrl+D. The key combination for the Copy Right command is Ctrl+R.

Using the Fill Series Dialog Box

If you want to specify a custom series, such as a number that increments in fractional portions or a maximum value for the series, enter the starting number, select your fill range, and choose Edit, Fill, Series. The dialog box shown in Figure 22-10 will appear. This dialog box allows you to specify the series type (linear, growth, date, or AutoFill) and—for a date value—the date unit (day, weekday, month, or year). These are characteristics that are usually set automatically when you use the AutoFill feature. A *linear* series is incremented by adding the *step value*; a *growth* series is incremented by multiplying by the step value.

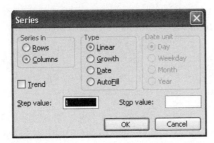

Figure 22-10. The Series dialog box lets you create custom fill sequences.

What makes the Series dialog box handy is the Step Value and Stop Value text boxes, which let you control how the specified series increments and specify its final value. For example, if you want to increment a numeric series by 1.5, type **1.5** in the Step Value text box. Similarly, if you want to set 10 as the highest number in the series, type **10** in the Stop Value text box. Figure 22-11 shows the results you get when you start with the number 1 and create a linear series that uses both the step and stop values mentioned above. Notice that although cells A8, A9, and A10 were selected in the fill range (just as a guess), they were left empty because the stop value in the Series dialog box (10) had been reached.

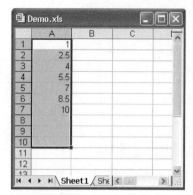

Figure 22-11. The Series dialog box lets you increment by an amount you specify and stop when a limit you set has been reached.

Checking for Errors

Checking your data entries for errors is a great way to maintain your professional profile! You'll locate mistakes that would trip up your users and avoid confusion (and embarrassment) down the road. Excel provides two tools that work in a smooth and well-integrated fashion with your worksheet-building efforts: Spell Checking and Error Checking.

Correcting Your Spelling

How often have you noticed a glaring spelling error just as you've begun to pass out copies of your document at a meeting? And you've sworn from that moment on to proofread and spell check without fail every document and e-mail you create. The resolve may crumble under time pressure, but spell checking in Excel is easy enough to do. You simply click the Spelling button on the Standard toolbar to check the current worksheet, or choose Tools, Spelling. Excel will check entries from the active cell to the end of the sheet, row by row. It will then prompt you before continuing to check from the top of the sheet.

To focus your efforts further, you can select a range of cells, and the Spelling command will check for errors only in the selection. Better yet, you can stop in the middle of entering data in a cell, click the Spelling button, and Excel will check only the current entry—the contents of the formula bar.

The Excel spelling checker works just like the full-featured dialog-box version of the spelling checker in Word. For complete instructions on using and customizing the spelling checker, see "Checking Spelling," on page 479. (You should, however, skip the subsection "Checking Your Spelling as You Type," because Excel doesn't have an as-you-type spelling checker. Note also that Excel doesn't have an option to check your grammar while you run a spelling check.)

Checking for Common Errors

After years of supporting customers using versions of Excel, Microsoft has identified eight of the most common errors that typically frustrate users. You can use Excel's error checking feature to locate, flag, and help rectify cell entries that possibly represent one of these eight errors. To set up error checking, choose Tools, Options, click the Error Checking tab in the Options dialog box, shown here, and select the particular potential errors that you want Excel to flag.

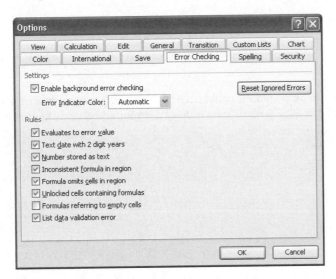

To have Excel check for possible errors while you work on a spreadsheet, select the Enable Background Error Checking option.

For instructions on dealing with possible errors that Excel has flagged while you work on a spreadsheet, see "Entering Text Values," on page 613.

Whether or not you've enabled background error checking, you can have Excel search the entire active spreadsheet for errors at any time by choosing Tools, Error Checking. If Excel detects a potential error during such an error check, it will display a dialog box like the one shown in Figure 22-12. This dialog box locates and identifies the potential error and suggests responses, including ignoring the situation. After you choose a response, you can navigate to other errors with the Previous and Next buttons.

Chapter 22

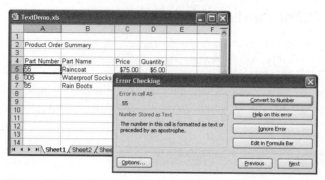

Figure 22-12. Error Checking alerts you to possible oversights that commonly plague Excel users.

Any of these potential error situations could occur intentionally, especially during the creation of a worksheet. But in general the errors deserve attention because they arise so commonly by accident.

Chapter 23

Expert Formatting Techniques

Formatting Cells 647
Changing Column Widths and Row
Heights 662
Creating Conditional Formatting 666

Using Styles 668
Creating and Modifying Templates 672
Changing Page Breaks 675

After you enter and edit the information in worksheet cells, you can format the data to highlight important facts and make the worksheet easier to read. In this chapter you'll learn how to format worksheet cells, change column widths and row heights, add and remove page breaks, use formatting styles, and work with predesigned workbook templates. You'll be surprised how easily you can improve the appearance of your Microsoft Office Excel 2003 worksheets by using the powerful techniques discussed in this chapter.

> Formatting the elements of a chart involves some different commands, which are discussed in "Formatting a Chart," on page 758.

Formatting Cells

Effective worksheet formatting is crucial when you present important information. Formatting the contents of a cell doesn't change how Excel stores the data internally; rather, it changes how the information looks on your screen and how it appears in print. In this section you'll learn the following techniques for formatting the data in cells:

- How to change the vertical and horizontal alignment of data in a cell
- How to change number formats
- How to change the font, text color, and background color
- How to add decorative borders and patterns to cells
- How to apply combinations of formatting effects using the AutoFormat command

Once you're familiar with these formatting options, you'll see (later in this chapter) how Excel can apply many formatting features automatically. This capability, called conditional formatting, means that Excel can format the contents of a cell depending on the value stored in the cell.

Changing Alignment

The gateway to Excel's formatting commands is the Cells command on the Format menu. To apply the command, you begin by highlighting the cell you want to format or by selecting a range of cells. Then choose Format, Cells or press Ctrl+1 to display the Format Cells dialog box, as shown in Figure 23-1. The Format Cells dialog box contains six tabs of formatting options that you can use to adjust the appearance of information in worksheet cells. You use the Alignment tab shown in Figure 23-1 to change the alignment and orientation of information in worksheet cells. You can also use the Formatting toolbar to set the most popular alignment options.

> **Tip** You can display the Format Cells dialog box by selecting the range of cells you want to format, right-clicking the range, and then choosing Format Cells from the shortcut menu.

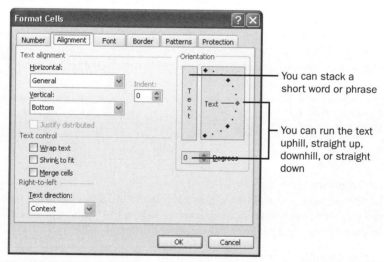

Figure 23-1.   This figure shows the Alignment tab of the Format Cells dialog box.

Adjusting Horizontal Alignment

To adjust the *horizontal* (side-to-side) alignment of data in a range of cells, select the range you want to align, choose Format, Cells or press Ctrl+1. Then, click the Alignment tab in the Format Cells dialog box and choose one of the eight alignment options in the Horizontal drop-down list. General alignment (the default) aligns information one of two ways, depending on the type of information you enter: it aligns text to the left edge of the cell, and it aligns numbers to the right edge. This basic alignment will be suitable for most entries. Left, Center, and Right enforce the indicated alignment in the cell, regardless of the type of information (text or numeric) you enter. You can also use toolbar buttons to set these common formatting options, as shown in Figure 23-2.

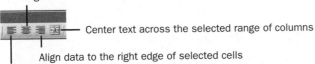

Align data to the center of selected cells

Center text across the selected range of columns

Align data to the right edge of selected cells

Align data to the left edge of selected cells

Figure 23-2.   Use the Formatting toolbar to set the more common cell formats.

The Fill option repeats the data in a cell to fill all the cells selected in the row, although the data is still stored only in the first cell. Note that this option applies only to a horizontal range, not to a vertical range. The Justify option aligns text evenly between the cell borders when longer entries wrap within a cell. (Turn text wrapping on and off using the Wrap text check box, which is also on the Alignment tab.) The next option in the Horizontal drop-down list is Center Across Selection, which centers the data in one cell across a range of adjacent cells. For example, to center the contents of cell A1 across columns A, B, C, and D, select cells A1 through D1, choose Format, Cells, click the Alignment tab, and select the Center Across Selection option in the Horizontal list. (For this option to work correctly, cells B1, C1, and D1 must be empty.)

To achieve a similar result (that is, similar to Center Across Selection alignment), you can select cells A1 through D1, and then click the Merge And Center button on the Formatting toolbar. The further effect of this command (which you can toggle on and off), is that Excel will treat the merged cells as a single cell. If you attempt to select cell C1, for example, after you have used the Merge And Center command in the example above, Excel will display your location (in the Name box) as cell A1.

Tip   For Horizontal alignment options that are followed by the word Indent (in parentheses), you can specify a measurement in the Indent box. For example, text that is formatted for Left alignment with an Indent value of 2 is aligned two picas from the left cell wall rather than immediately against the cell wall (the default).

The Horizontal drop-down list contains one final item, Distributed. This option, which is similar to Justify, evenly distributes text across the cell width and multiplies the height of the cell if necessary so that all the text is visible when wrapped. The appearance is similar to that of justified text except that incomplete lines are centered rather than left aligned. Figure 23-3 shows examples of several types of horizontal alignment formatting. (See the book's companion CD for a copy of the workbook Format.xls, shown in Figure 23-3.)

Chapter 23

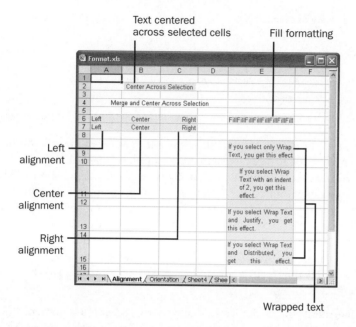

The Horizontal alignment options can create a variety of useful formatting effects.

Adjusting Vertical Alignment

The Alignment tab also allows you to adjust the *vertical* (top to bottom) alignment in cells. The default vertical alignment is Bottom, meaning that the cell contents are aligned to the bottom of the cell. However, if you change the row height to add additional white space to cells (you'll learn how to do this later in the chapter), you might enhance the appearance of your worksheet by selecting the Top or Center option in the Vertical drop-down list (see Figure 23-1).

> **Tip** An easy way to create multi-line text in a cell—and control where the text wraps—is to press Alt+Enter where you want a line break within the cell. The cell must, of course, be wide enough to accommodate the line lengths you specify.

If you have multiple lines of text in a cell, you can also use the Justify or Distributed alignment option to spread complete lines of text evenly between the top and bottom edges of the cell, multiplying cell height as necessary. If text is oriented vertically (as explained in the next section), the Justify and Distributed options differ just as they do for horizontal alignment: defaulting, respectively, to left (top) and centered alignment for incomplete lines of text.

Adjusting Text Orientation

A powerful formatting option on the Alignment tab is the Orientation setting, which changes the text orientation in the selected cells from the default horizontal orientation to an exact angle (measured in degrees) on a 180-degree semicircle. In the Orientation box, simply click the angle you want to use for the text or drag the word *Text* on the alignment compass. Excel will show you a preview of the orientation you select. This slick feature lets you create a ledger that includes space-saving, attractive column labels such as those shown in Figure 23-4. (See the book's companion CD for a copy of the workbook Format.xls, shown in Figure 23-4.)

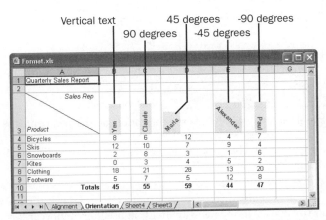

Figure 23-3.   The Orientation option in the Alignment tab lets you specify an exact angle for your text—just like using a protractor in art class.

> **Note**   Using the Degrees scroll box, you can specify an exact text angle from –90 degrees to +90 degrees.

One further option in this Orientation setting is the button you use to "stack" letters vertically in worksheet cells. To create this neat effect, click the vertical bar on the Alignment tab labeled *Text* (see Figure 23-1). When this bar is highlighted, Excel will create the stacked-letter effect shown in cell B3 in Figure 23-4. (The text orientation will be set to zero degrees.) This is a useful and visually interesting effect for labeling a column, especially if the text is brief.

Changing Number Formats

Excel allows you to change the appearance of your numeric entries by using several formatting options on the Number tab of the Format Cells dialog box, shown in Figure 23-5. To change the number format for a range of cells, begin by selecting the cells. If the first cell in the range contains a number, Excel will use that number in the Sample box to illustrate the changes in format. Next, choose Format, Cells or press Ctrl+1, click the Number tab, and select a category in the Category list.

Chapter 23

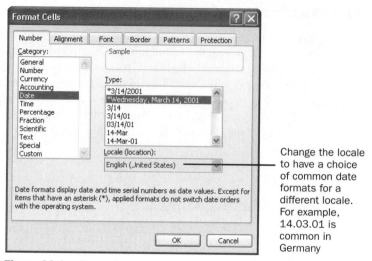

Figure 23-4. The Number tab lets you change the format of your numeric entries.

When you select a category, the tab changes, in most cases presenting additional format options that are appropriate to the category. If you select Currency, for example, you can specify a number of decimal places to display, a currency symbol, and a format for presenting negative amounts. On the other hand, if you're formatting a range of dates, the Date category presents a variety of date formats. Among them are five that use four-digit year formats. Excel includes these, of course, to eliminate the confusion that surrounded the Y2K rollover. After you make your format choices, you can click OK or move to another tab.

Table 23-1 describes the purpose of each numeric format category on the Number tab and shows examples of each.

Table 23-1. The Numeric Formats on the Number Tab

Category	Purpose	Examples
General	The default number format, right-aligned, with no special formatting codes.	15.75 5425
Number	A flexible numeric format that can be enhanced with commas, variable decimal places, and (for negative numbers) colors and parentheses.	3.14159 (1,575.32)
Currency	A general monetary format that can be enhanced with dollar signs, variable decimal places, and (for negative numbers) colors and parentheses. Excel supports the Euro format.	$75.35 ($1,234.10)
Accounting	A special currency format designed to align columns of monetary values along the decimal point. (The dollar sign appears along the left side of the cell.)	$ 75.00 $500.75

Table 23-1. The Numeric Formats on the Number Tab

Category	Purpose	Examples
Date	A general-purpose date format that displays calendar dates in several standard styles.	1/15/2000 15-Jan-01
Time	A general-purpose time format that displays chronological values in several standard styles.	3:30 PM 15:30:58
Percentage	A format that multiplies the value in the selected cell by 100 and displays the result using a percent sign (%).	175% 15.125%
Fraction	A format that expresses numbers as fractional values. (You specify the number of digits and denominator.)	1/8 2/16
Scientific	An exponential notation for numbers that contain a lot of digits.	1.25E-08 4.58E+12
Text	A format that treats numbers and formulas like text. (It aligns them on the left edge of the cell and displays them exactly as they are entered.)	500.35 12345.0
Special	A collection of useful formats that follow an alphanumeric pattern, including ZIP Code, Phone Number, and Social Security Number.	98109-1234 123-45-6789
Custom	A list of all standard formats (such as formats for foreign currency) and any custom numeric formats you create. (For more information, see "Creating a Custom Number Format," on page 654.)	INV-0075 £150.50

In addition to the options on the Number tab, you can use the Formatting toolbar buttons shown in Figure 23-6 to format the numeric entries in selected cells.

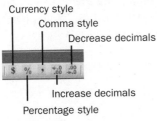

Currency style
Comma style
Decrease decimals
Increase decimals
Percentage style

Figure 23-5. The Formatting toolbar provides buttons for commonly used numeric formats.

Creating a Custom Number Format

If you routinely enter numeric values in a format that Excel doesn't recognize, you should consider creating a custom number format. For example, you might want to create a custom number format for part numbers or invoice numbers that include both letters and numbers or a monetary format that features international currency symbols. To create this type of custom format, choose Format, Cells or press Ctrl+1, click the Number tab, select Custom from the Category list, and then take either of the following steps:

- Modify an existing format by selecting it in the Type list and then editing it in the Type text box.

- Enter a new format in the Type text box using characters and one or more of Excel's special formatting symbols (given later).

Figure 23-7 shows the Custom option on the Number tab after a currency format using the British pound (£) symbol has been created.

If in creating a custom format you need to enter into the Type text box a symbol that isn't found on your keyboard (such as £), make sure Num Lock is turned on, hold down the Alt key, and type the appropriate four-digit code. Table 23-2 lists some of the most popular currency symbols and the keystrokes used to insert them.

Table 23-2. Currency Symbols and Keystrokes for Inserting Them

Country	Denomination	Symbol	Keystroke to Insert
United Kingdom	Pound	£	Alt+0163
Japan	Yen	¥	Alt+0165
United States	Cent	¢	Alt+0162

Tip When you create a custom format that contains special characters, you can use the Character Map utility included with Microsoft Windows XP to enter any available special character in the Type text box. In Character Map, select the character you want and copy it into the Clipboard. Then, paste the character into the Type text box. To run Character Map in Windows XP, choose Start, All Programs (or Programs), Accessories, System Tools, Character Map.

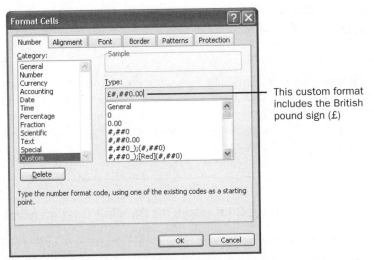

This custom format includes the British pound sign (£)

Figure 23-6. To create a custom number format, select the Custom option and either modify an existing format or create a completely new one.

Changing Excel's Default Currency Symbol

You can change the default currency symbol used in Excel and other Windows–based applications. In Windows XP, open the Control Panel, double-click the Regional And Language Options icon, and select the appropriate language and country or region in the drop-down list in the Standards And Formats area of the Regional Options tab. If you wish, you can then customize the format used to display monetary values for the selected language and country by clicking the Customize button in the Regional Options tab and selecting options in the Currency tab of the Customize Regional Options dialog box.

You can override the default currency formatting set through the Windows Control Panel in one or more specific cells by customizing the formatting using the Number tab of the Format Cells dialog box, as explained in this section.

To help you organize your custom number format, Excel lets you enter placeholders for digits, special symbols, and other useful characters using the formatting symbols shown in Table 23-3. You can also enter characters (such as currency symbols or useful abbreviations such as *Part* or *INV*) to be included in the format. For example, to create a custom part number format that translates the cell value 25 to the formatted part number *Part AA-025*, enter the code *Part AA-000* in the Type text box. To use the custom format later, click the Number tab, click the Custom Category, and then double-click the custom format in the list. You can also delete custom formats by highlighting the format and clicking the Delete button. (Excel won't let you delete the default formats.)

Chapter 23

Inside Out

Using custom and special formats

Custom and Special formats are especially useful if you need to enter a lot of data that combines numbers and punctuation, such as phone numbers or Social Security numbers. Creating a format can insert routine punctuation or prevent Excel from dropping a leading zero in a series of digits. The Special format for Social Security numbers, for instance, lets you enter the digits without the punctuation. Excel will insert the hyphens in their standard locations after you press Enter or move to a different cell.

Table 23-3. Useful Formatting Characters for Building Custom Number Formats

Character	Purpose	Example	Number Entered	Result
#	Creates a placeholder for significant digits, rounding to fit if necessary.	##.###	50.0048 2.30	50.005 2.3
0	Rounds numbers to fit like the # character, but fills any empty positions with zeros to align numbers and to fill all specified positions.	00.00	50.1 5	50.10 05.00
?	Also rounds numbers to fit, but fills any empty positions with spaces rather than extra zeros (if necessary) to align numbers and fill positions.	??.??	5.6 .70 73.27	5.6 .7 73.27
"text"	Adds the characters within the quotes to the value in the cell.	"ID " ##	75 2	ID 75 ID 2
comma (,)	Separates thousands in numbers.	#,###	5600	5,600
$, –, +, :, /, (,), space	Standard formatting characters. Each appears as specified in the custom numeric format.	$#.000	500.5	$500.500
%	Multiplies value by 100 and adds percent sign.	##%	.25	25%

Changing the Text Font and Text Color

To emphasize headings and distinguish different kinds of information in your worksheet, you can use the Font tab in the Format Cells dialog box, shown in Figure 23-8. The Font tab lets you change the font, style, size, and color of the text in selected cells. It also controls whether data is underlined and allows you to create special formatting effects such as strikethrough, superscript, and subscript. The fonts displayed on the Font tab depend on the type of printer you're connected to and the fonts installed on your system. Fonts preceded by a TrueType symbol are TrueType fonts designed to appear in print exactly as they do on the screen. You might also see fonts on the Font tab that have tiny printer icons in front of them; these are scalable fonts, which will look sharp when printed but might not display accurately on the screen. (The size will probably be right but the character shapes might not exactly match.)

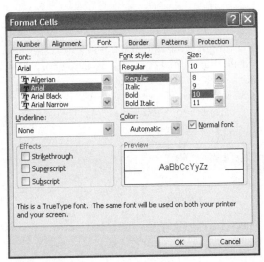

Figure 23-7. You can change the font and text color for selected cells in the Font tab of the Format Cells dialog box.

In addition to selecting formatting options in the Font tab, you can also use Excel's Formatting toolbar to change several font and text color options. Figure 23-9 shows the buttons you can use to increase your formatting speed.

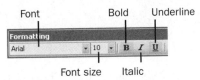

Figure 23-8. You can format selected text cells by using these Formatting toolbar buttons.

When you display the drop-down list of fonts on the Formatting toolbar, Excel shows each font in characters that match the font itself. If you don't need these visual cues, you can eliminate this somewhat cumbersome feature by choosing Tools, Customize and clicking the Options tab. Clear the option List Font Names In Their Font.

To change the text font and text color formatting in one or more cells, select the cells you want to format. (To format individual characters in a cell, see the sidebar called "Formatting Individual Characters in a Cell," on page 659.) Choose Format, Cells or press Ctrl+1, click the Font tab, and then use the lists and check boxes in the Font tab to adjust the font characteristics you want to change. The Preview area in the Font tab helps you verify that the appearance is what you want, especially if the font is unfamiliar. When you're finished, click the OK button.

> **Tip** If you want to return to the default font setting, select the Normal Font check box on the Font tab.

Adding Borders to Cells

Another useful technique for highlighting specific information in a worksheet is adding borders to important cells using the Border tab in the Format Cells dialog box, shown in Figure 23-10. The Border tab lets you place a solid or dashed line along one or more cell edges, and you can use the diagonal lines to divide cells from corner to corner. Borders help make the information in a worksheet easier to comprehend. You can emphasize particular cells, rows, and columns such as those containing headings or totals.

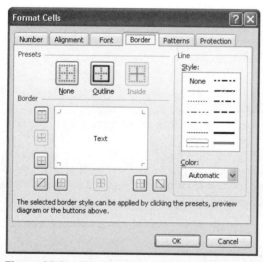

Figure 23-9. The Border tab lets you add borders and grids to selected cells.

To specify borders for the cells you've selected, first click one of the 14 line styles in the Style box (the None style removes existing borders). Then click the lines you want in the preview diagram in the Border box or click the buttons along the left and bottom of the Border box for the same result. As a shortcut, you can also use one of the three border styles in the Presets area: None (to remove existing borders), Outline (to place borders around the outside edges of the selected cells), or Inside (to place borders along the inside edges of the selected cells). You can also change the color of the border by selecting the desired color from the Color drop-down list. Remember to select the color before you select your borders.

Formatting Individual Characters in a Cell

You can also format individual characters in a cell if the cell contains a text value. (This technique won't work if the cell contains a numeric, date, or time value.) This useful feature lets you emphasize important words in a long text entry or create dramatic effects in headings. For example, you can italicize one word in a cell containing many words or change the first letter of a heading to a larger point size. To format individual characters in a cell, double-click the cell and select the character(s) you want to change. Then choose Format, Cells or press Ctrl+1 and change the attributes you want in the Font tab, or click the appropriate buttons on the Formatting toolbar. When you press Enter, the formatting will take effect.

Figure 23-11 shows an example of combined border styles. In the example we selected various ranges of cells and then applied outlines, partial outlines, and internal grids of different line weights as described in the labels. (See the book's companion CD for a copy of the workbook Orderfrm.xls, shown in Figure 23-11.)

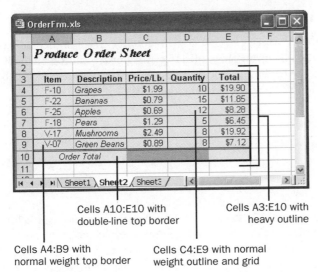

Cells A10:E10 with
double-line top border

Cells A3:E10 with
heavy outline

Cells A4:B9 with
normal weight top border

Cells C4:E9 with normal
weight outline and grid

Figure 23-10.   This worksheet uses a variety of border styles. You'll find a copy of this workbook on the book's companion CD, under the filename Orderfrm.xls.

Adding Instant Borders

A handy alternative to using the Border tab is clicking the Borders button on Excel's Formatting toolbar. In this case using the Formatting toolbar is much faster than using the Format Cells dialog box, and the toolbar also gives you single-step access to some formatting designs that require several steps using the Format Cells dialog box.

To use the Borders button, select the range of cells you want to highlight, click the down arrow to the right of the Borders button, and then pick from the 12 border options that appear on the drop-down menu, as shown in Figure 23-12 below. The bottom left style is useful for creating worksheet tables; it places a light border on the top of the cell and a heavier border on the bottom of the cell. Learning to use these border styles will save you considerable time as you format your worksheets.

Figure 23-11. The Borders button quickly applies commonly used border options to the selected range of cells.

Drawing Borders with the Borders Toolbar

If you're already comfortable with electronic drawing tools, you will immediately like the border drawing capability, which you can launch from the Borders button on the Formatting toolbar, shown in Figure 23-12 above. Choose the Draw Borders command from the Borders button drop-down menu to display the Borders toolbar shown here:

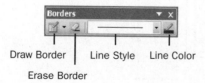

The Borders toolbar gives you access to all the features Excel offers for creating borders, and it lets you work directly on your worksheet cells. To draw borders, select the border style and color using the Line Style and Line Color controls, make sure that the Draw Border button is selected (highlighted), and then use the mouse to add borders (the mouse pointer will appear as a pencil). Either click the edge of a cell to apply a border to that edge, or click and drag to draw borders on several cell edges or to create a diagonal border across a cell. If you want to form a complete grid rather than just outside borders when you click and drag, click the down arrow on the Draw Border button and select the Draw Border Grid option from the drop-down menu. Click the Draw Border button itself to activate or deactivate border drawing mode.

Adding Shading to Cells

If you would like to create effects that complement the borders produced by the Border tab, the Patterns tab in the Format Cells dialog box shown in Figure 23-13 lets you add a solid background color, a colored background pattern, or both to one or more cells in your worksheet. To create effects, perform the following steps:

1 Select the cells you want to format.

2 Choose Format, Cells or press Ctrl+1 and click the Patterns tab.

3 To add a solid background color to the cells, click one of the colors shown in the Patterns tab.

4 To add a colored background pattern, first select the desired pattern from the Pattern drop-down list. Then, open the Pattern drop-down list again and select a color for the pattern.

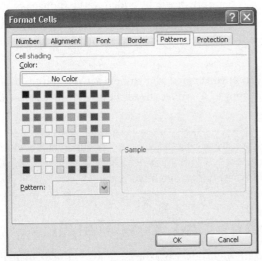

Figure 23-12. The Patterns tab lets you add color background shading and patterns to your cells.

> **Tip** An excellent practical use for background color is to shade every other row of a wide worksheet so that a reader can more easily glance across a row without confusion.

Color can make a striking addition to your worksheet and is ideal—if used in moderation—for documents created to be viewed electronically, such as status reports, departmental ledgers, sales projections, and the like. If you don't have a color printer, your color shading effects will be converted to gray tones when you print. (Not to worry, Excel usually does a good job at this.) To see what this conversion is like, you can view your worksheet using the File, Print Preview command.

Fill Color

You can also use the Fill Color button on the Formatting toolbar to apply a solid background color (but not a background pattern) to the selected worksheet cells. To remove an existing solid background color or background pattern from the selected worksheet cells, click the No Fill option.

Chapter 23

Copying Formatting Using the Format Painter Button

Occasionally you'll need to copy the formats from one cell to another cell without copying the data in the cell. For example, you might want to copy the cell formats you used to create a 14-point, bold, Times New Roman heading that has a thick border to a second heading you're creating later in the worksheet. Excel allows you to accomplish this task by using the Format Painter button on the Standard toolbar. To copy formatting using the Format Painter button, follow these steps:

1. Select the cell from which you want to copy formats.

2. Click the Format Painter button on the Standard toolbar. A marquee will appear around the selected cell and a paintbrush will be added to the mouse pointer.

Format Painter

3. Select the range of cells you want to change to the new format. You can switch to a different worksheet or workbook and navigate using the scroll bars without canceling the copying of the format.

If you decide you don't like the format you copied, remember that you can choose Edit, Undo to remove it. To cancel the format copy and remove the selection marquee before completing the operation, press Esc.

> **Tip** If you want to copy formats to cells or ranges that aren't contiguous, double-click the Format Painter button, and then select the cells you want to format one by one. When you've finished, click the Format Painter button again or press Esc.

Changing Column Widths and Row Heights

Excel gives you room for about eight digits in a worksheet cell if you use the default 10-point Arial font and the default column width. Worksheet cells are automatically resized whenever a number doesn't fit, unless you intentionally reduce a cell width so that a number won't fit—in that case Excel will display the number using the overflow characters, #######. Fortunately, it's easy to fiddle with your column widths and row heights if you want to format them in a special way. You can resize rows and columns by dragging with the mouse (the fastest method) or by using commands on the Format menu. We'll cover both techniques in this section.

> **Note** Different columns in a worksheet can be different widths, but all the cells in a particular column must be the same width. Likewise, different rows in the worksheet can have different heights, but all the cells in a particular row must be the same height.

Adjusting the Height or Width Manually

You can widen or narrow a column by dragging the right edge of the column heading with the mouse or by specifying a new width by using the Width command on the Format, Column submenu. Also, you can change a row's height by dragging the lower edge of the row heading or by specifying a new height by means of the Height command on the Format, Row submenu. Each method is described in the following sections.

For an automatic means of fitting spaces to dates, see "Using the AutoFit Command," on page 665.

Changing Column Width or Row Height Using the Mouse

Figure 23-14 shows how to change column width using the mouse. The process requires that you drag the right edge of the column heading at the top of the column. When the pointer is the right location for resizing, its shape changes to a sizing pointer with arrows pointing in opposite directions. To change row height using the mouse, follow a similar procedure: drag the lower edge of the row heading to increase or decrease the height.

 The Formula.xls example is on the companion CD to this book.

1 Position the mouse pointer at the right edge of the column heading and drag the column border, which appears as a dotted line

	A	B	C	D	E	F
1	Stock Watcher					
2						
3	Company	Ticker	Purchase	Last	Gain/Loss	
4	ABC Truck Parts	abct	$ 25.00	$ 27.50	10.0%	
5	Tasty Juice, Inc.	juce	$ 7.50	$ 7.50	0.0%	
6	FastChips Memory	fchp	$ 67.00	$ 39.50	-41.0%	
7	Internet Celebration	webc	$ 12.50	$ 75.00	500.0%	
8	Bouncy Balls, Ltd	bbbb	$ 18.00	$ 19.50	8.3%	
9	XYZ Steel	xstl	$ 38.00	$ 47.00	23.7%	
10						
11						
12						
13						
14						

Formula.xls — Width: 9.71 (73 pixels)

Sheet1 / Sheet2 / Sheet3

2 Release the mouse button to establish the new column width

Figure 23-13. Follow these steps to change the column width using the mouse. A ScreenTip displays the column width.

To change the width of several columns at one time with the mouse, select the columns you want to resize, and then drag and adjust one of the columns. When you release the mouse button, each of the columns will be the width of the one you changed. The same process applies to changing row heights. Select the rows and resize one of the rows in the selection.

Using the Column Width and Row Height Commands

The Width command on the Column submenu is useful if you want to type an exact width for the column you're resizing. Select a cell in the column you want to resize. To resize several columns at one time, select a cell in each of the columns you want to adjust. (Remember that you can select noncontiguous cells by pressing Ctrl while you click each cell.) Choose Format,

Chapter 23

Column, Width. The number you specify in the Cell Width dialog box is the average number of characters that will fit in the cell using the default font (defined as part of the Normal style, explained later in the chapter). Click the OK button to resize the column.

In a like manner, the Height command on the Row submenu is useful if you want to type an exact height for the row you're resizing. Highlight a cell in the row you want to resize. If you want to resize several rows at one time, select a cell in each of the rows you want to adjust. Choose Format, Row, Height. Specify the row height in the Row Height dialog box in points, and click the OK button. The standard height is based on the size of the default font.

Inside Out

Set your preferred column widths instantly

To set the default (or standard) width of columns in your worksheet, choose Format, Column, Standard Width and type the width you want. This command adjusts the width of every worksheet column that hasn't already been resized.

Hiding Columns and Rows

Note that you can use any of these resizing techniques to hide one or more columns or rows completely. Hiding a column, for example, is equivalent to setting its width to zero. Sometimes hiding data is desirable, either to shield the data from unauthorized glances or to keep it out of your way while you work.

Excel provides yet another way to hide one or more columns or rows: select the column or row you want to hide (or a cell in that column or row) and choose Hide from the Format, Column or Format, Row submenu. To restore the hidden column or row, select the columns or rows on both sides of the hidden entry (or cells in those columns or rows), and then choose Unhide from the Row or Column submenu. The hidden column or row will appear as you last saw it.

When you choose this command, the entire column or row, including the column letter or row number, will seem to disappear from the worksheet (though it hasn't actually been deleted).

Caution Hiding a column or row can be a great convenience but it can also be a risk. Be careful, for example, when deleting a range of columns and rows that you don't inadvertently delete hidden columns and rows in the process.

Although Excel doesn't permit you to specify different widths for cells in the same column (or different heights for cells in the same row), it does allow you to merge consecutive cells so that they're identified and treated as a single cell. (Also see "Adjusting Horizontal Alignment," on page 648.)

Using the AutoFit Command

If you want Excel to size your columns or rows automatically for you, use the AutoFit command on the Format, Column or Format, Row submenu. When you select a column and choose Format, Column, AutoFit Selection, Excel resizes the column to fit the widest entry in the column. This saves you the trouble of manually calculating point sizes or scanning every entry in a column as you drag the mouse. If you select a group of cells in a column, Excel adjusts the width based on the widest cell value in the selection, not the entire column.

Excel automatically resizes rows when you modify the font, so the row AutoFit command is less dramatic. When you select a row and choose Format, Row, AutoFit, Excel returns the row to the default height for the largest font being used in the row.

Applying a Combination of Effects Using AutoFormat

If you're formatting a block or table of cells, you can apply several formatting effects in one fell swoop by using the AutoFormat command on the Format menu. The AutoFormat command displays a dialog box that features several predesigned table styles in a list that you can scroll through. Figure 23-15 shows the AutoFormat dialog box displaying the two table formats that create a three-dimensional effect (3D Effects 1 and 3D Effects 2), as well as several other table formats. When you find the style you want, click OK to format the block of cells you selected as a table. You might try several styles on your own data to get the true visual effect and determine which one offers the most impact.

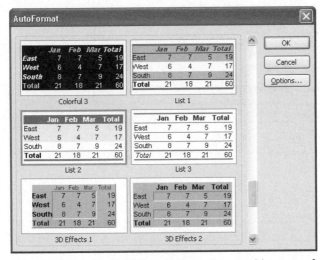

Figure 23-14. The AutoFormat dialog box provides many formats you can instantly apply to the selected cells in your worksheet.

By default, the AutoFormat command sets the Number, Border, Font, Patterns, Alignment, and Width/Height options to match the table style you select. You can limit the options used in AutoFormat by clicking the Options button in the dialog box and clearing the formatting

Chapter 23

features you don't want to change. For example, if you like a particular table style but don't want the border that's included, clear the Border check box, and click the OK button to apply the format's other characteristics.

Creating Conditional Formatting

Another slick feature of Excel is the ability it gives you to add *conditional formatting*—formatting that automatically adjusts depending on the contents of cells—to your worksheet. In plain English, this means that you can highlight important trends in your data—such as the rise in a stock price, a missed milestone, or a sudden spurt in your college expenses—based on conditions you set in advance using the Conditional Formatting dialog box. With this feature, an out-of-the-ordinary number "jumps out" at anyone who routinely uses the worksheet.

The following example shows how to add conditional formatting to a sample worksheet that tracks stock prices. If a stock in the Gain/Loss column rises by more than 20 percent, the conditional formatting will display numbers in bold type on a light blue background. If a stock in the Gain/Loss column falls by more than 20 percent, the number will appear in bold type on a solid red background. The worksheet is shown in Figure 23-16. (See the book's companion CD for a copy of the workbook CondForm.xls, shown in Figure 23-16.)

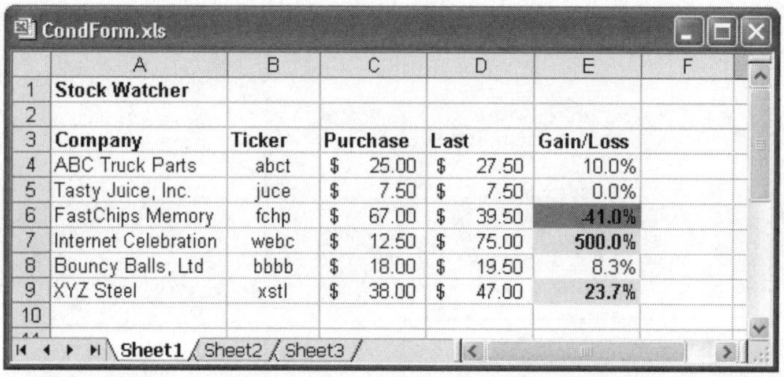

	A	B	C	D	E	F
1	**Stock Watcher**					
2						
3	**Company**	**Ticker**	**Purchase**	**Last**	**Gain/Loss**	
4	ABC Truck Parts	abct	$ 25.00	$ 27.50	10.0%	
5	Tasty Juice, Inc.	juce	$ 7.50	$ 7.50	0.0%	
6	FastChips Memory	fchp	$ 67.00	$ 39.50	**-41.0%**	
7	Internet Celebration	webc	$ 12.50	$ 75.00	**500.0%**	
8	Bouncy Balls, Ltd	bbbb	$ 18.00	$ 19.50	8.3%	
9	XYZ Steel	xstl	$ 38.00	$ 47.00	**23.7%**	
10						

CondForm.xls — Sheet1 / Sheet2 / Sheet3

Figure 23-15.   Conditional formatting highlights noteworthy numbers automatically, according to your specifications. You'll find a copy of this workbook on the book's companion CD, under the filename CondForm.xls.

To create such a conditional format, complete the following steps:

1   Create a worksheet containing one or more cells of numeric information. (The worksheet can be an invoice, a financial document, a sales report, or any other document with useful numeric data.)

2   Select the cell range to which you want to apply the conditional formatting. (Note that each cell can maintain its own, unique conditional formatting, so that you can set up several different conditions.)

3   Choose Format, Conditional Formatting. The Conditional Formatting dialog box will appear, displaying several drop-down lists, text boxes, and buttons.

4 In the first drop-down list, indicate whether you want Excel to use the current formula or the current value from the cells that you've selected. (In most cases you will want to use the cell value.) For our example, we chose to use the cell value.

5 In the second drop-down list, indicate the comparison operator you would like to use in the conditional formatting. For our example, we selected greater than, because we're looking for stock returns greater than 20 percent.

6 In the text box following the second drop-down list, type the number you want to use in the comparison. We typed 20%, or 0.2, because we want to isolate gains over 20 percent. (If you selected Between or Not Between in the second drop-down list, you'll need to enter low and high values into the *two* text boxes that appear.)

7 Click the Format button and specify the formatting you will use for the cells if the conditional statement you specified in steps 4 through 6 becomes true.

A modified Format Cells dialog box that has three formatting tabs will appear. We selected the Bold style on the Fonts tab and Light Blue on the Patterns tab and then clicked the OK button.

8 If necessary, click the Add button in the Conditional Formatting dialog box to add another condition to the scenario. (We took this opportunity to add a condition that highlighted losses of more than 20 percent in the worksheet.) The dialog box will expand to accept an additional condition.

> **Note** The Add button lets you add up to three conditions. The Delete button removes conditions you no longer want.

9 If you added a second condition, specify the features of the condition using the second set of drop-down lists, text box(es), and Format button as explained in steps 4 through 7.

We chose to use the cell value and the less than operator, and then typed –20%. (We could have typed –0.2 as well.) After clicking the Format button, we chose Bold for the font style on the Font tab, and then, using the Patterns tab, we specified solid red shading. Our screen looked like this:

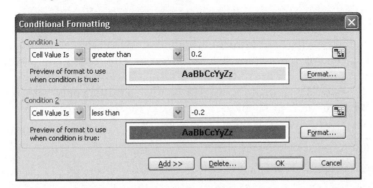

10 If necessary, add and define a third condition, as explained in steps 8 and 9.

11 Click the OK button to close the dialog box and the conditional formatting will be applied to the selected text. If any numbers fall into the ranges you specified, the formatting you specified will be applied. Figure 23-16 shows two gains and one loss highlighted by the conditional formatting we entered for this example. Our efforts certainly paid off, especially if we now act on the knowledge of our profits and losses!

Inside Out

Find the serial value for a date

You can use dates for comparisons, but Excel requires that you enter the date as a serial value, an integer incremented for each day beginning with January 1, 1900. To determine the appropriate value, enter the date in a cell and then reformat the cell to use General format. The date value will then be shown as a serial value. You can undo the formatting to restore the date to its previous formatting.

Tip   Find conditional formats

If you try to apply or remove cell formatting and find Excel strangely non-compliant, it might be that you've forgotten the conditional formatting that you've applied. (For example, if conditional formatting applies italics to a cell, you won't be able to remove the italics, nor will you be able to apply bold formatting, using the Formatting toolbar or the Font tab of the Format Cells dialog box.) Excel can help by finding all cells that have conditional formatting. To locate these cells, choose Edit, Go To, click the Special button, select Conditional Formats, and (below Data Validation) be sure All is selected. (Select Same rather than All to find all cells with conditional formatting identical to the conditional formatting of the currently selected cell.) When you click the OK button, Excel will indicate (with shading) all the cells with conditional formats.

Using Styles

If you routinely use the same formatting options for cells in your worksheets, you might want to consider creating a formatting *style* (a collection of formatting choices) that you can save with your workbook and use whenever you format information with the same attributes. After you create a new formatting style, or modify an existing one, you can use that style in any worksheet in your workbook, or you can copy the style to other open workbooks. In this section you will learn the following techniques:

- How to create your own styles
- How to apply existing styles
- How to copy or *merge* styles from other workbooks

Creating Your Own Styles

You create styles by using the Style command on the Format menu. When you choose this command, the Style dialog box will appear, as shown in Figure 23-17.

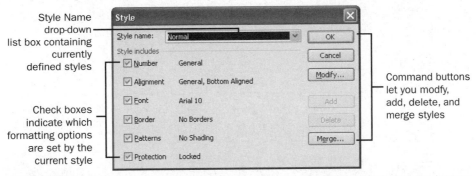

Style Name drop-down list box containing currently defined styles

Check boxes indicate which formatting options are set by the current style

Command buttons let you modfy, add, delete, and merge styles

Figure 23-16. You can use the Style dialog box to manage the formatting styles in your worksheet.

The easiest way to create a new style is by selecting a cell that has the formatting characteristics you want to assign to the style, choosing Format, Style, and giving the style a new name. This is called creating a style *by example*, because you use your own worksheet formatting to define the style.

If the cell you selected before choosing the Style command hasn't yet been formatted with a style, the Normal style will be displayed in the Style Name box. Excel predefines several styles in addition to the Normal style, including Comma, Currency, and Percent styles. If you want to modify one of these styles (or any other style that you previously defined) throughout the workbook, select the style in the Style Name drop-down list, click the Modify button, update the style using the tabs in the Format Cells dialog box, and click the OK button to return to the Style dialog box. When you click the OK button in the Style dialog box, the updated style will be changed throughout your workbook.

> **Tip** In the Style dialog box, you can also create a new style from scratch by typing a style name into the Style Name box and clicking the Modify button to set all the style's features. Then, either click the OK button to save the style and apply it to the selected range, or click the Add button to simply save the style.

The following steps show how to create a new style by example. The style we created is the vertically oriented column heading for Claude, shown in cell C3 in Figure 23-18. (See the book's companion CD for a copy of the workbook Format.xls, shown in Figure 23-18.) The heading is bold, dark blue, center-aligned, and rotated up 90 degrees in the cell. We call it Vertical Head.

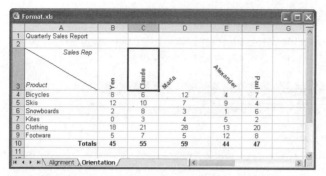

Figure 23-17. To create a new style by example, you select a cell in your worksheet that has the formatting you want to save for the new style. You'll find a copy of this workbook on the book's companion CD, under the filename Format.xls.

To create the Vertical Head style by example, follow these steps:

1 Format the cell you want to create your style from. For example, you could use the Alignment tab in the Format Cells dialog box to center the text horizontally and change the orientation, and then use the Font tab to change the font style to bold and dark blue.

2 Select the cell you just formatted.

3 Choose Format, Style.

4 Type *Vertical Head* (or another name of your choice) in the Sytle Name textbox

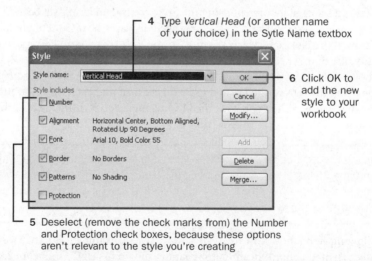

6 Click OK to add the new style to your workbook

5 Deselect (remove the check marks from) the Number and Protection check boxes, because these options aren't relevant to the style you're creating

If a style category (Number, Alignment, and so on) is cleared when you apply a style (there's no check mark in its check box), it means that the selected cells will keep their existing formatting for these categories.

Tip To delete a custom style you no longer want, select the style in the Style Name drop-down list and click the Delete button.

Applying Existing Styles

To apply an existing style in your workbook, either a predefined style or one that you've created, select the cell or range of cells to which you want to apply the style and choose Format, Style to open the Style dialog box. Then click the Style Name drop-down list to display the styles available in your workbook, select the style you want, check all the style categories (Number, Alignment, and so on) that you want to apply to the selected cell(s), and click the OK button.

Merging Styles from Other Workbooks

When you create a new style, you can use it only in the workbook where you create it—the new style is saved in the current workbook and won't appear in other workbooks. (This way, you won't mix up styles for your stock portfolio with those for your college expense budget.) However, you can copy or merge styles from other workbooks into the current workbook by using the Merge button in the Style dialog box.

> **Note**   Merging is a powerful tool, but use it with some caution. If the workbook into which you merge styles has matching style names, the new styles can override those existing styles and be applied throughout your workbook.

> **Tip**   Merging styles is a useful way to give your workbooks a consistent look. You can also use Excel templates (discussed in the next section) to format documents in a standard manner.

To merge styles from other Excel workbooks, follow these steps:

1   Open the *source* workbook (the workbook you want to copy styles from) and the *destination* workbook (the workbook you want to copy the styles to).

2   Activate the destination workbook and choose Format, Style.

3   Click the Merge button to display the Merge Styles dialog box shown below:

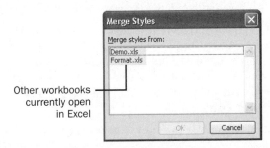

Other workbooks currently open in Excel

4   Select the name of the workbook you want to copy styles from (the source workbook), and then click the OK button.

Excel will copy all the styles from the source workbook to the destination workbook. If the source workbook contains formatting styles that have the same names as styles in the destination workbook, a warning message will appear asking whether you want to merge the styles with matching names anyway. If you click the Yes button, the styles will be merged, and the source styles will be applied throughout the workbook.

Note The Undo command does *not* reverse the effects of the Merge Styles dialog box. Be sure you want to copy over *all* the styles from the source workbook to the destination workbook before you click the Merge button. (Remember that you can delete unwanted styles before the merge by using the Delete button in the Style dialog box.)

Creating and Modifying Templates

Using formatting styles is a good way to organize existing data in a standard format. If you routinely create similar documents from scratch, however—such as monthly reports, purchase orders, or product invoices—consider creating an Excel template. A *template* is a file that serves as a model for creating new workbooks. The template can include workbook content as well as styles and macros. You can use the many preformatted templates that are included with the Microsoft Office 2003 software or available online from Office Online, or you can tell Excel to treat any of your own workbooks as a template. In this section, you'll learn

- How to create a new template file
- How to open and modify an existing template file

Tip   **Use an existing template**

If you want to use an existing Excel template to create a new workbook, choose File, New. Then use one of the three sources of templates that can be accessed through the New Workbook task pane:

- To use one of the templates provided with Office, click the On My Computer command in the Templates area and select the template in the Templates dialog box.

- To find, download, and use an online template from the Office Online site, either enter a keyword into the Search Online For text box and click the Go button, or click Templates On Office Online to run your browser and open the Templates home page of the Office Online Web site. You can also access this Web site by clicking the Templates On Office Online button at the bottom of the Template dialog box, which was mentioned in the previous instruction.

- To open a template that is stored on a Web site belonging to you or your company, click On My Web Sites.

For more information on using Office 2003 templates and wizards to create documents, see "Creating New Office Documents," on page 47. In particular, see "Downloading and Using Templates from Office Online," on page 55, for information on using Microsoft's expanded collection of online templates and the new Template Help task pane available in Office 2003 applications.

Inside Out

Create workbooks based on existing workbooks

Excel users have long recognized that using a template—or even an existing data file—to get a head start on file creation is simply smart and efficient. The only problem with using an existing data file rather than a template as a starting point was the danger that arose when you saved the new file—unintentionally overwriting the data file that you used as a head start.

Happily, Excel has finally adapted to the work habits of users by allowing you to create a new file based on an existing data file and then protecting you from inadvertently overwriting your original file. The provisional filename for the new file is a unique name, such as MyFile2, derived from, but not identical to, your original data file. To create a new workbook based on an existing one, choose File, New and then click the From Existing Workbook command in the New Workbook task pane.

Creating a New Template File

To make a new template file using one of your own workbooks as a model, complete the following steps. When you're finished, you will have a template you can use each time you want to create a workbook that has the formatting you've included.

1. Open the workbook you want to save as a template file.
2. Choose File, Save As. The Save As dialog box will appear.
3. Select Template (*.xlt) in the Save As Type drop-down list.
4. Enter a name for the template in the File Name text box, specify a folder location for the template by using the Save In list, and then click the Save button.

    When the Template (*.xlt) item is selected in the Save As Type drop-down list, the Save As dialog box automatically opens your current User Templates folder. If you want the Templates dialog box to display the new template you are creating, you must save it in the file folder designated as your User Templates folder, or in one of its subfolders. The default User Templates folder is C:\Documents and Settings*User Name*\Application Data\Microsoft\Templates, where *User Name* is the name you use for logging on to Windows. You can save the template directly within your User Templates folder; in this case, the template will appear in the General tab of the Templates (or New Office Document) dialog box. Alternatively, you can place it within a subfolder of your User

Chapter 23

Templates folder (an existing subfolder or a new one that you create); in this case, the template will be displayed in the Templates (or New Office Document) dialog box in a tab that's labeled with the name of the subfolder.

> You can change the location of your User Templates folder using Microsoft Word. The setting you make affects all Office applications that use templates. For instructions, see the tip "Choose locations for your templates," on page 415.

5 Close the workbook you saved as a template. The next time you want to use the template as a workbook model, choose File, New. Then, click the On My Computer command in the New Workbook task pane and select the template in the Templates dialog box.

Opening and Modifying an Existing Template File

To open and modify an existing workbook template—either a template included with Office 2003 or one you created on your own—follow these steps:

Open

1 Choose File, Open, or click the Open button on the Standard toolbar. The Open dialog box will appear.

2 In the Files Of Type drop-down list, select Templates (*.xlt).

3 Browse to the folder or Web site containing the template you want to open, select the template, and click the Open button. Excel will open the template file.

The templates supplied with Office are normally stored in a subfolder of the following folder on the hard disk in which you installed Office: \Program Files\Microsoft Office\Templates. For a description of the folder where you normally store the custom templates that you have created, see step 4 of the previous section, "Creating a New Template File."

If the template you opened was included with the Office 2003 software, it typically contains several worksheet tabs and operating instructions. It may also contain a useful template toolbar that has custom template commands and online Help for the template.

4 Unless you want to overwrite the original template file with the modified template that you create, choose File, Save As. When the Save As dialog box appears, give the template a new filename and possibly a new file location. For recommendations on where you should save a custom or modified template, see step 4 of the procedure in the previous section, "Creating a New Template File." Click the Save button to save the template file to disk.

> **Tip** When you modify a template, we strongly recommend saving your modified template to a new file rather than overwriting the original template file, by following the instructions in step 4. This way, you can still use the original template if you don't like the modifications you made or if the modifications aren't suitable for a particular application.

5 Your new template is now ready to be customized. When you're finished adding the touches you want, save your changes and close the template. Each time you open this template in the future, it will be ready to use as a boilerplate workbook.

Changing Page Breaks

After you format your worksheet, you might want to adjust where the page breaks fall, particularly for longer worksheets. A *page break* is a formatting code that tells your printer to stop printing information on one page and start printing on the next page. Excel adds a page break to your worksheet when a page is full and identifies the division with a light dashed line. (Excel adds both vertical and horizontal page breaks.) If you don't want to see these breaks as you work, choose Tools, Options. Then click the View tab and clear the Page Breaks option in the Window Options area.

You can set your own page breaks manually in the worksheet. For example, you might choose to place a page break between a table and a remittance form to keep all the table entries separate from the mail-back form. To set a manual page break in the worksheet, perform the following procedure. The result is shown in Figure 23-19:

1 Select the cell that you want to be located at the upper-left corner of the new page. (In the example shown in Figure 23-19, we selected cell G21. See the book's companion CD for a copy of the workbook Invoice.xls, shown in Figure 23-19.)

2 Choose Insert, Page Break.

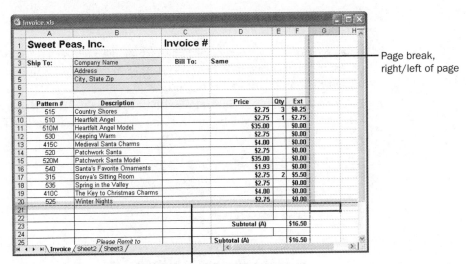

Page break, bottom/top of page

Figure 23-18. In Normal view, Excel indicates page breaks with bold dashed lines. You'll find a copy of this workbook on the book's companion CD, under the filename Invoice.xls.

The manual page break will appear as a bold dashed line (assuming that the Page Breaks view option is checked, as described previously in this section).

Tip   **Remove a manual page break**

To remove both the bottom and right edges of a manual page break, click the cell just below and just to the right of the page break (that is, the cell at the upper-left corner of the new page), and choose Insert, Remove Page Break.

To remove just the bottom of the page break or just the right side, before you choose the Insert, Remove Page Break command, select any cell directly below or directly to the right of the page break *except* the cell at the upper-left corner of the new page.

Using Page Break Preview

Excel also provides a special worksheet view called Page Break Preview that quickly identifies the page breaks in your worksheet and allows you to manipulate them easily. Page Break Preview shows you a miniature version of your worksheet (a little like the Print Preview command on the File menu), but marks page breaks with a thick bold line and highlights page numbers with giant labels so that you can quickly find your place (see Figure 23-20). To display the page break preview, choose View, Page Break Preview. To return to the Normal view of your workbook, choose View, Normal.

To view and modify page breaks in Page Break Preview, follow these steps:

1. Choose View, Page Break Preview. Excel will start Page Break Preview mode, as shown in Figure 23-20.

2. If you see a dialog box that displays a welcome message, read the instructions about modifying page breaks, and then click OK. (You can suppress this dialog box by clicking Do Not Show This Dialog Again.)

3. Examine the page breaks in your worksheet by using the vertical and horizontal scroll bars. Individual pages will be marked with large labels, and page breaks will be marked with bold lines.

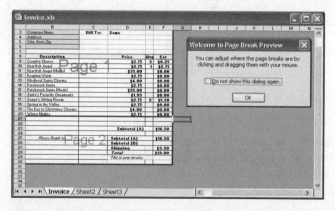

Figure 23-19. To change a page break, simply drag a break line to a new location.

> **Note** Page Break Preview is an active editing mode, so you can add information to worksheet cells, select ranges, choose commands, or edit individual entries while you preview your page breaks. However, you'll probably find it easier to read the contents of worksheet cells in Normal view.

4   To change a page break marked with a bold line, drag the break line with the mouse to a new location in the worksheet. When you release the mouse button, Excel will repaginate the worksheet and display the new page break. (If you want to reverse the change, you can reinstate the old page break by simply clicking the Undo button on the Standard toolbar.)

5   When you're finished working in Page Break Preview, choose View, Normal.

Chapter 23

Power Organizing with Workbooks

Managing Worksheets 679

Referencing Cells in Other
Worksheets 685

Using More Than One Workbook 687

Managing Shared Workbooks 693

Protecting Worksheets and
Workbooks 698

Worksheets are the basic building blocks used to store information in Microsoft Office Excel 2003, and workbooks are the organizational tools you can use to manage your worksheets effectively. By default, each Excel workbook contains three worksheets. In this chapter you'll learn how to switch between worksheets, name worksheets, add worksheets to a workbook, delete unwanted worksheets from a workbook, and rearrange worksheets. You'll also learn how to work with more than one workbook at a time, link information between worksheets and workbooks, create and manage shared workbooks on a network, and hide and protect worksheets and workbooks. When you're finished, you'll have all the tools you need to manage workbooks effectively.

Managing Worksheets

Workbooks help you organize the reports, ledgers, tables, and forms you use every day. In the early days of electronic spreadsheets, users typically created a new file for each worksheet they built. This approach worked fine for casual spreadsheet users, but experienced business users, who often worked with literally hundreds of worksheets, were soon swamped with files and folders. (If this sounds like you now, you'll like this section!)

Excel now provides the ability to create workbooks containing up to 255 worksheets. Although you're not actually required to save more than one worksheet in a workbook, this organizational feature gives you the option of collecting similar worksheets in one place. People use this capability in a variety of effective ways. For example, you can store all the annual worksheets related to product development costs (research, manufacturing, marketing, packaging, and so on) in one workbook entitled Development Costs 2003. Or you can break out the manufacturing cost estimates in one workbook, where each worksheet is a detailed cost estimate for a different product or a different estimate for the same product from a different vendor.

The value of worksheets is often apparent by the ease with which you can switch among them to print or edit information of different types. Changing worksheets is usually far easier than jumping or scrolling to locate subsections within the expanse of a single worksheet. Some workbooks, for example, have two or three sheets: the first for entering variable data, the second to present a chart or other analysis of the data, and perhaps a third that formalizes the results in a report.

In the first part of this chapter you'll learn the basic skills needed to manage worksheets in workbooks. You'll learn how to

- Switch between worksheets in a workbook
- Name your worksheets
- Delete worksheets from a workbook
- Add worksheets to a workbook
- Change the order of worksheets in a workbook
- Group worksheets for easier manipulation

Switching Between Worksheets

By default, each new Excel workbook contains three identical worksheets named Sheet1, Sheet2, and Sheet3. Each worksheet is identified by a *worksheet tab* at the bottom of the worksheet window, as shown in Figure 24-1. To switch between worksheets, you click the tab for the worksheet you want to display; and that worksheet then appears as the active worksheet in the workplace. To the left of the worksheet tabs are the *tab scroll buttons*, which you can use to display worksheet tabs not currently visible. Clicking the outside navigation arrows displays the first and last tabs in the workbook, and clicking the inside arrows displays tabs that aren't visible immediately to the left and right. To switch between worksheets in a workbook, follow the steps in Figure 24-1.

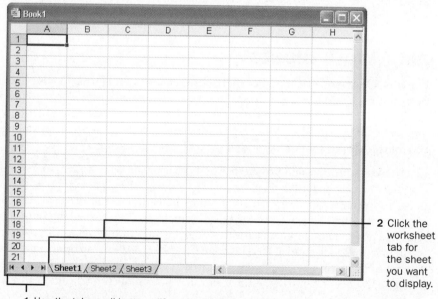

2 Click the worksheet tab for the sheet you want to display.

1 Use the tab scroll buttons (if necessary) to bring into view any worksheet tabs that may be hidden.

Figure 24-1. Use the worksheet tabs at the bottom of the window to switch between worksheets.

Naming Worksheets

The default names for worksheets—Sheet1, Sheet2, and so on—are just placeholders for more useful and intuitive names that you devise. You can name or rename a worksheet at any time by double-clicking the worksheet tab to select the title and then typing a new name (see Figure 24-1).

You can use up to 31 characters in your worksheet names (including spaces), but remember that the more characters you use, the fewer worksheet tabs you'll be able to see at one time. It's a good idea to strike a balance between meaningful and brief names.

You can also use a menu command to rename the worksheet that's currently visible. To do that, choose Format, Sheet, Rename and then type the new worksheet name and press Enter.

Changing Tab Color

Besides assigning a meaningful name to a tab, you can also change the tab color. This is useful for color-coding tabs for easier recognition or for indicating groups of worksheets that have a similar function. To change the tab color, choose Format, Sheet, Tab Color. Then, in the Format Tab Color dialog box that appears (shown below) select a color for the tab (or select No Color to remove a tab color) and click the OK button. Note that a worksheet's tab color will be fully apparent only when a different worksheet is active. While the worksheet itself is active, the tab will be white and the text will be underlined in the selected color.

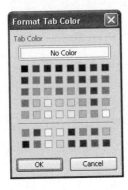

Deleting Worksheets

Although each empty worksheet in a workbook takes up only about 500 bytes of disk space, if you don't plan to use all the worksheets in a workbook, you can delete the unused worksheets to save space. (You can always add new worksheets later.) To delete a worksheet, activate it and then choose Edit, Delete Sheet.

Tip **Change the default number of worksheets**

By default, Excel displays three worksheets in a newly created workbook. However, you can adjust this number by choosing Tools, Options, clicking the General tab, and specifying a new number in the Sheets In New Workbook text box, either by typing a new number or by using the up or down arrow to increase or decrease the current value. You can specify any number from 1 through 255.

Caution Once you delete a worksheet—even if it contains several rows and columns of data—the worksheet will be permanently erased and you won't be able to undo the command.

Inserting Worksheets

Excel lets you add a new, empty worksheet to your workbook at any time by choosing the Insert, Worksheet command. When you insert a new worksheet, Excel places it before the active worksheet and assigns it an initial name, such as Sheet5. Figure 24-2 shows how a new sheet will be inserted if your workbook contains three worksheets and if Europe is the active worksheet. After you insert a new worksheet, you can change its name, as described in "Naming Worksheets," on the previous page.

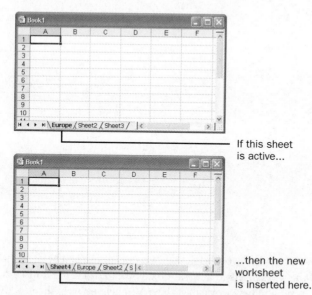

If this sheet is active...

...then the new worksheet is inserted here.

Figure 24-2. Excel inserts a new worksheet before the active worksheet in the workbook.

> **Tip** If you right-click a worksheet tab, a shortcut menu will appear with commands that let you accomplish common tasks with the active worksheet: deleting, renaming, copying, and the like. You can use this technique to speed up many of your workbook management tasks.

Moving or Copying Worksheets

If you don't like the placement of the worksheets you've created, you can easily move them within the workbook by using a simple drag-and-drop technique. To relocate a worksheet, click the tab for the worksheet you want to move, and then drag it to the desired new location. (A tiny down arrow will appear, indicating the location where the worksheet will be inserted if you release the mouse button.) Figure 24-3 shows how the three-step process works.

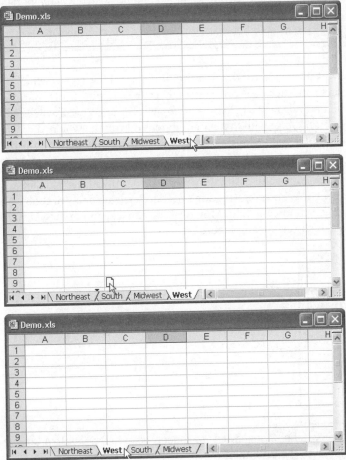

Figure 24-3. To move a worksheet, drag the worksheet tab to a new location.

Inside Out

Working with grouped worksheets

To select a group of worksheets, Excel uses a technique that's relatively consistent across the Microsoft Office System. First, activate one sheet in the group and then hold the Ctrl key as you click the tab for each additional sheet you want to select. To select a series of consecutive worksheets, activate the first sheet, hold the Shift key, and click the tab for the last sheet. A quick way to select all the worksheets in the workbook is to right-click a tab and then choose Select All Sheets from the shortcut menu. The word [Group] in the title bar indicates that several sheets are selected.

You can perform many actions on a selected group of worksheets rather than repeating the same action on each one individually. For example you can print, delete, move, or copy sheets, add headers and footers, or use many of the formatting commands on a group of sheets. To cancel the selection, click a tab that isn't in the selected group or right-click a selected tab and choose Ungroup Sheets from the shortcut menu. If all the sheets are selected, you can click any tab other than the one that's currently active.

You can copy a worksheet in a workbook by holding down the Ctrl key while you drag a tab from one location to another. This procedure will create a duplicate of the worksheet in the workbook. The name and any tab color will be copied also, and a "(2)" will be added to show that it's the second worksheet with that name. To remind you that you're duplicating a worksheet, the mouse pointer will include a plus (+) sign during the drag-and-drop operation.

Excel also makes it easy to move or copy a worksheet from one workbook to another. To begin, open both the source and destination workbooks. (If you want to move or copy the sheet to a new workbook, however, you don't need to open a blank workbook. You'll see the reason shortly.) Then choose the Edit, Move Or Copy Sheet command, which displays the Move Or Copy dialog box shown in Figure 24-4.

Figure 24-4. To copy rather than move a worksheet, be sure the Create A Copy check box is checked before you click the OK button.

From the To Book drop-down list, select the destination workbook. If you select (*new book*) for the destination, Excel will insert the sheet in an otherwise empty workbook—but it won't create the default number of blank sheets in addition to the moved or copied worksheet. If you want those default blank sheets to be included, click the New button on the Standard toolbar to create a new workbook before you begin the move or copy process; then, in the Move Or Copy dialog box select the new workbook as the destination.

After you specify the destination workbook in the To Book drop-down list, choose the location for the sheet in the Before Sheet list. Excel generates the list of sheets from the worksheet names in the destination workbook. Finally, if you want to copy rather than move the worksheet to the destination workbook, check the Create A Copy option.

Referencing Cells in Other Worksheets

When you create a workbook containing several worksheets, you will often want to reference the data in one worksheet when you build a formula in another worksheet. Setting up a connection between worksheets is sometimes called creating a *link* in Excel terminology, although nowadays the term tends to be associated with references in one file to objects located in another.

To learn how to link worksheets together in different workbooks, see "Linking Information Between Workbooks," on page 688.

Let's consider an example. If your workbook contains a separate worksheet for each sales region in the country, you could create a summary worksheet that includes sales data from each of the supporting worksheets. This use of references to other worksheets provides an additional advantage: when you change the source worksheet, Excel will update the related information in the dependent worksheet.

The following procedure shows you how to create formulas that reference other worksheets. The sample workbook contains five worksheet tabs—Summary, Northwest, South, Midwest, and West. Four of these tabs contain regional worksheets that present quarterly sales data for each of a company's sales representatives active in the region. (The sales reps are listed individually by name.) The Summary worksheet presents an overview of the sales activity throughout the year and uses several SUM functions to calculate the quarterly totals from each of the linked worksheets. You might want to use this worksheet structure in your own workbooks.

To create formulas that calculate totals from other worksheets and place them on a single summary worksheet, follow these steps:

1 Create your regional worksheets in a workbook or use your own data containing a similar pattern of detail-level worksheets that you want to sum up in a summary worksheet.

The following screen shows the sample worksheet named Northeast, which contains quarterly sales figures for the six sales reps active in the Northeast sales region.

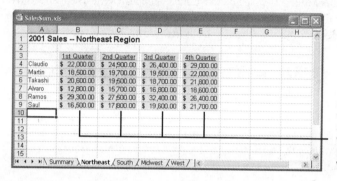

Each column of sales figures will be summed, and those sums will be displayed in the Summary worksheet.

 The SalesSum.xls example is on the companion CD to this book.

2 Add a new worksheet to your workbook to display the totals from the other worksheets. (Add the worksheet by choosing Insert, Worksheet, and then change the name to *Summary* or another appropriate name.)

3 Using the SUM function, add formulas to the Summary worksheet that compute totals. Begin each formula by typing =SUM(.

4 To specify a range for the SUM function, click the worksheet tab you want to include in the formula, and then select the range of cells you want to use within the link. For example, to add the six sales figures from the 1st Quarter column in the Northeast worksheet, click the Northeast worksheet tab, and then select cells B4 through B9. The customized formula will appear in the formula bar; the worksheet name and cell range will be separated by an exclamation mark (Northeast!B4:B9).

5 Press the Enter key to complete the formula. Excel will add a closing parenthesis to complete the function.

Excel will calculate the result and display it in cell B4 of the Summary worksheet, as shown in the following illustration. The completed formula will also appear in the formula bar.

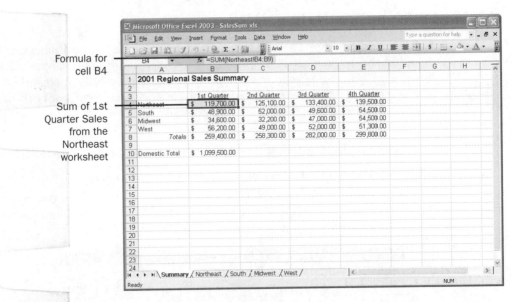

Formula for cell B4

Sum of 1st Quarter Sales from the Northeast worksheet

6 Repeat steps 2 through 5 to add linking formulas for the remaining summation cells.

Using More Than One Workbook

As you complete daily tasks with Excel, you'll often find it necessary to open additional workbooks to review sales figures, prepare an invoice, copy data, or complete other work. Excel allows you to load as many workbooks into memory as your system can handle. Each workbook appears in its own document window. Each workbook is given a separate icon on the Windows taskbar, provided that the Windows In Taskbar option is enabled (you can access this option by choosing Tools, Options and clicking the View tab). You can switch to any open workbook by clicking the workbook's icon on the taskbar or by choosing the workbook's filename from the Window menu. (Excel lists files on the Window menu in the order that you open them, from most recent to least recent.) You can also browse through opened workbooks by pressing Ctrl+F6. The following sections show you how to

- Link information between open workbooks
- Consolidate information from a series of similar sheets
- Use multiuser workbooks in a network setting

For information on opening multiple documents, working with document windows, and using Office 2003's new side-by-side document comparison feature, see "Working with Multiple Documents," on page 74.

Chapter 24

Linking Information Between Workbooks

Earlier in this chapter you learned how to build formulas that reference other worksheets in the workbook. You can also build formulas that reference worksheets in other workbooks. Before you create the linked formula, however, you must open each of the workbooks you plan to use. The following example adds the total revenue from a workbook named SalesLnk (containing international sales data) to the domestic sales total calculated in the SalesSum workbook.

If you want to create formulas that reference other workbooks, follow these steps:

1 Open the workbooks you plan to reference in your formulas.

You can practice by opening SalesSum and SalesLnk on your companion CD. The following screen shows the sample workbook named SalesLnk, which computes the total revenue received by a company from areas outside the United States:

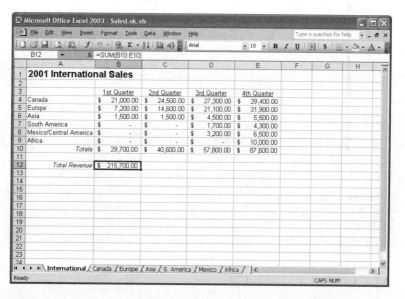

 The SalesLnk.xls, SalesSum.xls, South SalesSum.xls, and South SalesSum Completed.xls workbooks are on the companion CD to this book.

2 Add a formula to your worksheet that references cells in other workbooks.

For example, to copy a grand total from the International worksheet in the SalesLnk workbook to SalesSum, start in the cell in the Summary worksheet in SalesSum where you want to display the data, type an equal sign (=), click the SalesLnk workbook on the Windows taskbar (or press F6, repeatedly if necessary, to activate SalesLink if it doesn't appear in the taskbar), click the International worksheet tab, click the cell with the total you want to incorporate (B12 in this example), and press Enter. The linking formula will appear in the formula bar; if you examine the formula notation, you'll find the workbook filename enclosed in square brackets, followed by the worksheet name, an exclamation mark, and the linked cell's column letter and row number each preceded with a dollar sign ($). Your screen will look similar to this one:

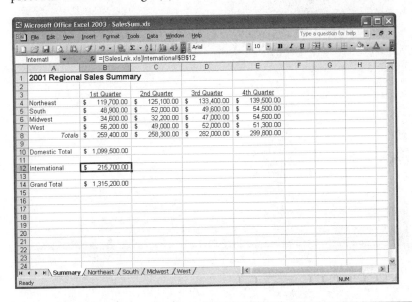

A dollar sign ($) preceding the column letter or the row number in a cell address indicates an *absolute reference*. For an explanation of absolute and relative references, see "Using Relative and Absolute Cell References," on page 730.

Consolidating Worksheets with Identical Formats

If you want to link several worksheets that share a common organizational format, you can also use the Data, Consolidate command to assemble workbook information. When you consolidate worksheets, you can use one or more *statistical functions* on the cell ranges you select to obtain useful information about your data. The statistical functions available include Sum, Count, Average, Max, Min, and StdDev.

You'll learn more about using statistical functions in Chapter 26, "Crunching Numbers with Formulas and Functions."

Consider, for example, a series of quarterly sales reports presented as a set of worksheets such as the ones shown here. You can load this workbook, South SalesSum.xls, from the companion CD. If each quarterly report has the same layout, as is the case in this sample workbook, you can create a consolidated view to present (for example) the total annual sales for each of the sales reps.

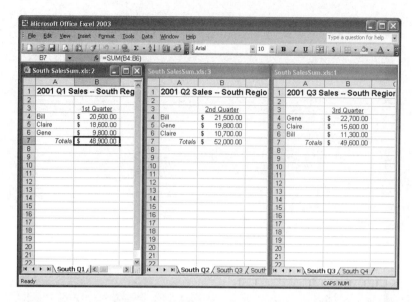

To use the Consolidate command to create a summary view, activate a blank worksheet or insert one at the front of the workbook. Rename the sheet Sales Summary. Now follow these steps:

1 Add the headings shown below to the blank worksheet.

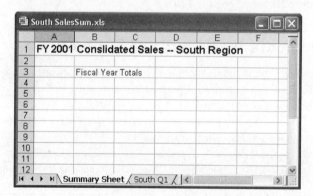

2 Make cell A4 the active cell and then choose the Data, Consolidate command.

3 In the Consolidate dialog box (shown in Figure 24-5), we'll use the Sum function, which is selected by default. This function sums data from corresponding cells in each of the ranges that you specify in the next step. You could open the drop-down list and choose another function if you wanted a different result, such as average quarterly sales.

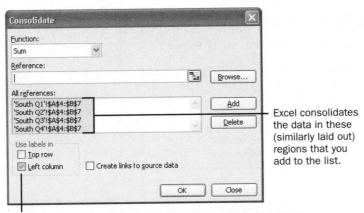

Excel consolidates the data in these (similarly laid out) regions that you add to the list.

Using column labels means that Excel associates rows with the same labels rather than those with exactly the same position.

Figure 24-5. The Consolidate command lets you identify the corresponding ranges of cells and the function to apply in the consolidation.

4 Click in the Reference box and then indicate the first reference by choosing the South Q1 tab and selecting the sales reps and results (including totals) in the first two columns, cells A4:B7. Click Add to add the range to the All References list.

5 Repeat the procedure in step 4 to add the same cell range from each of the other quarterly sales worksheets. (You'll notice that after you select the range in the South Q1 worksheet, Excel automatically selects the corresponding ranges in the three other worksheets. Therefore, you'll need only to switch to each of those three other worksheets and click the Add button in the Consolidate dialog box.) When all four ranges are specified, the dialog box will appear as shown in Figure 24-5.

6 Check the Left Column option to use the labels in the left column for correlating the data. Why is this important? In every quarter the sales reps are listed in order of performance, with the best sales results on top. This means that their order might change from quarter to quarter. To ensure that the sums, when consolidated, correctly follow the figures for each sales rep rather than simply totaling cell contents in corresponding locations, you specify that Excel should use the labels in the left column.

7 Click the OK button to generate the consolidation. The result is shown in the illustration given on the next page.

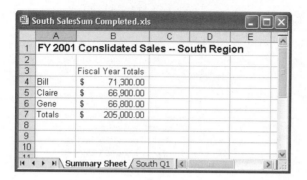

 Note You can open the South SalesSum Completed.xls workbook on the companion CD to see the results of completing these steps.

Saving a Workspace File

If you often use the same collection of workbooks in Excel, consider creating a *workspace file* to save information about which workbooks are open and how they appear on the screen. The next time you want to use the workbooks, simply open the workspace file, and each workbook will appear as it did when you last saved the workspace, including toolbars, cell selections, and other tools in the user interface. The workspace file doesn't include unsaved changes you make to your worksheets—you need to save these separately by using the Save or Save As command—but it *does* keep track of your open windows and worksheets, so that you can pick up right where you left off.

To save the arrangement of open workbooks in a workspace file, follow these steps:

1 Open and organize your workbooks as you would like them saved in the workspace file. (Creating a workspace file is a little like taking a picture, so get everything positioned just where you want it.)

2 Choose File, Save Workspace. The Save Workspace dialog box will appear. (It works basically like a Save As dialog box.)

3 Type a name for the workspace file in the File Name text box and specify a folder location if necessary. Either include the .xlw extension in the filename you type or omit the extension (in that case, Excel will provide it).

4 Click the Save button to save the workspace file. (You might also be prompted to save one or more of the open workbooks.)

When you're ready to open the workspace file later, locate the document and open it as you would any Excel document. Your workbooks and worksheets will appear just as you last saved them, including any cell selections you made.

Managing Shared Workbooks

If you have access to a shared folder on an attached network, you can create *shared workbooks* that several people can open and use simultaneously. This powerful feature allows you to distribute the responsibility for group tasks, such as revolving product inventories, incoming customer orders, or corporate mailing lists. The following steps show you how to create and maintain a shared workbook.

> If your workbook contains information arranged under uniform headings, you can set it up as an Excel database. See Chapter 28, "Power Database Techniques: Lists, Filters, and Pivot Tables."

 ## Troubleshooting

Features unavailable in shared workbooks

Excel does not support a feature that you want to use in a shared workbook.

If you work on a shared workbook, you'll eventually try to make a change that Excel doesn't allow or support for shared data. These limitations are detailed in Excel online Help under "Features That Are Unavailable in Shared Workbooks." As you'll see, this excellent Help item suggests alternatives for many situations. For example, although you can't insert or delete a block of cells, you can insert and delete entire rows and columns.

> **Tip**   To use a shared workbook, you need access to a shared folder on a computer network (not on an Internet server). If you or your colleagues don't have access to such a shared folder, ask your network system administrator how to get one or how to create one on your own computer.

Creating a Shared Workbook

To create a shared workbook, follow these steps:

1   Build the workbook you want to share as you normally would. Because a number of users will be working with the worksheets in your workbook, take extra care to format the contents clearly and concisely. You might also want to add cell comments that contain operation instructions and tips.

2   Choose Tools, Share Workbook. When the Share Workbook dialog box appears, click the Editing tab, as shown in the following illustration.

3 Check the Allow Changes By More Than One User At The Same Time option to designate the workbook as a shared workbook and then click the OK button. A message box will appear asking you if it's all right to save your workbook (a requirement if the workbook is to be shared).

4 Click the OK button in the message box to save the workbook.

To learn how to add comments to worksheet cells, see "Entering Comments," on page 616.

After you save the workbook, the word *Shared* will appear in the title bar between brackets, indicating that you're now editing a multiuser or shared workbook. As long as the Allow Changes By More Than One User At The Same Time option is checked on the Editing tab of the Share Workbook dialog box, you'll be able to save formulas in the workbook and modify any cell formatting.

Tip   For the shared workbook to operate properly, your coworkers need to open the same copy of the shared workbook from a shared network folder, *not* separate ones from their own individual hard disks. Users will know the workbook is shared if the word *Shared* appears in the title bar when it's loaded in Excel.

---

5 Use Windows Explorer to copy the shared workbook to a shared folder on your network and then notify your associates that the file is available for use. From now on, each time User A saves changes to the shared workbook, the changes will be copied to the shared list and any changes made by other users will be uploaded into User A's system as well. Excel handles and distributes the revisions automatically!

Monitoring a Shared Workbook

Once a shared workbook is active, you (as the owner of the file) can monitor it by choosing the Share Workbook command to find out who's using it. To see a list of the users working on the file, follow these steps:

1 Choose Tools, Share Workbook. The Share Workbook dialog box will appear.

2 A list of the users working on the file will be displayed on the Editing tab, as shown in Figure 24-6. The time displayed next to each user is the moment that user started editing the workbook.

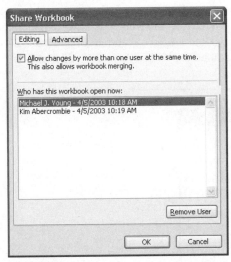

Figure 24-6. To see who is working on a shared workbook with you, use the Editing tab of the Share Workbook dialog box.

3 If you want to prohibit a user from working on the shared workbook, select the user's name and click Remove User. The user will be excluded from the editing session and won't be able to modify the shared copy of the file.

To turn off the shared workbook feature and disable multiuser editing in a workbook, choose Tools, Share Workbook, click the Editing tab, and clear the Allow Changes By More Than One User At The Same Time option.

Caution As owner of a shared worksheet, you should not disable the Share Workbook feature until each of your users has finished editing the workbook and has saved the changes, or you'll lock them out of the file. Disabling the Share Workbook feature discards any revision information in the file (known as the *change history*) and prohibits users from saving their changes to the multiuser copy of the workbook, even if you reopen sharing.

Chapter 24

Accepting or Rejecting Revisions

Each time you save a shared workbook, any changes you have made since the last time you saved the workbook are written to the shared workbook file. Also, when you save a shared workbook, if another user has changed a cell and has saved that change since the last time you saved your workbook, Excel copies into your workbook that cell's updated contents and displays a message box indicating that the workbook has been updated with another user's changes.

> **Tip** Rather than having Excel update your copy of a shared workbook with other users' changes whenever you save the workbook, as described in the previous paragraph, you can have Excel automatically update your copy of the workbook at regular intervals. To do this, choose Tools, Share Workbook, click the Advanced tab (shown in Figure 24-7), select the Automatically Every option—rather than the When File Is Saved option—and enter an interval time in the adjoining text box.

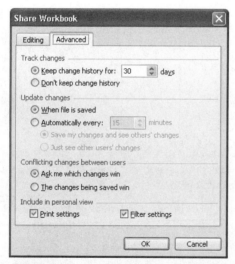

Figure 24-7. You can use the Advanced tab to customize how workbooks are shared.

Excel highlights each cell that has been updated with data coming from another user by drawing a dark-blue border around the cell and displaying a triangular change indicator in the cell's upper-left corner. Moving the cell pointer over a highlighted cell displays a Screen-Tip that provides information on the change, as shown here:

Change indicator   ScreenTip

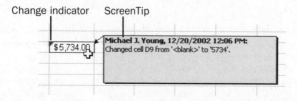

Later in this section you'll learn how to use the Highlight Changes dialog box to modify the way Excel highlights changed cells.

An exception to the scenario described so far in this section occurs if—since the last time you saved your workbook—you have updated a cell and also another user has updated this same cell and has saved that change. In this situation Excel's behavior depends on the option that's selected in the Conflicting Changes Between Users area of the Advanced tab of the Share Workbook dialog box, as follows:

- If the Ask Me Which Changes Win option is selected, Excel will display the Resolve Conflicts dialog box, which lets you decide whose changes will be saved in the shared workbook. This is a good option to select if you want to review the accuracy of each change as it occurs, or if you want to give one person's changes precedence over another's. (Although, as you'll see later in this section, you can later review changes and decide which version of the change to keep.)

- If the The Changes Being Saved Win option is selected, Excel will automatically save your version of the change because, in the scenario described, you are the last person to save the workbook. This is a good option to select when you feel confident that later changes are always more accurate than earlier changes, such as when tracking inventory quantities.

When you're ready to examine the list of editing activities in a shared workbook, choose Tools, Track Changes, and choose either Highlight Changes or Accept Or Reject Changes from the submenu. The Highlight Changes command displays a dialog box asking you to specify the editing changes you want Excel to highlight in the workbook, as shown in Figure 24-8. (If your workbook isn't currently shared, you can also use the Highlight Changes command to start sharing it as a workbook.)

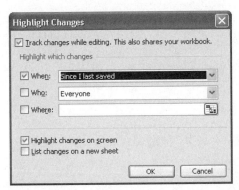

Figure 24-8. You can have Excel automatically highlight new edits in a shared workbook. To set options, use the Highlight Changes dialog box.

You can highlight changes that were made at a particular time, by a particular user, or in a particular worksheet range. When you click the OK button, Excel will outline in blue each modified cell in the workbook that matches your search criteria and will display a small triangle in the upper-left corner of each affected cell. To see how a highlighted cell was changed, place the mouse pointer over the cell, and Excel will display a ScreenTip containing the user name, date, time, and substance of the edit. (A highlighted cell and ScreenTip were shown near the beginning of this section.)

If you want to step through the list of revisions in the workbook and either accept or reject them, choose Tools, Track Changes, Accept Or Reject Changes. When you choose this command, Excel saves the workbook and then displays a dialog box asking for your search criteria.

As you do when you choose Highlight Changes, you specify the time, person(s), and location of the edits you're looking for using the drop-down lists in the dialog box. When you click the OK button, Excel will display the changes one at a time in the Accept Or Reject Changes dialog box, as shown in Figure 24-9. (If a cell has been changed more than once, the dialog box will list all the changes—the original value plus each changed value entered by one of the workbook's users.)

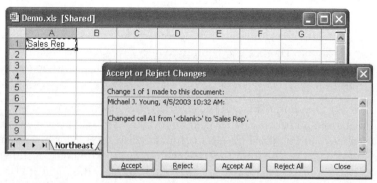

Figure 24-9. Excel tracks each edit in a shared workbook and lets you accept or reject it. If a change made by another user is inappropriate, you can discard it.

To accept an edit and store it in the shared workbook, click the Accept button. To reject the change, click the Reject button. (If a cell has been changed more than once and you want to reject the current change in favor of another change, select the change that you want to keep and click the Accept button.) After you accept or reject an edit, Excel will remove the revision highlighting from that cell.

Protecting Worksheets and Workbooks

In Chapter 23, "Expert Formatting Techniques," you learned how to hide rows and columns in your worksheet from unauthorized glances. (Turn to "Hiding Columns and Rows," on page 664, if you'd like a refresher.) Excel also lets you hide complete worksheets, as described in the tip below. But for a more powerful combination of openness and control, you can apply *password protection* to a worksheet or to an entire workbook. When you guard worksheets or workbooks by requiring a password, users can open the file but they can't change the parts you've protected. If you want to share your workbooks with others while protecting them from modification, this is the feature for you.

Chapter 24

You can even require a password from users when they open a workbook. See "Requiring a Password for File Access," on page 702.

Tip Hide individual worksheets
Being visible, as it turns out, is just another formatting option. To hide the active worksheet, choose Format, Sheet, Hide. Reverse the process by choosing Format, Sheet, Unhide and then selecting the sheet you want to unhide in the Unhide dialog box. Note that Excel doesn't let you hide a sheet in a workbook whose structure is protected (this detail is discussed later in this chapter).

Protecting Worksheets

To protect a worksheet in the workbook from modification, follow these steps:

1 Click the worksheet tab corresponding to the worksheet you want to protect.

2 Choose Tools, Protection, Protect Sheet. The Protect Sheet dialog box will appear, as shown in Figure 24-10.

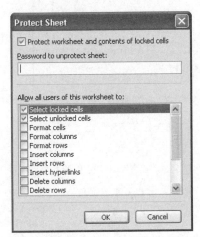

Figure 24-10. The Protect Sheet dialog box lets you protect a worksheet and assign specific permissions to users.

The Protect Sheet dialog box contains a password text box and a set of protection check boxes that list the ways in which you allow users to manipulate the worksheet. These range from selecting and reformatting cells to deleting entire columns and rows. By default, two options are checked, enabling users to select cells, both locked and unlocked. Note that the protection you apply affects only *locked cells* (unless you clear the Select Locked Cells option, which would cause all cells to be protected against all changes). Review the options and select any types of protection you *don't* require. (For more on protection, see the Troubleshooting sidebar "Protection unavailable" later in this section.)

> **Note** Initially, all cells in a worksheet are locked. For information on unlocking cells, see the Inside Out sidebar "Locking by not unlocking" later in this section.

3 Type a short (optional) password in the Password To Unprotect Sheet text box and click the OK button. Note that Excel distinguishes uppercase letters from lowercase letters, so remember any variations you make in your password's capitalization. If you forget this password, you won't be able to unprotect the worksheet. (For more on password use, see the Inside Out sidebar "Use a password (if any) with care" later in this section.)

4 When Excel asks you to verify your password, type it in again (and be sure to remember it). If anyone later attempts to modify this protected worksheet, Excel will display the following message box:

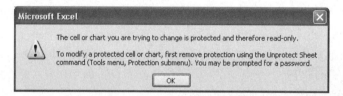

5 To remove worksheet protection later, choose Tools, Protection, Unprotect Sheet. If you didn't originally use a password, that's all there is to it! If you did, enter the worksheet password when the prompt appears.

Troubleshooting

Protection unavailable

You want to protect your worksheet or workbook, but the commands for doing so are dimmed.

Note that you won't be able to use the Protect Sheet or Protect Workbook command on a workbook that's shared. A separate command, Protect Shared Workbook, is available to let you enforce tracked changes (that is, prevent users from removing the shared workbook's change history; you set this option by checking Sharing With Track Changes in the Protect Shared Workbook dialog box). However, you won't be able to assign a password until the file is unshared. These three commands are all on the Tools, Protection submenu.

Inside Out

Use a password (if any) with care

A password isn't required to protect worksheets. And most users have had the experience of concocting a clever "easy-to-remember" password only to forget it an hour later. If you're afraid you'll forget the password, set worksheet protection without entering a password: You'll preserve the worksheet from accidental entries and mistakes, and you won't risk losing the ability to modify the file. (However, a renegade user could easily disable worksheet protection and then modify your document.)

Inside Out

Locking by not unlocking

If you want to let users modify some cells in your worksheet, Excel provides a rather circuitous route that requires you to think of protection as a tool and also as a format option. First, select the cells that you want to leave unprotected, choose Format, Cells, click the Protection tab, and clear the Locked option. As the note on the Protection tab explains, what you've just done has no immediate effect: locking or unlocking has no consequence until you protect the sheet. After you apply protection, all cells are locked except those that you explicitly formatted as unlocked.

This technique is useful (if confusing to apply) if you have a field for comments or an area in the worksheet that is typically used for data entry. And if you've ever wondered, protection isn't defeated if you selected the Format Cells option on the Protect Sheet dialog box. Remember, this would allow a user to format the cells on the protected sheet, which (you might have figured) enables the user to change the locked/unlocked setting and (voilà) get around protection. Nope. Excel eliminates the Protection tab from the Format Cells dialog box until the sheet is unprotected.

Protecting Workbook Structure

To protect the structure of an entire workbook from modification (that is, to guard the names and the order of the worksheets), follow these steps:

1 Choose Tools, Protection, Protect Workbook. The Protect Workbook dialog box will appear, as shown in Figure 24-11.

Chapter 24

Figure 24-11. The Protect Workbook dialog box lets you protect the structure of an entire workbook from modification.

The Protect Workbook dialog box contains a password text box and two protection check boxes. When the Structure check box is selected, users can't insert, delete, hide, rename, copy, or move worksheets in the workbook, although they *can* modify data in the worksheets if worksheet protection isn't set. When the Windows check box is selected, users can't resize the windows displaying the workbook.

2 Type a password in the password text box and click the OK button. Note any variations you make in your password's capitalization and take steps to remember the name. You can also click OK without typing a name to set workbook protection without a password.

3 Retype the password when Excel asks for it. From this point on, no user will be able to modify the worksheet's structure without first unprotecting the workbook by choosing the Tools, Protection, Unprotect Workbook (and supplying the password if you assigned one).

> **Tip**   If you work regularly in a multiuser environment, you might also enjoy the protection provided by the Protect Shared Workbook command on the Tools, Protection submenu. When you enable this toggle, it prevents users from modifying a shared workbook's change history.

Requiring a Password for File Access

If you're using Excel to track confidential information, you might want to limit access to your file by requiring a password to open it. This control goes further than protecting the workbook's content and structure: it prevents anyone lacking an entry key (the password) from viewing your workbook at all.

> **Caution**   Take care when using password protection. If you forget your password, you'll have no way to open the protected file.

To save a file that has password protection, follow these steps:

1 Create your workbook as you normally would. You don't need to hide or protect confidential parts of the file—your password protection limits access to every component.

2   Choose File, Save As to display the Save As dialog box. If you haven't already specified a filename, type one now in the File Name text box.

3   Open the Tools drop-down menu in the upper-right corner of the Save As dialog box, and then choose the General Options command.

4   The Save Options dialog box will appear, as shown in Figure 24-12. This dialog box contains two password protection text boxes: Password To Open, which prohibits users from opening the file unless they know the specified password, and Password To Modify, which prohibits users from saving changes to the file without knowing the password.

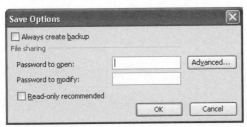

Figure 24-12.   To protect your file from unauthorized access, type a password in the Save Options dialog box.

> **Tip**   If you want to recommend—but not require—that users open the file as a read-only document, check the Read-Only Recommended option in the Save Options dialog box. Any user who subsequently opens the file will be given the option to open it in read-only mode but won't be required to do so. Users who modify a file opened in read-only mode can save their changes to a different file but are blocked from overwriting the original file.

5   To limit access to your workbook, type a password in the Password To Open text box and then click the OK button. When Excel asks for it, reenter the password to verify that you typed it as intended.

6   The next time you (or another user) tries to open the file, Excel will prompt for the password in a dialog box. To remove password protection, open the file (you'll need the password) and then choose File, Save As. Choose the General Options command from the Tools drop-down menu in the Save As dialog box (as in step 3). Then remove the password from the Password To Open text box.

> **Tip**   An alternative way to apply any of the file protections described in this section is to choose Tools, Options and click the Security tab. The Security tab also lets you digitally sign a workbook, remove personal information from a workbook, and set macro security options. For information on digital signatures and removing personal information, see "File-Sharing Protection," on page 474. For additional information on removing personal information, see the tip "Guard your privacy," on page 73. For information on macro security, see "Setting Macro Security," on page 229.

Chapter 24

Customizing Excel to Work the Way You Do

Adjusting Views. 705

Setting Printing Options 708

Using Multiple Panes 718

Customizing Excel Using the Options
Dialog Box 720

Installing Add-In Commands
and Wizards 725

A short time ago one of the editors of this book moved into a new office. Our first visit to her new digs was a shock; in place of the familiar, delightfully idiosyncratic workspace stood an empty desk, a computer wrapped in packing tape, several boxes of books and supplies, and four white walls bathed in pale, phosphorescent light. However, after several hours of patient adjustment and tinkering, her simple 10' × 10' room again reflected her personality and interests. Books and treasures lined the walls, a soft lamp replaced the cold overhead lighting, and the computer displayed a familiar electronic photograph. In a way, this routine relocation reminded us of one of the many aspects we really like about Microsoft Office 2003 applications—they're eminently adaptable to your preferences and work style.

> You can also change how toolbars and menus are presented in the Microsoft Excel interface. For more information about these and other customization options, see Chapter 9, "Customizing the Office 2003 Application Interface."

This chapter gives you several techniques for customizing Microsoft Office Excel 2003 and making it work the way you want it to. As you read about each technique, notice that some affect a particular worksheet or workbook and others apply across Excel to each workbook you open or create. You'll learn how to magnify the worksheet and save your favorite views, set your typical printing options, and configure a timesaving feature called AutoComplete. You'll also learn how to control recalculation and adjust other hidden settings using the Options dialog box, and how to install add-in commands and wizards. When you're finished, you'll have all the techniques you need to create your own personalized Excel interface.

Adjusting Views

In Chapter 23, "Expert Formatting Techniques," you learned how to increase the point size in worksheet cells to make numbers and headings more readable. You can also change the magnification of the worksheet to zoom in on information or back up to view it from a distance. In this section you'll learn how to use the Zoom command to vary the magnification in your workbook, and you'll discover how to save different views using the Custom Views command.

Using the Zoom Command

The Zoom command on the View menu changes the magnification of the selected worksheets. You can enlarge the worksheet temporarily to examine a group of cells, or you can shrink the worksheet so that you can judge its overall appearance. (This change doesn't affect any of your data or formatting, and it doesn't alter the way your worksheets appear when printed.) When you choose View, Zoom, the Zoom dialog box will appear, as shown in Figure 25-1.

Zoom
Magnification
200%
100%
75%
50%
25%
Fit selection
Custom:
100
%
OK
Cancel

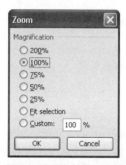

Figure 25-1. The Zoom dialog box lets you enlarge or shrink the selected worksheets without changing cell formatting.

The default worksheet magnification is 100%, or Normal view. To enlarge the worksheet to twice its normal size, select the 200% option. To shrink the worksheet, select the 75%, 50%, or 25% option. After you select a magnification percentage and click the OK button, your worksheet will be resized. If you save the workbook to disk and close the file, the zoomed view will appear when you reopen the workbook.

Perhaps the most useful option is Fit Selection, which adjusts the magnification to display only the cells you select before choosing the Zoom command. Its effect is illustrated in Figure 25-2. Finally, the Custom option lets you specify an exact magnification percentage, from 10% reduction to 400% enlargement.

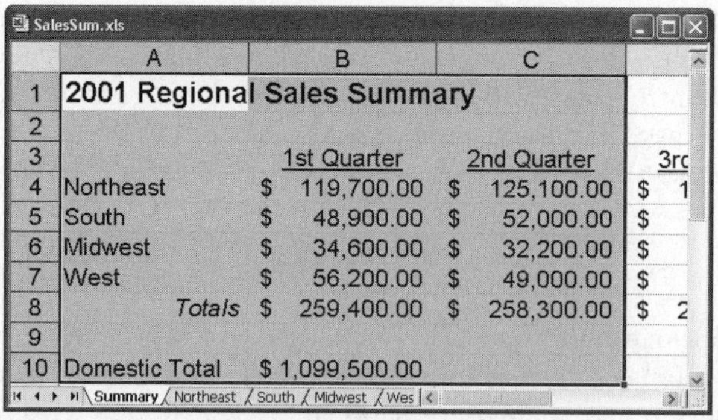

SalesSum.xls
A
B
C
1 2001 Regional Sales Summary
2
3 1st Quarter 2nd Quarter 3rc
4 Northeast $ 119,700.00 $ 125,100.00 $ 1
5 South $ 48,900.00 $ 52,000.00 $
6 Midwest $ 34,600.00 $ 32,200.00 $
7 West $ 56,200.00 $ 49,000.00 $
8 Totals $ 259,400.00 $ 258,300.00 $ 2
9
10 Domestic Total $ 1,099,500.00
Summary
Northeast
South
Midwest
Wes

Figure 25-2. The Fit Selection option zooms the worksheet to show only the selected cells. Before we chose the Zoom command, we selected cells A1 through C10.

The Zoom control on Excel's Standard toolbar also gives you access to many of the magnification options in the Zoom dialog box. To use the Zoom control, follow these steps:

1 If you plan to magnify your worksheet based on a selection, highlight a range of cells in the worksheet. If you want to magnify several worksheets in the workbook, hold down Ctrl and click the worksheet tabs you want resized.

2 Click the down arrow on the Zoom control. Your toolbar will look similar to the one shown here:

3 Select the magnification option you want. Excel will resize the selected worksheets.

> **Tip** Not all the worksheets in a workbook need to be viewed at the same magnification. Occasionally, you might want to vary how your worksheets appear within the workbook.

Saving Views Using the Custom Views Command

If you find you like rotating between two or three different views when you work in your workbook, you can save your views to disk and switch between them freely by using the Custom Views command on the View menu. Custom Views is a replacement for the View Manager add-in available in versions of Excel prior to 2000. Note, however, that Custom Views are not saved in the workbook when you convert a file to XML (Extensible Markup Language) using the Save As command and that the Custom Views are deleted from your workbook.

When you save a view, you give it a name, and Excel records the display options, window settings, printing options, and current selection(s) in your entire workbook. (Settings that apply to an individual worksheet, such as the current selection and zoom factor, are saved for each worksheet in the workbook.) You can quickly switch back and forth between saved views. To save a view using the Custom Views command, follow these steps:

1 Set the view and display settings you want to save as a custom view. For example, set the magnification of each worksheet, select a cell or range in each worksheet to make it the current selection each time you use the view, hide columns that are unnecessary for a given update task, or resize the workbook window.

2 Choose View, Custom Views (any worksheet can be active). The Custom Views dialog box will open, and any custom views you've previously defined will appear in the Views list.

3 Click the Add button. You'll see the Add View dialog box shown here:

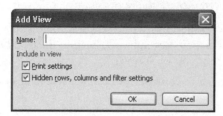

4 Type a descriptive name for your workbook view, such as Sales Update. Check one or both of the options for the optional items you can save in your view: the Print Settings option and the Hidden Rows Columns And Filter Settings option. Then click the OK button. Excel will save your custom view and store it in the current workbook.

> Print settings are covered in the next section. Filters are explained in Chapter 28, "Power Database Techniques: Lists, Filters, and Pivot Tables."

To display a custom view later, perform the following steps:

1 Open the workbook, and choose Views, Custom Views. The Custom Views dialog box will appear, as shown here:

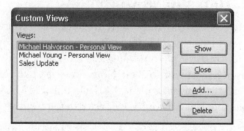

2 Double-click the view you want to show. The dialog box will close and all worksheets in the workbook will adjust to your custom settings.

> **Note** To delete a custom view, select the view in the Custom Views dialog box, and then click the Delete button.

Setting Printing Options

Few changes to a workbook turn out to be as noticeable as the options you select before printing. Using the Page Setup command on the File menu, which displays the Page Setup dialog box, you can control the orientation of your page, the width of your margins, the text or pictures placed in headers and footers, and the presence of extra worksheet elements such as gridlines and cell comments. The Page Setup dialog box contains four tabs (Page, Margins, Header/Footer, and Sheet) that control how worksheets are printed. We'll cover each tab in this section.

As you go through the following sections, keep in mind that all settings you make in the Page Setup dialog box affect only the active worksheet within your workbook. Therefore, before you change any of the settings described, be sure to activate the worksheet that you want to modify.

Controlling Page Orientation

To customize your printing options, choose File, Page Setup and click the Page tab. The Page tab, shown in Figure 25-3, lets you control orientation and other options related to the physical page you will be printing on. Orientation governs the direction in which your worksheet appears on the printed page. Portrait, the default, is a vertical orientation designed for worksheets that are longer than they are wide. If your worksheet is too wide to fit on one page in this orientation, which is often the case, choose the Landscape option to orient the worksheet horizontally.

The Scaling options let you reduce or enlarge your worksheet so that it fits in the specified number of pages. The percentage you enter in the Adjust To text box is similar to the percentage you specify when you create custom views using the View, Zoom command. For a description, see "Using the Zoom Command," on page 706. In this case, however, the scaling affects the printed page, not the view on your screen.

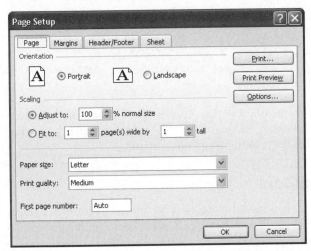

Figure 25-3. The Page tab lets you adjust page orientation and other paper options.

The Paper Size and Print Quality options let you specify the size of the paper you're printing on, as well as the desired printing resolution. These options are drawn from the settings of your selected Microsoft Windows–based printer. To set the unique attributes of your printer, click the Options button in the Page Setup dialog box and make your changes in the dialog box tabs.

Adjusting the Margins

The Margins tab of the Page Setup dialog box allows you to adjust the margins in the active worksheet (see Figure 25-4). Typical margin settings are 1 inch for the top and bottom, and 0.75 inch for the left and right. As you change the margins, Excel shows you in the preview window which margin in your document will be affected. Customizing the margin settings is especially useful if you're printing on letterhead paper or other sheets that contain graphics or text you don't want to overprint.

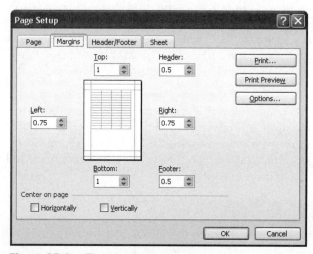

Figure 25-4. The Margins tab gives you control over the placement of your worksheet relative to the edges of the paper you print it on.

If you want to center your worksheet between the margin settings, check the Horizontally option at the bottom of the Margins tab to center the printout from left to right. Check the Vertically option to center the printout from top to bottom.

Adding Headers and Footers

The Header/Footer tab of the Page Setup dialog box (shown in Figure 25-5) lets you add a header or a footer to your worksheet when it prints. Headers and footers typically contain reference information about a document, such as the worksheet name, the time or date, or the current page number. Excel permits you to pick headers and footers from a predefined list in the Header/Footer tab, or you can create your own custom entries by clicking the Custom Header or Custom Footer button. Excel offers the option of inserting and formatting a picture as part of a custom header or footer. Like other settings made in the Page Setup dialog box, you define headers or footers separately for each worksheet within a workbook.

> **Tip** An alternative way to display the Header/Footer tab of the Page Setup dialog box is to choose View, Header And Footer.

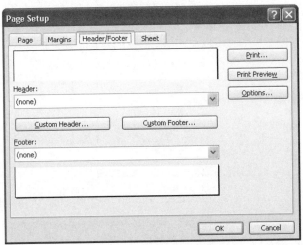

Figure 25-5. The Header/Footer tab lets you choose a header or footer from a predefined list or create your own version.

To choose predefined headers and footers from the Page Setup dialog box, complete the following steps:

1 Choose File, Page Setup. When the Page Setup dialog box opens, click the Header/Footer tab.

2 To pick a new header, select one of the formats from the Header drop-down list. The first format—(None)—removes the header. Note that commas between items separate the header or footer components, which are aligned at the left margin, in the center of the page, and at the right margin.

When you select a format, the header will be shown in the preview area above the Header drop-down list.

3 To pick a new footer, select one of the formats from the Footer drop-down list. Again, the (None) option removes the footer from the document.

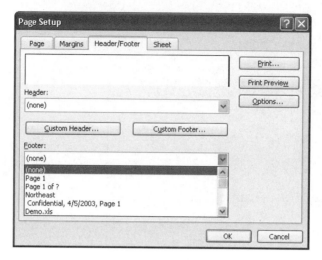

After you set headers and footers, your screen should resemble the following:

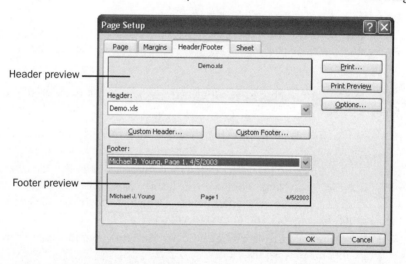

Header preview

Footer preview

4 When you're finished, click the OK button. The specified headers and footers will appear on each page of the worksheet when you print it.

If you don't like the predefined headers and footers, you can create your own by clicking the Custom Header or Custom Footer button in the Header/Footer tab. To create a custom header, complete the following steps:

1 Choose File, Page Setup. When the Page Setup dialog box opens, click the Header/Footer tab.

2 In the Header drop-down list, select the predefined header that comes closest to the custom header you want to create. This header will serve as a starting point for your new header. If no predefined header comes close to what you want, leave (None) selected.

3 Click the Custom Header button. The following dialog box will appear:

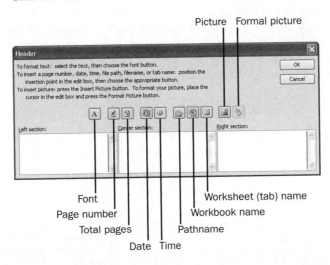

The Header dialog box lets you specify your header in three sections: left, center, and right.

4 Click in one of the sections, and then type the text you want.

For details on working with templates, see "Creating and Modifying Templates," on page 672.

You can supplement the text you type by clicking any of the special buttons to enter codes in your header. For example, if you click the eighth button (the Worksheet Name button), the code *&[Tab]* will be placed in the header. This is Excel's special formatting code for inserting the name of the current worksheet.

5 To change the text formatting, select the portion you want to format and click the Font button (the first one). Selecting and formatting the code for an element (such as *&[Tab]*) causes Excel to format the text that the code generates at print time.

6 To insert a picture in the header, place the cursor in the desired header field and click the Picture button. Then select the file containing the picture and click the Insert button.

7 When the insertion point is within a section that contains a picture, the Format Picture button is enabled. To adjust the picture's scale, cropping, and other attributes (color, brightness, and contrast), click this button to open the Format Picture dialog box.

The Format Picture dialog box has two tabs. The first, the Size tab, lets you scale the picture: the entire image is sized to fit the dimensions you specify. Don't cancel the Lock Aspect Ratio unless you want the picture to be distorted as it's scaled. After you decide on the proper scaling factor for the image, go to the second tab, the Picture tab. Here you have settings for cropping and other effects. Cropping (as opposed to scaling) eliminates part of the picture. Figure 25-6 shows the Picture tab.

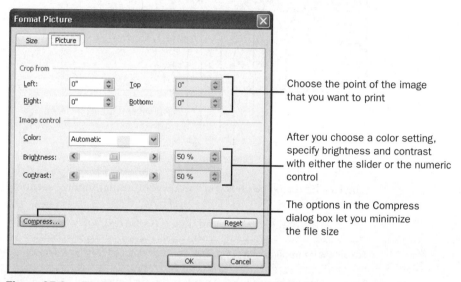

Choose the point of the image that you want to print

After you choose a color setting, specify brightness and contrast with either the slider or the numeric control

The options in the Compress dialog box let you minimize the file size

Figure 25-6. The Picture tab provides a number of ways to fine-tune a graphic for presentation in the header or footer.

For a discussion on the differences between scaling an image and cropping it, see "Cropping a Picture," on page 122.

8 If you want Excel to save the embedded picture in ways that optimize the file size, click the Compress button in the Picture tab of the Format Picture dialog box. This might mean matching the saved resolution to the printer, discarding the cropped regions from the file, and so forth.

9 When you've finished creating the custom header in the Header dialog box, click the OK button to view your customized header in the preview area of the Header/Footer tab of the Page Setup dialog box. If you don't like the results, repeat steps 3 through 8 and make further changes.

Inside Out

Customizing default printer options

The options in the Page Setup dialog box affect the current worksheet. When you save your workbook, the printer options are saved with it, but the default values are used whenever you create a new workbook with the standard Workbook template. Excel doesn't exactly invite you to open this Workbook template to modify it—say, with your own preferred header or footer—but you can do the next best thing. Open a new document with the Workbook template in the Templates dialog box (or click Blank Workbook in the New Workbook task pane); make changes that reflect your preferences for view, toolbars, headers and footers, margins, orientation, and the like; and then save the document as a template, calling it perhaps My Blank Workbook.xlt. Select this template when you create a new document using the File, New command.

Tip If you want to include an ampersand in header or footer text, be aware that you'll need to type two of them, like this: &&. Excel treats the first ampersand as an escape character to initiate special formatting codes. Also, you cannot format text in headers and footers for color. A possible workaround is to apply the desired colors to cells in the worksheet and then designate those cells as print titles, as explained in "Repeating Row or Column Headings," on page 718.

That's the procedure for creating a custom header. If you want to create a custom footer, click the Custom Footer button in the Header/Footer tab of the Page Setup dialog box and follow steps 4 through 9 as you would for creating a custom header.

To see the printed appearance of the active worksheet, choose File, Print Preview or click the Print Preview button in the Page Setup dialog box or on the Standard toolbar to activate Print Preview view. This view is especially helpful if you insert a picture that's larger than the preview area in the Header/Footer tab of the Page Setup dialog box. (In Print Preview view, you can click the Setup button on the toolbar to return to the Page Setup dialog box and adjust the page settings.)

Tip To create multiline headers or footers, press Enter at the end of the line in the section portion of the Header or the Footer dialog box.

Adding Gridlines and Other Options

The Sheet tab of the Page Setup dialog box (see Figure 25-7) lets you include visual or interpretive aids such as gridlines, comments, and repeating row and column headings in your printout. *Gridlines* are the dividing lines you normally see on your screen that run down each column and across each row, identifying the cells in the worksheet. To print gridlines with your worksheet, simply check the Gridlines option in the Print category. *Cell comments* are special notes you create by using the Comments command on the Insert menu. You can specify how they're printed by choosing a selection in the Comments drop-down list. The default (None) is not to print any comments the worksheet might contain.

To learn more about using comments in your worksheet, see "Entering Comments," on page 616.

Tip To remove gridlines from your screen, choose Tools, Options, click the View tab, and clear the Gridlines option. To print only certain gridlines, outline cells using the Border tab in the Format Cells dialog box, as discussed in "Adding Borders to Cells," on page 658.

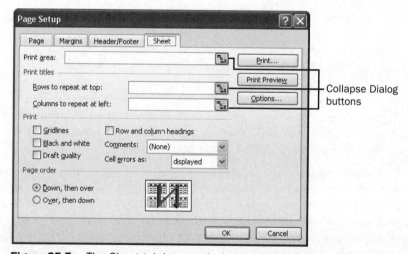

Figure 25-7. The Sheet tab lets you include extras such as gridlines and cell comments in your printout.

Two other useful features in the Sheet tab are the Print Area and Print Titles text boxes. Both these features let you select ranges for printing. In the Print Area text box, you specify the worksheet range to be printed. In the two Print Titles text boxes, you can choose to repeat either row or column headings (or both) on multipage printouts.

Specifying a Print Area

To have Excel print a specified region of your worksheet, rather than printing all its contents, use the Print Area feature as follows:

1 Choose File, Page Setup.

2 When the Page Setup dialog box opens, click the Sheet tab.

3 Click the Collapse Dialog Box button at the right end of the Print Area text box, as shown here:

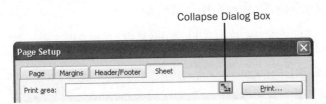

Collapse Dialog Box

The dialog box will temporarily shrink to let you to see your worksheet. If it still obscures your view, drag its title bar to move it out of the way.

4 Select the cells you want to print in the worksheet.

As you select the cells, a marquee will appear around the range, a pop-up box will show the number of rows and columns you're selecting, and a description of the cells will appear in the Print Area text box, as shown here:

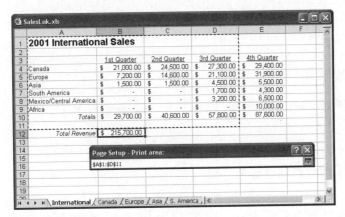

5 When you've selected the cells you want, click the Collapse Dialog Box button again.

6 After making any other changes, click the Print button, and then click the OK button in the Print dialog box to print the cells you selected.

> **Tip** To delete a print area or to choose a different one (without changing your data), click the Sheet tab of the Page Setup dialog box and delete the cell range in the Print Area text box. Leave it blank or draw a new range on your worksheet.
>
> An alternative way to specify a print area is to select the range and choose File, Print Area, Set Print Area. An alternative way to remove an existing print area is to choose File, Print Area, Clear Print Area.

Repeating Row or Column Headings

To repeat row or column headings (or both) on each printed page of a long (or wide) worksheet, follow these steps:

1 Choose File, Page Setup.

2 When the Page Setup dialog box opens, click the Sheet tab.

3 Click one of the Collapse Dialog Box buttons in the Print Titles area to select repeating rows or repeating columns.

4 Select the rows or columns you want to have repeated on each page. Excel will highlight all of the rows or columns you select by surrounding them with a marquee.

5 Click the Collapse Dialog Box button again to complete your selection.

6 You can repeat steps 3 through 5 if you want to repeat both rows and columns on your printed worksheet.

7 After making any other changes, click the OK button to close the Page Setup dialog box, or click the Print button to print the worksheet.

> **Tip** You can verify how your print options look by clicking the Print Preview button in the Page Setup dialog box or by choosing File, Print Preview. This allows you to decide whether to make cosmetic adjustments and ensures that you've chosen the portion of the worksheet you want.

Using Multiple Panes

In the previous section you saw how you can repeat rows and columns when you print a worksheet, which is useful when you want to see the headings or refer to a summary column while you review a multipage document. You can achieve the same convenience when you edit or review a worksheet on your screen by splitting the worksheet into multiple panes. The panes let you see different parts of a worksheet at the same time.

Excel saves the pane divisions that you create in each worksheet when you save the workbook, and restores them when you reopen the workbook. The pane divisions of each worksheet are also saved as part of a custom view, described in "Saving Views Using the Custom Views Command," earlier in the chapter.

Splitting a Worksheet into Panes

To split a sheet, first highlight a cell in the column or row to the right of or below the pane division that you want to establish. Next, point with your mouse to one of the *split boxes*, inconspicuous rectangles in the scroll bars that are located above the up scroll arrow and to the right of the right scroll arrow. When your mouse pointer is located on a split box, it changes to a double line with opposing arrows, as shown in Figure 25-8.

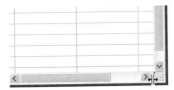

Figure 25-8.   The mouse pointer appears as a double-headed arrow when you place it over the split box. Drag the box or double-click to create a new pane.

> **Note**   When you split a sheet, Excel doesn't prevent you from scrolling in one pane to the same rows or columns that are displayed in another pane. This can be confusing when you find repetition on the screen, such as a duplicate column A or row 1. Freezing panes prevents this duplication, as you'll learn in the next section.

Double-click a split box to establish two panes at the selected cell. The split box on the horizontal scroll bar creates a vertical split; the split box on the vertical scroll bar creates a horizontal split. You can also drag the split box to specify a dividing line between two panes. Using both split boxes (or using the Window, Split command), you can create four separate panes in a worksheet. When you're ready to remove a split, double-click the pane divider or choose Window, Remove Split.

Freezing Panes in a Worksheet

Freezing a pane is a variation on splitting panes: columns or rows to the left of or above a certain line remain visible while the rest of the worksheet scrolls indefinitely. This is a useful feature when you're working on a large database and want to keep the row headings (field names) visible as you scroll through the rows (records). Alternatively (or additionally), you can freeze the first column or two to keep a key field visible as you scroll to the right.

To freeze a pane, select the entire row or column immediately below or to the right of the region to be frozen and choose Window, Freeze Panes. Select a single cell, as shown in Figure 25-9, to freeze both the rows above and the columns to the left of the cell.

Scrolling a frozen pane is limited until you unfreeze the pane. To do so, choose Window, Unfreeze Panes.

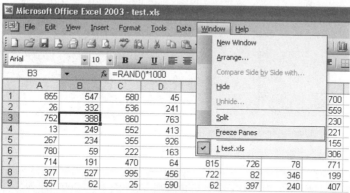

Figure 25-9. Select cell B3 and then choose Freeze Panes from the Window menu to freeze column A and rows 1 and 2.

Customizing Excel Using the Options Dialog Box

To change the way Excel looks and works, experiment with the customization choices in the Options dialog box shown in Figure 25-10. As you do in Microsoft Word, you display the Options dialog box by choosing Tools, Options. The Options dialog box contains tabs that control virtually every aspect of the Excel interface. Although some tabs customize features that you might be unfamiliar with, such as the settings that help you transfer data from other spreadsheet programs, you can often learn a lot about how Excel works just by browsing through the tabs in this dialog box. In this section you'll experiment with the following options:

- Formula calculation settings, such as manual recalculation and updating remote references
- Worksheet appearance options, such as scroll bars and colors
- Editing options, such as drag-and-drop settings and default decimal places

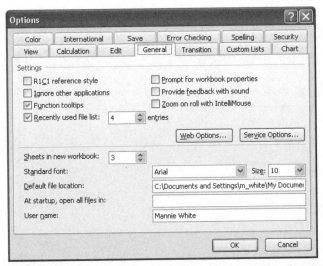

Figure 25-10. The Options dialog box lets you customize many of Excel's commands and options. The General tab controls basic options such as the standard font.

Controlling Calculation

When you enter a formula, Excel automatically computes the result or recalculates. Most of the time you'll want Excel to recalculate automatically when you modify cells that are included in formulas—it makes sense to keep your numbers up to date. But occasionally you'll want to configure Excel so that it recalculates only at your command. For example, you might want to refer to the previous result of a calculation while you enter new values in a worksheet. Or, you might want to disable recalculation temporarily if you're entering a relatively large amount of data into cells that are referenced in complex formulas in other cells. (Otherwise Excel would need to recalculate one or more formulas every time you enter new data, which can take some time to finish.)

To customize formula calculation in your worksheet, choose Tools, Options, and then click the Calculation tab of the Options dialog box. You will see the dialog box shown in Figure 25-11.

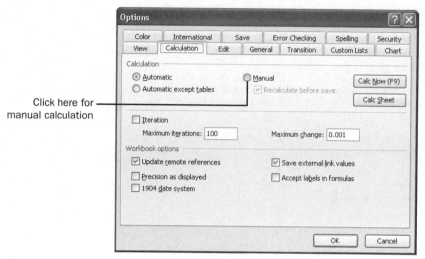

Click here for manual calculation

Figure 25-11. To control recalculation in a worksheet, click the Calculation tab.

For manual calculation, select the Manual option in the Calculation area, and then click the OK button. From this point on, Excel will recalculate formulas only when you enter or edit them, when you press F9 to calculate manually, or when you return to the Calculation tab and click the Calc Now (F9) button. If you're disabling automatic recalculation, you might also want to disable automatic updating from other documents linked to your worksheet. To remove this option, clear the Update Remote References option in the Workbook Options area of the Calculation tab, and Excel won't update links that rely on other documents for data.

> **Tip** Remember to reselect the Automatic option in the Calculation area and to reselect the Update Remote References check box when you're finished entering data. Otherwise your workbook might display out-of-date information and present incorrect results.

Customizing Worksheet Appearance

You've already learned how to add toolbars to your workspace and change the layout of workbook windows. Using the View tab in the Options dialog box, you can further adjust your worksheet's appearance. The View tab includes option buttons and check boxes that enable and disable several visual characteristics, as shown in Figure 25-12. If you prefer not to have the task pane visible when you launch Excel, for example, clear the Startup Task Pane option. Or you can remove the formula bar and status bar from the screen, giving you more real estate for your worksheet, by clearing the Formula Bar and Status Bar check boxes. If you don't like the red triangle that signifies that a comment has been placed in a cell, you can choose None in the Comments category. The red indicators will disappear, but the comments will remain.

For a refresher course on using toolbars and working with document windows, see Chapter 4, "Working with Office 2003 Applications, Documents, and Program Windows."

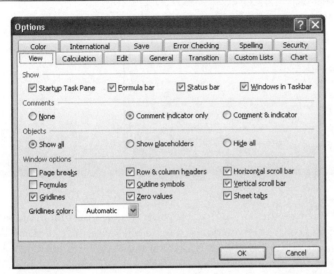

Figure 25-12. The View tab controls how your worksheet appears on the screen.

You might also find it useful to examine the selections in the Window Options category of the View tab. You can use these options to choose whether to view automatic page breaks, gridlines (you can also alter their color), scroll bars, and other visual features of your worksheet. When you're finished customizing your worksheet's appearance, click the OK button to close the Options dialog box.

Customizing Editing Options

If you want to change how Excel responds to your editing instructions, you can modify several special settings, including the way the drag-and-drop technique works, the way Excel responds to the Enter key, and the action the AutoComplete feature takes. Figure 25-13 shows the Edit tab in the Options dialog box, which controls these customizations and more.

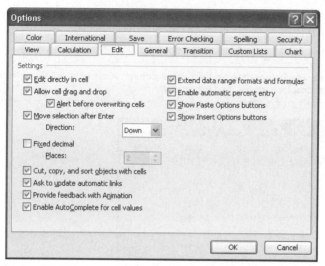

Figure 25-13. You can personalize Excel's editing behavior by enabling or disabling options in the Edit tab.

To disable direct cell editing—the option that lets you move the insertion point within cells (as you can in the formula bar) after you double-click a cell—clear the Edit Directly In Cell option. You might want to clear this option if you often accidentally double-click cells when selecting ranges. When this option is turned off, you must edit the cell's contents in the formula bar.

A related option is Allow Cell Drag And Drop, which enables the drag-and-drop method for copying and moving cells. If you tend to drag cells unintentionally, you might want to clear this option.

> **Caution**   We recommend that you *never* disable the Alert Before Overwriting Cells safety feature, which protects you from inadvertently copying one piece of data over another.

If you spend a lot of time keying in data a row at a time, you might prefer that Excel move the selection box to the right when you press Enter (rather than down, which is the default). To make this change, the Move Selection After Enter option must remain checked, and you'll need to select Right from the drop-down list associated with that option. Clearing the Move Selection After Enter check box indicates that you want to "lock in" the entry but not change the active cell when you press Enter.

You might consider disabling the AutoComplete feature if you grow weary of Excel automatically entering data for you based on your last entry. Although this capability is extremely useful, it can also be tiresome if Excel doesn't guess your intentions correctly. To stop Auto-Complete, clear the Enable AutoComplete For Cell Values option. When you're finished selecting your editing choices, click the OK button to close the Options dialog box.

Installing Add-In Commands and Wizards

You can use the Add-Ins command on the Tools menu to install useful tools known as *add-in commands* and *wizards*, which further extend the functionality of Excel. Typical add-in commands included with Excel 2003 are Solver and Analysis ToolPak, which appear on the Tools menu after you install them. You can also acquire add-in commands and wizards from third-party software developers.

To install add-in commands and wizards, complete the following steps:

1 Choose Tools, Add-Ins. The Add-Ins dialog box will appear, as shown in Figure 25-14.

2 Select the add-in command or wizard that you want to have appear as a menu command. To locate a command that doesn't appear in this dialog box, click the Browse button and find it on your hard disk.

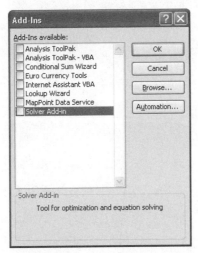

Figure 25-14. The Add-Ins command on the Tools menu allows you to add and remove add-in commands and wizards.

> **Tip** To remove an add-in command or wizard from a menu, clear the add-in or wizard in the Add-Ins dialog box. The add-in command will be removed when you next start Excel.

3 Click the OK button to save your changes and reconfigure the menu. Excel will then search for the tool on your system and prompt you for your Office 2003 installation CD, if necessary.

> To see the Solver Add-In at work, see Chapter 29, "Advanced Business Analysis."

Most add-in commands appear on the Tools menu after you've installed them. However, occasionally the utility's designer will opt to locate it someplace else in the menu structure after installation.

Chapter 26

Crunching Numbers with Formulas and Functions

Building a Formula 727
Using Built-In Functions 733
Using Functions to Analyze Finances. . . 737
Using Names in Functions 742

A *formula* is an equation that calculates a new value from existing values. In Chapter 21, "Excel Fundamentals," you learned how to build simple formulas using numbers and cell references, and in Chapter 24, "Power Organizing with Workbooks," you expanded your skills by creating formulas that referenced cells from other worksheets and workbooks. In this chapter you'll discover how to build more sophisticated formulas. You'll learn how to use arithmetic operators and parentheses to control how your formulas are evaluated, you'll explore techniques for replicating (copying) formulas, and you'll practice using names to make your formulas easier to read and modify.

In addition, you'll learn how to use Microsoft Office Excel 2003's impressive collection of built-in functions for specialized tasks such as totaling rows and columns, computing averages, and calculating monthly loan payments. Using well-organized formulas and functions, you can evaluate business data in new ways, spot important trends, and plan your financial future.

Building a Formula

Figure 26-1 shows two basic Excel formulas. The first calculates a value by adding the contents of a series of cells, and the second uses an Excel function to find the sum of a range of cells and then multiplies that sum by a number. These formulas have several characteristics in common:

- Each begins with an equal sign (=). The equal sign tells Excel that the following characters are part of a formula that should be calculated and that the result should be displayed in a cell. (If you omit the equal sign, Excel will treat the formula as plain text and won't compute the result.)

- Each formula uses one or more arithmetic operators. An arithmetic operator is not required, however; you might easily create a formula that uses one or more functions to do all the necessary calculating. Each formula includes values that are being combined by using arithmetic operators. When you use Excel formulas, you can combine numbers, cell references, results of functions, and other values.

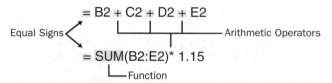

$$= B2 + C2 + D2 + E2$$

Equal Signs ———— Arithmetic Operators

$$= SUM(B2:E2)* 1.15$$

└─ Function

Figure 26-1. Simple formulas can include numeric values, operators, cell references, and Excel functions.

The examples in this chapter feature an order-form worksheet that catalogs the merchandise sold in a small pet shop. It's the type of worksheet that pet shop employees might use to take orders over the phone or that customers might use to purchase mail-order items. As you work through this chapter, you'll see how to use Excel formulas and functions to add information to the order-form worksheet. You can load the worksheet from the companion CD (or create it yourself) and follow the examples exactly if you want to, or you can customize the worksheet for your own purposes.

Multiplying Numbers

Formulas that multiply the numbers in two cells are among the most basic and easy to enter. To multiply a price cell and a quantity cell to create a subtotal, complete the following steps:

1 Create a product order form, price list, or another worksheet containing well-organized Price, Quantity, and Subtotal columns. The order-form worksheet we'll use looks like this:

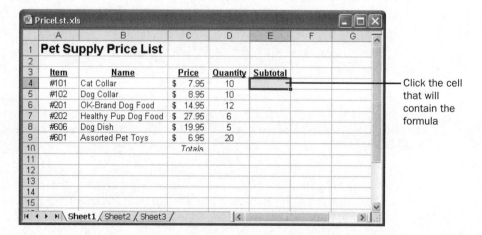

Click the cell that will contain the formula

For your convenience as you follow the example, the PriceLst.xls example workbook is on the companion CD.

2 In the Subtotal column, click the cell that will contain the multiplication formula (E4, in our example).

3 Type the equal sign (=) to begin the formula.

An equal sign will appear in the formula bar and in the highlighted cell. From this point on, any numbers, cell references, arithmetic operators, or functions that you type will be included in the formula.

> To learn more about entering simple formulas, referencing cells, and using the formula bar, see "Entering Formulas," on page 618.

4 In the Price column, click the cell containing the first number to be multiplied (C4, in this example). A dotted-line marquee will appear around the highlighted cell, and the cell's reference will appear in the cell you're editing and in the formula bar.

5 Type an asterisk (*) to add the multiplication operator to the formula.

6 In the Quantity column, click the cell containing the second number to be multiplied (D4, in this example). The complete formula will now appear in the selected cell and in the formula bar. Your worksheet should look similar to this one:

The formula bar records your formula as you build it

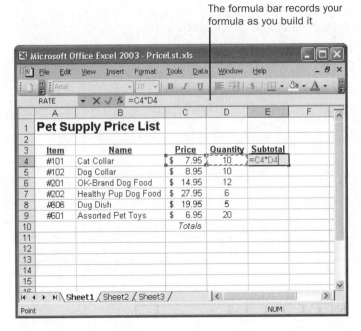

7 Press Enter to end the formula. Excel will calculate the result (79.5, in this example), and display it in the cell containing the formula. The number will automatically appear in a monetary format.

Replicating a Formula

Excel makes it easy to copy, or *replicate*, a formula into neighboring cells, using the Fill submenu of the Edit menu. The slick thing about the Fill submenu is that its commands automatically adjust the cell references in your formula to match the rows and columns you're copying to. For example, if you replicate a formula (that averages the values in the row) down a column with the Down command, Excel adjusts the row numbers so that the formula includes appropriate references in each cell. (Excel automatically adjusts cell references when you delete cells, too.)

For more information about the commands on the Fill submenu, see "Using the Fill Commands," on page 642.

The following example uses the same order-form worksheet to demonstrate formula replication. To replicate a formula, complete the following steps:

1 Highlight the cell that has the formula and expand the selection to include the empty cells you want to fill.

To control how Excel calculates formulas, see "Controlling Calculation," on page 721.

2 Choose Edit, Fill. Then choose Down from the submenu if your formula is at the top of the selected range (or choose Right, Left, or Up as appropriate). Your formula will be replicated within the selected cells, as shown here:

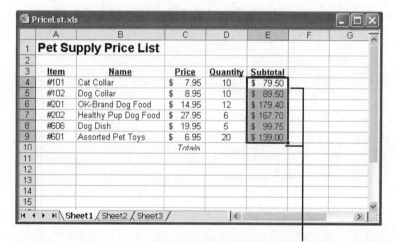

Excel replicates the formula

Tip You can also replicate a formula by using the AutoFill mouse technique. Simply select the cell you want to replicate, click the tiny box in the lower-right corner of the cell, and drag it over the cells you want to fill.

Using Relative and Absolute Cell References

When you replicate a formula, Excel adjusts cell references relative to each new location of the formula. So a formula in cell D8 that references cell C8 is, as a matter of *relative* location, referencing the cell immediately to the left of the cell containing the formula. Copy the formula to D9, and the cell that's referenced becomes C9; paste the formula to G12, and the referenced cell in the formula becomes F12—the cell located to the left of the one containing the formula.

To override this behavior, you need to indicate that a cell location in a formula is *absolute* rather than *relative*, and you do this by inserting a dollar sign ($) before the column and row designations. So as an absolute reference, H8 becomes *H8*. The formula =*H8 *2* when copied to any other cell in the worksheet remains =*H8 *2*.

The example below calculates a mileage reimbursement for trips taken in a personal vehicle. The formula in cell C6 references the reimbursement rate as an absolute cell reference, *B3*, and the miles driven as a relative reference to cell B6. When you replicate the formula to other cells in column C, the reimbursement rate correctly references the same location while the location referenced in column B changes to match the current row.

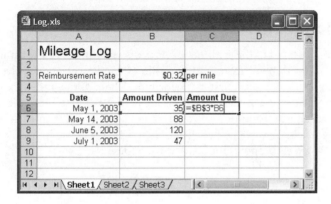

 (A copy of the example workbook shown here is provided on the book's companion CD, under the filename Log.xls.)

A third type of cell reference is called a *mixed* reference because it mixes relative and absolute notation. The cell referenced as $C8, for instance, has an absolute column location. Wherever you replicate a formula that contains a reference to $C8, it continues to reference column C, although the relative row indicator might change. Similarly, C$8 is a mixed reference, although here the row number is fixed, whereas the column reference is subject to change.

Tip   Cycling through reference types

When you're entering or editing a formula in the formula bar, pressing F4 changes the reference type for the cell reference nearest the insertion point. Thus, if the cell reference is relative (A5, for example), press F4 to change it to absolute (A5); press F4 again to change it to a mixed reference (A$5), again to change it to the other mixed reference ($A5), and yet again to change it back to a relative reference again.

Chapter 26

Editing Formulas

Excel allows you to edit formulas in the same way that you edit any other cell entry. Simply double-click the cell, move the insertion point to the mistake using the mouse or the arrow keys, make your correction, and press Enter. To cancel an edit, press Esc before pressing Enter.

> **Note** You can edit within a cell as described in this section only if the Edit Directly In Cell option is checked. To access this option, choose Tools, Options and then click the Edit tab. An alternative way to edit a cell's contents, which you can use whether or not the Edit Directly In Cell option is checked, is to select the cell, click in the formula bar, make your edit within the formula bar, and press Enter.

Combining Arithmetic Operators

Table 26-1 shows a complete list of the arithmetic operators you can use in a formula. When you enter more than one arithmetic operator, Excel follows standard algebraic rules to determine which calculations to accomplish first in the formula. These rules—called Excel's *order of evaluation*—dictate that exponential calculations are performed first, multiplication and division calculations second, and addition and subtraction last. If more than one calculation exists in the same category, Excel evaluates them from left to right. For example, when evaluating the formula =6–5+3*4, Excel computes the answer using these steps:

=6–5+3*4

=6–5+12

=1+12

=13

Table 26-1. Excel's Arithmetic Operators, in Order of Evaluation

Operator	Description	Example	Result
( )	Parentheses	(3+6)*3	27
^	Exponential	10^2	100
*	Multiplication	7*5	35
/	Division	15/3	5
+	Addition	5+5	10
–	Subtraction	12–8	4

Parentheses and Order of Evaluation

As you can see in Table 26-1, parentheses come first, letting you override Excel's normal order of evaluation. For example, consider how parentheses create a difference in evaluation between these two formulas:

=10+2*0.25

=(10+2)*0.25

The first formula produces a result of 10.5, while the second formula produces a result of 3. By modifying Excel's order of evaluation in the second formula, you wind up with a different answer.

Troubleshooting

Enforcing operator precedence

A complicated mathematical formula calculates unexpected results.

Parentheses can make a formula easier to read and therefore easier to troubleshoot or revise. If you get unexpected results from a formula, the problem might be that your assumptions about the order of evaluation are incorrect. You can add parentheses to enforce the order of evaluation you expect, even if you believe the expected order is the one Excel would normally use.

In fact, you can add any number of parentheses to a formula as long as you use them in matching pairs. For example, although the following formulas both produce the answer 15, the first formula is a bit easier to decipher.

=((5*4)/2)+(10/2)

=5*4/2+10/2

If you specify an uneven number of parentheses in a formula or a pair of parentheses that don't match, Excel will display a message saying that it found an error in the formula and will propose a correction. Click the Yes button in the message box to accept Excel's proposed correction or click the No button so you can correct the mistake in the formula bar or in the cell directly.

Using Built-In Functions

To accomplish more sophisticated numerical and text processing operations in your worksheets, Excel allows you to add functions to your formulas. A *function* is a predefined equation that operates on one or more values and returns a single value. Excel includes a collection of more than 200 functions in several useful categories, as shown in Table 26-2. For example, you can use the PMT (payment) function from the Financial category to calculate the periodic payment for a loan based on the interest rate charged, the number of payments desired, and the principal amount.

For more information on the PMT function, see "Using PMT to Determine Loan Payments," on page 738.

Table 26-2. Categories of Excel Functions

Category	Used For
Financial	Loan payments, appreciation, and depreciation
Date & Time	Calculations involving dates and times
Math & Trig	Mathematical and trigonometric calculations like those found on a scientific calculator
Statistical	Average, sum, variance, and standard-deviation calculations
Lookup & Reference	Calculations involving tables of data
Database	Working with lists and external databases
Text	Comparing, converting, and reformatting text in cells
Logical	Calculations that produce the result TRUE or FALSE
Information	Determining whether an error has occurred in a calculation

You must enter each function with a particular *syntax*, or structure, so that Excel can process the results correctly. For example, the PMT function has a function syntax that looks like this:

PMT(**rate,nper,pv,**fv,type)

The abbreviated words shown between the parentheses are called *arguments*; these are the values that you supply so that the function can return its result, enabling your formula to complete its calculations. In this function, *rate* is the interest rate, *nper* is the number of payments you will make, and *pv* (present value) is the principal amount. To use a function correctly, you must specify a value for each of these required (**boldfaced**) arguments, and you must separate the arguments with commas. The arguments *not* shown in bold are optional. For the PMT function, the arguments *fv* (future value) and *type* are optional. (Each is explained in online Help.)

To use the PMT function to calculate the monthly loan payment on a $1,000 loan at 19 percent annual interest over 36 months, for example, you could type the following formula:

=PMT(19%/12,36,1000)

When Excel evaluates this function, it places the answer ($36.66) in the cell containing the formula. (The answer is negative, as indicated by the parentheses, because it's money you must pay out.) Note that the first argument (the interest rate) is divided by 12 in this example to create a monthly rate for the formula. This demonstrates an important point—you can use other calculations, including other functions, as the arguments for a function. Although it takes a little time to master the way these arguments are structured, you'll find that functions produce results that can otherwise take hours to calculate by hand.

The Versatile SUM Function

Perhaps the most commonly used function in Excel's collection is SUM, which totals the range of cells you select. Because SUM is used so often, the Standard toolbar includes an AutoSum button to make adding numbers faster. In the following example, we will use the AutoSum button to sum the values in the Subtotal column in our order-form worksheet.

To total a column of numbers using the SUM function, follow these steps:

1 Click the cell in which you want to place the SUM function. (If you're totaling a column of numbers, select the cell directly below the last number in the column.)

2 Click the AutoSum button.

Excel will place the SUM function in the selected cell and in the formula bar, and (if possible) will automatically select a range of neighboring cells as an argument for the function. If you selected a cell directly below a column of numbers, your screen will look similar to the one in Figure 26-2.

Figure 26-2. The AutoSum button inserts the SUM function and automatically suggests the cells to use for the argument.

3 If Excel selected the range you want to total, press Enter to complete the function and compute the sum. If Excel didn't select the range you want to add up, select a new range by dragging the mouse over the range and pressing Enter. (You can specify any block of cells in any open workbook to be an argument to the SUM function.) To cancel the AutoSum command, press the Esc key before pressing Enter.

Tip   Use SUM to add nonadjacent ranges

You can use the SUM function to add multiple noncontiguous ranges by separating the cell ranges with commas. For example, =SUM(A3:A8,C3:C8) adds six cells in column A to six cells in column C and displays the total. To select noncontiguous cells or ranges, click each cell or drag over each range while pressing the Ctrl key.

Chapter 26

The Insert Function Command

With so many functions to choose from, it might seem daunting to experiment with unfamiliar features on your own. Excel makes it easier by providing the Insert, Function command, which opens the Insert Function dialog box, where you can learn about functions and enter them into formulas.

The Insert Function dialog box, shown in Figure 26-3, lets you either search for a function based on a general description you enter or browse through the function categories and then pick just the function you want. When you highlight a function, the dialog box displays a brief description of the function that explains its syntax and purpose.

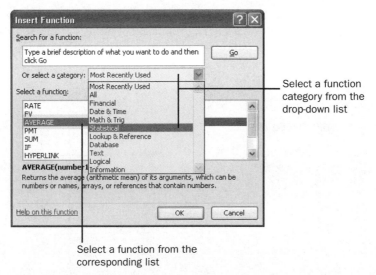

Figure 26-3. The Insert Function dialog box lists functions by category.

> **Note** In the Insert Function dialog box, all arguments in the function syntax appear in bold, but not all are required. Use the Excel online Help for more detailed documentation of each function and its arguments.

When you double-click a function in the Select A Function list, Excel displays a second dialog box prompting you for the arguments. If the note for an argument says that it can be omitted, the argument is optional. Give it a try now with a useful statistical function called AVERAGE.

To use AVERAGE to calculate the average of a list of numbers, follow these steps:

1 Click the cell in which you want to place the results of the AVERAGE function. (In the pet shop example, this is C12. The label Avg. Price has been added in B12.)

2 Choose Insert, Function to display the Insert Function dialog box.

3 Open the drop-down list of categories and select Statistical. The mathematical functions in the Statistical category will appear in the Select A Function list.

Chapter 26

4   Click the AVERAGE function, and then click the OK button. A second dialog box will appear, titled Function Arguments, which asks you for the arguments in the function. In the AVERAGE function, you can specify either individual values to compute the average or a cell range. In our example you'll specify a cell range.

5   Click the Collapse Dialog Box button (at the right end of the Number1 text box shown below), and the dialog box will shrink to show only the text box you're about to fill.

6   Select the cells you want to average. In our example we selected the numbers in the Price column (cells C4 through C9) to determine the average price of pet supplies in the store.

7   After you release the mouse button, press Enter or return to the collapsed dialog box and click the button at the right of the argument field. The dialog box will return to its normal size, and the cell range you selected will appear in the dialog box and in the AVERAGE function in the selected cell and in the formula bar. Our dialog box looks like this:

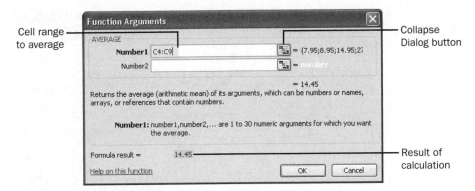

Cell range to average

Collapse Dialog button

Result of calculation

8   Click the OK button in the Function Arguments dialog box to complete the formula and calculate the result. The average, $14.45, will appear in the cell containing the AVERAGE formula.

> **Tip**   You can include one function as an argument in another function if the result is compatible. For example, the formula =SUM(5,SQRT(9)) adds together the number 5 and the square root of 9, and then displays the result (8).

Using Functions to Analyze Finances

Although Excel includes too many functions to discuss exhaustively in this book, we thought you might enjoy seeing a few more examples of functions and formulas to prompt your own exploration. We've decided to highlight three of Excel's most useful financial functions: PMT, FV, and RATE. Using these functions, you can precisely calculate loan payments, the future value of an investment, or the rate of return produced by an investment.

Using PMT to Determine Loan Payments

The PMT function returns the periodic payment required to amortize a loan over a set number of periods. In plain English, this means that you can estimate what your car payments will be if you take out an auto loan or what your mortgage payments will be if you buy a house. Try using the PMT function now to determine what the monthly payments will be for a $10,000 auto loan at 9 percent interest over a 3-year period.

To use the PMT function, follow these steps:

1 Click the worksheet cell in which you want to display the monthly payment.

2 Choose Insert, Function to display the Insert Function dialog box.

3 Choose the Financial category from the drop-down list of categories, and then double-click PMT in the list of function names. The Function Arguments dialog box will appear. You will enter numeric values for rate (the interest rate), nper (the number of payments), and pv (the present value, or loan principal).

4 Type **9%/12** into the Rate text box and press Tab, type **36** into the Nper text box and press Tab, and type **10000** into the Pv text box. The dialog box should look like the one shown here:

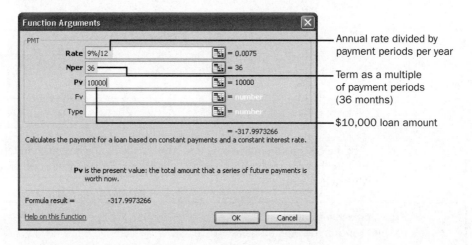

The result of the calculation (-317.9973266) will appear near the bottom of the dialog box.

> **Tip** As you grow accustomed to using functions, you might simply type them in your formula without using the Insert Function command. As you begin to type the arguments for the function, Excel provides pop-up help that walks you through the syntax.

> **Tip** To calculate monthly payments, be sure to type the annual interest using a percent sign and divide it by 12 to create a monthly interest rate. Likewise, be sure to specify the number of payments in months (36), not years (3).

Chapter 26

5 Click the OK button in the Function Arguments dialog box to complete the function and display the result. Your monthly loan payment, less any applicable loan fees, will appear in the cell you highlighted. The result, formatted as currency, appears as ($318.00) in the worksheet (Excel has rounded off the original number). The amount appears in red and between parentheses because it represents money that you must pay out.

Using FV to Compute Future Value

Although monthly loan payments are often a fact of life, Excel can help you with more than just debt planning. If you enjoy squirreling away money for the future, you can use the FV (future value) function to determine the future value of an investment. Financial planners use this tool when they help you determine the future value of an annuity, Individual Retirement Account (IRA), or Simplified Employee Pension (SEP) account. The following example shows you how to compute the future value of an IRA in which you deposit $2,000 per year for 30 years at a 10 percent annual interest rate—a possible scenario if you invest $2,000 per year between the ages of 35 and 65.

To use the FV function to calculate the value of your investment at retirement, follow these steps:

1 Click the worksheet cell in which you want to display the investment total.

2 Choose Insert, Function to open the Insert Function dialog box.

3 Select the Financial category, and then double-click FV for the function name.

The Function Arguments dialog box will appear, which contains a description of the FV function and five text boxes for the function arguments. (The arguments are related to those of the PMT function, but now a Pmt field is added so that you can enter the amount you're contributing each period.)

4 Type **10%** in the Rate text box and press Tab, type **30** in the Nper text box and press Tab, type **-2000** in the Pmt text box and press Tab twice, and then type **1** in the Type text box (indicating that the payments will be made at the beginning of each year). Your dialog box should look like the following:

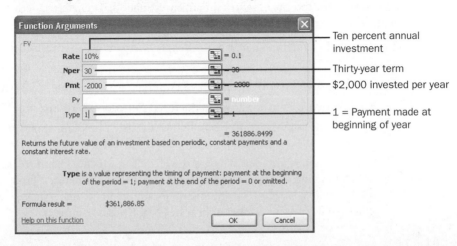

Ten percent annual investment

Thirty-year term

$2,000 invested per year

1 = Payment made at beginning of year

5 Click the OK button to display the result. In our example the 30-year IRA has a future value of $361,886.85. Not bad for a total investment of $60,000.

> **Note**   By placing a 1 in the Type text box, you direct Excel to start calculating each year's interest at the beginning of the year—a sensible move if you place one lump sum in your IRA at the same time each year. If you omit this argument, Excel calculates each year's interest at the end of the year, and because of the lost compounding the total future value will be smaller—about $33,000 less in this example.

Troubleshooting

Money troubles

The results of a financial formula are way off.

If you use a financial function and get results that are far different than you expected, consider the following common sources of error:

- Rate and Nper arguments must be based on the same units of time. In the previous examples, months were the basis in one case, years in another.

- Payments and loans are treated as negative or positive in the sense of a ledger: incoming amounts are positive, and outgoing amounts are negative.

Using the RATE Function to Evaluate Rate of Return

You will often want to evaluate how a current investment is doing or how a new business proposition looks. For example, suppose that a contractor friend suggests you lend him $10,000 for a laundromat/brew pub project and agrees to pay you $3,200 per year for four years as a minimum return on your investment. So what's the projected rate of return for this investment opportunity? You can figure it out quickly using the RATE function, which allows you to determine the rate of return for any investment that generates a series of periodic payments or a single lump-sum payment.

To use the RATE function to determine the rate of return for an investment, follow these steps:

1 Click the worksheet cell in which you want to display the rate of return.

2 Choose Insert, Function to open the Insert Function dialog box.

3 Select the Financial category, scroll down the list of function names, and double-click RATE.

The Function Arguments dialog box will appear, which contains a description of the RATE function and six text boxes for the function arguments. (Scroll down to see the sixth text box, Guess.) The arguments are similar to the ones you've used in previous financial functions, but they appear in a slightly different order.

4 Type **4** in the Nper text box and press Tab, type **3200** in the Pmt text box and press Tab, and type **-10000** in the Pv text box. Be sure to enter the third argument—the loan value—as a negative number. Your dialog box should look like this:

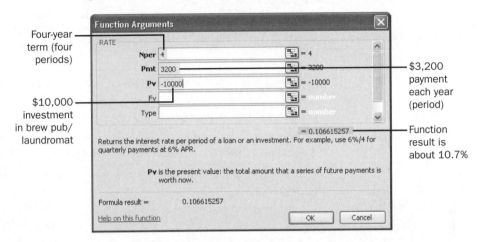

Four-year term (four periods)

$10,000 investment in brew pub/laundromat

$3,200 payment each year (period)

Function result is about 10.7%

Chapter 26

5 Click the OK button in the Function Arguments dialog box to display the result. In this example, your investment of $10,000 today will return 11 percent. With this information in hand, you can decide whether the projected rate of return is enough for you or whether you would rather try something less risky—or renegotiate the deal.

In short, Excel functions can't guarantee your financial success, but, when used correctly, they can help you analyze your choices.

Using Function Error Values

The Insert Function dialog box makes entering functions relatively straightforward. If you do make a mistake when typing a function, you might receive a code called an *error value* in one or more cells. Error values begin with a pound (#) symbol and usually end with an exclamation point. For example, the error value #NUM! means that the function arguments you supplied aren't appropriate to calculate the function—one of the arguments might be too big or too small.

If you see an error value in a cell, simply double-click the cell and fix your mistake in the cell (or select the cell and fix the error in the formula bar), or delete the formula and enter it again. Also, if you have enabled background error checking, you can select the cell, click the error button that appears, and choose an option from the drop-down menu, such as using online Help, ignoring the error, or displaying the Formula Auditing toolbar. Table 26-3 shows the most common Excel error values and their meanings.

For more information on using Excel's error checking feature, see "Entering Text Values," on page 613, and "Checking for Common Errors," on page 645.

> **Tip** If you want to suppress the error values when you print a worksheet, choose File, Page Setup. Then click the Sheet tab and in the Cell Errors As drop-down list select an option other than *displayed* (such as *<blank>*).

Table 26-3. Common Error Values in Excel Formulas

Error Value	Description
#DIV/0!	You're dividing by zero in this formula. Verify that no cell references refer to blank cells.
#NA	You might have omitted a function argument. No value is available.
#NAME?	You're using a name in this formula that hasn't been defined in the workbook. (See the next section, "Using Names in Functions.")
#NULL!	In a formula, you referred to the intersection of two ranges that don't intersect.
#NUM!	Your function arguments might be out of range or otherwise invalid, or an iterative function you're using might not have computed long enough to reach a solution. (Entering a rough answer in the *Guess* argument might reduce the number of iterations Excel needs.)
#REF!	Your formula includes range references that have been deleted.
#VALUE!	Your formula is using a text entry as an argument.
######	Your calculation results were too wide to fit in the cell. Increase the column width.

Using Names in Functions

To make your functions more readable and easier to type, you can name a cell or range of cells in your worksheet and then use the name in place of cell references throughout your workbook. For example, you could give the cells E4 through E9 the name Subtotal and then use the SUM function to add the six cells by entering the following formula:

=SUM (Subtotal)

After you assign a name to a cell or range, you can use the name in any formula in your workbook.

Creating Cell and Range Names

Excel gives you two techniques for creating names in a workbook: you can click the Name box and type a name or you can use the Insert, Name, Create command. If you have a column heading already in place, using the Create command is slightly faster.

Names must begin with a letter and can't include spaces. We recommend that you limit your names to 15 characters or fewer so they fit easily into the Name box and you can type them quickly in formulas.

Chapter 26

Assigning Names with the Create Command

To create a name using the Create command, follow these steps:

1 Select a range of cells, and include a label or heading in the selection to define the name. For example, the following selection includes the text label Subtotal for the range name:

2 Choose Insert, Name, Create.

The Create Names dialog box will appear, prompting you for the location of the name within your selection:

3 Click the OK button to accept Excel's default selection if you included a row or column heading in your range; otherwise, click the option to tell Excel where to find the name.

In this example Excel detected the text label Subtotal at the top of your selection. You can use this name in computations in any worksheet in the workbook.

Assigning Names with the Name Box

To create a name by selecting, clicking, and typing, follow the steps shown in Figure 26-4. This direct approach is handy if you want to name cells in a different, perhaps more economical, way than the headings used in the worksheet. If you name an individual cell, the name will appear in the Name Box whenever you select the cell. If you assign a name to a range of cells, the name won't appear unless you select the complete range.

1 Select the cell or range you want to name

2 Click the Name box and type an unused name with no spaces

3 Press Enter

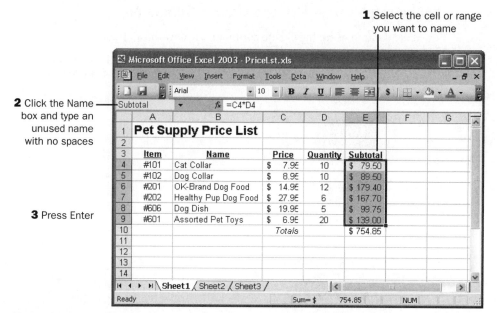

Figure 26-4. You can create a named range by hand.

Putting Names to Work

You can use names as arguments in functions wherever they're appropriate. For example, you could use the Subtotal range name in the SUM and AVERAGE functions because they accept ranges as arguments, but you couldn't use Subtotal in the PMT function because each of the PMT arguments must be a single number.

To insert a name into a formula or function, follow these steps:

1 Create the formula or function as you normally would. For example, to determine the average of the cells in the Subtotal range, begin your formula as follows:

=AVERAGE (

2 When it's time to specify a range of cells as an argument, type the named range in the formula:

=AVERAGE(Subtotal)

When you've finished entering the formula, press Enter.

Troubleshooting

Trouble with names

A formula returns the error code #NAME?.

If your formula returns the error code #NAME?, you might have incorrectly remembered a name you assigned in the workbook.

To be safe, you can choose names from a list by using the Paste Name dialog box. To insert names in this manner, type your formula, and when it's time to insert a name, choose Insert, Name, Paste, and then double-click the name that you want to include. The error might also arise if you delete or modify a name that you used in the formula (as described in the next section). Redefine the name or update the reference in your formula to correct the error.

Deleting and Modifying Names

Names are an important component of well-documented formulas. They also make your formulas easy to revise. When you modify the name, Excel automatically updates all your formulas. If you delete a name that's used in a formula, the error value #NAME? will appear in the cell containing the formula.

Tip You can't undo a name deletion. To fix the problem, you will need to replace the name in the formula with an actual cell reference or with a valid name.

To define or delete a name, or to modify the cells referenced by a name, follow these steps:

1 Choose Insert, Name, Define to display the Define Name dialog box.

This dialog box displays a list of the names in your workbook and a Refers To text box describing the cell(s) that each name references, as shown here:

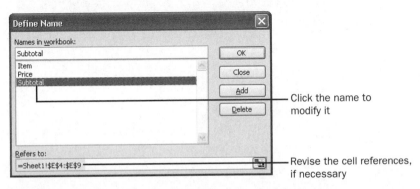

2 Perform one of the following actions in the Define Name dialog box:

- To define a new name, type it into the Names In Workbook text box. Then either type a description of the referenced cell(s) into the Refers To text box or (usually easier) click the Collapse Dialog button at the right end of this box and select the cell(s) directly in the worksheet.

- To delete a name, select it in the Names In Workbook list and click the Delete button.

- To modify a name, select it in the Names In Workbook list and either edit the description of the referenced cell(s) in the Refers To box or (often easier) click the Collapse Dialog button at the right end of this box and select a new range of cell(s) directly in the worksheet.

Chapter 27

Advanced Worksheet Charts

Planning a Chart 747
Creating a Chart 751
Formatting a Chart 758
Adding Labels and Arrows 766
Printing a Chart 768

When you have worksheet data that you need to present to others, it often makes sense to display some of the facts and figures as a *chart.* Charts are graphical representations of data that transform rows and columns of information into meaningful images. Charts can help you to identify numerical trends that can be difficult to spot in worksheets, and they can add color and flair to an important presentation. In this chapter you'll learn how to create a Microsoft Office Excel 2003 chart from worksheet data, format your chart's appearance, add special effects, and print your chart. If it's your job to plan for the future or analyze the past, you'll find Excel's charting tools both useful and addictive.

Planning a Chart

Before you can create a chart, you need to do some planning. You create an Excel chart from the data in an existing Excel worksheet, so before you build a chart, you need to create a worksheet that contains the necessary facts and figures. Excel can create a chart from data that's distributed throughout a worksheet, but you'll make the process easier if you organize your numbers so that they can be combined and selected easily. For example, Figure 27-1 shows a sales worksheet that contains rows and columns of data you can easily convert into several types of charts.

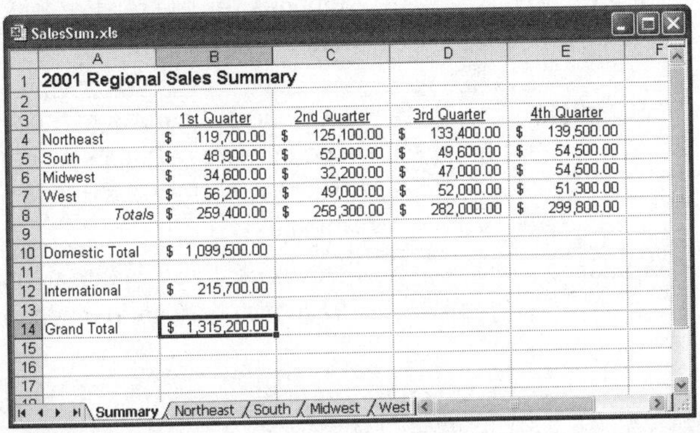

SalesSum.xls

	A	B	C	D	E
1	2001 Regional Sales Summary				
2					
3		1st Quarter	2nd Quarter	3rd Quarter	4th Quarter
4	Northeast	$ 119,700.00	$ 125,100.00	$ 133,400.00	$ 139,500.00
5	South	$ 48,900.00	$ 52,000.00	$ 49,600.00	$ 54,500.00
6	Midwest	$ 34,600.00	$ 32,200.00	$ 47,000.00	$ 54,500.00
7	West	$ 56,200.00	$ 49,000.00	$ 52,000.00	$ 51,300.00
8	*Totals*	$ 259,400.00	$ 258,300.00	$ 282,000.00	$ 299,800.00
9					
10	Domestic Total	$ 1,099,500.00			
11					
12	International	$ 215,700.00			
13					
14	Grand Total	$ 1,315,200.00			

Figure 27-1. Creating charts is easier when you make neatly organized rows and columns of data.

Choosing a Chart Type

As you plan, give some thought to the type of chart you'll be creating. Excel provides 14 chart types that you can use to present worksheet data, and there are several variations for each chart type. The basic chart types are shown in Table 27-1 along with each one's typical uses. For example, you can use a pie chart to describe the relationship of parts to a whole or a bar chart to compare different categories of data with each other. If you're gathering information for an annual sales report, you might want to try out both of these chart types.

> If you have your worksheet set up with fields and records like a database, you can also create an interactive chart called a *PivotChart*. For more information about this powerful charting feature, see "Creating PivotTables and PivotCharts," on page 789.

Table 27-1. Excel Chart Types and Typical Uses for Each One

Chart Symbol	Chart Type	Typical Use
	Column	Compares categories of data with each other vertically
	Bar	Compares categories of data with each other horizontally
	Line	Shows trends by category over a period of time
	Pie	Describes the relationship of the parts to the whole in a single group
	XY (Scatter)	Depicts the relationship between two kinds of related data
	Area	Emphasizes the relative importance of values over a period of time
	Doughnut	Compares the parts to the whole in one or more data categories; a more flexible pie chart that has a hole in the middle
	Radar	Shows changes in data or data frequency relative to a center point

Table 27-1. Excel Chart Types and Typical Uses for Each One

Chart Symbol	Chart Type	Typical Use
	Surface	Tracks changes in two variables as a third variable (such as time) changes; a three-dimensional (3-D) chart
	Bubble	Highlights clusters of values; similar to a scatter chart
	Stock	Plots stock or commodity trading data, including the volume and the open, high, low, and close prices
	Cylinder	Uses a unique cylinder shape to present bar or column chart data
	Cone	Emphasizes the peaks in data; a bar or column chart drawn with cones
	Pyramid	Emphasizes the peaks in data; a bar or column chart drawn with pyramids

Measure Twice, Chart Once

Charting requires some up-front planning to get the best results. Just as a carpenter measures a length of wood twice before cutting it, you would be well advised to take your time and think about your goals for a chart before creating it. As you plan your charting strategy, ask yourself the following questions:

- Which worksheet data would I like to highlight in a chart? Can I build my worksheet so that I can copy data directly to the chart?

- How will I present my chart? Do I want to store it as a separate chart sheet in my workbook, embedded in an existing worksheet, or as part of a Microsoft Word document or a Microsoft PowerPoint presentation?

- Which chart type do I plan to use? Do I want to show one category of data (such as first-quarter sales by geographic region), or several (such as the four most recent quarters of sales by geographic region)?

Understanding Chart Elements, Excel-Style

Finally, to help you map your data to the representation in the various chart types, you need to master the terms that Excel uses—terms that apply to the worksheet data that it charts and terms that apply to the various chart elements that you can format or otherwise modify.

As an example, you might create a standard column chart from the data selected in Figure 27-2. For a column chart, Excel assumes initially that the columns of values that you select are the *data series*, and the column headings become the *series names* in the Legend box, as shown in Figure 27-3. (You can correct these assumptions as necessary.) The *legend* explains the way Excel uses colors or patterns to correspond to particular names of data values or data series.

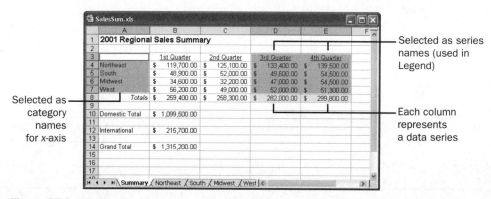

Figure 27-2. Select the data that you want to be represented graphically.

In a two-dimensional chart, Excel refers to the horizontal axis, or *x*-axis, as the *Category axis* and it refers to the vertical axis, or *y*-axis, as the *Value axis*. The chart in Figure 27-3 uses the row headings in column A to identify the values on the Category axis. Lines that mark distance along the axes are called *tick marks*, and the horizontal and vertical extensions of these marks within the plot area are *gridlines*. The chart also illustrates the use of *labels*, which refer here to the text attached to the plotted values themselves.

> **Note** In a 3-D chart, the vertical axis is the *z*-axis—and is still called the Value axis—whereas the "depth" axis is the *y*-axis, which Excel refers to as the *Series axis*.

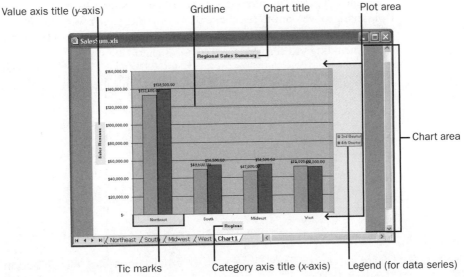

Figure 27-3. Understand the terms Excel applies to chart elements so that you can use the various tools to modify and format them.

When you create a chart, you can either embed it within an existing worksheet, along with the cells and any data that is contained in them, or you can display it in a separate workbook tab known as a *chart sheet*, which displays only a chart with no cells.

Creating a Chart

When you have a well-organized worksheet in place, you're ready to create a chart. In the following examples we'll use the 2001 Regional Sales Summary workbook (SalesSum.xls) shown earlier in Figure 27-1 to create a pie chart and a column chart. Because charting often involves experimenting with different chart types, feel free to follow your own impulses as you complete the instructions.

 The SalesSum.xls example is on the companion CD to this book.

To create a pie chart in a new chart sheet in the workbook, follow these steps:

1   Prepare a worksheet that has rows and columns of information that you can use in the chart. Add row and column labels if you want them included in the chart.

> **Tip**   If you select headings along with the data for your chart before you create the chart, Excel will add the names to the chart automatically.

2 Select the cell range containing the data to be plotted. In this example we'll be creating a pie chart, so we want to select one series of values (one row or column). The following screen shows how you would select numbers in the 1st Quarter column for a pie chart, including text that you want to use as chart labels:

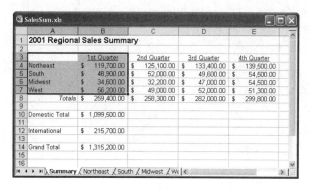

Chart Wizard

3 Create the chart. Choose Insert, Chart, or click the Chart Wizard button on the Standard toolbar.

The Chart Wizard will start, and you will see the Step 1 page, shown here, which asks you to select a chart type:

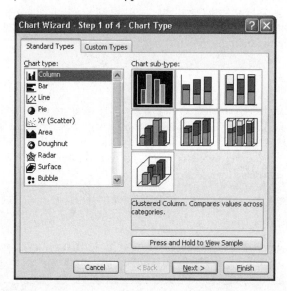

4 In the Chart Type list, click the Pie chart type. Then, in the Chart Sub-Type area, click the chart with the description "Exploded pie with a 3-D visual effect." (The descriptions of the subtypes appear as you click each one.)

5 Click the Next button to display the Chart Wizard Step 2 dialog box, which prompts you for the worksheet cells to include in the chart. The cells you selected in step 2 will appear in the Data Range text box (cells A3 through B7).

> **Note** If you organized your worksheet well, and if you selected the proper data, your chart should now contain the correct information (although the names might be too small to see). If your chart doesn't look right, use the options and lists in the tabs of the Chart Wizard Step 2 dialog box to change the cells used for the data series, names, and chart title.

6 Click the Next button to display the Chart Wizard Step 3 page, which controls the chart's titles, legend, and data labels. Your pie chart will appear in a preview area with the default settings, as shown here:

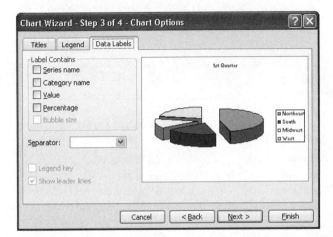

7 Starting from the Titles tab, change the chart title by typing **2001 Regional Sales Summary** in the Chart Title text box. Click the Legend tab and clear the Show Legend option. Then click the Data Labels tab and check both the Category Name and the Value options in the Label Contains area. Clear the Show Leader Lines option because the pie sections are few and the labels should be clear without leader lines.

> **Tip** It's often wise to use labels rather than relying on the legend if you will be printing and photocopying a chart and you fear that the distinctions in grayscales will be lost.

8 Click the Next button to proceed to the Step 4 dialog box (the final step). This dialog box asks you for the location of your new chart. You can either create a new chart sheet for the chart or embed it as an object in one of your existing worksheets. Select the As New Sheet option, type **Summary Chart** in the highlighted text box, and then click the Finish button.

Chapter 27

Excel will complete the pie chart and display it in a new chart sheet with the name you assigned, Summary Chart. Excel will adjust the Zoom control on the Standard toolbar so that the entire chart is visible. The Charting toolbar will also appear; we will cover that feature in "Formatting a Chart," on page 758.

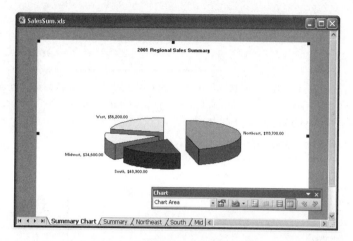

9   Choose File, Save to save your new chart to disk as part of your open workbook. You can now display the pie chart at any time by clicking the Summary Chart tab.

> **Tip**   To get a better look at the title, labels, and data in your new chart, click the Zoom control on the Standard toolbar, and select a higher viewing percentage. You will find that 75% or 100% usually works well for reading the text in your chart and for formatting names.

Creating an Embedded Chart

Excel also allows you to create an in-place, or *embedded*, chart in an existing worksheet. This technique allows you to closely associate graphical images with the data in your worksheet. For example, within a bakery worksheet that contains inventory and sales data, you could create an area chart depicting bagel production. In the following example, we will show you how to add a column sales chart to a sales summary worksheet.

To create an embedded chart in a worksheet, follow these steps:

1   Prepare a worksheet that has rows and columns of data that you can chart. As you create the worksheet, set aside some room for a rectangular column chart.

2   Select the cell range containing the data that you want to plot. In our example we'll be creating a chart similar to the one in Figure 27-3, which has groups of columns representing sales regions, so if you want to follow our example, you will need to select several columns of data. (The chart in Figure 27-3 is contained in its own chart sheet,

while our chart will be embedded in an existing worksheet.) For this example, let's select two columns, as shown here:

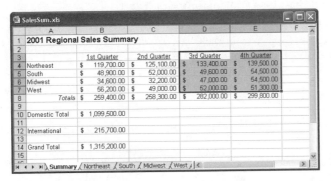

3 Click the Chart Wizard button on the Standard toolbar. (Creating an embedded chart is exactly like creating a stand-alone chart, except for specifying the chart location in the last step of the Chart Wizard.)

4 In the Chart Type dialog box, specify the chart type you want to use and click Next. (In this example, we'll use the default column chart type.)

5 The Chart Source Data dialog box reflects the data range selected in step 2. To add region names for the Category axis, click the Series tab and click the Collapse Dialog Box button in the Category (X) Axis Labels text box. Select cells A4:A7 and press Enter so that the dialog box appears as shown here. Click the Next button to proceed to the next step.

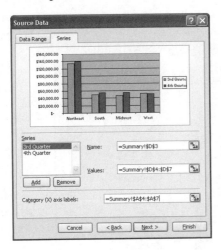

Chapter 27

6 Customize your chart by choosing from the options presented in the Chart Options dialog box or accept Excel's settings. Notice that you have a different set of options for the column chart than you did for the pie chart.

In our chart, let's add a title for the chart and for each axis. In the Titles tab, type **Regional Sales Summary** in the Chart Title text box, **Regions** in the Category (X) Axis text box, and **Sales Revenue** in the Value (Y) Axis text box.

> To modify fonts and numeric formats as shown in Figure 27-3, use the techniques described in "Formatting a Chart," on page 758.

7 When you're finished, click the Next button to display the Chart Location dialog box:

8 Select the As Object In option button, and then specify the worksheet in which you want to place the new chart by using the adjacent drop-down list. (We placed our chart in the Summary worksheet.)

9 Click the Finish button to complete the chart.

The Chart Wizard will build the chart to your specifications and place it in the middle of the worksheet, as shown in the following illustration. (Note that the chart is currently selected and has eight selection handles.)

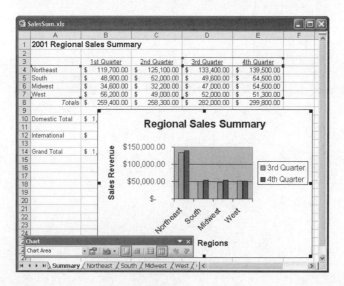

Chapter 27

10 Drag the chart to the desired location in the worksheet and resize it to display the amount of detail you want. (Drag the chart by one of its edges so that you don't inadvertently rearrange the chart components.)

> **Tip** Excel creates embedded charts small to make them easy to move and format. However, your chart usually looks better if you enlarge it.

11 When you're finished, click outside the chart to remove the selection handles and lock it in place on your worksheet. (Click the chart to reactivate the selection handles in the future.)

Working with Embedded Charts

When you embed an Excel chart in a worksheet, you create an object that can be resized, formatted, moved, and deleted like clip art or any other object. You can use the following editing techniques on embedded charts:

- To resize an embedded chart, move the mouse pointer to the edge of the chart and drag one of the selection handles.

- To format an embedded chart, double-click the chart (in its background area), and the Format Chart Area dialog box will appear. Add borders to the chart from the Patterns tab or choose other commands from the Font or Properties tabs.

> **For more information, see "Formatting a Chart," on page 758.**

- To move an embedded chart from one location to another in the worksheet, click within the object and drag it to a new location. To move the chart to a new worksheet, click the chart, and then choose Chart, Location. To move the chart to another workbook or Microsoft Office 2003 application, click the chart, choose Edit, Cut; open or switch to the destination document; and then choose Edit, Paste.

- To delete an embedded chart, select the chart and press the Delete key.

 The Charts.xls example workbook, provided on the book's companion CD, includes both the pie chart and the embedded bar chart that you created following the steps given in this chapter.

Chapter 27

Inside Out

Freeze a chart

Whether you embed a chart or create it in a new chart sheet, Excel changes the chart as you change its data. In general, this automatic updating is a good thing: your chart remains current without your making a deliberate effort. But what if you *want* to freeze the chart? You can copy the chart to another workbook, but even then, Excel updates the chart (as long as you choose to update links when prompted) because the program establishes a link between the chart and its external data set.

Should you want to freeze the chart, your best bet is to break the link. Copy the chart to a separate workbook. While the second workbook is active, choose Edit, Links. In the Edit Links dialog box, select the link between the chart and its data (if more than one link is present), and click the Break Link button. When Excel warns you about the consequences of breaking the link, click the Break Links button in the message box.

Formatting a Chart

If you're content to use Excel's default formatting for your chart, you're all finished—just tidy up your chart and print it. If you're like most people, however, you probably can't resist adding a label here or changing the point size there. In this section you will learn how to format charts by changing the chart type, editing titles and gridlines, adjusting the legend, adding text, and controlling character formatting. What you learn will apply both to embedded charts and to stand-alone chart sheets in the workbook.

> **Tip**   To reverse the order of the items on an axis, you can make the change in the Format dialog box. Select the axis by clicking it, choose Format, Selected Axis, and click the Scale tab. Check the option for reversing the order, which is labeled to reflect the axis itself, whether it contain values, categories, or series (for 3-D charts only).

Exploring the Chart Menu

When you created the pie chart in the first example in this chapter, you might not have noticed that a Chart menu replaced the Data menu on the menu bar and that several commands on the remaining menus changed. Excel's Chart menu includes commands that are specifically designed for charting, as shown on the next page. (Note that your Chart menu might be customized differently.)

> **Note** The Chart menu replaces the Data menu whenever a chart is the active object—either because you activate a chart sheet or because you click on some element of an embedded chart.

Using the Chart Toolbar

The Chart toolbar shown in Figure 27-4 contains several buttons designed to help you format your chart. This toolbar also contains the Chart Objects drop-down list, which you can use to select different components of your chart for editing (such as the chart title, legend, and plot areas). Many of the buttons on the Chart toolbar correspond to commands on the Chart menu, as you will see in the following sections. Display the Chart toolbar at any time by choosing it from the Toolbars submenu of the View menu.

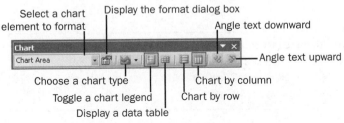

Figure 27-4. The Chart toolbar appears when a chart is active in the workbook. To remove it, click the Close button.

Changing the Chart Type

Even after you create a chart, you're not locked in to one particular chart type. If your data supports it, you can reformat your chart to use any of Excel's 14 chart types. (For example, you can change your pie chart into a column chart.) To switch between chart types, click the Chart Type button on the Chart toolbar or choose Chart, Chart Type.

To change the pie chart you created earlier into a column chart by using the Chart toolbar, follow these steps:

1 If the chart is embedded, click it to select it. If the chart appears in its own chart sheet, simply activate that chart sheet.

2 Click the down arrow on the Chart Type button on the Chart toolbar to display pictures of the various chart types.

3 Click the 3-D Column Chart button. (When you move the pointer over each chart type, its name appears.)

Your chart changes shape to match the selected chart type. The following screen shows how your pie chart looks when it's changed into a 3-D column chart. (The value labels for the data points were moved—by dragging them using the mouse—for better visibility.)

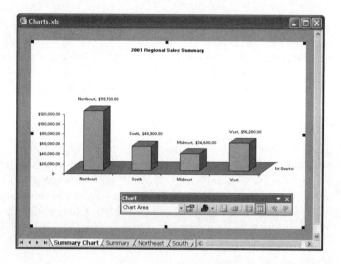

> **Tip** **Choosing additional chart subtypes**
>
> For a wider selection of chart types (for example, to change from 3-D view to 2-D view), select the chart, and choose Chart, Chart Type. Here you can pick from over 70 different combinations of chart types and subtypes.

Changing Titles and Data Labels

You can edit the text in your chart's titles and data labels and modify the font, alignment, and background pattern. If you select a data label, you can change its numeric formatting.

To edit title or data label text, follow these steps:

1 Display the chart that you want to modify. If the chart is embedded in a worksheet, click the chart to activate it. Excel will display its charting commands and tools.

2 Use the Zoom control to zoom in on the title or data label so that you can read it, if necessary. The best view for editing text is usually 100%.

3 Click the title or data label in the chart. (If you're selecting a data label, click a second time to select a particular label in the series.) Selection handles will surround the text.

4   Click again to place the insertion point at the spot you want to edit. You can insert new text and use the Backspace and Delete keys to delete unwanted text.

Tip   You can check the spelling of the text in a chart by selecting the text object and choosing Tools, Spelling.

---

5   When you've completed your edits, press the Esc key once to remove the insertion point and then press Esc a second time to remove the selection handles. (You can also click outside the chart to remove the selection handles.)

Changing Character Formatting

To change a title or data label font, alignment, or pattern, follow these steps:

1   Click the title or data label. (If you're selecting a data label, click a second time to select a particular label rather than selecting the entire series.) Selection handles will appear around the text.

2   Choose Format, and then Selected Chart Title or Selected Axis Title (for a title) or Selected Data Labels (for a data label). Only one of the commands will be available. You will see a dialog box similar to the one shown in Figure 27-5.

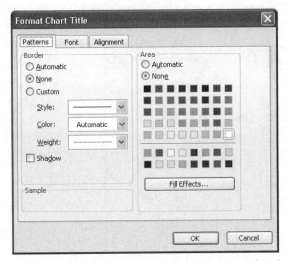

Figure 27-5.   You can format chart titles and data labels in the same way as regular worksheet text.

Note   If you're formatting a data label, the dialog box will also have a Number tab. We'll discuss this tab in the next example.

---

3 Use the Patterns, Font, and Alignment tabs to modify the borders or colors, adjust the character formatting in the text, or adjust the text orientation. For example, if you plan to print your chart, you might want to increase the text's point size using the Font tab.

4 When you've finished formatting the text, click the OK button.

> To learn more about formatting text, see Chapter 23, "Expert Formatting Techniques."

Adjusting Numeric Formatting in Data Labels

If you selected a data label in the instructions given in the previous section, the formatting dialog box (titled Format Data Labels) will include a Number tab, as shown in Figure 27-6. To use the Number tab to adjust the numeric formatting in data labels, complete the following steps:

1 Click a data label or an axis that contains numeric data such as percentages or dollar amounts. By selecting an axis, you also select the numeric values associated with the intersection of the gridlines and the axis.

> **Tip** To add or change data labels, choose Chart, Chart Options and click the Data Labels tab.

2 Choose Format, Selected Axis. Or, if you selected a data label, choose Format, Selected Data Labels.

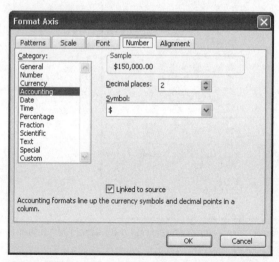

Figure 27-6. The Number tab lets you change the number formatting in an axis or data label.

3 Click the Number tab of the Format dialog box, shown in Figure 27-6. (If you're formatting an axis, the dialog box will also have a Scale tab, which you can use to adjust the numbers and tick marks along the axis.)

4 Click the numeric category that you want to use and specify a new number of decimal places if necessary.

5 When you finish formatting, click the OK button.

Adjusting Gridlines

With most chart types (the exceptions being pie and doughnut charts), you can include gridlines that extend vertically from the *x*-axis or horizontally from the *y*-axis. Gridlines help you to associate numbers accurately with the pictures in your chart, and they're especially useful if you need to make exact comparisons between categories of data.

To add gridlines to your chart, follow these steps:

1 Display the chart. If your chart is embedded in a worksheet, click the chart to activate Excel's charting commands and tools.

2 Choose Chart, Chart Options to display the Chart Options dialog box. Then click the Gridlines tab (see Figure 27-7).

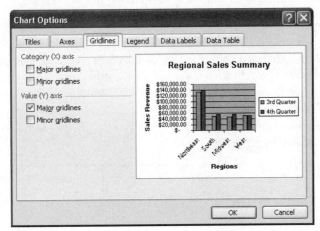

Figure 27-7. The check boxes in the Gridlines tab determine which gridlines appear.

3 To add gridlines to one or more axes, check the corresponding Major Gridlines options. If you want to create a denser pattern of gridlines, check one or more Minor Gridlines options also.

4 Click the OK button to add the gridlines. To remove the gridlines, simply clear all of the Gridlines options and click the OK button.

> **Tip** You can also remove gridlines by clicking the gridlines in your chart and pressing Delete.

Modifying the Chart Legend

A chart *legend* describes what each color or pattern represents in a chart so that you can compare the values in a category. Excel lets you change the font, colors, and location of an existing chart legend by using a special dialog box. You can add a legend to a chart when you first build the chart using the Chart Wizard, or later by clicking the Legend button on the Chart toolbar. Because the Legend button is an on or off toggle, you can add or remove a chart legend quickly to see whether you like it. If you remove the chart legend, you will have more room on your chart for graphing the data.

To modify the font, colors, or location of a chart legend, follow these steps:

1 Display the chart and click the legend, which will then be surrounded by selection handles. (You can resize the legend by dragging any of these handles.)

2 Choose Format, Selected Legend to display the Format Legend dialog box. This dialog box contains three tabs that let you control the border, colors, and patterns used for the legend box; the font used for the legend text; and the location of the legend in relation to the chart.

3 Use the Patterns, Font, and Placement tabs to customize the legend. When you finish, click the OK button.

> **Tip** To quickly format the text in a chart legend, you can also select the legend and use the Font, Font Size, Bold, Italic, Underline, Fill Color, and Font Color buttons on the Formatting toolbar.

Changing the Viewing Angle in 3-D Charts

Excel offers you 3-D chart types in the Area, Bar, Column, Line, Pie, Surface, Cylinder, Cone, and Pyramid categories. Three-dimensional charts have much in common with two-dimensional charts, but they add a feeling of depth that brings realism and visual interest to your data. You can change the orientation, or *viewing angle*, of a 3-D chart by selecting the chart and choosing Chart, 3-D View to display the 3-D View dialog box shown here:

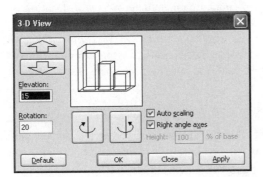

To tilt the chart up or back, click the large up or down buttons in the 3-D View dialog box above the Elevation text box. To rotate the chart left or right, click the clockwise or counterclockwise buttons beneath the chart preview area. You can also change the perspective or line-of-sight angle by clicking the up or down buttons above the Perspective text box (these buttons are available only if the Right Angle Axes option is cleared).

Copying Chart Formats

If you're creating a number of charts that you intend to present as a set, you can ensure that they are formatted consistently by copying the formats of one to each of the others. This technique is similar to format painting as you might use it in worksheets or in other Office 2003 applications. To copy chart formats, complete the following steps:

1 Select the chart area (rather than a specific element) of the chart that you want to model the other charts after. To do this, click within the chart but not within a specific chart element. Or, select Chart Area in the Chart Objects drop-down list on the Chart toolbar.

2 Choose Edit, Copy.

3 Activate the chart to which you want the new formatting to apply.

Chapter 27

4 Choose Edit, Paste Special. In the Paste Special dialog box, select the Formats option and click the OK button.

Excel will reformat the second chart to match the first, possibly including some aspects that you didn't intend to change, such as the chart type or the scaling of the axis. You can undo the Paste Special operation or reverse the unwanted changes individually.

Adding Labels and Arrows

Have you ever been lost in a shopping mall, unable to determine your location or find the store you're looking for? When this happens, it's comforting to find the mall map, with its familiar "You Are Here" arrow and message that identify your location and help you get your bearings. As you design your charts, you can use Excel's charting commands to add similar pointers to your own pictures. If you have important aspects that you want to highlight, this could be the perfect tool.

To highlight a chart attribute by adding an arrow, follow these steps:

1 Display the chart that you want to embellish with an arrow. If the chart is embedded in a worksheet, click the chart to activate Excel's charting commands and tools.

Drawing

2 Click the Drawing button on Excel's Standard toolbar.

Excel will then display its multipurpose Drawing toolbar (typically in the lower part of the screen, just above the status bar), as shown here:

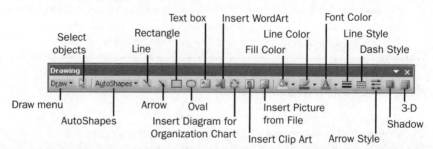

3 Click the Arrow button on the Drawing toolbar. The mouse pointer will change to drawing crosshairs.

4 Draw the line that will be your arrow—clicking and holding at the arrow's tail, dragging and then releasing at the arrow's head. When you release the mouse button, a default-style arrow will appear.

5 Customize the arrow by adjusting the line's weight with the Line Style button, selecting a dashed line style with the Dash Style button, or adjusting the arrow's head and tail with the Arrow Style button.

Chapter 27

The Drawing toolbar contains several tools to further embellish your charts and worksheets. For more information, see Chapter 6, "Adding Professional Graphics and Special Effects to Office 2003 Documents."

To add text to the arrow, follow these steps:

1 Click the Text Box button on the Drawing toolbar.

2 Use the drag technique to draw a rectangle to hold your label text. When it's approximately the right size, release the mouse button.

3 Type the label text and click near the border of the text box to select the entire text box (removing the insertion point from within the text box).

4 Use the Formatting toolbar to set the text's font, size, style (bold, italic, or underline), background (fill) color, or font color. Use the Drawing toolbar to change the background (fill) color or font color, to add a border to the text box (click the Line Style button), or to set the border color (click the Line Color button).

Tip You can reposition free-floating text boxes and arrows in your chart by selecting them and dragging them with the mouse. To delete a text box or arrow, select the object and press Delete.

5 Resize the text box using the selection handles and place the text box where you want it by dragging a border. Then click outside the chart area to remove the selection handles. The following is an example of an arrow and text box added to a chart:

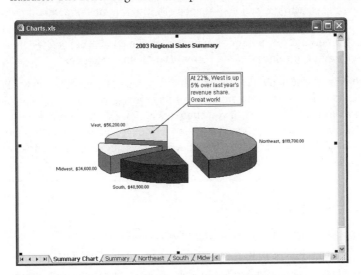

6 Click the Close button on the Drawing toolbar to remove it from the screen. (If you don't see a Close button, right-click the Drawing toolbar and deselect the Drawing option on the shortcut menu.)

Chapter 27

Printing a Chart

When you've finished creating attractive charts, you will most certainly want to print them. Printing charts isn't much different from printing worksheets, but you have a few extra options. If you're using a black-and-white printer, you will want to examine your chart in Print Preview to verify that its colors have been properly converted to grayscale shading. If you're printing an embedded chart, you have the option of printing the chart with or without the worksheet data around it.

To double-check chart colors in Print Preview, follow these steps:

1 Display the chart that you want to print. If the chart is in its own chart sheet, activate that sheet. If the chart is embedded in a worksheet, click the chart to select it.

Print Preview

2 Click the Print Preview button on the Standard toolbar.

3 Verify the chart shading—you should be able to distinguish one shade of gray from another. (If you're using a color printer, you will, of course, see everything in color.)

4 Click the Close toolbar button to exit Print Preview.

Troubleshooting

Move beyond shades of difference

Differences in shading are not sufficient to distinguish data series in printed charts.

If you're not happy with the shading—especially with any lack of contrast between supposedly distinct data series or data points—double-click the chart piece you want to change and specify a new color or pattern. Depending on the chart type, you will be working with either the Format Data Series or the Format Data Point dialog box.

In the Patterns tab, click the Fill Effects button and look at the options in the Pattern tab of the Fill Effects dialog box. These are effective for creating readily distinguishable regions for black-and-white printing. In fact, if you choose File, Page Setup when a chart is selected, and then click the Chart tab, you will find a check box for black-and-white printing under the Printing Quality options. This option goes beyond grayscaling; it substitutes patterns for colors to provide clear distinctions in the printed output.

To print a chart, follow these steps:

1 Display the chart that you want to print, as follows:

■ If the chart is in its own chart sheet, activate that sheet.

■ If the chart is embedded in a worksheet, activate the worksheet. If you want to print the chart only, and not the surrounding worksheet data as well, you must also click the chart to select it (otherwise, both the worksheet data and the embedded chart will be printed).

2 Choose File, Print to open the Print dialog box.

3 Specify the print options that you want and then click the OK button to send your chart to the printer.

Troubleshooting

Chart "scalability"

Excel is printing the chart larger than expected.

By default, if Excel prints only a chart (that is, it doesn't include a containing worksheet), it scales the chart to fill the entire printed page. If you want your printed chart to be the same size as the chart in your worksheet, select the chart, choose File, Page Setup, click the Chart tab, and then select the Custom option. This option tells Excel to render the chart on paper exactly as it appears in your worksheet. Use Print Preview to get an idea of the size differences.

Chapter 27

Power Database Techniques: Lists, Filters, and PivotTables

Using a List as a Database 771
Sorting Rows and Columns. 778
Using AutoFilter to Find Records 783
Analyzing a List with the Subtotals
Command 785

Converting an Excel List into an
Access Database 788
Creating PivotTables and PivotCharts . . 789
NEW FEATURE! Using the New Excel List Commands. . . 800

If you routinely track large amounts of information in your business—customer mailing lists, phone lists, product inventories, sales transactions, and so on—you can use the extensive list-management capabilities of Microsoft Office Excel 2003 to make your job easier. A *list* is a table of data stored in a worksheet, organized into columns of *fields* and rows of *records*. A list is essentially a *database*, but because lists are stored in Excel workbooks and not in formatted files created by database programs such as Microsoft Access or Microsoft Visual FoxPro, Microsoft has chosen to use the word *list* as the preferred term.

In this chapter you'll learn how to create a list in a workbook, sort the list based on one or more fields, locate important records by using filters, organize and analyze entries by using subtotals, and create summary information by using PivotTables and PivotCharts. The lists that you create will be compatible with Access, and, if you're not already familiar with Access, the techniques that you learn here will give you a head start on learning several database commands and terms. The chapter concludes with a discussion on the new List commands provided by Excel 2003.

Using a List as a Database

A list is a collection of rows and columns of consistently formatted data adhering to somewhat stricter rules than an ordinary worksheet. To build a list that works with all of Excel's list-management commands, you need to follow a few guidelines. Figure 28-1 shows a simple sales-history list that has five columns, or fields, and a dozen sales transaction records. This list is saved in Pivot.xls, which you can load from this book's companion CD.

Each row represents
a record in the list

Each column represents a field
containing one type of information

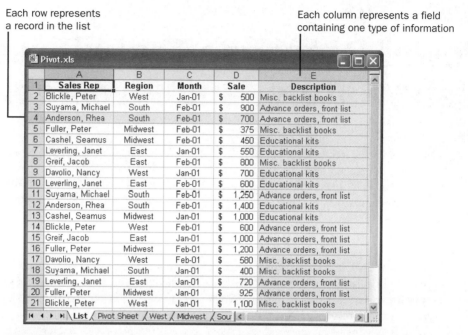

Figure 28-1. In an Excel worksheet, a list typically includes column headers, for easier manipulation.

When you create a list, keep the following in mind:

- Maintain a fixed number of columns (that is, fields) of information; you can alter the number of rows as you add or delete records to keep your list up to date.

- Use each column to hold the same type of information.

- Don't leave blank rows or columns in the list area. You can leave blank cells, if necessary.

- Make your list the only information in the worksheet so that Excel can more easily recognize the data as a list.

- Maintain your data's integrity by entering identical information consistently. For example, don't enter an expense category as *Ad* in one row, *Adv* in another, and *Advertising* in a third if all belong to the same classification.

To create a list in Excel, follow these steps:

1 Open a new workbook or a new worksheet in an existing workbook.

2 Create a column header for each field in the list, format the headers in bold type, and adjust their alignment.

Chapter 28

3 Format the cells below the column headers for the data that you plan to use. This can include number formats (such as currency or date), alignment, or any other formats.

The Pivot.xls example workbook is on this book's companion CD.

For information about sharing a list with other users over a network, see "Managing Shared Workbooks," on page 693.

4 Add new records (your data) below the column headers, taking care to be consistent in your use of words and titles so that you can organize related records into groups later. Enter as many rows as you need, making sure that no empty rows are in your list, not even between the column headers and the first record. See Figure 28-1 for a sample list of information. When you've finished, save your workbook. If your list grows to include many records, consider keeping a separate backup copy in a safe place as an extra precaution.

Inside Out

Let AutoComplete finish typing your words

Excel's AutoComplete feature helps you insert repetitive list entries consistently by recognizing the words you type and finishing them for you. A nice alternative is to right-click the cell and choose Pick From List from the shortcut menu to reuse an entry that was previously typed in the same column.

To activate the AutoComplete feature, choose Tools, Options, click the Edit tab, and check the Enable AutoComplete For Cell Values option. It's important that repeated names and other data (such as January, Midwest Region, and so on) be entered identically from record to record to enable Excel to recognize the data for grouping, sorting, and calculating.

Using a Form for Data Entry

To make it easy to manage the data in your list, Excel lets you add, delete, and search for records by using the Data, Form command. When you choose this command, a customized dialog box will appear, showing the fields in your list and several list-management command buttons (see Figure 28-2). The name of the current worksheet will also appear on the dialog box title bar.

Chapter 28

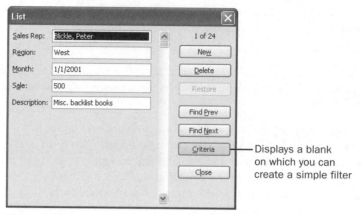

Figure 28-2. The Form command gives you another way to enter data into the rows and columns of a list.

When you choose the Data, Form command, the first record in the list will appear. You can scroll to other records by using the vertical scroll bar. To display a blank record, you can scroll to the bottom of the list or click the New button. Excel adds new records to the end of the list. Although you'll often add records by typing them directly into the worksheet, using the Form command is a useful alternative (for, say, a less-experienced colleague you've asked to help enter data), and in some cases you'll find that it works faster.

The Criteria button lets you limit the records that you see in the Form window by applying a simple filter. When you click it, Excel lets you enter search criteria on a blank form to match entries in the corresponding field; your search criteria can include relational operators, such as < and >. When you specify criteria for fields that contain text, Excel finds matches when you supply only the initial letters in an entry (*St* matches *Stevens* or *Stewart*), much as it would if you were using the Find command. It also accepts the familiar wildcard characters *?* (to match any single character) and * (to match any string).

> **Note** Excel won't find strings of text *within* an entry. For instance, in the example list, entering *Kim* as a search criterion into the Sales Rep text box wouldn't find records containing *Abercrombie, Kim* in the Sales Rep column. Rather, you would need to use the * character to match any leading text. That is, entering **Kim* would match *Abercrombie, Kim*.

In Figure 28-3, three sample criteria are entered. Click the Find Prev button to move to the first matching record that precedes the current record (row); click the Find Next button to move to the first matching record after the current record. Click the Criteria button to refine your search text. Click the Close button to remove the form (clearing any criteria you entered) and return to the list in the worksheet.

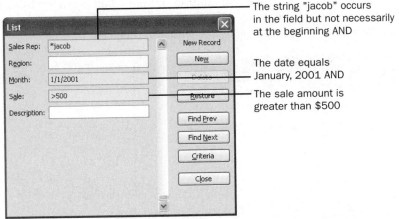

Figure 28-3.   The Criteria button displays a blank form with fields into which you can enter search information.

Validating Data as You Enter It

If several people are using your Excel list, you might want to control the type of information they're allowed to enter into worksheet cells in order to minimize typing mistakes. For example, you might want to require that only January or February dates can be entered into the Month column or that only dollar values in a particular range (say, $0–$5,000) can be entered into the Sale column. With Excel you can enforce input requirements such as these by using a formatting option called *data validation*. When you use data validation, you protect part or all of your worksheet from invalid input that might cause formulas or list-management tools to produce incorrect results.

> **Tip**   Remember too that Excel also lets you protect parts of your sheet from changes by a user. See "Protecting Worksheets and Workbooks," on page 698.

To enforce data validation of a particular range of worksheet cells, follow these steps:

1   Select the cells in the column that you want to protect with data validation. This should include cells already containing data as well as the blank cells below, where you'll be adding new records. (If you're not sure how long your list will be, you may want to select the entire column.)

2   Choose Data, Validation to open the Data Validation dialog box. Click the Settings tab.

3   In the Allow drop-down list, specify the input format you want to require for the selected cells. Your options are Any Value (used to remove existing data validation), Whole Number, Decimal, List, Date, Time, Text Length, and Custom (a format you specify by writing your own formula).

When you select a value in the Allow drop-down list, additional text boxes will appear, as shown below, that let you specify extra input conditions or *restrictions*, such as the smallest number and the largest number Excel will accept.

4 Click the Input Message tab, as shown below, and select Show Input Message When Cell Is Selected to specify a message that will appear when the cell is selected.

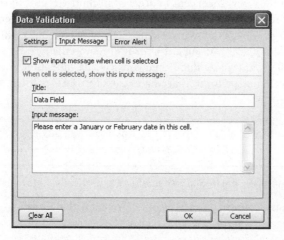

In the Title and Input Message text boxes, type the title and text you want displayed in the pop-up box that appears when a user selects a cell containing the data validation formatting. (Entering text into these boxes is optional, but doing so will help your users discover the requirements you've established *before* they make a mistake.)

5   Click the Error Alert tab, as shown below, and check the Show Error Alert After
    Invalid Data Is Entered option to have Excel display an error message if a user enters
    inappropriate information into a cell.

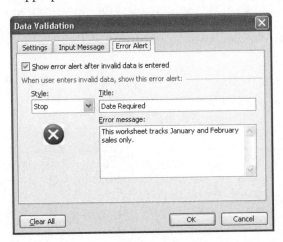

6   In the Style drop-down list, select one of the following options:

   ■   Stop (to block the input)

   ■   Warning (to caution the user but allow the input)

   ■   Information (to display a note but allow the input)

7   In the Title and Error Message text boxes, type the title and text you want displayed in
    the error message box that appears if the user enters invalid data. For example, a useful
    title and text might be *Date Required* and *This worksheet tracks January and February
    sales only*.

8   Click the OK button to close the Data Validation dialog box. If you specified the
    options given in steps 5 through 7, you'll see a gentle error message similar to the
    following if you enter the wrong type of data in a cell that has active data validation:

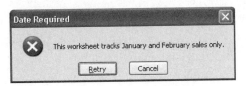

Sorting Rows and Columns

Once your records are organized into a list, you can use several commands on the Data menu to rearrange and analyze the data. The Sort command allows you to arrange the records in a different order based on the values in one or more columns. You can sort records in ascending or descending order or in a custom order, such as by days of the week, months of the year, or job title.

 The Pivot.xls example is on this book's companion CD.

To sort a list based on one column, follow these steps:

1 Select a cell in the column that you want to use as the basis for sorting the list.

> **Caution** If you select an entire column before sorting, Excel will display a dialog box that lets you either sort the entire list (by expanding the selection to include the entire list) or sort only the entries in the column. If you sort only the column entries, they won't remain in the same rows with the records to which they belong.

2 Choose Data, Sort. Excel will select all the records in your list and will display the Sort dialog box, shown here:

3 The Sort By drop-down list contains the header for the column you selected. If you like, you can now select a different column in the list box for the sort.

4 Click one of the sort order option buttons to specify ascending order (A to Z, lowest to highest, earliest date to latest) or descending order (Z to A, highest to lowest, latest date to earliest).

5 If the first row of your list is a header (the usual case), select the Header Row option so that Excel will leave the header row at the top of the list and exclude it from the sort. If your list doesn't have a header row, select the No Header Row option.

6 Click the OK button to run the sort. If you sorted the first column in ascending order, your screen will look similar to this:

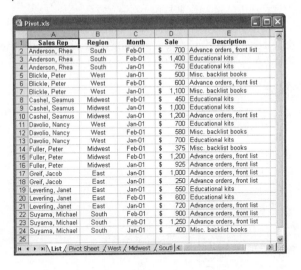

> **Tip** Click a cell, sort a list
>
> To quickly sort a list based on a single column, select a cell in the column, and then click either the Sort Ascending or Sort Descending button on the Standard toolbar.
>
>
>
> Sort Ascending   Sort Descending

Sorting on More than One Column

If you have records in your list that have identical entries in the column you're sorting with, you can specify additional criteria to sort those records. To sort a list based on two or three columns, follow these steps:

1 Select a cell in the list that you want to sort.

> **Caution** If you select an entire column before sorting, Excel will display a dialog box that lets you either sort the entire list (by expanding the selection to include the entire list) or sort only the entries in the column. If you sort only the column entries, they won't remain in the same rows with the records to which they belong.

2 Choose Data, Sort. Excel will select the records in your list and display the Sort dialog box, shown in the previous section.

3 Select the primary field for the sort in the Sort By drop-down list. Specify ascending or descending order for that column.

4 Click the first Then By drop-down list and pick a second column for the sort to further sort any records that have identical entries in the primary field. Specify ascending or descending order for the second sort as well.

5 If it's required, click the next Then By drop-down list and pick a third column for the sort. Once more, specify ascending or descending order. (Your sorts needn't all be in the same direction.) A Sort dialog box that has three levels of sorting is shown here:

6 If the first row of your list is a header (the usual case), select the Header Row option so that Excel will leave the header row at the top of the list and exclude it from the sort. If your list doesn't have a header row, select the No Header Row option.

7 Click the OK button to run the sort.

The example given here shows how a sort would look based on the options shown above:

These three records demonstrate how the three sort fields
are applied; the primary field is Sales Rep (ascending),
followed by Description (ascending), and then Sale (descending)

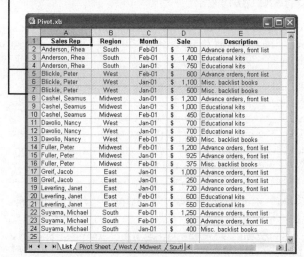

Chapter 28

Note that the columns you specify in the Then By sections are used only to arrange records that are otherwise identical for sorting purposes—not to control the entire sort. (For this reason, numbers in the Sale column are only in descending order when both the Sales Rep and the Description fields are identical.)

Troubleshooting

Cell reference roulette

Sorting a list created invalid results or error values for cells containing formulas.

Sorting a list that contains formulas can make a fine mess of the cell references within the formulas. If you sort by row, you'll be all right only if the formulas in each row refer only to other cells in the same row. Otherwise, undo the sort and change cell references in formulas to absolute references to cells outside the list, preferably on a different worksheet. To restore a list to its original order after a sort, choose Edit, Undo Sort immediately after running the sort or display the Undo button's drop-down list and click an earlier sort action to reverse it. (Keep in mind that selecting an earlier sort action using the Undo list will reverse all actions up to and including the sort.)

Creating Your Own Custom Sort Order

Excel allows you to create custom sort orders so that you can rearrange lists that don't follow predictable alphanumeric or chronological patterns. For example, you can create a custom sort order for the regions of the country (West, Midwest, East, South) to tell Excel to sort the regions in the way *you* want rather than by strict alphabetic rules. When you define a custom sort order, it will appear in the Options dialog box and will be available to all the workbooks in your system.

To create a custom sort order, follow these steps:

1 Choose Tools, Options and then click the Custom Lists tab.

2 Click the NEW LIST item in the Custom Lists list, and the text pointer will appear in the List Entries list. This is where you'll type the items in your custom list. (In this example you'll create the custom order West, Midwest, South, East.)

3 Type **West, Midwest, South, East**, and then click the Add button. You can either separate each value with a comma or type each one on a separate line.

The new custom order will appear in the Custom Lists list, as shown in Figure 28-4. You can now use this sorting order to sort your columns, as described in the next section of this chapter, "Using a Custom Sort Order."

Chapter 28

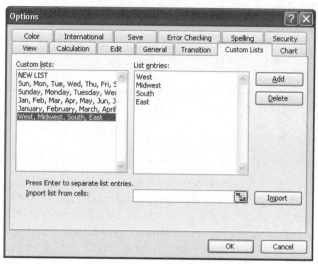

Figure 28-4. The Custom Lists tab lets you add, delete, and edit Excel's collection of custom sorting orders.

4 Click the OK button to close the Options dialog box.

Using a Custom Sort Order

When you want to sort based on an order that isn't alphabetical or numerical—the days of the week, for example, or the months of the year that have been entered as text rather than dates—you can click the Options button in the Sort dialog box and specify a custom sort order to use for the comparison. To use a custom sort order, follow these steps:

1 Click any cell in your list.

2 Choose Data, Sort. Excel will select the records in your list and display the Sort dialog box.

3 Select the primary field for the sort in the Sort By drop-down list. Specify ascending or descending order. (The direction you specify also applies to the custom sort, where Ascending is the custom order as shown and Descending is the reverse order.) In our example, we selected the Region field, ascending order.

4 Click the Options button to display the Sort Options dialog box, as shown here:

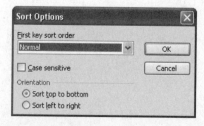

5 Click the First Key Sort Order drop-down list and select the custom order that you want to use.

6 Click the OK button in each dialog box to run the sort. Your list will appear sorted with the custom criteria you specified.

Using AutoFilter to Find Records

When you want to hide all the records (rows) in your list except those that meet certain criteria, you can use the Data, Filter, AutoFilter command. The AutoFilter command places a drop-down list at the top of each column in your list (in the header row). To display a particular group of records, select the criteria that you want in one or more of the drop-down lists. For example, to display the sales history for all employees who had $1,000 orders in January, you could select January in the Month column drop-down list and $1,000 in the Sale drop-down list.

To use the AutoFilter command to find records, follow these steps:

1 Click any cell in the list.

2 Choose Data, Filter, AutoFilter. Each column header will now display a down arrow.

3 Click the down arrow next to the header above the column that you want to use for the filter. A list that contains filter options will appear. It will be similar to the one shown in Figure 28-5.

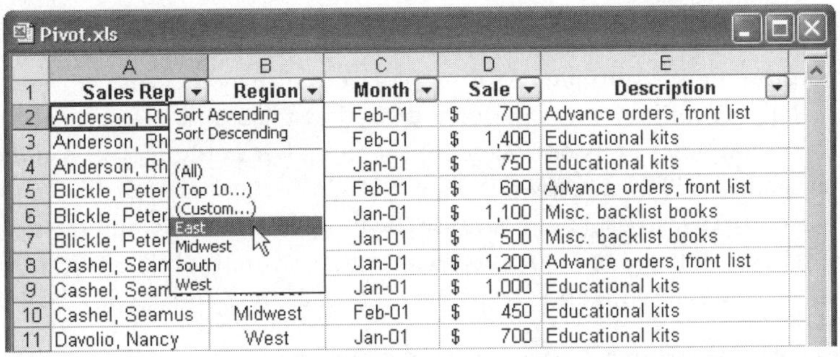

Figure 28-5. The AutoFilter command places filter arrows at the top of each column in your list.

4 If a column in your list contains one or more blank cells, you'll also see (Blanks) and (NonBlanks) options at the bottom of the list. The (Blanks) option displays only the records containing an empty cell (blank field) in the filter column so that you can locate any missing items quickly. The (NonBlanks) option displays the opposite—all records that have an entry in the filter column. Click the value that you want to use for the filter.

Excel will hide the entries that don't match the criterion you specified and will highlight the down arrow on the header above the column used in the filter. Figure 28-6 shows the results of using East as the criterion in the Region column.

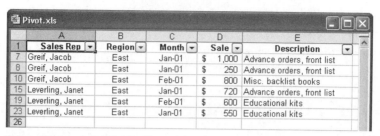

Figure 28-6. A list that's filtered for East region entries hides all records that don't match.

You can apply more than one filter to further narrow your list—a useful strategy if your list is many records long. To continue working with AutoFilter but to redisplay all your records, choose Data, Filter, Show All. Excel will display all your records again but will leave the drop-down lists in place. To remove the AutoFilter drop-down lists, deselect the Data, Filter, AutoFilter command.

NEW FEATURE! **Tip** When AutoFilter is turned on, you can quickly sort your list using the values in any column by clicking the down arrow in the column's header and clicking either Sort Ascending or Sort Descending on the drop-down list.

Creating a Custom AutoFilter

When you want to display a numeric range of data or customize a column filter in other ways, click Custom in the AutoFilter drop-down list to display the Custom AutoFilter dialog box. The dialog box contains two relational drop-down lists and two value drop-down lists that you can use to build a custom range for the filter. For example, you could display all sales greater than $1,000 or, as shown in Figure 28-7, all sales between $500 and $800. The drop-down lists are easy to deal with because the most useful values and relationships are already listed in them—all you have to do is select the ones you want. You can further fine-tune your criteria by using the And and Or options as well as the ? and * wildcard characters.

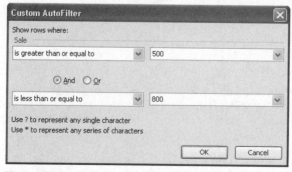

Figure 28-7. The custom AutoFilter dialog box lets you build your own filter.

To create a custom AutoFilter, follow these steps:

1 Click any cell in the list.

2 If AutoFilter isn't already enabled, choose Data, Filter, AutoFilter. A drop-down list will appear at the top of each column in the list.

3 Click the arrow next to the header belonging to the column that you want to use for the customized filter and click (Custom) on the drop-down list. The Custom AutoFilter dialog box will open.

4 Click the first relational operator drop-down list and select the relationship (equals, is greater than, is less than, and so on) that you want to use for the filter, and then click the first value drop-down list and specify the boundary that you want to set. (For example, you could specify *is greater than or equal to $500*.)

5 If you want to specify a second range, click And to indicate that the records must meet both criteria or click Or to indicate that the records can match either criterion. Then select a relationship in the second relational operator drop-down list and a range boundary in the second value drop-down list. Figure 28-7 shows a Custom AutoFilter dialog box with two range criteria specified.

6 Click the OK button to apply the custom AutoFilter. The records selected by the filter will be displayed in your worksheet.

Inside Out

Refining the filter

If the Custom AutoFilter dialog box doesn't provide enough options to create the filter you need, the Data, Filter, Advanced Filter command might offer adequate flexibility. Using advanced criteria, you can specify more than two criteria for a single column, joined with AND or OR, and you can include calculations in your criteria. You might, for example, filter a portfolio list to find only those investments that have increased in value by 20 percent over the last year. For details, see the online Help topic "Filter by Using Advanced Criteria."

Analyzing a List with the Subtotals Command

The Subtotals command on the Data menu helps you organize and analyze a list by displaying records in groups and inserting summary information, such as subtotals, averages, maximum values, or minimum values. The Subtotals command can also display a grand total at the top or bottom of your list, letting you quickly add up columns of numbers. As a bonus, Subtotals displays your list in Outline view so that you can expand or shrink each section in the list simply by clicking.

Inside Out

Subtotals vs. PivotTables

Be sure to sort and filter your list as much as you require before you add subtotals, because Excel sorts and filters the subtotal rows as if they were individual records (and yes, this can get messy). PivotTables (discussed in "Creating PivotTables and PivotCharts," on page 789) are generally more useful than the Subtotals command if you want to continue experimenting with sorts and filters. With a PivotTable, unlike subtotals, you can continue to make changes that affect the sorting, such as swapping the primary and secondary sort fields.

To add subtotals to a list, follow these steps:

1 Arrange the list so that the records for each group are located together. An easy way to do this is to sort on the field on which you're basing your groups. For example, you could sort based on employee, region, or store.

2 Choose Data, Subtotals. Excel will open the Subtotal dialog box and select the list.

3 In the At Each Change In drop-down list, select a group whose subtotal you want to define. This should be the same column that you sorted the list with. Each time this value changes, Excel will insert a row and compute a subtotal for the numeric fields in this group of records.

4 In the Use Function drop-down list, select a function to use in the subtotal. SUM is the most popular, but other options are available, as described in Table 28-1.

5 In the Add Subtotal To drop-down list, select the column or columns to use in the subtotal calculation. You can subtotal more than one column by selecting multiple boxes, but you'll apply the same function in all columns. The following screen shows the settings for a typical use of the Subtotals command:

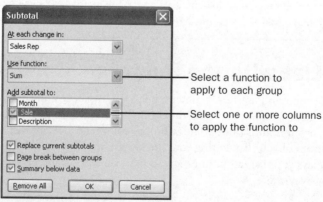

6 Click the OK button to add the subtotals to the list. You'll see a screen similar to the one in Figure 28-8, complete with subtotals, outlining, and a grand total.

Chapter 28

> **Note** You can choose the Subtotals command as often as necessary to modify your groupings or calculations. When you've finished using the Subtotals command, click the Remove All button in the Subtotal dialog box.

Table 28-1. Summary Functions in the Subtotal Dialog Box

Function	Description
SUM	Add up the numbers in the subtotal group
COUNT	Count the number of records in the group
AVERAGE	Calculate the average of the numbers in the group
MAX	Display the largest number in the group
MIN	Display the smallest number in the group
PRODUCT	Multiply together all the numbers in the group
COUNT NUMS	Count the number of cells containing numeric values in the group
STDDEV	Estimate the standard deviation based on a sample
STDDEVP	Calculate the standard deviation for an entire population
VAR	Estimate the variance in the group based on a sample
VARP	Calculate the variance for an entire population

Click the minus button to collapse the subtotal details

These three buttons give the display options: 1=Grand Total Only,
2=Grand Total and Subtotals, 3=All Records

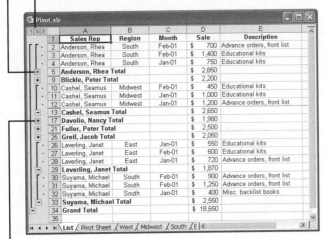

Click the plus button to expand the subtotal to show details

Figure 28-8. The Subtotals command creates an outline view of your list.

Working in Outline View

When you use the Subtotals command in Excel to create outlines, you can examine different parts of a list by clicking buttons in the left margin, as shown in Figure 28-8. Click the numbers at the top of the left margin to choose how many levels of data you want to see. Click the plus or minus button to expand or collapse specific subgroups of data. (Note that this is similar to the way you expand and collapse parts of a Microsoft Word document in its Outline view.)

> **Tip**   You can group any contiguous set of rows or columns in a list without adding subtotals. To do this, select the rows or columns (they don't need to have matching entries) and then choose Data, Group And Outline, Group. Excel will display the list as an outline, and you'll be able to expand or collapse individual groups, or all groups, as you can with an outline created with the Subtotals command. To remove rows or columns from a group, select them and choose Data, Group And Outline, Ungroup.

Converting an Excel List into an Access Database

Access 2003, Microsoft's relational database management system, is a member of the Office 2003 family and is covered in Part 7 of this book. If you've been working with lists in Excel for a while, you might be wondering whether your lists are compatible with Access, and when, if ever, you should move up to a more sophisticated database. What are the real differences between these two products? The short answer is that Excel is perfectly suited to list management as long as your databases don't become too large and you don't need to track unusual data or run especially advanced commands. However, Excel has the following limitations when it's dealing with databases:

- Worksheets are limited to 65,536 rows, meaning that you can't have more than 65,535 records (names in your mailing list, sales transactions, and the like).

- Fields can't contain more than 256 characters, which limits you to shorter descriptions or notes in your lists.

- Excel can't store pictures, sounds, and other types of special data in fields.

- Excel lacks advanced data protection or sophisticated backup features.

- You can't create custom data entry forms without using Access.

If you'd like to move your list into Access in the future, be assured that the transition will be relatively painless. To convert your Excel list into an Access database, start Access and choose File, Open. Then in the Open dialog box, select Microsoft Excel (*.xls) in the Files Of Type drop-down list and locate and open your Excel workbook.

When you open an Excel workbook in Access, Access launches a wizard that saves your list as an Access table. (To complete the conversion, you need to specify the worksheet that the list is in.) Figure 28-9 shows the Pivot.xls worksheet used in this chapter organized as an Access database. You'll find a copy of the database on the book's companion CD under the filename Pivot.mdb.

788

After you import and save the table, you'll find many familiar data management and formatting commands on the Access menus. You can learn more about specific Access commands in Part 7 of this book.

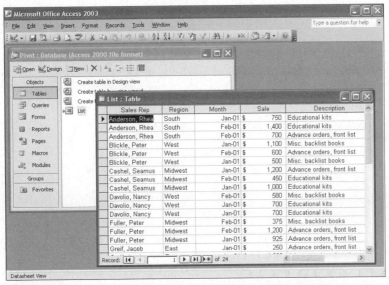

Figure 28-9. Excel lists appear as database tables in Access.

Creating PivotTables and PivotCharts

The most sophisticated data-analysis feature in Excel is the *PivotTable*, an organization and analysis tool that displays the fields and records in your list in new and potentially useful combinations. PivotTables are made easy in Excel by a powerful wizard on the Data menu. The wizard goes further to create not only tables but also colorful *PivotCharts*: compelling graphical reports that display PivotTable information visually.

In this section you'll learn how to create both PivotTables and PivotCharts by using the Pivot-Table And PivotChart Wizard, and you'll learn how to connect to external data sources to apply this command in powerful new ways.

Using the PivotTable And PivotChart Wizard

The best way to learn about a PivotTable is to create one. Fortunately, the PivotTable And PivotChart Wizard gives you complete control over the position of row and column headers in your table so that you can rearrange all the important variables down the road. To create a PivotTable, follow these steps:

1 Click a cell in the list that you want to view as a PivotTable.

2 Choose Data, PivotTable And PivotChart Report. The PivotTable And PivotChart Wizard will start and will display the Step 1 page, which prompts you for the source of data for the table, as shown here:

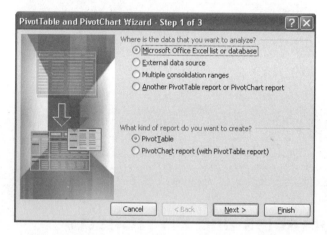

> **Tip**   On the Step 1 page, verify that the Microsoft Excel List Or Database option and the PivotTable option are both selected, and click the Next button to display the Step 2 page.

3 In this example you'll create a PivotTable from a list in your worksheet. However, you can also create PivotTables from external data (such as records received by Microsoft Query), multiple consolidation ranges, or another PivotTable or Pivot-Chart. After you select a data source, Excel will prompt you for a data range.If you had selected a cell in a list when you started the wizard, Excel will select the entire list for you when it displays the Step 2 page. If the list data you want to analyze in the PivotTable is not already selected, select it now using the mouse. (Be sure to include the column headers.)

Don't worry about the Step 2 page getting in the way—Excel will minimize it when you start selecting cells, giving you a full-window look at your data. Our sample screen looks like this:

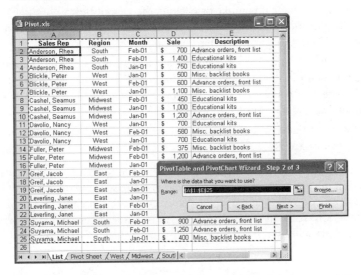

When the selection you want appears in the Range text box of the Step 2 page, click the Next button to display the Step 3 page (the final one).

4 By default, Excel creates PivotTables in new worksheets, although on the Step 3 page, shown here, you can specify an existing worksheet and even an exact location within a worksheet.

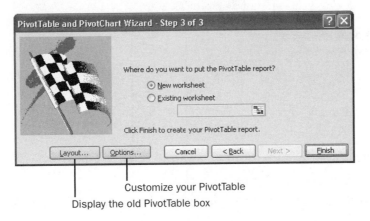

Customize your PivotTable

Display the old PivotTable box

Chapter 28

In Excel 97, the PivotTable Wizard displayed a layout grid at this point to help you build your PivotTable, but this feature is now provided directly in the worksheet by means of an enhanced PivotTable toolbar. However, you can use the old PivotTable "construction" page if you like by clicking the Layout button on the Step 3 wizard page. In addition, you can use the Options button now or in the future to fine-tune how your PivotTable or PivotChart appears.

5 Click the Finish button on the Step 3 page to accept the default settings and continue building your PivotTable. The PivotTable And PivotChart Wizard will open a new worksheet, create a blank PivotTable and a list of available data fields, and display the PivotTable toolbar, as shown in Figure 28-10.

6 Define the initial layout of your PivotTable by dragging fields from the PivotTable Field List into the Row, Column, Data, and Page Fields areas in the worksheet.

In Figure 28-10, the Month field has been placed in the Row area and the Region field has been placed in the Column area. The Sale field is being selected on the PivotTable Field List and will be dragged to the Data area. Fields placed in the Data area are added together with the SUM function. You can arrange, or *pivot*, these values later, so don't worry too much about the final placement of fields now. (We'll look at the Page area in "Using the Page Area," on page 794.)

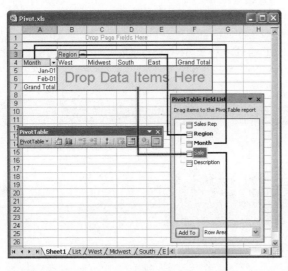

The Sale field is being dragged to the Data area

Figure 28-10. A PivotTable lets you try new arrangements of the data in your worksheet.

After you place a field in the Data area, Excel finalizes the PivotTable, as shown below:

Evaluating a PivotTable

It might take you a moment to recognize the data in your PivotTable, because it presents an entirely new view of your list. It's almost as if you had created new row and column headers, typed all the data again, and used the Subtotals command to summarize the results! However, you didn't have to rearrange your worksheet manually—the PivotTable And PivotChart Wizard did it for you. Best of all, you can easily transpose one or more fields and use new functions to highlight other trends in your list.

To help you work with the PivotTable and create PivotCharts, Excel displays the PivotTable toolbar, shown in Figure 28-11. You'll find this toolbar useful when evaluating and customizing your PivotTables and PivotCharts. Take a moment to examine the buttons and commands on the PivotTable toolbar, and then read the summary data in your new PivotTable, especially the Grand Total row and column.

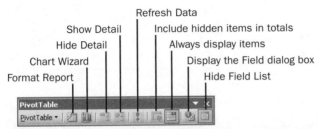

Figure 28-11. The PivotTable toolbar contains commands and buttons specifically designed for manipulating PivotTables.

Rearranging Fields in a PivotTable

To rearrange, or pivot, the data in your PivotTable, just drag the buttons for the fields in the table and move them to new locations. You can also remove unwanted fields by dragging their buttons out of the PivotTable, and you can add new fields by dragging field names from the PivotTable Field List onto the PivotTable.

To demonstrate this capability, let's first swap the Row and Column fields in the PivotTable we created above. Drag the Month button from the Row area to the Column area and the Region button from the Column area to the Row area. Then drag the Sales Rep field from the PivotTable Field List to the Row area, being sure to drop it to the right side of the Region button. (If the table gets confusing, you can always drag a field button—or all the field buttons—out of the PivotTable.) The resulting table is shown in Figure 28-12.

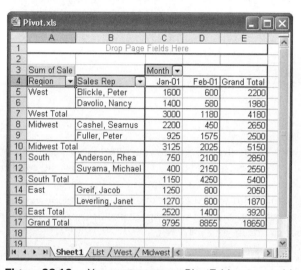

Figure 28-12. You can rearrange PivotTables to provide new views and new insights on the same data.

> **Tip**   **A degree of independence**
> As you edit or rearrange the data in the PivotTable, note that your changes don't affect the data in your list (which is in its own worksheet)—your original rows and columns remain the same. However, if you change the cells in your list, you'll need to click the Refresh Data button on the PivotTable toolbar to see the changes.

Using the Page Area

Even a well-designed table can present an overwhelming amount of information—or at least more information than a person can focus on at a given moment. The Page area lets you interact with the PivotTable to choose the data series you want to display. It lets you view multiple data series as if each were on a separate page. Alternatively, you can use the Show

Pages command to send each of the page views to its own worksheet. Let's see how the Page area works in an example.

If you've followed the steps in the foregoing sections, you've created a PivotTable and then rearranged the fields to develop the version shown in Figure 28-12. To use the Page area, you can simply drag the Region button from the Row area to the Page area (at the top of the worksheet). When you release the field, Excel will change the PivotTable to the simplified version shown in Figure 28-13.

Inside Out

Dividing, but not always conquering

Moving a field to the Page area gives you the powerful option of viewing the pages individually. But it also limits your options. When the same field was in the Row area, you could drop down a list of field entries and select any combination of items. The drop-down list for the Page area lets you choose one at a time or all at once, but not the combination of your choice.

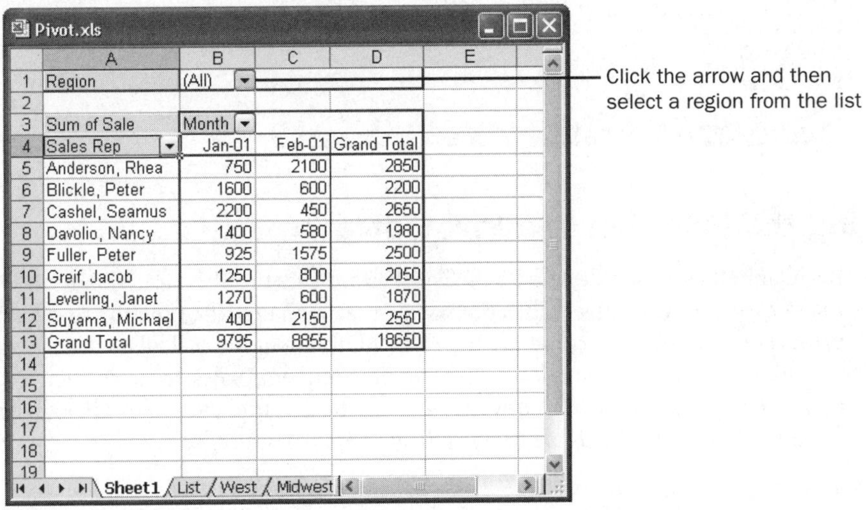

	A	B	C	D	E
1	Region	(All) ▾			
2					
3	Sum of Sale	Month ▾			
4	Sales Rep ▾	Jan-01	Feb-01	Grand Total	
5	Anderson, Rhea	750	2100	2850	
6	Blickle, Peter	1600	600	2200	
7	Cashel, Seamus	2200	450	2650	
8	Davolio, Nancy	1400	580	1980	
9	Fuller, Peter	925	1575	2500	
10	Greif, Jacob	1250	800	2050	
11	Leverling, Janet	1270	600	1870	
12	Suyama, Michael	400	2150	2550	
13	Grand Total	9795	8855	18650	

Click the arrow and then select a region from the list

Figure 28-13. Moving a field to the Page area lets you see your data all at once or as a series of separate pages.

In this latest version of the PivotTable, the data for all the regions is presented, but you can easily focus the table on any one region. Click the down arrow beside the Region button. Although the initial value is (All), the drop-down list lets you select any region and view its data separately.

After you've experimented with this feature, click the PivotTable button at the left end of the PivotTable toolbar to open the pop-up menu and choose Show Pages. (Be sure that the active cell is within the PivotTable.) Excel will then display the Show Pages dialog box. Notice that the Region field is selected (it's the only field in the Page area; if two or more fields were in the Page area, you would need to select one). Then click the OK button. The command will create four new worksheets, one for each page, labeled *West*, *Midwest*, *South*, and *East*. On each sheet is a PivotTable, linked to the original, that contains the page for the corresponding region. The following table, for example, is on the tab labeled *East*.

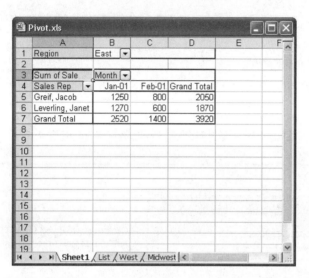

Changing the Function in a PivotTable

By default, the PivotTable And PivotChart Wizard uses the SUM function to add up values in the Data area of your PivotTable, but you can easily change the function to calculate another value. For example, you could use the AVERAGE function to calculate the average sales in a month or the COUNT function to total up the number of sales orders written by a particular employee. The list of functions available is identical to the set employed by the Subtotals command, described in Table 28-1, on page 787.

To change the function used in a PivotTable, follow these steps:

1 Open the worksheet containing your Excel PivotTable, if it isn't already open. (This should be the worksheet containing your primary PivotTable, not a worksheet created using the Show Pages command discussed in the previous section.)

2 In the upper-left corner of your PivotTable (the cell above the Row field and to the left of the Column field), double-click the button displaying the Data field name. In our example, the cell's location is A3 and contains the title Sum of Sale.

You'll see the PivotTable Field dialog box, as shown in Figure 28-14.

Double-click this cell in the PivotTable...

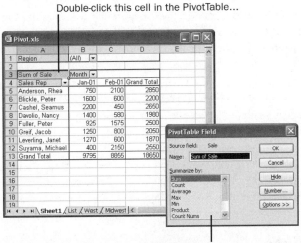

...to display this list of analysis functions

Figure 28-14. Double-click the cell containing the current function and field to display the PivotTable Field dialog box.

3 In the Summarize By list, select the new function that you want to use. (For example, select the MAX function to display the largest sales total in the field.) Notice that after you click the OK button, the field's button will be relabeled to reflect the new function. (For example, if you selected the MAX function for the Sale field in the Data area, the button would be relabeled "Max Of Sale.")

> **Tip**   An alternative way to modify the function used for summarizing data is to select the button displaying the Data field name by clicking it and then click the Field Settings button on the PivotTable toolbar to display the PivotTable Field dialog box. The PivotTable Field dialog box displays different options, depending on the type of cell selected.

Adjusting the Formatting in a PivotTable

When you use the PivotTable And PivotChart Wizard to modify a PivotTable, Excel automatically reformats the table to match the data in your list and to calculate the result of the function that you're using. Avoid making manual changes to the table formatting, because the AutoFormat table feature overwrites them each time you rearrange the PivotTable.

However, you can make lasting changes to the numeric formatting in the Data area by following these steps:

1 Click any numeric data cell in the PivotTable (not a row or column header).

2 Click the Field Settings button on the PivotTable toolbar. The PivotTable Field dialog box will open.

3 Click the Number button. The familiar Number tab of the Format Cells dialog box will appear, which allows you to adjust the formatting of the numbers in the Data area.

4 Select a type of numeric format in the Category list and then use the other controls to specify a formatting style. For example, to apply currency formatting to numbers, select the Currency category, specify the number of decimal places you want, and specify a style for negative numbers.

5 Click the OK button to close the Format Cells dialog box and then click the OK button to close the PivotTable Field dialog box. Excel will change the numeric formatting in the table, and these changes will persist each time you modify the PivotTable.

Tip   **Use AutoFormat for fast style makeovers**

To change the header and line style, highlight a cell in the PivotTable, and choose Format, AutoFormat. Excel will display a list of table styles for you to choose from. Select the style you want, and then click the OK button to reformat the PivotTable.

Displaying PivotCharts

If you find PivotTables addictive, you'll want to take advantage of a closely related data analysis tool, the PivotChart. A PivotChart is a graphical version of an Excel PivotTable. PivotCharts are created from existing PivotTables and are placed in new chart sheets in the workbook. Like PivotTables, PivotCharts have dynamic, customizable fields that you can drag from the PivotTable Field List, move around the charting area, or remove. You can also modify the functions used to analyze data in a PivotChart.

To analyze an Excel list using a PivotTable chart, follow these steps: (If you already have an existing PivotTable in your workbook, click a cell in the PivotTable, and start with step 4.)

1 If you haven't already created a PivotTable for the list you want to analyze, create one now following the instructions given in "Using the PivotTable And PivotChart Wizard," on page 790.

Note   Although the PivotTable And PivotChart Wizard gives you the option of creating a PivotChart in the first wizard step, you'll still be required to create a PivotTable in the third wizard step to base the PivotChart on. For this reason, we recommend that you simply follow the default wizard options and first create a PivotTable and then create a PivotChart based on that PivotTable. (You won't lose any time doing so.)

Chart Wizard

2 Click any cell within your PivotTable and, on the PivotTable toolbar, click the Chart Wizard button to open a new chart sheet and build a new PivotChart based on the selected PivotTable. You'll see a chart that looks similar to the one in Figure 28-15.

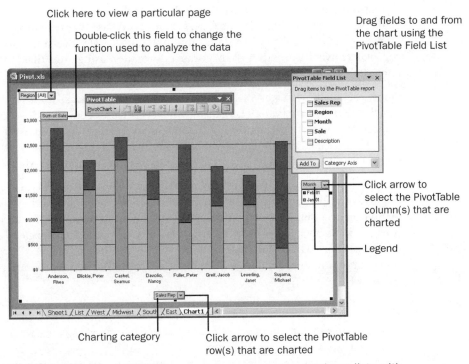

Click here to view a particular page

Double-click this field to change the function used to analyze the data

Drag fields to and from the chart using the PivotTable Field List

Click arrow to select the PivotTable column(s) that are charted

Legend

Charting category

Click arrow to select the PivotTable row(s) that are charted

Figure 28-15. Excel 2002 allows you to analyze your database lists with customizable PivotCharts.

3 You're now free to customize and format the PivotChart as you see fit. The labels in Figure 28-15 suggest some ways to customize the chart.

> **Tip** In a PivotChart, the *legend* represents the PivotTable column field and the *charting category* represents the PivotTable row field. To customize either of these values, right-click the associated field button in the chart and choose a command from the shortcut menu that appears.

Using External Data Sources in PivotTables

When you created your PivotTable by using the PivotTable And PivotChart Wizard, you had the option of using external data as the source of your information. One method of extracting external data for your PivotTable is by using Query, a program shipped with Office that you can use to connect to external data sources using an open database connectivity (ODBC) software driver. Query acts as a link between Excel and database files that have diverse data formats, such as Access, Visual FoxPro, SQL Server, dBASE, Paradox, and Btrieve. With Excel 2000, you gained the ability (using Query) to access yet another type of external data source, known as an *OLAP cube*. OLAP stands for online analytical processing, a format designed to consolidate massive amounts of corporate information using units that are sometimes referred to as *data warehouses*.

Query uses ODBC to translate complex data-filtering questions, or *queries*, into a language called SQL (structured query language), which is usually pronounced "sequel." As a result, you can use Query to extract information about compatible database files in sophisticated ways. For example, your query might be, "How many sales reps do we have who sell more than $20,000 in products per year and who work in the South or the Midwest?"

When you want to work with external database files, consider using Query as a stand-alone tool or as a utility to import your data into Excel. Start Query in Excel by choosing a command from the Data, Import External Data submenu. To use Query for accessing data in constructing a PivotTable, select External Data Source in the Step 1 page of the PivotTable And PivotChart Wizard, and then click the Get Data button in the Step 2 page. (Query is an add-in program, so you'll have to install it using the Office Setup program before it can be accessed.)

> **Tip** For more information about using Query to manage external data sources, search for "Query (Microsoft)" in the Excel Help Index. You can also access a series of helpful cue cards from within the Query Help menu.

Using the New Excel List Commands

Excel 2003 provides a set of new commands for working with a List, most notably the ability to publish a List on a on a team Web site on a server that runs Microsoft Windows SharePoint Services.

> For information on Windows SharePoint Services, see Chapter 8, "Using Windows SharePoint Services in Professional Workgroups."

Any block of cells in a spreadsheet that conforms to the list guidelines described in "Using a List as a Database," at the beginning of the chapter, is considered to be a *list* in the general sense of the term, and you can work with such a list using any of the techniques given in the previous sections of this chapter. To use the new Excel 2003 List commands, however, you must employ a new command to explicitly mark the data as an Excel 2003 List. This book capitalizes the word *List* when it refers to an explicitly marked Excel 2003 List, to distinguish it from a list that hasn't been so marked.

The following is the general procedure for marking an Excel 2003 List and for using the new Excel 2003 List commands:

1 Select the range of worksheet cells that you want to covert to a List. (Include the header row, if any.)

2 Choose Data, List, Create List or press Ctrl+L. When the Create List dialog box appears, as shown here, verify that the desired range is specified in the text box, check the My List Has Headers option if the range you selected has a header row, and click the OK button.

Excel will then covert the specified range to an Excel 2003 List, which is marked with a surrounding border, and it will turn on the AutoFilter feature (described earlier in the chapter). When you select one or more cells in a List, the border is highlighted and a blank row appears at the bottom, which is marked with an asterisk (*) and allows you to add a new record. Figure 28-16 shows the data in the Pivot.xls example workbook after it has been converted to an Excel 2003 List.

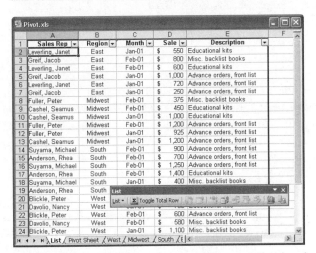

Figure 28-16. This figure shows a data range that has just been converted to an Excel 2003 List.

3 To work with the List, you can use the commands on the Data, List submenu, shown here:

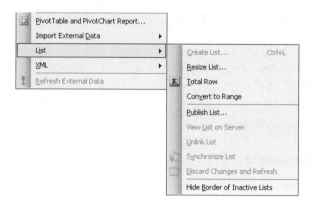

You can also use the new List toolbar:

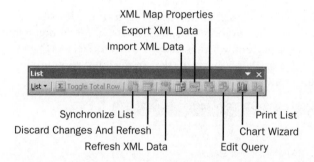

Some of the commands on the List submenu and on the List And XML toolbar are used to manage a List that has been published on a SharePoint team Web site and has been linked to the SharePoint list (these commands are disabled when you first create a List).

> Some of the commands on the List toolbar are used for working with XML data in Excel, as explained in "Working with XML Data in a Worksheet," on page 838.

Publishing an Excel 2003 List to a SharePoint site copies your local Excel List to a new SharePoint list that all members of the team Web site can share. (For an explanation of SharePoint lists, see Chapter 8.) The following are the basic steps for publishing a List on a SharePoint site:

1 Select a cell within the List and choose Data, List, Publish List.

2 In the Publish List To SharePoint Site Step 1 page, enter an address, name, and description for your SharePoint list. For the address, you should supply the URL (Uniform Resource Locator) of the root of your SharePoint site; Excel will place the new SharePoint list within an appropriate subfolder on this site. If you want to be able to synchronize your local Excel List with the shared SharePoint list, check the Link To The New SharePoint Team Services List option. When you're done, click the Next button. If prompted, you'll then need to enter your SharePoint user name and password.

3 In the Publish List To SharePoint Site Step 2 page, verify that each column will be converted to the appropriate data type in the SharePoint list and click the Finish button. Your Excel List will now be copied to the SharePoint site, where it will appear as a custom SharePoint list. Figure 28-17 shows a SharePoint list that was created by publishing the example Excel List you saw previously in this section.

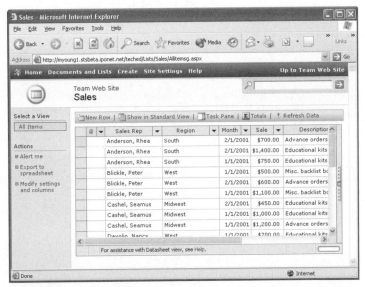

Figure 28-17. This is a SharePoint list, viewed in Internet Explorer, which was created by publishing the Excel List shown in Figure 28-16.

4 If you opted to link your Excel List to the new SharePoint list in step 2, you can now use the commands on the Data, List submenu and on the List toolbar (both shown earlier in this section) to view the SharePoint list, synchronize the Excel List with the SharePoint list, refresh the Excel List (discarding any changes), set the properties of the Excel List, or remove the link between the Excel List and the SharePoint list.

Advanced Business Analysis

Using the Goal Seek Command
to Forecast 805

Using the Solver to Set Quantity
and Pricing 808

Using the Scenario Manager
to Evaluate What-If Questions 815

Running a successful business requires many important skills. One of your best management tools is the capacity to build what-if models to help you plan for the future. How many $1.75 coffees do you need to sell to gross $30,000? What will happen to your bottom line if you lower the price of caffe latte but increase advertising expenses? Fortunately, Microsoft Office Excel 2003 provides several planning tools to help you map out a robust future. In this chapter you'll learn how to use the Goal Seek command to find an unknown value that produces a desired result; the Solver add-in to calculate an optimum solution based on several variables and constraints; and the Scenario Manager to create and evaluate a collection of what-if scenarios containing multiple input values.

Using the Goal Seek Command to Forecast

Excel's basic forecasting command is Goal Seek, which is located on the Tools menu. The Goal Seek command determines the unknown value that produces a desired result, such as the number of $14 compact discs a company must sell to reach its goal of $1,000,000 in CD sales. Goal Seek is simple because it's streamlined—it can calculate only one unknown value. If you need to determine additional unknowns in your forecasting, such as the effects of advertising or quantity discounts on pricing, use the Solver command (described in "Using the Solver to Set Quantity and Pricing," on page 808).

To use Goal Seek, set up your worksheet to contain the following:

- A formula that calculates your goal (for example, a formula that calculates the total CD sales revenue)

- An empty variable cell for the unknown number that will produce the desired outcome (for example, a cell to hold the number of CDs you must sell to reach $1 million in sales)

- Values in any cells (other than the empty cell) that the formula refers to (for example, a cell that stores the price of a CD)

The empty cell should be referenced in your formula; it serves as the variable that Excel changes.

When the Goal Seek command starts to run, it repeatedly tries new values in the variable cell to find a solution to the problem you've set. This process is called *iteration*, and it continues until Excel has run the problem 100 times or has found an answer within .001 of the target value you specified. (You can adjust these iteration settings by choosing Tools, Options and adjusting the Iteration options in the Calculations tab.) Because it calculates so fast, the Goal Seek command can save you significant time and effort over the brute force method of trying one number after another in the formula.

To forecast using the Goal Seek command, follow these steps:

1 Create a worksheet that contains a formula, an empty *variable* cell that will hold your solution, and any data you need to use in your calculation. For example, Figure 29-1 shows how you might set up a worksheet to determine the number of cups of coffee priced at $1.75 that you would have to sell to gross $30,000.

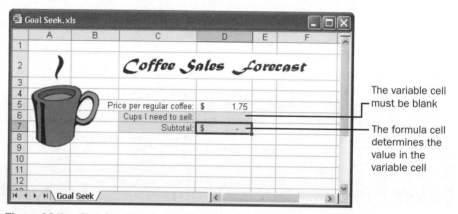

Figure 29-1. The Goal Seek command requires a formula and a blank variable cell.

The Goal Seek.xls example worksheet is on the companion CD to this book.

2 In your worksheet, select the cell containing the formula.

3 Choose Tools, Goal Seek. The Goal Seek dialog box will open, as shown here. The dialog box asks you to complete a sentence, "Set cell <blank_1> to value <blank_2> by changing cell <blank_3>." The cell name you selected before you chose the command will appear in the first text box, and a marquee will appear around the cell in your worksheet.

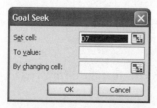

4 Press Tab, and then type the goal that you want to reach in the To Value text box. For example, to reach $30,000 in sales, type **30000** in the To Value text box.

Press Tab to select the By Changing Cell text box, collapse the Goal Seek dialog box, if necessary, and then click the blank cell that is to contain your answer (the variable cell). The Goal Seek command will calculate the value for this blank cell using your goal in the To Value text box and the formula in the cell referenced in the Set Cell text box. The variable cell will be indicated by a selection marquee (cell D6 in this example):

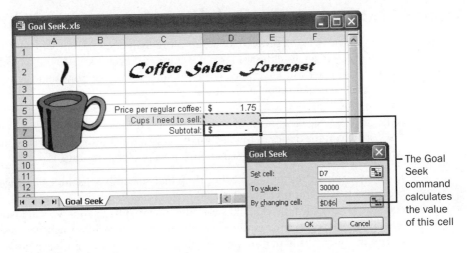

5 Click the OK button to find a solution for your sales goal.

Excel will display the Goal Seek Status dialog box when the iteration is complete, and the result of your forecast will appear in the worksheet, as shown in Figure 29-2. This forecast shows that you need to sell 17,143 coffees at $1.75 per cup to reach your sales goal of $30,000.

6 Click the OK button to close the Goal Seek Status dialog box.

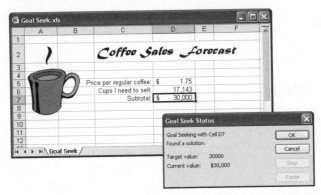

Figure 29-2. The Goal Seek command displays its result in the empty variable cell that you specified in your worksheet.

Chapter 29

> **Tip** In a time-consuming calculation, such as a computation that involves several financial functions, you can click the Pause button in the Goal Seek Status dialog box to stop the iteration or the Step button to view one iteration at a time.

Using the Solver to Set Quantity and Pricing

When your forecasting problem contains more than one variable, you need to use the Solver add-in utility to analyze the scenario. Veterans of business school will happily remember multivariable case studies as part of their finance and operations management training. While a full explanation of multivariable problem solving and optimization is beyond the scope of this book, you don't need a business school background to use the Solver command to help you decide how much of a product to produce, or how to price goods and services. We'll show you the basics in this section by illustrating how a small coffee shop determines which types of coffee it should sell and what its potential revenue is.

In our example we're running a coffee shop that currently sells three beverages: regular fresh-brewed coffee, premium caffe latte, and premium caffe mocha. We currently price regular coffee at $1.25, caffe latte at $2.00, and caffe mocha at $2.25, but we're not sure what our revenue potential is and what emphasis we should give to each of the beverages. (Although the premium coffees bring in more money, their ingredients are more expensive and they take more time to make than regular coffee.) We can make some basic calculations by hand, but we want to structure our sales data in a worksheet so that we can periodically add to it and analyze it using the Solver.

> **Note** The Solver is an add-in utility, so you should verify that it's installed on your system before you get started. If the Solver command isn't on your Tools menu, choose Tools, Add-Ins, and select the Solver Add-In option in the Add-Ins dialog box. If Solver isn't in the list, you'll need to install it by running the Office Setup program again and selecting it from the list of Excel add-ins. For more information, see "Installing Add-In Commands and Wizards," on page 725.

Setting Up the Problem

The first step in using the Solver command is to build a Solver-friendly worksheet. This involves creating a *target cell* to be the goal of your problem—for example, a formula that calculates total revenue—and assigning one or more *variable cells* that the Solver can change to reach your goal. Your worksheet can also contain other values and formulas that use the target cell and the variable cells. In fact, for the Solver to do its job, each of your variable cells must be *precedents* of the target cell. (In other words, the formula in the target cell must reference and depend on the variable cells for part of its calculation.) If you don't set it up this way, when you run the Solver you'll get the error message, "The Set Target Cell values do not converge."

Figure 29-3 shows a simple worksheet that we can use to estimate the weekly revenue for our example coffee shop and to determine how many cups of each type of coffee we will need to sell. The worksheet in the figure appears in Formula Auditing mode, which was enabled by choosing Tools, Formula Auditing, Formula Auditing Mode. Cell G4 is the target cell that calculates the total revenue that the three coffee drinks generate. The three lines that converge in cell G4 were drawn by selecting that cell and choosing Tools, Formula Auditing, Trace Precedents. The arrows show how the formula in cell G4 depends on three other calculations for its result. (To remove the arrows, choose Tools, Formula Auditing, Remove All Arrows.)

The three variable cells in the worksheet are cells D5, D9, and D13—these are the blank cells whose values we want the Solver to determine when it finds a way to maximize our weekly revenue.

 The Solver.xls example workbook is on the companion CD to this book.

In the bottom-right corner of our screen is a list of constraints we plan to use in our forecasting. A *constraint* is a limiting rule or guiding principle that dictates how the business is run. For example, because of storage facilities and merchandising constraints, we're currently able to produce only 500 cups of coffee (both regular and premium) per week. In addition, our supply of chocolate restricts the production of caffe mochas to 125 per week, and a milk refrigeration limitation restricts the production of premium coffee drinks to 350 per week.

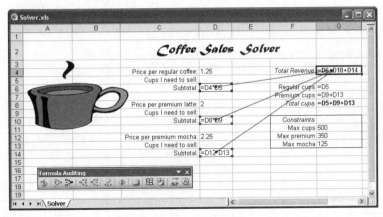

Figure 29-3. The commands on the Tools, Formula Auditing submenu help you visualize the relationship between cells. Here the target cell depends on three other cells, each of which contains a formula.

These constraints structure the problem, and we'll enter them in a special dialog box when we run the Solver command. Your worksheet must contain cells that calculate the values used as constraints (in this example, G8, G7, and D13). The limiting values for the constraints are listed in cells G11 through G13. Although listing the constraints isn't necessary, it makes the worksheet easier to follow.

> **Tip** Name key cells
>
> If your Solver problem contains several variables and constraints, you'll find it easiest to enter data if you name key cells and ranges in your worksheet by using the Insert, Name, Define command. Using cell names also makes it easy to read your Solver constraints later. For more information about naming, see "Using Names in Functions," on page 742.

Running the Solver

After you've defined your forecasting problem in the worksheet, you're ready to run the Solver add-in. The following steps show you how to use the Solver to determine the maximum weekly revenue for your coffee shop given the following constraints:

- No more than 500 total cups of coffee (both regular and premium)
- No more than 350 cups of premium coffee (both caffe latte and caffe mocha)
- No more than 125 caffe mochas

In addition to telling you the maximum revenue, the Solver calculates the optimum distribution of coffees in the three coffee groups. To use the Solver, complete the following steps:

1   Click the target cell—the one containing the formula that's based on the variable cells you want the Solver to determine. In Figure 29-3, the target cell is G4.

2   Choose Tools, Solver. The Solver Parameters dialog box will open, as shown here:

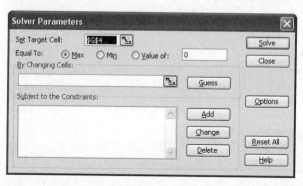

3   If the Set Target Cell text box doesn't already contain the correct reference, select the text box and then click cell G4 to insert *G4* as the target cell.

4   Select the Max option following the Equal To label, because you want to find the maximum value for the target cell.

5   Click the button at the right end of the By Changing Cells text box to collapse the dialog box. Select each of the variable cells. If the cells adjoin one another, simply select the group by dragging across the cells. If the cells are noncontiguous, as in our example, hold down the Ctrl key and click each cell (this will place commas between the cell entries in the text box).

For our example, select cells D5, D9, and D13 (the three blank cells reserved for the number of cups of coffee that need to be sold in each category), which will place the following value in the By Changing Cells text box: *D5,D9,D13*, as shown here:

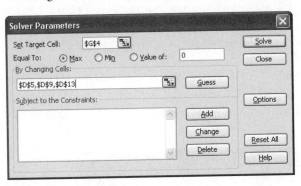

> **Tip   Use the Guess button to preview the result**
> If you click the Guess button, the Solver tries to guess at the variable cells in your forecasting problem. The Solver creates the guess by looking at the cells referenced in the target cell formula. Don't rely on this guess, though—it's often incorrect!

6   Constraints aren't required in all Solver problems, but this problem has three. Click the Add button to add the first constraint using the Add Constraint dialog box.

The first constraint is that you can sell only 500 cups of coffee in one week. To enter this constraint, click cell G8 (the cell containing the total cups formula), select <= in the operator drop-down list, and with the insertion point in the Constraint text box, click G11 or type **Max_cups**, using the underline character to link the words. (Max_cups is the name of cell G11 in our example.) The Add Constraint dialog box should look like this:

When you're done, click the Add button in the Add Constraint dialog box to enter the first constraint.

> **Note**   You have the option of typing a value, clicking a cell, or entering a cell reference or name in the Constraint text box. If you click a cell that has a defined name, Excel will use that name when you add the constraint.

7 Define the second constraint—you can sell only 350 premium coffees in one week. With the insertion point in the Cell Reference text box, click cell G7 (the cell containing the premium cups formula), select <= in the operator drop-down list, and in the Constraint text box, type **Max_premium** (the name of cell G12) or click cell G12. When you're finished, click the Add button to enter the second constraint.

8 Define the third constraint—you can sell only 125 caffe mochas in one week. Click cell D13 (the variable cell containing the number of mocha cups), select <= in the operator drop-down list, and in the Constraint text box, type **Max_mocha** (the name of cell G13) or click cell G13.

9 Click the OK button in the Add Constraint dialog box to display all three constraints in the Solver Parameters dialog box. It should look like the one shown here:

> **Tip** To modify one of the constraints that appears in the Solver Parameters dialog box, select the constraint and click the Change button. To customize the iteration and calculation parameters in the Solver utility, click the Options button and make your adjustments.

10 Your forecasting problem is ready to go, so click the Solve button to calculate the result.

After a brief pause the Solver will display the Solver Results dialog box describing how the optimization analysis went. If the Solver runs into a problem, you'll see an error message, and you can click the Help button to learn more about the difficulty. If the Solver finds a solution, you see the following dialog box:

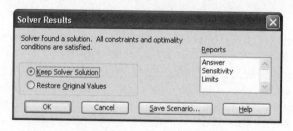

11 To display the new solution in your worksheet, select the Keep Solver Solution option in the Solver Results dialog box and then click the OK button. The Solver will place an optimum value in the target cell and will fill the variable cells with the solutions that best match the constraints you specified, as shown in Figure 29-4.

In this example, you've learned that if you're limited to selling 500 cups of coffee per week, you can expect a maximum of $918.75 in revenue and your optimum drink distribution is 150 cups of regular coffee, 225 cups of caffe latte, and 125 cups of caffe mocha. Although this financial model doesn't consider several realistic business variables, such as the costs associated with running a shop and the benefits of making volume purchases, it does help you to forecast much more easily and quickly than you could using pencil and paper.

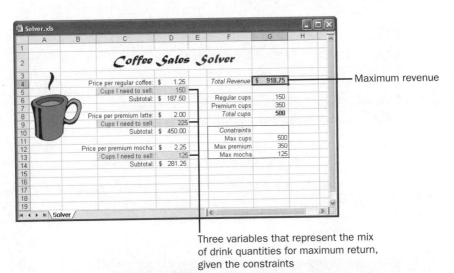

Maximum revenue

Three variables that represent the mix of drink quantities for maximum return, given the constraints

Figure 29-4. When the Solver finishes, the values that produce the optimum result in the target cell will appear in the variable cells.

Editing Your Solver Forecast

Perhaps the best feature of a Solver forecast is that you can easily edit it to evaluate new goals and contingencies. For example, if you decide that you want to earn exactly $700 per week from coffee drinks, you can use the Solver to tell you what the optimum combination of drinks would be. Setting a target value in the Solver is a little like using the Goal Seek command to determine a value for an unknown variable, although with Solver you can use more than one variable.

To edit the Solver forecast you created in the previous exercise to find the variables needed to reach a specific goal, follow these steps:

1 Activate the worksheet in which you previously used the Solver. In the variable cells, leave the values that were generated by the Solver in the previous exercise (namely, 150 in D5, 225 in D9, and 125 in D13).

2 Choose Tools, Solver. The Solver Parameters dialog box will appear, still displaying the target, variables, and constraints from your last Solver problem. You'll adjust these to compute a new forecasting goal.

3 Select the Value Of option and type **700** in the text box to the right. The Value Of option sets the target cell to a particular goal so that you can determine the variable mix you need to reach your milestone. (In this example, the variable cells represent the numbers of cups of different types of coffee.) Your dialog box should look like this:

4 Click the Solve button to find a solution to your forecasting problem. When the Solver has finished, click the OK button in the Solver Results dialog box.

Figure 29-5 shows the solution the Solver generates if, before you ran the Solver, the variable cells had contained the values that were generated in the previous exercise (namely, 150, 225, and 125). The new Solver results indicate that you can make $700 by selling 100 mochas, 175 lattes, and 100 regular coffees.

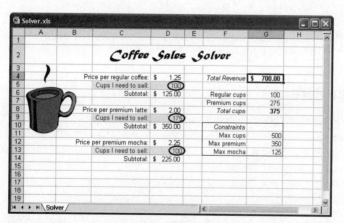

Figure 29-5. When you specify a target goal, the Solver computes an optimum product mix that meets your constraints.

What if There Is More Than One Solution to the Problem?

In the previous example, the Solver determined that you could sell 100 mochas, 175 lattes, and 100 regular coffees to reach your sales goal of $700. But you can also reach the $700 mark using a different product mix; for example, you could sell 94 regular coffees, 151 lattes, and 125 mochas to reach $700. (Using this mix, your revenue would actually be $700.75.) So, how *did* the Solver decide what the optimum product mix would be? The Solver simply started with the current numbers in the variable cells and adjusted them until it found an acceptable solution (subject to the constraints described in the previous example). This is why, if you use different starting values in the variable cells before you run the Solver, you can get different results from a problem with multiple solutions.

Troubleshooting

Solver doesn't find a solution

Solver reaches its iteration limit without finding a solution.

The starting values in the variable cells can affect the solution: Solver might fail to find a solution or it might time out before reaching a solution. Enter values in variable cells that fall close to what you believe the final values will be. If Solver still reaches its iteration limit without arriving at a solution, you can adjust the starting values and restart or click Continue to use the maximum solution time. You can adjust both the maximum iterations and maximum time by using the Options button in the Solver Parameters dialog box.

If you would like to use a particular product mix, you can take advantage of the way the Solver reaches its results. Enter the values that you think might be acceptable in the variable cells before you run the Solver, and Excel will use those as starting values when it computes the solution.

Using the Scenario Manager to Evaluate What-If Questions

Although the Goal Seek and Solver commands are extremely useful, if you run several forecasts you can quickly forget the results for each forecast. More important, you have no real way to compare the results of the Goal Seek and Solver commands. Each time you change the data, the previous solution is lost. To address this limitation, the Scenario Manager helps you keep track of multiple what-if models. Using the Tools, Scenarios command, you can create new forecasting scenarios, view existing scenarios, run scenario management commands, and display consolidated scenario reports. We'll show you each technique in this section.

Creating a Scenario

A *scenario* is a named what-if model that includes variable cells linked together by one or more formulas. Before you create a scenario, you must design your worksheet so that it contains at least one formula that's dependent on cells that can be fed different values. For example, you might want to compare best-case and worst-case scenarios for sales in a coffee shop based on the number of cups of coffee sold in a week. Figure 29-6 shows a worksheet that contains three variable cells and several formulas that can serve as the basis for several scenarios. (This coffee sales worksheet is the same one we used in the Solver example.) In the following example, we will use this worksheet to show how to create a best-case and a worst-case sales scenario.

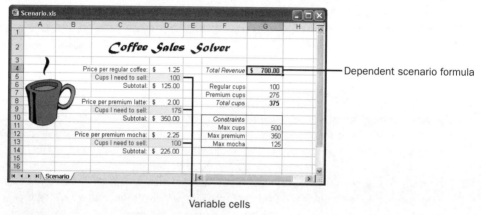

Figure 29-6. Before you create a scenario, you need to build a worksheet with one or more formulas that depend on variable cells.

 The Scenario.xls example workbook is on the companion CD to this book.

To create a scenario using the active workbook, follow these steps:

1 Choose Tools, Scenarios. The Scenario Manager dialog box will appear, as shown here:

2   Click the Add button in the Scenario Manager dialog box to create your first scenario. You'll see the Add Scenario dialog box.

3   Type **Best Case** (or another suitable name) in the Scenario Name text box, and press the Tab key.

4   In the Changing Cells text box, specify the variable cells that you want to modify in your scenario. You can type cell names, highlight a cell range, or hold down the Ctrl key and click individual cells to add them to the text box. (If you hold down the Ctrl key, Excel will automatically place commas between the cells that you click.) To follow our example, hold down the Ctrl key and click cells D5, D9, and D13. Your screen should look like the one shown here:

> **Tip**   You might want to define cell names for your variable cells. That way, you'll have an easier time identifying your variables when you create your scenarios and when you type in arguments later.

5   Click the OK button in the Add Scenario dialog box to add your scenario to the Scenario Manager. You'll see the Scenario Values dialog box, which asks you for your model's variables. The default values are the numbers that were already in the cells.

6   Type **150**, press Tab, type **225**, press Tab, and type **125**. These are the values (derived by the Solver in the previous section) that will produce the revenue in your best-case scenario based on the constraints described in "Setting Up the Problem," on page 808. Your screen will look like the one here:

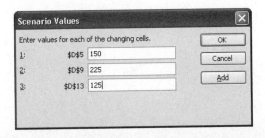

Chapter 29

7   Click the Add button in the Scenario Values dialog box to return to the Add Scenario dialog box, where you'll create a second scenario. Type **Worst Case** in the Scenario Name text box and click the OK button to display the Scenario Values dialog box again.

8   In the Scenario Values dialog box, type **50**, **40**, and **30** in the text boxes for the variable cells, and then click the OK button. (These values represent our guess at the worst case.) The Scenario Manager dialog box will reappear and list the Best Case and Worst Case scenarios you just created. Now you're ready to view the results of your forecasting models.

9   Click the Close button to close the Scenario Manager dialog box.

> **Tip**   You can save Solver problems as scenarios for future trials by clicking the Save Scenario button in the Solver Results dialog box when the Solver computes a new forecast. The Solver prompts you for a name, which you can use later to view the scenario in the Scenario Manager.

Viewing a Scenario

Excel keeps track of each of your worksheet scenarios. You can view them by choosing the Tools, Scenarios command whenever your worksheet is open.

Inside Out

Save your workbook before loading a scenario

When you view a scenario, Excel replaces the current values in your worksheet with the values stored in the scenario. If you want to load a scenario but still be able to restore the previous values in the worksheet, be sure to save your file before loading the scenario.

To view a scenario, follow these steps:

1   Choose Tools, Scenarios. You'll see the Scenario Manager dialog box, shown in Figure 29-7.

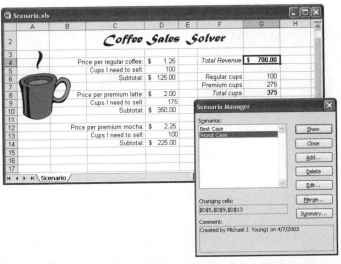

Figure 29-7. The Show button lets you compare the results of different what-if scenarios in your worksheet.

2 In the Scenarios list, select the scenario that you want to view.

3 Click the Show button. Excel will substitute the values in the scenario for the variables in your worksheet and display the results in your worksheet, as shown in Figure 29-7. (The Scenario Manager dialog box will remain visible. You might need to move it to view the results.)

4 Select additional scenarios and click the Show button to compare and contrast the what-if models in your worksheet. When you're finished, click the Close button to remove the Scenario Manager dialog box. The last active scenario will remain in your worksheet.

Creating Scenario Reports

Although you can easily compare different scenarios by switching between them using the Show button in the Scenario Manager dialog box, you might occasionally want to view a report that contains consolidated information about the scenarios in your worksheet. You can accomplish this quickly by clicking the Summary button in the Scenario Manager dialog box. Excel will automatically format the summary report and copy it to a new worksheet in your workbook.

To create a scenario report, follow these steps:

1 Activate the worksheet containing the scenario(s) you want to use for your report.

2 Choose Tools, Scenarios to display the Scenario Manager dialog box.

Chapter 29

3 Click the Summary button to open the Scenario Summary dialog box, shown here:

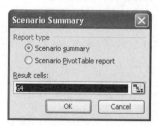

The Scenario Summary dialog box prompts you for a result cell to total in the report and also for a report type. A *scenario summary report* is a formatted table that appears in its own worksheet. A PivotTable is a special summary table whose rows and columns can be rearranged, or *pivoted*.

For more information about viewing PivotTable reports, see "Rearranging Fields in a PivotTable," on page 794.

4 Select the result cell that you want to total (cell G4 in this example), click the report option button that you want to use (accept the Scenario Summary default if you're not sure), and then click the OK button.

After a short pause, a new Scenario Summary tab will appear in your workbook, as shown in Figure 29-8. The outlining buttons in your report's left and top margins will help you shrink or expand the rows and columns in your scenario summary.

Note Each time you click the Summary button in the Scenario Manager dialog box, Excel creates a new summary worksheet in your workbook. To delete unwanted summary reports, activate the worksheet containing the unwanted scenario summary, and then choose Edit, Delete Sheet.

Excel uses the defined names for variable cells D5, D9, and D13, which results in a more comprehensible summary

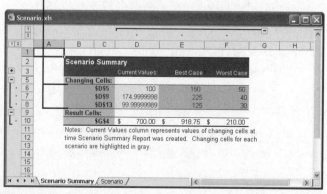

Figure 29-8. The Summary button creates a scenario summary report in a new worksheet in your workbook.

Managing Your Scenarios

Once you've defined a scenario using the Add button, luckily you're not stuck with that scenario forever. You can edit and delete scenarios by clicking the Edit and Delete buttons in the Scenario Manager dialog box. The Edit button lets you change the name of the scenario, remove existing variable cells, add new variable cells, or even choose a completely new group of variables. To assign different values to the variable cells in a scenario, clear the Prevent Changes option in the Edit Scenario dialog box. After you click the OK button, Excel will display the Scenario Values dialog box. Make any changes you want to make, and then click the OK button.

To remove a particular scenario permanently, simply select it in the Scenario Manager dialog box and click the Delete button.

Finally, you can copy scenarios into the active worksheet from any other worksheet in a currently open workbook. To do this, click the Merge button in the Scenario Manager dialog box and specify a source workbook and worksheet in the Merge Scenarios dialog box.

Publishing on the Web and Working with XML in Excel

Designing an Excel Web Page. 824

Publishing an Excel Web Page 825

Running an Excel Web Page
on the Internet 830

Using Web Queries. 832

NEW FEATURE! Working with XML Data
in a Worksheet. 838

So far in this book you've used Microsoft Office Excel 2003 to create reports, invoices, charts, lists, and PivotTables that are ready for use on your own computer or for traditional printing and paper distribution. However, with Excel you can also save your worksheets in HTML (Hypertext Markup Language) or XML (Extensible Markup Language) format for electronic circulation on the World Wide Web. Several new features make this process straightforward and useful.

And it's a two-way street: another feature of Excel lets you import data from the Internet into a worksheet. This capability is not only easy to use, but it's also powerful in that it allows for regular updates to reflect the volatile nature of Web content.

In this chapter you'll learn how to prepare your worksheet so that it can be saved in a Web page format, and you'll learn how to set special publication options that make your work-book more accessible and useful on the Internet. You'll also learn the simple commands that both save and preview completed Web pages, and you'll learn how to use Microsoft Office Web toolbars to issue Excel commands in Microsoft Internet Explorer. You'll step through the process of creating and revising Web queries. When you're finished, you'll have the skills necessary to create and distribute your own Excel Web pages and to import data from the Internet. Finally, you'll learn how to use Excel 2003's new XML features that allow you to import, view, analyze, edit, and export any type of XML data from within an Excel worksheet.

Designing an Excel Web Page

Web pages are documents that are written in the HTML format, which is optimized for displaying information attractively in Web browsers, such as Internet Explorer and Netscape Navigator. In the past, only special-purpose application programs such as Microsoft Front-Page allowed you to create HTML documents for the Web, but now you can create Web pages using each of the applications in the Office 2003 software suite. The program you choose depends on the features you want to provide and the type of Web site you're constructing. Naturally, the most effective Excel Web pages use Excel's rich worksheet formatting, calculation, and data analysis capabilities.

Creating an Excel Web page is no different from building a regular worksheet from scratch. You enter information in rows and columns, edit the data, and use formulas and formatting commands as you normally would. However, take care to use fonts and colors in a way that's aesthetically compatible with the other documents on your Web site and use hyperlinks when necessary to connect your Excel Web page to other Internet sites. And be sure to preview your documents carefully to verify that the HTML file conversion created a Web page that matches your expectations.

In addition, be aware that some of the features in your Excel worksheet might not be available to your users when the document is published on the Web. For example, when a user views an Excel Web page in a browser, change tracking, macros, and forms will be disabled, and Excel add-in programs such as the Solver won't be available. However, if users will be viewing the Excel Web page using Internet Explorer 4.01 or later, you can use Office Web Components to allow them to work interactively with formulas, filters, PivotTables, charts, and worksheet formatting commands. (You'll learn more about these options later in this chapter.)

Static Pages vs. Interactive Pages

Fundamentally, you have two options when presenting Excel Web pages: you can display a static, noninteractive Excel spreadsheet (in other words, a snapshot of your worksheet that can't be modified), or you can display a working, interactive spreadsheet that users can modify directly in Internet Explorer. The option you select depends on your Web site's purpose and your particular design goals. Static Web pages are best for showing purchase orders, sales data, and other tabular information that should be viewed but not modified. Interactive Web pages are best for budgeting, calculation, and analysis tools that invite remote colleagues and other Internet users to experiment with their own facts and figures. (For example, a mortgage calculator that prompts users for their own loan information.)

Inside Out

Interactive Web page limitations

Before you decide to publish a particular type of Excel workbook data as an interactive Web page, consider the following limitations on this type of Web page:

- To view an interactive Web page, the user must have installed the Office Web Components on his or her computer and have the required license to run them. The Office Web Components are included with Office 2003 and are an optional feature that you can install when you set up the Office suite.

- The user can't effectively save any changes made to an interactive spreadsheet or print an interactive spreadsheet without exporting the spreadsheet to Excel (as explained later in the chapter).

- The user can't submit any data entered into an interactive spreadsheet to a Web server.

Because of these limitations, you probably wouldn't want to interactively publish an order form, a questionnaire, an invoice, or other item that would need to be saved, printed, or submitted to a Web server to be useful. Although if a user has Excel installed he or she could export the interactive spreadsheet to Excel and then save or print the results, doing so would eliminate much of the convenience of working with the data in a browser. (In this case it would be easier for the user to simply download the original workbook.)

Interactive Excel Web pages work best for publishing data that's primarily meant to be viewed and perhaps analyzed on an ad hoc basis (for example, finding the total or average of various numbers). Interactive Web pages are also useful for publishing an Excel utility, such as a loan amortization calculator, in which the user can enter the required parameters and derive a simple result.

Publishing an Excel Web Page

The Save As Web Page command on the Excel File menu saves an existing Excel worksheet, chart sheet, or complete workbook as a Web page and allows you to set a number of useful publication options. Before you use this command, verify that your workbook contains the proper document style and content for your Web page and that it presents information in a clear format that includes the necessary operating instructions. And remember: Users with no knowledge of you or your workbook will open and run this document on the Internet or an intranet, so take care to make the workbook user interface simple and intuitive.

To save or publish an Excel worksheet, chart sheet, or workbook as a Web page, follow these steps:

1. Open the workbook that contains the data you want to save as an Excel Web page. If you want to save a specific worksheet or chart sheet, activate that sheet.

Chapter 30

For the example given in these instructions, activate the Payment Calculator work-sheet in the Payment.xls workbook, shown here. This worksheet contains a simple loan payment calculator, which we will publish as an interactive spreadsheet. You enter the annual interest rate, loan term in months, and loan amount, and the calculator displays the monthly payment (using the Excel PMT function).

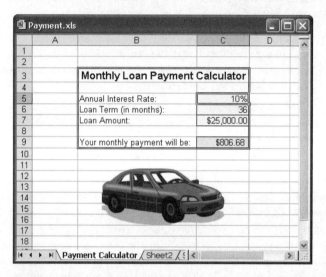

 The Payment.xls example workbook is on the Microsoft Office System Inside Out—2003 Edition companion CD.

2   Choose File, Save As Web Page. Excel will display the Save As dialog box and will select the Single File Web Page (*.mht; *.mhtml) format in the Save As Type drop-down list (see Figure 30-1).

Figure 30-1. The Save As Web Page command displays the Save As dialog box, which offers options that control how your Excel worksheet will be converted into an HTML document.

When a Web page format is selected in the Save As Type drop-down list in the Save As dialog box, you'll see the following four options related to Web publishing:

- You can specify which part of your workbook you want to publish (the entire workbook or the active sheet).

- You can specify whether you want the document to be interactive or not.

- You can add or modify the HTML document title. When the document is viewed in a browser, this title appears in the browser's title bar.

- You can select advanced options by clicking the Publish button.

3 Select a Web page format in the Save As Type drop-down list, as follows:

- To save the data in a single Web page file, which will include any supplemental data, select Single File Web Page (*.mht; *.mhtml). For the example, you should select this option.

- To save the data in a conventional Web page, select Web Page (*.htm; *.html). With this option, Excel might create additional files for storing supplemental data. It will store these files in a subfolder that is assigned a name based on the Web page's filename (for instance, if the Web page is named Invoice.htm, the folder will be named Invoice_files).

> **Note** You won't be able to change the selection in the Save As Type drop-down list unless the Entire Workbook option is selected and the Add Interactivity option is cleared. So if you want to change the Web page format, select Entire Workbook and clear Add Interactivity if necessary (at least temporarily).

4 To save the complete workbook as a Web page, select Entire Workbook. To save just the active worksheet or chart sheet, select Selection: Sheet (if you've already published the active sheet, this option will be named Republish: Sheet).

For the example, select the Selection: Sheet option.

5 If you want to make your worksheet interactive, verify that the Add Interactivity option is checked.

This option should be checked for the current example.

6 If you want to add a Web page title (or modify an existing title), click the Change Title button, and type the title text into the Set Title dialog box.

For the example, click the button and type "Loan Payment Calculator."

7 Type a new filename in the File Name text box or just accept the default name. It's easiest to omit the filename extension and let Excel add an appropriate one. (Excel will add .mht for the single-page Web page format or .htm for the conventional Web page format.)

Chapter 30

8 Click the Publish button to display all Web publishing options in the Publish As Web Page dialog box, shown in Figure 30-2. These options are described below. For the example, you don't need to alter any of these options, except possibly the last one mentioned (Open Published Web Page In Browser).

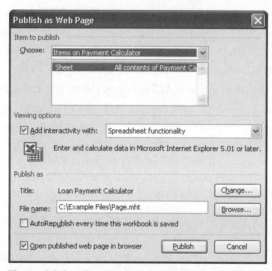

Figure 30-2. The Publish As Web Page dialog box lists the entire collection of Web page publishing options available to you.

- The Item To Publish lists at the top of the dialog box give you the option of selecting only a portion of your sheet for the Web page. Although you would typically include the whole sheet in an interactive Excel Web page to allow the user some maneuvering room, this option is useful if you want to limit what users can see and do on the screen.

- The Viewing Options control what the user can do with the worksheet when it appears in the browser. To make the Web page interactive when it's displayed in a browser, check the Add Interactivity With option. To specify the type of interactivity you want to use, select an option in the adjoining drop-down list. Excel Web pages support general spreadsheet functionality, PivotTable functionality, and charting functionality (provided the corresponding items are included in the published Web page).

Interestingly, the interactivity features listed here aren't provided by the Excel application itself, but by small ActiveX controls called *Office Web Components* that Excel places in the HTML document when it builds the Web page. When your completed page is viewed in Internet Explorer version 4.01 or later, these components spring to life as toolbars and simulate many of the capabilities of a real Excel worksheet.

- The Publish As options let you change the HTML document title and file-name—the same options you saw in the Save As dialog box earlier.

- You can check the AutoRepublish Every Time This Workbook Is Saved option to assure that any changes you save to the workbook also get propagated to the Web page.

- Finally, the Open Published Web Page In Browser option gives you a chance to display the completed Web page in Internet Explorer. (If you check this option, Excel will start Internet Explorer when you click the Publish button.) We recommend that you habitually use this preview option whenever you publish Web pages so that you can see early in the development process how the page will appear to users on the Web.

9 Check the Open Published Web Page In Browser check box and then click the Publish button. Excel will launch your browser and display the Web page.

Figure 30-3 shows the result for the Payment Calculator example worksheet we've been working with, displayed in Internet Explorer 6.0. If you have a different browser installed, you'll get different results. If you want to redisplay the page in your browser later, just double-click the page's filename in Windows.

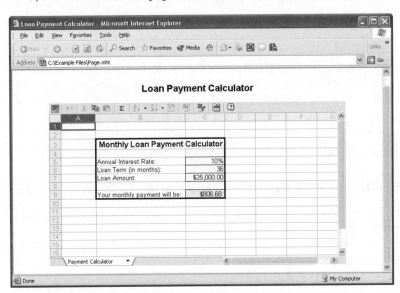

Figure 30-3. The Open Published Web Page In Browser option lets you preview your worksheet in your browser—Internet Explorer in this case.

10 If you want to publish your Web page on your company's intranet or on the World Wide Web, you'll need to copy the file to the Web server. If in step 3 you selected the conventional Web page format [Web Page (*.htm; *.html)] rather than the single-file format [Single File Web Page (*.mht; *.mhtml)], you'll also need to copy the subfolder—if any—containing the page's supplemental files. For instructions on transferring your file(s) to the Web server, confer with your network administrator, webmaster, or Web hosting company.

Running an Excel Web Page on the Internet

If you created a static Excel Web page, your options for manipulating the Web page in your Internet browser are rather limited. You can use the scroll bars to view all aspects of the page, and you can copy cell data from the page to the Clipboard by selecting the desired cells, right-clicking the selection, and choosing Copy from the shortcut menu. However, if you requested an interactive Web page when you saved the Excel worksheet using the Save As Web Page command, you can perform a number of useful editing and calculation activities on your Web page, including filling the worksheet with data, editing and formatting cells, adding new formulas, running filters, modifying charts (if you included one), and manipulating PivotTables (if included).

As mentioned earlier, the spreadsheet functionality that Excel Web pages provide comes not from Excel itself, but from a collection of ActiveX controls used in the worksheet called Office Web Components. Internet Explorer versions 4.01 and later recognize these components, which offer a subset of Excel's data analysis features to users working with an Excel spreadsheet on the Web. You can identify the presence of Office Web Components in Internet Explorer by the special toolbars that appear directly above Excel HTML documents and by the Office Web icon that appears on the left side of Office Web toolbars. If you click this icon in Internet Explorer, you'll see an Office Web Components dialog box.

Working with an Interactive Web Page in Your Browser

Interactive Excel Web pages allow you to move the cell pointer around the worksheet to enter and edit data. If you enter data into cells that are linked to a formula, a new result will be calculated immediately in the worksheet when you press the Enter key. In addition, the Office Web Components toolbars (such as the Office Spreadsheet Component toolbar described here) allow you to manipulate your data in other ways.

The following exercise will give you some experience in working with an interactive spreadsheet in Internet Explorer:

1 In Internet Explorer (version 4.01 or later), open the example interactive Excel Web page (the loan payment calculator) that you created in the exercise given in "Publishing an Excel Web Page," on page 825. You can do this by double-clicking the page's filename in Windows. Or, if the page has been posted to an intranet or Web server, you can open it from the server by entering its URL (Uniform Resource Locator) into your browser. Here's how the page appears in Internet Explorer 6.0:

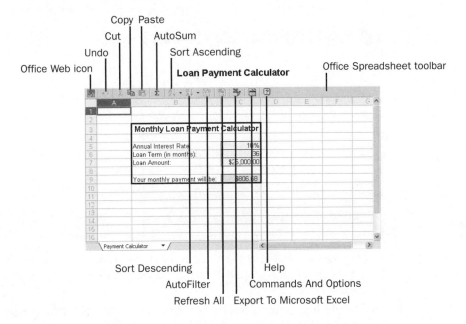

2 To experiment with editing cells, enter an interest rate, loan term, and loan amount into the corresponding cells of the interactive spreadsheet. You can't edit or format any of the other cells because the original spreadsheet was protected except for these three cells. (Try it!) The spreadsheet will then display your monthly loan amount.

Note that when editing cells, you can use the Undo, Cut, Copy, and Paste buttons on the Office Spreadsheet Component toolbar.

Note To create the example interactive Excel Web page, you need to open the Payment.xls example workbook from the companion CD and save the Payment Calculator worksheet as an interactive spreadsheet by choosing the File, Save As Web Page command. The detailed steps were given in the numbered procedure in "Publishing an Excel Web Page," on page 825.

Tip To read complete instructions on working with an interactive spreadsheet in your browser, click the Help button on the Office Spreadsheet Component toolbar.

---

3 To experiment with formatting cells, select the cell where you enter the interest rate (C5), click the Commands And Options button on the Office Spreadsheet Component toolbar, open the Format tab of the Commands And Options dialog box, shown here, and click the Italic button to apply italics to the text in the selected cell.

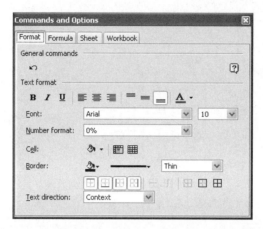

You can use the tabs of the Commands And Options dialog box to modify many other features of an interactive spreadsheet, as well as to find data or change viewing options.

4 To print the interactive spreadsheet or to save its contents (including any changes you have made), click the Export To Microsoft Excel button on the Office Spreadsheet Component toolbar. A copy of the spreadsheet will be opened in Excel, and you can use any of the Excel's commands to work with it.

Of course, the Export To Microsoft Excel command will be available only if Excel is installed on the user's computer. Although you can print an interactive spreadsheet by choosing File, Print in the browser window, this will print the entire page, including the toolbar and scroll bars. Also, you won't be able to control what portion of the spreadsheet is printed, and for a spreadsheet that is too large to view at once only the currently visible portion will be printed.

Without exporting an interactive spreadsheet to Excel, the only way to save data you have entered is to manually select the cells, use the Copy command (for example, choose Edit, Copy), and paste the data into a permanent document. Using the browser's File, Save As command will save the original Web page, *not* including any data you have entered or edited.

Using Web Queries

Excel not only publishes to the Web, it also gives you convenient ways—through Web queries—to pull data seamlessly from the Web into Excel worksheets. With the explosion of data available on the Web, this is a crucial capability to exploit. And because data on the Web is often valuable for its timeliness, Excel builds automatic background refresh capabilities into Web queries, so that you can be sure that the external data you import from the Web is up-to-the-minute.

Importing Data from the Web

You can use Web queries to import data from the Web into Excel. The process is interactive and easy to follow, much like a wizard, enabling you to select just the information you want. Of course, you need Internet access to display the data source you intend to use and make your selection. As an example, let's import some stock data from MSN to see how the process works.

To begin, establish an Internet connection and open a new Excel worksheet. (You also can use this process to import data to an already-existing worksheet.) Then complete the following steps:

1 Select cell A1 on the worksheet. Then, choose Data, Import External Data, New Web Query. Excel will display the New Web Query dialog box, shown here:

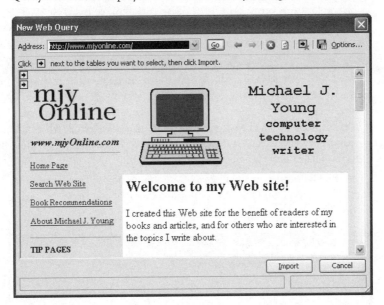

2 In the Address text box, enter the Web address for the site you want to display and then press Enter or click the Go button next to the Address box. For this example, enter **http://moneycentral.msn.com/scripts/webquote.dll**. The site will appear in the browser window within the dialog box.

3 In the Name Or Symbol text box on the Web site, enter the following ticker symbol (or a symbol of your own choosing): **MSFT**. Then click the Go button next to the Name Or Symbol box to display the current trading price for the stock.

If the market is open at the time of the query, the price reflects a 15-minute delay. If the market is closed, the price is the last trading price at the closing bell.

> **Caution** Web sites seem to be constantly in flux. So although this example was devised with stability in mind, there is no guarantee that the MSN screens will match or that eventual redesign of the Web site won't invalidate the specific instructions. If you can't find the symbol lookup features described here, look around the site a little and you might find equivalent features you can use.

4 In the browser window of the New Web Query dialog box, each block of information on the MoneyCentral screen will be displayed with a small selection box in its upper left corner: a square yellow icon that contains a black arrow. In this example, click the arrow or arrows for the blocks of stock data that you want to include in your worksheet. Each icon you check will become green (with a check mark instead of an arrow), and the block of data will be highlighted.

5 Click the Options button on the toolbar at the top of the New Web Query dialog box to display the Web Query Options dialog box. From among the Formatting options, make sure that the None option is selected under Formatting, and then click the OK button.

6 You're now ready to import the selected information into your worksheet. Click the Import button near the bottom of the New Web Query dialog box. Excel will display the Import Data dialog box to verify the target area for the imported information. In this example, leave the Existing Worksheet option selected, with the reference A1 in the adjoining text box. For now, ignore the Properties button, which displays the External Data Range Properties dialog box.

7 Click the OK button in the Import Data dialog box to finish the import process. Excel will fetch the data and then present it in a block of cells in your worksheet, as shown in Figure 30-4.

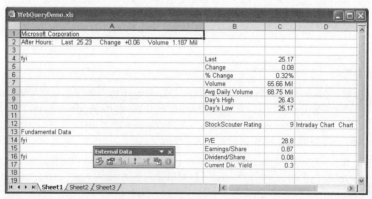

Figure 30-4. The Web query results in a block of imported data, which can be unformatted, as shown here, or can retain formatting.

If you chose to retain the HTML formatting, the imported data will have a full set of formatting features: colored backgrounds, font formatting—even hyperlinks that display related pages. Also notice that Excel displays the External Data toolbar. We'll look at some of these tools in the next section.

Revising Web Queries

To revise a Web query, select any of the cells containing imported data and then click the appropriate button in the External Data toolbar, shown here:

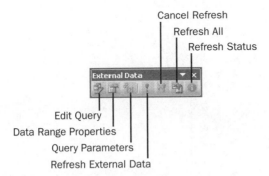

You can edit the query itself or change the properties assigned to the data range, as explained in the next two sections. You can also use your mouse to right-click a cell in the data table and choose a command from the shortcut menu.

Editing Web Queries

When you click the Edit Query button on the External Data toolbar, Excel displays the Edit Web Query dialog box. You can navigate to a different Web page or select different blocks of data at the current site. Click a green, checkmarked icon to clear a selection; click additional yellow icons to add them to the current selection. If no table is selected before you click the Import button, Excel will import all the selectable items on the current Web page.

Click the Options button on the toolbar in the Edit Web Query dialog box to change the Web query options. You can change the formatting that's preserved in the external data or alter other import settings. Among the Web query formatting options, Rich Text Formatting Only is generally a good middle-of-the-road choice. It preserves most character formatting but does not retain hyperlinks and other attributes that might be overkill in a simple presentation.

Changing Data Range Properties

Click the Data Range Properties button on the External Data toolbar to display the External Data Range Properties dialog box, shown here:

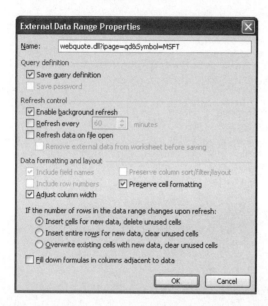

This dialog box is particularly valuable for setting the refresh options you want for the Web data. You might want to experiment using the Web query defined in the previous example (for tracking a stock price). When you finish adjusting the options, click the OK button to save your changes.

By default, the Save Query Definition option is checked. If you clear this option, the rest of the options will be dimmed: without a saved query, Excel has no query definition to consult for refreshing the data. The Save Password is available only for external database queries, not Web queries (if you use a password to access the data source, this option retains a copy of your password so you don't have to reenter it).

Troubleshooting

External data tools unavailable

The commands available through the External Data toolbar are dimmed.

The External Data toolbar has seven toolbar buttons. Various buttons are dimmed at different times. Here are some clues to what's going on. All the buttons except Refresh All are dimmed if the sheet is protected (via the Tools, Protection, Protect Sheet command) or if the selected cell is not part of external data. Query Parameters is always dimmed for Web queries.

Cancel Refresh and Refresh Status are available only if a refresh is in progress. During a refresh, Edit Query and Data Range Properties are dimmed so that you can't redefine a query that's currently being applied.

The Refresh Control options in the External Data Range Properties dialog box let you modify the way the Web query is updated from the original source. If you clear the Enable Background Refresh option, once a refresh process starts you won't be able to use Excel until the process is finished. The other options let you turn on automatic refreshing of the Web query data and determine the frequency at which your data is automatically refreshed. Only integer values (minutes) are accepted for the refresh interval. If you haven't enabled automatic refreshing, you can manually refresh the data using the External Data toolbar: click Refresh to refresh the block of data that includes the currently selected cell or click Refresh All to refresh all blocks of external data in the workbook.

Among the formatting options, don't worry about the dimmed items. They generally apply to external database queries rather than Web queries. Preserve Cell Formatting can be a useful option. If you check it, when you refresh data, cells within the block of imported data will retain any formatting you directly applied to them (if the option is cleared, the formatting you applied will be lost).

Inside Out

Keeping a snapshot of Web data

If you want to save a snapshot of Web data such as stock price information, you'll need to frustrate the automatic refresh features that will change the data right out from under you. It might occur to you to save a copy of the external data to a new worksheet, so you could then format the table and present the snapshot of Web data later. But you'd be in for a surprise: the copy would be refreshed whenever the original data is refreshed.

To freeze the data, you need to choose Edit, Paste Special when you paste the Web data to a new worksheet. Among the Paste options, select Values And Number Formats and then click the OK button. You can use Paste Special a second time with the same selected range to paste the Column Widths as well. Then, you might want to do some additional cell formatting by hand, but the values will remain static.

NEW FEATURE! Working with XML Data in a Worksheet

XML is an increasingly important format for storing and exchanging structured data, primarily on the Internet. XML is ideally suited for representing lists and other types of data that are stored in an Excel worksheet. To gain a general understanding of the features and importance of XML, you should start by reading "Creating, Editing, and Viewing XML Documents," on page 594. Pay particular attention to the definitions of the words *element* and *schema*. (You might want to stop reading that section when you reach the subsection "Creating XML Documents in Word," which begins the coverage of the Word-specific XML features.)

> **Note** For a comprehensive general introduction to XML, see *XML Step by Step, Second Edition* (Michael J. Young, Microsoft Press, 2002).

Beginning with version 2002, Excel has provided the ability to save an Excel workbook in XML format. The basic advantage of saving a workbook in XML format is that XML is a universal, open, nonproprietary, text-based format that is rapidly becoming the common medium for data exchange. Therefore, a workbook saved in XML isn't limited to being processed by Excel. Rather, it can be displayed and updated, or have its data extracted, by software written by any third party.

> **Note** To save the active workbook in XML format, choose File, Save As. Then, in the Save As dialog box, select XML Spreadsheet (*.xml) in the Save As Type drop-down list and specify a filename and location. (Either include the .xml extension in the filename or omit the extension and let Excel add it.)

When you save a workbook in the XML Spreadsheet format, the resulting document contains *all* the workbook information (including the document properties, the size and dimensions of the document window, the workbook styles, the cell formats, as well as the actual cell data). The document uses a specific set of elements and is given a highly specialized structure. (The elements and structure conform to Excel's own XML schema.) Saving a workbook in XML format allows you to reopen the workbook without loss of features, just as if you had saved it in the proprietary Excel .xls format.

Excel 2003 has added an important new XML capability: Within an Excel worksheet, you can now import, view, analyze, modify, and export XML data that uses *any* set of elements and has *any* structure—that is, XML data that conforms to any specified schema. In the worksheet, the XML data is contained in an XML list (which is explained later). You can import XML data from a variety of sources, including XML documents, Web services, or databases that can return data in XML format. You can now also work directly with the XML elements within the worksheet.

For general information on working with lists, see Chapter 28, "Power Database Techniques: Lists, Filters, and PivotTables."

The following is a basic, general procedure you can use for importing, working with, and exporting XML data in a worksheet:

1. Open the workbook and activate the worksheet in which you want to work with XML data.

2. Choose Data, XML, Import to import the XML data into the active worksheet. In the Import XML dialog box (which is similar to the standard Open dialog box), locate and select the XML document that contains the XML data you want to work with and then click the Import button. If the XML document you selected doesn't refer to an XML schema, Excel will display a message box indicating that it will create a schema based on the selected XML document. To continue, click the OK button in this message box.

Excel will then display the Import Data dialog box, shown here:

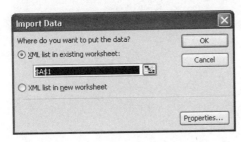

In the Import Data dialog box, select the XML List In Existing Worksheet option, use the adjoining text box to indicate where you want to place the block of XML data in your worksheet (or just accept the default location), and click the OK button. Excel will then insert the XML data at the specified location. The data will be placed within an *XML list* (also known as an *XML map*), which is a special type of Excel 2003 List designed for working with XML data.

Note For an explanation of Excel 2003 Lists, see "Using the New Excel List Commands," on page 800.

The following is an example of an XML document that you might import into a worksheet. This document describes an inventory of books and is named Inventory.xml. It's a good example of the type of XML document that you can effectively work with in an Excel list because, like a typical list, it consists of a series of records (the BOOK elements), each of which contains the same set of fields (TITLE, AUTHOR, BINDING, PAGES, and PRICE).

```xml
<?xml version="1.0"?>
<!-- File Name: Inventory.xml -->
<INVENTORY>
   <BOOK>
      <TITLE>The Adventures of Huckleberry Finn</TITLE>
      <AUTHOR>Mark Twain</AUTHOR>
      <BINDING>mass market paperback</BINDING>
      <PAGES>298</PAGES>
      <PRICE>5.49</PRICE>
   </BOOK>
   <BOOK>
      <TITLE>Leaves of Grass</TITLE>
      <AUTHOR>Walt Whitman</AUTHOR>
      <BINDING>hardcover</BINDING>
      <PAGES>462</PAGES>
      <PRICE>7.75</PRICE>
   </BOOK>
   <BOOK>
      <TITLE>The Legend of Sleepy Hollow</TITLE>
      <AUTHOR>Washington Irving</AUTHOR>
      <BINDING>mass market paperback</BINDING>
      <PAGES>98</PAGES>
      <PRICE>2.95</PRICE>
   </BOOK>
   <BOOK>
      <TITLE>The Marble Faun</TITLE>
      <AUTHOR>Nathaniel Hawthorne</AUTHOR>
      <BINDING>trade paperback</BINDING>
      <PAGES>473</PAGES>
      <PRICE>10.95</PRICE>
   </BOOK>
   <BOOK>
      <TITLE>Moby-Dick</TITLE>
      <AUTHOR>Herman Melville</AUTHOR>
      <BINDING>hardcover</BINDING>
      <PAGES>724</PAGES>
      <PRICE>9.95</PRICE>
   </BOOK>
   <BOOK>
      <TITLE>The Portrait of a Lady</TITLE>
      <AUTHOR>Henry James</AUTHOR>
      <BINDING>mass market paperback</BINDING>
      <PAGES>256</PAGES>
      <PRICE>4.95</PRICE>
   </BOOK>
```

```
<BOOK>
    <TITLE>The Scarlet Letter</TITLE>
    <AUTHOR>Nathaniel Hawthorne</AUTHOR>
    <BINDING>trade paperback</BINDING>
    <PAGES>253</PAGES>
    <PRICE>4.25</PRICE>
</BOOK>
<BOOK>
    <TITLE>The Turn of the Screw</TITLE>
    <AUTHOR>Henry James</AUTHOR>
    <BINDING>trade paperback</BINDING>
    <PAGES>384</PAGES>
    <PRICE>3.35</PRICE>
</BOOK>
</INVENTORY>
```

The Inventory.xml example XML document is on the *Microsoft Office System Inside Out—2003 Edition* companion CD.

Here's how the data looks when it has been imported into a worksheet:

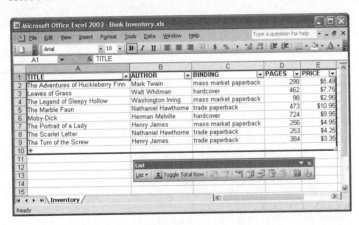

When Excel imports a block of XML data that's structured like that in Inventory.xml into an XML list, using the procedure described here, it does the following:

- It creates a schema for the XML document and attaches the schema to the XML list. To do this, it analyzes the document and infers the schema based on the document's structure. The schema is stored within the workbook.

- It *maps* each of the XML document's repeating "field" elements (for the example document, TITLE, AUTHOR, BINDING, PAGES, and PRICE) to a separate column. Each mapped column is used for displaying and editing the contents of a specific repeated XML field element.

- It copies the data from the XML document and displays it in the appropriate cells, according to the mapping. Each of the "record" elements in the XML document (for the example document, each BOOK element) is displayed in a separate row.

■ It normally stores—within the workbook—the location of the XML data source. (This allows you to refresh the XML data from the original source by choosing a single command, as explained later.)

3 In the XML list you can add or delete rows, sort or filter rows, edit or format cells, and perform other manipulations on the data, using the techniques discussed in the previous chapters in this part of the book. You'll find the methods given in Chapter 28 particularly useful.

For instance, in the example worksheet (shown under the previous step) you might want to assign currency formatting to the cells in the PRICE column. You might want to sort the rows by author. Or you might want to add a total row at the bottom (you can do this by clicking the Toggle Total Row button on the List toolbar).

4 If you have modified the data in your XML list—for example, you have added or removed records or edited the contents of fields—you can save the modified data back to the original XML source document (overwriting the document's current contents), to another existing XML document (overwriting its contents), or to a new XML document. To do this, select a cell in the XML list and choose Data, XML, Export. Then, in the Export XML data dialog box (which is similar to the Save As dialog box), choose a file location, select or enter a filename, and click the Export button. Excel will write the current contents of the XML list to the destination file as a well-formed XML document. This document will store the raw XML data, but not the formatting or other workbook features.

Using the Export command is generally useful if you are using your XML list as a tool for *editing* XML (as opposed to just viewing or analyzing XML data).

Caution   Keep in mind that when you export an XML list to an existing XML document, the document's contents will be *overwritten* with the data you're saving.

5 If the original XML source document has been modified since you imported it and you want to view the modified document, or if you have changed the XML list in Excel and you want to discard your changes, you can copy the current contents of the source document to the XML list in your worksheet, replacing the current contents of the XML list. To do this, select a cell in the XML list and choose Data, XML, Refresh XML Data.

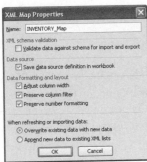

Figure 30-5. You can use the XML Map Properties dialog box to modify features of an XML list.

Using the Refresh XML Data command is generally useful if you're using your XML list as a tool for viewing or analyzing (rather than editing) the XML data contained in a source document that other software is updating. Consider, for example, that an order entry system stores orders in an XML document and that you're using an Excel XML list to view and analyze these orders. If this document is the XML source document for your XML list, you would use the Refresh XML Data command to view an up-to-date list of orders.

Caution When you use the Refresh XML Data command, the contents of your XML list are *replaced* with the current contents of the original XML source document. If you use the Refresh XML Data command and then realize you've made a big mistake, choose Edit, Undo Import immediately after refreshing. Your previous XML list contents will be restored.

6 To save the entire workbook itself, including any XML data that it currently contains, use the usual File, Save command or File, Save As command.

Inside Out

Working with import options

If you disable the Save Data Source Definition In Workbook option (described later), Excel will discard the location of the XML source document and the Refresh XML Data command will no longer be available. You can still refresh the document, however, by selecting a cell in the XML list, choosing Data, XML, Import, and selecting the XML source document in the Import XML dialog box.

You can set the Save Data Source Definition In Workbook option, as well as several other options that affect refreshing and importing data, by selecting a cell in your XML list and choosing Data, XML, XML Map Properties to open the XML Map Properties dialog box, shown in Figure 30-5.

Note You can save an entire workbook that contains an XML list and other data in native Excel format or in XML format. You can also save it as an Excel template if you want to use it as the basis for creating other workbooks. Keep in mind that this is a distinct process from exporting the XML data contained in a specific XML list to an XML document. As explained, saving a workbook in XML format always saves all workbook features including formatting and uses Excel's own schema to structure the output document. In contrast, exporting the XML data from a particular XML list saves only the raw data contained in that list and structures the data according to the schema that is attached to that list, creating a "pure" XML document (*pure* in the sense that Excel workbook information isn't mixed in).

Customizing an XML List

When you create an XML list by importing an XML document as described in the previous section, Excel maps *all* the repeating field elements, in the order they occur in the document, to successive columns in the XML list, and it reads *all* the document's character data into the list. If, however, you wish to work with only a portion of the data from an XML document, or if you want to arrange the fields in a different order from that in which they occur in the document, you can customize the XML list by using the XML Source task pane to remap the field elements to columns in your XML list.

Note You can also create a mapping for an XML list from scratch (rather than modifying an existing mapping as described in this section). One way to do this is to use the Open dialog box to directly open an XML document. Then, when Excel displays the Open XML dialog box, select the third option: Use The XML Source Task Pane.

As an example, if you had imported the demonstration XML document given in the previous section (Inventory.xml) into an XML list, you might want to customize the list. You might, for instance, want to display only the AUTHOR element followed by the TITLE element (rather than displaying all five repeating field elements in their original order). The following are the steps you would need to perform:

1 Select a cell in the XML list and choose Data, XML, XML Source to display the XML Source task pane with the design tools shown here:

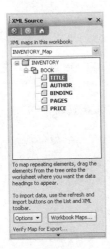

The XML Source task pane displays a hierarchical list of all the XML source document's elements, indicating that document's structure. (Excel stores this structure internally in the schema that it generated when you imported the document.) When you click an element (say, AUTHOR), Excel will highlight the column in the XML list that's mapped to this element.

2 Remove the mappings for the AUTHOR, BINDING, PAGES, and PRICE elements. To remove these mappings, you can simply delete the corresponding columns (B, C, D, and E) in the worksheet. One way to remove these four columns is to click the heading for column B, hold down the mouse button, drag to the right to highlight all four columns, and then choose Edit, Delete. In the XML Source task pane, you will now notice that the AUTHOR, BINDING, PAGES, and PRICE elements are no longer displayed in bold type, indicating that these elements are not currently mapped.

3 Insert a new column to the left of column A (the only remaining column in the XML map). Recall from previous chapters that you can do this by selecting column A and choosing Insert, Columns.

4 Map the AUTHOR element to the new column you inserted (now column A) by dragging the AUTHOR element from the hierarchical list in the XML Source task pane and dropping it on the top cell of column A (cell A1).

You now have the XML elements displayed in the desired order in the XML list, but you'll notice that the AUTHOR column no longer contains data. That's because you deleted the AUTHOR mapping from its original position and remapped it to a new column.

> **Note** XML elements have a one-to-one relationship with worksheet ranges. That is, you can map a given element to only a single range, and a given range can be mapped to only a single element.

5 To restore the data, select any cell in the XML list and choose Data, XML, Refresh XML Data. With your customized XML list, the Refresh XML Data command will read in only the data for the mapped elements (AUTHOR and TITLE), rather than reading in all the document's character data. The final result is shown here:

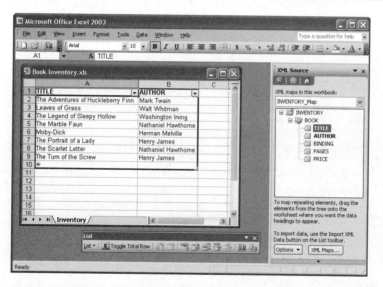

> **Note** When you export a customized XML list, the resulting XML document will contain just the elements that are actually mapped to the list (including the parents of those elements). In the example, the XML document would contain only the INVENTORY, BOOK, TITLE, and AUTHOR elements. Exporting XML lists was discussed in the previous section.

Part 5

PowerPoint

31 PowerPoint Fundamentals   849

32 Advanced Presentation Formatting   877

33 Mastering Tables, Graphics, Video, and Sound 895

34 Adding Special Effects to a Presentation   909

35 Setting Up and Presenting the Slide Show   923

Chapter 31

PowerPoint Fundamentals

Exploring the PowerPoint Window 849
Understanding PowerPoint Views 852
Creating a Presentation 856
Entering and Editing Text 866
Using Outlines 870
Adding Comments 873
Checking Spelling and Style......... 874
Saving a Presentation 876

Microsoft Office PowerPoint 2003 is presentation graphics software. Using PowerPoint, you can create and display sets of slides that combine text with diagrams, photos, clip art, media files, and animated special effects. You can then turn your work into 35-mm slides, transparencies, or printed handouts. Or, you can present your work electronically or interactively on the World Wide Web.

Furthermore, because PowerPoint is part of the Microsoft Office System, you can easily combine Microsoft Word outlines, Microsoft Excel worksheets, and Microsoft Clip Organizer illustrations into your own original PowerPoint text and graphics.

When you need to teach, persuade, or explain, PowerPoint can help you create clear, attention-getting presentations.

In this introductory chapter, you'll learn the following features of PowerPoint:

- The main features of the PowerPoint window
- How to build a simple presentation quickly
- How to add and edit text in placeholders and in an outline
- How to add comments to slides
- How to check your spelling and writing style
- How to select a file format to save a presentation

For a description of the new features included in PowerPoint 2003, see "New PowerPoint Features," on page 13.

Exploring the PowerPoint Window

The PowerPoint window, shown in Figure 31-1, opens by default in Normal view, which displays a slide and three work areas—an Outline tab, a Slides tab, and a pane for notes. Also by default, PowerPoint initially displays the Getting Started task pane, which contains tools for opening an existing presentation, creating a new presentation, or finding information or resources on the Microsoft Office Online Web site.

For details on using task panes, including the new Getting Started and Research task panes, see "Using the Task Panes in Office Applications," on page 42.

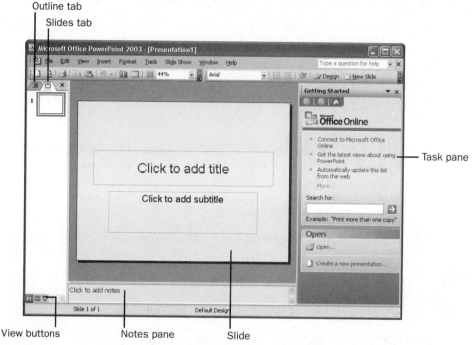

Figure 31-1. Important parts of the PowerPoint window are shown in Normal view.

The PowerPoint interface elements, many of which are shared with other Office programs, include the following:

- A menu bar provides access to the most important commands in PowerPoint.

- The toolbars provide one-click access to frequently used commands. Placing the mouse pointer on a tool displays a ScreenTip that briefly describes the tool's function. The Common Tasks toolbar—found in versions of PowerPoint earlier than 2002—has been replaced by two new buttons on the Formatting toolbar: Design (for slide design options) and New Slide (with slide layout options), both of which open a task pane that contains the required commands.

- The task panes are where you find options for creating a new presentation or working with existing presentations. Although you can also access many of these commands from the menu bar, you'll find it convenient to work with the task panes' Web-like interface, particularly when creating presentations in a hurry.

- Like most Office application windows, the PowerPoint application window also contains sizing buttons that you can use to minimize, maximize, restore, and close windows, plus a status bar at the bottom of the screen that displays the number of the slide you're working on as well as the type of presentation you're creating.

- A vertical scroll bar appears on the right side of the slide when you have more than a single slide in your presentation. The scroll box moves you from slide to slide, not up or down through the slide's text (as happens in a Word document, for example). In addition, PowerPoint displays the number and title of each slide as you drag the scroll box.

- The two buttons displaying double arrows at the bottom of the vertical scroll bar give you another way to move through slides. Click the button with the upward-pointing arrows to go to the previous slide; click the button with the downward-pointing arrows to move to the next slide.

- The View buttons below the Slide and Outline tabs let you quickly switch to different PowerPoint views. Each view is designed to make some aspect of creating and viewing a slide show as effective as possible. Views are described in more detail in "Understanding PowerPoint Views," on page 852.

- The Microsoft PowerPoint Help button at the right end of the Standard toolbar displays the new Help task pane, which is described in Chapter 3, "Getting Expert Help on Office 2003."

Elements of a Slide

After you're comfortable with the PowerPoint window, take a look at what is typically included on a slide, shown in Figure 31-2.

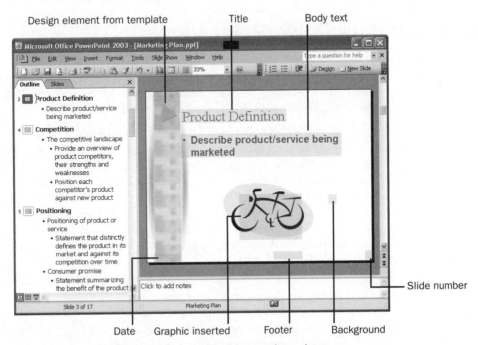

Figure 31-2. The contents of a typical slide are shown here.

A basic slide contains the following elements:

- **A background**   A slide with a design template applied comes with predesigned background graphics, fills, and color schemes, all of which can be modified or scrapped if you choose to create your own.

- **A title**   Each slide generally has a title, as shown in Figure 31-2. Each presentation usually also has a title slide that contains the title of the presentation, the subtitle, and information about the presentation, such as what audience it was created for.

- **Body text**   This consists of content that you enter, often formatted as a bulleted or numbered list.

- **Placeholders**   These are boxes outlined with dotted lines that serve as containers for text and objects (such as diagrams, tables, photos, or media files) that you can add to the slide. Some placeholders also contain a rotate handle so you can manipulate the position of the placeholder.

- **Footer**   This is an area at the bottom of a slide that you can use to specify your organization name or slide show theme. You can also delete this section.

- **Date and time**   Also appearing at the bottom of a slide, this setting can be set to update automatically or can be deleted.

- **Slide number**   By default, this appears at the bottom of a slide, although you can move it anywhere you like or delete it.

Understanding PowerPoint Views

To use PowerPoint effectively to create and modify presentations, you need to become comfortable with PowerPoint's views. By default, PowerPoint opens in Normal view, but you can display the other views by clicking their buttons in the lower left corner of the PowerPoint window. PowerPoint displays your slides in any of four basic views:

- Normal view is the default view in this version of PowerPoint. It contains three main panes. One pane displays the current slide. Another pane contains an Outline tab, displaying an outline view of the entire presentation, and a Slides tab, displaying thumbnails of all the slides in the presentation. The third main pane is for adding notes. When PowerPoint is in Normal view, a task pane that gives you options for working with text, graphics, sound, animation, and other effects can also be displayed (as shown in Figure 31-1). You can change the size of any of these panes by dragging one of the borders between panes. (For more on setting the default view, see the Inside Out sidebar "Start out with your favorite view," later in this section.)

- Slide Sorter view, shown in Figure 31-3, arranges all your slides across and down the screen so that you can see the entire presentation. Use Slide Sorter view when you want to see your presentation as a whole and when you want to view or add transitions (visual effects) between slides, although the newly enhanced Normal view lets you apply transitions and animations without leaving that view.

PowerPoint Fundamentals

Slide number   Preview Transition Effect

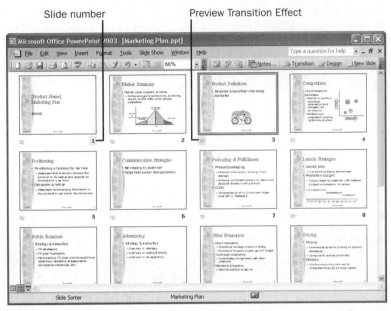

Figure 31-3. Slide Sorter view is useful for working on a presentation as a whole.

● Slide Show view, shown in Figure 31-4, lets you preview the show itself by displaying each slide on a full screen. In Slide Show view, you can see the results of transitions as well as any animation or sound effects you have added to the presentation. PowerPoint provides many ways to navigate through your slides.

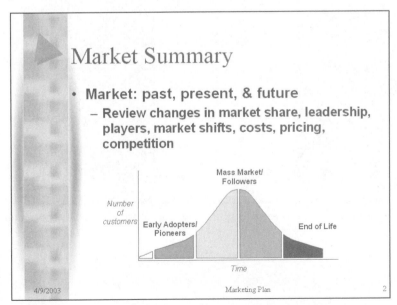

Figure 31-4. Slide Show view lets you view each slide on a full screen.

● Notes Page view, shown in Figure 31-5, gives you a large working area in which to add notes to a slide. To turn on this view, choose View, Notes Page. When you print your notes pages, PowerPoint prints each slide plus its accompanying notes on a single page, so you should use the Print Preview button on the Standard toolbar to preview your notes pages and see if all the slide's notes fit on a page. You can make the slide smaller in Notes Page view to fit more notes on each page.

Keep in mind that you can also add notes to a slide using the small notes pane that appears in Normal view. However, this pane provides a smaller working area and offers fewer formatting options than Notes Page view (for example, you can't apply a background).

Inside Out

Start out with your favorite view

You can specify in which view you want PowerPoint to always open. Choose Tools, Options, and then click the View tab. In the Default View drop-down list in the View tab, select the view you are most comfortable using to create presentations.

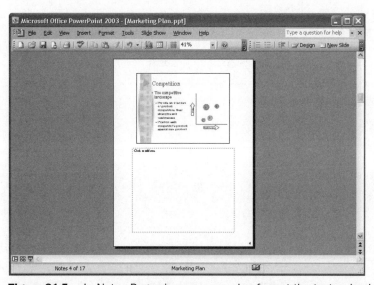

Figure 31-5. In Notes Page view, you can also format the text or background of your notes.

Using a Web Browser to View a Presentation

You can make your PowerPoint presentations available for viewing on the Web by saving or publishing them as Web pages. If you are working on a presentation that you know will be viewed on the Web, choose File, Web Page Preview to check how the slides look in a browser.

Chapter 35, "Setting Up and Presenting the Slide Show," discusses formatting a presentation for the Web in greater detail.

Note   By default, PowerPoint presentations saved as Web pages are optimized for viewing in Microsoft Internet Explorer 4.0 or later. Be aware that aspects of your presentation, such as animations, slide scaling to fit the browser window, or media files, can be adversely affected when viewed in other browsers.

Using Print Preview to View a Presentation

You can view your slides as they will look in printed form by choosing the File, Print Preview command. Print Preview opens in its own window. It is a streamlined view in which to set options for printing not just slides, but also handouts, notes pages, and outlines. If you aren't using a color printer, you'll be printing your presentations in black and white or grayscale, but viewing them on your computer screen in color. It will therefore be useful to preview how they will actually look in black and white or grayscale before you print them.

The Print Preview toolbar also provides quick access to options for setting the orientation for handouts, notes, or an outline; adding a frame around each slide when printed; determining how many slides to print per page in handouts; printing hidden slides; and editing the slide headers and footers. A slide in Print Preview is shown here:

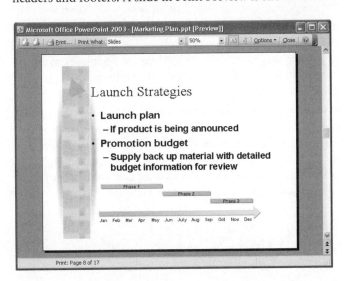

Creating a Presentation

After you're comfortable with the PowerPoint window and its views, the next step is creating a presentation. PowerPoint, like most Office 2003 applications, offers you a variety of choices, which are summarized below. You'll see these options listed in the New Presentation task pane, shown here, which you can open by choosing File, New. The following sections discuss these options in greater detail.

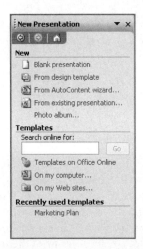

- Clicking Blank Presentation under New, or clicking the New button on the Standard toolbar, gives you a plain canvas on which to create a single slide. This option offers the most flexibility but, as you'd expect, it also assumes that you know what you want to do and how to do it. You start with a single blank slide and create additional slides chosen from the suggestions in the Slide Layout task pane. Then you can add color, background, and any objects that you choose.

- Clicking From Design Template under New creates a presentation that initially consists of a single slide and lets you apply a PowerPoint design template to your presentation. A design template includes a predesigned font, color scheme, background, and other features that create a cohesive design for your slides.

- Clicking From AutoContent Wizard under New is by far the easiest approach to creating a new presentation. The AutoContent Wizard asks for information and then creates a set of slides built around the theme you specify. The wizard applies an initial color scheme most suitable for the type of output you specify, although you can change the suggestions for content as well as the formatting and color scheme. You can also add your own presentations to the AutoContent Wizard.

- Clicking From Existing Presentation under New lets you choose a PowerPoint presentation that you have already created and saved, and build a new presentation on it. Clicking this option opens the New From Existing Presentation dialog box, where you can search for presentations on your computer, network, or on an Internet or intranet site. PowerPoint will create a copy of the selected presentation so that you can enhance it and save it as a new, different presentation.

- Clicking PhotoAlbum under New displays a dialog box that lets you create a new presentation consisting of a collection of graphics. You can obtain the images from graphics files or from a scanner or digital camera attached to your computer.

- Using the Search Office Online text box and the Go button or clicking the Templates Home Page command, all under Templates in the New Presentation task pane, lets you locate and use an online template from the Office Online Web site.

- Clicking On My Computer under Templates opens the New Presentation dialog box, where you can browse through and select any of the PowerPoint templates that are stored on your computer (those supplied with PowerPoint as well as any custom templates you have created).

- Clicking On My Web Sites under Templates lets you open a PowerPoint template that is stored on a Web site belonging to you or your company.

- Clicking the name of a template under Recently Used Templates lets you quickly reuse the template.

> Most of the methods for creating a presentation base the new presentation on a PowerPoint *template*, which is a file with the *.pot* filename extension that contains content and formatting and serves as a starting point for a new presentation. For general information on using Office 2003 templates to create documents, see "Creating New Office Documents," on page 47. For information on creating your own PowerPoint templates, see "Creating a Custom PowerPoint Template," on page 865.

To open an existing presentation, choose File, Open or click the Open button on the Standard toolbar. For details, see "Opening Existing Office Documents," on page 56.

Using the AutoContent Wizard

The AutoContent Wizard is often the simplest way to start a new presentation when you're either new to the software or working under deadline pressure. The AutoContent wizard generates a set of 8 to 12 slides with a design that is suitable for a particular type of presentation. To use the AutoContent Wizard, perform the following steps:

1 Choose File, New to open the New Presentation task pane. In the task pane, click From AutoContent Wizard under the New heading. After reading the information in the introductory wizard dialog box, click the Next button.

2 In the second AutoContent Wizard page, select the general category of the presentation you're going to give by clicking one of the five buttons: All, General, Corporate, Projects, or Sales/Marketing. For example, to see a list of the types of business presentations, click the Corporate button. The dialog box will then appear as shown here:

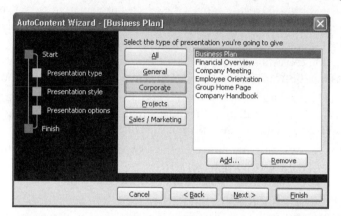

3 Select a specific presentation type in the list for the category you selected, and then click the Next button.

> **Note** You might select a presentation based on a template that has not been installed. When prompted by PowerPoint, you can install the template, but you must have the Office 2003 CD or network connection to install from. To avoid doing this each time you select an uninstalled template, you can go back to Office Setup and install all the templates at once.

> **Tip** Add your own presentation type
>
> You can add a presentation type to any of the categories that appear in the second AutoContent Wizard page. The presentation type you add can be based on an existing presentation or PowerPoint template to which you have access. To add a presentation type, in the second AutoContent Wizard page, click the button for the appropriate category, click the Add button, and then in the Select Presentation Template dialog box select the PowerPoint presentation or template you want to use and click the OK button.
>
> To remove a presentation type from the category that is displayed in the second AutoContent dialog box, select it in the list and then click the Remove button.

4 In the next dialog box, select the output style for the presentation you'll be making. The wizard will customize your presentation according to the type of output you select. You can choose to play your presentation either on-screen or on the Web, and you can specify whether you need black-and-white or color overheads, or 35-mm slides. Then click the Next button.

5 Enter the information that you want to appear on the opening, or title, slide. By default, the wizard includes your name. You provide the title of your presentation and the information you want included in the footer on each slide. (The footer might actually appear at the top of a slide, depending upon the slide's layout.) When you're done, click the Next button and then click the Finish button in the final wizard page.

The AutoContent Wizard will create a basic set of slides built around the choices you made, and will display the presentation in Normal view, as shown in Figure 31-6.

With the preliminary work done, you can add or remove slides, modify the initial text and graphics, and change the formatting to make the presentation your own.

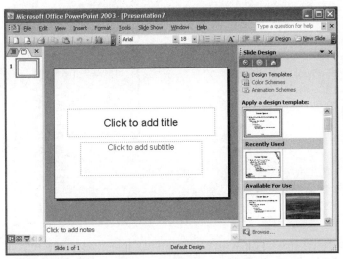

Figure 31-6. The AutoContent Wizard creates a new presentation with options for modifying the design or color scheme or adding animation schemes.

Starting a Blank Presentation

When you want to opt for full creativity instead of relying on the AutoContent Wizard, follow these steps:

1 Choose File, New to display the New Presentation task pane. Then click Blank Presentation under New. Or, simply click the New button on the Standard toolbar. A title slide with a white background will appear.

2 If you want to keep the title slide that appears by default, add your text directly to the title and subtitle placeholders on the slide or in Outline view. You can also select a different layout in the Slide Layout task pane that PowerPoint displays when it creates the new presentation.

3 To add slides, use the Slide Layout task pane. Place your mouse pointer over the layout you want to use, and when the down arrow button appears, click it to view the drop-down menu, and then choose Insert New Slide. The following figure shows a newly added slide:

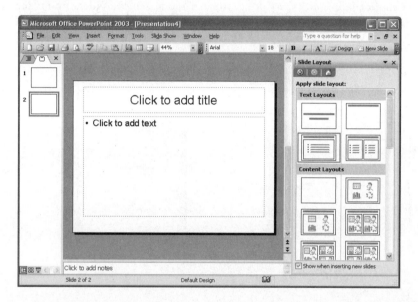

Once you have chosen the basic layout for your blank slide, you can enter, edit, and format its contents, as well as add design elements and animations. PowerPoint uses certain fonts and font sizes by default even in a blank presentation, but you can easily change them. Following basic design guidelines can make your slides eye-catching and easy to read:

● Apply no more than two fonts per slide.

● Obey the 6 by 6 rule: No more than six words per line and no more than six lines per slide.

● Select fonts that suit your audience: Tempus Sans ITC is casual, Times New Roman is conservative, and Verdana is good for the Web.

● Select dark backgrounds for on-screen slide shows and light backgrounds for overhead transparencies.

You'll learn more about text formatting in Chapter 32, "Advanced Presentation Formatting."

Using a Design Template

PowerPoint uses the term *design template* to refer to a PowerPoint template (a *.pot* file) that provides the design for only a single slide. You can use a design template as the basis for creating a new presentation consisting initially of a single slide, or you can use a design template to apply a design to individual slides—or to all slides—in an existing presentation.

Design templates help you apply a consistent design and color scheme to an entire set of slides. They have names such as Compass, Glass Layers, Digital Dots, and Blends. These templates combine a background color and design with a set of eight complementary colors that PowerPoint uses for elements such as titles, backgrounds, slide text, shadow effects, and so on.

The following illustration shows a title slide based on the Crayons design template—suitably whimsical for a children's clothing business, but unsuitable for a stockholders' meeting:

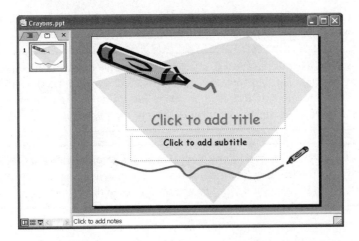

To create a new presentation and apply a design template, follow this procedure:

1 Choose File, New to open the New Presentation task pane and click From Design Template under New.

PowerPoint will create a new presentation consisting of a single (title) slide with a plain design, just as it does when you click Blank Presentation or click the New button on the Standard toolbar. However, in this case it begins by displaying the Slide Design task pane, shown here, rather than going immediately to the Slide Layout task pane.

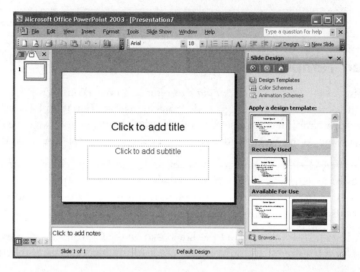

2 In the Apply A Design Template list in the Slide Design task pane, click the design template that you want to use as the basis for the design of the slides in your presentation.

 Tip You can click the Design Templates On Microsoft Office Online item at the bottom of the Apply A Design Template list to display the Templates home page of the Office Online Web site, where you can locate and download an online template. For more information, see "Downloading and Using Templates from Office Online," on page 55.

Note An alternative method for performing steps 1 and 2 is to open the New Presentation dialog box, click the Design Templates tab, and select a design template, as explained in "Other Ways to Start a Presentation from a Template," later in the chapter.

3 Click the down arrow button next to the design template thumbnail to view options for applying the template to all slides or selected slides, or to change the size of the thumbnail previews.

Although your new presentation consists of only a single slide, for a presentation that contains two or more slides, you can use the drop-down menu to apply a design template to all slides in the presentation (which is what happens if you simply click the template name) or to apply the design template to only the selected slide or slides.

4 To continue building a presentation, choose Format, Slide Layout to display the Slide Layout task pane. Apply a new layout to the title slide, if you wish, and then insert new slides using the desired layout or layouts, as explained in the previous section.

5   Click the back arrow at the top of the Slide Layout task pane to return to the Slide Design task pane. Here you'll find additional options for editing the color scheme or adding animation schemes.

Animation schemes were introduced with PowerPoint 2002. They are a combination of animations and transitions that can be applied without leaving the Normal view.

> For more information on animation schemes and transitions, see Chapter 34, "Adding Special Effects and Hyperlinks."

Using an Existing Presentation as a Model

In PowerPoint 2003, you can use the From Existing Presentation command in the New Presentation task pane to open a copy of any PowerPoint presentation you'd like to use as the basis for a new presentation. This command makes creating custom templates, as discussed later in the chapter, less critical.

To create a new presentation based on an existing one, perform the following steps:

1   Choose File, New to open the New Presentation task pane and click From Existing Presentation under New. The New From Existing Presentation dialog box will open, as shown here:

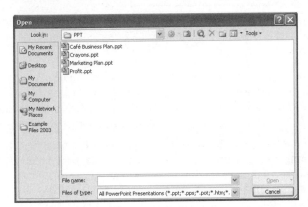

2   Select the presentation you want and click the Create New button.

3   Modify the existing presentation, and then choose File, Save or File, Save As. Either command will open the Save As dialog box so that you can specify a filename and location for your new presentation file.

Other Ways to Start a Presentation from a Template

Most of the methods for creating a presentation that are discussed in the previous sections of this chapter use a PowerPoint template as the basis for the new presentation. The following are three additional ways to create a presentation based on a template. All the methods use commands in the New Presentation task pane, which you can open by choosing File, New.

● To use a template stored on your computer—either one supplied with PowerPoint or a custom template you've created—click On My Computer under Templates. This will display the New Presentation dialog box, shown in Figure 31-7. (This dialog box is equivalent to the Templates dialog box that appears in Word and Excel.) Select the template you want to use and click the OK button.

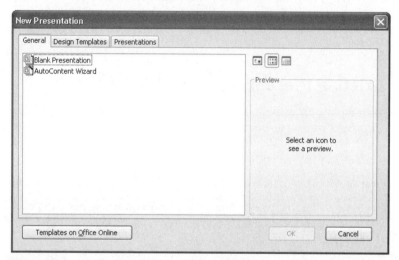

Figure 31-7. In the New Presentation dialog box you can select a PowerPoint template—either one supplied with PowerPoint or a custom template you have created.

By selecting an item in the General tab of the New Presentation dialog box, you can create a blank presentation or run the AutoContent Wizard, as discussed previously in the chapter. You can also select any custom template that you have created and stored directly in your User Templates folder (as discussed later in the chapter).

By selecting a template in the Design Templates tab, you can create a new presentation containing a single slide (a title slide) that is based on a design template, as explained in "Using a Design Template," earlier in the chapter. When the new presentation opens, PowerPoint will display the Slide Layout task pane so that you can change the layout of the title slide or add new slides with specified layouts.

In the Presentations tab, you can select a *presentation template*. While a design template contains only a single slide, a presentation template contains an entire set of slides. Basing a new document on a presentation template creates a complete presentation in a single step. You need only customize the individual slides.

If you have created custom PowerPoint templates in subfolders in your User Templates folder, those templates will appear in other tabs in the New Presentation dialog box.

> **Tip** You can quickly reuse a template that you've recently used by clicking its name under Recently Used Templates in the New Presentation task pane.

- To find, download, and use an online PowerPoint template from the Office Online Web site, use the controls at the top of the Templates area of the New Presentation task pane. Either enter a keyword into the Search Office Online text box and click the Go button, or click Templates Home Page to run your browser and open the Templates home page of the Office Online site.

> For information on using Microsoft's expanded collection of online templates and the new Template Help task pane available in Office 2003 applications, see "Downloading and Using Templates from Office Online," on page 55.

- To open a PowerPoint template that is stored on a Web site belonging to you or your company, click On My Web Sites under Templates.

Creating a Custom PowerPoint Template

If you find that many of the presentations you produce have the same basic content—for example, business plan presentations that all share a common design—you might want to create a custom template that you can use as the basis for building these presentations. If your template contains the common content and formatting for your presentations, generating a new presentation will be simply a matter of customizing the content and formatting. The following steps are used to create a custom template:

1. Create or open the presentation you want to use as a template.
2. Choose File, Save As to display the Save As dialog box.
3. In the Save As Type drop-down list, select Design Template (*.pot).
4. Select a folder location, enter a filename for your template, and click the Save button.

When the Design Template (*.pot) item is selected in the Save As Type drop-down list, the Save As dialog box automatically opens your current User Templates folder. If you want the New Presentation dialog box to display the new template you are creating, you must save it in the file folder designated as your User Templates folder, or in one of its subfolders. The default User Templates folder is C:\Documents and Settings*User Name*\Application Data\Microsoft\Templates, where *User Name* is the name you use for logging on to Windows. You can save the template directly within your User Templates folder; in this case, the template will appear in the General tab of the New Presentation dialog box. Alternatively, you can place it in a subfolder in your User Templates folder (an existing subfolder or a new one that you create); in this case, the template will appear in the New Presentation dialog box in a tab that's labeled with the name of the subfolder.

> You can change the location of your User Templates folder using Word. The setting you make affects all Office applications that use templates. For instructions, see the tip "Choose locations for your templates," on page 415.

Entering and Editing Text

No matter which method you use to create a new presentation, entering text is a matter of replacing the text that PowerPoint provides in each slide placeholder with your own text. This section describes ways to build the body of a presentation using text. The text you enter in placeholders, such as titles, subtitles, and bulleted lists, can be entered and edited in the slide itself or in the Outline tab.

> **Note** This section deals with adding text to placeholders on a slide. PowerPoint also lets you add text to an AutoShape, add text to a text box for use as a caption or label for graphics, and insert WordArt. However, these three options treat text as an object and are created using the Drawing toolbar, which is covered in Chapter 33, "Mastering Tables, Graphics, and Drawings."

Entering Text in Placeholders

Dotted or shaded borders surround placeholders, which come preformatted with a particular font and font size. Placeholders contain text that you replace with your own text. They can be resized using the sizing handles that appear when the placeholder is selected, rotated using the rotate handle (present on only certain placeholders), or moved when the mouse pointer becomes a four-headed arrow. By default, PowerPoint automatically wraps text within the placeholder as you type, so press Enter only when you want to start a new paragraph. To enter text in placeholders, perform the following steps:

1 Select the placeholder by clicking in it.

2 Type your own text.

3 When you have finished typing text, click anywhere outside the placeholder to make the border disappear.

Tips for Positioning Placeholders

When you're working with placeholders, here are some tips to keep in mind:

- If you're having trouble fitting text onto a slide, try resizing or repositioning another placeholder before enlarging the one in which you want more text. To reposition a placeholder, point to a part of the border other than a sizing handle and, when the pointer becomes a four-headed arrow, drag the placeholder up or down on the slide. Moving a title placeholder higher or reducing its size, for example, results in extra space for a bulleted list below it.

- Because PowerPoint automatically wraps text, you can use placeholder resizing as a quick-and-dirty way to realign text. To turn a two-line paragraph into a one-line paragraph, for instance, widen the placeholder box. To force text to fill more vertical space, make the box narrower and taller.

- You can resize or move placeholders to make room for an object, such as a graphic, that isn't provided for on your slide layout.

You can also choose a new anchor point for your text to change its alignment within the placeholder. Normally, PowerPoint adds text from the top down. By choosing a different anchor point, you can have PowerPoint add text from the bottom or from the middle of an object instead. This feature is useful when text doesn't completely fill the placeholder. To select a new anchor point for a placeholder, follow these steps:

1   Select the placeholder you want to modify, and then choose Format, Placeholder to open the Format AutoShape dialog box.

2   In the Text Box tab, select a new text anchor point in the Text Anchor Point drop-down list, as shown here:

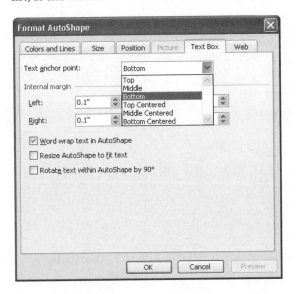

Working with Automatic Text Formatting

When you type more text than the placeholder can hold, PowerPoint, by default, doesn't expand the placeholder to contain the overflow. Instead, it automatically reduces the font size of the text in the placeholder. If you later delete some of the text, PowerPoint will increase the font size until it reaches its original size.

After this kind of automatic formatting action, what Office refers to as a smart tag appears. *Smart tags* are buttons that display a menu of options that you can choose from to control the automatic formatting or layout decisions that PowerPoint makes. The smart tag buttons that you'll run into when entering and editing text are likely to include the following:

● AutoCorrect Options button
● Paste Options button

● AutoFit Options button (This button appears when PowerPoint changes the font size as described above.)

● Automatic Layout Options button

You can use these buttons to undo the automatic formatting in this instance, turn it off completely, or go to the AutoCorrect Options dialog box (also available from the Tools menu) to set your own AutoCorrect and AutoFormat options. The AutoFormat As You Type tab of the AutoCorrect Options dialog box is shown in Figure 31-8.

Figure 31-8. The AutoFormat As You Type tab in the AutoCorrect dialog box allows you to customize PowerPoint's automatic text formatting features.

For more information on the AutoCorrect dialog box options, see "Checking Spelling and Style," on page 874.

Using Smart Tag Recognizers

The current version of PowerPoint lets you use smart tag *recognizers* to convert specific types of data in your presentations—such as dates, financial (stock ticker) symbols, and names—to smart tags that you can use to perform useful actions on the data—such as looking up a stock quote for a financial symbol. To enable one or more smart tag recognizers, choose Tools, AutoCorrect Options and click the new Smart Tags tab. Details on working with smart tags and using the Smart Tags tab are given in "Using Smart Tags in Word," on page 276.

Editing Text

To edit text, you must first select it. In PowerPoint, in addition to dragging the mouse over the text you want to select, you can use the following mouse shortcuts:

- In Normal view, click on a slide icon in the Outline or Slide tab to select the entire slide (this doesn't select text within the slide).
- In Normal view, select any bulleted item by clicking anywhere in the placeholder, and then moving the mouse pointer to the left of the item and clicking when the pointer becomes a four-headed arrow.

Using the keyboard, you can choose one of these methods:

- To move to the beginning of a line, press Home; to move to the end, press End.
- To select to the beginning or to the end of a line from the insertion point, press Shift+End or Shift+Home.
- To select consecutive lines, hold down Shift and press End or Home repeatedly.

You can replace any amount of text just by selecting it and typing something else. You can also duplicate text quickly, using the standard Office cut-and-paste technique. When you use the Paste command, the Paste Options button will sometimes appear. The options available on its menu might let you choose whether you want the item or items you're pasting to retain their own formatting or to use the formatting specified by the design template. You can also choose Edit, Paste Special to more precisely control how and in what format data is transferred, which can be particularly useful when pasting Excel files or graphics files.

Note   The Paste Options button will appear only if the Show Paste Options Buttons option is checked. You access this option by choosing Tools, Options and clicking the Edit tab.

For more information on copying and moving data among Office programs and on using the Office Clipboard, see Chapter 7, "Exchanging Data in Office 2003."

To move text, select it, and then use one of the following methods:

- Select the text and drag it to its new location.
- Right-click the selected text and use the Cut and Paste commands on the shortcut menu.
- To delete text, select it and press Delete or choose Edit, Clear.
- To delete an entire slide, display it (in Normal view) or select it (in Slide Sorter view), and choose Edit, Delete Slide.

Using Outlines

Instead of—or in addition to—entering text into placeholders provided by templates and built-in layouts, you can organize your thoughts in outline form and then turn your outline into slides. An outline provides a summary of a presentation arranged in headings and sub-headings. If you're creating a complex presentation or if you're a person who values structure and likes to see how the parts contribute to the whole, working with an outline is probably a good choice for you.

Outlines in PowerPoint are created or edited using the Outline tab in Normal view, as shown in Figure 31-9, with the splitter bar moved to the right to reveal more of the outline pane.

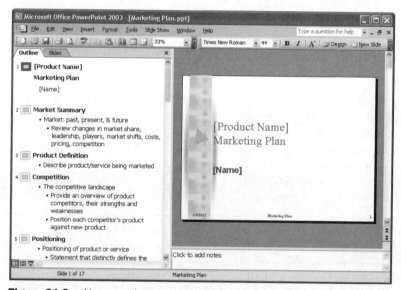

Figure 31-9. You can shape presentation content using the Outline tab.

If you have opened an existing presentation or if you're using a presentation template, the text will appear in outline form, as shown in Figure 31-9. If you're working on a blank pre-sentation, you'll see a slide number and a slide icon, but no text will appear until you type some.

When you begin entering text in the Outline tab, you can use the tools on the Standard and Formatting toolbars to help you order your content. Using these tools lets you increase or decrease an indent, which moves the selected text to a higher or lower outline level, collapse or expand content so that you can see only headings or all subheads too, and also show or hide formatting. It's useful at this point to open the Outlining toolbar in its default position, docked on the left side of the PowerPoint window next to the Outline tab area. To open the Outlining toolbar, choose View, Toolbars, Outlining. The Outlining toolbar will open, as shown here:

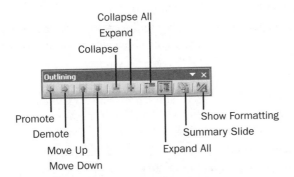

Entering an Outline from Scratch

When you have displayed a blank presentation in the Outline tab, generating an outline feels as if you're working on a cross between a Microsoft Word document and a PowerPoint slide. The outline tab shows a numbered slide icon. You can enter text next to the icon for a heading to be used as a title, and enter your body text under the title. Body text can be formatted in up to five outline levels.

- Pressing Enter creates a new paragraph exactly like the preceding one. For example, if the last character you typed was in a bulleted item, press Enter to create another bulleted item; if the last character you typed was in a slide title, press Enter to create a new slide.

- If the last text you typed was a slide title, pressing Ctrl+Enter creates a bulleted item. If the last text you typed was a paragraph within a slide (such as a bulleted or numbered item), pressing Ctrl+Enter creates a new slide.

- If you want to create an outline that has several sublevels, use the Promote and Demote buttons on the vertical Outlining toolbar.

- Click the Promote button to raise the importance of a paragraph one heading level.

- Click the Demote button to lower the importance of a paragraph one heading level. You can also use the Demote button to move the top-level heading (next to the slide icon) on one slide to the previous slide.

Modifying an Outline

When you're comfortable creating an outline in Normal view, use the following procedures to control and refine either an outline that you have created from scratch or one that you're revising by using the suggestions in a template or the headings in another document that you're inserting into PowerPoint:

- To select a single paragraph (slide title or body text paragraph within a slide) in an outline, drag the mouse pointer over the text.
- To select a paragraph plus all its subitems, click to the left of the paragraph, where the pointer becomes a four-headed arrow. (To select a bulleted or numbered paragraph plus its subitems, click the bullet or number.)
- To select an entire slide, click the slide icon.
- To select several consecutive paragraphs or slides, press Shift as you click. (Although pressing Ctrl while you click lets you select nonconsecutive items in other Office 2003 applications, it doesn't work that way in PowerPoint.)
- To move a paragraph, select it and either drag it to its new location or use the Move Up and Move Down buttons on the Outlining toolbar.

> **Note** When you drag text, a small empty box appears over the lower portion of the pointer when you click the pointer to drag the text. If it doesn't, make sure that drag-and-drop editing is turned on. Choose Tools, Options. In the Edit tab, check the Drag-and-Drop Text Editing check box.

- Use the buttons on the Outlining toolbar to change outline levels and to control how much of the outline you see on screen.

Rearranging Slides on the Outline Tab

As you're working with your slides, you might find that you need to rearrange some of them. You can easily do so by dragging them to new locations in Slide Sorter view, but when you're working in the Outline tab in Normal view, the drag-and-drop technique works just as well. To reorder your slides, follow these steps:

1. Place the mouse pointer on the slide icon and, when the pointer becomes a four-headed arrow, drag the slide to a new location.

   As you drag, watch the horizontal line that shows where you're dragging the slide. To avoid inserting the slide into the body of another slide, don't release the mouse button until the line is completely above or below your target.

2. To undo a move, either choose Edit, Undo Move, or click the Undo button.

   When you move slides, PowerPoint automatically renumbers them for you.

Expanding and Duplicating Slides

Other useful slide management capabilities that PowerPoint 2003 offers you are the ability to expand one slide into several slides and the ability to quickly duplicate a slide.

Using the Outlining toolbar, you can easily turn one or more paragraphs on a slide into new, separate slides. To expand one slide into several slides, follow these steps:

1 Display the slide you want to expand in the Outline tab of Normal view.

2 In the Outline tab, select one or more paragraphs in a slide.

3 Click the Promote button on the Outlining toolbar—repeatedly if necessary—until the highest level paragraph or paragraphs that you selected become separate slides.

4 Repeat these steps to expand as many paragraphs as you choose into separate slides.

To create an identical copy of a slide in your presentation, perform the following steps:

1 Select the slide in the Outline tab.

2 Choose Insert, Duplicate Slide. PowerPoint will create a copy of the slide and place it immediately after the selected slide in the presentation. If you want to move the duplicated slide to a new location, you can use the drag-and-drop technique.

Creating a Summary Slide

You can use a summary slide, a bulleted list of all or selected slide titles, to introduce your presentation; this is often called an *agenda slide*. You can also insert a summary slide at the end of your presentation to recap the points you covered. To create a summary slide, perform the following steps:

1 In the Outline tab, select the slides you want to include on the summary slide.

2 Click the Summary Slide button on the Outlining toolbar. The summary slide will appear before the first slide you selected. If you selected several slides, the summary slide may be more than one slide.

3 If you want to customize the summary slide, delete, add, or edit text as necessary.

4 If you want the summary slide to appear in a different position, move it to the desired position.

Adding Comments

If you plan to share your presentations with other authors or editors, you might want to annotate a few important slides with comments to provide instructions or highlight critical information. In PowerPoint, you can add a comment and post it to a slide by following these steps:

1 Display the slide in Normal view and choose Insert, Comment. This will display a comment box that contains your name, the date, and the insertion point.

2 Type your comment text in the comment box.

   If you type or receive a lengthy comment, use the scroll bars that appear on the right side of the comment box to view the entire comment.

3 When you finish typing the comment, click another object on your slide to lock in the comment. The comment box will close and only a small marker containing your initials plus the comment number will remain.

4 To display the comment text again, click the comment marker.

5 To edit the comment text, double-click the comment marker to open the comment box and place the insertion point in it.

6 To move the comment, drag the comment marker with the mouse. To delete the comment, click the marker and press Delete.

> **Tip** To change the reviewer name and initials that appear on any comments that you subsequently insert, Choose Tools, Options. Click the General tab and then edit the Name and Initials fields.

The comment will appear on your slide in each view as long as the View, Markup menu option is selected. This option is selected when you enter your first comment. You can also use the Reviewing toolbar to manage your comments; it appears when you create your first comment.

Here's what a comment looks like on a slide after you enter your text into it:

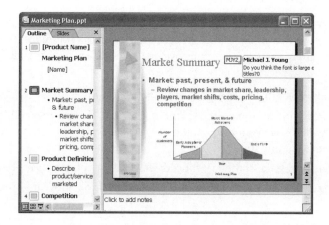

Checking Spelling and Style

Misspellings loom large when your slide show is projected onto a big screen. PowerPoint's Spelling feature finds and highlights misspellings in your outlines, notes (less important, because they're not being projected), and text on slides, such as titles and bulleted lists.

By default, PowerPoint checks your spelling as you type and marks any misspelled words with a wavy red underline. Right-click the word and choose an option from the shortcut menu to correct the spelling at that moment.

> **Note** To modify the way PowerPoint's spelling checker works, choose Tools, Options and click the Spelling And Style tab.

For more information on using the Spelling feature, see "Checking Spelling," on page 479.

You can also have PowerPoint check the style of the text you enter in your slides. When this feature is enabled, PowerPoint will notify you if you enter text that violates one of its style rules. To turn on style checking and to view or modify PowerPoint's style rules, perform the following steps:

1 Choose Tools, Options and click the Spelling And Style tab.

2 Check the Check Style option.

   When you check this option, if the Office Assistant isn't already enabled, PowerPoint will prompt you to enable it. *Style checking requires the Office Assistant to be enabled.*

3 To view or modify PowerPoint's style rules, click the Style Options button to open the Style Options dialog box, shown here:

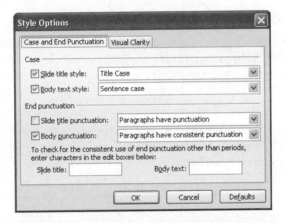

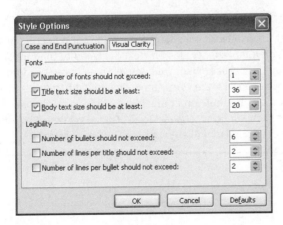

4 If you subsequently enter text that violates a style rule, a light bulb will appear next to the Office Assistant. Click the light bulb to see a choice of options for dealing with the style rule infraction: change the text according to the style suggestion; ignore the current infraction; stop checking for violations of the current rule (that is, stop showing the same tip); or display the Style Options dialog box, where you can change the rule settings.

Tip You can use the AutoCorrect feature in PowerPoint to correct common errors, such as typing two initial capital letters in a word, forgetting to capitalize the first word of a sentence, or making a common spelling error. To set AutoCorrect options, choose Tools, Auto-Correct Options and click on the AutoCorrect tab. To learn more about AutoCorrect, see "Automatically Fixing Your Text with AutoCorrect" on page 271.

Saving a Presentation

By default, PowerPoint saves your presentations as native format (.ppt) files, which saves and opens them as typical presentations, but you can use the Save As dialog box to specify in what format you want to save a particular presentation. You can also choose Tools, Options, and in the Save tab, set options that change the default type of file that PowerPoint uses to store your presentations.

The Save As dialog box also lists other file formats for saving presentations, such as HTML for Web presentations, or for saving a PowerPoint 2003 presentation to a format suitable for opening in an earlier version of PowerPoint.

Inside Out

Remove personal information

You can have PowerPoint remove personal information from your presentations when you save them. The information removed includes any text assigned to the Author, Manager, and Company presentation properties. Also, your actual name is removed from all comments and macros and replaced with the word Author. You might find this a useful option if you are creating presentations for the Web or a public kiosk, and would prefer not to have your name visible. To set these options, choose Tools, Options. In the Security tab, check the Remove Personal Information From File Properties On Save option.

Chapter 32

Advanced Presentation Formatting

Formatting Text. 878

Working with Color and
Color Schemes 886

Changing the Background 888

Working with Presentation
Masters 890

An effective Microsoft PowerPoint presentation communicates information and affects your audience in some way. The effect varies with your presentation's purpose, but what doesn't vary is the importance of arranging content on your slides so that your message has the greatest impact.

You want the text to be clearly readable, titles quickly grasped, lists well placed, and related information logically aligned. To support the words in your presentation, you want to select color, backgrounds, and repeating design elements that enhance your presentation's feeling and theme.

PowerPoint comes with templates that make all the design choices for you. However, the more familiar you (and your audience) are with PowerPoint, the more interested you'll become in crafting original presentations.

In this chapter you'll learn about:

- Formatting text
- Formatting bulleted and numbered lists
- Working with paragraph indentation, alignment, and line spacing
- Modifying color and color schemes
- Working with backgrounds and creating custom backgrounds
- Working with presentation masters

Formatting Text

Font, font size, style, and color are defined by settings in the design template assigned to each slide in your presentation. You can reformat text properties by making changes on an individual slide or by making global changes to a slide master. In this section you'll learn to make formatting changes to individual slides.

> **Working with slide masters and multiple masters is covered in "Working with Presentation Masters," on page 890.**

To apply a different formatting to text, perform the following steps:

1 Make a selection, as follows:

   ■ To change the formatting of all text in a placeholder, click the placeholder's border to select it. (When you have correctly selected a placeholder, a thick dotted border will appear around the placeholder, but the insertion point will *not* appear inside the placeholder.)

   ■ To change the formatting of just some of the text in a placeholder, select (highlight) the text you want to change.

2 Issue your formatting command.

You can format text by working in the Font dialog box or by using the buttons on the Formatting toolbar, which control many of the most common changes that you might want to make.

Formatting Text Using the Formatting Toolbar

The Formatting toolbar contains the Font drop-down list, which displays samples of the fonts; the Font Size box; Increase Font Size and Decrease Font Size buttons; and the Font Color button. You can also apply different font styles (bold or italic) or effects (underline or shadow) by clicking the appropriate button on the Formatting toolbar. Although it's best to use no more than two fonts for all the text in your presentation, you can often add variety and emphasis by changing the font style.

You can use the bold and italic font styles for drawing attention to text in a presentation. However, avoid using italics for emphasis or to define a word because they can look blurry when projected on a screen. Instead, consider underlining the text. But rather than simply using the underline text effect, consider drawing a decorative line below the text using the Drawing toolbar, as shown in Figure 32-1 and discussed in the following Inside Out element.

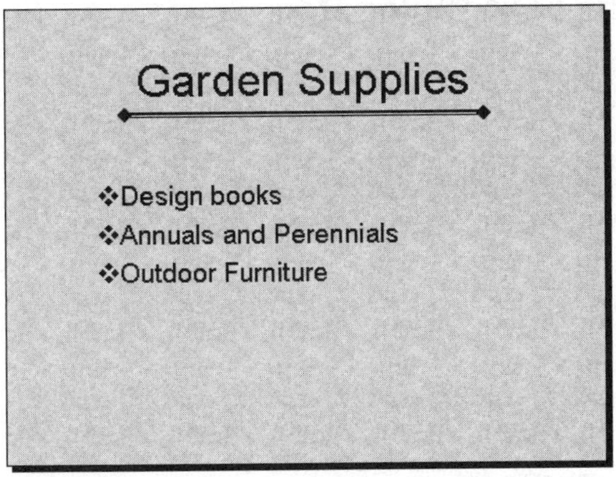

Garden Supplies

- ❖Design books
- ❖Annuals and Perennials
- ❖Outdoor Furniture

Figure 32-1. If the title had been underlined using the underline font effect, it would have cut off the characters' descenders.

Inside Out

Draw a line rather than applying underlining

Drawing a line to underline text is generally a better choice than applying the underline font effect. Assigning the underline effect in the Font dialog box (or by using the Underline button on the Formatting toolbar) doesn't permit you to specify where to put the line in relation to the text above it. Most often, the result is a line that is too close to the text, which can cut off the characters' descenders (the tail of a lowercase *g* or *p*, for example). Also, unlike the versatile underline font effect in Word, in PowerPoint you can apply only single-thickness, plain underlining.

To create more effective underlining, draw a line under the text using the Line tool on the Drawing toolbar. Choose View, Toolbars, Drawing to display the Drawing toolbar. Click the Line button on the toolbar and drag the pointer under the text to draw the line, while holding down the Shift key to make it easier to make the line exactly horizontal. Then, select the line, choose Format, AutoShape, and in the Format AutoShape dialog box, click the Colors and Lines tab to format its style, color, and size using the available options. You can position the line using the mouse or the options on the Position tab of the Format AutoShape dialog box.

Text Formatting Using the Font Dialog Box

When you want to create several formatting effects at once, you can also use the Font dialog box, shown here, by choosing Format, Font.

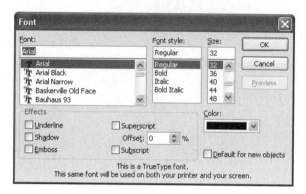

You can use this standard dialog box to make all the formatting changes covered in the previous section. In addition, you can use this dialog box to apply a few other special effects—embossing, superscript, and subscript.

To format the selected text using the Font dialog box, do one or more of the following:

● To change the text color, pick a new color in the Color drop-down list. By adding color to your text, you can emphasize important words or phrases on your slide.

● To add a shadow effect, check the Shadow option. The shadow effect adds a shadow at the bottom and to the right of each character, making the text appear three-dimensional. However, it's more effective when applied to graphics and objects than to text used in presentations.

● To add embossing to text, check the Emboss option. PowerPoint surrounds each character with a combination of light and dark outlines so the letters appear to be raised. The color depends on the slide's background color. Embossing generally works best with fonts that produce thick characters or with headline-sized text that is formatted as bold.

Replacing Fonts

To replace one font with another throughout an entire presentation, you'll typically want to use the slide master, as explained later in this chapter. However, if you've added individual formatting to some slides, the slide master may not be linked to every instance of the font in your presentation.

> For more details on making changes to slide masters, see "Working with Presentation Masters," on page 890.

To make sure that you're replacing all the instances of the font, select the text and then perform the following steps:

1 Choose Format, Replace Fonts.

2 In the Replace Font dialog box, verify that the font you want to replace is selected in the Replace drop-down list, which contains only fonts used in your presentation.

3 Specify the new font in the With drop-down list, shown here, which contains all available PowerPoint fonts:

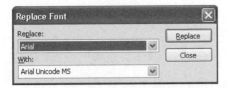

4 Click the Replace button and then click the Close button to return to your presentation.

All instances of the font will be replaced in the presentation with the replacement font you selected, except for fonts in WordArt objects.

Copying Formatting

When you want to copy the look and style of text or other formatting, use the Format Painter button on the Standard toolbar. This technique also works with other PowerPoint objects, such as AutoShapes, pictures, clip art, and WordArt objects. To copy text formatting from one word, phrase, or placeholder to another, follow these steps:

1 Select the first item, and then click the Format Painter button on the Standard toolbar.

2 Click the item you want to copy the formatting to.

Working with Bullets and Numbering

Bulleted lists are frequently used to organize information on slides in PowerPoint. When you use a bulleted-list placeholder, PowerPoint enters the bullets automatically. You can also insert a bullet in front of any paragraph. Simply place the insertion point within the paragraph (or select several paragraphs) on the slide and then click the Bullets button on the Formatting toolbar. PowerPoint will add a bullet at the beginning of your paragraph (or paragraphs).

If you want to remove bullet(s), click anywhere in a paragraph that contains a bullet (or select several bulleted paragraphs), and then click the Bullets button again.

To insert a numbered list on a slide, follow the same procedure, but instead of clicking the Bullets button, click the Numbering button on the Formatting toolbar.

Using the Bullet button on the Formatting toolbar applies standard bullets selected by PowerPoint. To choose a different bullet style, perform the following steps:

1 Select the text to reformat, choose Format, Bullets And Numbering, and then click the Bulleted tab, shown here:

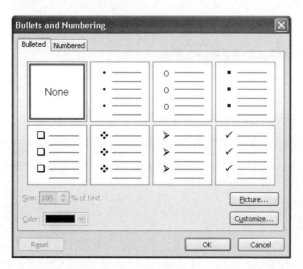

2 In the Size text box, specify the size of the bullets as a percentage of the text size.

3 Select a bullet style, as follows:

  ■ To use one of the standard bullet styles shown, select it. Then, select the bullet color in the Color drop-down list and click the OK button.

  ■ To use a custom character or symbol for the bullets, click the Customize button and select the character or symbol in the Symbol dialog box. After closing the Symbol dialog box, select the bullet color in the Color drop-down list and click the OK button.

Chapter 32

Advanced Presentation Formatting

■ To use a graphic image for the bullets, click the Picture button. Then, in the Picture Bullet dialog box, either select one of the images provided by PowerPoint or click the Import button to select a graphics file containing the bullet image. When you click the OK button in the Picture Bullet dialog box, PowerPoint will immediately apply the selected picture bullet and return you to the presentation window.

> For information on using the Symbol dialog box, see "Inserting Symbols and Foreign Characters," on page 260.

You can also apply custom numbering to one or more paragraphs by selecting them, choosing Format, Bullets And Numbering, and clicking the Numbered tab, shown here:

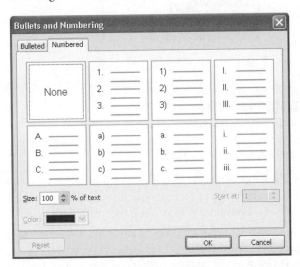

Formatting Indents and Tab Settings

An indent is a paragraph formatting attribute. When you work with bulleted and numbered lists in PowerPoint, you often need to adjust the paragraph indentation in the template so that enough space exists between the text and bullets and the text aligns correctly. To do this, follow these steps:

1 Choose View, Ruler to display the horizontal and vertical rulers.

2 Click within the paragraph you want to modify. The ruler will show the markers for the paragraph indentation.

A slide title paragraph has a single set of indentation settings. A body text paragraph, however, has five different sets of indentation settings—one for each of the five possible indentation levels. (PowerPoint, however, displays only the indentation-setting markers for the current indentation level and for any higher indentation levels. Thus, if a paragraph is at the highest indentation level, you'll see only a single set of markers, but if it's at the lowest level, you'll see all five sets of markers.)

3 Drag the upper triangle-shaped marker to adjust the indent of the first line of a paragraph.

4 Drag the lower triangle-shaped indent marker to move the text following a bullet or number and to align any additional lines in the paragraph at the same point, as shown in Figure 32-2.

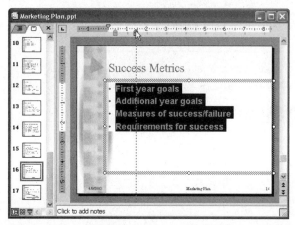

Figure 32-2. Creating custom bullets often requires formatting the paragraph indentation in the list.

As you drag, you'll see a vertical dashed line, which helps you position the marker. You'll typically be dragging these first two markers in opposite directions when you're adding space between a bullet or number and the text following it.

5 Drag the lower rectangular indent marker to adjust the indent of the entire paragraph, without changing the relative indents of the different parts of the paragraph. (Dragging this marker moves both of the triangular markers simultaneously.)

> **Tip** Adjust the indentation level of a paragraph
>
> As you learned in Chapter 31, "PowerPoint Fundamentals," you can change a paragraph's indentation level by using the Demote and Promote buttons on the Outlining toolbar. You can also change the indentation level by clicking the Increase Indent or Decrease Indent button on the Formatting toolbar.

A *tab stop* is one of the positions where text is aligned when you press the Tab key. The default tab stops are indicated with small gray markers just below the horizontal ruler (see Figure 32-2). You can adjust the spacing of the default tab stops by dragging one of these markers to the right to increase the spacing or to the left to decrease it. As in Word, you can also set custom tab stops to left-align text at the tab stop, to center text at the tab stop, or to right-align text at the tab stop. You can use the decimal tab stop to align decimal points at the tab stop. To set a tab stop, click the button at the left end of the horizontal ruler until you see the symbol for the type of tab you want to use. Then click the position on the ruler where you want to locate the tab stop (this will remove all default tab stops to the left). To move a custom tab stop, drag it to a new position on the ruler. To remove a custom tab stop, drag it off the ruler.

Changing Text Alignment and Line Spacing

PowerPoint templates apply default text alignment settings for placeholders. Titles are often centered and body text is usually aligned flush left. When you want to modify alignment, choose from among the Align Left, Center, Align Right, and Justify (both margins even) alignment options.

To change text alignment, follow these steps:

1 Select the text you want to align. (Either select individual lines of text using the mouse or select entire text placeholders.)

2 Click one of the alignment buttons on the Formatting toolbar (Align Left, Center, or Align Right).

3 To apply justified alignment—a formatting option that aligns text to both left and right margins—choose Format, Alignment, Justify.

You can also adjust the vertical space before or after selected paragraphs and change the amount of line spacing between the lines within paragraphs. For example, to increase the vertical space between each item in a bulleted or numbered list or to adjust the line spacing within each bulleted or numbered paragraph, perform the following steps:

1 Select the paragraphs you want to modify.

2 Choose Format, Line Spacing to display the Line Spacing dialog box, shown here, and then make your formatting selections.

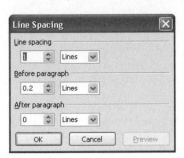

Working with Color and Color Schemes

The design template you apply to a presentation controls the color scheme of the slides. The color scheme, which consists of eight colors selected by PowerPoint, affects the background, text, lines, shadows, fills, accents such as bullets, and hyperlinks on your slides. You can use color to add contrast, to attract attention to a particular slide or element such as a table or chart, or to create a mood or feeling in your audience.

Whatever the goal involved in your color choices, the first factor you should consider is the medium you will use to display the slide show. When giving an electronic presentation, using a display device to project the image in a well-darkened room, you are safe in relying on this basic rule: use a darker background and a lighter foreground to hold your audience's attention. Too much light color on the screen ultimately annoys your viewers: their eyes can't quickly adjust to a white background in a dark room and they get tired of looking at it for too long. When using overheads, slides, or printed presentations, use the opposite tenet: keep the foreground dark and the background light.

To change the color scheme, select the slide and display the color scheme tools in the Slide Design task pane by choosing Format, Slide Design and then clicking the Color Schemes command in the Slide Design task pane. The Slide Design task pane will then display thumbnails of suggested color schemes, as seen here:

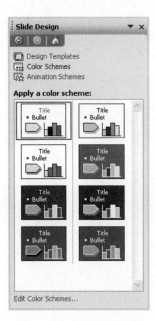

- To apply a new color scheme to all the slides in your presentation, click the desired scheme in the Apply A Color Scheme list.
- To apply a new color scheme to only the currently selected slide or slides, click the down arrow that appears when you point to a color scheme and choose Apply To Selected Slides from the drop-down menu.

Tip You can also apply a new color scheme to notes pages or handouts. To apply a color scheme to notes pages, choose View, Notes Page before selecting the color scheme as explained. To apply a color scheme to handouts, choose View, Master, Handout Master before selecting the color scheme.

Creating a Custom Scheme

When you want to create your own color scheme, you can select the colors from PowerPoint's version of the color wheel, like the one illustrated here in the Standard tab of the Colors dialog box:

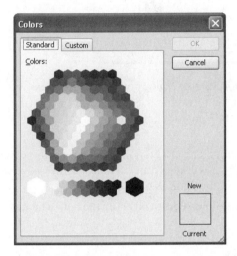

A color wheel shows relationships among colors. Choosing colors that are adjacent on the color wheel creates more harmonious schemes, but with little contrast. (When you hear designers say that a color combination really "pops," they're usually referring to the effect of contrast.) Choosing colors that are located opposite each other on the color wheel creates contrast. Professional designers often achieve successful contrast by choosing three colors about equidistant from each other on the color wheel; for example, red, yellow, and blue work well together.

To create your own color scheme, perform the following steps:

1 If the color schemes aren't already displayed in the task pane, choose Format, Slide Design and then click the Color Schemes command in the Slide Design task pane.

2 Click the Edit Color Schemes command at the bottom of the Slide Design task pane. The Edit Color Scheme dialog box will appear, as shown here:

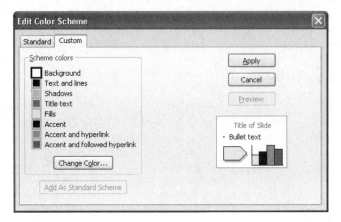

3 In the Custom tab of the Edit Color Scheme dialog box, click the presentation element you want to adjust—Background, Text And Lines, Shadows, and so on (the current color is displayed in a box beside the element name). Then click the Change Color button and pick a new color.

4 When you're finished choosing colors for presentation elements, click the Add As Standard Scheme button. PowerPoint will save your custom scheme and display it in the list of available color schemes in the Slide Design task pane.

5 Click Apply to close the dialog box. PowerPoint will apply the new scheme to all the slides in your presentation.

Changing the Background

PowerPoint templates come with ready-made background designs that include some or all of these elements: color, shading, pattern, texture, and pictures.

You'll want to change the background of a slide or slides in many instances—when you're inserting a chart, diagram, picture, or table that won't show up well against the prescribed background; when you want your audience to really focus on a slide or section of a presentation.

When you make changes to the background, you can apply them to individual slides, to notes pages, to handouts, and to the slide masters.

For more details on making changes to slide masters, see "Working with Presentation Masters," on page 890.

To modify the background color of a slide, perform the following steps:

1 In Normal or Slide Sorter view, select the slide or slides to which you want to apply a background color.

2 Choose Format, Background. The Background dialog box will appear.

3 In the Background dialog box, click the down arrow in the lower-right corner of the Background Fill area to open the drop-down menu of background options, as shown in Figure 32-3.

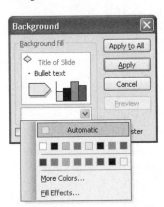

Figure 32-3. Here, the drop-down menu of background options has been opened.

4 From the drop-down menu, choose one of the displayed colors. Or choose More Colors to select from a broader range of standard colors or to specify a custom color.

5 In the Background dialog box, click the Apply button to apply the background color to the selected slide(s) or click the Apply All button to apply it to all the slides in your presentation.

Now you can apply PowerPoint fill effects (or import your own) to add to the background color. Fill effects add pattern and texture to a background, which in turn adds depth to your slide design. As you apply fill effects, remember that the background is the *backdrop* for the message of your presentation. It's not the whole story and shouldn't overshadow the foreground, where you'll do the job of spelling out your message.

Fill effects let you apply a gradient (a color transition effect), a texture (a standard texture or one you import from a graphics file), a pattern (for example, horizontal hash marks), or a background picture (which you import from a graphics file, which will be automatically scaled to fit the background of a PowerPoint slide). To apply a background fill effect, follow these steps:

1 In Normal or Slide Sorter view, select the slide or slides to which you want to apply a background fill effect.

2 Choose Format, Background. The Background dialog box will appear.

3 In the Background dialog box, click the down arrow in the lower-right corner of the Background Fill area to open the drop-down menu of background options and then choose Fill Effects. The Fill Effects dialog box will appear, as shown here:

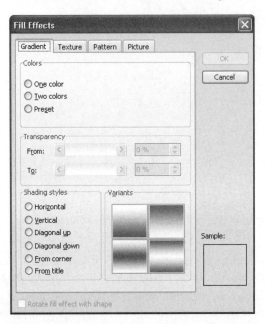

4 Click the tab for the particular type of fill effect you want to apply, choose the specific effect, and click the OK button to return to the Background dialog box, where you'll see a preview image of a slide showing both the selected background and the fill effect you just created.

5 In the Background dialog box, click the Apply button to apply the background color and fill effect to the selected slide(s) or click the Apply All button to apply it to all the slides in the presentation.

Tip Changing the background of notes pages or handouts

You can also change the background of notes pages or handouts. To change the background of notes pages, choose View, Notes Page and then choose Format, Notes Background. You can apply changes to the background of notes pages to the selected notes page or to all notes pages.

To change the background of handouts, choose View, Master, Handout Master and then choose Format, Handout Background. Background changes to handouts apply to all handout pages for that presentation, as well as to the printed outline.

Working with Presentation Masters

In a PowerPoint presentation you can globally change the default formatting and layout of a particular type of presentation element by modifying the corresponding *master*. Modifying a master to effect global changes in a presentation is somewhat analogous to customizing a style in Word to change a particular text element throughout a document. PowerPoint provides four different types of master:

- A *title master* controls the default formatting and layout of the presentation's *title slide*. Usually the first slide in a presentation is a title slide, which is used for introducing the presentation and has a unique design. However, you can designate any slide as a title slide (or remove that designation) by displaying the slide, choosing Format, Slide Layout, and applying the Title Slide layout (or applying a different layout to remove the title slide designation). You might want to use more than one title slide within a presentation to separate major sections or to summarize what you've covered in different groups of slides.
- A *slide master* controls the default formatting and layout of the nontitle slides in the presentation (usually all slides except the first one).
- A *notes master* controls the default formatting and layout of the notes pages.
- A *handout master* controls the formatting and layout of the presentation handout. A *handout* is a printed version of your presentation that displays one to nine slides per page. You can print a presentation handout by choosing File, Print Preview, choosing a handout layout in the Print What drop-down list on the toolbar, and then clicking the Print toolbar button.

The following is the basic procedure for working with a title master or a slide master:

1 Choose View, Master, Slide Master to switch into *slide master view*, shown in Figure 32-4.

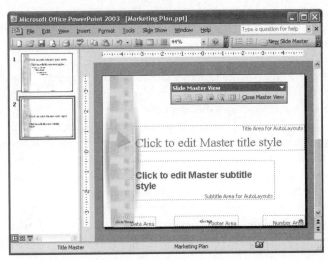

Figure 32-4. This figure shows a presentation opened in slide master view.

2 In the pane at the left of the presentation window, click the thumbnail image for the title master to work with the title master or click the thumbnail image for the slide master to work with the slide master (as shown in Figure 32-4). To identify a thumbnail image, hold the mouse pointer over it and PowerPoint will display a ScreenTip indicating the master's name and type, as well as which slides in the presentation it controls.

Most presentations have both a title master and a slide master. However, a presentation to which only the Default Design design template has been applied (for example, a presentation you created by clicking the New button on the Standard toolbar) will have just a slide master. In this case the slide master will control the default formatting and layout of all the slides in the presentation.

Also, if you have applied more than one design template to the slides in a presentation, that presentation will have several pairs of title and slide masters, one pair contributed by each design template that has been used. This feature, introduced with PowerPoint 2002, is known as *multiple masters*. Again, if you hold the mouse pointer over the thumbnail image for a particular master in the left pane, a ScreenTip will reveal the type of the master and which slides it controls.

Tip   If you find working with multiple masters confusing, you can disable this feature by choosing Tools, Options, clicking the Edit tab, and checking the Multiple Masters option in the Disable New Features area. Subsequently, you'll be able to apply a design template (with its masters) only to the entire presentation, not to individual slides.

3   Adjust the formatting and layout of the title or slide master just as if you were working with an individual slide. Your changes will affect the *default* formatting and layout of the associated slides. Keep in mind that if you directly change the formatting or layout of one or more individual slides, your direct changes will override the default formatting and layout defined in the associated title or slide master.

You can adjust the font or paragraph formatting of the text in any of the master's five placeholders by selecting that text and using the formatting the techniques given in previous sections of this chapter. In a slide master, these placeholders are labeled Title Area, Object Area (the text area), Data Area, Footer Area, and Number Area. A title master has a Subtitle Area placeholder rather than an Object Area placeholder. In a slide master, you can format any of the five levels of body text by selecting the corresponding paragraph in the Object Area placeholder.

Note   When you modify the font or paragraph formatting of a particular type of text (for instance, the text in the Title Area or the top-level text in the Object Area) in the slide master, the title master will inherit the change. However, you can then override that change by opening the title master and directly applying different formatting.

You can adjust the slide color scheme and background using the methods given earlier in this chapter.

You can use the mouse to move or resize any of the five placeholders. You can change the selected placeholder's formatting by choosing Format, Placeholder. Your changes will affect the corresponding placeholders on the slides.

> **Note** To remove a placeholder from a title or slide master, select it and press Delete. When you remove a placeholder from a master, the master no longer controls the formatting of the corresponding placeholders on the individual slides. However, placeholders are not actually removed from slides. To restore a placeholder you've removed from a master, click the Master Layout button on the Slide Master View toolbar, described later, and check the removed placeholder in the Master Layout dialog box.

You can modify the visibility and content of the Date Area, Footer Area, and Number Area by choosing View, Header And Footer. The changes you make will appear on all the slides in the presentation.

While working on a title or slide master, you can use the commands on the Slide Master View toolbar, shown here:

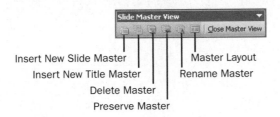

4 When you're done modifying the title or slide master, click the Close Master View button on the Slide Master View toolbar to return to your former presentation view.

You can use similar techniques to modify the formatting and layout of the notes master or handout master, thereby changing the formatting and layout of the notes pages in your presentation or the presentation handout. (You'll be able to override the notes master formatting or layout for one or more individual notes pages by working in Notes Page view.) To work with the notes master, choose View, Master, Notes Master. To work with the handout master, choose View, Master, Handout Master.

Mastering Tables, Graphics, Video, and Sound

Creating Tables 896
Adding Graphics 898
Adding Video Clips and Sound 902

The basic formatting effects in Microsoft Office PowerPoint 2003 create solid, compelling presentations. To further enliven your presentations, however, you can add tables and graphics. The types of graphics you can add include pictures that you insert, drawings that you create yourself (AutoShapes), ready-made Microsoft Office diagrams, special text effects (WordArt), and charts. Tables and the different types of graphics all work to illustrate conceptual information and help you make your point quickly and effectively. You can also enliven your slide shows by adding one or more video or sound clips or background music to your presentation. When you use well-chosen tables, graphics, video, and sound to support the information you're presenting, you can make complicated information clear and intelligible to your audience.

In this chapter, you'll learn how to

- Create and format PowerPoint tables
- Add different types of graphic objects to a presentation
- Save PowerPoint elements in graphics files
- Use grids and drawing guides to align elements on a slide
- Display digital pictures in a photo album presentation
- Add video and sound clips to a presentation
- Play tracks from an audio CD during a slide show

Creating Tables

Adding tables to your slide presentation is an excellent way to show important trends and relationships among groups of data. Typically, PowerPoint tables look best when they're kept small and concise, with no more than two or three columns and three or four rows, as shown in Figure 33-1.

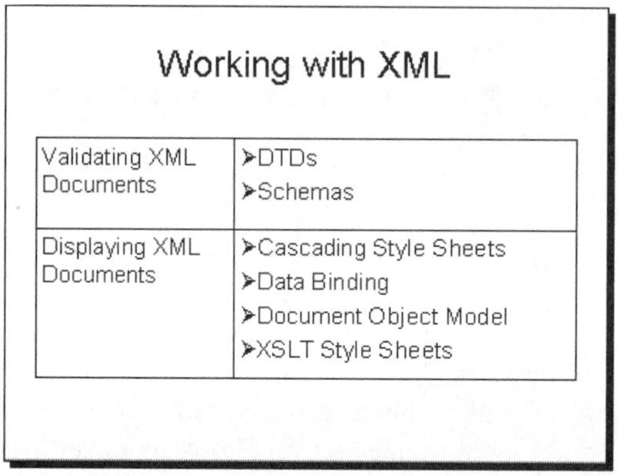

Figure 33-1. It's good design practice to keep tables simple when including them on a slide.

You can create a table that has numbers, words, or both in a PowerPoint slide. To insert a basic table, perform the following steps:

1 Display the slide in which you're going to create the table.

2 Click the Insert Table button on the Standard toolbar.

3 In the table grid that drops down from the Insert Table button, move the mouse pointer to select the number and arrangement of columns and rows that you need. When you click, the blank table will be inserted into the current slide.

4 Add your data to the cells.

Another way to add a table to your presentation is to add a slide with one of the content layouts that includes a table icon. Click the table button in the placeholder, and specify the number of columns and rows that you need in the Insert Table dialog box.

You can quickly perform simple editing tasks by clicking within the table area and making your changes, as follows:

- To move from one cell to another within the table, press the Tab or Shift+Tab keys.

- To correct typos and make simple changes to the data, use the standard editing operations such as insert, delete, copy, and move.

- To change the size of cells, drag one of the internal vertical or horizontal borders between cells.

- To add or remove a row, right-click within a table row and choose Insert Rows or Delete Rows from the shortcut menu. To insert a row at the end of the table, place the insertion point in the last cell and press Tab.

- To resize the entire table, drag the sizing handles that appear on the outer edges of the table when it is selected.

- To move the table, place the mouse pointer over an outside border and, when the pointer becomes a four-headed arrow, drag the table to a new location.

- To remove a table, click on an outside border to select the entire table and press Delete.

To create a more complex table, follow these steps:

1   If the Tables And Borders toolbar isn't visible, click the Tables And Borders button on the Standard toolbar. Make sure that the Draw Table button is selected on the Tables And Borders toolbar.

2   Use the pointer, which is a pencil now, to draw the boundaries of your table, and then drag the pointer to create the columns and rows.

3   To remove an inside border from a table, click the Eraser button on the Tables And Borders toolbar, and then click the border you want to remove.

The Tables And Borders toolbar includes two useful buttons to help you resize table elements on slides: Distribute Rows Evenly and Distribute Columns Evenly. If necessary, you can use these buttons to revise the row and column widths in your table.

Formatting a Table

Use table formatting to add clarity to your presentations; for example, you can emphasize relationships among groups of data by adding shading to a column heading, or you can distinguish groups of cells by giving them their own color scheme.

You can make changes to your table (inserting and deleting rows and columns, adding fill colors to cells, applying borders, or changing the text alignment within cells, and so on) by using the formatting options available on the Tables And Borders toolbar.

To format a table, select the particular cells you want to modify, click the Table button on the Tables And Borders toolbar, and then choose Borders And Fill from the drop-down menu. The Borders tab of the Format Table dialog box will appear, as shown in Figure 33-2.

Chapter 33

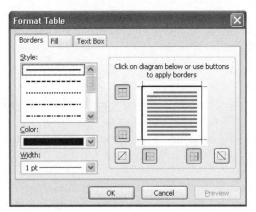

Figure 33-2. Apply borders to a table using the Borders tab of the Format Table dialog box.

Use the appropriate tab to make changes:

- To modify the style, color, and width of the border around the selected cell(s), use the Border tab.
- To apply a background color or fill effect to the selected cell(s), use the Fill tab.
- To adjust the text alignment, change the internal margins, or rotate the text within the selected cell(s), use the Text Box tab. (Rotating text in a column or row is often a convenient way to make information fit into a cell and keep it readable.)

> PowerPoint tables are similar to Microsoft Word tables. For detailed information on working with tables in Word, much of which you can apply to PowerPoint, see Chapter 13, "Arranging Text Using Tables, Columns, and Lists."

Adding Graphics

The techniques for adding graphics to slides in PowerPoint are basically the same as those used for adding graphics to documents in other Microsoft Office 2003 programs, although PowerPoint does have a few unique graphics features, such as grids, drawing guides, and photo albums. In this chapter, the term *graphics* is meant to include pictures (inserted clip art or graphics files), AutoShapes (individually drawn objects), Office diagrams, WordArt objects, charts, and other linked or embedded objects.

You can enhance a PowerPoint presentation by using the shared Office 2003 graphics tools to add any of the following types of graphic objects to a slide:

- You can insert a picture into a slide using the Microsoft Clip Organizer program, which allows you to locate pictures stored on a local or network disk or to download pictures from the extensive collection of clip art on the Office Online Web site. You can also import a picture into a slide directly from a graphics file stored on a local, network, or Internet location. For information, see "Inserting Pictures into Office Documents," on page 107.

Chapter 33

- You can create your own drawings in a slide by using AutoShapes. An AutoShape is a predefined or free-form figure—such as a line, oval, cube, flowchart symbol, banner, or free-form scribble—that you can quickly insert into a document and then customize. For instructions, see "Using AutoShapes to Create Drawings," on page 123.

- You can add a conceptual drawing—such as an organization chart or a Venn diagram—to a slide by inserting a ready-made Office diagram. Office diagrams are covered in "Generating Conceptual Drawings Using Office Diagrams," on page 127.

- You can create special text effects in a slide—such as curved, slanted, or three-dimensional text—by inserting a WordArt object. Instructions are given in "Using WordArt to Produce Special Text Effects," on page 133.

- You can build a chart that graphically represents numerical data in a slide by using the Microsoft Graph program. You can find out how in "Constructing Charts Using Microsoft Graph," on page 136.

Tip **Save time by using content layouts**

As you read the general instructions for inserting graphic objects, keep in mind that Power-Point provides a unique way to insert a clip from Clip Organizer, a picture from a graphics file, an Office diagram, or a chart: Choose Format, Slide Layout to open the Slide Layout task pane. In the task pane, apply a *content* layout, which is one that contains one or more collections of icons representing graphic objects you can insert. Corresponding buttons will then appear within one or more placeholders in the slide—Insert Clip Art, Insert Picture, Insert Diagram Or Organizational Chart, and Insert Chart. You can insert a graphic object by clicking one of these buttons. (You can also insert a table or an audio or video clip by clicking the Insert Table button or the Insert Media Clip button.)

- You can link or embed data from another Office application in a PowerPoint slide. For example, you could link or embed a Microsoft Excel worksheet range or an Excel chart. For general information, see Chapter 7, "Exchanging Data in Office 2003." For an example showing how to embed an Excel worksheet range in a PowerPoint slide, see "An Embedding Example," on page 174.

Note To insert one of the graphic objects described in this list into a notes page, you must first switch to the Notes Page view. (Choose View, Notes Page.) When you switch back to Normal view, the graphic objects you just added won't be displayed, but they will print and display in Notes Page view.

For information on modifying any of the types of graphic objects mentioned in this list, including instructions for controlling the overlapping order of different graphic objects that intersect on a slide, see "Modifying Graphic Objects," on page 142.

Saving PowerPoint Elements as Pictures

You can save a snapshot of any object contained in a slide—for example, a placeholder and its text, a picture, an AutoShape object, an Office diagram, or a chart—in a graphics file. You can then edit the graphics file (if you have an appropriate vector or bitmap graphics editor), insert it in another program, display it in a Web page, or even insert it back into a PowerPoint slide as an imported picture. Use the following procedure:

1 Right-click the object, and then choose Save As Picture from the shortcut menu.

2 In the Save As Picture dialog box, type a filename for the picture, specify the folder you want to store it in, and select an appropriate type of file format.

Using Grids and Drawing Guides

The grids and drawing guides are viewable, nonprinting guidelines that you can use to help position objects on a slide. To view the grid or the drawing guides on all slides, follow these steps:

1 Choose View, Grid And Guides.

2 In the Grid And Guides dialog box, check the Display Grid On Screen option, the Display Drawing Guides On Screen option, or both options.

A slide with both the grid and the drawing guides turned on looks like this:

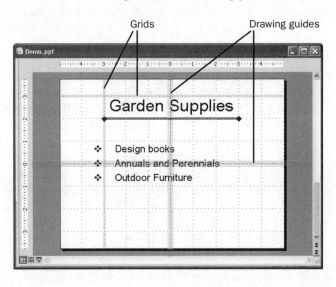

The drawing guides, consisting of a horizontal and a vertical line that initially intersect in the middle of the slide, are helpful in arranging objects evenly on a slide. To manipulate the drawing guides, perform the following steps:

● To move a guide, select it and then drag it to another location on the slide. When you drag a guide, a measurement appears, telling you where on the vertical or horizontal ruler you are moving the guide.

● To add a new guide, press Ctrl while dragging the guide.

● To delete a new guide that you added, drag it off the slide.

The grid, which consists of a set of many intersecting lines, helps you position objects precisely on a slide. To manipulate the grid, perform the following steps:

1 Choose View, Grid And Guides. The Grid And Guides dialog box will appear, as shown here:

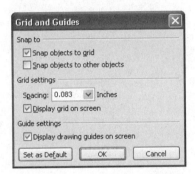

2 In the Grid And Guides dialog box, select the spacing you want to use between gridlines in the Spacing drop-down list under Grid Settings.

3 By default, Snap Objects To Grid is checked, which causes PowerPoint to align an object on one of the grid dots—or halfway between dots—when you drag it on the slide. If you want to be able to drag an object to any position, clear this option or override it on an ad hoc basis by pressing Alt as you drag the object.

4 Check the Snap Objects To Other Objects check box to align objects with each other when you drag them.

In addition to positioning objects by using the grid or the drawing guides, you can align or evenly distribute several objects by selecting them, clicking the Draw button on the Drawing toolbar, and then choosing an appropriate command from the Align Or Distribute submenu. Or, you can choose a command from the Nudge submenu to move the selected object(s) in small increments.

Creating a Photo Album

PowerPoint lets you quickly create a *photo album*, which is a presentation that consists of a title slide and a collection of graphic images, one or more per slide. You can obtain the images from graphics files or from a scanner or digital camera attached to your computer. To create a photo album, perform the following steps:

1 Choose Insert, Picture, New Photo Album. Or, if the New Presentation task pane is displayed, click Photo Album under New. PowerPoint will then display the Photo Album dialog box, shown here:

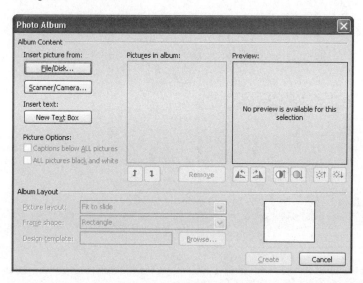

2 In the Photo Album dialog box, build your photo album presentation. You can use the controls to insert pictures; to insert a text box (a slide for displaying text); to preview, modify, or rearrange the pictures; to adjust the layout of the pictures on the slides; and to add captions.

3 Click the Create button to create the Photo Album you have built.

Adding Video Clips and Sound

You can also enhance a slide by adding a video clip or sound. Inserting a video clip or adding sound to a slide can add interest to your presentation, but relying on multimedia effects to carry your presentation often backfires. Too much sound and motion during a presentation is ultimately confusing to your audience. Used judiciously, however, video and sound effects can quickly catch your viewers' attention.

Inserting Video Clips

You can insert one or more video clips—that is, movies—into any slide. You might want to play a video quote from your product manager, for example, or run a short documentary movie for a fund-raising event. You could even create a video for product tutorials and educational materials.

> **Note** Most of the movie clips stored in the Clip Organizer are simply animated .gif files, small files that contain an animated sequence of images. If you imported your own movie files into the Clip Organizer, you will find them there, too, generally stored in .avi format. You might be able to find additional movie clips on your network, intranet, or the Internet.

Before you insert video clips, think about the environment you'll be presenting in. Does the computer you'll use have the necessary hardware (such as a sound card, speakers, and an enhanced video card) for playing the multimedia items during your presentation? You might consider adding a few multimedia elements just in case. If the machine you give your presentation on doesn't support them, plan an alternate way to make your presentation compelling. With this basic detail considered, you'll find that adding video and sound is the same as adding any other object to your slides, and the special effects are truly exciting.

To insert a movie into a slide, follow these steps:

1. Display the slide in which you want to add a video clip.

2. If you want to browse the Clip Organizer for a movie clip, choose Insert, Movies And Sounds, Movie From Clip Organizer. PowerPoint will open the Clip Art task pane and will select the Movies option in the Results Should Be drop-down list. You can use the Clip Art task pane to locate a video clip stored on your computer or on the Office Online Web site. Click the movie you want to add to your slide.

> **Note** Some of the layouts you can apply to a slide (using the Slide Layout task pane) add a group of buttons to the slide for inserting various types of objects. These are known as *content* layouts or *text and content* layouts. If you've applied such a layout to your slide, you can insert a video clip from the Clip Organizer by clicking the Insert Media Clip button and selecting a video clip in the Media Clip dialog box (which displays both movie and sound clips). However, the Clip Art task pane (or the freestanding Clip Organizer program) provides more features for locating and inserting a video clip and usually makes the task easier.

3. If you want to insert a movie from a movie file on a local disk, a shared network location, or an Internet site, choose Insert, Movies And Sounds, Movie From File. Select the movie file in the Insert Movie dialog box that appears, and then click the OK button.

Chapter 33

4 If you selected a movie clip in animated .gif format, the animation will run automatically the entire time the slide is displayed in a slide show. If, however, you selected a movie in another format (such as .avi), PowerPoint will display a message box letting you choose when the movie will play. To have the movie play automatically when the slide is displayed in a slide show, click the Automatically button. To have the movie play only after you click the movie object, click the When Clicked button. PowerPoint will then add the video object to your slide.

5 Resize the video object, if necessary, by selecting it in the slide and dragging the sizing handles that are displayed around the object. To maintain the object's original proportions, drag one of the corner sizing handles. To change the original proportions, drag one of the sizing handles in the center of a border. To change the object's size without displacing the center of the object (that is, to resize it symmetrically about the center), press Ctrl while you drag a sizing handle. To move the video object, drag it to a new location.

For a movie clip that isn't in animated .gif format, you can modify the way the video plays during a slide show by right-clicking the video object in your slide and choosing a command from the shortcut menu, as follows:

- To adjust the volume or to change the video object display options, choose Edit Movie Object to open the Movie Options dialog box. Note that this dialog box will also indicate where the movie clip is stored. If it's stored within the presentation file, the dialog box will display the location "Contained In Presentation." If it's stored in a separate linked file, it will display the file path. In the latter case, if you are going to present your slide show on another computer, you'll need to take the linked file with you.

> **Tip** The easiest way to copy a presentation plus all linked files to a portable medium that you can bring to another computer is to use the new Package for CD feature described in "Using the Package For CD Feature," on page 932.

- To modify the way the video clip plays during a slide show, choose Custom Animation and use the controls in the Custom Animation task pane.

> For information on working with the Custom Animation task pane, see "Customizing Animation," on page 911.

- To control the action that takes place when you either click the video object or move the mouse pointer over it, choose Action Settings.
- To preview the video clip, choose Play Movie.

> For more information on slide shows, see Chapter 35, "Setting Up and Presenting the Slide Show."

Chapter 33

Inserting Sound Clips

Sound effects, such as music and voice recordings, can add another level of professionalism to your slide presentations. Music is an effective way to introduce or end a presentation and it gives your audience something to listen to as they enter and leave the presentation room. You could play a movie theme song as background music for several slides, or play a voice recording that contains advertising slogans to insert on a single slide, for example.

You can find sound files in several places—in the Clip Organizer, in the folder where you've chosen to store your audio files, on the Internet, or from a network folder. There are many sound file formats; two common ones are wave files (with the .wav filename extension) and MIDI files (with the .mid, .midi, or .rmi filename extension). After you add a sound to a slide, you'll see a Sound icon, as shown in Figure 33-3.

Sound object

Figure 33-3.   PowerPoint inserts a Sound object in your slide when you add a sound clip.

To add a sound clip to your slide show, perform the following steps:

1   Display the slide to which you want to add sound.

2   Use one of the following three methods to insert the sound clip:

- If you want to browse through the Clip Organizer for a sound clip, choose Insert, Movies And Sounds, Sound From Clip Organizer. PowerPoint will display the Clip Art task pane and will select Sounds in the Results Should Be drop-down list. You can use the Clip Art task pane to locate a sound clip stored on your computer or on the Office Online Web site.

- If you want to insert a sound clip from an existing sound file on a local disk, a shared network location, or an Internet site (if you haven't imported the file into the Clip Organizer), choose Insert, Movies And Sounds, Sound From File. The Insert Sound dialog box will appear. Select the sound file that you want, and then click the OK button.

■ If you have a microphone attached to your computer and you want to record your own sound clip and add it to the slide, choose Insert, Movies And Sound, Record Sound. PowerPoint will display the Record Sound dialog box. Use the controls in this dialog box to record your sound and then click the OK button.

> **Note** Some of the layouts you can apply to a slide (using the Slide Layout task pane) add a group of buttons to the slide for inserting various types of objects. These are known as *content* layouts or *text and content* layouts. If you've applied such a layout to your slide, you can insert a sound clip from the Clip Organizer by clicking the Insert Media Clip button and selecting a sound clip in the Media Clip dialog box (which displays both movie and sound clips). However, the Clip Art task pane (or the freestanding Clip Organizer program) provides more features for locating and inserting a sound clip and usually makes the task easier.

3 If you recorded the sound clip, the sound will play during a slide show only when you click the sound object. (You can modify this behavior using the Custom Animation task pane, as explained later in this section.) If, however, you inserted a sound clip from the Clip Organizer or from a sound file, PowerPoint will display a message box letting you choose when the sound clip will play. To have the clip play automatically when the slide is displayed in a slide show, click the Automatically button. To have the clip play only after you click the sound object, click the When Clicked button. Power-Point will then add to your slide a sound object displaying a speaker icon.

4 Resize the sound object, if you wish, by selecting it in the slide and dragging the sizing handles that are displayed around the object. To maintain the object's original proportions, drag one of the corner sizing handles. To change the original proportions, drag one of the sizing handles in the center of a border. To change the object's size without displacing the center of the object (that is, to resize it symmetrically about the center), press Ctrl while you drag a sizing handle. To move the sound object, drag it to a new location.

You can modify the way the sound clip plays during a slide show by right-clicking the sound object in your slide and choosing a command from the shortcut menu, as follows:

● To adjust the volume or change the sound object display options, choose Edit Sound Object to open the Sound Options dialog box. Note that this dialog box will also indicate where the clip is stored. If it's stored within the presentation file, the dialog box will display the location "Contained In Presentation." If it's stored in a separate linked file, it will display the file path. (PowerPoint normally stores a sound clip in a separate file if it's larger than 100 KB.) In the latter case, if you are going to present your slide show on another computer, you'll need to take the linked file with you.

> **Tip** The easiest way to copy a presentation plus all linked files to a portable medium that you can bring to another computer is to use the new Package for CD feature described in "Using the Package For CD Feature," on page 932.

- To modify the way the sound clip plays during a slide show, choose Custom Animation and use the controls in the Custom Animation task pane.

> For information on working with the Custom Animation task pane, see "Customizing Animation," on page 911.

- To control the action that takes place when you either click the sound object or move the mouse pointer over it, choose Action Settings.
- To preview the sound clip, choose Play Sound.

Playing CD Audio Tracks

PowerPoint can locate and play a particular track from a CD during your presentation. You can choose to have an entire track play or specify a segment of it.

To insert a CD audio selection, perform the following steps:

1 Choose Insert, Movies And Sounds, Play CD Audio Track. The Insert CD Audio dialog box will appear, as shown in Figure 33-4.

Figure 33-4. Set play options in the Insert CD Audio dialog box.

2 In the Insert CD Audio dialog box, enter a start and end track number in the Start At Track and End At Track boxes. If you want, enter a particular time within each track at which playing should start or stop. Use the other controls to adjust the playing volume and set the display options.

3 Click the OK button to insert the CD play specifications.

4 PowerPoint will now display a message box letting you choose when the CD will play. To have the CD play automatically when the slide is displayed in a slide show, click the Automatically button. To have the CD play only after you click the sound object, click the When Clicked button. PowerPoint will add to your slide a sound object that displays a CD icon.

Chapter 33

5 Resize the sound object, if you wish, by selecting it in the slide and dragging the sizing handles that are displayed around the object. To maintain the object's original proportions, drag one of the corner sizing handles. To change the original proportions, drag one of the sizing handles in the center of a border. To change the object's size without displacing the center of the object (that is, to resize it symmetrically about the center), press Ctrl while you drag a sizing handle. To move the sound object, drag it to a new location.

You can modify the way the CD tracks play during a slide show by right-clicking the sound object in your slide and choosing a command from the shortcut menu, as follows:

- To adjust the volume or change the sound object display options, choose Edit Sound Object to open the CD Audio Options dialog box.

- To modify the way the sound clip plays during a slide show, choose Custom Animation and use the controls in the Custom Animation task pane.

For information on working with the Custom Animation task pane, see "Customizing Animation," on page 911.

- To control the action that takes place when you either click the sound object or move the mouse pointer over it, choose Action Settings.

- To preview the selected CD tracks, choose Play Sound.

Chapter 33

Adding Special Effects to a Presentation

Applying Animation. 910
Applying Transitions 917
Creating Hyperlinks 918
Assigning Actions to Objects 920

The animation effects in Microsoft Office PowerPoint 2003 can help you focus your audience's attention on a particular slide or element on a slide. Animating a text item or an object means adding a special visual or sound effect to it. For example, you can have each slide title zoom in to the sound of a drum roll or each bullet point fly in to the sound of wind. Using PowerPoint's animation schemes, you can apply predesigned animation effects and transitions to selected slides or an entire slide show with one click. When you use transitions, you can have one slide appear to dissolve or wipe into another or choose from other filmlike transition effects.

In addition, you can create hyperlinks and action buttons that let you move to a specific slide, a custom show, a particular file, or a Web page during your presentation. By carefully balancing this combination of special effects—animation, sounds, transitions, and links to network and Web resources—you can fill your slide show with life and energy.

In this chapter you'll learn about

- Applying animation schemes
- Customizing animation by adding or changing individual animation effects
- Animating separate elements in a diagram or chart
- Creating an animation motion path
- Adding transitions to individual slides
- Creating hyperlinks
- Assigning an action to an object so that PowerPoint performs the specified action when the object is clicked

Applying Animation

When you animate the text and objects in your presentations, you can help focus your audience's attention on your major points and give them something interesting to look at in the process.

PowerPoint 2002 introduced more sophisticated tools for controlling how information appears on a slide, which are contained in animation schemes. Animation schemes apply a set of animation effects and transitions to an entire presentation. You no longer have to animate each bullet point or apply a transition between each slide in your presentation. You can select a preset scheme and simply click to apply it to selected slides or to your whole presentation. To get an idea of what is included in a predefined animation scheme, move your mouse pointer over the scheme name in the Slide Design task pane when it displays the animation schemes. A ScreenTip will appear, as shown in Figure 34-1, containing information about which elements on the slide are animated (the title or body) and whether a transition is included in the scheme.

Figure 34-1. A ScreenTip provides a description of the components of an animation scheme.

To apply an animation scheme to a slide show, perform the following steps:

1 Open the presentation you want to animate and display it in Normal view.

2 Choose Slide Show, Animation Schemes to open the Slide Design task pane and display the animation schemes in this task pane.

3 Apply an animation scheme, as follows:

   ■ To apply an animation scheme to one or more individual slides, select the slide thumbnails in the Slides tab in the pane at the left of the presentation window. (To select multiple slides, press Ctrl while you click each thumbnail.) Then, in the Apply To Selected Slides list in the Slide Design task pane, click the animation scheme you want to apply. The animations are organized in Subtle, Moderate, and Exciting categories.

■ To apply an animation scheme to all the slides in the presentation, click the scheme in the list and then click the Apply To All Slides button.

If the AutoPreview option is checked in the Slide Design task pane, PowerPoint will run the animation on the currently displayed slide when you first apply an animation effect or change an animation effect setting. To preview the animation scheme that has been applied to any slide, display that slide and click the Play button at the bottom of the Slide Design task pane.

Customizing Animation

To customize an animation scheme that you have applied, display the slide in Normal view and choose Slide Show, Custom Animation. You'll see the Custom Animation task pane, presenting animation options, as shown in Figure 34-2.

Figure 34-2. You can use the Custom Animation task pane to customize an animation scheme applied to a slide.

The large list in the task pane lists each animation effect that has been applied to a slide element (for example, to a paragraph of text, a picture, a chart, or a Microsoft Office diagram). If you hold the mouse pointer over an item in the list, you'll see a ScreenTip that indicates when the effect starts, the name of the effect, and a description of the slide element to which the effect has been applied.

You can use the animation effect list to set the order in which the animation effects take place. For example, you might want to first have the title move onto the slide to let the viewers know what the subject is, then display a piece of clip art to plant a visual image in viewers' minds, **911** and finally show a bulleted list to flesh out the image with text. Effects are listed in the order in which they occur, from top to bottom in the list. To change the order of an effect in this list, use the mouse to drag it up or down in the list. Or click an effect to select it and then use the up arrow button or down arrow button at the bottom of the list (these buttons are labeled Re-Order). The numbers displayed in the effect list, as well as on the slide, indicate the order of the animation effects.

You can customize a particular animation effect by clicking it to select it in the effect list and then using the other controls in the Custom Animation task pane, as follows:

- To replace the effect with a different effect, click the Change button and choose the effect you want from one of the submenus on the drop-down menu that appears. The commands on these submenus are described in more detail later in this section.

- To remove the effect from the slide element, click the Remove button.

- To specify how and when the effect takes place, select an item in the Start drop-down list. To have the effect run automatically, select With Previous (the effect will run simultaneously with the previous effect) or After Previous (the effect will run after the previous effect). If you select With Previous or After Previous for the first animation in a slide, the animation will run automatically when the slide is first shown. If you select On Click, when it's time to run the effect, PowerPoint will pause until you click the slide.

- For certain effects, you can select a setting in the Property drop-down list to customize the effect in some way. The list will be labeled according to the property that it sets. For example, with the Checkerboard effect the list is labeled Direction and allows you to select the direction in which the checkerboard effect moves (down or across the element).

- To adjust the speed of the animation, select an item in the Speed drop-down list.

- To set a variety of options for the selected animation effect, click the down arrow and choose a command from the drop-down menu, shown here:

Choosing Effect Options opens a dialog box (labeled according to the animation effect—for example, Checkerboard), where you can enhance the effect (for instance, add sound), fine-tune the effect's timing, and control the way the animation is applied to a group of objects (for instance, the group of lower-level paragraphs under an upper-level paragraph or the separate bars in a bar chart). In the next section you'll learn more about using the Effect Options command to enhance an animation effect that is applied to a diagram or chart. Choosing the Timing command opens the Timing tab of the same dialog box that is opened by the Effect Options command.

> **Tip** To preview all animations assigned to the current slide, click the Play button at the bottom of the Custom Animation task pane. To run an actual slide show, starting with the current slide, click the Slide Show button.

You can also use the Custom Animation task pane to add a new animation effect to an element on the current slide—for instance, to a text paragraph, a picture, or a chart. You can add an effect to an element that has not yet been animated or you can add a new effect to an element that already has one or more effects (a single element can exhibit *several* animation effects that take place at different times). You can use this technique to customize the animation in a slide to which you've assigned an animation scheme (as discussed in the previous section) or to manually animate a slide that doesn't have an animation scheme. To add a new animation effect, perform the following steps:

1 In the slide, select the element you want to animate.

2 In the Custom Animation task pane, click the Add Effect button and then choose an animation effect from the submenus on the drop-down menu that appears, shown here:

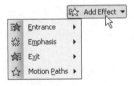

(When you select an element in the slide rather than an animation effect in the Custom Animation task pane, the Add Effect button replaces the Change button.)

- Choose from the Entrance submenu to select an animation effect that occurs as the item appears on the slide.

- Choose from the Emphasis submenu to select an animation effect that occurs after the item appears on the slide.

- Choose from the Exit submenu to select an animation effect that occurs as the item is removed from view on the slide.

■ Choose from the Motion Paths submenu to specify the exact route the element will take as it moves through its animation sequence. These commands are discussed later in the chapter.

3 Customize the newly added animation effect, if desired, following the instructions given previously in this section.

Animating Diagrams and Charts

If you have added an Office diagram (such as an organization chart or Venn diagram) or a Microsoft Graph chart to a slide, you can apply an animation effect to the object following the instructions given in the previous section. You can also add an interesting enhancement to the animation effect that causes PowerPoint to animate each part of the diagram or chart separately. For example, if a slide contains a bar chart, you can have PowerPoint run an animation that is applied to one bar at a time, rather than simply animating the display of the entire chart as a unit.

For information on adding an Office diagram or a Graph chart to a slide, see "Adding Graphics," on page 898.

To animate the individual elements of an Office diagram or Graph chart, perform the following steps:

1 Select the diagram or chart and apply an animation effect as explained in the previous section. Leave the Custom Animation task pane open.

2 In the animation effect list in the Custom Animation task pane, select the animation that you applied, click the down arrow, and choose Effect Options from the drop-down menu.

3 In the dialog box that PowerPoint displays (which is labeled according to the name of the effect—for example, Checkerboard), click the Diagram Animation or the Chart Animation tab.

4 In the Group Diagram or Group Chart drop-down list, select the way you want PowerPoint to animate the individual components of the diagram or chart. The available options depend on the type of the object and the particular animation effect that is applied. For example, with a Graph Chart and the Box animation effect, you can select As One Object, By Series, By Category, By Element In Series, or By Element In Category.

Creating Motion Paths

One of the new features that was introduced in PowerPoint version 2002 gives you the ability to draw the motion path that you want an object to follow during an animation. Creating a custom motion path is useful when you're creating several custom animation effects and you need to bring in another element that must navigate among the pieces you've already placed on the slide. You can use a predefined motion path or you can create a custom motion path by using the mouse to draw the path on the slide.

Chapter 34

Adding Special Effects to a Presentation

To add a predefined motion path, perform the following steps:

1 Display the slide you want to add a motion path to.

2 Choose Slide Show, Custom Animation to open the Custom Animation task pane, if necessary.

3 If you want to modify an existing animation effect, in the Custom Animation task pane select the effect in the animation effect list and click the Change button. If you want to create a new animation effect, select the element in the slide that you want to animate and click the Add Effect button in the Custom Animation task pane. In either case, a drop-down menu of animation effects will appear.

4 From the Motion Paths submenu on the drop-down menu, choose one of the predefined paths listed or choose More Motion Paths to apply one of PowerPoint's additional predefined motion paths. Figure 34-3 shows a slide containing a title that follows the Diagonally Down Right predefined motion path.

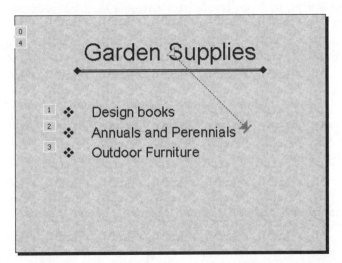

Figure 34-3. The predefined motion path applied to the title in this slide is indicated by a dotted line, with an arrow marking the end of the path.

Inside Out

Hide an object after animation

When you create a motion path for text or an object, typically you want it to move off the slide and disappear after it follows its path. To do so, you must either draw a custom path and drag the line off the slide or apply an effect option that makes the text or object appear to exit. To apply the effect option, in the Custom Animation task pane select the animation effect in the list, click the arrow next to the effect name, and then choose Effect Options from the drop-down menu to open the Effect Options dialog box. Click the Effect tab, select Hide After Animation in the After Animation drop-down list, and then click the OK button.

Chapter 34

PowerPoint also makes it easy for you to draw your own motion path for an object. To create a custom motion path, follow the preceding procedure, but in the Custom Animation task pane, click the Change or Add Effect button, choose Motion Paths, Draw Custom Path to open the submenu, and then choose a command from the submenu as follows:

- Choose Line to draw a straight path. Drag to draw the path. Press the Shift key while dragging the pointer to create perfectly horizontal or vertical lines.

- Choose Curve to draw a smoothly curved path. Click where you want the path to start, move the pointer and click at each point along the path where you want to add another curved segment. Double-click or press Esc to end drawing.

- Choose Freeform to draw a path that contains both curved and straight segments. To draw a curved segment, drag the pointer. To draw a straight segment, move the pointer without holding down the mouse button and then click the end point. Double-click or press Esc to end drawing.

- Choose Scribble to draw a curved path that looks like it has been drawn with a pen. Drag to draw the path.

Tip   To gain more control over mouse movements when drawing shapes, you can adjust the tracking speed of your mouse in Microsoft Windows Control Panel to make it move more slowly.

Whether you have added a predefined motion path or have drawn one yourself, you will see an outline of the path on your slide in Normal view when the Custom Animation task pane is open, as shown in Figure 34-4.

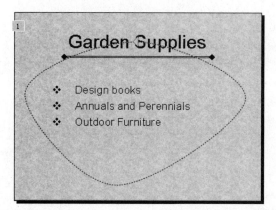

Figure 34-4.   The custom motion path shown here moves around the other elements on the slide.

To edit a custom-drawn path, you can right-click it and then choose from the options on the shortcut menu. If you choose Edit Points from the shortcut menu, you can change the shape of the path by dragging the small black squares that appear along the path, which are called *edit points*, as shown here:

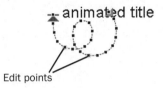

You can move the entire animation path by dragging it to a new location on the slide.

Applying Transitions

The purpose of a transition is to add visual interest as you move from one slide to the next. If you choose an animation scheme for your presentation, your slide show might already have transitions. (As mentioned previously in the chapter, some animation schemes include transitions in addition to animation effects.) However, you might wish to fine-tune the look of your show by changing the default transition between one or more slides, or you might want to add transitions to a presentation that doesn't already have them. The best way to do this is in Normal view, where you can select one or more slides using the Slides tab and then select transition effects using the Slide Transition task pane.

To add or change transitions in a presentation, follow these steps:

1   Choose View, Normal, if it's not already selected.

2   To apply a transition to selected slides, select those slides in the Slides tab. (To select multiple slides, press Ctrl while you click each one.) To apply a transition to all slides, you can select any slide or slides—you don't need to select all of them.

3   Choose Slide Show, Slide Transition to open the Slide Transition task pane, shown in Figure 34-5.

Figure 34-5. The Slide Transition task pane includes options for adding and customizing slide transitions.

4 Select a transition in the Apply To Selected Slides list. PowerPoint will assign that transition to just the selected slide(s); if you want to assign it to *all* slides in the presentation, you must then click the Apply To All Slides button.

5 If you want to customize the transition, you can use the other options in the Slide Transition task pane to change the transition speed, to add sound, or to control the way the slides advance during a slide show.

> **Note** If the AutoPreview option is checked in the Slide Transition task pane, whenever you add or change the transition, or modify a transition option, PowerPoint automatically runs the transition on the slide in Normal view. You can run the transition this way at any time by clicking the Play button. You can also preview the transition by running an actual slide show, starting with the current slide, by clicking the Slide Show button.

You can apply different transitions to different slides or groups of slides, so you may want to select groups of similar slides and assign each group a transition type. The transition effect appears when the slide is first opened, although if you add a similar exit animation effect, it can mimic the transition that introduces the slide.

Creating Hyperlinks

Hyperlinks can provide connections between a slide and other slides, other PowerPoint presentations, documents created in other Office programs, and Web pages.

Hyperlinks can be either text, which is underlined in a color you specify, or a graphic object, such as a picture or a chart. You can add action settings for hyperlinks so that a sound plays or highlighting occurs when you click or move your pointer over the hyperlink. By default, PowerPoint creates a hyperlink every time you type an e-mail address or URL (Uniform Resource Locator) on a slide.

To create a hyperlink, perform the following steps:

1 Select the text or object to which you want to assign a hyperlink (or just place the insertion point where you want to insert new hyperlink text).

2 Choose Insert, Hyperlink, or click the Insert Hyperlink button on the Standard toolbar to open the Insert Hyperlink dialog box.

3 Select the target location or enter its address into the Address text box.

4 If you're assigning the hyperlink to text, you can edit the text (or enter new text) in the Text To Display text box. (If you're linking an object, the Text To Display box is not available.)

5 You can provide custom ScreenTip text, which will be displayed when you hold the mouse pointer over the hyperlink in a slide show (or in a browser if you publish your presentation as a Web page). To do this, click the ScreenTip button and enter your text into the Set Hyperlink ScreenTip dialog box, shown here:

> **Note** If you don't assign custom ScreenTip text, the ScreenTip will simply display the hyperlink's target address.

The link between the destination file and the hyperlink can be broken in several ways. For example, it will be broken if you move a target file, if the address (URL) of a target Web page changes, or if the location of a shared folder changes. Always click each link in Slide Show view to test it before you present your show. Make sure that an Internet link opens correctly in your browser. (A hyperlink isn't active in Normal view, but when you run your presentation in Slide Show view, you can navigate to the target location by clicking it.)

> For much more detailed information on using the Insert Hyperlink dialog box, see "Adding and Using Hyperlinks," on page 580.

Assigning Actions to Objects

You can assign an *action* to a block of text or to a graphic object so that when you click the text or object during a slide show, PowerPoint will perform the specified action. This action can be one of the following: "hyperlink" to a target location, run a program, run a macro, or play a sound. Although you can assign an action to any text or graphic object in a slide, PowerPoint provides a type of graphic object known as an *action button* that's specifically designed for carrying out an action. You can use one of a set a predefined action buttons (which have images indicating typical actions) or you can insert a blank action button and then add custom text to it.

Action buttons, as well as actions assigned to other objects, are especially useful for creating slide shows that users run themselves—for example, in a trade-show booth or kiosk. Action buttons let users interact easily with a presentation.

To create an action button or to assign an action to an existing object in a slide, perform the following steps:

1 In Normal view, display the slide in which you want to assign an action.

2 Do one of the following:

    ■ To create an action button, choose Slide Show, Action Buttons and then choose a particular button from the submenu, shown here:

    Then place the mouse pointer at the position on your slide where you want to display the button and drag to mark the button dimensions. When you release the mouse button, PowerPoint will display the Action Settings dialog box.

    ■ If you want to assign an action to an existing block of text or graphic object, select the text or object and choose Slide Show, Action Settings. PowerPoint will display the Action Settings dialog box.

3 Define the action or actions in the Action Settings dialog box, as follows:

■ To define an action that occurs when you click the text or object, use the Mouse Click tab, shown here:

■ To define an action that occurs when you move the mouse pointer over the text or object, use the Mouse Over tab, which is almost identical to the Mouse Click tab.

If you wish, you can define both a mouse click action and a mouse over action. Also, for either a mouse click or a mouse over action, you can have PowerPoint play a sound *in addition* to performing another action. The Run Macro action will be available only if you have defined one or more macros in the presentation.

For information on macros, see "Recording and Running Macros," on page 224.

Note The Object Action option will be available only if you selected a movie or sound clip prior to opening the Action Settings dialog box. In fact, this is the only action option (other than None) that you can assign to a movie or sound clip.

4 If you chose the blank ("custom") action button in step 2, you can now add text to it. (You can actually add text to any type of action button.) To add text, right-click the button, choose Add Text from the shortcut menu, and type the text on the button. When you finish typing the text, click the slide outside the button.

Chapter 34

Setting Up and Presenting the Slide Show

Picking a Presentation Medium 923
Preparing an Electronic
Presentation 926
Giving an Electronic Presentation 933

Printing Slides, Notes Pages,
and Handouts 936
Publishing Your Presentation
on the Web 938

After you've created a slide show that makes your points as clearly as possible, you must decide on the medium that you'll use to present your slides. You can deliver your presentation on-screen, using a computer and a projector, or over the Web. You can also transform your slides into overhead transparencies, 35-mm slides, or printed handouts. You should then rehearse your presentation so that you are comfortable with the content, flow, and timing of your material.

If you travel and you want to run your slide show from another computer, just use the new Package for CD feature to copy one or more presentations to a CD or to a folder on another medium, optionally including a PowerPoint viewer. Then you or any other presenter can run the slide show from another computer, even if it doesn't have PowerPoint installed on it.

This chapter discusses how you can fine-tune your presentation before you run your slide show, how to actually run a presentation, how to create notes and handouts to accompany it, and how to publish your presentation on the Web.

In this chapter, you'll learn about

- Choosing the presentation medium you'll use
- Preparing and running an electronic slide show
- Creating hard copies of slides, note pages, and handouts
- Publishing a slide show on the Web

PowerPoint provides several different ways to display your slide show. You can deliver an electronic slide show, typically presented from a notebook computer connected to a projector; a presentation of overhead transparencies or 35-mm slides projected on a large screen; a Web-based presentation of slides saved in HTML; or a live presentation broadcast over the Web.

If you choose an electronic presentation, you can set up your slide show in three ways:

- To be presented full screen by an individual—the most common method. With this method, you'll have complete control of the slide show from beginning to end. You can skip slides, stop the presentation, add meeting minutes, and so on.

- To be presented in a window along with navigation controls—designed for presentations that you want to distribute to colleagues or send out over a network.

- To be presented at an automated kiosk—a method that creates a self-running presentation suitable for a demonstration at a kiosk or trade show booth.

In addition, you can control which slides are included in the final presentation, how narration and animation are used, and how the slides advance.

To pick the show type, complete the following steps:

1 Choose Slide Show, Set Up Show. You'll see the following dialog box:

2 Select an option in the Show Type area to specify the show type—Presented By A Speaker (Full Screen), Browsed By An Individual (Window), or Browsed At A Kiosk (Full Screen).

3 Select an option in the Show Slides area to specify which slides you want included in the show. You can include all the slides (the default), a range of slides, or a custom slide show if you've created one. (For more information about custom shows, see "Creating a Custom Show," on page 930.)

4 Check any of the options you want in the Show Options area. These options control the way the slide show is run. If you selected the Presented By A Speaker (Full Screen) option in step 2, you can also select a different default color for the pen that is used for annotating slides during a show. (You'll be able to change the pen color during a show.)

5   Under Advance Slides, specify whether you want to advance the slides manually or by using timings if they're present. (You create slide timings by using the Rehearsal toolbar, as you'll learn in "Rehearsing the Show," on page 926.)

6   If you have two monitors attached to your computer, you can check the Show Presenter View option to have PowerPoint display the Slide Show view on a monitor that's visible to your audience while it displays the Presenter view of the slide show on your personal monitor. The Presenter view provides additional features for controlling a presentation; for instance, you can see thumbnail images of all slides in the show, easily navigate to a particular slide, or view your speaker notes. After you check Show Presenter View, in the Display Slide Show On drop-down list, select the monitor you want to use to display the Slide Show view of the presentation.

7   In the Performance area, you can check an option to use hardware graphics acceleration if it's available and to change the graphics resolution used for the slide show. Click the Tips button to get help on the options in this area.

8   When you're finished setting up the show, click the OK button. To see how your choices have affected the presentation, choose Slide Show, View Show, or press F5.

Using Overheads

If you have an inkjet or laser printer, you can load the printer's paper tray with overhead transparencies made especially for such printers. Before you print your slides on overheads, you must check the page setup. Choose File, Page Setup to open the Page Setup dialog box, shown here:

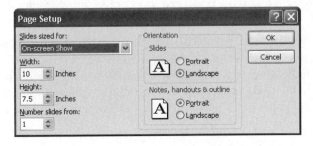

Use the options here to change to Overhead as the medium for which the slides are sized, and adjust the dimensions of the printed page to fit your overheads, as well as specify the orientation of the slides and other pages.

You can print your slides in grayscale, black and white, or color on transparencies, just as if they were paper. When you're ready to print, choose File, Print. To print your presentation in color on transparencies, you must choose a color printer from the Name drop-down list in the Printer section of the Print dialog box. You'll produce a set of high-quality transparencies that you can project on an overhead projector. However, if you need higher resolution and richer color reproduction than your printer provides, you can send your presentation file to a service bureau to have digital color overheads made.

Ordering 35-mm Slides

When your slide show includes technical images that require high-quality image resolution and contrast, your solution is to project 35-mm slides onto a large screen. Make sure that the room in which you're going to use the slide projector is darkened as much as possible. For high-quality image resolution, have a service bureau turn the presentation files into professional 35-mm slides for you. Before you do this, contact the service bureau, and ask if they have any special instructions for preparing your files. You can often send your files electronically and get your presentation materials back via overnight delivery.

Preparing an Electronic Presentation

A professional-looking electronic presentation fills a computer screen with your slides and keeps the audience interested with various special effects such as animation, transitions, and timings. For a small audience, you can use a desktop or notebook computer. For a large audience, you'll need a larger monitor or projection technology such as an LCD (liquid crystal display) projector that connects directly to your computer, as well as a non-glare projection screen.

Rehearsing the Show

Rehearsals are the backbone of any professional production, whether it's a Broadway play or a company slide show. Rehearsing your presentation is important so that you know what to say and when to say it, as well as to make sure that you don't run over or under your allotted time. You don't want to have to improvise if you run short or race through your material if you run long. Even worse, if you run over your time limit at a busy conference, you could be asked to leave the podium whether you're finished or not.

You can add a *timing* to some or all the slides in a presentation so that during a slide show, PowerPoint will automatically advance to the next slide after the specified time expires. (You can also manually move to the next slide before the time elapses.) Adding timings to your slides can help keep you on track when you present your slide show.

You can add timings to your slides by having PowerPoint automatically measure the length of time it requires you to display each slide while you rehearse your presentation. To do this, follow these steps:

1 If you haven't already done so, use the Set Up Show dialog box to set up your slide show, as explained in "Picking a Presentation Medium," on page 923.

2 Choose Slide Show, Rehearse Timings. When the full-screen version of your first slide appears on screen, rehearse exactly what you'll tell your audience about this slide, using your notes and moving through any animation effects you've applied. The Rehearsal toolbar, shown here, counts the seconds that the slide remains on screen.

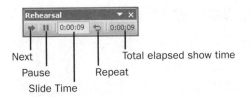

Next
Pause
Slide Time
Repeat
Total elapsed show time

> **Tip** Your audience's attention can wander if you spend too much time on a slide. If you intend to spend more than two or three minutes on the topic covered on one slide, make two or three slides for this subject. On the other hand, if a slide takes only a few seconds to discuss, it's probably too elementary and could be combined with another slide.

To move to the next element on your slide (a paragraph or graphic object that has an animation effect that is triggered by a mouse click) or to the next slide, click the Next button on the Rehearsal toolbar to advance the slides manually. If you move to the next slide, PowerPoint resets the Slide Time counter in the center of the toolbar, which measures the time spent on the current slide.

To pause a slide and temporarily stop both time counters, click the Pause button on the Rehearsal toolbar. When you want to continue, click the Pause button again.

To start over with a slide, click the Repeat button.

3 To stop rehearsing and return to Normal view, press Esc or right-click on the screen and choose End Show from the shortcut menu. PowerPoint will then display a message box that indicates the total elapsed time for the slide show and asks if you want to save the timings.

4 If you want to save the recorded timings, click the Yes button in the message box. If you want to discard the timings (perhaps because you want to run the rehearsal again), click the No button. If you click Yes, PowerPoint will save the recorded timing for each slide that you viewed during the rehearsal. It will also open the slides in Slide Sorter view and display the recorded timing beneath each viewed slide, as shown in Figure 35-1.

When you subsequently run a slide show, PowerPoint will automatically advance each timed slide after the time period elapses. If you want to remove the timing from one or more slides—so that they won't advance automatically—or if you want to manually adjust the timings, use the Slide Transition task pane as explained in the next section.

Chapter 35

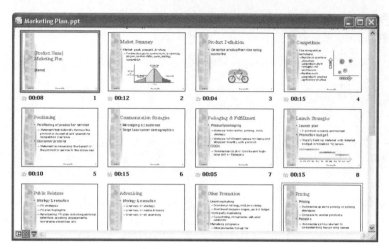

Figure 35-1. You can see the rehearsal timings in Slide Sorter view.

Setting Timings Manually

As an alternative to using the Rehearse Timings command described previously, you can use the Slide Transition task pane to add timings to one or more slides manually so that these slides will advance automatically during a slide show after an interval that you specify. This allows you to set precise target times for presenting each slide, rather than going by the actual amount of time each slide took during a rehearsal. You can also use the Slide Transition task pane to adjust or remove timings added by the Rehearse Timings command.

To set slide timings manually, perform the following steps:

1 In Normal view, display the slide you want to set timings for.

> **Note** You can also set timings simultaneously for a group of slides by using the Slides tab to select all of them. Remember that to select multiple slides, you must press Ctrl while you click each slide thumbnail.

2 Choose Slide Show, Slide Transition. The Slide Transition task pane will appear.

3 If you want to add a timing to the slide, check the Automatically After option in the Advance Slide area of the task pane and enter or modify the timing period in the adjoining text box, in the format *hh:mm:ss* (or use the arrows in the list box to set the time).

> **Note** If you previously viewed the slide when you ran the Rehearse Timings command, the Automatically After option will already be checked and the measured time will appear in the text box.

If you want to remove the timing from the slide, so that it will no longer advance automatically, clear the Automatically After option.

Check the On Mouse Click option if you want to be able to manually move to the next slide by clicking the current slide. If you check both the Automatically After and On Mouse Click options, you'll be able to click the slide before the automatic advance time expires and advance immediately to the next slide.

4   Repeat the above steps for each slide in your show for which you want to add or modify a timing.

Recording Narration

If you want to include narration during your slide show, a feature typically used in presentations that are self-running or Web-based, you can easily do this. With PowerPoint, you can add voice narration to a slide show so that you can prepare a final presentation in advance, complete with recorded material in your own voice.

To record a voice narration, you'll need a sound card, a microphone, and a set of speakers.

Complete these steps:

1   Choose Slide Show, Record Narration. The Record Narration dialog box will appear, showing the amount of free disk space and the number of minutes you can record, as shown here:

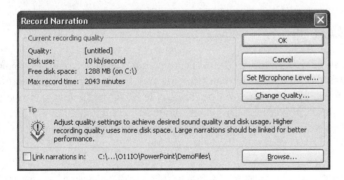

2   Click the Set Microphone Level button to calibrate your microphone.

3   Click the Change Quality button and use the options in the Sound Selection dialog box to select the format and attributes used for storing the recorded sound.

4   To begin recording, click the OK button in the Record Narration dialog box.

5   Record voice content for each slide in your presentation, clicking to move from one slide to the next. PowerPoint records the narration with timings for each slide.

6   If you want to stop the narration for any reason, right-click anywhere in the slide, and then choose Pause Narration from the shortcut menu. When you're ready to resume, right-click and then choose Resume Narration.

7 When you complete or close the slide show, PowerPoint will display a message box asking whether to save the slide timings along with your narration. To save the timings, click the Save button. To save the narration only, click the Don't Save button. If you want to synchronize your narration with each slide it accompanies, you must click the Save button. Your presentation will then open in Slide Sorter view, and a moving star icon will appear in the lower-left corner of each slide that you viewed (along with the slide's timing, if you saved timings), indicating the presence of a voice narration.

If you open a slide with a narration in Normal view, you'll notice a sound icon in the slide's lower-right corner, representing the narration. When you run the slide show, the narration will play automatically (although you can use the Custom Animation task pane, described in Chapter 34, to have the narration attached to a particular slide play only after the user clicks the slide).

> **Tip**   You can run the slide show without playing the narration by choosing Slide Show, Set Up Show and then checking the Show Without Narration option.

If you saved the timings in step 7, when you run the slide show, each slide will advance automatically after the recorded time expires. If you want to change this behavior, use the Slide Transition task pane as explained in "Setting Timings Manually," on page 928.

> For information on recording sound clips and adding them to individual slides, see "Inserting Sound Clips," on page 905.

Creating a Custom Show

The Custom Shows command on the Slide Show menu lets you create a short list of alternate slide shows based on the slides in your presentation. For example, in a presentation for sales reps, you might want to drop a few slides that are irrelevant to them, such as slides presenting your production staff's editorial policies. After you create a custom show, you can then specify it when you're configuring your show's presentation options in the Set Up Show dialog box.

> The Set Up Show dialog box is described in "Picking a Presentation Medium," on page 923.

To create a custom show:

1 Open the presentation you want to select slides from, and choose Slide Show, Custom Shows. The Custom Shows dialog box will appear, as seen here, listing your current collection of custom shows (if any).

Setting Up and Presenting the Slide Show

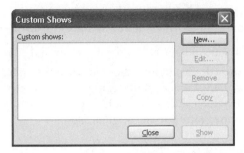

To define a new custom show, click the New button to display the Define Custom Show dialog box, shown here:

Type a name for your custom show in the Slide Show Name text box. To specify each slide you want to include in the custom show, select it in the Slides In Presentation list and click the Add button to copy it to the Slides In Custom Show list. (To add several slides in a single step, select them all before clicking Add.) Click the OK button when you're finished.

2 To edit, remove, copy, or show one of your custom shows, click the appropriate button in the Custom Shows dialog box. Click the Close button when you're finished.

Hiding Slides

You can put information you want to reveal only to a certain audience or only at a certain time on a hidden slide. To hide a slide, select the slide on the Slides tab in Normal view, and choose Slide Show, Hide Slide. The slide will appear on the Slides tab with a strikethrough on its slide number, as shown here:

Chapter 35

When a hidden slide is selected, you can unhide it by choose Slide Show, Hide Slide again, to deselect the option. To reveal a hidden slide when you run a slide show, do one of the following:

● From the slide that precedes the hidden slide, press H to unveil the hidden slide.

● In the slide that logically precedes the hidden slide (for example, in the slide that asks the question you answer with the hidden one), create an action button or other type of hyperlink that displays the hidden slide. (You could also add an action button or hyperlink to the hidden slide to return to the original slide.)

Using the Package for CD Feature

If you want to take your presentation on the road and run a slide show on other computers, you can manually copy the presentation file to a CD or other portable medium, but you'll face two possible problems. First, if the presentation is linked to external files (such as movie and sound clip files), you'll have to find out what those files are and copy them to the CD. Also, if the file path of a linked file on the CD differs from its original file path, you'll need to manually relink the file (for example, reinsert a movie clip). Second, if the computer on which you want to run the slide show doesn't have PowerPoint installed, you'll be in trouble.

The solution to both of these problems is to use the new Package for CD feature (which replaces the Pack and Go feature in previous PowerPoint versions) to copy your presentation to a CD or other portable medium. You can have Package for CD copy all linked files (automatically relinking them to the presentation if necessary) and include a complete PowerPoint viewer program that you can use to run a slide show on a computer that doesn't have PowerPoint itself installed.

To use the Package for CD feature, perform the following steps:

1 Open the presentation you want to package.

2 Choose File, Package For CD to display the Package For CD dialog box, shown here:

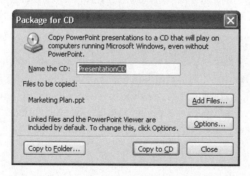

3 In the Package For CD dialog box, you can customize the packaging of your presentation by performing any of the following actions:

■ To change the name of the destination CD or folder on another medium, edit the contents of the Name The CD box.

Chapter 35

- By default, only the active presentation will be packed. To include other presentations, click the Add Files button.

- To choose whether to include the PowerPoint viewer, linked files, or embedded TrueType fonts, or to add password protection to the packed presentation(s), click the Options button.

4 Start the copy process by doing one of the following:

- If you have a CD recorder on your computer and want to copy the files to a CD, insert a recordable CD into the recorder and click the Copy To CD button.

- If you want to copy the files to a folder on a local disk, network disk, or portable medium other than a CD, click the Copy To Folder button and in the Copy To Folder dialog box, specify a name and location for the folder and click the OK button. PowerPoint will *create* a folder that has the name and location you specify. (You can't have PowerPoint use an existing folder.)

5 Click the Close button in the Package For CD dialog box.

If you packaged your presentation to a CD and AutoRun is enabled on the computer you're using to run your slide show, the PowerPoint viewer will run automatically when you insert the CD. Otherwise, you'll need to manually start the viewer by running the *Pptview.exe* program on the CD or in the folder you created on another medium, and then select the file that contains the presentation you want to show.

Giving an Electronic Presentation

To launch your presentation on the big screen, use one of the following methods:

- From Windows Explorer, right-click the PowerPoint presentation file, and choose Show from the shortcut menu. During the presentation, your slides appear in Slide Show view. When you finish the show, you'll be returned to Windows Explorer.

- Within PowerPoint, open your show in Normal view and display the slide that you want to show first. To start the slide show, choose View, Slide Show or choose Slide Show, View Show. Alternatively, you can press F5 or click the Slide Show button at the bottom left of the PowerPoint window.

- If you are running the slide show from a CD or folder prepared by the Package for CD feature, see the instructions on running the show at the end of the previous section.

Whichever method you use to start your slide show, the first slide will appear on the screen. You'll talk about your first slide, and then, if your show is automatically timed, the slide will disappear from the screen and the next slide will immediately appear, using the transition effect you've specified, if any. If your show doesn't have timings, you can advance to the next slide by pressing Enter, Spacebar, or the Right Arrow key, or by clicking the slide. To return to the previous slide, you can press the Left Arrow key. To move to a specific slide, you can type the slide number and then press Enter. To end the show, press Esc.

Note You can advance a slide by clicking it only if the On Mouse Click option is checked for that slide in the Slide Transition task pane, described in "Setting Timings Manually," on page 928. If this option isn't checked, you'll need to use one of the other navigation options discussed in this section.

By default, when you display a slide the mouse pointer is initially hidden. When you first move the mouse, however, PowerPoint displays both the pointer and a small slide show toolbar in the lower left corner of the screen, shown here:

Show previous slide   Show next slide

Display Pointer Options menu   Display Navigation menu

If you stop moving the mouse for four seconds, the pointer and toolbar will again be hidden. This describes the default, or "automatic," pointer and toolbar behavior. To have the pointer and toolbar be either shown all the time or hidden all the time, click the toolbar button for displaying the Pointer Options menu and then choose Arrow Options, Visible or choose Arrow Options, Hidden.

The other commands on the Pointer Options menu are discussed in the next section.

To navigate through your slides or to perform other tasks during a slide show, you can click the slide show toolbar button that displays the Navigation menu, shown here, and choose an appropriate command, as follows:

- To navigate to another slide, choose the Next, Previous, or Last Viewed command, or choose a specific slide from the Go To Slide submenu.
- To switch to a custom show, if you've created one, choose a command from the Custom Show submenu.

Custom shows are explained in "Creating a Custom Show," on page 930.

- To temporarily display an all-black or all-white screen (the normal screen will be restored when you click the screen or press a key), to view or edit the speaker notes for the current slide, or to reduce the slide size so that you can access the Windows task bar to switch to another program, choose a command from the Screen submenu.

- To view a concise list of keyboard and mouse click shortcuts that you can use while you run a slide show, choose Help or press F1.

- If the current slide has a timing assigned to it, you can stop it from automatically advancing to the next slide by choosing Pause. To resume automatic advancing, choose this command again (it will be labeled Resume).

- To end the slide show, choose End Show.

> **Tip** As an alternative to using the slide show toolbar to display the Pointer Options or Navigation menu, you can right-click the screen to display the shortcut menu, which includes all the commands from both of these menus. (The Pointer Options menu commands all appear on the Pointer Options submenu.)

Annotating Slides

You can use the mouse or a pen input device to annotate a slide during a slide show. For example, you can use a pen tool to circle or underline an important point, to draw an arrow to emphasize an element, or to add lines to connect related items. Or, you can use a highlighter tool to highlight areas of the screen in yellow. To use a pen or the highlighter, perform the following steps:

1   Click the button on the slide show toolbar that displays the Pointer Options menu, shown here:

2   To use a pen, choose Ballpoint Pen or Felt Tip Pen. To use a yellow highlighter, choose Highlighter. To change the ink color for a pen, choose a new color from the Ink Color submenu. (The highlighter is always yellow.)

3   Draw on the slide by dragging.

4 To remove a particular annotation, choose Eraser and then drag across the annotation. To remove all annotations from the slide, choose Erase All Ink On Slide or press E.

5 To go to the next slide, you'll need to press Enter, Spacebar, or the Right Arrow key (or use one of the other navigation methods discussed in the previous section), because clicking the slide will start an annotation rather than advancing the slide show.

6 If you want to stop drawing and restore the normal mouse pointer, choose Arrow (or one of the options on the Arrow Options submenu, discussed in the previous section), or press Ctrl+A.

7 When the slide show ends, PowerPoint will display a message box asking whether to keep your ink annotations. Click the Keep button to save them, or click the Discard button to let them go.

Printing Slides, Notes Pages, and Handouts

In many cases, you'll want to print your entire presentation, including your slides, outline, speaker notes, or audience handouts. Even when you're presenting your material electronically, you can print your notes and handouts to rehearse with, to pass around to colleagues for a critique, or to fill information gaps.

To print your presentation, follow these steps:

1 Open the presentation that you want to print, choose File, Page Setup, and specify the size of the output medium you're using and the desired printing orientation (portrait or landscape) for your slides and for your outline, notes, or handouts. Click the OK button.

2 Choose File, Print to display the Print dialog box, shown here:

3 In the Name drop-down list select the printer you want to use.

4   Specify the slides that you want to print in the Print range area. You can print your entire presentation, the current slide, selected slides, a custom show, or a set of slides that you specify by entering slide numbers.

5   In the Print What drop-down list, select the material to be printed. Your options are slides, handouts, notes, or the outline of your presentation.

6   Use the other controls to specify the number of copies, the printing color, options for handouts (if that's what you're printing), and other features.

7   To preview the printed result, showing all the options you have selected, click the Preview button to switch into Print Preview. To return to the Print dialog box, click the Print button on the Print Preview toolbar.

For more information on the Print Preview view, see "Using Print Preview to View a Presentation," on page 855.

8   Click the OK button to begin printing.

Creating Handouts

You can create handouts, which are printed pages containing one or more slides (up to nine) that you can distribute to your audience to help them follow along with your presentation. When you choose the layout that features three slides to a page, PowerPoint also prints lines on the right side of the page for your audience to take notes. The lined space is not visible until you view the handout in Print Preview, as shown in Figure 35-2.

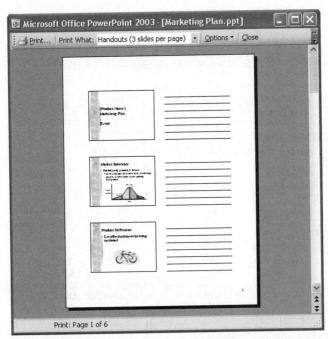

Figure 35-2.   Switch to Print Preview to see the lined notes area.

Chapter 35

Publishing Your Presentation on the Web

To widen the distribution of your presentation, you can save it as a Web page, which you can publish on a company intranet or on the Web. When you create the Web page, you can include any graphics, video, sound, animations, transitions, or hyperlinks that you have added to your slides. When your presentation is viewed in a browser, the browser will display each slide together with its notes. The browser will also display an outline of the slide show and navigation controls, making it easy to move through the different slides. PowerPoint makes giving a presentation on the Web as easy as giving one on your laptop in a conference room down the hall.

Tip   Create a workgroup collaboration Web site

Publishing a typical PowerPoint presentation essentially creates a slide show on the Web. As an alternative, you can use PowerPoint to create a more traditional Web site that is designed to enable a workgroup to collaborate on a project. To do this, create a presentation based on the Group Home Page presentation template. You'll find this template in the Presentations tab of the New Presentation dialog box. (For instructions on creating a new presentation using a template in the New Presentation dialog box, see "Other Ways to Start a Presentation from a Template," on page 863.) Once you've created and customized the presentation, publish it as a Web page using the instructions given in the following sections.

Previewing Your Presentation in a Browser

To see how the current presentation will look as a Web page, choose File, Web Page Preview. The slide show will open in your browser, as shown in Figure 35-3.

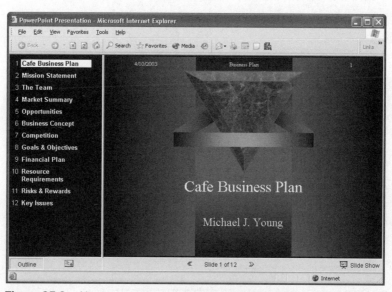

Figure 35-3.   You can preview a slide as a Web page.

Web Page Preview might give you some ideas on how to improve your presentation for a Web audience. To edit your slide show, close the browser window and switch back to PowerPoint. Make any changes to your slides before you save your presentation as a Web page.

Saving Your Presentation as a Web Page

You can save your presentation as a Web page in one of two ways. First, you can use the Save As dialog box to quickly convert the current presentation to a Web page format and save the page file (or files) to disk, using a default set of publishing options. Second, you can use the Publish As Web Page dialog box to select from a large number of publishing options and create a separate copy of the current presentation as a Web page.

To use the Save As dialog box to quickly convert a presentation to a Web page, perform the following steps:

1 Open the presentation you want to make ready for the Web.

2 Choose File, Save As Web Page. The Save As dialog box will appear, as shown here:

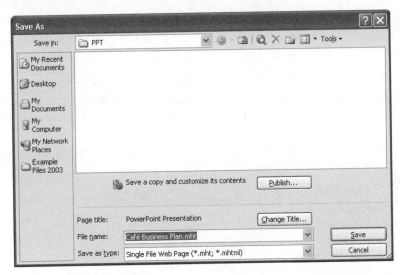

3 In the Save As dialog box, select the folder in which you want to save the Web page, and enter a filename in the File Name text box (or accept the default name). You should omit the filename extension because PowerPoint will add an appropriate extension in the next step.

4 Select a Web page format in the Save As Type drop-down list, as follows:

■ To save the entire presentation in a single Web page file, select Single File Web Page (*.mht; *.mhtml). Choosing this option makes it easier to publish or move your Web presentation.

■ To save the presentation in a conventional Web page, select Web Page (*.htm; *.html). With this option, PowerPoint will create a single main Web page that you open to view the presentation, plus a collection of subsidiary Web page files and supplemental data files (for instance, files storing the graphics that appear in the slides). It will store the subsidiary and supplemental files in a subfolder that is assigned a name based on the filename of the Web page (for instance, if the Web page is named *MarketingPlan.htm*, the folder will be named MarketingPlan_files). If you copy the resulting Web page to a server, you'll have to copy this folder along with it.

5   To modify the Web page title, which will appear in the title bar of the browser used to view the page, click the Change Title button.

6   Click the Save button in the Save As dialog box. PowerPoint will save the current contents of the presentation in the selected Web format, renaming the open presentation to indicate the new format. (For instance, if you save *MarketingPlan.ppt* as a single file Web page, the new presentation name you'll see on the PowerPoint title bar will be *MarketingPlan.mht*.)

7   If you want to publish your Web page on your company's intranet or on the Web, you'll need to copy the file to the Web server. If in step 4 you selected the conventional Web page format [Web Page (*.htm; *.html)] rather than the single-file format [Single File Web Page (*.mht; *.mhtml)], you'll also need to copy the subfolder containing the additional files. For instructions on transferring your file(s) to the Web server, confer with your network administrator, webmaster, or Web hosting company.

To use the Publish As Web Page dialog box to create a separate copy of a presentation as a Web page, and to fine-tune the Web page features, perform the following steps:

1   Open the presentation you want to publish on the Web.

2   Choose File, Save As Web Page to display the Save As dialog box with the Web publishing controls. (You can see how the Save As dialog box appears under step 2 of the previous instructions.)

3   In the Save As dialog box, click the Publish button to display the Publish As Web Page dialog box, shown here:

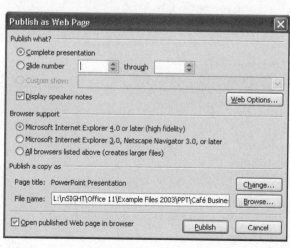

> **Note** Don't bother to select a folder, enter a filename, or select a format in the Save As dialog box, because if you've previously used the Publish As Web Page dialog box, it will open with the settings you formerly entered there, rather than those you entered in the Save As dialog box.

4 Select the options you want in the Publish As Web Page dialog box.

PowerPoint will customize the Web page according to the Browser Support option you select so that the page doesn't include any features that aren't supported by the specified browser versions. To select the folder in which you want to store the Web page, and to choose the Web page format (Single File Web Page or Web Page), click the Browse button. For an explanation of the two Web page formats, see step 4 in the preceding list of instructions.

To select further options that affect the Web page that PowerPoint will create, click the Web Options button and enter your choices in the tabs of the Web Options dialog box, shown here, and then click the OK button to return to the Publish As Web Page dialog box.

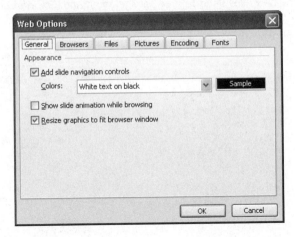

5 Click the Publish button in the Publish As Web Page dialog box. PowerPoint will immediately create your Web page and, if you checked the Open Published Web Page In Browser option in the Publish As Web Page dialog box, it will display the page in your default browser.

PowerPoint will save a *copy* of the current presentation as a Web page, but will leave the original presentation format open in PowerPoint so you can modify and save it separately. (For instance, if you publish MarketingPlan.ppt by using the Publish As Web Page dialog box, a separate Web page file will be created but the open presentation in PowerPoint will still be MarketingPlan.ppt.)

Chapter 35

> **Note** PowerPoint will save the options you enter in the Publish As Web Page and Web Options dialog boxes so that they will appear in these dialog boxes if you later publish your page again.

6 If you want to publish your Web page on your company's intranet or on the Web, see step 7 in the preceding list of instructions.

Other Ways to Disseminate Your Presentation

Another way to share a PowerPoint presentation you've created is to e-mail it to members of your workgroup for their reviews. To do this, you can use the File, Send To, Mail Recipient (For Review) command, or the File, Send To, Mail Recipient (As Attachment) command. For an explanation of these two commands, see "Sharing Word Documents Using E-Mail," on page 470.

You can also fax your document to one or more recipients using a fax service on the Internet by choosing the new File, Send To, Fax Service command. For information on this command, see "Using An Internet Fax Service," on page 1025.

Part 6

Outlook

36   Outlook Fundamentals   945

37   Working with Outlook Items and Folders   955

38   Managing Messages and Appointments   999

39   Managing Contacts, Tasks, and
     Other Types of Information   1047

40   Customizing Outlook   1077

Outlook Fundamentals

A Rundown on Outlook 945   Viewing Information in Outlook 947
Setting Up Outlook 946

A Rundown on Outlook

You can use Microsoft Office Outlook 2003 to organize and track your personal information, to communicate with other people in your organization or anywhere on the Internet, and to share information with members of your workgroup. The following are some of the important tasks you can perform with Outlook:

- Send, receive, store, and systematize e-mail messages.
- Maintain a personal calendar of appointments, events, and meetings.
- Schedule meetings with your coworkers.
- Store names, addresses, and other information about your business and personal contacts. Quickly communicate with any of your contacts.

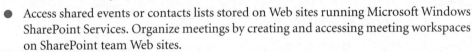

- Access shared events or contacts lists stored on Web sites running Microsoft Windows SharePoint Services. Organize meetings by creating and accessing meeting workspaces on SharePoint team Web sites.
- Use Instant Messaging to communicate in real time with friends and associates on the Internet.
- Create to-do lists and manage personal or group projects.
- Keep a journal of messages you send or receive, Microsoft Office 2003 documents you access, or other business or personal events.
- Jot down miscellaneous information on electronic "sticky notes."
- Explore sites on the Internet and your company's intranet.

For a description of the new features included in Outlook 2003, see "New Outlook Features," on page 14.

Setting Up Outlook

If Outlook requires information to set itself up or to create an account for sending and receiving e-mail message, the first time you run the program you'll see one or more dialog boxes prompting you for the required information. The specific dialog boxes and options that Outlook displays depend on whether you previously had Outlook or another e-mail program installed on your computer and on that program's configuration. The dialog boxes also vary according to the choices you make during the setup process. When Outlook has gathered the required configuration information, it will start running.

If Outlook already has all the information it requires, it will just begin running without displaying setup dialog boxes.

When Outlook runs for the first time, it inserts a welcome message into your Inbox. It also adds a convenient shortcut for running Outlook to the Quick Launch toolbar displayed on the Windows taskbar, as shown here:

Launch Microsoft Outlook

Inside Out

Customize your Outlook setup

During the initial setup Outlook uses any previous configuration settings on your computer. Or, if Outlook wasn't previously set up on your computer, it prompts you for only the minimum amount of information that's required to run the program and it makes a number of configuration choices for you—such as the type, name, and location of the file that stores your Outlook data. Presumably, it does this to get you started using the program as quickly as possible, although some of the choices Outlook makes might not be the ones you prefer. Later, however, you can add, remove, or modify Outlook accounts or data files. For information, see "Adding, Modifying, and Removing Outlook Accounts," on page 1080, and "Managing Outlook Data Files," on page 1088.

Outlook vs. Outlook Express

Don't confuse Outlook 2003 with Outlook Express. Outlook is a full-featured personal information manager and messaging client, and it's one of the major applications in the Microsoft Office System. Outlook Express, by contrast, is a specialized e-mail and news-reader program that's included with Internet Explorer.

Viewing Information in Outlook

Each type of information that Outlook manages is stored in a separate *Outlook folder*. Table 36-1 lists the type or types of information stored in each of the default Outlook folders that Outlook initially sets up. (As explained in Chapter 37, "Working with Outlook Items and Folders," you can create one or more additional folders for storing each information type.) A particular piece of information stored in an Outlook folder is known as an *item*—for example, an e-mail message stored in the Inbox folder, an appointment stored in the Calendar folder, or a task description stored in the Tasks folder.

> **Note** In this book the names of the default Outlook folders—Inbox, Calendar, Contacts, and so on—are capitalized. In contrast, the expressions used to describe a general type of folder—such as *a calendar folder, a contacts folder,* or *a tasks folder*—are not capitalized. The expression *a contacts folder*, for instance, describes any folder that contains contact descriptions—either the Contacts default folder or a custom contacts folder you've created.

Table 36-1. Information Stored in Default Outlook Folders

Default Outlook Folder	Type(s) of Outlook Items Stored in the Folder
Calendar	Appointments, all-day events, and meetings.
Contacts	Contact descriptions (names, addresses, phone numbers, and other information on your personal or business contacts) and distribution lists (each of which stores an entire set of contact descriptions).
Deleted Items	Outlook items and folders that you've removed, before they're permanently deleted.
Drafts	E-mail messages. The Drafts folder stores a message that you're writing before you send it.
Inbox	E-mail messages. The Inbox receives your incoming e-mail messages.
Journal	Records of events that have occurred, such as accessing an Office file, sending an e-mail message, or making a phone call.
Junk E-mail	Stores suspected junk e-mail messages.
Notes	Electronic "sticky notes," each of which stores text information.
Outbox	E-mail messages. The Outbox folder temporarily stores a message that you've sent before it's uploaded to the outgoing e-mail server and transmitted to the recipient.
Sent Items	E-mail messages. The Sent Items folder stores a copy of each message after it has been sent and uploaded to the outgoing e-mail server.
Tasks	Descriptions of tasks you need to perform or personal or group projects you're managing.

Table 36-1. **Information Stored in Default Outlook Folders**

Default Outlook Folder	Type(s) of Outlook Items Stored in the Folder
Search folders	Outlook initially creates three search folders: For Follow Up, Large Mail, and Unread Mail. Search folders don't actually store Outlook items. Rather, when you open one of them, it shows all the items that are in one of your e-mail folders and that meet specified criteria, such as messages that are unread. For more information on search folders, see "Using Search Folders to Categorize Your Messages," on page 1019.
Outlook Today	Displays an overview of the current information in other Outlook folders.

Figure 36-1 shows the Outlook window as it might appear when you first run the program. (In this figure the Outlook Today folder is open in Outlook. If you've customized Outlook, you might see a different folder when Outlook first starts.)

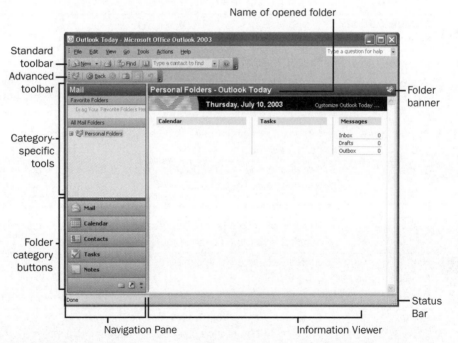

Figure 36-1. This figure shows the Outlook program window as it might appear when you first start Outlook.

To view and work with the items of information stored in a particular folder, you need to *open* that folder. Outlook will then display the folder's items in the Information Viewer of the Outlook window, and the Outlook menu commands, toolbar buttons, and the upper portion of the Navigation pane will change to provide the commands you need to manage the type of information kept in that folder.

> **Note** You can hide or display the Navigation pane by choosing View, Navigation Pane or by pressing Alt+F1.

The fastest way to open an Outlook folder is to use the Navigation pane. The Outlook 2003 Navigation pane is a radically modified version of the Outlook Bar found in previous Outlook versions. Rather than simply displaying groups of shortcuts that you click to open specific folders, the upper portion of the Navigation pane (labeled "Category-specific tools" in Figure 36-1) now displays tools for working with different types of information. The tools change according to the type of folder you have open. Also, opening a particular folder is now a two-step process:

1. In the lower portion of the Navigation pane, click the button corresponding to the category of the Outlook folder you want to open: Mail, Calendar, Contacts, Tasks, Notes, or Journal. For example, if you want to open a folder that stores e-mail messages, select that folder category by clicking the Mail button; and if you want to open a folder that stores contacts, click the Contacts button.

   Outlook will then open the folder belonging to the selected category that was most recently opened. For instance, if Outbox is the e-mail folder you had open most recently and you click the Mail button, Outlook will reopen the Outbox folder.

   Outlook provides six default folders for storing e-mail messages: Inbox, Drafts, Outbox, Sent Items, Junk E-mail, and Outlook Today. (Although you don't normally store an e-mail message in Outlook Today, it can be done. Therefore this folder is considered to be an e-mail folder.) In addition, Outlook provides three default search folders, listed in Table 36-1, which allow you to view items in other e-mail folders.

   Outlook, however, provides only a *single* default folder for storing each of the other types of information: calendar items, contacts, tasks, notes, and journal entries. So if you clicked the button for one of these categories, the folder you want will now be open (unless you've created or made available additional folders in that category).

> **Note** You can change the sizes of the upper portion of the Navigation pane (containing the category-specific tools) and the lower portion (containing the category buttons) by using the mouse to drag the border between the two areas. If not all the category buttons fit in the available space, Outlook will display the set of buttons that didn't fit as a single row of small buttons at the bottom of the Navigation pane.

2. The upper part of the Navigation pane will now list the names of the folders belonging to the selected category. Click the name of the folder you want to open.

If you clicked the Mail category button, you'll see both a Favorite Folders list of frequently used e-mail folders and a hierarchical list of all your e-mail folders, labeled All Mail Folders

Chapter 36

(see Figure 36-1). (All Mail Folders is a smaller version of the Folder List that contains just the e-mail folders and the Deleted Items folder. The Folder List is described in the next section.)

If you clicked one of the other category buttons, the folders belonging to that category will be displayed in a list labeled My Calendars, My Contacts, My Tasks, and so on. Also, if you've opened one or more SharePoint contacts lists, you'll see them when you click the Contacts button in a separate list titled Other Contacts. Likewise, if you've opened one or more SharePoint events lists, you'll see them when you click the Calendar button in a separate list titled Other Calendars.

Note If you clicked the Calendar category button and if you have more than one calendar folder, you'll be able to check two or more of the folder names to have Outlook display all of them, side-by-side.

For information on customizing the Favorite Folders list of e-mail folders or the lists of folders belonging to other categories (My Calendars, My Contacts, and so on), see "Customizing the Navigation Pane," on page 1077.

After you click a folder category button, you'll also see tools—in the upper portion of the Navigation pane—for working with that type of folder. For instance, if you clicked the Calendar button, you might see the Date Navigator for going to specific dates and a command for opening a shared calendar. Likewise, if you click the Contacts button, you might see options for changing or customizing the current folder view, as well as a command for opening shared contacts. The tools displayed for a particular folder vary according to the folder's option settings. These tools will be explained in the following chapters.

Tip View a folder in a separate window

You can open an Outlook folder in a separate Outlook window, rather than closing the currently opened folder. To do this, right-click the name of the folder displayed in the upper portion of the Navigation pane. Then choose Open In New Window from the shortcut menu. The second window will be the same as the originally opened Outlook window. This technique allows you to have several folders opened at once and is especially useful if you want to view another folder without disturbing your view of the current folder. For instance, if you're reading your appointments for a day next week in the Calendar folder, you could view another folder without losing your place by opening it in a separate window (switching folders in the current Outlook window would move the calendar back to today's date).

Chapter 37 explains the general techniques for viewing and working with the Outlook items contained in the opened Outlook folder. Chapter 38, "Managing Messages and Appointments," and Chapter 39, "Managing Contacts, Tasks, and Other Types of Information," then describe the methods for working with the items in specific Outlook folders, namely Inbox (and other e-mail folders), Calendar, Contacts, Tasks, Journal, and Notes.

NEW FEATURE! Using Other Methods to Open Folders

The following are additional ways to open folders in Outlook:

- **Using the Folder List** The Folder List displays *all* your Outlook folders in a single, hierarchical list (see Figure 36-2). The advantage of using the Folder List is that you can readily locate and open *any* Outlook folder in a single step (rather than having to first click a category button and then click a specific folder). To display this list in the upper portion of the Navigation pane, click the Folder List category button in the lower portion of the Navigation pane.

Notes | Configure Buttons
Journal | Shortcuts
Folder List

Figure 36-2. When the Folder List is displayed in the Navigation pane, it replaces the category-specific tools that are normally shown.

You use the Folder List just like the list in the left pane of Microsoft Windows Explorer. To expand or contract a branch, click the square button displaying the plus (+) or minus (−) symbol; to open a folder, click the folder name.

If your Inbox, Sent Items, or Deleted Items folder contains one or more unread messages, the Folder List indicates the presence of these messages by displaying the folder name in bold and it shows the number of unread messages in parentheses following the folder name. Likewise, if your Drafts, Outbox, or Junk E-mail folder contains one or more messages—read or unread—the Folder List indicates the presence of the messages by displaying the folder name in bold and it shows the total number of messages in square brackets following the folder name. Also, if a search folder displays one or more messages, the Folder List displays the folder name in bold and indicates the total number of messages in square brackets following the search folder name.

> **Note** As you can see in Figure 36-2, Outlook folders—like file folders—are arranged in a hierarchy of folders and subfolders. Outlook Today (which is labeled by default as "Personal Folders" if you store your Outlook data on a local hard disk) is at the top of the hierarchy and the other Outlook folders fall within it. (Therefore, one way to open Outlook Today is to click the folder at the hierarchy root.) As explained in Chapter 37, when you create a new Outlook folder, you can make it a subfolder of any other Outlook folder.

- **Using shortcuts** You can click the Shortcuts category button in the lower portion of the Navigation pane to display any shortcuts that have been defined for opening an Outlook folder (or a Web site, file, or file folder). Shortcuts are arranged in groups, as shown here. Simply click one to open the corresponding Outlook folder (or Web site, file, or file folder).

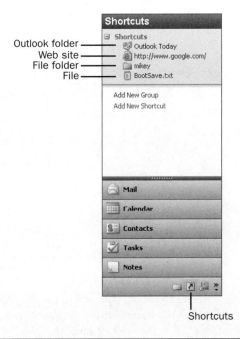

Shortcuts

> Outlook initially displays only a shortcut for opening the Outlook Update Web site. For instructions on creating other shortcuts and shortcut groups, see "Customizing the Navigation Pane," on page 1077.

- **Using the Go menu** You can choose one of the commands (except Folder) on the Go menu, shown here, or press the equivalent keystroke, to select a folder category and display the folders belonging to that category (as well as the category-specific tools) in the upper portion of the Navigation pane. Choosing one of these commands is equivalent to clicking a category button in the lower portion of the Navigation pane.

- **Using the Go To Folder dialog box**   Choose Go, Folder or press Ctrl+Y to open the Go To Folder dialog box, which displays all your Outlook folders, as shown here. In the dialog box, select the folder you want to open, using either the drop-down list of recently opened folders at the top or the hierarchical list of all your folders displayed below, and click the OK button.

- **Using the Advanced toolbar**   You can display the advanced toolbar, shown here, by choosing View, Toolbars, Advanced. It provides three buttons that you can use to quickly open specific folders:

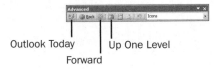

Outlook Today   Up One Level

Forward

- ■ To open Outlook Today, click the Outlook Today button.

- ■ To reopen the folder you previously had open, click the Back button.

- ■ After you've gone back one or more times, you can go forward again by clicking the Forward button.

- ■ You can open the next folder up in the hierarchy by clicking the Up One Level button. For example, if the Inbox folder is open, clicking Up One Level opens Outlook Today—because Outlook Today is the next folder up in the hierarchy of Outlook folders.

- ● **Using the keyboard**   To quickly open the Inbox, press Ctrl+Shift+I.

Working with Outlook Items and Folders

Working with Outlook Items 955
Working with Outlook Folders 991

Printing Outlook Information 994
Using Outlook Today to Get
an Overview 995

Working with Outlook Items

An individual piece of information stored in a Microsoft Office Outlook 2003 folder is known as an *item*—for example, an e-mail message stored in the Inbox, a contact description stored in the Contacts folder, or a record of an event stored in the Journal folder. For a summary of the different type or types of items that are stored in each of the default Outlook folders, see Table 36-1, on page 947.

The first step in working with a particular type of Outlook item is to open the folder that contains the items. To open a folder, you can use any of the techniques discussed in "Viewing Information in Outlook," on page 947. The following sections in this chapter explain how to work with the items in the currently opened folder in the following ways:

- Creating new items
- Editing items
- Moving and copying items
- Removing and archiving items
- Changing the folder view and sorting, filtering, and grouping items
- Finding items
- Organizing items

Creating New Items

The way you enter information into an Outlook folder is to create a new item. Although Outlook sometimes lets you create a new item right in the Information Viewer of the main Outlook window, you usually create an item by opening an Outlook *form*. A form is a separate window that displays a set of controls—text boxes, buttons, drop-down lists, check boxes, and so on—in which you enter each piece of information that's to be stored in the item, such as the recipient of an e-mail message, the name of a contact, or the subject of a task. Each of these pieces of information is known as a *field*.

To create a new Outlook item, complete the following steps:

1 Open the Outlook folder where you want to store the item.

> **Note** To create an e-mail message, open any e-mail folder. The default e-mail folders are Inbox, Drafts, Outbox, Sent Items, Junk E-mail, and Outlook Today. Or, open one of the e-mail search folders. The default search folders are For Follow Up, Large Mail, and Unread Mail.

New Form

2 Open a form for defining the new item using either of the following methods:

- To create the most common type of item stored in the open folder, click the New button on the Standard toolbar or press Ctrl+N. Table 37-1 shows the types of items that this command creates in each of the default Outlook folders.

- To create a specific type of item in a folder that manages several item types, choose the appropriate command from the Actions menu. For example, in the Calendar folder, you can create a new appointment, all-day event, meeting request, recurring appointment, or recurring meeting by choosing the corresponding command from the Actions menu:

Table 37-1. Types of Items Created by the New Command

Default Outlook Folder	Type of Item Created by the New Command
Inbox, Drafts, Outbox, Sent Items, Junk E-mail, Outlook Today, or one of the search folders (For Follow Up, Large Mail, and Unread Mail)	E-mail message
Calendar	Appointment
Contacts	Contact
Tasks	Task
Journal	Journal entry
Notes	Note

Outlook will then open a blank form for you to fill in. The form that Outlook displays is designed specifically for defining the type of item you're creating. Figures 37-1 to 37-3 show three examples of these forms.

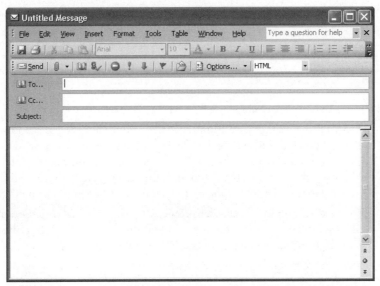

Figure 37-1. This is the form that Outlook displays for creating a new e-mail message (here, Microsoft Word is used as the Outlook e-mail editor).

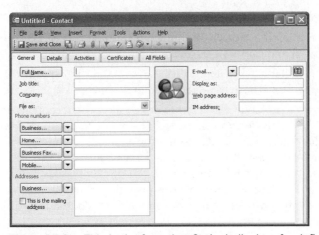

Figure 37-2. This is the form that Outlook displays for defining a new contact in the Contacts folder.

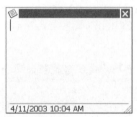

4/11/2003 10:04 AM

Figure 37-3. This is the form that Outlook displays for entering a new note into the Notes folder.

3   Enter the information for the item in the controls in the form.

A form provides toolbar buttons and menu commands to assist you in completing the form and formatting your text. For convenience, a form also provides general-purpose menu commands that are the same as menu commands found in the main Outlook window—for example, the commands on the File, New submenu for creating new Outlook items. (The Notes form provides only a few menu commands and no toolbars.)

The next section in this chapter provides some general information on entering or editing information in a form, and the following chapters describe the specific information that you enter in each type of Outlook item.

4   Close the form and save the item as follows:

■   For an e-mail message, meeting request, or assigned task, click the Send button to save the item and send it to the recipient. The item will be saved in your Outbox folder for sending later or it will be sent immediately (depending on your current option settings).

■   For a note, click the Close button in the form's upper-right corner. The item will be saved in the open notes folder.

■   For all other types of items, click the Save And Close button on the form's Standard toolbar. The item will be saved in the open folder.

■   For any item except a note, you can save the current contents of the form without closing the form by choosing File, Save or by pressing Ctrl+S. For any type of item except an e-mail message, the item will be saved in the open folder. An e-mail message will be saved in the Drafts folder. To close the form and discard the information you've entered, choose File, Close, click the Close button in the upper-right corner of the form, or press Esc or Alt+F4. (Outlook will warn you and let you save your changes if you want.) Outlook automatically saves the text you type into a note.

The next section explains how to reopen an item in a form so that you can view all of the item's information or edit that information.

> **Tip** **Use an item to create an item of a different type**
>
> You can use an existing item to quickly create a new item of a different type by dragging the existing item from the Information Viewer and dropping it on a Navigation pane shortcut for an Outlook folder of a different type. You can also drag it to the destination folder's name in the Folder List. (To display your shortcuts or the Folder List, click the Shortcuts or the Folder List button in the lower portion of the Navigation pane.) The new item will contain information from the existing item. For example, dragging an appointment from the Calendar folder and dropping it on a shortcut or the folder name for the Tasks folder will create a new task that contains the description and date (which becomes the task's due date) from the appointment. Dragging an e-mail message from the Inbox and dropping it on a shortcut or the folder name for the Contacts folder will create a new contact containing the name and e-mail address of the person who sent the message as well as the body of the message (which is stored in the contact item's large text box). And dragging an item from the Contacts folder to a shortcut or the folder name for the Inbox will create a new e-mail message addressed to the contact. (You can then fill in the subject and message text.)

An alternative way to create a new Outlook item, which you can use regardless of which folder is currently open, is to choose a command from the File, New submenu, or from the equivalent drop-down menu that appears when you click the down arrow on the New button on the Standard toolbar:

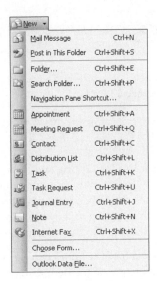

(The icon and ScreenTip text on the New button on the Standard toolbar change to match the open folder, for example "New Mail Message" or "New Contact.")

Or, you can press the equivalent shortcut key. The shortcut keys are displayed on the New drop-down menu, shown in the previous illustration, but note that to create a new e-mail message when an e-mail folder is *not* open, you need to press Ctrl+Shift+M. (The above figure shows the menu as it appears when the Inbox, or another e-mail folder, is opened. The menu indicates that you can create an e-mail message by pressing Ctrl+N because that's the shortcut key for creating the default item type for the currently open folder.)

> **Note** If you create an item using File, New, the New drop-down menu, or the equivalent keystroke, and a matching type of folder is *not* open, the item will be saved in the default folder for that type of item (Calendar, Contacts, Journal, Notes, or Tasks). For instance, if you create a new contact when the Calendar folder is open, it will be saved in your Contacts folder. If you've created several contacts folders and want to save a new contact in a specific one, you'll need to have that contacts folder open when you create the new item. (Exceptions: When you click the Send button in the form for an e-mail message, meeting request, or assigned task, the item will be saved in your Outbox folder or will be sent immediately. When you issue the Save command in the form for an e-mail message, the message will be saved in your Drafts folder.)

If the open folder appears in a table view (a view consisting of rows and columns), you can create a new item right in the Information Viewer of the main Outlook window by clicking in the top row, typing information in each column, and pressing Enter:

Create a new item by entering it into the top row —

> Views are discussed in "Changing the Way You View Items," on page 973.

> **Note** You can also open an empty form by double-clicking in the top row.

To add items to a particular folder in this way, the Allow In-Cell Editing and Show "New Item" Row options must be selected for the current view. To find these options, choose View, Arrange By, Current View, Customize Current View, click the Other Settings button, and look in the Column Headings And Rows area of the Other Settings dialog box. See the next section for a discussion on entering or editing item information in the Information Viewer.

Typically, however, the Information Viewer doesn't show all of the item's fields. If one or more fields you want to define aren't shown, you'll need to create the item using a form, as described previously in this section.

> Alternatively, if one or more fields that you want to define or view aren't shown in a table view, you can add those fields to the view, possibly eliminating the need to open items in a form. For instructions, see "Modifying Columns in a Table View," on page 977.

> **Tip** **Use an item to create an item of the same type**
>
> If you want to create a new item that's similar to an existing item of the same type (for example, if you want to create a new contact for a person in the same household), make a copy of the existing item (as explained later in the chapter) and then edit the copy.

Editing Items

With most views, you can directly edit an item in the Information Viewer in the main Outlook window without opening the item in a form, provided that the Allow In-Cell Editing option is checked for that view. (To access this option for a view, switch to that view, choose View, Arrange By, Current View, Customize Current View, click the Other Settings button, and look in the dialog box that appears, the title of which varies according to the view.) To edit an item, click in the field you want to enter or change, and type the new text:

Click in Full Name field to edit it

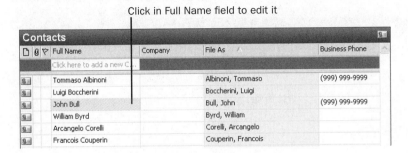

You can set the value of some fields by clicking in the field and selecting a value from a drop-down list:

And you can set the value of other fields (such as the completion status of a task) by checking a check box.

> Views are discussed in "Changing the Way You View Items," on page 973.

The Information Viewer, however, typically shows only a subset of an item's fields, and you can't edit some of those fields in the Information Viewer (such as the File As field of a contact). Also, some views don't allow you to edit any of the fields (such as a timeline or icons view).

To view or edit *any* field, you can open the item. When you open an item, Outlook displays it in the same form that's used to create that type of item (see Figure 37-4). You can open an item using one of the following methods:

- Double-click the item in the Information Viewer.
- Click the item to select it and press Ctrl+O or Enter.
- Right-click the item and choose Open from the shortcut menu.

Note You can open several items simultaneously by selecting all of them and then using either of the last two methods in the list above. To select several adjoining items, click the first and then click the last while pressing Shift. To select nonadjoining items, click the first and then click each additional one while pressing Ctrl. To select *all* items in the open folder, choose Edit, Select All or press Ctrl+A.

To close all open items, choose File, Close All Items from the main Outlook window.

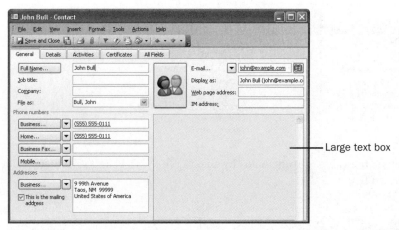

Large text box

Figure 37-4. This figure shows a contact opened for editing in the Contact form.

Tip   Use a form to browse items
Once you've opened an item in a form, you can open other items in the same Outlook folder without leaving the form. To open the previous or next item, click the Previous Item or Next Item button on the form's Standard toolbar, shown here, or press Ctrl+< or Ctrl+>.

Previous Item —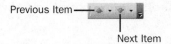

Next Item

Chapter 37

> **Tip** To open the first or last item in the folder, click the down arrow on the Previous Item or Next Item button and choose the First Item In Folder or Last Item In Folder command from the drop-down menu, as shown here:
>
>

The commands that the form provides for entering, editing, selecting, formatting, moving, copying, or finding text, as well as those for checking your spelling or undoing your actions, are similar to commands available in Word and other Microsoft Office applications. For detailed instructions, see the Outlook online help topic "Working with Text."

> **Tip** Enter a date using English
>
> You can enter a date or time into a form's date or time field (such as a task's due date or an appointment's start time) by typing a normal English expression into the text box, such as "one week from now" or "midnight." Entering "noon" or "midnight" is useful if you've never quite figured out whether these times are 12 A.M. or P.M.!

Most Outlook forms provide a large, unlabeled text box where you can enter free-form information—such as the body of an e-mail message, a description of an appointment, or comments about a contact (see Figure 37-4). When entering information in this text box, you can insert a file, another Outlook item, or a linked or embedded item as follows:

● To insert a file, choose File from the form's Insert menu or click the Insert File button on the form's Standard toolbar, and select the file in the Insert File dialog box. Click the Insert button to insert the file as an attachment to the item, or click the down arrow on this button to select an alternative way to insert the file:

Clicking the button, choosing Insert, or choosing Insert As Attachment causes Outlook to store a copy of the file within the item but to display it as an icon that you must double-click to view the copy. Choosing Insert As Text causes Outlook to insert and display all the text from the file in the text box. Choosing Insert As Hyperlink causes Outlook to insert just a hyperlink to the file without storing the contents of the file in the item.

> **Note** The Insert button in the Insert File dialog box for an e-mail message doesn't provide the Insert As Hyperlink command. And if you're using Word as your e-mail editor, the Insert button also omits the Insert As Attachment command (although simply clicking the Insert button or choosing Insert will insert the file as an attachment).

Inserting a file is a common way to send information with an e-mail message.

> **Note** An alternative way to insert a file as an attachment is to drag the file from a file folder that's displayed in Microsoft Windows and drop it in the large text box.

- To Insert an Outlook item, choose Item from the form's Insert menu and select the item in the Insert Item dialog box. In the Insert As area of the dialog box, you can choose to insert the file as text only, as an attachment, or as a shortcut. Inserting as text only adds the entire contents of the item. Inserting as an attachment stores a copy of the inserted item within the receiving item but displays the inserted item as an icon. Inserting as a shortcut causes Outlook to insert just a link to the inserted item. Alternatively, to insert the item as an attachment, you can drag the item from the Information Viewer in the main Outlook window and drop it in the large text box.

> **Note** If you're using Word as your e-mail editor, to insert an Outlook item into the body of an e-mail message, you need to click the down arrow on the Insert File button in the message header and choose Item from the drop-down menu. You can insert the item only as an attachment.

For example, you might attach an appointment to an e-mail message so that the recipient can add that appointment to his or her Calendar folder (by dragging it from the e-mail message to the Calendar folder).

> **Note** In a note, you can insert an Outlook item as text by dragging the item and dropping it in the note form.

> **Tip** Insert an item into an e-mail message quickly
> If you've selected an Outlook item in the Information Viewer or opened it in a form, you can create an e-mail message and insert that item as an attachment using a single command. Just choose Forward from the Actions menu in Outlook or in the form, or press Ctrl+F.
>
> Also, in the Calendar and Contacts folders, Outlook provides commands for attaching an item to an e-mail message using a generic format that can be read by some personal information managers in addition to Outlook. Namely, if you've selected an appointment or other item in the Calendar folder, you can choose Actions, Forward As iCalendar; and, if you've selected a contact in the Contacts folder, you can choose Actions, Forward As vCard.

- To insert a linked or embedded item, choose Object from the form's Insert menu and select the object and insertion options in the Insert Object dialog box. For details on linked and embedded items, see Chapter 7, "Exchanging Data in Office 2003."

Chapter 37

Tip   Include hyperlinks in your Outlook items

In the large text box of an Outlook form (including the body of a note), you can insert a hyperlink that opens an Internet site or sends an e-mail address by simply typing the URL. For a hyperlink target other than a Web site, be sure to type the full URL, including the protocol (such as *mailto:* or *ftp:*), as in this example:

mailto:someone@microsoft.com

Outlook will automatically convert your text to a blue, underlined hyperlink.

Alternatively, if you use Word as your e-mail editor, you can create a hyperlink by choosing Insert, Hyperlink, clicking the Insert Hyperlink button on the Standard toolbar, or pressing Ctrl+K. Adding hyperlinks in Word is discussed in "Adding and Using Hyperlinks," on page 580.

For instructions on closing the form and saving (or discarding) your changes, see step 4 of the procedure for creating a new item, on page 958. (But keep in mind that when you issue the Save command, the item will be saved back to its original folder, regardless of which folder is currently open.)

Tip   Save Outlook information to disk

You can save a copy of an Outlook item in a disk file. To do this, select the item in the Information Viewer or open it in a form, and choose Save As from the File menu in Outlook or in the form. Before saving the item, select the desired format from the Save As Type drop-down list in the Save As dialog box.

You can also save a copy of an item in a disk file with the Message Format (that is, as an *.msg* file) by dragging it from the Information Viewer and dropping it on a file folder or on the Windows Desktop. Opening such a file (for example, by double-clicking it) opens the saved copy of the Outlook item in a form, even if Outlook isn't currently running.

Keep in mind that a copy of an Outlook item stored in a disk file *isn't* linked to the original item and won't be updated if the original item is changed.

Also, you can export an entire Outlook folder to a disk file in a variety of different formats, and you can import data from a range of file types (such as a Microsoft Access database or another Outlook data file) to an Outlook folder. To import or export items, run the Import And Export Wizard by choosing File, Import And Export in Outlook.

Moving and Copying Items

You can move an Outlook item to a different folder, and you can copy an item to the same folder or to a different folder. With either operation the destination folder can be of the same type as the folder storing the original item or it can be of a different type. Copying or moving an item to a folder of a different type creates a new item in the destination folder; the new item will contain information from the original item.

Moving or copying items can be useful in a variety of situations. For example, you could organize the e-mail messages you've received by creating several new e-mail folders (perhaps named Business Messages, Personal Messages, and Mailing List Messages) and then moving messages to these folders from your Inbox. Also, you could make a copy of an item in the same folder as the original item (or in a different folder of the same type) to get a head start in creating a new item that will contain much of the same information (perhaps a contact who works for the same company as an existing contact). And, you could copy an item to a different type of folder to create a new item based on an existing one, as explained in the tip "Use an item to create an item of a different type," on page 959.

To move or copy an item, complete the following steps:

1 In the Outlook window, select the item or items you want to move or copy.

> **Note** To select several adjoining items, click the first and then click the last while pressing Shift. To select nonadjoining items, click the first and then click each additional one while pressing Ctrl. To select *all* items in the open folder, choose Select All from the Edit menu or press Ctrl+A.

2 Choose Edit, Move To Folder or Edit, Copy To Folder to move or copy the item. (To move the item, you can also press Ctrl+Shift+V.) This will display the Move Items or the Copy Items dialog box (see Figure 37-5).

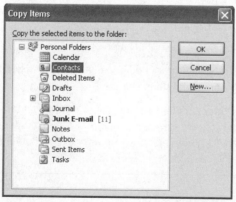

Figure 37-5. You can use the Copy Items dialog box to copy an item.

> **Note** An alternative way to display the Move Items dialog box is to click the Move To Folder button on the Standard toolbar and choose Move To Folder from the drop-down menu. (The Move To Folder button isn't available when you're viewing the Calendar.) Also, you can immediately move the selected item or items to one of the folders that you've recently moved or copied an item to, by choosing the folder name from this menu:
>
>

3 In the Move Items or Copy Items dialog box select the destination folder, or click the New button to create a new destination folder.

4 Click the OK button.

When you move or copy an item to a destination folder of a different type, the method just given uses a default method to move or copy. For example, if you copy an e-mail message from the Inbox to your Contacts folder, Outlook creates a new contact containing text from the e-mail message. (It copies the message sender's name to the contact's Full Name and File As fields; the sender's e-mail address to the contact's E-Mail field; and the body of the message to the contact form's large text box). As another example, if you use the Move Items dialog box to "move" a contact to your Tasks folder, Outlook creates a new task request that's addressed to the contact and leaves the original contact in place (thus, the "move" operation actually performs a copy).

To choose the exact way the item is transferred from the source folder to the destination folder, use the right mouse button to drag the item from the Information Viewer in the Outlook window, drop it on the name of the destination folder in the Folder List or in your Shortcuts list in the Navigation pane, and choose the transfer method you want from the shortcut menu that appears. (To display the Shortcuts list or the Folder List, click the Shortcuts button or the Folder List button in the lower portion of the Navigation pane.)

The following is the shortcut menu that Outlook displays when you right-drag an e-mail message from an e-mail folder to the Contacts folder:

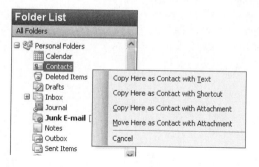

Note If you've opened an item in a form, you can move or copy it by choosing File, Move To Folder or File, Copy To Folder. These commands work just like the identically named commands on the Edit menu in the Outlook window, which are explained in this procedure.

Undo

Tip Undo moving or copying an item

Issuing the Undo command *immediately* after moving or copying an item reverses the move or copy operation. Either choose Edit, Undo Move (or Undo Copy), or click the Undo button on the Advanced toolbar.

Troubleshooting

Attached item not updated

You created an appointment in your Calendar folder, and you inserted an item from your Contacts folder into the appointment's large text box as an attachment, using one of the methods discussed in "Editing Items," on page 961, or in "Moving and Copying Items," on page 966. Your purpose was to provide ready access to information on the person with whom you have the appointment. However, when you updated the contact in your Contacts folder, the copy of that contact attached to your appointment wasn't updated.

Attaching an item creates a separate copy of that item, which isn't updated when the original item is changed. If you want to insert an item and have it updated when the original item changes, you should insert it as a *shortcut* rather than as an attachment. If you're using the Insert Item dialog box to insert the contact (as described in "Editing Items"), select the Shortcut option in the Insert As area. (A shortcut's icon is marked with a curved arrow.) If you're creating a new appointment by copying a contact to your Calendar folder, right-drag the contact, drop it on a shortcut for the Calendar folder or on the Calendar folder name in the Folder List, and choose Copy Here As Appointment With Shortcut, as explained in "Moving and Copying Items."

Removing and Archiving Items

Delete

You can remove one or more items from an Outlook folder by selecting the item or items in the Information Viewer of the Outlook window and then choosing Edit, Delete, clicking the Delete button on the Standard toolbar, or pressing Ctrl+D. If you've opened an item in a form, you can remove it by clicking the Delete button on the form's toolbar, choosing File, Delete, or pressing Ctrl+D (a particular form might not have all of these commands).

> **Note** To select several adjoining items, click the first and then click the last while pressing Shift. To select nonadjoining items, click the first and then click each additional one while pressing Ctrl. To select *all* items in the open folder, choose Edit, Select All or press Ctrl+A.

Inside Out

Delete key produces different results

If you've selected an entire item in the Information Viewer, you can remove it by pressing Delete. However, if you've selected only an individual field in an item (that is, the insertion point is within a field), the Delete key will remove only the character following the insertion point.

When you remove an item, it's not permanently deleted right away. Rather, it's initially moved to the Deleted Items folder. As long as an item is still in the Deleted Items folder, you can restore it to the folder that originally contained it by simply moving it back to that folder using any of the methods described in the previous section in this chapter.

If you want to permanently delete the item, remove it from the Deleted Items folder using any of the methods just described. You can also permanently delete *all* items in the Deleted Items folder by choosing Tools, Empty "Deleted Items" Folder. Or, you can have Outlook permanently delete all items in the Deleted Items folder each time you exit the program by choosing Tools, Options, clicking the Other tab in the Options dialog box, and checking Empty The Deleted Items Folder Upon Exiting. To see a message before an item is permanently deleted, click the Advanced Options button in the Other tab and make sure that the Warn Before Permanently Deleting Items option is checked.

Also, if you archive your Outlook folders, as discussed next, you can have Outlook permanently delete all items in the Deleted Items folder that are older than a specified age. This method is usually safer for permanently deleting items because it generally gives you a longer period of time in which you can recover removed items from the Deleted Items folder.

Archiving Items

You can clean up your Outlook folders by *archiving*. Archiving removes Outlook items either by moving them to a separate Outlook data file, from which you can later recover them, or by permanently deleting them. You can have Outlook archive automatically at specified intervals, or you can archive manually.

To have Outlook archive automatically, complete the following steps:

1 For each folder you want to archive, right-click the folder's name in the Navigation pane, choose Properties from the shortcut menu, click the AutoArchive tab (shown in Figure 37-6), and do one of the following:

   ■ To use Outlook's default AutoArchive settings, select the Archive Items In This Folder Using The Default Settings option. (You can change these default settings for all folders by clicking the Default Archive Settings button to display the AutoArchive dialog box, described in the next two steps.)

   ■ To override the default AutoArchive settings for the current folder, select Archive This Folder Using These Settings, and then select the specific AutoArchive options you want.

   This procedure enables archiving for the particular folder and tells Outlook how to do it. Click the OK button when you're finished.

> **Note** Because items in a Contacts folder don't normally become obsolete with time—as messages, appointments, and other items do—you can't have Outlook automatically archive your Contacts folder (its Properties dialog box doesn't have an AutoArchive tab). You can, however, manually archive this folder, as described later.

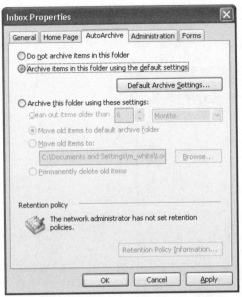

Figure 37-6. You can set up automatic archiving for a folder using the AutoArchive tab in the Properties dialog box.

2 Choose Tools, Options, click the Other tab in the Options dialog box, and click the AutoArchive button to display the AutoArchive dialog box. In this dialog box, check the Run AutoArchive Every option, and in the adjoining text box enter the desired frequency of automatic archiving in days. This will cause Outlook to begin automatically archiving at the specified frequency all folders for which you turned on archiving in step 1.

3 In the AutoArchive dialog box, choose any other automatic archiving options you want and click the OK button. Note that you can override the settings in the Default Folder Settings For Archiving area for a particular folder by selecting Archive This Folder Using These Settings in the AutoArchive tab in that folder's Properties dialog box, as explained in step 1.

To archive manually, complete the following steps:

1 Choose File, Archive to display the Archive dialog box (shown in Figure 37-7).

2 Do one of the following:

- To archive all folders for which archiving is enabled in the AutoArchive tab of the folder's Properties dialog box, using the settings made in that tab (as explained in step 1 of the previous procedure), select the Archive All Folders According To Their AutoArchive Settings option.

971

■ To archive a single folder, select Archive This Folder And All Subfolders and then select the folder and any other archiving options that you want to apply.

3 Click the OK button to start archiving.

Figure 37-7. The Archive dialog box lets you archive your Outlook folders manually.

Tip Preserve individual items

You can exempt an important item from being automatically archived by opening the item in a form, choosing Properties from the form's File menu, and checking Do Not AutoArchive This Item. Note, however, that if you perform a manual archiving, you can override this setting by checking Include Items With "Do Not AutoArchive" Checked in the Archive dialog box.

To recover an archived item, you can choose File, Open, Outlook Data File and select the Outlook data file where you stored the archived item (you specify this folder when you set up automatic archiving or perform a manual archive). Outlook will open the archive file and display its contents (together with the contents of your main data file) in the Folder List. You can then use the Folder List to open the folder containing the archived item and copy it back to its original folder.

For information on opening and working with Outlook data files, see "Managing Outlook Data Files," on page 1088.

Changing the Way You View Items

You can change the way you view Outlook items displayed in the Information Viewer of the main Outlook window in the following ways:

- Switching and customizing views
- Sorting, filtering, and grouping items
- Using the Reading pane

These techniques are discussed in the following three sections.

Switching and Customizing Views

You can work with an Outlook folder using a variety of different *views*, which vary—often radically—in the way the information is organized and in the amount of detail that's shown in the Information Viewer of the main Outlook window. For example, Figure 37-8 shows the Contacts folder in the Phone List view, which displays all contacts in a table, with each contact in a separate row and each contact field (such as Full Name, Company, File As, and so on) in a separate column. Figure 37-9 shows Contacts in the By Category view, which also displays the contacts in a table but groups them according to the contents of their Category fields. And Figure 37-10 shows the Contacts folder in the Address Cards view, which displays each contact in a business card format.

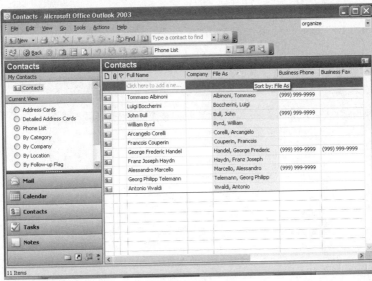

Figure 37-8. This figure shows the Contacts folder in the Phone List view.

Note You can assign each of your Outlook items one or more different categories, which you can use to group, filter, sort, or find items. The following chapters explain the details of assigning categories to different types of items. Sorting, filtering, and grouping items are covered in the next section of this chapter.

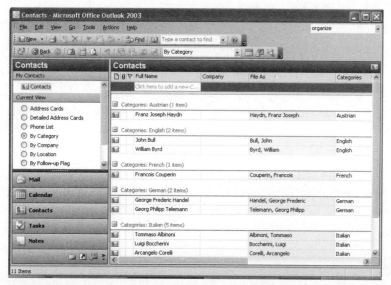

Figure 37-9. This figure shows the Contacts folder in the By Category view.

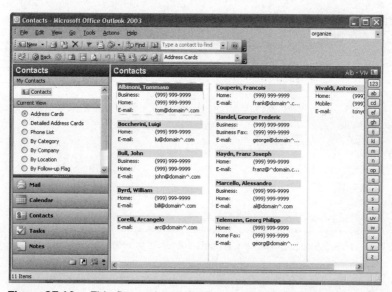

Figure 37-10. This figure shows the Contacts folder in the Address Cards view.

Each folder has available a set of default views that are appropriate for the type of information stored in that folder. To change the view of the open folder, simply select another item in the Current View drop-down list on the Advanced toolbar. (If the Advanced toolbar isn't visible, choose View, Toolbars, Advanced.) For example, the available views for the Contacts folder are shown here:

Alternatively, you can choose the view from the View, Arrange By, Current View submenu. Also, if the View, Arrange By, Show Views In Navigation Pane menu option is selected, you can select a view in the Current View list in the Navigation pane, as shown here:

For certain views, such as the Day/Week/Month view of the Calendar folder and the Message Timeline view of the Inbox folder, you can control the number of days that appear on the screen by choosing the Day, Week, or Month option from the View menu, or by clicking the Day, Week, or Month button on the Standard toolbar. Some views (such as the Day/Week/ Month view of the Calendar folder) also have a Work Week option.

You can modify any view by activating that view and then choosing View, Arrange By, Current View, Customize Current View to display the Customize View dialog box (the actual title of this dialog box includes the name of the active view—for example, Customize View: Phone List or Customize View: Address Cards). This dialog box contains a set of buttons you can click to change various features of the current view. Note that in certain views, some of these buttons are disabled because the corresponding features don't apply to that view. For example, if Day/Week/Month is the current view of the Calendar folder, the Group By, Sort, and Format Columns buttons are disabled. Also, the information that appears to the right of each button depends on the particular view that's active and the options that have been selected for that view. This information either gives the current settings or describes the types of settings you can apply by clicking the button. Figure 37-11 shows the Customize View dialog box as it appears when the Phone List view of the Contacts folder is active, using default settings.

> **Tip**   A quick way to display the Customize View dialog box is to right-click in a blank area within the Information Viewer of the Outlook window and choose Customize Current View from the shortcut menu.

Figure 37-11.   Displaying the Customize View dialog box is the first step in modifying the current view.

You can click the Other Settings button in the Customize View dialog box to change the fonts used in the view and to modify other features, which vary according to the current view. In some views—such as the Messages view of the Inbox folder or the Day/Week/Month view of the Calendar folder—you can click the Automatic Formatting button in the Customize View dialog box to apply distinguishing formatting to certain items. For example, in the Messages view of the Inbox folder, you could have the headings for all unread messages displayed in an italic green font. Or, in the Day/Week/Month view of the Calendar folder, you could have all meetings organized by your boss appear in red text to indicate their importance.

The features set by using the Fields button are discussed in the sidebar "Modifying Columns in a Table View," on this page, while those set by using the Group By, Sort, and Filter buttons are discussed in the next section of this chapter. The features set by clicking the new Format Columns button are summarized in Table 37-2.

 You can restore any of the settings that you've made by using the Customize View dialog box to their default values by clicking the new Reset Current View button.

Finally, you can choose View, Arrange By, Current View, Define Views to display the Custom View Organizer dialog box (shown in Figure 37-12), in which you can modify any of the views available for the current folder, restore any of these views to its default settings, rename a view, or create a new custom view.

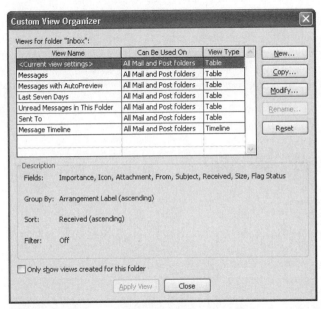

Figure 37-12. The Custom View Organizer dialog box allows you to work with any of the views available for the current folder.

Modifying Columns in a Table View

In many of the Outlook views, the information is arranged in a table consisting of rows and columns (for instance, the Messages view of the Inbox folder shown in Figure 36-1 on page 948 and the Phone List view of the Contacts folder shown in Figure 37-8). Each column displays the values of a given field of information. A *field* is an individual unit of information in an Outlook item—for example, the subject or received date of a message in the Inbox folder.

In a table view, you can modify the columns in a variety of ways. For example, you can change the width of a column by dragging the right border of the *column heading* (the button-like bar, containing a label, at the top of the column).

> **Note** The column headings won't appear if the folder items are currently displayed in the Outlook window using *multi-line layout* (the text belonging to one or more items spans more than a single line). To prevent Outlook from using multi-line layout, choose View, Arrange By, Current View, Customize Current View. Then click the Other Settings button, clear the Use Multi-Line Layout... option, and select the Always Use Single-Line Layout option.

You can adjust the width of a column to accommodate its contents by double-clicking the column heading's right border. You can move a column by dragging its heading to a new position in the column heading row. And you can remove a column by dragging the heading to any position on the screen outside the column heading row. (When the mouse pointer turns into an X, releasing the mouse button will remove the column.)

You can add, remove, or rearrange columns in a table view by choosing options in the Show Fields dialog box. To display this dialog box, choose View, Arrange By, Current View, Customize Current View. Alternatively, you can right-click in a blank area in the Information Viewer of the Outlook window and choose Customize Current View from the shortcut menu. Then click the Fields button in the Customize View dialog box (shown in Figure 37-11).

To modify a column from within the Information Viewer, right-click the column's heading to display the following shortcut menu:

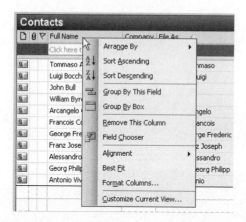

Then choose a command as described in Table 37-2.

Table 37-2. Modifying Columns Using the Shortcut Menu

To Modify the Column Like This	Do This on the Shortcut Menu
Delete the column	Choose Remove This Column.
Display a dialog box that lets you add a new column by simply dragging a field name from the dialog box to the desired position in the heading row	Choose Field Chooser.

Table 37-2. Modifying Columns Using the Shortcut Menu

To Modify the Column Like This	Do This on the Shortcut Menu
Apply left (the default), right, or centered alignment to the contents of the column	Choose a command from the Alignment sub-menu.
Make the column just wide enough to display the column contents	Choose Best Fit. This command has the same effect as double-clicking the right border of the column heading.
Change the format, label, width, or alignment of one or more columns in the table	Choose Format Columns and select options in the Format Columns dialog box. You can also display this dialog box by choosing View, Arrange By, Current View, Format Columns or by clicking the new Format Columns button in the Customize View dialog box.
Display the Customize View dialog box	Choose Customize Current View.

Sorting, Filtering, and Grouping Items in Folders

You can further refine the way information appears in a particular view of an Outlook folder by sorting, filtering, or grouping the items in the folder. You can assign different sorting, filtering, or grouping settings to each view, and the settings will stay with the view until you explicitly change them.

For a fast new method that you can use to sort or group items in an Outlook 2003 table view, see "Quickly Arranging Folder Items," on page 983.

Note You can sort, filter, or group items in any table view (that is, any view consisting of rows and columns with a row of column headings at the top). You can also perform one or more of these operations in certain other views. For example, in the Address Cards view of the Contacts folder, you can sort or filter items, and in the By Type view of the Journal folder, you can filter or group items. You can tell which operations are possible in a particular view by the buttons that are enabled in the Customize View dialog box. (These buttons are discussed next.)

To sort, filter, or group items in the current view, choose View, Arrange By, Current View, Customize Current View to display the Customize View dialog box (shown in Figure 37-11). Alternatively, you can display this dialog box by right-clicking anywhere in the heading row of a table view, or in a blank area of any type of view, and then choosing the Customize Current View command from the shortcut menu.

To sort the items in a folder, click the Sort button in the Customize View dialog box. This will display the Sort dialog box (shown in Figure 37-13), which lets you sort the items by the values of one or more fields, in either ascending or descending order. Alternatively, you can sort the items in a table view by the values in one of the columns by simply clicking the heading above that column. Each click of the heading toggles between an ascending and a descending sort. An arrow appears in the heading of a column currently used for sorting—an up arrow for an ascending sort or a down arrow for a descending sort. (If the column is too narrow, however, the arrow won't appear in the heading.) You can use several fields for sorting by clicking each heading while pressing Shift; Outlook will sort using the fields in the order you click them.

Figure 37-13. The Sort dialog box lets you sort the items in a folder.

When you open a folder, Outlook normally displays all items stored in that folder. However, you can click the Filter button in the Customize View dialog box to display the Filter dialog box (Figure 37-14), where you can set conditions to determine which items will appear. For example, you could display only those messages in the Inbox that contain the word *manuscript* in the message text, or only those messages that are marked as high importance. The criteria you can select are the same as those in the Advanced Find dialog box, which is discussed in "Finding Outlook Items," on page 986.

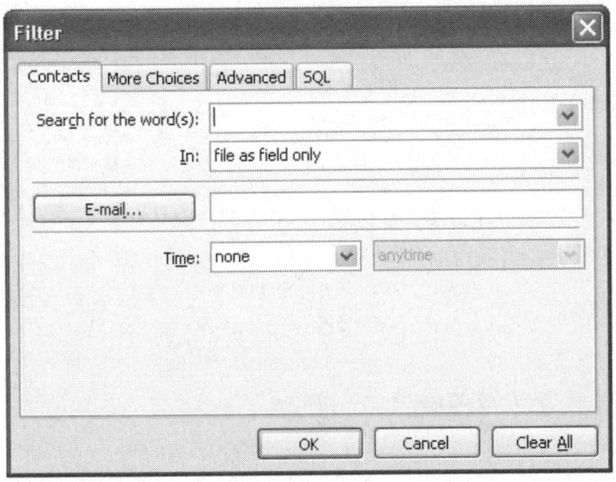

Chapter 37

Figure 37-14. The Filter dialog box lets you control the items that appear in a folder.

You can click the Group By button in the Customize View dialog box to display the Group By dialog box (Figure 37-15). In the Group By dialog box, first make sure that the Automatically Group According To Arrangement option is cleared. (Outlook checks this option when you use the new Arrange By submenu, discussed in the next section, rather than creating a custom grouping as explained here.) You can then use the Group By dialog box to group items by the values of one or more fields, rather than displaying the items in a simple list. For example, if you were to group the messages in your Inbox by the Importance field, Outlook would list all high-importance messages in one group, followed by all normal-importance messages in a second group, followed by all low-importance messages in a third group. You can define groups within groups, creating up to four levels of nested groups. For instance, in the previous example, within each importance group you could group the messages by their sensitivities. Figure 37-9 shows the Contacts folder grouped by the Category field (in this case, the grouping is part of the definition of the By Category view).

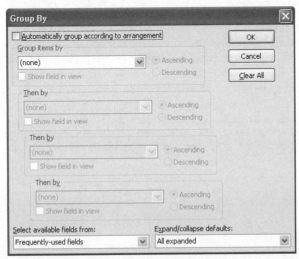

Figure 37-15. The Group By dialog box lets you group items by one or more fields.

⚙ Troubleshooting

Outlook items mysteriously disappear

You switched to a different view and some of the items in the Outlook folder disappeared.

When you apply a filter (or a sort or grouping), you're actually modifying the definition of the current view. The filter (or the sort or grouping) will stay with the view and will be reapplied whenever you switch back to that view. If you suspect that Outlook isn't displaying all of the items in the open folder, look for the words "Filter Applied" at the right end of the Folder Banner:

("Filter Applied" also appears at the left end of the Outlook status bar.)

To remove the filter, choose View, Arrange By, Current View, Customize Current View, click the Filter button, and click the Clear All button in the Filter dialog box (as shown in Figure 37-14). (Likewise, you can remove sorting and grouping by clicking the Clear All button in the Sort or Group By dialog box.)

Outlook provides the following two alternative ways to group items in a table view:

- You can group the items by the values in a column by right-clicking the column's heading and choosing Group By This Field from the shortcut menu.

Group By
Box

- You can choose Group By Box from this same shortcut menu (or click the Group By Box button on the Advanced toolbar) to display the Group By box at the top of the Information Viewer. (This box isn't labeled, but when it's empty it contains the message "Drag a column header here to group by that column.") Once this box appears, you can drag one or more column headings into the box to group the items by the associated field or fields. You can change the order of the groupings by dragging the field names within the Group By box. To remove a grouping, drag the field name outside the Group By box and, when the mouse pointer becomes a large X, release the mouse button.

When items are grouped, you can expand or collapse groups by clicking the + or – button at the top of the group, or by using the commands on the Expand/Collapse Groups submenu on the View menu.

> **Tip** Another way to display the Sort, Filter, or Group By dialog box is to right-click in a blank area in the Information Viewer in the Outlook window and choose Sort, Filter, or Group By from the shortcut menu.

You can use the Categories command on the Edit menu to assign categories to the selected item or items in the open Outlook folder. For example, you might assign some messages to the Business category and others to the Personal category. (As explained in Chapter 38, "Managing Messages and Appointments," and Chapter 39, "Managing Contacts, Tasks, and Other Types of Information," you can also assign a category to an item when you create or edit it in a form.) You can then sort, filter, or group the items based on their categories. You can also locate and display items that belong to a given category using the Advanced Find command, which is covered in "Using the Advanced Find Dialog Box," on page 988.

Quickly Arranging Folder Items

You can use the commands on the new View, Arrange By submenu to quickly sort or group Outlook items displayed in a table view, such as the Messages view of Inbox, the Active Appointments view of Calendar, or the Phone List view of Contacts. The commands on this submenu sort or group the items using a set of 13 standard categories—Date, Conversation, From, To, and so on—which are the same for all folders. When you choose one of these categories, Outlook uses the folder's most appropriate field to sort or group the items. For example, if you choose the Date category to sort e-mail messages in the Inbox, Outlook uses the Received field (the date each message was received).

To arrange items in the open folder, which must be displayed in a table view, perform the following steps:

1 Choose View, Arrange By to display the Arrange By submenu, shown on the next page. You can also display this submenu by right-clicking a heading and choosing Arrange By from the shortcut menu.

> **Note** If the folder items are currently displayed in the Outlook window using *multi-line layout* (the text belonging to one or more items spans more than a single line), Outlook will display a special bar at the top of the list, rather than displaying the usual row of headings. This bar displays the item that is currently selected on the Arrange By submenu (for example, "Arranged By: Date"). To open the Arrange By submenu, simply click (rather than double-click) the bar.

2 Do either of the following:

■ To sort the items, choose one of the 13 sorting categories from the top portion of the submenu (Date, Conversation, From, To, and so on) to specify the particular information that is to be used to sort the items. Make sure that the Show In Groups menu option is deselected.

■ To group the items, choose one of the 13 sorting categories and make sure that the Show In Groups menu option is selected.

> **Note** If you use the Sort or Group By dialog box (described in the previous section) to sort or group the items by a field that doesn't match one of the 13 standard sorting categories on the Arrange By submenu (for example, you sort contacts in the Phone List view using the File As field), Outlook will select the Custom option on this submenu. You can also choose the Custom option to display the Customize View dialog box.

Using the Reading Pane

Reading
Pane

You can use the new Reading pane to view the contents of an Outlook item without having to open it in a form. The Reading pane replaces the Preview pane provided in previous versions of Outlook, which you could display only at the bottom of the Outlook window. In Outlook 2003, however, you can display the Reading pane at the right side of the window or at the bottom of the window by choosing View, Reading Pane, Right or View, Reading Pane, Bottom. To hide the Reading pane, choose View, Reading Pane, Off. You can also display the Reading pane at its previous position, or hide the Reading pane, by clicking the Reading Pane button on the Advanced toolbar. Once you display the Reading pane within a particular view, the pane will appear whenever you use that view—until you hide it. Setting the position of the Reading pane sets its position for *all* views of the current folder.

If you've opened the Tasks folder, the Notes folder, or an e-mail folder such as Inbox, the Reading pane works just as the Preview pane did in Outlook 2000. That is, it shows selected item fields in a header and it displays the contents of the item's large text box (such as the body of an e-mail message) below that (see Figure 37-16).

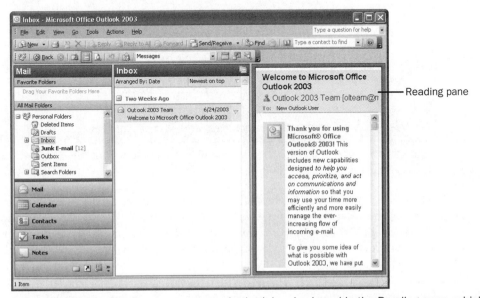

Figure 37-16. In this figure, a message in the Inbox is viewed in the Reading pane, which appears at the right side of the Outlook window.

If, however, you've opened one of the other default Outlook folders, the Reading pane in Outlook 2003 displays the selected item in the item's form—that is, within the form used to display the item when you open it (see Figure 37-17). The Reading pane shows only the main tab of the form and doesn't let you edit its contents. If you can't see the entire form, try expanding the Reading pane by dragging the pane's upper or left border, or try changing the position of the form (right or bottom).

Figure 37-17. In this figure, a Contacts item is viewed in the Reading pane, which appears at the bottom of the Outlook window.

When the Reading pane is displayed, you can display different items by pressing the Spacebar to display the next item or by pressing Shift+Spacebar to display the previous item, provided that the Single Key Reading Using Space Bar option is checked. To modify this option or other features of the Reading pane, choose Tools, Options, click the Other tab, and click the Reading Pane button.

Tip Preview an item's text

Auto-Preview

In a table view, you can display the text contained in each item's large text box—or at least the first part of that text—below each item in the Information Viewer by turning on the Auto-Preview feature. You can turn AutoPreview on or off by choosing View, AutoPreview or by clicking the AutoPreview button on the Advanced toolbar.

If you want to perform another search, click the New Search button to remove the items that have been found and to clear the search criteria you've specified.

Finding Outlook Items

The fastest way to find Outlook items that contain specified text—in any field—is to use the Find pane, which is displayed at the top of the Information Viewer. To use the Find pane, follow these steps:

1 Open the Outlook folder that you want to search and switch to the view you want to use to display the found items.

Find

2 To display the Find pane (see Figure 37-18), click the Find button on the Standard toolbar, choose Tools, Find, Find, or press Ctrl+E. (To hide the Find pane, click the Find button or choose Tools, Find, Find again, or click the Close button at the right of the pane.)

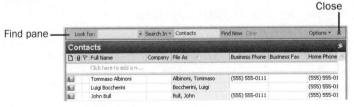

Figure 37-18. This figure shows the Find pane that appears when the Contacts folder is open.

3 Type the text you want to find in the Look For box, or select previously entered search text from the drop-down list.

4 To search a folder other than the one that's currently open, click the Search In button and choose the folder from the drop-down menu, or choose Choose Folders and select one or more folders in the Select Folder(s) dialog box. In the text box to the right of the Search In button, Outlook will list the folder or folders that will be searched (this text box initially contains only the name of the folder that is currently open). (For more information, see the Inside Out sidebar, "Open a folder before searching it.")

Options

5 To look for your search text in all item fields, click the Options button and make sure that the Search All Text In Each Message option is selected on the drop-down menu. To speed up the search, you can deselect this option to search only the most frequently used fields.

6 Click the Find Now button.

Inside Out

Open a folder before searching it

Although the Find pane lets you search in one or more folders besides the one that is currently open, it uses the current view of the open folder to display the search results; this view might not show much of the information for the items that are found. Consider, for example, that the Contacts folder is open and the Phone List view is active. If you search for items in the Inbox folder, the Phone List view won't show the information belonging to the items that are found because this view displays the wrong fields (Full Name, Company, and so on, rather than From, Subject, and so on). So if you're searching a single folder, you should open that folder before you use the Find pane.

Outlook will then display any found items within the Information Viewer. (Outlook may switch to a different view to better present the results.) To clear the found items from the Information Viewer and redisplay the items that were listed there before you performed the search, click the Clear button in the Find pane.

Using the Advanced Find Dialog Box

The main advantages of using the Advanced Find dialog box rather than the Find pane are that you can fine-tune your search criteria, you can stop the search at any time, and because an Advanced Find search runs in the background, you can continue working in Outlook during a long search.

You can search for items in one or more Outlook folders, and you can search either for items of a particular type (such as messages, contacts, or journal entries) or for items of any type. For example, you could search the Inbox folder for all messages that were sent by a given person. Or, you could search all your Outlook folders for items of any type that are assigned a particular category, such as Business or Personal. The Advanced Find dialog box lets you specify a wide variety of search criteria.

To use the Advanced Find dialog box, complete the following steps:

1   Display the Advanced Find dialog box (shown in Figure 37-19) by choosing Tools, Find, Advanced Find, by pressing Ctrl+Shift+F, or by right-clicking a folder name in the Navigation pane and choosing Advanced Find from the shortcut menu. Also, if the Find pane is displayed, you can click the Options button and choose Advanced Find from the drop-down menu.

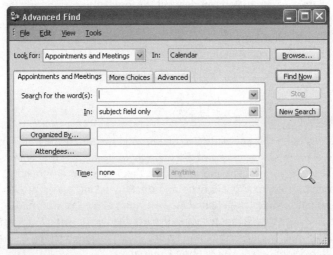

Figure 37-19. The Advanced Find dialog box provides the most powerful way to search for Outlook items.

2 In the Look For drop-down list, select the type of Outlook item or items that you want to search for.

> **Note** Selecting the Files (Outlook/Exchange) item in the Look For drop-down list searches for files that are stored in an e-mail folder. Although the technique isn't covered in this book, it's possible to store entire files directly in an e-mail folder such as the Inbox, where they are listed along with any messages in the folder. Storing files in an e-mail folder is typically used to share files on Exchange Server. (Using Outlook as an Exchange Server client isn't covered in this book.)

3 Click the Browse button and select the specific Outlook folders that you want to search. The folder or folders you select will appear in the In box. Or you can just accept the default folder that appears in the In box.

4 Specify basic search criteria in the first tab, which is labeled according to the item you've selected in the Look For list, such as "Contacts" or "Messages." You can specify more advanced search criteria in the other tabs. The particular search options that appear on the tabs of the Advanced Find dialog box depend on the type of item you're searching for (which is selected in the Look For drop-down list).

5 Click the Find Now button to start the search.

You can resume working in Outlook while a search takes place. If you want to stop a search before it has finished, click the Stop button.

After the search is completed, Outlook will display all matching items in a list that's added to the bottom of the Advanced Find dialog box. You can open an Outlook item by double-clicking it in this list. Keep in mind that the Advanced Find dialog box provides many of the same commands that the main Outlook window provides for customizing the view, sorting and grouping the items, and so on.

You can also save all of the criteria you've entered in the Advanced Find dialog box by choosing Save Search from the File menu in the dialog box and then specifying the name of the file in which you want to store the search criteria. (The file will be given the *.oss* extension.) You can quickly rerun the same search later by choosing File, Open Search and selecting this file. Or, if the Advanced Find dialog box doesn't currently appear, you can display it and rerun the search by double-clicking the *.oss* file in Windows.

> **Note** In Office 2003 you can also search for Outlook items, as well as disk files, by using the Basic File Search or Advanced File Search task pane in Word, Microsoft Excel, Microsoft PowerPoint, Microsoft Access, or Microsoft FrontPage. Or you can use the similar features in the Search dialog box, which you display by choosing Search from the Tools drop-down menu in the Open dialog box and related dialog boxes. For more information, see "Finding Office Files or Outlook Items Using the File Search Feature," on page 63.

Organizing Items Using the Organize Pane

The Organize pane is a Web-style page that you can display at the top of the Information Viewer and use for working with Outlook items. Although it doesn't let you do anything you can't do by using the program's conventional commands, it provides fast, easy alternative methods for performing some of the more common tasks.

You can perform the following tasks in the Organize pane. These tasks aren't available in all folders. In the Organize pane that appears for each folder, Outlook provides only the capabilities that are most useful for working with the types of items stored in that folder.

- Move selected items in the folder to another folder. Or have Outlook automatically move e-mail messages in the future, according to rules that you specify. For example, you could have all future e-mail messages that your boss sends automatically moved to a specific folder.
- Assign categories to items—such as Business or Personal—or create new categories.
- Change the current view.
- Organize messages by color-coding certain ones.

The techniques for moving e-mail messages using rules and for color-coding e-mail messages are discussed in "Organizing Your E-Mail Messages," on page 1021 and "Handling Junk E-Mail," on page 1022.

To use the Organize pane, follow these steps:

1 Open the folder you want to work with.

2 Choose Tools, Organize. The Organize pane will then appear at the top of the Information Viewer. The features that the Organize pane includes vary depending on the current folder. Figure 37-20 shows the Organize pane for the Calendar folder.

You can remove the Organize pane by choosing the Tools, Organize command again or by clicking the Close button in the pane's upper-right corner.

Figure 37-20. This figure shows the Organize pane that appears when the Calendar folder is open.

3 Click a command at the left of the Organize pane—such as Using Categories or Using Views—to indicate the way you want to organize the folder. This will open a tab on the right that contains the necessary controls.

4 Use the controls on the right side of the pane to carry out the organizing tasks.

Working with Outlook Folders

The Outlook folders described in this book are the default folders created by the Outlook program. You can create additional folders to store specific types of Outlook items. For example, you might create one or more folders for storing saved e-mail messages, rather than keeping them all in your Inbox. Also, you might create a new folder for storing appointments so that you can have one calendar for your personal appointments and another for your business appointments.

To create a new Outlook folder, complete the following steps:

1 Choose File, New, Folder; choose File, Folder, New Folder; or press Ctrl+Shift+E. This will display the Create New Folder dialog box, shown in Figure 37-21.

Figure 37-21.   Use the Create New Folder dialog box to create a new Outlook folder.

2   Type a name for your new folder in the Name text box.

3   In the Folder Contains drop-down list, select the type of Outlook item the new folder will contain, as follows:

- To create a folder for storing e-mail messages, select Mail And Post Items.

- To create a folder for storing appointments, events, or meetings, select Calendar Items.

- To create a folder for storing contact descriptions and distribution lists, select Contact Items.

- To create a folder for storing tasks, notes, or journal entries, select Task Items, Note Items, or Journal Items.

> **Note**   Although the technique isn't covered in this book, you can store discussion postings in an e-mail folder along with messages—hence the description "Mail And Post Items." Discussion postings are typically placed in a shared e-mail folder on an Exchange Server network computer, where they allow network users to conduct a discussion.

4   In the Select Where To Place The Folder list, click the folder in which you want to store the new folder. Your new folder will be made a subfolder of the folder you select and will appear under that folder in the Folder List.

Note Outlook folders—like file folders—are arranged in a hierarchy of folders and sub-folders. This hierarchy is shown in the Folder List. Outlook Today (which also has a data file name, usually "Personal Folders") is at the top of the hierarchy. The default Outlook folders are all direct subfolders of Outlook Today. You can store your new folder at the same level as the default Outlook folders by selecting the top item (usually labeled "Personal Folders") in the Select Where To Place The Folder list in the Create New Folder dialog box.

5 Click the OK button.

You can also create a new Outlook folder by making a copy of an existing folder and its contents. To do this, open the folder you want to copy, choose File, Folder, Copy "*Folder*" (where *Folder* is the name of the open folder). You'll then have to select the folder where you want to store the copy. Outlook will copy the folder plus any subfolders it contains, together with the contents of these folders, and it will assign the copy a default name. You can rename it later.

You can't move, rename, or remove any of the default Outlook folders (Inbox, Calendar, and so on), but you can move, rename, or remove an Outlook folder that you've created. To perform one of these operations, open the folder, and then on the Folder submenu of the File menu, choose Move "*Folder*," Rename "*Folder*," or Delete "*Folder*" (where *Folder* is the name of the open folder).

As when you remove an Outlook item, when you remove an Outlook folder, it isn't permanently deleted at that moment. Rather, it's moved to the Deleted Items folder, where it becomes a subfolder of Deleted Items. You can permanently delete it using the same techniques described for removing items in "Removing and Archiving Items," on page 969. And you can restore a folder by moving it back to its original location in the folder hierarchy. Be aware that if you've selected the Empty The Deleted Items Folder Upon Exiting option on the Other tab of the Options dialog box (displayed by choosing Tools, Options), the items in your Deleted Items folder will be permanently deleted when you exit Outlook.

Note Rather than choosing the menu commands discussed in this section from the Folder submenu of the File menu, you can choose them from the shortcut menu that appears when you right-click the Folder Banner above the Information Viewer.

Tip Use the folder list to work with folders

An alternative way to perform the operations explained here is to click the Folder List button in the lower portion of the Navigation pane to display the Folder List, right-click an Outlook folder name in the Folder List, and then choose a command from the shortcut menu that appears. Using the Folder List, you can also move an Outlook folder by simply dragging it or copy a folder by pressing Ctrl while you drag. And you can remove an Outlook folder by selecting it and pressing the Delete key. (Outlook will ask you to confirm the deletion.) For information on displaying the Folder List, see "Using Other Methods to Open Folders," on page 951.

Printing Outlook Information

Outlook lets you print the information stored in any of your Outlook folders. For example, you could print a message stored in the Inbox folder, a day (or a range of days) in the Calendar folder, or, to create an address book that you can carry with you, the entire contents of your Contacts folder.

Outlook provides a variety of methods for printing. The following is a flexible, general procedure that you can use for printing any kind of Outlook information:

1 Open the folder containing the information you want to print and switch to the view that displays the items the way you want to print them. (The current view affects the printing options that the Print dialog box provides when you display it.)

2 If you want to print one or more specific items—for example, messages in the Inbox folder or contacts in the Contacts folder—select the item or items. To select an item, click it; to select additional items, press Ctrl while you click each one.

3 Choose File, Print, or press Ctrl+P to display the Print dialog box, which is shown in Figure 37-21.

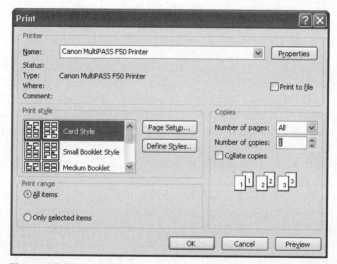

Figure 37-22. This figure shows the Print dialog box as it would appear if you had opened the Contacts folder in the Address Cards view and selected a single contact before you displayed the dialog box.

4 In the Print Style list near the center of the dialog box, select a printing style to specify the general way the information will be organized on the printed copy and the level of detail that will be shown.

5 If you want to modify the selected printing style for the current print job, click the Page Setup button to display the Page Setup dialog box, which lets you modify the fonts, paper size, headers or footers, and other features of the printed pages. If you want to permanently modify one of the default printing styles or create a custom style, click the Define Styles button in the Print dialog box.

6 Change other print options in the Print dialog box, as necessary. The specific options available depend on the folder you opened, its view, and the items you selected before you displayed the dialog box. For example, if you opened the Contacts folder, you can choose whether to print all contacts or only the contact or contacts that you selected by using the Print Range area.

7 To preview the appearance of the printed output and to see the effect of all the options you've selected, click the Preview button. When you're finished previewing, click the Print button on the Print Preview toolbar to return to the Print dialog box.

8 To begin printing, click the OK button in the Print dialog box.

Inside Out

Use the Print dialog box for predictable results

Print

Printing by simply clicking the Print button on the Standard toolbar creates somewhat random results. In some situations Outlook prints immediately, while in other situations it first displays the Print dialog box so that you can select the print settings you want. To get predictable results, it's generally better to use the Print dialog box as discussed in the preceding instructions.

Using Outlook Today to Get an Overview

The Outlook Today folder displays a Web page that provides you with an overview of some of your current Outlook information and allows you to access other Outlook folders. It's shown in Figure 37-23.

Figure 37-23. The Outlook Today folder displays a Web page that gives you an overview of your Outlook information.

You can use Outlook Today as your starting point for working in Outlook. You can use the default Outlook Today folder shown in Figure 37-23 in the following ways:

● To open the Calendar, Tasks, or Inbox folder, click Calendar, Tasks, or Messages.

● The Calendar area displays your appointments, all-day events, and meetings for the next five days. To open one of these items, click it.

● The Tasks area lists all your pending tasks, showing their subjects and due dates. To mark a task as completed, check the check box (Outlook will then draw a line through the task). To open a task, click the task subject or due date.

● The Messages area shows the number of unread messages in your Inbox, as well as the total numbers of messages in your Drafts and Outbox folders. To open one of these folders, click the folder name.

● To customize the Outlook Today folder, click the Customize Outlook Today command near the upper-right corner of the page to open the Customize Outlook Today page. Here you can check the When Starting Go Directly To Outlook Today option to have Outlook display the Outlook Today folder when you first run the program. You can also modify the information that Outlook Today displays from your Calendar, Tasks, and E-mail folders. And, you can select an alternative page style.

Tip You can have Outlook open *any* of your Outlook folders when it first starts. To do this, choose Tools, Options, click the Other tab, and click the Advanced Options button. Then, in the Advanced Options dialog box, check the Browse button next to the Startup In This Folder box, and in the Select Folder dialog box select a new startup folder.

Inside Out

Use a shortcut to display a Web page

The Web page that appears in the Outlook Today folder is known as the folder's *home page*. You can assign a home page to *any* Outlook folder. A home page might be useful for displaying instructions or other information about the folder. Unfortunately, however, Microsoft removed the View, Show Folder Home Page command, which made it relatively easy to switch between viewing the folder's home page and viewing its contents in Outlook 2000. In Outlook 2003, a better way to display a Web page in the Outlook window is to add a shortcut to the Navigation pane for opening that page. You can then easily display the page by clicking the Web-page shortcut, and then quickly switch to viewing a folder's contents by clicking the folder's name in the Navigation pane. For information on adding a shortcut to the Navigation pane for opening a Web page, see "Customizing the Shortcuts List," on page 1079.

If you still want to assign a home page to a folder, right-click the folder's name in the Navigation pane, choose Properties from the shortcut menu, click the Home Page tab, and either type in the file path of the Web page you want to use as the home page or click the Browse button to locate and select the page. To display the folder's home page rather than its contents, check the Show Home Page By Default For This Folder option. To display the page's contents, you have to go back to this tab and clear this option.

Managing Messages and Appointments

Receiving and Sending E-Mail Messages
Using the E-Mail Folders 999

Maintaining Your Schedule with
the Calendar Folder 1026

Receiving and Sending E-Mail Messages Using the E-Mail Folders

If you've set up one or more e-mail accounts in Microsoft Office Outlook 2003, you can use Outlook to receive and send e-mail and to organize your e-mail messages. Outlook uses the default e-mail folders it has created as follows:

- Incoming e-mail messages are delivered to your Inbox folder.

- While you compose a message using the e-mail editor, Outlook normally stores the message in your Drafts folder.

- When you send a message, Outlook temporarily stores it in your Outbox folder until the message is transmitted to your outgoing e-mail server and delivered to the recipient. (In some cases, when you send a message it's transmitted immediately to the outgoing server rather than being stored in the Outbox.)

- When a message is transmitted to the outgoing e-mail server, Outlook normally stores a copy of the message in your Sent Items folder.

Note You can control whether Outlook automatically saves unsent messages that you are composing and whether it saves copies of your outgoing messages in the Sent Items folder, and you can set other e-mail handling options, by choosing Tools, Options, and clicking the E-Mail Options button in the Preferences tab of the Options dialog box to open the E-Mail Options dialog box (shown in Figure 38-1).

You can specify the folder where Outlook saves unsent messages and how often it saves them, as well as set other advanced e-mail processing options, by clicking the Advanced E-Mail Options button in the E-Mail Options dialog box to open the Advanced E-Mail Options dialog box (shown in Figure 38-2).

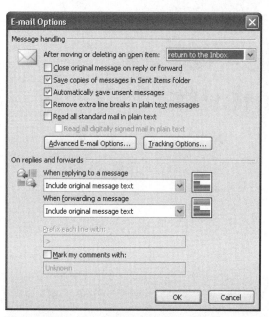

Figure 38-1. The E-Mail Options dialog box provides a basic set of e-mail options.

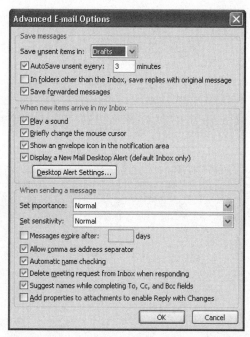

Figure 38-2. Further e-mail options are available in the Advanced E-Mail Options dialog box.

For information on sending messages in real time using instant messaging, see "Using Your Contacts Folder," on page 1055. For information on setting up an e-mail account when you first run Outlook, see "Setting Up Outlook," on page 946. For information on working with e-mail accounts at any time, see "Adding, Modifying, and Removing Outlook Accounts," on page 1080.

Receiving and Viewing E-Mail Messages

To receive and view your e-mail messages, complete the following steps:

1 In Outlook, open the Inbox folder.

2 Click the Send/Receive button on the Standard toolbar; choose Tools, Send/Receive, Send/Receive All; or press F9.

Outlook will then download all messages from your incoming e-mail server and add them to your Inbox. (It will also transmit any outgoing messages in your Outbox folder, as discussed in "Composing and Sending E-Mail Messages" later in the chapter.) Figure 38-3 shows how messages are displayed in your Inbox if you've selected the Messages view.

> **Note** In an e-mail folder such as the Inbox, the descriptions of incoming messages you haven't read or replied to are displayed in bold type. You can mark any message as read (nonbold) by selecting it and choosing Edit, Mark As Read or by pressing Ctrl+Q. You can mark the selected message as Unread (bold) by choosing Edit, Mark As Unread. And you can mark all messages in your Inbox as read (nonbold) by choosing Edit, Mark All As Read. Outlook always automatically marks a message as read if you open it in a Message form or if you reply to or forward the message. To control the way Outlook marks messages as read when you view them in the Reading pane, choose Tools, Options, click the Other tab, and then click the Reading Pane button.

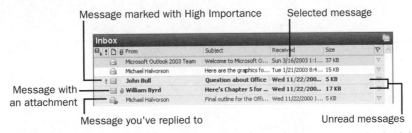

Figure 38-3. This figure shows a set of incoming e-mail messages in the Inbox folder, displayed with the Messages view

3 You can read your messages by viewing them in the Reading pane (see Figure 38-4 and "Using the Reading Pane," on page 984) or by opening them in the Message form (see Figure 38-5 and "Editing Items," on page 961). The Message form provides commands for replying to or forwarding the message, printing it, moving it to a different Outlook folder, deleting it, or adding a message flag (a comment such as *Call* or *Follow Up* attached to the message). In the Message form, you can also open other messages, create new messages, and perform additional operations.

1001

For more information on adding flags to messages, see "Using Quick Flags," on page 1007.

Figure 38-4. You can view an e-mail message in the Reading pane.

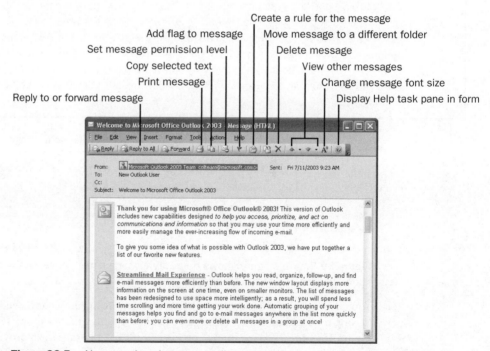

Figure 38-5. You can also view an e-mail message by opening it in the Message form.

> **Note** If you have more than one e-mail account, be sure to read "Using Groups to Manage Several E-Mail Accounts," on page 1008.

If a message includes an attachment, it's marked with a paper-clip icon (shown in Figure 38-3) in the Outlook window. When you've opened a message in the Message form, you can open the attachment by double-clicking it (the attachment is represented by an icon and filename). If the format of the message is Rich Text, the icon and filename for an attachment will appear in the body of the message, as shown here:

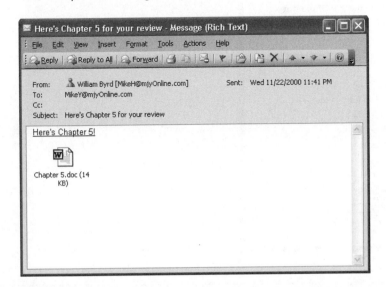

If the format of the message is HTML (Hypertext Markup Language) or plain text, the icon and filename will appear below the Subject line in the message header. You can save an attachment to a disk file by selecting the message in the Outlook window and choosing the appropriate command from the File, Save Attachments submenu. Or you can open the message in a form and choose Save Attachments from the form's File menu.

> **Caution** Certain types of message attachments can contain viruses. Although Outlook automatically blocks some types of potentially unsafe attachments (such as directly executable files), it does allow you to open other types of attachments that might contain viruses (for example, Office documents, which can carry macro viruses). In general, you should never open or save an attachment in a message from an unknown source. And even if the message is from someone you know, you should verify with that person that they have intentionally sent you a file with an attachment. (Certain viruses cause messages to be sent out to the addresses in the user's address book without the user's knowledge.) For more information, see "Setting Macro Security," on page 229.

When you view an incoming or outgoing message in the Reading pane or open it in a Message form, Outlook now displays a smart tag button next to any name or e-mail address that appears in the message header. You can click this button to schedule a meeting with that person (using the Meeting form, described later in the chapter), to contact the person using instant messaging, to add the person to your Contacts folder, or to perform other tasks. Here's the menu that's displayed when you click the smart tag button next to the sender's name in the Reading pane:

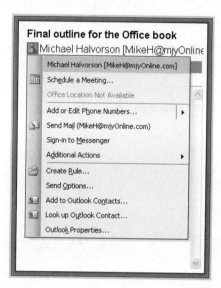

Note You'll see the smart tag buttons described here only if the Enable The Person Names Smart Tag option is checked. To access this option, choose Tools, Options and click the Other tab.

Tip View a message's Internet headers

With most types of e-mail accounts, you can view the Internet header for a message by right-clicking the message in the Outlook window, choosing Options from the shortcut menu, and looking in the Internet Headers area near the bottom of the Message Options dialog box. Internet headers reveal interesting information (if you know how to interpret it!) regarding the sending and routing of the message on the Internet.

Reading HTML Messages Privately and Safely

HTML is a popular format for e-mail messages because it allows a message to include graphics, background pictures, and full formatting (such as bulleted lists and paragraph alignment). Most popular e-mail programs support HTML, and, as explained later in the chapter, it's now the default format for the messages you send in Outlook. However, receiving HTML messages from unknown sources can create risks to your privacy and your computer's safety. Outlook 2003 therefore includes two new features that help you read incoming HTML messages privately and safely.

First, by default Outlook blocks external content contained in incoming HTML messages. The term *external content* refers to pictures or sound clips that are not actually embedded in the e-mail message, but rather are downloaded from a Web site when you read the message. (In other words, the message contains links to the pictures or sounds rather than the actual data.) Legitimate senders use external content to reduce the size of e-mail messages. However, a sender of junk e-mail sometimes includes an external content link that sends back a signal indicating that someone has received and has viewed the message (this link is known as a *Web beacon*). Your e-mail address might then be included on their list of "live" addresses and become the target for additional unsolicited messages.

When you receive an HTML message, Outlook blocks external content by default. It displays a red X in place of each external picture and includes a note in the message header (as well as in each blocked picture) indicating the presence of the blocked content. You can click the note in the header (or right-click the note in a blocked picture) and, from the drop-down menu, choose a command to download the blocked pictures, to change the settings for external content blocking, or to add the message sender or the sender's domain to your e-mail Safe Senders list (see Figure 38-6). For information on the e-mail Safe Sender's list, see "Handling Junk E-Mail," on page 1022.

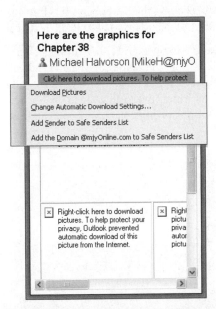

Figure 38-6. You can override blocking of external content on a per-message basis.

Chapter 38

If you choose the Change Automatic Download Settings command, Outlook will display the Automatic Picture Download Settings dialog box, shown here, where you can read about and modify external content blocking. You can also open this dialog box by choosing Tools, Options, clicking the Security tab, and clicking the Change Automatic Download Settings button in the Download Pictures area.

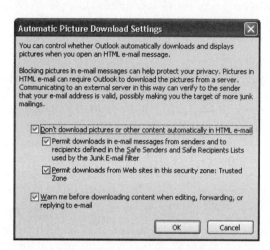

The second new HTML safety feature in Outlook is an option that allows you to view all HTML messages in plain text. HTML messages can contain harmful scripts. Although with the usual security settings, Outlook prevents scripts from running in HTML messages, the most secure way to be certain that scripts can't run is to display all HTML messages in plain text. By default, the option for displaying HTML messages in plain text is off. You can turn it on by choosing Tools, Options, clicking the Preferences tab, clicking the E-Mail Options button, and, in the E-Mail Options dialog box, checking the Read All Standard Mail In Plain Text option.

When the plain-text display option is on and you open an HTML message, Outlook will show only the message text and will display a note in the message header indicating that the message was converted to plain text. You can click this note, as shown here, and choose a command to display the message in HTML format (overriding the plain-text feature for the current message) or to open the E-Mail Options dialog box (where you can turn off the plain-text option for all messages).

Using Quick Flags

If you've collected a large number of messages in your Inbox, you can flag those messages that need further attention. As explained earlier in the chapter, you can add a flag by opening a message in the Message form and clicking the Follow Up button on the form's Standard toolbar. In Outlook 2003 you can now quickly add a flag to a message displayed in the Information Viewer of the Outlook Window by simply clicking the Flag Status button at the right end of the message. The first click adds a standard "Follow Up" flag without a due date. The second click changes the flag to a "Follow Up Completed" flag, indicating that you have replied to or otherwise attended to the message. You can see the flag's icon in the Information Viewer. You can view the full text for the flag ("Follow Up" or "Follow Up Completed" for a simple flag) in the header when the message is viewed in the Reading pane or in the Message form. And all messages that have been flagged—but not marked as completed—will appear in the new For Follow Up search folder. (By default, the messages appearing in this folder will be grouped by the flag color.)

Search folders are explained in "Using Search Folders to Categorize Your Messages," on page 1019.

If you want to clear (that is, remove) the flag from a message, to assign a flag that has a specific color, to change the default flag color, or to customize the flag in other ways, right-click the Flag Status button and choose a command from the drop-down menu, shown here:

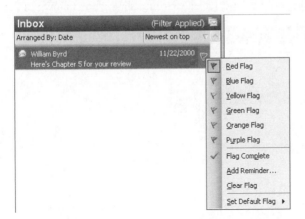

An alternative way to choose one of these commands is to select the message, choose Actions, Follow Up, and choose the command from the submenu.

Choosing the Add Reminder command opens the Flag For Follow Up dialog box, shown here, where you can type or select the flag's text (for instance, "Forward," "Read," or "Reply," rather than the default "Follow Up" text), change the flag type (that is, its color), set a due date and time for the flag, mark the task associated with the flag as completed, or clear the flag.

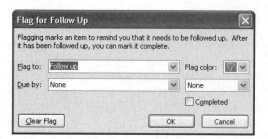

Using Groups to Manage Several E-Mail Accounts

If you have more than one e-mail account (perhaps one provided by your company for business e-mail and another you use for personal messages), you can set up account *groups*. These groups let you control exactly which accounts Outlook uses to send and receive e-mail when you initiate a send and receive operation. Groups also let you have Outlook automatically send and receive e-mail at fixed intervals using specific accounts.

Initially, Outlook creates a single group called All Accounts that includes all your e-mail accounts. To create a new group, complete the following steps:

1. Choose Tools, Send/Receive, Send/Receive Settings, Define Send/Receive Groups, or press Ctrl+Alt+S to open the Send/Receive Groups dialog box (shown in Figure 38-7).

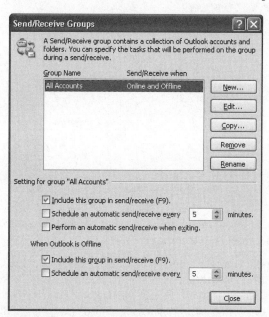

Figure 38-7. The Send/Receive Groups dialog box lets you set up and modify e-mail account groups.

2 Click the New button, and in the dialog boxes that Outlook displays, enter a name for the group, add the accounts you want to belong to the group, and select the options you want for each account in the group.

3 When you get back to the Send/Receive Groups dialog box, you can select your new group in the list and select options for the entire group. These options let you include or exclude the group from the accounts that Outlook uses when you click the Send/Receive button or press F9 (described in "Receiving and Viewing E-Mail Messages," on page 1001), or when you choose Tools, Send/Receive, Send And Receive All. You can also have Outlook automatically send and receive messages using the group's accounts at specified intervals. Notice that you can set separate options for working online or offline in Outlook. You switch between working offline and online by choosing File, Work Offline. (At the right end of the status bar, Outlook indicates whether you're currently working online or offline.)

> **Note** Outlook initially defines the All Accounts group so that Outlook will always use all your e-mail accounts (whether you're working online or offline) when you click the Send/Receive button, press F9, or choose Tools, Send/Receive, Send/Receive All. If you want to control the specific accounts that Outlook uses when you issue one of these commands, you can redefine this group (or delete it).

Once you've set up groups, you can send and receive your e-mail messages selectively by choosing the appropriate command from the Send/Receive submenu of the Tools menu, as shown here:

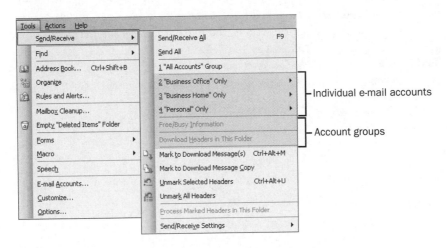

Note If you've set up one or more groups for automatic sending and receiving of e-mail, you can turn off (or turn back on) automatic transfers by choosing Tools, Send/Receive, Send/Receive Settings, Disable Scheduled Send/Receive.

Inside Out

Understanding which groups are included by Send And Receive All

Keep in mind that the Send And Receive All command, in spite of its name, does *not* necessarily send and receive e-mail using all your e-mail account groups. Rather, it uses only those groups that are enabled. An enabled group is one for which the Include This Group In Send/Receive (F9) option is checked in the Send/Receive Groups dialog box for the current online/offline mode. (This dialog box is shown in Figure 38-7 and is explained in step 3 on page 1009.) For example, if a group has the Include This Group In Send/Receive (F9) option checked in the When Outlook Is Online area of the Send/Receive Groups dialog box, that group will be enabled when Outlook is online.

- Choose Send And Receive All to send and receive e-mail using all enabled account groups.
- Choose the name of an individual e-mail account to send and receive e-mail using just that account, regardless of the groups that are set up and their settings.
- Choose the name of an account group to send and receive e-mail using all accounts defined and enabled in that group. (Sending or receiving can be disabled for a particular account in a group by settings you make when you add the account to the group.)

Note If you receive and send e-mail using a dial-up service (that is, a service you access with a modem and telephone line), you can control the way Outlook connects to your account by choosing Tools, Options, clicking the Mail Setup tab, and selecting or checking options in the Dial-Up area at the bottom of the tab (see Figure 38-8).

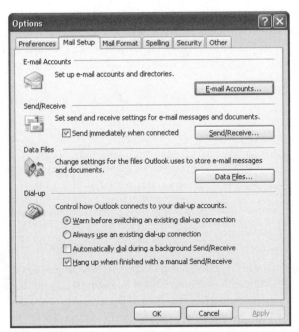

Figure 38-8. You can use the Mail Setup tab of the Options dialog box to manage your e-mail accounts, accounts groups, and data files, and to modify the way Outlook connects to dial-up accounts.

Setting the E-Mail Format and Editor

When you create a new e-mail message by choosing Actions, New Mail Message, by pressing Ctrl+N, or by using an equivalent command, Outlook creates the new message using your default e-mail format—plain text, rich text, or HTML—and it opens the message in your default e-mail editor—Outlook or Microsoft Word. (When you reply to or forward a message, Outlook uses the format of the original message you received and opens it in your default e-mail editor.) When you first install Outlook 2003, the default e-mail format is set to HTML, and, if Word is installed, it will be your default e-mail editor. You can change both these defaults—and set other e-mail formatting options—by choosing Tools, Options and clicking the Mail Format tab (shown in Figure 38-9 on page 1015).

If you select HTML as your default e-mail format, you can also select default HTML *stationery* that will be used as the basis for the new e-mail messages you create. HTML stationery adds initial content to new messages, which might include a background color, background graphics, or boilerplate text. After you create a message using stationery, you can customize these elements if you wish and then add your own text. To specify default stationery, select the name of the stationery from the Use This Stationery By Default drop-down list in the Mail Format tab or click the Stationery Picker button to select stationery in the Stationery Picker dialog box, which lets you preview each stationery style.

You can create a new message and override either your default format or your default editor by choosing a command from the Actions, New Mail Message Using submenu. If your default format is HTML and your default editor is Word, this submenu appears as follows:

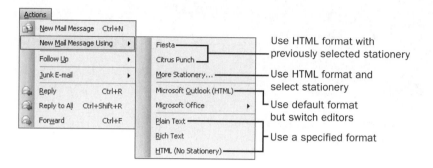

You can also override your default format after you've opened a new message in Word by selecting a format from the Message Format drop-down list in the message header (see Figure 38-10). If you've opened the new message in the built-in Outlook editor, you can change the format by choosing a command from the form's Format menu (although this menu might not include all three of the Outlook e-mail formats). Table 38-1 provides details on using the buttons on your message headers (in Word) or the Standard toolbar (in Outlook).

Table 38-1. Using the Buttons on the Message Header (in Word) or the Standard Toolbar (in Outlook)

To Do This	Perform This Action Using the Message Header (or Standard Toolbar) Buttons
Specify the account you want Outlook to use to send your message, if you have more than one account.	Choose an account from the Accounts drop-down menu. (This button will appear only if you've set up more than one e-mail account.)
Insert a file or an Outlook item into the message.	In the Word editor, choose Insert File or Insert Item from the Insert File drop-down menu and then select the file or item in the Insert File or Insert Item dialog box. In the Outlook editor, to insert a file, click the Insert File button or choose File from the form's Insert menu. To insert an Outlook item, choose Item from the form's Insert menu.
Open the Select Names dialog box (the same dialog box opened by clicking the To or Cc button).	Click the Address Book button.

Table 38-1. **Using the Buttons on the Message Header (in Word) or the Standard Toolbar (in Outlook)**

To Do This	Perform This Action Using the Message Header (or Standard Toolbar) Buttons
Have Outlook replace names you've typed into the To or Cc boxes with the e-mail addresses from your Contacts folder.	Click the Check Names button.
NEW FEATURE! Use the Information Rights Management feature in Office 2003 to allow the recipient to read the message, but not forward, print, or copy the message. (For more information, see "Using Information Rights Management to Restrict Document Permissions," on page 80.	Click the Permission button.
Mark the message as *high importance*.	Click the Importance: High button.
Mark the message as *low importance*.	Click the Importance: Low button.
Add a flag (such as *Follow Up* or *No Response Necessary*).	Click the Message Flag button and select the flag in the Flag For Follow Up dialog box. (For more information on flagging a message, see "Using Quick Flags," on page 1007.
NEW FEATURE! Create a rule that causes Outlook to display a notice in an alert window, play a selected sound, move the message, or perform other actions when you receive a message from a recipient entered into the To or Cc box, or a message that contains the same Subject text as the current message.	Click the Create Rule button and fill in the Create Rules dialog box. (You must already have entered a recipient into the To or Cc box, or entered text into the Subject box.)
Display the Message Options dialog box (shown in Figure 38-12). This dialog box lets you modify many message features, including assigning associated contacts and categories to the message.	Click the Options button. In Word only, you can also click the down arrow on this button and choose several additional e-mail options from the drop-down menu.
Change the message's format.	In the Word editor, select a format in the Message Format drop-down list. In the Outlook editor, choose an option from the form's Format menu.
NEW FEATURE! Add a digital signature to the message or encrypt the message.	Click the Digitally Sign button or the Encrypt Message button. These buttons appear at the right end of the Message Header (or Standard Toolbar) only if the Add Digital Signature To Outgoing Messages option is checked. To access this option, in the Outlook window (not in the message form) choose Tools, Options and click the Security tab.

Composing and Sending E-Mail Messages

To create and send an e-mail message, complete the following steps:

1 Create the message using one of the following methods:

- To reply to a message you've received, select the message in the Outlook window and click the Reply button on the Standard toolbar; choose Actions, Reply; or press Ctrl+R. Outlook will create a new message and open it in the Message form. The message will be addressed to the sender of the original message, will have the same Subject field as the original, prefaced with *RE:*, and the body of the message will contain information from the original message's header (usually, the sender, the sending date, and the recipient) plus the original message's text. (You'll add your message above the header information.) The message, however, won't contain any file attachments from the original message.

  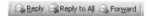

- To send a message reply to all people, other than you, who received the selected message, click the Reply To All button; choose Actions, Reply To All; or press Ctrl+Shift+R.

- To forward the selected message, click the Forward button; choose Actions, Forward; or press Ctrl+F. Outlook will create a new message and open it in the Message form. The message will have the same Subject field as the original, prefaced with *FW:*, and the body of the message will contain information from the original message's header (usually, the sender, the sending date, and the recipient) plus the original message's text and any attachments that were included in the original message. (You'll add your message, if any, above the header information and enter the message recipient in the To text box.)

New Mail Message

- To create a new message, make sure that an e-mail folder is open and choose Actions, New Mail Message; click the New button on the Standard toolbar; or press Ctrl+N. (If don't have an e-mail folder open, you can create a new message by clicking the down arrow on the New button and choosing Mail Message from the drop-down menu or by pressing Ctrl+Shift+M.) Outlook will open a blank Message form for you to fill in. (For more information, see the "Setting the E-Mail Format and Editor" sidebar on page 1011.)

> **Note** You can also issue almost all of the commands described here for creating a message by opening a message in a form and choosing the command from within the form.

2 Complete the message header in the Message form and type your message into the large text box. Figure 38-10 shows the Message form displayed by Word.

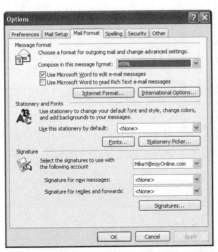

Figure 38-9. The Mail Format tab of the Options dialog box lets you select the format, editor, stationery, fonts, signature, and other features of your e-mail messages.

> **Note** To hide or show the message header in the Message form, click the E-Mail button on the Standard toolbar (in Word) or choose View, Message Header (in the Outlook e-mail editor).

You can type the recipient's address directly into the To or Cc text box (such as *someone@microsoft.com*), or you can click the To or Cc button to open the Select Names dialog box (see Figure 38-11), where you can select a recipient or a distribution list (a collection of recipients) from your Contacts folder or—if you've set up a directory account—look up an e-mail address using an Internet directory service. You can use the buttons at the top of the message header in Word (or the buttons in the form's Standard toolbar in the Outlook editor) to work with your message, as explained in Table 38-1 on page 1012.

> For information on setting up and using directory accounts for looking up e-mail addresses on the Internet, see "Adding, Modifying, and Removing Outlook Accounts," on page 1080.

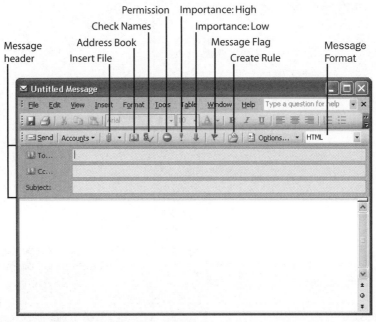

Figure 38-10. When you use Word as the e-mail editor, you'll see a blank Message form like this one.

Figure 38-11. You can select a recipient or look up an e-mail address in the Select Names dialog box.

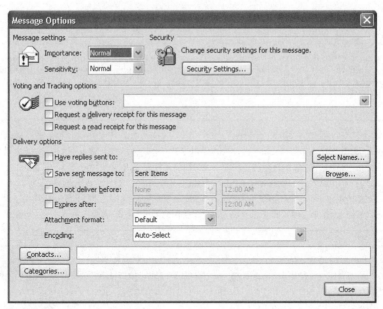

Figure 38-12. The Message Options dialog box lets you change message settings.

Tip   Preserve your recipient's anonymity

If you're sending an e-mail message to several recipients and you don't want to reveal the list of e-mail addresses to each message recipient, insert each of the recipient's addresses into the Bcc text box rather than into the To or Cc box. (If you wish, you can insert your own e-mail address into the To box or just leave that box blank.) To display the Bcc text box in the message header, choose Bcc from the Options drop-down menu on the message header (in Word), or choose View, Bcc Field (in the Outlook e-mail editor).

---

3   When you've completed entering the message content and setting message options, click the Send button on the message header (in Word) or on the Standard toolbar (in the Outlook editor) to move your message to the Outbox and mark it for delivery.

Note   The description of the message in your Outbox that's marked for delivery is formatted in italics. If you reopen the message, be sure to click the Send button again. Otherwise, it will no longer be marked for delivery and will just sit in your Outbox when you perform a send and receive operation.

---

4   Transmit your message (plus any other messages in your Outbox) to your outgoing e-mail server for delivery as follows:

■   To send messages only, choose Tools, Send/Receive, Send All. If you have more than one e-mail account, Outlook will transmit each message in your Outbox using the account designated for that message (see the first item in Table 38-1).

■ To send and receive messages, click the Send/Receive button on the Standard toolbar; choose Tools, Send/Receive, Send/Receive All; or press F9.

> If you have more than one e-mail account, see "Using Groups to Manage Several E-Mail Accounts," on page 1008, for important information on using account groups, along with the commands on the Send/Receive submenu of the Tools menu, to control exactly which accounts are used to send and receive e-mail.

> **Note**   If the Send Immediately When Connected option is checked and you're working online, Outlook will immediately transmit a message when you click the Send button in the Message form, rather than storing it in the Outbox. (If you access your e-mail server using a dial-up connection, Outlook will dial that connection if you're not already connected.) You'll find this option by choosing Tools, Options and clicking the Mail Setup tab (shown in Figure 38-8). You switch between working offline and online by choosing File, Work Offline.

> **Tip**   **Resend a message**
> If you want to resend a message (perhaps to remind the recipient to reply), open the copy of the message stored in your Sent Items folder and choose Resend This Message from the Message form's Actions menu.

Sending Shared Attachments

General instructions for attaching a file to an e-mail message or other Outlook item were given in "Editing Items," on page 961. For an e-mail message, Outlook now allows you to add either a regular file attachment (as discussed in "Editing Items") or a *shared attachment*. Sending an Office document as a shared attachment creates a new document workspace on a SharePoint team Web site and adds a shared copy of the attached document to a document library within that workspace. Each message recipient receives a personal copy of the document and can also access the shared copy in the document workspace. A recipient can update his or her personal copy with changes that are made by other recipients.

> For general information on SharePoint document workspaces, see "Sharing Documents Using a Document Workspace," on page 190.

To send a shared document attachment, first open and fill in a Message form and attach the desired Office document using any of the methods for adding a regular file attachment that are described in "Editing Items" (for example, you can drag the document from Windows Explorer and drop it in the Message form's large text box). Next, click the Attachment Options button in the Message form to display the new Attachment Options task pane. Then in the task pane, select the Shared Attachments option and enter the URL of your SharePoint team Web site. See Figure 38-13.

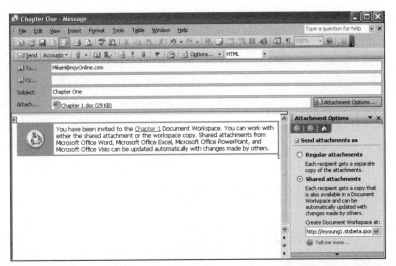

Figure 38-13. The new Shared Attachment task pane lets you convert an attached Office document to a shared attachment, which creates a shared copy of the document in a SharePoint document workspace.

Using Search Folders to Categorize Your Messages

Search folders are another new feature that Outlook 2003 provides to help you deal with overflowing e-mail folders. A search folder is a "virtual folder" in the sense that it doesn't actually store messages but rather lists every message that's stored in an e-mail folder and that meets a specific criterion or set of criteria.

> **Note** The default search folders list conforming messages contained in any of your e-mail folders (default e-mail folders as well as e-mail folders you've created). However, you can customize a default search folder or create a new search folder, so that the folder will list only the conforming messages contained in one or more specified Outlook e-mail folders.

For example, the Unread Mail default search folder provided with Outlook lists every message that is contained in one of your e-mail folders and that is marked as unread. As soon as one of these messages is marked as read, it automatically disappears from the list in the Unread Mail search folder. This doesn't mean that the message has been deleted (it will still be stored in its original folder), but rather that it no longer meets the search folder's criterion.

Outlook provides three default search folders, which work as follows:

- For Follow Up lists all messages that are assigned a flag but aren't marked as completed, as explained in "Using Quick Flags," on page 1007.
- Large Mail lists all messages that are greater than 100 KB in length.
- Unread Mail lists all messages that are marked as unread.

When you click the Mail category button in the lower portion of the Navigation pane, the search folders are listed in the Navigation pane, along with the regular e-mail folders. In the All Mail Folders list (or the general Folder List), the search folders are all listed within the Search Folders branch of the folder hierarchy. You can also add them to your Favorite Folders list, as explained in "Customizing the Navigation Pane," on page 1077.

You can create a new search folder that uses the criteria you specify by following these steps:

1 Click the Mail category button in the lower portion of the Navigation pane.

2 Choose File, New, Search Folder or press Ctrl+Shift+P to open the New Search Folder dialog box, shown here:

3 In the New Search Folder dialog box, do one of the following:

- To use a standard search criterion for choosing the items that will be displayed in the search folder, select one of the criteria in the Reading Mail, Mail From People And Lists, or Organizing Mail categories. Then, if the particular criterion you selected has options, click the Choose button to set those options.

- To create a search folder that uses one or more new criteria that you specify, select the Create A Custom Search Folder item at the end of the list, click the Choose button, and then in the Custom Search Folder dialog box enter a search folder name and specify your search criteria. In this dialog box you can also select one or more specific e-mail folders to search. If you don't specify one or more particular e-mail folders to search, your new search folder will search all e-mail folders (just like the default search folders supplied by Outlook or a new search folder you create using a standard search criterion).

To rename or remove a search folder, right-click the folder name in the Navigation pane and choose Delete "*Folder*" or Rename "*Folder*" from the shortcut menu (where *Folder* is the name of the search folder). To modify a search folder, right-click its name and choose Customize This Search Folder.

Organizing Your E-Mail Messages

You'll probably want to move all messages that you've read or replied to out of your Inbox and into one or more other folders to store and categorize them. If you don't do this on a regular basis, the number of messages in your Inbox can rapidly get out of hand. The techniques for creating new folders and moving items between folders are explained in "Working with Outlook Folders," on page 991, and "Moving and Copying Items," on page 966.

Outlook's Organize pane can help you manage your e-mail messages. The general techniques for using the Organize pane are discussed in "Organizing Items Using the Organize Pane," on page 990. The following are some additional tasks you can perform with the Organize pane that are unique to e-mail folders:

● You can create a rule that automatically moves messages that are sent from or to a particular person as soon as each message is delivered to the Inbox. To do this, select a message from or to the person whose e-mail you want to have moved (if no such message is available, don't worry—you can enter the name later), open the Using Folders tab of the Organize pane, and select and enter appropriate values in the Create A Rule item (shown in Figure 38-14).

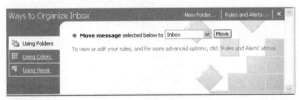

Figure 38-14. When the Inbox folder is open, the Using Folders tab of the Organize pane appears as shown in this figure.

● You can have Outlook automatically color-code messages from or to a particular person or messages that are sent only to you. To do this, select an e-mail message from or to the person whose e-mail you want to color-code (if no such message is available, don't worry—you can enter the name later), open the Using Colors tab of the Organize pane (shown in Figure 38-15), and select and enter the appropriate values into the controls.

Figure 38-15. When the Inbox folder is open, the Organize pane includes a Using Colors tab.

Chapter 38

Also, if your Inbox starts growing out of control, you can choose Tools, Mailbox Cleanup to display the Mailbox Cleanup dialog box (shown in Figure 38-16). This dialog box can help you find old or large e-mail messages so that you can move or delete them. You can also use it to display the current sizes of all of your Outlook folders, to run the AutoArchive feature, to empty your Deleted Items folder, and to delete alternate versions of items in your mailbox.

> For information on archiving and on the Deleted Items folder, see "Removing and Archiving Items," on page 969.

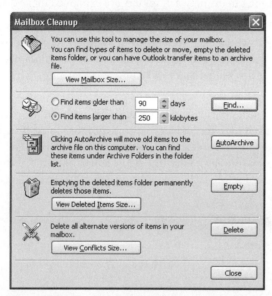

Figure 38-16. The new Mailbox Cleanup dialog box helps you find large or old e-mail messages and perform other maintenance tasks.

 ## Handling Junk E-Mail

Outlook 2003's new junk e-mail filter replaces the rules-based junk and adult-content e-mail feature that was accessed through the Junk E-Mail tab in the Organize pane of previous Outlook versions. The new junk e-mail filter allows you to fine tune the level of junk e-mail protection and to construct lists of known junk e-mail senders (whose messages are always filtered) as well as lists of safe (that is, trusted) e-mail addresses or domains (which are exempt from filtering).

To use the new junk e-mail filter, perform the following steps:

1 Set up the junk e-mail filter by choosing Tools, Options, clicking the Junk E-Mail button in the Preferences tab of the Options dialog box, and selecting the options you want in the tabs of the Junk E-Mail Options dialog box, shown on the next page.

- In the Options tab, you set the general level of junk e-mail protection. If you select the Low or High option, Outlook will analyze the content of all messages you receive to identify suspected junk e-mail.

  Note that even if you select the No Protection option, Outlook will still classify messages received from addresses or domains on your blocked senders list (explained later) as suspected junk e-mail.

  If the Permanently Delete Suspected Junk E-Mail Instead Of Moving It To The Junk E-Mail Folder option is cleared, Outlook will move all suspected junk e-mail messages to your Junk E-mail folder. If this option is checked, Outlook will delete all suspected junk e-mail messages.

Caution   We recommend that you do *not* check the Permanently Delete Suspected Junk E-Mail Instead Of Moving It To The Junk E-Mail Folder option. If this option is cleared, Outlook will move all suspected junk e-mail messages to your Junk E-mail folder, where you can periodically review the messages and recover any messages that you want to read. If you check this option, however, Outlook will immediately delete any suspected junk e-mail message, without moving it to the Deleted Items folder. You therefore won't be able to review or recover suspected junk e-mail messages. (If you do feel that you need to check this option, you should at least wait until you've seen the junk e-mail filter in action before doing so.)

The remaining steps in this procedure assume that you haven't checked the Permanently Delete Suspected Junk E-Mail Instead Of Moving It To The Junk E-Mail Folder option.

- In the Safe Senders tab, you can add, edit, remove, import, or export e-mail addresses or domains on your safe senders list. When you receive a message *from* an address or domain on your safe senders list, Outlook will *not* classify the message as suspected junk e-mail regardless of its content.

- In the Safe Recipients tab, you can add, edit, remove, import, or export e-mail addresses or domains on your safe recipients list. When you receive a message that is addressed *to* an address or domain on your safe recipients list, Outlook will *not* classify the message as suspected junk e-mail regardless of its content. Many Outlook users receive e-mail at more than one address. If you have a particular incoming e-mail address that you use to receive important e-mail messages (for example, your work e-mail address) or an incoming e-mail address that is not publicized (and therefore isn't likely to be the target of junk e-mail), you might want to add it to your safe recipients list.

- In the Blocked Senders tab, you can add, edit, remove, import, or export e-mail addresses or domains on your blocked senders list. When you receive a message *from* an address or domain on your blocked senders list, Outlook *will* classify the message as suspected junk e-mail regardless of its content.

2 You should periodically examine the contents of your Junk E-mail folder to check whether it contains any messages that you want to read or save. You can recover a message in Junk E-Mail by using any of the standard methods to move the message back to the Inbox or to another e-mail folder.

Alternatively, you can select the message and then either choose Actions, Junk E-Mail, Mark As Not Junk or click the Not Junk button on the Standard toolbar. Outlook will then move the message back to the Inbox and will also display a dialog box that gives you the opportunity to add the message's "from" address to your trusted senders list or to add the message's "to" address to your trusted recipients list.

3 You can build up your safe senders, safe recipients, or blocked senders list by adding a received message's "from" or "to" address to one of these lists. (You can also add the message's "from" domain to your safe senders list.) To do this, select the message and then choose one of the four commands from the top section of the Actions, Junk E-Mail submenu, shown here:

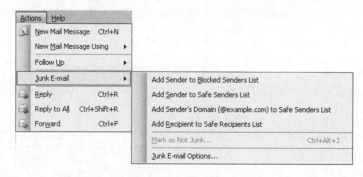

Outlook 2003's junk e-mail filter is considerably more sophisticated and complex than the rules-based junk e-mail system included in previous Outlook versions. This section provides only an introduction to its basic features. For more information, see the Outlook online help topic "Junk E-Mail Filter."

 ## Using an Internet Fax Service

Although Outlook 2002 eliminated the integrated fax feature that was formerly a part of the program, Outlook 2003 has reintroduced faxing capability. This time, however, the fax feature uses e-mail and a third-party Internet fax service rather than a fax modem installed in your computer.

You can use Outlook 2003 to both send and receive faxes. To send a fax, you fill out a fax form, including the fax's content and the recipient's telephone number. You then e-mail the form to an Internet fax service provider, who forwards the fax to the recipient using the telephone system. To receive faxes, the service provider gives you a personal incoming fax telephone number. When someone sends a fax to that number, the service provider converts the fax to an e-mail message, which it sends to you so that you receive the fax in your Outlook Inbox.

To send a fax using an Internet fax service, perform the following steps:

1 Start the process in one of the following ways:

   ■ In Outlook, choose File, New, Internet Fax or press Ctrl+Shift+X.

   ■ In Word, Excel, or PowerPoint, open a document that you want to fax and then choose File, Send To, Recipient Using Internet Fax Service.

2 If you haven't already signed up with an Internet fax service provider, Outlook will now display a message box that gives you the opportunity to visit a Web page where you can choose a provider. Click the OK button in the message box to open this page in your browser. After you select a fax service provider and open an account with the company, Outlook faxing will be activated on your computer. Whenever someone sends a fax to the personal fax telephone number that the provider has given you, a copy of the fax will be e-mailed to your Inbox. To send your first fax, you must now return to step 1.

3 Outlook will open a fax form containing a default cover sheet (as shown in Figure 38-17). If you opened the form in Word, Excel, or PowerPoint, the document you had open will already be attached to the fax message. Fill out the fax form, as follows:

   ■ Type the fax recipient's name and fax telephone number into the first row in the message header. If you want to send the fax to more than one recipient, click the Add More command at the end of the first header row.

   ■ If you want to include a cover sheet, make sure that the Use Cover Sheet option is checked in the Fax Service task pane. Then, either fill in the fields in the default cover sheet, including a message if you want, or use the controls in the Fax Service task pane to select an alternative cover sheet.

Chapter 38

- If you opened the fax form in Outlook and want to attach an Office document or other file to the fax, click the Attach command at the beginning of the third header row.

- You can use the tools in the Fax Service task pane to preview your fax, to calculate the cost of sending the fax, or to contact your fax service provider.

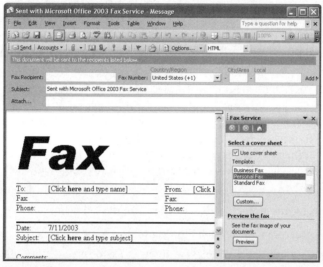

Figure 38-17. The fax form lets you specify the recipient's name and fax telephone number, include a cover sheet and message, and attach a file.

4 Select an e-mail account (if you have more than one) from the Accounts drop-down menu on the e-mail header toolbar. Then click the Send button on the e-mail header toolbar to send the fax. The content of the fax form will be e-mailed to your Internet fax service provider like any other type of e-mail message. When the service provider receives the message, it will forward it over the telephone lines to the recipient fax number or numbers that you provided on the form.

Maintaining Your Schedule with the Calendar Folder

You can use the default Outlook Calendar folder—or any other calendar folder that's available in Outlook—to schedule appointments, events, or meetings—terms that have specific meanings in Outlook. An *appointment* is an activity that can be scheduled for any time period and consumes a block of your own time. For example, an interview that you're planning to conduct next Wednesday morning from 9 to 9:30 would be an appointment. An *event* (sometimes called an *all-day event*) is an occurrence that lasts for one or more entire days but doesn't necessarily fully consume your time. For example, your birthday next May 21 would be an event. A *meeting* is similar to an appointment but involves other people and resources that you schedule using Outlook. For example, a conference with your team of programmers that takes place in a conference room and uses a computer projector and that you've sched-

Chapter 38

uled using Outlook would be a meeting. The following sections explain how to work with each of these three types of calendar items.

 If you have more than one calendar folder available in Outlook 2003, keep in mind that you can now open several of these folders at the same time and view them side-by-side in the Outlook window. When you click the Calendar button in the lower portion of the Navigation pane, you'll notice that each of your calendar folders is displayed with a check box, rather than as a simple folder name that you click. Check the box for each calendar folder that you want to view.

Scheduling Appointments

You can schedule a one-time appointment, which is added to a single time slot in your Calendar folder, or you can schedule a recurring appointment, which is added to a series of time slots in your Calendar according to a daily, weekly, monthly, or yearly recurrence pattern that you specify. In either case, begin by opening your default Calendar folder or another calendar folder in which you want to schedule the appointment.

Then, to schedule a one-time appointment, complete the following steps:

1 Select the time period for the appointment in the Information Viewer of the Outlook window (shown in Figure 38-18). (If you do this, Outlook will save you time by filling in the appointment times when it displays the Appointment form. However, this step is optional because you can specify any time period you want in the form.)

New
Appoint-
ment

2 Choose Actions, New Appointment; click the New button on the Standard toolbar; or press Ctrl+N. Outlook will then open an empty Appointment form, as shown in Figure 38-19.

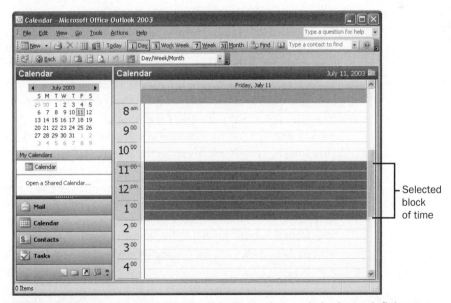

Figure 38-18. You can save time by selecting a time period prior to defining an appointment for that time.

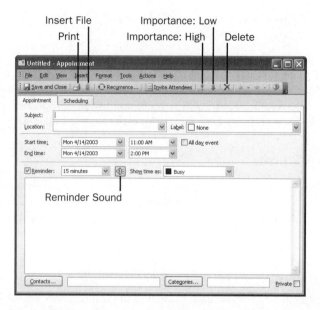

Figure 38-19. This figure shows an empty Appointment form for scheduling a new appointment.

3 Fill in the Appointment form as follows:

> **Note** Don't check the All Day Event option unless you want to convert the appointment to an event. An event is a different type of calendar item and is described in the next section.

■ Describe the appointment by entering a short description into the Subject text box. You can also enter a longer appointment description, comments, or other information into the large text box.

■ To indicate where the appointment will take place, type a location into the Location text box or select a previously entered location from the drop-down list.

■ If you didn't select the meeting time in step 1, enter the starting and ending dates and times for the meeting into the Start Time and End Time controls. (You can click the down arrow in one of these controls to select a date from a Calendar or a time from a list of times.)

■ To have Outlook display a message to remind you of the appointment, check the Reminder option and in the adjoining text box enter the amount of time in advance of the appointment that the message should be displayed, or select a time from the drop-down list. To modify or turn off the sound Outlook plays when it displays the message, click the Reminder Sound button.

- To specify your availability during the appointment time, select an item in the Show Time As drop-down list, as shown here:

Blue ——
Purple ——

In certain views of the Calendar folder, Outlook will indicate your availability by displaying a border around the appointment time using the pattern shown on the drop-down menu (a white border for free time, a cross-hatched border for tentative time, a blue border for busy time, or a purple border for out-of-office time).

- To color-code your appointment, select an item other than None in the Label drop-down list, as shown here:

In the Outlook window, the appointment text will be displayed with a background using the color you select: red for an important appointment, blue for a business appointment, green for a personal appointment, and so on.

- To enter one or more contacts who are associated with the appointment (perhaps the person you're going to interview), click the Contacts button and select one or more items from your Contacts folder (or from another contacts folder that's available in Outlook). Outlook will then display the contact(s) in the adjoining text box. Entering a contact here links the appointment to the contact; as a result, the Activities tab of the form for that contact will list the appointment as well as other linked Outlook items. You can double-click a contact name in the box to open the contact.

- To assign one or more categories to the appointment, click the Categories button and in the Categories dialog box (shown in Figure 38-20) check any of the predefined categories you want to assign in the Available Categories list. To add a custom category to the list (and check it), type it into the Item(s) Belong To These Categories text box and click the Add To List button. You can use categories for finding, sorting, filtering, or grouping Outlook items (see "Finding Outlook Items," on page 986, and "Sorting, Filtering, and Grouping Items in Folders," on page 979).

Figure 38-20. Use the Categories dialog box to assign one or more categories to an appointment.

■ To mark your appointment as private, check the Private option. (The appointment will then be hidden if you share your Calendar folder with others.)

4 Click the Save And Close button on the form's Standard toolbar.

Troubleshooting

Trouble with custom categories

You've been assigning custom categories (for example, Foreign and Domestic) to your Outlook items by typing them directly into the Categories text box in the item forms. However, when you sort, filter, group, or search by category, some of the items are missing from categories and extraneous categories appear.

Outlook lets you assign new custom categories by typing them directly into the Categories text box. However, if you make a minor typo, you inadvertently create a new category, so that items you want in the same category end up in different categories. A better way to create a custom category is to click the Categories button and enter it into the Categories dialog box (shown in Figure 38-20), as explained on page 1029. With this method, the category is added to the *master category list*, and subsequently it will always appear in the Categories dialog box (like all items in the master category list). To assign the same category to additional items, open this dialog box and check the category in the list, rather than typing it directly into the form.

Note that you can also assign categories to the selected item or items in the Outlook window—without opening the item(s) in a form—by choosing Edit, Categories, which also opens the Categories dialog box.

Note also that in the Categories dialog box, you can click the Master Category List button to open the Master Category List dialog box, where you can add or remove categories from the master list or reset the master list back to the original set of categories defined by Outlook.

To create a recurring appointment, perform the steps given above, *except* rather than entering the starting and ending times in the Appointment form, click the Recurrence button on the Standard toolbar (shown in Figure 38-19) and enter the desired recurrence pattern into the Appointment Recurrence dialog box (shown in Figure 38-21). Or, you can create the appointment by choosing Actions, New Recurring Appointment (rather than New Appointment); Outlook will then display the Appointment Recurrence dialog box before it displays the Appointment form.

Note To change the recurrence pattern, click the Recurrence button in the form. Then, in the Appointment Recurrence dialog box, enter new information or click the Remove Recurrence button to convert the recurring appointment to a one-time appointment.

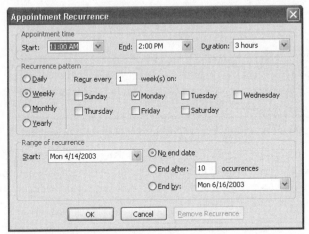

Figure 38-21. Use the Appointment Recurrence dialog box to create a recurring appointment.

Setting Up Events

To schedule a one-time or recurring event, complete the following steps:

1 In the Calendar folder, select the day or days on which the event will occur. (If you do this, Outlook will save you time by filling in the event days when it displays the Event form. However, this step is optional because you can specify any day or range of days in the form.)

2 Choose Actions, New All Day Event. Outlook will then open an empty Event form, as shown in Figure 38-22.

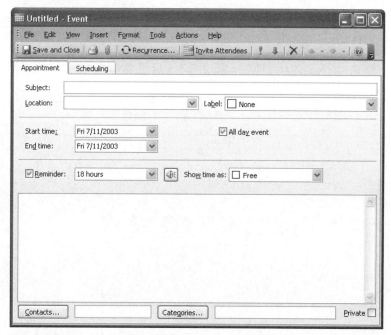

Figure 38-22. You use an empty Event form for scheduling a new event.

3 Fill in the form as described (for an appointment) in step 3 of the previous section, but be sure to leave the All Day Event option checked. Also, because an event is always scheduled for one or more complete days, the form doesn't include controls for specifying starting and ending times.

> **Note** To create a recurring event, which is analogous to a recurring appointment, click the Recurrence button and fill in the (mislabeled) Appointment Recurrence dialog box rather than entering starting and ending dates in the form. To remove the recurrence, which converts the item to a one-time event, click the Recurrence button again and click the Remove Recurrence button in the Appointment Recurrence dialog box.

4 Click the Save And Close button on the form's Standard toolbar.

> **Note** You can convert an appointment to an event by simply checking the All Day Event option in the Appointment form.

Scheduling Meetings

To schedule a meeting with one or more people, do the following:

1 Select the time period for the meeting in the Information Viewer of the Outlook window. (If you do this, Outlook will save you time by filling in the meeting times when it displays the Meeting form. However, this step is optional because you can specify any time period you want in the form.)

2 Choose Actions, New Meeting Request, or press Ctrl+Shift+Q. Outlook will then open an empty Meeting form, as shown in Figure 38-23.

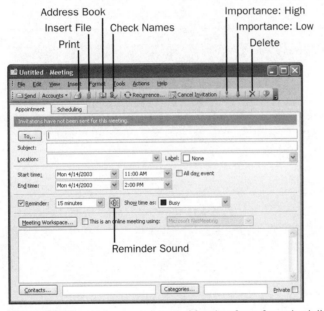

Figure 38-23. You use an empty Meeting form for scheduling a new meeting.

> **Note** To schedule a recurring meeting (analogous to a recurring appointment), create the meeting by choosing Actions, New Recurring Meeting rather than choosing Actions, New Meeting Request. Then, before Outlook displays the Meeting form, it will then display the (mislabeled) Appointment Recurrence dialog box in which you can specify the recurrence pattern (shown in Figure 38-21, on page 1031).
>
> Also, you can convert a one-time meeting to a recurring one by clicking the Recurrence button on the form's Standard toolbar and entering the recurrence pattern into the Appointment Recurrence dialog box. (And you can convert a recurring meeting to a one-time meeting by clicking the Remove Recurrence button in this same dialog box.)

3 Type the e-mail addresses of the people you want to invite to the meeting (the meeting *attendees*) into the To text box, separating each address with a semicolon. Or click the To button to select the addresses from your Outlook Contacts folder.

> For information on entering or selecting addresses, see "Composing and Sending E-Mail Messages," on page 1014.

4 Fill in the other controls in the Meeting form following the instructions given under step 3 in "Scheduling Appointments," on page 1028 (see Figure 38-24).

To schedule an online meeting, check the This Is An Online Meeting Using option and then select the online meeting software you're using in the following drop-down list (for example, Microsoft NetMeeting) and enter information about the meeting into the other controls that appear as soon as you check This Is An Online Meeting Using.

> **Note**   To invite other people to an all-day event, rather than a meeting, check the All Day Event option in the Event form. This coverts the meeting to an *invited event*.

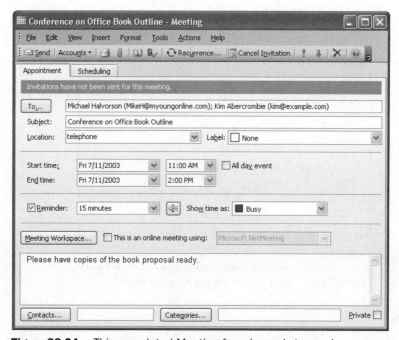

Figure 38-24.   This completed Meeting form is ready to send.

> The Meeting Workspace button in the Meeting form is explained in "Creating and Linking to a SharePoint Meeting Workspace," on page 1039.

5   Select an e-mail account (if you have more than one) from the Accounts drop-down menu on the Standard toolbar. Then click the Send button on this same toolbar to place a meeting-request e-mail message in your Outbox and then transmit this message to your outgoing e-mail server so that the requests will be delivered to the attendees, as explained in "Composing and Sending E-Mail Messages," on page 1014.

Outlook will place a copy of the meeting in the scheduled time slot in your Calendar folder, and a meeting request will appear in the Inbox of each attendee you invited. An attendee can open the meeting request or just view the request in the Reading pane of the Inbox (shown in Figure 38-25), and the attendee can reply by opening the meeting request and clicking the Accept, Tentative, or Decline button in the form.

If the attendee has Outlook version 2002 or later, he or she can simply view the meeting request message in the Reading pane of the Inbox and click the Accept, Tentative, or Decline button in the Reading pane header (shown in Figure 38-25). Also, with Outlook 2002 or later, the attendee can click the Propose New Time button (in the Reading pane or in the form) to send a reply with a proposal for a new time. (To help the attendee pick a suitable new time, when the attendee clicks this button, Outlook displays the Propose New Time dialog box, which lets the attendee use the meeting planner as discussed in the sidebar "Planning a Meeting," on page 1037.)

If the attendee clicks any of the reply buttons except Decline, a copy of the meeting will be added to the scheduled time slot in the attendee's Calendar folder. Whichever button the attendee clicks, the meeting request will be removed from the attendee's Inbox.

The attendee's reply will be e-mailed back to you, and as soon as you open the reply message or view it in the Reading pane, Outlook will record the response in the copy of the meeting in your Calendar folder.

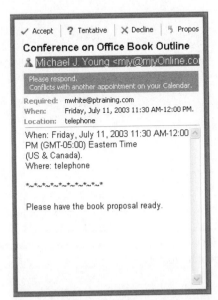

Figure 38-25.   This figure shows the meeting request in the Inbox of one of the invited attendees, viewed in the Reading pane.

Chapter 38

Note   Your attendees can propose new meeting times only if the Allow Attendees To Propose New Times For Meetings You Organize option is checked. To find this option, choose Tools, Options, click the Calendar Options button in the Preferences tab of the Options dialog box, and look in the Calendar Options area of the Calendar Options dialog box (shown in Figure 38-26).

In the Calendar Options dialog box, you can also customize the way the Calendar folder displays weeks, add standard holidays to your Calendar folder, and make other settings that affect the look or operation of your Calendar folder.

Tip   Reach a wider audience by using iCalendar

If you send out your meeting requests using the standard iCalendar Internet format—rather than the proprietary Outlook meeting format—you can invite anyone who uses a calendaring program that supports iCalendar, including Outlook version 2002 or later. To use iCalendar, choose Tools, Options, click the Calendar Options button in the Preferences tab of the Options dialog box and make sure that the When Sending Meeting Requests Over The Internet Use iCalendar Format option is checked in the Calendar Options dialog box (as shown in Figure 38-26). Before you send a particular meeting request, you can override this option by choosing Send As iCalendar from the Tools menu in the Meeting form to deselect the menu option.

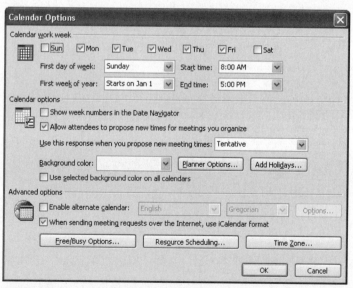

Figure 38-26.   In the Calendar Options dialog box you can make settings that affect the operation of your Calendar folder.

6 To view the records of the meeting replies, so you can see at a glance which attendees have replied and what their responses are, open your copy of the meeting in your Calendar folder and open the Tracking tab of the Meeting form (shown in Figure 38-27).

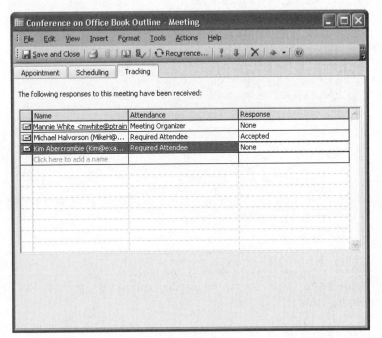

Figure 38-27. You can view the replies to your meeting requests in the Tracking tab of the Meeting form.

Note You can convert an appointment to a meeting by clicking the Invite Attendees button on the Appointment form's Standard toolbar. And you can convert a meeting to an appointment by clicking the Cancel Invitation button on this same toolbar *before* you click the Send button to transmit the request.

Planning a Meeting

If you and all your attendees connect to the same Microsoft Exchange Server network, or if you and all attendees have published your free/busy times on the Internet, you can use Outlook's meeting planner to quickly select a time for the meeting when all attendees (and all required resources) are free. You can use the meeting planner in the following ways:

● When you've opened a Meeting form to define a meeting (as described previously), you can click the Scheduling tab of the meeting form to access the meeting planner (as shown in Figure 38-28).

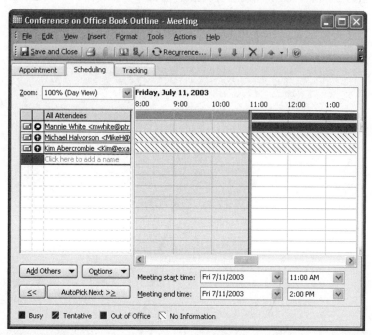

Figure 38-28. You can use the meeting planner through the Scheduling tab of the Meeting form.

- When you schedule a new meeting, you can choose Actions, Plan A Meeting (rather than choosing New Meeting Request). Outlook will then display the Plan A Meeting dialog box, which lets you use the meeting planner. When you click the Make Meeting button in the Plan A Meeting dialog box, Outlook will then display the Meeting form, where you can define the meeting and send out meeting requests.

- If an attendee opens a meeting request in his or her Inbox—or views it in the Reading pane—and clicks the Propose New Time button, Outlook opens the Propose New Time dialog box, which displays the meeting planner.

- You can consult the meeting planner whenever a calendar folder is open, without actually scheduling a meeting, by choosing Actions, View Group Schedules.

If you want to schedule meetings over the Internet (rather than using Exchange Server) you and your attendees must publish your free/busy times, and you must tell Outlook where to locate each attendee's free/busy information by completing the following basic steps:

1 To publish free/busy times, you (as well as each attendee) should choose Tools, Options, click the Calendar Options button in the Preferences tab of the Options dialog box to open the Calendar Options dialog box (shown in Figure 38-26), click the Free/Busy Options button, and fill in the publishing options in the Free/Busy Options dialog box (shown in Figure 38-29). If you check the Publish And Search Using Microsoft Office Internet Free/Busy Service option, and if you haven't previously signed up with this service, you'll need to click the Manage button to connect to Microsoft's Free/Busy service site and register for the service.

Note that you can have Outlook update your free/busy information at any time by opening the Calendar folder and choosing Tools, Send/Receive, Free/Busy Information.

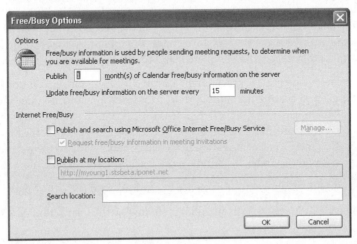

Figure 38-29. The Free/Busy Options dialog box lets you control the way Outlook publishes your free/busy information.

2 To tell Outlook where to look for each attendee's free/busy information, you can enter a default free/busy location into the Search Location text box in the Free/Busy Options dialog box. You can also enter a free/busy location for a specific contact by opening that contact, opening the Details tab in the Contact form, and entering the URL (Uniform Resource Locator) of the contact's free/busy location into the Address text box in the Internet Free-Busy area. If you provide a free/busy location for a contact, Outlook will look for that contact's free/busy schedule at that location rather than at the default free/busy location.

Creating and Linking to a SharePoint Meeting Workspace

If you're a member of a team Web site on a Web server running Microsoft Windows Share-Point Services, you can create a meeting workspace on that site and link it to an Outlook Meeting form to help organize the meeting that you're planning. A meeting workspace is a specialized type of SharePoint Web site that's designed specifically for arranging and coordinating a meeting—a meeting recorded in an events list on a SharePoint team site or a meeting that you schedule in Outlook by sending out meeting requests as explained in the previous section.

For general information on SharePoint team Web sites, see Chapter 8, "Using Windows SharePoint Services in Professional Workgroups." For a summary of the methods for creating a meeting workspace from within a team Web site that you've opened in your browser (rather than from within Outlook), see "Exchanging Information on a SharePoint Site," on page 198.

Like other types of SharePoint Web sites, a meeting workspace can contain lists, document libraries, and other components. A typical meeting workspace includes a document library for sharing documents related to the meeting, plus a collection of custom lists—for example, lists to delineate meeting objectives, to keep track of attendees, to record an agenda of topics, to follow tasks that need to be completed, and to catalog decisions that need to be made.

You can create a meeting workspace right within a Meeting form in Outlook. The new meeting workspace will acquire the subject, date, time, location, and attendee information from the Meeting form, and Outlook will update the information in the meeting workspace when the corresponding information changes in your Meeting form. Also, the Meeting form (your copy, as well as the copies sent to attendees) will contain a link to the meeting workspace, allowing you or any attendee to visit the workspace by clicking the link.

To create and link to a meeting workspace in Outlook, complete the following steps:

1 Open a new Meeting form and fill it in, following the instructions given in the previous section.

2 Click the Meeting Workspace button in the Meeting form and use the controls in the Meeting Workspace task pane that appears to create a new meeting workspace on your SharePoint team Web site. You'll need to specify your site's address (URL) and the workspace template you want to use. See Figure 38-30.

After you create the meeting workspace, the Meeting form will be linked to that workspace, which means that you can open the meeting workspace from the form, and that, when you change information in the form, Outlook will update the corresponding information in the meeting workspace.

Tip If a meeting workspace already exists on your SharePoint team Web site, you can link the Meeting form to that workspace—rather than creating a new one—by clicking the You Can Also Link To An Existing Workspace command in the Tip area at the bottom of the initial Meeting Workspace task pane.

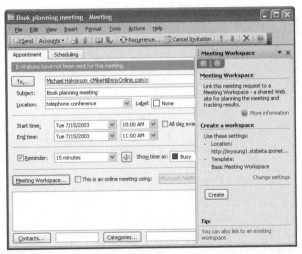

Figure 38-30. You can use the new Meeting Workspace task pane in a Meeting form to create a meeting workspace on a SharePoint team Web site and to link the form to that workspace.

3 Send the meeting request as described in the previous section.

4 To open the linked meeting workspace in your browser, click the hyperlink (bearing the name of the meeting workspace) in the large text box of the Meeting form, or click the Go To Workspace command in the Meeting Workspace task pane (see Figure 38-31).

Figure 38-32 shows a meeting workspace created from an Outlook Meeting form and opened in a browser.

> **Note** The hyperlink to the meeting workspace will be available in your copy of the Meeting form, as well as in the copies you send to other attendees, so that all meeting attendees will have ready access to the workspace.

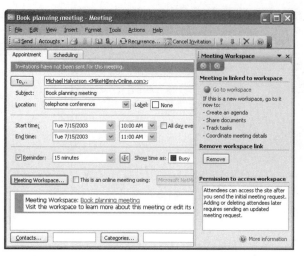

Figure 38-31. When a Meeting form is linked to a SharePoint meeting workspace, the large text box of the form includes a hyperlink and the task pane includes a command, either of which you can click to open the workspace in your browser.

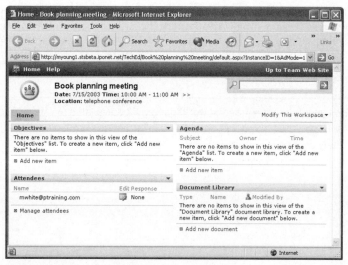

Figure 38-32. This figure shows the meeting workspace, opened in Internet Explorer, that was created from the Meeting form shown in Figures 38-29 and 38-30.

5 After you've opened the meeting workspace in your browser, you can add items to the site's lists, upload meeting documents, customize the site, or perform other tasks using the techniques explained in Chapter 8.

Working with Your Calendar Folder

Chapter 37, "Working with Outlook Items and Folders," describes the general methods for working with Outlook views, items, and folders. In the Calendar folder, the most common view is Day/Week/Month, which displays your calendar items (appointments, events, and meetings) in the Information Viewer in a layout that resembles a printed calendar or appointment book. In this view (shown in Figure 38-33), you can click the Day, Work Week, Week, or Month button on the Standard toolbar to adjust the view's range.

Icon indicates that this item is a meeting   Date Navigator

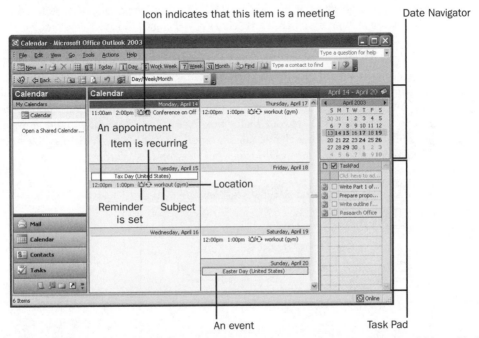

An event   Task Pad

Figure 38-33. This figure shows the Day/Week/Month view of the Calendar folder, with the Week range displayed.

The following are some unique techniques you can use in the Day/Week/Month view of the Calendar folder (some of these techniques aren't available in all ranges):

- You can quickly view particular time slots by clicking objects within the Date Navigator. You can view any date by choosing Go, Go To Date or pressing Ctrl+G and entering the date into the Go To Date dialog box. And you can select the current day by clicking the Today button on the Standard toolbar.

- You can view, open, or add items in your Tasks folder (described in Chapter 39, "Managing Contacts, Tasks, and Other Types of Information") by using the Task Pad. If the Task Pad isn't visible, choose View, Task Pad. To control the particular tasks that are shown in the Task Pad, choose commands from the View, Task Pad View submenu.

● You can add a new appointment or event (the item type depends on the current range and where you click) by clicking a time slot and typing the subject. And you can edit an item's subject by clicking it and typing.

● You can change an item's time by dragging it to a new time slot (press Ctrl while you drag to make a copy). And you can change an item's duration by dragging its border.

> **Tip** **Publish your Calendar on the Web**
> You can publish a snapshot of your Calendar folder on the Web by choosing File, Save As Web Page to save your Calendar in an HTML file and then posting that file to your Web server. Keep in mind that if any items change, you'll have to repeat this process to update your published Calendar.

If you specified a reminder for an appointment, event, or meeting, when the item is nearly due (or if it's past due but you just started Outlook), Outlook will display a reminder message. All reminders are displayed in a single dialog box (shown in Figure 38-34), so you don't have to view and close a separate dialog box for each due item (as you did in previous versions of Outlook). To view all due calendar items that you haven't dismissed, you can display this dialog box at any time by choosing View, Reminders Window.

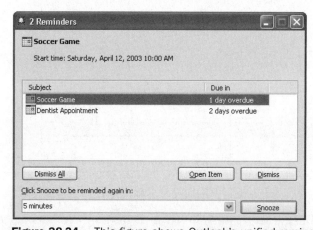

Figure 38-34. This figure shows Outlook's unified reminder dialog box.

In addition to the Calendar folder options you can set in the Calendar Options dialog box (shown in Figure 38-26), you can make the following settings to customize your Calendar folder:

● To have the reminder feature turned on by default when you open a new Appointment, Event, or Meeting form and to specify the default reminder time, choose Tools, Options, check the Default Reminder option in the Preferences tab of the Options dialog box, and select the time in the adjoining drop-down list.

● To modify the font used in the Date Navigator or to customize the reminder feature, click the Other tab of the Options dialog box, click the Advanced Options button, and click the Font button to set the Date Navigator font or click the Reminder Options button to change the reminder feature.

Opening a SharePoint Calendar in Outlook

If you're a member of a team Web site on a Web server running Windows SharePoint Services, you can open and view a SharePoint events list in Outlook as a calendar folder. (A SharePoint events list is similar to an Outlook calendar folder.) This feature allows you to view and work with a shared calendar belonging to your SharePoint team within the convenient and familiar Outlook environment. Furthermore, using Outlook's new side-by-side calendar viewing option, you can view the shared folder alongside your personal calendar and perhaps look for conflicting appointments or copy appointments from the events list into your personal calendar.

When you open a SharePoint events list in Outlook, Outlook creates a separate copy of the list as an Outlook calendar folder and stores it on a local disk, so you can view the calendar items even when you're not connected to the Internet. However, your Outlook calendar folder remains linked to the SharePoint events list so that you can update your calendar folder using a single command. Keep in mind that the update goes only one way: it copies the latest version of the SharePoint events list to your Outlook calendar folder but does *not* copy changes from your Outlook calendar folder back to the SharePoint events list. In fact, you can't make any changes to your linked Outlook calendar folder—it's strictly read-only.

> For general information on SharePoint team Web sites, see Chapter 8.

To open a SharePoint events list as a linked Outlook calendar folder, perform the following steps:

1 Following the instructions given in Chapter 8, use your browser to open the Web page for the SharePoint events list that you want to view in Outlook and click the Link To Outlook command in the toolbar near the top of the page. Outlook will ask you to confirm the request and will then create and open a linked calendar folder. It will list the calendar folder in the Other Calendars list in the Navigation pane. The calendar folder will also appear in the Folder List under the heading "SharePoint Folders."

2 To copy the current contents of the SharePoint events list to your linked Outlook calendar folder, right-click the calendar folder name in the Navigation pane and choose Refresh from the shortcut menu. You should do this whenever a team member updates the SharePoint events list. Figure 38-35 shows an Outlook calendar folder that's linked to a SharePoint events list.

Chapter 38

> **Tip** To receive an e-mail message notifying you whenever the SharePoint events list is updated, you can sign up for an alert for that list by clicking the Alert Me command in the Actions area at the left of the list's Web page (as explained in Chapter 8). Alternatively, you can sign up for the alert from within Outlook by clicking the Mail button in the lower portion of the Navigation pane, choosing Tools, Rules And Alerts, clicking the Manage Alerts tab, and then clicking the New Alert button.

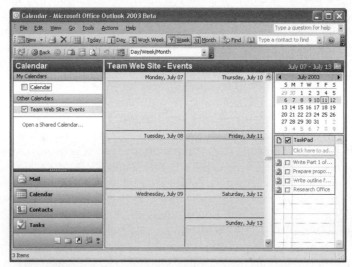

Figure 38-35. You can refresh an Outlook calendar folder that's linked to a SharePoint events list to view the latest list contents. You can't, however, make changes to the calendar folder in Outlook.

3 To quickly view the linked SharePoint events list in your browser, right-click the name of the linked calendar folder in the Navigation pane and choose Open In Web Browser.

> **Tip** Export individual events from your SharePoint site to Outlook
>
> If you have access to a team Web site on a Web server running Windows SharePoint Services, you can copy an individual event from the site to your default Calendar folder so that you'll have a personal copy of the event description. To do this, use your browser to open the Web page for the events list that contains the event you want to copy, click the event item to display it in a separate Web page, and then click the Export Event command on the toolbar near the top of the page. If prompted, choose to open the file (rather than to save it on disk). The event will then be opened in an Outlook Appointment form, which you can use to read, modify, and save the item in your default Calendar folder.

Managing Contacts, Tasks, and Other Types of Information

Maintaining Your Address List with the
Contacts Folder 1047

Managing Tasks and Projects with the
Tasks Folder 1060

Recording Events with the
Journal Folder. 1068

Storing Miscellaneous Information
in the Notes Folder. 1074

Maintaining Your Address List with the Contacts Folder

You can use the default Contacts folder—or any other contacts folder that's available in Outlook—to store names, mailing addresses, phone numbers, e-mail and Web addresses, and many other types of information for your business or personal contacts. Once you've added a collection of contacts to your Contacts folder, you can use Microsoft Office Outlook 2003 commands to quickly find a contact, and then send an e-mail message or an instant message to the contact, write the contact a letter, telephone the contact, visit the contact's Web site, or communicate with the contact in other ways.

> **Note** Although for simplicity this chapter often refers to just the default *Contacts folder*, you can also use the techniques with any other contacts folder that's available in Outlook.

Defining Contacts and Distribution Lists

You can add individual contacts as well as distribution lists to your Contacts folder. A *distribution list* is a single item that contains an entire set of contact descriptions (known as *members* of the distribution list)—for example, everyone in your department or all the members of your rowing club. A member of a distribution list can be a reference to one of the contacts already stored in your Contacts folder, or it can be an independent description consisting of just a person's or company's name, e-mail address, and preferred e-mail format. When you address an e-mail message (or a meeting request or task assignment), you can send it to all of the members of a distribution list as easily as you can send it to a single e-mail address. You can do that by clicking the To (or Cc or Bcc) button in the message header and selecting the distribution list in the Select Names dialog box.

> For information on addressing e-mail messages, see "Composing and Sending E-Mail Messages," on page 1014.

To define a new contact, complete the following steps:

1 Open a blank Contact form (shown in Figure 39-1) using one of the following methods:

New
Contact

- Open the Contacts folder and choose Actions, New Contact; click the New button on the Standard toolbar; or press Ctrl+N.
- With any folder open, choose Contact from the New drop-down list on the Standard toolbar or press Ctrl+Shift+C.

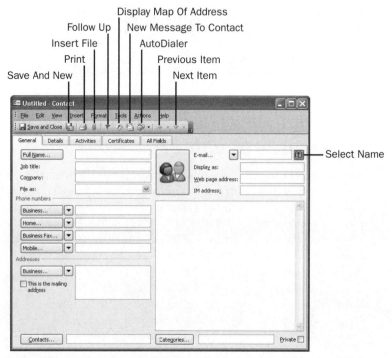

Figure 39-1. This is a blank Contact form, which you use for defining a new contact.

> **Tip** Use an existing contact
>
> If you want to create a new contact that has some of the same information as an existing contact (perhaps a contact who works for the same company), select the existing contact in the Contacts folder, and then choose Actions, New Contact From Same Company (rather than New Contact). When the Contact form is opened, it will initially contain the company name, business address, business telephone number(s), and Web page address from the existing contact.

Chapter 39

2 Fill in the Contacts form as follows:

■ If the contact is an individual (rather than a company), type the contact's full name into the Full Name text box.

> **Note** Outlook stores the name you type in the Full Name text box as a set of separate fields—Title, First, Middle, Last, and Suffix. This feature allows you to search, sort, filter, or group items by one of these individual fields. To see how Outlook has divided the name you typed into separate fields, and to make corrections if necessary, click the Full Name button to display the Check Full Name dialog box. (If Outlook can't decipher the name you've typed, it will display this dialog box automatically.)

■ If the contact has a job title, type it in the Job Title text box.

■ If the contact is associated with a company, or if you're defining the item for a company rather than an individual, type the name in the Company text box.

■ After you enter text in the Full Name or Company text box, Outlook fills in the File As text box. Outlook displays the File As field at the top of each contact in Address Cards view and uses this field (by default) to sort the contacts. If you want to change this field, select a new choice (for example, *John Smith* rather than *Smith, John*) in the File As drop-down list, or type a new value.

■ You can enter up to four telephone numbers for the contact, one in each of the Phone Numbers text boxes. To enter each, click the Down Arrow next to a box, select the type of phone number (Business, Business Fax, Home, Home Fax, Pager, and so on), and then type the number in the box. If you skip the area code, Outlook will insert your current area code (which you can set using the Phone And Modem Options item in the Control Panel and in other places in Windows).

■ You can enter up to three different street or post office box addresses for the contact. To enter each one, click the down arrow to the left of the Addresses text box and select a description for the address—Business, Home, or Other. Then type the full address into the Addresses text box.

To designate one of the addresses you enter as the contact's mailing address, check the This Is The Mailing Address option when that address is displayed. If you use Microsoft Word to print an individual envelope or label for the contact, or if you use Word's mail merge feature to create form letters or other output documents using your Contacts folder as the recipient list, Word will use the designated mailing address.

■ If you have a graphics file containing a picture of the contact or some other image that you would like to display in the Contact form, click the new Add Contact Picture button and select the file in the Add Contact Picture dialog box.

■ You can enter up to three e-mail addresses for the contact. To enter each one, click the down arrow to the left of the E-Mail text box and select E-Mail, E-Mail 2, or E-Mail 3. Then, either type the address in the E-Mail text box or click the adjoining Select Name button to select the address in the Select Name dialog box.

■ When you address an e-mail message to the contact, Outlook will display the contents of the Display As text box in the To, Cc, or Bcc field of the Message form. When you enter an e-mail address in the Contact form, Outlook will add default display text (the contact's name followed by the e-mail address) to the Display As text box, but you can change this text if you wish.

■ If the contact has a Web page, type the URL in the Web Page Address text box.

■ If the contact has an address for receiving Instant Messaging messages, type it in the IM Address text box. (Using Instant Messaging is described in "Using Your Contacts Folder," on page 1055.)

■ Type any free-form information you wish in the Contact form's large text box.

■ To enter one or more other contacts who are associated with the current contact (perhaps members of the same family), click the Contacts button and select one or more other contacts from your default Contacts folder (or from another available contacts folder). Outlook will then display the contact(s) you selected in the adjoining text box. (See the tip, "Link a contact to related information," on page 1052.)

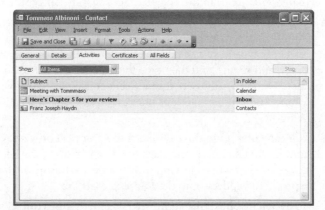

Figure 39-2. You can view linked Outlook items and files in the Activities tab in the Contact form.

■ To assign one or more categories to the contact, click the Categories button, and in the Categories dialog box (see Figure 39-3), check any of the predefined categories you want to assign in the Available Categories list. To add a custom category to the list (and check it), type it in the Item(s) Belong To These Categories text box and click the Add To List button. You can use categories for finding, sorting, filtering, or grouping Outlook items. (To learn more about using categories for finding, sorting, filtering, or grouping Outlook items, see "Finding Outlook Items," on page 986, and "Sorting, Filtering, and Grouping Items in Folders," on page 979. For important information on creating custom categories, see the troubleshooting sidebar "Trouble with custom categories," on page 1030.)

Figure 39-3. Use the Categories dialog box to assign one or more categories to the contact.

■ To mark the contact as private, check the Private option. (The contact will then be hidden if you share your Contacts folder with others.)

■ To enter additional information about the contact—such as the contact's department, profession, nickname, birthday, or Microsoft NetMeeting settings—display the Details tab of the Contacts form.

■ To view, modify, or add certificates for the contact, use the Certificates tab. A contact's certificate is a digital ID that Outlook uses to send encrypted e-mail to that contact.

■ To access all fields that contain information about the contact, or to create custom fields, use the All Fields tab.

Note   Outlook stores each phone number you enter as a set of separate fields—Country/Region, City/Area Code, Local Number, and Extension. This feature allows you to search, sort, filter, or group items by one of these individual fields. To see how Outlook has divided a phone number you typed into separate fields, and to make corrections if necessary, click the button next to the phone number, which is labeled according to the type of the phone number (Business, Home, and so on). This will display the Check Phone Number dialog box.

Note   Outlook stores an address you type in the Address text box as a set of separate fields—Street, City, State/Province, ZIP/Postal Code, and Country/Region. This feature allows you to search, sort, filter, or group items by one of these individual fields. To see how Outlook has divided the address you typed into separate fields and to make corrections if necessary, click the button next to the Addresses text box, which will be labeled Business, Home, or Other. This will display the Check Address dialog box. (If Outlook can't decipher an address you've typed, it will display this dialog box automatically.)

> **Note** The Select Name dialog box is similar to the Select Names dialog box that appears when you click the To, Cc, Bcc, or Address Book button in a Message form. If you've set up a directory account, you can search an Internet directory service for the contact's e-mail address. Directory accounts are discussed in "Adding, Modifying, and Removing Outlook Accounts," on page 1080.

3 Click the Save And Close button on the form's Standard toolbar.

> **Tip** Link a contact to related information
>
> Entering one or more other contacts into the Contacts text box in the Contacts form *links* those contacts to the current contact (and also links the current contact to the other contacts). You can link any other Outlook item to the current contact by entering the current contact in the Contact text box of the other Outlook item.
>
> You can also link any Outlook item or disk file to the current contact by choosing Actions, Link, Items or choosing Actions, Link, File in the Contact form (or in the main Outlook window if the contact is selected in the Information Viewer). The following are a few examples of items or files you might want to link to the current contact:
>
> - An appointment you have with the contact
> - An item in the Notes folder containing free-form information relating to the contact
> - A Word document the contact sent you
>
> If you send or receive a message to or from a contact, Outlook *automatically* links the message to the contact in your Contacts folder (this includes a regular e-mail message, as well as a meeting or task request or reply and the corresponding item in the Calendar or Tasks folder).
>
> If one or more items or files are linked to the current contact, you can view them by displaying the Activities tab in the Contact form (shown in Figure 39-2). To open an item or file, double-click it in the Activities tab.

To define a distribution list, follow these steps:

1 Open a blank Distribution List form (shown in Figure 39-4) using one of the following methods:

- Open the Contacts folder and choose Actions, New Distribution List.
- With any folder open, choose Distribution List from the New drop-down list on the Standard toolbar or press Ctrl+Shift+L.

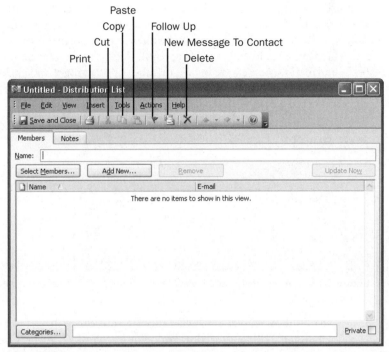

Figure 39-4. This is a blank Distribution List form, which you use for defining a new distribution list.

2 Type a name for the distribution list in the Name text box.

3 Add members to the distribution list. To add each member, do one of the following in the Members tab in the Distribution List form:

- To add one or more members from the contacts stored in a contacts folder, click the Select Members button. Then, in the Select Members dialog box, select a particular contacts folder in the Show Names From The drop-down list (if you have more than one contacts folder) and choose the contact or contacts from the list. A member you add this way will be linked to the contact, so that if you change any of the information about the contact in the contacts folder, the member in the distribution list will reflect that change.

- To add a new member, click the Add New button and enter the person's or company's name, e-mail address, e-mail address type, and preferred e-mail format in the Add New Member dialog box (see Figure 39-5). If you leave the Add To Contacts option clear, the new member will consist of an independent description and will not be linked to a contact in the Contacts folder. If you check Add To Contacts, Outlook will create a new contact in your Contacts folder containing the information you supplied and it will link the new member to that contact, as described above.

The new members you add will appear in the list in the Distribution List form. If you double-click a member based on a contact, Outlook will open the linked contact in the

Contact form. If you double-click a new, independent member, Outlook will open the member in the E-Mail Properties dialog box, which displays the same controls as the Add New Member dialog box in which you originally created the member (except that it doesn't have an Add To Contacts option). In either case, you can modify the member's information. You can remove a member by selecting it and clicking the Remove button in the Distribution List form (this removes only the distribution list member, *not* a contact to which it's linked).

Figure 39-5. You use the Add New Member dialog box to create a new distribution list member.

4 If you wish, add categories to the Categories box or check the Private option, as explained in step 2 of the procedure for defining a contact, given previously in this section.

5 If you wish, you can enter free-form information about the distribution list by clicking the Notes tab and typing the information in the large text box.

6 Click the Save And Close button on the form's Standard toolbar.

In the Information Viewer, Outlook marks a distribution list using a double-head icon. Here's how one would appear in the Address Cards view:

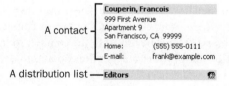

Tip   **Keep your distribution list private**

Unless you want to reveal to all message recipients the entire list of e-mail addresses in your distribution list, add the distribution list to the Bcc field when you address an e-mail message, rather than adding it to the To or Cc field. To display the Bcc field in the Message form's header, choose Bcc from the Options drop-down menu in the message header (in Word), or choose Bcc Field from the View menu (in the Outlook e-mail editor).

Troubleshooting

Distribution list displays out-of-date information

You've added members from your Contacts folder to a distribution list. However, when you change or delete a contact and then open the distribution list, the information displayed in the Distribution List form doesn't show your changes.

Although a distribution list member you create from a contact is linked to that contact, and Outlook will use the current e-mail address contained in the contact if you address a message using the distribution list, the information that appears in the Distribution List form will become out of date if you change the contact's Display As or E-Mail field (these are the two fields that appear in the Distribution List form). Also, if you delete the contact a member is linked to, the member will continue to appear in the Distribution List form. To update all the information that appears in the Distribution List form, click the Update Now button in the form. (Update Now will remove a deleted contact from the distribution list only if you've deleted the contact not only from the contacts folder but also from the Deleted Items folder.)

Using Your Contacts Folder

Figure 39-6 shows a set of contacts that have been added to the Contacts folder as they appear in the commonly used Address Cards view. This section explains how to quickly find or communicate with a contact you've added to your Contacts folder and how to set several Contacts folder options.

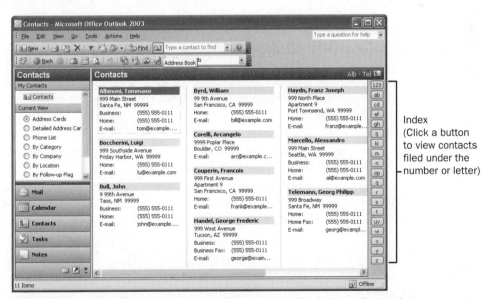

Figure 39-6. This figure shows the Contacts folder in the Address Cards view.

In addition to the general methods for finding Outlook items discussed in "Finding Outlook Items," on page 986, you can quickly locate a contact when working in any folder by typing the contact's name (or part of the name) in the Find A Contact box on the Standard toolbar and pressing Enter:

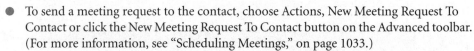

You can also select a previously entered name from the drop-down list.

You can communicate with a contact in a variety of ways by selecting the contact in the Information Viewer and then using Outlook commands, as follows:

- To send an e-mail message to the contact, choose Actions, New Message To Contact. (For more information, see "Receiving and Sending E-Mail Messages with the E-Mail Folders," on page 999.)

- To use Word and the Word Letter Wizard to write a letter to the contact, choose Actions, New Letter To Contact. (See the tip, "Have Word write your letters," on page 567.)

- To run Word's mail-merge feature from within Outlook, select the contacts you want to receive the form letter (or other mail-merge output document), choose Tools, Mail Merge, fill in the Mail Merge Contacts dialog box, and then complete the mail merge operation in Word. Once Outlook transfers you to Word, the easiest way to complete the merge is to choose Tools, Letters And Mailings, Mail Merge Wizard in Word to display the Mail Merge task pane. For details on using mail merge in Word, see "Using the Mail Merge Wizard to Automate Large Mailings," on page 549.

New
Meeting
Request To
Contact

- To send a meeting request to the contact, choose Actions, New Meeting Request To Contact or click the New Meeting Request To Contact button on the Advanced toolbar. (For more information, see "Scheduling Meetings," on page 1033.)

- To schedule an appointment with the contact, choose Actions, New Appointment With Contact. Outlook will open a new appointment in a form and will link the appointment with the contact by entering the contact's name in the Appointment form's Contacts box. (For more information, see "Scheduling Appointments," on page 1027.)

New Task
For
Contact

- To assign a task to the contact, choose Actions, New Task For Contact or click the New Task For Contact button on the Advanced toolbar. (See "Managing Tasks and Projects with the Tasks Folder," on page 1060.)

- To create a new journal entry that's linked to the contact (and has the contact's name as the subject), choose Actions, New Journal Entry For Contact. (See "Recording Events with the Journal Folder," on page 1068.)

- If you have a modem attached to the same line as your telephone, you can place a call to the contact by using the commands on the Call Contact submenu of the Actions menu:

Dial

Alternatively, you can use the menu that appears when you click the down arrow on the Dial button on the Standard toolbar.

Call Using
NetMeeting

- If you've defined NetMeeting settings for the contact (in the Contact form's Details tab) you can establish a NetMeeting connection with that contact by choosing Actions, Call Using NetMeeting or by clicking the Call Using NetMeeting button on the Advanced toolbar.

- If both you and the contact have instant messaging accounts and if you've entered the contact's instant messaging address in the IM Address text box in the General tab in the Contact form, you can use instant messaging to communicate with the contact in real time—provided that the person is currently logged on—by opening the contact in the Contact form and choosing Actions, New Instant Message in the form.

Explore
Web Page

- If you've entered a URL in the Web Page Address text box in the contact's form, you can open that Web page in your browser by clicking the Explore Web Page button on the Advanced toolbar or by pressing Ctrl+Shift+X.

Display
Map Of
Address

- You can display a map showing the location of the contact's address by opening the contact and choosing Actions, Display Map Of Address in the Contact form or by clicking the Display Map Of Address button on the form's Standard toolbar. Outlook will then connect to the Microsoft MapPoint Web Service on the Web and attempt to locate and display the map.

> **Note** If you've opened a contact in the Contact form, keep in mind that most of the commands mentioned in this list are also available in the form. (The Display Map Of Address and New Instant Message commands are available *only* in the Contacts form.)

Tip Customize the Contacts folder

To specify the order in which you enter contact names in the Full Name text box (such as "First (Middle) Last" or "Last First") so that Outlook knows how to divide the names into separate fields, or to change the default way Outlook files contacts ("Last, First," "First Last," "Company," and so on), choose Tools, Options, click the Contact Options button in the Preferences tab in the Options dialog box, and make your changes in the Contact Options dialog box (shown in Figure 39-7). You can also use this dialog box to display an additional contacts index using a specified language. A contacts index is a vertical list of numbers and letters that appears in an address cards view, along the right side of the Information Viewer, to help you navigate to a particular contact (see Figure 39-6).

Figure 39-7. The Contact Options dialog box lets you change the order in which you enter names and other features of the Contacts folder.

Opening a SharePoint Contacts List in Outlook

If you are a member of a team Web site on a Web server running Microsoft Windows SharePoint Services, you can open and view a SharePoint contacts list in Outlook as a contacts folder. This feature allows you to view and work with a shared list of contacts belonging to your SharePoint team within the convenient and familiar Outlook environment.

When you open a SharePoint contacts list in Outlook, Outlook creates a separate copy of the list as an Outlook contacts folder and stores it on a local disk, so you can view the contacts even when you're not connected to the Internet. However, your Outlook contacts folder remains linked to the SharePoint contacts list so that you can update your contacts folder using a single command. Keep in mind that the update goes only one way: it copies the latest version of the SharePoint contacts list to your Outlook contacts folder, but does *not* copy changes from your Outlook contacts folder back to the SharePoint contacts list. In fact, you can't make any changes to your linked Outlook contacts folder—it's strictly read-only.

> **For general information on SharePoint team Web sites, see Chapter 8, "Using Windows SharePoint Services in Professional Workgroups."**

To open a SharePoint contacts list as a linked Outlook contacts folder, perform the following steps:

1   Following the instructions given in Chapter 8, use your browser to open the Web page for the SharePoint contacts list that you want to view in Outlook, and click the Link To Outlook command on the toolbar near the top of the page. Outlook will ask you to confirm the request and will then create and open a linked contacts folder. It will list the contacts folder in the Other Contacts list in the Navigation pane. The contacts folder will also appear in the Folder List under the heading "SharePoint Folders."

2   To copy the current contents of the SharePoint contacts list to your linked Outlook contacts folder, right-click the contacts folder name in the Navigation pane and choose Refresh from the shortcut menu. You can do this whenever a team member updates the SharePoint contacts list. While you are working online, Outlook will also automatically update the folder every 20 minutes. Figure 39-8 shows an Outlook contacts folder that's linked to a SharePoint contacts list.

> **Tip**   To receive an e-mail message notifying you whenever the SharePoint contacts list is updated, you can sign up for an alert for that list by clicking the Alert Me command in the Actions area at the left of the list's Web page (as explained in Chapter 8). Alternatively, you can sign up for the alert from within Outlook by clicking the Mail button in the lower portion of the Navigation pane, choosing Tools, Rules And Alerts, clicking the Manage Alerts tab, and then clicking the New Alert button.

Chapter 39

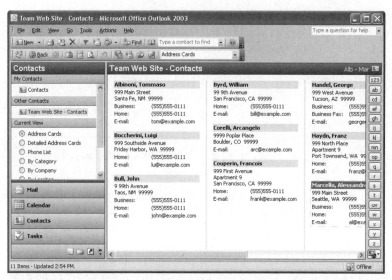

Figure 39-8. You can refresh an Outlook contacts folder that's linked to a SharePoint contacts list to view the latest contents of the list. You can't, however, make changes to the contacts folder in Outlook.

3 To quickly view the linked SharePoint contacts list in your browser, right-click the name of the linked contacts folder in the Navigation pane and choose Open In Web Browser.

Tip Import contacts from Outlook to a SharePoint team Web site

You can import one or more contacts from an Outlook contacts folder to a SharePoint contacts list. To do this, open the Web page for the SharePoint contacts list in your browser and click the Import Contacts command on the toolbar near the top of the page. Outlook will then display the Select Users To Import dialog box, where you can choose one of your contacts folders (by selecting it in the Show Names From The drop-down list) and then select one or more contacts from that folder to import into the SharePoint contacts list.

Managing Tasks and Projects with the Tasks Folder

Each item in the default Tasks folder—or in any other tasks folder—stores information about a task or project that needs to be completed, including a description of the task, as well as the task's due date, priority, completion status, and other details. You can create a *personal task* to keep tabs on a task you're undertaking by yourself. A personal task is stored in your Tasks folder only and you are the *owner* of the task.

Note Although for simplicity this chapter often refers to just the default *Tasks folder*, you can also use the techniques with any other tasks folder that's available in Outlook.

You can also create an *assigned task* by sending a task request to someone else, who becomes the task owner and is responsible for completing the task. The task itself is stored in the owner's Tasks folder, although Outlook places a copy of the task in your Tasks folder and updates your copy whenever the owner changes the task information (for example, if the owner changes the value in the % Complete field). All task requests, replies, and updates are transmitted using e-mail messages.

You can manage a group project by assigning the individual project tasks to different members of your workgroup (as well as to yourself). For a complex project, you might want to create a separate tasks folder to store all of the project's tasks.

Defining Tasks

To create a personal task, complete the following steps:

1 Open a blank Task form (shown in Figure 39-9) using one of the following methods:

New Task

■ Open the Tasks folder and choose Actions, New Task, click the New button on the Standard toolbar, or press Ctrl+N.

■ With any folder open, choose Task from the New drop-down list on the Standard toolbar or press Ctrl+Shift+K.

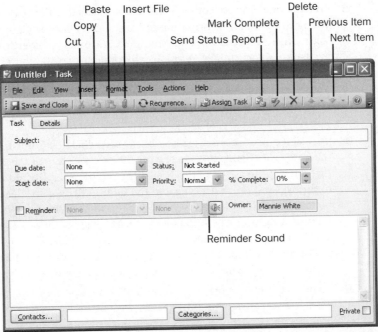

Figure 39-9. This figure shows a blank Task form as it appears when you define a new personal task.

Chapter 39

2 Fill in the Task form as follows:

- Enter a brief description of the task in the Subject text box. If you want, you can type a more complete task description, as well as instructions, comments, or any free-form information, in the large text box.

- If the task has specific starting and due dates, enter those in the Due Date and Start Date text boxes. (You can click the down-arrow button on either box to select the date from a drop-down calendar.)

- Select a priority for the task—Low, Normal, or High—in the Priority drop-down list.

- If you've already started working on the task, indicate its current completion status by selecting a value in the Status drop-down list and entering the completion percentage in the % Complete box. If you haven't started the task, just leave the default values—Not Started and 0%—in these controls and update their values as you begin working on the task.

- To have Outlook display a message to remind you when the task is due, check the Reminder option and in the following controls, type or select the date and time you want Outlook to display the reminder (by default, Outlook displays it at 8 A.M. on the day the task is due). To modify or turn off the sound Outlook plays when it displays the reminder message, click the Reminder Sound button.

- To enter one or more contacts who are associated with the task (perhaps people you need to ask for information or assistance), click the Contacts button and select one or more items from your default Contacts folder (or from another available contacts folder). Outlook will then display the contact(s) in the adjoining text box. Entering a contact here links the task to the contact; as a result, the Activities tab in the form for that contact will list the appointment as well as other linked Outlook items. You can double-click a contact name in the Contacts box to open the contact.

- To assign one or more categories to the task, click the Categories button and in the Categories dialog box (see Figure 39-3), check any of the predefined categories you want to assign in the Available Categories list. To add a custom category to the list (and check it), type it in the Item(s) Belong To These Categories text box and click the Add To List button. You can use categories for finding, sorting, filtering, or grouping Outlook items (see "Finding Outlook Items," on page 986, and "Sorting, Filtering, and Grouping Items in Folders," on page 979). (For important information on creating custom categories, see the troubleshooting sidebar "Trouble with custom categories," on page 1030.)

- To mark the task as private, check the Private option. (The task will then be hidden if you share your Tasks folder with others.)

- To enter additional task information, display the Details tab. Here you can add the names of companies associated with the task, billing information, and mileage for the task. When you complete the task, you can also enter in this tab the date completed, the total estimated work hours, and the actual work hours.

Note If the task you're defining is one that repeats—that is, it needs to be completed at regular intervals—click the Recurrence button on the Standard toolbar in the Task form and specify the daily, weekly, monthly, or yearly recurrence pattern in the Task Recurrence dialog box (see Figure 39-10). Outlook will add only the first task in the series to your Tasks folder. When you mark that task as completed (by selecting Completed in the Status drop-down list in the Task form or by simply checking the Completed column displayed in the task's description in the Information Viewer of the Outlook window), Outlook will add the next task in the repeated series. And it will keep on adding tasks like this one at a time.

You can have Outlook change a recurring task's due date to the due date for the *next* task in the series by opening the task and choosing Skip Occurrence from the form's Actions menu. (This command won't be available if you selected the Regenerate New Task option in the Task Recurrence dialog box.) This is a convenient way to extend the deadline for a particular task in the series.

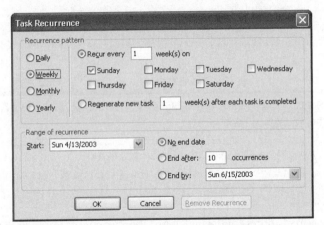

Figure 39-10. Use the Task Recurrence dialog box when the task you're defining is one that repeats.

3 Click the Save And Close button on the form's Standard toolbar.

To create an assigned task, complete the following steps:

1 Open a blank Task form for an assigned task (shown in Figure 39-11) by opening the Tasks folder and choosing Actions, New Task Request or by pressing Ctrl+Shift+U.

Chapter 39

Paste   Insert File

Copy   Address Book   Delete

Cut   Check Names

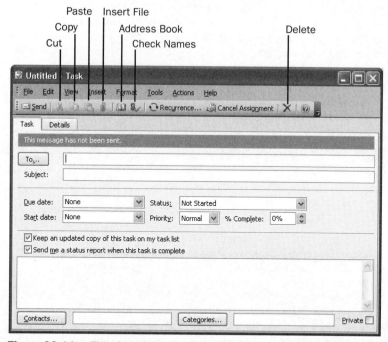

Figure 39-11. This figure shows a blank Task form as it appears when you define a new assigned task.

Note You can convert a personal task to an assigned task by clicking the Assign Task button on the form's Standard toolbar, and you can convert an assigned task to a personal task by clicking the Cancel Assignment button.

2   Enter the e-mail address of the person to whom you want to assign the task. This person will become the task owner. Either type the address in the To text box or click the To button to select the address from your Outlook Contacts folder.

For information on entering or selecting addresses, see "Composing and Sending E-Mail Messages," on page 1014.

Note To store a copy of the assigned task in your own Tasks folder, check the Keep An Updated Copy Of This Task On My Task List option. Although you won't be able to directly modify this copy of the task, Outlook will automatically update it when the task owner changes the task in his or her Tasks folder. (You will, however, be able to convert your copy of the task to a task that you own by displaying the Details tab in the Task form and clicking the Create Unassigned Copy button. If you do this, you'll no longer receive updates, but you'll be able to use the task yourself or to click the Assign Task button on the form's Standard toolbar to assign the task to someone else.)

To receive an e-mail message when the task owner marks the task as completed, check the Send Me A Status Report When This Task Is Complete option.

3 Fill in the remaining controls in the tabs of the Task form, following the instructions in step 2 of the procedure for creating a personal task, given on page 1062. However, note the following:

- The Task form doesn't contain the Owner text box because you aren't the owner of a task you assign. This box appears only in the actual task, which will be stored in the owner's Tasks folder.

- The Task form doesn't include the Reminder controls. Only the task owner will be allowed to set a reminder.

4 Select an e-mail account (if you have more than one) from the Accounts drop-down menu on the Standard toolbar. Then click the Send button on this same toolbar to place a task assignment e-mail message in your Outbox, and then transmit the message to your outgoing e-mail server as explained in "Composing and Sending E-Mail Messages," on page 1014. Typically, the following series of events now occurs:

- Outlook stores a copy of the task in your Tasks folder, provided that you checked the Keep An Updated Copy Of This Task On My Task List option.

- The task owner receives a task request as an e-mail message.

- The task owner opens the task request message and clicks the Accept or Decline button in the form to accept or relinquish ownership of the task. If the owner has Outlook version 2002 or later, he or she can simply view the task request in the Reading pane and click the Accept or Decline button that appears in the Reading pane header (see Figure 39-12). You'll receive an e-mail message indicating the owner's reply, and your copy of the task (if you have one) will indicate the owner's acceptance.

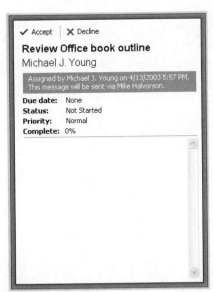

Figure 39-12. This figure shows a task request received in the owner's Inbox, viewed in the Reading pane.

- If the owner accepted the task request, the task is added to the owner's Tasks folder (and the task request is removed from the Inbox). Whenever the owner modifies the task, your copy of the task—if you have one—will be updated (by means of a special e-mail message).

- When the owner marks the task as completed, you'll receive an e-mail message notifying you, and your copy of the task (if you have one) will be marked as completed, provided that you checked the Send Me A Status Report When This Task Is Complete option in the original task request form.

> **Note** The task owner can click the Assign Task button on the Task form's Standard toolbar to assign the task to someone else. All people who have assigned the task to another person and who have checked the Keep An Updated Copy Of This Task On My Task List option in the Task form will be included in the Update List for the task stored in the current owner's Tasks folder (the Update List appears in the Details tab in the Task form).

Working with Your Tasks Folder

The Task Timeline view of the Tasks folder arranges your tasks in a timeline according to their due dates. All of the other views display the tasks in a table, some of them applying a filter or grouping the tasks (see Figure 39-13).

> **Tip** Navigate quickly through the Task Timeline
>
>
>
> In the Tasks Timeline view, you can go directly to a particular time period by clicking in the shaded heading at the top of the Information Viewer (which displays the months and years) and choosing a date from the calendar that drops down. Or, you can choose Go, Go To Date or press Ctrl+G to display the Go To Date dialog box. To go to the time period displaying the current date, you can click the Today button on the Standard toolbar. You can change the range of days shown in the window by clicking the Day, Week, or Month button on the Standard toolbar.

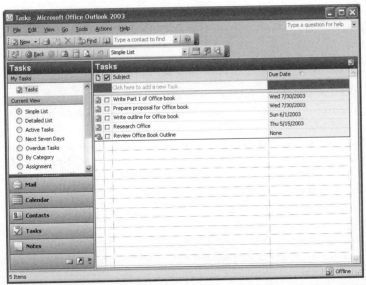

Figure 39-13. The Tasks folder in the Simple List view displays the Subject and Due Date of all tasks and has check boxes that you can click to mark tasks as completed.

Tip **Arrange tasks in any order**

If you remove all sorting from a table view of the Tasks folder, you can drag the tasks to arrange them in any order you want. If the tasks are currently sorted, you can remove sorting by choosing View, Arrange By, Custom. Then click the Sort button in the Customize View dialog box, and click the Clear All button in the Sort dialog box.

You can modify the appearance or behavior of the Tasks folder in the following ways:

● To change the default time of day when a reminder appears for a task due on that date, choose Tools, Options and select a time in the Reminder Time drop-down list in the Preferences tab. You can modify task colors and other features by clicking the Task Options button in this same tab to display the Task Options dialog box (see Figure 39-14).

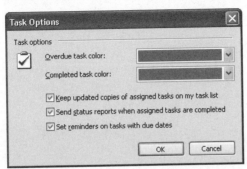

Figure 39-14. Use the Task Options dialog box to modify task colors and other features of the Tasks folder.

● You can set additional options that affect the Tasks folder by clicking the Other tab in the Options dialog box and clicking the Advanced Options button.

Recording Events with the Journal Folder

Each item in the default Journal folder—or in any other journal folder—stores a journal entry that contains information on a particular event that occurred, such as receiving an e-mail message or a task request, creating a Microsoft Excel 2003 workbook or editing a Word document, sending a letter, or making a phone call. You can have Outlook *automatically* create a journal entry whenever you send or receive a message (e-mail message, meeting request, task request, and so on) to or from a particular contact or whenever you open a document in a particular Microsoft Office 2003 application. You can also *manually* create a journal entry to record any type of event.

> **Note** Although for simplicity this chapter often refers to just the default *Journal folder*, you can also use the techniques with any other journal folder that's available in Outlook.

 Inside Out

Take advantage of automatic message links

If you simply want to keep track of messages for one or more contacts, you do *not* need to turn on automatic journaling, because when you send or receive a message to or from a contact, Outlook *automatically* links the message to that contact (this includes a regular e-mail message as well as a meeting or task request or reply and the corresponding item in the Calendar or Tasks folder). You can view all of the contact's messages by opening the contact and looking in the Activities tab in the Contact form.

Recording Entries in Your Journal Folder

To have Outlook begin automatically recording journal entries, do the following:

Inside Out

Keep automatic journaling under control

Turning on automatic journal recording can slow Outlook's response time and also rapidly expand the size of your Outlook data file. Therefore, if you use automatic recording, you should enable it for only the messages and document accesses you truly need to record. Keep in mind that you can use the Activities tab in the Contacts form to view all of a contact's messages without incurring the overhead of automatic journaling, as explained in the "Inside Out" on page 1068. To control the growth of your Outlook data file that's caused by automatic journaling, archive your Journal folder regularly, using the instructions given in "Archiving Items," on page 970.

1   Open your Journal folder. If automatic recording of journal entries isn't currently enabled, Outlook will display a message box giving you the option to turn on automatic journaling. Click the Yes button in this message box to display the Journal Options dialog box (shown in Figure 39-15). You can display this dialog box at any time by choosing Tools, Options and clicking the Journal Options button in the Preferences tab.

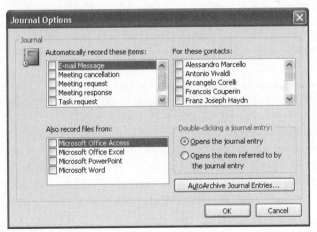

Figure 39-15.   The Journal Options dialog box lets you set up automatic recording of journal entries.

2   To have Outlook automatically create a journal entry whenever you receive or send a message from or to a contact, check the specific types of messages you want to record in the Automatically Record These Items list and then check the contacts whose messages you want to record in the For These Contacts list. (This list shows all the contacts in your default Contacts folder. You won't be able to select contacts in another contacts folder.)

3 To have Outlook automatically record a journal entry whenever you open a document in an Office application, check the specific Office applications whose documents you want to record in the Also Record Files From list, which will display the applications currently installed on your computer.

Tip   Control the way you open journal entries

When Outlook automatically creates a journal entry, it inserts into the entry's large text box a shortcut to the message (which is an Outlook item) or to the disk file that's associated with the entry. (When you create a manual journal entry using the method described in the next section, you can also insert an Outlook item shortcut or a file shortcut, as explained in "Editing Items," on page 961.)

If you select the Opens The Journal Entry option in the Journal Options dialog box (shown in Figure 39-15), whenever you double-click a journal entry that contains a shortcut (or use any other method to open the item), Outlook will open the journal entry itself in the Journal Entry form. To open the item or file targeted by the shortcut, you can right-click the entry and choose Open The Item Referred To from the shortcut menu. An Outlook item will be opened in the appropriate form and a file will be opened in the application that was used to create it.

If, however, you select Opens The Item Referred To By The Journal Entry, double-clicking an entry with a shortcut will immediately open the item or file targeted by the shortcut. To open the entry itself, right-click it and choose Open Journal Entry from the shortcut menu.

---

4 Click the OK button.

Tip   View automatically recorded entries for a contact

When Outlook automatically records a journal entry for a contact, it links the entry to that contact (by inserting the contact's name in the Contacts text box, discussed later in this section). You can therefore view at a glance all of the automatically recorded journal entries for a contact by opening that contact and looking in the Activities tab in the Contact form. You can select Journal in the Show drop-down list at the top of the Activities tab to display only the linked journal entries and not other linked Outlook items.

 Troubleshooting

Journal entries for document accesses don't appear

You turned on automatic journal entries for accessing Office documents, but the entries don't appear in your Journal folder.

If the Journal folder is currently open in Outlook, automatically recorded journal entries for document accesses won't appear until you close the Journal folder by opening another folder in Outlook and then reopen the Journal folder.

Chapter 39

To manually record any type of event, complete the following steps:

1. Open a blank Journal Entry form (shown in Figure 39-16) using one of the following methods:

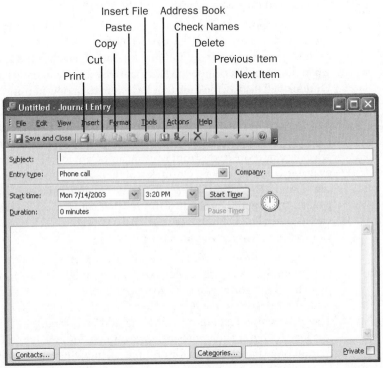

New
Journal
Entry

■ Open the Journal folder and choose Actions, New Journal Entry; click the New button on the Standard toolbar; or press Ctrl+N.

■ With any folder open, choose Journal Entry from the New drop-down list on the Standard toolbar or press Ctrl+Shift+J.

Figure 39-16. This figure shows a blank Journal Entry form, which you use for manually recording a new journal entry.

2. Fill in the Journal Entry form as follows:

> **Note** The By Type view of the Journal folder groups your journal entries by the value of the Entry Type field.

■ Enter a short description for the entry in the Subject text box. If you wish, you can enter a full description, comments, or any free-form information in the large text box.

Chapter 39

- Select the item from the Entry Type drop-down list that most closely describes the event you're recording—Conversation, Document, E-Mail Message, Fax, Phone Call, and so on. (For more on the Journal Entry form, see the Inside Out sidebar, "Use categories to get around journal folder limitations," on page 1073.)

- If a company is associated with the entry, enter its name in the Company text box.

- If the event occurs during a specific period of time, enter or select the starting date and time in the Start Time controls (Outlook initially sets these controls to the date and time when you opened the form).

  Then enter the event duration in the Duration text box or select a duration from the drop-down list. Or, click the Start Timer button when the event starts (for example, when you initiate a phone call) and then click the Pause Timer button when the event has completed (for example, when you hang up the phone), and Outlook will display the time that has expired, in one-minute increments, in the Duration box.

- To enter one or more contacts who are associated with the journal entry (perhaps the person you're speaking to on the phone), click the Contacts button and select one or more items from your default Contacts folder (or from another available contacts folder). Outlook will then display the contact(s) in the adjoining text box. Entering a contact here links the journal entry to the contact; as a result, the Activities tab in the form for that contact will list the journal entry as well as other linked Outlook items. You can double-click a contact name in the Contacts box to open the contact.

- To assign one or more categories to the journal entry, click the Categories button and in the Categories dialog box (shown in Figure 39-3), check any of the predefined categories you want to assign in the Available Categories list. To add a custom category to the list (and check it), type it in the Item(s) Belong To These Categories text box and click the Add To List button. You can use categories for finding, sorting, filtering, or grouping Outlook items. (For more information on using categories for finding, sorting, filtering, or grouping Outlook items, see "Finding Outlook Items," on page 986, and "Sorting, Filtering, and Grouping Items in Folders," on page 979. For important information on creating custom categories, see the troubleshooting sidebar "Trouble with custom categories," on page 1030.)

- To mark the journal entry as private, check the Private option. (The journal entry will then be hidden if you share your Contacts folder with others.)

3 Click the Save And Close button on the form's Standard toolbar.

Inside Out

Use categories to get around journal folder limitations

Surprisingly, the Journal Entry form doesn't let you create custom types, which would make the Journal folder more useful as a general-purpose journaling tool. And the collection of built-in types is quite limited. If an event you want to record (such as selling shares of a mutual fund at a particular time and price) doesn't fit one of the built-in types, the best you can do is to choose one of the less specific types, such as note, and then possibly assign a custom category (such as Sale Of Shares) to indicate a more precise classification. You could then find, sort, filter, or group your Journal entries using the categories. Categories are described later in this list.

 Tip Dial and record a call using a single command

You can telephone one of your contacts and create a journal entry to time and record the call using a single command. To do this, select the contact in your Contacts folder, click the Dial button on the Standard toolbar, and before placing your call, check the Create New Journal Entry When Starting New Call option in the New Call dialog box (shown in Figure 39-17).

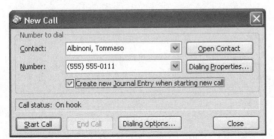

Figure 39-17. The New Call dialog box allows you to automatically create a record of every call you make.

 Tip Navigate quickly through a journal timeline

If you switch to the By Type, By Contact, or By Category view of the Journal folder, Outlook will display your journal entries in a timeline, grouping the items differently with each view. In a timeline view of the Journal folder, you can go to a particular time period by clicking in the shaded heading at the top of the Information Viewer (which displays the months and years) and choosing a date from the calendar that drops down. Or, you can choose Go, Go To Date or press Ctrl+G to display the Go To Date dialog box. To go to the time period displaying the current date, you can click the Today button on the Standard toolbar. You can change the range of days shown in the window by clicking the Day, Week, or Month button on the Standard toolbar.

Chapter 39

Storing Miscellaneous Information in the Notes Folder

You can use the default Notes folder—or any other available notes folder—to quickly jot down free-form information on any topic. An individual note in the Notes folder is an electronic equivalent of a "sticky note."

> **Note** Although for simplicity this chapter often refers to just the default *Notes folder*, you can also use the techniques with any other notes folder that's available in Outlook.

To enter a new note, complete the following steps:

1   Open a blank Note form (shown in Figure 39-18) using one of the following methods:

New Note

- Open the Notes folder and choose Actions, New Note, click the New button on the Standard toolbar, press Ctrl+N, or double-click in a blank spot in the Notes folder.

- With any folder open, choose Note from the New drop-down list on the Standard toolbar or press Ctrl+Shift+N.

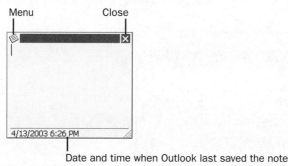

Date and time when Outlook last saved the note

Figure 39-18.   This figure shows a blank Note form for entering miscellaneous information.

2   Type any text you want into the note form, which consists of a single text box.

3   To set options for the note, click the Menu button to display the note's drop-down menu, as shown here:

Then choose a command as follows:

- To change the background color of the note, choose a color from the Color submenu.

- To enter one or more contacts who are associated with the note (perhaps the person you're speaking to on the telephone while you're jotting down information), choose Contacts, click the Contacts button in the Contacts For Note dialog box (shown in Figure 39-19) and select one or more items from your default Contacts folder (or from another available contacts folder). Outlook will then display the contact(s) in the adjoining text box. Entering a contact here links the note to the contact; as a result, the Activities tab in the form for that contact will list the note as well as other linked Outlook items. You can double-click a contact name in the Contacts box in the Contacts For Note dialog box to open the contact.

Figure 39-19. You use the Contacts For Note dialog box to enter contacts associated with a note.

- To assign one or more categories to the note, choose Categories and in the Categories dialog box (see Figure 39-3) check any of the predefined categories you want to assign in the Available Categories list. To add a custom category to the list (and check it), type it in the Item(s) Belong To These Categories text box and click the Add To List button. You can use categories for finding, sorting, filtering, or grouping Outlook items. (For information on using categories for finding, sorting, filtering, or grouping Outlook items, see "Finding Outlook Items," on page 986, and "Sorting, Filtering, and Grouping Items in Folders," on page 979. For important information on creating custom categories, see the troubleshooting sidebar "Trouble with custom categories," on page 1030.)

Chapter 39

- To save the contents of the note in a disk file, choose Save As.
- To create a new e-mail message that contains the note as an attachment, choose Forward.
- To create another note, choose New Note.
- To delete, print, or close the Note form, choose Delete, Print, or Close.

4 You can leave the note open while you work in other programs, so that you can quickly add more information. Or you can close the note by clicking the Close button or pressing Esc; the note will then appear only as an item in the Notes folder. In either case, Outlook will automatically save the text you add; you don't have to issue a save command (as you do with other Outlook items or in a note editor such as Microsoft Notepad).

Tip   Organize your notes using colors

To organize your notes into topics, you can assign the notes on each topic a different color. You can assign any of five colors from the menu in the Notes form, as described under step 3, or you can right-click the note in the Information Viewer and choose a color from the Color submenu on the shortcut menu. Once you've marked your notes using different colors, you can have Outlook group the notes by color; just switch to the By Color view.

Note   To change the default note color or size applied to the new notes you create, or to change the font used in all existing and new notes, choose Tools, Options, click the Note Options button in the Preferences tab in the Options dialog box, and choose the settings you want in the Note Options dialog box (see Figure 39-20). To remove the date and time stamp from the bottom of your notes, display the Other tab in the Options dialog box, click the Advanced Options button, and clear the When Viewing Notes Show Time And Date option.

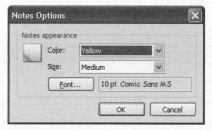

Figure 39-20.   You can change the appearance of notes by using the Note Options dialog box.

Chapter 40

Customizing Outlook

Customizing the Navigation Pane.... 1077

Adding, Modifying, and Removing
Outlook Accounts 1080

Managing Outlook Data Files........1088

NEW FEATURE! Customizing the Navigation Pane

The previous chapters in this part of the book explained how to use the new multipurpose Navigation pane to open and work with your Outlook folders. The following sections describe the different ways you can modify the Navigation pane to suit your working style.

Configuring the Navigation Pane Buttons

As explained in the previous chapters, the lower portion of the Navigation pane—also known as the *button bar*—includes a button corresponding to each category of Outlook folder. You click one of these buttons to display a list of the folders belonging to that category, as well as category-specific tools. The button bar also includes a button to display the Folder List and one to display your shortcuts.

To customize the button bar, click the Configure Buttons button in the lower-right corner of the Navigation pane and choose a command from the pop-up menu, as follows:

- To change the size of the button bar, you can use the Show More Buttons or Show Fewer Buttons command, although it's easier to just drag the button bar's upper border up or down.

- To specify which buttons are displayed in the button bar, to change the order of the buttons, or to restore the button bar to its "factory" configuration, choose Navigation Pane Options to open the Navigation Pane Options dialog box. (You can also open this dialog box by choosing Tools, Options, clicking the Other tab, and clicking the Navigation Pane Options button.)

● An alternative way to specify which buttons are displayed in the button bar is to select or deselect the button options on the Add Or Remove Buttons submenu.

Customizing the My *Folders* Lists

When you click the Calendar, Contacts, Tasks, Notes, or Journal category button in the button bar, the Navigation pane displays a list of folders belonging to that category, which is labeled My Calendars, My Contacts, My Tasks, My Notes, or My Journals. If you've opened a SharePoint list as an Outlook Calendar or Contacts folder, you'll also see an Other Calendars or Other Contacts list. You can modify one of these lists as follows:

● To remove a folder from the list, right-click the folder name in the list and choose Remove From My *Folders* or Remove From Other *Folders* from the shortcut menu (where *Folders* is the folder category, such as Calendars or Contacts).

● To change the position of a folder name in the list, right-click it and choose Move Up In List or Move Down In List from the shortcut menu. Or, drag the folder to a new position in the list.

● To add a folder to the list, click the Folder List button in the button bar, right-click the folder name in the Folder List, and choose Add To My *Folders* or Add To Other *Folders* from the shortcut menu (where *Folders* is the folder category, such as Calendars or Contacts). The folder will be added to the list corresponding to the folder's category; for example, an Outlook calendar folder (one that's *not* a SharePoint folder) will be added to the My Calendars list.

Customizing the Favorite Folders List

When you click the Mail category button in the button bar, the Navigation pane displays the Favorites Folders list showing selected e-mail folders, as well as the All Mail Folders hierarchical list showing all your available e-mail folders. You can customize the Favorites Folders list as follows:

● To add a folder to the Favorite Folders list, click the Mail button in the button bar, right-click the folder name in the All Mail Folders list, and choose Add To Favorite Folders from the shortcut menu. Or, drag a folder from the All Mail Folders list and drop it on the Favorite Folders list.

● To change the position of a folder name in the Favorite Folders list, right-click it and choose Move Up In List or Move Down In List from the shortcut menu. Or, drag the folder to a new position in the list.

● To remove a folder from the Favorite Folders list, right-click the folder name in the list and choose Remove From Favorite Folders from the shortcut menu.

Customizing the Shortcuts List

When you click the Shortcuts button in the button bar, the Navigation pane displays your Shortcuts list, which contains groups of shortcuts. You can click a shortcut in one of these groups to open an Outlook folder, a file, a file folder, or a Web page. An Outlook folder or a Web page will be opened in the Outlook window. A file will be opened in the program that's registered to open the file type. And a file folder will be opened in Microsoft Windows Explorer.

You might want to customize your Shortcuts list to display a carefully selected list of short-cuts to the Outlook folders, files, file folders, and Web pages that you access most frequently. You might also want to organize your shortcuts into logical shortcut groups—for example, you might place your shortcuts into groups named Personal Outlook Folders, Shared Outlook Folders, Office Documents, and Web Pages.

You can customize your Shortcuts list in the following ways:

- To create a new shortcut group, click the Add New Group command in the Navigation pane below the Shortcuts list.

- To rename or remove a shortcut group, or to change its position in the list, right-click the name of the group and choose a command from the shortcut menu, shown here:

- To add an Outlook folder shortcut to a particular group in the Shortcuts list, click the Add New Shortcut command in the Navigation pane below the Shortcuts list (or choose the Add New Shortcut command on the shortcut menu described in the previous item) and select the Outlook folder in the Add To Navigation Pane dialog box.

- To add a file or file folder shortcut, display your Shortcuts list. Then drag the file or folder name from Windows Explorer and drop it in the Shortcuts list group where you want to display it. To add a Web page shortcut, you can display your Favorites folder in Windows Explorer, drag a Web page shortcut from Windows Explorer or from the Favorites menu displayed in Windows Explorer or in Internet Explorer, and drop it on the group where you want to display it. If the Outlook window is hidden when you start dragging the file or folder, hold the pointer over the Outlook button in the Windows Taskbar until the Outlook window appears, and then complete the drag operation.

- To rename or remove a shortcut, right-click it and choose Rename Shortcut or Delete Shortcut from the shortcut menu.

Chapter 40

> **Note** If you delete an Outlook folder, a file, or a file folder, or if a Web site is no longer available, it's a good idea to remove any shortcut that opens that object. (You can leave the shortcut, but clicking it will only display an error message.)

- To move a shortcut to a different group or to another position in the same group, drag it using the mouse and drop it at the desired position. To make a copy of a shortcut in a different group, press Ctrl while you drag.

Adding, Modifying, and Removing Outlook Accounts

"Setting Up Outlook," on page 946, discussed setting up an e-mail account the first time you run Outlook. The Outlook setup program gets you started using Outlook by creating a single e-mail account either by importing settings (as well as messages and addresses) from an e-mail program already installed on your computer or by defining a new e-mail account. This section explains how to add one or more additional e-mail accounts and how to modify or remove e-mail accounts. (You would need two accounts, for example, if you have one e-mail service provided by your company for business use and another that your family uses for personal messages.)

You can also add (or modify or remove) directory accounts or address book accounts. A *directory account* lets you access an Internet or intranet directory service, such as VeriSign Internet Directory Service, for looking up people's names and e-mail addresses. (An Internet or intranet directory service is also known as an LDAP [Lightweight Directory Access Protocol] server.) Once you install a directory account, you can look up e-mail addresses by choosing Tools, Address Book or by pressing Ctrl+Shift+B to display the Address Book dialog box, selecting the name of the directory account in the Show Names From The drop-down list (shown in Figure 40-1), and then choosing Tools, Find. Outlook will also use the directory account to look up the e-mail address of a name you type into the To (or Cc or Bcc) text box in a Message form (as well as looking them up in your contacts folder or folders), or you can use the directory account to look up e-mail addresses in the Select Names dialog box that appears when you click the To, Cc, Bcc, or Address Book button on the form. Finally, you can use the directory account to look up a contact's e-mail address in the Select Name dialog box that appears when you click the button to the right of the E-Mail text box in the Contact form.

> **Note** To use a directory account in Outlook, you must be working online. To start working online, deselect the File, Work Offline menu option.

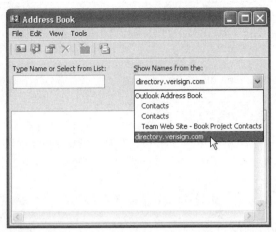

Figure 40-1. You can look up a name using a directory service in the Address Book dialog box.

Check
Names

Note Outlook automatically looks up names you type into the To, Cc, or Bcc text boxes in a message header if the Automatic Name Checking option is checked. (If this option isn't checked, you can look up the addresses of names you've typed by clicking the Check Names button on the message header or on the Standard toolbar.) To access the Automatic Name Checking option, choose Tools, Options, click the E-mail Options button in the Preferences tab, click the Advanced E-Mail Options button, and look in the When Sending A Message area of the Advanced E-Mail Options dialog box (see Figure 38-2).

Troubleshooting

Address lookups too slow

You added a directory account for an LDAP server on the Internet. It now takes a long time for Outlook to look up names you type into a message header.

Having Outlook look up names you enter into your outgoing messages using a directory account can be quite useful if that account connects to a small, fast LDAP server on your company's intranet. But if the directory account connects to an LDAP server on the Internet, it will probably be too slow (especially if you have a slow Internet connection) and it will come up with too many "hits" for it to be practical for looking up names you type into message headers.

Fortunately, you can prevent Outlook from using a directory account for looking up names in the Message form, while still keeping the account available on your system (so that you can use it to look up names through the Address Book or Select Names dialog box, as discussed earlier in this section) and having Outlook automatically look up addresses in your Contacts folder. To do this, complete the following steps:

1   Choose Tools, Address Book or press Ctrl+Shift+B to open the Address Book dialog box (shown in Figure 40-1).

2   In the dialog box, choose Tools, Options to open the Addressing dialog box.

3   Select the directory account in the When Sending Mail list at the bottom of the dialog box and click the Remove button (as shown in Figure 40-2).

Alternatively, you can select the account and click the down arrow to move it down in the list. Outlook uses any address books and directory accounts in the order they're listed. If it finds a name in an address book, it won't go on to search the directory service.

Figure 40-2. The Addressing dialog box lets you control the way Outlook handles addresses in the Address Book and e-mail messages.

An *address book account* lets you use the Address Book or Select Names dialog box to look up names in your Contacts folder or in a Personal Address Book, and it also allows Outlook to automatically look up names you type into the To, Cc, or Bcc text boxes in a Message form. The Outlook setup program adds an address book account called Outlook Address Book that lets you look up names in your default Contacts folder. If you add one or more new contacts folders (including a contacts folder linked to a SharePoint contacts list), the Outlook Address Book account will let you look up names in any of these folders, as well as in the default Contacts folder.

> **Note** To be able to access your default Contacts folder or another contacts folder through the Outlook Address Book account, the folder's Show This Folder As An E-mail Address Book property must be checked. To access this option, right-click the folder's name in the Navigation pane, choose Properties from the shortcut menu, and open the Outlook Address Book tab.

You can create one additional address book account for looking up names in a Personal Address Book. You can use an existing Personal Address Book or create a new empty one. (Note that rather than being stored in your Outlook data file, as your Contacts folder is, a Personal Address Book is stored in a separate file with the .pab extension.) Unless you already have addresses stored in a Personal Address Book that you want to use, you don't need to create a Personal Address Book account; you'll find it much simpler and more convenient to store all your addresses in a contacts folder and use the address book account that Outlook has already set up.

Inside Out

Use a Contacts folder rather than a Personal Address Book

With former versions of Outlook, using a Personal Address Book was an attractive alternative because it let you define groups of addresses called *personal distribution lists*, and the Contacts folder didn't have this feature. However, now that the Contacts folder provides distribution lists, there's little reason to start using a Personal Address Book.

To add, modify, or remove an e-mail account, complete the following steps:

1. Choose Tools, E-Mail Accounts to display the first page of the E-Mail Accounts wizard (see Figure 40-3).

> **Note** Another way to start the E-mail Accounts wizard is to choose Tools, Options, click the Mail Setup tab, and click the E-Mail Accounts button. Or you can double-click (or click, in Category View) the Mail item in the Windows Control Panel and click the E-Mail Accounts button in the Mail Setup–Outlook dialog box.

Chapter 40

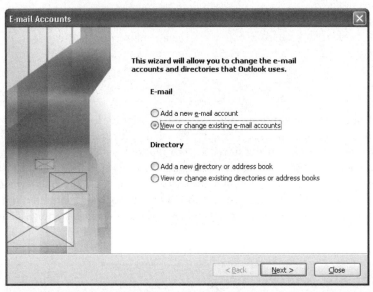

Figure 40-3. This figure shows the first page of the E-Mail Accounts wizard.

2 Select the View Or Change Existing E-Mail Accounts option and click the Next button. (This option lets you add accounts as well as view, modify, or remove them. If you want only to add an account, you can choose Add A New E-Mail Account instead.) Outlook will display the second page of the E-Mail Accounts wizard (shown in Figure 40-4).

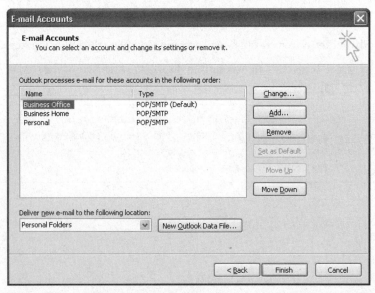

Figure 40-4. This is the second page that the E-Mail Accounts wizard displays when you work with e-mail accounts.

3 In the second wizard page, do one or more of the following:

> **Note** POP3 (Post Office Protocol version 3) is the most common nonproprietary server protocol used for receiving e-mail from the Internet. An Outlook account that uses a POP3 e-mail server for *receiving* messages uses an SMTP (Simple Mail Transfer Protocol) e-mail server for *sending* messages on the Internet.

- To add a new account, click the Add button and in the pages the wizard displays, select the e-mail account type and fill in the account details.
- To modify or remove an account, select it in the list and click the Change or the Remove button.
- To mark an account as your default e-mail account, select it and click the Set As Default button. When you send an outgoing e-mail message, Outlook uses your default e-mail account unless you choose a different account from the Accounts drop-down menu on the message header or Standard toolbar. (This option doesn't affect the accounts used for receiving e-mail.)
- To change the order in which accounts are used for receiving e-mail (when you use multiple accounts for a send and receive operation), select an account and click the Move Up or Move Down button.
- To specify the Outlook data file to which incoming e-mail messages will be delivered (if more than one data file is opened) choose the name of the data file in the Deliver New E-Mail To The Following Location drop-down list. Data files are discussed in the next section.

4 Click the Finish button.

> **Tip**   Import e-mail settings
> Another way to create an e-mail account is to import the settings from an e-mail program that's already installed on your computer. You can also import the e-mail messages and addresses you've stored using the previously installed e-mail program. The e-mail programs from which Outlook can import settings, messages, and addresses include Outlook Express and Eudora Pro and Light. To import, choose File, Import And Export. Then, in the first Import And Export Wizard page (shown in Figure 40-5), select Import Internet Mail Account Settings or select Import Internet Mail And Addresses, click the Next button, and fill in the requested information.

Chapter 40

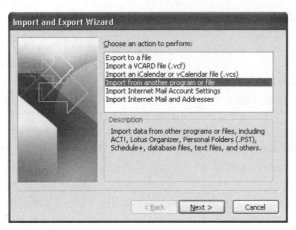

Figure 40-5. This figure shows the first page of the Import And Export Wizard.

To add, modify, or remove a directory service or address book account, follow these steps:

1 Choose Tools, E-Mail Accounts to display the first page of the E-Mail Accounts Wizard (see Figure 40-3).

2 Select the View Or Change Existing Directories Or Address Books option and click the Next button. (This option lets you add accounts as well as view, modify, or remove them.) Outlook will display the second page of the E-Mail Accounts Wizard (shown in Figure 40-6).

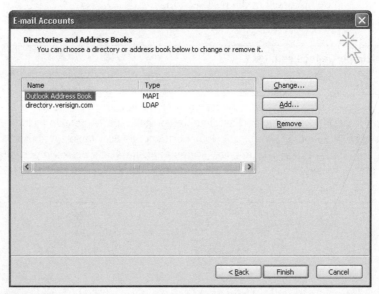

Figure 40-6. This is the second page that the E-Mail Accounts Wizard displays when you work with directories or address books.

3   To define a new account, click the Add button. In the pages the wizard displays, select an account type and fill in the account details. If you're adding an address book account, keep in mind that you can have only one Outlook Address Book account and one Personal Address Book account.

Tip   Find information on Internet directory services

Some installations of Windows have a set of Internet directory services installed, which you can use in Windows to look up people on the Internet. Although these services aren't initially accessible to Outlook, you can look up the properties of any of the services and use that information to define an Outlook directory account to access the same service. To do this in Windows XP, choose Start, Search. Then, in the Search Companion pane at the left of the Search Results dialog box, click Computers Or People and then click People In Your Address Book. Next, right-click any directory service listed in the Look In drop-down list in the Find People dialog box, and choose Properties from the shortcut menu. Windows will display a Properties dialog box listing the directory service's properties. You can copy or write down these property settings and use the same values to set up that service in Outlook.

Using Separate Profiles

The accounts and the Outlook data file that the Outlook setup program creates, as well as any that you define as described in this chapter, are all part of the current Outlook *profile*. The Outlook setup program creates a single profile. If, however, you want to create one or more distinct Outlook setups, including different e-mail and other types of accounts as well as different Outlook data files (each of which would contain different folders and items), you can create one or more new profiles. You can then have Outlook load any profile when it starts. If, for example, two or more people used Outlook on the same computer and wanted separate accounts, folders, and items, each person could create and use a separate profile.

To create a new profile in Windows XP, perform the following steps:

1   Double-click the Mail item in the Windows Control Panel (or *click* the item if you are in the Category View of the Control Panel).

2   Click the Show Profiles button in the Mail Setup – Outlook dialog box.

3   Click the Add button in the Mail dialog box (shown in Figure 40-7) and type a name for the new profile when prompted.

Figure 40-7. You use the Mail dialog box of the Mail program in the Control Panel to work with profiles.

4 Define accounts for the profile using the E-Mail Accounts wizard, as explained previously in this chapter (the wizard will automatically create a new data file for the profile).

When you've finished defining the new profile, you'll be returned to the Mail dialog box. As you can see in Figure 40-7, this dialog box lets you copy or remove a profile, change its properties (the accounts or data file), and control which profile Outlook uses. If you want to be able to switch profiles easily, select Prompt For A Profile To Be Used so that you can choose a profile each time you start Outlook.

Managing Outlook Data Files

Your Outlook information—consisting of your Outlook folders plus all items and item attachments contained in these folders—is stored in an *Outlook data file* on your computer. An Outlook data file is also known as a *personal folders file*, and it is assigned the .pst extension. The personal folders file that the Outlook setup program automatically creates uses the new Outlook 2003 data file format, which provides larger size limits and better support for multilingual Unicode data but which isn't compatible with previous versions of Outlook. However, if you create a new Outlook data file, as explained later in this section, you can optionally choose to use the format that was also used in Outlook versions 97, 98, 2000, and 2002 so that you'll be able to freely share this data file with users of previous Outlook versions.

Note If you have created an Outlook folder that's linked to an events or contacts list on a SharePoint team Web site, Outlook will store a local copy of the list or lists in a separate .pst file (named by default SharePoint Folders.pst). Also, if you are using Outlook as a client for Microsoft Exchange Server, Outlook will access the information that's stored in your mailbox on the network computer that runs Exchange Server (in this case, however, you can also create and store information in a .pst file on a local disk).

The Outlook setup program creates a single personal folders file named Outlook.pst, adds the default Outlook folders to it, and adds the data file to the current profile so that it's opened whenever you start Outlook. Although this is the only Outlook data file you need, in some cases you might want to create one or more additional data files, as explained in the following section.

Note Like the accounts that are set up in Outlook (which are discussed in the previous sections) the Outlook data file or files that are opened in Outlook are part of your current Outlook profile. For information on creating and using more than one profile, see the sidebar "Using Separate Profiles," on page 1087.

Tip **Back up your Outlook data file!**
Because your Outlook data file contains all the information you've entered into Outlook and because it could become corrupted or be deleted accidentally, it's important to back it up regularly. You can probably use your current backup system (you do have one, right?), provided that your backup medium has sufficient capacity (Outlook data files can become quite large).

If backing up your Outlook data file starts taking too much time and too much space on your backup medium, it's time to archive your folders. Archiving copies older items into a different Outlook data file, which you can back up separately if you want. For information on archiving, see "Archiving Items," on page 970.

Chapter 40

Do You Know Where Your Outlook Data File Is?

It's important to know your Outlook data file's name and location so that you can back it up regularly. (See the tip "Back Up Your Outlook Data File!" on page 1089.) You might also need to know the location of your Outlook data file so that you can copy it to another computer that has Outlook installed, allowing you to access your Outlook information on that computer. For example, you might want to copy your data file from your desktop computer to your notebook computer before leaving on a trip (and then copy it back when you return). Note that you need to quit Outlook before you can copy an opened data file.

To find the name and full file path of your Outlook data file, choose File, Data File Management and look in the list in the Outlook Data Files dialog box (see Figure 40-8). To see the full file path of the data file, you'll probably need to widen the Filename column by dragging the right border of the column heading and then scroll the list. Or select the data file, click the Settings button, and look in the Filename text box.

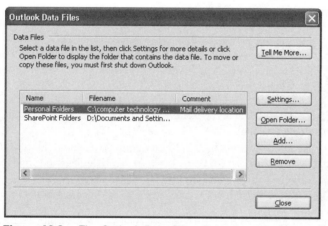

Figure 40-8. The Outlook Data Files dialog box lets you work with the file or files storing your Outlook data.

You can even view the entire contents of the folder containing your Outlook data file by clicking the Open Folder button in the Outlook Data Files dialog box.

Note that if you've used the Outlook archiving feature, you might find an additional Outlook data file, which is used to store your archived items, listed in the Outlook Data Files dialog box. You specify the name and location of this file when you set up the archiving feature, as explained in "Archiving Items," on page 970. (The archiving data file appears in the Outlook Data Files dialog box only if the Show Archive In Folder List option is checked in the AutoArchive dialog box, which causes Outlook to open that data file every time you run Outlook.) Also, if you've created an Outlook folder that's linked to an events or contacts list on a SharePoint team Web site, you'll see the file that stores a local copy of the list(s), which by default is named SharePoint Folders.

Creating and Modifying Outlook Data Files

You can create one or more Outlook data files in addition to the one added by the Outlook setup program (or by creating a linked folder or by using the archive feature). You might, for example, want to create a new Outlook data file and copy some of your Outlook items into that file so that you can keep them safe, use them on a different computer, or share them with a coworker.

To create or modify Outlook data files, complete the following steps:

1 Choose File, Data File Management to open the Outlook Data Files dialog box (shown in Figure 40-8).

2 In the Outlook Data Files dialog box, do one or more of the following:

■ To create a new Outlook data file and open it in Outlook, click the Add button. Then, in the New Outlook Data File dialog box, select the format you want to use for your new data file and click the OK button. Next, in the Create Or Open Outlook Data File dialog box, specify a filename and location for the file and click the OK button. Outlook will then display the Create Microsoft Personal Folders dialog box, where you can specify a "friendly" name for your data file in the Name text box (this name is distinct from the actual filename; Outlook will display this name in the Outlook Data Files dialog box and in the Folder List) and specify other data file options. When you click the OK button, Outlook will create and open your new data file, which will initially have only the default Deleted Items folder and an empty folder for storing new search folders; you can later add Outlook folders of any type.

■ To compact an Outlook data file, to change its "friendly" name in Outlook, to add a comment, or to add or change a password, select the file in the list and click the Settings button.

■ To close an Outlook data file, select it in the list and click the Remove button. Clicking this button doesn't delete the Outlook data file but merely closes it in Outlook, so you'll be able to reopen it later. Opening and closing Outlook data files is discussed in the next section.

> **Note** Initially, Outlook delivers your incoming e-mail to the Inbox of the Outlook data file created by the Outlook setup program. In the Outlook Data Files dialog box, this file is indicated with the text "Mail Delivery Location" in the Comment column. To have Outlook deliver your incoming e-mail to the Inbox of a different Outlook data file, choose Tools, E-Mail Accounts, select View Or Change Existing E-Mail Accounts, click the Next button, and select the name of the Outlook data file in the Deliver E-Mail To The Following Location drop-down list. The next time you start Outlook, your change will take effect. Outlook will then create a complete set of default Outlook folders (Calendar, Contacts, Journal, and so on) and default search folders within the newly designated e-mail destination data file. Note that the Outlook data file where Outlook delivers your e-mail is also known as the *default* Outlook data file.

Chapter 40

> **Note** You can't close the Outlook data file designated as your e-mail delivery location (that is, your default Outlook data file).

3 Click the Close button in the Outlook Data Files dialog box.

Opening, Closing, and Working with Outlook Data Files

The Outlook data file where Outlook delivers your incoming e-mail (that is, the *default* Outlook data file) is always opened in Outlook. You can open one or more additional Outlook data files to work with the folders and items they contain or to copy or move folders or items between Outlook data files. For example, if a coworker sent you an Outlook data file containing a set of items you need, such as contacts or appointments, you would have to open that data file to access those items. Or to recover archived items, you would need to open the Outlook data file to which you archived your folders (if it isn't already open).

To open an Outlook data file, choose File, Open, Outlook Data File and select the file in the Open Outlook Data File dialog box. As mentioned in the previous section, when you create a new Outlook data file, it's automatically opened in Outlook.

When an Outlook data file is opened in Outlook, it appears in the Folder List along with the other opened data file or files. You can use the Folder List to open the data file's folders and to view its items (see Figure 40-9). You can also move either an Outlook folder (together with all its items and subfolders) or an individual item from one data file to another by dragging it in the Folder List. (To copy the folder or item, press Ctrl while dragging.)

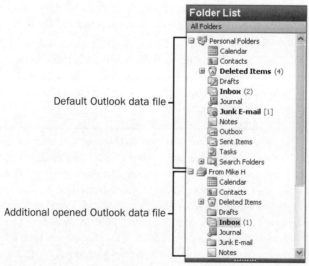

Default Outlook data file ┤

Additional opened Outlook data file ┤

Figure 40-9. In this figure the Folder List displays the default Outlook data file, plus an additionally opened data file.

> **Note** When an Outlook data file is opened in Outlook, it's also listed in the Outlook Data Files dialog box (shown in Figure 40-8), which was discussed in the previous section.

For information on using the Folder List, see "Using Other Methods to Open Folders," on page 951.

To close an additional Outlook data file that's been opened (you can't close the default one), right-click the name of the data file in the Folder List and choose Close "*Data File Name*" from the shortcut menu (where *Data File Name* is the "friendly" name of the data file), as shown here:

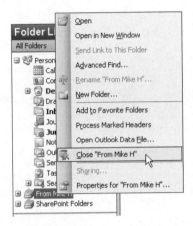

You can also close an Outlook data file by selecting it in the Outlook Data Files dialog box and clicking the Remove button, as explained in the previous section.

Chapter 40

Part 7

Access

41 Access Fundamentals   **1097**

42 Setting Up Tables and Relationships   **1113**

**43 Using Queries to Select and
Combine Information**   **1149**

**44 Creating Forms and Data Access Pages
for Working with Data**   **1171**

**45 Generating Reports to
Present Information**   **1199**

Access Fundamentals

A Rundown on Access. 1097
Designing and Planning
an Access Database 1100
Creating a New Database 1104

Using the Database Window
and Object Views 1107
Saving, Closing, and Opening Databases
in Access 1110

A Rundown on Access

Microsoft Office Access 2003 is the premier Microsoft Office 2003 application for managing data. Access, however, can also be fairly challenging to learn and might have more power than you really need. If the information you want to store is fairly simple—for example, an uncomplicated product inventory, a list of names and addresses, or a log of events—you might well be able to use an Office application that's more familiar to you.

> For a description of the new features in Access 2003, see "New Access Features," on page 15.

For example, Microsoft Office Excel 2003 is ideal for storing basic lists of information. Each row in a worksheet can hold one record (for instance, the information on one product in your inventory), each cell in a row can hold one field (such as the description or price of a product), and the top row in the worksheet can display a label for each field. Excel lets you sort, find, filter, automatically fill, summarize, group, outline, subtotal, and work with the data in other ways. Furthermore, Excel 2003 now lets you publish your data on a Web server that runs Microsoft Windows SharePoint Services. For more information, see Chapter 28, "Power Database Techniques: Lists, Filters, and PivotTables."

> **Note** Database information is divided into *records*, and records are divided into *fields*. Each record stores the information about one of the individual items that the database tracks, such as a product, a client, or an expense. Each field stores an individual piece of information within a record (for example, the description or number of a product, the name or e-mail address of a client, or the amount or date of an expense). When database information appears in a tabular list, typically each row displays a single record and each column displays a particular field for all of the records.

Microsoft Office Outlook 2003 is superb for storing and sharing names and addresses, task descriptions, journal entries, appointments, and free-form notes, as well as messages. And, if you create custom forms and new folders in Outlook, you can use Outlook to store and share almost any type of information.

Microsoft Word 2003 is ideal for recording free-form information, such as research notes, especially when you use its outlining feature. And you can use Word tables to store and display reasonable amounts of numeric or textual data. Word even provides mathematical functions for working with numbers in tables, as well as database tools for working with data fields and records in tables.

However, if you want to store large amounts of information, if your data is fairly complex or interrelated, or if you spend much of your time working with information, you'll probably want to use Access. Access is a dedicated data management application. More than any other Office application, Access provides specialized data management tools, options for connecting to external databases, customization features, and facilities for publishing live data on the Web or on a company intranet.

One feature in particular sets Access apart from the other Office applications in storing data: Access lets you create a *relational database*. In contrast, information stored in an Excel worksheet, an Outlook folder, or a Word table, is stored as a *flat-file database*. A flat-file database consists basically of a single list of records, where each record stores *all* of the information on a particular item. For example, Figure 41-1 shows an inventory of books stored in a flat-file organization, where each record (row) stores all the information on a particular book. (Although this list was actually created in Access, it's similar to an Excel list or a Word table and *doesn't* take advantage of the Access relational database capabilities.)

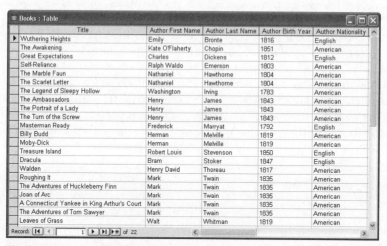

Figure 41-1. In a flat-file database, each record in a list stores all the information on a particular item. The data shown here is from the Book Inventory01 example database.

 (Many of the examples in the Access chapters are based on various versions of the Book Inventory example database. These versions are named Book Inventory01, Book Inventory02, and so on. You'll find copies of these databases on the companion CD provided with this book under the filenames Book Inventory01.mdb, Book Inventory02.mdb, and so on.)

One major problem with a flat-file database organization is that information is usually duplicated in separate records. For example, in the list shown in Figure 41-1, wherever one author has written more than one book, all of that author's information—first name, last name, birth year, and nationality—is duplicated in the record for each book. Not only does this arrangement waste storage space, but also it requires unnecessary data entry; it increases the likelihood of errors (the more times you need to enter "1835" the more likely it is you'll make a typo); and it makes the data more difficult to maintain (for example, if you discover that an author's birth year is incorrect, you'll need to fix it in every record where it occurs).

> **Note** In Access an individual list of records is known as a *table*. The number of records entered into a table is limited only by storage capabilities, but each record has a fixed number of fields.

A relational database solves the problem of duplicated data by storing a *single* copy of each set of duplicated fields in a separate list and then using identifiers to *relate* the lists. In Access, for example, the information shown in Figure 41-1 could be stored more efficiently by using two related Access tables, one table containing a list of book records and the other table a list of author records. Each record in the author table would have a unique identifier, and each record in the book table would include the unique identifier of the record for the book's author. The matching identifiers allow you to locate the information on each book's author and form the basis of the relationship between the tables (see Figure 41-2). You can then pull the separated data back together again in very flexible ways by using queries, reports, and other Access database objects (discussed later in the chapter), which can display data belonging to several tables according to the criteria you specify.

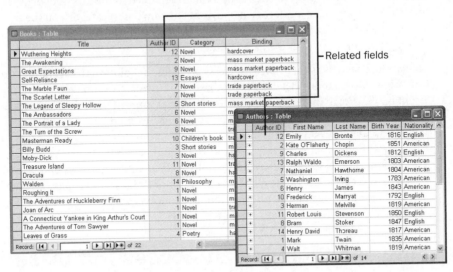

Figure 41-2. In Access you can eliminate duplicated information by storing data in two related tables, rather than in a single flat-file list. The tables shown here are from the Book Inventory02 example database.

Furthermore, if a field stores the unique identifier of a record in a related table (as does the Author ID field in the Books table shown in Figure 41-2), rather than requiring you to look

Chapter 41

up and type the correct identifier (as was done in the Books table), Access lets you define a field so that it displays a drop-down list of the records in the related table. A field that displays a drop-down list of choices is known as a *lookup field*. For example, in the Books table you could convert the Author ID field to a lookup field that lists all author names, so that rather than typing the unique identifier for an author, the user would simply select the author's name from the list, as shown here. (Even though the field displays a value from another table, internally it still stores only a numeric identifier.)

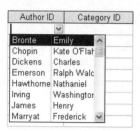

The next steps in consolidating the information displayed in the example Books table would be, first, to create a separate related table for storing the values displayed in the Category field (Novel, Essays, Short Stories, and so on), because these values are also repeated in many records, and, second, to convert Category to a lookup field. Using a related table and a lookup field is especially valuable for storing an information item such as a category, because the lookup field permits users to enter only a value contained in the drop-down list and prevents them from misspelling a category name or making up a new category on the fly. (Unofficial or misspelled categories would pose serious problems if you use the Category field to sort, filter, group, or work with the data in other ways.)

A relational database system such as Access provides the solution to yet another problem that you might encounter with a flat-file database. To illustrate this problem, consider the flat-file list of books shown in Figure 41-1 and imagine that some of the books have several authors. To store multiple authors in the flat-file database, you would have to add an arbitrary number of extra fields to store additional author information (wasting a great deal of space for the majority of books that have only a single author and possibly still not having room to store the authors for a book with many authors). In a relational database system, you can solve this problem by creating a separate related table of authors, plus an intermediate related table that stores book-author pairs. For information on this topic, see the Troubleshooting sidebar "Need a many-to-many relationship," on page 1133.

Designing and Planning an Access Database

The previous section should have helped you decide whether Access is the appropriate application to use for managing your information and should have given you an understanding of some of the unique benefits that Access offers, primarily its relational database capabilities. If you've decided to use Access to store and manage your data, the following are the basic steps you need to follow. The details are given in the remainder of this chapter and in the following chapters in this part of the book.

1 Create a new database. An Access database stores a body of related information—for example, an inventory of assets, a set of customer descriptions, a product inventory, a ledger, a time and billing system, a collection catalog, a membership roster, an investment portfolio, or a set of class enrollment records. You can start with a blank database and design the entire database yourself. Or, you can use one of the database wizards provided with Access, which will build the basic structure for a particular type of database for you. Details are given in "Creating a New Database," on page 1104.

> **Note** Using the various types of Access wizards can eliminate many of the steps in this list. However, it's important to understand these steps so that you can modify the designs created by wizards or build your own designs when you can't find an appropriate wizard.

2 Add tables to the database. A table is a *database object* that stores data. (The other types of database objects, described later, are used to view, enter, edit, retrieve, and summarize the data contained in tables and to work with that information in other ways.) Each table contains a list of records that store information on one of the types of items that are tracked in your database. For example, in a book inventory database, you might add tables for listing books, authors, book categories, and binding types. You can create a blank table and then manually define the table's fields and specify the types of information stored in each field (such as Text, Number, Date/Time, or Currency). Or you can use the Table Wizard to create a table with predefined fields and then customize that table. Be sure to design your tables and their fields in a way that minimizes duplicated information, for all the reasons discussed in "A Rundown on Access," on page 1097. Tables are covered in Chapter 42, "Setting Up Tables and Relationships."

> **Tip** **Let Access perform your calculations**
> If you need to display values that Access can derive by performing math on information stored in your tables, *don't* include these values as table fields. Instead, in your queries, forms, and reports you can define fields that display the results of calculations based on existing table fields, without permanently storing these values in tables. Using calculated fields in queries, forms, and reports allows Access (rather than the person entering the data) to perform the calculation and eliminates storing unnecessary information. For example, if you want to display an inventory of office supplies, your table needs only two fields: Units On Hand (for example, number of boxes of pencils) and Measure Of Unit (for example, the number of pencils in a box). Access can do the multiplication and display the total number of each item in a query, form, or report.

3 Define or modify table relationships. Having your data optimally divided into separate, related tables isn't enough. Before Access can work with related data, the relationships between tables must be explicitly defined. In some cases Access will automatically define relationships for you. Sometimes, however, you'll need to use the Relationships window to explicitly define the relationships between tables or to modify the properties of the relationships that Access has set up. (Instructions for doing

Chapter 41

this are given in "Setting Up Table Relationships," on page 1128.) Figure 41-2 shows two related Access tables, which appear in Datasheet view.

4   Create other database objects for working with the data stored in the database tables. The following are brief descriptions of the main types of database objects, other than tables, that you can add to your database:

■ **Query**   A tool for extracting, combining, and displaying data from one or more tables, according to criteria you specify. For example, in a book inventory database you could create a query to view a list of all hardcover books with more than 500 pages that you purchased in the last five months. In a query, you can sort information, summarize data (display totals, averages, counts, and so on), display the results of calculations on data, and choose exactly which fields are shown. You can view the results of a query in a tabular format (that is, Datasheet view, as shown in Figure 41-3) or you can view the query's data through a form or on a report. You can even use a query to update data automatically in one or more tables. The techniques for creating, modifying, and using queries are covered in Chapter 43, "Using Queries to Select and Combine Information."

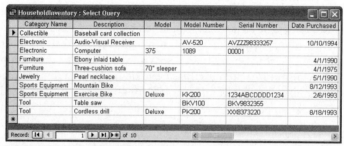

Category Name	Description	Model	Model Number	Serial Number	Date Purchased
Collectible	Baseball card collection				
Electronic	Audio-Visual Receiver		AV-520	AVZZZ98333257	10/10/1994
Electronic	Computer	375	1089	00001	
Furniture	Ebony inlaid table				4/1/1990
Furniture	Three-cushion sofa	70" sleeper			4/1/1975
Jewelry	Pearl necklace				5/1/1990
Sports Equipment	Mountain Bike				8/12/1993
Sports Equipment	Exercise Bike	Deluxe	KK200	1234ABCDDDD1234	2/6/1993
Tool	Table saw		BKV100	BKV9832355	
Tool	Cordless drill	Deluxe	PK200	XXX8373220	8/18/1993

Figure 41-3.   This query, displayed in Datasheet view, shows fields from four different database tables.

■ **Form**   A window, similar to a dialog box, that contains a set of controls (such as labels, text boxes, and check boxes) that allow you to view, enter, or edit database information, typically one record at a time, as shown in Figure 41-4. In a form, you can display data obtained directly from one or more tables or data that has been extracted using a query. Although it's possible to directly enter and edit the information in tables in Datasheet view, a database usually includes a set of forms that can make entering and editing data considerably easier and can limit the fields that can be viewed or modified. The methods for creating, modifying, and using forms are described in Chapter 44, "Creating Forms and Data Access Pages for Working with Data."

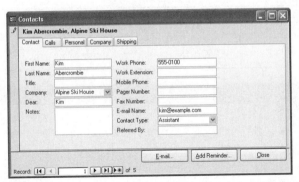

Figure 41-4. This form, displayed in Form view, lets you view and enter data belonging to two different tables one record at a time.

■ **Data access page** A Web page, similar in appearance to a form, that you can publish on your organization's intranet (see Figure 41-5). Users can open a data access page in their browsers and use it to view and update data from one or more tables in the database. Unlike other database objects, a data access page is stored in a set of separate files rather than incorporated into the database file. You'll find an introduction to creating data access pages in "Creating a Data Access Page," on page 1195.

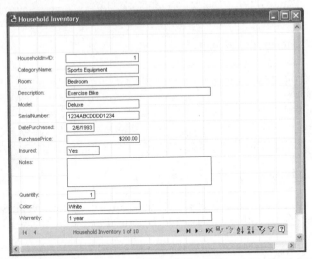

Figure 41-5. This data access page lets you view and modify the records belonging to a single table. It's displayed in Access in Page view.

■ **Report** Used primarily for printing selected database information. A report lets you label, sort, group, or summarize the data it presents (see Figure 41-6). And, like a form, a report can display data directly from one or more tables or it can display the results of a query. Access provides a variety of attractive, easy-to-read formats that you can apply to your reports.

> **Note** As with a database or table, you can build a query, form, data access page, or report from scratch. Or you can use an Access wizard to create a fully functional database object that you can later customize.

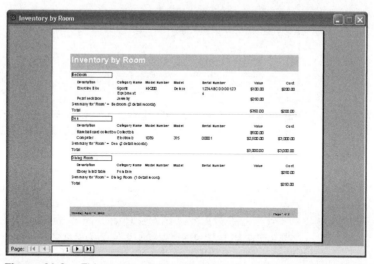

Figure 41-6. This report labels, groups, and summarizes (in total lines) data from an Access table. It's displayed in Access in Print Preview view.

5 Enter data in the database.

> **Note** Keep in mind that queries, forms, data access pages, and reports provide tools for viewing, adding, modifying, selecting, combining, sorting, summarizing, and printing database information and working with that data in other ways. None of these objects actually stores data. In a database, all data is stored in one or more tables.

Creating a New Database

If you want to build a database from scratch, you can create a blank database and then manually add tables and other database objects one at a time. To create a blank database, follow these steps:

1 If the New File task pane (shown in Figure 41-7) isn't visible, show it by clicking the New toolbar button; choosing File, New; or pressing Ctrl+N.

New

Figure 41-7. This figure shows the New File task pane that's displayed in Access.

2 Click the Blank Database command in the New area of the New File task pane.

3 Select a location and enter a name for your database file in the File New Database dialog box, which works just like the standard Save As dialog box.

Access will then save the new, blank database in the specified database file (which will have the *.mdb* extension), and it will open the Database window in the main Access window.

4 Add database objects as explained in the chapters in this part of the book.

If you can find an appropriate database wizard, you can gain a significant head start by using that wizard to create your database. To use a database wizard, follow these steps:

1 If the New File task pane isn't visible, show it by clicking the New toolbar button; choosing File, New; or pressing Ctrl+N.

2 Click the On My Computer command in the Templates area of the New File task pane to display the Templates dialog box.

New

3 Click the Databases tab in the Templates dialog box (shown in Figure 41-8), select a database wizard in the list, and click the OK button.

> **Tip** Access lists your recently used database wizards in the Recently Used Templates area of the New File task pane. To use one of these wizards, you can simply click it rather than performing steps 2 and 3.

Chapter 41

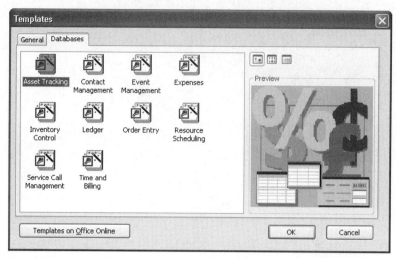

Figure 41-8. The Databases tab in the Templates dialog box lets you select a database wizard for creating a new Access database.

Tip To find, download, and use an online Access wizard from the Office Online Web site, use the controls at the top of the Templates area of the New File task pane. Either type a keyword in the Search Online For text box and click the Go button, or click Templates On Office Online to run your browser and open the Templates home page of the Office Online site. (You can also open the Templates home page by clicking the Templates On Office Online button at the bottom of the Templates dialog box, described in this section.)

For information on using Microsoft's expanded collection of online templates and wizards, and on using the new Template Help task pane available in Office 2003 applications, see "Downloading and Using Templates from Office Online," on page 55.

4 Select a location and enter a name for your database file in the File New Database dialog box, which works just like the standard Save As dialog box. The database wizard will then display a series of dialog boxes.

5 In the wizard dialog boxes, select the features you want for your new database. Typically, you'll get to select one or more optional fields for each table that the wizard generates, the style of the forms and reports, and the database title. You can click the Finish button at any time to create the database using default settings for any options you haven't set.

Access will then generate the new database, adding a complete set of tables. Depending on the database design, it may also add queries, forms, and reports. It will automatically save the database in the database file you specified in step 4 (the file will have the *.mdb* extension), and it will open the Database window. Usually, the wizard will also create and open a Switchboard window (a special type of database form), which provides a friendly interface that lets you open various database objects or close the database.

Access Fundamentals

6 Modify the database objects using the techniques explained in the chapters in this part of the book.

Note You can use an existing Access database to create a new one by clicking the From Existing File command in the New area of the New File task pane. The new database will be an exact copy of the existing one but will have a new name that Access automatically assigns when it opens the new database. You can modify the filename using Windows Explorer.

Tip **Create a database in Windows**
You can create a new database without first running Access by choosing the All Programs (or Programs), New Office Document command from the Start menu in Microsoft Windows. To create a blank database, double-click the Blank Database item in the General tab of the New Office Document dialog box. To create a database using a wizard, click the Databases tab. For more information, see "Creating a Document Using the New Office Document Dialog Box," on page 47.

Access Projects vs. Access Databases

The New File task pane (shown in Figure 41-7) includes commands for creating a new *Access project file*—Project Using Existing Data and Project Using New Data. You'll also find similarly named items for creating Access projects in the General tab in the Templates dialog box (shown, but not opened, in Figure 41-8).

Creating an Access project file, rather than an Access database, is an alternative way to set up database access. Rather than containing the actual data, an Access project file (which has the *.adp* file extension) stores settings for connecting to an external Microsoft SQL Server database. It's typically used to create a client–server application.

In contrast, an Access database (which has the *.mdb* file extension) contains the actual data, as well as definitions of database objects such as tables and queries. This data is managed by the Microsoft Jet database engine, which is included with the Access application.

The information in this book pertains to Access databases, *not* Access projects.

Using the Database Window and Object Views

Whenever a database is open, Access displays the Database window (shown in Figure 41-9), which serves as the central program location for working with the database objects (tables, queries, forms, and so on) in the open database.

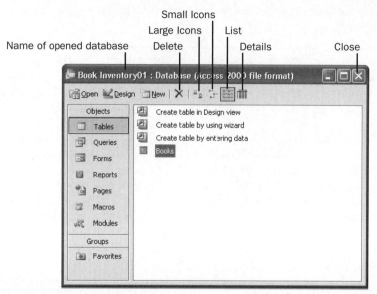

Figure 41-9. In the Database window, you can view, open, create, copy, move, rename, delete, organize, and perform other operations on the database objects in the open database.

If the Database window is hidden by another window or is minimized, you can display it using one of the following methods:

● Click the button for the Database window on the Windows taskbar. This button will be labeled with the name of the database that you're working with, followed by a colon, the word *Database*, and the file format. (The label is the same as the title of the Database window.) For example, if you're working with the Contact database, the label might be *Contact : Database (Access 2000 File Format)*.

> **Note** The Windows taskbar displays a button for the Database window *only* if the Windows In Taskbar option is checked. You can find this option by choosing Tools, Options and looking in the View tab in the Options dialog box.

● Choose the item for opening the Database window from the Window menu in Access. The item is labeled the same way as the Database window title and the corresponding button on the Windows taskbar.

● Click the Database Window toolbar button.

● Press F11.

Database Window

The following procedures are among the important ways you can work with database objects using the Database window:

● To work with a particular type of database object, click the corresponding button in the left column of the Database window—Tables, Queries, Forms, Reports, Pages, and so on.

- To view a database object, click it to select it and then click the Open button on the Database window toolbar (if the object is a report, this button will be labeled Preview). Or, just double-click the object.

- To change the design of a database object, select it and click the Design button.

- To create a new database object of the type that currently appears in the Database window, click the New button to display the New *Object* dialog box (New Table, New Query, New Form, New Report, or New Data Access page). The New *Object* dialog box will display a list of all the ways to create a new database object (the list varies according to the type of object you're creating). The remaining chapters in this part of the book give details on using each of the New *Object* dialog boxes.

- To make a copy of a database object, right-click it and choose Copy from the shortcut menu. Then right-click a blank spot in the Database window and choose Paste from the shortcut menu. You can also copy (or move) a database object to another database that is opened in a separate Access window by right-clicking the object and choosing the Copy (or Cut) command, and then right-clicking in the Database window for the target database and choosing the Paste command.

- To rename a database object, select it and press F2.

- To delete a database object, select it and press the Delete key or click the Delete button in the Database window.

- You can perform several additional operations on a database object by right-clicking it and choosing a command from the shortcut menu. For example, you can choose commands from the following shortcut menu when you right-click a table listed in the Database window:

- To close the current database, together with the Database window, click the Close button in the upper-right corner of the window.

Access provides several different *views* for working with database objects. When you select a database object in the Database window and click the Open button (or the Preview button for a report) or when you double-click an object, Access opens the object in a view that's appropriate for examining and modifying the object's data—Datasheet view for a table or query, Form view for a form, Page view for a data access page, and Print Preview view for a report. If you click the Design button, Access will open the object in Design view, where you can modify the object's design (for instance, for a table, change the fields and their data types).

Once you've opened a database object in any view, you can switch to any other available view by choosing a different view from the View menu or by clicking the down arrow on the View toolbar button and choosing a different view from the drop-down menu. The available views depend on the type of the database object. With a table, for example, you can choose any of the following views:

The chapters that follow explain the details of the commonly used views.

Saving, Closing, and Opening Databases in Access

The way an Access database is saved on disk is different from the way a typical Office document is saved, in the following respects:

- When you modify the *data* stored in the database in Datasheet or Form view—for example, when you add, change, or delete a record in the Datasheet view of a table— Access automatically saves your changes in the database file.

Save

- When you modify the *design* of a database object—for instance, when you add, modify, or remove fields in the Design view of a table or when you change the columns in the Datasheet view of a query—you have to manually save your changes. You can save these changes using the usual commands—that is, by choosing File, Save, by clicking the Save toolbar button, or by pressing Ctrl+S.

- Because of the automatic data-saving feature of Access, when you create a new database, Access saves it to a disk file *before* it lets you start working on the database, as explained previously in this chapter.

To close the current database (and leave Access running), activate the Database window and either click the Close button in the upper-right corner of that window, or choose Close from the File menu in the Access window. Creating a new database, or opening an existing one, also causes Access to close the current database.

> **Tip**   **Select the best database format**
>
> When you create either a blank database or one based on a wizard, Access 2003 stores the database in an Access database file (an *.mdb* file) that has the same format that was used by Access 2000. This format works fine for smaller databases and offers the advantage of letting you easily share your database file with Access 2000 users.
>
> If, however, you're creating a relatively large database, you may be able to obtain better performance by converting your database to the new format that was introduced with Access 2002. To do this, choose Tools, Database Utilities, Convert Database, To Access 2002 - Access 2003 File Format. Access will create a separate database file in the new format, leaving your original database file intact. Although you won't be able to immediately share an Access 2002 format database with users of Access versions earlier than 2002, you can convert it back to an earlier format by choosing Tools, Database Utilities, Convert Database, To Access 2000 File Format or by choosing Tools, Database Utilities, Convert Database, To Access 97 File Format.

Opening a Database

To open an existing database, use one of the standard techniques for opening an Office document:

Open

- In Access, choose File, Open, click the Open toolbar button, or press Ctrl+O. Or in Windows, choose Start, All Programs (or Programs), Open Office Document. Then, select the database file in the Open or Open Office Document dialog box.

   Or

- Choose a recently opened database file from the bottom of the File menu or click the name of a recently opened database file in the Open area at the bottom of the Home task pane. (You can click the More command in this area to display the Open dialog box.)

> For details on these as well as other ways to open Office documents, see "Opening Existing Office Documents," on page 56.

Unlike most other Office applications, however, if you open a database from within Access, it will close any database that's already opened. To have more than one database open at the same time, you can open an additional database outside Access (for example, by using the Open Office Document dialog box or by double-clicking a database file in Windows Explorer). Or, you can start another Access instance by choosing All Programs (or Programs), Microsoft Access from the Start menu in Windows, and then open the database from within Access.

Chapter 41

Backing Up Your Database

The automatic saving of data in Datasheet or Form view can help safeguard against the loss of information you've added. Keep in mind, however, that because of this feature you *can't* reverse changes you've made by simply abandoning the database without saving, as you can with a Word document or an Excel workbook. For example, if you accidentally delete a large group of records or fields, you can't reverse that change by simply closing the database without saving, because the change will already have been written to the database disk file. Nor can you reverse the deletion of one or more records or fields by issuing the Undo command. Although Access generally warns you before it deletes the data, such deletions are permanent. And Access has commands that are capable of quickly deleting large amounts of data!

The best way to safeguard against loss of data in Access is to make frequent, regular backups of the database file and to always create a backup copy of the database before you make any significant changes to the data or design. That way you can revert to the previous state of the database if necessary.

Access 2003 now provides the following convenient method for backing up the database that is currently open:

1   Choose File, Back Up Database. (If one or more of your database objects are still open, Access will automatically close them. Access can't back up your database if any objects remain open.)

Access will then display the Save Backup As dialog box, which is basically the same as the standard Save As dialog box displayed by Office applications.

In the Save Backup As dialog box, Access will open the folder containing the current database file and, in the File Name text box, it will enter a default filename for the backup copy of the database. Each time you back up the database, Access will generate a new default backup filename based on the filename of the current database and the date. For example, if the current database is saved in *Inventory.mdb*, Access will name the first backup you make on 5/21/2003 *Inventory_2003-05-21.mdb*, the second backup you make on that day *Inventory_2003-05-21_(1).mdb*, and so on.

2   If you wish, select a new folder for your backup file. Also, if you want to use a different naming scheme, edit the contents of the File Name text box. Note, however, that it's generally easiest and safest just to accept the default backup filename that Access proposes. Click the Save button to create the backup.

If you use your own naming scheme, be careful to give each backup file in a given folder a unique name, rather than overwriting a previous backup file or the database file itself. The idea is to create several generations of backup files, so that if anything goes wrong with a particular backup file, you can revert to a previous one.

Setting Up Tables and Relationships

Creating a Table 1113
Customizing a Table in Design View . . 1118

Setting Up Table Relationships 1128
Working in Datasheet View 1134

Creating a Table

To create a new table in Microsoft Office Access 2003, open the New Table dialog box (shown in Figure 42-1) by selecting the Tables object type and clicking the New button in the Database window, as explained in "Using the Database Window and Object Views," on page 1107. Then select an option in the list, as follows, and click the OK button:

Figure 42-1. In the New Table dialog box you can select one of five ways to create a new table.

● To create a table containing a basic set of fields and to open that table in Datasheet view so you can begin adding data immediately, select the Datasheet View option. The table will initially have 10 fields (named Field1 through Field10), as shown in Figure 42-2. You'll need to save the table design before you close the table or switch to another view (Access will prompt you if you forget). When you first save the table, Access will assign a data type to each field according to the type of information you entered into that field (such as Text, Number, Date/Time, or Currency) and it will discard any of the initial fields in which you haven't entered data.

For information on adding data and performing limited customizations to the table design in Datasheet view, see "Working in Datasheet View," on page 1134. For instructions on extensively modifying the table using Design view, see "Customizing a Table in Design View," on page 1118.

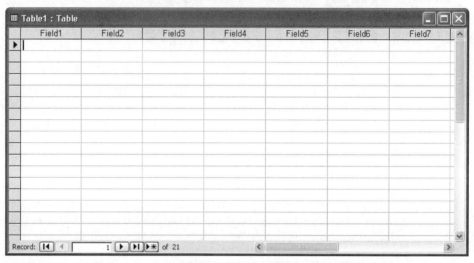

Figure 42-2. The Datasheet View option creates a new table containing 10 initial fields in which you can immediately start entering data. Only some of the fields are shown here.

- To open a new, blank table in Design view, where you can add fields and define their properties, select the Design View option. For more information, see "Customizing a Table in Design View," on page 1118.

- To create a new table using the Table Wizard, which will greatly assist you in adding fields to your new table and in assigning appropriate properties to these fields, select the Table Wizard option (see Figure 42-3). Once the wizard has generated your new table, you can open it in Datasheet view to immediately begin adding data or to perform limited modifications to the table design, as explained in "Working in Datasheet View," on page 1134. Or you can open it first in Design view to customize the table design more extensively, as described in "Customizing a Table in Design View," on page 1118. Or you can enter data into the table using a form the Table Wizard creates.

Note You can have the Table Wizard automatically designate a *primary key* for the new table. See "Designating a Primary Key," on page 1127. If your database contains other tables, the wizard might also allow you to define relationships between your new table and existing tables. See "Setting Up Table Relationships," on page 1128.

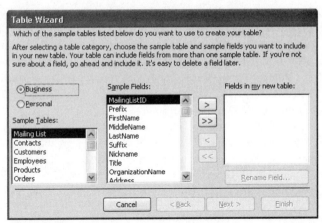

Figure 42-3. The Table Wizard helps you quickly add fields to a new table. It assigns an appropriate data type and other properties to each field it adds.

● To create a new table in your Access database by importing data from an external database file or other external data source, select the Import Table option, click the OK button, and then select the database file or data source in the Import dialog box. You can import data from an Access, Lotus 1-2-3, Paradox, or dBASE database file; from a Microsoft Excel workbook; from a Microsoft Outlook or Microsoft Exchange folder; from an XML (Extensible Markup Language) document or an HTML (Hypertext Markup Language) Web page; from a text file; from an ODBC (open database connectivity) data source; or from a list on a team Web site running Microsoft Windows SharePoint Services. The new table and its data will become an integral part of your Access database, just as if you had entered it within Access, and the data won't be affected by subsequent changes made to the data source after you import it.

> For information on importing an Access table from an XML document, see the next section, "Importing and Exporting XML Documents."

Note The Import and Link dialog boxes are similar to the standard Open dialog box. However, in the Files Of Type drop-down list, you can select either a file type (such as Microsoft Excel) or a data source (such as Windows SharePoint Services). As soon as you select a data source, Access immediately displays a wizard (for example, the Import SharePoint Team Services wizard) that you'll use to import or link the data, rather than continuing to use the Import or Link dialog box.

● To create a new table that's linked to an external database file or other external data source, select the Link Table option, click the OK button, and select the database file or data source in the Link dialog box. You can link a table to data in an Access, Paradox, or dBASE database; in an Excel workbook; in an Outlook or Exchange folder; in an

HTML Web page; in a text file; in an ODBC data source; or in a list on a SharePoint team Web site. Rather that storing the data itself, a linked table stores only a connection to the data source, and you can use the table to view or modify the data within that source. You should use linking rather than importing if a separate application maintains the data and you want to use Access to tap into the current data.

Tip **Export Access data to XML or other formats**

You can export a table or other database object to an external file by selecting the object in the Database window and choosing File, Export, which displays the Export *Object* To dialog box (where *Object* is a description of the selected database object). You can export a database object to a variety of formats—for example, to an Access database; to an Excel workbook; to an XML document or an HTML or ASP (Active Server Pages) Web page; to a text or RTF (Rich Text Format) file; or to Microsoft IIS .htx and .idc files.

You can also export a table, query, form, or report to another Microsoft Office 2003 application by selecting the object in the Database window and then choosing a command from the Office Links submenu on the Tools menu:

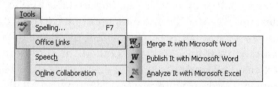

The Merge It With Microsoft Word command is available only for a table or query. It runs a mail merge operation in Microsoft Word 2003, using the table or query as the recipient list. See Chapter 19, "Using Word to Automate Mailings."

For information on exporting an Access table to an XML document, see the next section, "Importing and Exporting XML Documents."

Importing and Exporting XML Documents

If you're creating a new table by importing an XML document, as explained in the previous section, you'll need to select the XML (.xml) file in the Import dialog box and click the Import button. Access will then display the Import XML dialog box, shown here, where you can set import options. Click the Options >> button to display all the options.

You can click the Transform button in the Import XML dialog box to have Access convert the XML document to a new structure as it imports the data, according to a transform (.xsl or .xslt) file that you specify.

When you import the XML file, Access infers a schema from the structure of the XML document. (As explained later in this section, you can save this schema in a separate schema [.xsd] file if you export the table.) You can also import an XML schema (.xsd) file—rather than an XML document—to create an empty table that has the set of fields and field properties that are specified in the schema.

For general information on XML, transforms, and schemas, see "Creating, Editing, and Viewing XML Documents," on page 594.

If you're exporting an Access table or other database object to an XML document, as explained in the tip at the end of the previous section, in the Export *Object* To dialog box you'll need to select XML (*.xml) in the Save As Type drop-down list and specify a filename and location for the XML file. When you click the Export button in the Export *Object* To dialog box, Access will display the Export XML dialog box, shown here, where you can select export options, as follows:

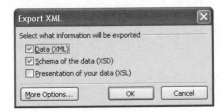

- To export all data in the table to a well formed XML (.xml) file, select the Data (XML) option.

- To export the table's schema (which specifies the table's structure but doesn't include the data) to an XML schema (.xsd) file, select the Schema Of The Data (XSD) option.

- To export the table's data to an XML (.xml) file and also generate a Web page (.htm) file and a transform (.xsl) file for viewing the table's data, select the Data (XML) option *and* the Presentation Of Your Data (XSL) option (you can't select the second option without selecting the first). You can then view your data by opening the resulting Web page (.htm) file in your browser (this file is linked to the .xml and .xsl files).

- To customize any of three exporting options listed above, click the More Options button and then click the corresponding tab—Data, Schema, or Presentation—in the Export XML dialog box.

Customizing a Table in Design View

You can use Design view to define the design of a new, blank table you've created using the Design View option in the New Table dialog box. You can use it to customize the design of a new table you've created using one of the other options in the New Table dialog box. And you can use it to modify an existing table that already contains data. Design view allows you to add, remove, or rearrange fields; to define the name, the data type, and other properties of each field; and to designate a primary key for the table.

To open a table in Design view, follow the instructions given in "Using the Database Window and Object Views," on page 1107. Figure 42-4 shows the Books table in the Book Inventory03 example database, opened in Design view. The top portion of the Design view window lists the fields in the table, one per row, and gives the name, data type, and an optional description for each field. (These are three of the field's *properties*, which are explained in "Setting the Field Properties," on page 1122.) If you're using Design view to create a new table, this list will initially be empty.

The tabs in the bottom portion of the window show all the other properties for the current field. (The *current field* is the one that's selected in the field list—it's marked with an arrow in the box at the left end of the row.) Each property is displayed in a separate box within the grid.

Save

To save the changes you make in Design view choose File, Save; or click the Save toolbar button; or press Ctrl+S.

Row selectors   A property box   Field list

The current field

Properties for the
current field are
displayed on
these tabs

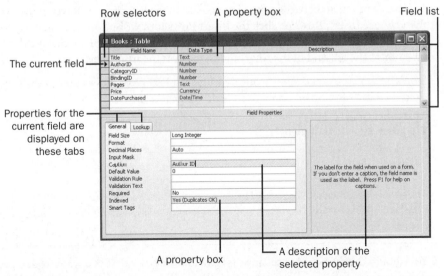

A property box   A description of the
selected property

Figure 42-4. The Design view of a table lets you modify the table's fields and their properties. This table belongs to the Book Inventory03 example database.

> **Tip** You can rapidly toggle a table between Design view, in which you can modify the table design, and Datasheet view, in which you can view the table data, by simply clicking the View toolbar button.

Adding, Removing, and Rearranging Fields

Using Design view, you can add new fields to a table, remove fields, or move or copy fields from one position in the field list to another.

Adding a Field

To add a new field to a table at the end of the list, click in the Field Name column of the first blank row in the field list in the top portion of the Design view window and enter a field name. You can type up to 64 characters for the field name, including spaces. Ideally, however, you should make the name short and descriptive of the field's contents. It's also best to avoid including spaces in field names if you want to be able to easily access those fields from VBA (Visual Basic for Applications) code. If you want the field to be labeled with a "friendlier" name in Datasheet view, including spaces if you wish (for example, Type Of Binding rather than BindingID), you can assign that name to the field's Caption property (as described later in the chapter). If the Caption property has a value, Access will use it to label the field's column in Datasheet view; if the Caption property is blank, Access will label the column using the field name.

Insert Rows

To insert a new field between two existing fields in the list, click the lower of the two fields and then choose Insert, Rows or click the Insert Rows toolbar button. Another way to insert a field is to select the entire row below the desired insertion position by clicking the row selector (the box at the left end of the row), and then press the Insert key.

Don't be too concerned about your new field's initial position— you can easily move it (as described in "Moving or Copying a Field," on page 1121).

> **Tip**   Use the shortcut menu
>
> As you work in Access, keep in mind that you can often display a shortcut menu of useful commands by right-clicking a field, title bar, column or row heading, or other object. The shortcut menu will provide commands that are appropriate for working with the particular object that you clicked. For example, you can insert a new field into a table by right-clicking the row below the desired insertion position and then choosing Insert Rows from the shortcut menu.

You should then proceed to set any of the field properties that you want to change from their default values, following the instructions that will be given in "Setting the Field Properties," on page 1122.

Build

> **Tip**   Have Access build your field
>
> When you add a field, you may be able to save time by using the Field Builder, which lets you select and insert a predefined field suitable for a particular purpose (such as a telephone number in a table of contacts or a serial number in a table of products). The primary advantage of using the Field Builder is that a field you insert will have all its properties set to appropriate values. (The field builder offers the same list of predefined fields as the Table Wizard, described earlier in the chapter.)
>
> To use the Field Builder, click the row in the field list below the position where you want to insert the new field and click the Build toolbar button.

Removing a Field

Delete Rows

To remove a field from the table, click anywhere in the field's row in the field list and choose Edit, Delete Rows or click the Delete Rows toolbar button. Another way to delete a field is to select its entire row by clicking the row selector (the box at the left end of the row) and then press the Delete key. You won't be able to delete a field that's used to create a relationship with another table; you must first remove the relationship (relationships are covered later in this chapter).

> **Caution** If a particular field already contains data, be aware that deleting the field will delete its data for every record in the table.

Undo

> **Caution** Access lets you undo multiple actions in Design view. (To undo an action, choose Edit, Undo; or click the Undo toolbar button; or press Ctrl+Z.) However, once you save the table design (which you must do before changing views), you won't be able to undo your deletion and the data will be permanently deleted.

Moving or Copying a Field

Access uses the order in which the fields are listed in Design view as the default order of the fields in Datasheet view or in a form or report that you generate from the table. Therefore, you should arrange the fields in a logical order. Keep in mind, however, that in Datasheet view or in a form or report you can override the default field order and arrange the fields any way you want (without affecting their order in the Design view of the table).

To move a field to a different position in the field list, first select its entire row by clicking the row selector (the box at the left of the row). Then perform either of the following actions:

- Use the mouse to drag the row selector up or down to the new position:

Drag the row selector to move the selected field up or down in the list

⊞ Books : Table	
Field Name	Data Type
Title	Text
AuthorID	Number
CategoryID	Number
BindingID	Number
Pages	Text
Price	Currency
DatePurchased	Date/Time

- Choose Edit, Cut (or press Ctrl+X). Then click in the row below the desired new position of the field and choose Edit, Paste (or press Ctrl+V). Be sure to just click in the row below the desired insert position so that it contains the insertion point; if you select this entire row, it will be deleted when you paste. (Note that this method won't work if the field is currently part of one or more relationships. Also, if the field already contains data, that data will be lost.)

> **Note** If you want to make a copy of a field, use the second method for moving a field, but choose the Copy command (or press Ctrl+C) rather than choosing the Cut command (or pressing Ctrl+X). After the field is copied, click the field name and type in a different, unique name. (You won't be able to save your modifications if two fields have the same name.) Note that although the original field's properties will be duplicated in the copy of the field, any data contained in the original field will *not* be transferred to the copy.

Chapter 42

1121

Setting the Field Properties

Each of the fields in a table is described by a set of *properties*. The field's properties determine how the field's data is stored, handled, or displayed. The properties include the field name, the data type, the description, and other features such as the field size, format, and caption. You can view and set a field's properties within the boxes in the Design view window (both in the field list at the top of the window and on the tabs in the bottom portion). (See Figure 42-4, for example.) Note that when the insertion point is within a property box, Access displays information about that property in the lower-right corner of the window, and you can get detailed information by pressing F1.

When you add a new field, you must enter a name for it. Access will assign all the field's other properties a default setting. (For some fields the default setting is no value; that is, the property box will initially be blank.) You can modify any of these properties, or you can simply accept the default setting.

Renaming a Field

To change a field's name property, click in the Field Name column for that field and type in the name you want. Follow the naming instructions given at the beginning of "Adding a Field," on page 1119. Changing the field name won't affect any of the table's relationships.

Setting the Data Type

Every field is assigned a specific data type, which determines the kind of data that can be entered into the field. The default data type of a new field is Text. To change a field's data type, click in the Data Type column for that field, and select a new data type from the drop-down list:

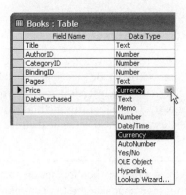

Setting Up Tables and Relationships

The available data types are described in Table 42-1.

Table 42-1. **Data Types You Can Assign to Table Fields**

Data Type	Usage
Text (default)	Holds any type of characters, either letters or numbers. The number of characters that can be stored depends on the value (0 to 255) assigned to the Field Size property (described later). Note that even if you set Field Size to 255, Access will use only the amount of memory required by each entry.
Memo	Similar to Text, but holds up to 64,000 characters.
Number	Holds a numeric value that you can use to perform calculations or comparisons. The size and type of number you can store is determined by the current setting of the Field Size property (described later).
Date/Time	Holds valid calendar dates for the years 100 through 9999 and clock times in either 12-hour or 24-hour format. This data type lets you sort and calculate data chronologically.
Currency	Accurately stores monetary values for use in financial calculations and comparisons.
AutoNumber	Stores a unique number that Access assigns as each new record is added. Access either increments the number by one with each new record, or it assigns a unique random number, according to the setting of the New Values property. These numbers aren't reused when you delete records, and you can't change the value of an AutoNumber field.
Yes/No	Efficiently stores one of two values: true or false, yes or no, on or off (according to the setting of the Format property). You can set the field using a check box in Datasheet view or on a form.
OLE Object	Holds an OLE (object linking and embedding) object (such as an Excel spreadsheet, a Word document, or a picture, sound, animation, or video clip) that you insert by using the Insert, Object command. See Chapter 7, "Exchanging Data in Office 2003," for information on OLE objects.

Table 42-1. Data Types You Can Assign to Table Fields

Data Type	Usage
Hyperlink	Holds a hyperlink—that is, the location of another database object, an Office document, or a page on the Web. You insert the hyperlink into the field by choosing Insert, Hyperlink. You can then open the target object, document, or Web page by clicking the hyperlink in the field.
Lookup Wizard	Selecting this item runs the Lookup Wizard, which assists you in converting the field to a lookup field, which is described in "A Rundown on Access," on page 1097. Before you select this item, you should first set the field's data type by selecting Text, Number or Yes/No from the list. (A field must have one of these three data types before you can convert it to a lookup field.) In Datasheet view a lookup field displays a drop-down list that contains values from another table or query or a fixed list of values that you specify when you use the Lookup Wizard. You can later modify the properties of a lookup field's list by changing values in the Lookup tab at the bottom of the table Design view window.

Caution If a field already stores data, changing its data type can result in loss of information. For instance, if you change a field's data type from Text to Number, Access will permanently delete the contents of any field that doesn't contain a valid numeric value, and it may alter the values of numbers according to the field's Field Size property (for instance, if Field Size is set to Long Integer, Access will convert 29.95 to 30).

Adding a Description

If you wish, you can assign a description to a field by entering it into the Description column for that field. When a field is selected in Datasheet view, Access displays the field's description, if any, in the status bar. You might therefore want to create a description containing instructions or other information that would be useful to the person entering data into the table.

Setting Other Field Properties

You set the remaining field properties using the General and Lookup tabs in the bottom portion of the table Design view window. To set additional properties for a field, complete the following steps:

1 Click anywhere within the field's row in the upper part of the Design view window or select the row. (It will then become the current field and will be marked with an arrow in the row selector.)

2 Click the General tab in the lower half of the window to set general-purpose properties or click the Lookup tab to modify the properties that apply specifically to a lookup field (as described in the last item in Table 42-1).

3   Click in the box for any property that you want to modify and enter a new value or select it from the drop-down list, if available. Consult the property description displayed in the help area on the right or press F1 for detailed information about the current property.

> **Note**   When you click in certain property boxes, an ellipsis (…) button appears to the right of the box. You can click this button to display a dialog box that will assist you in entering a value into the field. Which dialog box Access displays depends on the particular field. For example, it might show the Expression Builder dialog box, the Input Mask Wizard, or the SQL Statement : Query Builder window.

The set of additional properties that are available for a field depends on the field's data type. In general, these properties control the way data is entered, stored, and displayed in the field. The following sections describe some of the important properties.

Field Size Property   The Field Size property controls the amount of space that's allocated for a particular field. It's available only for a field that has the Text, Number, or AutoNumber data type. For a Text field, the Field Size specifies the maximum number of characters that can be stored in the field; you can enter a value between 0 and 255. (The default value is 50.) For a Number field, you can select a value from the drop-down list that determines the size and type of number that the field can store:

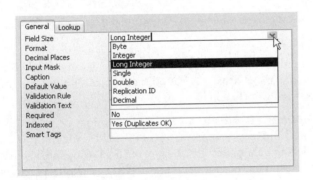

For example, you can use the Long Integer value (the default) to store whole numbers ranging from approximately –2 billion to +2 billion, or you can select the Double value to store numbers with decimal components (such as 3.14). For an AutoNumber field, you can select Long Integer or Replication ID. (A Replication ID is a 16-byte globally unique identifier.)

Format Property   The Format property determines how the data is displayed on the screen or how it's printed. Choose the format that you want from the drop-down list. For example, for a field that has the Date/Time data type, you can choose to display the date as a Long Date (for example, Monday, December 1, 2003), as a Short Date (for example, 12/1/2003), or using other date and time formats.

Chapter 42

Decimal Places Property   The Decimal Places property lets you choose the number of decimal places that Access displays for a field that has the Number or Currency data type. (It affects only the way the number is displayed, not the precision of the value that's stored internally.) Choose a specific number of decimal places from the drop-down list or choose Auto (the default value) to display the default number of decimal places for the field's Format property setting.

Input Mask Property   Most data types also give you the option to define an *input mask*. (By default, there is no input mask.) An input mask assists you in entering valid data into a field. It displays placeholder characters showing you the number of characters you need to enter (usually _ characters, which are replaced by the characters you type); it includes separator characters so you don't have to type them (such as the parentheses and dash in a telephone number); and it prevents you from typing an inappropriate character (for example, a letter when you're entering a phone number). Figure 42-5 shows an input mask applied to a field with the Date/Time data type, as it's displayed in Datasheet view.

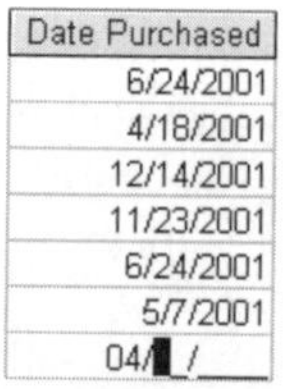

Date Purchased
6/24/2001
4/18/2001
12/14/2001
11/23/2001
6/24/2001
5/7/2001
04/█ /___

Figure 42-5.   This input mask makes it easier to enter a valid date in the mm/dd/yyyy format.

The fastest way to define an input mask for a Text or Date/Time data-type field is to run the Input Mask Wizard by clicking the ellipsis (…) button that appears at the right end of the Input Mask property box when you click in it.

Caption Property   If you enter text into the box for the Caption property, Access will use this text to label the field in Datasheet view, at the top of the field's column. If you leave the Caption box empty (the default value), Access will label the field using the field name. This property gives you flexibility in the way your fields are labeled in Datasheet view, without your having to change the actual field name.

Default Value Property   If you're creating a database in which a field usually contains the same value—for example, the City field in an address database in which most of the addresses are in the same city—you can assign that value to the Default Value property. (By default, this property is blank.) Then, whenever Access creates a new record, it will insert the value into the field for you (for example, *New Orleans*). You can then change the value if necessary.

Required Property   If you select Yes in the Required property box, Access will require that a value be entered into the field when the record is created or modified. If you choose No (the default value), the field can be left empty.

Indexed Property   This property controls whether a field is *indexed*—that is, whether Access builds an index for the field. Indexing a field significantly speeds up searching, sorting, or running queries on that field, but it requires more space for storing the information and can make adding, deleting, or updating records slower. The primary key for a table (discussed in the next section) is automatically indexed. The choices in the drop-down list in the Indexed property box are the following:

- **Yes (Duplicates OK)**   The field will be indexed, and you'll be able to enter the same value into more than one record.

- **Yes (No Duplicates)**   The field will be indexed, and you must enter a unique value into the field for each record. (This is the default for a field that's designated as the primary key, discussed next.)

- **No**   The field won't be indexed, and you'll be able to enter the same value into more than one record. (This is the default for all fields except one designated as the primary key.)

Smart Tags Property   You can use the new Smart Tags property to add a smart tag recognizer to a field. If a field has been assigned a smart tag recognizer (such as the Financial Symbol recognizer) and if—in Datasheet or Form view—you enter the type of data into that field that the recognizer looks for (such as a financial symbol), Access will display a smart tag indicator in the field's lower-right corner. When you click in the field or just hold the mouse pointer over it, a smart tag button will appear. You can click this button to perform an action on the data (such as looking up a stock quote for a financial symbol), as shown here:

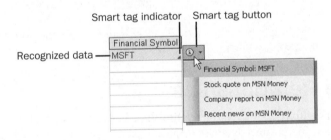

To add a smart tag recognizer to the current field, click the ellipsis to the right of the Smart Tags property box and select one or more recognizers in the Smart Tags dialog box.

For general information on smart tag recognizers, see "Using Smart Tags in Word," on page 276.

Designating a Primary Key

Primary
Key

The primary key consists of one or more fields that Access can use to uniquely identify the records contained within the table. A table must have a primary key if it's on the "one" side of a one-to-many relationship, as explained in "Setting Up Table Relationships," on page 1128.

When you designate a single field as the primary key, the field's Indexed property is automatically set to Yes (No Duplicates) and you won't be able to change this setting. Thus, you can quickly sort or retrieve the records using the primary key field, and you'll be barred from entering duplicate values into this field. Also, when you enter or modify the data in a record, Access won't let you leave a primary key field blank.

In most cases a single field is used as the primary key, although in situations where the data in a single field can't be unique for each record, two or more fields can be designated. In this case the data in all the primary key fields combined must be unique for each record. (For example, an inventory table might contain a part number field and a subpart number field, where neither field is unique by itself but when taken together, they form a unique combination.) When multiple fields are used to create a primary key, the Indexed property for each component of the primary key will not be changed and remains editable, unlike a single field that's designated as the primary key.

To designate a field, or a group of fields, as the primary key, select the field or fields in the field list and choose Edit, Primary Key or click the Primary Key toolbar button. (To select several fields, click the row selector for the first one, and then click the row selector for each additional one while holding down the Ctrl key.) Access will mark the primary key field(s) with a key icon, as shown here:

Field designated as the primary key

To remove the primary key designation from a field, select it and choose the Edit, Primary Key command or click the Primary Key toolbar button again.

Setting Up Table Relationships

Before Access can work with related data, the relationships between related tables must be explicitly defined. When you create a database using a database wizard or when you add a table using the Table Wizard, Access will define relationships for you.

If the required relationships between tables aren't defined, in some cases Access will define them for you as they're needed—for instance, when you add a lookup field or when you insert a subdatasheet (discussed later in this chapter). In other cases, you must explicitly define the required relationships before Access can combine the related data—for example, when you use a wizard to create a query that displays data from two or more related tables. Explicitly defining a relationship also allows Access to maintain integrity of the related data.

> **Note** Although this section focuses on tables, you can also define relationships for queries, and you may need to do so if you use a query as the basis for a report or for another query.

To view existing relationships, to define new ones, or to change relationship properties, follow these steps:

1 Close any tables that are opened. (You won't be able to make certain changes to a relationship if one of the related tables is open.)

2 Open the Relationships window by choosing Tools, Relationships or—if the Database window is active—by clicking the Relationships toolbar button. Figure 42-6 shows the relationships that are defined in the Book Inventory03 example database.

Relation-ships

> **Note** If no relationships have yet been defined in your database, when you open the Relationships window, Access will first display the Show Table dialog box, explained in step 4 in this procedure.

The lines between the field lists in the Relationships window indicate relationships between specific fields. In a typical relationship, the field in one of the two tables has a unique value. Two types of fields store unique values: a single field designated as the primary key and any field whose Indexed property is set to the value Yes (No Duplicates). The other table's field in a typical relationship has a nonunique value; that is, its Indexed property is set to No or to Yes (Duplicates OK). The table containing the unique field is commonly known as the *primary table* in the relationship, and the table containing the non-unique field is commonly known as the *related table* in the relationship.

> **Note** The term *related table* is also used in a more general sense to refer to *any* table that has a relationship with another table.

A single record in the primary table (for example, the record for Mark Twain in the Author table) can match several records in the related table (for example, the records for all books written by Mark Twain in the Books table). However, a record in the related table (for example, *The Adventures of Huckleberry Finn*) can match only a single record in the primary table (Mark Twain). Accordingly, the relationship between the related fields in the two tables (in the example, AuthorID) is called a *one-to-many* relationship. The *one* side of a relationship line is marked with a "1" and the *many* side is marked with an infinity symbol (∞) (but only if you've chosen to enforce referential integrity, as explained in the sidebar "Enforcing Referential Integrity," on page 1132).

Chapter 42

1129

A relationship

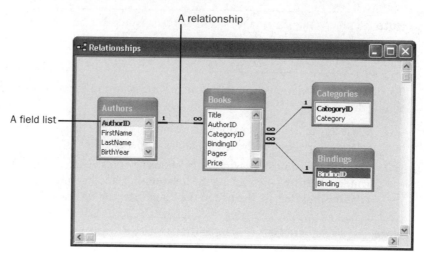

A field list

Figure 42-6. The Relationships window shows the relationships that have been defined between tables in the database. These relationships belong to the Book Inventory03 example database.

Note In the one-to-many relationship between the Authors and Books tables in the Book Inventory03 example database (shown in Figure 42-6), the field containing unique data (AuthorID) is in the Authors table, which is therefore the primary table. The field containing nonunique, related data (also named AuthorID) is in the Books table, which is therefore the related table.

Like the author descriptions, the book categories and binding types are also stored in primary tables in the Book Inventory03 database, so that categories and binding types aren't duplicated in the Books table. Placing the categories and binding types in separate primary tables also allows the user to select categories and binding types from lookup fields, rather than having to type in the values. See the discussion on the advantages of storing data in separate tables that are connected by relationships in "A Rundown on Access," on page 1097.

3   If necessary, arrange the field lists shown in the Relationships window so that you can see the relationship lines clearly. You can move a field list by using the mouse to drag its title bar.

Note If *both* fields in a relationship are unique, the relationship is known as *one-to-one*. For instance, in an employee database, if employee descriptions were stored in one table and their social security numbers were stored in a related table, the relationship would be one-to-one (each employee record would match a single social security record and vice versa). Breaking apart information like this is uncommon because it doesn't prevent duplicated data, and it would be more efficient to simply place all the data in a single table. One possible reason for doing it, however, would be to keep some information (such as a social security number, password, or birth date) confidential by placing it in a separate one-to-one related table that has limited access.

Show Table

4   If one or more tables whose relationships you want to view or work with aren't shown in the Relationships window, choose Relationships, Show Table or click the Show Table toolbar button and select the table or tables in the Tables tab of the Show Table dialog box.

Show All Relation- ships

Note   You can hide a field list by clicking it and pressing Delete or choosing Relation-ships, Hide Table. Doing so won't remove any relationships that are associated with this table but will merely hide the field list and its relationships from view. You can show the field lists for all tables involved in relationships by choosing Relationships, Show All or by clicking the Show All Relationships toolbar button.

5   To define a new relationship, drag the related field from the field list for one of the tables, drop it on the related field in the field list for the other table, and click the Cre-ate button in the Edit Relationships dialog box that Access shows (see Figure 42-7). Note that related fields don't need to have the same name, only the same data type (although they're often given the same name to clarify the relationship).

Notice that the Edit Relationships dialog box displays the type of the relationship, which is based on the related fields: One-To-Many, One-To-One, or Indeterminate. An Indeterminate relationship is one for which Access can't explicitly determine the nature of the relationship (neither related field can be determined to be unique). For information on the Enforce Referential Integrity and related options, see the sidebar "Enforcing Referential Integrity," on page 1132. For a brief explanation of the options you can select by clicking the Join Type button, see the sidebar "Modify Table Rela-tionships for a Query," on page 1158.

If you later want to change the features of a relationship, you can reopen the Edit Rela-tionships dialog box for that relationship by double-clicking the relationship's line in the Relationships window.

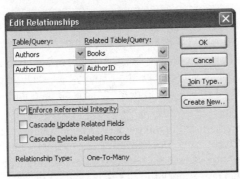

Figure 42-7.   The Edit Relationships dialog box lets you add or change a relationship's features.

Chapter 42

6 To delete a relationship, click the line to select it and then press the Delete key.

7 When you've finished working with relationships, close the Relationships window. If you've modified the window's layout (that is, the tables that are included and their arrangement), Access will ask if you want to save the layout. (Rest assured that the relationships themselves have already been saved.) Be sure to click the Yes button if you want to reuse this same layout.

Enforcing Referential Integrity

When you define a relationship, you can check the Enforce Referential Integrity option in the Edit Relationships window to have Access make sure that the correspondence between the tables is maintained as you enter data and work with the database. Specifically, this option ensures that each record in the related table will properly match a record in the primary table. To select this option, the data types of the related fields must be the same, and the relationship can't be *indeterminate* (an invalid relationship for enforcing referential integrity in which neither related field can be explicitly determined to be unique). If the option is enabled, Access will control changes you attempt to make to the related fields in the following ways:

- Access won't allow you to enter a value into the related table field that lacks a matching value in the primary table field. For instance, in the Book Inventory03 example database (shown in Figure 42-6 and other figures), you couldn't enter into the Books table an AuthorID value that isn't found in the Authors table. You can, however, leave the related table field blank (indicating that it doesn't refer to any record).

- Access won't permit you to change the value in the primary table field if matching records are already in the related table field. For instance, in the Book Inventory03 example database, you wouldn't be able to change the value of the AuthorID field in any of the records in the Authors table because each of the AuthorID values is already used in the Books table. (Actually, in this example you couldn't change this field anyway because it has been assigned the AutoNumber data type.)

  However, if you check the Cascade Update Related Fields option in the Edit Relationships dialog box, Access will let you change the primary table field and will automatically update all the matching values in the related table field so that referential integrity is maintained between the two tables.

- Access won't let you delete a record in the primary table if matching records are in the related table. For instance, in the Book Inventory03 example database, you couldn't delete any of the Authors records because each one has matching records in the Books table. However, if you check the Cascade Delete Related Records option in the Edit Relationships dialog box, Access will enforce referential integrity by deleting all the matching records in the related table for each record you delete in the primary table.

Troubleshooting

Need a many-to-many relationship

You need to connect two tables with a many-to-many relationship, but Access doesn't provide this type of relationship.

In Access you can indirectly set up a many-to-many relationship by creating an intermediate table. Consider, for instance, the Book Inventory03 example database (shown in Figure 42-6 and other figures in this part of the book). If some of the books have more than one author, and you want to be able to link a book to all the book's authors and to link an author to all the author's books, you need to set up a many-to-many relationship. You could set up this relationship, thereby allowing the book inventory database to support more than one author for each book, by performing the following steps:

1 Add a unique identifying field to the Books table (perhaps named BookID), so that each record in the intermediate table can reference a specific book record (and make this field the primary key while you're at it). Also, eliminate the AuthorID field in the Books table because it's no longer needed.

2 Create an intermediate table (perhaps named BookAuthors) in which each record contains the unique identifier of a book record plus the unique identifier of an author record, thereby linking a book to one of its authors and an author to one of his or her books.

3 Define a relationship between the Books and BookAuthors tables and a relationship between the BookAuthors and Authors tables, as shown in Figure 42-8. Both these relationships will be one-to-many, but the overall result will be to connect Authors and Books in an indirect many-to-many relationship.

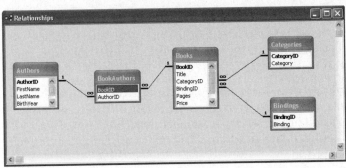

Figure 42-8. The BookAuthors table effectively creates a many-to-many relationship between the Books table and the Authors table. These relationships and tables belong to the Book Inventory04 example database.

Chapter 42

Working in Datasheet View

Using Datasheet view is the most common way of viewing a table or a query. You can also view a form in Datasheet view, although you almost always work with forms in Form view. Figure 42-9 shows the Books table in the Book Inventory03 example database displayed in Datasheet view. In this view each column represents a single field in the database, and each row represents a record. To open a table (or a query or form) in Datasheet view, follow the instructions given in "Using the Database Window and Object Views," on page 1107.

Title	Author ID	Category ID	Binding ID	Pages	Price
Wuthering Heights	Bronte	Novel	hardcover	424	$12.95
The Awakening	Chopin	Novel	mass market paperback	195	$4.95
Great Expectations	Dickens	Novel	mass market paperback	639	$6.95
Self-Reliance	Emerson	Essays	hardcover	249	$8.79
The Marble Faun	Hawthorne	Novel	trade paperback	473	$10.95
The Scarlet Letter	Hawthorne	Novel	trade paperback	253	$4.25
The Legend of Sleepy Hollow	Irving	Short stories	mass market paperback	98	$2.95
The Ambassadors	James	Novel	mass market paperback	305	$5.95
The Portrait of a Lady	James	Novel	mass market paperback	256	$4.95
The Turn of the Screw	James	Novel	trade paperback	384	$3.35
Masterman Ready	Marryat	Children's book	trade paperback	425	$12.89
Billy Budd	Melville	Short stories	mass market paperback	195	$4.49
Moby-Dick	Melville	Novel	hardcover	724	$9.95
Treasure Island	Stevenson	Novel	trade paperback	283	$11.85
Dracula	Stoker	Novel	hardcover	395	$17.95
Walden	Thoreau	Philosophy	mass market paperback	523	$6.95
Roughing It	Twain	Novel	mass market paperback	324	$5.25
The Adventures of Huckleberry Finn	Twain	Novel	mass market paperback	298	$5.49
Joan of Arc	Twain	Novel	trade paperback	465	$6.95
A Connecticut Yankee in King Arthur's Court	Twain	Novel	mass market paperback	385	$5.49
The Adventures of Tom Sawyer	Twain	Novel	mass market paperback	205	$4.75
Leaves of Grass	Whitman	Poetry	hardcover	462	$7.75
*					$0.00

Record: I◄ ◄ 1 ► ►I ►* of 22

Figure 42-9. Datasheets provide an easy way to work with the data stored in your database. This table belongs to the Book Inventory03 example database.

Entering and Editing Data in Datasheet View

New Record

The last row in Datasheet view is available for adding new records and is marked with an asterisk (*) in the row selector (the box at the left end of the row) to indicate where the new record goes (as shown in Figure 42-9). You can quickly move to the last row by clicking the New Record toolbar button.

To enter data into a new record or to modify an existing record in the table, click the field that you want to fill in or modify. If you prefer using the keyboard, you can press the Enter or Tab key to move from left to right through the columns in a record. To move back a column, press Shift+Tab. You can enter or modify text in a field using the standard editing methods that all Office applications provide.

As soon as you begin entering or changing information in a record, the row selector to the left of the row displays a pencil icon, indicating that the record contains unsaved changes, as shown in Figure 42-10. Access will automatically save your changes (and remove the pencil icon) when you move to a different record. You can save your changes before then by pressing Shift+Enter. (The Save command on the File menu, the Save toolbar button, and the Ctrl+S shortcut key save any changes you've made to the layout of Datasheet view, *not* changes you've made to the current record.) You can abandon any unsaved changes you've made to a record, restoring it to its original state, by pressing Esc. When you first enter data into a new record in the last row, Access immediately creates a new blank row below the one that you're editing.

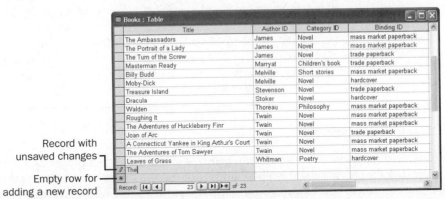

Record with unsaved changes

Empty row for adding a new record

Figure 42-10. Access uses a pencil icon to mark a record containing unsaved changes, and it uses an asterisk to mark the empty row at the end of the table where you enter the next new record.

To enter a value into a lookup field, select a value from the drop-down list, as shown here:

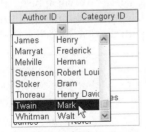

(If the Limit To List property has been set to Yes for the lookup field, if you type a value, it must match one of the items in the list. One of the purposes of a lookup field is to limit the values you can enter.)

If a field's Format property has been assigned a specific format, all you have to do is enter the value that goes into that field, in any convenient form, and move to another field. Access will then properly format the entry for you. For example, if a numeric field is formatted for currency, when you type **2.1** and move out of the field, Access will display the information in the field as $2.10.

A field that has an input mask, such as a date field, will display a template for you to fill in with the actual values, as shown in Figure 42-5.

Chapter 42

1135

Tip   Zoom a field

If you find entering data into a cell in Datasheet view a bit confining, or if the font is a little too small to see clearly, press Shift+F2 to open the Zoom dialog box, which lets you enter the field's data into a spacious, scrollable list box, and to select any font. (The font you select will be used only in the Zoom dialog box; it won't affect the text in the Datasheet view.) Zooming is especially useful for entering a large amount of text into a field with the Memo data type (which can hold up to 64,000 characters!). The Zoom dialog box will allow you to enter more data than is allowed for the field; however, when you click the OK button in the Zoom dialog box, Access will warn you that it's going to truncate the data. Also, the Zoom dialog box is not available for fields with the Date/Time data type.

Deleting Records

Delete
Record

To delete a record, select it by clicking its row selector, and then choose Edit, Delete Record; or click the Delete Record toolbar button; or press the Delete key. (If you use the menu command or toolbar button, you can just click anywhere in the record; you don't need to select the entire record.)

To delete an entire group of adjoining records, first select all the records by clicking the row selector of one record and dragging the highlight up or down over the other records, and then issue the Delete command.

The record or records will be removed from view and a dialog box will appear, telling you exactly what you're deleting. If you realize that you're deleting something by mistake, click the No button to stop the deletion process. To proceed with the deletion, click the Yes button.

Caution   Once you delete a record and click the Yes button to confirm your action, you won't be able to restore the record. You *can't* undo a record deletion using the Undo command. If you ever want to restore a deleted record, you'll have to reenter it from scratch. (Or copy the record from a backup copy of the database.)

Find

Tip   Find or replace text quickly

You can quickly find specified text in Datasheet view by choosing Edit, Find; or by clicking the Find toolbar button; or by pressing Ctrl+F. Then enter your search criteria into the Find tab of the Find And Replace dialog box (see Figure 42-11). To replace text, choose Edit, Replace or press Ctrl+H to open the Replace tab of the Find And Replace dialog box.

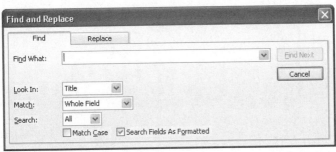

Figure 42-11. The Find And Replace dialog box lets you search for text in a single field or in an entire table.

Customizing Datasheet View

This section explains several ways to modify the design of the Datasheet view of the currently displayed table, query, or form. Some of the changes you can make affect only the layout of the Datasheet view and don't alter other views or the underlying structure of the table, query, or form. These changes include adjusting the column width or row height and rearranging the order of the columns. Other changes affect a table's underlying structure and alter the way the table appears in other views, such as Design view. These changes include renaming, adding, and deleting fields. (You can make these changes only to a table viewed in Datasheet view, not to a query or form.) Note that many of the techniques for modifying the design of the Datasheet view resemble techniques used in Excel worksheets.

You can change the width of a column in Datasheet view by dragging the right border of the column heading, as shown below:

Dragging a column border to a new position

Books : Table		
Title	Author ID	Category ID
Wuthering Heights	Bronte	Novel
The Awakening	Chopin	Novel
Great Expectations	Dickens	Novel
Self-Reliance	Emerson	Essays
The Marble Faun	Hawthorne	Novel
The Scarlet Letter	Hawthorne	Novel
The Legend of Sleepy Hollow	Irving	Short stories
The Ambassadors	James	Novel
The Portrait of a Lady	James	Novel

Original column border

You can change the height of *all* rows by dragging the bottom border of any row selector (one of the buttons to the left of the rows). You *can't* change the height of individual rows.

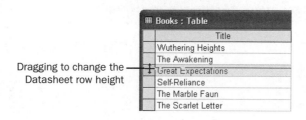

Dragging to change the Datasheet row height

Tip **Let Access adjust the width of a column**

You can have Access determine the most appropriate width for a column by double-clicking the right border of the column heading. Access will then adjust the column width to the smallest possible size that can display all the information contained within that column (including the caption in the column heading).

The columns in Datasheet view are initially arranged in the order in which the corresponding fields are listed in Design view. However, you can rearrange the columns in Datasheet view any way you want. To move a particular column, select the column by clicking the column heading. Be sure to release the mouse button. Then drag the column heading right or left to the new location. (If you don't release the button after you first click the column heading, dragging will simply select multiple columns.) Note that changing the order of columns in Datasheet view doesn't change the underlying order of the fields as displayed in Design view or other views.

In Datasheet view, each column heading displays the Caption property of the field shown in that column, unless the Caption property is blank. In that case the heading displays the name of the field (the Field Name property). No matter which property is displayed in the heading, you can change the *field name* by double-clicking the column heading, typing a new name, and pressing Enter. The Caption property will be set to blank (if it wasn't already blank), and the heading will display the field name. (You can't assign a new value to the Caption property in Datasheet view.)

You can also add or delete columns in the Datasheet view of a table, thereby adding fields to or removing fields from the table. To add a column, click anywhere in the column to the right of the position where you want the new column, and then choose Insert, Column. Access will create a new column and will assign it an initial name; it will name the first column you add Field1, the second column Field2, and so on. You can then change the field name as described previously.

To delete a column, click anywhere in the column and choose Edit, Delete Column. You'll have the opportunity to confirm your action.

Inside Out

Deleting a column deletes data!

Keep in mind that when you delete a column, you're permanently removing a field—together with all its data—from the table. You *can't* issue the Undo command to reverse this action. If you delete a column and then realize later that you should have left that information where it was, you'll have to recreate the field and reenter that field's information for every record in the database, perhaps thousands! In short, be careful about deleting a column, and always make a backup copy of your database before making any major changes.

Tip **Temporarily hide columns**

You can also temporarily hide one or more columns by selecting them and choosing Format, Hide Columns. To select a single column, click its heading. To include additional columns, keep the mouse button pressed and drag left or right (if you release the button after clicking, you'll move the initial column rather than extending the selection).

You can later make one or more hidden columns visible again by choosing Format, Unhide Columns and checking all the columns that you want to reappear.

Save

Access automatically saves any changes that affect a table's underlying structure (renaming, adding, or deleting a field, as well as edits to each record). If, however, you adjust the Datasheet view *layout* (the column width, row height, or column arrangement), you must save your changes by choosing File, Save; or clicking the Save toolbar button; or pressing Ctrl+S. If you haven't saved your layout changes, you'll be asked whether you want to do so when you close the table. If the changes aren't necessary, click No and the next time you open the table in Datasheet view, it will be displayed in its original layout.

Adding and Using Subdatasheets

If the table displayed in Datasheet view is the primary table in a one-to-many relationship, you can display the matching records in the related table by using a *subdatasheet*. For instance, if a subdatasheet were added to the Datasheet view of the Authors table in the Book Inventory03 example database, you could display a list of all books written by a particular author by clicking the plus (+) symbol in the first column to open the subdatasheet for that record, as shown in Figure 42-12.

Chapter 42

Subdatasheet displaying records in the Books
table that match author "Mark Twain"

Author ID	First Name	Last Name	Birth Year	Nationality
1	Mark	Twain	1835	American

Title	Category ID	Binding ID	Pages	Price
Roughing It	Novel	mass market paperback	324	$5.25
Joan of Arc	Novel	trade paperback	465	$6.95
A Connecticut Yankee in King Arthur's Court	Novel	mass market paperback	385	$5.49
The Adventures of Tom Sawyer	Novel	mass market paperback	205	$4.75
The Adventures of Huckleberry Finn	Novel	mass market paperback	298	$5.49
				$0.00

2	Kate O'Flaherty	Chopin	1851	American
3	Herman	Melville	1819	American
4	Walt	Whitman	1819	American
5	Washington	Irving	1783	American
6	Henry	James	1843	American
7	Nathaniel	Hawthorne	1804	American
8	Bram	Stoker	1847	English

Record: ◀◀ ◀ 1 ▶ ▶◀ ▶* of 5

Figure 42-12. You can display or hide the subdatasheet for a particular record by clicking
the + or – in the first column. This table belongs to the Book Inventory03 example database.

If a table displayed in Datasheet view is the primary table in a *single* relationship, Access automatically adds a subdatasheet that displays the related table. If, however, the table is the primary table in more than one relationship, you must explicitly add the subdatasheet and
specify the particular relationship you want to use by performing the following steps. (Before
beginning this procedure, you might open the Relationships window so that you can see
which fields and tables are related.)

1 Choose Insert, Subdatasheet. Access will open the Insert Subdatasheet dialog box
(shown in Figure 42-13).

Figure 42-13. You can add or modify a subdatasheet using the Insert Subdatasheet dialog box.

2 In the list within the appropriate tab of the Insert Subdatasheet dialog box, select the
related table (or query) you want to display in the subdatasheet.

3 In the Link Child Fields drop-down list, select the name of the related field in the related table (the table you want to display in the subdatasheet), if it isn't already selected.

4 In the Link Master Fields drop-down list, select the name of the related field in the primary table (the table currently displayed in Datasheet view), if it isn't already selected.

5 Click the OK button.

You can use this same procedure to modify an existing subdatasheet.

Sorting and Filtering in Datasheet View

The fastest way to sort the records in Datasheet view is to right-click the heading of the column you want to use as the sort key, and then choose Sort Ascending or Sort Descending from the shortcut menu, as shown here:

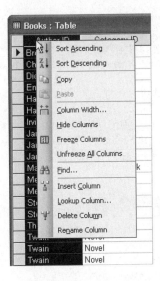

An ascending sort arranges number fields from smallest to largest (for example, –3, 0, 1, 2, 10), date fields from earliest to most recent (for example, 5/21/1948, 6/15/1994, 3/15/2001), and text fields in alphabetical order. A descending sort arranges fields in the opposite order.

You can also *filter* the records in a table to display only those records that match your criteria, rather than displaying all the records in the table. You can apply a filter by selection or by using a form.

Applying a Filter By Selection

The fastest way to filter records is by finding a field in a record that contains the information you want to use as a filter criterion and then having Access list only those records that contain the same entry in that field. For example, in the Books table (in the Book Inventory03 example database), you might want to list all the hardcover books in stock. To do so, you first locate a record containing the entry that you want to use to select your records—in this case, a record that has the entry *hardcover* in the Binding ID field, as shown in Figure 42-14.

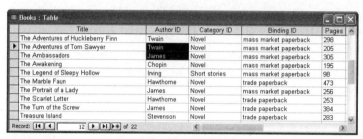

Figure 42-14. To start a Filter By Selection, you must first select the information you want to use as the filter criterion. This table belongs to the Book Inventory03 example database.

Filter By
Selection

Either click anywhere within the field or select the whole entry to tell Access to match the field's entire contents. Then choose Records, Filter, Filter By Selection. Or click the Filter By Selection toolbar button. Access will then show only the records that meet the filter criterion—that is, records that have the same value in the selected field. The Datasheet view of the Books table shown in Figure 42-14 would then appear as shown in Figure 42-15, where only hardcover books are displayed.

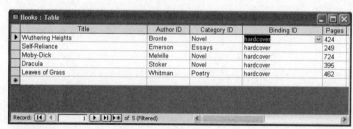

Figure 42-15. This figure shows the same table as Figure 42-14 after applying a filter to show only hardcover books.

> **Note**   To show all records *except* those that have the value of the field you selected, choose Records, Filter, Filter Excluding Selection.

**Remove/
Apply Filter**

To return to viewing all your records, choose Records, Remove Filter/Sort or click the Remove/Apply Filter toolbar button. You can later reapply your most recently defined filter by simply choosing Records, Apply Filter/Sort or by clicking the Remove/Apply Filter toolbar button. (When a filter is applied, this button is selected, its ScreenTip label is Remove Filter, and clicking it removes the filter. After the filter has been removed, the button is deselected, its label is Apply Filter, and clicking it reapplies the previous filter.)

> **Note**   When a filter is currently applied, Access displays "(Filtered)" at the bottom of the Datasheet window, and it displays "FLTR" on the Access status bar. These indicators warn you that not all the table's records are displayed.

If you select a portion of a field entry before issuing the Filter By Selection command, Access will use only the selected text in determining which records to display. For example, in the Books table shown in Figure 42-14, if you select the word *paperback* in one of the entries in the Binding ID field and you then apply Filter By Selection, both *mass market paperback* and *trade paperback* books will be included in the list.

Note, however, that if your selection includes the first letter in an entry, Access will match only fields that *start* with the selected text. For example, if you select the *M* in the Author ID field of the *Moby-Dick* record, Access will display only books with author names that start with *M*.

You can also filter records using the entries from several fields in a record. In this case Access will display only records that match *all* the selected entries. To do this, first be sure that the fields that have the values you want to use are next to each other. (You can move columns in the Datasheet window if necessary.) Then select all the entries to be used for the match and issue the Filter By Selection command. To select several adjoining field entries in a record, click the left end of one entry to select it (click when the pointer becomes a large plus sign) and, without releasing the mouse button, drag the highlight left or right over the other entry or entries. For example, if you made the following selection:

Title	Author ID	Category ID	Binding ID	Pages
The Adventures of Huckleberry Finn	Twain	Novel	mass market paperback	298
The Adventures of Tom Sawyer	Twain	Novel	mass market paperback	205
A Connecticut Yankee in King Arthur's Court	Twain	Novel	mass market paperback	385
Joan of Arc	Twain	Novel	trade paperback	465
Roughing It	Twain	Novel	mass market paperback	324
The Awakening	Chopin	Novel	mass market paperback	195
Billy Budd	Melville	Short stories	mass market paperback	195
Moby-Dick	Melville	Novel	hardcover	724
Leaves of Grass	Whitman	Poetry	hardcover	462
The Legend of Sleepy Hollow	Irving	Short stories	mass market paperback	98

Record: 1 of 22

Access would display only the books that are mass market paperback novels.

Finally, you can select entries across adjoining records, rather than fields, and then use the Filter By Selection command. In this case Access will list records that match *any* of the selected field values. For instance, if you made the following selection:

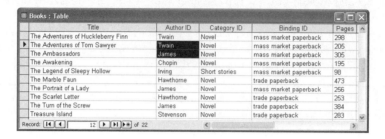

Access would display all Mark Twain's books, all Henry James's books, and no others. If the values you want to select don't happen to be in adjoining fields, you'll have to use one of the filtering methods described next.

Applying a Filter by Form

Filter By
Form

When you want to use more than one value to filter records, a more versatile approach is to use Filter By Form. The following are the steps of this procedure:

1 Choose Records, Filter, Filter By Form. Or click the Filter By Form toolbar button. The records will be hidden and the Datasheet window will be converted to the Filter By Form window, which is shown in Figure 42-16.

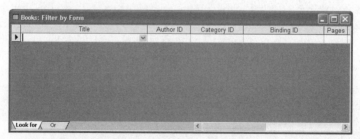

Figure 42-16. The Filter By Form window replaces the Datasheet window when you issue the Filter By Form command. (The Books table belongs to the Book Inventory03 example database.)

The Filter By Form window displays a single blank row in the same format as one of your records. (Note, however, that if you previously applied a filter to the table, in the Filter By Form window the fields used in the previous filter will initially contain the values you had assigned them.) The information in the Filter By Form window is divided into separate tabs: the Look For tab (the one that's displayed initially), plus one or more Or tabs. You display a particular tab by clicking the tab's label at the bottom of the window.

2 Begin defining your filter by choosing entries in the fields shown in the Look For tab. When you click in a field, a down arrow appears at the right end. Click this arrow to display a drop-down list of the different values that are currently contained in that field within all the records of the table. Select the one you want to use for your filter.

You can select a value in more than one field to *reduce* the number of records shown. When you apply the filter, Access will display the records that match *all* the selected entries. For instance, in the Books example table, if you wanted to display all trade paperback novels, you would select *Novel* in the Category ID field and *trade paperback* in the Binding ID field, as shown here:

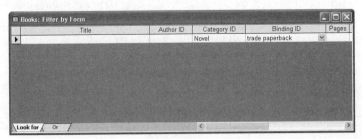

3 After you've selected all the values you want from the Look For tab, you can define alternative filter criteria to *expand* the number of records shown. You do this by displaying the first Or tab, which will show another row of fields. Select one or more values in these fields the same way you did in the Look For tab. When you apply the filter, Access will display all records that match *either* the values in the Look For tab *or* the values in the Or tab. For instance, in the Books example table, you could list all hardcover novels as well as all trade paperback novels by first selecting the values shown above on the Look For tab, and then on the first Or tab, selecting *Novel* in the Category ID field and *hardcover* in the Binding ID field:

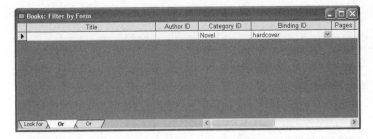

You can expand the number of listed records even further by selecting values from additional Or tabs. Each time you select one or more values from an Or tab, another Or tab becomes available for you to display.

Rather than selecting a value in a field, you can specify a filter criterion by typing an expression containing a comparison operator. Table 42-2 shows the six standard comparison operators.

Chapter 42

To use a comparison operator, enter the operator, followed by the comparison value, into the field that contains the value to be evaluated. For example, to find all books that cost more than $20, you would enter the greater-than operator and the value **20** (that is, **>20**) into the Price field. If you don't use an operator and you just select a value in a field, Access assumes that you're searching for exact matches.

Clear Grid

If you select a value in a field or type in a comparison expression and then decide that you don't really want to use it, you can delete the entry, remove the entire tab, or clear the entire filter. To delete a single entry, select it and press the Delete key. To remove a tab that you've created, display it and then choose Edit, Delete Tab. You can clear all the entries in the filter by choosing Edit, Clear Grid or by clicking the Clear Grid toolbar button.

**Remove/
Apply Filter**

4 Once you have specified all the values for your filter, you can activate the filter by choosing Filter, Apply Filter/Sort or by clicking the Remove/Apply Filter toolbar button. Access will then return you to the standard Datasheet window, showing only those records that match your filter.

Table 42-2. The Standard Comparison Operators

Operator	Definition
>	Greater than
<	Less than
=	Equal to
<=	Less than or equal to
>=	Greater than or equal to
<>	Not equal to

For instance, here's how the example Book table would appear after you choose the filter values from the Look For and Or tabs described and shown in the preceding instructions:

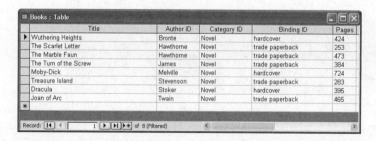

To remove the filter and display all records, choose Records, Remove Filter/Sort or click the Remove/Apply Filter toolbar button. You can later reapply your most recently defined filter by simply choosing Records, Apply Filter/Sort or by clicking the Remove/Apply Filter button. (When a filter is applied, this button is selected, its ScreenTip label is Remove Filter, and clicking it removes the filter. After the filter has been removed, the button is deselected, its label is Apply Filter, and clicking it reapplies the previous filter.)

**Remove/
Apply Filter**

Other Ways to Sort and Filter

If you want to filter *and* sort the records in a table rather than perform the two-step process of first applying a filter and then sorting the records, you can use the Records, Filter, Advanced Filter/Sort menu command. This command opens a window that's quite similar to the Design view window showing a query, except that it allows you to work with fields within the current table only. In the Advanced Filter/Sort window, you can define criteria for sorting and filtering the records in the table, using one or more fields.

Better yet, you can create a query, which allows you to use fields from several tables for sorting and filtering and to control exactly which fields are displayed. The next chapter explains the techniques for creating, modifying, and using queries.

Using Queries to Select and Combine Information

Creating a Query 1149

Modifying a Query 1154

Creating a Crosstab Query 1166

Creating and Running Queries
to Modify Data 1168

Creating a Query

Queries and other database objects are described in "Designing and Planning an Access Database," on page 1100. To create a new query, display the New Query dialog box (shown in Figure 43-1) by selecting the Queries object type and clicking the New button in the Database window, as explained in "Using the Database Window and Object Views," on page 1107, and then select an option in the list, as follows:

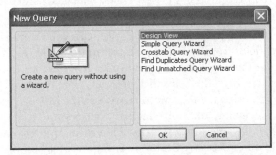

Figure 43-1. In the New Query dialog box you can select one of five ways to create a new query.

- To create your query from scratch in Design view, choose the Design View option. For information on designing the query in Design view, see "Modifying a Query," on page 1154.

- To have Microsoft Office Access 2003 assist you in designing the query, choose the Simple Query Wizard option. Using this wizard is the easiest way to create a new, general-purpose query, and it's discussed in "Creating a Basic Query with the Simple Query Wizard," on page 1150.

- To create a special-purpose query, known as a *crosstab query*, for comparing different subsets of the information in the database, choose the Crosstab Query Wizard option. See "Creating a Crosstab Query," on page 1166.

● To create a special-purpose query that can help you maintain your data, choose the Find Duplicates Query Wizard option or the Find Unmatched Query Wizard option. These two options are discussed in "Creating a Maintenance Query," on page 1154.

Once you have selected the option you want, click the OK button.

> **Note** Keep in mind that a query database object stores only the query definition—field names, data selection criteria, sorting orders, grouping information, and so on. It *doesn't* store the actual data that it displays; that data is stored only in the database tables. Consequently, every time you run a particular query, it shows the *current* state of the data stored in the database tables.

Creating a Basic Query with the Simple Query Wizard

The following procedure creates a general-purpose query using the Simple Query Wizard. (The figures show the steps for creating a query that lists all the books written by each author in the Book Inventory03 example database. The query lists the author's first and last names and each book's title, price, and category, drawing information from the Authors, Books, and Categories tables. If you want to see the final result as you read these steps, look ahead to Figure 43-5.)

1 Select the Simple Query Wizard option in the New Query dialog box and click the OK button. The Simple Query Wizard will start running.

2 In the first Simple Query Wizard dialog box, select all the fields you want to include in your query. You can select fields from one or more tables or other queries. To begin, select a table or query in the Tables/Queries drop-down list that has one or more fields you'd like to include. Then move all the fields that you want from the Available Fields list to the Selected Fields list, using the four buttons between the lists. Repeat this operation to include fields from any additional tables or queries you need to use. (In Figure 43-2, we chose the First Name and Last Name fields from Authors; the Title and Price fields from Books; and the Category field from Categories.) When you finish selecting fields, click the Next button to open the second wizard dialog box. (For more on creating queries, see the Inside Out sidebar, "Define relationships *before* creating a query," later in this section.)

> **Tip** Include all necessary fields
>
> Be sure to include all the fields that you need—for displaying information in the query, for selecting the data that is displayed, or for sorting the results of the query.

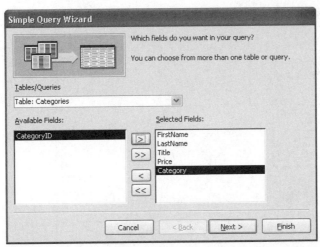

Figure 43-2. In the first Simple Query Wizard dialog box, you select all the fields that you need. The fields selected here were used to create the example query described in the text.

3 If you selected one or more numeric fields in addition to the primary key (such as the book price in the example query), Access will display the second Simple Query Wizard dialog box shown in Figure 43-3. (If you didn't select a numeric field in the first dialog box, the wizard will immediately display the final dialog box, discussed in the next step.) In this dialog box, select the type of query, as follows:

- To show the information on the query from *every* matching record, select Detail.

- To display summary information from each group of matching records, rather than showing the information from all matching records, select Summary. Then click the Summary Options button, and in the Summary Options dialog box, select the type of summary value you want to be calculated—sum, average, minimum, or maximum. For example, if you selected the Summary option and the average summary value for the example query, the query would display a single line for each book category for each author. That line would show the author's first and last names, the category name, the name of the first book belonging to that category, and the average price of all of the author's books in that category. For more information, see "Summarizing Your Information," on page 1160.

When you're finished, click the Next button.

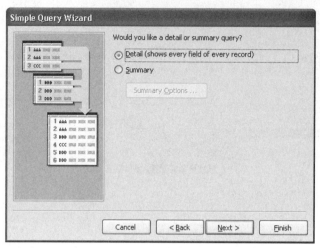

Figure 43-3. If you've selected a numeric field, the second Simple Query Wizard dialog box lets you choose the type of query you want. Here, the Detail option was selected for the example query.

4 In the final Simple Query Wizard dialog box, enter a new title for your query in the text box (as shown in Figure 43-4) or accept the default title. If you're ready to view your query immediately, select the Open The Query To View Information option to open the query in Datasheet view. If you want to examine and possibly modify the query design before you view the results, select the Modify The Query Design option to open the query in Design view, which is discussed in "Modifying a Query," on page 1154. Click the Finish button to proceed.

Inside Out

Define relationships *before* creating a query

If you've selected fields belonging to two database objects (tables or queries) that don't have a formal relationship defined in the Relationships window, when you click the Next button, Access will display a message box and will require you to explicitly define the relationship in the Relationships window and then restart the wizard and reselect the fields you want. For some reason, Access doesn't simply create the necessary relationships for the current query, as it does when you add tables or queries without defined relationships to the query Design window (explained in "Modifying a Query," on page 1154). To avoid this problem, be sure to explicitly define relationships between all tables or queries that you want to use in your query, following the instructions given in "Setting Up Table Relationships," on page 1128.

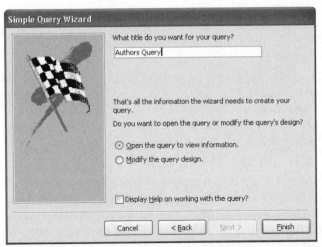

Figure 43-4. In the final Simple Query Wizard dialog box, you give the query a name and specify how it's to be opened. This figure shows the name given to the example query.

Figure 43-5 shows the example query displayed in Datasheet view. Notice that the rows aren't sorted in this query. (Because it lists the books written by each author, you would probably want the query to be sorted by the authors' last names.) For information on applying a sorting order or on making other customizations to a query, see "Modifying a Query," on page 1154.

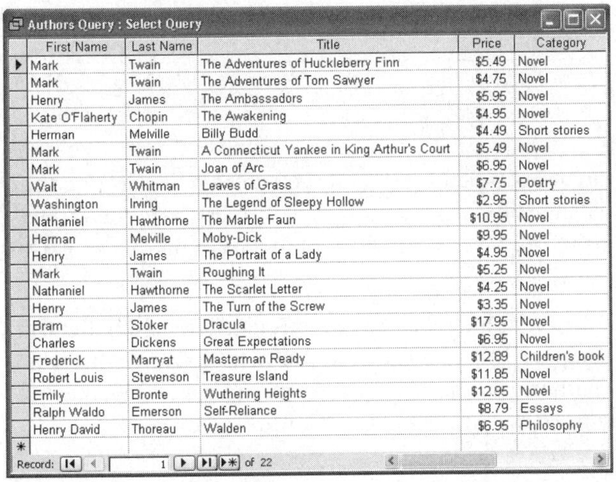

First Name	Last Name	Title	Price	Category
Mark	Twain	The Adventures of Huckleberry Finn	$5.49	Novel
Mark	Twain	The Adventures of Tom Sawyer	$4.75	Novel
Henry	James	The Ambassadors	$5.95	Novel
Kate O'Flaherty	Chopin	The Awakening	$4.95	Novel
Herman	Melville	Billy Budd	$4.49	Short stories
Mark	Twain	A Connecticut Yankee in King Arthur's Court	$5.49	Novel
Mark	Twain	Joan of Arc	$6.95	Novel
Walt	Whitman	Leaves of Grass	$7.75	Poetry
Washington	Irving	The Legend of Sleepy Hollow	$2.95	Short stories
Nathaniel	Hawthorne	The Marble Faun	$10.95	Novel
Herman	Melville	Moby-Dick	$9.95	Novel
Henry	James	The Portrait of a Lady	$4.95	Novel
Mark	Twain	Roughing It	$5.25	Novel
Nathaniel	Hawthorne	The Scarlet Letter	$4.25	Novel
Henry	James	The Turn of the Screw	$3.35	Novel
Bram	Stoker	Dracula	$17.95	Novel
Charles	Dickens	Great Expectations	$6.95	Novel
Frederick	Marryat	Masterman Ready	$12.89	Children's book
Robert Louis	Stevenson	Treasure Island	$11.85	Novel
Emily	Bronte	Wuthering Heights	$12.95	Novel
Ralph Waldo	Emerson	Self-Reliance	$8.79	Essays
Henry David	Thoreau	Walden	$6.95	Philosophy

Record: 1 of 22

Figure 43-5. This query is the result of the Simple Query Wizard choices shown in Figures 43-2 through 43-4.

Creating a Maintenance Query

In the New Query dialog box, Access provides two wizards that create queries to help you maintain the integrity of the data in your tables.

The Find Duplicates Query Wizard creates a query that scans through a selected table or query and lists all records containing duplicate values for a given field. If you want to create a relationship between two tables, you can use this wizard to determine whether the related field in the primary table has duplicate values. (Recall from Chapter 42, "Setting Up Tables and Relationships," that the related field in the primary table in a relationship must have unique values.)

The Find Unmatched Query Wizard creates a query that compares two tables and locates any records in the first table that lack a related record in the second. This wizard can be useful for simply locating special cases within your data. (For instance, in the Book Inventory03 example database, you could find all authors for whom you have no books in your inventory. That is, you could obtain a list of all records in the Authors table that have no matching records in the Books table.) Also, if you're redesigning your database and want to define a one-to-many relationship between two existing tables, you can use this wizard to make sure that every record in the related table has a matching record in the primary table, which is required for maintaining referential integrity. (For instance, if you were just setting up the relationship between the Books and Authors tables in the Book Inventory03 example database, you could use this wizard to obtain a list of any records in the Books table that lack a matching record in the Authors table.)

> For information on relationships between tables and referential integrity, see "Setting Up Table Relationships," on page 1128.

Modifying a Query

You can use Design view to define a new query (one you created by selecting the Design View option in the New Query dialog box), to customize a new query (one you created by selecting one of the Wizard options in the New Query dialog box), or to modify an existing query of any type.

To open a query in Design view, follow the instructions given in "Using the Database Window and Object Views," on page 1107. Figure 43-6 shows the example query described in "Creating a Basic Query with the Simple Query Wizard," on page 1150, opened in Design view. You can see the results of this query in Figure 43-5.

Using Queries to Select and Combine Information

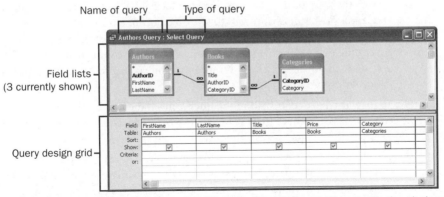

Figure 43-6. This query was created using the Simple Query Wizard with the choices shown in Figures 43-2 through 43-4 and was opened in Design view.

The top portion of the query Design view window displays field lists for one or more tables or other queries in the database and shows the relationships between these objects in the same way these relationships are shown in the Relationships window. (We rearranged the lists shown in Figure 43-6 to make the relationships easier to see.) You can use any of these fields in the query. The query is defined in the grid in the lower portion of the window. Each column in the query design grid defines a field that's displayed in the query, or is used to sort rows or select records, or is both displayed and used to sort or select.

In the query Design view window, you can perform one or more of the following actions to define or modify the query:

- If the table or query that contains a field you want to display or use in the query doesn't appear in the top portion of the Design window, choose Query, Show Table and select one or more tables or queries in the Show Table dialog box. Note that if you create a new query by selecting the Design View option in the New Query dialog box, Access automatically displays the Show Table dialog box before it opens the query Design window so you can add the field lists you'll need. See the sidebar "Modify Table Relationships for a Query," on page 1158. To remove a field list, click it, and then either choose Query, Remove Table or press the Delete key.

- To add a field to a column, select it in the drop-down list in the Field row. Or, drag the field from the field list that displays it and drop it on the query design grid; this will insert a new column for that field to the left of the column where you dropped the field. To display on your query *all* fields belonging to a particular table or other query, select or drag the asterisk (*) item. For example, to display all fields contained in the Books table, select "Books.*" in the drop-down list, or drag the "*" from the top of the Books field list. When you add a field to the Field row in a column, Access automatically adds the field's table to the Table row in that column. (You can show or hide the Table row in the query design grid by selecting or deselecting the View, Table Names menu option.)

Note The primary key field (or fields) for a table is formatted in **bold** in the field list.

- To sort the rows of the query by a particular field, select a sort type—Ascending or Descending—in the Sort row of the field's column. For instance, to sort the rows in the example query shown in Figure 43-6, by the authors' last names, you would select Ascending or Descending in the Sort row of the LastName column (see Figures 43-7 and 43-8). If you select a sort in more than one column, Access will apply the sorts in the order of the columns.

- To display a particular field in the query, check the box in the Show row of the field's column. If you want to use a field to sort rows or select records, but don't want the field to appear in the query, clear the box.

- To select the records that appear in the query, you can enter a value in the Criteria row of a particular field. For instance, to display only novels in the example query of Figure 43-6, you would type **Novel** in the Criteria row of the Category column. (For a Text type field, Access will add quotation marks around the text when you move to another cell or save the query.) Also, with a numeric or date field, you can enter a comparison using the standard operators (>, <, >=, <=, and <>, as explained in Table 47-2). For instance, in the example query, to display only books that cost more than $10, you would type >10 in the Criteria row of the Price column.

> **Note**   You can use the Boolean *And* operator to create a more complex expression. For example, to show books that cost more than $10 but less than $15, you could type **>10 And <15**. The expression *Between 10 And 15* is equivalent to *>=10 And <=15*.

- To combine several selection criteria using *And* logic, enter them all in the Criteria row. For example, to show books that cost more than $10 *and* are novels, you would enter both of the criteria described in the previous item in the Criteria row. These criteria are shown in Figure 43-7, and the resulting query (listing the expensive novels) is shown in Figure 43-8.

> **Tip**   Get help creating an expression
>
> To create a complex expression, you can use the Expression Builder dialog box, which provides buttons for inserting operators (arithmetic, comparison, Boolean, and grouping). It also contains lists that let you quickly insert any field in the database, as well as any available function, constant, operator, or common expression. To use the Expression Builder, right-click in the box where you want to enter the expression and choose Build from the shortcut menu. You can click the Help button in the Expression Builder dialog box to get information on its features.

- To add a selection criterion using *Or* logic, enter the criterion in the Or row. For instance, to display books that either cost more than $10 dollars *or* are novels, you could enter >10 in the Criteria row of the Price column and enter **Novel** in the Or row of the Category column. The query would list all of the novels, plus all of the books over $10. To add further *Or* criteria you can use additional rows at the bottom of the query design grid.

- To delete all your entries in a particular row or column, click in that row or column and choose Edit, Delete Rows or Edit, Delete Columns. To delete all entries in the query design grid (make sure that you want to!), choose Edit, Clear Grid.

Run

- To display the results of your query (that is, to *run* the query using the database's current contents), choose View, Datasheet View; choose Query, Run; or click the Run toolbar button.

Tip **Run or modify a query quickly**

You can rapidly toggle a query between Design view, in which you can modify the query design, and Datasheet view, in which you can view the query results, by simply clicking the View toolbar button.

View Datasheet   View Design

For information on working with a query (as well as a table or form) in Datasheet view, see "Working in Datasheet View," on page 1134.

Save

- To save your query design, so that after you close the query you can later run or modify it from the Database window, choose File, Save; or click the Save toolbar button; or press Ctrl+S.

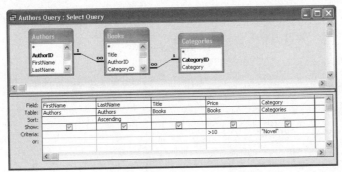

Figure 43-7. This query definition adds sorting and selection criteria to the example query in Figure 43-6. The results are shown in Figure 43-8.

Figure 43-8. These are the results of the query definition in Figure 43-7.

Modify Table Relationships for a Query

When you create a new query, it acquires the default relationships and the properties of those relationships that are defined in the Relationships window, as explained in "Setting Up Table Relationships," on page 1128. These relationships are initially displayed in the top portion of the query Design window. (If two tables shown in the query Design window can be related, but *don't* have a relationship defined in the Relationships window, Access will add the relationship to the Design window. This relationship will be available only for the current query—it won't be added to the Relationships window.)

You can add, remove, or modify relationships within the query Design window using methods similar to those described in "Setting Up Table Relationships" on page 1128. The changes you make here affect only the current query—they won't change the default relationships set up in the Relationships window and used elsewhere in the database.

When you double-click a relationship line in the query Design window, Access displays the Join Properties dialog box (shown in Figure 43-9), which lets you change the *join type* of the relationship. A query always displays a row when it encounters a record in one table with a matching record in the other table (for instance, when the query finds a record in the Authors table with a matching record in the Books table). The join type controls whether or not the query will display a row when one of the tables has a record that *doesn't* have a matching record in the other table (for example, if the query finds an Authors record without a matching Books record).

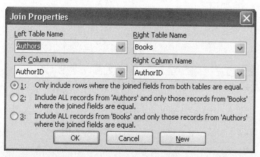

Figure 43-9. The Join Properties dialog box lets you change the join type of a relationship, affecting the current query only.

Using Top-Value Queries

Access provides a useful enhancement to its sorting feature that allows you to look at the highest or lowest values for a field in a query. For instance, in the Authors Query example described in the previous section, you might be interested in looking at only the three least expensive titles. To look at the highest or lowest values, follow these steps:

1 Open the query in Design view.

2 Designate the field to be used for sorting the rows in the query. To look at the lowest values in the list, sort by selecting Ascending in the Sort row of the field's column. To look at the highest values in the list, sort by selecting Descending in the Sort row. (In the example, you would select an Ascending sort for the Price field, and remove any sort specifications from other fields, as well as any selection criteria left in the query design.)

3 In the Top Values drop-down list on the toolbar, select the number of top or bottom values that you want to see. If the number you want isn't listed, type your own number in the box at the top of the list and press Enter. (In the example, you would need to type 3, as shown in Figure 43-10.)

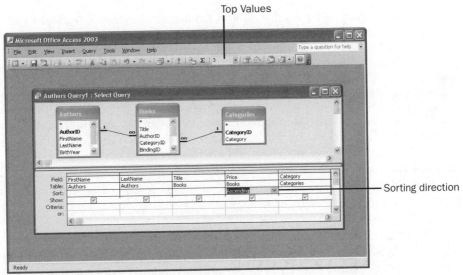

Figure 43-10. You can list just the top or bottom values in a sorted query by selecting a number or percentage in the Top Values drop-down list on the toolbar.

Tip View the top or bottom percentage

The Top Values drop-down list also lets you select or type a percentage rather than an absolute number of values to be displayed. For example, in a query listing students and their test scores, you could select a Descending sort on the score field and enter 15% in the Top Values list box to retrieve a list of the students in the top 15 percent of the class (perhaps the ones who get As).

---

4 To view the query results, use any method to switch to Datasheet view. (Figure 43-11 shows the results of the example query, which lists the three least expensive books.)

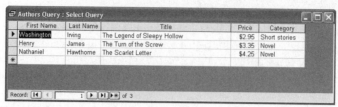

Figure 43-11. This figure shows the results of the query definition shown in Figure 43-10.

Summarizing Your Information

You can create a query that displays summary information for each group of matching records, rather than showing the information from all matching records. As explained in step 3 in "Creating a Basic Query with the Simple Query Wizard," on page 1150, if your query contains a numeric field, you can use the Simple Query Wizard to generate a query that displays summary information.

Totals

You can also use Design view to convert any *select query* (see the following note) to one that displays summary information. To do this, open the query in Design view and choose View, Totals or click the Totals toolbar button to display the Total row in the query design grid. (To remove the Total row, choose the command or click the button again.)

> **Note** Most queries, and all of the queries described so far in this chapter, are *select queries*. A select query displays rows of information extracted from one or more tables or other queries. Other types of queries are described later in this chapter.

To summarize the values in a particular field, open the drop-down list in the Total row in the field's column (see Figure 43-12) and select one of the functions listed in Table 43-1. For a field that has the Number or Currency data type, you can select any of these functions. For a field that has a nonnumeric data type, such as text, you can use only the Count function (which displays the total number of matching records that have any value in that field) or First or Last (which displays the first or the last field value encountered).

> **Note** The functions Sum, Avg, Min, Max, Count, StDev, and Var are known as the *aggregate* functions.

Chapter 43

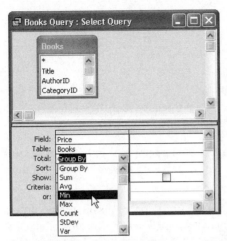

Figure 43-12. Adding the Total row lets you create a query that displays summary information. This query is included in the Book Inventory03 example database.

Table 43-1. Functions You Can Select in the Total Row

Function	Description
Sum	Adds up all the values within the group
Avg	Finds the average for all the values within the group
Min	Finds the lowest value within the group
Max	Finds the highest value within the group
Count	Determines the number of matching records within the group
StDev	Determines the standard deviation for the population defined by the group
Var	Determines the variance for the population defined by the group
First	Displays the first matching value in the group
Last	Displays the last matching value in the group
Expression	To use a custom expression that employs one or more of the aggregate functions to summarize the values in the group (rather than using one of the built-in functions described in this table), enter the expression in the Field row and select Expression in the Total row in the same column. (Expressions are discussed in the next section.)

If you have only a single field in your design grid, and you select a summary function in the Total box (as shown in Figure 43-12), the resulting datasheet will display a single number that summarizes all matching values and will look similar to the datasheet shown in Figure 43-13.

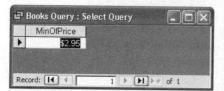

Figure 43-13. This figure shows the results of the query definition shown in Figure 43-12, with the Min function selected in the Total row of the Price column.

Notice that the query that appears in Datasheet view contains only an answer to your query and a column heading identifying the function and field that were used—in the example, MinOfPrice (the minimum value in the Price field).

More commonly, you use the Total row to perform calculations on *groups* of values within the matching records (as the function descriptions in Table 43-1 imply). To do this, you need to add a field to the grid that will be used to group the records, and then select the Group By option in that field's Total row. (This option is the default.) For instance, in the example query shown in Figure 43-12, you might want to determine the average price of each category of books (novels, essays, short stories, and so on). To do this, you would need to have two fields in your design grid: the CategoryID field, which is used for grouping the records, and the Price field, which is used for the calculation, as shown in Figure 43-14.

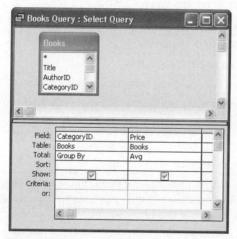

Figure 43-14. Adding a field and selecting Group By in the Total row provides a summary of each group of records.

When you run this type of query, Access lists each group together with the calculation result for the values within that group, as shown in Figure 43-15.

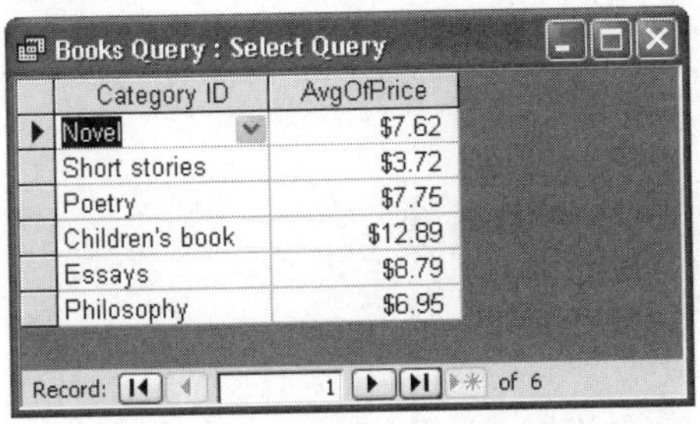

Books Query : Select Query

Category ID	AvgOfPrice
Novel	$7.62
Short stories	$3.72
Poetry	$7.75
Children's book	$12.89
Essays	$8.79
Philosophy	$6.95

Record: 1 of 6

Figure 43-15. This figure shows the results of the query definition in Figure 43-14.

Keep in mind that you can control the order of the rows displayed in the query by using the Sort row, as explained in "Modifying a Query," on page 1154.

You can also use a field to select the specific records that are used in the summary calculation. You do this by choosing the Where option in the Total row in the field's column and then adding one or more selection criteria to that field's Criteria or Or rows. If you do this, the field will be used only to select records; it won't be used to group records and it won't be displayed in the query (Access won't allow you to check the Show box for the field).

Adding Calculated Fields

Sometimes you might want to display the result of a calculation that has been performed on information within the record or records that appear, within each row of a query, rather than summarizing values across records as described in the previous section. To do this, the best approach is to create a calculated field. You can create such a field within a query, on a form, or within a report. For example, perhaps you'd like to see the purchase price of books if their prices were all increased by 15 percent. To include this information in a query, you would add a field to the query design grid that would perform this calculation. This new field is called a *calculated field* because it performs a computation rather than simply displaying the value of a field in a table.

To create a calculated field, click in the Field row in a blank column in the query design grid and enter the expression for calculating the value. Rather than typing the name of a field to be used in your calculation, you can click the down arrow to the right of the box and select the field name from the drop-down list; you can then type the remainder of the expression. Formulas for calculating fields are similar to formulas entered in cells in Microsoft Excel 2003 worksheets—the main difference is that rather than referring to cell addresses, you refer to field names. The formula will be calculated and its result displayed in every row of the query (or in every row of a report or on every record shown in a form).

Figure 43-16 shows an expression that calculates a 15 percent increase in the purchase price of each book, as the expression would appear immediately after you type it, before you press Enter or run the query.

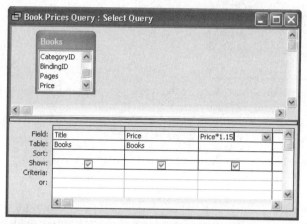

Figure 43-16. A calculated field contains an expression that computes a value based on other fields. This query is included in the Book Inventory03 example database.

When you run this query, you see the results shown in Figure 43-17. Notice that the field name consists of the letters *Expr* followed by a digit, indicating the sequence in which the calculated field was created, and that the results of the calculation aren't formatted appropriately for monetary amounts. (When you display a field from a table, it acquires the field's formatting. But when you create a calculated field, it's initially unformatted.)

Title	Price	Expr1
The Adventures of Huckleberry Finn	$5.49	6.3135
The Adventures of Tom Sawyer	$4.75	5.4625
A Connecticut Yankee in King Arthur's Court	$5.49	6.3135
Joan of Arc	$6.95	7.9925
Roughing It	$5.25	6.0375
The Awakening	$4.95	5.6925
Billy Budd	$4.49	5.1635
Moby-Dick	$9.95	11.4425
Leaves of Grass	$7.75	8.9125
The Legend of Sleepy Hollow	$2.95	3.3925
The Ambassadors	$5.95	6.8425
The Portrait of a Lady	$4.95	5.6925
The Turn of the Screw	$3.35	3.8525
The Marble Faun	$10.95	12.5925
The Scarlet Letter	$4.25	4.8875
Dracula	$17.95	20.6425
Great Expectations	$6.95	7.9925
Masterman Ready	$12.89	14.8235
Treasure Island	$11.85	13.6275
Wuthering Heights	$12.95	14.8925
Self-Reliance	$8.79	10.1085
Walden	$6.95	7.9925

Record: 1 of 22

Figure 43-17. This figure shows the results of the query design in Figure 43-16.

Fortunately, you're not stuck with the default name and format that Access initially assigns. It's quite easy to change both the name of the calculated field and its formatting. If you return to Design view, you'll notice that the expression you originally typed in the Field box for the calculated field (in the example, Price*1.15) has been reformatted to include a field name. In the example query the expression would now appear as follows:

```
Expr1: Price*1.15
```

To change the field name, just select the text that precedes the colon and type the new name. For instance, in this example you could replace *Expr1* with *Expected Price*.

To format the calculated field, right-click anywhere in the column for the field in the query design grid, and choose Properties from the shortcut menu to display the field's *property sheet*. (A property sheet is a dialog box, usually tabbed, that lets you view or modify an object's properties.) In the General tab, click the Format property box, and from the drop-down list, select an appropriate format. For the example, you would choose Currency. Switch to Datasheet view to see the result of the formatting option you selected, as shown in Figure 43-18.

Title	Price	Expected Price
The Adventures of Huckleberry Finn	$5.49	$6.31
The Adventures of Tom Sawyer	$4.75	$5.46
A Connecticut Yankee in King Arthur's Court	$5.49	$6.31
Joan of Arc	$6.95	$7.99
Roughing It	$5.25	$6.04
The Awakening	$4.95	$5.69
Billy Budd	$4.49	$5.16
Moby-Dick	$9.95	$11.44
Leaves of Grass	$7.75	$8.91
The Legend of Sleepy Hollow	$2.95	$3.39
The Ambassadors	$5.95	$6.84
The Portrait of a Lady	$4.95	$5.69
The Turn of the Screw	$3.35	$3.85
The Marble Faun	$10.95	$12.59
The Scarlet Letter	$4.25	$4.89
Dracula	$17.95	$20.64
Great Expectations	$6.95	$7.99
Masterman Ready	$12.89	$14.82
Treasure Island	$11.85	$13.63
Wuthering Heights	$12.95	$14.89
Self-Reliance	$8.79	$10.11
Walden	$6.95	$7.99

Figure 43-18. This figure shows the first part of the example query of Figures 43-16 and 43-17, after the calculated field has been renamed and formatted.

Troubleshooting

Access won't run a query with a calculated field

You created a query containing a calculated field, but whenever you try to switch to Datasheet view to see the query results, Access displays a mysterious dialog box titled Enter Parameter Value rather than running the query.

If you enter a name that isn't the name of one of the fields in the table or tables used in your query, Access will assume that the name is a parameter that must be entered each time the query is run. For instance, in the example query described in "Adding Calculated Fields," on page 1163, if you erroneously entered Cost rather than Price into the expression in the calculated field, Access would treat Cost as a parameter and prompt you for its value when you run the query, because the Books table used in this query doesn't contain a field named Cost.

Keep this behavior in mind for situations where you actually want to have Access prompt you for a parameter each time you run the query. For instance, in the Book Inventory03 example database, if you wanted to create a query that displays books that cost less than a specified amount, you could enter the expression <[Cost] into the Criteria row of the Price field. (The brackets are needed in this context to indicate that Cost is a name rather than a literal text value.) Because the Books table doesn't contain a field named Cost, Access will treat Cost as a parameter and will prompt you for its value each time you run the query.

Creating a Crosstab Query

All the queries discussed so far in this chapter are known as *select* queries. A select query is the most common type of query; it displays rows of information extracted from one or more tables or other queries. This section introduces a second type of query, the *crosstab query*.

Sometimes the information in a database can be organized by two different types of groupings, and you might want to extract information about the various subsets formed by the different groupings. Imagine, for example, that you've collected test results from a group of students. The students can be grouped based on gender (male or female) as well as age (15, 16, or 17). It might be useful to know the average test score for each of the possible subsets (15-year-old boys, 15-year-old girls, 16-year-old boys, 16-year-old girls, 17-year-old boys, and 17-year-old girls). You can accomplish this by using a statistical matrix called a *cross-tabulation*. In Access, you can generate a cross-tabulation by creating a crosstab query. The results of a crosstab query for the test score scenario just described are shown in Figure 43-19.

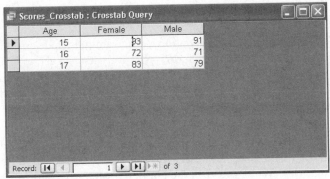

Figure 43-19. This crosstab query is based on data from a table of test scores.

 The crosstab query used in this example is included in the Scores.mdb example database on the companion CD.

The following summary describes the steps for creating a crosstab query using the Crosstab Query Wizard:

1 Open the New Query dialog box (shown in Figure 43-1) as explained in "Using the Database Window and Object Views," on page 1107.

2 In the New Query dialog box, select the Crosstab Query Wizard option and click the OK button.

3 In the first Crosstab Query Wizard dialog box, select the table or query containing the fields you want to include.

For instance, to create the Scores_Crosstab example query shown in Figure 43-19, you would select the name of the table that stores the gender, age, and test score for each student. (This table is named Scores.) Here's how the table used by the example query appears in Design view:

Field Name	Data Type
StudentID	AutoNumber
Name	Text
Gender	Text
Age	Number
Score	Number

4 In the second dialog box, select from one to three fields to be used for row headings. (For the example query, you would select only the Age field.)

5 In the third dialog box, select a single field to be used for the column headings. (For the example query, you would select the Gender field.)

6 In the fourth dialog box, select the field and the function you want to use to calculate the values that appear in the query for each subset—that is, for each column and row intersection. (For the example query, you would select the Score field and the Avg function to display the average test score for each subset.)

Also, check the Yes Include Row Sums option if you want to include an additional column that summarizes the values in each row—the average of all values if you chose the Avg function, the sum of all values if you chose the Sum function, and so on. For instance, if you selected this option for the example query, the query would include a column that displays the average of the female value and the male value for each age. (To create the example query, you would clear this option.)

7   In the fifth and final dialog box, enter a name for the query (or accept the default name), and choose whether the new query should initially be opened in Datasheet view or in Design view. When you click the Finish button, the wizard will create the query.

Tip   Convert a query to a crosstab

You can also convert an existing query to a crosstab query. To do so, open it in Design view and choose Query, Crosstab Query. This command will add a Total and a Crosstab row to the query design grid and will convert the query to a crosstab query. In the Crosstab row, select Row Heading for one or more fields to designate the row headings, select Column Heading for one field to designate the column headings, and select Value for one field to designate the field you want to use to display the values in the row–column intersections. In the Total row, select Group By for the fields used for headings, and select a function (Sum, Avg, and so on) for the field used to display the values. The easiest way to learn how to set up a crosstab query in Design view is to study the design of a crosstab query generated by the Crosstab Query Wizard.

Creating and Running Queries to Modify Data

So far, this chapter has described two major types of queries: the select query and the crosstab query. Four additional types of queries, which are known as *action queries*, can actually change your data: a make-table query, an append query, a delete query, and an update query.

Caution   Before running any of the queries discussed in the following sections, make a backup copy of your database. (See "Backing Up Your Database," on page 1112.) These queries can permanently modify your database, possibly removing a large amount of data. You can also back up the specific table or tables that will be modified by making copies of these tables using the Database window, as described in "Using the Database Window and Object Views," on page 1107.

The following procedure describes the general steps for creating and running an action query. The next sections of the chapter discuss the particulars of each type of action query.

1   Open a new or an existing query in Design view, as described previously in this chapter.

Using Queries to Select and Combine Information

2 Convert the query to an action query by choosing the query type—Make-Table Query, Update Query, Append Query, or Delete Query—from the Query menu. Or choose the query type from the Query Type drop-down list on the toolbar:

Query Type

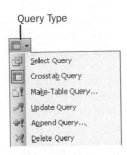

When you convert a query to an action query, the rows in the query design grid will change according to the type of information that must be specified. For two of the query types (make-table and append), Access will display a dialog box to obtain more information before returning you to the Design window.

3 Fill in the query design grid. The particular rows that are available depend upon the type of query you're creating.

4 To preview the results of running the query, switch to Datasheet view by choosing Datasheet View from the View menu or from the View drop-down menu on the toolbar. (Do *not* choose the Query, Run menu command or click the Run toolbar button at this stage.) The query will display a list of the records that it will append, delete, update, or add to a new table—without actually changing any data. (Unfortunately, however, when you preview an update query, it lists the records that it will modify but shows the current values, not the new values that the query will generate.)

> **Note** With a select or crosstab query, the Run command on the Query menu and the Run toolbar button have the same effect as choosing Datasheet View from the View menu or from the View drop-down menu on the toolbar—that is, Access will simply switch to Datasheet view. With these types of queries, *running* a query is synonymous with *viewing a query in Datasheet view*.
>
> With an action query, however, the Run command and the Run toolbar button cause the query to perform its intended action—appending, deleting, updating, or inserting into a new table. In contrast, choosing Datasheet View from one of the View menus merely switches to Datasheet view so that you can preview the query's effect without actually changing data.

Run

5 Choose Query, Run or click the Run toolbar button to carry out the data modification.

Make-Table Query

The make-table query type creates a new table and adds to this table all of the information that the query selects. The new table can be in the current database or in a different one. A make-table query is especially useful for archiving information in a database. For instance, you could first use a make-table query to copy older records from the current table to an archive table. You could then convert the query to a Delete query, and use it to remove the older records from the current table.

Append Query

Like the make-table query type, the append query type adds the information it selects to another table, which can be either in the current database or in a different one. However, rather than creating and adding the information to a new table, it appends the information to an existing table, thereby adding new records at the end of the existing table. You often use this query to add a new batch of records to update an existing table; for instance, you might receive a database of new books published in the present year that you want to integrate into your existing books table.

Delete Query

The most dangerous of these four queries is the delete query, which removes from your tables all records that match your conditions. This query can be useful for housekeeping—for example, you might use it to eliminate from your database all records with dates earlier than January 1, 1999—but it can be dangerous if you make a mistake in defining your conditions. Be certain to back up your data and to preview the results in Datasheet view before clicking the Run button with this type of query!

Update Query

An update query provides a powerful way to change the value of any fields in your database for those records that match the conditions you specify. When you convert a query to an update query, Access adds an Update To row to the query design grid. You can use that row to specify a value or an expression that indicates how the value in a field should be changed.

You enter expressions using the same general guidelines that you follow when creating calculated fields. See "Adding Calculated Fields," on page 1163, for more information. The example query given there included a field that showed the result of increasing the purchase price by 15 percent. If you decided to actually raise the price of books by 15 percent, you could use an update query to change the value of the Price field in every record in the Books table to 115 percent of its previous value, permanently changing the data in your database.

Creating Forms and Data Access Pages for Working with Data

Creating a Form 1171
Customizing a Form 1178

Viewing and Modifying Data
in a Form 1189
Publishing Data on an Intranet Using
a Data Access Page 1193

Creating a Form

Forms and other database objects in Microsoft Office Access 2003 are described in "Designing and Planning an Access Database," on page 1100. To create a new form, open the New Form dialog box (shown in Figure 44-1) by selecting the Forms object type and clicking the New button in the Database window, as explained in "Using the Database Window and Object Views," on page 1107, and then select an option in the list, as follows:

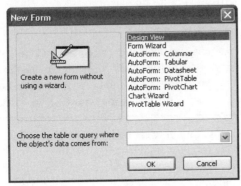

Figure 44-1.   In the New Form dialog box, you can select one of nine ways to create a new form.

- To create the form yourself by adding controls one at a time in Design view, select the Design View option. For information on using Design view, see "Customizing a Form," on page 1178.

- To have Access create the form for you according to your specifications, select the Form Wizard option. The Form Wizard lets you choose the specific fields to include, which can belong to one or more tables or queries. See "Creating a Form Using the Form Wizard," on page 1173.

● To have Access quickly create a form that has a particular configuration (Columnar, Tabular, Datasheet, PivotTable, or PivotChart), based on the record source table or query you select in the drop-down list, select one of the five AutoForm options. Access will immediately create the form, including all fields from the record source and using default options without asking for your specifications.

> **Note** A form is usually associated with a specific table or query in the database, which is known as the *record source*. A typical form displays the records belonging to the record source one at a time and lets you add, modify, or delete these records.
>
> If you select any of the AutoForm options or the Chart Wizard option in the New Form dialog box, you *must* specify the table or query that will be the record source for the form by selecting that table or query in the drop-down list at the bottom of the dialog box, which displays all of the tables and queries in the database.
>
> If you select any of the other options, you can also specify a record source. Or you can omit this step, leave the drop-down list blank, and then define the record source later in the process. (With the Design View option, you can even leave the form without a record source. You might do this to create a form that simply displays information and performs actions, such as the Switchboard form that some database wizards create as an alternative interface for accessing database objects.)

● To use the Chart Wizard to create a form that contains a Microsoft Graph chart, select the Chart Wizard option. The chart will graph data from the data source that you select in the drop-down list. For information on charts generated by the Graph program, see "Constructing Charts Using Microsoft Graph," on page 136.

> **Tip** Insert a chart into any form
> No matter how you create a form, you can use the Chart Wizard to insert a chart into it by opening the form in Design view, choosing Insert, Chart, and dragging to mark the rectangular area on your form where you want to display the chart. The Chart Wizard will then start running and will guide you through the process of designing your chart.

● To have Access take information from one or more tables or queries and create a form containing a Microsoft Office Excel 2003 PivotTable, select the PivotTable Wizard option. For information on Excel PivotTables, see Chapter 28, "Power Database Techniques: Lists, Filters, and PivotTables."

Once you have selected the option you want, click the OK button.

In general, it's easiest to use the Form Wizard or one of the AutoForm options to create at least a rough draft of your form. You can then customize the form, using the techniques described in "Customizing a Form," on page 1178.

Creating a Form Using the Form Wizard

The following is the procedure for generating a new form using the Form Wizard. (The figures show the steps for creating a form for viewing and editing a single table, Books, in the Book Inventory03 example database. If you want to see the final result as you read these steps, look ahead to Figure 44-6.)

1 In the New Form dialog box, select the Form Wizard option and click the OK button. (You *don't* need to select a record source in the drop-down list in the New Form dialog box.) The Form Wizard will start running.

2 In the first Form Wizard page, shown in Figure 44-2, select all the fields you want to display on your form. The resulting form will contain a separate control for accessing each of the fields that you pick. To begin, in the Tables/Queries drop-down list, select the table or query that has the fields you want to include. This table or query will become the record source for the table, and all the fields that belong to it will be displayed in the Available Fields list. Then move all the fields that you want from the Available Fields list to the Selected Fields list, using the four buttons located between the lists. When the Selected Fields list has all the fields you want, click the Next button to display the second Form Wizard page.

> For information on selecting fields from more than one table or query, see the sidebar "Accessing Several Tables or Queries in a Form," on page 1176.

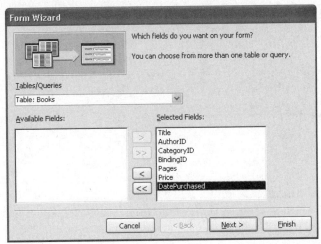

Figure 44-2. In the first Form Wizard page, select all the fields you want to access from your new form. The fields selected here are for creating the example form.

Tip **Control the field order**

The order in which the fields are listed in the Selected Fields list is the order in which the wizard will arrange the fields in the form. Although you can't rearrange fields that have already been added to the Selected Fields list, you can control the position where the next field is added. To do this, first select the field in the Selected Fields list that is immediately above the position where you want to add the new field. Then add the new field; it will be placed just below the field you selected. If you don't like the position of a particular field in the Selected Fields list, select it, click the < button to remove it, and then add it back to the list at the desired position.

3 In the second Form Wizard page, shown in Figure 44-3, choose the basic arrangement of the controls on the form. To make your choice, select each option and observe the way the selected layout will look on your form, as shown in the dialog box. The Columnar layout is the most common and usually enables you to view one complete record at a time in Form view. The Tabular layout lets you view multiple records at the same time in Form view, while the Datasheet layout generates a form that's intended to be displayed in Datasheet view. The Justified layout arranges the form's objects to fill the form window. When you've selected the layout you want, click the Next button.

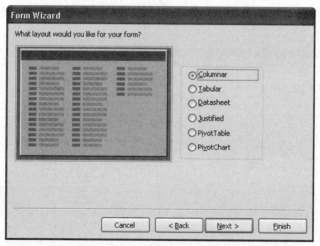

Figure 44-3. In the second Form Wizard page, choose the form's layout. The layout selected here, Columnar, is used in the example form.

4 In the third Form Wizard page, shown in Figure 44-4, choose the form's style, which affects the background color or pattern, the fonts, the look of the controls, and other features. Again, to help you make your choice, the page shows how the form will look with each style option. When you've made your choice, click the Next button to open the final wizard page.

> **Tip** You can change the style you selected in the Form Wizard after the form has been created. To do this, display the form in Design view, select the entire form, choose Format, AutoFormat, and then select a new style in the AutoFormat dialog box. To select the entire form, click the form selection button in the upper-left corner of the form, as shown in "Formatting a Form," on page 1183.

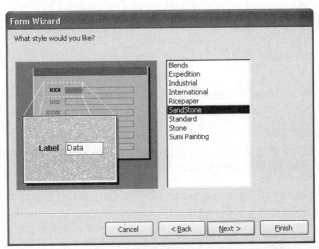

Figure 44-4. In the third Form Wizard page, choose the form style. The style selected here, SandStone, is used in the example form.

5 In the final Form Wizard page, shown in Figure 44-5, assign a name to the form and choose the way the form will initially be opened. If you select the first opening option, the form will be opened in Form view (or Datasheet view if you selected the Datasheet layout) so that you can immediately begin using the form to view or modify data, as discussed later in the chapter. If you select the second opening option, the form will be opened in Design view so that you can modify its design, as described in the next section, "Customizing a Form."

When you've made all your choices, click the Finish button to have Access create the form. (As you can with the other Access wizards, you can click the Finish button within any of the pages to create the form using the options you've set and the default choices for the options you haven't set.)

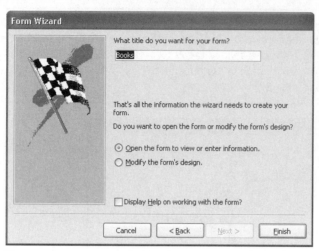

Figure 44-5. In the fourth Form Wizard page, enter a name and select a form opening option. These are the options selected for the example form.

Figure 44-6 shows the example form, opened in Form view. (The example form is included in the Book Inventory03 example database on the companion CD to this book.)

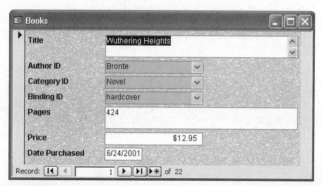

Figure 44-6. This form is the result of the Form Wizard choices shown in Figures 44-2 through 44-5.

Accessing Several Tables or Queries in a Form

When you select the fields for your form in the first Form Wizard page, shown in Figure 44-2, you can add fields from several tables or queries. To add fields from each table or query, select it in the Tables/Queries drop-down list and then use the buttons to move the fields you want to the Selected Fields list.

If you add fields from several tables or queries, the wizard will display one or two additional pages that weren't shown in this section: one page in which you specify the table or query by which you want to view your data (for example, if you selected fields from the Authors and the Books tables, you would choose to view your data either "by Authors" or "by Books") and possibly another page in which you select a layout for a subform. The choices you make determine the form's record source.

If your form includes fields from two tables that are related in a one-to-many relationship and if you selected to view your data by the *primary* table, the wizard will let you display the records from the related table in a *subform* contained within the form. For instance, in the Book Inventory03 example database, if you chose to view your data by the Authors table (the primary table) and included one or more fields from the Books table (the related table), you could add the subform shown in Figure 44-7. As an alternative, the wizard will let you set up a *linked form*, which is an entirely separate form that displays the related data and which you open by clicking a button on the main form.

On the other hand, if you chose to view your data by the *related* table in the one-to-many relationship, when the form displays a record in the related table, it will simply display the unique matching fields from the primary table along with the fields from the current record in the related table. For instance, in the example described in the previous paragraph, if you chose to view your data by the Books table (the related table), when the form displays a Books record, it would display the unique matching Author information along with the book title, as shown in Figure 44-8. (In this case the record source is actually a SQL (structured query language) query statement that selects fields from both tables.)

A form that accesses data from several tables or queries can be complex to design from scratch or to modify. However, if you create the form using the Form Wizard, almost everything is set up for you.

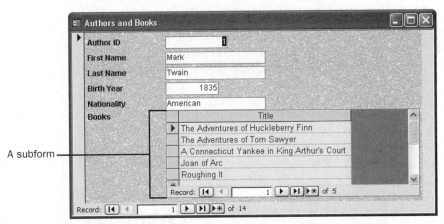

A subform ———

Figure 44-7. This form shows the fields of the Authors primary table (the record source) and includes a subform for displaying the Title field of each matching record in the Books related table. The form is included in the Book Inventory03 example database.

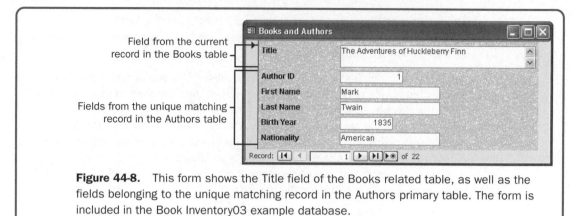

Field from the current record in the Books table

Fields from the unique matching record in the Authors table

Figure 44-8. This form shows the Title field of the Books related table, as well as the fields belonging to the unique matching record in the Authors primary table. The form is included in the Book Inventory03 example database.

Customizing a Form

You can use Design view to complete a new form that you created by selecting the Design View option in the New Form dialog box, to customize a new form that you created by selecting one of the Wizard or AutoForm options in the New Form dialog box, or to modify an existing form of any type. Design view lets you add, remove, or modify the controls that make up the form, as well as change the properties of the form itself.

To open a form in Design view, follow the instructions given in "Using the Database Window and Object Views," on page 1107. Figure 44-9 shows the example form described in the previous section, "Creating a Form Using the Form Wizard," opened in Design view. You can see the appearance of this form in Form view in Figure 44-6.

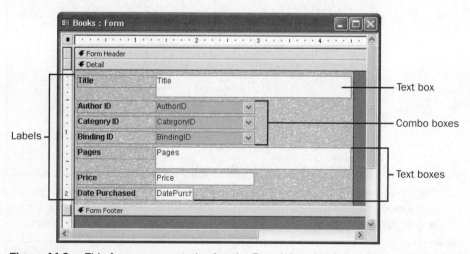

Figure 44-9. This form was created using the Form Wizard with the choices shown in Figures 44-2 through 44-5 and was opened in Design view.

In the form Design view window, you can perform one or more of the following actions to design or customize a form:

Field List

- To add a control that accesses a specific field in the form's record source, which is known as a *bound control*, drag the name of the field from the *field list* (see Figure 44-10), and drop it at the position on the form where you want to display the control. If the field list isn't visible, choose View, Field List or click the Field List toolbar button.

  Access will add a control that's appropriate for the type of the field, together with an attached text label. For example, if you drag a field with a text, numeric, or date data type, Access will add a text box. If you drag a field with the Yes/No data type, Access will add a check box. Or, if you drag a lookup field, Access will add a combo box that displays the lookup field values in its drop-down list.

For information on lookup fields, see Table 47-1, on page 1242.

Figure 44-10.   This field list is displayed when the Books example form is opened in Design view.

Toolbox

- To add a bound control of a particular type, first click the button for the type of control you want in the Toolbox toolbar, and *then* drag the field from the field list. The Toolbox toolbar is shown in Figure 44-11 and its buttons are described in Table 44-1. If this toolbar isn't currently displayed, either choose View, Toolbox, or click the Toolbox toolbar button.

  For example, if you'd prefer to access a Yes/No field using a toggle button rather than a check box, you could click the Toggle Button button on the Toolbox toolbar and then drag the field from the field list to the form. Clicking a Toolbox button has an effect only if the type of control you click is appropriate for the data type of the field that you drag to the form. (For instance, clicking Command Button has no effect if you drag a text field, because you can't use a command button to access a text field.)

Chapter 44

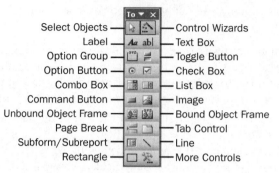

Select Objects — Control Wizards
Label — Text Box
Option Group — Toggle Button
Option Button — Check Box
Combo Box — List Box
Command Button — Image
Unbound Object Frame — Bound Object Frame
Page Break — Tab Control
Subform/Subreport — Line
Rectangle — More Controls

Figure 44-11. This figure shows the Toolbox toolbar buttons and their functions.

- To add an unbound control, click the button for the control on the Toolbox toolbar, and then click the position on the form where you want to display the control. (Click the button and then click the form. Don't try to drag the button to the form as you do with fields in the field list!) An unbound control is one that *doesn't* access a field in the form's record source. Its value and appearance doesn't change as you display different records in the form, although you can alter the state of an unbound control, for example, by clicking a check box or typing in a text box.

  You can use unbound controls for a variety of purposes. For example, you can use a label (always unbound) to label other controls or to display information, or you can use a command button (also always unbound) to perform an action. Also, you can use an unbound object frame, image, line, or rectangle to decorate the form or provide constant information that doesn't change from record to record.

- To delete a control, click it to select it and press the Delete key.

- To move, copy, or resize a control, or to modify its appearance or properties, follow the instructions given in the next section, "Formatting a Form."

Table 44-1. Toolbox Buttons for Modifying a Form's Design

Button	Name	Description
	Select Objects	Lets you select a single control by clicking it or multiple controls by pressing Shift while clicking each one. When this button is selected, you can also select controls by dragging a selection rectangle around them.
	Control Wizards	When this button is selected, Access will automatically run a wizard when you insert one of the following types of controls: an option group, a combo box, a list box, a command button, or a subform/subreport. The wizard will assist you in assigning the essential properties to the control or group of controls (such as the items displayed in a combo box, the action performed by clicking a command button, or the data shown in a subform/subreport). If you don't use a wizard, you'll probably need to assign appropriate properties manually using the control's property sheet, as discussed in "Formatting a Form," on page 1183.
Aa	Label	Lets you display descriptive text for labeling a control or providing instructions. To add or edit the text in a label control, click the control once to select it and then click again to place the insertion point within the control. With most types of controls, when you add the control, Access automatically adds a text label that's attached to the control. (The behavior of attached controls is described in "Formatting a Form," on page 1183.)
ab|	Text Box	Adds a box for displaying, entering, or modifying data.
	Option Group	Adds a set of option buttons, check boxes, or toggle buttons in which you can select only one control at a time. If an option group is bound to a field, a numeric value is stored in the field to indicate which control in the group is selected. When you add an option group, you can use the Option Group Wizard to choose the settings you want. (Control wizards are discussed in the "Control Wizards" item in this table.)
	Toggle Button	Adds a rectangular push button that can be used to turn an option on or off. It appears pressed in when the option is on. A toggle button is suitable for binding to a field that has the Yes/No data type.

Table 44-1. **Toolbox Buttons for Modifying a Form's Design**

Button	Name	Description
⦿	Option Button	Adds a round button (also known as a *radio button*) that can be used to turn an option on or off. The button contains a black dot when the option is on. Although you can add an independent option button and bind it to a field with the Yes/No data type, an option button is usually used within an option group for selecting one of a set of mutually exclusive options (see previous table item).
☑	Check Box	Adds a small square box that can be used to turn an option on or off. Contains a check mark when the option is on. When you drag a field with the Yes/No data type from the field list onto the form, by default Access adds a check box that is bound to the field.
▤	Combo Box	Adds a control that consists of a text box plus a drop-down list. You can either type text into the text box or select an item from the list.
▤	List Box	Adds a permanently displayed list of items (in contrast to a combo box, which displays a drop-down list). You set the control's value by selecting an item in the list.
▭	Command Button	Adds a rectangular button that you click to perform an action, such as going to the next record, printing the current record, or running a program. When you add a command button, you can use the Command Button Wizard to select the specific action that the button performs. (Control wizards are discussed under the "Control Wizards" item in this table.)
🖼	Image	Adds a constant picture to a form. (The picture doesn't change when you switch records.)
⬚	Unbound Object Frame	Displays an OLE (object linking and embedding) object such as an Excel spreadsheet. The object is constant; it doesn't change with each record.
⬚	Bound Object Frame	Displays OLE objects that are stored in the records of a table, such as employee photos. This control is intended to be bound to a field that has the OLE Object data type. The object will change as you view various records.
▤	Page Break	Marks the position of a page break, which will cause the following text to be printed at the top of the next page if you print the form.

Chapter 44

Table 44-1. Toolbox Buttons for Modifying a Form's Design

Button	Name	Description
	Tab Control	Lets you divide the form into separate tabs. After you add and adjust the size of a tab control, you can add controls to any of its tabs. (For an example of a form that uses tabs, see Figure 41-4.)
	Subform/ Subreport	Adds information from an additional table or query to a form or report so that you can view or modify its data. (See the sidebar "Accessing Several Tables or Queries in a Form," on page 1176.)
	Line	Lets you draw a single straight line on a form.
	Rectangle	Draws a rectangle on the form.
	More Controls	Allows you to add an ActiveX control to your form. When you click this button, you can select from a menu listing the ActiveX controls that are installed on your computer.

For information on embedded OLE objects, see Chapter 7, "Exchanging Data in Office 2003."

Troubleshooting

Embedded OLE object isn't displayed

You added an Unbound Object Frame control to display an embedded OLE object in your form. However, all you see is an icon for the program that created the object.

To display the content of the embedded object, rather than just an icon, click the control to select it, and choose Edit, *X* Object, Convert (where *X* is the object type, such as *Equation*). Then, in the Convert dialog box, clear the Display As Icon option.

Formatting a Form

The following is the general procedure for modifying the controls in a form or for changing the properties of a form section or of the form itself. You can also use these same steps for formatting a report, so if you're working with a report, substitute the word *report* for *form* as you read these instructions.

1 Open the form in Design view.

Toolbox

2 Make sure that the Select Objects button is selected on the Toolbox toolbar. (See Figure 44-11. If this toolbar isn't displayed, either choose View, Toolbox, or click the Toolbox toolbar button.)

1183

3 Select the control or controls you want to modify, as follows:

> **Note** The first click on a text or combo box selects the control, and the second click places the insertion point within the control (if you want to select the control again at this point, you'll have to click on one of the control's borders).

> **Note** You can change the way a selection rectangle selects controls. If the Partially Enclosed option is selected, the rectangle will select all controls that are completely or partially contained within the rectangle. If the Fully Enclosed option is selected, the rectangle will select only the controls that are completely contained within the rectangle. You can access these options by choosing Tools, Options and clicking the Forms/Reports tab.

- To select a single control, click it. Access will display seven small sizing handles, plus one large moving handle around the selected control, as shown here:

- To select several controls, click each one while pressing Shift. Or you can select all the controls in a rectangular area by using the mouse to drag a selection rectangle around the controls, as shown here:

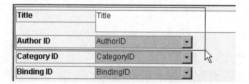

  If you have selected several controls but want to exclude just one or two controls from the selection, hold down the Shift key and click each control you want to deselect.

- To select the form (*not* all the controls in the form, but the form itself), click the form selection button in the upper-left corner of the form. This will deselect any selected control or form section, as shown here:

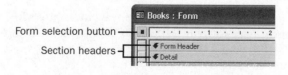

Form selection button
Section headers

Chapter 44

> **Note** If you know the name of a control, you can select it by choosing its name in the Object drop-down list at the left end of the Formatting toolbar. (The Formatting toolbar is explained later in this section.) You can also select a form section by choosing FormHeader, Detail, or FormFooter in the Object drop-down list. Or you can select the entire form by choosing Form in this list.

- To select a specific form section—Form Header, Detail, or Form Footer—click the section's header, or click the button to the left of the header, or click on a blank spot within the section. This will deselect any selected controls. (Form sections are discussed later in this section.)

4 Modify the selection according to the instructions in the following list:

- To change the size of a selected control, point to one of the seven sizing handles, and drag when the pointer becomes a two-headed arrow, as seen here:

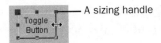

A sizing handle

Alternatively, to change the size of one or more selected controls, choose a command from the Format, Size submenu, as shown here:

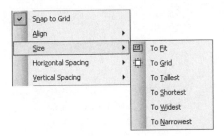

- If a single control is selected, you can move it by pointing to either the moving handle or to one of the borders (but *not* to a sizing handle) and dragging when the pointer assumes the image of a hand, as seen here:

Moving handle — Border — Sizing handle

If several controls are selected, you can move all of them simultaneously by pointing to one of the controls (but *not* to a moving handle or to a sizing handle) and dragging when the pointer assumes the image of an open hand, as shown here:

If several controls are selected, you can move one of them independently of the others by pointing to its moving handle and dragging when the pointer assumes the image of a hand with an extended index finger, as shown here:

Recall that for many types of controls, when you insert the control Access automatically *attaches* a label to the control. When you click either the control or its label to select it, the moving handle appears *both* on the control and on the label (even though only one is selected). To move the control and the label together, drag a border on the selected object; to move either the control or the label independently, drag its moving handle.

- To make a copy of the selected control or controls, choose Edit, Copy, and then choose Edit, Paste (or use the equivalent toolbar buttons or shortcut keys).

- To align a group of selected controls, you can choose a command from the Format, Align submenu, as shown here:

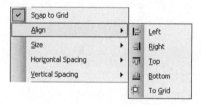

- To adjust the spacing of a group of selected controls, choose a command from the Format, Horizontal Spacing submenu:

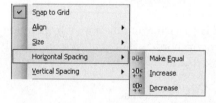

or from the Format, Vertical Spacing submenu:

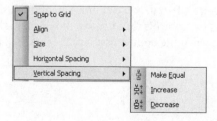

■ To alter the text formatting, background color, text color, border color or width, or visual effects (such as Raised or Shadowed) of the selected control(s), form section, or form, use the controls on the Formatting toolbar shown in Figure 44-13.

Properties

■ To change the properties of the selected control or controls, the selected form section, or the form itself if the form is selected, choose View, Properties, or click the Properties toolbar button, or press F4 or Alt+Enter to display the *property sheet* for the selected object. A property sheet is a dialog box that contains a set of tabs for the different categories of properties available for the currently selected object. (See Figure 44-14.) You can leave the property sheet open while you work in Design view, and it lets you view or modify the properties of whatever object is currently selected.

> **Note** You can move a control (or add a new one) to any position within the three sections of a form: Form Header, Detail, or Form Footer. Controls that you place in the Detail section appear in the main part of the form in Form view. Controls placed in the Form Header or Form Footer section appear in the Form Header or Form Footer section at the top or bottom of the form in Form view. (See Figure 44-12.) If the Form view window is made too small to show all the controls, scroll bars will appear that scroll the Detail section but not the Form Header or Form Footer sections. Note that the Form Header and Form Footer sections appear in Design view only if the View, Form Header/Footer menu option is selected.

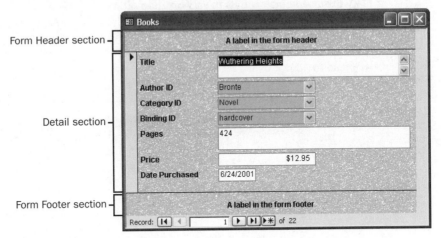

Figure 44-12. You can place controls in any of the three form sections that are displayed in Form view.

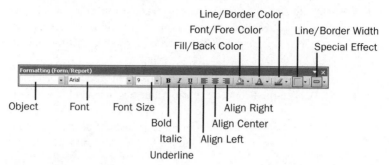

Figure 44-13. The Formatting toolbar lets you change the appearance of controls and any text they contain.

Note Choosing To Grid from the Format, Size submenu moves each of the boundaries of the selected control(s) to the nearest gridline on the form. If the Snap To Grid option on the Format menu is selected, resizing or moving a control always moves the control edge or edges that are repositioned to the nearest gridline. Gridlines are visible in Design view only if the View, Grid menu option is selected (gridlines are active whether or not they're visible). In the figures in this section, gridlines were hidden for clarity.

Tip Use separate controls to vary text formatting

Sometimes you might want to have a label that has two different text formats—for example, a label reading "*Full* Address." You can't apply multiple text formats to a control, although you can achieve the same result in a label by creating two label controls that are lined up to appear as if they were only one. Because each portion of the label is in a separate control, you can assign different formats to each.

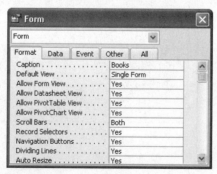

Figure 44-14. This figure shows the property sheet for the form itself.

> **Tip** Explore properties
>
> To learn how the many properties listed in the property sheet affect different types of controls, select a control, open the property sheet, and click in any property box that you're curious about. Press F1 and Access's online Help system will take you directly to a complete explanation of the property.

> **Tip** Create a calculated control
>
> You can define the properties of a text box control so that it displays the result of a calculation performed on one or more of the fields in the record source, rather than simply displaying or setting the contents of a single field. To do this, display the text box's property sheet, click the Data tab, and enter the expression for the calculation you want to perform into the Control Source property box. (For a bound control, the Control Source property is normally set to the name of the field that the control is bound to.) For instance, in the Books example form shown in this chapter, if you wanted to display a text box control that shows the total book price including sales tax, you could enter the following expression (assuming the sales tax rate is 7 percent):
>
> =[Price]*1.07
>
> To properly format the calculated result, you could then select the Currency format in the Format property box in the property sheet's Format tab.
>
> For help in entering a complex expression, you can click the ellipsis (...) button that appears at the right of the Control Source property box when it's active. This will run the Expression Builder.
>
> A calculated control in a form is analogous to a calculated field in a query, which is discussed in "Adding Calculated Fields," on page 1163.

Viewing and Modifying Data in a Form

To use a form to view or modify the data that it accesses, open the form in Form view using any of the methods described in "Using the Database Window and Object Views," on page 1107. Figure 44-15 shows a form opened in Form view displaying an existing record.

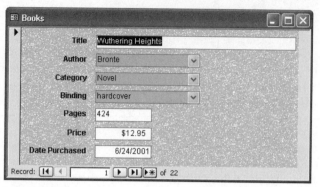

Figure 44-15. This form was generated using the Form Wizard and then customized in Design view. It accesses the records in the Books table of the Book Inventory03 example database.

The techniques you use in a form for entering information into a new record or for modifying an existing record are basically the same as the techniques you use in standard Microsoft Office 2003 dialog boxes. When entering or editing a record in a form, keep in mind the following points:

- When you add or modify data within the current record, Access displays a pencil icon on the vertical bar at the left of the form. This icon indicates that the record contains unsaved changes. When you move to a different record (using one of the methods described later in this section) or close the form, Access automatically saves the original record's contents. You can also save the current record's contents at any time by choosing Records, Save Record.

> **Note** You can also press Shift+Enter to save the record, unless the insertion point is within a text box for which the Enter Key Behavior property is set to New Line In Field. You'll find this property in the Other tab of the control's property sheet.

Undo

- You can reverse changes you've made in the currently displayed record (or in the previously displayed record if you haven't yet changed the current record) by issuing the Undo command (choose Edit, Undo, or click the Undo toolbar button, or press Ctrl+Z) or by pressing Esc.

Spelling

- You can check the spelling of the text in *all* records by choosing Tools, Spelling, or clicking the Spelling toolbar button, or pressing F7. You can also have Access automatically replace specific text as you type by using the AutoCorrect feature; to set it up, choose Tools, AutoCorrect. The Spelling and AutoCorrect features work in essentially the same way they do in Microsoft Word 2003. For general instructions, see "Checking

Spelling," on page 479, and "Automatically Fixing Your Text with AutoCorrect," on page 271.

In a form, you can view any of the records belonging to the record source, and you can add new records to the record source or delete records from it. Access provides a small toolbar permanently positioned in the lower-left corner of the form (see Figure 44-16). You can use this toolbar to navigate through the existing records or to add new records.

> **Note** In Access, you can modify the way the spelling checker works by choosing Tools, Options and opening the Spelling tab in the Options dialog box.

Figure 44-16. This toolbar, displayed at the bottom of a form, displays the current record number and lets you navigate to any record or add a new record.

If you prefer to use the keyboard rather than the mouse, press Page Down to move forward a single record or Page Up to move back a single record. To jump to the first field of the first record, press Ctrl+Home, and to jump to the last field of the last record, press Ctrl+End. (If pressing Ctrl+Home or Ctrl+End moves the insertion point within a control or does nothing, instead of moving between records, press the Tab key once and try again.)

The Current Record text box displays the number of the currently displayed record. To open a specific record, you can type the record number into this box and press Enter.

Find

> **Tip** Find or replace text quickly
> You can quickly find specified text in any of the records by choosing Edit, Find, or by clicking the Find toolbar button, or by pressing Ctrl+F, and then entering your search criteria into the Find tab of the Find And Replace dialog box (see Figure 47-11, on page 1258). To replace text, choose Edit, Replace, or press Ctrl+H to open the Replace tab of the Find And Replace dialog box.

New
Record

To create a new record, click the New Record button on the toolbar at the bottom of the form (see Figure 44-16) or click the New Record button on the main Access toolbar. The new record will be added to the form's record source and will be displayed in the form so that you can enter information into it.

Rather than entering mostly repetitive information for a new record, you can copy the data from another, similar record into the new record and then just modify the data as necessary. You can also copy information from one record over another record's data, replacing the original contents of the target record. To copy a record, complete the following steps:

1 Select the record that's the source of the information by displaying that record in the form and clicking the vertical bar at the left of the form to select the entire record. (This bar is equivalent to the row selector you see in Datasheet view, and it's highlighted when you click it.)

Click anywhere in this bar to select the entire record

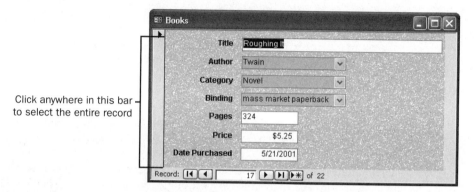

2 Choose Edit, Copy or press Ctrl+C. (If you want to move the source record's contents, choose Cut or press Ctrl+X instead.)

3 Display the target record in the form. (This record can be an existing one or a newly created one.) Make sure the vertical bar at the left is still highlighted, indicating that the entire record is selected.

4 Choose Edit, Paste or press Ctrl+V. The value of every control in the source record will be copied into the same control in the target record, except for any control that accesses a primary key field or other field that must have a unique value.

Delete Record

To permanently delete a record, display the record in the form, and then choose Edit, Delete Record, or click the Delete Record toolbar button. Access will require you to confirm the deletion before it removes the record. If the deletion will result in additional cascading deletions in related tables, a dialog box will inform you of that and give you an opportunity to stop. Just as when you delete a record in Datasheet view, once you confirm a deletion, the data is permanently lost—you can't restore it using the Undo button, and you'll have to manually reenter it if you want to restore it later.

Tip Sort or filter records viewed in a form

You can sort or filter the records you view in a form in the same way that you sort or filter records when you view a table, query, or form in Datasheet view. For general instructions, see "Sorting and Filtering in Datasheet View," on page 1141.

Note that you can also display a form in Datasheet view. Each row in the Datasheet view of a form displays the controls (that is, fields) for a particular record, one control per column. Although Datasheet view is generally much less convenient for working with a form than Form view, it has the advantage of allowing you to view multiple records at a time.

Troubleshooting

All records have disappeared

While viewing a form in Form view, you chose the Data Entry command from the Records menu to see what it does. Now all your records seem to be missing, and you can't get them back.

The Data Entry command switches on a special mode that allows you to enter new records but hides existing records in the data source. The confusing thing about the command is that you can't toggle it off by choosing the same menu option that turns it on (as you can with most commands that turn on special modes). Although the Data Entry command doesn't actually apply a filter (you don't see the Filtered message on the form or the FLTR message on the Access status bar), the way you turn data entry mode off is to choose Records, Remove Filter/Sort. Once you choose Remove Filter/Sort, you'll see all your records again.

Publishing Data on an Intranet Using a Data Access Page

A data access page is similar to a form. Like a form, it displays a collection of controls and allows you to access fields in one or more tables or queries in a database. Unlike a form, however, it's stored in a separate file rather than within the database. Because this file is in HTML (Hypertext Markup Language) format, it can be opened in a Web browser as well as in Access. And when it's opened in a browser, it doesn't merely display static information but rather allows you to navigate through the records in the record source table or query and to add, modify, or remove information, just as you can in Access. If you place the data access page and its supplemental files on a Web server on your organization's intranet and if you store the Access database on a shared network drive, other users in your organization can work with the database by opening the page in their Web browsers. Figure 44-17 shows a data access page viewed in Access, and Figure 44-18 shows the same page viewed in the Microsoft Internet Explorer Web browser.

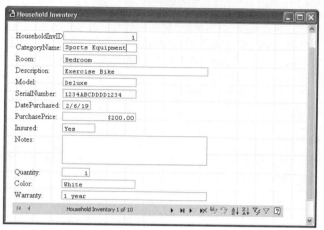

Figure 44-17. In Access a data access page functions like a form. This page is part of the Inventry.mdb example database.

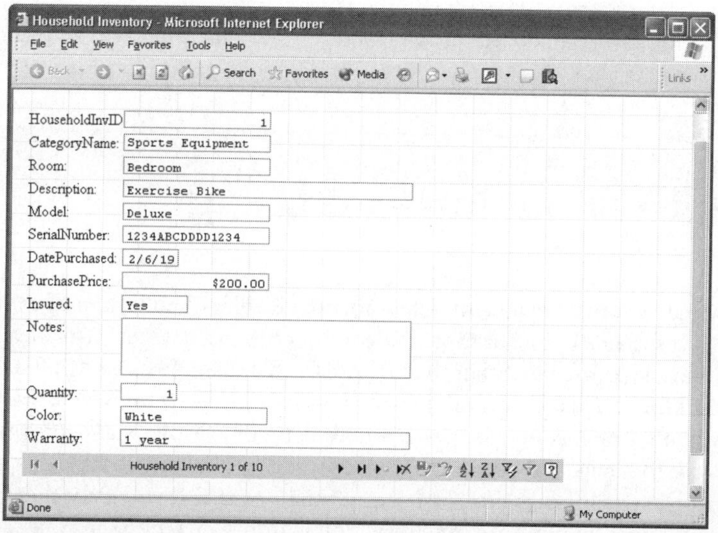

Figure 44-18. You can also open a data access page in a Web browser.

To use a particular data access page in Access, open the page using the instructions given in "Using the Database Window and Object Views," on page 1107. This will open the page in Page view (as shown in Figure 44-17), which is analogous to Form view for using a form. To open a data access page in a Web browser, you'll need to run your browser and enter the file path or URL (Uniform Resource Locator) where the page is stored on a local disk, shared network drive, or intranet Web server. (If you've already opened a data access page in Access, you can preview its appearance in your browser by choosing File, Web Page Preview.)

> For more information on opening a data access page from an intranet location, see "Publishing a Data Access Page," on page 1197.

To view or modify records in a data access page, you use the same basic techniques that were described for forms in "Viewing and Modifying Data in a Form," on page 1189. Notice, however, that a data access page typically contains a more complete toolbar than a form, as shown in Figure 44-19.

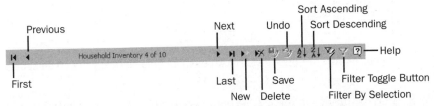

Figure 44-19. This is the toolbar displayed at the bottom of a data access page when it's viewed in Page View in Access or when it's opened in a Web browser.

> **NEW FEATURE!** **Caution** If you create a data access page in Access 2003, you won't be able to modify its design (by opening it in Design view) using Access 2000 or Access 2002. However, if you install the Microsoft Office 2003 Web Components feature on the computer that runs the previous version of Access (Access 2000 or 2002), you'll be able to open the data access page in Page view in the previous Access version, or in a browser, so that you can view and modify the records. You can install the Microsoft Office 2003 Web Components by running the setup program on the Office 2003 CD.

Creating a Data Access Page

To create a new data access page that connects to the currently opened Access database, follow these steps:

1 Open the New Data Access Page dialog box (shown in Figure 44-20) by selecting the Pages object type and clicking the New button in the Database window, as explained in "Using the Database Window and Object Views," on page 1107.

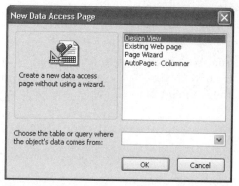

Figure 44-20. In the New Data Access Page dialog box, you can select one of four ways to create a new data access page.

2 In the drop-down list near the bottom of the New Data Access Page dialog box, select the table or query that you want to use as the record source.

3 Select an option in the list to specify the way the new page will be created, and click the OK button. The options, listed below, are similar to those you can select in the New Form dialog box when you create a new form:

- To create a data access page from scratch in Design view, select the Design View option.

- To create a new data access page based on a Web page you already have, select the Existing Web Page option.

- To run a wizard that creates a new data access page for you, according to your specifications, select the Page Wizard option.

- To quickly generate a new data access page based on the selected record source, where the controls are arranged in a single column, using default options, select the AutoPage: Columnar option.

> **Note** You can also create a data access page from scratch in Design view by clicking the Blank Data Access Page command in the New File task pane. (You can open this task pane by choosing File, New.)

In general, the easiest way to create a new data access page that has the features you want is to select the Page Wizard option. Using the Page Wizard is simple yet flexible. It works much like the Form Wizard, which was discussed in "Creating a Form Using the Form Wizard," on page 1173. You might be able to use it to create your final page—or at least a preliminary version of your page that you can then customize, as discussed next.

> **Tip** Convert another database object to a data access page
>
> You can create a data access page by saving a copy of a table, query, form, or report as a data access page. To do this, select the database object in the Database window and choose File, Save As. Then, in the Save As dialog box, select Data Access Page in the As drop-down list and enter a name for the data access page into the Save text box at the top.

Modifying a Data Access Page

To modify a data access page, open it in Design view using any of the methods explained in "Using the Database Window and Object Views," on page 1107.

Figure 44-21 shows the same form shown in Figures 44-17 and 44-18, opened in Design view. Design view lets you add, remove, resize, or rearrange the controls that make up the page. You can also modify the properties of any of the controls or of the page itself. The techniques for using Design view to modify a data access page are similar to those for customizing a form in Design view, which were described in "Customizing a Form," on page 1178.

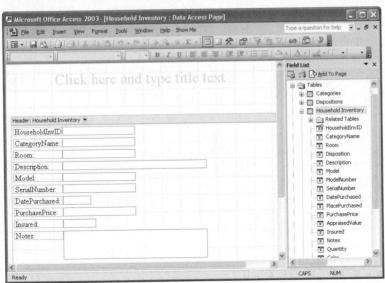

Figure 44-21. Design view provides an extensive set of tools for customizing a data access page.

Publishing a Data Access Page

The typical way to share a data access page with others in your organization is to store the data access page—together with its supplemental files—on a Web server on your intranet, and to store the Access database file on a shared network drive.

> **Note** The folder where you store the data access page and the folder where you store the Access database file can be the *same* folder, provided that the folder can be accessed by the intranet's Web server *and* has been set up as a shared network folder.

If your data access page and its supplemental files aren't already stored on your intranet's Web server, you'll need to copy the files to the appropriate folder on the server. (If you're uncertain about where you need to post these files or how to transfer them to the server, contact your company Webmaster or network administrator.) Be sure to copy all of the following files to the server:

- The HTML file containing the data access page. (For the example data access page shown in Figures 44-17 and 44-18, this is Household Inventory.htm.)

- The graphics and other supplemental files used by the data access page. These files are stored in a subfolder bearing the same name as the data access page, followed by *_files*. (For the example data access page, this subfolder is named Household Inventory_files.) You should store these files in a subfolder of the server folder in which you store the data access page; this subfolder should have the same name as the original subfolder that Access created. For instance, if you copied the example data access page, Household Inventory.htm, to the Household folder on your intranet server, you should copy the supplemental files to the folder Household\Household Inventory_files on this server.

If the database file itself (Inventory.mdb for the example data access page) isn't already stored in a shared network folder, you'll need to copy it to one.

You'll probably also need to edit the *page connection* property of the data access page to properly indicate the location of the database file that the page connects to. To do this, open the data access page in Design view, right-click the page's title bar (if the page's window is maximized, you'll need to restore it to a non-maximized window), and choose Page Connection from the shortcut menu. Then type the full file path of the database file into the Select Or Enter A Database Name text box in the Connection tab of the Data Link Properties dialog box, or click the adjoining ellipsis (…) button to select the file. Be sure to specify the location of the database file using a UNC (Universal Naming Convention) path (for example, \\Inventory\C\Stock\Widgets.mdb) so that everyone on the intranet will be able to access it. (A local file path, such as C:\Stock\Widgets.mdb, will work only if the data access page is opened on the computer where the database file is stored.)

Generating Reports to Present Information

Creating a Report 1199   Previewing and Printing a Report 1215
Modifying a Report 1210

Creating a Report

Reports and other database objects are described in "Designing and Planning an Access Database," on page 1100. To create a new report, display the New Report dialog box (shown in Figure 45-1) by selecting the Reports object type and clicking the New button in the Database window, as explained in "Using the Database Window and Object Views," on page 1107, and then select an option in the list, as follows, and click the OK button:

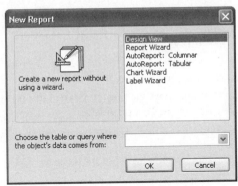

Figure 45-1. In the New Report dialog box you can select one of six ways to create a new report.

- To create a report from scratch using Design view, select the Design View option. Design view is discussed in "Modifying a Report," on page 1210.

- To have Microsoft Access 2003 help you design the report, select the Report Wizard option. Instructions for using the Report Wizard are given in "Using the Report Wizard," on page 1201.

- To use default settings to quickly create a report based on a single table or query, with a columnar or tabular layout, select the AutoReport: Columnar or the AutoReport: Tabular option. Either report will include all the fields belonging to the record source table or query that you select in the drop-down list at the bottom of the New Report dialog box.

In a *columnar report*, each field is presented in a separate row that has the field name on the left and the contents of the field on the right. Depending on the number of fields in your database, each record might fit on a single sheet of paper or might extend onto several sheets; you might even be able to fit several records on one page.

A *tabular report* organizes the information in rows and columns, where each record is displayed in a separate row, with each of its fields in a separate column. (To see an example of a tabular report generated by the Report Wizard, look ahead to Figure 45-11.)

> **Note** If you select an AutoReport option, the Chart Wizard option, or the Label Wizard option, you must also select a table or query in the drop-down list at the bottom of the New Report dialog box. This list shows all the tables and queries in the database. The report will display the fields belonging to the table or query you select, which is known as the report's *record source*.
>
> If, however, you select the Design View or Report Wizard option, you can leave the drop-down list blank and specify the record source later in the process. With either of these options, you can display fields belonging to *several* related tables or queries. If the report displays records from several tables or queries, the record source is actually an SQL query statement that selects the desired information. If you use the wizard, Access will create this statement for you. If you create the report in Design view, you must assign the statement to the report's Record Source property (the easiest way to do this is to click the ellipsis button next to the Record Source property box to run the SQL Statement: Query Builder). Properties are discussed in "Modifying a Report," on page 1210.

- To use the Chart Wizard to create a report that contains a Microsoft Graph chart, select the Chart Wizard option. The chart will graph data from the data source that you select in the drop-down list. For information on charts generated by the Graph program, see "Constructing Charts Using Microsoft Graph," on page 136.

> **Tip** Insert a chart in any report
> No matter how you create your report, you can use the Chart Wizard to insert a chart into it by opening the report in Design view, choosing Insert, Chart, and dragging to mark the rectangular area on your report where you want to display the chart. The Chart Wizard will then start running and will guide you through the process of designing your chart.

- To use the Label Wizard to create mailing labels or other types of labels, select the Label Wizard option. The labels will display the information from the data source that you select in the drop-down list.

> **Tip**   **Use Word to print labels**
>
> Microsoft Word lets you print labels, form letters, envelopes, and other types of mail-merge output documents directly using an Access database as the recipient list (that is, as the data source). For printing labels, Word offers more features, greater flexibility, and perhaps a more familiar interface than the Access Label Wizard. If you've already opened the Access database you want to use for printing merge documents, a quick way to run Word's Mail Merge Wizard is to select the table you want to use as the recipient list in the Database window and then choose Tools, Office Links, Merge It With Microsoft Word. For information on using Word's mail-merge feature, see "Using the Mail Merge Wizard to Automate Large Mailings," on page 549.

Using the Report Wizard is the easiest way to design a report, and yet the wizard is quite flexible. Although selecting one of the AutoReport options is a faster way to create a columnar or tabular report based on the fields in a single table or query, you can use the Report Wizard to create these same types of reports and have much greater flexibility in the choice of fields and in the report design.

Using the Report Wizard

The following steps describe the procedure for creating a report using the Report Wizard. (The figures show the steps for creating a report that displays a list of books, organized by binding type and author, in the Book Inventory03 example database. If you want to see the final result as you read these steps, look ahead to Figure 45-10.)

1   Select the Report Wizard option in the New Report dialog box and click the OK button. (You don't need to select a record source in the drop-down list in the New Report dialog box.)

2   In the first Report Wizard page, shown in Figure 45-2, select the fields to be included in the report. You have the option of selecting from several related tables or queries, as you do when you use other Access wizards. Be sure to include all the fields that have any relevance to your report, whether the field values are to appear in each detail line, to be summarized, or to be used for grouping the records.

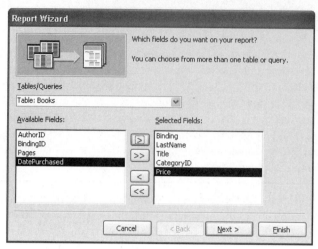

Figure 45-2. In the first Report Wizard page, you select all the fields to be used in the report. This figure shows the fields selected for the example report (they're from the Bindings, Author, and Books related tables).

Move the fields you want from the Available Fields list into the Selected Fields list by using, as necessary, the four buttons between the lists. To access fields from different tables or queries, select each one in the Tables/Queries drop-down list, and then move the fields you want. This list includes all the tables and queries defined in your database. When you've finished selecting fields, click the Next button to display the next Report Wizard page.

3 If you selected fields from more than one table or query in the previous step, the second Report Wizard page, shown in Figure 45-3, asks you to choose one table or query that will be used for grouping the information in the report, if possible. (You'll be able to select further grouping levels, based on individual fields, in the next Report Wizard page.) After you've selected a grouping table, click the Next button.

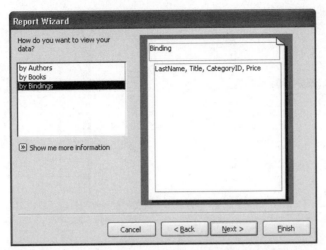

Figure 45-3. In the second Report Wizard page (which appears only if you selected fields from more than one table or query), select a table or query to be used for grouping. This figure shows the selection for the example report, in which the top-level grouping is by binding types.

> **Note** In the Book Inventory03 example database, Bindings and Authors are both *primary tables* in one-to-many relationships with the Books table. Therefore, each record in the Bindings or Authors table can match many records in the Books table, and thus you can easily use the Bindings or Authors table for grouping records in the Books table. This isn't true for the Books table, however, because it constitutes the *related table* in both the relationships. Accordingly, if you selected the Books table, the Report Wizard wouldn't attempt to group your records for you. In the next Report Wizard page, however, you would have the opportunity to specify grouping on the basis of individual fields. For information on relationships and the differences between primary and related tables, see "Setting Up Table Relationships," on page 1128.

4 In the third Report Wizard page, shown in Figure 45-4, you can add grouping levels to your report by selecting one or more fields to be used to group the records.

In the example shown in Figure 45-4, because the Bindings table was selected in the second wizard page, the field from this table, Binding, is already selected as the main grouping field in the third page. (If the Books table had been selected in the previous page, no grouping field would be defined yet.) In this example you could now add one or more fields to create *additional* grouping levels.

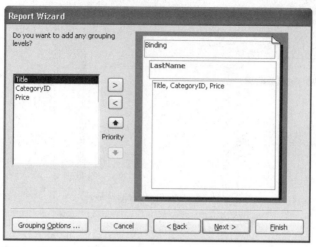

Figure 45-4. In the third Report Wizard page, you can add grouping levels to your report. In the example report the LastName field was added as the second grouping level, as shown in this figure.

To add a grouping field, select it in the list at the left, and click the > button to move it into the report model at the right. To remove the field that's selected on the right, click the < button to move it back to the left. You can add up to three fields, which—when combined with an initially selected grouping field—would generate up to four grouping levels in your report. You can change the priority level of a grouping field that you've chosen by clicking the field name in the report model and then clicking the up arrow or down arrow Priority button. When you've finished defining the grouping of your records, click the Next button to move to the fourth Report Wizard page.

Tip Use grouping levels to summarize information

An important reason for including grouping levels is that they allow you to summarize numeric information within each group. For instance, including the Binding and LastName grouping levels in the example report would allow you to display the total cost of the books that have a particular binding type, as well as the total cost of all books by a particular author within a binding category. Instead of the sum, you could also display the average, minimum, or maximum book cost. Defining summary calculations is discussed in the sidebar "Setting Summary Options," on page 1207.

5 The fourth Report Wizard page, shown in Figure 45-5, lets you choose the sorting order for the Detail section in the report. Note that the report groups are automatically sorted on the fields used for grouping. In this page, however, you can choose one or more fields that will be used for sorting the detail lines falling within each group. Choose the primary sort field by selecting it from the top drop-down list (labeled 1). You can then choose one or more additional sort fields in the remaining drop-down lists. (Note that each list contains the names of only those report fields that aren't used for grouping.) For an explanation of the Summary Options button, see the sidebar "Setting Summary Options." When you're finished with the fourth Report Wizard page, click the Next button to move on to the next page.

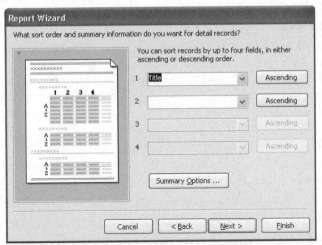

Figure 45-5. In the fourth Report Wizard page you specify how to sort the detail lines in your report. In the example report, Title is selected in the first list to sort the detail records by book title.

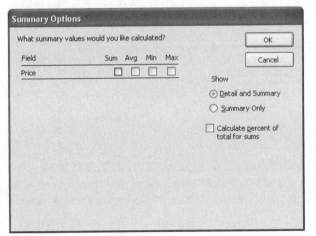

Figure 45-6. In the Summary Options dialog box you can have Access summarize numeric information for each group. For the example report, none of the summary functions are selected.

6 The fifth Report Wizard page, shown in Figure 45-7, allows you to select your report's layout and orientation. Each layout option in this page specifies how much of the database information is repeated at each level of the report. When you select an option, the model at the left of the page gives you an idea of how your report will look:

- The Stepped layout places each new group header in its own section of the report, putting no other information on the same line.

- The Block layout compresses the information for the group header onto the same line as the information for the first detail listing in that group. This makes

Chapter 45

for a more vertically compact report, but often it's somewhat difficult to find the information you need.

- The Outline 1 and Outline 2 layouts overlap the columns used for the grouping values but keep the text for each value on a separate line. These layouts are useful when you have a report that's too wide to fit legibly on a single page. Alternatively, you can consider changing the page orientation from the Portrait option to the Landscape option, which gives you a wider page to work with.

- The Align Left 1 and Align Left 2 layouts position the grouping fields flush with the left margin and repeat the detail headers at the top of each Detail section. These options provide the largest area across your page for your detail records, although they make distinguishing the different groups a bit more difficult.

When you're finished setting options in the fifth Report Wizard page, click the Next button to go to the sixth page.

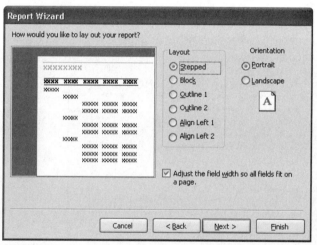

Figure 45-7.   In the fifth Report Wizard page, select your report's layout and orientation. This figure shows the settings used for the example report.

7   The sixth page of the Report Wizard, shown in Figure 45-8, lets you choose a formatting style for your report. These styles automatically apply fonts, borders, and spacing to your report design. When you're finished selecting the style, click the Next button to move on to the seventh page.

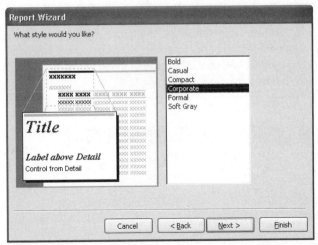

Figure 45-8. In the sixth Report Wizard page, choose the style of the elements in your report. The example report uses the Corporate style.

8 In the seventh and final Report Wizard page, shown in Figure 45-9, you can name your report and choose whether to immediately preview the report's printed appearance or open it in Design view so that you can modify its design, as explained next. Click the Finish button to generate and open your report.

Setting Summary Options

One button in the fourth Report Wizard page is crucial but easy to overlook: the Summary Options button. Click this button to display the Summary Options dialog box, shown in Figure 45-6. This dialog box lists each of the numeric or currency fields included in your report's Detail section. As you can see in Figure 45-6, in the example report only the Price field (which has the Currency data type) qualifies as a summary field.

You can choose to have Access summarize the values in one or more of these fields for each group in the report. If you want a summary to appear in your report, simply check one or more of the summary value functions for the field that you want to summarize. Access can calculate the sum, average, minimum, or maximum value.

By selecting one of the Show options, you can specify whether the records within each group or only the summary information will be shown. In general, the first time you produce a report, you'll probably want to select Detail And Summary so that you can see clearly how Access is organizing the information. Later you might want to hide the detail information so that your report is more concise and contains fewer distractions. (You can do this by using Design view, described in "Modifying a Report," on page 1210.)

You can also select the Calculate Percent Of Total For Sums option to have Access calculate the percent of the grand total represented by each group's total. In the example report you could determine what percentage of the total cost of the inventory was contributed by each group of books. When you've finished setting the summary options, click the OK button to return to the fourth Report Wizard page.

Figure 45-9. In the seventh (and last) Report Wizard page, decide on a report name and choose how to open the report. The example report is named Books by Binding Type.

Figure 45-10 shows the example report, opened in Print Preview view. As is typical of a report generated by the Report Wizard, the field sizes and positions need some adjustment so that text isn't cut off. Also, the column headings would benefit from friendlier names. Figure 45-11 shows the same report, also opened in Print Preview view, after it has been modified slightly using Design view, which is discussed in the next section of the chapter.

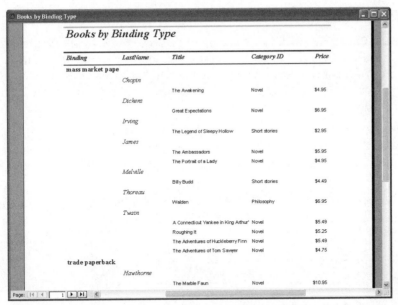

Figure 45-10. This report is the result of the Report Wizard choices shown in Figures 45-2 through 45-9.

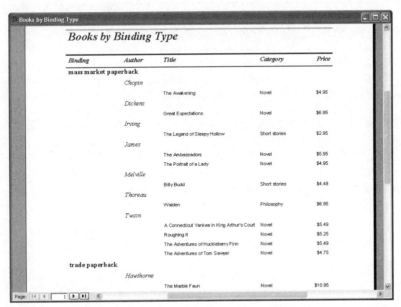

Figure 45-11. This is the report shown in Figure 45-10 after some minor customizations were made in Design view.

Modifying a Report

You can use Design view to design a new report that you created by selecting the Design View option in the New Report dialog box; to customize a new report that you created by selecting one of the Wizard or AutoReport options in the New Report dialog box; or to modify an existing report of any type. Design view lets you add, modify, or remove the controls that make up a report, work with report sections, and change the properties of the report itself.

To open a report in Design view, follow the instructions given in "Using the Database Window and Object Views," on page 1107. Figure 45-12 shows a report opened in Design view. In Figure 45-11 you can see how this report appears in Print Preview view.

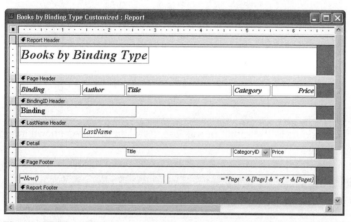

Figure 45-12. This report was created using the Report Wizard with the choices shown in Figures 45-2 through 45-10. It was then opened in Design view and slightly modified (headings were edited and control widths were adjusted).

As you can see in Figure 45-12, Design view for a report is essentially the same as Design view for a form. Like a form, a report consists of various controls added to different sections in Design view. In the example report, the controls in the Report Header and Page Header sections are all labels, which display constant values wherever they appear on the report. The controls in all the other sections are text boxes (except CategoryID, as explained in the following note).

> **Note** The CategoryID control in the example report's Detail section is a combo box control. The Report Wizard used a combo box rather than a text box because CategoryID in the Books table is a lookup field. When bound to a lookup field, a combo box displays the values from the related Categories table (Novel, Short Stories, and so on). A text box would display the field's actual contents, namely, the *identifiers* of the records in the related Categories table (1, 2, 3, and so on).

The controls in the BindingID Header, LastName Header, and Detail sections are bound to various fields in the report's record source, and, when the report is printed, they display the different values of the field. The two controls in the Page Footer section are calculated controls; that is, they display the results of the expressions that they contain. The left field displays the current day and date. The right field displays the current report page and the total number of pages in the report.

> For information on creating calculated fields, see the tip "Create a calculated control," on page 1189.

In Design view for a report, you work with controls and format the report using the same basic techniques you use in Design view for a form. For a description of these techniques, see "Customizing a Form," on page 1178, and "Formatting a Form," on page 1183. The following sections of the chapter cover several topics that apply specifically to reports.

Understanding Report Sections

As you can see in Figure 45-12, Design view divides the report into separate sections. The information defined within each section will appear at a specific position on the printed report. The Report Header information appears at the beginning of the first page, and the Report Footer information appears at the end of the last page. The contents of the Page Header section appear at the top of each page, and the contents of the Page Footer section appear at the bottom of each page.

If you chose to group the information in your report using one or more fields (in the second and third Report Wizard pages), there will also be a header section for each of these fields. And if you chose to calculate summary values for one or more fields (using the Summary Options button in the fourth Report Wizard page), there will be a footer section corresponding to each of the group header sections. The next section, "Controlling the Groupings," explains several ways to modify the group headers and footers in your report.

Chapter 45

Finally, the information in the Detail section is displayed for each detail record that is printed on the report. You can study Figures 45-13 and 45-14 to see where the different sections displayed in Design view will appear on a printed report. These figures show the printed appearance of the report opened in Design view in Figure 45-12.

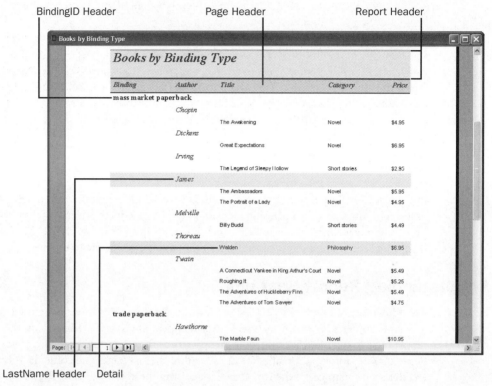

Figure 45-13. This report is based on the design shown in Figure 45-12 and shows the location of each of the report sections (except Page Footer) on the printed report.

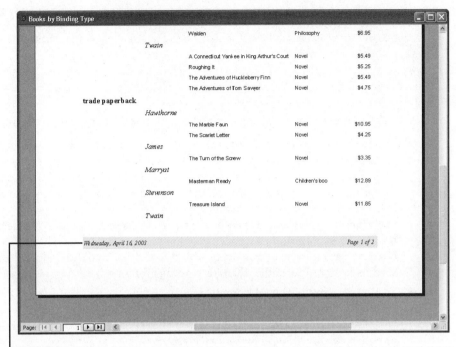

Page Footer

Figure 45-14. This report is based on the design shown in Figure 45-12 and shows the location of the Page Footer section on the printed report.

Controlling the Groupings

Sorting And Grouping

When a report is open in Design view, you can control the way the records in your report are grouped and sorted by choosing View, Sorting And Grouping or clicking the Sorting And Grouping toolbar button to display the Sorting And Grouping dialog box, shown in Figure 45-15.

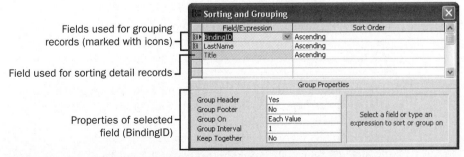

Fields used for grouping records (marked with icons)

Field used for sorting detail records

Properties of selected field (BindingID)

Figure 45-15. The Sorting And Grouping dialog box shown here contains the sorting and grouping settings for the example report.

> **Note** Figure 45-15 shows the sorting and grouping settings for the example report described in the previous sections. These options are the direct result of the choices that were made when the report was created using the Report Wizard—specifically, the choices made in the second, third, and fourth wizard pages, which are described in "Using the Report Wizard," on page 1201, and are shown in Figures 45-3 through 45-5.

In the Sorting And Grouping dialog box, you can do one or more of the following:

- To add another grouping level to the report, add a new field to an empty row in the Field/Expression column by selecting the field name in the drop-down list in that row. Then select a sorting order for the group in the Sort Order column. And, select Yes in the Group Header property box to display a header section for the group, or select Yes in the Group Footer property box to display a footer section for the group, or select Yes in both property boxes to display both a header and a footer section. The field will then be marked with a grouping icon. (If you don't select Yes in either of these two property boxes, the grouping icon won't appear next to the field and the field will be used for sorting detail records rather than for creating groupings.)

- To remove a grouping level from the report, click in the box to the left of the row containing the grouping field to select the entire row, and then press Delete. Note that this will remove the associated grouping section or sections from the report (header, footer, or both) *plus any fields contained in these sections.*

- The order in which the grouping fields are listed in the Sorting And Grouping dialog box is the order in which they are used to group records in your report. To change the grouping order, you can move a field in the list by clicking the box to the left of the field's row and then dragging the box up or down.

- To add or remove a field for sorting detail records in the report, use the same techniques, except be sure that No is selected in both the Group Header and the Group Footer property boxes. If more than one sorting field is listed, Access will sort detail records in the order in which these fields appear in the list; change this order if you want to change the sorting order.

- The Group On and Group Interval properties are important options that work together.

  For a grouping field, when the Group On property is set to Each Value (the most common setting), the report creates a new group for every distinct value of the grouping field. In this case the Group Interval setting has no effect. To change to a different grouping, select a new setting for the Group On property from the drop-down list. The available settings depend on the grouping field's data type. Then type a number in the Group Interval property box to quantify the Group On setting. For example, if the grouping field is numeric, you could select Interval in the Group On box and type 2 in the Group Interval box. As a result, the report would create a new group for every *other* distinct value, rather than for every distinct value.

As another example, if the grouping field is text, you could select Prefix Characters in the Group On box and then type 1 in the Group Interval box. This would create a group for all records in which the grouping field starts with *A*, another group for the *B*s, a third for the *C*s, and so on. To organize the information in smaller groups (*Aa*, *Ab*, *Ac*), you would type 2 in the Group Interval box.

● To ensure that a group—including the header, detail section, and footer—is always printed on the same page if possible, select the Whole Group setting in the Keep Together property box for the grouping field. Note that this setting tends to create blank space at the bottom of pages. By selecting the With First Detail setting, you can save paper and still ensure that the header is always printed on the same page with at least one of the following detail records. This avoids having a new header appear at the bottom of a page with no data below it. For either of these settings, if there isn't room on a page to fit what's requested (a whole group, or a header plus at least one detail record), Access will ignore the setting.

> **Tip Get help on properties**
> For some group properties, you can obtain detailed information by placing the insertion point within the property box in the Sorting And Grouping dialog box and pressing F1.

Chapter 45

You can also remove or add the Report Header and Report Footer sections, or the Page Header and Page Footer sections, by deselecting or selecting options on the View menu. To remove both the Report Header and the Report Footer sections, deselect the Report Header/Footer option on the View menu. Likewise, to remove both the Page Header and Page Footer, deselect the Page Header/Footer option. Note, however, that removing a header and footer in this way deletes any controls that they contain! (Access will ask for your confirmation first.) If you select one of these menu options again, the corresponding header and footer sections will reappear in Design view, but they will be empty of controls.

Previewing and Printing a Report

To preview your report's printed appearance, you can switch to either the Print Preview or Layout Preview view, using any of the methods discussed in "Using the Database Window and Object Views," on page 1107. To see the actual data that will print on the report, including all the report pages, switch to Print Preview view. To get a quick look at your report's general layout, you can switch to Layout Preview view, which shows only a sampling of the lines that will print. (Clicking the Preview button in the Database window opens the selected report in Print Preview view.)

> **Note** In addition to the general ways of switching to Print Preview view, if the report is open in Design view, you can open it in Print Preview by choosing File, Print Preview or by clicking the Print Preview toolbar button.

To set the margins, page orientation, paper source, column layout, and other page layout and printing settings, open the report in any view or select it in the Database window and choose

File, Page Setup to display the Page Setup dialog box (see Figure 45-16). (You can also display this dialog box, minus the Page tab, by clicking the Setup button in the Print dialog box just before you print, as described next.)

Figure 45-16. You can display the Page Setup dialog box for the selected or opened report by choosing File, Page Setup.

When you're ready to print your report, open it in any view or select it in the Database window, and then choose File, Print or press Ctrl+P to display the standard Print dialog box, which lets you select printer settings and print options. Or click the Print toolbar button to immediately print your report using default options.

Troubleshooting

Report includes blank pages

When you print your report, unwanted blank pages are included.

If your report is too wide for the paper size specified in the Page tab of the Page Setup dialog box (shown in Figure 45-16), your printer might produce an unwanted blank page after every printed page. Try reducing the width of the margins in the Margins tab of the Page Setup dialog box or switching to the Landscape orientation in the Page Tab of the same dialog box. If neither remedy works, change your report's layout in Design view to reduce its width.

If you're getting an unwanted blank page at the end of your report and you don't have information in your report footer, make sure that the footer height is set to zero. To do this, open the report in Design view, right-click the band for the Report Footer section, choose Properties from the shortcut menu, and in the Format tab of the ReportFooter property sheet, set the Height property to 0".

Part 8

FrontPage Fundamentals

46 FrontPage Fundamentals   1219

47 Managing Your Web Site with FrontPage   1239

48 Creating and Editing Web Pages   1279

49 Formatting Your Web Pages   1321

50 Adding Advanced Features to Your Web
    Pages and Working with Source Code   1363

FrontPage Fundamentals

A Rundown on FrontPage 1219   NEW FEATURE! Navigating in FrontPage 1233
Creating and Opening Web Sites 1221

A Rundown on FrontPage

Although most of the Microsoft Office 2003 Edition applications allow you to create Web pages and publish documents on the Web, the ultimate Office tool for Web publishing is Microsoft Office FrontPage 2003. FrontPage provides a set of site management tools that let you create, manage, and publish Web sites. It also includes a full-featured, integrated Web page editor. Here are some of the things you can do with the FrontPage Web site management tools:

- Quickly create an entire Web site using a template or wizard. Each template or wizard creates a set of coordinated and interlinked Web pages suitable for a particular purpose, such as establishing a corporate presence, conducting an online discussion, displaying personal information, managing a group project, or collaborating with your workgroup on a Web site that's based on Microsoft Windows SharePoint Services. The template or wizard formats the pages consistently and adds link bars, images, text, and other initial elements to get you started. FrontPage 2003 includes several new templates, known as *packages*, that you can use to create data-driven Web sites—an issue tracking site, a news and product review site, or a Web log—on a Web server running Windows SharePoint Services.

- Manage the folders and files in your Web site using an interface similar to Microsoft Windows Explorer.

- View reports that show the status of all files, shared content (such as stylistic themes), hyperlinks, Web components, and other constituents of your Web site; identify potential problems; and summarize the usage of a SharePoint team Web site (explained later in this chapter).

- Use graphic views of your Web site to visualize, modify, and verify the hyperlinks that tie the pages together and let users navigate through your site and explore other sites.

- Apply stylistic themes to your Web site. Each theme instantly applies consistent styling to the background, text, lists, page banners, link bars, and other elements within every page in your site.

- Manage your Web site projects by keeping a list of the tasks that each team member needs to perform. Assign files, categorize files, control the site's source files, and use other workgroup techniques.

- Open and edit a Web site directly on a Web server. Or work offline on a copy of your site stored on a local or network disk, and then publish your site to a Web server. Use FrontPage's new Remote Web Site view to copy and synchronize files between a local and a remote Web site.

The FrontPage site management tools are discussed primarily in this chapter and in Chapter 47, "Managing Your Web Site with FrontPage."

Here's a sample of how you can use FrontPage to create and edit Web pages:

- Modify and add content to the pages in your Web site or create new pages. You can get a head start in creating a new page by using a template or wizard that adds an initial set of elements to the page and formats these elements consistently. Some templates or wizards create pages suitable for specific uses, such as a bibliography, a feedback form, or a table of contents. Others generate frames pages with different patterns. (A frames page allows you to view several pages at once, each in a separate frame.)

- On a SharePoint team Web site, create a *Web part page*, which is a free-from Web page that you can quickly build by adding and customizing predefined components known as *Web parts*.

- Attach a page to a *dynamic template*, which provides content and formatting, restricts the areas where the page can be modified, and keeps the page up-to-date with template modifications. On a SharePoint team Web site, create a *Web part page*, which is a free-form Web page that you can quickly build by adding and customizing predefined components known as *Web parts*.

- Use the new layout tables and cells to quickly arrange and format the content on your pages. You can choose from a variety of predefined layout tables or draw your own.

- Add document libraries, lists, or other information components to a SharePoint team Web site.

- Add and format text, symbols, images (now including Shockwave Flash files), video clips, horizontal dividing lines, hyperlinks, tables, forms, frames, and other standard Web page elements.

- Precisely format Web page elements by modifying, creating, and using Cascading Style Sheet styles.

- Add Web components such as date and time stamps, comments, dynamic effects (such as animated *interactive buttons* that change when you click or point to them), forms for searching the site, spreadsheets or charts, hit counters, photo galleries, included files, link bars, tables of contents, site usage statistics, and controls that display information from Web sites such as MSN or Expedia.

- Add Java Applets, ActiveX controls, and other advanced Web page controls.

- Check the spelling in your pages and consult a thesaurus.

- Find or replace text. Search for and replace specific HTML (Hypertext Markup Language) elements. Save and reuse your search criteria.

- Preview your Web pages in one or more browsers or print them. Simulate different browser resolutions when designing or previewing a page.

- Work directly with your Web page's underlying HTML source code using the new Quick Tag Selector and other tools. Use FrontPage's enhanced source code editor to edit any type of source code file or other plain-text file.

Using FrontPage to create and edit Web pages is covered mainly in Chapter 48 through Chapter 50.

For a list of the new features included in FrontPage 2003, see "New FrontPage Features," on page 15.

Creating and Opening Web Sites

When you first run FrontPage (for example, by choosing Start, All Programs, Microsoft Office, Microsoft Office FrontPage 2003 in Microsoft Windows), it displays a new, empty Web page, as shown in Figure 46-1.

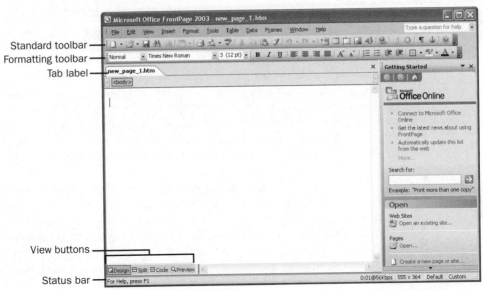

Figure 46-1. This figure shows the FrontPage window as it appears when you first start running the program.

> **Note** A *Web page* is a file in HTML format. A *Web browser*, such as Microsoft Internet Explorer, downloads and displays a Web page from a *Web server* program installed on a computer attached to the World Wide Web or to your company's intranet. A Web page usually has the .htm or .html file extension.

With the tools that are available when you first run FrontPage, you can use the program as a full-featured Web page editor. You can create new Web pages or open and edit existing pages using the techniques explained in Chapter 48, "Creating and Editing Web Pages." Each open page appears in a separate tab, and you can view a particular page by clicking its tab label (see Figure 46-1).

However, to use FrontPage's many Web site management and publishing tools and to gain access to all of FrontPage's Web page features (such as link bars and other Web components), you need to create a new FrontPage Web site or open an existing one. A FrontPage Web site consists of a home page (stored in a file named Index.htm or Default.htm); other Web pages that are accessed from the home page; as well as image, multimedia, document, and other types of files that the Web pages display. A FrontPage Web site also includes support folders and files that FrontPage uses for managing the site.

When a Web site is open in FrontPage, the program interface includes a Web Site tab, which provides access to the Web site management and publishing tools, in addition to a tab for each open Web page (or other type of file). The Web Site tab is described in "Navigating in FrontPage," near the end of the chapter.

Chapter 46

Creating a Web Site Offline or Online

You can create or open a FrontPage Web site that's stored on a local or network disk location. In this case, you access the Web site using its file path. When your site is ready to view, you can use FrontPage's Web site publishing feature to copy the site to the Web server that will be used to deliver your site to the World Wide Web or to your company's intranet. FrontPage 2003 now lets you publish directly to Web servers that use the FTP (File Transfer Protocol) or DAV (Distributed Authoring and Versioning) protocol, as well as servers that have the Microsoft FrontPage Server Extensions or Windows SharePoint Services or that are on a local or network disk. This is the best way to create a FrontPage Web site if your server is maintained by a separate Internet service provider or Web hosting company or if you connect to it using a dial-up connection. Working on a Web site stored on a disk location is faster, saves you connect time, and provides you with a complete backup copy of the Web site in case something happens to the site's files on the server. Also, while you modify an existing page, visitors to your site can continue to view the original version of the page on the server, and you won't have to worry about them seeing a page that's "under construction."

> FrontPage's Web site publishing feature is discussed in Chapter 47, "Managing Your Web Site with FrontPage."

Alternatively, you can create or open a FrontPage Web site that's stored directly on the Web server computer used to deliver your site to the Web or intranet, provided that the Web server has the FrontPage Server Extensions or Windows SharePoint Services. In this case you access the Web site in FrontPage using the site's URL (Uniform Resource Locator) and the HTTP protocol (Hypertext Transfer Protocol, normally used for delivering Web pages to browsers). This is a good way to create a Web site if you have a fast, full-time connection to the server and you're confident that the site's files are being backed up routinely on the server. This method also makes it fast to test Web components, such as hit counters, that function only when the Web site is delivered from a Web server (and not just opened in the browser from a disk). Finally, this approach lets you easily use FrontPage's workgroup features to collaborate on building the site with your coworkers.

Whether it's on a disk or a server location, a Frontpage Web site is stored in a specially marked folder that contains—in addition to the site's pages and other files you create—a set of subfolders (such as _vti_cnf and _vti_pvt) and files that FrontPage creates to allow it to manage the site. In Windows Explorer, a folder used to store a FrontPage Web site is marked with a globe icon (see Figure 46-2).

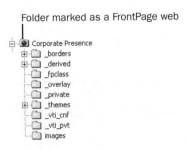

Figure 46-2. This figure shows a folder on a local disk that stores a FrontPage Web site named Corporate Presence, as viewed in Windows Explorer.

To create a new Web site, perform the following steps:

1 Open the Web Site Templates dialog box using one of the following methods:

■ Choose File, New to display the New task pane, shown in Figure 46-3. Then click the More Web Site Templates command in the New Web Site area of the task pane.

■ Click the down-arrow on the Create A New Normal Page button at the left end of the Standard toolbar and choose Web Site from the drop-down menu, as shown here:

Note You can open the Web Site Templates dialog box by clicking *any* of the commands in the New Web Site area of the New task pane. The commands differ only in the tab of the Web Site Templates dialog box they initially display or in the template they initially select.

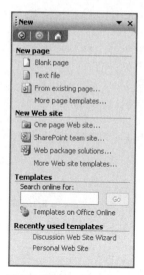

Figure 46-3. You can use the New Page Or Web Site task pane to create a new Web site or a new Web page.

NEW FEATURE!

Tip To find, download, and use an online FrontPage template from the Office Online Web site, use the controls in the Templates area of the New task pane. Either enter a keyword into the Search Online For text box and click the Go button, or click Templates On Office Online to run your browser and open the Templates home page of the Office Online site.

For information on using Microsoft's expanded collection of online templates and wizards and on using the new Template Help task pane available in Office 2003 applications, see "Downloading and Using Templates from Office Online," on page 55.

Both of these methods display the Web Site Templates dialog box, shown in Figure 46-4.

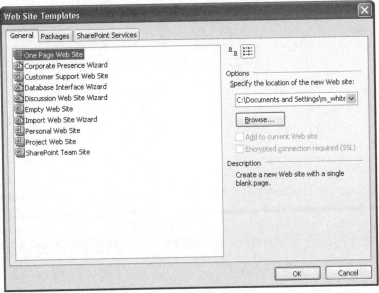

Figure 46-4. The Web Site Templates dialog box allows you to create a Web site based on a template.

2   Select a Web Site template or wizard from the General or Packages tab in the Web Site Templates dialog box, as described in Table 46-1.

> **Tip** You can quickly reuse a Web site template by clicking its name in the Recently Used Templates area near the bottom of the New task pane, rather than performing steps 1 and 2. FrontPage will immediately open the Web Site Templates dialog box and select the template, so that you can enter the site's location and specify other options. Keep in mind that the Recently Used Templates area lists both Web site templates and Web page templates.

3   Type the location where you want to create your new Web site into the Specify The Location Of The New Web Site text box in the Web Site Templates dialog box.

> **Note**   If you enter into the Specify The Location Of The New Web Site text box a folder that's already designated as a FrontPage Web site, when you click the OK button, FrontPage will display an error message and won't let you overwrite the existing site.
>
> If you want to add the content supplied by a template or wizard to an existing Web site (you will be asked whether you want to overwrite any existing file that has the same name as a file supplied by the template or wizard), open that site before displaying the Web Site Templates dialog box. Then, in the Web Site Templates dialog box, check the Add To Current Web Site option rather than entering a location into the Specify The Location Of The New Web Site text box.

To store your Web site on a local or network disk location, enter the full path of the folder where you want to save it. To store your Web site directly on a Web server (one that has appropriate Microsoft server extensions), enter the full URL of the folder where you want to post your site. Keep in mind that when you create a new Web site, you specify only the *folder* where the site's files are stored, *not* a specific file. If the folder you enter doesn't exist, FrontPage will create it.

> **Note** If you enter into the Specify The Location Of The New Web Site text box the URL of a secure site that uses the SSL (Secure Sockets Layer) protocol, check the Encrypted Connection Required (SSL) option. (When connecting to this type of site, your URL will begin with *https://* rather than *http://*.)

You can click the Browse button to locate and open an existing folder using the New Web Site Location dialog box, which is similar to the standard Open dialog box and lets you navigate to and open a folder on a disk or Web site. When you click the Open button in the New Web Site Location dialog box, you'll be returned to the Web Site Templates dialog box and the folder you opened will be entered into the Specify The Location Of The New Web Site text box. If you want FrontPage to create a new subfolder within that folder for storing your new Web site, you need to type the folder name at the end of the path or URL in the text box.

4 Click the OK button in the Web Site Templates dialog box.

Table 46-1. Creating a New Web Site by Selecting a Template in the Web Site Templates Dialog Box

To Create This Type of Web Site	Select This Template or Wizard (in This Tab of the Web Site Templates Dialog Box)
A Web site consisting initially of a single, blank page. You can later add content to this page and create additional pages as described in the following chapters.	One Page Web Site (General)
A Web site that provides information and services for your customers, including pages for describing products, catalogs, or manuals, or for presenting frequently asked questions (FAQs); pages that allow customers to request service or leave suggestions; and a support forum. This template is designed primarily for software companies.	Customer Support Web Site (General)
A Web site that initially contains no pages, so that you can create your own pages (using the page templates of your choice) as described in the following chapters.	Empty Web Site (General)
A Web site built from a set of existing Web pages or other files located on a local or network disk or on a Web site.	Import Web Site Wizard (General)

Table 46-1. Creating a New Web Site by Selecting a Template in the Web Site Templates Dialog Box

To Create This Type of Web Site	Select This Template or Wizard (in This Tab of the Web Site Templates Dialog Box)
A custom team Web site on a server running Windows SharePoint Services. (See "Customizing and Creating SharePoint Team Web Sites," on page 1231.)	SharePoint Team Site (General)
A Web site for yourself, including pages for providing information about yourself and your interests, for listing links to your favorite Web sites, for displaying photos, and for obtaining feedback from visitors (using a form).	Personal Web Site (General)
A Web site for managing a group project, including pages containing a membership roster, a schedule, a file archive, a site search feature, a discussion forum, and contact information.	Project Web Site (General)
A Web site that allows visitors to view and update data in a database on the Web server.	Database Interface Wizard (General)
A Web site for managing an online discussion group, including a table of contents, threads, and a search feature.	Discussion Web Wizard (General)
A general-purpose corporate Web site, including a table of contents, forms for searching the site or providing feedback, and pages for presenting news and describing products and services.	Corporate Presence Wizard (General)
NEW FEATURE! An issue-tracking Web site on a Web server that is running Windows SharePoint Services, including a report feature and a document library.	Issue Tracker (Packages)
NEW FEATURE! A news Web site on a Web server that is running Windows SharePoint Services, including features for reviews, previews, discussions, and voting.	News And Reviews Site (Packages)
NEW FEATURE! A Web log ("blog") site on a Web server that is running Windows SharePoint Services, including features for searching the site, listing hot topics and links, and conducting discussions.	Web Log (Packages)

Chapter 46

Selecting a template or wizard other than One Page Web Site or Empty Web Site will create a new Web site that includes an initial set of pages. (One Page Web Site creates only a single, blank, unformatted page.) These pages will be given consistent formatting (by applying a theme, as explained later) and will include hyperlinks that let visitors navigate through the pages, as well as page banners, headings, tables, text, horizontal dividing lines, lists, and other initial elements that are appropriate for the particular type of Web site that the template or wizard creates. A wizard, such as the Corporate Presence Wizard, asks a series of questions and customizes the Web site according to your choices. A template immediately generates the Web site without customization.

Tip How to use subsites

If you create a new Web site in a subfolder of a folder that's already designated as a FrontPage Web site, your new site is termed a *subsite*.

Another way to create a subsite is to right-click the name of an existing subfolder within a Web site folder (in the FrontPage Folder List or in the Folders view of the Web Site tab, described later in this chapter) and choose Convert To Web from the shortcut menu. FrontPage will then convert the subfolder to a Web site by adding the special folders and files that it uses to manage the site. It will also mark the subfolder with a globe icon to indicate that it's a FrontPage Web site folder and not just a regular file folder.

Rather than creating a single huge FrontPage Web site, it might be better to place some of the site's content into one or more subsites. You can separately open each subsite, which will be small and fast to work with. If you publish the main Web site (as described in Chapter 47), you can publish any subsites it contains at the same time. If you've opened a Web site that contains a subsite, you can open the subsite in a separate FrontPage window by simply double-clicking the subsite folder in the FrontPage Folder List or Folders view.

After you close the Web Site Templates dialog box, and after the wizard has finished (if you chose one), your new Web site will be opened in FrontPage. If you create a new Web site while an existing site is open, the new site will be displayed in a separate top-level FrontPage window. You can now modify the initial pages in the Web site, add or delete pages, and customize your site in other ways using the techniques given in the following sections and chapters. Figure 46-5 shows the home page (index.htm) of a new Web site created using the Personal Web Site template, ready for your customizations.

Tip Change a Web site's name

The name of a Web site is actually the name of the folder that contains the site's files and subfolders. You can change the Web site's name by choosing Tools, Site Settings, and entering a new name into the Web Name text box in the General tab of the Site Settings dialog box. Note that this will change the name of the folder in which the Web site is stored as well as the site's name displayed in FrontPage. The FrontPage title bar, as well as many of the FrontPage views, identifies the Web site by displaying the full file path (such as C:\Web Sites\Personal) or the full Web address (such as *http://www.example.net/personal*) of the folder where the site's files are stored. Note, however, that you can't change the name of a Web site that contains a subsite.

Figure 46-5. This figure shows the home page of a new Web site created using the Personal Web Site template.

> **Tip** Delete a Web site with caution
>
> If you want to delete the current FrontPage Web site, open the Folder List, if it isn't already visible, by choosing View, Folder List (see Figure 46-5). Then, in the Folder List, right-click the top-level folder (in Figure 46-5, that would be C:\Web Sites\Personal Site), and select Delete from the shortcut menu. FrontPage will then display a Confirm Delete dialog box that lets you choose whether to delete all the files belonging to the Web site, to delete only the files that FrontPage uses to maintain the site (leaving the pages, graphics files, and other files and subfolders that contain the actual site content and converting the folder to a regular file folder), or to cancel the deletion. Keep in mind that if you select one of the deletion options, the change will be permanent, and you won't be able to restore the deleted files or folders (unless you have made backup copies, which is always a good idea). FrontPage doesn't place these files and folders in the Recycle Bin folder.

If you want to open a Web site in FrontPage—either one you created previously or a FrontPage Web site from another source that you want to modify—perform the following steps:

1 Choose File, Open Site. (Resist the temptation to choose File, Open, which will open an individual file, not a Web site.) Or click the down-arrow on the Open button on the Standard toolbar and choose Open Site from the drop-down menu, shown here:

Either method displays the Open Site dialog box, shown in Figure 46-7.

Note To modify a Web page or Web site that wasn't created in FrontPage, rather than opening the site directly in FrontPage, you need to select the Import Web Site Wizard in the General tab of the Web Site Templates dialog box, as explained previously in this section.

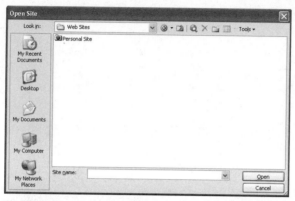

Figure 46-6. You can open an existing FrontPage Web site using the Open Site dialog box.

2 Select the folder in the Open Site dialog box (which works like the standard Open dialog box displayed in Office applications) using one of the following methods:

- Open the Web site folder in the Open Site dialog box so that its contents are displayed.

- Open the folder that contains the Web site folder and then click the Web site folder in the dialog box to select it.

- Enter the full path or URL of the Web site folder into the Site Name text box.

You can select a folder on a local or network disk, or on a Web or intranet site that has appropriate Microsoft server extensions (as discussed earlier in the chapter).

3 Click the Open button.

Tip You can quickly reopen a Web site that you recently had open by choosing the site's name from the File, Recent Sites submenu. You can also open a recently opened Web site by clicking its name in the Web Sites area of the Getting Started task pane. (Clicking the More command in this area is another way to display the Open Site dialog box.)

Note When you restart FrontPage, it will reopen the Web site that was opened when you last quit the program, if any, if the Open Last Web Site Automatically When FrontPage Starts option is checked. You can find this option by choosing Tools, Options, clicking the General tab, and looking in the Startup area (see Figure 46-7).

Chapter 46

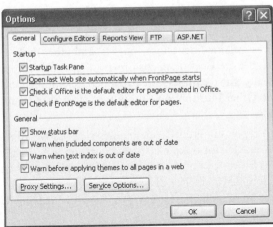

Figure 46-7. The General tab of the Options dialog box lets you select startup and general FrontPage options.

Customizing and Creating SharePoint Team Web Sites

A Web server on which the Windows SharePoint Services server extensions are installed can host one or more *team Web sites*. A team Web site provides collaboration features that allow workgroups to share documents, exchange information, and work together on projects. These features are described in Chapter 8, "Using Windows SharePoint Services in Professional Workgroups."

> Chapter 8 explains how to access a team Web site from Office applications or from a browser. It also describes how to make routine modifications to the site when accessing it in a browser.

Because a team Web site is actually a FrontPage Web site, you can modify it extensively using FrontPage.

To modify a team Web site in FrontPage, perform the following main steps:

1 Follow the general steps given in the previous section for opening a FrontPage Web site. In the Open Site dialog box, type the site's full URL into the Site Name text box and click the Open button. Alternatively, if you have created a shortcut to the site in your My Network Places folder, you can select that shortcut in the Open Site dialog box and click the Open button.

2 Manage the site, apply a theme, modify the Web pages in other ways, or create new Web pages using any of the general FrontPage techniques given in this part of the book.

In addition, you can use the following FrontPage features, which are available only when you work on a Web site that resides on a server running Windows SharePoint Services:

- You can add new custom document libraries, lists, and other types of information components to the site, or you can customize information components that are already on the site. The techniques are explained in "Adding Document Libraries, Lists, and Other Information Components to a SharePoint Team Web Site," on page 1243.

- You can view usage reports in FrontPage's Reports view (provided that usage reporting has been enabled for the site). These reports provide usage summaries and page hit counts for various time periods; list the operating systems, browsers, and referring domains and URLs of site visitors; and display other statistics. For information on using the Reports view, see "Viewing Web Site Reports," on page 1265.

- You can insert and customize a predesigned form for adding, editing, or displaying items in a document library, list, or other component by choosing Insert, Form, List Form. For general information on working with forms, see "Creating Interactive Forms to Collect Information," on page 1363.

- You can add a new, custom Web part page to the site. A Web part page consists of a matrix of content areas, known as *zones*, in which you can insert predefined components called *Web parts*. Web part pages are explained in "Creating a Web Part Page on a SharePoint Team Web Site" on page 1286.

You can also create a new team Web site on a server running Windows SharePoint Services as a nested Web site (subsite) within an existing team Web site. To do this, follow the general instructions for creating a new Web site given in the previous section. However, in the Web Site Templates dialog box, do the following:

1. Select one of the templates for creating a SharePoint team Web site, as follows:
   - To create a general-purpose team Web site, select the SharePoint Team Site template in the General tab.

   - To create a more specialized team Web site, select one of the templates in the Packages tab. These templates are described in Table 46-1.

2. In the Specify The Location Of The New Web Site box, type the full URL of an existing team Web site, followed by the name of the folder where you want to store the new subsite you're creating. For instance, if a team Web site is set up at *http://www.example.com* and you want to create a subsite that's stored in a folder named *Research*, you would type **http://www.example.com/Research**. FrontPage would then create the new subfolder and make it a subsite of the existing Web site without overwriting or disturbing the existing site.

> **Note** When you create a new team Web site, you must create it directly on the Web server using the server's URL. You can't create it at a disk location and later publish it to the server.

3. Customize your site, as explained in step 2 of the previous procedure (see Figure 46-8).

Tab labels

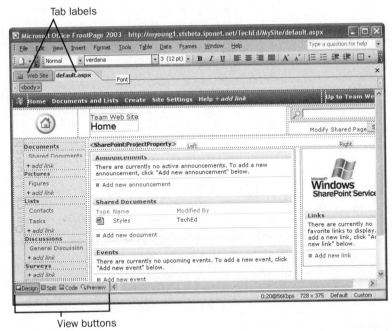

View buttons

Figure 46-8. This figure shows the home page of a newly created team Web site opened in FrontPage.

 Note In Office 2003 you can also create highly specialized subsites of a SharePoint team Web site known as *document workspaces* and *meeting workspaces*. Document workspaces are discussed in "Sharing Documents Using a Document Workspace," on page 190, and meeting workspaces are covered in "Creating and Linking to a SharePoint Meeting Work-space," on page 1039.

Navigating in FrontPage

 In FrontPage 2003, accessing the specific tools you want to work with is now a two-step process:

1 Open the tab that corresponds to the general task you want to accomplish. You open a tab by clicking its tab label at the top of the working area of the FrontPage window:

■ FrontPage provides a tab for each open Web page or other file. To work on the page or file, click the corresponding tab label. See Figure 46-9.

■ When a Web site is open, FrontPage also provides the Web Site tab. To access the Web site management and publishing tools, click the Web Site tab label. See Figure 46-10.

Chapter 46

Tab labels

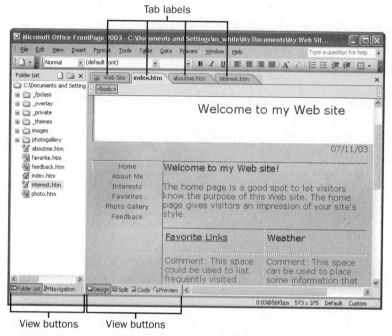

View buttons   View buttons

Figure 46-9. In this figure, the tab for a Web page (index.htm) has been opened and Design view activated.

Tab labels

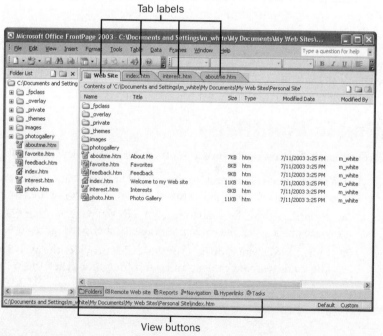

View buttons

Figure 46-10. In this figure, the Web Site tab has been opened and Folders view activated.

Chapter 46

2   Activate the required view of the tab by clicking one of the view buttons displayed at the bottom of the tab:

- If you've opened a tab for working on a Web page, you can choose one of the views described in Table 46-2. You can see the view buttons in Figure 46-10. (If you've opened a text file that isn't a Web page, only one view will be available and you won't see view buttons.)

- If you've opened the Web Site tab, you can choose one of the views explained in Table 46-3. You can see the view buttons in Figure 46-10.

> **Note**   As mentioned previously in the chapter, you can display the Folder List in a pane at the left of the FrontPage window by choosing View, Folder List (see Figure 46-9 or 46-10). The Folder List lets you see and work with your Web site's folders and files while you're working in any tab. (Details on using the Folder List are given in the next chapter.) When the tab for a Web page or other file has been opened, you can click the Navigation view button at the bottom of the Folder List to display a compact version of the Navigation view of your Web site in the left pane (this view is explained in Table 46-3). You can click the Folder List view button at the bottom of the left pane to restore the Folder List. Also, you can use the Toggle Pane button on the Standard toolbar to toggle the left pane on or off, or—by opening the button's drop-down menu and choosing a command—to switch between the left pane's Folder List and Navigation views.

An alternative way to activate one of the views available in the Web Site tab is to choose the view name from the View menu, as shown here:

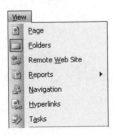

To open Reports view from the View menu, you have to choose a specific report name from the Reports submenu. Note that the View, Page command redisplays your most recently displayed Web page or other file.

The available toolbar buttons and menu items change according to the currently active view, so that you can choose only the commands appropriate for each view. All the views are discussed in greater detail in the chapters that follow.

Table 46-2. The Views Available in a Tab Displaying a Web Page

View	Description and Purpose	Discussed in
Design	A WYSIWYG view that allows you to edit a Web page as it appears in a Web browser.	Chapter 48, "Creating and Editing Web Pages," Chapter 49, "Formatting Your Web Pages," and Chapter 50, "Adding Advanced Features to Your Web Pages and Working with Source Code"
Code	Allows you to view and edit the underlying HTML source code for a Web page.	"Directly Editing Source Code Files," on page 1384
Split	Displays the Design view of the page in one pane and the Code view in another pane.	"Directly Editing Source Code Files," on page 1384
Preview	Renders the page almost as if it were opened in a Web browser.	"Previewing and Printing Your Page," on page 1317

Table 46-3. The Views Available in the Web Site Tab

View	Description and Purpose	Discussed in
Folders	Shows all the Web site's folders and the site's files contained in these folders. This view lets you work with the folders and files using commands similar to those of Windows Explorer.	"Working with Your Web Site's Folders and Files," on page 1239
Remote Web Site	Allows you to exchange and synchronize files between the opened FrontPage Web site and a remote Web site. This task pane is most commonly used to publish (that is, copy) a Web site stored on disk to a Web server. (This view replaces the Publish Web dialog box found in previous FrontPage versions.)	"Publishing Your Web Site," on page 1273
Reports	Displays a variety of different reports, which show the status of all files, shared content (such as themes), hyperlinks, Web components, and other constituents of your Web site; identify potential problems; and summarize the usage of a SharePoint team Web site	"Viewing Web Site Reports," on page 1265

Table 46-3. The Views Available in the Web Site Tab

View	Description and Purpose	Discussed in
Navigation	Graphically displays and allows you to modify the hierarchical navigation structure used by the link bars in your Web pages. Link bars allow visitors to move from page to page.	"Using Navigation View," on page 1255
Hyperlinks	Graphically displays information about all the hyperlinks in your Web pages and lets you check the integrity of those hyperlinks.	"Using Hyperlinks View," on page 1260
Tasks	Lets you manage tasks that you and other members of your workgroup need to perform to create or maintain the current Web site.	"Managing Your Web Site Projects," on page 1262

Managing Your Web Site with FrontPage

Working with Your Web Site's Folders
and Files 1239

Setting Up Your Web Site's
Navigation Structure 1254

Managing Your Web Site Projects 1262

Viewing Web Site Reports 1265

NEW FEATURE! Publishing Your Web Site 1273

Working with Your Web Site's Folders and Files

To work with the files that make up the current FrontPage Web site, as well as the folders that contain these files, start by performing the following two steps:

1 If the Folder List doesn't appear at the left of the FrontPage window, open it by choosing View, Folder List or by pressing Alt+F1.

2 Activate Folders view by clicking the Web Site tab label at the top of the working area of the FrontPage window and then clicking the Folders view button at the bottom of the tab.

> **Note** Although you can work with the folders and files in your Web site by using either the Folder List or Folders view by itself, the most powerful way to manage your folders and files is to have both of these tools open simultaneously. When the Folder List and Folders view are both displayed, they work together to provide much of the functionality offered by Windows Explorer.
>
> Keep in mind that you can display the Folder List while you have any other tab or view open in FrontPage, giving you somewhat limited but readily available access to your Web site's folders and files.

The files contained in a FrontPage Web site include Web pages (HTML files) as well as the graphics, multimedia, and other types of files that the Web pages display.

> **Tip** Use FrontPage, not Windows Explorer, to manage your Web site files
>
> You *could* use Windows Explorer to manage your Web site's files and folders. However, it's much better to use FrontPage to perform all file management tasks, such as moving, renaming, or importing folders and files, because FrontPage maintains information on the current contents of the Web site and performs automatic tasks to keep your Web site files synchronized. For example, if you use Windows Explorer to move or rename a file that's the target of a hyperlink, the hyperlink will no longer work. In contrast, if you work with files and folders using FrontPage's Folder List or Folders view, FrontPage will automatically modify hyperlinks as necessary so that they continue to function.

Figure 47-1 shows a Web site with both the Folder List visible and Folders view activated. The Folder List shows a simple hierarchical list of the Web site folders and the files in each folder. You can expand or collapse a branch of the hierarchy by clicking the box that displays the plus (+) or minus (–) symbol. The FrontPage Folder List works much like the Folders pane that you can optionally display at the left of the Windows Explorer window (although unlike Windows Explorer, the Folder List in FrontPage also displays the names of the files in each folder).

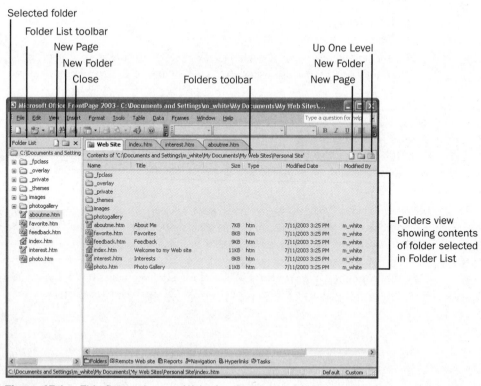

Figure 47-1. This figure shows a Web site that was created using the Personal Web Site template.

Folders view shows the contents of only a single folder at a time (both the files and the subfolders in the folder). However, it displays much more information for each file—the name, title, size, file type, date and time of the last modification, modification author, and file comments. Folders view resembles the right pane of Windows Explorer in Details view.

> **Tip** You can change the title of or add comments to a file that appears in the Folder List or Folders view by right-clicking the filename, choosing Properties from the shortcut menu, and then clicking the General tab to change the title or clicking the Summary tab to add comments.

The easiest way to work with the files in a particular folder is to first locate and click the name of the folder in the Folder List; this will select the folder in that list. Folders view will then open that folder and show a detailed list of the files and subfolders in the folder.

> **Note** Although it's more difficult than using the Folder List, you can use Folders view alone to navigate to a particular folder. To open a subfolder that appears in Folders view, double-click it. To open the next folder up in the hierarchy—if any—click the Up One Level button on the Folders toolbar. Note that FrontPage doesn't let you view the contents of folders that are higher in your file system hierarchy than the root folder for your Web site. (Forget about using FrontPage as a replacement for Windows Explorer!)

In Folders view, you can sort the file list using the values in a particular column by clicking the button-like heading at the top of that column. Each click toggles between an ascending and a descending sort. (You can use this same technique to sort the task list in Tasks view, which is explained later in this chapter.)

 Troubleshooting

Some Web site folders aren't listed

Quite a few of the Web site folders that you can see in Windows Explorer, such as _derived, _fpclass, and _overlay, don't appear in FrontPage.

If the Show Hidden Files And Folders option isn't checked, in the Folder List and in Folders view FrontPage shows only the Web site folders containing the files that you work directly with in creating and modifying your site. It hides the folders containing the files that it uses internally for managing the site. The folders it hides are marked as hidden folders in the file system. Therefore, you can see them in Windows Explorer only if you've chosen to view hidden files and folders in Windows.

If, however, the Show Hidden Files And Folders option is checked, FrontPage shows most of the hidden folders and the files they contain. (Some folders are still hidden; for example, _derived, _vti_cnf, and _vti_pvt.) To access the Show Hidden Files And Folders option, choose Tools, Site Settings and click the Advanced tab.

Working with Folders

In the Folder List or in Folders view, you can create, delete, rename, move, or copy folders using the same basic methods as in Windows Explorer. The commands for performing these operations are summarized in Table 47-1. Unless otherwise specified, you can use a technique in either the Folder List or in Folders view. (See Figure 47-1.) To "select" a folder means to click the folder's name so that it's highlighted. To "open" a folder means to display the folder's contents (this applies to Folders view only). The bulleted items in the right column represent alternative methods—use whichever one you prefer. You'll need to select a specific folder before using some of these commands.

Table 47-1. Techniques for Working with Web Site Folders in FrontPage's Folder List or Folders View

To Do This with Web Site Folders	Perform This Action
Create a new folder	● Select a folder in the Folder List and then click the New Folder button on the Folder List toolbar at the top of the list. The new folder will be made a subfolder of the selected one.
	● Open a folder in Folders view and then click the New Folder button on the Folders toolbar. The new folder will be made a subfolder of the opened one.
	● Select a folder in the Folder List or open it in Folders view, click the down arrow on the Create A New Normal Page button at the left end of the Standard toolbar, and choose Folder from the drop-down menu, shown here:

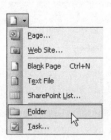

The new folder will be made a subfolder of the selected or opened folder.

● Right-click a blank area in the Folder List or in Folders view and choose New, Folder from the shortcut menu. The new folder will be made a subfolder of the folder that is selected in the Folder List (if you right-clicked there) or opened in Folders view (if you right-clicked there).

Table 47-1. Techniques for Working with Web Site Folders in FrontPage's Folder List or Folders View

To Do This with Web Site Folders	Perform This Action
Delete a folder	● Right-click the folder name and choose Delete from the shortcut menu.
	● Select the folder and press Delete.
Rename a folder	● Right-click the folder name and choose Rename from the shortcut menu.
	● Select the folder and press F2.
Move (or copy) a folder	● Select the folder and choose Edit, Cut (or Copy). Then, specify the destination folder and choose Edit, Paste. You can specify the destination folder either by selecting the folder in the Folder List, or by opening the folder in Folders view.
	● Use the Cut (or Copy) and Paste toolbar buttons in the same way.
	● Use the Ctrl+X (Cut) or Ctrl+C (Copy) and the Ctrl+V (Paste) shortcut keys in the same way.
	● Use the mouse to drag the folder to the destination folder. (To copy the folder, press Ctrl while you drag.)

 Inside Out

Be careful when deleting in FrontPage

Use caution when deleting a Web site, a Web site folder, or a file in FrontPage. Although FrontPage asks for confirmation before deleting one of these items, for some reason, it deletes the item permanently and *doesn't* put it in your Recycle Bin. You therefore won't be able to recover a deleted Web site, folder, or file (unless you've made a backup copy, which is always a good idea!).

Adding Document Libraries, Lists, and Other Information Components to a SharePoint Team Web Site

If you are using FrontPage to modify a team Web site on a server running Microsoft Windows SharePoint Services—or if you've created a new team Web site—you can add new information components to the Web site. The types of information components you can add are document libraries, picture libraries, form libraries, lists (links, announcements, contacts, events, tasks, issues, or custom lists), discussion boards, and surveys. Adding one of these components creates a new folder in your Web site that contains a set of default Web pages used to display, create, and modify the information items stored in the component. For a library type information component—document, picture, or form—this folder also stores the files and subfolders that belong to the library.

For general information on Windows SharePoint Services and a description of the different types of SharePoint information components, see Chapter 8, "Using Windows SharePoint Services in Professional Workgroups." For an overview of the techniques for customizing and creating SharePoint team Web sites in FrontPage, see "Customizing and Creating SharePoint Team Web Sites," on page 1231.

To create any of the types of information components mentioned, perform these basic steps:

1 In the Folder List, select the folder in which you want to create the folder for your new information component. The new folder will be a subfolder of the folder you select.

2 Click the down arrow on the Create A New Normal Page button at the left end of the Standard toolbar and then choose SharePoint List from the drop-down menu, shown here:

Then, in the SharePoint List dialog box, click the tab for the type of information component you want to create, as follows:

■ To create a document library, picture library, or form library, click the Document Libraries tab, shown in Figure 47-2.

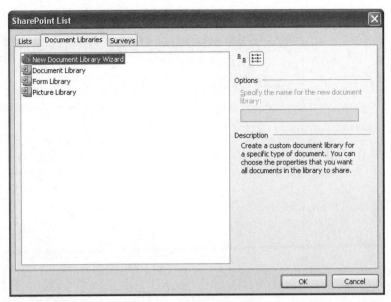

Figure 47-2. You create a new document library, picture library, or form library using the Document Libraries tab of the SharePoint List dialog box.

■ To create a list (a links, announcements, contacts, events, tasks, or custom list) or a discussion board, click the Lists tab, shown in Figure 47-3.

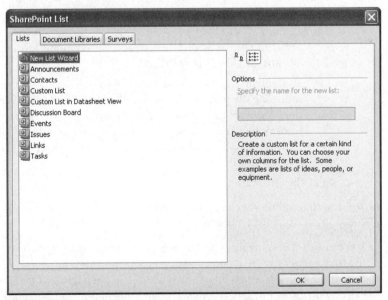

Figure 47-3. You create a new list or discussion board using the Lists tab of the SharePoint List dialog box.

- To create a survey, click the Surveys tab, shown in Figure 47-4.

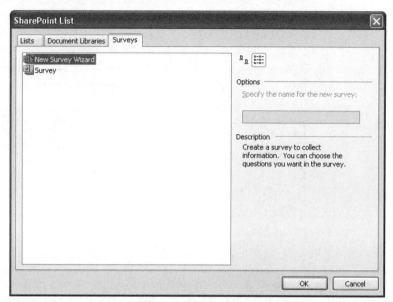

Figure 47-4. You create a new survey using the Surveys tab of the Share-Point List dialog box.

3 In the Document Libraries, Lists, or Surveys tab of the SharePoint List dialog box, do one of the following:

- To use a wizard to create a customized information component, select the wizard at the beginning of the list—New Document Library Wizard, New List Wizard, or New Survey Wizard.

- To immediately create a particular type of list, choose one of the templates listed following the wizard. Notice that the SharePoint List dialog box displays a description of the wizard or template you select. Then, type a name for the new information component in the text box on the right (which is labeled according to the type of list you're creating, for example, Specify The Name For The New Document Library).

4 Click the OK button.

You can then modify the supporting Web pages in the folder for your new information component using the techniques given in this part of the book.

You can also change many of the features of the new information component by right-clicking the folder used to store it and choosing Properties from the shortcut menu to display the Properties dialog box (as shown in Figure 47-5). Keep in mind that you can also modify an existing document library or other type of information component on a SharePoint team Web site by changing its properties in the same way. The specific properties you can view or set depend on the type of the information component. The following properties are some of the most common:

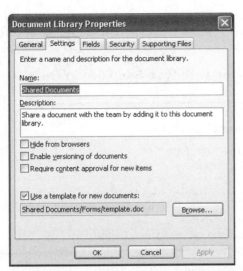

Figure 47-5. You can view or modify the properties of a document library by using the Document Library Properties dialog box.

- The folder permissions (for example, whether scripts can be run) in the General tab
- The name and description of the information component in the Settings tab
- The fields—that is, properties—that all items in the component will have (for example, ID, Title, Modified, and Created) in the Fields tab
- The component's security settings (which items users can read and which items users can edit) in the Security tab
- The names and locations of the component's supporting Web pages (for example, the default Web page used to view the information, and the Web pages containing the forms for displaying, creating, or editing items) in the Supporting Files tab

Note In FrontPage, when you have opened a Web page that's located on a SharePoint team Web site, you can insert a custom form that can be used to display, create, or edit items in a particular document library or other type of information component that's located on the same site. To do this, place the insertion point at the position in the page where you want to locate the form and then choose Insert, Form, List Form. For general information on working with forms, see "Creating Interactive Forms to Collect Information," on page 1363.

Working with Files

You can also use Windows Explorer methods in the Folder List or in Folders view to select, delete, rename, move, copy, or open Web site files. Table 47-2 summarizes the commands for performing these operations. Unless otherwise specified, you can use a technique in either the Folder List or in Folders view. (See Figure 47-1.) To "select" a file means to click the filename so that it's highlighted. To "open" a folder means to display the folder's contents (this applies to Folders view only). The bulleted items in the right column represent alternative methods—use whichever one you prefer. You will need to select a specific file before using some of these commands.

Table 47-2. Techniques for Working with Web Site Files in FrontPage's Folder List or Folders View

To Do This with Web Site Files	Perform This Action
Select all files in the folder that's currently open in Folders view	Choose Edit, Select All. Press Ctrl+A.
Delete a file	Right-click the filename and choose Delete from the shortcut menu. Select the file and press Delete.
Rename a file	Right-click the filename and choose Rename from the shortcut menu. Select the file and press F2.
Move (or copy) a file	Select the file and choose Edit, Cut (or Copy). Then, specify the destination folder and choose Edit, Paste. You can specify the destination folder either by clicking the folder name in the Folder List, or by opening the folder in Folders view. Use the Cut (or Copy) and Paste toolbar buttons in the same way. Use the Ctrl+X (Cut) or Ctrl+C (Copy) and the Ctrl+V (Paste) shortcut keys in the same way. Use the mouse to drag the file to the new location. (To copy the file, press Ctrl while you drag.)
Open a file using the default editor	Double-click the filename. Right-click the filename and choose Open from the shortcut menu. Select the file and press Enter.

Table 47-2. Techniques for Working with Web Site Files in FrontPage's Folder List or Folders View

To Do This with Web Site Files	Perform This Action

Open a file using a specific editor	Inventory.xml Inventory.xml 2KB xml 7/
	  Open
	  Open With ►
	    1 FrontPage (Open as XML)
	    2 FrontPage (Open as Text)
	  Open in New Window
	    3 Notepad
	  New From Existing Page
	    4 FrontPage (Open as HTML)
	  Preview in Browser
	    Choose Program...
	  Cut
	  Copy
	  Paste
	  Set as Home Page
	  Rename
	  Delete
	  Publish Selected Files...
	  Don't Publish
	  Properties...

Create a new Web page	See the instructions given in "Creating a New Web Page," on page 1279.
Create a new text file	See the instructions in "Directly Editing Source Code Files," on page 1384.

If you move a file that is the target of one or more hyperlinks in your Web site's pages, FrontPage updates the hyperlinks so that they point to the correct location. Likewise, if you move a graphics file, FrontPage updates all image elements in the Web site's pages that display the image.

As indicated in Table 47-2, you can open a file using either the default editor or a different editor program that you specify. You can change the default editor for a specific file type (as identified by its filename extension), or add a new file type and default editor, by choosing Tools, Options and clicking the Configure Editors tab, shown in Figure 47-6.

> **Note**   If no default editor is designated in FrontPage for a particular file type, when you double-click a file of that type (or use a comparable opening method), FrontPage will open the file using the program—if any—that's registered in Windows to open the file type. If no program is registered in Windows to open the file type, FrontPage will display the Open With dialog box to let you select a program.

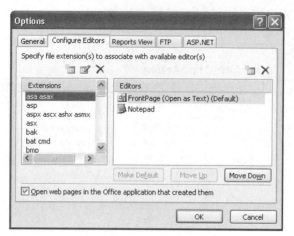

Figure 47-6. In the Configure Editors tab of the Options dialog box you can designate which programs open different types of Web site files.

If the Open Web Pages In The Office Application That Created Them option is checked in the Configure Editors tab, FrontPage will open a Web page that is marked as having been created in another Microsoft Office application by using that Office application. If this option isn't checked, FrontPage will open all Web pages using the designated default editor (which for most types of Web pages is, of course, FrontPage itself).

Note that for some types of plain-text files, you can open them in FrontPage in more than one way. For example, you can open an XML (*.xml*) file in FrontPage either "as XML" or "as text." In either case, the file is opened for editing in an editing tab. In the first case, however, FrontPage provides special tools for working with XML (such as the XML View toolbar), while in the second case, it provides only basic text editing tools.

> For a discussion on using FrontPage to directly edit source code files and other plain text files, see "Directly Editing Source Code Files," on page 1384.

Importing Web Site Files and Folders

In addition to creating Web site files and folders within FrontPage, you can also import them from local or network disk locations or from the Internet. Importing files is especially important if you've been using another program to create Web pages, graphics files, or other Web site files and you now want to make those files part of a FrontPage Web site. Be sure to use one of the importing techniques discussed here rather than using Windows Explorer to copy files into one of your site's folders; doing this will ensure that FrontPage is properly apprised of the files you're adding to the site.

To import one or more files, or folders together with the files they contain, into the currently open Web site, perform the following steps:

1   In the Folder List, select the folder in which you want to store the file(s) or folder(s) you're importing.

2 Choose File, Import to display the Import dialog box (shown in Figure 47-7).

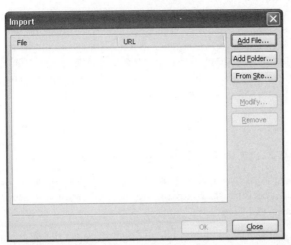

Figure 47-7. The Import dialog box allows you to import files or folders into a Web site.

3 To the list in the Import dialog box (known as the import list) add each of the files or folders that you want to import, as follows:

- To add one or more individual files from a local or network disk location or from the Internet, click the Add File button and select one or more files in the Add File To Import List dialog box.

- To add a folder—plus all the files it contains—from a local or network disk location (but not from the Internet), click the Add Folder button and select the folder in the File Open dialog box.

When all files or folders you want to import appear in the list in the Import dialog box, click the OK button. FrontPage will make a *copy* of the imported folders or files, leaving the originals intact.

> **Note** If a Web site isn't open when you choose the File, Import command, FrontPage will run the Import Web Site Wizard rather than display the Import dialog box. You can also run this wizard by clicking the From Site button in the Import dialog box, or by selecting the Import Web Site Wizard item in the General tab of the Web Site Templates dialog box, which is discussed in "Creating and Opening Web Sites," on page 1221.
>
> The Import Web Site Wizard lets you import one or more files from an existing Web site or from a file folder on a local or network disk. If you import from a Web site, you can specify the server type (for example, FrontPage Server Extensions Or Windows SharePoint Services or FTP). You can import the files to the currently open FrontPage Web site (if any), to another existing FrontPage Web site, or to a new FrontPage Web site. When the wizard finishes running, it turns over control to the new Remote Web Site view, which you can use to select the specific files you want to import into your Web site. (The Remote Web Site view is discussed in "Publishing Your Web Site," on page 1273.)

Chapter 47

1251

> **Tip** Use dragging to import
>
> Another way to import a file or folder into your Web site is to drag it from Windows Explorer, and then drop it on the destination folder in the FrontPage Folder List. The file will be *copied* into the Web site folder. (Unlike copying a file to a folder displayed in Microsoft Internet Explorer, you don't need to press Ctrl to make a copy.) If the FrontPage window is hidden when you start dragging the file or folder, hold the pointer over the FrontPage button on the Windows taskbar until the FrontPage window appears, and then complete the drag operation.

Importing a Web Page and Its Graphics Files

To import a Web page into the current Web site, including all or most of the graphics files that appear on the page, perform the following steps, whether you are importing from a disk location or Internet address.

1   Choose File, Open and in the Open File dialog box, select the Web page you want to import and click the Open button. You can select a Web page on a local or network disk or on a Web site or other Internet location. FrontPage will now open the page in a tab for editing.

   If the page is on a Web server with the Microsoft FrontPage Server extensions, FrontPage will display a message box asking for a user name and password. You can click the Cancel button in that message box and then click the Yes button when FrontPage asks if you want to open a read-only copy of the page.

> **Note** If the Web page you open was created in an Office application other than FrontPage, it might be opened in the creating application. You can open these Web pages in FrontPage, provided that the format of the Web page is one for which FrontPage is designated as the default editor. By default, FrontPage is designated as the default editor for standard Web page (*.htm*, *.html*, and so on) files. However, by default FrontPage is not designated as the default editor for a Single File Web Page (*.mht*) file (you can create these files in other Office 2003 applications, such as Microsoft Word and Microsoft Excel). If you wish, you can designate FrontPage as the default editor for any type of Web page using the method explained in "Working with Files," earlier in the chapter.
>
> To have FrontPage open any type of Web page for which it is the default editor—even if that page was created in another Office application—choose Tools, Options, click the Configure Editors tab, and clear the Open Web Pages In The Office Application That Created Them option (see Figure 47-6).

2   Choose File, Save As and in the Save As dialog box, save the page in the current Web site folder or in one of its subfolders. (If you save the file outside the Web site folder, it won't become part of the current Web site.) Click the Change Title button if you want to give the imported copy of the page a different title.

When you click the Save button in the Save As dialog box, if the imported page contains one or more embedded images, FrontPage will display the Save Embedded Files dialog box (see Figure 47-8). For each of the graphics files displayed by the page, this dialog box lets you choose whether or not to save a local copy of the file in one of the folders in your Web site. (If you choose not to save a local copy, the page will reference the original copy of the graphics file, which must be accessible for the image to appear.) FrontPage will adjust the image references in the page according to your choices in the Save Embedded Files dialog box.

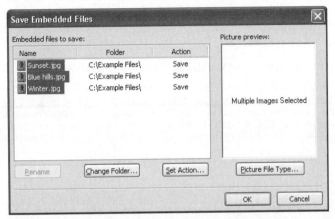

Figure 47-8. The Save Embedded Files dialog box lets you choose whether to save local copies of the files for embedded images.

This procedure makes a *copy* of imported page and graphics files, leaving the originals intact.

Troubleshooting

Graphics files not saved

You used the technique presented in this section to import a Web page. However, FrontPage didn't save copies of all the graphics files within your Web site.

When you use this technique, FrontPage saves only graphics files that are located within the same domain and that are referenced using relative paths. An image is displayed using the HTML IMG element, and the location of the graphics file is assigned to the SRC attribute of this element. FrontPage, for example, will save a graphics file for an IMG element where SRC is set to /library/images/curve.gif, but it won't save a graphics file for an IMG element where SRC is set to *http://www.example.com/library/images/arrow.gif*.

You can manually save any graphics file by opening the page in Internet Explorer, right-clicking the image, choosing Save Picture As, and selecting a folder within your Web site. (Other browsers should have similar commands.)

Working with Imported Web Site Files

After you import a Web page into your Web site, you can modify it in FrontPage using the techniques described in the chapters in this part of the book. You can provide hyperlinks to the imported page to make it an integral part of the Web site and to allow visitors to access the page. (You can provide hyperlinks to the imported page either by manually inserting hyperlinks into other pages in the Web site or by adding the imported page to the navigation structure maintained in Navigation view, as explained later in this chapter.) To make the imported page look like other pages in your Web site, you'll need to explicitly apply the Web site's theme (if any) to that page. And if the site uses shared borders and you want them to appear in the imported page, you'll need to explicitly include the default shared borders by choosing Format, Shared Borders.

If you import an image file, you can display the image within any of your Web site pages.

For details on applying Web site themes, see "Using Themes to Quickly Change the Overall Page Format," on page 1353. For information on shared borders, see "Working With Shared Borders," on page 1313. For details on importing and using graphics, see "Inserting Images," on page 1300.

Inside Out

Use the Save As command instead of the Export command to save a page with graphics

You can export a file from a Web site to a location outside the site by selecting the file in the Folder List or in Folders view, choosing the File, Export command, and selecting a target folder in the Export Selected As dialog box. This will make a copy of the file in the target directory, leaving the file in your Web site intact. (You can export only a single file at a time using this method.) If, however, the page contains embedded images, FrontPage exports only the page itself and not the graphics files referenced by the image elements.

A better way to export a page that contains images is to open the page for editing in FrontPage. Then choose File, Save As and select the target location in the Save As dialog box. When you click the Save button, FrontPage will display the Save Embedded Files dialog box, which lets you export any or all of the graphics files referenced by the page, in addition to the page itself. Keep in mind, however, that if you then edit the page and use the normal Save command, your changes will be saved to the *exported copy* of the page, *not* the copy of the page within the Web site. To open the Web site's copy, close the current page and then reopen the page from the file within the site.

Setting Up Your Web Site's Navigation Structure

FrontPage provides two views that let you work with the hyperlinks in the Web pages of your FrontPage Web site: Navigation and Hyperlinks. The following sections explain how to use each of these views to examine and modify hyperlinks.

> "Viewing, Verifying, and Repairing Hyperlinks," on page 1270, shows how to work with hyperlinks using the Hyperlinks report that you can display in FrontPage's Reports view. For information on manually adding hyperlinks to a Web page, see "Including Internal and External Hyperlinks," on page 1306.

> **Note**   A hyperlink can be either internal or external. An *internal* hyperlink links to a location within the current Web site—either to a different location in the current page, or to a different page or file stored in the site. An *external* hyperlink links to a location outside the current Web site—for example, to a page on the World Wide Web.
>
> Note that FrontPage sometimes uses the word *hyperlink* to refer to an *embedded image* (an HTML IMG element) in a Web page, which displays the contents of a graphics file in the page. However, unless otherwise stated, in this book *hyperlink* refers only to a true hyperlink element, which opens and displays a different file or a different part of the current page.

Using Navigation View

Navigation view lets you visualize and modify the Web site's *navigation structure* (see Figure 47-9). You open Navigation view by clicking the Web Site tab label at the top of the working area of the FrontPage window and then clicking the Navigation view button at the bottom of the tab.

The navigation structure is a hierarchical arrangement of the pages in the Web site that controls the way *link bars* within the site's pages work. Specifically, it controls the functioning of all link bars that are of the type "Bar based on navigation structure". A link bar of this type contains a set of automatically generated hyperlinks that let the visitor navigate to other pages in the Web site. In this type of link bar, you don't have to manually add links and specify their target locations. Rather, you simply assign the link bar a property such as Same Level or Back And Next (as described later in this section, and shown in Figure 47-11), and FrontPage automatically generates the links required to navigate to other pages according to the Web site's navigation structure. For example, the Favorites page (favorite.htm) generated by the Personal Web Site template contains a link bar with the Same Level property. Using the navigation structure (shown in Figure 47-9) as a map, FrontPage generates links to the About Me, Interests, Favorites, Photo Gallery, and Feedback pages. (It also adds a link to the Welcome To My Web Site home page because the link bar's Home Page property is checked.)

Navigation toolbar

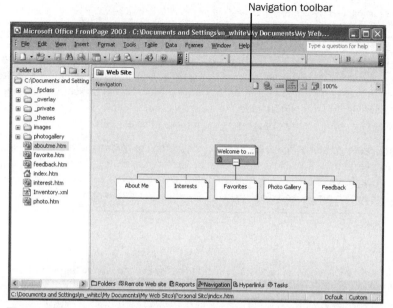

Figure 47-9. In this figure, Navigation view shows the navigation structure of a Web site created by using the Personal Web Site template.

Note You can also create *custom* link bars with the "Bar with custom links" type or the "Bar with back and next links" type. These types aren't affected by the Web site's navigation structure. Rather, you have to add links manually, specifying the target location of each link. The links you have added to a custom link bar also appear in Navigation view; however, these links are shown in an area that's completely separate from the Web site's navigation structure.

Custom link bars aren't covered in this book. In this section, the term *link bar* is used to refer specifically to the "Bar based on navigation structure" type.

The pages created by a Web site wizard or template, such as Corporate Presence Wizard or Personal Web Site, typically contain link bars that are based on the navigation structure, and the Web site's pages are added to the navigation structure. By changing the Web site's navigation structure, you can immediately change the targets of all affected link bars in the pages without having to edit each page and adjust individual hyperlinks.

You can add a link bar based on the navigation structure to any page by performing the following steps.

1 Open the page for editing and place the insertion point at the position in the page where you want to insert the link bar.

Opening pages is discussed in "Opening an Existing Web Page," on page 1288.

2 Choose Insert, Navigation. This will open the Insert Web Component dialog box and select the Link Bars component in the Component Type list.

3 In the Choose A Bar Type list, select the Bar Based On Navigation Structure type (shown in Figure 47-10), and click the Next button.

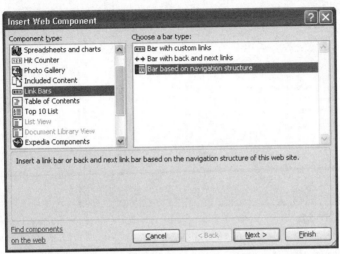

Figure 47-10. This figure shows the selections for inserting a link bar that's based on the navigation structure.

In the next two Insert Web Component dialog boxes that appear, select the link bar's style and orientation, and then click the Finish button. FrontPage will now display the General tab of the Link Bar Properties dialog box, which lets you set properties that specify the part of the navigation structure that FrontPage uses to generate the links on the link bar (see Figure 47-11).

Chapter 47

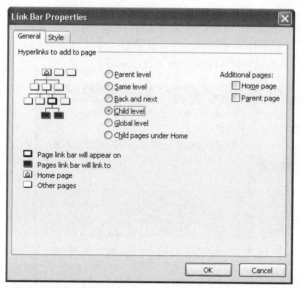

Figure 47-11. The General tab of the Link Bar Properties dialog box lets you select the part of the Web site's navigation structure that the link bar will link to.

For general information on inserting Web components, see "Adding Dynamic Content with Web Components," on page 1374.

4 Add the page to the Web site's navigation structure, if the page isn't already shown in Navigation view, as explained in the remainder of this section.

Note You can have FrontPage add link bars to the top, left, or right shared border when you set up shared borders, as explained in "Working with Shared Borders," on page 1313.

Tip Customize link bar labels
You can modify the default labels that appear in link bars for links that navigate to the home page, the parent page, the previous page, or the next page. To do this, choose Tools, Site Settings and click the Navigation tab.

You can collapse or expand a branch of the navigation hierarchy displayed in Navigation view by clicking the box that displays the (–) or (+) symbol at the top of that branch.

You can also adjust the display by right-clicking a blank spot in Navigation view and choosing Zoom, Portrait/Landscape, or Expand All from the shortcut menu shown here:

Or, for a page that isn't at the top of the hierarchy, you can right-click in the page and choose View Subtree Only from the shortcut menu to display only that page plus all its "descendant" pages below it in the hierarchy. To show the full hierarchy again, click the View All button that will appear above the subtree.

You can also perform any of the shortcut menu actions that were described—except Expand All—by clicking equivalent buttons on the Navigation toolbar, shown in Figure 47-12.

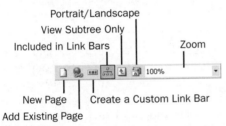

Figure 47-12. The Navigation toolbar allows you to perform many of the same actions as the Navigation view shortcut menu.

To change the position of a particular page in the navigation structure, simply drag it to the new position. You can add a page to the structure (perhaps a new page you added to the Web site) by dragging it from the Folder List to the desired position in the structure. (If the Folder List isn't visible, choose View, Folder List or press Alt+F1.) As you drag a page, temporary lines show the effect of dropping it at each position.

> **Caution** Make sure that the Included In Link Bars option is enabled for all pages in the navigation hierarchy. If this option is disabled, both link bars and page banners on the page are hidden. (The option is enabled by default for all of the pages that a Web site template or wizard adds to a new Web site.) You can enable or disable this option by selecting a page in Navigation view and then clicking the Included In Link Bars button on the Navigation toolbar. Alternatively, you can right-click a page and choose Included In Link Bars from the shortcut menu.

> **Note** Many of the Web site templates and wizards also add a FrontPage component known as a *page banner* to each page. A page banner displays the page's title in a decorative box at the top of the page, but only if the page is included in the Web site's navigation structure shown in Navigation view and if the Included In Link Bars option is selected for that page. (Page banners are discussed in "Adding Dynamic Content with Web Components," on page 1374.)

To remove a page from the navigation structure, click it to select it and press Delete, or right-click it and choose Delete from the shortcut menu. Then, if prompted, select Remove Page From The Navigation Structure. (Note that selecting the other option, Delete This Page From The Web Site, deletes the actual Web page file in addition to removing the page from the hierarchy.) Once you remove a page from the navigation structure, it will no longer be the target of link bars in other pages, and any link bar or page banner that it contains will be hidden.

> **Tip** Apply your navigation structure changes
>
> FrontPage might not immediately implement a change that you make to the navigation structure. To force it to immediately apply your change or changes to all affected pages in the Web site, right-click a blank spot in Navigation view and choose Apply Changes from the shortcut menu.

In Navigation view, you can also change a page's title by selecting the page and pressing F2, or by right-clicking it and choosing Rename from the shortcut menu. (The title appears on the browser's title bar, on the page banner—if the page has one—and in various views in FrontPage.) You can open a page in a tab for editing by double-clicking it. Finally, you can undo or redo many actions that you performed in Navigation view by choosing Edit, Undo or Edit, Redo.

> **Tip** View the Web site's navigation structure while you edit a Web page
>
> When you have a page open in a tab for editing, you can view and work with the Web site's navigation structure by displaying the Navigation pane. To display it, select the View, Navigation Pane menu option. If the Folder List was previously displayed, the Navigation Pane will replace it. (You can switch back and forth between the two panes by clicking the Folder List or the Navigation button at the bottom of the pane.) Although the Navigation pane doesn't provide as many features for working with the navigation structure as Navigation view, you can modify the view or change certain features of the navigation structure by right-clicking a file or a blank area in the pane and choosing commands from the shortcut menu. You can also rearrange the hierarchy by using the mouse to drag the pages.

Using Hyperlinks View

Hyperlinks view graphically displays all the hyperlinks in your Web pages: those in link bars, as well as individual hyperlinks that a template or wizard included in your pages or that you added yourself (see Figure 47-13). You open Hyperlinks view by clicking the Web Site tab label at the top of the working area of the FrontPage window and then clicking the Hyperlinks view button at the bottom of the tab.

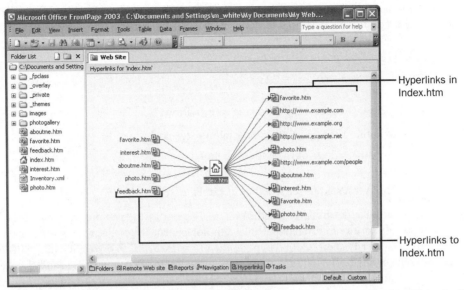

Figure 47-13. In this figure, Hyperlinks view shows the initial hyperlinks in a Web site that was created using the Personal Web Site template.

When you click a Web site file in the Folder List to select it, it appears in the center of Hyperlinks view. (You can also display a file in the center by right-clicking its name in Hyperlinks view and choosing Move To Center from the shortcut menu.) Hyperlinks view graphically shows all files containing hyperlinks *to* the central page (to the left of that page) and the targets of all hyperlinks *in* the page (to the right of that page). You can display more or less information in Hyperlinks view by clicking the plus (+) or minus (–) box next to the name (or title) of a file.

To modify the way hyperlinks are displayed, right-click a blank spot in Hyperlinks view to display the following shortcut menu:

Then choose a command to select or deselect an option, as follows:

- To display the title of each page rather than its filename, select Show Page Titles.
- To show the graphics files referenced by embedded images (IMG elements), as well as true hyperlinks, select Hyperlinks To Pictures.
- If a page contains more than one hyperlink to a single target, to show all these hyperlinks, select Repeated Hyperlinks.

Chapter 47

If you use the mouse to point to a file or target site to the left or right of the central file, FrontPage displays additional information about the hyperlink in a ScreenTip, as shown here:

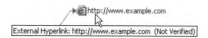

The ScreenTip displays the following information:

- Whether the hyperlink is internal or external
- The full address of the hyperlink target
- An indication if the hyperlink is *broken* (its target cannot be found) or if it's *not verified* (not yet tested to see whether its target exists)

An external hyperlink is marked as *not verified* until you explicitly verify it. (FrontPage automatically verifies internal hyperlinks, but not external ones, because doing so can take a long time.) To verify an unverified hyperlink, or to retest a *broken* or verified hyperlink, right-click the file or site to the left or right of the central file in Hyperlinks view, and choose Verify Hyperlink from the shortcut menu. FrontPage will then attempt to open the target file. If it finds the target, it removes the *not verified* tag from the ScreenTip. If it doesn't find the target, it tags the hyperlink as *broken* in the ScreenTip and also adds a break to the line that extends to the hyperlink target in Hyperlinks view.

 Tip Halt a long process

Verifying external hyperlinks or embedded images can take a long time because it requires connecting with one or more other Web servers. If you want to halt the process, click the Stop button on the Standard toolbar. You can also click the Stop button to halt other potentially lengthy operations, such as importing files into your Web site.

You can repair a broken hyperlink by opening the page that contains it and then editing the hyperlink. (You can open any file or Web site that appears in Hyperlinks view by double-clicking it.) Also, you can efficiently repair all broken hyperlinks in the Web site by using the Hyperlinks report.

For information on editing hyperlinks, see "Including Internal and External Hyperlinks," on page 1306. For details on using the Hyperlinks report, see "Viewing, Verifying, and Repairing Hyperlinks," on page 1270.

Managing Your Web Site Projects

You can use Tasks view to manage tasks that you or your co-workers must complete to finish or to maintain a FrontPage Web site (see Figure 47-14). You open Tasks view by clicking the Web Site tab label at the top of the working area of the FrontPage window and then clicking the Tasks view button at the bottom of the tab.

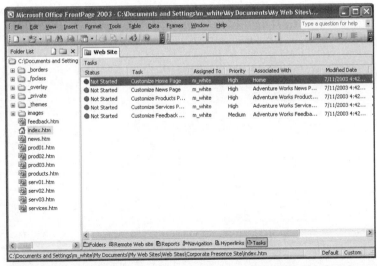

Figure 47-14. In this figure, Tasks view shows the tasks that the Corporate Presence Wizard adds to a new Web site.

Sometimes FrontPage automatically adds tasks to the list in Tasks view to inform you of unfinished jobs you need to complete. For example, if you create a new Web site using the Corporate Presence Wizard, FrontPage adds tasks to show you where you need to customize the site. Also, if you use FrontPage to find or replace text or to check the spelling in your pages, you can have it add a task for each page that contains matching text or misspellings.

For information on finding and replacing text, see "Finding and Replacing Text in Your Web Pages," on page 1293. For information on checking your spelling, see "Proofing Text in Your Web Pages," on page 1297.

In any FrontPage view, you can manually add a task to the list in Tasks view by clicking the down arrow next to the Create A New Normal Page button at the left end of the Standard toolbar and choosing Task from the drop-down menu shown here:

In Tasks view, you can also create a new task by right-clicking a blank area in the view and choosing Add Task from the shortcut menu. Then, define the new task by filling in the New Task dialog box that FrontPage displays (see Figure 47-15).

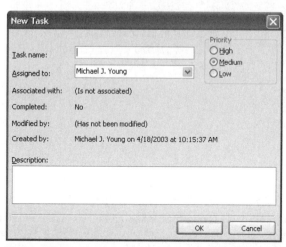

Figure 47-15. You can manually add a new task by defining it in the New Task dialog box.

If completing a task requires you to work with a particular file in your Web site, you can create a new task that is associated with that file. You can do this by first selecting the file's name in the Folder List and then opening the New Task dialog box by choosing the Tasks command from the Create A New Normal Page drop-down menu, as described previously. The filename of the associated file will appear in the New Task dialog box, and the title or filename will appear in Tasks view in the Associated With column. (In Figure 47-14, notice that all of the tasks added by the wizard are associated with files.)

When a task is associated with a file, you can open that file by selecting the task in Tasks view and then choosing Edit, Tasks, Start Task. Alternately, you can right-click the task and choose Start Task from the shortcut menu. FrontPage will open the file in the same way that it opens a file you double-click in the Folder List, as explained in "Working with Files," on page 1247.

To modify a task, double-click it in Tasks view, or right-click it and choose Edit Task from the shortcut menu, or select it and press Enter. FrontPage will open it in the Task Details dialog box, which has the same layout as the New Task dialog box shown in Figure 47-15. You can then change the task name, the person who is assigned the task, the task's priority, and its description. Also, clicking the Start Task button in the Task Details dialog box provides another way to open the file associated with the task, if there is one.

When you have finished a task, you can change its status from Not Started to Completed (and change the dot to the left of the task from red to green) by selecting the task in Tasks view and then choosing Edit, Tasks, Mark Complete. Or, you can right-click the task and choose Mark Complete from the shortcut menu. (Once you've marked a task as completed, you can't change that designation.)

To delete a task, right-click it and choose Delete Task from the shortcut menu, or select it and press Delete. To display all tasks that you haven't deleted, select the Edit, Tasks, Show History menu option. Or, right-click a blank spot in Tasks view and select the Show History option on the shortcut menu. Unless this option is selected, completed tasks will be hidden (although not until you close and reopen the Web site, press F5, or deselect the Show History menu option).

Viewing Web Site Reports

Reports view allows you to display a variety of different reports that provide detailed information on the files, problems, and workflow status of your Web site, and—if the Web site is on a server running Windows SharePoint Services—statistics on the site's usage. You can use this information to get an overview of the contents of your Web site; to spot potential problems, such as pages that load slowly, broken hyperlinks, and malfunctioning FrontPage components; and to ascertain the number of visitors your Web site is receiving and which pages are most popular. Figure 47-16 shows Reports view displaying the Site Summary report.

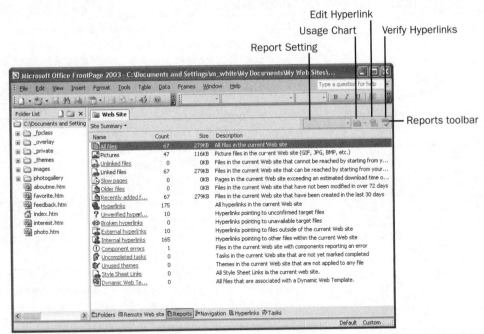

Figure 47-16. This figure shows the Site Summary report in FrontPage Reports view. This Web site was created using the Personal Web Site template.

To display a particular report, activate Reports view by clicking the Web Site tab label at the top of the working area of the FrontPage window and then clicking the Reports view button at the bottom of the tab. Then, select the particular report you want to see from the drop-down

Chapter 47

menu at the left end of the Reports toolbar (the menu button is labeled with the name of the currently displayed report, such as Site Summary):

Alternatively, in any FrontPage view you can choose the particular report you want to see from the View, Reports submenu. This will activate Reports view and show the selected report. The available reports are briefly described in Table 47-3.

Table 47-3. The Reports You Can Display in Reports View

Report	Description
Site Summary	Displays the total numbers (and total sizes, where applicable) of files, pictures (embedded images), unlinked files, linked files, slow pages, older files, recently added files, hyperlinks, and other elements in your Web site.
Files Category	
All Files	Lists all the pages, graphics files, and other types of files in your Web site. For each file, it gives the name, title, folder location, size, type, modification date, author, comments, and—if available—the total number of page hits.
Recently Added Files	Lists the Web site files that have been created within the number of days currently selected in the Report Setting drop-down list on the Reporting toolbar (ranging from 1 to 365 days).
Recently Changed Files	Lists the Web site files that have been modified within the number of days currently selected in the Report Setting drop-down list on the Reporting toolbar (ranging from 1 to 365 days).
Older Files	Lists the Web site files that have not been modified within the number of days currently selected in the Report Setting drop-down list on the Reporting toolbar (ranging from 0 to 365 days).
Shared Content Category	
Dynamic Web Templates	Lists the Web pages in your Web site, and for each page gives the name of any dynamic Web-page template that's attached to the page. For information on dynamic Web-page templates, see "Working with Dynamic Templates," on page 1284.

Table 47-3. The Reports You Can Display in Reports View

Report	Description
Shared Borders	Lists the Web pages in your Web site, and for each page indicates any shared borders assigned to the page—Top, Left, Bottom, or Right. For information on shared borders, see "Working with Shared Borders," on page 1313.
Style Sheet Links	Lists the Web pages in your Web site, and for each page gives the filename of any external cascading style sheet (CSS) linked to the page. For information on cascading style sheets, see "Modifying, Creating, and Using Cascading Style Sheet Styles," on page 1358.
Themes	Lists the Web pages in your Web site, and for each page gives the name of any theme attached to the page, as well as the current theme settings (that is, whether or not the page has vivid colors, active graphics, or a background picture). For information on themes, see "Using Themes to Quickly Change the Overall Page Format," on page 1353.
Problems Category	
Unlinked Files	Lists any Web site files that cannot be opened by starting from the home page and following hyperlinks.
Slow Pages	Lists any pages in the Web site that have an estimated download time greater than the time selected in the Report Setting drop-down list on the Reporting toolbar (ranging from 0 to 600 seconds). In calculating the download times, FrontPage by default assumes a connection speed of 56 Kbps. To change the assumed speed, choose Tools, Options, click the Reports View tab, and select a new speed in the Assume Connection Speed Of drop-down list.
Hyperlinks	Lists all individual hyperlinks in your Web site, or optionally just the external and broken internal hyperlinks, indicating the status of each. For more information, see the next section, "Viewing, Verifying and Repairing Hyperlinks."
Component Errors	Lists any Web site files that contain Web components that are reporting errors. (If your Web site is stored on a disk location, this list will include Web components, such as hit counters, that won't function until your site is published to a Web server.) Web components are discussed in "Adding Dynamic Content with Web Components," on page 1374.

Chapter 47

1267

Table 47-3. **The Reports You Can Display in Reports View**

Report	Description
Workflow Category	
Review Status	Displays the current review status of each file in the Web site, indicating whether the file has been reviewed, and if so, the result of that review. You can assign a review status to a file by selecting the filename in the Folder List, choosing File, Properties, clicking the Workgroup tab, and selecting an item in the Review Status drop-down list box. (The default choices for status are Approved, Denied, and Pending Review.)
Assigned To	Displays, for each file in your Web site, the name of the person in your workgroup who has been assigned the responsibility for completing the file. You can assign a file to a person by selecting the filename in the Folder List, choosing File, Properties, clicking the Workgroup tab, and typing or selecting the person's name in the Assigned To box.
Categories	Displays the category of each file in your Web site. You can assign one or more categories to a file by selecting the filename in the Folder List, choosing File, Properties, clicking the Workgroup tab, and checking one or more standard categories in the Available Categories list or by clicking the Categories button to add one or more custom categories.
Publish Status	Displays the publishing status of each file in your Web site. The publishing status of a file is set to either Publish or Don't Publish, indicating whether or not that particular file will be included when you publish your Web site. You can change the publishing status of a file by selecting the filename in the Folder List, choosing File, Properties, clicking the Workgroup tab, and either checking or clearing the Exclude This File When Publishing The Rest Of The Web option. You can also right-click the file in the Folder List and choose Don't Publish from the shortcut menu.

Table 47-3. The Reports You Can Display in Reports View

Report	Description
Checkout Status	If you've enabled the document check-in and check-out feature, you can display this report to view version control information on each file: the person—if any—who has checked out the file (that is, opened it), the file version number, and the date the file was locked if it has been locked. The document check-in and check-out feature provides basic version control for files in a Web site in environments where the site is stored on a shared network disk or Web server and several people are working on it. To enable check-in and check-out, choose Tools, Site Settings and check the Use Document Check-In And Check-Out option on the General tab.
Usage Category	If your Web site is published on a server running Windows Share-Point Services and if usage reporting has been enabled for the site, you can select from a large number of reports in this category. These reports provide usage summaries and page hit counts for various time periods; list the operating systems, browsers, and referring domains and URLs (Uniform Resource Locators) of site visitors; and display other statistics. If usage reporting isn't enabled for your SharePoint team Web site, see the server administrator.

When you display certain reports, you can modify the information that appears by selecting options in the Report Setting drop-down list on the Reporting toolbar. For example, in the Recently Added Files report, you can select the number of previous days for which files are shown; and in the Slow Pages report, you can select the minimum download time for the files that are listed.

Also, if you double-click an item in a report (or single-click an underlined item), FrontPage performs a related action, if appropriate. The particular action depends on the type of item. For example, if you click the All Files item in the Site Summary report, it displays the All Files report. If you click the Uncompleted Tasks item in the Site Summary report, it activates Tasks view. And if you double-click the name of a Web page in the All Files report, it opens the page for editing.

Note You can modify features of Reports view in the Reports View tab of the Options dialog box (shown in Figure 47-17), which you open by choosing Tools, Options.

Chapter 47

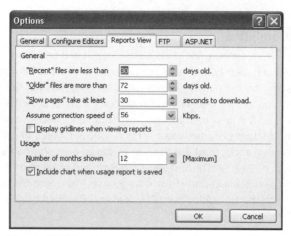

Figure 47-17. You can modify the features of Reports view using the Reports View tab of the Options dialog box.

Tip **Publish a report**

You can publish a report by displaying it in a Web page in your Web site. To do this, open the report, right-click anywhere in the report, and choose Copy Report from the shortcut menu. Then, place the insertion point within the page in which you want to display the report and choose Edit, Paste. FrontPage will insert a copy of the report, and display it within a table. Note, however, that for some reason FrontPage doesn't provide a shortcut menu in the Site Summary page, so you can't use this method to publish that particular report.

Viewing, Verifying, and Repairing Hyperlinks

This chapter has described two FrontPage views that let you work with hyperlinks: Navigation and Hyperlinks. The Hyperlinks report, shown in Figure 47-18, provides yet another way to view the hyperlinks in your Web site, as well as to verify hyperlinks and to repair broken ones.

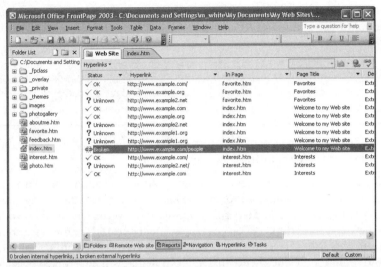

Figure 47-18. The Hyperlinks report shown here lists all external and broken hyperlinks.

> **Caution** If you have one or more open Web pages with unsaved changes, you should save your changes before showing the Hyperlinks report or checking hyperlinks, because FrontPage looks for hyperlinks in the disk files for the pages, not in unsaved versions of pages opened for editing.

The first column of the Hyperlinks report displays the status of each hyperlink. The following types of status are the most common.

- **OK**   The hyperlink has been *verified*—that is, tested to see whether the target exists—and the target has been found.

- **Broken**   Verification was attempted on the hyperlink, but the hyperlink target couldn't be found. (This doesn't necessarily mean the target doesn't exist—a bad Internet connection or a Web server problem or a canceled verifying operation could be at fault.)

- **Unknown**   The hyperlink hasn't yet been verified. This status is equivalent to the *not verified* tag that appears in Hyperlinks view. It applies to external hyperlinks only, because FrontPage automatically verifies all internal hyperlinks when it first compiles the report. An external hyperlink is marked as Unknown until you explicitly verify it.

> **Note**   The Hyperlinks report lists embedded images in addition to actual hyperlinks, and the comments in this section apply to embedded images as well as hyperlinks.

Unlike the Navigation and Hyperlinks views, the Hyperlinks report shows only the individual hyperlinks in your Web site pages—that is, the hyperlinks that *aren't* part of link bars. If the Show Internal Hyperlinks option is enabled, it shows all such hyperlinks; otherwise, it shows only external hyperlinks (with any status) and broken internal hyperlinks. You can enable or disable this option by right-clicking anywhere in the report and choosing Show Internal Hyperlinks from the shortcut menu.

> **Note** When you first display the Hyperlinks report, FrontPage may display a message box asking whether you want to verify the hyperlinks in your Web site. If you click the Yes button in this message box, FrontPage will verify all unknown external hyperlinks in your Web site.

You can verify or re-verify an external hyperlink—OK, broken, or unknown—by right-clicking it and choosing Verify Hyperlink from the shortcut menu.

You can also verify all external hyperlinks with any status, or all unknown external hyperlinks, by clicking the Verify Hyperlinks button on the Reporting toolbar (shown in Figure 47-16) and then selecting the Verify All Hyperlinks option or the Verify Only Unknown Hyperlinks option in the Verify Hyperlinks dialog box (shown in Figure 47-19). You can also use the Verify Hyperlinks dialog box to verify just the selected hyperlink or hyperlinks. In addition, you can use it to resume a previous hyperlink verification that you interrupted by clicking the Stop button on the Standard toolbar.

Figure 47-19.   You can verify or resume verification of hyperlinks with the Verify Hyperlinks dialog box.

You can fix a broken hyperlink by double-clicking it in the Hyperlinks report, by right-clicking it and choosing Edit Hyperlink from the shortcut menu, or by selecting it and clicking the Edit Hyperlink button on the Reporting toolbar. FrontPage will then display the Edit Hyperlink dialog box (shown in Figure 47-20), which lets you quickly fix the hyperlink without having to open and edit the page that contains it. The Edit Hyperlink dialog box lets you change a broken hyperlink in all pages where it occurs or in just one or more selected pages. You can either type the new hyperlink address or click the Browse button to open the standard Office 2003 Edit Hyperlink dialog box to locate a new link target (this is a different Edit Hyperlink dialog box from the one that first appears in FrontPage).

> For instructions on using the standard Office 2003 Edit Hyperlink dialog box (which has the same features as the Insert Hyperlink dialog box), see "Adding and Using Hyperlinks," on page 580.

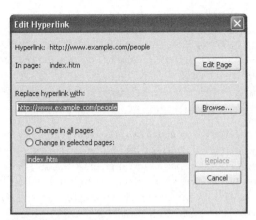

Figure 47-20. You can use the Edit Hyperlink dialog box to repair a broken hyperlink in any of the pages where it occurs.

 # Publishing Your Web Site

You can use the new Remote Web Site view, which replaces the Publish Web dialog box found in previous versions of FrontPage, to copy Web site folders and files between the Web site that's currently open in FrontPage (the *local Web site*) and a remote site (the *remote Web site*). Earlier versions of FrontPage required that the remote site be on a server running FrontPage Server Extensions or Windows SharePoint Services, or be located on a local or network disk. The FrontPage 2003 Remote Web Site view supports these two types of remote sites, as well as remote FTP servers and WebDAV (Web Distributed Authoring and Versioning) servers.

You can use Remote Web Site view to copy your entire Web site—all folders, pages, graphics files, other supporting files, and folders and files used internally by FrontPage—to a remote site. You can then use Remote Web Site view to keep the remote Web site or the local Web site up-to-date, in any of the following ways:

- You can copy from the local Web site to the remote Web site all files that have been created or changed on the local Web site since the last time you published.

- You can copy from the remote Web site to the local Web site all files that have been created or changed on the remote Web site since the last time you published.

- You can *synchronize* the local Web site and the remote Web site. This performs both of the preceding processes: It copies all new or changed files on the local Web site to the remote Web site, and it copies all new or changed files on the remote Web site to the local Web site. The result of synchronizing is that both the local Web site and the remote Web site are made the same and are brought up-to-date with the changes that have been made on either Web site.

> **Note**   If a file has been changed on *both* the local Web site and the remote Web site since the last time you published, it won't be copied when you publish using any of the three methods explained above. However, you can force FrontPage to copy the file by using the individual file copying method, mentioned next.

- You can copy individual files in either direction.

If you create and maintain your Web site on a local disk location that serves as a staging area, you can use Remote Web Site view when your Web site is complete to copy the Web site to a server on the World Wide Web or on your company's intranet, allowing others to view the site. You can subsequently use Remote Web Site view whenever you modify your local Web site to update the remote copy of the Web site on the server. Although this is the most typical use for Remote Web Site view, you can also use it to create a backup copy of your Web site for safekeeping. Additionally, if you and one or more other authors are creating and maintaining a Web site located on a server, each author could work on a personal local copy of the Web site and use Remote Web Site view's synchronization feature to copy changes in the local copy to the server and to copy other authors' changes on the server back to the local copy.

For information on places where you can store your Web site, see the sidebar "Creating a Web Site Offline or Online," on page 1222.

The following are the basic steps for using Remote Web Site view:

1 Open Remote Web Site view by clicking the Web Site tab label at the top of the working area of the FrontPage window and then clicking the Remote Web Site view button at the bottom of the tab. Alternatively, you can choose either of the following menu commands: File, Publish Site or View, Remote Web Site.

2 If you haven't yet set up a remote site, click the Remote Web Site Properties button on the Remote Web Site toolbar at the top of the view. Then, in the Remote Web Site tab of the Remote Web Site Properties dialog box (shown in Figure 47-21), provide the address (URL or folder path) of the remote site and specify the type of the server that's located on that site (select File System if the remote site is on a local or network disk). If the folder you specify doesn't exist, FrontPage will create it and add the files necessary to convert it to a FrontPage Web site. You can use the Optimize HTML and Publishing tabs to select additional publishing options. Figure 47-22 shows Remote Web Site view after a remote site has been set up.

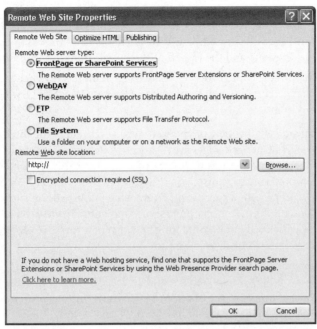

Figure 47-21.   You use the Remote Web Site Properties dialog box to set up a remote Web site and select publishing options.

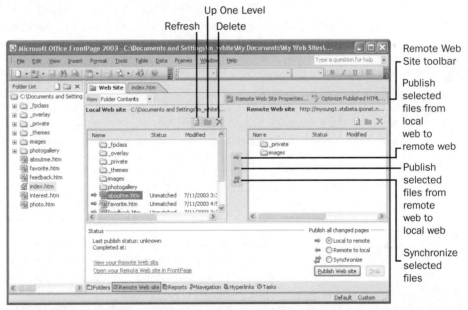

Figure 47-22.   This figure shows Remote Web Site view after a remote site has been set up, but before files have been published to the remote site.

3 If you haven't yet copied your local Web site to the remote site, select the Local To Remote option in the Publish All Changed Pages area and click the Publish Web Site button. FrontPage will copy all your Web site folders and files to the remote site, so that the local Web site and the remote Web site will contain the same contents.

4 After you've initially copied your Web site to the remote site, whenever files have been added or changed on either site, you can use Remote Web Site view to update one or both sites, as follows:

- To copy *all* eligible new or changed files, select one of the three options in the Publish All Changed Pages area—Local To Remote, Remote To Local, or Synchronize. These options were explained earlier in this section. When you select an option, FrontPage displays an arrow to the left of each file that will be published. To prevent a specific file from being published, right-click it and select the Don't Publish option on the shortcut menu. (FrontPage will then replace the arrow with a red circle containing an X.) When you're ready to start copying files, click the Publish Web Site button.

- To copy one or more individual files in either direction, select the file(s) on the local or on the remote Web site and click the button displaying a *single*-headed arrow that points to the other Web site. These buttons are located between the two file lists and are labeled in Figure 47-22.

- To synchronize one or more individual files, select the file(s) on the local Web site or on the remote Web site and click the button between the lists that displays *two* arrows pointing toward each Web site (see Figure 47-22). When you synchronize an individual file, the selected file will be copied to the other Web site if it has been changed since the last time you published. However, if the corresponding file on the other Web site has been changed since the last time you published, that file will be copied instead, replacing the selected file. (If *both* files have changed, FrontPage will flash a few message boxes but won't copy either file.)

Note If a file has been changed on *both* Web sites since the last time you published, FrontPage will mark it with a question mark and set its status to Conflict. When you publish, FrontPage will display the Conflicts dialog box, which lets you cancel the publishing operation, or continue publishing all of the files that are *not* in conflict. To copy a file that's in conflict, you can use the method for publishing individual files, described next. (When a conflicting file is involved, FrontPage will ask you to confirm the copy operation.)

Publish Web

Caution If you've already set up a remote Web site for the current Web site, clicking the Publish Site button on the Standard toolbar doesn't merely open Remote Web Site view (which would allow you to select publishing options and publish in various ways). Rather, it opens Remote Web Site view and automatically begins the publishing process using the Local To Remote option. So if this isn't the way you want to publish, be sure to use one of the other methods for opening Remote Web Site view.

Chapter 47

Tip Find a hosting service with FrontPage Server Extensions

To take advantage of FrontPage's features it's important to publish your Web site to a Web server that has the Microsoft FrontPage Server Extensions or Windows SharePoint Services. Fortunately, many Web hosting companies now provide FrontPage Server Extensions, including services using the Unix operating system as well as services using Windows. In the Remote Web Site tab of the Remote Web Site Properties dialog box (shown in Figure 47-21), you can click the Click Here To Learn More link to connect to a Microsoft site that helps you find a registered "Web presence provider" (that is, Web hosting service) that offers the FrontPage Server Extensions. You can also find a wealth of comparisons, ratings, reviews, and additional information on a large number of Web hosts by consulting other Web host directories on the Web, computer magazines, and Internet newsgroups where webmasters congregate. Because of the great differences in the terms, services, and ratings of various hosts, it pays to shop carefully.

Chapter 48

Creating and Editing Web Pages

Creating a New Web Page 1279
Opening an Existing Web Page 1288
Common Editing Tasks 1289
Adding the Text Content 1291
Inserting Images 1300
Separating Content with
Horizontal Dividing Lines 1305

Including Internal and
External Hyperlinks 1306
Using Tables Effectively 1308
Working with Shared Borders 1313
NEW FEATURE! Previewing and Printing
Your Page 1317

Creating a New Web Page

You can create a new Web page to add to the Microsoft Office FrontPage 2003 Web site you're currently working on. You can also use FrontPage as a general-purpose HTML (Hypertext Markup Language) editor and create a Web page that isn't part of a Web site. You can use the methods given in this section to create a new Web page whether or not a FrontPage Web site is currently open, unless stated otherwise. (At the end of the section you'll learn how to use two methods for creating and saving a page in a single step, which are available only if a Web site is open.)

Note Keep in mind that if you haven't opened a FrontPage Web site, many FrontPage features won't be available—for example, publishing, reports, hyperlink management, tasks, shared borders, and many of the FrontPage Web components.

To create a new blank page, use any of the following techniques:

- Click the Create A New Normal Page button at the left end of the Standard toolbar, shown here:

- Press Ctrl+N.
- Choose File, New to open the New task pane (shown in Figure 48-1). Then click the Blank Page command in the New Page area of the task pane.

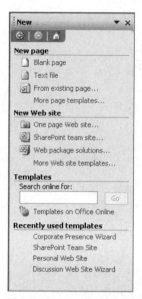

Figure 48-1. The New task pane provides a variety of ways to create or open Web pages.

Tip Designate a home page

When a visitor navigates to the root folder of your Web site without specifying a particular file in the URL (Uniform Resource Locator), the visitor's browser opens the page designated as your home page. In a FrontPage Web site created on a local or network disk, FrontPage designates the Web page file Index.htm in the root Web site folder as your home page. In a FrontPage Web site created directly on a Web server, FrontPage designates the Web page file Default.htm as the home page. In the Folder List and in Folders view, FrontPage marks the designated home page with a home icon. If you want to designate a different page as your home page, you can right-click that page in the Folder List or in Folders view and choose Set As Home Page from the shortcut menu. FrontPage will rename your former Index.htm (or Default.htm) file to Index-old.htm (or Default-old.htm) and then rename the file you clicked Index.htm (or Default.htm).

To get a head start in creating a particular type of Web page, you can create it using one of FrontPage's Web page templates by performing the following steps:

1 Open the Page Templates dialog box using one of the following techniques:

■ Click the down arrow on the Create A New Normal Page button on the Standard toolbar, and choose Page from the drop-down menu, as shown here:

- Choose File, New to open the New task pane (shown in Figure 48-1). Then, click the More Page Templates command in the New Page area.

2   In the General tab of the Page Templates dialog box (shown in Figure 48-2), select the template or wizard you want to use as the basis for your new Web page. To help you choose a template, the dialog box shows a description and—for most templates—a preview image of the page that will be created using the selected template.

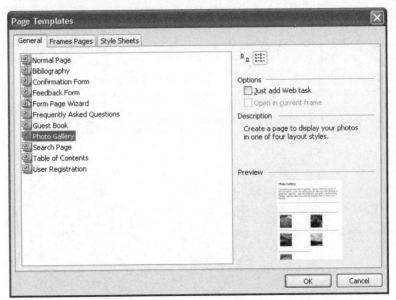

Figure 48-2.   The General tab of the Page Templates dialog box presents a list of templates and wizards you can use as the basis for a new page.

> **Note**   If you don't want to work on the new page immediately, you can check the Just Add Web Task option. FrontPage will create the page, prompt you to save it, and add a task to Tasks view for finishing the page. To open the page, you can right-click the task in Tasks view and choose Start Task from the shortcut menu (as well as use any of the other methods for opening a page). Tasks are discussed in "Managing Your Web Site Projects," on page 1262.

> The Frames Pages tab is discussed in "Using Frames to Display Multiple Pages," on page 1367. The Style Sheets tab is explained in "Modifying, Creating, and Using Cascading Style Sheet Styles," on page 1358.

3 Click the OK button.

> **Note** You can quickly create a Web page based on a recently used Web page template by clicking the template name in the Recently Used Templates area near the bottom of the New task pane (shown in Figure 48-1). Keep in mind that the recently used templates list includes Web site templates as well as Web page templates.
>
> You can also use an existing Web page to create a new one by clicking the From Existing Page command in the New Page area of the New task pane. The new page will be an exact copy of the existing page but will have a new name (a temporary name that FrontPage assigns when it opens the page for editing and a permanent name you assign the first time you save the page).

FrontPage will then open your new page in an editing tab so that you can start adding content and customizing the page. The page will contain all the content supplied by the template or wizard you chose. Also, if a Web site is currently opened, any theme assigned to the site will be applied to the new page, and any default shared borders used in the site—plus the shared border contents—will be added to the page (see Figure 48-3).

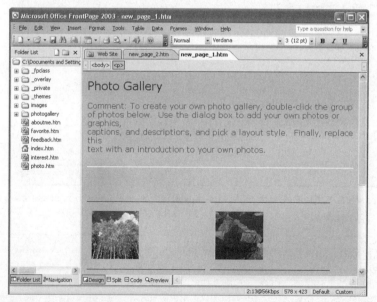

Figure 48-3. This figure shows a new page created using the Photo Gallery template.

> Themes are explained in "Using Themes to Quickly Change the Overall Page Format," on page 1353. Shared borders are discussed in "Working with Shared Borders," on page 1313.

Tip To find, download, and use an online FrontPage template from the Office Online Web site, use the controls in the Templates area of the New task pane. Either enter a keyword into the Search Online For text box and click the Go button or click Templates On Office Online to run your browser and open the Templates home page on the Office Online site.

For information on using Microsoft's expanded collection of online templates and wizards and on using the new Template Help task pane available in Office 2003 applications, see "Downloading and Using Templates from Office Online," on page 55.

Save

To save your new Web page, or any Web page you've modified in FrontPage, choose File, Save. Alternatively, you can click the Save button on the Standard toolbar or press Ctrl+S. Then select a filename and location in the Save As dialog box. Although the Save As dialog box lets you save a Web page anywhere, if a Web site is opened and you want the page to be part of that site, be sure to save it in the Web site folder or one of its subfolders. If you want to change the page's title, click the Change Title button in the Save As dialog box and type a new title before you click the Save button.

Note If you don't save a new Web page within the Web site folder or one of its subfolders, that page won't be part of the Web site. As a result, it won't appear in the Folder List or Folders view, it won't be published to a remote site if you publish the Web site, and you won't be able to use FrontPage's Web site maintenance tools with the page (reports and hyperlink maintenance, for example).

Tip Create and save a new page with a single command
If a Web site is currently open in FrontPage, you can use either of the following two methods to create a new page and save it under a default filename with a single command. (You can later rename the page.)

- In the Folder List, select the folder where you want to store the page and click the New Page button on the Folder List toolbar at the top of the list. Or, in Folders view, open the folder where you want to store the page and click the New Page button on the Folders toolbar at the top of the view. (See Figure 47-1.)

- In the Folder List, right-click the folder where you want to store the page and choose New, Blank Page from the shortcut menu. Or, in Folders view, open the folder where you want to store the page, click a blank area in the view, and choose New, Blank Page from the shortcut menu.

Creating Your Own FrontPage Templates

If you have created a Web page that you would like to use as the basis for creating additional pages, you can save the page as a custom, standard FrontPage template. Your custom template will then appear in the My Templates tab of the Page Templates dialog box so that you can use

Chapter 48

it to create new pages in the same way you can use one of the built-in templates supplied with FrontPage. To save a page as a FrontPage template, perform the following steps:

1 Choose File, Save As.

2 Select FrontPage Template (*.tem) in the Save As Type drop-down list in the Save As dialog box.

3 Click the Save button. You don't need to specify either a filename or a location for saving the template. FrontPage will later prompt you for the template filename and it will automatically save the template in the required location on your hard drive.

4 Type new text or accept the default text when FrontPage prompts you for a title, name, and description in the Save As Template dialog box. When you later open the My Templates tab of the Page Templates dialog box to create a new page, you'll see the title and description of your custom template, along with a preview image of the template. Click the OK button when you're done.

> **Note** If you're working together with other authors on a Web site stored on a Web server, you can check the Save Template In Current Web Site option to have FrontPage save a copy of the template files within a hidden folder in the Web site, so that other authors can use the template. (A copy of the template will be stored on the hard drive of every other author who subsequently opens the Web site.)

5 If your page contains images, FrontPage will display the Save Embedded Files dialog box. Here, just click the OK button to save all the page's graphics files along with the template.

 ## Working with Dynamic Templates

FrontPage 2003 provides a new type of template, known as a *dynamic Web page template* (or just *dynamic template*), which you can use to add predefined content and formatting to a Web page, as an alternative to using a standard FrontPage Web page template as described previously. Dynamic templates have the following unique features:

● You attach a dynamic template to an existing page after that page has been created rather than using it to create a new page.

● A dynamic template remains attached to the page. If you later change the template, you can have FrontPage automatically update the attached page so that it acquires the changes made in the template.

● When a page is attached to a dynamic template, you're allowed to edit only those parts of the page that are designated in the template as *editable regions*. For example, an organization could create a dynamic template to serve as a blueprint for a standard Web page; the template could be designed so that a page author could enter content into the body of the page (which would be made an editable region) but not alter the organization's standard heading, logo, links, and copyright message (which would be parts of the template not designated as editable regions).

> **Note** Dynamic templates in FrontPage are syntax compatible with Macromedia Dreamweaver 4 templates, making it easy to convert a Dreamweaver site to FrontPage or to collaborate with Dreamweaver users on the same site.

The following are the basic steps for creating and using a dynamic template:

1 Create, add content, and format the page you want to use as a dynamic template using the standard techniques given in this part of the book.

2 Designate as an editable region each area of the page where you want template users to be able to add or change content or formatting. To create each editable region, place the insertion point at the position where you want to insert the region (or select text that you want to incorporate in the region) and choose Format, Dynamic Web Template, Manage Editable Regions. Then, in the Editable Regions dialog box, type a region name into the Region Name text box, click the Add button, and then click the Close button.

3 Save your dynamic template by choosing File, Save As. In the Save As dialog box, select Dynamic Web Template (*.dwt) in the Save As Type drop-down list, specify a name and location for the template file, and click the Save button. Figure 48-4 shows a Web page that has been saved as a dynamic template.

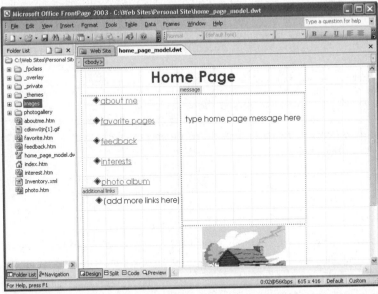

Figure 48-4. This is a dynamic Web template that could be used as a blueprint for creating a home page. It contains two editable regions, named "message" and "additional links." A copy is provided on the companion CD in the file home_page_model.dwt.

4 To apply the dynamic template to a Web page, first create a new Web page. Then choose Format, Dynamic Web Template, Attach Dynamic Web Template, and select the dynamic template in the Attach Dynamic Web Template dialog box.

Note It's best not to add content to a page until *after* you have attached the dynamic template to that page. However, if a page already has content when you attach a dynamic template, FrontPage will let you insert that content within one of the template's editable regions.

The page will acquire the content and formatting from the template. You'll be able to add or change content or formatting within the designated editable region(s).

5 If you later modify the dynamic template, when you save your changes, FrontPage will ask if you want to update any attached pages within the same Web site. Click the Yes button to update the attached page or pages with the latest changes to the template. If an attached page is stored outside the current Web site, you can update that page by opening it in FrontPage for editing and choosing Format, Dynamic Web Template, Update Selected Page.

Tip You can choose Format, Dynamic Web Template, Update All Pages to update *all* pages within the current Web site that are attached to dynamic templates.

Creating a Web Part Page on a SharePoint Team Web Site

The previous chapter ("Managing Your Web Site with FrontPage") explained how to use FrontPage to create a new document library, list, or other information component in a team Web site on a server running Microsoft Windows SharePoint Services. You can also use FrontPage to add a free-form Web page, known as a *Web part page*, to a SharePoint team Web site.

The techniques for creating a document library, list, or other information component in a SharePoint team Web site are covered in "Adding Document Libraries, Lists, and Other Information Components to a SharePoint Team Web Site," on page 1243.

The following are the basic steps for using FrontPage to create a Web part page on a Share-Point team Web site:

1 Open the team Web site in FrontPage and then open the Page Templates dialog box using one of the techniques given previously in the chapter. For instance, you can click the down arrow on the Create A New Normal Page button on the Standard toolbar and choose Page from the drop-down menu.

2 In the Web Part Pages tab of the Page Templates dialog box (see Figure 48-5), select the template that has the layout you want to use for creating your page and click the OK button.

The new page will consist of a matrix of *zones*, in which you can add content. You add content to a zone by inserting and customizing one or more predefined components known as *Web parts*.

For information on Web part pages, zones, Web parts, and the techniques for adding a Web part page to a SharePoint team Web site using your browser, see "Creating New Site Components," on page 201.

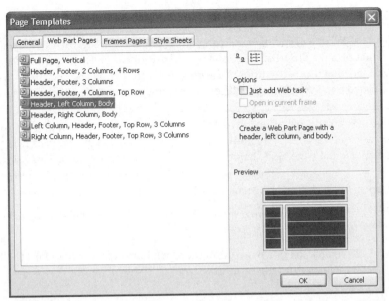

Figure 48-5. The Web Part Pages tab of the Page Templates dialog box lets you select a template for creating a free-form Web page on a SharePoint team Web site.

3 To add content to a zone, click the Click To Insert A Web Part command displayed within the zone and use the Web Parts task pane that appears to select and insert a Web part. (See Figure 48-6.)

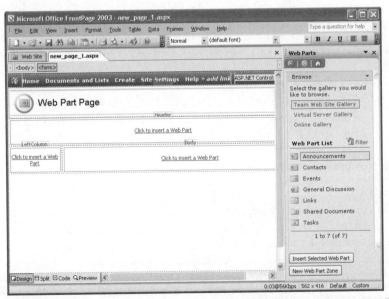

Figure 48-6. This figure shows a newly created Web page with the Web Parts task pane.

Opening an Existing Web Page

To edit a Web page, you open it in an editing tab in FrontPage. You can open and edit a page whether or not a FrontPage Web site is currently open. The page might be a new one you created following the instructions in the previous section, a page you want to customize that was generated by a Web site template, or an existing page outside a Web site.

> **Note** Opening a page outside of the current Web site and then saving it in the Web site is a convenient way to import into your site both the page and the graphics files for all images displayed in the page. See "Importing a Web Page and Its Graphics Files," on page 1252.

To open any Web page, perform the following steps:

1 Use any of the following methods to display the Open File dialog box:

- Choose File, Open.

- Click the down arrow on the Open button on the Standard toolbar and choose Open from the drop-down menu, as shown here:

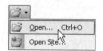

- Press Ctrl+O.

- If the Getting Started task pane is displayed, click the More command in the Pages area. Also, FrontPage displays your two most recently opened Web pages above the More command. You can quickly reopen one of these pages, bypassing the Open File dialog box, by clicking its name.

> **Tip** You can also reopen a recently opened page choosing the filename from the File, Recent Files submenu.

2 In the Open File dialog box, which works just like the standard Open dialog box in Office applications, make sure that the Web Pages item is selected in the Files Of Type drop-down list, locate and select the page, and then click the Open button.

> The Open Office Document and Open dialog boxes are explained in "Opening Existing Office Documents," on page 56.

You can also open a Web page that's part of the current Web site by double-clicking the filename in the Folder List or in a view that lists Web site files (Folders, Remote Web Site, Reports, Navigation, or Hyperlinks).

> In FrontPage 2003, you can now open and edit a text file—for example, a file containing XML (Extensible Markup Language) source code. For information on editing text files, see "Directly Editing Source Code Files," on page 1384.

If you have several Web pages opened at once in FrontPage, you can activate a particular page by clicking the page's tab label at the top of the working area of the FrontPage window, as shown here:

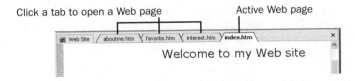

Click a tab to open a Web page   Active Web page

Welcome to my Web site

Or you can use the old method of choosing a page's name from the Window menu. You can close all open Web pages and text files by choosing the new Window, Close All Pages command.

Common Editing Tasks

You can use the editing techniques described in the following sections when you work with any of the basic page elements discussed in this chapter, as well as the more advanced elements covered in Chapter 50, "Adding Advanced Features to Your Web Pages and Working with Source Code." Most of these techniques are described briefly because they're quite similar to those used in Microsoft Office Word 2003 and other Microsoft Office 2003 applications. To use these techniques, you must be working on a Web page in Design view or in the design pane of Split view. To activate one of these views, display the page in an editing tab and click the Design or Split view button at the bottom of the tab.

Selecting

You can select blocks of text—including any embedded images, horizontal dividing lines, or other elements—by holding down the Shift key while you press an arrow key, or by dragging over the area with the mouse.

> You can also use almost any of the Word selection methods discussed in "Selecting the Text," on page 282.

You can select individual nontext elements, such as images, horizontal dividing lines, or Web components, by simply clicking them. Choosing Edit, Select All, or pressing Ctrl+A, selects all text and other elements in the main body of the page (but not in shared borders).

> Shared borders are discussed in "Working with Shared Borders," on page 1313.

Moving, Copying, and Deleting

You can move or copy selected blocks of text or other elements (such as images, horizontal dividing lines, and Web components) using the same basic methods that are used in Word. Namely, you can move the selected item by dragging it with the mouse or copy it by pressing

Ctrl while you drag. You can also use the Clipboard to move or copy it by means of the standard Cut, Copy, and Paste commands. You can move or copy within a single page, between separate pages, or between documents. For example, you could use any of these methods to copy a block of text or an image from a document in Word to a Web page in FrontPage.

> For details on copying and moving methods, see "Moving and Copying Text Using the Mouse," on page 287, and "Moving and Copying Text Using the Clipboard," on page 289. Keep in mind that you can use these methods with other selected page elements besides text.

When you paste text into a page, FrontPage chooses a default formatting option but displays the Paste Options button so that you can select a different option. The available formatting options depend on the source and formatting of the text. For example, if you paste a paragraph copied from a Word document, the Paste Options button gives you the choices shown here:

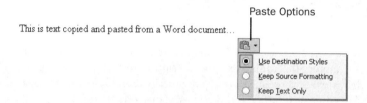

You can switch between choices to see which one creates the effect you want.

> **Note** FrontPage displays the Paste Options button only if the Show Paste Options Buttons option is checked. You'll find this option by choosing Tools, Page Options and looking in the General tab.

You can select from a greater number of formatting options by using the Convert Text dialog box, rather than using the standard Paste command and the Paste Options button. To paste, choose Edit, Paste Special to open the Convert Text dialog box, shown here:

Then, select one of the following options:

● To insert the text as a single paragraph assigned the Formatted style, converting each paragraph break within the original text to a line break and preserving all line breaks in the original text, select One Formatted Paragraph or Formatted Paragraphs.

> **Note** The Formatted style displays the text in a monospace font, without wrapping the lines, and preserves all space characters and line breaks in the original text. (FrontPage embeds the text assigned this style in an HTML PRE element.) For general information on FrontPage styles, see "Formatting Paragraphs," on page 1322.

- To insert the text as a single paragraph, applying the current formatting at the position in the page where you insert the text and removing paragraph and line breaks within the original text, select Normal Paragraphs.

- To insert the text as a single paragraph, applying the current formatting at the position in the page where you insert the text, converting each paragraph break within the original text to a line break, and preserving all line breaks in the original text, select Normal Paragraphs With Line Breaks.

- To insert the text as a single paragraph, applying the current formatting at the position in the page where you insert the text, removing paragraph and line breaks within the original text, and rendering any HTML elements in the pasted text (rather than displaying the tags as literal text, as do the other paste options), select Do Not Convert. For example, if the text contained <b>important</b>, FrontPage would display the word *important* in bold and wouldn't display the <b> and </b> tags.

Finally, you can delete the selected block of text, image, horizontal dividing line, Web component, or other element by choosing Edit, Delete or by pressing the Delete key.

Undoing and Redoing Editing Actions

Undo

You can undo or redo your recent editing actions by choosing the usual Undo or Redo commands from the Edit menu or by clicking the Undo or Redo buttons on the Standard toolbar. FrontPage also provides the following unique way to undo *all* editing changes you have made since the page was last opened or saved. Make sure that you really want to discard all your changes, because you won't be able to restore them.

Redo

1   Choose View, Refresh or press F5.
2   Click the Yes button when FrontPage displays a message box asking whether you want to revert to the saved version of the page. (It will display this message only if you've made changes since the page was last opened or saved.)

The page will now be restored to its most recent saved version, removing your changes.

Adding the Text Content

You can enter, edit, and navigate through text in FrontPage using the same basic methods as in Word, which are described in Chapter 11, "Efficient Editing in Word." To use these techniques, you must be working on a Web page in Design view or in the design pane of Split view. To activate one of these views, display the page in an editing tab and click the Design or Split view button at the bottom of the tab.

As in Word, you should let the text wrap automatically as you type a paragraph and press Enter only to create a new paragraph. (The position where each line in a paragraph wraps will ultimately be determined by the width of the browser window used to view the page.) You can insert a line break *within* a paragraph by pressing Shift+Enter. Most browsers insert extra vertical space between separate paragraphs, but not between lines separated by line breaks, so you can use a line break rather than a paragraph break to space separate lines more closely.

As explained in "Modifying Image Properties" on page 1337, when you assign left or right alignment to an image, the adjoining lines of text are placed to one side of the image. You can insert a special type of line break in one of these lines that forces the following line to be placed below the image rather than to one side of it (even if there's plenty of room for the line to the side of the image). To do this, choose Insert, Break to display the Break dialog box, shown here:

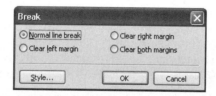

Then, select one of the options other than Normal Line Break, as follows:

- To move the following line below a left-aligned image only, select Clear Left Margin.
- To move the following line below a right-aligned image only, select Clear Right Margin.
- To move the following line below either a left-aligned or a right-aligned image, select Clear Both Margins.

Show All

Tip Show or hide breaks

Click the Show All button on the Standard toolbar to show or hide the symbols that indicate the position of paragraph marks (¶) and line breaks (ø).

You can insert one of a selection of symbol characters not found on the keyboard by choosing Insert, Symbol. Then, in the Symbol dialog box, select the symbol you want and click the Insert button.

For complete instructions on using the Symbol dialog box, see "Inserting Symbols and Foreign Characters," on page 260.

You can also insert the contents of an entire file by choosing Insert, File and then selecting the filename in the Select File dialog box, as seen here:

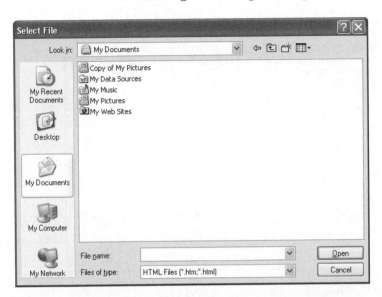

The Files Of Type list box displays the different file types you can insert, which include HTML files, Rich Text Format (RTF) files, text files, and Word documents. When you insert the file, FrontPage converts it to HTML format and makes it an integral part of your page.

Finding and Replacing Text in Your Web Pages

When you're working on a Web page or other type of text file in an editing tab, you can search for text within that page by performing the following steps:

Find

1   Click the Find button on the Standard toolbar; choose Edit, Find; or press Ctrl+F to open the Find And Replace dialog box.

2   In the Find tab of the Find And Replace dialog box (shown here), enter your search text into the Find What text box (or click the Most Recently Used button to select previously entered search text), make sure that the Current Page option is selected, and select the other search options that you want to use.

Regular Expressions   Most Recently Used

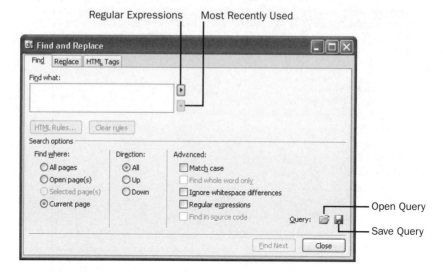

Open Query

Save Query

The following new search options deserve mention:

- To search for an expression, ignoring the number of space, tab, or line breaks within the text, check the Ignore Whitespace Differences option.

- To search using *regular expressions* in your search text (for example, + to match one or more characters), check the Regular Expressions option. You can insert a regular expression into the Find What text box by clicking the Regular Expressions button and choosing the expression from the pop-up menu.

- To specify that the search text must be located inside (or not inside) a specific type of HTML element, click the HTML Rules button and create one or more rules in the HTML Rules dialog box. For example, you could search for italicized text by creating an HTML rule that states that the text must be within an italics (I) element. (Note that the HTML Rules dialog box uses the expression *inside tag*, although the more accurate expression would be *inside element*.) To remove any HTML rules you created, click the Clear Rules button in the Find tab.

- To save your search criteria or to restore criteria you saved previously, click the Save Query or Open Query button.

- You can search for text within any of the page editing views: Design, Split, Code, or Preview. If you're working in Split view, you can check the Find In Source Code option to search the code pane or clear this option to search the design pane.

3 Each time you click the Find Next button in the Find tab, FrontPage will highlight the next occurrence of your search text within the active page.

Tip Once you have used the Find And Replace dialog box to locate one or more occurrences of your search text, you can close the dialog box and continue searching by pressing F3 to find the next occurrence or Shift+F3 to find the previous occurrence.

When you're working on a Web page or other type of text file in an editing tab, you can replace text within that page by choosing Edit, Replace or by pressing Ctrl+H, and then carrying out the operation using the Replace tab of the Find And Replace dialog box, shown here. Again, be sure to leave the Current Page option selected.

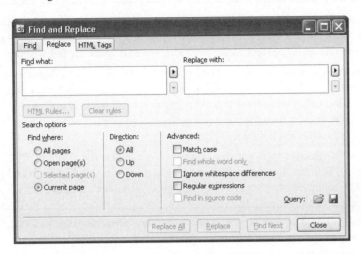

You can leave the Find And Replace dialog box open while you work on the page.

For information on using the HTML Tags tab of the Find And Replace dialog box, see "Finding and Replacing HTML Elements," on page 1389.

Note If the page contains one or more shared borders (discussed in "Working with Shared Borders," on page 1313), you can search for or replace text within all shared borders (omitting the main part of the page) by placing the insertion point within one of the shared border areas prior to using the Find or Replace command. (If the insertion point or selection is in the main part of the page, FrontPage will search or replace only within the main part.)

Alternatively, to use FrontPage to find or replace text in one or more pages belonging to the current Web site, in a single operation, in any view, perform the following steps:

1 If you want to find or replace text in one or more specific Web pages, select the file or files in the Folder List. If you select a folder name, FrontPage will search all Web pages in that folder. If you want to search all pages in the current Web site or all pages that are opened for editing, you can skip this step.

> **Note** If you use the method described in these steps, FrontPage will search Web pages, but *not* other types of text files. To search a text file that isn't a Web page, you'll need to open that file in FrontPage and use the search method given in the previous numbered steps.

2 To find text, click the Find button on the Standard toolbar; choose Edit, Find; or press Ctrl+F; FrontPage will display the Find tab of the Find And Replace dialog box. To replace text, choose Edit, Replace or press Ctrl+H to display the Replace tab.

3 Carry out the operation in the Find or Replace tab. If you selected files in step 1, you can find or replace text within just those pages by selecting the Selected Page(s) option. To find or replace text within all pages that are currently opened for editing in FrontPage, select the Open Page(s) option. To find or replace text within *all* pages in your Web site, select the All Pages option.

4 The Find or Replace tab will list all pages that contain text matching your criteria (see Figure 48-7). You can now open the pages one at a time in an editing tab and complete your find or replace operation. To open a page, double-click it in the list.

> **Note** If text is found in a shared border, the Find And Replace dialog box will list the page containing the shared border text (Left.htm, Right.htm, Top.htm, or Bottom.htm).

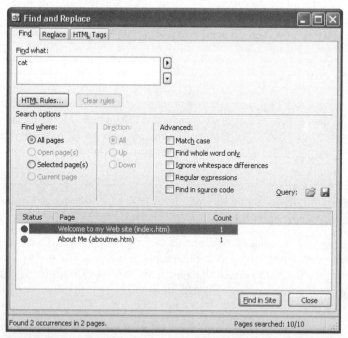

Figure 48-7. In this figure, the Find command is used to search for text in all pages in the current Web site.

Proofing Text in Your Web Pages

FrontPage provides tools for checking your spelling and looking up synonyms. You can check your spelling or look up synonyms for words in the active page in the FrontPage editor, or you can check the spelling in an entire group of pages in your Web site.

> **Note** If your page contains text in a foreign language, you can set the language of a block of text so that FrontPage will use the correct dictionary for checking spelling and looking up synonyms within the text. To do this, select the text and choose Tools, Set Language. For information on setting the language of text, see "Marking the Language," on page 236.

The easiest way to check your spelling in pages opened in the editor is to use the as-you-type spelling checker. If this feature isn't already enabled, you can turn it on by choosing Tools, Page Options and checking the Check Spelling As You Type option in the General tab. If this feature is enabled and you type a word in a page that the spelling checker doesn't recognize, FrontPage will mark the word with a red, wavy underline. You can then do one of the following:

- Ignore the word.
- Correct the word manually.
- Right-click the word and choose an option from the shortcut menu, as shown here:

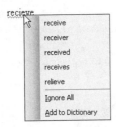

- If the correct spelling is displayed on the top section of the menu, you can choose that spelling to correct the word.
- To have FrontPage stop marking the word in the current page (until you close the page), choose Ignore All.
- To add the word to a supplemental dictionary so that FrontPage will stop marking the work permanently in all pages, choose Add To Dictionary.

If you clear the Check Spelling As You Type option in the General tab of the Page Options dialog box, FrontPage will stop marking newly typed misspellings, and any existing wavy underlines will be removed. You can hide the wavy underlines on all pages by checking the Hide Spelling Errors In All Documents option in this same tab.

If you would rather not deal with misspellings as you type text, you can check the spelling of a block of text or an entire page in an editing tab *after* you have entered it. If you're planning to use this method, you'll probably want to turn off the as-you-type spelling checker so you won't be bothered with the wavy underlines while you type. To check the spelling of text within the active page, perform the following steps:

1 To check spelling within a specific block of text, select the block. To check all text in the main text area, place the insertion point anywhere in the text.

> **Note** To check spelling within a shared border, you must select the text you want to check (it's not sufficient to simply place the insertion point within a shared border). FrontPage won't check spelling within any shared border if the insertion point or selection is in the main part of the page, or if you haven't selected text in a shared border. Shared borders are discussed in "Working with Shared Borders," on page 1313.

Spelling

2 Choose Tools, Spelling; click the Spelling button on the Standard toolbar; or press F7.

3 For each word it doesn't recognize, the spelling checker will display the Spelling dialog box, which you can use to change the spelling or to ignore the word and proceed with the check. This dialog box works very much like the Spelling And Grammar dialog box in Word.

> For details on Word's Spelling And Grammar dialog box, see "Checking the Spelling of Existing Text," on page 482.

You can also look up a synonym for a word or expression by selecting it—or by just placing the insertion point within a single word—and choosing Tools, Thesaurus Dialog or pressing Shift+F7. FrontPage will display the Thesaurus dialog box, shown here, which displays synonyms for various meanings of the word and allows you to replace the word with a synonym or to look up additional synonyms.

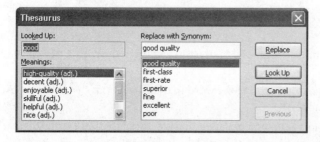

To check the spelling in an entire group of pages in FrontPage, perform the following steps:

1 If you want to check spelling in one or more specific pages, select the file or files in the Folder List. If you select a folder name, FrontPage will check all Web pages within that folder. If you want to check all pages in the Web site, you don't need to select any particular folder. However, if a Web page or other type of text file is currently displayed in an editing tab, either click the Web Site tab or click anywhere within the Folder List so that the editing tab isn't active. (If the insertion point or selection is within a Web page in an editing tab, you'll check just the spelling in that file. If it's within another type of text file, the spelling feature won't be available.)

> **Note** FrontPage will check spelling only within Web pages, not within other types of files in your Web site.

2 Choose Tools, Spelling; or click the Spelling toolbar button; or press F7. FrontPage will display the Spelling dialog box, which will appear as shown here:

3 If you selected files in step 1, you can check spelling in just those pages by selecting the Selected Page(s) option in the Spelling dialog box. To check spelling within all pages in your Web site, select the Entire Web Site option. You can check the Add A Task For Each Page With Misspellings option to create a task in the Tasks view for every page that contains misspellings so that you can correct all misspellings later by following up on those tasks (if you check this option, you can still correct the spelling in the pages immediately, if you wish, as described in these instructions). Click the Start button to begin the check.

4 The Spelling dialog box will list all pages containing misspellings (see Figure 48-8), giving the title (followed by the filename in parentheses) for each page. You can now open the pages one at a time in an editing tab and correct your misspellings. To open a page, double-click it in the list in the Spelling dialog box.

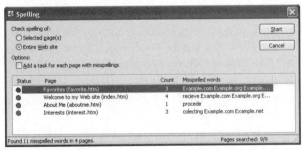

Figure 48-8. You can check spelling in all pages in the current Web site using the Spelling dialog box.

Inside Out

Correcting Misspellings in a Shared Border

If a shared border contains a misspelling, FrontPage flags that misspelling for each page that displays the shared border. However, if you double-click one of these pages to correct the misspelling, FrontPage ignores the shared border and bypasses the misspelled word.

Chapter 48

To work with misspellings in a shared border, you can later open any page that displays that shared border, select the shared border's text, and run another spelling check.

Alternatively, if you check the spelling in *all* pages in the Web site, you can open the actual page containing the shared border content from the Spelling dialog box and correct its spelling. The contents of the shared borders are stored in separate page files, named Left.htm, Top.htm, Right.htm, and Bottom.htm, which are stored in the _borders hidden subfolder of your Web site. Shared borders are discussed in "Working with Shared Borders," on page 1313. Note, however, that the Spelling dialog box shows shared border pages only if the Show Hidden Files And Folders option is checked. You can access this option by choosing Tools, Site Settings and clicking the Advanced tab.

Inserting Images

FrontPage provides more ways than ever to insert embedded images into your pages. The following are the different ways to add an image to a page:

- To add an image (or a movie or sound clip) from the collection of media files maintained by the Microsoft Clip Organizer program, choose Insert, Picture, Clip Art or click the Insert Clip Art button on the Drawing toolbar. FrontPage will display the Clip Art task pane. For information, see "Inserting Pictures with the Clip Organizer," on page 107.

Drawing

Note If the Drawing Toolbar isn't displayed, you can show it by clicking the Drawing button on the Standard toolbar.

Insert
Picture
From File

- To insert an image from a graphics file, choose Insert, Picture, From File, or click the Insert Picture From File button on the Standard toolbar or on the Drawing toolbar. For instructions, see "Importing Pictures," on page 117.

- To add an image that's displayed in another program, copy the graphics into the Clipboard and paste the graphic data into the page in FrontPage. For details, see "Importing Pictures," on page 117.

- If you have a scanner or digital camera attached to your computer, you can insert a scanned image or a digital photograph by choosing Insert, Picture, From Scanner Or Camera.

- To add and arrange a collection of images quickly, choose Insert, Picture, New Photo Gallery. For information on inserting a photo gallery, see "Adding a Photo Gallery," on page 1304.

- To insert a Shockwave Flash (.spl, .swf, or .swt) file, choose Insert, Picture, Movie In Flash Format.

- To insert a drawing canvas, choose Insert, Picture, New Drawing. Drawing canvases are explained in the sidebar "Drawing Canvases," on page 126.

- To create your own drawing within FrontPage by adding one or more AutoShapes, choose Insert, Picture, AutoShapes, or use the Drawing toolbar. For complete information on creating drawings, see "Using AutoShapes to Create Drawings," on page 123.

Insert WordArt

- To add decorative text, choose Insert, Picture, WordArt, or click the Insert WordArt button on the Drawing toolbar. For instructions on adding decorative text, see "Using WordArt to Produce Special Text Effects," on page 133.

- To add a video clip, choose Insert, Picture, Video. For details on working with video clips, see "Inserting a Video Clip," on page 1305.

For each embedded image you insert, FrontPage normally adds an HTML image element (an IMG element) to the page. An image element doesn't store the actual data for the image; rather, it stores the URL of a separate graphics file, which the browser loads and displays when it processes the image element.

If you insert one or more images from the Clip Organizer, from graphics or video files located outside of the current Web site, or from the Clipboard, the next time you save the page, FrontPage will display the Save Embedded Files dialog box (see Figure 48-9), which lets you control the way FrontPage saves the graphics file for each embedded image. In this dialog box, you can perform one or more of the following actions:

- To control whether FrontPage saves a copy of the selected file within the Web site, click the Set Action button to open the Set Action dialog box. If you choose not to save the file, FrontPage will use a reference to the original file rather than creating a copy of the file within the Web site.

- To rename the selected file, click the Rename button.

- To change the location of the selected file within the Web site, click the Change Folder button.

- To select the format of the selected file, click the Picture File Type button and in the Picture File Type dialog box, select the desired format (GIF, JPEG, PNG-8, or PNG-24), as well as the options you want for the selected format. You can insert into a page an image in almost any format—for example, GIF, JPEG, bitmap, TIFF, Windows metafile, Postscript, and PCX. However, if FrontPage saves a copy of the file in the Web site, it will convert the graphics to GIF, JPEG, or PNG format (a .gif, .jpg, or .png file).

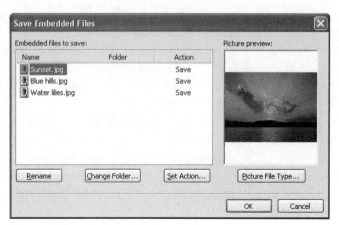

Figure 48-9. The Save Embedded Files dialog box lets you control the way FrontPage saves graphics files.

Note GIF (Graphics Interchange Format) and JPEG (Joint Photographic Experts Group) are the two most common graphics formats used on the Internet. GIF is ideal for efficiently storing an image that contains a moderate number of colors (typically 256 or less), while JPEG is best for storing an image based on a photograph that has many colors (more than 256). The PNG (Portable Network Graphics) formats are less common, and fewer browsers support them. PNG-8 is similar to GIF but provides better color support. PNG-24 is similar to JPEG; it stores the image without loss of detail (unlike JPEG) but creates a larger file than JPEG.

If you insert an image from a graphics file that's already stored in the current Web site (perhaps one supplied by the Web site template that you used to create the site or one that you imported into the site), FrontPage won't display the file in the Save Embedded Files dialog box. Nor will FrontPage display in this dialog box a file for an AutoShape or a WordArt object that you insert; rather, it will automatically save the graphics.

Note If the VML Graphics Office Drawing option is enabled, FrontPage will save an AutoShape or WordArt image directly within the Web page in VML (Vector Markup Language) format, which is a plain-text, XML-based description of a drawn image. If the Downlevel Image File option is checked, FrontPage will also include a regular IMG (image) element that refers to a stored .gif file as an alternative format for browsers that don't support VML. If the page is part of a Web site, FrontPage automatically saves the .gif file in a subfolder within the site, which FrontPage hides but which you can view in Microsoft Windows Explorer. If the page isn't part of a Web site, FrontPage stores the .gif file in a subfolder of the folder containing the page. (In either case the name of the subfolder is based on the name of the page that contains the image.)

You can set the VML Graphics Office Drawing and Downlevel Image File options by choosing Tools, Page Options and clicking the Authoring tab. See the tip "Ensure Compatibility" and Figure 48-19.

For information on changing an image's properties, as well as modifying an image using the Pictures toolbar, see "Formatting Images," on page 1336.

Creating a Thumbnail Image

A large image can take up a lot of space in a page and can also require an undue amount of time to download. To solve this problem, you can have FrontPage replace the full image with a *thumbnail image*, which is a smaller version of the image. A thumbnail image is assigned a hyperlink to the full image so that when you view the page in a browser, you can click the thumbnail image to display the full image by itself in the browser window.

Auto
Thumbnail

To convert an image to a thumbnail image, display the page that contains the image, select the image by clicking it, and then click the Auto Thumbnail button on the Pictures toolbar, or choose Auto Thumbnail from the Tools menu or from the shortcut menu that appears when you right-click the image, or press Ctrl+T. FrontPage will replace the image with a smaller version of the same image, and it will assign the small image a hyperlink to the full image.

You can modify the appearance—the size, border, and edge treatment—of the thumbnail images you create by choosing Tools, Page Options and clicking the AutoThumbnail tab (see Figure 48-10). (The changes you make here will affect only the thumbnail images you subsequently generate, not those that have already been created.) In this tab, you can change the size and border thickness of a thumbnail image and you can add a beveled edge.

Figure 48-10.   The AutoThumbnail tab of the Page Options dialog box allows you to set options for thumbnail images.

Adding a Photo Gallery

If you want to display a collection of images—derived from graphics files, a scanner, or a digital camera—you can quickly insert and arrange the images and create thumbnail images by adding a Photo Gallery component to your page (see Figure 48-11).

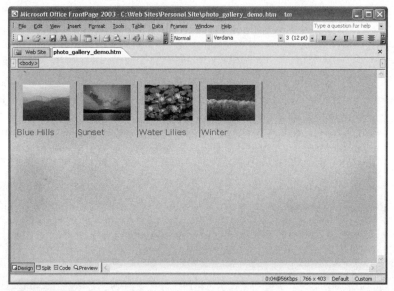

Figure 48-11. This Web page contains a single Photo Gallery component displaying the thumbnail versions of four images in FrontPage's Preview pane.

To insert a Photo Gallery component, perform the following steps:

1 Choose Insert, Picture, New Photo Gallery to open the Photo Gallery Properties dialog box.

2 To add the images, use the Pictures tab of the Photo Gallery Properties dialog box. To add each image, click the Add button and choose an image source from the drop-down menu. To work with each added image, select it in the list and use the controls in the Pictures tab (see Figure 48-12).

Figure 48-12. The Pictures tab of the Photo Gallery Properties dialog box is shown as it was filled in to create the Photo Gallery shown in Figure 48-11.

3 Use the Layout tab to select the general arrangement of the images in the Photo Gallery.

> A Photo Gallery is a type of FrontPage Web component. For general information on inserting and working with Web components, see "Adding Dynamic Content with Web Components," on page 1374.

Inserting a Video Clip

You can insert a video clip into a Web page at the position of the insertion point by choosing Insert, Picture, Video and selecting a video file in the Video dialog box, which works just like the standard Open dialog box.

You can also add a video clip from the Clip Organizer by inserting a Movies type clip. See "Inserting Pictures with the Clip Organizer," on page 107. The video sequence is normally played when the page is first opened in a browser. However, "Modifying a Video Clip," on page 1344, explains how to modify the behavior of a video clip.

Separating Content with Horizontal Dividing Lines

A horizontal dividing line is an attractive element you can use to separate different parts of your page. If the page has a theme, horizontal dividing lines are given a style that blends with the page's overall look. To insert a horizontal dividing line, place the insertion point at the position where you want to divide the page content and choose Insert, Horizontal Line. The line will occupy an entire row on the page.

Chapter 48

For information on modifying a horizontal dividing line, see "Formatting Other Page Elements," on page 1349.

Including Internal and External Hyperlinks

You can assign a hyperlink to a block of text, an image, a video clip, or a Web component. When the page is displayed in a browser, clicking an element that has been assigned a hyperlink causes the browser to display a different page, a different location within the same page, or a file such as an Office document or an image file. The file and the location that's displayed are known as the hyperlink's *target*. If the target is a file other than a Web page, the browser might open it in a different application or let you save it in a disk file.

Note This section explains how to add individual hyperlinks to a page. Another way to add hyperlinks is to insert a link bar Web component, which contains a set of hyperlinks for navigating to other pages in the Web site. With link bars that are based on the Web site's navigation structure, FrontPage automatically creates and maintains the hyperlinks contained in the bar. For more information, see "Using Navigation View," on page 1255.

Hyperlink

To add a hyperlink or to modify a hyperlink you have already assigned to an element, select the text, image, or other element. Or just place the insertion point at the position where you want the hyperlink (you'll be able to supply the hyperlink text that's displayed in your page when you define the hyperlink). Then choose Insert, Hyperlink; or click the Hyperlink button on the Standard toolbar; or press Ctrl+K. (The command won't be available if you've selected an element that can't be assigned a hyperlink, such as a horizontal dividing line.) Then, specify the hyperlink's target in the Insert Hyperlink dialog box (which is labeled Edit Hyperlink if you're modifying an existing hyperlink; see Figure 48-13). Follow the instructions for using Word's Insert Hyperlink dialog box given in "Adding and Using Hyperlinks," on page 580. The Insert Hyperlink dialog box in FrontPage is the same as that in Word, except that it has a Parameters button that you can click to add information for querying a database and a Style button you can click to modify the style of the hyperlink.

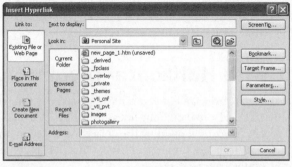

Figure 48-13. The Insert Hyperlink dialog box lets you add a hyperlink to a page.

> **Caution**   If you specify a hyperlink to a local or network file using a full file path specification (such as C:\Documents\Summary.htm or file:///C:/Documents/Summary.htm), the hyperlink won't work if the page is viewed on a different computer (unless the same file happens to exist in the same folder on that computer). To make your hyperlinks portable, you should use a Web address—either a relative address to another file within the Web site, such as *images/sunset.htm*, or a full Web address such as *http://www.example.com/mypage.htm*.

Normally when a hyperlink is clicked, the browser displays the beginning of the target file. If, however, your hyperlink's target is a Web page—either the same page that contains the hyperlink or a different one—you can have the browser display a particular location within that page by doing the following:

1   Open the target page in FrontPage.

2   Select text at the target location within the page.

3   Assign a bookmark to that text by choosing Insert, Bookmark or pressing Ctrl+G and typing a bookmark name. (You can include spaces in the name.) The text you selected in step 2 will be marked with a dashed underline.

4   When you define the hyperlink (in the same page or in a different one), select the target page in the Insert Hyperlink dialog box, click the Bookmark button, and in the Select Place In Document dialog box, select the bookmark you just defined.

> **Tip**   **Open a hyperlink target in a separate window**
>
> You can force browsers to open the hyperlink target in a separate browser window, rather than replacing the contents of the current window. This can be a useful way to let visitors to your Web site view another Web site without closing your page, which would encourage them to leave your site. To do this, click the Target Frame button in the Insert Hyperlink (or Edit Hyperlink) dialog box (shown in Figure 48-13), and select the New Window item in the Common Targets list of the Target Frame dialog box. (The other options in this dialog box—other than Page Default (None), which causes the browser to open the target using its default method—apply only if the hyperlink is contained in a page that's displayed within a frame. For more information on frames, see "Using Frames to Display Multiple Pages," on page 1367.)

To remove a hyperlink from a block of text or other element, select the element (or just place the insertion point anywhere within a block of text), open the Edit Hyperlink dialog box, and click the Remove Link button.

> **Note**   If the hyperlink's target is a page or file within your Web site, and you later use FrontPage to move or rename the target, FrontPage will automatically update the hyperlink so you don't need to edit it manually.

Chapter 48

If the page is open in FrontPage's Design or Split view, you can follow a hyperlink in a page by clicking it while pressing the Ctrl key or by right-clicking it and choosing Follow Hyperlink from the shortcut menu. (The Follow Hyperlink command isn't available for a hyperlink in a link bar. For this type of hyperlink, you'll need to use the Ctrl+click method.) For a page displayed in Preview view, you can simply click the hyperlink.

Following a hyperlink in Design or Split opens the file that's the target of the hyperlink. If the target is a page (within the Web site, on a disk or network, or on the Web), it's opened and displayed in an editing tab so you can view and edit it. If it's a different type of file (such as an image file or Office document), it's opened in the associated editor program. If the page is in a read-only location (for example on a Web server without Microsoft extensions for which you have a password), you won't be able to save the page back to its original location; however, you'll be able to save a separate copy of the page. Following a hyperlink in Preview view (or in a Web browser) merely displays the target document.

For information on using the Hyperlinks or Reports view to work with the hyperlinks in the pages in your Web site, see "Using Hyperlinks View," on page 1260, or "Viewing, Verifying, and Repairing Hyperlinks," on page 1270. For information on assigning hyperlinks to specific areas within an image to create an image map, see "Enhancing Images Using the Pictures Toolbar," on page 1340. For information on setting colors for text hyperlinks, see "Modifying Page Properties," on page 1350.

Using Tables Effectively

You can arrange text, images, and other page elements in rows and columns using tables, which are almost identical to tables in Word documents. Tables are a very effective way to organize information and enhance the appearance of a Web page. They are potentially more important in Web pages than in Word documents because Web pages lack some of the other formatting features that are available for Word documents, such as multiple columns and tab characters for aligning text (in FrontPage, the Tab key just inserts spaces). Fortunately, when creating Web pages in FrontPage, you can use tables to accomplish many of the same effects.

In FrontPage, you can insert a table by clicking the Insert Table button on the Standard toolbar and dragging to select the number of rows and columns, as shown here:

You can also insert and work with tables using the commands on the Table menu shown here:

You can also use the Tables toolbar seen here:

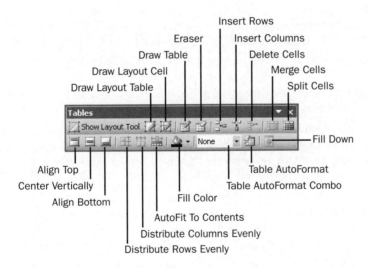

And you can apply or remove borders from a table using the Border button on the Formatting toolbar shown here:

You can apply borders with greater control over the formatting and apply a background color or picture by using the Borders And Shading dialog box.

The Borders And Shading dialog box is discussed in "Applying Borders and Shading," on page 1329.

The techniques for creating and modifying tables are substantially the same as those used in Word. For details, see "Arranging Text with Tables," on page 345, and "Adding Borders and Shading," on page 361. As you read that material, however, keep in mind the following differences in the way that you work with tables in FrontPage:

- In FrontPage, if you've added text to one cell, you can have FrontPage automatically copy that text to all cells in the same row to the right of that cell or to all cells in the same column below that cell. To do this, select the cell with the content you want to duplicate, plus all cells to the right or below to which you want to copy the content. Then choose Table, Fill, Right or choose Table, Fill, Down; or, click the Fill Right or Fill Down button on the Tables toolbar.

- In FrontPage, you can't adjust the width of individual cells in a column. You can adjust the width of only the entire column.

- In FrontPage, you can't select a entire cell by clicking on its left edge. To select a cell, you need to choose Table, Select, Cell. (You can select several entire cells by dragging over them.)

- FrontPage doesn't display end-of-cell or end-of-row marks. To insert a column at the right end of the table, select the right column and choose Table, Insert, Rows Or Columns. Then select the Right Of Selection option in the Insert Rows Or Columns dialog box and click the OK button.

- In FrontPage, you can't change the orientation of text in table cells; that is, you can't make it read from bottom to top or from top to bottom.

- In FrontPage, you can't designate a row as a heading. (If a page break occurs within a table, Word repeats the heading row(s) at the top of the next page.) You can, however, display a caption above or below the table by choosing Table, Insert, Caption. You can modify the caption position (top or bottom of table), as well as its style, by choosing Table, Table Properties, Caption.

  You can also designate one or more cells as a table *header*, which normally centers the cell's text and displays it in bold. To do this, select the cell(s) and choose Table, Table Properties, Cell. Then check the Header Cell option in the Cell Properties dialog box.

- FrontPage offers only a single AutoFit option (AutoFit To Contents, on the Table menu). It doesn't offer the AutoFit To Window or Fixed Column options available in Word.

- The Table menu in FrontPage doesn't provide Sort, Formula, or Show Gridlines commands. (Gridlines are always visible in FrontPage when borders aren't applied.)

- FrontPage 2003 provides a new set of tools, not found in Word, designed especially for working with tables that are used to arrange content on a Web page. You access these tools through the new Table, Layout Tables And Cells menu command; through the new Show Layout Tool, Draw Layout Table, and Draw Layout Cell buttons on the Tables toolbar; and through the new Layout Tables And Cells and Cell Formatting task panes. These tools are discussed in the next section.

Using Layout Tables and Cells

Because a table is so often used as the basic framework for arranging and organizing the content on a Web page, FrontPage 2003 provides a new set of tools designed specifically for creating and formatting the tables and table cells that are used to arrange Web page content. You can use these tools to work with a specially designated table, known as a *layout table*, which can have one or more cells. Or you can use these tools to work with a specially designated single-celled table known as a *layout cell*.

The following is a summary of the basic steps for working with layout tables and cells:

1   After you have created a new Web page, but before you have begun adding content to it, choose Table, Layout Tables And Cells to display the Layout Tables And Cells task pane.

> **Note**   If the Show When Creating A New Page option is checked at the bottom of the Layout Tables And Cells task pane, this task pane will appear automatically when you create a new page.

2   To create a layout grid for arranging your page's content, insert a layout table using one of the following methods:

- To insert a layout table having a specific arrangement of cells, click one of the table models in the Table Layout list.

- To insert a layout table consisting of a single cell, click the Insert Layout Table command.

- To use the mouse to draw a layout table, click the Draw Layout Table button.

Figure 48-14 shows a newly created Web page in which a layout table has been inserted.

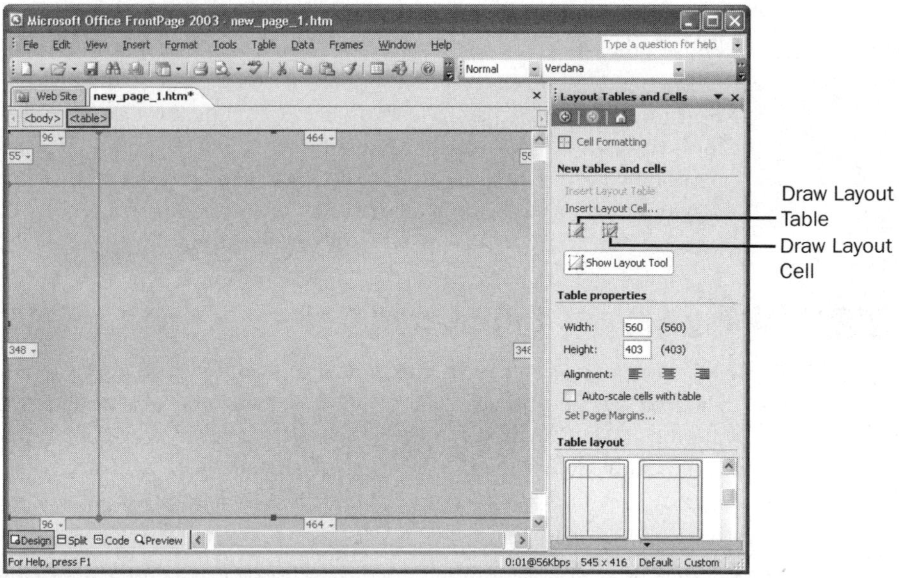

Figure 48-14. The "Corner, Header, Left, and Body" layout table has been inserted into the new Web page shown in this figure.

> **Tip** Because you typically use a layout table to hold all your page's content, it is, of course, much better to insert the table first and then add the page content into the appropriate cells. You can, however, effectively add a layout *cell* (as described in step 4) to a page with existing content. You can use a layout cell to highlight a specific block of text or graphics within the page.

3 To modify the features of the layout table, use the controls in the Table Properties area of the Layout Tables And Cells task pane.

4 To create a single-celled table that you can use to contain and highlight text or graphics within your page, insert a layout cell using one of the following methods:

- To insert a layout cell having exact measurements that you enter using a dialog box, click Insert Layout Cell.

- To use the mouse to draw a layout cell, click the Draw Layout Cell button.

5 To adjust the dimensions of a layout table, of cells within a layout table, or of a layout cell, or to add new cells, you can click the different table or cell borders and use the mouse to drag the various handles that appear.

6 To format a cell within a layout table, or to format a layout cell, click the Cell Formatting command at the top of the Layout Tables And Cells task pane to display the Cell Formatting task pane, shown here:

Then, click within the cell you want to format and use the controls in the Cell Formatting task pane to apply the desired formatting features. You can change the cell size, padding, vertical alignment, background color, and margins; apply borders, a header, or a footer; or add rounded corners or shadows. To modify a layout table or cell, you can also use many of the FrontPage techniques for working with regular tables, which were described in the previous section.

Working with Shared Borders

A page in a FrontPage Web site can display one or more shared borders on the top, bottom, left, or right of the page. The contents of a shared border are identical in all Web site pages that display that shared border. If you add or edit an element in a shared border in one page, your modification affects the content of that shared border in all pages in the Web site that display it. You might, for example, use a top shared border to display a page banner, a left shared border to display a link bar, and a bottom shared border to display an e-mail address, modification date, copyright notice, or other information.

A Web site has a *default* arrangement of shared borders; for instance, the default might be for all pages to display a top and a left shared border. A particular page can also have *individual* shared border settings, which override the default Web site settings.

To set the default shared borders, perform the following steps:

1 In any view, choose Format, Shared Borders.

> **Note** If the Format, Shared Borders command isn't available, see the Troubleshooting sidebar "Shared Borders Command Is Unavailable," later in this section.

2 In the Shared Borders dialog box, select the All Pages option (see Figure 48-15).

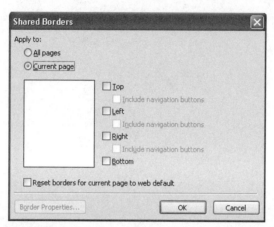

Figure 48-15. The Shared Borders dialog box provides options for working with shared borders.

3 Check the options for the particular shared borders you want to include. If you select a top, left, or right shared border, you can also check the adjoining Include Navigation Buttons option to have FrontPage automatically add a link bar that's based on the Web site's navigation structure to the shared border.

4 To assign a background color or picture to any of the shared borders you selected in step 3, click the Border Properties button.

Troubleshooting

Shared Borders command is unavailable

You want to apply shared borders to a set of pages you're creating, but the command is dimmed on the Format menu and you can't choose it.

Shared borders are one of the Web page features that are unavailable if you haven't opened a Web site but rather are using FrontPage to edit individual pages. Other unavailable features include publishing (the Publish Site command on the File menu); link bars, tables of contents, and several other Web components; and the Web site management tools provided through the Web Site tab.

If you've opened a Web site and the Format, Shared Borders command is still unavailable, you can enable it by choosing Tools, Page Options, clicking the Authoring tab, and checking the Shared Borders option.

To assign individual shared border settings to one or more pages, perform the following steps:

1 Select the page(s) you want to modify in the Folder List. Alternatively, for a single page, you can open it and display it in an editing tab.

2 Choose Format, Shared Borders and in the Shared Borders dialog box, select the Selected Page(s) option. (If you opened a page in step 1, the option will be Current Page rather than Selected Page(s).) Then check the options for the shared borders you want to apply.

> **Note** When you're applying individual shared border settings, you can't check the Include Navigation Buttons options.

3 To assign a background color or picture to any of the shared borders you selected in step 2, click the Border Properties button.

4 To remove the individual shared border settings and use the default settings for the selected pages, check the Reset Borders For Current Page To Web Default option.

When you work in the main area of the page, the shared border areas are marked with dotted lines. To add or edit elements in a shared border, click anywhere within it; the dotted lines will become solid lines. You can then work within the shared border the same way you work within the page's main area.

> **Note** FrontPage stores the shared border content in Web page files named Bottom.htm, Left.htm, Right.htm, and Top.htm, which are kept in the hidden _borders subfolder within your Web site. If you wish, you can open and directly edit any of these pages.

Troubleshooting

Shared borders offer little control

You've added shared borders to the pages in your Web site to display common content that you want to appear in every page, but you have little control over the width, height, and text alignment of the shared border areas and you can't add visible borders to define these areas.

Shared borders were enhanced in FrontPage 2002 to let you assign a separate background color or picture to any of the shared borders or to the main area of the page. (In earlier versions of FrontPage, the page background was applied to all shared borders as well as to the main area of the page.) However, you still have little control over the size of the shared borders or the alignment of text within them. The following alternative method lets you create border areas that contain shared content, but provide all the sizing, alignment, and visible border choices offered by FrontPage tables:

1 In each page in your Web site, follow the instructions given in the previous section to add a layout table that provides one or more cells that you can use as border areas.

For example, to create top, left, and bottom border areas, you could use a layout table with the "Header, Body, Footer, and Left" style, shown in Figure 48-16.

Cell used for top border area

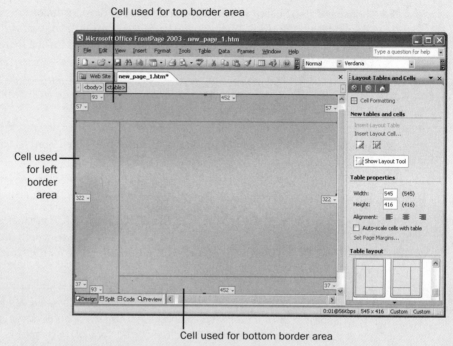

Cell used
for left
border
area

Cell used for bottom border area

Figure 48-16. In the layout table applied to this page, you could use the top, left, and bottom cells as border areas.

2 To include shared content in one of the cells used as a border area, create a separate page that contains the content that is to be displayed in that border area in all pages (perhaps a title and logo for a top border area and a list of hyperlinks for a left border area). Save the page within the Web site.

3 In each page, place the insertion point in the cell used for the border area, choose Insert, Web Component, and in the Insert Web Component dialog box, select Included Content in the Component Type list and select Page in the Choose A Type Of Content list. (See Figure 48-17.) Then click the Finish button and type the name of the page you created in step 2 into the Include Page Properties dialog box.

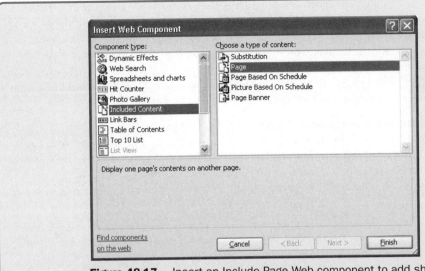

Figure 48-17. Insert an Include Page Web component to add shared content to a table cell used as a border area.

 Previewing and Printing Your Page

You can quickly preview the way a page opened in FrontPage will appear in your browser by displaying that page and clicking the Preview view button at the bottom of the editing tab. This will display the page in Preview view, which will render the page almost as if it were opened in your browser. To resume editing the page, click the Design view button to return to Design view.

Alternatively, you can preview a page by opening it within any browser installed on your computer. If you use this method, you can also have FrontPage adjust the size of the browser window to show exactly how much of the page will be displayed in a maximized browser window under a particular video resolution. Another reason for using this method is that some Web components—such as a table of contents—are displayed correctly only in a browser and not in the Preview view.

To preview your page in a browser, perform the following steps:

1 If the page has unsaved changes, be sure to save it so that you'll see the latest version when you preview it.

2 Open and display the page in an editing tab or select the page's filename in the Folder List.

3 Choose File, Preview In Browser to display the submenu. Or click the down arrow next to the Preview button on the Standard toolbar to display the drop-down menu. Then, from the submenu or drop-down menu (shown in Figure 48-18), choose a command for the browser you want to use (if you have more than one). If you choose a command that includes a video resolution (such as 800 x 600), FrontPage will adjust the size of the browser window to show you how much of the page would fit within a maximized browser window under the indicated resolution.

 To add or remove browsers from the menu (the File, Preview In Browser submenu as well as the Preview drop-down menu), choose the Edit Browser List command. If two or more browsers have been added to the menu, the menu will include a Preview In Multiple Browsers command for each resolution. You can choose one of these commands to have FrontPage run *all* the browsers and display the page in each of them, making it easy for you to quickly check the appearance of your page in several browsers.

> **Tip**   To quickly redisplay the selected or displayed page using the previous single-browser option you choose from the Preview In Browser submenu or from the Preview drop-down menu, press F12. Or right-click the filename in the Folder List and choose Preview In Browser from the shortcut menu. (To open the page in all browsers on the menu list, using the last chosen resolution, choose Preview In Multiple Browsers from this shortcut menu.)

Preview

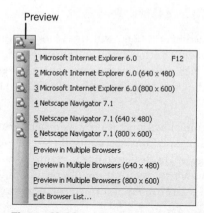

Figure 48-18.   You can preview a Web page by selecting a browser and resolution from the Preview drop-down menu on the Standard toolbar.

Tip Simulate a browser resolution in the FrontPage editor

When you view a page in the Design, Split, or Preview view, you can have FrontPage adjust the size of the view to show how much of the page would be visible in a browser under a specific video resolution. To do this, click the resolution displayed at the right end of the FrontPage status bar and select the desired target resolution from the pop-up menu, shown here:

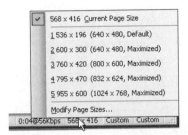

To change the list of resolutions that are displayed on the pop-up menu, choose Modify Page Sizes.

You can print a hard copy of the page opened in the Design, Split, or Code view by choosing commands from the File menu, as follows:

- To set a header, footer, or margins for the printed page, or to select the printer and printer settings, choose Page Setup.
- To preview the printed appearance of the page, choose Print Preview.
- To display the Print dialog box, which lets you select the printer and printing options and then print the page, choose Print or press Ctrl+P.
- To print the page immediately using your default printer and printing options, click the Print button on the Standard toolbar.

Print

 Tip Ensure compatibility

If you know the features of the Web server on which your page is published (specifically, the FrontPage and Windows SharePoint Services technologies provided, if any), or if you know the type or types of browsers that will be used to view your pages, you can have FrontPage allow you to add only those page elements and features that the available server and browser technologies support. To do this, choose Tools, Page Options and click the Authoring tab (see Figure 48-19). Then, to specify available server technologies, do either of the following:

- In the drop-down list at the top (FrontPage And SharePoint Technologies), select Default, None, or Complete to specify the available server support for FrontPage and SharePoint technologies. FrontPage will then automatically check or clear the options for the appropriate specific server technologies.

or

Chapter 48

- Check just the options for the specific server technologies that are available and clear all the others. FrontPage will then select the Custom item in the drop-down list.

To specify the available browser technologies, do one of the following:

- In the Browsers and Browser Versions drop-down lists, select the specific browsers and browser versions that your visitors will use. FrontPage will then automatically check or clear the options for the appropriate specific browser technologies.

    or

- Check just the options for the specific browser technologies that are available to your prospective site visitors and clear all the others.

After you do this, FrontPage will dim and disable the commands and options for adding features that rely on technologies that are cleared in the Authoring tab.

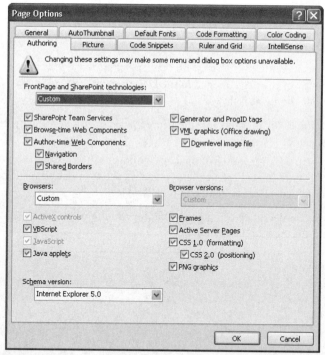

Figure 48-19. The Authoring tab of the Page Options dialog box lets you specify the server and browser technologies that will be available when users view your web.

Chapter 49

Formatting Your Web Pages

A Page Formatting Overview 1321
Formatting Paragraphs 1322
Formatting Characters 1332
Formatting Images 1336
Positioning Paragraphs, Images,
Tables, and Other Elements 1346

Formatting Other Page Elements 1349
Formatting the Whole Page 1350
Modifying, Creating, and Using
Cascading Style Sheet Styles 1358

A Page Formatting Overview

The previous chapter explained how to use Microsoft Office FrontPage 2003 to add the most basic elements to your Web pages. This chapter explains how to use the FrontPage editor to format many of these elements, as well as the entire page and the more advanced elements discussed in Chapter 50, "Adding Advanced Features to Your Web Pages and Working with Source Code." In this chapter, to *format* means to modify the appearance, behavior, or other characteristics of the element or page.

The most common way to format an element is by displaying its *properties* dialog box. For example, you can format text in the Font dialog box, a paragraph in the Paragraph dialog box, an image in the Picture Properties dialog box, and the entire page in the Page Properties dialog box. The methods for displaying the properties dialog box depend on the particular element.

You can also format certain elements using special-purpose toolbars provided by FrontPage: the Formatting toolbar for formatting paragraphs, tables, and characters; the Positioning toolbar for positioning paragraphs, images, tables, and other elements; the DHTML Effects toolbar for applying animation and formatting effects to paragraphs; and the Pictures toolbar for formatting images. If the toolbar you want to use isn't currently visible, you can show it by choosing its name from the View, Toolbars submenu.

Finally, you can apply additional formatting features by using various menu commands (in addition to those that display properties dialog boxes or toolbars). For example, you can use the Format, Borders And Shading command to add borders or background colors or images to paragraphs and tables, and the Format, Page Transition command to assign transition effects to the entire page.

> **Note**   If a theme has been applied to your page, FrontPage won't let you directly change some of the formatting defined by the theme. For instance, in a page that has a theme, you can't use the techniques presented in this chapter to directly modify the page background or the default font displayed when the page is open for editing in FrontPage. You can, however, indirectly modify these formatting features by customizing the theme. (See "Using Themes to Quickly Change the Overall Page Format" on page 1353.)

Formatting Paragraphs

Applying paragraph formatting changes the appearance of one or more entire paragraphs of text. This section describes the following essential paragraph formatting techniques:

- Changing the paragraph style or format using the Formatting toolbar
- Changing the paragraph format using the Paragraph dialog box
- Applying bullets or numbering using the Bullets And Numbering dialog box
- Removing paragraph formatting

The following sections explain how to modify the format of a paragraph by adding borders or shading or applying dynamic HTML (Hypertext Markup Language) effects.

> For information on placing a paragraph at any position on the page, see "Positioning Paragraphs, Images, Tables, and Other Elements," on page 1346.

To change the paragraph style or alignment, or to apply bullets, numbering, or borders using the Formatting toolbar, perform the following steps:

1   Select the paragraph or paragraphs you want to format. Or, to format a single paragraph, simply place the insertion point anywhere within it.

2   Use the controls on the Formatting toolbar (shown in Figure 49-1) as follows:

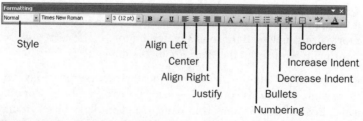

Figure 49-1.   This figure labels the controls on the Formatting toolbar that can be used for formatting paragraphs.

> **Note** Formatting a paragraph by applying the appropriate style—rather than assigning individual paragraph and character formatting features—saves you time (you may not need to apply any further formatting), promotes formatting consistency throughout your document (for example, all headings with the Heading 1 style will look the same), and gives the browser greater latitude in applying formatting that's appropriate and that conforms to the user's preferences.

- To change the paragraph style, choose an item in the Style drop-down list (other than Default Character Style), as shown here:

The best way to begin formatting a paragraph is to select the style from the Style drop-down list that most closely matches the function of the paragraph. For example, if the paragraph serves as body text, you should select the Normal style. (This style is applied by default to the text in a new, blank page.) Or, if the paragraph serves as a top-level heading, you should select the Heading 1 style. Applying a style converts the paragraph to the appropriate HTML element (see Table 49-1). Then, even if you apply no further paragraph or character formatting, the browser will display the paragraph using appropriate formatting features. (For instance, it might format a Heading 1 paragraph using a 24-point Times New Roman font, and a Normal paragraph using a 12-point Times New Roman font.)

If you wish, you can then refine the formatting of the paragraph by applying specific paragraph or character formatting features, which will override the features of the style. The techniques for refining formatting are described in the remainder of this section and in the following sections. You can also refine the formatting of the paragraphs in your page by globally modifying the formatting of specific page elements or by creating and applying custom character or paragraph styles, as explained in "Modifying, Creating, and Using Cascading Style Sheet Styles," on page 1358.

- To quickly convert the selected paragraphs to a bulleted or numbered list (or to remove existing bullets or numbers), click the Bullets or Numbering button. But for greater control over the list's formatting, use the Bullets And Numbering dialog box, as described later in this section.

■ To adjust the left indent of the selected paragraph, click the Increase Indent or Decrease Indent button. If you select an item within a bulleted or numbered list (a list that consists of more than one paragraph) and click the Increase Indent button, the paragraph will be indented and will become a *nested* list item. Each click Increase Indent will increase the level of nesting, and each click Decrease Indent will decrease it. In a bulleted list, nested items will display different bullet characters, and in a numbered list, they will start a new numbering sequence. (After the first click, the bullet or number will disappear; it will reappear after subsequent clicks. So keep clicking!)

■ To adjust the alignment of the selected paragraph or paragraphs, click the Align Left, Center, Align Right, or Justify button. Clicking one of these buttons when it's already selected deselects the button, removes the alignment style, and assigns the paragraph the Default alignment style, meaning that the browser will display the paragraph using the alignment style set in the browser.

■ To quickly apply (or remove) one or more borders around the selected paragraph or paragraphs, or cell(s) in a table, click the down arrow on the Border button and choose a border style from the palette shown here:

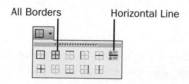

All Borders   Horizontal Line

Note The Horizontal Line button on the right side of the Border drop-down palette inserts a horizontal dividing line rather than applying a border.

To apply borders with more formatting options, or to apply a background color or picture, use the Borders And Shading dialog box, explained in "Applying Borders and Shading," on page 1329.

Table 49-1. The Built-In FrontPage Styles

Built-In FrontPage Style	HTML Element(s) Applied to the Text	Description/Comment
Address	ADDRESS	For formatting a name, initials, an address, an author list, or other identifying information, typically at the bottom of a page.
Bulleted List	UL and LI	You can create a bulleted list by applying this style to each item. For greater control over the list's formatting, use the Bullets And Numbering dialog box, described later in this section.

Table 49-1. The Built-In FrontPage Styles

Built-In FrontPage Style	HTML Element(s) Applied to the Text	Description/Comment
Default Character Style	None	This style *doesn't* apply an HTML element. Rather, it is used to remove a custom character style as explained in "Modifying, Creating, and Using Cascading Style Sheet Styles," on page 1358.
Defined Term	DL and DT	To create a glossary or other list of term and description (or definition) pairs, format each term using Defined Term and each definition or description using Definition.
Definition	DL and DD	See the previous item.
Directory List	DIR and LI	For formatting a list of short items. Most browsers, however, treat this style as though it were Bulleted List.
Formatted	PRE	Displays the text in a monospace font, preserving all space characters and line breaks, without wrapping the lines. This style is often used to display program code.
Heading 1 through Heading 6	H1 through H6	For formatting top-level through level 6 headings.
Menu List	MENU and LI	For formatting a list of short menu items in a compact format. Most browsers, however, treat this style as though it were Bulleted List.
Normal	P	For formatting a normal paragraph of body text.
Numbered List	OL and LI	You can create an automatically numbered list by applying this style to each item. For greater control over the list's formatting, use the Bullets And Numbering dialog box, described later in this section.

To modify the paragraph alignment, indentation, or spacing using the Paragraph dialog box, perform the following steps:

1 Select the paragraph or paragraphs you want to format. Or, to format a single paragraph, simply place the insertion point anywhere within it.

2 Choose Format, Paragraph or right-click the selection or paragraph you want to format and choose Paragraph from the shortcut menu. This will display the Paragraph dialog box (shown in Figure 49-2).

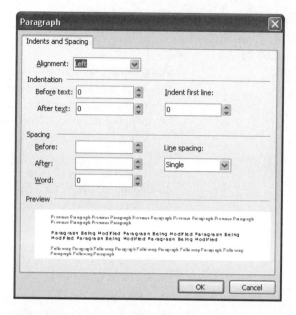

Figure 49-2. The Paragraph dialog box allows you to change the alignment, indentation, and spacing of a paragraph.

3 Select options in the dialog box until the sample paragraph in the Preview area has the look you want.

To convert paragraphs into a bulleted or numbered list using the Bullets And Numbering dialog box, perform the following steps:

1 Select the paragraphs containing the list items. (Or, to convert a single paragraph to a bulleted or numbered item, place the insertion point anywhere within it. When you press Enter at the end of a list paragraph, the next paragraph is given the same list formatting.)

2 Choose Format, Bullets And Numbering to display the Bullets And Numbering dialog box.

3 Select options in the tabs of the Bullets And Numbering dialog box, as follows:

■ To apply bullets consisting of an image from a graphics file, use the Picture Bullets tab (shown in Figure 49-3).

Figure 49-3. The Picture Bullets tab of the Bullets And Numbering dialog box allows you to apply bullets consisting of an image from a graphics file.

- To apply one of the standard bullet styles that are built into browsers, use the Plain Bullets tab (shown in Figure 49-4).

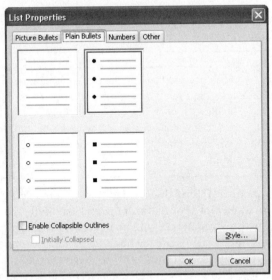

Figure 49-4. The Plain Bullets tab of the Bullets And Numbering dialog box appears only if the page has no theme.

■ To create an automatically numbered list, use the Numbers tab to select a numbering style and to specify the starting number (as shown in Figure 49-5).

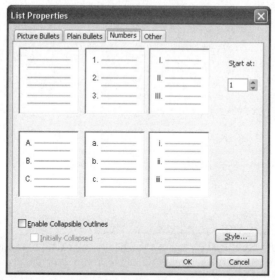

Figure 49-5. The Numbers tab of the Bullets And Numbering dialog box allows you to select a numbering style and a starting number.

> **Note** If a theme is applied to the current page, the Bullets And Numbering dialog box won't include the Plain Bullets tab, and you'll be able to apply only graphics bullets.

> **Note** As explained earlier, you can use the Increase Indent and Decrease Indent buttons on the Formatting toolbar to adjust the level of indentation of different list items, thereby converting a simple list into a multilevel outline. If you want the page visitor to be able to collapse or expand the outline by clicking it in a browser, check the Enable Collapsible Outlines option in the Bullets And Numbering dialog box. To start with a collapsed outline, also check the Initially Collapsed option.

To remove most of the formatting features discussed in this section, select *all the text in the paragraph* and choose Format, Remove Formatting or press Ctrl+Shift+Z or Ctrl+Spacebar. The paragraph will revert to the Normal style, with no bullets or numbering, no indentation (of the type applied through the Paragraph dialog box), the Default alignment style, single line spacing, and no extra spacing between lines or words. Keep in mind that this command will also remove character formatting. This command, however, won't remove borders or shading.

> **Note**   The Remove Formatting command won't remove paragraph formatting from a paragraph unless you've selected *all the characters* in the paragraph. Also, this command will remove indentation that you've applied using the Paragraph dialog box (which indents by adding a CSS margin style to the paragraph element), but *not* indentation that you've applied using the Increase Indent button on the Formatting toolbar (which indents a non-list paragraph by nesting the paragraph within one or more BLOCKQUOTE elements).

Applying Borders and Shading

You can emphasize one or more paragraphs or cells in a table by applying borders or shading using the Borders And Shading dialog box. Perform the following steps:

1   Select the paragraph(s) or table cell(s). (To select a single table cell, place the insertion point within it and choose Table, Select, Cell. If the entire cell isn't selected, you'll apply borders or shading to the paragraph within the cell, rather than to the cell itself.)

> **Note**   If you select several paragraphs prior to applying borders, a single set of borders will be drawn around the entire group of paragraphs. To draw separate borders around each paragraph, select and apply borders to each paragraph individually, or choose the All Borders option from the Border drop-down palette on the Formatting toolbar, described in the previous section, to apply all the borders at once.

2   Choose Format, Borders And Shading to display the Borders And Shading dialog box.

3   Select options in the tabs of the Borders And Shading dialog box until the sample paragraph in the Preview area has the look you want. (The Preview area on either tab shows the effects of the options selected on both tabs.) See Figures 49-6 and 49-7.

A foreground color you select on the Shading tab is applied to the text characters, while a background color fills the paragraph's background. Clicking the down arrow on the Background Color or Foreground Color control displays the same color palette shown by the Highlight and Font Color buttons on the Formatting toolbar.

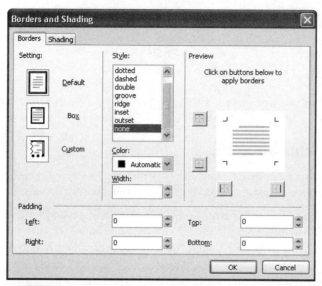

Figure 49-6. Apply borders using the Borders tab of the Borders And Shading dialog box.

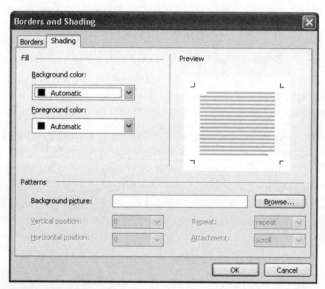

Figure 49-7. Apply shading using the Shading tab of the Borders And Shading dialog box.

For more information on choosing a color from a color palette, see "Formatting Characters," on page 1332.

After you have applied a border or shading, you can adjust the size of the area that is enclosed by the border or that is shaded by clicking the paragraph and then dragging one of the sizing handles that appear, as shown here:

Creating Dynamic HTML Effects

You can use the DHTML Effects toolbar to animate a paragraph. The animation is known as a *dynamic HTML effect*, and it can consist of the paragraph's "flying" off the page in a particular direction, an instant change in the paragraph's format (the font, border, or shading), or another effect. You can have the animation occur when the page is first loaded into a browser, when you click the paragraph, when you double-click the paragraph, or when you place the mouse pointer over the paragraph.

To animate a paragraph, perform the following steps:

1 Display the DHTML Effects toolbar, shown here, by choosing View, Toolbars, DHTML Effects.

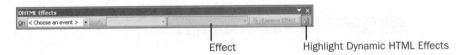

Effect   Highlight Dynamic HTML Effects

2 Place the insertion point anywhere within the paragraph you want to animate (or select several paragraphs).

3 To specify when the animation occurs, select an item in the On drop-down list on the DHTML Effects toolbar: Click, Double Click, Mouse Over, or Page Load.

4 To specify the general type of animation that occurs, select an item in the Apply drop-down list: Fly Out (to have the paragraph "fly" off the page) or Formatting (to have the formatting change). If you selected Mouse Over in step 3, only Formatting will be available. If you selected Page Load, a variety of additional effects will be available (Drop In By Word, Elastic, Fly In, and others).

5 To further specify the type of animation that occurs, select an item in the Effect drop-down list. The available items depend on your previous choices. For example, if you selected Fly Out in the Apply drop-down list, you can select To Left, To Top, To Bottom-Left, or another value, to specify the direction of the animation.

Chapter 49

If the Highlight Dynamic HTML Effects button is selected on the DHTML Effects toolbar, any paragraph that has been assigned an effect will be highlighted in Design and Split view (but not in Preview view or in a browser). You can test an effect by clicking the Preview button at the bottom of the editing tab to switch to Preview view, or by displaying the page in a browser. (The animation won't be displayed in Design or Split view.) If you want to remove an effect from a paragraph, click the paragraph, and then click the Remove Effect button on the DHTML Effects toolbar.

Formatting Characters

You can apply character formatting to change the appearance of one or more individual characters in your page. To format characters, either select a block of existing characters or place the insertion point at the position where you are going to type new characters. Then, choose either Format, Font or Format, Properties, or press Alt+Enter. (As a general rule, choosing the Format, Properties command displays the properties dialog box for the currently selected element. If you have selected a block of characters, it will display the properties dialog box for characters, which is labeled Font.) Or, you can right-click the selected characters or insertion position and choose Font from the shortcut menu. FrontPage will then display the Font dialog box, shown in Figures 49-8 and 49-9. Select options in the Font and Character Spacing tabs in this dialog box until the text sample in the Preview area has the look you want, and then click the OK button.

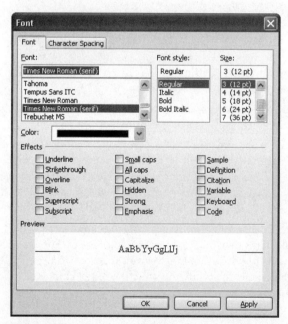

Figure 49-8. The Font tab of the Font dialog box is used to set the text font, style, size, color, and effects.

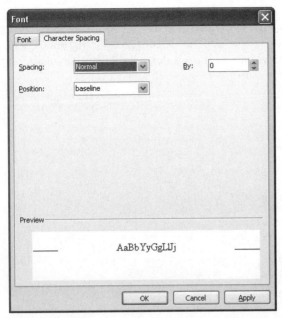

Figure 49-9. The Character Spacing tab of the Font dialog box is used to set the text spacing and position.

You can also quickly apply some of the available character formats to the selected text—or to the characters you will type at the current position of the insertion point—by using the Formatting toolbar shown here:

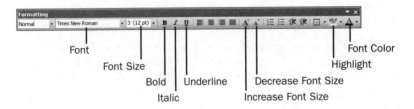

The buttons not labeled in this graphic are used for formatting paragraphs or tables, and are explained in "Formatting Paragraphs," on page 1322.

The Font Color button (as well as the Color drop-down list in the Font dialog box) sets the color of the text characters themselves, while the Highlight button sets the color of the background surrounding the characters. To apply a specific text or background color, click the Font Color button (or the equivalent Color drop-down list in the Font dialog box) or the Highlight button to display the color palette shown here:

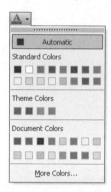

Then, select an item on the palette as follows:

- To display the text using the default color defined by the theme, choose Automatic. If the page doesn't have a theme, this option will display the text using the text or background color defined in the Formatting tab of the Page Properties dialog box for the page.

> The Formatting tab of the Page Properties dialog box is explained in "Modifying Page Properties," on page 1350.

- To apply a commonly used color, select a color in the Standard Colors area.
- To apply one of the colors defined by the page's theme, select a color in the Theme Colors area (which appears only if the page has a theme). Using one of these colors instead of selecting a new one can help ensure that your text blends into the theme's overall color scheme.
- If you've previously applied specific colors to elements in the current page, you can reapply one of these colors by choosing a color in the Document Colors area. This area of the palette helps you reuse colors and maintain a consistent color scheme.
- To choose from a much larger selection of standard colors, to define a custom color, or to use a color that appears anywhere on your screen, choose More Colors.

To reapply the previously applied text or background color, you can just click the Font Color or Highlight button rather than displaying the palette.

Tip   Match a color
If you see a color you like anywhere on your screen (perhaps in a Web page that you've opened in your browser), you can apply that exact color to an element in FrontPage by clicking the More Colors option on the color palette (for example, on the palette displayed by the Font Color or Highlight button on the Formatting toolbar). Then, in the More Colors dialog box, click the Select button and then click the color you want to use wherever it appears on your screen.

If you select the (Default Font) item in the Font list of the Font dialog box or in the Font drop-down list on the Formatting toolbar, the selected text will be displayed using the default font specified by the page's theme. If the page doesn't have a theme, then each browser will display the text using the font set in the browser.

Note   You can select the fonts that FrontPage uses in Design view (and in the design pane of Split view) to display all text assigned the (Default Font) formatting in any page that doesn't have a theme. To do this, choose Tools, Page Options and click the Default Fonts tab (shown in Figure 49-10). For each available language, you can then select—in the Design View area—a font for proportional text and one for fixed-width text. (The fixed-width font is used in a paragraph that's assigned the Formatted style.)

Also for each available language, you can select—in the Code View area—the font and font size that FrontPage uses in Code view, in the code pane of Split view, and also when you're editing a text file in the source code editor.

Keep in mind that your choices affect only the way the page appears in the FrontPage editing views, *not* the way it is shown in the FrontPage Preview view or the way it appears in a browser.

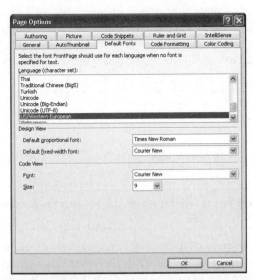

Figure 49-10.   The Default Fonts tab of the Page Options dialog box allows you to select default fonts that FrontPage uses for displaying text.

Also, if you select the Normal item in the Size list of the Font dialog box or in the Font Size drop-down list on the Formatting toolbar, the browser will display the text using the font size set in the browser for the style assigned to the paragraph that contains the text. The font size for the Normal paragraph style (in HTML, a P element) is typically 12 points, and the font size for the Heading 1 paragraph style (an H1 element) is typically 24 points. (The exact size depends on the particular browser and the settings made in that browser.)

> Paragraph styles are discussed in "Formatting Paragraphs," on page 1322.

To remove any character formatting that has been applied to a block of text (by you or by the template used to create the page), select the characters and choose Format, Remove Formatting or press Ctrl+Shift+Z or Ctrl+Spacebar. The character format will revert to the (Default Font) font, the Regular font style, the Normal size, and the Automatic font and highlight colors, and any effects will be removed. Keep in mind that if an entire paragraph is selected, this command will also remove most types of paragraph formatting from that paragraph.

> You can also format characters by defining and applying user-defined character styles, as explained in "Modifying, Creating, and Using Cascading Style Sheet Styles," on page 1358.

Troubleshooting

Kerning isn't available

You would like to apply kerning to your characters as you can in Microsoft Word, but the feature isn't available in FrontPage.

Although FrontPage won't automatically kern your text, you can manually kern a specific letter pair (such as *Ta*) by selecting the characters and choosing Format, Font. Then, click the Character Spacing tab, select Condensed in the Spacing drop-down list, and in the By box enter the amount (in pixels) by which you want the spacing between the characters to be reduced.

Formatting Images

The following sections describe how to modify images using the Picture Properties dialog box and the Pictures toolbar.

> "Inserting Images," on page 1300, explains how to insert an image in a page and how to convert an image element to a thumbnail image.

The first step is always to select the image, which you do by clicking it. FrontPage will display a set of sizing handles around the selected image. (You can also select an image by selecting one or more adjoining text characters and extending the selection highlight across the image. In this case, FrontPage will reverse the image colors rather than displaying sizing handles. However, using this method for selecting an image won't let you perform many of the formatting operations discussed in the next two sections.)

Modifying Image Properties

To modify an image's properties, perform the following steps:

1 Click the image to select it.

2 Choose Format, Properties; press Alt+Enter; right-click the image and choose Picture Properties from the shortcut menu; or double-click the image. This will display the Picture Properties dialog box.

3 To modify the size and position of the image, set options as follows in the Appearance tab (shown in Figure 49-11):

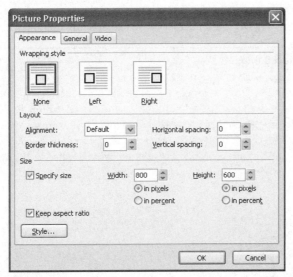

Figure 49-11. You can modify the wrapping style, layout, or size of an image, or add a border, in the Appearance tab of the Picture Properties dialog box.

- To change the size of the image from its original size specified in the image file, check the Specify Size option and enter the size and size options using the controls in the Size area.

  Changing the size here *scales* the image—that is, it makes everything in the image larger or smaller. In the next section, you'll learn how to reduce the overall dimensions of an image by cropping it, which discards parts of the image rather than making all parts of the image smaller. You can also quickly scale an image by clicking it and dragging a sizing handle; if you drag a corner handle, the image proportions will be preserved. To restore an image to its original size, just clear the Specify Size option in the Appearance tab.

- To adjust the alignment of the image with respect to the adjoining text, select an option in the Alignment drop-down list. If you select the Left or the Right alignment option—or if you select the Left or Right wrapping style, which has the same effect—the image will be aligned with the left or right page margin, and the adjoining lines of text will wrap around the image. If you select any of the other alignment options, the image will be placed within a line of text and will be treated like a single text character; the particular option you select will affect the vertical alignment of the image with respect to the line of text that contains it. (The Default option is the same as Baseline.) ("Positioning Paragraphs, Images, Tables, and Other Elements," on page 1346, explains how to position an image anywhere on a page rather than aligning it with text.)

- To display a border around the image, enter a thickness greater than 0 in the Border Thickness text box.

- To adjust the spacing between the image and the surrounding elements, enter a value in the Horizontal Spacing or Vertical Spacing text box.

Tip   **Resample a reduced image**

When you reduce the size of an image in the Picture Properties dialog box, you reduce its *displayed* size, but not the size of the image file. (The file still stores the complete data for the full image.) To reduce the size of the file to match the displayed image size, you can *resample* the image. In FrontPage 2003 there are now two ways to resample an image. First, whenever you select an image that you have resized, FrontPage will display the Picture Actions button. To resample, you can click this button and choose the Resample Picture To Match Size option on the drop-down menu, shown here:

(Once you've selected the Resample Picture To Match Size option, the Picture Actions button will no longer appear, because resampling is an irreversible action.)

Second, you can use the Resample button on the Pictures toolbar, described in "Enhancing Images Using the Pictures Toolbar," on page 1340.

Resampling will produce an image file that is smaller and faster to download. However, because graphics data is permanently removed from the file, you won't be able to scale the image back to its original size without loss of image quality. (For this reason, before you resample an important image, it's a good idea to make a backup copy of the image file.)

---

4 To change other image settings, use the General tab (shown in Figure 49-12) as follows:

Figure 49-12. The General tab of the Picture Properties dialog box allows you to change other image settings.

- To change the image file, type a new file path or URL in the Picture text box or click the Browse button to select the file.

- To edit the image in Microsoft Picture Library (or an alternative graphics editor you've configured FrontPage to use), click the Edit button. (If the graphics file is in the current FrontPage Web site, you can also open it for editing by double-clicking its filename in the Folder List.) (For information on configuring FrontPage to use a specific graphics editor that you have installed for editing a particular type of graphics file, see "Working with Files," on page 1247.)

- To change the image format, click the Picture File Type button and select a format in the Picture File Type dialog box. (For information on the Picture File Type dialog box and the different graphics formats, see "Inserting Images," on page 1300.)

- To specify the location of a low-resolution version of the image file, which the browser can quickly download and display while the full image file is downloading, enter the file path or the URL of the file in the Low-Res text box or click the Browse button to select the file. (In FrontPage, you can create a low-resolution version of an image file by using either the Auto Thumbnail feature or the Resample command.) (The Auto Thumbnail feature is described in "Creating a Thumbnail Image," on page 1303. The Resample command is explained in the tip "Resample a reduced image," on page 1338.)

- To specify alternative text, type it in the Text text box. Some browsers will display this text while the image file is downloading, when the pointer is held over the image (the text will appear in a ScreenTip), or if images are disabled in the browser.

- If you have a file that contains a description of the image, you can enter the file's path or URL into the Long Description text box or click the Browse button to select the file. According to the HTML 4.01 specification, this file should contain a more detailed description of the image, which complements any alternative text that you specified. However, Microsoft Internet Explorer 6 doesn't actually display the description.

- To assign a hyperlink to the image, use the controls in the Default Hyperlink area.

> For information on assigning hyperlinks to an image, see "Working with Image Maps," on page 1344. You use the Video tab for formatting video clips, as explained in "Modifying a Video Clip," on page 1344.

> **Tip** Use the Formatting toolbar to align an image quickly
>
> You can assign the selected image the Left or Right alignment style by clicking the Align Left or Align Right button on the Formatting toolbar. (When an image is selected, these two buttons don't have their usual effect of aligning a paragraph. The Center button, however, will affect the paragraph alignment, as usual.)

Enhancing Images Using the Pictures Toolbar

The Pictures toolbar lets you modify an image in a variety of unique ways not available through other FrontPage commands. To use this toolbar, first click the image to select it. If the Pictures toolbar doesn't appear automatically, choose View, Toolbars, Pictures to display it. The toolbar is shown in Figure 49-13, and its buttons are described in Table 49-2.

Figure 49-13. The Pictures toolbar provides many tools for working with images.

Table 49-2. The Buttons on the Pictures Toolbar

Button	Button Name	Description
	Insert Picture From File	Displays the Picture dialog box for inserting an image. (See "Inserting Images," on page 1300.)
	Text	Adds a text label to the image. If you want, you can assign a hyperlink to a text label so that the label functions as a hotspot. (See "Working with Image Maps," on page 1344.) FrontPage will convert a non-GIF image to the GIF format before it adds the text.

Table 49-2. The Buttons on the Pictures Toolbar

Button	Button Name	Description
	Auto Thumbnail	Converts the image to a thumbnail image. See "Creating a Thumbnail Image," on page 1303.
	Position Absolutely	Position Absolutely converts the image to a positioned image that you can move anywhere on the page. Bring Forward and Send Backward change the overlapping order for a positioned image. For details, see "Positioning Paragraphs, Images, Tables, and Other Elements," on page 1346.
	Bring Forward	
	Send Backward	
	Rotate Left 90°	Rotates the image counterclockwise or clockwise by 90 degrees.
	Rotate Right 90°	
	Flip Horizontal	Flips the image horizontally or vertically, creating a mirror image.
	Flip Vertical	
	More Contrast	Adjusts the image contrast. Increasing the contrast makes the dark parts darker and the light parts lighter, while decreasing the contrast does the opposite.
	Less Contrast	
	More Brightness	Adjusts the image brightness. Increasing or decreasing the brightness makes all parts of the image lighter or darker.
	Less Brightness	
	Crop	Crops the image—that is, reduces the overall dimensions of the image by discarding parts of the image (in contrast to scaling the image to make it smaller, as discussed in the previous section). See the next section, "Cropping an Image."
	Line Style	Lets you change the style of the lines used to draw an AutoShape or the border around a text box. (This button isn't available for an image.)
	Format Picture	Displays the Format dialog box for formatting an AutoShape, text box, or WordArt object. (This button isn't available for an image.)

Table 49-2. **The Buttons on the Pictures Toolbar**

Button	Button Name	Description
	Set Transparent Color	Makes one of the colors in an image transparent, so that the page background colors show through wherever the image has the transparent color. See "Controlling Transparency," on page 1343.
	Color	Converts the color format of the image to Automatic, Grayscale, Black & White, or Wash Out.
	Bevel	Creates a beveled effect around the edges of the image to give it a three-dimensional look.
	Resample	Rewrites the image file based on the current displayed size of the image. When you *scale* an image (not crop it), its displayed size becomes different from the size defined in the image file. Resampling makes both sizes the same. If you've scaled an image down, resampling will make the image file smaller and faster to download and display. (See the tip "Resample a reduced image," on page 1338.)
	Select	When this button is enabled, you can click a hotspot to select it, and then you can use the mouse to resize or move the hotspot, or press Delete to delete it. (See "Working with Image Maps," on page 1344.)
	Rectangular Hotspot	Draws a rectangular, circular, or polygonal hotspot within the image. After you've drawn the hotspot, the Insert Hyperlink dialog box will appear, where you can enter the target of the hyperlink. You can later edit the hyperlink by selecting the Select button and double-clicking the hotspot. (See "Working with Image Maps," on page 1344.)
	Circular Hotspot	
	Polygonal Hotspot	
	Highlight Hotspots	Displays the hotspots only, without the image, making it easier to locate hotspots within a busy image. (See "Working with Image Maps," on page 1344.)
	Restore	Reverses any scaling you have done, or any changes you have made to the image using the Pictures toolbar since the image was inserted or last saved.

Cropping an Image

To crop an image, perform the following steps:

1 Click the image to select it.

2 Click the Crop button on the Pictures toolbar (see Figure 49-13). FrontPage will then display cropping borders and handles on the image, as shown here:

Cropping border   Cropping handle

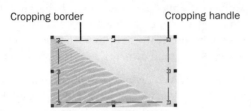

3 Drag one or more of the cropping handles to define the new image size.

4 Click the Crop button again or press Enter.

Note that you can't restore the discarded parts of a cropped image after you save the page. (Before you save the page, you can restore the image by clicking the Restore button on the Pictures toolbar, as described in Table 49-2.) Therefore, before cropping, you might want to make a backup copy of the image.

Controlling Transparency

You can make a color in an image transparent by clicking the Set Transparent Color button on the Pictures toolbar (see Figure 49-13). For a non-GIF image, FrontPage will ask whether you want to convert the image to the GIF format; you'll need to click the OK button to create a transparent color (only GIF images support transparent colors). Then, within the image, click the color you want to make transparent. To make an image nontransparent and restore the transparent color to its original value, click the Set Transparent Color button and then click the color again. (Or click the Restore button on the Pictures toolbar to reverse *all* formatting changes you made since you inserted the image or last saved the page.)

Tip   **Modify a background image**

If the page doesn't have a theme and if you assigned it a background image (as discussed in "Modifying Page Properties," on page 1350), you can modify the background image by using one of the following buttons on the Pictures toolbar when no image is selected: Rotate Left 90°, Rotate Right 90°, Flip Horizontal, Flip Vertical, More Contrast, Less Contrast, More Brightness, Less Brightness, Color, or Bevel. Caution: Even though the Restore button is available, it *won't* reverse changes you have made to the background image.

Working with Image Maps

As you can see in Figure 49-13 and Table 49-2, the Pictures toolbar includes a set of buttons that let you create and work with *image maps*: Select, Rectangular Hotspot, Circular Hotspot, Polygonal Hotspot, and Highlight Hotspots. An image map is an image that contains *hotspots*. A hotspot is a rectangular, circular, or polygonal area that is assigned a hyperlink. When you click a hotspot in the image, the browser opens the hyperlink target. An image map is commonly used as a graphical alternative to a set of text hyperlinks. For example, a Web page giving instructions on using a computer program could display an image of the program window with hotspots on various features of the window (menus, buttons, the status bar, and so on). Clicking a hotspot could display a page that describes the feature.

A hotspot is invisible in the browser. However, the mouse pointer changes—typically to a hand—when it's moved over a hotspot. You can define a hotspot by using the Rectangular Hotspot, Circular Hotspot, or Polygonal Hotspot button. The Polygonal Hotspot button is especially useful for creating a hotspot covering an irregularly shaped area of the image. Instructions on using these buttons are given in Table 49-2.

In an image map, you can also assign a *default* hyperlink to the entire image (as you can with an image that isn't an image map), using the standard techniques used to assign a hyperlink to text or other elements. Or you can assign a default hyperlink in the Default Hyperlink area in the General tab of the Picture Properties dialog box. A default hyperlink is activated by clicking anywhere in the image *except* on a hotspot.

> Standard techniques for assigning hyperlinks are explained in "Including Internal and External Hyperlinks," on page 1306. The General tab of the Picture Properties dialog box is described in "Modifying Image Properties," on page 1337 and shown in Figure 49-12.

Modifying a Video Clip

"Inserting a Video Clip," on page 1305, explains how to add a video clip to a page, either from a video file or from the Clip Organizer. After you have inserted a video clip, you can modify its appearance and behavior using the Image Properties dialog box.

To modify a video clip, perform the following steps:

1 Select the video clip by clicking it and then choose Format, Properties or press Alt+Enter. Or, right-click the clip and choose Picture Properties from the shortcut menu. Or, double-click the clip. This will display the Video tab of the Picture Properties dialog box (shown in Figure 49-14).

Figure 49-14. You can modify video clip settings using the Video tab of the Picture Properties dialog box.

2 Enter settings in the Video tab, as follows:

- To display a different video file or to repair the reference to the current file, type the file path or URL in the Video Source text box or click the Browse button to select the video file.

- To specify *when* the video is played, select On File Open or On Mouse Over.

- To specify *how many times* the video plays once it starts, use the controls in the Repeat area. Enter the desired pause, in milliseconds, between each repetition in the Loop Delay text box.

3 You can set any of the options in the General or Appearance tab of the Picture Properties dialog box. Note, however, that if you enter the path or URL of a picture file in the Picture text box in the General tab, that picture will be displayed only in FrontPage Preview view and not in the Internet Explorer browser. (Also, the Edit and Picture File Type buttons in the General tab affect only the picture specified in the Picture text box, not the video clip.)

The General and Appearance tabs of the Picture Properties dialog box are explained in "Modifying Image Properties," on page 1337. Another way to scale a video clip is by dragging a sizing handle, as explained with regard to images in "Modifying Image Properties," on page 1337.

You can also position a video clip by using the techniques explained in the next section.

Positioning Paragraphs, Images, Tables, and Other Elements

Normally, the paragraphs of text, the images, the tables, and the other elements in a Web page are arranged in sequence down the page—one element follows another and each element has its own space. (One minor exception is that you can assign an image or a table a wrapping style that makes it float to the left or right of the adjoining text.)

In recent versions of FrontPage, however, you can *position* a text paragraph, image, table, or other element such as a horizontal dividing line—that is, you can place it anywhere on the page, outside the normal flow of elements. A positioned element can occupy the same area as another element (positioned or unpositioned), and you can control the order in which the different elements overlap. Figure 49-15 shows a positioned paragraph used to create a margin note on a page.

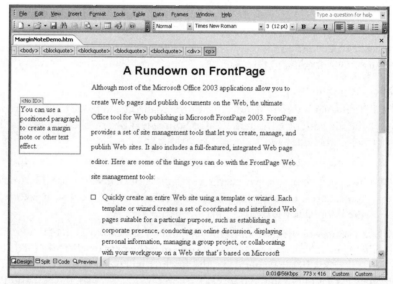

Figure 49-15. You can use a positioned paragraph on a page to create a margin note.

The following is the fastest way to position an element:

1. Make sure that positioning is enabled in FrontPage by choosing Tools, Page Options, clicking the Authoring tab, and verifying that the CSS 2.0 (Positioning) option is checked.

2 Choose View, Toolbars, Positioning to display the Positioning toolbar, shown here:

Position Absolutely   Bring Forward Bring Backward

3 Select the element you want to position. (You can simply place the insertion point anywhere within a paragraph that you want to position.)

4 Click the Position Absolutely button on the Positioning toolbar so that the button is selected. FrontPage will then draw a border around the element to indicate that the element is positioned and to show the boundaries of the positioned area. When you click the border, the border will be highlighted in blue and blue sizing handles will appear around it, indicating that the positioned area is selected.

5 If you want to change the dimensions of the positioned area around the element, drag the appropriate blue sizing handle, as shown here:

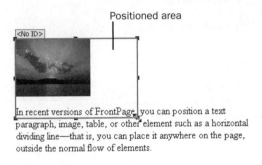

Positioned area

Note A copy of the Web page shown in the previous figure, as well as the following figures, is included on the companion CD in the file named PositionDemo.htm.

Alternatively, you can change the dimensions of the positioned area by entering values in the Width and Height text boxes on the Positioning toolbar. Changing one of these dimensions doesn't change the size of the element itself, but rather changes the size of the positioned area surrounding the element. (You can't make the positioned area smaller than the element.) Since the positioned area outside the element is normally transparent, changing its dimensions won't have a visual effect in a browser unless you assign the positioned area a visible border or a background color other than Automatic.

Note   To assign a visible border or a background color to a positioned area, click the positioned area's border to select the area (the border will be highlighted in blue and blue sizing handles will appear). Then use the Format, Borders And Shading command, as explained previously in the chapter. (You can also use the Highlight button on the Formatting toolbar to assign a background color to a positioned area, but you can't use the Borders button to assign a border to a positioned area.) The following figure shows a positioned image, displayed in Preview view, where the positioned area has been expanded and assigned a background color (it was also given a negative Z-index, as explained later, so that the overlapping text would show on top of the background):

In recent versions of FrontPage, you can position a text paragraph, image, table, or other element such as a horizontal dividing line—that is, you can place it anywhere on the page, outside the normal flow of elements.

6   If you want to move the positioned element, make sure the positioned area is still selected so the border is highlighted in blue and blue sizing handles are visible, place the mouse pointer over one of the borders, and when the pointer turns into a four-headed arrow, drag the element to the desired location on the page, as shown here:

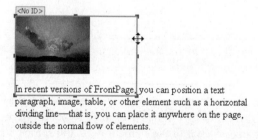

In recent versions of FrontPage, you can position a text paragraph, image, table, or other element such as a horizontal dividing line—that is, you can place it anywhere on the page, outside the normal flow of elements.

Alternatively, you can assign the positioned paragraph a precise position by typing the coordinates of the position in the Left and Top text boxes on the Positioning toolbar.

7 If you want to change the overlapping order for the positioned element, make sure the positioned area is still selected and click the Bring Forward or Send Backward button on the Positioning toolbar.

Alternatively, you can set the overlapping order by typing a value into the Z-Index text box on the Positioning toolbar. A positioned element that has a higher index will be displayed on top of any positioned paragraph that has a lower index. And a positioned paragraph that has an index greater than or equal to 0 will be displayed on top of unpositioned text, while one that has a negative index will be displayed behind unpositioned text.

> **Tip** The Position Absolutely, Bring Forward, and Send Backward buttons are also on the Pictures toolbar (which is shown in Figure 49-13).

> **Tip** **Position text using a text box**
> You can also use a *text box* to position text, to draw a border around the text, to add shading, or to apply a wrapping or positioning style. Add a text box by clicking the Text Box button on the Drawing toolbar and then clicking the position within the page where you want to insert the text box. FrontPage automatically makes a newly inserted text box a positioned element, as explained previously in this section. Set a text box's properties by clicking it and choosing Format, Text Box. For details on working with text boxes, see "Using Text Boxes to Create Precise Page Layouts," on page 510.

Formatting Other Page Elements

You can format several additional types of page elements by displaying the properties dialog box for the element. To display the properties dialog box for any of the elements mentioned in this section, click the element to select it and choose Format, Properties or press Alt+Enter. Or, you can right-click the element and choose *X* Properties from the shortcut menu, where *X* is a description of the element (for example, Horizontal Line, Form Field, Link Bar, or ActiveX Control).

You can format a horizontal dividing line in the Horizontal Line Properties dialog box, shown here:

You can also modify the properties of any of the following types of page elements, which are discussed in Chapter 50, "Adding Advanced Features to Your Web Pages and Working with Source Code":

- Form fields, such as text boxes, check boxes, and push buttons
- Web components, such as link bars, page banners, and hit counters
- Advanced elements, such as Java applets, plug-ins, and ActiveX controls

> Form fields are discussed in "Creating Interactive Forms to Collect Information," on page 1363. A general explanation of Web components is given in "Adding Dynamic Content with Web Components," on page 1374. Advanced elements are described in "Inserting Advanced Controls," on page 1379.

Formatting the Whole Page

In the following sections, you'll learn various ways to modify the appearance, behavior, and other characteristics of the entire page. All these changes affect the active page—that is, the one currently displayed in FrontPage.

Modifying Page Properties

To modify the properties of the active page displayed in an editing tab, do the following:

1. Make sure that you're viewing the page in Design or Split view and choose File, Properties or right-click anywhere on the page (in Split view, be sure to right-click in the design pane) and choose Page Properties from the shortcut menu. This will display the Page Properties dialog box.

2. To change the page's title, to modify the effect of clicking hyperlinks in the page, to add a background sound, or to make other changes, use the General tab (see Figure 49-16).

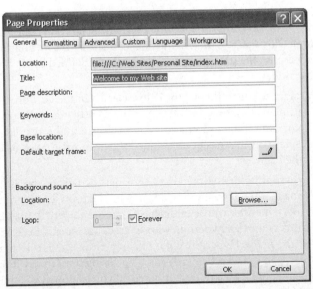

Figure 49-16. The General tab of the Page Properties dialog box allows you to add a background sound or to modify a page's title, hyperlinks, and other features.

3 To add a background picture to the page, to specify a solid background color, or to define text colors, use the Formatting tab (shown in Figure 49-17), taking note of the following points:

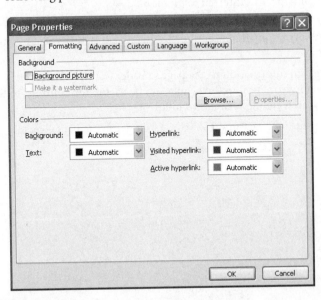

Figure 49-17. The Formatting tab of the Page Properties dialog box allows you to add a background color or picture, or define text colors, in a page that has no theme.

- The controls in the Formatting tab are enabled *only* if the page doesn't have a theme. Another way to display the Formatting tab is to choose Format, Background. (For a page with a theme, the controls in the Formatting tab are disabled because the properties set in this tab are defined by the theme and cannot be overridden.)

- For a page without a theme, the color selected in the Text drop-down list in the Formatting tab is applied to all text in the page that is assigned the Automatic text color. And if the Automatic color is selected in the Text list, each browser will display text that has been assigned the Automatic color using the text color set in the browser.

- The hyperlink colors selected in the Formatting tab are applied to all hyperlinks on the page when it's viewed in a browser. The browser assigns the Hyperlink color to a hyperlink whose target hasn't yet been opened. It assigns the Visited Hyperlink color to a hyperlink whose target has already been opened, and it assigns the Active Hyperlink color to a hyperlink that is selected. (In Internet Explorer, you can select a hyperlink by pressing the Tab key; the hyperlink will then be marked with a dotted outline and you can open its target by pressing Enter.) Selecting the Automatic color value causes the browser to use the hyperlink color set in the browser.

4 To add one or more margins to the page, use the Advanced tab (shown in Figure 49-18). You can create a top, left, bottom, or right margin by entering the desired margin width in the Top Margin, Left Margin, Bottom Margin, or Right Margin text box. Values entered in the Margin Width and Margin Height text boxes have no effect on the margins that appear in Internet Explorer 6.

In the Advanced tab, you can also define a hyperlink *rollover effect*, which consists of alternative formatting that is applied to the hyperlink text when the mouse pointer is held over it.

5 To add custom information to the page's header (its HEAD element), use the Custom tab. Adding information to the header can be useful, for example, to list key words that Web search engines can use to index the page.

6 To set the page language and HTML encoding, use the Language tab.

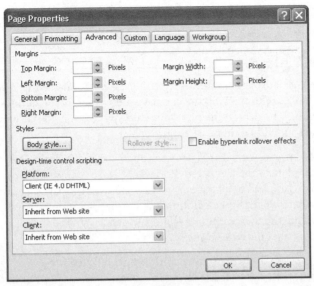

Figure 49-18. Use the Advanced tab of the Page Properties dialog box to add one or more margins to the page, to define a hyperlink rollover effect, or to make other page settings.

Using Themes to Quickly Change the Overall Page Format

Applying a theme to a Web page assigns a set of consistent formatting features to all elements in that page, and applying the same theme to all pages in a FrontPage Web site gives the entire site a consistent look.

FrontPage supplies a large collection of predefined themes. The following are just a few examples:

- Blueprint, which applies an architectural drawing motif
- Nature, for a bucolic look
- Topo, which makes your Web pages resemble topographical maps

The Web page characteristics that are affected by a theme include the following:

- The page background color or image.
- The colors and fonts used for text with various paragraph styles (Normal and Heading 1 through Heading 6). The color or font is used only if the text is assigned the Automatic color setting or the (Default Font) font setting; you can override the theme color or font by assigning other settings.
- The colors of text hyperlinks (regular, visited, and active).
- The images used for the bullets in bulleted lists.
- The text color, text font, and images used in page banners and link bars.
- The color of borders in tables.

1353

> **Note** Applying a theme to a page is the only way to format certain FrontPage components, such as a page banner. Without a theme, a page banner is displayed in plain text, and you have no way to enhance its appearance.

Every FrontPage Web site has default theme settings: It is assigned either a specific theme or no theme. Also, a page within a Web site can have individual theme settings (a particular theme or no theme). The default theme settings are applied only to those pages in the Web site that don't have individual theme settings.

With most of the templates or wizards you can use to create a Web site (for example, the Personal Web Site template or the Corporate Presence Wizard), your new Web site is assigned a default theme that is applied to all pages. (Initially, none of the pages has individual theme settings.) You can later change the default theme settings—removing the theme, applying a new one, or changing the theme options—and you can assign individual theme settings to one or more of the pages in the Web site.

You can modify the default theme settings for the current Web site—adding, changing, or removing a default theme, as well as altering the theme options. Your changes will affect all pages in the Web site that don't have individual theme settings. Use the following procedure:

1 Choose Format, Theme to display the Themes task pane (shown in Figure 49-19). You can be in any FrontPage view when you do this.

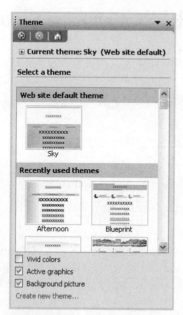

Figure 49-19. The Themes task pane allows you to work with themes.

A thumbnail image of the Web site's current default theme will appear at the top of the Select A Theme list in the Theme task pane. (If the Web site isn't assigned a default theme, you'll see an empty thumbnail image labeled No Theme at the top of the list.)

2 To assign a new default theme to the Web site, first check each of the theme options that you'd like to apply; they appear at the bottom of the Theme task pane: Vivid Colors, Active Graphics, or Background Picture. Then, in the Select A Theme list, locate the thumbnail image for the theme that you want, click the down arrow that appears when you hold the pointer over the thumbnail, and choose Apply As Default Theme from the drop-down menu, shown here:

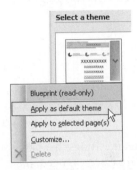

3 To have no default Web site theme, choose Apply As Default Theme from the drop-down menu for the No Theme thumbnail in the Select A Theme list.

Tip   Create or customize a theme

If none of the themes supplied with Microsoft Office 2003 precisely matches your needs or your sense of aesthetics, you can create a new theme from scratch or customize an existing theme. To create a new theme, click the Create New Theme command at the bottom of the Theme task pane and fill in the theme's features in the Customize Theme dialog box. To customize an existing theme, click the down arrow next to the theme's thumbnail image in the Select A Theme list in the Theme task pane, choose Customize from the drop-down menu, and modify the theme's features in the Customize Theme dialog box. If you customize one of the themes supplied with FrontPage, you will be prompted to save your customized version of the theme under a new name. (The themes supplied with FrontPage are read-only.)

A new or customized theme will appear in the Select A Theme list. You can remove a new or customized theme you've created by clicking the down arrow next to the theme's thumbnail in the list and choosing Delete from the drop-down menu.

To assign individual theme settings to a page in your Web site, perform the following steps:

1 Open and display the page in an editing tab, or select the page in the Folder List.

2 Choose Format, Theme to display the Themes task pane. The page's current theme settings will appear at the top of the Themes task pane: the name of the page's current theme (or No Theme if the page doesn't have a theme) and the specific theme options that have been assigned to the page (vivid colors, active graphics, or a background picture), as shown here:

The theme settings that appear are either theme settings that have been individually applied to the page, or, if no theme settings have been applied, the Web site's default theme settings.

3 To assign a new theme to the page, first check each of the theme options that you want; these appear at the bottom of the Theme task pane: Vivid Colors, Active Graphics, or Background Picture. Then, in the Select A Theme list, click the thumbnail image for the theme that you want to apply.

4 To remove the current theme from the page, click the No Theme thumbnail in the Select A Theme list.

> **Tip** To change the theme options (Vivid Colors, Active Graphics, or Background Picture) without changing the Web site's default theme or the page-specific theme, first check just those options you want at the bottom of the Theme task pane, and then *reapply* the current default theme or page-specific theme, following the instructions given in this section. (To reapply a theme, *don't* click the Web Site Default Theme thumbnail at the top of the list; rather, click the thumbnail found below in the list.)

Applying Dynamic Page Transition Effects

A final formatting touch is to add one or more *transition effects* to a page. A transition effect is an animated action that occurs when the page is either opened or closed in a browser.

To add transition effects to the active page in FrontPage, perform the following steps:

1 Choose Format, Page Transition to display the Page Transitions dialog box (shown in Figure 49-20).

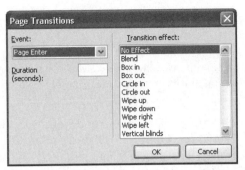

Figure 49-20. The Page Transitions dialog box lets you apply various page transition effects.

2 You can define up to four transition effects. To define each one, select an event in the Event drop-down list (see later descriptions), enter an effect duration in seconds in the Duration text box (see the following Note), and in the Transition Effect list select the effect you want to take place when the event occurs.

> **Note** If you don't enter a value in the Duration text box, the effect duration will default to 1 second.

You can select any of the following events in the Event drop-down list:

- Page Enter, to have the effect occur when the user navigates *to* the page from any other page
- Page Exit, to have the effect occur when the user navigates *away from* the page to any other page
- Site Enter, to have the effect occur when the user navigates to the page from a page at a different Web site
- Site Exit, to have the effect occur when the user navigates away from the page to a page at a different Web site

To preview the transition effects you assigned to the page, open the page in a browser (for example, by clicking the Preview button on the Standard toolbar), and then navigate back and forth between that page and another page or site. (It's normally difficult to navigate back and forth in FrontPage's Preview view because the view doesn't provide navigation commands.)

Modifying, Creating, and Using Cascading Style Sheet Styles

This section gives a brief introduction to cascading style sheet (CSS) styles, which provide the ultimate tool for precisely formatting the elements in one or more pages in your Web site. In FrontPage, you can define CSS style settings at the following three levels:

- **Inline**   An inline CSS style setting is applied to an individual page element, such as a paragraph, heading, table, or image. FrontPage will use an inline CSS style setting when you apply certain formats to an element. For example, if you assign a block of text the Small Caps character style or if you assign a paragraph a "before text" indentation using the Paragraph dialog box, FrontPage will implement the format by applying an inline CSS style setting to the block of text or to the paragraph.

> **Note**   An inline CSS style setting is added directly to the element's start-tag. For example, if you assign a paragraph a "before text" indentation of 10 pixels using the Paragraph dialog box, FrontPage will generate the following start-tag for that paragraph:
>
> <p style="margin-left: 10px">
>
> And if you assign the Small Caps character style, FrontPage will embed the characters in a SPAN element that has the following start-tag:
>
> <span style="font-variant: small-caps">

FrontPage also generates one or more inline CSS style settings whenever you click the Style button in the Properties dialog box for an element and apply one or more formatting features in the Modify Style dialog box. For example, you'll see a Style button in the Table Properties dialog box and the Picture Properties dialog box, and you'll see a Body Style button in the Advanced tab of the Page Properties dialog box. The settings you make in the Modify Style dialog box will affect only the specific element whose Properties dialog box you've displayed. (Clicking the Body Style button in the Advanced tab of the Page Properties dialog box applies an inline style to the page's BODY element.)

- **Embedded**   An embedded CSS style setting is stored in a style sheet located in the page's header (the HEAD element) rather than in a particular element. You can create embedded CSS style settings that customize the formatting of a particular element— such as a top-level heading (an H1 element)—everywhere it occurs in the document, by performing the following steps:

  1   Choose Format, Style to display the Style dialog box (shown in Figure 49-21).

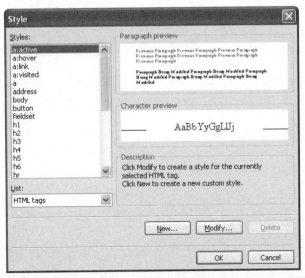

Figure 49-21. The Style dialog box allows you to create and modify embedded CSS styles.

2 Select HTML Tags in the List drop-down list to display HTML elements, and in the Styles list, select the particular element you want to customize. For example, you would select H1 to customize the formatting of all top-level headings (H1 elements) in the document.

3 Click the Modify button and select the desired formatting features in the Modify Style dialog box.

You can also add embedded CSS style settings that create a user-defined style that you can apply to any paragraph or block of characters in the document (much like a user-defined style in Word), by performing the following steps:

1 Choose Format, Style to display the Style dialog box (see Figure 49-21).

2 Click the New button to display the New Style dialog box.

3 In the New Style dialog box, enter a name (also known as a *selector*) for your style, select Paragraph or Character to indicate the type of element the style will be applied to, and choose the desired formatting features.

Your new user-defined style will subsequently appear in the Styles drop-down list on the Formatting toolbar and you can use it just like one of the built-in FrontPage styles, such as Normal or Heading 1. (The style name you entered will be prefixed with a period and sometimes with an element name, such as SPAN, to indicate the element to which the style is applied.) Also, if you click the Style button in an element's Properties dialog box, you can format that element by selecting or typing the user-defined style name in the Class box in the Modify Style dialog box.

To remove a user-defined character style from text you've assigned it to, select the text and then select Default Character Style in the Style drop-down list on the Formatting toolbar, or choose Format, Remove Formatting.

> **Note** Embedded CSS style settings are added to a STYLE element within the page's HEAD element. For example, if you create a style that modifies H1 elements by adding italic formatting, FrontPage will insert the following declaration in the STYLE element:
>
> *h1 {font-style: italic}*
>
> And if you create a user-defined paragraph style that you name CenteredDouble, which applies centered alignment and double spacing to a paragraph, FrontPage will add the following declaration to the STYLE element:
>
> *.CenteredDouble {text-align: center; line-height: 200%}*
>
> If you assign this user-defined style to a paragraph in the page, FrontPage will set the P element's CLASS attribute to the name of the style, as in this example:
>
> *<p class="CenteredDouble">*

- **External**   An external CSS style setting is stored in a separate CSS file (with the .css filename extension) that is linked to one or more Web pages. Like an embedded CSS, an external CSS can contain styles that globally modify an HTML element, as well as user-defined styles that you can apply to individual elements in the page. The advantage of using an external CSS is that by attaching the same CSS to several pages (perhaps all the pages in a FrontPage Web site) you can easily give them uniform formatting. To create an external CSS and attach it to a Web page, perform the following basic steps:

  1 Choose File, New and then click More Page Templates in the New task pane.

  2 Click the Style Sheets tab of the Page Templates dialog box, select a template for your new CSS, and click the OK button. The CSS will be opened in a tab for editing.

  3 If you wish, you can customize the style sheet by creating styles that modify HTML elements or by adding user-defined styles. You can directly edit the CSS file, or you can click the Style button on the Style toolbar that appears when you open a CSS file and use the Style dialog box to add or modify style settings, as explained under the description of embedded styles earlier in this section.

  4 Save the CSS file within the current Web site.

  5 To attach the CSS to a page, open the page and choose Format, Style Sheet Links. In the Link Style Sheet dialog box, select the Selected Page(s) option, click the Add button, and in the Select Style Sheet dialog box, select the new CSS file you created. Click the OK button, and then click the OK button in the Link Style Sheet dialog box.

Once you link an external CSS to a page, the styles in the CSS that modify elements will globally alter the formatting of basic elements throughout your page. Also, any user-defined styles defined in the linked CSS will be listed in the Style drop-down list on the Formatting menu so you can apply them to elements in the page. And, if you click the Style button in an element's Properties dialog box, displaying the Modify Style dialog box, you can format that element by typing the name of a user-defined style in the attached style sheet into the Class box.

The term *cascading* in cascading style sheet derives from the fact that you can define style settings at various levels. If conflicting style settings are defined at different levels, an inline style setting takes precedence over an embedded style setting, and an embedded style setting takes precedence over an external style setting.

Troubleshooting

Formatting features are unavailable

When you format your document, quite a few formatting features are disabled, such as Small Caps and several other character format settings, most paragraph formatting features, and the Borders And Shading and Position commands on the Format menu. Also, you can't apply a theme. Nor can you use any of the CSS methods described in "Modifying, Creating, and Using Cascading Style Sheet Styles," on page 1358.

None of these features will be available if the CSS 1.0 (Formatting) option isn't checked in the Authoring tab of the Page Options dialog box. To display this dialog box, choose Tools, Page Options. These features all use CSS styles. If some of your page visitors will be using older browsers without support for CSS, then you should clear the CSS 1.0 (Formatting) authoring option so that all features that rely on CSS will be disabled in FrontPage and you won't inadvertently use them. If, however, your visitors will be using browsers with CSS support, you should definitely check this option so that you can take full advantage of FrontPage's formatting capabilities. Furthermore, element positioning (as discussed in "Positioning Paragraphs, Images, Tables, and Other Elements," on page 1346) requires support for CSS version 2.0. Therefore, if your target browsers support CSS 2.0, you should also make sure that the CSS 2.0 (Positioning) option is checked in the Authoring tab so that you can position paragraphs. Note that Internet Explorer began supporting CSS 1.0 with version 3.0 of the browser, and CSS 2.0 with version 4.0.

For more information on the Authoring tab of the Page Options dialog box, see the tip "Ensure compatibility" on page 1319 and Figure 48-15 on page 1314.

Adding Advanced Features to Your Web Pages and Working with Source Code

Creating Interactive Forms
to Collect Information 1363

Using Frames to Display
Multiple Pages 1367

Adding Dynamic Content
with Web Components 1374

NEW FEATURE! Working Directly with Source Code . . . 1382

Creating Interactive Forms to Collect Information

A form consists of a collection of *fields* (sometimes known as *controls*)—such as text boxes, check boxes, and push buttons—that are used to collect information from visitors to your Web page. Each form normally includes a Submit button that the user clicks after filling in the fields to transmit the information, plus a Reset button that the user can click to clear all fields prior to entering new information. Figure 50-1 shows an example form as it appears in Microsoft Office FrontPage 2003, and Figure 50-2 shows the same form displayed in Microsoft Internet Explorer.

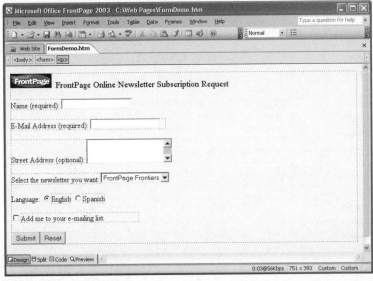

Figure 50-1. This figure shows a simple form displayed in Design view. This form is provided on the companion CD under the filename FormDemo.htm.

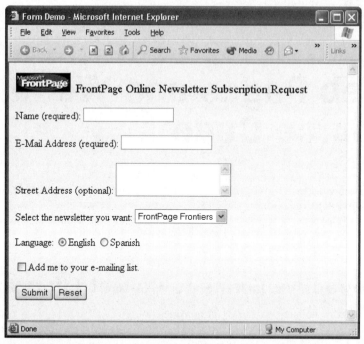

Figure 50-2. Here, the form shown in Figure 50-1 is displayed in Internet Explorer.

To create a form in Design view, perform the following steps:

1 Place the insertion point at the position in your page where you want to add the form.

2 Insert the first form field by choosing the appropriate command from the Insert, Form submenu, shown here:

Table 50-1 briefly explains how to use the commands on the Insert, Form submenu and describes the different fields you can insert. When you insert the first field, FrontPage draws a dotted rectangle defining the form's boundaries (browsers don't display this line) and automatically adds a Submit button and a Reset button to the form.

> **Note** FrontPage adds form boundaries and Submit and Reset buttons when you insert a field only if the Automatically Enclose Form Fields Within A Form option is checked. You'll find this option by choosing Tools, Page Options and clicking the General tab.

3   Use the Insert, Form submenu to insert any additional fields that you want. Be sure to insert each additional field *within* the dotted rectangle marking the form. Otherwise the new field will belong to a separate form and its information won't be submitted when the user clicks the Submit button. (Clicking a Submit button sends only the information within the same form as the button.)

You can arrange the fields as you like. Fields are a part of the normal flow of text and you can move or copy them just like text characters.

4   Add any text or other elements that you want in the form.

You can type in text to create a title, a label, instructions for completing the form, or other information. If you type a label next to a field (for example, if you type **Add me to your mailing list** following a check box), be sure to link the label and the associated field. Doing this makes the label and the field function as a unit when the form is displayed in a browser; for example, users will be able to check or clear a check box by clicking on the linked label as well as on the box itself. To link a label and a field, select both of them and then choose Insert, Form, Label. FrontPage draws a dotted rectangle around each linked label.

You can also insert tables, images, and almost any other element that can be inserted into a page.

5   Set the table properties.

Table 50-1. Using the Commands on the Form Submenu of the Insert Menu

To Do This with Forms	Choose This Command
Insert the form boundaries, a Submit button, and a Reset button for a regular Web form	Form
Create a *list form*, which is a special-purpose form for adding, editing, or displaying items in a document library, list, or other information component on a SharePoint team Web site	List Form This command is available only if you've opened a team Web site on a server running Microsoft Windows SharePoint Services.
Insert a form into a Web part page belonging to a SharePoint team Web site.	Form Web Part This command is available only if you're working on a Web part page within a SharePoint team Web site.

Table 50-1. **Using the Commands on the Form Submenu of the Insert Menu**

To Do This with Forms	Choose This Command
Insert a one-line text box	Textbox
Insert a multiline, scrolling text box	Text Area
Insert a one-line text box, plus a Browse button that opens the Choose File dialog box, so that the user can either type in a filename or select a file in the dialog box	File Upload
Insert a check box	Checkbox
Insert an option button	Option Button
Insert a box for grouping and labeling a set of fields	Group Box
Insert a drop-down list	Drop-Down Box
Insert a button	Push Button
Insert a button that allows you to type the label directly on the button and customize the button's width and height	Advanced Button
Insert an image	Picture
Link the selected text label and control (explained later in this section)	Label
Open the Form Properties dialog box for viewing or setting the form's properties	Form Properties

You can change the properties of an individual field by selecting it and then choosing Format, Properties or pressing Alt+Enter to open the Properties dialog box. Or you can right-click the field and choose Form Field Properties from the shortcut menu. The properties you can set in the Properties dialog box depend on the type of the field. For example, for a drop-down list, you can enter the values that will be displayed in the list. And for a push button, you can change the button's label or designate the button as a Submit or Reset button.

To set the properties of the entire form, open the Form Properties dialog box (shown in Figure 50-3) by placing the insertion point anywhere within the form and choosing Insert, Form, Form Properties. Or you can right-click anywhere on the form and choose Form Properties from the shortcut menu. To control where the information from the form fields is sent when a user clicks the Submit button, choose an option in the Where To Store Results area and type in the required information. You can click the Options button to control the way the information is saved and to specify a confirmation page that the browser will display after the user clicks the Submit button.

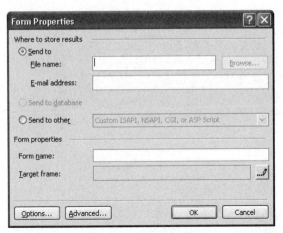

Figure 50-3. You can set the properties of the entire form in the Form Properties dialog box.

Tip **Use a template to create a form**

To get a head start in designing a form, you can create a new page using the Feedback Form template, which adds a complete feedback form that you can customize, or the Form Page Wizard, which generates a custom form, laying out all the fields for you based on the choices you enter. For information on creating new pages using templates and wizards, see "Creating a New Web Page," on page 1279.

Using Frames to Display Multiple Pages

You can show several pages simultaneously in the browser window by displaying each page in a separate *frame*. Figure 50-4 shows an example of a set of frames, viewed in Internet Explorer. The frame on the left serves as a table of contents. When the user clicks one of the hyperlinks on the link bar contained in the left frame, the target page is displayed in the right frame.

Figure 50-4. In this figure, frames are used to display two pages at once.

> **Note** FrontPage won't let you create frames unless the Frames option is checked in the Authoring tab of the Page Options dialog box (which you can open by choosing Tools, Page Options). See the tip "Ensure compatibility," on page 1319, and Figure 48-15 on page 1314.

To use frames, you must create a *frames page*, which defines the number and layout of the frames and optionally specifies the initial page to be displayed within each frame. When the user opens the frames page, the frames appear within the browser window, and each frame displays its initial page (if one has been specified for it). To create a frames page, perform the following steps:

1. Choose File, New and then click More Page Templates in the New task pane to open the Page Templates dialog box.

2. Click the Frames Pages tab in the Page Templates dialog box (shown in Figure 50-5), select the template that defines the number and layout of frames that you want, and click the OK button. (Keep in mind that you'll be able to adjust the number or layout of the frames later.)

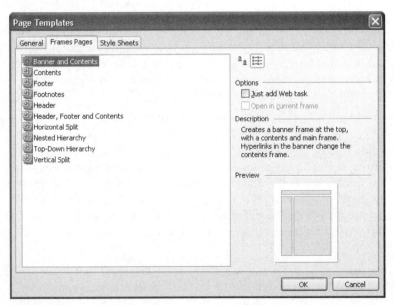

Figure 50-5. Select a template for creating a frames page in the Frames Pages tab of the Page Templates dialog box.

After you perform these steps, FrontPage will open the new frames page. An example is shown in Figure 50-6.

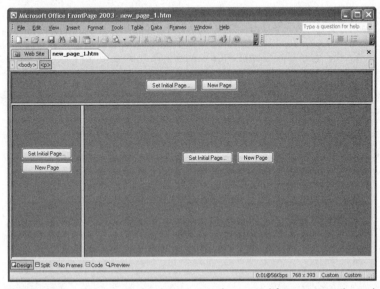

Figure 50-6. This example shows a newly created frames page based on the Banner And Contents template.

To have a particular frame initially display an existing page, click the Set Initial Page button within that frame and then select the page. To have a frame initially display a newly created page, click the New Page button in the frame. If you don't add an existing or new page to a particular frame, that frame will initially be empty when the frames page is opened in a browser; however, a page could be displayed in that frame when the user clicks a hyperlink in one of the other frames (as explained shortly).

A page you add to a frame will be displayed within that frame in Design view, where you can use FrontPage commands to edit it. (If you want, you can also open and edit the page in a separate editing tab by right-clicking in the frame and choosing Open Page In New Window from the shortcut menu.) When you issue the Save command (by choosing File, Save, by clicking the Save button on the Standard toolbar, or by pressing Ctrl+S), FrontPage saves the frames page itself, plus all new or modified pages displayed in the individual frames. (The Save As dialog box displays a model of the frames page and highlights the frame FrontPage is about to save. When no frame is highlighted, FrontPage is about to save the frames page itself.)

You can modify a particular frame by clicking it to activate it (FrontPage will highlight its border) and then choosing a command from the Frames menu as shown here:

- To divide the frame horizontally or vertically into two frames, choose Split Frame.
- To remove the frame, choose Delete Frame.
- To edit the page contained in the frame within a full, separate editing tab, choose Open Page In New Window.
- To save only the page displayed in the frame, choose Save Page or Save Page As.
- To change the frame's properties, choose Frame Properties to open the Frame Properties dialog box (shown in Figure 50-7).

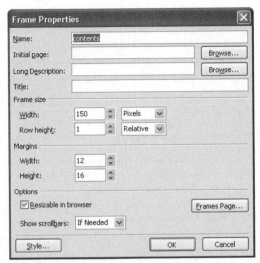

Figure 50-7. You can use the Frame Properties dialog box to change the properties of the selected frame within a frames page.

> **Note** When you click within a particular frame, that frame is selected and FrontPage draws a blue border around it. You can also select the entire frames page by clicking on this border; the border will then be drawn around the entire editing tab, enclosing all frames. Alternatively, you can select the entire frames page by pressing F6, repeatedly if necessary. When the entire frames page is selected, most of the commands on the Frames menu are unavailable. However, you need to select the entire frames page before issuing certain commands. For instance, if you want to preview the frames page in your browser (rather than previewing just the page in an individual frame), you'll need to select the entire frames page before issuing the Preview command.

You can also change a frame's initial size by simply dragging a border in the FrontPage editor. And you can split a frame by holding down Ctrl while you drag.

You can change the properties of the frames page itself by choosing Frames, Frame Properties and then clicking the Frames Page button at the bottom of the Frame Properties dialog box to open the Page Properties dialog box. This dialog box includes the usual tabs for setting page properties (described in "Modifying Page Properties," on page 1350), plus a Frames tab that allows you to adjust the spacing between frames and to show or hide the borders around the frames.

If you include a hyperlink on a page displayed within a frame, you can specify the particular frame in which the target is to be opened. For example, on a frames page that has two frames, the frame on the left could contain a page that has a list of hyperlinks and serves as a table of contents. The target of each hyperlink could be opened in the frame on the right. This way, the table of contents is always immediately accessible while the user views various pages in the right frame.

To specify a target frame when you create (or edit) a hyperlink, click the Target Frame button in the Insert Hyperlink (or Edit Hyperlink) dialog box (see Figure 48-10), and then select the target frame in the Target Frame dialog box. This dialog box displays a diagram of the frames; to select a frame, just click on it in the diagram. Also, in the General tab of the Page Properties dialog box for a page displayed in one of the frames, you can specify a default target frame for all hyperlinks on the page.

For further details, see "Including Internal and External Hyperlinks," on page 1306. For more information on specifying a default target frame for hyperlinks, see "Modifying Page Properties," on page 1350, and Figure 44-16.

Tip   Provide an alternative for browsers that don't support frames

When you create a frames page, FrontPage also creates an accompanying "no frames" page. If you attempt to open the frames page in a browser that doesn't support frames, the browser will display the "no frames" page instead. The "no frames" page can furnish an explanatory note or provide alternative content that doesn't rely on frames. To view or edit this page, click the No Frames view button at the bottom of the editing tab (this button appears only when the editing tab displays a frames page).

Adding Inline Frames

In FrontPage, as an alternative to creating a frames page to view multiple pages, you can simply insert an *inline frame* into any page. An inline frame is a rectangular element in a page that displays another page and lets you scroll through it (see Figure 50-8).

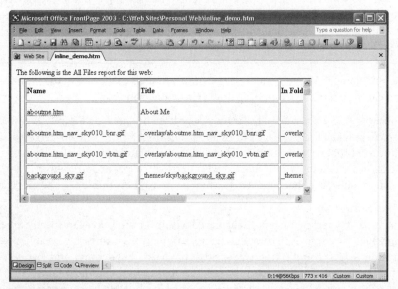

Figure 50-8.   A Web page can contain an inline frame showing the contents of another page, as seen here in the Preview pane.

To add an inline frame to a Web page, perform the following steps:

1 Place the insertion point at the position in the page where you want to display the inline frame and choose Insert, Inline Frame. FrontPage will then insert a blank inline frame, as shown here:

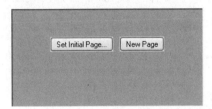

2 To select an existing page or to create a new page to display in the inline frame, click the Set Initial Page button or the New Page button in the blank inline frame.

3 To customize the inline frame, click a border (not the inside of the frame), so that sizing handles appear around the frame. Then you can change the size of the inline frame by dragging a sizing handle, and you can set the inline frame's properties by choosing Format, Properties or by pressing Alt+Enter, and then entering settings into the Inline Frame Properties dialog box (shown in Figure 50-9).

In the Inline Frame Properties dialog box, notice that the inline frame has an identifying name (I1 in Figure 50-9). If you add a hyperlink to the main page, you can make the browser display the hyperlink target within the inline frame by clicking the Target Frame button in the Insert Hyperlink (or Edit Hyperlink) dialog box and then selecting that name in the Target Frame dialog box.

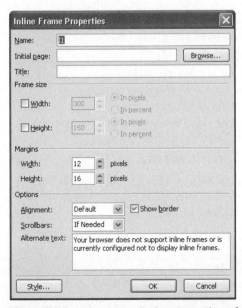

Figure 50-9. You can edit the properties of an inline frame in the Inline Frame Properties dialog box.

For general information on defining hyperlinks, see "Including Internal and External Hyperlinks," on page 1306.

Adding Dynamic Content with Web Components

A FrontPage *Web component* is an element that you can quickly insert into a Web page to automatically generate and display information or to add a feature. Many of these ready-to-run components let you add sophisticated capabilities to your Web pages and require little effort. The different types of Web components are described in Table 50-2.

Table 50-2. Web Components You Can Add to a Page

FrontPage Component Type	Description of Component(s)
Advanced Controls	● These components are described in the next section, "Inserting Advanced Controls."
Comment	● Comment: Lets you add text commentary that you can see when the page is opened in Design view, but that is hidden when the page is displayed in a browser.
Date And Time	● Date And Time: Displays the date and time when you last edited the page or when the page was last automatically updated (for example, when FrontPage updates a hyperlink).
Document Library View	● Document Library View: In a Web page within a SharePoint team Web site, displays the contents of a document library belonging to that site. This component was supported by the previous SharePoint version (SharePoint Team Services from Microsoft), but isn't supported by the current SharePoint version (Windows SharePoint Services).
Dynamic Effects	● Interactive Button: A button that you click to open a hyperlink target. The button colors change when you either hold the mouse pointer over the button or click the button. You can choose from a collection of predesigned buttons and then customize the button's appearance and behavior.
	● Marquee: Displays text that scrolls horizontally across the page.
Expedia Components	● Link To A Map: Inserts a link to a map on the Expedia Web site. When you define the component, you specify the location that's shown in the map.
	● Static Map: Inserts a copy of a map that's displayed within your Web page.
Hit Counter	● Hit Counter: Keeps track of and displays the number of times someone has opened the page.

NEW FEATURE!

Table 50-2. **Web Components You Can Add to a Page**

FrontPage Component Type	Description of Component(s)
Included Content	● Page: Displays the contents of another page. If you want to display a block of text or other elements in several locations in your Web site, you can add the content to a single page and then use this Web component to insert that page in all the locations. With this method, you need to maintain only a single copy of the repeated content. See the Troubleshooting sidebar "Shared borders offer little control," on page 1315.
	● Page Banner: Displays the page title. The banner's style is controlled by the page theme, and the page must be included in the Web site's navigation structure shown in Navigation view (otherwise, the banner will be hidden).
	● Page Based On Schedule: Displays a specified page for a specified time period. This component is like a Page component, except that after the specified period, the included page is no longer displayed. It's useful for showing textual information that will expire on a certain date.
	● Picture Based On Schedule: Displays a specified image for a specified time period, after which the image is hidden. This component is useful for showing graphical information that will expire on a certain date.
	● Substitution: Displays the current value of a standard or user-defined Web site variable. The standard variables are Author (the person who created the page), Modified By (the person who most recently changed the page), Description (a description of the page), and Page URL (the full Web address or file path of the page). You can create user-defined variables for the current Web site by choosing Tools, Site Settings and then clicking the Parameters tab in the Site Settings dialog box.

Chapter 50

Table 50-2. Web Components You Can Add to a Page

FrontPage Component Type	Description of Component(s)
Link Bars	● Bar Based On Navigation Structure: Displays a set of hyperlinks that FrontPage automatically generates based on the Web site's current navigation structure shown in Navigation view. (For more information, see "Using Navigation View," on page 1255.) The component's style is controlled by the page theme.
	● Bar With Back And Next Links: Displays "Back" and "Next" custom hyperlinks.
	● Bar With Custom Links: Displays a collection of custom hyperlinks. For a Bar With Back And Next Links component or a Bar With Custom Links component you must specify each of the custom hyperlinks. You do this in the Link Bar Properties dialog box that's displayed when you insert the link bar. You can add links later by clicking the Add Link command that appears to the right of the link bar in Design view. Also, FrontPage will display a separate page hierarchy for the custom link bar in Navigation view; you can add or remove links by working with that hierarchy in Navigation view.
List View	● List View: In a Web page within a SharePoint team Web site, displays the contents of a list or other information component belonging to that site. This component was supported by the previous SharePoint version (SharePoint Team Services from Microsoft), but isn't supported by the current SharePoint version (Windows SharePoint Services).
MSN Components	● Search The Web With MSN: Lets the visitor perform a Web search using Microsoft Network.
	● Stock Quote: Obtains and displays stock quotes from the MoneyCentral Web site.
MSNBC Components	● A set of components that obtain and display news headlines (business, technology, and so on) or weather forecasts from the MSNBC Web site.
Photo Gallery	● Photo Gallery: Displays a collection of images, automatically generating thumbnail images for each. For more information, see "Adding a Photo Gallery," on page 1304.

Table 50-2. Web Components You Can Add to a Page

FrontPage Component Type	Description of Component(s)
Spreadsheets And Charts	● Office Chart: Charts data that you enter or data obtained from a database in a column, bar, line, pie, or other type of chart.
	● Office Pivot Table: Displays data from a database in an interactive pivot table. (For information on pivot tables, see Chapter 28, "Power Database Techniques: Lists, Filters, and Pivot Tables.")
	● Office Spreadsheet: Displays the data you enter in a spreadsheet that the visitor can view or edit.
Table Of Contents	● Based On Page Category: Generates and automatically updates a list of hyperlinks to other pages in the current Web site that belong to the category or categories you specify when you define the component. (You assign categories to a page by selecting or opening the page, choosing File, Properties, and clicking the Workgroup tab.)
	● For This Web Site: Generates and automatically updates a list of hyperlinks to all other pages in the current Web site.
Top 10 List	● Components that display Web site usage statistics in the form of top-10 lists: the 10 most visited pages in the Web site, the 10 most common referring visitor domains, the 10 most common visitor browsers, and so on.
Web Search	● Current Web: Generates a form that lets the user search through all the text on the pages of your Web site. The search results are displayed as a list of hyperlinks to the pages that contain matching text.

To add a Web component to a page, perform the following steps:

1 Place the insertion point at the position in the page where you want to display the Web component.

2 Insert the Web component as follows:

■ To insert a Date And Time or Comment component, choose Insert, Date And Time or Insert, Comment.

■ To insert any of the other types of components listed in Table 50-2, choose Insert, Web Component. Then, in the Insert Web Component dialog box (shown in Figure 50-10), select the component type in the Component Type list and then select a specific component or component style in the list to the right (the label on the right list depends on the component type you've selected; for example, Choose An Effect, Choose A Control, or Choose A Counter Style).

Then, click the Finish button. Or, with components that allow you to make additional settings (such as Link Bars), you can click the Next button to select settings or—if the button is enabled—click the Finish button to accept the default settings. In any case, FrontPage might now display one or more additional dialog boxes to gather required information for creating the Web component.

> **Note** An alternative way to insert a link bar, a page banner, or an interactive button is to choose Insert, Navigation; or Insert, Page Banner; or Insert, Interactive Button.

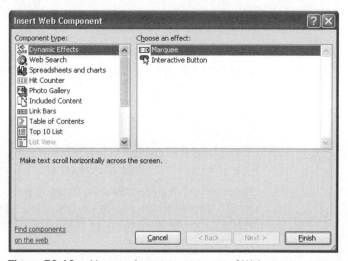

Figure 50-10. You can insert most types of Web components using the Insert Web Component dialog box.

> **Tip** **Obtain additional Web components**
> To look for additional Web components that you can download and add to your Web pages, click the Find Components On The Web link at the bottom of the Insert Web Component dialog box. This command will connect you to a page on the Office Online Web site.

3 After the component is installed, you can change its properties by clicking the component and choosing Format, Properties or pressing Alt+Enter. Or you can double-click the component. FrontPage will then display the properties dialog box for the component, which lets you view and adjust properties (see Figure 50-11).

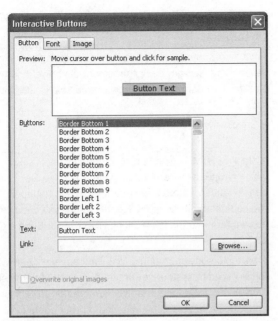

Figure 50-11. The Interactive Buttons dialog box is typical of the properties dialog boxes that let you view and change the properties of Web components.

Inserting Advanced Controls

You can add several Web components to your page that FrontPage classifies as *advanced controls*. These components don't necessarily provide more advanced features than the Web components discussed in the previous section and shown in Table 50-2. Instead, they're considered advanced because they require you either to write program code or to obtain software from a third party. These controls are summarized in Table 50-3.

Table 50-3. The Advanced Controls You Can Add to a Page

Advanced Control	Description
ActiveX Control	A portable software module that you can insert in a Web page to perform a specific task or set of tasks. For example, an ActiveX control might display a calendar, run a multimedia presentation, or generate a chart. Before you can add an ActiveX control to a page, you must install the control on your computer.
Confirmation Field	Displays the contents of a specific field in a form that the visitor has submitted to the Web server. This component must be placed on the form's *confirmation page*, which is displayed when a visitor successfully submits the form. You can use a custom confirmation page for a form by clicking the Options button in the Form Properties dialog box (shown in Figure 50-3), clicking the Confirmation Page tab, and entering the name and location of the custom page (or clicking the Browse button to select the page).

Table 50-3. **The Advanced Controls You Can Add to a Page**

Advanced Control	Description
Design-Time Control	An ActiveX control that you use while designing or editing a page. If you haven't installed any design-time controls on your computer, the Design-Time Control item will be unavailable in the Choose A Control list.
Movie In Flash Format	A Shockwave Flash movie.
HTML	A block of HTML (Hypertext Markup Language) source that you type, which FrontPage inserts directly into the page file. This component lets you add features that FrontPage doesn't support. You must enter the code carefully because FrontPage doesn't check or modify it. (For more information, see "Working Directly with Source Code," on page 1382.)
Java Applet	A portable software module that you can insert in a Web page to perform a specific task or set of tasks. A Java applet is similar to an ActiveX control, except that it offers greater portability and security and it doesn't have to be installed on your computer.
Plug-In	Another type of software module that extends the browser's capabilities. Plug-ins were originally designed for Netscape Navigator 2, but Internet Explorer version 3 and later also support them.

To insert an advanced control, follow the general instructions for adding a Web component given in the previous section. In the Insert Web Component dialog box, select Advanced Controls in the Component Type list, and then select the specific control you want to insert in the Choose A Control list (shown in Figure 50-12).

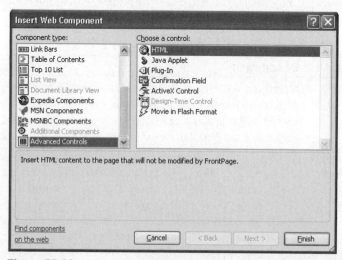

Figure 50-12. You insert advanced controls using the Insert Web Component dialog box.

> **Note** After you insert an HTML control, the results of the HTML source it contains won't be visible until you view the page in the Preview pane or open it in a browser. Design view shows only a question mark between angle brackets to mark the location of an HTML control.

Troubleshooting

Web component doesn't work!

FrontPage lets you add Web Search, Hit Counter, and Top 10 List Web components to your page. However, when you save the page and view it in your browser, none of these components work.

Each of these Web components will work only if the page is delivered—over an intranet or on the World Wide Web—from a Web server that has the FrontPage Server Extensions or Windows SharePoint Services installed. These components *won't* work if the page is opened in a browser from a local or network disk location.

If you've created your Web site on a disk location, these Web components will work correctly once you publish your site to a server that has the FrontPage Server Extensions or Windows SharePoint Services.

> For details, see the sidebar "Creating a Web Site Offline or Online," on page 1222, and the tip "Find a hosting service with FrontPage Server Extensions," on page 1277.

If your Web server doesn't have either the FrontPage Server Extensions or Windows Share-Point Services, it's best to disable these components so you don't inadvertently insert one of them. You can do this by choosing Tools, Page Options, clicking the Authoring tab, and clearing the Browse-Time Web Components option.

Troubleshooting

Can't insert Web component!

The Web component you want to add is dimmed in the Insert Web Component dialog box, so you can't insert it.

FrontPage doesn't let you insert a Web component if the required support isn't present. If a Web site isn't currently opened in FrontPage, you won't be able to insert any of the following types of Web components:

- Included Content, except Substitution
- Link Bars
- Table of Contents
- Top 10 List

Chapter 50

- List View
- Document Library View
- Advanced Controls, Confirmation Field (You can insert the other types of Advanced Controls.)

You can't insert either of the following components unless you have opened a Web site that resides on a server running Windows SharePoint Services:

- List View
- Document Library View

Each of the following Web components requires one or more of the Web technologies that you can have FrontPage enable or disable by choosing Tools, Page Options, clicking the Authoring tab, and checking or clearing options. If a technology that a particular Web component requires is disabled in this tab, FrontPage won't let you insert it.

> For details on the Authoring tab of the Page Options dialog box, see the tip "Ensure compatibility," on page 1319, and Figure 43-15.

- Web Search
- Spreadsheets And Charts
- Hit Counter
- Photo Gallery
- Included Content
- Link Bars
- Table of Contents
- Top 10 List
- List View
- Document Library View
- Advanced Controls, except HTML and Plug-In

Working Directly with Source Code

If you are familiar with HTML, the underlying language of Web pages, you can use FrontPage's extensive tools for working directly with a page's HTML source code. You could create an entire Web page from scratch by using the FrontPage source code editor to enter the page's HTML source code, element by element. More commonly, however, you use the WYSIWYG (What You See Is What You Get) view of the page provided by Design view, as discussed previously in this part of the book, to enter the bulk of the Web page content and then use the HTML tools to optimize, fine-tune, or enhance the page's underlying HTML source. (Examining a page's source code is also a good way to increase your knowledge of HTML.)

FrontPage provides tools for accessing a page's HTML while you work in Design view (or the design pane of Split view). It also provides an integrated source code editor that you can use to edit the HTML source code for a Web page or to edit other types of source code files such as CSS (cascading style sheet) files or XML (Extensible Markup Language) documents. Additionally, FrontPage includes the new HTML Tags tab in the Find And Replace dialog box, which you can use to find and replace specific HTML tags in a Web page. The following sections provide an introduction to each of these features.

Working with HTML Source Code in Design View

FrontPage provides the following methods for working with HTML while you create or edit a page in Design view (or in the design pane of Split view):

- You can display the page's HTML tags by choosing View, Reveal Tags, or by pressing Ctrl+/. FrontPage will display the start-tag and the end-tag (if present) on either side of each page element. For example, the editor will display a <P> tag at the beginning of each paragraph, and a </P> tag at the end of each paragraph (assuming the paragraph has an end-tag). If you place the mouse pointer over a tag, a ScreenTip will show the complete content of the start-tag, including any attributes defined within that tag (for example, the target address for a hyperlink element). And if you click a start-tag or end-tag, FrontPage will highlight the matching tag and all content between the two tags. To hide the tags, choose Reveal Tags or press Ctrl+/ again. See Figure 50-13.

- You can add a block of HTML source directly to the page at the position of the insertion point by inserting an HTML Web component, described in Table 50-3.

- To work with the HTML tags in the page, you can display the new Quick Tag Selector, shown in Figure 50-13, by selecting the View, Quick Tag Selector menu option.

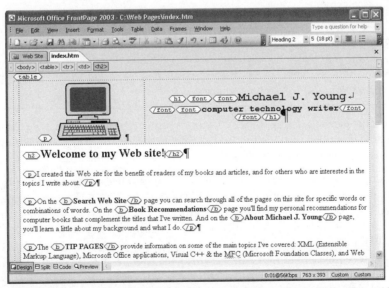

Figure 50-13. This page is opened in Design view with both the Reveal Tags option enabled and the Quick Tag Selector shown.

The Quick Tag Selector shows all the HTML element tags that surround the current selection or position of the insertion point. For example, in the page shown in Figure 50-13, the insertion point is at the beginning of the "Welcome to my Web site!" heading and the Quick Tag Selector shows that this point is within an H2 (second level heading) element, within a TD (table cell) element, within a TR (table row) element, within a TABLE element, within the page's BODY element.

When you hold the mouse pointer over a tag displayed in the Quick Tag Selector, FrontPage draws a border around the corresponding element in the page and displays a down arrow on the tag. To work with the tag, click the down arrow and choose a command from the drop-down menu, shown here:

NEW FEATURE! Directly Editing Source Code Files

You can now use FrontPage's integrated source code editor to edit any type of source code file or other plain-text file. (In the previous FrontPage version, you could edit only a Web page file or a CSS file.)

> **Note** FrontPage is configured by default to open most of the types of text files that you might work with while building a Web site (for example, files with the .htm, .html, .css, .xml, .java, .c, and .cpp filename extensions). To configure it to open additional types of plain-text files, see "Working with Files," on page 1247.

You can open an existing source code file or other type of plain-text file using any applicable method described in "Opening an Existing Web Page," on page 1288. For instance, you can choose File, Open and select the file in the Open File dialog box.

When you open a file, FrontPage looks at the filename extension and displays the tools that are appropriate for working with that file type. If the file has the .htm, .html, or other configured Web page filename extension, FrontPage provides the Design, Split, Code, and Preview views and all the Web page creation tools and features described previously in this part of the book. If the file has any other type of extension, FrontPage provides only a source code editing view (equivalent to the Code view of a Web page). However, it does provide a special toolbar if you open a CSS file (the Style toolbar) or an XML document (the XML View toolbar), and it offers commands that are appropriate for the type of file you've opened (described later).

To create a new source code file, or other type of plain-text file that isn't a Web page, perform the following steps:

1 Click the down arrow on the Create A New Normal Page button at the left end of the Standard toolbar and choose Text File from the drop-down menu. FrontPage will open a blank text file in an editing tab.

2 Before you enter text into the file, choose File, Save and then select a location for the file and enter a filename in the Save As dialog box. You should include the filename extension in the name you type, and, to prevent FrontPage from appending another extension to the end of your filename, surround the entire name in quotation marks (for example, *"Inventory.xml"*). It's a good idea to save the empty file before adding text, because for certain file types (specifically, .css and .xml files), the source code editor will provide special tools once it has identified the type of the file (which it determines from the filename extension you specify when you save the file).

For instructions on using a style template to create a new CSS file, see "Modifying, Creating, and Using Cascading Style Sheet Styles," on page 1358.

Using the Source Code Editor

When you work on a text file in the FrontPage source code editor, you can use many of the same editing techniques that are provided in Design view for editing Web pages. These techniques are discussed in "Common Editing Tasks," on page 1289, "Adding the Text Content," on page 1291, and "Previewing and Printing Your Page," on page 1317.

You can access a useful set of tools for working with the particular type of file you've opened by right-clicking within the file and choosing a command from the shortcut menu (see Figures 50-14 and 50-15). The commands available on the shortcut menu depend upon the type of file you've opened. You can also use the new Code View toolbar, shown here, which you can display by choosing View, Toolbars, Code View.

Additionally, FrontPage provides a set of commands for working in the source code editor on the Edit, Code View submenu, shown here:

To edit the source code for a Web page file, you can work in Code view or in the new Split view, which shows both a code pane (equivalent to Code view) and a design pane (equivalent to Design view) and synchronizes the two panes (see Figure 50-14). In both the Code view and the code pane of Split view, FrontPage's IntelliSense feature makes it easier to work with HTML source code. For example, if you type < to begin inserting an HTML tag, FrontPage displays a pop-up list of all tags that are legal in the current context. You can double-click a tag in the list to quickly insert it. The list is shown here:

You can also access the IntelliSense tools through the Edit, IntelliSense submenu, shown here:

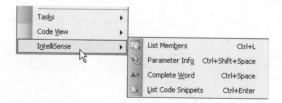

> **Note** The HTML source code that you see in Code view or in the code pane of Split view might differ somewhat from the source in the HTML file that FrontPage saves on disk. For example, if the page displays a shared border, the table that creates the border won't be included in the source code shown in Code or Split view. Also, a FrontPage component— such as a Date And Time component or an Include Page—will not yet be expanded into the actual content that will be added to the HTML file on disk.

When you edit a CSS or XML file, the source code editor supplies a toolbar with commands that are useful for working with these types of files (the Style toolbar for a CSS file and the XML View toolbar for an XML file, which is shown in Figure 50-15).

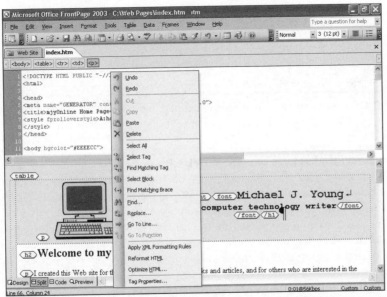

Figure 50-14. Here, a Web page is opened in the new Split view, and the shortcut menu has been displayed by right-clicking in the code pane. (This is the same Web page that was shown in Design view in Figure 50-13.)

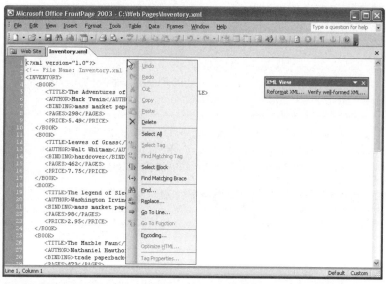

Figure 50-15. Here, an XML document is opened in the FrontPage source code editor and the shortcut menu has been displayed by right-clicking in the editor tab.

Tip Make your HTML source conform to XML rules

XML doesn't define a specific set of elements, but it does enforce a fairly strict, consistent syntax to help eliminate incompatibilities. HTML, on the other hand, defines a specific set of elements so that browsers can universally interpret the language, but it has relatively loose rules of syntax. You can create the best of both languages by having FrontPage convert the HTML source for your Web page so that it conforms to the stricter syntax rules of XML. For example, if your page contains a start-tag for an element (such as <P> for a paragraph) but no matching end-tag (</P> for a paragraph), FrontPage will add the missing end-tag. (In XML, every element must have both a start-tag and an end-tag, or use an empty element tag, such as <HR/> for a horizontal dividing line.) Enforcing XML rules may eliminate ambiguities in your page's HTML source and reduce incompatibilities and differences in the way various browsers or other programs interpret and display the page.

To make your HTML source comply to XML rules, click the Code view button at the bottom of the editing tab to display your page's HTML source code, right-click anywhere within the page, and choose Apply XML Formatting Rules from the shortcut menu.

For more information on XML and XML syntax rules, see Michael J. Young, *XML Step by Step, Second Edition* (Microsoft Press, 2002).

Customizing the Source Code Editor

You can customize many features of the FrontPage source code editor by choosing Tools, Page Options and making settings in the tabs of the Page Options dialog box, as follows:

- **General tab**   Use the options in the Code View Options area to modify word wrapping, line numbering, and other features of the source code editor.
- **Default Fonts tab**   Use the drop-down lists in the Code View area to change the font and font size that's displayed in the source code editor.
- **Code Formatting tab**   The options in this tab let you change the way FrontPage formats the text you enter into the source code editor—for example, the tab size, the formatting of specific HTML elements, and whether FrontPage converts all tag names to uppercase or lowercase.
- **Color Coding tab**   Use the drop-down lists to modify the way FrontPage color codes specific objects within the source code editor, such as normal text, tags, and comments.
- **IntelliSense tab**   Use these options to customize the IntelliSense feature in the source code editor. (IntelliSense was discussed in the previous section.)
- **Code Snippets tab**   Use this tab to add, modify, or remove *code snippets*, which are frequently used blocks of source code that you can insert into the source code editor by pressing Ctrl+Enter and then double-clicking the snippet description in the pop-up list that appears.

Finding and Replacing HTML Elements

The section "Finding and Replacing Text in Your Web Pages," on page 1293 explained the general features of the Find And Replace dialog box. When you work with a Web page, you can use the new HTML Tags tab of this dialog box, shown in Figure 50-16, to find or to find and replace specific HTML elements. You can use this tab in Design, Split, or Code view of a Web page.

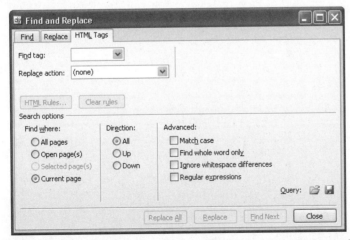

Figure 50-16.   You can use the new HTML Tags tab to find or to find and replace specific HTML elements in a Web page.

You can click the HTML Rules button to create rules for refining your search. For example, you could locate all right-aligned paragraphs by searching for P elements and creating a rule specifying that a matching element must include an *align* attribute set to the value *right*.

To replace each matching element, select an item other than (None) in the Replace Action drop-down list.

Part 9

InfoPath

51   InfoPath Fundamentals   1393

52   Designing Forms in InfoPath   1399

53   Filling Out and Delivering Forms in InfoPath   1417

InfoPath Fundamentals

A Rundown on InfoPath 1393

Opening a Form Template
in Design Mode 1394

A Rundown on InfoPath

Most of the applications in the Microsoft Office System allow you to create and edit special-purpose forms for entering and exchanging information. However, by far the most versatile and powerful Office application for collecting and delivering information using electronic forms is Microsoft Office InfoPath 2003. InfoPath provides a complete set of tools for designing and customizing forms, for filling out and editing forms, and for delivering forms to various destinations. The following are some of InfoPath's most important unique features:

- InfoPath allows you to design highly dynamic and flexible forms. For example, you can add repeating tables or sections to a form that the user can expand to enter multiple items (for instance, a table in an invoice form might initially display only a single row but allow the user to insert additional rows to enter multiple invoice items). You can hide parts of a form, allowing the user to display them only as needed. And you can provide various views of a form (for instance, a resume form might provide one view that's optimized for entering information and another view that displays the information in an attractive format for printing).

- The data that a user enters in a form is stored in XML (Extensible Markup Language), a universal, plain-text format that can be processed by a wide variety of applications. Furthermore, a form can be designed to store its data using the XML document structure specified by any standard XML schema that the designer provides. These features mean that the data associated with a form can be stored in a format that is immediately compatible with an organization's databases, Web services, or other applications and repositories of information. Therefore, once data has been entered in an InfoPath form, it will never need to be rekeyed, scanned, converted, or cut and pasted into another program.

For general information on XML and XML schemas, see "Creating, Editing, and Viewing XML Documents," on page 594.

- Like Microsoft Word and most other Office applications, InfoPath uses a document model. While filling out a form, the user can store the form—temporarily or permanently—in a file on a local disk and later reopen and continue working on the form. The user, therefore, doesn't need to complete the form in a single session, as is required with a Web page form.

- Once the user has completed a form, InfoPath provides a variety of ways to directly deliver the form to the next destination in the organization's workflow. For instance, the form can be printed, sent in an e-mail message, or saved in an XML document on a shared network or Internet location (such as a Microsoft SharePoint team Web site); or the data can be directly submitted to a linked database, Web service, or other data source.

- An InfoPath form is based on a *form template*, also known as a *solution*. Although each user needs to have a personal copy of the InfoPath program (or have access to a shared copy on a server), form templates can be stored on a network or Internet location (such as a SharePoint form library) so that they can easily be shared by all users in an organization or workgroup.

- An organization can easily update all existing and new forms that are based on a shared template by simply modifying the shared copy of the template. A form remains linked to its template, so that each time a user opens the form, the form is automatically updated with the latest changes made to the template. Also, whenever a user opens a new form based on a shared template, InfoPath creates a local copy of the template so that the user can work on the form even when access to the shared template isn't available (for example, when a user is traveling and isn't connected to the network).

> **Note** For a comprehensive general introduction to XML, see Michael J. Young, *XML Step by Step, Second Edition* (Microsoft Press, 2002). This book explains how to write well-formed and valid XML documents and how to display XML documents on the Web. It includes complete instructions for writing XML schemas and transforms.

Opening a Form Template in Design Mode

The following three sections provide overviews of the three main stages in working with a form in InfoPath: designing the form, filling out the form, and delivering the form. The next two chapters in this part of the book explain the details of these three steps.

1. Design the Form

Every InfoPath form is based on a *form template*—also known as an InfoPath *solution*—that defines the design of the form. When you open a new form, you must select a particular form template, which specifies the content, the layout, the formatting, the data type of each control (text box, list box, option button, and so on), and many other features of the form. The template remains permanently linked to the form, so that if the template is modified, you'll see those changes the next time you open the form.

In InfoPath, *designing a form* means creating or modifying a form template. InfoPath provides a basic set of sample form templates. These form templates are designed for creating forms for asset tracking, expense reports, invoices, purchase orders, resumes, and many other common types of forms. However, even if one of the sample form templates closely meets your needs, your organization will probably want to make at least minor customizations to the template. Accordingly, InfoPath lets you customize any of the sample form templates provided with the program, as well as any other form template that's stored on a local or network disk or on the Internet. (If you customize an InfoPath sample form, you must save your customized version separately from the original template, which you can't overwrite.) For example, Figure 51-1 shows a form based on the Invoice (Single Tax Rate) sample form template provided with InfoPath. Obviously you wouldn't want to have to enter your company's information in the "From" controls each time you fill out an invoice. Figure 51-2 shows a form based on a customized version of this form template in which the company information has been made a permanent part of the template.

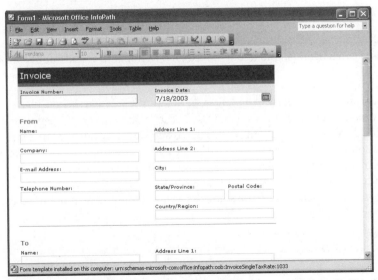

Figure 51-1. This figure shows a newly opened form in InfoPath. The form is based on the sample Invoice (Single Tax Rate) form template.

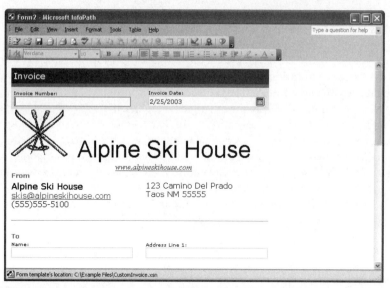

Figure 51-2. This figure shows a form based on a customized version of the Invoice (Single Tax Rate).

You can also create a new form template in InfoPath. You can start with a blank form template and design the form from scratch. Or, you can create a new form template that's based on a specific data source, so that the data entered and stored by the form matches the format of the data source, and can be exchanged directly with that source. The data source can be an XML document or schema, a database (Microsoft SQL Server or Microsoft Access), or a Web service. In the latter two cases, the form can be linked to the data source so that the user can view (that is, query) data in the data source as well as submit new or modified records directly to the data source.

> **Note** Included in a form template is an XML schema that describes the structure of the underlying XML elements that store the data entered in the form's controls. If you base a form template on a schema file, you explicitly supply the template's schema. If you create a form template from scratch, InfoPath builds a schema as you add controls to the form. And, if you base a new form template on an XML document, database, or Web service, InfoPath infers the schema from the structure of the data source. As you'll learn in Chapter 52, you can work directly with the template's schema using the Data Source task pane.

Whether you are customizing an existing form template or creating a new one, you work in InfoPath's *design mode*, which provides extensive interactive tools for adding and formatting layout tables, controls, text, graphics, and other form elements; for applying color schemes;

for working with the underlying data fields (that is, the XML elements); for designing separate form views; and for performing many other design tasks.

A form template consists of a collection of related files. When you save a form template that you've customized or created, InfoPath stores all these files in a single compressed file with the .xsn filename extension. You can save a form template on a local drive for your personal use, or you can save it on a network drive or on the Internet so that it can be used by other members of your organization or workgroup. An ideal place to store a shared template is in a form library on a SharePoint team Web site.

The details on customizing and creating form templates are described in Chapter 52, "Designing Forms in InfoPath." If you aren't planning to be involved in customizing forms, but simply want to know how to fill out and deliver forms, you can skip Chapter 52 and go directly to Chapter 53, "Filling Out and Delivering Forms in InfoPath."

2. Fill Out the Form

To fill out a new form, you must select a form template. You can use one of the sample form templates provided with InfoPath, or you can use a custom form template stored on a local disk or on a shared network or Internet location.

You then fill out the form in InfoPath's *edit mode*, using the extensive tools provided for entering information in the form's controls. These tools include standard Office editing commands (cut, copy, paste, drag-and-drop, undo, redo, and so on), find and replace commands, spelling checking, error checking (for controls that require specific data types), adding digital signatures, displaying or hiding optional sections, and inserting additional repeating sections or rows in repeating tables.

In addition, when you enter information in a rich text box control, InfoPath provides a full range of editing and formatting commands: You can insert text, pictures, tables, horizontal dividing lines, or hyperlinks. You can format characters or paragraphs. And you can create bulleted or numbered lists.

When you fill out a form, you can save your work at any time by using the standard Save or Save As command. When you save a form, InfoPath writes the contents of the form's controls to an XML document (a file with the .xml filename extension). This file includes only the text and formatting you've entered in the form's controls, *not* any text, pictures, tables, or other content defined in the form template that lies outside the controls.

To resume filling out a form in InfoPath, you simply reopen the XML document that contains the form's data. InfoPath then automatically reopens the form's template, displays the form according to the template design, and inserts the data from the XML document back into the form's controls. You can then continue where you left off.

> **Note** You might wonder how InfoPath identifies a form's template when you open the XML document that contains the form data. It does this by inserting a processing instruction in the XML document. The processing instruction includes the address (file path, URL, or other identifier) of the form's template.
>
> When you double-click a form's XML document file in Windows Explorer, another processing instruction in the XML document tells Windows to open the file in InfoPath rather than in the default application that's registered to open an XML file (usually, your browser).

The details on filling out a form are described in Chapter 53, "Filling Out and Delivering Forms in InfoPath."

3. Deliver the Form

Once you've finished filling out a form, you'll probably need to deliver the form to another person, application, or data repository in your organization. InfoPath provides several ways to deliver your report:

- Use the standard Save or Save As command, mentioned in the previous section, to write the form's data to an XML document on a shared network drive or Internet site where other people or applications can access and process it. (For example, you could store the XML document in a form library on a SharePoint team Web site.)
- Use Microsoft Outlook to send the form in an e-mail message to one or more recipients.
- If the form is set up for submitting, you can directly submit the data to a database, Web service, Web site, or other destination.
- Save the form as a static Web page (HTML file) that you can post to a Web server. Although the data in the form can't be modified in a Web page, this format allows people who don't have InfoPath to read the form.
- If your organization hasn't quite reached the paperless stage, you can print the form and deliver the hardcopy.
- Export the form's data for analysis in Microsoft Excel.

The details on delivering a form are described in Chapter 53, "Filling Out and Delivering Forms in InfoPath."

Designing Forms in InfoPath

Opening a Form Template
in Design Mode 1399

Customizing a Form Template 1403
Saving a Form Template 1412

Opening a Form Template in Design Mode

To create a new form template or to customize an existing one, you must first use the Design A Form task pane, shown in Figure 52-1, to open the form template in design mode. You can display the Design A Form task pane by choosing File, Design A Form.

Recently opened form templates —

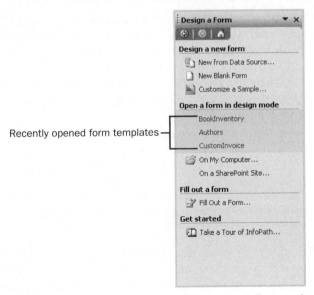

Figure 52-1. You can use InfoPath's Design A Form task pane to open a form template in design mode.

In the Design A Form task pane, you can open a form template in design mode using one of the following methods:

- To create a new form template entirely from scratch, click the New Blank Form command in the Design A New Form area. InfoPath will open an empty form template. Your typical next steps would be to use the techniques given later in this chapter to add one or more layout tables or sections and then to insert text, graphics, and controls (such as text boxes, list boxes, and option buttons). Each time you insert a control into the form, you can have InfoPath automatically add a corresponding field (that is, an XML [Extensible Markup Language] element) to the template's underlying schema. (Or, you can add a field manually.) Thus, InfoPath builds the form template's schema step-by-step as you design the form.

> **Tip** You can quickly open a blank form template without using the Design A Form task pane by clicking the Design A Form button at the left end of the Standard toolbar. This button is available, however, only if InfoPath is already in design mode.

- To modify one of the sample form templates provided with InfoPath, click the Customize A Sample command in the Design A New Form area and then select a template in the Customize A Sample dialog box. InfoPath will open a copy of the form template in design mode. You can then use the design tools described later in this chapter to customize the template. Figures 51-1 and 51-2 show one of the sample forms before and after customization. When you save the customized form template, you'll need to store it separately from the original sample template, which you aren't allowed to overwrite.

- To modify a custom form template that you or someone else has created, click one of the commands in the Open A Form In Design Mode area. You can open any form template by clicking On My Computer and then selecting the template file in the Open In Design Mode dialog box. The template can be located on a local or network disk or on the Internet, and it will have the .xsn filename extension. Files of this type will appear in the Open dialog box when the InfoPath Form Templates (*.xsn; *.xsf) item is selected in the Files Of Type drop-down list.

  To quickly open a form template that's assigned to a form library on a SharePoint team Web site, you can click On A SharePoint site. You can also immediately reopen a form template by clicking one of the recently opened templates listed at the top of the Open A Form In Design Mode area.

> For information on working with InfoPath forms on a SharePoint team Web site, see the sidebar "Working with Form Libraries on a SharePoint Team Web Site," on page 1415.

  You can then use the design tools, described later in the chapter, to modify the form template. When you save the template, you can use the File, Save command to overwrite the original template or use the File, Save As command to create a new copy of the template.

- To create a new form template that's based on an existing data source, click the New From Data Source command in the Design A New Form area to open the Data Source Setup Wizard dialog box, shown in Figure 52-2. In this dialog box, select one of the three options, described here, and then click the Next button and supply the additional requested information.

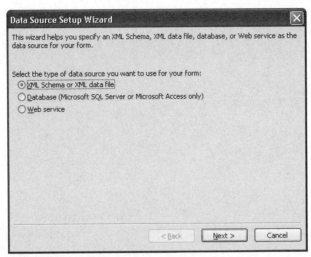

Figure 52-2. You use the Data Source Setup Wizard to create a new form template based on an existing data source.

- To create a new form template that has a schema matching an existing XML schema (.xsd) file or an existing XML document (.xml) file, select the XML Schema Or XML Data File option. After you click the Next button, you'll need to specify the location of the schema or XML file. When InfoPath opens the new form template, you won't see any initial controls or other content. However, if you look in the Data Source task pane (described later in the chapter), you'll see that the form's schema contains all the XML elements (known as *groups* and *fields* in the task pane) that were defined in the schema or document that the template was based upon. You can use the Data Source task pane to quickly add to the form controls that are bound to these elements.

  The form template does *not* retain a link to the schema or document used for creating it. Therefore, you can freely add or remove groups or fields from the form. Keep in mind, however, that if you do so, the form's schema will no longer match that of the schema or document file used as its basis.

  Figure 52-3 shows a form template that was based upon the Inventory.xml example XML document. Two additional fields (that is, fields not contained in the XML document) were added to the form: Review for typing in a review and Cover for displaying an image of the book's cover. (The Inventory.xml XML document is listed in "Working with XML Data in a Worksheet," on page 838, and is provided on the book's companion CD.)

Chapter 52

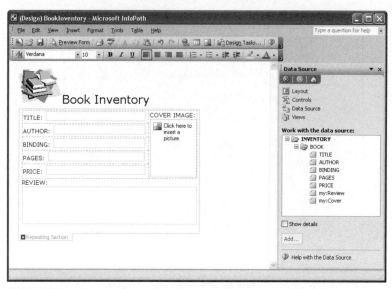

Figure 52-3. Here, a form template based upon the XML document Inventory.xml is opened in InfoPath's design mode.

- To create a new form template that is based upon a SQL (structured query language) Server or Access database, select the Database (Microsoft SQL Server Or Microsoft Office Access Only) option.

- To create a new form template that's based upon a Web service, select the Web Service option.

  If you select either the Database (Microsoft SQL Server Or Microsoft Office Access Only) option or the Web Service option, the form's schema will contain an element (known as a *field* in InfoPath) corresponding to each of the fields of the data source, and you'll be able to use the Data Source task pane to quickly add to the form controls that are bound to these fields.

  Because the form template retains a link to the database or Web service used as its basis, the form user will be able to view (that is, query) data from the data source. (InfoPath will create a separate form view designed for querying data. Views are discussed later in the chapter.) However, because of the link, you won't be able to remove groups or fields from the form (doing so would make the form's underlying schema incompatible with the linked data source).

  Also, if you select the Database (Microsoft SQL Server Or Microsoft Office Access Only) or Web Service option, InfoPath will, if possible, automatically turn on the Enable Submit option, which allows a form user to choose the File, Submit command to write a new or modified record back to the data source.

> **Note** You can control the Enable Submit option for a form by choosing Tools, Submitting Forms.

Figure 52-4 shows a form template that was based on the Authors table in the Book Inventory03.mdb Access database. (This database was presented in this book in Part 7, "Access," and is one of the example Access databases provided on the companion CD.)

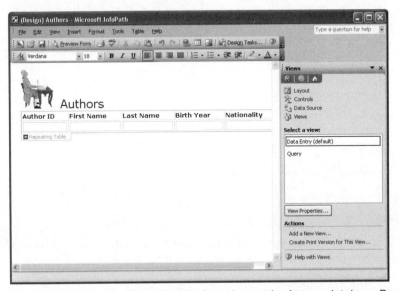

Figure 52-4. Here, a form template based upon the Access database Book Inventory03.mdb is opened in InfoPath's design mode. This figure shows the Data Entry view of the form.

Tip If you're filling out a form in edit mode, you can quickly open the form's template by clicking the Design This Form button on the Standard toolbar.

Customizing a Form Template

When you first open a form template in design mode, InfoPath displays the Design Tasks task pane, shown in Figure 52-5, which provides ready access to the four main task panes that you use in designing a form template: Layout, Controls, Data Source, and Views. The following sections explain how to use each of these task panes. The Design Tasks task pane also provides a command for running the Publishing Wizard, which is discussed in the last section of this chapter.

Note You can display the Design Tasks task pane at any time by clicking the Design Tasks button on the Standard toolbar.

Chapter 52

Figure 52-5. The Design Tasks task pane serves as the main switchboard for accessing the most commonly used task panes employed in designing a form template.

Adding a Layout to a Form

If you started with a blank form template and are designing the template from scratch, your first step is usually to use the Layout task pane, shown in Figure 52-6, to insert tables or sections to contain and arrange the form's content. You can also use this task pane to modify existing tables in a form.

Figure 52-6. You use the Layout task pane to insert tables or sections or to modify tables.

> **Tip**   A convenient way to display the Layout task pane is by choosing Format, Layout.

InfoPath allows you to insert the following different types of tables and sections. You can insert any of these items using the Layout task pane, except where noted otherwise.

- An InfoPath *table* is similar to a table in Word and other Office applications. It can be used to contain and arrange any type of content.

- A *section* is somewhat similar to a text box in other Office applications. It's generally used to contain and display the fields that belong to a single group. (Fields and groups are explained in "Working with a Form's Data Source," later in this chapter.) You need to use the Controls task pane, described in the next section, to insert a regular section (a section that isn't repeating or optional).

- A *repeating table* is one that initially consists of a header and a single data row but allows the form user to insert additional rows when the form is filled out. A repeating table is generally used to display a repeating set of fields. For instance, the Authors.xsn example template shown in Figure 52-4 uses a repeating table in which each data row displays all the fields for a given author (Author ID, First Name, Last Name, and so on). The form user can add more rows as needed to define additional authors. You need to use the Controls task pane, described in the next section, to insert a repeating table.

- A *repeating section* initially consists of a single section, but allows the form user to insert additional sections. A repeating section is generally used to display a repeating field or a repeating set of fields in a group. For instance, the BookInventory.xsn example template shown in Figure 52-3, includes a repeating section in which each section displays all the fields for a given book. The form user can add more sections as needed to define additional books.

- An *optional section* is initially hidden on the form, but allows the user to display it if it's needed. For instance, the Invoice (Single Tax Rate) sample template provided by InfoPath includes two optional sections, one that displays invoice terms and another that lets the user add freeform notes. (A form based on this template is shown in Figure 51-1.)

> **Tip**   A good way to learn how to use the different types of tables and sections effectively is to open some of the InfoPath sample tables in design mode and study how these elements are employed. Design mode clearly labels the type of each element—Section, Repeating Table, and so on. (Although it doesn't label a nonrepeating table.)

 You can also insert or work with tables by using the Insert Layout Table button on the Standard toolbar; the Table menu; the Tables toolbar (which you can display by choosing View, Toolbars, Tables); or the Insert, Layout Table menu command.

You can apply borders or background shading to a table by selecting the table, choosing Format, Borders And Shading, and working in the Borders And Shading dialog box. The techniques are similar to those used in Word, as explained in "Adding Borders and Shading," on page 361.

Chapter 52

Inserting Controls in a Form

You can use the Controls task pane, shown in Figure 52-7, to insert the individual controls—such as text boxes, list boxes, and option buttons—into which the user enters information when filling out the form. To insert a control, place the insertion point at the position in your form where you want to display the control and then click the description of the control you want in the Insert Controls list in the Controls task pane. Alternatively, you can drag a control description from the list and drop it on the target location within the form.

Figure 52-7. You use the Controls task pane to insert the controls that allow the form user to enter information into the form.

> **Tip** An alternative way to insert a text box, a drop-down list, or a repeating table is to choose the corresponding command from the Insert menu. You can choose More Controls on this menu to display the Controls task pane.

Once you have inserted a control, you can use standard mouse techniques to resize or move it. You can set a control's properties by right-clicking the control and choosing *Control* Properties from the shortcut menu (where *Control* is a description of the control, such as Text Box or Picture), by double-clicking the control, or by selecting the control and pressing Alt+Enter. InfoPath will display the Properties dialog box for the particular type of control (for instance, the Text Box Properties dialog box or the Picture Properties dialog box), as shown in Figure 52-8.

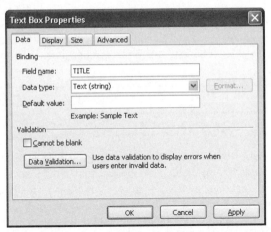

Figure 52-8. This Properties dialog box lets you set the properties of a text box.

You can convert a control to an entirely different type of control by selecting it and choosing a command from the Edit, Change To submenu. For example, you could convert a text box control to a check box control.

If the Automatically Create Data Source option is checked in the Controls task pane when you insert a control, InfoPath will automatically add a new field or group to the form's underlying schema and it will bind the control to that field or group. You can see the new field or group in the Data Source task pane, described in the next section. If you select or hold the pointer over a control, InfoPath will display the name of the field or group that the control is bound to (the name will appear in a box in the control's upper-right corner). You can change the binding by selecting the control and choosing Edit, Change Binding.

> **Note** A control such as a text box or check box is bound to a *field*, meaning that the data entered into the control will be stored in the XML element that corresponds to that field when the user saves the form. A repeating table or any type of section is bound to a *group*, meaning that all the controls within the table or section are bound to fields contained within the group.

If the Automatically Create Data Source option is cleared when you insert a control, InfoPath will prompt you to select an existing field or group to which the control will be bound.

> **Note** If the form template is linked to a database or Web service, or if the template is based on one of the sample templates provided with InfoPath, you won't be able to check the Automatically Create Data Source option. In these cases, when you insert a control, you'll need to specify the field or group to which the control will be bound. (If the form template doesn't yet include this field or group, you'll have to first define the field or group using the Data Source task pane, as described in the next section.)

Tip If a form template is based upon a data source, as described earlier in this chapter, and therefore already has a fully defined underlying schema, you can use the Data Source task pane to quickly add controls that are bound to the form's existing fields and groups, as explained in the next section.

Picture Controls vs. Static Pictures

A *picture control* allows the form user to insert a picture from a graphics file while filling out the form. You can insert a picture control by clicking the Picture item in the Insert Controls list in the Controls task pane, or by choosing Insert, Picture, Control. An example of a picture control is the control labeled COVER IMAGE in the BookInventory.xsn example form template shown in Figure 52-3. This picture control lets the user enter a picture showing the cover for each book.

 In contrast, InfoPath displays a *static picture* permanently in the form and doesn't allow the user to replace it. You can insert a static picture by clicking the Insert Picture button on the Standard toolbar; by choosing Insert, Picture, From File; or by choosing Insert, Picture, Clip Art. An example of a static picture is the picture showing a collection of books in the upper-left corner of the BookInventory.xsn example form template shown in Figure 52-3. This picture is always displayed in the form and can't be modified when the user fills out the form.

Working with a Form's Data Source

The Data Source task pane, shown in Figure 52-9, lets you work directly with the form template's underlying schema. Recall that a form template's schema defines the elements and the element structure in the XML document that is used to store the data that the user enters into the form. In the Data Source task pane, an XML element that contains other (nested) elements is called a *group* and an XML element that doesn't contain other elements is called a *field*.

If you're building a form template from scratch, or if you're customizing the schema of an existing template, you can add a group or field by first selecting—in the Work With The Data Source list—the existing group that you want to contain your new group or field. Then, click the Add button and define your new group or field in the Add Group Or Field dialog box.

Figure 52-9. The Data Source task pane lets you work directly with the form's XML elements—that is, its groups and fields.

You can add to your form a control, set of controls, table, or section that's bound to a particular group or field by clicking the group or field name in the Work With The Data Source list, clicking the down arrow that appears, and then choosing a command from the top section of the drop-down menu. Here's the drop-down menu that's displayed for a group:

In the example shown in this figure, choosing Repeating Section With Controls would insert a repeating section containing an entire set of controls, each control bound to one of the fields within the BOOK repeating group (TITLE, AUTHOR, BINDING, and so on). The resulting repeating section is shown in Figure 52-3. (In the repeating section shown in this figure, however, a layout table has been added and the controls have been resized and rearranged.)

You can also modify the form template's schema by using the drop-down menu on a group or field, shown on the previous page, to add, delete, move, or create a reference to a group or field. *Moving* a group or field moves it to a different group. *Creating a reference* to a group or field makes a copy of the group or field within a different group.

Finally, you can choose the Properties command from the drop-down menu to modify the group's or field's property settings.

> **Tip** If you check the Show Details option in the Data Source task pane, the list will display the data type of each field, plus any default value that's assigned to a field.

Managing Form Views

A form can have several different *views*, or ways of displaying and entering the form's data. When filling out a form, the user can switch to a different form view by choosing the name of the view from InfoPath's Views menu.

You work with a form template's views using the Views task pane, shown in Figure 52-10. Here, you can perform the following tasks:

Figure 52-10. The Views task pane lets you create or modify form views.

- To create a new view, click the Add A New View command in the Actions area and supply a view name when prompted. A newly created view will initially be blank; however, keep in mind that you can easily copy and paste content from an existing view into a new view to get a head start in designing the new view.

- To open a particular view in the design mode window so that you can work on its content, click the name of the view in the Select A View list.

- To modify a view's property settings, including the view name, the background color, the character formatting used for the controls in the view, and the view's print settings, select the view in the list and then click the View Properties button to open the View Properties dialog box.

> **Tip** Another way to set the properties of the view that's currently displayed in design mode is to choose Format, View Properties.

- To add a *print view* to a view, select the view in the list and then click the Create Print Version For This View command in the Actions area. If the form user issues the Print command when working with a particular view, InfoPath will automatically print the print view if one has been assigned.

> **Tip** To assign an existing print view to a particular view (rather than creating a new print view), open the View Properties dialog box for the view, click the Print Settings tab, and select the print view in the drop-down list at the top of the tab.

Using Other Form Design Tools

The following are among the additional useful design tasks that you can perform while working on a form template in InfoPath's design mode:

- To insert a hyperlink in a form, click the Insert Hyperlink button on the Standard toolbar; choose Insert, Hyperlink; press Ctrl+K; or click the Hyperlink item in the Controls task pane.

- To insert a horizontal dividing line at the current position of the insertion point, choose Insert, Horizontal Line.

- To format characters or paragraphs in the form, use the Font task pane (which you can display by choosing Format, Font) or use the Formatting toolbar (which you can display by choosing View, Toolbars, Formatting).

- To create bulleted or numbered lists, use the Bullets And Numbering task pane, which you can display by choosing Format, Bullets And Numbering. Or use the Bullets or the Numbering button on the Formatting toolbar.

- To globally modify the text colors, table border colors, table background (shading) colors, and possibly other colors used in the form, select a color scheme in the Color Schemes task pane (which you can open by choosing Format, Color Schemes). The effect of applying a color scheme (if any) depends upon the way the form was designed.

- To check the spelling of the text you've entered into a form template, click the Spelling button on the Standard toolbar; choose Tools, Spelling; or press F7. You can also have InfoPath check the spelling of words as you type them. To turn the as-you-type spelling checker on or off, or to set other spelling options, choose Tools, Options and click the Spelling tab.

> InfoPath's spelling checkers work like those in Word, which are explained in "Checking Spelling," on page 479.

● To see how the form looks when its controls contain data, you can have InfoPath display sample data by selecting the View, Sample Data menu option.

● To see how the form looks and behaves when it's being filled out, you can view the form in edit mode in a separate window by clicking the Preview Form button on the Standard toolbar; by choosing a command from the File, Preview Form submenu; or by pressing Ctrl+Shift+B. To close the edit mode window in which you are previewing the form, click the Close Preview button on the Standard toolbar.

● To set options that affect the entire form, choose Tools, Form Options and enter your settings into the tabs of the Form Options dialog box, as shown in Figure 52-11.

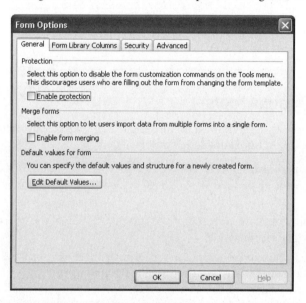

Figure 52-11. You can set a variety of options that affect the entire form by using the Form Options dialog box.

Saving a Form Template

When you have finished creating or modifying a form template in design mode, you of course need to save it. You can use the following procedure to save the template on a local disk. You would use this procedure to store a template that is intended for your personal use, or to preserve your work while you're developing a template that you will ultimately save in a shared location.

1 Choose File, Save As. (Or, if you haven't yet saved the form, you can choose File, Save or click the Save button on the Standard toolbar.) In the message box that InfoPath displays, click the Save button, as shown here:

Chapter 52

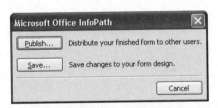

InfoPath will then display the standard Save As dialog box.

2   Select a file name and location for your form template in the Save As dialog box. It's easiest to omit the extension from the file name you enter and let InfoPath append the appropriate extension for a form template file, .xsn.

Note that in the Save As dialog box, you can click the Change Name button to add a friendly name for the template (or to modify an existing friendly name), which Info-Path will display in the recently used templates list in the Fill Out A Form task pane, as well as in the Forms dialog box (explained in the next chapter).

3   To resave a form template to its current location, choose File, Save; or click the Save button on the Standard toolbar.

Extracting a Form Template's Files

A form template actually comprises a collection of separate files. When you save a form template as described in this chapter, these files are all stored in compressed format within a single form template file that has the .xsn file name extension.

You can, however, extract the individual files from a form template that's opened in design mode by choosing File, Extract Form Files and then, in the Browse For Folder dialog box, selecting the file folder where you want to store the template's individual files.

A form template's files include a manifest (.xsf) file that defines much of the functionality behind the template, a schema (.xsd) file representing the template's underlying XML schema, and an XSLT (Extensible Stylesheet Language Transformations) style sheet (.xsl) file—also known as a transform file—for each view, which contains the instructions for displaying the view.

If you have extracted a form template's files, you can examine and work with the individual files. You can also open the form template in design mode by choosing the template's manifest (.xsf) file in the Open In Design Mode dialog box (described earlier in this chapter). And, you can fill out a new form based on the template by selecting the manifest file in the Open dialog box, as explained in Chapter 53, "Filling Out and Delivering Forms in InfoPath."

You can also save your form template to a shared location on a network or on the Internet so that other users will be able to access the template. To do that, follow these steps:

1   Choose File, Publish. Or, if the Design Tasks task pane is currently displayed, you can click the Publish Form command near the bottom of the pane. InfoPath will then run

the Publishing Wizard. (You can also run the Publishing Wizard by using the more roundabout method of choosing File, Save As and then clicking the Publish button in the message box, which was shown previously in this section.)

2 In the second Publishing Wizard dialog box (shown in Figure 52-12), you must select the type of location where you want to save your form template, as follows:

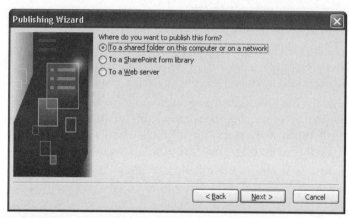

Figure 52-12. In the second Publishing Wizard page, you select the type of shared location where you want to save your form template.

- To save the form template where it will be accessible through your organization's network, select To A Shared Folder On This Computer Or On A Network. After you click the Next button you'll need to specify a file path, a file name, and a friendly name (the "form name") for your template.

- To save the form template in a new or existing form library on a SharePoint team Web site and to assign the template as the library's default form template, select To A SharePoint Form Library. For more information on this option, see the sidebar "Working with Form Libraries on a SharePoint Team Web Site," later in this section.

- To save the form template to a shared Internet location, select To A Web Server. After you click the Next button you'll need to specify a URL (Uniform Resource Locator), a file name, and a friendly name (the "form name") for your template.

If you store your form template in a shared location, other users will be able to fill out new forms based on your template. Furthermore, you'll be able to quickly update all the forms that users have created from your template, as well as new forms that they will subsequently create, by simply editing the shared form template (for example, you might want to add a new company logo or modify a telephone number). The next time any user opens in edit mode an existing or new form based on that template, your modifications will appear. (Each time the user opens the form in edit mode, InfoPath opens the form's template and uses the information in the template to display the form.)

However, because all existing forms based on your shared form template remain linked to the template, you must exercise caution when you make template changes. For example, you shouldn't move or rename a shared template. Also, you should avoid making changes to a shared template's design that could impair or cause data loss in existing forms that were created from your template—for instance, you shouldn't remove or rename a field or group. For more information on this important but complex issue, see the InfoPath online help.

After you've saved a form template and are done working with it, you can close the template but leave the InfoPath window open by choosing File, Close.

Working with Form Libraries on a SharePoint Team Web Site

With the latest version of Windows SharePoint Services, a SharePoint team Web site can include *form libraries*. A form library is similar to a SharePoint document library, and when you view the site in a browser, it's listed along with the site's document libraries in the Document Libraries area of the Documents And Lists page. A form library, however, is designed specifically for filling out and storing forms that are based on the library's form template. When you create a new form library using your browser (through the Create page, as explained in Chapter 8, "Using Windows SharePoint Services in Professional Workgroups"), you select the form template that will be assigned to that library. All forms that are created in the library will be based upon this template.

For information on Windows SharePoint Services, see Chapter 8.

Using InfoPath, you can open and modify a form library's template by clicking the On A Share-Point Site command in the Design A Form task pane, as explained previously in this chapter.

You can also *replace* a form library's current form template with the template that's open in InfoPath design mode. To do this, use the Publishing Wizard (described in this section) and select both the To A SharePoint Form Library option (in the second wizard page) and the Modify An Existing Form Library option (in the third wizard page). Note, however, that replacing a form library's template can result in the permanent loss of data in existing forms stored in that library.

More commonly, however, you use the Publishing Wizard to create a *new* form library that's assigned the form template that's open in InfoPath design mode. To do this, select the To A SharePoint Form Library option (in the second wizard page) and the Create A New Form Library option (in the third wizard page).

To fill out and save a form in a SharePoint form library, use your browser to connect with the library's page (as described in "Accessing SharePoint Document Libraries Using Your Browser," on page 183). Then, click the Fill Out This Form button on the toolbar near the top of the page. This will run InfoPath on your computer and open a new form in edit mode so that you can fill out the form and save it within the form library, where other team members can access it. The commands for working with a form library in your browser are similar to those provided for a document library, as described in "Accessing SharePoint Document Libraries Using Your Browser."

Filling Out and Delivering Forms in InfoPath

Opening a New Form in Edit Mode... 1417
Filling Out a Form............... 1419

Saving and Delivering a Form 1423

Opening a New Form in Edit Mode

To fill out a new form, you must first use the Fill Out A Form task pane, shown in Figure 53-1, to select a form template and open the form in edit mode. You can display the Fill Out A Form task pane by choosing File, Fill Out A Form.

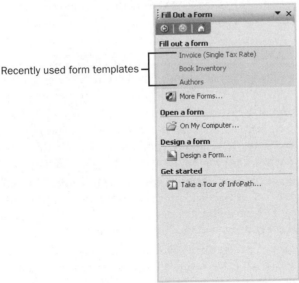

Figure 53-1. You can use InfoPath's Fill Out A Form task pane to open a new form in edit mode.

In the Fill Out A Form task pane, you can use one of the following methods:

- To base your new form on one of the sample form templates supplied with InfoPath, click the More Forms command in the Fill Out A Form area to display the Forms dialog box. Then, click the Sample Forms tab (shown in Figure 53-2), select the template you want to use, and click the OK button.

> **Tip** To use a form template from the collection of templates provided on the Microsoft Office Online Web site, click the Form Templates On Office Online button at the bottom of the Forms dialog box.

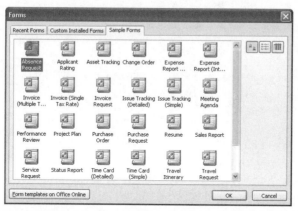

Figure 53-2. The Sample Forms tab in the Forms On My Computer dialog box lets you use one of the sample form templates supplied with InfoPath to open a new form.

- To base your new form on a recently used form template, click the template name in the list of recently used templates at the top of the Fill Out A Form area. The templates listed here are the ones that were recently edited, created, or used to create a form.

- To base your new form on a custom form template that's stored on a local or network disk or on the Internet, click On My Computer in the Open A Form area. Then, in the Open dialog box select Form Templates (*.xsn; *.xsf) in the Files Of Type drop-down list, select the template's .xsn (or .xsf file), and click the Open button.

- Once you have used a custom form template to create a new form, the template will appear in the Recent Forms tab of the Forms dialog box. You can reuse one of these templates by clicking the More Forms command in the Fill Out A Form task pane and then clicking the Recent Forms tab of the Forms dialog box.

- If a form is currently open in edit mode, you can click the Fill Out A Form button on the Standard toolbar to open a new form based on the same form template as the one used for the currently open form. If you're in edit mode but a form isn't currently open, clicking this button will display the Fill Out A Form task pane.

After you complete one of these procedures, InfoPath will use the selected form template to structure a new form and to display it in the InfoPath window in edit mode. Figure 53-3 shows a newly opened form that was based on the BookInventory.xsn example template. (This template was shown in design mode in Figure 52-3.)

Chapter 53

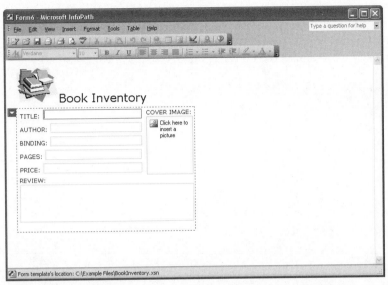

Figure 53-3. This figure shows a form newly opened in edit mode.

Filling Out a Form

When you open a form in edit mode, InfoPath provides a wealth of tools to help you fill out the form. Most of the tools are similar to features provided in other applications in the Microsoft Office System, and using them is quite straightforward. The following summary is intended primarily to make you aware of the tools that are available, rather than to provide detailed instructions on using them.

- If more than one view has been defined for the open form, you can switch to any view by choosing its name from the top section of the View menu.

- To move from one control to another, you can either click each control, or you can press Tab or Shift+Tab to move forward or backward through the controls.

- When you enter text in a control, InfoPath provides the standard editing commands for the Office System, many of which are listed on the Edit menu, shown here:

● You can use the Find task pane, shown in Figure 53-4, to search through the text you've entered in a form, or you can use the Replace task pane to find and replace text. You can display the Find task pane by choosing Edit, Find or pressing Ctrl+F. You can display the Replace task pane by choosing Edit, Replace or pressing Ctrl+H.

Figure 53-4. You can use the Find task pane to search through the text entered in the controls in a form.

● To check the spelling of the text entered in the form's controls, click the Spelling button on the Standard toolbar; choose Tools, Spelling; or press F7. You can also have InfoPath check the spelling of words as you type them in controls. To turn the as-you-type spelling checker on or off, or to set other spelling options, choose Tools, Options and click the Spelling tab. You can specify the particular dictionary that InfoPath uses to check all the text entered in controls in the current form by choosing Tools, Set Language and selecting a language in the Language dialog box.

Note The spelling checker will work in a control only if the Enable Spelling Checker property option was checked for that control when the form's template was designed. This option is found in the Display tab of the Properties dialog box for the control.

● If a control has a data type other than Text (Text allows any input) or has been assigned a data validation rule, InfoPath will check for errors, displaying a dashed red border around the control when an inappropriate value is entered. You can select the next control in the form that has been tagged with an error by choosing Tools, Go To Next Error or by pressing Ctrl+Shift+E. You can view a description of the error in the current control by choosing Tools, Show Error Message or pressing Ctrl+Shift+S.

> **Note** When you design a form template, you can designate the data type of a control (and its underlying field), or you can add a data validation rule (for example, not allowing a numeric control to contain a value greater than 100), using the Data tab of the control's Properties dialog box.

- If digital signatures have been enabled for the form, you can digitally sign the form by choosing Tools, Digital Signatures or by clicking the Digital Signatures button on the Standard toolbar.

> **Note** When you design a form template, you can enable digital signing of the form by choosing Tools, Form Options, clicking the Security tab, and checking the Allow Users To Digitally Sign This Form option.

- If a form contains an optional section, you can display it by clicking the section description, as shown here:

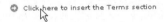

To hide the optional section again, click the down arrow in the section's upper-left corner and choose Remove *Section* (where *Section* is the name of the optional section) from the drop-down menu, as shown here:

- You can insert or remove a copy of a repeating section or a row in a repeating table by clicking the down arrow in the section's or table's upper-left corner (the down arrow appears when you hold the pointer over the section or table), and choosing the appropriate command from the drop-down menu, as shown here:

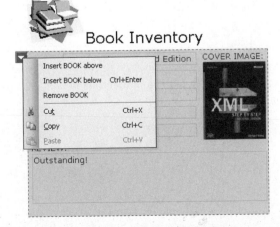

Chapter 53

An alternative way to insert a copy of a repeating section or a row in a repeating table is to choose Insert, Section, *Group* where *Group* is the name of the group that appears in the repeating section or table (such as BOOK in the example shown in the preceding figure).

● When you enter information in a rich text box control, InfoPath provides a full range of editing and formatting commands, including the following:

■ To insert a picture from a graphics file, click the Insert Picture button on the Standard toolbar or choose Insert, Picture, From File. To insert a picture from the Microsoft Clip Organizer, choose Insert, Picture, Clip Art.

■ To insert a table or to work with a table, use the Table menu, the Tables toolbar, or the Insert Table button on the Standard toolbar. To apply borders or shading to a table, choose Format, Borders And Shading.

■ To insert a horizontal dividing line, choose Insert, Horizontal Line.

■ To insert a hyperlink, click the Insert Hyperlink button on the Standard toolbar; choose Insert, Hyperlink; or press Ctrl+K. Keep in mind that if you type a valid URL or e-mail address in a rich text box control, InfoPath will automatically convert it to a hyperlink.

■ To format characters, use the Font task pane (which you can display by choosing Format, Font or by pressing Ctrl+D) or the Formatting toolbar. (The Font task pane is shown in Figure 53-5.)

Figure 53-5. You can use the Font task pane to format characters entered in a rich text box control.

- To modify a paragraph's alignment or indentation, use the Formatting toolbar.

- To create a bulleted or numbered list, use the Bullets And Numbering task pane (which you can display by choosing Format, Bullets And Numbering) or the Bullets button or Numbering button on the Formatting toolbar. Note that you can click the down arrow on the Bullets button or on the Numbering button to select a particular bullet or numbering style.

- To modify the form template that the form is based on, click the Design This Form button on the Standard toolbar or choose Tools, Design This Form.

Saving and Delivering a Form

You can use the following methods to save your work while you fill out a form, to store the final copy of a completed form, or to deliver a finished form to another person or application:

- To save your form to a form file on a local or network disk, or on the Internet, click the Save button on the Standard toolbar; choose File, Save; or choose File, Save As. As explained in Chapter 51, a form file is in XML format and has the .xml filename extension.

- To close the active form, but leave the InfoPath window displayed, choose File, Close. To reopen and resume working on a form that you saved and closed, choose File, Fill Out A Form (if necessary) to open the Fill Out A Form task pane, and then click the On My Computer command in the task pane's Open A Form area. Then, in the Open dialog box, select Forms (*.xml) in the Files Of Type drop-down list and select the XML file containing your saved form.

> **Tip** A quick way to reopen a recently opened form is to choose its name from the recently opened files list near the bottom of the File menu.

- To use Outlook to send the form in an e-mail message to one or more recipients, click the Send To Mail Recipient button on the Standard toolbar or choose File, Send To Mail Recipient. InfoPath will then display an e-mail header at the top of the form window. Fill out the header and click the Send button. (See Figure 53-6.)

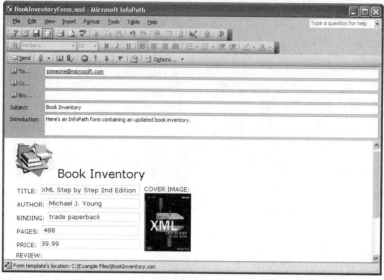

Figure 53-6. The e-mail header lets you send a completed form to one or more recipients using Outlook.

- If the form's template was set up for submitting, you can directly submit the form's data to the designated database, Web service, Web site, or other destination by choosing File, Submit. (The form's designer might also have included a Submit button that you can click in the form.)

- To save the form as a static Web page (HTML file) that you can post to a Web server, choose File, Export To, Web. Then, select a location and name for the Web page file, which InfoPath will save in the Single File Web Page format, with the .mht or .mhtml filename extension.

- To print the form, use the following commands:

  - To set the paper size and source, the printing orientation (portrait or landscape), and the margins displayed on the printed page, choose File, Page Setup.

  - To preview the printed appearance of the form, click the Print Preview button on the Standard toolbar; choose File, Print Preview; or press Ctrl+F2.

  - To print the form, choose File, Print to open the Print dialog box, where you can set printing options, or click the Print button on the Standard toolbar to print immediately using default options.

  Keep in mind that if a print view has been defined for the active view, InfoPath will print the print view instead of the active view.

> Print views are explained in "Managing Form Views," on page 1410.

- To export the form's data for analysis in a Microsoft Excel worksheet, choose File, Export To, Microsoft Office Excel and then supply the required information in the Export To Excel Wizard.

Part 10

Customizing Office 2003 Using VBA

54	VBA Fundamentals	1427
55	Using Variables, Operators, and Functions to Manage Information	1439
56	Adding Logic and Computing Power with Control Structures	1461
57	Using Toolbox Controls to Create a User Interface	1477

VBA Fundamentals

Using the Visual Basic Development
Environment to Edit a Macro 1427

Learning the Visual Basic Programming
Tools 1431

A Microsoft Office 2003 Edition *macro* stores a sequence of Office commands, allowing you to execute those commands at any time by *running* the macro. Macros are written in a computer language known as Visual Basic for Applications, or VBA. You should begin your study of VBA by reading "Recording and Running Macros," on page 224 in Chapter 9. That section explains how to create a macro by recording it, which is the easiest way to build a relatively simple macro if you're working in Microsoft Word, Microsoft Excel, or Microsoft PowerPoint. It also explains how to run macros and covers the important topic of macro security.

The chapters in this part of the book explain how to use the Visual Basic development environment—also known as the Visual Basic Editor—to edit existing macros or to write new ones from scratch with the VBA programming language. There are several advantages to learning how to use the Visual Basic development environment and VBA, rather than relying on recording macros. You can use the Visual Basic Editor to customize and fine-tune the macros you record. You can create much more sophisticated macros—for example, macros that include variables, operators, and control structures and that display custom dialog boxes. You can write macros that use the facilities of several Office System applications, creating integrated Office solutions. And finally, you can create macros for Office applications that don't permit you to record macros (Microsoft Outlook, Microsoft Access, and Microsoft FrontPage).

In this chapter you'll learn the basic techniques for using the Visual Basic Editor to edit existing macros (for instance, macros that you have recorded). You'll also learn how to use the essential programming tools provided by the development environment.

Using the Visual Basic Development Environment to Edit a Macro

In the Microsoft Office System, you can edit your recorded macros and create new macros from scratch by using the Visual Basic development environment, a special utility that has its own windows, menus, and programming tools. Word, Excel, PowerPoint, Outlook, Access, and FrontPage all allow you to use this program to create or edit macros that you can run from within the application. In this section you'll learn how to use the Visual Basic development environment to edit a recorded Word macro named InsertAddress. (You won't be able to use the Visual Basic development environment to edit a recorded macro in Outlook, Access, or FrontPage, because these applications don't allow you to record macros.) Feel free to experiment a little in this section—the skills you learn will come in handy each time you work with macros.

 Note   The InsertAddress macro is contained in the Word document MacroDemo.doc provided on this book's companion CD.

If, however, you wish to record your own copy of the InsertAddress macro, follow the instructions given in "Recording and Running Macros," on page 224 in Chapter 9. If you do this, be sure to save the macro in a document named MacroDemo.doc, which is referenced in the instructions that follow. (Don't save it in a template.)

To edit the InsertAddress macro using Visual Basic, perform the following steps:

1   In Word, open the document MacroDemo.doc, which contains the InsertAddress macro.

2   Choose Tools, Macro, Macros. You'll see the Macros dialog box, which lists the Insert-Address macro in the Macro Name list.

Note   Depending on where you saved your recorded macro, you might need to change the selection in the Macros In drop-down list in order to see your macro listed in the Macro Name list. To show all available macros, select All Active Templates And Documents in the drop-down list.

In the example document, MacroDemo.doc, the InsertAddress macro is stored in the document itself, so you would need to select either the All Active Templates And Documents item or the MacroDemo.doc (Document) item.

3   Click the InsertAddress macro and then click the Edit button. The Visual Basic development environment will start, as shown in Figure 54-1.

Code window

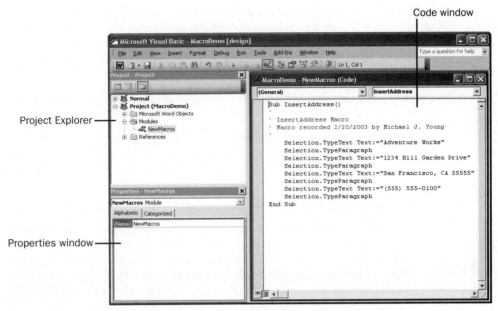

Project Explorer

Properties window

Figure 54-1. The Visual Basic development environment allows you to create new macros and modify existing ones.

The Visual Basic development environment includes a variety of programming tools to help you write, edit, test, and manage your Office application macros. The most important tools to identify now are the Project Explorer window, the Properties window, and the Code window. (We'll discuss each in this chapter.) You might see these tools in a slightly different arrangement on your screen if someone else has used your computer or if your setup options were different than ours.

The Code window is a large text-editing window that displays the contents of your Office macro in the VBA programming language. Each program statement in this macro follows a particular programming rule, and the trick to learning macro programming in Office is understanding the syntax principles and program logic behind each of the Visual Basic statements.

> **Note** Another name for the exact spelling, order, and spacing of keywords in a macro statement is *syntax*.

The macro is stored in a special program code container called a *subroutine*, which is part of the more comprehensive container called a *module*. This particular subroutine is called InsertAddress, and it is delimited (or enclosed as a block of macro text) by the Sub and End

Chapter 54

Sub statements, respectively. Within the body of the subroutine, you'll see descriptive comments, which appear in green type, and the Visual Basic program statements that do the work of the macro, which appear in black type. In this macro, the Sub and End Sub statements appear in blue type, because they're special reserved words in the Visual Basic programming language called *keywords*.

To add a descriptive comment to the macro and edit the business phone number, perform the following steps:

1 Press the Down arrow key until the insertion point is on the fourth line that begins with a single quotation mark (') character (the line immediately below the line that begins '*Macro recorded*). Then, press the right arrow key once to move the insertion point past the single quote that begins the line.

2 Press Spacebar once, type **My first macro**, and press Enter.

Visual Basic will insert your new comment and display it in green type. A comment line begins with a single quote character and is for documentation purposes only, not to be used by the macro when it runs. You should use comments as informal notes about how your macro works if you plan to share your macro with friends and work associates. (Comments are especially useful when you write complicated program statements.) Your Code window should look like this illustration:

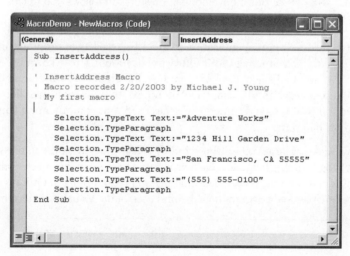

3 Now move the insertion point to the program statement containing the phone number you entered, and change the last four digits to **0150**. Your Code window should look like this:

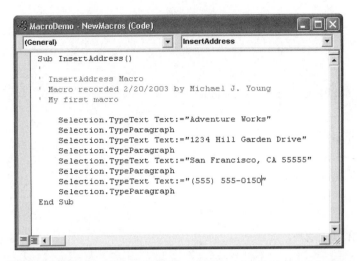

This simple edit changes the content of your macro each time you run it. Although we're not focusing on the exact details of the Visual Basic program statements right now, you might find it interesting to know what the words *Selection* and *TypeText* are doing in the program code. Selection is an *object*, or a component of the current document or application that can be programmatically controlled. The Selection object designates a particular location in your document for action—either the text block that is highlighted or the current position of the insertion point. TypeText is a *method*, or a command that can be executed using the specified object. When the TypeText method is used with the Selection object, Word inserts the specified text at the current insertion point—exactly what your InsertAddress macro does when you run it! Similarly, the *Selection.TypeParagraph* statement inserts a new paragraph at the current position of the insertion point.

4   While the Code window containing your edited macro is active, save your changes by choosing File, Save or by clicking the Save button on the Visual Basic Editor's Standard toolbar.

You're finished editing the InsertAddress macro for now. Leave the Visual Basic development environment open. In the next section you'll run the macro again.

Learning the Visual Basic Programming Tools

The Visual Basic development environment contains a number of useful programming tools to help you construct and manage your macros in Word, Excel, PowerPoint, Outlook, Access, and FrontPage. In this section you'll learn how to use the most important programming tools. As you work through the remaining chapters of this part of the book, you'll gain additional experience with the tools by constructing practical, working macros.

Chapter 54

> **Note** If you're not interested in all the details about programming tools right now, just skim this section and move on to the next chapter. You can use this information later as reference material.

The essential Visual Basic tools include:

- Menu bar
- Toolbars
- Project Explorer
- Properties window
- Online Help system

Using the Menu Bar

The menu bar in the Visual Basic development environment contains commands that are specifically designed to edit and manage your macros. Table 54-1 describes the functionality of the menus.

Table 54-1. Menus in the Visual Basic Development Environment

Menu Name	Purpose
File	Saves macros, imports and exports useful routines, removes macro modules, prints the contents of the active Code window, and closes the development environment (returning you to the Office application from which you ran it).
Edit	Edits and searches for text in the active Code window, formats code, and displays information about available properties, methods, and constants.
View	Displays the various tools in the development environment.
Insert	Extends your macro or project by adding new objects or features: a new code procedure, a custom dialog box (UserForm), a module, or a supporting file.
Format	Formats the objects and text in a custom UserForm dialog box.
Debug	Detects and fixes programming errors in your macros.
Run	Executes your macros. A special command, Break, is useful for debugging.

Table 54-1. Menus in the Visual Basic Development Environment

Menu Name	Purpose
Tools	Customizes the project containing your macro (each document or template has an associated *project* that stores macros): provides references to other libraries, controls, or Web services; allows you to change the project's properties or add a digital signature; and sets program options. The Macros command is identical to the Macros command on your Office application's Tools menu.
Add-Ins	Runs add-in commands and uses the Add-In Manager dialog box.
Window	Adjusts the size and orientation of the windows in the development environment and switches between open code windows.
Help	Displays online Help and connects to frequently used Visual Basic Web sites.

To run the InsertAddress macro using the Run Sub/UserForm command, perform the following steps:

1 If you followed the tutorial instructions in "Using the Visual Basic Development Environment to Edit a Macro," earlier in this chapter, you will have opened the Macro-Demo.doc Word document, run the Visual Basic development environment, edited the InsertAddress macro, and saved your changes.

2 In the Visual Basic Editor, choose Run, Run Sub/UserForm or press F5. Word will run your macro in the MacroDemo.doc document.

3 Because the InsertAddress macro has no visible user interface, you won't see it run in the Visual Basic development environment. You'll need to switch back to the Macro-Demo.doc Word document to see the results. To do this, click the View Microsoft Word button at the left end of the Standard toolbar in the Visual Basic Editor or use any standard Windows method to switch to the Word document.

4 Verify that the InsertAddress macro correctly displayed your address text.

5 Switch back to the Visual Basic development environment and leave this program running so that you can explore the features described in the following sections.

Using the Visual Basic Toolbars

The Visual Basic toolbars provide rapid access to the most common commands and procedures in the Visual Basic development environment. By default, only the Standard toolbar appears, but you can add special-purpose Visual Basic toolbars by choosing View, Toolbars. Figure 54-2 shows the purpose of the buttons and controls on the Standard Visual Basic toolbar.

Chapter 54

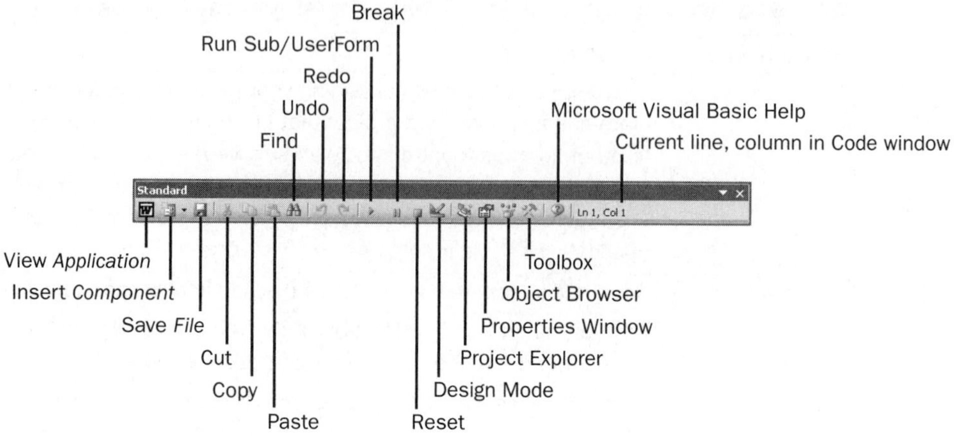

Break
Run Sub/UserForm
Redo
Undo
Find

Microsoft Visual Basic Help
Current line, column in Code window

View *Application*
Insert *Component*
Save *File*
Cut
Copy
Paste

Toolbox
Object Browser
Properties Window
Project Explorer
Design Mode
Reset

Figure 54-2. The Standard toolbar is a convenient way to issue commands in the Visual Basic development environment.

Using the Save Button to Save Your Changes

Save

After you modify a macro in the Visual Basic development environment, it makes good sense to save your changes to prevent accidental data loss because of a power failure or system crash. To save your macro, make sure that the Code window displaying the macro is active and then click the Save button on the Standard toolbar or choose File, Save.

Visual Basic saves a macro on disk by saving the file in which the macro is stored. For example, if you stored your macro in a Word document named MacroDemo.doc, Visual Basic will save that document. If, however, you stored your macro in the Normal template, Visual Basic will save the Normal.dot file.

> **Note** If the Project Explorer window is currently active (see Figure 54-1), the Save toolbar button and the File, Save menu command will save the file containing the module (or other component) that's currently selected in the Project Explorer.
>
> In any case, the ScreenTip on the Save button, as well as the label on the File, Save command, will indicate the name of the file that will be saved (for example, *Save MacroDemo* or *Save Normal*).

Using Project Explorer

Project
Explorer

The Visual Basic Project Explorer is an organizational tool that displays a hierarchical list of the documents and templates—or *projects* as they're known in Visual Basic—that are currently open in your Office application, along with their supporting components. Using Project Explorer, you can add or delete components from a project, compare elements and reorganize them, and display items of interest. If the Project Explorer window isn't visible, you can display it by choosing View, Project Explorer, or by clicking the Project Explorer toolbar button.

When you first start using Project Explorer, you might find its assortment of folders and components a bit confusing, but stick with it. Project Explorer is a useful programming tool, and its secrets can be readily comprehended. Each project name corresponds to a document or template that's currently open in your application. In the Project Explorer window shown in Figure 54-3, the projects for the Normal.dot template and the MacroDemo.doc document are shown, along with their supporting components. (If you've been following the examples to this point, these are the files you'll see.) You'll see additional projects in your Project Explorer window if you have other documents open.

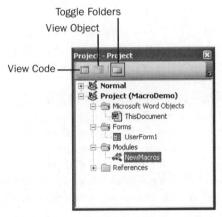

Figure 54-3. The Project Explorer window allows you to manage the components of Visual Basic projects.

When you use Visual Basic, you can customize several different components of an Office document or template. As we demonstrated earlier in the chapter, you can record a macro and store it in a document or template file. In Project Explorer, you'll see that Word stores the macro within a standard module named NewMacros. You can also add one or more of the following components to your project:

- Additional standard modules, which can contain macros and other useful program code
- Class modules, which define classes and the methods and properties used to control objects belonging to the classes
- Custom dialog boxes, called *forms* or *UserForms*
- References to commands and objects in other projects or Windows applications

Project Explorer keeps track of all these different components and provides access to them through two special buttons: View Code and View Object. To view or work with a particular component, expand the hierarchy, if necessary, and click the component name. If the component contains program code (such as a module or a UserForm), you can examine it by clicking the View Code button. If the component contains a user interface (such as a Word document or a UserForm), you can examine it by clicking the View Object button.

To use Project Explorer to examine the project for the example document, MacroDemo.doc, perform the following steps:

1   If you've been following the tutorial instructions in this chapter, the MacroDemo.doc document will be open in Word and you will have run the Visual Basic development environment.

2   If Project Explorer isn't visible in the Visual Basic development environment, click the Project Explorer button on the Standard toolbar.

3   If the Toggle Folders button at the top of Project Explorer isn't selected (highlighted), click the button to select it.

4   Click the plus sign (+) next to the project for the example document, Project (Macro-Demo), to view all the project's components if they are not already visible. You'll see a folder named Microsoft Word Objects, a folder named Modules, and a folder named References.

5   Click the plus sign (+) next to the Microsoft Word Objects folder if its contents aren't currently visible, and then select the object named ThisDocument. Each project you work with that is based on a Word document or template has a ThisDocument object. You can write general-purpose macros and store them within this object (rather than within a module). But more importantly, you can create special-purpose macros within this object that Word automatically runs when you open or close the document, or—for a template project—when you create a new document based on that template.

View
Object

6   To view the example document in Word, click the View Object button at the top of the Project Explorer window.

7   When you're finished viewing the example document, switch back to the Visual Basic development environment.

8   Open the Modules folder within the MacroDemo project (if its contents aren't currently visible), and click the NewMacros module.

View Code

9   Click the View Code button at the top of the Project Explorer window to display in a Code window the VBA source code for the InsertAddress macro that's contained in the NewMacros module.

Using the Properties Window

The Properties window lets you change the characteristics, or *property settings*, of a project or of a document, module, or UserForm contained in a project. For example, the Name property of the module in the Project (MacroDemo) project that contains the example InsertAddress macro is set to NewMacros. (Whenever you record a macro, Word automatically places it in the NewMacros module of the document or template where you store the macro.) If you'd like to change the name of this module to reflect its new contents, you can change it using the Properties window.

At the top of the Properties window, you'll find an object drop-down list, which you can use to switch between objects. If the Properties window is displaying the properties of a project, module, or document object, the object drop-down list will contain only a single item (the name of the project, module, or document object). If, however, the Properties window is displaying the properties of a UserForm, the drop-down list will include an item for each interface object (each control contained in the UserForm, plus the UserForm itself), and you can use the list to view or set the properties of the different objects.

The main part of the Properties window is a two-tabbed properties list with scroll bars, which contains property settings that you can modify while your macro is being built (a construction phase programmers call *design time*). In the Properties window you can view property settings alphabetically or by category. As you'll learn in the next chapter, you can also set properties while your macro is running (at *run time*) if you modify property settings appropriately using program code.

Take a moment now to change the Name property setting for the NewMacros module in the Project (MacroDemo) project. By changing this setting from NewMacros to InsertAddress, you can clearly identify the contents of your address macro later, and your NewMacros module won't become too unwieldy. (If you record additional macros, Word will store them in the NewMacros module, creating a module with this name if one doesn't already exist.)

> **Note** You can keep all your macros in the NewMacros module if you like, but we recommend that you save at least some of them in separate modules.

To change the Name property setting for the NewMacros module, perform the following steps:

Properties Window

1 In the Project Explorer, select the NewMacros module in the Project (MacroDemo) project.

2 If the Properties window isn't currently visible, click the Properties Window button on the Standard toolbar. Your Properties window should look similar to this example:

The Properties window lists only one property for the NewMacros module, the Name property. Later you'll work with objects that contain dozens of property settings.

3 Double-click the NewMacros name in the Properties window and press Delete to erase the current property setting.

4 Type **InsertAddress**, and then press Enter.

The setting of the Name property will change from NewMacros to InsertAddress, and the new name will appear in the Properties window and in the Modules folder in Project Explorer.

Tip   Getting help in the Visual Basic Editor

As in the other Office applications, you can access help in the Visual Basic Editor by using the Help task pane or the Ask A Question list (the Office Assistant isn't available). Note, however, that the Visual Basic Help component must be installed on your computer. In the Office Setup program, you'll find this component under the Visual Basic For Applications item within the Office Shared Features component group.

For information on using the Help task pane and the Ask A Question list, see Chapter 3, "Getting Expert Help on Office 2003." For information on running the Office Setup program, see Chapter 2, "Installing and Configuring Office 2003."

Exiting Visual Basic

When you're finished working on a Visual Basic macro, you have two options: you can switch back to your Office application and leave the Visual Basic development environment running, or you can exit Visual Basic and return to your application. Unless you plan to edit another macro soon, you don't need to leave Visual Basic running. If you want to use it again, you can easily restart it using the Macros dialog box or by choosing Tools, Macro, Visual Basic Editor in an Office application.

To exit from the Visual Basic development environment and return to the Office application from which you started Visual Basic, choose File, Close And Return To *Application* (where *Application* is the name of the Office application, such as Word). Or just click the Close button at the right end of the Visual Basic title bar.

Note   The keyboard shortcut for exiting Visual Basic and returning to your Office application is Alt+Q.

Using Variables, Operators, and Functions to Manage Information

Reading a Visual Basic Program
Statement 1439
Using Office Constants 1442
Declaring Variables 1447

Using Visual Basic Functions 1448
Using Object Variables
to Process Text 1454
Building Formulas 1456

What are the mysterious commands that make Microsoft Office 2003 Edition macros run? In this chapter, you'll learn about many of the Microsoft Visual Basic program statements that collectively constitute a macro. You'll learn how to use special values called constants to execute Office commands, and how to use storage containers called variables to store data temporarily in your macro. You'll also learn how to use Visual Basic functions to transfer information back and forth between Office documents, and how to use mathematical operators to perform tasks such as addition and multiplication. With this essential grounding in program syntax, you'll be ready to tackle more sophisticated Office management tasks.

Reading a Visual Basic Program Statement

As you learned in Chapter 54, "VBA Fundamentals," a line of code in a Visual Basic program is called a *program statement*. A program statement is any combination of Visual Basic keywords, objects, properties, methods, functions, operators, and symbols that collectively create a valid instruction recognized by the Office macro interpreter. A complete program statement can be a simple keyword such as *Beep*, which sounds a note from your computer's speaker, or it can be a combination of elements, such as the Word 2003 program statement shown in Figure 55-1, which uses the TypeText method of the Selection object to insert the text *Adventure Works* into the current document.

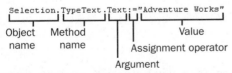

Figure 55-1. This figure shows an example of a typical Microsoft Word Visual Basic program statement.

The rules of construction that you must use when you build a program statement are called *statement syntax*. Visual Basic for Applications (VBA) shares many of its syntax rules with earlier versions of the Basic programming language and with other computer languages. The trick to writing good program statements is learning the syntax of the most useful language elements and then using those elements correctly, in conjunction with programming constructs called objects, properties, and methods, to manage Office's features.

What Is an Object?

Objects are the fundamental building blocks of Visual Basic; nearly everything you do in Visual Basic involves modifying objects. When you write Visual Basic macros for Office, your first task is to learn about the objects Office uses to represent its commands and features. For example, in Word the current, open document is stored in the Document object, and each document contains a Paragraph object corresponding to each paragraph.

A *collection* is an object that contains several other objects, usually of the same type. For example, the Documents object contains all the documents that are currently open in Word, and the Paragraphs object contains all the paragraphs in the current document or selection, as illustrated in Figure 55-2. By using properties and methods, you can modify a single object or an entire collection of objects.

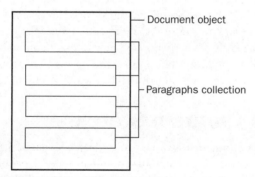

Figure 55-2. This illustration shows a Document object and its Paragraphs collection.

What Are Properties and Methods?

Properties and *methods* are special keywords you use to manipulate Visual Basic objects. Using a bicycle metaphor, properties are attributes like the color or style of a bicycle (mountain bike, touring, or tandem), and methods are the actions a bicycle can perform (pedaling, jumping, or coasting). Some more specific examples follow.

Properties Are Attributes

A *property* is an attribute of an object or an aspect of its behavior. For example, the properties of a document include its name, its contents, its save status, and which windows are currently open to view it. To change the characteristics of an object, you change the values of its properties.

Here's how it works. To set the value of a property, write a program statement that contains the following elements, in this order: a reference to one or more objects, each followed by a period; the property name; an equal sign; and the new property value. For example, this program statement uses the SplitSpecial property to open a separate pane in the active window to display all the footnotes in a document:

```
ActiveWindow.View.SplitSpecial = wdPaneFootnotes
```

In this case, both ActiveWindow and View are objects. (The View object is contained in the ActiveWindow object.) SplitSpecial is a property that can be assigned one of 18 values associated with split windows. In this example, the value we assigned to SplitSpecial is a constant named wdPaneFootnotes, a special value used to identify footnotes in Word's object library. (You'll learn more about properties and constants in the next section of the chapter.)

Methods Perform Actions

A *method* is an action that an object can perform. For example, you can use the Save method to save all the open documents in Word by writing the following program statement:

```
Documents.Save
```

In most cases, methods are actions and properties are characteristics. Using a method causes something to happen to an object, whereas using a property returns information about the object or causes a quality of the object to change.

Learning More About the Office Object Model

Each chapter in Part 10 explores a new aspect of the Office object model, so you'll be getting lots of practice using objects, properties, and methods to streamline your document management tasks. However, you can also learn about the object model for each Office application on your own by using the features discussed in the following sections.

Object Browser

Object
Browser

The Visual Basic Editor includes a tool called the Object Browser that lets you display the properties and methods associated with all the objects in your system, including those supported by Office applications. You can display the Object Browser window by clicking the Object Browser button on the Standard toolbar; by choosing View, Object Browser; or by pressing F2.

Microsoft Visual Basic Online Help

Office fully describes each object, property, and method in the online Visual Basic Help file for each application. You can access these Help topics by clicking the Help button on the Standard toolbar or by choosing Help, Microsoft Visual Basic Help to display the Microsoft Visual Basic Help task pane, and then entering the name of the object, property, or method in the Search text box and clicking the adjoining Start Searching button. Alternatively, you can select the name of the object, property, or method in the Code window or in the Object Browser and press F1 to immediately display a descriptive Help topic.

Code Window Auto List Feature

When you type the name of an Office application object followed by a period in a Code window, the Visual Basic Editor automatically lists all the properties and methods that you can use with the object. For example, if you type "ActiveDocument" and a period, a drop-down list of all the methods and properties associated with the ActiveDocument object appears, as shown here:

To insert one of the elements into your program code, simply double-click the desired method or property, and it will be appended to the statement.

In the following chapters, you'll learn more about using Office objects, properties, and methods in program statements. First, you'll learn how to assign values to properties by using Office constants.

Using Office Constants

A common characteristic of many Word macros is a program statement that changes the structure of a document or a command option in the word processor itself. For example, you might choose to change the line spacing in a particular paragraph to double spacing, or you might change Word's document view to Print Layout view. To make such a change in a Visual Basic macro, you need to use a *constant* in your program statement, a special value supplied by Office to adjust settings in each Office application.

True to its name, a constant is a named value that doesn't change while your macro runs. It replaces a number or word in your macro with a coded label that you can easily remember. You can create your own constants to store information, as you'll learn later in this chapter, but the most useful constants are special values called *intrinsic constants* that Office applications define in object libraries for your use.

For example, to change Word's document view to Print Layout, you could use the wdPrint-View constant, as shown in the following program statement:

```
ActiveWindow.View.Type = wdPrintView
```

This example contains the following elements:

- The ActiveWindow object, which represents the currently active document window in Word
- The View property, which returns an object representing the active view in the active window
- The Type property, which sets the document view type for the window (options include Normal, Web Layout, Print Layout, Outline, Print Preview, and Master)
- The wdPrintView Word constant, which sets the view to Print Layout view (other useful constants include wdNormalView, wdWebView, wdMasterView, wdPrintPreview and wdOutlineView)

 Inside Out

Prefixes identify the object library

The letters *wd* at the beginning of the wdPrintView constant identify it as an intrinsic constant in the Word object library. The Word object library is a special file that defines objects, properties, methods, and constants; it is automatically included in Word macros. Constants in the Word object library actually represent simple numbers; for example, wdPrintView contains the number 3. However, when you write Word macros, you'll find the constant names much easier to remember.

Other Office applications have their own constant prefixes and object libraries, including *xl* (Microsoft Office Excel object library), *ac* (Microsoft Office Access object library), and *vb* (VBA object library).

Using Constants to Create Custom Formatting

Take a moment now to try a simple example using Word constants. In this exercise, you'll create a macro, called CenterHeading, which uses Word constants to format selected text with shading, border formatting, and center alignment. You'll also learn how to type a new macro from scratch using the Visual Basic Editor, a technique you'll return to often in Part 10.

 Note A copy of the macro you'll create in this section, CenterHeading, is stored in the Chap55.doc document on the companion CD to this book.

To create the CenterHeading macro, follow these steps:

1 Start Word and open a new, blank document. (In this exercise, you'll store the Center-Heading macro within a document file, not in a template.)

2 Choose Tools, Macro, Macros. Word will display the Macros dialog box, where you create and run Visual Basic macros.

3 Type **CenterHeading** in the Macro Name text box, and then click the Macros In drop-down list and select your new, blank document in the list.

4 Click the Create button.

Word will start the Visual Basic Editor and create a new macro procedure named CenterHeading in the NewMacros module belonging to the document's project. It will display this procedure in a Code window. When you create a new macro from scratch, use the Code window to type the program statements that make up the macro. You enter your code between the Sub and End Sub statements, which mark the beginning and ending of the macro, respectively.

5 Begin your macro now by typing the object name **Selection** followed by a period.

When you type a period after an object name that the Visual Basic Editor recognizes, a drop-down list will appear containing a list of the properties and methods that are compatible with it, as shown here:

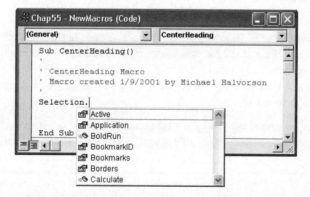

Each program statement in this macro begins with the Selection object, because you are formatting selected text in your Word document.

6 Scroll down the drop-down list and double-click the Shading property. Type a period to display a second drop-down list, as seen here:

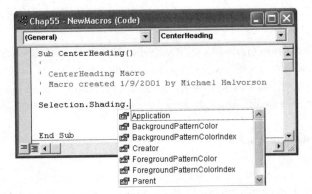

7 Double-click the Texture property in the drop-down list to build a program statement that adjusts the shading formatting of the selected text in your document. The Visual Basic Editor will now display the expression *Selection.Shading.Texture* in the Code window.

8 Finish your program statement by typing an equal sign (=), double-clicking on the wdTexture10Percent constant in the drop-down list, and pressing Enter.

Congratulations! You have now completed your first program statement, a command that adds 10 percent background shading to the selected text in your Word document.

9 Complete your macro by entering the following three program statements. You can either use the drop-down lists to pick properties and constants (as you did earlier), or you can type the program statements directly into the Code window.

```
Selection.Borders(wdBorderBottom).LineStyle = wdLineStyleSingle
Selection.Borders(wdBorderBottom).LineWidth = wdLineWidth150pt
Selection.ParagraphFormat.Alignment = wdAlignParagraphCenter
```

When you run the macro, the first two program statements, which use the Borders property, format the selected paragraph using a single underline border that is 1.5 points wide. Notice that two Word constants are used in each of the first two program statements, a constant that identifies which border is being formatted (wdBorderBottom), and a constant that selects the formatting options you have chosen (wdLineStyleSingle and wdLineWidth150pt). The final program statement uses the ParagraphFormat property to set the paragraph alignment of the selected paragraph to center alignment. The result is a window that looks like the following:

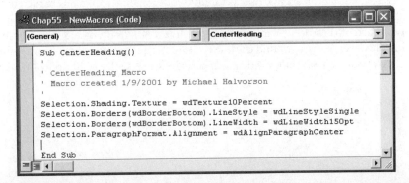

To run the CenterHeading macro in your Word document and create the custom formatting effect, follow these steps:

1 Click the Save button on the Visual Basic Editor's Standard toolbar to save the document (your new macro will be saved within the document).

2 Click the View Microsoft Word button at the left end of the Visual Basic Editor's Standard toolbar. Word will display the blank document containing the CenterHeading macro.

3 Type **Table of Contents**, and press Enter to create some text that you can use to test your macro.

4 Select the entire line or paragraph that you typed, and change the point size to 16 points. (Your macro will function perfectly at any point size, but a medium-sized font looks best for a heading.)

> **Note** The CenterHeading macro is designed for formatting paragraphs only, so you need to select everything you typed, including the end-of-paragraph mark. Alternatively, you can simply place the insertion point anywhere within the paragraph, without making a selection. If you select only a portion of the characters in the paragraph you'll get different results than those shown here.

5 Choose Tools, Macro, Macros.

6 Click the CenterHeading macro if it's not already selected, and then click Run.

Word will run your macro and format the Table of Contents heading by using shading, border, and center alignment commands, as shown here:

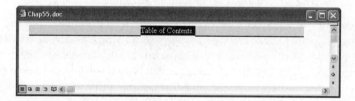

In the remaining chapters in Part 10 of this book, you might see line continuation characters at the end of some Visual Basic code lines. The line continuation character (_) is simply a device used to indicate line breaks for lines that are longer than 60 characters (for better readability). These breaks are acceptable to the Visual Basic interpreter. If you choose, you can type each of these long statements on one line if you don't include the continuation character. However, you might find the line continuation character useful if you want to see all your code at once. (The Code window can actually scroll to the right up to 1,024 characters.)

Troubleshooting

Breaking strings in VBA macro code causes problems

You're in the middle of a Visual Basic macro and you decide to break one long line of code into two lines using the line continuation character (_). Unfortunately, the line of code contained a literal string value (text between quotation marks), and your edit has produced a compilation error and stopped the macro from running.

You cannot use a line continuation character to break a string that is enclosed in quotation marks. If you try to do this, Visual Basic will halt the execution of your macro and you'll need to fix it before you can continue. To troubleshoot the problem, find a way to place the entire string on one line, even if it extends well into the right margin of the VBA Editor. Or, you can break the string into separate parts and then join those parts using the string concatenation operator (&), which is described in Table 55-1 and illustrated in the following example statement:

```
MsgBox "This is the first part of the message" _
& " -- and this is the second part."
```

Declaring Variables

In the previous section, you learned how to use unchanging values called constants to specify formatting options in your macros. In this section, you'll learn how to create temporary storage containers called *variables* to store information that is updated periodically as your macro runs. Variables are useful because they let you assign a short, easy-to-remember name to a piece of data you plan to work with. Variables can hold the following types of information:

- Numbers or words that you assign to your macro when you create it, such as an age or important date
- Special values that the user enters when the macro runs, such as a name or heading title
- Information from an Office document, such as words, paragraphs, cells, or slides
- The result of a specific calculation, such as the amount of sales tax that is due on a purchase

The process of declaring and using variables is covered in the following sections.

Making Reservations for Variables: The Dim Statement

Before you use a variable, you need to make a reservation, or *dimension*, for it in your macro. You accomplish this by placing the Dim keyword and the name of the variable at the beginning of your macro. Such an action reserves room in memory for the variable when the macro runs, and it lets Visual Basic know what type of data it should expect to see later. For example, the statement Dim FullName creates space for a variable in a macro named FullName.

By default, Office creates variables in a general-purpose format, or *type*, called Variant. The Variant type can adapt itself to a variety of data formats, including numbers, words, dates, and so on. Although you can specifically declare your variables to be of an exact type to save memory, you'll rarely need to do so in Office macros.

Putting Variables to Work

After you declare a variable, you are free to assign information to it in your code. For example, the following program statement assigns the string *Clare of Assisi* to the FullName variable:

```
FullName = "Clare of Assisi"
```

After this assignment, you can use the FullName variable in place of Clare of Assisi in your code. For example, the assignment statement

```
Selection.TypeText Text:=FullName
```

would insert *Clare of Assisi* into the current document using the TypeText method of the Selection object.

Using Visual Basic Functions

An excellent use for a variable is to hold information in your macro that has been entered by the user. One way to manage this input is to use special Visual Basic keywords called *functions* that perform useful work and then return important values to the macro. In the following sections, you'll learn how to use the InputBox and MsgBox functions to manage input and output in an Office document, and how to use arguments to pass information to a function.

Using a Variable to Store Input

The InputBox function is designed as a simple way to receive input from the user and store it temporarily in a variable. In the following example, you'll enhance the CenterHeading macro by adding a dialog box that prompts the user for the name of a new heading. You'll also learn how to make a *procedure call* in a macro.

 Note A copy of the macro you'll create in this section, InsertHead, is in the Chap55.doc document on the companion CD to this book.

To add a dialog box that prompts a user for a new heading name, perform the following steps:

1 In Word, open the document in which you stored the CenterHeading macro in the exercise given earlier in the chapter. Then, choose Tools, Macro, Macros. Word will display the Macros dialog box.

2 In the Macros In drop-down list in the Macros dialog box, select the document you opened in step 1.

Because the new macro you are creating uses the CenterHeading macro that you created earlier in the chapter, you should save the new macro in the same document that CenterHeading is stored in.

3 Type **InsertHead** in the Macro Name text box, and then click the Create button. Word will start the Visual Basic Editor and open a new macro procedure named InsertHead in a Code window.

4 Inside the procedure displayed in the Code window, type the following program statements to declare two variables and use the InputBox function:

```
Dim Prompt, Heading
Prompt = "Please enter your heading text."
Heading = InputBox$(Prompt)
Selection.Font.Size = 16
Selection.TypeText Text:=Heading
```

This time you're declaring two variables by using the Dim statement: Prompt and Heading. The second line in the procedure assigns a group of characters, or a *text string*, to the Prompt variable. The macro then uses this message as a text argument for the InputBox function. (An *argument* is a value or expression passed to a subprocedure or a function.)

The next line *calls*, or *runs*, the InputBox function and assigns the result of the call—the text string the user enters—to the Heading variable. InputBox is a special Visual Basic function that displays a dialog box on the screen and prompts the user for input. In addition to supporting a prompt string, the InputBox function supports other arguments that you might want to use occasionally. Consult the Visual Basic online Help for details.

After InputBox has returned a text string to the macro, the fourth statement in the procedure changes the font size to 16 points (suitable for a heading), and the fifth statement inserts the text into your document using the TypeText method.

Now you'll use the commands in the CenterHeading macro to add some formatting interest to your new heading. Rather than typing the CenterHeading statements again in your macro, you can accomplish the same effect by simply adding the name of the CenterHeading procedure at the end of your routine.

5 Below the second Selection statement, type **CenterHeading**, and press Enter.

Adding the name of another procedure to your macro is known as *calling a procedure*. When the Visual Basic interpreter encounters this particular statement, it will run the CenterHeading macro in the InsertHead macro. Figure 55-3 shows the completed macro.

```
Chap55 - NewMacros (Code)

(General)                          ▼   InsertHead                        ▼

Sub CenterHeading()
'
' CenterHeading Macro
' Macro created 1/9/2001 by Michael Halvorson
'
Selection.Shading.Texture = wdTexture10Percent
Selection.Borders(wdBorderBottom).LineStyle = wdLineStyleSingle
Selection.Borders(wdBorderBottom).LineWidth = wdLineWidth150pt
Selection.ParagraphFormat.Alignment = wdAlignParagraphCenter

End Sub
Sub InsertHead()
'
' InsertHead Macro
' Macro created 1/9/2001 by Michael Halvorson
'
Dim Prompt, Heading
Prompt = "Please enter your heading title."
Heading = InputBox$(Prompt)
Selection.Font.Size = 16
Selection.TypeText Text:=Heading
CenterHeading
|
End Sub
```

Figure 55-3.   The InsertHead macro calls the CenterHeading macro.

Inside Out

Making procedures accessible

If you want to call one procedure from another procedure, you must place the called procedure either in the same module as the calling procedure, or in another module that is either in the same project as the calling procedure or in the Normal project. Otherwise, Visual Basic won't be able to find the procedure you call.

Now run the InsertHead macro in your Word document to try out the InputBox function and your two variables. To do so, follow these steps:

1   Click the View Microsoft Word button on the Standard toolbar in the Visual Basic Editor. Word will display the document you opened in step 1 of the previous numbered instructions.

2   Move the insertion point to a blank line.

3   Choose Tools, Macro, Macros.

4   Click the InsertHead macro if it's not already selected, and then click the Run button. Word will run your macro and display an InputBox using the prompt string you specified, as shown here:

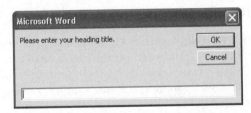

5 Type **Visual Basic is Fun!** and press Enter.

The InputBox function will return your heading to the macro and place it in the Heading variable. The program will then use the variable and the CenterHeading procedure to apply some custom formatting, as seen here:

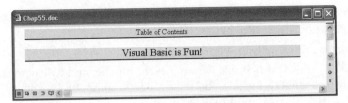

Anytime you want to prompt the user for information in your programs, you can use the InputBox function. It provides a nice complement to the more sophisticated dialog boxes called UserForms. In the next example, you'll see how to use a similar function to display text in a dialog box.

You can find more information about UserForms in Chapter 57, "Using Toolbox Controls to Create a User Interface."

6 Click the Save button on Word's Standard toolbar to save the document, together with the InsertHead macro that's contained in the document.

Inside Out

What are arguments?

As you learned using InputBox, Visual Basic functions often use one or more arguments to define their activities. For example, the InputBox function uses the Prompt variable as an argument to display dialog box instructions for the user. When a function uses one or more arguments, separate the arguments using commas and enclose the whole group of arguments in parentheses. The following example shows a function call that has two arguments:

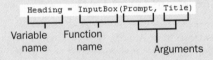

Using a Variable for Output

You can display the contents of a variable by passing the variable to a method (such as the TypeText method of the Selection object) or by passing the variable as an argument to a dialog box function. One useful dialog box function for displaying output is the MsgBox function. Like InputBox, MsgBox takes one or more arguments as input, and you can assign the results of the function call to a variable.

The syntax for the MsgBox function is as follows:

```
ButtonClicked = MsgBox(Prompt, ButtonStyle, Title)
```

The following items are important:

- *ButtonClicked* represents a variable that receives the result of the function. It indicates which button was clicked in the dialog box.
- *Prompt* is the text to be displayed on the screen.
- *ButtonStyle* is a constant that determines the number and style of the buttons in the dialog box. Options include VbOKOnly, VbOKCancel, VbAbortRetryIgnore, VbYesNoCancel, VbYesNo, and VbRetryCancel.
- *Title* is the text displayed in the title bar of the message box.

> **Note** In Visual Basic syntax listings, items in italics are placeholders for variables or other values in your program code. By convention, programmers use italics to highlight the parts of program syntax that you need to customize with your own instructions. (You'll also see this convention in the Visual Basic online Help.)

If you're just displaying a message using MsgBox, the *ButtonClicked* variable, the assignment operator (=), and the *ButtonStyle* and *Title* arguments are optional. (MsgBox has two more optional arguments.) Note that when you omit the *ButtonClicked* variable and the assignment operator, you must also omit the parentheses around the arguments (you'll see an example later in the chapter). For more information about MsgBox and its arguments, enter the word "MsgBox" in the Code window and then click the word and press F1.

In the following exercise, you'll use the MsgBox function to display the user name associated with your copy of Word. This name is stored in the Options dialog box's User Information tab, and you can modify it in Word by choosing Tools, Options. Word places the registered user name in comments and change marking, so it's a good idea to check this setting periodically using a macro.

Using MsgBox to Display the Registered User

> **Note** A copy of the macro you'll create in this section, DisplayUser, is located in the Chap55.doc document on the companion CD to this book.

Often you'll find it handy to display a status message about a document by using a macro. To create a macro that displays information about the registered user, perform the following steps:

1 In Word, open the document in which you want to store the macro. Then, choose Tools, Macro, Macros.

2 In the Macros In drop-down list in the Macros dialog box, select the document you opened in step 1.

3 Type **DisplayUser** in the Macro Name text box, and then click the Create button. Word will start the Visual Basic Editor and open a new macro procedure named DisplayUser in a Code window.

4 Inside the procedure displayed in the Code window, type the following program statements to declare one variable and use the MsgBox function:

```
Dim DialogTitle
DialogTitle = "The current user name is"
MsgBox Application.UserName, , DialogTitle
```

The first statement declares the variable DialogTitle to hold some descriptive text for the MsgBox function. The second statement assigns a text value to the variable. The third statement displays a message box on the screen, places the UserName property of the Application object inside the message box, and places the contents of the DialogTitle variable in the title bar. (When you don't use the ButtonClicked argument with MsgBox, you add an extra comma to indicated the missing argument. Also, when you don't assign the value returned by the function to a variable, you omit the parentheses around the argument list.)

> **Note** You can also use the UserName property to set the user name in Word. For example, to change the user name to Michael Halvorson, you would type **Application.UserName = "Michael Halvorson"**.

To run the DisplayUser macro in your Word document and try out the MsgBox function, follow these steps:

1 Click the View Microsoft Word button on the Standard toolbar in the Visual Basic Editor. Word will display the document you opened in step 1 of the previous numbered instructions.

2 In Word, choose Tools, Macro, Macros.

3 Click the DisplayUser macro, and then click the Run button. Word will run your macro, which will display the current user name for your copy of Word, as shown in this example:

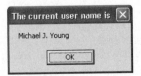

If the user name is incorrect, change it now by choosing Tools, Options and clicking on the User Information tab, or write a macro to do it!

4 Click the Save button on Word's Standard toolbar to save the document, together with the DisplayUser macro that's contained in the document.

Using Object Variables to Process Text

Another useful application for variables is holding portions of your document while your macro runs. For example, you might use a variable to hold a copy of a paragraph temporarily while you rearrange the paragraph's contents or move it to a new location. However, because documents and their contents are represented by objects in Visual Basic, you'll need to create a special container called an *object variable* when you want to reference an object in Office.

To declare an object variable in Visual Basic, use the following syntax:

```
Dim ObjectVar As Object
```

In the Dim statement, *ObjectVar* is the name of the variable you'll assign the object to later in your program code. For example, to create an object variable to hold text, you might use the following Dim statement:

```
Dim myText As Object
```

After you dimension an object variable, you can use it to reference an Office object by creating a Set statement, following this syntax:

```
Set ObjectVar = ObjectName
```

In the Set statement, *ObjectVar* is the name of your object variable, and *ObjectName* is an expression that returns an Office object. For example, to assign a Word Range object containing the text from the first paragraph in the active document to the myText object variable, you might use the following Set statement:

```
Set myText = ActiveDocument.Paragraphs(1).Range
```

After you assign an object to the object variable, you can use the variable just as you would use the object. Thus, object variables save you typing time because the object variable names are usually shorter than the full object names. You'll see this method used to work with Office objects regularly in Part 10 of this book.

Using an Object Variable to Copy Text

 Note A copy of the macro you'll create in this section, CopyParagraph, is located in the Chap55.doc document on the companion CD to this book.

One practical use for an object variable is to hold a range reference when you copy text from one location to another. To create a macro that copies the first paragraph of the active document to a new document, perform the following steps:

1. In Word, open the document in which you want to store the macro. Then, choose Tools, Macro, Macros.

2. In the Macros In drop-down list in the Macros dialog box, select the document you opened in step 1.

3. Type **CopyParagraph** in the Macro Name text box, and then click the Create button. Word will start the Visual Basic Editor and open a new macro procedure named Copy-Paragraph in a Code window.

4. Type the following program statements inside the procedure displayed in the Code window:

```
Dim myText As Object
Set myText = ActiveDocument.Paragraphs(1).Range
Documents.Add
Selection.InsertAfter myText
```

The first statement declares a variable, myText, of type Object to hold the reference to a Range object. The second statement then assigns a Range object representing the first paragraph in the active document to myText. The object expression contains a collection index (1), which specifies the first paragraph in the Paragraphs collection. (The second paragraph has an index of 2, the third paragraph has an index of 3, and so on.)

> **Note** The Range object contains only the text of the first paragraph, not the formatting. If you also want to copy the formatting of the paragraph, create a second object variable and use the Duplicate property of the Range object to copy the formatting.

Next, the Add method adds a new document to the Documents collection, and the InsertAfter method inserts the current value of the myText object variable into the new Word document.

To run the CopyParagraph macro in your Word document, follow these steps:

1. Click the View Microsoft Word button on the Visual Basic Editor toolbar. Word will display the document you opened in step 1 of the previous numbered instructions. If the document is currently empty, type or paste in several paragraphs of text. The Copy-Paragraph macro will copy the first paragraph to a new document.

2. In Word, choose Tools, Macro, Macros.

3. Select the CopyParagraph macro, and then click the Run button. Word will run your macro, which will create a new document containing the first paragraph from the originally opened document (the text only, not the formatting).

4. After you have verified the operation of your macro, close the new document and discard your changes. (You won't need to save the new document in this chapter.)

5 Open the Word document that contains your new macro, and then click the Save button on Word's Standard toolbar to save the document, together with the CopyParagraph macro that's contained in the document.

Building Formulas

A *formula* is a statement that combines variables, operators, and keywords—or some of these elements—to create a new value. Visual Basic contains several language elements designed for use in formulas. In this section, you'll practice working with mathematical operators, the symbols used to tie together the parts of a formula. With a few exceptions, the mathematical symbols you'll use are the ones you use in everyday life, and their operations are fairly intuitive.

Visual Basic provides the mathematical operators shown in Table 55-1.

Table 55-1. Visual Basic Mathematical Operators

Operator	Mathematical Operation	Example
+	Addition	Sum = 15.95 + 22.50
−	Subtraction	Balance = 100 − 75
*	Multiplication	Product = 88 * 2
/	Division	Ratio = 6 / 5
\	Integer (whole number) division	FullDinners = 8 \ 3
Mod	Remainder division	Scraps = 8 Mod 3
^	Exponentiation (raising to a power)	AreaOfSquare = 5 ^ 2
&	String concatenation (joining text strings together)	FullName = "Bob" & "James"

Computing Formulas in Your Documents

Periodically, you might have to total numbers in an Office document or perform some sort of numeric calculation. The following exercise demonstrates how you can compute the sales tax for a number that is selected in the active document.

Word includes a formula feature that lets you total numbers in a table and perform other simple calculations. However, it doesn't contain a command that lets you make numeric computations on the fly using a selected number. Complete the following steps to build a macro that computes the total cost of an item including sales tax.

 Note A copy of the macro you'll create here, SalesTax, is located in the Chap55.doc document on the companion CD to this book.

1 In Word, open the document in which you want to store the macro. Then, choose Tools, Macro, Macros.

2   In the Macros In drop-down list in the Macros dialog box, select the document you opened in step 1.

3   Type **SalesTax** in the Macro Name text box, and then click the Create button. Word will start the Visual Basic Editor and open a new macro procedure named SalesTax in a Code window.

4   Type the following program statements inside the procedure in the Code window:

```
Dim CostOfItem, TotalCost, TaxRate
TaxRate = 1.091
CostOfItem = Selection.Text
TotalCost = CostOfItem * TaxRate
MsgBox Format(TotalCost, "$#,##0.00"), , "Total Cost with Tax"
```

Inside Out

Copying macros to Word's Normal template

The five macros presented in this chapter are all contained in the NewMacros module in the Chap55.doc document on the companion CD to this book. If you'd like to copy one or more of these macros to your Normal.dot template (so that you can use them in Word without having the Chap55.doc document open), perform the following steps:

Open the Chap55.doc document in Word.

1   Choose Tools, Macro, Macros to open the Macros dialog box, and then click the Organizer button.

2   In the Macro Project Items tab in the Organizer dialog box, verify that the Chap55.doc document is open in the left list, and then select the NewMacros module in it.

3   Click the Rename button and change the name of the NewMacros module to Chap55. (You can't copy one NewMacros module over another.)

4   Verify that the Normal template is open in the right list, and then click the Copy button to copy the Chap55 module into the Normal template.

5   When you're finished, click the Close button.

The Dim statement declares three variables of the Variant type: CostOf Item, TotalCost, and TaxRate. Variant is a good choice in this case because the exact format of two numbers in your Word document is unknown: They could be large or small, integers or floating-point values, and so on. The third variable holds the current sales tax rate (in this example, 9.1 percent). You can change this number to reflect your local sales tax rate, if you wish.

The third statement in the macro uses the Text property of the Selection object to return the currently selected text to the CostOf Item variable. The fourth statement then uses a formula and the multiplication operator to compute the total cost of the item plus sales tax. Finally, the MsgBox function displays the total with the help of the Format function, so the total appears with the proper currency formatting.

> **Note** The Format function can display the results of a calculation in a variety of formats, including percent, integer, date, string, and other custom formats. For more information, search for "Format Function" in the Visual Basic online Help.

To run the SalesTax macro in your Word document, follow these steps:

1   Click the View Microsoft Word button on the Visual Basic Editor toolbar. Word will display the document you opened in step 1 of the previous numbered instructions.

2   The SalesTax macro requires that you select a number in your document, so clear some room and type the following test values (one per line) so that you can evaluate the macro:

```
      10
   $1,000.00
   five bucks
```

3   Select 10 as the first test number.

4   Run the SalesTax macro using the Macros dialog box. Word will immediately display a message box containing the total cost of a $10 item with 9.1 percent sales tax, as seen here:

5   Click the OK button to close the dialog box, and then select $1,000.00 and run the macro again. (You should verify that the macro can handle currency formatting.)

Fortunately, you are using Variant variables in your macro, which can handle the switch between different types of numbers, resulting in the following display:

6   Click the OK button, and then select the text *five bucks* and run the macro.

This time, Visual Basic generates a run-time error that stops the macro and displays a dialog box explaining the problem, as shown here:

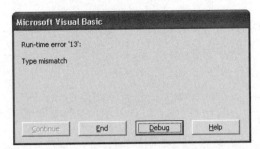

The words *type mismatch* mean that the value selected in the document (*five bucks*) cannot be multiplied by the value in the TaxRate constant (1.091). Unfortunately, this macro works only with numbers, not text.

7   Click the Debug button. In the Code window, Visual Basic will highlight the program statement that caused the run-time error.

Reset

8   Click the Reset button on the Visual Basic toolbar to stop the program.

9   Click the View Microsoft Word button on Visual Basic's Standard toolbar to return to Word, and then click the Save button on Word's Standard toolbar to save the document, together with the SalesTax macro.

Adding Logic and Computing Power with Control Structures

Writing Conditional Expressions 1461
Writing If...Then Decision Structures . 1462

Writing Select Case
Decision Structures 1466
Writing For...Next Loops 1469

Now it's time to make your macros sizzle with speed and power! In Chapter 55, "Using Variables, Operators, and Functions to Manage Information," you learned how to write Microsoft Office 2003 macros from scratch using several essential keywords in the Microsoft Visual Basic for Applications (VBA) programming language. In this chapter you'll learn how to add logic and efficiency to your macros by writing conditional expressions, decision structures, and loops that manage the information in your documents. These skills allow you to write macros that rapidly format text elements, change settings in Office applications, manipulate collections, automate tables, and quickly open common documents.

Writing Conditional Expressions

One of the most useful tools for processing information in a procedure is a conditional expression. A *conditional expression* is a part of a complete program statement that asks a true-or-false question about a property, a variable, or another piece of data in a macro. For example, the conditional expression

```
NumberOfWords < 100
```

evaluates to True if the NumberOfWords variable contains a value that is less than 100, and it evaluates to False if NumberOfWords contains a value that is greater than or equal to 100. Table 56-1 shows the comparison operators you can use in a conditional expression.

Table 56-1. The Heart of a Conditional Expression Is the Comparison Operator

Comparison Operator	Meaning
=	Equal to
< >	Not equal to
>	Greater than
<	Less than
> =	Greater than or equal to
< =	Less than or equal to

> **Note** Expressions that can be evaluated as true or false are also known as *Boolean expressions,* and the True or False result can be assigned to a Boolean variable or property.

Table 56-2 shows some conditional expressions and their results. You'll work with these expressions later in the chapter.

Table 56-2. **Sample Conditional Expressions and Their Results**

Conditional Expression	Result
10 < > 20	True (10 is not equal to 20)
Pages < 20	True if Pages is less than 20; otherwise, False
Application.UserName = "Kim Abercrombie"	True if the registered user name for your copy of Office is Kim Abercrombie; otherwise, False
Selection.Text = CityName	True if the selected text in your Word document matches the contents of the CityName variable; otherwise, False

Writing If...Then Decision Structures

Conditional expressions can control the order in which statements are executed when they're used in a special block of statements known as a *decision structure.* An If...Then decision structure lets you evaluate a condition in the program and control the flow of execution based on the result. In its simplest form, an If...Then decision structure is written on a single line, in the form "If *condition* Then *statement*," where the *condition* placeholder represents a conditional expression and *statement* represents a valid VBA macro statement. For example,

```
If Application.UserName = "Kim Abercrombie" Then MsgBox "Welcome, Kim!"
```

is an If...Then decision structure using the conditional expression Application. UserName = "Kim Abercrombie" to determine whether the macro should display the message "Welcome, Kim!" in a message box on the screen. If the UserName property of the Application object contains a name that matches "Kim Abercrombie," Office will display the message box; otherwise, it will skip the MsgBox statement and execute the next line in the macro. Conditional expressions always result in a True or False value, never in a maybe.

Testing Several Conditions in an If...Then Decision Structure

VBA also supports an If...Then decision structure that allows you to include several conditional expressions. This block of statements can be several lines long and contains the important keywords ElseIf, Else, and End If.

```
If condition1 Then
    statements executed if condition1 is True
```

```
ElseIf condition2 Then
    statements executed if condition2 is True
[Additional ElseIf clauses and statements can be placed here]
Else
    statements executed if none of the conditions is True
End If
```

In this structure, *condition1* is evaluated first. If this conditional expression is True, the block of statements below it is executed, one statement at a time. (You can include one or more program statements.) If the first condition is not True, the second conditional expression (*condition2*) is evaluated. If the second condition is True, the second block of statements is executed. (You can add additional ElseIf conditions and statements if you have more conditions to evaluate.) Finally, if none of the conditional expressions is True, the statements below the Else keyword are executed. The whole structure is closed at the bottom by the End If keywords.

In the next section you'll use an If...Then decision structure to convert a selected heading style in Microsoft Word 2003 to formatted text in the Normal style.

Using an If...Then Decision Structure to Convert Styles

Note A copy of the macro you'll create in this section, ConvertStyles, is located in the Chap56.doc document on the companion CD to this book.

Word's Normal template includes three default formatting styles for headings: Heading 1, Heading 2, and Heading 3. To write a macro that converts a Heading 1 paragraph to all caps, a Heading 2 paragraph to underline, and a Heading 3 paragraph to italic formatting, setting the paragraph's style to Normal, perform the following steps:

1 Start Word and open a new, blank document.

2 Choose Tools, Macro, Macros. Word will open the Macros dialog box, where you create and run Visual Basic macros.

3 Type **ConvertStyles** in the Macro Name text box, and then select your new, blank document in the Macros In drop-down list. (In these exercises, you want to store your macro in a document file rather than in a template.)

4 Click the Create button. Word will start the Visual Basic Editor and open a new macro procedure named ConvertStyles in a Code window.

5 Type the following program statements inside the procedure displayed in the Code window:

```
If Selection.Type = wdSelectionIP Then
    MsgBox "No text selected."
ElseIf Selection.FormattedText.Style = "Heading 1" Then
    Selection.FormattedText.Style = wdStyleNormal
    Selection.Font.AllCaps = True
ElseIf Selection.FormattedText.Style = "Heading 2" Then
    Selection.FormattedText.Style = wdStyleNormal
    Selection.Font.Underline = True
```

```
    ElseIf Selection.FormattedText.Style = "Heading 3" Then
        Selection.FormattedText.Style = wdStyleNormal
        Selection.Font.Italic = True
    End If
```

6 Click the Save button on the Visual Basic Editor's Standard toolbar and then specify a filename for your document.

This macro consists entirely of an If…Then decision structure that contains one If statement and three ElseIf clauses. The first If statement uses the Selection object's Type property to see whether text is selected in the document that can be evaluated by the macro. If there is a text selection, the structure determines which heading style is active, converts the head back to the Normal style, and applies some simple text formatting to preserve the meaning of the heads. (Heading 1 becomes all caps, Heading 2 is underlined, and Heading 3 is formatted as italic.)

By changing the style and formatting constants used in this example, you could easily modify the Word macro to convert other styles or formatting options. Your Code window should look like Figure 56-1.

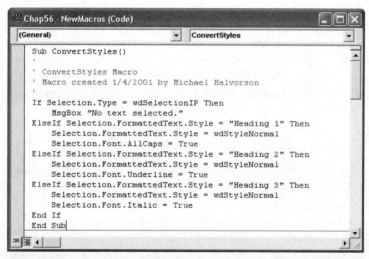

Figure 56-1. The ConvertStyles macro is shown in the Visual Basic development environment.

Running the ConvertStyles Macro

To run the ConvertStyles macro to convert Word styles, follow these steps:

1 Click the View Microsoft Word button at the left end of the Visual Basic Editor toolbar.

2 At the top of the document, type **First Head**, **Second Head**, and **Third Head** on three lines. Place the heads on separate lines so you can test each level of formatting.

3 Select the first head, and apply the Heading 1 style by using the Style drop-down list on Word's Formatting toolbar.

4 Format the second head using the Heading 2 style and the third head using the Heading 3 style.

5 Now select First Head in your document and run the ConvertStyles macro.

Be sure to select all the text in the head and to select one head only and not multiple lines. When you run the macro, Word will convert the selected head to all caps.

> At this point, we assume you know how to start a macro. To review the four techniques you can use to run a macro in Office 2003, see "Running a Macro," on page 227.

6 Select Second Head and run the macro. Word will convert the second style to under-lined type.

7 Select Third Head and run the macro. Word will convert the third style to italic type.

Figure 56-2 shows the three heads before and after the macro conversion.

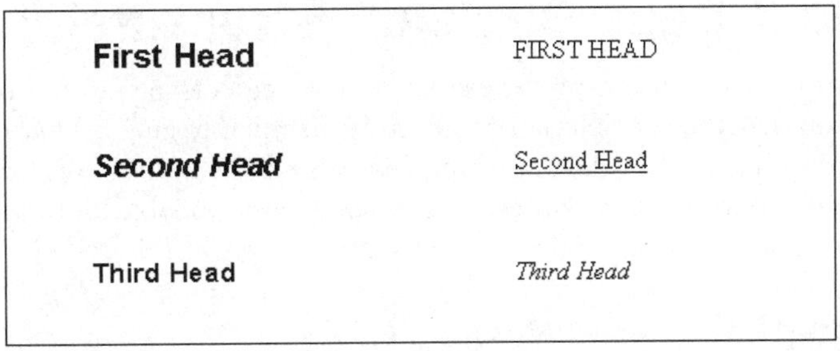

First Head	FIRST HEAD
Second Head	<u>Second Head</u>
Third Head	*Third Head*

Figure 56-2. The ConvertStyles macro converts Word headings from their default formatting to more compact formatting.

8 Click the Save button on Word's Standard toolbar to save the changes to your document.

Inside Out

Using Logical Operators in Conditional Expressions

Visual Basic lets you test more than one conditional expression in your If...Then and ElseIf clauses if you want to include more than one selection criterion in your decision structure. The extra conditions are linked together by using one or more of the logical operators shown in Table 56-3.

For example, the following decision structure uses the And logical operator to test an Office object:

```
If Application.UserName = "Michael Halvorson" _
        And Price < 300 Then
    MsgBox "Buy the product."
End If
```

You'll see an example of this operator later in the chapter.

Table 56-3. Useful Logical Operators in VBA

Logical Operator	Meaning
And	If and only if both conditional expressions are True, then the result is True.
Or	If either conditional expression is True or if both are True, then the result is True.
Not	If the conditional expression is False, then the result is True. If the conditional expression is True, then the result is False.
Xor	If one and only one of the conditional expressions is True, then the result is True. If both are True or both are False, then the result is False.

Writing Select Case Decision Structures

Visual Basic also lets you control the execution of statements in your macros by using Select Case decision structures. A Select Case structure is similar to an If…Then…ElseIf structure, but it's more efficient when the branching depends on one key variable, or *test case*. In addition, Select Case structures make your macro code more readable for others and easier to update later. The syntax for a Select Case structure looks like this:

```
Select Case variable
Case value1
    program statements executed if value1 matches variable
Case value2
    program statements executed if value2 matches variable
Case value3
    program statements executed if value3 matches variable
.
.
.
End Select
```

A Select Case structure begins with the Select Case keywords and ends with the End Select keywords. You replace the *variable* placeholder with the variable, property, or other expression that is to be the key value, or test case, for the structure. You replace *value1*, *value2*, and *value3* with numbers, strings, or other values related to the test case being considered. If one of the values matches the variable, the statements below its Case clause are executed, and then Visual Basic continues executing program code after the End Select statement. (If more than one value matches the variable, Visual Basic will execute the statements following the first matching value.)

You can include any number of Case clauses in a Select Case structure, and you can include more than one value in a Case clause. If you list multiple values after a case, separate them with commas. A Select Case structure also supports a Case Else clause that you can use to control how Visual Basic handles cases not captured by the preceding cases.

The following example shows how you can use a Select Case structure in an Office macro to display an appropriate message about a person's age. If the Age variable matches one of the Case values, an appropriate message is displayed by using a message box. If not, the Else clause is executed.

```
Select Case Age
Case 16
    MsgBox "You can drive now!"
Case 18
    MsgBox "You can vote now!"
Case 21
    MsgBox "You can drink wine with your meals."
Case 65
    MsgBox "Time to retire and have fun!"
Case Else
    MsgBox "You're a great age! Enjoy it!"
End Select
```

A Select Case decision structure is usually much clearer than an If…Then structure and is more efficient when you're making three or more branching decisions based on one variable or property. However, when you're making two or fewer comparisons or when you're working with several different values, you'll probably want to use an If…Then decision structure.

Using Select Case to Determine a Document's Paper Size

The following exercise demonstrates how you can use a Select Case structure to display the current Word document's paper type. You can accomplish this task by using a macro to compare the PageSetup object's PaperSize property to three different Office constants associated with paper.

Note A copy of the macro you'll create in this section, PaperSize, is located in the Chap56.doc document on the companion CD to this book.

To write this macro, complete the following steps:

1 In Word, open the document in which you want to store the macro.

2 Choose Tools, Macro, Macros.

3 In the Macros In drop-down list, select the document you opened in step 1.

4 Type **PageSize** in the Macro Name text box and then click the Create button. Word will start the Visual Basic Editor and open a new macro procedure named PageSize in a Code window.

5 Type the following program statements inside the procedure displayed in the Code window:

```
Dim PaperType
PaperType = ActiveDocument.PageSetup.PaperSize
Select Case PaperType
Case wdPaperLetter
    MsgBox "Document type is Letter (8 1/2 x 11)."
Case wdPaperLegal
    MsgBox "Document type is Legal (8 1/2 x 14)."
Case wdPaperEnvelope10
    MsgBox "Document type is Envelope 10 (4 1/8 x 9 1/2)."
Case Else
    MsgBox "Type unknown. Check File/Page Setup/Paper Size."
End Select
```

6 Click the Save button on the Visual Basic Editor's Standard toolbar to save the macro, together with the document that contains the macro.

The PageSize macro requires no user input. It simply stores the current paper size in a Variant variable named PaperType and then uses a Select Case structure to determine which type of paper is in use. The results are then displayed in a message box for the user.

The default paper size in Word is Letter (8½-inch × 11-inch), but you can adjust this setting by choosing File, Page Setup and clicking the Paper tab. If you're ever uncertain about the page size, just run this macro.

Running the Macro

To run the PageSize macro and determine your document's paper size, perform the following steps:

1 Click the View Microsoft Word button on the Visual Basic Editor's Standard toolbar. Word will display the document you opened in step 1 of the previous numbered instructions.

2 Run the PageSize macro. Word will display a message box that describes the current document's paper type, as shown here:

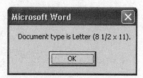

3 Experiment with the macro if you like by changing the paper type by choosing File, Page Setup and clicking the Paper tab.

Troubleshooting

Your Macro Doesn't Account for Each Possibility in a Select Case Statement

You've written a useful macro that quickly reports the type of paper your document requires for a printout. But your paper size is set to a value that you didn't plan for in your macro.

Select Case statements can supply dozens of Case arguments that test constants such as the ones you used in this paper-testing macro. You can add additional constants to this macro by searching for "PaperSize property" in the Visual Basic online Help and adding statements. However, all "open-ended" Select Case statements should end with an Else clause that handles possibilities your code doesn't specifically test for. In this macro, for example, we displayed the message "Type unknown. Check File/Page Setup/Paper Size." Use Else as a troubleshooting solution whenever there are document attributes, however unlikely, that you're not testing for.

Writing For...Next Loops

A For...Next loop lets you execute a specific group of program statements a set number of times in a macro. This control structure can be useful if you're performing several related calculations, working with collections of Office objects, or processing several pieces of user input. A For...Next loop is really just a shorthand way of writing out a long list of program statements. Because each group of statements in the list would perform essentially the same work, Visual Basic lets you define one group of statements and request that it be executed as many times as you want. The syntax for a For...Next loop looks like this:

```
For variable = start To end
    statements to be repeated
Next variable
```

In this syntax statement, For, To, and Next are required keywords, and the equals to (=) is a required operator. You replace the *variable* placeholder with the name of a numeric variable that keeps track of the current loop count, and you replace *start* and *end* with numeric values representing the starting and stopping points for the loop. The line or lines between the For and Next statements are the commands that are repeated each time the loop is executed.

For example, the following For...Next loop uses the TypeParagraph method to insert four carriage returns in a Word document:

```
For i = 1 To 4
    Selection.TypeParagraph
Next i
```

This loop is the functional equivalent of writing the Selection.TypeParagraph statement four times in a procedure. It looks the same to the Visual Basic interpreter as this:

```
Selection.TypeParagraph
Selection.TypeParagraph
Selection.TypeParagraph
Selection.TypeParagraph
```

The variable used in the loop is *i*, a single letter that, by convention, stands for the first integer counter in a For...Next loop. Each time the loop is executed, the counter variable is incremented by one. (The first time through the loop, the variable contains a value of 1, the value of *start*; the last time through, it contains a value of 4, the value of *end*.) As you'll see in the following sections, you can use this counter variable to great advantage in your loops.

Using a Loop to Manage Tables

For...Next loops work best when you're processing information that conforms to a particular pattern. For example, For...Next loops are handy when you want to add, remove, or modify information in tables. Each Word document and Microsoft PowerPoint 2003 presentation contains a Tables collection that holds each of the tables in a particular document. By using a combination of table methods and properties, you can create tables, insert information, remove information, format the entries, and so forth.

Creating a Macro That Automatically Builds Tables

The macro introduced here inserts a new table in the active Word document at the insertion point. The macro first prompts you for the number of rows and columns in the table and then creates the table if it's at least 2 × 2 in size. The macro uses a For...Next loop to add entries to each of the cells in the first column and then uses the AutoFormat command to format the entire table.

Note A copy of the macro you'll create in this section, AutoTable, is located in the Chap56.doc document on the companion CD to this book.

To build the macro, follow these steps:

1. In Word, open the document in which you want to store the macro.
2. Choose Tools, Macro, Macros.
3. In the Macros In drop-down list, select the document you opened in step 1.
4. Type **AutoTable** in the Macro Name text box and then click the Create button. Word will start the Visual Basic Editor and open a new macro procedure named AutoTable in a Code window.
5. Type the following program statements inside the procedure displayed in the Code window:

```
Dim iRows As Integer, iColumns As Integer
Dim myTable

iRows = InputBox("Number of Rows?")
iColumns = InputBox("Number of Columns?")

If iRows > 1 And iColumns > 1 Then '2x2 table required
    Set myTable = ActiveDocument.Tables.Add(Selection.Range, _
        iRows, iColumns)
    For i = 2 To iRows
        myTable.Cell(i, 1).Range.InsertAfter "Item " & i - 1
    Next i
    myTable.AutoFormat Format:=wdTableFormatColorful2
Else
    MsgBox "Sorry, minimum table size 2 rows and 2 columns."
End If
```

6 Click the Save button on the Visual Basic Editor's Standard toolbar to save the macro, together with the document that contains the macro.

This macro declares three important variables: iRows, an integer that contains the number of rows in the table; iColumns, an integer that contains the number of columns; and myTable, an object variable that represents the new table in the document. The main part of the macro is contained in an If…Then decision structure that uses the And logical operator to verify that the user has specified a large enough table. This bounds checking prevents the macro from crashing if the user enters a number that's too small to define a usable table.

Inside the If…Then decision structure, the For…Next loop uses a starting value of 2 so that text entry begins in the second row. (The first row is reserved for table headings.) The loop then uses the InsertAfter method to add text following the pattern Item 1, Item 2, Item 3, and so forth, until no more rows exist in the table.

Running the AutoTable Macro

To run the AutoTable macro you just created, follow these steps:

1 Click the View Microsoft Word button on the Visual Basic Editor's Standard toolbar. Word will display the document you opened in step 1 of the previous numbered instructions.

2 Move the insertion point to a place where you'd like to create a table and then run the AutoTable macro. Word will display an input box prompting you for the number of rows in your table, as seen here:

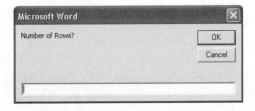

3 Type 5 and click the OK button. Word will display a second input box prompting you for the number of columns, as shown here:

4 Type 4 and click the OK button. Word will create a 5-row by 4-column table in the current document, fill the first column with text entries, and apply automatic formatting (as shown in Figure 56-3).

Item 1			
Item 2			
Item 3			
Item 4			

Figure 56-3. The AutoTable macro instantly creates a preformatted table in your document.

5 If you plan to use this macro often, return to the Visual Basic Editor and customize the macro code to insert appropriate table headings and column text using the InsertAfter method and specify your own preferences for table formatting using the AutoFormat method.

Using For...Each Loops

For...Next loops are useful if you know exactly how many times a particular group of statements should run, but what if you simply want to process each object in a collection? Fortunately, the designers of VBA included a special loop called For...Each that is specifically designed to march through each item in a collection. You'll find this especially useful when you're working with the Documents, Tables, Fields, Footnotes, Paragraphs, and Words collections.

The For...Each loop has the following syntax:

```
For Each element In collection
    statements to be repeated
Next element
```

The following items are important:

- The *element* placeholder represents a variable name that you enter of type Variant. When the loop runs, *element* stands for each item in the collection one by one.

- The *collection* placeholder represents the name of a valid collection in Office, such as Documents or Paragraphs.

Processing a Collection Using For...Each

The macro introduced here uses a For...Each loop to check each open Word document in the Documents collection for a file named MyLetter.doc. If the file is found in the collection, the macro makes it the active document in Word. If the file is not found, the macro loads the file from the root folder (C:\) on your hard disk.

> **Note** This macro runs correctly only if you put a file named MyLetter.doc in the root folder on drive C (C:\). Because such a file doesn't exist in that location by default, you'll need to create a simple one there to get this example to work, or you'll need to specify a new path location in the macro.

>   **Note** A copy of the macro you'll create in this section, ShowLetter, is located in the Chap56.doc document on the companion CD to this book. A sample MyLetter.doc file that you must place in C:\ to test the macro is also included on the CD.

To create the ShowLetter macro, perform the following steps:

1 In Word, open the document in which you want to store the macro.

2 Choose Tools, Macro, Macros.

3 In the Macros In drop-down list, select the document you opened in step 1.

4 Type **ShowLetter** in the Macro Name text box and then click the Create button. Word will start the Visual Basic Editor and open a new macro procedure named ShowLetter in a Code window.

5 Type the following program statements inside the procedure displayed in the Code window:

```
Dim aDoc, docFound, docLocation
docFound = False
docLocation = "c:\myletter.doc"

For Each aDoc In Documents
    If InStr(1, aDoc.Name, "myletter.doc", 1) Then
        aDoc.Activate
        docFound = True
        Exit For
    End If
Next aDoc

If docFound = False Then Documents.Open FileName:=docLocation
```

6 Click the Save button on the Visual Basic Editor's Standard toolbar to save the macro, together with the document that contains the macro.

The macro begins by declaring three variables, all of type Variant. The aDoc variable represents the current collection element in the For…Each loop, docFound is initialized to a Boolean value of False and is assigned a Boolean value of True only if the document is found in the Documents collection, and docLocation contains the file path of the MyLetter.doc file on disk.

The For…Each loop cycles through each document in the Documents collection, searching for the MyLetter.doc file. If the InStr function (which detects one text string within another) detects the file, the file is made the active document. If the file isn't found, the macro opens it by using the Documents object's Open method.

The InStr function's first argument (1) is an optional numeric start argument that sets the starting position for a search. The next two arguments, which are required, specify the text string being searched and the text string that you're looking for within the first string, respectively. The last argument, which is also optional, establishes the type of comparison. In this case, 1 represents a text comparison, which is the type of string you're looking for. If you want to see more information about the InStr function's arguments, search for InStr in Visual Basic's online Help.

Also note the Exit For statement, which we use to exit the For…Next loop when the MyLetter.doc file has been found and activated. Introduced here for the first time, Exit For is a special program statement that you can use to exit a For…Next loop when continuing causes unwanted results or unnecessary processing. Periodically, you'll want to use Exit For in your own macros.

Running the ShowLetter Macro

To run the ShowLetter macro, perform the following steps:

1. Click the View Microsoft Word button on the Visual Basic Editor's Standard toolbar. Word will display the document you opened in step 1 of the previous numbered instructions.

2. Click the New button twice to open two more Word documents. You should add a few documents to the Documents collection to test the macro properly.

3. In Word, activate the document in which you saved the ShowLetter macro (the document you opened in step 1 of the previous numbered instructions).

4. Run the ShowLetter macro to load the MyLetter.doc file.

    Word will open MyLetter.doc from the root folder when the macro doesn't locate the file in the Documents collection. Figure 56-4 shows our MyLetter.doc file, a short essay about the Italian Renaissance.

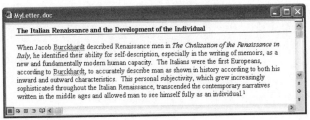

Figure 56-4. The ShowLetter macro opens the MyLetter.doc file if it's not in the current Documents collection.

5 Once again, activate the document in which you saved the ShowLetter macro and then run the ShowLetter macro. This time Word will find the MyLetter.doc document in the Documents collection and will display it using the Activate method.

6 Close the MyLetter.doc document and the two empty Word documents and then click the Save toolbar button to save any changes you've made to the document containing the ShowLetter macro.

Chapter 56

Using Toolbox Controls to Create a User Interface

Getting Started with UserForms 1477

Using the TextBox Control to Process
Paragraphs. 1487

Can macros have their own sharp-looking user interfaces? Something more than the Microsoft Office 2003 dialog boxes you've been using so far in Part 10? The answer is yes! In this chapter, you'll learn how custom macro interfaces, or *UserForms*, are designed and how they run in the Microsoft Visual Basic development environment. You'll also learn how to build UserForms, create programmable objects on them, configure UserForms using property settings, and customize UserForms using event procedures. The toolbox controls you'll use to accomplish this work include Label, CommandButton, Image, and TextBox. When you're finished, you'll have all the tools you need to build the ultimate user interface for any Office macro.

Getting Started with UserForms

The best way to get started with UserForms is to create a simple macro that displays a custom dialog box and uses it to display information. In this section, you'll create a music trivia macro that asks the user a simple question about a popular rock and roll instrument. Along the way, you'll learn the three fundamental steps for creating a Visual Basic UserForm: designing the user interface, setting properties, and writing event procedures.

Designing the User Interface

A UserForm is simply a custom dialog box that you create in the Visual Basic Editor by using programmable interface objects called *toolbox controls*. To open a UserForm in the Visual Basic Editor, first, in the Project Explorer, select the project in which you want to use the form. Then, choose Insert, UserForm. Each UserForm will appear in a separate UserForm window in the Visual Basic Editor. Also, the Project Explorer will list each UserForm in the Forms folder of the project to which you added the form. The first UserForm you add to a particular project will be named UserForm1, and subsequent UserForms will be named UserForm2, UserForm3, and so on.

Whenever a UserForm window is active in the Visual Basic Editor, a palette of toolbox controls also appears in a window, which allows you to add programmable interface objects to your UserForm (as shown in Figure 57-1). If you have used a drawing program such as

Microsoft Paint, you have many of the skills you need to use toolbox controls. To build the interface objects, click a control in the toolbox, and then draw the interface object by dragging with the mouse. This task is usually a simple matter of clicking to position one corner of the object and then dragging to create a rectangle that's exactly the size that you want. After you create the object—a text label, for example—you can resize it using the selection handles or you can relocate it by dragging. You can also resize the UserForm itself to create a dialog box with the exact size you want.

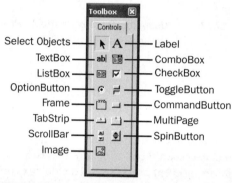

Figure 57-1. You create interface objects on your form using toolbox controls.

Building a Custom Dialog Box

Note A copy of the macro you'll create in this section, MusicTrivia, is located in the Chap57.doc document on the companion CD to this book. The Guitar.bmp file (a supporting bitmapped graphic) is also included on the CD.

To create a UserForm that uses the Label, Image, and CommandButton controls, perform the following steps:

1 Start Microsoft Word and open a new, blank document.

2 Choose Tools, Macro, Macros. Word will display the Macros dialog box, where you create and run Visual Basic macros.

3 Type MusicTrivia in the Macro Name text box, and then select your new, blank document in the Macros In drop-down list.

4 Click the Create button. Word will start the Visual Basic Editor and open a new macro procedure named MusicTrivia in a Code window.

5 Inside the procedure displayed in the Code window, type the following program statements to load and open the UserForm:

```
Load UserForm1
UserForm1.Show
```

Every macro that opens a UserForm needs these two program statements to bring the UserForm into memory and display it. In this simple macro, you'll type only two lines in the macro. You'll type the remaining program statements into event procedures associated with the objects on the UserForm. (Event procedures are discussed in greater detail in "Writing Event Procedures," on page 1484.)

6 Choose Insert, UserForm.

The Visual Basic Editor will open a new UserForm in a window and display the toolbox controls. The UserForm will be named UserForm1, as seen here:

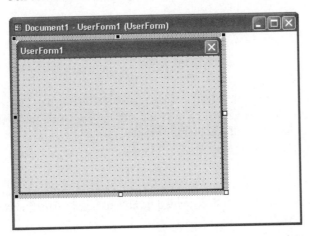

Note Make sure that the Code window displaying your macro is active when you choose Insert, UserForm, so that the UserForm is added to the project containing the macro you're writing. Alternatively, you could select the project or any of its components in the Project Explorer before you choose Insert, UserForm.

7 Click the Label button in the toolbox and then place the mouse pointer over the User-Form.

The mouse pointer will change to crosshairs when it rests on the form. The crosshairs are designed to help you draw the rectangular shape of a label. When you hold down the left mouse button and drag, the label object will take shape and snap to the grid formed by the intersection of the dots on the form.

Tip To learn the name of a control in the toolbox, hold the mouse pointer over the control until its ScreenTip appears.

8 Move the mouse pointer to a point near the upper left corner of the UserForm, hold down the left mouse button, and then drag down and to the right. Stop dragging and release the mouse button when your label object looks like the one shown here:

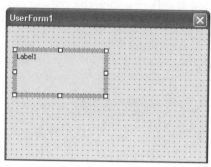

The purpose of a label object is to display formatted text on a UserForm. The first label object on a form is named Label1, and subsequent labels are named Label2, Label3, and so forth. You'll add text to the label object later.

9 Click the Label button in the toolbox again, and then create a second, smaller label object below the first one.

Each label object on a UserForm maintains its own set of properties and methods. By creating two separate label objects, you'll be able to manipulate them individually using program code.

10 Click the Image button in the toolbox. Then create a large, square image object on the right side of the form, as shown here:

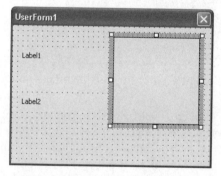

The purpose of an image object is to display clip art, photographs, bitmaps, and other electronic artwork on a UserForm. Specifically, an image object can display .ico, .wmf, .bmp, .cur, .jpg, and .gif files. You'll use this image object to display a photograph of the musical instrument that demonstrates the answer to the music trivia question.

11 Click the CommandButton button in the toolbox. Then create a command button object at the bottom of your UserForm on the left side.

The purpose of a command button object is to create dialog box buttons on a User-Form. Typical command buttons include OK and Cancel, but you can also create your own button types.

12 Click the CommandButton button in the toolbox again, and then create a second command button object at the bottom of your UserForm on the right side.

You're finished creating objects on your UserForm. If the final dialog box doesn't look like the one shown in Figure 57-2, use the mouse to fine-tune the size and location of your objects.

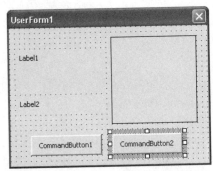

Figure 57-2. This UserForm includes five objects.

13 Click the Save button on the Visual Basic Editor's Standard toolbar, and then specify a filename for your new document.

Setting Properties

After you create objects on your UserForm using toolbox controls, your next step is customizing the objects using property settings. As you learned in Chapter 54, "VBA Fundamentals," a property setting is a quality or characteristic of an object that can change as your macro runs. You can change the property settings for objects on a UserForm by using the Properties window at design time (when your macro is being built), or by using program code at run time (while your macro is executing).

To set properties for the MusicTrivia macro's UserForm, follow these steps:

1 If the Properties window isn't currently visible, show it by clicking the Properties Window button on the Standard toolbar; choosing View, Properties Window; or pressing F4.

2 Click the first label object on the UserForm.

Chapter 57

Before you can set a property for an object, you must select the object on the User-Form. When you select the first label object, its name (Label1) appears at the top of the Properties window in the Object drop-down list, as seen here:

3 In the Properties window, double-click the text (Label1) to the right of the Caption property to select it, and press Delete.

The default text setting for the Caption property is deleted.

4 Now enter a new caption. In the box for the Caption property, type **What rock and roll instrument is often played with sharp, slapping thumb movements?** and press Enter.

The contents of the Label1 object on the form change to match your trivia question. Because the label object's WordWrap property is set to True by default, the text wraps inside the label object.

5 Click the Label2 object on the UserForm, and follow the same steps to change its Caption property to **The Bass Guitar**.

6 With the Label2 object still selected, click the Visible property, and change its setting to False. That will keep the answer hidden until the first command button is pressed.

7 Click the Image1 object on the form. Now you'll set the PictureSizeMode, Picture, and Visible properties of the image object to display a photograph of a bass guitar when the user clicks a command button.

8 Click in the PictureSizeMode property box in the Properties window, and select 1-fmPictureSizeModeStretch in the drop-down list. This property setting resizes artwork in an image box so that it fits exactly.

9 Click in the Picture property box, and then click the button containing three dots that appears at the right end of the box. A dialog box will appear, as shown here, prompting you to select a piece of artwork for the image box.

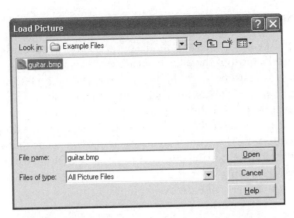

10 Browse to find a picture file on your system, and then click the Open button.

We recommend that you use the Guitar.bmp graphic located on this book's companion CD, but you can also select a piece of artwork from your own computer.

If you select the Guitar.bmp file, you'll see the photograph of a hip Seattle bass player in the image box. (Look closely—he's currently demonstrating the slap-bass technique.)

11 Click in the Visible property box for the image object, and set it to False. You'll keep the photograph hidden until the user clicks the first command button.

12 Now select the first command button object on the form, and change its Caption property to **Answer**.

13 Change the Caption property of the second command button to **Quit**.

14 Click in the UserForm itself (not an object), and then set the Caption property of the UserForm to **Music Trivia**.

You're finished setting properties for the macro, and your UserForm should look similar to the one shown in Figure 57-3.

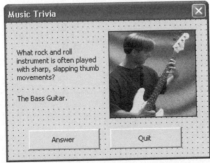

Figure 57-3. This is the completed user interface of the MusicTrivia UserForm.

Writing Event Procedures

The final step in creating a UserForm is writing the program code for the interface objects on the UserForm. Fortunately, most of the objects on a UserForm already know how to work when the macro runs, so you just need to add the final touches using a few carefully designed event procedures. An *event procedure* is a special routine that runs when an object on your form is manipulated at run time. (Technically, event procedures run when a specific *event* is triggered in the UserForm, such as a click, a double-click, or a drag-and-drop operation.) UserForm event procedures use the same Visual Basic macro language that you're familiar with, so you'll have little trouble figuring out what to do. Like Office macros, the trick to learning the ropes is understanding what the most important properties and methods do and then running them in the proper sequence using program code.

Using the Code Window to Write Event Procedures

To write click event procedures for the two command button objects on the UserForm, CommandButton1 and CommandButton2, perform the following steps:

1 Double-click the CommandButton1 object (the button that has the Answer caption). The Visual Basic Editor will open the click event procedure for the CommandButton1 object in a Code window, as seen here:

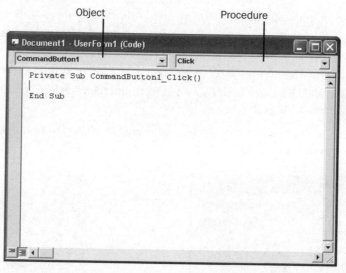

2 Type the following code between the Private Sub and End Sub statements:

```
Image1.Visible = True
Label2.Visible = True
```

These program statements make the Image1 and Label2 objects visible on the User-Form when the user clicks the Answer button.

3 Click the Object drop-down list in the Code window and select the CommandButton2 object.

4 Type **Unload UserForm1** between Private Sub and End Sub, as shown here:

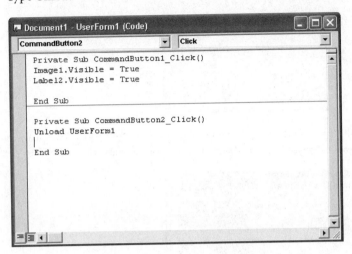

This line unloads the Music Trivia UserForm and closes the macro when the user clicks the Quit button.

> **Note** Use the Unload statement whenever you want to close a UserForm and return to the Word macro that opened it.

5 Now click the Save button on the Visual Basic Editor's Standard toolbar to save the document, together with your UserForm and macro.

Running the MusicTrivia Macro

Congratulations! You have built your first UserForm. Now return to Word and run the macro. To do so, follow these steps:

1 Click the View Microsoft Word button on the Visual Basic Editor's Standard toolbar.

2 In Word, press Alt+F8, and double-click MusicTrivia.

Alt+F8 is the keyboard shortcut to display the Macros dialog box. After you double-click the macro name, Office will start the macro and display the UserForm on the screen, as seen here (pretend you don't know the answer to our little puzzler):

Chapter 57

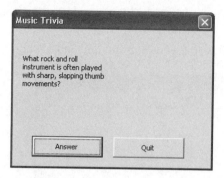

3 Click the Answer button. The answer and photograph will appear on the form, as shown here, just as you stipulated in the CommandButton1 event procedure.

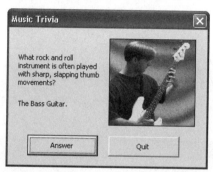

4 Click the Quit button to close the macro. The UserForm will unload and the macro will stop.

Troubleshooting

Images don't disappear as you requested

If a macro you're writing displays images on a UserForm, how and when those images appear is probably very important to you. What do you do if an image or control you want hidden doesn't disappear when you run the macro?

UserForms provide VBA programmers with several exciting opportunities—you can create a user interface that makes objects appear and disappear at set times or when you get specific feedback from the person using your macro. In this example, if you forgot to set the Image1 and Label2 Visible properties to False when you created the macro, Visual Basic won't hide the picture of the bass guitar and the second label (the answer to your puzzler) when the macro starts—spoiling the whole point of the program. If this happened to you, change the Visible properties for those objects using the Properties window. To manage how objects appear and disappear on UserForms, check the Visible property for each object to be sure that you get the right results when the macro starts. Then, as the macro runs, you can adjust the Visible settings programmatically to create interesting visual effects!

Using the TextBox Control to Process Paragraphs

The Label control is useful if you want to display a short sentence on a UserForm, but if you want to display or solicit large amounts of text, you'll want to use the TextBox control. A TextBox is a rectangular storage container for words, sentences, and paragraphs—the basic stuff of Office documents. You can receive text from the macro user via a TextBox control, and provide your macro with raw material for text processing, comparing, or printing. You can also display text using the TextBox control; this text may be material from an existing document, or information from the operating system or the macro itself. Best of all, the TextBox control is designed with ease of use in mind—you can display it with or without scroll bars, and you can select, copy, and paste information to and from a TextBox just as with an Office document.

You can configure a text box object to handle several lines of text by setting three properties in the Properties window. Before you set these properties, be sure the text box object is selected.

- Set Multiline to True (to display more than one line).
- Set ScrollBars to 2-fmScrollBarsVertical (to provide scroll bar access to lines that are not visible in the TextBox).
- Set WordWrap to True (to force text wraps at the right margin).

Processing Text in a Word Document

 Note Chap57.doc, located on the companion CD to this book, contains the two macros developed in this chapter: MusicTrivia (a trivia macro) and ParaScan (a Word paragraph formatting utility). Detailed construction steps for the ParaScan macro are not included because of its length. The Chap57.doc document also contains sample text for the ParaScan macro.

The ParaScan macro displays a UserForm that uses a text box object to show each paragraph in a Word document, one by one. The UserForm contains Next, Format, and Delete buttons so that you can quickly scan the document and make formatting adjustments or delete unwanted material. As you practice using the utility, you'll learn more about using program code to manipulate the contents of an Office document. To run this macro, perform the following steps:

1. Start Word and open the Chap57.doc example document on the companion CD.

2. Press Alt+F8 to display the Macros dialog box, and then double-click the ParaScan macro. Word will run the macro, which displays the ParaScan UserForm, shown on the next page.

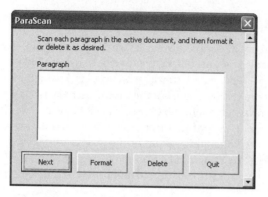

3 Click the Next button on the UserForm to select the first paragraph in the Chap57.doc document and copy it to the text box object on the UserForm, as seen here:

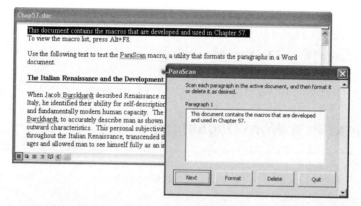

The four buttons at the bottom of the UserForm describe your options in this macro: You can scan the next paragraph by clicking Next; you can format the current paragraph by clicking Format; you can delete the current paragraph by clicking Delete; or you can close the macro by clicking Quit.

4 Click the Next button seven more times to select the eighth paragraph in the document.

This paragraph is too long to fit entirely in the text box, but if you click the text box, a vertical scroll bar will appear to let you see the hidden text.

5 Now click the Format button to change the font formatting in the paragraph. The macro will display the Font dialog box, as shown here, so that you can quickly make the formatting changes you want.

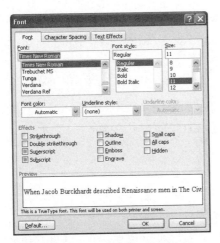

6 Change the font to 9 point, change the color to Blue, and then click the OK button. The macro will format the selected paragraph as you requested.

7 Click the Next button again, and then click the Delete button. The macro will highlight a new paragraph and then delete it when you click the Delete button.

8 Click Next a few more times to see how the ParaScan macro works, and then click the Quit button to close the macro.

> **Note** The ParaScan macro was written primarily for demonstration purposes, but if you'd like to use it to manage your own documents, copy it to your Normal template using the Organizer tool so that you can use it with all your documents. (Right now, it's available only in the Chap57.doc document.) For detailed instructions on using the Organizer, see the Inside Out element "Copying macros to Word's Normal template," on page 1457.

Reviewing the ParaScan Macro Code

ParaScan is a two-part macro. The first part is a simple two-line procedure named ParaScan that uses the Load statement and the Show method to open and display the UserForm2 dialog box on the screen. The real work of the macro happens in the second part, a custom User-Form containing an event procedure for each command button object in the user interface: Next, Format, Delete, and Quit.

Something new you'll see in this macro is a global, or *public*, variable named Num, which keeps track of the current paragraph in the document. A public variable is declared at the top of a module using the Public keyword, in a special section called Declarations. When you declare a public variable in a macro, the variable holds its value in all event procedures in the macro. By way of contrast, variables declared within an event procedure are *local* to the event procedure, meaning they are reset each time an event procedure is finished.

Chapter 57

Loading Text in a Text Box Object

When the user clicks Next, the CommandButton1 Click event procedure runs, as shown here:

```
Private Sub CommandButton1_Click()
Num = Num + 1
ActiveDocument.Paragraphs(num).Range.Select
TextBox1.Text = ActiveDocument.Paragraphs(Num).Range
Label1.Caption = "Paragraph " & Num
If Num = ActiveDocument.Paragraphs.Count Then
    CommandButton1.Enabled = False
End If
End Sub
```

This event procedure increments the Num variable, which tracks the current paragraph number in the document. Using the paragraph number, the routine then selects the current paragraph and copies it to the Text property of the TextBox1 object. The number of the current paragraph is also displayed in the Label1 caption, and if the paragraph is the last one in the document, the Next button is disabled. (Clicking the Next button when there are no more paragraphs would cause a run-time error.)

Opening the Font Dialog Box

The second command button object (Format) displays Word's built-in Font dialog box so that the user can format the selected paragraph. When the user clicks the button, the following code runs and displays the Font dialog box:

```
Private Sub CommandButton2_Click()
Dialogs(wdDialogFormatFont).Show
End Sub
```

A built-in dialog box is displayed when you use one of Word's dialog box constants with the Dialogs collection and the Show method.

> **Tip** The Dialogs collection contains a constant name for each dialog box that Word can display. To learn more about these constants, search for "displaying built-in Word dialog boxes" in the Word Visual Basic online Help.

Deleting a Paragraph

The third command button (Delete) deletes the paragraph that is currently selected in the Word document and is visible in the TextBox1 object. Deleting the text is the easy part—a simple matter of using the Delete method and the active range, as the first line of the event procedure demonstrates:

```
Private Sub CommandButton3_Click()
ActiveDocument.Paragraphs(Num).Range.Delete
If Num >= 2 Then Num = Num - 1
```

```
ActiveDocument.Paragraphs(Num).Range.Select
TextBox1.Text = ActiveDocument.Paragraphs(Num).Range
Label1.Caption = "Paragraph " & Num
If Num = ActiveDocument.Paragraphs.Count Then
    CommandButton1.Enabled = False
End If
End Sub
```

The rest of the event procedure clarifies what happens next. If the document contains two or more paragraphs, the new selected paragraph simply becomes the paragraph directly above the one you deleted (or the paragraph directly below if you deleted the first paragraph in the document). However, if the document contains only one paragraph, the paragraph's text is deleted and an empty paragraph (that is, one consisting of only an end-of-paragraph mark) remains; the paragraph count stays the same, because in a Word document there can never be zero paragraphs. Finally, if the new active paragraph is the last paragraph in the document, the Next button is disabled so that the user cannot specify a paragraph outside the valid range. (Such an action would produce a run-time error.)

Unloading the UserForm

Finally, the Quit command button on the UserForm ends the macro by unloading the User-Form. This technique is always the best way to close a UserForm:

```
Private Sub CommandButton4_Click()
Unload UserForm2
End Sub
```

The ParaScan macro demonstrates the unique interplay among UserForms, event procedures, and document elements in an Office macro. You have learned several of the skills necessary to write your own professional-looking macros. Take this accomplishment as your starting point, and continue learning about the objects and statements that you can use in Visual Basic for Applications. The wide world of macro programming awaits you!

Chapter 57

Index of Troubleshooting Topics

	Error	Description	Page
A	Access	Creating many-to-many relationships	1133
	Access	Inability to run queries with calculated fields	1166
	Access	Embedded OLE objects not displayed in forms	1183
	Access	All records have disappeared from forms	1193
	Access	Reports include blank pages	1216
	Address Lookups	Address lookups too slow	1081
	Attachments	Attached item not updated in Outlook	968
	AutoCorrect	Turning off AutoCorrect	279
	AutoFormat	Turning off AutoFormat	279
	AutoShapes	AutoShapes disappear in Word	127
	AutoText	Missing entries	417
B	Background Sound	Inability to remove background sound	588
	Backgrounds	Shared borders and backgrounds	1315
	Balloons	Needing to scroll to view balloons	465
	Business Analysis	Solver does not find a solution	815
C	Calculated Fields	Inability to run queries with calculated fields	1166
	Calculations	Formulas and calculations	619
	Calendar	Attached item not updated in calendar	968
	Categories	Problems with categories	1030
	Charts	Excel prints larger than expected	769
	Charts	Shading lacks sufficient contrast	768
	Clipboard	Missing Clipboard blocks	162
	Comments	You need to scroll to see change or comment balloons	465
	Comments	Comments have disappeared	466
	Contents Folder	Distribution list displays out-of-date information	1055
	Copying	Missing AutoText, macros, or customization	417
	Copying	You have trouble copying outline headings	433
	Copying	Lost document versions	579
	Custom Categories	Trouble with custom categories	1030

Error	Description	Page
D Data Entry Command	Records disappear when using Data Entry command	1193
Design View	Report layout and design view	1216
Distribution Lists	Distribution list displays out-of-date information	1055
Drag-and-Drop	Drag-and-drop editing doesn't work	289
E Editing	You would rather do it yourself	279
Editing	Undo unavailable in Excel	634
Embedded Objects	Embedded OLE object isn't displayed	1183
Equations	Can't enter spaces into an equation	141
Excel	Errors after installing Excel	607
Excel	Creating fractions in numeric entry	612
Excel	Formulas do not compute	619
Excel	Can't insert a hyperlink in Excel	625
Excel	Undo unavailable	634
Excel	Features unavailable in shared workbooks	693
Excel	Protection for worksheet or workbook unavailable	700
Excel	Enforcing operator precedence	733
Excel	Errors in financial formulas	740
Excel	Formulas return error code with names	745
Excel	Protection commands unavailable	700
Excel	Chart prints larger than expected	769
Excel	Shading on chart lacks sufficient contrast	768
Excel	Sorting of list creates invalid results or errors	781
Excel	Solver doesn't find a solution	815
Excel	External data tools unavailable	837
F Formatting	Cannot underline trailing spaces	317
Formatting	Formatting changes mysteriously	338
Formatting	Creation fraction in numeric entry	612
Formatting	Shading on chart lacks sufficient contrast	768
Formatting	Formatting features are unavailable	1361
Formulas	Do not compute	619
Formulas	Enforcing operator precedence	733
Formulas	Errors in financial formulas	740
Formulas	Formulas return error code with names	745
Formulas	Sorting Excel list creates invalid results or errors	781

Error	Description	Page
FrontPage	Some Web folders aren't listed in Folders view	1241
FrontPage	Graphics files not saved	1253
FrontPage	Shared Borders command is unavailable	1314
FrontPage	Shared borders offer little control	1315
FrontPage	Kerning isn't available	1336
FrontPage	Formatting features are unavailable	1361
FrontPage	Web component doesn't work	1381
FrontPage	Can't insert Web component	1382
G Graphics Files	Graphics files not saved in FrontPage	1253
H Headers	Access report layout and headers	1216
Headers and Footers	Headers or footers cut off	531
Hyperlinks	Can't insert a hyperlink in Excel	625
I Indexes	Spelling errors in index	442
Indexes	Edits to index or tables of contents are lost	446
Installation	Errors after installing Excel	607
Items	Outlook items disappear in different view	982
J Journal Entries	Journal entries for document access don't appear	1070
K Kerning	Kerning isn't available	1336
Kerning	Manual kerning vs. automatic	1336
L Linking Data	Can't link data from PowerPoint	164
Lists	Problems sorting lists in Excel	781
Lost Documents	Lost Web page document	579
M Macros	Reversing the effects of an Office macro	229
Macros	Enabling macro security for all Office applications	232
Macros	Missing entries in macro	417
Macros	Breaking strings in macros causes problems	1447
Macros	Macro doesn't account for each possibility in Select Case statement	1469
Moving	Missing AutoText, macros, or customizations	417
O Office Techniques	Speech recognition is slow or unreliable	86
Office Techniques	Speech recognition inserts extra spaces	91

Error	Description	Page
Office Techniques	Missing Clipboards blocks	162
Office Techniques	AutoShapes disappear in Word	127
Office Techniques	Can't enter spaces into an equation	141
Office Techniques	Can't link data from PowerPoint	164
Office Techniques	Reversing the effects of an Office macro	229
Office Techniques	Enabling macro security for all Office applications	232
OLE Objects	OLE objects not displayed in Access forms	1183
Online Documents	Lost document versions	579
Online Documents	Can't remove a background sound	588
Outlook	Attached item not updated	968
Outlook	Items disappear in different view	982
Outlook	Trouble with custom categories	1030
Outlook	Distribution list displays out-of-date information	1055
Outlook	Journal entries for document accesses don't appear	1070
Outlook	Address lookups too slow	1081
P PowerPoint	Can't link data from PowerPoint	164
Printing	Excel charts larger than expected	769
Protecting Cells	Protection for worksheet or workbook unavailable	700
Q Queries	Queries with calculated field don't calculate in Access	1166
R Records	All records have disappeared	1193
Reports	Access report includes blank pages	1216
S Saving	Lost document versions	579
Saving Documents	You would like to save a document quickly	256
Saving Documents	Your document is too big to save	429
Security	Enabling macro security for all Office applications	232
Select Case Statements	Macro doesn't account for each possibility in Select Case statement	1469
Shared Borders	Shared Borders command is unavailable	1314
Shared Borders	Shared Borders offer little control	1315
Sharing Workbooks	Features unavailable in shared workbooks	693
Solver	Solver doesn't find a solution	815
Sorting	Trouble sorting lists in Excel	781
Sound	Can't remove a background sound	588

Error	Description	Page
Speech Recognition	Speech recognition is slow or unreliable	86
Speech Recognition	Speech recognition inserts extra spaces	91
Spelling Errors	The index has spelling errors	442
Split Boxes	The Split Box is not visible	251
Strings	Breaking strings in VBA macros causes problems	1447
T Tables	Table text is cut off	361
Tables	Creating a many-to-many relationship in Access	1131
Tables of Contents	Edits to tables of contents are lost	446
Text Boxes	Text boxes disappeared	514
U Undo	Undo unavailable in Excel	634
Undo	Reversing the effects of an Office macro	229
UserForms	UserForm images not disappearing as requested	1486
V VBA	Breaking strings in VBA macro code causes problems	1447
VBA	Macro doesn't account for each possibility in Select Case statement	1469
VBA	UserForm images not disappearing as requested	1486
Viewing Documents	Document is too wide to view	254
W Web Components	Web component doesn't work	1381
Web Folders	Some Web folders aren't listed in FrontPage Folders view	1241
Web Pages	Lost document versions	579
Web Pages	Can't remove a background sound	588
Web Pages	Kerning isn't available	1336
Web Pages	Formatting features are unavailable	1361
Web Pages	Web component doesn't work	1381
Web Pages	Can't insert Web component	1382
Word	AutoShapes disappear in Word	127
Word	Can't enter spaces into an equation	141
Word	Can't link data from PowerPoint	164
Word	The Split Box isn't visible	251
Word	Document is too wide to view	254
Word	You would like to save a document quickly	256
Word	You would rather edit document yourself	279
Word	Drag-and-drop editing doesn't work	289

Error	Description	Page
Word	Cannot underline trailing spaces	317
Word	Formatting changes mysteriously	338
Word	Table text is cut off	361
Word	Missing AutoText, macros, or customizations	417
Word	Your document is too large to save	429
Word	You have trouble copying outline headings	433
Word	Spelling errors in index	442
Word	Edits to index or tables of contents are lost	446
Word	You need to scroll to see Change or Comment balloons	465
Word	Comments have disappeared	466
Word	Text boxes have disappeared	514
Word	Headers or footers cut off	531
Workbooks	Features unavailable in shared workbooks	693
Workbooks and Worksheets	Protection unavailable in workbooks and worksheets	700

Index

Symbols and Numbers

+ (addition operator), 732
/ (division operator), 732
= (equals sign), 618–19, 727
^ (exponential operator), 732
* (multiplication operator), 729, 732
( ) (parentheses), arithmetic operators and, 732
(pound sign), error values, 741
- (subtraction), 732
35 mm slides, projecting, 926
3-D charts, 750, 765

A

absolute cell references, Excel, 731
Access
    backing up, 1112
    calculations, 1101
    converting Excel lists to, 788–89
    data access pages. See data access pages, Access
    database creation, 1103–07
    database design, 1100–1103
    Database window, 1107–10
    exporting data, 1116
    forms. See forms, Access
    InfoPath form template based on Access database, 1403
    linking and embedding and, 173
    mapping to tasks, 9
    New command, 52
    new features, 14–15
    opening databases, 1111
    overview, 1097–1100
    projects compared with databases, 1107
    queries. See queries, Access
    reports. See reports, Access
    saving databases, 1110–11
    tables. See tables, Access
Access Label Wizard, 1201
Access project files (.adp), 1107
action buttons, 920
action queries
    creating, 1168–70
    types of, 1170
actions, assigning to PowerPoint objects, 920–21
Activation Wizard, Office 2003, 19–21
active cell, Excel, 608
ActiveX controls, 828
Add Or Remove Buttons command, 219–20
Add Text command, 152
add-ins
    Excel, 725
    Solver, 808
    Word, 416
addition operator (+), 732
address book accounts
    adding, 1080
    looking up addresses, 1082
    Outlook account types, 1082–83
    working with, 1086
Address Cards view, Outlook, 974, 1055
address lists, Word, 549
addresses, storing in Outlook, 1051
.adp files, 1107
adult content, e-mail filters, 1022–24
advanced controls, Web pages, 1378–82
    inserting, 1380–82
    list of, 1379–80
    overview, 1379
Advanced File Search task pan, 66
Advanced Find, Outlook items, 988–89
agenda slides, 873
Alert Before Overwriting Cells, 724
aliases, styles and, 397, 400
alignment
    Access forms, 1186
    InfoPath forms, 1423
    PowerPoint text, 885
alignment, Excel
    Format Cells dialog box, 648
    horizontal, 648–50
    text, 651
    vertical, 650
alignment, FrontPage
    images, 1292
    Web page images, 1338
Web page paragraph formats, 1324–26
alignment, Word
    cells in Word tables, 354–55
    page numbers, 520
    paragraph formats, 319
    vertical options, 542
all-day events. See events
alphabetical sorts, Excel lists, 778–79
Alt key
    table selection (Alt+5), 348
    text selection, 286
And logic, queries, 1156
animation
    character formats, 311
    DHTML effects, 1331
animation, PowerPoint
    creating new effect, 913
    customizing, 911–14
    diagrams and charts, 914
    motion paths, 914–16
    schemes, 910–11
    speed of, 912
annotation, PowerPoint slide shows, 935–36
antonyms, 497
appearance options
    Outlook tasks, 1067–68
    table of contents, 443–44
    worksheets, 722–23
append queries, 1170
application interface, 209–38
    adding/removing toolbar buttons, menu items, or menus, 214–15, 219–20
    customizing icons, 218–19
    customizing shortcut menus, 214
    customizing toolbars, 210–12
    displaying toolbars, 212
    image menus, 220
    macro security, 229–32
    macros, when to build, 224–25
    modifying toolbar buttons, menu items, or menus, 216–17
    overview, 209–10
    Rearrange Commands dialog box and, 220–21
    recording macros, 225–27
    running macros, 227–28

application interface, *continued*
saving and restoring settings,
235–37
setting options, 232–35
shortcut key assignments,
222–23
application interface, Excel,
606–08
application interface, FrontPage,
15
application interface, PowerPoint,
849–51
application interface, Word, 248
Application Recovery utility, 70
applications
integration features, 6
macro security, 232
mapping to tasks, 7–10
methods for running, 39–41
new features by application,
13–16
new features shared by, 11–12
Office 2003, 3
opening documents from within,
62–63
selecting during installation of
Office 2003, 19–20
application window. *See*
application interface
appointments
defined, 1026
recurring, 1031
scheduling, 1027–31, 1056
archiving
journal entries, 1069
Outlook data, 1089
Outlook items, 970–72
arguments
Excel functions, 734
VBA functions, 1451
arithmetic operators. *See*
mathematical operators
Arrange By submenu, 14, 983–84
arrow indicators, adding to charts,
766–67
arrow keys
navigating Excel worksheets,
608, 613
navigating to headers/footers,
525
arrows (double), slide navigation
and, 851
ASCII character set, 261
Ask A Question list, Office Help, 29
assigned tasks, Outlook, 1061

Assistant. *See* Office Assistant
attachments
adding to e-mail message, 964
shared attachments, 14,
1018–19
viruses and, 1003
attendees, Outlook meetings,
1034–37
attributes, VBA, 1440–41
audio and video, Power Point,
902–08
playing CD audio tracks, 907–08
sound clips, 905–07
video clips, 903–04
authors, of comments, 462
AutoArchive, Outlook, 971
AutoCalculate box, Excel, 607
AutoComplete
AutoText entries, 268
Excel and, 614, 724
list entries, 773
style aliases, 400
AutoContent Wizard, PowerPoint
presentations, 857–59
AutoCorrect, 271–76
applying, 275–76
checking spelling with, 276, 481
enabling, 272
exceptions, 274
PowerPoint errors, 876
symbols and, 273
text replacements, 273
turning off, 279
AutoFill, series in worksheets,
641–42
AutoFilter command
customizing, 784–85
Excel lists, 783–84
AutoFit command
formula replication, 730
PowerPoint text, 868
Word tables, 351–52
worksheet rows and columns,
665
AutoForm options, Access forms,
1172
AutoFormat
overview, 340
PivotTables, 798
PowerPoint, 867–68
turning off, 279
worksheets, 665–66
AutoFormat As You Type, 341
AutoLayout option, AutoShapes,
129

Automatic Update
links, 166
styles, 399
Automatically Update Document
Styles option, 338
AutoPlay, 17
AutoPreview, Outlook, 986
AutoRecover feature, 69–70
AutoReport, 1199–1200
AutoShapes, 124–27
adding text to, 152
AutoLayout option, 129
clips, 125
drawing canvases, 126
inserting, 124–25
PowerPoint drawings, 899
transforming, 148
Web page images, 1301
Word and 127
worksheet images, 621
AutoSum, 735
AutoText, 266–69
creating entries, 266, 269
inserting entries, 267–68, 270
modifying entries, 269
templates, 409
toolbar, 271
turning off, 279
viewing entry content, 270–71
AutoText submenu, 268
AutoThumbnail, 1303
AVERAGE function, Excel, 689,
736–37
axes, Excel charts, 750

B

Back button, navigating among
task panes, 44
background saves, Word
documents, 255–56
backgrounds, Access, 1174
backgrounds, Excel, 621–22
backgrounds, InfoPath, 1405
backgrounds, PowerPoint, 852,
888–90
backgrounds, Web pages
color formats, 591–92,
1334–35, 1351
sounds, 588
backups
data files, 1088–89
databases, 15, 1112
Web pages, 576
balloons
Balloons drop-down list, 451
margin balloons, 448
scrolling to view, 465

batch processing, tracked changes,
457
Bcc box, Outlook, 1017
blank presentations, PowerPoint,
859–61
body text, PowerPoint slides, 852
Body Text style, 336, 420
Bold button, Formatting toolbar,
317
bold text
PowerPoint and, 878–79
shortcut key for, 318
bookmarks
functions of, 301
text, 300–301
books/booklets, 539–43
adjusting page layout for,
541–43
creating, 539–40
paper size and source, 540–41
boolean expressions, 1462
borders, Excel, 658–60
drawing, 660
instant, 659–60
styles, 659
borders, FrontPage
images, 1338
positioned elements, 1348
Web pages, 1324
borders, InfoPath tables, 1405
borders, Word, 361–71
applying to entire document,
370–71
applying to selected areas of
document, 364–65
Borders And Shading dialog box,
366–69
cells, 346
changing existing, 365
character formats, 311
defaults, 360
overview, 361–63
paragraph formats, 321
properties, setting before applying, 357
Tables and Borders toolbar,
363–64
Borders And Shading dialog box,
366–69, 401, 1329–31, 1348
bound controls, Access forms,
1179
brochures, Word, 241
browse buttons
document navigation, 303–05
Word, 248

browse commands
Go To command, 304
searches, 297
browsers. See Web browsers
built-in functions, Excel formulas,
733–34
bulleted lists
converting to an outline, 282
creating, 379–80
Format Menu, 401
InfoPath forms, 1411, 1423
outline heading, 424
paragraph formats, 322
PowerPoint, 881–83
Web pages, 1323, 1326–28
business analysis tools, Excel,
805–21
Goal Seek forecasts, 806–07
Goal Seek worksheets, 805–06
scenario creation, 816–18
scenario management, 821
scenario reports, 819–20
scenario views, 818–19
Solver, running, 810–13
Solver forecasts, 813–14
Solver worksheets, 808–10
button bar, Outlook, 1077–78
Button Editor, 218
By Category view, Outlook, 974

C

calculated controls, Access forms,
1189
calculated fields, queries, 1163–65
calculations
Access, 1101
Excel, 721–22
Calendar folder, Outlook, 1028–46
Day/Week/Month views, 975
event setup, 1032
information stored in, 947
overview, 1026–27
planning meetings, 1037–39
scheduling appointments,
1027–31
scheduling meetings, 1033–37
SharePoint calendars, 1047–48
SharePoint meeting workspace,
1039–42
working with, 1043–46
calendars
iCalendar, 1036
publishing to Web, 1044
SharePoint, 1047–48
side-by-side calendar folders, 14

cameras, adding artwork to charts,
621
canvases. See drawing canvases
capitalization
case styles, 287
shortcut keys for, 318
styles, 315
Caption property, Access tables,
1126
Cascading Style Sheets. See CSS
(Cascading Style Sheets)
case, capitalization styles, 287
categories, Outlook
assigning to appointments,
1031
assigning to contacts, 1050
custom, 1030–31
distribution lists, 1054
journal entries and, 1072, 1073
notes, 1075–76
tasks, 1062
category axis, Excel charts, 750
Cc box, Outlook, 1015
CD, installation from, 17–19
CD audio tracks, PowerPoint,
907–08
CD presentations, PowerPoint side
shows, 932–33
cell references, Excel, 607, 781
formulas and, 619–20
sorting problems and, 781
cells, Excel worksheets
active cell, 608
adding, 640
cell pointers, 608–09
cell references, 607, 619–20,
730–31, 781
clearing or deleting, 630–32
comments. See comments,
worksheets
drag-and-drop, 638
formats. See formats, Excel
replicating formulas between,
729–31
selecting, 608, 627–29
Solver setup, 808
cells, Word tables
adding blocks, 349
adding individual, 348–49
alignment, 354–55
deleting, 350
gridlines, 346
numbering, 378
resizing, 350–53
text or graphics in, 347
text orientation, 354
width of, 351

centimeters, units of measurement, 316
chapter numbers, adding to page numbers, 521
character formats, Excel charts, 761–62
character formats, InfoPath forms, 1411, 1422
character formats, Web pages, 1332–36
    fonts, 1335–36
    Formatting toolbar, 1333
    overview, 1332
    removing, 1336
    text and background color, 1334–35
character formats, Word
    applying, 330–32
    applying directly to characters, 308–09
    borders and shading, 362
    fonts, 312–15
    Formatting toolbar, 317
    levels of, 307
    scaling, 252
    shortcut keys, 318
    spacing, 310, 313
    styles, 328
    types of, 309–11
    units of measurement, 316
character styles, 328
    applying, 330–33
    customizing, 393
    emphasis, 396
    modifying, 397
    page numbers, 527
Chart menu, 758–59
chart sheet, Excel, 751
Chart toolbar, Excel, 759
Chart Wizard, Excel
    creating charts, 751–54
    embedded charts, 754–57
    PivotCharts, 798
charts, Excel, 747–69
    adding to Access forms, 1172
    adding to Access reports, 1200
    advantages of, 747
    changing type of, 759–60
    character formats, 761–62
    Chart menu, 758–59
    Chart toolbar, 759
    copying formats, 765–66
    creating, 751–54
    elements, 750–51
    embedded charts, 754–57
    freezing data, 758

gridlines, 763–64
labels and arrows, 766–67
legends, 764
numeric formats, 762–63
Pie Chart example, 752–54
planning, 747, 749
printing, 768
titles and labels, 760–61
types of, 748–49
charts, PowerPoint, 914
charts, Word
    constructing with Microsoft Graph, 136–38
    creating from Word tables, 138
    not linked to tables, 138
Check For Updates command, 23
Clear command, worksheet cells, 631
Clear Formatting command, 333–34
Clip Art, 109–11, 621
Clip Gallery, Microsoft Office 2000, 107
Clip Organizer
    adding images to Web pages, 1301
    adding pictures to PowerPoint slides, 898
    assigning keywords to clips, 117
    freestanding mode, 113–16
    importing clips, 116–17
    inserting clips, 111–12
    managing movie or sound clips with, 588
    online clips, 112
    overview, 107–09
    searching for clips, 109–10
Clipboard
    icon, 158
    moving and copying text with, 289–91
    Office Clipboard vs. Windows Clipboard, 158
    options, 292
    saving large documents, 429
    task pane, 158
clips. See media clips
code. See source code, HTML
Code View toolbar, 1385–87
Code window, VBA
    auto list feature in, 1442
    Visual Basic development environment, 1429
    writing event procedures, 1484–85
collections, VBA objects, 1440

color-based organization, Outlook notes, 1076
color options
    character formats, 310
    InfoPath forms, 1411
    PowerPoint, 887–88
    shading, 369
    text color in Excel, 656–58
    Web page backgrounds, 591–92
    Window Font color, 368
color underlining, 310
column breaks, 375–76
columns, Access
    forms, 1174
    reports, 1200
    tables, 1138–39, 1155
columns, Excel worksheets, 662–64
    adding, 639
    adjusting width manually, 662–63
    adjusting width with mouse, 663
    hiding, 664
    printing options, 718
    selecting, 627–28, 630
    Width command, 663–64
columns, Outlook
    heading, 977–78
    modifying with shortcut menu, 978–79
columns, Word documents, 371–76
    applying with Columns button, 372–73
    applying with Columns dialog box, 373–74
    arranging text with, 371–72
    fine tuning, 374–76
columns, Word tables
    adding, 346, 348–49
    deleting, 350
    modifying width of, 351–53
Columns button, 372–73
Columns dialog box, 373–74
CommandButton, UserForms, 1481
commands
    list commands, 13, 800–803
    mail merge, 558
    voice command mode, 93–94
comments, document
    adding voice comments, 463–64
    inserting to workgroup documents, 459–61
    scrolling to view, 465

comments, PowerPoint

viewing, editing, and deleting
workgroup documents,
462–64
comments, PowerPoint, 873–74
comments, worksheets
entering, 616–17
managing, 617
printing, 716
**common errors list, worksheets,
645–46**
comparison operators
conditional expressions and,
1461
queries and, 1156
sorting and filtering records,
1146
compound documents, 154
compression, pictures, 122
**conditional expressions, 1461–62,
1465–66**
**conditional formats, Excel work-
sheets, 666–68**
constants, VBA, 1442–47
custom formatting, 1443–47
intrinsic constants, 1442
constraints, Solver, 809, 811–12
Contacts folder, Outlook, 1047–60
addresses in, 1082
archiving, 970
communicating with contacts,
1056–57
Contacts form, 1049–51
customizing, 1058
distribution lists, 1052–54
e-mailing contacts, 1056
existing contacts, 1048
information stored in, 947
journal entries, 1070, 1072
linking contacts to related information, 1052
mail merge, 553, 561
new contacts, 1047–48
Personal Address Book compared with, 1083
scheduling appointments, 1031
SharePoint contacts list, 1058–
60
Contacts form, Outlook, 1049–51
**content layouts, Power Point, 903,
906**
**continuation character (_), VBA
macros, 1446–47**
controls, Access forms
alignment and spacing, 1186
bound, 1179
calculated controls, 1189

copying, 1186
properties, 1187, 1189
selecting, 1184–85
text formats, 1187–88
unbound, 1180
controls, InfoPath forms, 1406–08
Conversion Wizard, 256
**Convert command, Object sub-
menu, 174**
**Copy command (Ctrl+C). _See also_
moving and copying**
Access fields, 1121
Access forms, 1192
Clipboard and, 158
embedding data, 171
Excel data, 637
linking data, 163
static data exchange, 155
Word text, 289
**Count function, Excel worksheets,
689**
crashes, computer, 69
cropping
pictures, 122–23
Web page images, 1343
crosstab queries, 1166–68
converting existing query to,
1168
creating, 1167
overview, 1166
CSS (Cascading Style Sheets)
embedded setting, 1358–60
external setting, 1360
inline setting, 1358
Ctrl key
Ctrl+C. _See_ Copy command
(Ctrl+C)
Ctrl+CC (Office Clipboard), 163
Ctrl+D. _See_ deleting
Ctrl+F6 (browse open work-
books), 687
Ctrl+G (Go To), 302–04
Ctrl+H (replace), 298
Ctrl+N (New), 1104
Ctrl+O (Open), 62–63, 1111
Ctrl+P (print), 544
Ctrl+Q (removing paragraph
formats), 322, 334
Ctrl+S (Save), 69–70
Ctrl+Shift+Z (clear formatting),
334
Ctrl+Spacebar (clear format-
ting), 334
Ctrl+V (Paste), 289, 635–37,
1121, 1192

data exchange

Ctrl+X (cut). _See_ Cut command
(Ctrl+X)
Ctrl+Y (Go To). _See_ Go To com-
mand (Ctrl+Y)
Ctrl+Y (Repeat), 265, 285, 635
Ctrl+Z (Undo). _See_ Undo (Ctrl+Z)
selecting multiple ranges, 629
**currency symbols, Excel, 654,
655–56**
**Custom View Organizer, Outlook,
977**
**Custom Views command, Excel,
707–08**
Customize dialog box
Commands tab, 213–14, 216
customizing application inter-
face, 210
Options tab, 232–35
toolbars, 210–12
Toolbars tab, 212–13
Cut command (Ctrl+X)
Access fields, 1121
Clipboard and, 158
embedding data and, 171
Excel worksheets, 635–37
static data exchange and, 155
Word text, 289

D

data access pages, 1193–98
Access, 1193–98
creating, 1195–97
database objects, 1103
editing, 1197
overview, 1193–95
publishing, 1197–98
toolbars, 1195
**data analysis. _See_ PivotTables,
Excel**
data entry
Access forms, 1190
Access tables, 1134–36
Excel lists, 773–75
data exchange, 153–76
Clipboard and, 158–62
copying and moving data statically, 155–58
editing embedded objects, 173
editing linked data, 166–67
embedding by creating new data,
172–73
embedding example, 174–76
embedding from a portion of an
existing document, 171

data exchange, *continued*
  embedding from entire
    document, 171–72
  embedding overview, 170
  hyperlinks, 168
  linking entire document, 163–64
  linking example, 168–70
  linking overview, 162
  linking parts of a document, 163
  methods, 153–55
data files, Outlook, 1088–93
  backing up, 1088–89
  creating, 1091–92
  location of, 1090
  overview, 1088–89
  working with, 1092–93
Data menu, Excel, 785
data series, Excel charts, 750
data sources
  Excel, 799–800
  InfoPath forms, 1406–08
data types, Access fields, 1122–24
data validation
  Excel lists, 775–77
  InfoPath forms, 1420
database objects, 1101
  Data access page, 1103
  Form, 1101–02
  Query, 1101–02
  Report, 1103–04
  view options, 1110
  working with, 1108–09
Database window, Access,
  1107–10
  displaying, 1108
  working with database objects,
    1108–09
databases. *See also* **Access**
  backing up, 15
  creating, 1103–07
  designing, 1100–1103
  Excel lists. *See* lists, Excel
  formats, 1111
  opening, 1111
  projects compared with, 1107
  relational vs. flat-file, 1098
  saving, 1110–11
  view options, 1110
  working with database objects,
    1108–09
data warehouses, 800
Datasheet view, Access, 1134
  creating tables, 1113–14
  data entry, 1134–36
  deleting records, 1136–37

options, 1137–39
queries, 1169
sorting and filters records,
  1141–47
subdatasheets, 1139–41
Date Navigator, Outlook Calendar,
  1043
dates
  Excel, 614–16, 641–44
  Outlook forms, 963
  PowerPoint slides, 852
  as serial value, 668
  Word, 263–64
Day/Week/Month view, Outlook
  Calendar, 975, 1043
decimals
  Access tables, 1126
  Excel numeric values, 612
decision structures, 1462
  If...Then, 1462–66
  Select Case, 1466–69
Deleted Items folder, Outlook, 947
deleting
  clearing worksheet cells,
    631–32
  FrontPage and, 1243
  Outlook items, 969
  paragraphs, Word, 1490–91
  queries, 1170
  records, Access forms, 1192
  Web pages, 1291
  Web sites, 1229
design, page layout, 509–10
design mode, InfoPath, 1396
  creating new form templates,
    1399–1402
  design tasks, 1411–12
  modifying form templates,
    1400–1401
Design Tasks task pane, InfoPath,
  1403–04
design templates, PowerPoint
  color schemes, 886
  overview, 861
  text formats, 878
design time, VBA, 1437
Design view, Access, 1118–28
  adding fields, 1119–20
  creating forms, 1171
  creating queries, 1149
  creating reports, 1199
  customizing forms, 1178
  editing data access pages,
    1197
  editing queries, 1155–57
  editing reports, 1210

field properties, 1122–26
moving and copying fields, 1121
overview, 1118–19
primary keys, 1127–28
removing fields, 1120–21
report layout, 1216
sorting and grouping report
  records, 1213–15
Design view, FrontPage
  creating forms, 1364–65
  navigation, 1234
  source code, 1383–84
  WYSIWYG, 1382
desktop, adding shortcuts to, 41
DHTML effects, 1331–32
Diagram Gallery, 131
Diagram toolbar, 131
diagrams, animating in
  PowerPoint, 914
diagrams, Office, 127–33
  converting, 133
  disappearing in Word, 127
  labels and text, 132
  organization charts, 128–29
  overview, 127
  selecting and inserting, 130–31
dialog boxes
  building custom, 1478–81
  compared with task panes, 42
dictation mode, speech recogni-
  tion, 89–93
  inserting extra spaces, 91
  punctuation characters, 90–91
  turning on, 89
dictionaries, Word
  activating, 488–89
  adding words to, 490
  creating custom, 487–88
  Dictionary Language drop-down
    list, 484
  removing, 489
digital cameras, 1300
digital certificates, 475
digital IDs, 1051
digital signatures
  e-mail messages, 1013
  InfoPath forms, 1421
  workbook protection, 703
dim (dimension) statements, VBA
  macros, 1447–48
directories, mail merge, 549,
  558–59
directory service accounts
  adding, modifying, removing,
    1086
  functions of, 1080

LDAP and, 1080
Outlook account types,
    1080–81
discussion boards
adding to SharePoint team Web
    site, 1243–47
customizing, 204–05
information managed by, 183
overview, 178
participating in, 193–95
discussions, online
discussion boards, 193–95
document discussions, 195–98
display options, Word, 251–54
distribution lists
adding categories, 1054
adding members, 1053–54
creating, 1052–53
defined, 1047
members, 1047
privacy, 1054
.doc format, 573
document libraries, WSS
accessing from applications,
    187–88
accessing from browsers,
    183–87
adding to SharePoint team Web
    site, 1232, 1243–47
customizing, 204–05
folder associated with, 182
overview, 178
properties, 1247
saving documents in, 188
Document Map, 430–32
document model, InfoPath forms,
    1393
Document Recovery pane, 69–70
documents. *See also* **Word**
borders. *See* borders, Word
columns of text. *See* columns,
    Word documents
creating, opening, saving, 255
data exchange. *See* data
    exchange
footnotes and endnotes,
    434–37
formats. *See* formats, Word
indexes, 438–42
lists. *See* lists, Word
managing large/complex. *See*
    Outline view
multiple, 74–76
online, 569–73
page layout. *See* page layout,
    Word

permissions, 80–81
previewing, 77
printing. *See* printing options,
    Word documents
proofing. *See* proofing docu-
    ments
properties, 76–79
removing personal information
    from, 73
saving in XML format, 597
shading. *See* shading, Word
sharing, 190–93
side by side views, 11
smart documents, 11
specialized, 241–42
statistics, 495
storing different versions of
    Word, 257–58
table of contents, 443–46
templates. *See* templates, Word
too wide to view, 253–54
workgroups. *See* workgroup doc-
    uments
XML. *See* XML documents
documents, creating, 47–56
New command, 52–53
New Document task pane,
    53–55
New Office Document dialog
    box, 47–52
Office Online templates for,
    55–56
documents, opening, 56–63
from within applications, 62–63
nonnative formats, 58
Open Office Document dialog
    box, 57–62
overview, 56–57
reopening recently opened docu-
    ments, 58
on Web sites and FTP sites,
    58–59
from Windows Explorer, 57
documents, saving, 69–74
AutoRecover feature, 69–70
document too large, 429
fast saves and background
    saves, 256
locations for, 71–72
Save As dialog box, 70–73
Save button (Ctrl+S), 69–70
Save command, 429
as Web pages, 73–74
document window, 251
document workspaces, WSS
creating, 191, 1233

overview, 178
sharing documents, 190–93
.dot files, 411
., 414
double-clicking, 246–47
draft font option, Word, 253–54
Drafts folder, Outlook, 947
drag-and-drop
documents, 55
media clips, 115
PowerPoint slides, 872
text editing, 289, 354
Web sites, importing, 1252
worksheets, 638, 683, 724
Draw menu, Word, 146–47
Draw Table button, Tables And Bor-
    ders toolbar, 355
drawing, Word tables, 355–57
drawing canvases
adding to Web pages, 1300
discarding, 512
overview, 126
drawing guides, Power Point,
    900–901
Drawing Pad window
creating sketch in, 103–04
tasks performed with, 104–05
Drawing toolbar
Arrow button, 766
AutoShapes compared with,
    126
modifying graphic objects,
    144–49
drop-down menus, 114
dynamic HTML effects, 1331–32
dynamic templates, 1284–86
creating, 1285–86
features of, 1284
FrontPage, 15, 1220

E

editing options, Access
data access pages, 1197
forms, 1189–92
reports, 1210–11
editing options, Excel, 723–24
formulas, 732
queries, 1155–57
editing options, FrontPage
Web pages, 1289–91
Web sites, 1231–32
editing options, Outlook
items, 961–65
views, 961–62
editing options, PowerPoint, 869

editing options, Word, 259–305
AutoCorrect, 271–76
AutoText, 266–71
bookmarking text, 300–301
Clipboard options, 292
date, 263–64
editing modes, 259
Find command, 293–96
Find command with wildcards, 296–97
foreign characters, 261–64
insertion points, moving with Go To command, 302–04
insertion points, positioning, 281
macros for saving place in documents, 301–02
moving and copying with Clipboard, 289–91
moving and copying with mouse, 287–89
navigating with browse buttons, 304–05
repeating editing actions, 265
Replace command, 298–99
smart tags, 276–79
symbols, 260–61
text addition, 259–60
text deletion, 282
text selection, 282–84, 286
time, 263–64
transferring multiple blocks of text, 291–92
undoing/redoing editing and formatting actions, 285–87
edit mode, InfoPath
filling out forms, 1419–23
filling out new forms, 1397–98
opening forms in, 1417–19
edit points, motion paths, 917
effects, character formats, 310
electronic forms, InfoPath, 16
Electronic Mail command, mail merge, 557
electronic postage, 561
elements, Web pages
formats, 1349–50
positioning, 1346–49
Word, 580
elements, XML, 594, 599, 838
Else, keywords, 1462
Else If, keywords, 1462
e-mail
automatic mailings, 557
delivery of InfoPath forms, 1423
filtering, 14

importing settings, 1085
mail delivery locations, 1091
PowerPoint presentations, 942
protocols for sending and receiving, 1085
shared documents, 470–71
e-mail accounts
adding, modifying, and removing, 1083–85
grouping, 1008–10
options, 1010
Outlook account types, 1080–81
e-mail messages, Outlook, 999–1027
attachments, 964, 1003
categorizing with search folders, 1019–20
creating, 1014–18
default folders, 999–1000
formats, 1011–13
HTML messages, 1005–06
Internet headers, 1004
junk e-mail, 1022–24
options, 1000–1001
organizing, 1021–22
quick flags, 1007–08
receiving, 1001–02
recipient anonymity, 1017
sending, 1014
sending to contacts, 1056
shared attachments, 1018–19
task assignments, 1065
viewing in Message form, 1001–02, 1004
viewing in Reading pane, 1001–02, 1004
embedded charts, 754–57
embedded images, FrontPage, 1255
embedded objects, 170
embedded setting, CSS (Cascading Style Sheets), 1358–60
embedding data, 170–76
by creating new data, 172–73
editing, 173
from entire document, 171–72
example, 174–76
overview, 154, 170
from a portion of an existing document, 171
in PowerPoint, 899
when to use, 154
encryption
file-sharing, 475
SSL, 1226

End If, keywords, 1462
endnotes
converting, 437
inserting, 434–35
moving, 435
numbering format, 435
reformatting, 437
shortcut keys, 436
envelopes
creating, 552
electronic postage, 561
formats, 563
options, 562
printing single, 560
equals sign (=), 618–19, 727
equations
formats, 142
inserting into documents, 139–42
error checking, Excel
background error checking, 614
common errors list, 644
spelling, 644
error checking, PowerPoint, 876
error values, Excel functions, 741–42
event procedures, UserForms, 1484–86
overview, 1484
writing in Code window, 1484–85
events
defined, 1026
journal entries, 1072
setup, 1032
Excel, 605–26
annotating, 618
application interface, 606–08
business analysis tools. See business analysis tools, Excel
charts. See charts, Excel
comments, 616–17
Compare Side By Side mode, 75–76
date settings, 614–16
embedding worksheet in PowerPoint, 174–76
formats. See formats, Excel
formulas. See formulas, Excel
functions. See functions, Excel
graphics, 621–22
hyperlinks, 622–26
InfoPath data, analyzing in, 1398
IRM and, 80–81

linking spreadsheet to Word
report, 168–70
lists. *See* lists, Excel
mapping to tasks, 8
multiple documents, 74–75
New command, 52
new features, 13
New Workbook task pane, 53
numeric values, entering,
611–13
overview, 605
Personal Macro Workbook, 225
PivotCharts. *See* PivotCharts,
Excel
PivotTables. *See* PivotTables,
Excel
Research task pane, 44
saving workbooks, 626
smart documents, 47
starting, 605–06
text values, entering, 613–14
time settings, 614–16
toolbars, 606
Web publishing. *See* Web
publishing, Excel
worksheet editing options. *See*
worksheets, editing
worksheet navigation, 608–11
XML data. *See* XML data, in
Excel
Excel, customizing, 705–25
calculations, 721–22
editing options, 723–24
installing add-in commands and
wizards, 725
multiple panes, 718–20
printing options, 708–18
views, 705–08
worksheet appearance, 722–23
**exceptions to document permis-
sions, 473–74**
exchanging data. *See* data
exchange
exponential operator (^), 732
**Export command, Web sites files,
1254**
**exporting XML documents,
1116–18**
expressions
Access queries, 1156
boolean expressions, 1462
conditional expressions,
1461–62, 1465–66
regular expressions, 1294
Extend mode, 283–84

Extensible Markup Language. *See*
XML (Extensible Markup
Language)
**Extensible Stylesheet Language
Transformations (XSLT), 596**
extensions, file. *See* file extensions
**external content blocking, Outlook,
1005–06**
**external data source, Excel lists,
800**
External Data toolbar, 835–36
external hyperlinks, 1306–08
**external setting, CSS (Cascading
Style Sheets), 1360**

F

F4 (repeat), 285
F5 (Go To), 302–04
F8 (text selection), 284
fast saves, 255–56
fatal errors, 69
Favorites Folders, 1078
faxes
creating in mail merge, 558–59
Internet fax service, 11,
1025–26
new Outlook features, 14
field code switches
indexes, 442
table of contents, 445
fields, Access
databases, 1097
field list, 1179
forms, 1174
queries, 1155, 1163–65
reports, 1201–02
fields, Access tables
adding, 1119–20
building, 1120
descriptions, 1124
moving and copying, 1121
properties, 1122–26
removing, 1120–21
zooming, 1136
fields, InfoPath data sources, 1408
fields, Outlook forms, 955
fields, PivotTables, 794
fields, Web forms, 1363
**fields, Word online documents,
570–71**
file extensions
.adp files, 1107
.dot files, 411, 414
.gif files, 904
.mdb files, 1105, 1107

.mid (.midi) files, 905
.pot files, 865
.ppt files, 876
.pst files, 1088–89
.rmi files, 905
template and wizard files, 50
.wav files, 905
.xml files, 594, 838
file formats
converting, 63, 256–57
converting during saves, 71
new Word features, 13
opening documents in nonnative
format, 58, 63
files. *See also* folders
converting groups of files,
256–57
Open Office Document dialog
box, 60
Save As dialog box, 72–73
sharing, 474
template files (.dot), 411, 414
File Search task pane, 63–69
accessing, 64
advanced, 66–67
compared with Find command,
63
refining search criteria, 67
searching for files or items, 64
tasks performed with, 65
files, Web sites
importing, 1250–51
Windows Explorer compared
with FrontPage for managing,
1239–41
working with, 1247–50
working with imported, 1254
File Transfer Protocol. *See* FTP (File
Transfer Protocol)
Fill Color button, 661
Fill commands, 642–43
fill handle, 641
Fill Series dialog box, 643–44
**Fill submenu, replicating formulas,
729–30**
filters. *See also* sorting
AutoFilter command, 783–85
Graphics Filters feature, 118
junk e-mail, 1022–24
tracking changes, Word documents, 450
filters, Access tables, 1141–47
filtering by form, 1144–46
filtering by selection, 1142–44
filters, Outlook, 979–83

Final change marking mode, track change markup modes, 454
Final Showing Markup, track change markup modes, 454
finances, functions for analyzing, 737–42
Find All command, Excel _worksheets, 633
find and replace
  Access, 1136–37, 1191
  Excel, 632–33
  Find command, 293–97
  formatting, 293–96
  FrontPage, 15
  HTML elements on Web pages, 1389–90
  Outlook, 986–89
  Replace command, 298–99
  search options, 295–96
  text, 293–96, 1136–37
  text elements on Web pages, 1293–96
  wildcards, 296–97
  Word, 293–96, 298–99
Find Duplicates Query Wizard, 1154
Find pane, Outlook, 986–88
Find Unmatched Query Wizard, 1154
flags, quick flags, 15, 1007–08
flat-file databases, 1098–99
Folder items, Outlook, 983–84
Folder List
  activating for FrontPage, 1239–41
  creating new Web pages, 1283
  displaying Outlook folders, 951
  FrontPage, 1235
  importing Web site files and folders, 1250–52
  locations for, 992
  Outlook folders in, 1092
  working with FrontPage folders, 1242–43
  working with Outlook folders, 993
  working with Web site files, 1247–48
Folder view, FrontPage
  activating, 1239–41
  Web site views, 1234
  working with files, 1247–48
  working with folders, 1242–43
folders. See also files
  starting applications from, 40–41

storing linked documents in same folder, 167
vertical scroll bar, 1092
folders, Outlook, 991–97
  creating, 991–93
  default for e-mail messages, 999–1000
  Folder List, 951–52, 993
  hierarchy, 993
  information stored in default folders, 947–48
  opening, 949–53
  opening with Go menu, 952–53
  removing items from, 969
  shortcut to Inbox, 954
  shortcuts for opening, 952
  viewing, 950
folders, Web sites
  importing, 1250–51
  Windows Explorer compared with FrontPage for managing, 1239–41
  working with, 1242–43
Font dialog box, 313–15
  Character Spacing tab, 313
  Font tab, 313
  Format Menu, 400
  opening, 1490
  PowerPoint formatting, 880
  subscripts and superscripts, 315
  Text Effects tab, 314
fonts
  changing in Excel, 656–58
  changing in PowerPoint, 880–81
  character formats, 309
  character formats in Web pages, 1335–36
  characters in, 261
  font substitution, 312
  InfoPath forms, 1411, 1422
  PowerPoint presentations, 860
  sharing, 477
  shortcut keys for managing size of, 318
  size and color options in PowerPoint, 878
  TrueType fonts, 314, 477
  Web pages and, 579
  Window Font color, 368
footers. See headers and footers
footnotes
  converting, 437
  inserting, 434–35
  numbering format, 435
  reformatting, 437
  shortcut keys, 436

For...Each loop, 1472–75
forecasts, business
  editing Solver forecasts, 813–14
  Goal Seek, 806–07
  Solver, 808
foreign characters, 261–64
Form, database objects, 1101–02
Form command, Excel lists, 773–74
form design tasks, InfoPath, 1411–12
form letters, mail merge, 558–59
form libraries, WSS
  adding to SharePoint team Web site, 1243–47
  customizing, 204–05
  document libraries, 178, 182
  picture libraries, 178, 182
Form Properties dialog box, 1366–67
Form submenu commands, 1365–66
form templates, InfoPath
  based on SQL (structured query language), 1402
  basing new form on, 1418
  creating new, 1396, 1399–1402
  designing InfoPath forms, 1394–95
  extracting files from, 1413
  file structure of, 1397
  modifying, 1400–1401
  overview, 1394
Form Wizard, 1173–76
Format dialog box, 514–15
Format Menu of Modify Style dialog box, 400–402
Format Object dialog box, 149–51
Format Painter
  copying formats between worksheet cells, 662
  copying PowerPoint formats, 881
Format Picture dialog box, 714
Format Settings dialog box, 259, 332
formats, Access
  databases, 1111
  forms, 1183–89
  reports, 1205–06
formats, Excel
  alignment, 648–51
  AutoFit command, 665

AutoFormat command, 665–66
borders, 658–60
cell formats, 647
characters, 659
column width, 662–64
conditional formats, 666–68
copying with Format Painter, 662
currency symbol, 655–56
date, 615
numbers, 651–54
page breaks, 675–77
PivotTables, 797–98
row height, 662–64
shading, 660–61
styles, 668–72
templates, 672–75
text font and color, 656–58
time, 615
formats, Excel charts, 758–66
character formats, 761–62
Chart menu, 758–59
Chart toolbar, 759
chart type, 759–60
copying, 765–66
gridline adjustments, 763–64
legends, 764
numeric, 762–63
titles and labels, 760–61
formats, FrontPage, 1301
formats, graphics, 118, 1301
formats, Outlook
e-mail messages, 1011–13
HTML e-mail messages,
1005–06
notes, 1075
formats, PowerPoint, 877–93
alignment, 885
backgrounds, 888–90
bulleted lists, 881–83
color schemes, 887–88
copying, 881
fonts, 880–81
indents, 883–85
line spacing, 885
numbered lists, 881–83
presentation masters, 890–93
sound clips, 905
Tab settings, 883–85
tables, 897–98
text, 867–68, 878–80
formats, Word, 307–43
applying, 330–33
automatic formats, 340–43
character. See character
formats, Word
envelopes, 563

equations, 142
formatting consistency checker,
330
graphic objects, 149–51
horizontal dividing lines, 585
hyperlinks, 582
labels, 564
movie clips, 586
page numbers, 520, 527
paragraph. See paragraph formats
removing, 333–34
replacing, 299
Reveal Formatting task pane,
338–40
saved formats, 329–33, 337
searches for, 299
searching for, 295
selecting text with same formatting or style, 335–36
Show/Hide, 260
styles. See styles, Word
table styles, 357–59
undoing/redoing, 285–87
Web pages, 591–93
formatting consistency checker,
330
Formatting Restriction dialog box,
473
Formatting toolbar, Excel
Fill Color button, 661
fonts and text color options, 657
numeric formats, 653
setting format options, 649
Formatting toolbar, PowerPoint
indentation, 884
text formats, 878–79
Formatting toolbar, Web pages
character formats, 1333
paragraph formats, 1322–24
Formatting toolbar, Word
Border button, 365
bulleted lists, 377–78
character formats, 317
numbered lists, 377–78
overview, 248
paragraph formats, 325
saved formats, 337
styles, 337
forms, Access, 1171–93
adding fields from tables or
queries, 1176–78
AutoForm options, 1172
copying data in, 1192–93
customizing, 1178–81
data entry, 1190
editing data, 1189–92

formats, 1183–89
Form Wizard, 1173–76
options for creating, 1171–72
toolbox buttons for modifying,
1181–83
forms, Excel lists, 773–75
forms, FrontPage
interactive Web forms, 1363–67
predesigned, 1232
forms, InfoPath
adding controls, 1406–08
data source, 1408–10
delivering, 1398, 1423–24
designing, 1398, 1411–12
electronic forms, 16
filling out, 1397–98, 1419–23
form libraries, 1415
laying out, 1404–05
saving, 1423
views, 1410–11
forms, Outlook
browsing Outlook items with,
962
Contacts, 1049–51
dates, 963
fields, 955
Tasks, 1062
forms, Word documents, 473
formula bar, Excel, 611
formulas, Excel, 727–46
arithmetic operators, 732–33
building, 727–28
built-in functions, 733–34
calculation options, 721–22
cell references, 619–20
creating, 620
editing, 732
entering, 618
function error values, 741–42
FV function, 739–40
Insert Function command,
736–37
multiplying numbers, 728–29
naming functions, 742–46
PMT function, 738–39
RATE function, 740–41
replicating between cells,
729–31
SUM function, 735
formulas, inserting into Word
tables, 361
formulas, VBA, 1456–59
macros for computing formulas
in documents, 1456–59
mathematical operators, 1456

For...Next loops, 1469–72
managing tables with, 1470–72
overview, 1469–70
Forward button, task pane navigation, 44
fractions, Excel numeric values, 612
Frame Properties dialog box, 1371
frames, text positioning, 401, 528
frames, Web pages, 1367–74
creating frames page, 1368–70
hyperlinks, 1371–72
inline frames, 1372–74
properties, 1370–71
in Word, 590–91
frames document, 591
frames page, 591, 1368–70
free/busy options, planning meetings, 1039
free-form Web pages
adding to Web sites, 202
customizing, 203–04
freestanding mode, Clip Organizer, 113–16
FrontPage, 1219–37. See also Web sites
deleting Web sites, 1229
editing Web sites, 1231–32
mapping to tasks, 9
naming Web sites, 1228
navigation tools, 1233–35
new features, 15–16
opening Web sites, 1229–31
overview, 1219–21
positioning elements in Web pages, 1346–49
Server Extensions, 1222
SharePoint team Web site, 1232–33
styles, 1324–25
subsites, 1228
templates and wizards, 49
themes, 1353–56
transition effects, 1356–57
usage reports, 1232
as Web page editor, 1221–22
Web pages. See Web pages, FrontPage
Web site templates, 1223–27
Web site views, 1236–37
working offline or online, 1222–23
working with HTML source code in Design view, 1383–84
FrontPage Server Extensions, 1277

FTP (File Transfer Protocol)
FrontPage support for, 1222, 1273
opening documents from FTP sites, 58–59
saving documents to FTP sites, 72
functions, Access, 1161
functions, Excel
built-in, 618, 733–34
categories of, 734
changing in PivotTables, 796–97
defined, 733
error values, 741–42
FV function, 739–40
Insert Function command, 736–37
naming, 742–46
PMT function, 738–39
RATE function, 740–41
Subtotals command, 787
SUM function, 735
functions, VBA, 1448–51
arguments, 1451
Format, 1458
InputBox, 1448–51
MsgBox, 1452–54
FV function (future value), 739–40

G

Gallery tab, Office Assistant, 28–29
Getting Started task pane
functions of, 44
Office 2003 new features, 11
opening, 34
GIF (Graphics Interchange Format)
.gif extension, 904
graphic file formats, 1301–02
global entries, indexes, 440
global templates, 409, 416
Go menu, Outlook, 952–53
Go To command (Ctrl+Y)
dates, 1066
moving insertion point, 302–04
Outlook folders, 953
worksheet navigation, 610
Goal Seek command, 805–07
forecasting with, 806–07
setting up worksheets for, 805–06
grammar checking
customizing, 496–97
existing text, 493–95
while typing, 490–92

graphics, 107–51
adding to Web pages, 1300–1302
alignment in Web pages, 1292
for charts, 136–38
combining with text boxes in page layout, 514–16
diagram templates. See diagrams, Office
drawing toolbar, 144–49
drawings. See AutoShapes
format changes, 149–51
formats for, 1301–02
headers and footers, 529, 714
importing pictures, 117–19
importing Web site graphics files, 1252–53
mouse and, 142–44, 284
object modifications, 142
picture modifications, 119–23
pictures, inserting. See Clip Organizer
positioning in Web pages, 1346–49
for presentations. See presentations, PowerPoint
scaling, 252
shortcut menu, 152
templates, 409
text effects, 133–36
for Word tables, 347
for worksheets, 621–22
graphics, PowerPoint, 898–902
adding to slides, 898–99
grids and drawing guides, 900–901
photo album, 902
saving PowerPoint elements as pictures, 900
Graphics Filters feature, 118
Graphics Interchange Format (GIF)
.gif extension, 904
graphic file formats, 1301–02
graphs. See Microsoft Graph
gridlines, Excel
adding, 763–64
charts, 750
printing options, 716
gridlines, Power Point, 900–901
gridlines, Word cells
drawing tables, 356
overview, 346
resizing table cells, 350
grouping levels, Access reports, 1203–04, 1214

groups
Access reports, 1202–03, 1213–15
e-mail accounts, 1008–10
InfoPath data source, 1408
Outlook items, 981–83
performing calculations on, 1162
shortcut group, 1079
Guess button, Solver, 811

H

handout masters, PowerPoint, 891
handouts
defined, 891
PowerPoint slide shows, 937
handwriting interface
accessing, 97
character formats, 99
functions of, 96–97
handwriting recognition, 99–101
ink mode, 98–99
inserting sketches, 103–05
On-Screen keyboards, 105
text mode, 101–02
Writing Pad window, 98
hard page breaks, 547
headers and footers
Access reports, 1211, 1216
creating, 524–27
defined, 519
Excel printing options, 710–14
graphic objects in, 529
Internet headers, 1004
PowerPoint slides, 852
sizing and positioning, 527–29
symmetric, 537
varying within documents, 529–30
Word formats, 527
headings
changing levels, 422–23
copying, 433
navigating document, 430–32
outlines, 425
printing options, Excel, 718
styles, 337, 420
Height command, worksheet rows, 664
Help, 23
Ask A Question list, 29
Excel Help button, 607
Help task pane, 30–33
Office Assistant, 25–29
online resources, 33–35

Help task pane, 30–33
asking a question, 30–32
browsing, 32–33
displaying, 30
Office 2003 new features, 11
hiding
Hide Grammatical Errors In This Document, 492
Hide Spelling Errors In This Document, 482
rows and columns in worksheets, 664
slides in PowerPoint presentations, 931–32
text highlighting, 466
worksheets, 699
highlighting text, 466–68
blocks of text, 466
finding, 467
hiding, 466
PowerPoint slide shows and, 935
printing, 466
removing, 468
home pages
customizing, 203–04
designating, 1280
Outlook Today, 997
WSS task options, 179–81
horizontal alignment, Excel, 648–50
horizontal dividing lines
formatting, 585, 1350
functions of, 583
InfoPath forms, 1411, 1422
inserting, 583–85
separating Web page content with, 1305
text alignment, 387
horizontal rulers
adjusting columns, 374–75
headers and footers, 528
paragraph formats, 326
setting margins, 537–39
horizontal scroll bar, 608
Horizontal Spacing, Web page images, 1338
hosting services, 1277
hotfixes, Office, 23
hotspots, image maps, 1344
.htm or .html formats, 576, 939–40, 1221
HTML (Hypertext Markup Language)
data access pages and, 1193

e-mail security and, 14, 1005–06
Excel and, 823
FrontPage as HTML editor, 1279
online documents and, 569
saving InfoPath forms as, 1398, 1424
source code. See source code, HTML
Web pages and, 576, 1221
Word formats, 573
HTML IMG element, 1253, 1255
HTTP (Hypertext Transfer Protocol), 1222
hung applications, 70
hyperlinks
adding to Web pages, 1306–08
creating, 580–82
display options, 1261–62
formats, 334, 582
frames, 1371–72
internal or external, 1255
linking data, 168
modifying, 583
removing, 1307
rollover effects, 1352
targets, 1306
verifying and repairing, 1262, 1270–73
hyperlinks, Access forms, 1177
hyperlinks, Excel
activating, 625–26
creating in worksheets, 622–24
editing and removing, 626
hyperlinks, InfoPath forms, 1411, 1422
hyperlinks, Outlook items, 965
hyperlinks, PowerPoint presentations, 918–19
Hyperlinks reports, Web sites, 1270–73
Hyperlinks view, Web sites, 1260–62
Hypertext Markup Language. See HTML (Hypertext Markup Language)
Hypertext Transfer Protocol (HTTP), 1222
hyphenation
automatic, 501–02
inserting hyphen characters, 504–05
manual, 503–04
methods, 500–501
paragraph formats, 321
hyphenation zone, 502

I

iCalendar, 1036
icons
  customizing, 218–19
  displaying data as, 165
If...Then decision structures, 1462–66
  converting Word styles, 1463–65
  keywords (ElseIf, Else, and End If), 1462
  overview, 1462
Image button, UserForms, 1480
image formats, Web pages, 1336–45
  cropping images, 1343
  image maps, 1344
  overview, 1336–37
  Picture Properties dialog box, 1337–40
  Pictures toolbar, 1340–42
  resampling reduced images, 1338
  transparency controls, 1343
  video clips, 1344–45
image maps, 1344
image menus, 220
images. *See* graphics
IM (Instant Messaging), 1050
importing
  data with queries, 833–35
  e-mail settings, 1085
  media clips, 116–17
  Outlook contacts, 1060
  pictures, 117–19
  Web site files and folders, 1250–52, 1254
  XML data, 839–43
  XML documents, 1116–18
In Line With Text, wrapping style, 121
Inbox folder, Outlook
  information stored in, 947
  shortcut to, 954
inches, units of measurement, 316
Include Text field, 429
indentation
  compared with margins, 538–39
  paragraph formats, 320, 324, 325
  paragraph formats, Web pages, 1324
  PowerPoint, 883–85
  Word lists and, 378, 382

indeterminate data, 1132
indexes, 438–42
  Access fields, 1127
  compiling, 440–41
  customizing entries, 441–42
  entries, 438–40
  field code switches, 442
  global entries, 440
  spelling errors, 442
  subentries, 438–40
Indexing Service, 65–66
InfoPath
  adding controls to forms, 1406–08
  data sources for forms, 1408–10
  delivering forms, 1398, 1423–24
  designing forms, 1394–97, 1411–12
  edit mode, 1417–19
  extracting files from form templates, 1413
  features, 1393
  filling out new forms, 1397–98, 1419–23
  form libraries, 1415
  form views, 1410–11
  laying out forms, 1404–05
  mapping to tasks, 9
  modifying form templates, 1400–1401
  new features in Office 2003, 16
  new form templates, 1399–1402
  printing forms, 1424
  saving form templates, 1412–15
  saving forms, 1423
information exchange, WSS, 198–201
information gathering. *See* InfoPath
information pages, WSS
  customizing, 204–05
  document libraries, 182
  form libraries, 182
  functions of, 182–83
  lists, 181–82
  picture libraries, 182
Information Rights Management (IRM), 11, 80–81, 1013
Information Viewer, Outlook, 973, 1054

ink annotations, 466, 618
inline frames, Web pages, 1372–74
inline graphic objects, Word, 144
inline setting, CSS (Cascading Style Sheets), 1358
InputBox function, VBA, 1448–51
INS Key For Paste option, 292
Insert Function command, Excel, 736–37
Insert mode, Word, 259
Insert Table button, Standard toolbar, 346
insertion points
  moving, 302–04
  positioning, 281
installing Office 2003, 17–20
  activation, 19–21
  application selection and configuration, 19–20
  installation type, 18
  revisiting Setup, 22–23
Instant Messaging (IM), 1050
integers, Excel numeric values, 612
IntelliSense, 1386
interactive forms, Web pages, 1363–67
interactive Web pages
  compared with static Web pages, 824–25
  limitations of, 825
  working with in browser, 830–32
interface. *See* application interface
internal hyperlinks, Web pages, 1306–08
Internet directory services, 1087
Internet Explorer
  displaying Web pages in, 824
  Save Picture As option, 1253
Internet fax service, 11, 1025–26
Internet headers, e-mail messages, 1004
investments, calculating rate of return, 740–41
IRM (Information Rights Management), 11, 80–81, 1013
Italic button, Formatting toolbar, 317
italic text
  PowerPoint and, 878–79
  shortcut key for, 318
items, Outlook, 955–91
  adding to e-mail message, 964
  archiving, 970–72

columns in Table view, 977–79
copying, 966–68
creating, 956–60
creating from existing items, 959
creating items similar to existing items, 961
editing, 961–65
filtering, 979–83
finding, 986–89
Folder items, 983–84
grouping, 979–83
hyperlinks, 965
methods for defining, 956
moving, 966–68
organizing, 990
Reading pane, 984–86
removing, 969–70
saving to disk, 965
sorting, 979–83
switching views, 973–77
types of, 956
view options, 973
iteration process, Goal Seek, 805–06

J

Joint Photographic Experts Group (JPEG), 1301–02
join types, relationships, 1158
Journal Entry form, 1071–73
Journal folder, Outlook, 1068–73
automatic journaling, 1069
categories and, 1073
information stored in, 947
Journal Entry Form, 1071–72
linking entry to contacts, 1056
manual journaling, 1071
navigating journal timelines, 1073
opening journal entries, 1070
overview, 1068
recording entries, 1068–70
viewing entries for a contact, 1070
JPEG (Joint Photographic Experts Group), 1301–02
junk e-mail, 1022–24
Junk E-mail folder, Outlook, 947

K

kerning, 311, 315
keyboard commands, spoken versions of, 94
keyboard shortcuts
assigning to styles, 399

character formats, 318
currency symbols, 654
defining in Word, 222–23
deleting text, 282
editing text in PowerPoint, 869
footnotes and endnotes, 436
for frequently used symbols, 264
inserting characters, 263
moving insertion point, 281
navigating Excel worksheets, 609–10
opening Outlook Inbox, 954
paragraph formats, 326–27
running macros, 228
selecting ranges of cells, 629
selecting text, 283
series in worksheets, 643
templates, 410
tracking changes in Word documents, 449
keyboards
On-Screen Standard Keyboard, 105
On-Screen Symbol Keyboard, 105
keywords
Elself, Else, and End If, 1462
imported media clips and, 117
searching for clips by, 109

L

Label button, UserForms, 1479–80
labels, 563–67
Access reports and, 1200–1201
adding to Office diagrams, 132
creating, 552
customizing, 566
formats, 564
graphic images on, 566
postal bar codes, 566
series in worksheets, 641–44
labels, Excel
changing chart labels, 760–61
charts, 750
worksheets, 613
landscape orientation
page layout, 534
worksheet print outs, 709
Language Bar
buttons on, 88–89
customizing, 96
Handwriting button, 97
Tools button, 95

Language dialog box, 401, 506
Language indicator, on Word status bar, 245
languages
automatic detection, 507–08
character formats, 311
currency symbols, 655
manual formatting, 508
marking to exclude from proofing, 505–07
spell checking, 484
Web pages, 578, 1352
layout
Access reports, 1205–06, 1216
InfoPath forms, 1404–05
layout cells, FrontPage, 15, 1312–13
Layout Preview, Access reports, 1215
layout tables, FrontPage, 15, 1311–13
LCD (liquid crystal display), 926
LDAP (Lightweight Directory Access Protocol), 1080
legends
Excel charts, 750, 764
PivotCharts, 799
letters, Word options for writing, 567
libraries
form libraries. See form libraries, WSS
Microsoft Office Picture Manager, 1339
object library, 1443
Schema Library, 601
Lightweight Directory Access Protocol (LDAP), 1080
line breaks, paragraph formats, 320
line numbers
adding, 542
documents, 303
paragraph formats, 321
reformatting, 543
line spacing
paragraph formats, 320, 324–25
PowerPoint, 885
lines, units of measurement, 316
link bars
adding, 1256–57
customizing labeling of, 1258
Web site navigation, 1255–56

linking data, 162–70
  editing links, 166–67
  entire document, 163–64
  Excel spreadsheet to Word
    report, 168–70
  hyperlinks, 168
  overview, 154, 162
  parts of a document, 163
  PowerPoint, 164
  storing linked documents in
    same folder, 167
  updates, 166
  when to use, 154
links
  breaking chart links to freeze
    data, 758
  text boxes, 513
  workbooks, 688–89
  worksheets, 685
liquid crystal display (LCD), 926
List Bullet style, 337
list commands, Excel 2003, 13,
  800–802
list styles
  modifying, 397, 406
  outline numbered list, 383–84
  types of styles and, 329
List submenu, 802
List toolbar, 802
lists
  adding to SharePoint team Web
    site, 1243–47
  creating, 1245
  WSS information components,
    181–82
lists, Excel, 771–803
  analyzing with PivotCharts. *See*
    PivotCharts, Excel
  analyzing with PivotTables. *See*
    PivotTables, Excel
  commands for working with,
    800–803
  converting to Access database,
    788–89
  creating, 771–73
  data entries forms, 773–75
  data validation, 775–77
  finding records, 783–85
  limitations when dealing with
    databases, 788
  list commands, 800–803
  sorting lists of more than one
    column, 779–81
  sorting one column lists,
    778–79

sort order, 781–83
Subtotals command and,
  785–88
lists, Word, 377–84
  bulleted, 379–80
  Bullets And Numbering dialog
    box, 377
  converting bulleted or numbered
    list to an outline, 282
  Formatting toolbar, 377–78
  indentation, 382
  numbered, 380–81
  ordering text, 377
  outline numbered list, 381–84
  sorting paragraphs, 384–86
lists, WSS, 178
  creating, 202
  customizing, 204–05
  participating in, 198–201
loans
  FV function (future value),
    739–40
  PMT function, 738–39
locked cells, 699
logical operators, 1465–66

M

macros
  adding, 1428
  CenterHeading macro, 1444–47
  command for running, 218
  computing formulas in docu-
    ments, 1456–59
  conditional expressions,
    1461–62
  continuation character (_),
    1446–47
  copying to Word's normal tem-
    plate, 1457
  defined, 224
  descriptive statements, adding
    to, 1430–31
  dim statements for variables,
    1447–48
  For...Each loops, 1472–75
  For...Next loops, 1469–72
  If...Then decision structures,
    1462–66
  online documents, 569
  for printing current selection,
    547–48
  procedure calls, 1448–50
  recording, 225–27
  running, 227–28, 1433
  saving place in documents,
    301–02

security, 229–32
Select Case decision structures,
  1466–69
templates, 409
undoing, 229
UserForms. *See* UserForms
when to build, 224–25
workbook security, 703
magnification, 705. *See also* zoom
Mail Delivery Location, Outlook,
  1091
mailings, Word, 549–67
  creating main document,
    551–52
  editing main document, 554–55
  envelopes, 560–63
  generating output documents,
    557
  labels, 563–67
  recipient list, 553
  types of output documents, 549
  working with output documents,
    556
mail merge, 549–59
  commands, 558
  creating faxes, form letters, and
    directories, 558–59
  creating main document,
    551–52
  editing main document, 554–55
  generating output documents,
    557
  Mail Merge toolbar, 554
  Mail Merge Wizard, 550
  Outlook and, 1056
  printing output documents,
    1201
  recipient list, 553
  types of output documents, 549
  working with output documents,
    556
Mail Setup tab, 1011
main document, mail merge, 549,
  551–52, 554–55
maintenance mode, Office, 22–23
maintenance queries, 1154
make-table queries, 1170
Manual Update, 166
many-to-many relationships, 1133
margin balloons, 448
margins
  compared with indentation,
    538–39
  Excel printing options, 710
  marking, 537
  paragraph formats, 324

setting with Margins tab,
533–37
setting with rulers, 537–39
Web pages, 1352
**marquees, adding to Web pages,
588–89**
Master Document view, 426–28
**masters, PowerPoint presenta-
tions, 890–93**
types of, 891
working with, 891–93
**mathematical equations, inserting
into documents, 139–42**
**mathematical functions, Access,
1101**
**mathematical functions, Word,
242**
**mathematical operators, Excel,
732–33**
formulas, 618, 727
list of, 732
order of evaluation, 732–33
**mathematical operators, VBA,
1456**
mathematical symbols, Excel, 612
**Max function, Excel worksheets,
689**
.mdb files, 1105, 1107
media clips. *See also* **Clip Organizer**
accessing online, 112
defined, 107
drop-down menu, 114
importing, 116–17
inserting, 111–12, 125
inserting using drag-and-drop,
115
keyword searches, 109
searching for, 109–10
meetings
creating workspace for, 1233
defined, 1026
planning, 1037–39
requesting of contacts, 1056
scheduling, 1033–37
SharePoint workspace, 178,
1039–42
**members, distribution lists, 1047,
1053–54**
menu items
adding/removing, 214–15
modifying, 216–17
overview, 213
menus
accessing in full-screen mode,
253
adding/removing, 214–15

application interface, 219–20
Arrange By submenu, 14,
983–84
customizing, 12
drop-down menus, 114
image menus, 220
Microsoft Office submenu, 39
Microsoft Office Tools submenu,
41
Modify Selection menu, 216–17
Object submenu, 174
overview, 213
Rearrange Commands dialog
box and, 220–21
shortcut menus. *See* shortcut
menus
Start menu, 39
menus, Excel
Chart menu, 758–59
Data menu, 785
Fill submenu, 729–30
List submenu, 802
Picture submenu, 621
menus, FrontPage, 1365–66
menus, Outlook, 952–53
menus, PowerPoint, 850
menus, VBA, 1432–33
menus, Word
AutoText submenu, 268
Draw menu, 146–47
Table menu, 359–60
templates and, 410
merge fields, 549
merging documents, 458
Merging styles, 671–72
Message form, 1001–02, 1004
methods, VBA, 1441
.mht, 576
.mhtml, 576
.mht or .mhtml, 940
microphone
adding voice comments,
463–64
recording narration for slide
shows, 929
speech recognition, 83, 86
Microphone Wizard, 84
Microsoft Access. *See* **Access**
Microsoft Equation, 139–42, 173
Microsoft Excel. *See* **Excel**
Microsoft FrontPage. *See*
FrontPage
Microsoft Graph
adding to Access forms, 1172
animating in PowerPoint, 914
constructing charts, 136–38

embedding data, 173
PowerPoint presentations and,
899
**Microsoft Office Picture Manager,
1339**
Microsoft Office submenu, 39
Microsoft Office Tools submenu, 41
Microsoft Outlook. *See* **Outlook**
Microsoft PowerPoint. *See*
PowerPoint
**Microsoft Visual Basic Help,
1441–42**
Microsoft Windows, 1107
Microsoft Word. *See* **Word**
.mid (.midi) files, 905
**millimeters, units of measurement,
316**
**Min function, Excel worksheets,
689**
Mirror Margins, 534, 536–37
mixed cell references, 731
modems, 1057
Modify Selection menu, 216–17
Modify Style dialog box, 394–402
accessing, 394–95
Automatically Update option,
280
default styles in, 395–97
Format Menu, 400–402
options , 394, 397–99
**module containers, for macros,
1429**
motion paths, 914–16
mouse
handwriting with, 105
managing columns and rows in
Excel, 663
modifying graphic objects,
142–44
moving and copying text with,
287–89
moving cells, rows, and columns
in Word tables, 353
rearranging PowerPoint slides,
872
selecting ranges of cells,
627–28
selecting text, 286
selecting worksheets rows and
columns, 627–28
selection techniques, 284
movie clips
adding to Web pages, 585–87,
1300
formats, 586
PowerPoint, 903–04

moving and copying
  data statically. *See* static copy-
    ing/moving data
  fields, Access tables, 1121
  Outlook items, 966–68
  rows, columns, or cells in Word
    tables, 353
  text boxes, 512–13
  text, with Clipboard, 289–91
  text, with mouse, 287–89
  Web pages, 1289–90
  worksheets, 683–85
MsgBox function, VBA, 1452–54
multi-line layout, Outlook, 978
multiple documents, 74–76
  comparing side by side, 75–76
  managing, 74–75
multiple masters, PowerPoint, 892
multiple panes, worksheets,
  718–20
multiplication operator (*), 729,
  732
multiplying numbers, Excel,
  728–29
multivariable forecasting. *See*
  Solver
My Folders, 1078
My Network Places
  accessing team Web site, 178
  opening shared documents, 58
  saving documents to shared
    drives, 71
My Places, 61
My Recent Documents, 11, 58

N

names, Access
  fields, 1122
  reports, 1207
names, Excel functions, 742–46
  cell and range names, 742–44
  deleting/modifying, 745–46
  errors, 745
  inserting into formulas or func-
    tions, 744
names, Web sites, 1228
names, worksheets, 681
narration, PowerPoint slide shows,
  929–30
navigation, Web sites
  Hyperlinks view, 1260–62
  Navigation view, 1255–60
  options for Web sites, 1254–55
navigation
  browse buttons, 304–05

  Excel worksheets, 608–11
  FrontPage, 1233–35
  link bars, 1255–56
  PowerPoint slide shows, 934
  with scroll bars, 281
  through an outline, 429–32
  viewing, 1260
  Web toolbar, 583
navigation keys, 525
Navigation pane, Outlook, 14,
  1077–78
Navigation view, Web sites,
  1255–60
negative indents, Word tables, 361
NetMeeting, 1057
Netscape Navigator, 824
New command
  creating empty Office document,
    52–53
  creating new database, 1104
New Document task pane, 53–55
"new from existing" feature, 59
New Office Document command,
  39
New Office Document dialog box,
  47–52
newsletters, Word, 241
newspaper-style columns. *See* columns, Word documents
New Style dialog box, 404–06
nonbreaking space, 505
nonprinting characters, Show/
  Hide, 260
Normal style
  shortcut key, 337
  text, 336
Normal template, Word, 1457
Normal view
  adding comments, 459–61
  PowerPoint, 849, 852
  viewing, editing, or deleting
    comments, 462–66
  Word, 249
Normal.dot template, 225
notation, cell ranges, 628
Notes folder, Outlook
  categories, 1075–76
  entering notes, 1074
  formats, 1075
  information stored in, 947
  organizing with colors, 1076
notes masters, PowerPoint, 891
Notes Page view, PowerPoint, 854
numbered lists
  Bullets and Numbering dialog
    box, 380–81

  converting to an outline, 282
  creating, 380–81
  Format Menu, 401
  InfoPath forms, 1411, 1423
  outline numbered list, 381–84
  PowerPoint, 881–83
  Web pages, 1323, 1326–27
numbers
  Excel chart formats, 762–63
  Excel formats, 651–54
  paragraph formats, 322
  series in worksheets, 641–44
numbers, page. *See* page numbers
numeric values, Excel, 611–13

O

Object Browser, VBA, 1441
object linking and embedding
  (OLE), 41, 570
object model, Office, 1441–42
Object submenu, 174
objects, VBA, 1440, 1443
object types, converting, 174
Office 2003 suite
  advantages of, 4
  applications in, 3
  features, 4–7
  mapping applications to tasks,
    7–10
  new application: InfoPath, 16
  new features by application,
    13–16
  new features shared by most
    applications, 11–12
  utilities, 3
Office Assistant, 25–29
  asking a question, 26
  customizing interface, 210
  hiding, 28
  options, 28–29
  Search Results task pane, 27
  turning on or off, 25–26
Office Clipboard
  activation methods, 158–59
  compared with Windows Clip-
    board, 158
  pasting blocks of data from,
    160–61
  pasting data in Excel, 637
  shortcut menu, 162
Office diagrams. *See* diagrams,
  Office
Office object model, 1441–42
Office Online
  Clip Art, 112

document templates from, 55–56
getting help online, 33–35
Office 2003 new features, 11
Search text box, 55
Office Shortcut Bar, 41
Office Web Components, 828
OLAP (online analytical processing) cubes, 800
OLE (object linking and embedding), 41, 570
one-to-many relationships, Access fields, 1130
one-to-one relationships, Access fields, 1130
online analytical processing (OLAP) cubes, 800
online documents, 569–73
fields in, 570–71
macros, 569
object linking and embedding, 570
overview, 569–70
Reading Layout view, 571–73
online resources, 33–35, 112
On-Screen Standard Keyboard, 105
On-Screen Symbol Keyboard, 105
Open As Copy command, 59
Open command (Ctrl+O), 62–63, 1111
Open dialog box, 62–63
Open Office Document command, 40
Open Office Document dialog box
customizing My Places, 61
documents, opening, 57–62
file and folder management, 60
opening
Access databases, 1111
documents. See documents, opening
Font dialog box, 1490
Outlook folders, 949–52
Outlook Inbox, 954
Outlook journal entries, 1070
SharePoint team Web site, 188
Web pages, 1288–89
Web sites, 1229–31
Word, 255
operators
comparison operators, 1146, 1156, 1461
logical operators, 1465–66
mathematical, 140, 1456
optional hyphens, 504–05
optional sections, InfoPath, 1405, 1421

Options tab of Customize dialog box, 232–35
organization charts
adding artwork to worksheets, 621
adding to PowerPoint slides, 899
animating in PowerPoint, 914
creating, 128–29
disappearing in Word, 127
Organize pane, Outlook, 990–91, 1021–22
Organizer
copying macros and templates, 417
templates and, 407, 412–13
Or logic, 1156
Other Corrections tab, 274
Outline level, paragraph formats, 321
outline numbered list
converting bulleted or numbered lists to, 382
creating, 381–82
list styles, 383–84
outlines, PowerPoint
creating, 871
modifying, 871–72
overview, 870–71
Outline view
adding comments, 459–61
advantages of, 419
changing outline levels, 422–24
collapsing/expanding outline text, 426–29
Document Map, 430–32
headings using outline levels, 425
Master Document view, 428
moving blocks of text, 425–26
navigating through an outline, 429–32
paragraph formats, 419
printing outlines, 432
Subtotals command, 788
switching to, 420–21
symbol in, 421
trouble copying outline headings, 433
Word and, 249
working with comments, 462–66
Outlining toolbar
collapsing/expanding outline text, 426–28
expanding and duplicating PowerPoint slides, 873

heading levels, 422–23
illustration of, 420
PowerPoint, 871
Outlook
Advanced toolbar, 953–54
archiving data, 1089
calendars. See Calendar folder, Outlook
compared with Outlook Express, 946
contacts. See Contacts folder, Outlook
e-mail messages. See e-mail messages, Outlook
e-mailing InfoPath forms, 1398, 1423
Folder List, 951
folders. See folders, Outlook
forms, 955
Go menu, 952–53
Go To Folder, 953
Internet fax service, 1025–26
items. See items, Outlook
journal entries. See Journal folder, Outlook
mapping to tasks, 8
new features, 14–15
notes. See Notes folder, Outlook
overview, 945
printing, 994–95
setup, 946
shortcuts, 952
tasks. See Tasks folder, Outlook
viewing information in, 947–50
Outlook, customizing, 1077–93
address book accounts, 1082–83, 1086
address lookups, 1081–82
data files, 1088–93
directory accounts, 1080, 1086
e-mail accounts, 1083–85
Favorites Folders list, 1078
My Folders list, 1078
Navigation pane buttons, 1077–78
profiles, 1087–88
Shortcuts list, 1079–80
Outlook Express, 946
Outlook Today folder, Outlook
customizing, 996
functions of, 995–97
home pages and, 997
information stored in, 948
output documents
mail merge, 549
printing, 1201
overhead transparencies, 925

Overtype mode, Word, 259
OVR indicator, 259
owner, of tasks, 1060

P

Package for CD, PowerPoint, 13, 932–33
packages, FrontPage, 16, 1219
Page area, PivotTables, 794–96
page banners, 1260
Page Break Preview, 676–77
page breaks
  adjusting, 546–47
  paragraph formats, 321
  worksheets, 675–77
page connection properties, data access pages, 1198
page elements. *See* elements, Web pages
page layout, Word, 509–39
  books/booklets, 541–43
  creating headers and footers, 524–27
  designing, 509–10
  graphics, 514–16
  margin settings with Margins tab, 533–37
  margin settings with rulers, 537–39
  options, 532–33
  page numbers, 519–22, 531
  printer-ready publications, 241
  sectioning documents, 522–23
  sizing and positioning headers and footers, 527–29
  text boxes, 510–16
  text orientation, 534–36
  varying headers and footers within a document, 529–30
  watermarks, 517–19
page numbers, 519–22
  applying to document sections, 521, 531
  automatic, 519–21, 531
  formats, 527
  reformatting, 522
  section breaks, 531
page orientation
  Excel printing options, 709
  Word page layout, 534
Page Properties dialog box, 1350–53
page setup
  Access reports, 1216

borders and shading in Word documents, 362
  templates, 409
  worksheets, 710–14
pagination adjustments, 546–47
Paint program, 119
paper
  options for printing books/booklets, 540–41
  options for printing worksheets, 709
Paper Orientation drop-down list, 451
Paragraph dialog box
  Format Menu, 400
  headers and footers, 528
  paragraph formats, 323–24, 1325–26
paragraph formats, Web pages, 1322–32
  alignment, 1324–26
  borders, 1324, 1329–31
  bulleted lists, 1323, 1326–27
  dynamic HTML effects, 1331–32
  Formatting toolbar, 1322–24
  indentation, 1324
  numbered lists, 1323, 1326–27
  overview, 1322
  paragraph styles, 1323–25
  removing formatting, 1328–29
  shading, 1329–31
paragraph formats, Word, 318–27
  applying directly to paragraphs, 319
  bulleted lists, 377
  Formatting toolbar, 325
  headers and footers, 527
  horizontal ruler, 326
  indentation, 883
  line spacing options, 325
  numbered lists, 377
  Outline view, 419
  page breaks, 546–47
  Paragraph dialog box, 323–24
  paragraph styles, 328
  shortcut keys, 326–27
  types of, 319–22
paragraph marks, Show/Hide, 260
paragraph styles, 328
  applying, 330–33
  creating by example, 403–04
  customizing, 393
  deleting, 403
  headers and footers, 527

modifying, 397
  Web pages, 1323–25
  working with, 336
paragraphs, Word
  applying borders and shading to, 362
  creating new line within, 259
  deleting, 1490–91
  sorting lists of, 384–86
ParaScan macro, TextBox control, 1487, 1489
parentheses [()], arithmetic operators and, 732
Password To Modify text box, 475
passwords
  document protection, 475–76
  workbook security, 702–03
  worksheet protection, 701
Paste command (Ctrl+V)
  Access fields, 1121
  Access forms, 1192
  Excel worksheets, 635–37
  Word text, 289
Paste Link option, 163
Paste Options button, 156–57
Paste Special command
  embedding data, 171
  linking data, 163
  static data exchange, 155–57
patterns
  Access forms, 1174
  Web pages, 591–92
  Word shading, 369
pen, handwriting with, 105
percentages, sort results, 1159
permissions
  documents, 80–81, 127
  IRM, 1013
Personal Address Book, 1082–83
personal distribution lists, 1083
personal folders file. *See* data files, Outlook
personal information
  removing from documents, 73
  removing from PowerPoint presentations, 876
Personal Macro Workbook, 225
personal tasks, 1060
Phone List view, Outlook, 973
phone numbers, storing in Outlook, 1051
photo album, Power Point, 902
photo galleries, 1300, 1304–05
Photo Gallery template, 1282
picas, units of measurement, 316

picture controls, InfoPath, 1408
picture libraries, WSS
    accessing, 189–90
    adding to SharePoint team Web
        site, 1243–47
    customizing, 204–05
    folder associated with, 182
    overview, 178
pictures. *See also* graphics
    compressing, 122
    cropping, 122–23
    defined, 107
    importing, 117–19
    InfoPath, 1408
    inserting into InfoPath forms,
        1422
    inserting with Clip organizer,
        107–12
    methods for modifying, 119–21
    saving PowerPoint elements as,
        900
Pictures toolbar, 1340–42
Picture submenu, 621
Picture toolbar, 119
Pie Chart example, 752–54
PivotCharts, Excel
    displaying, 798–99
    overview, 789
PivotTable toolbar, 793
PivotTables, Excel
    Access forms and, 1172
    compared with Subtotal
        command, 786
    creating, 790–92
    evaluating, 793
    external data sources, 799–800
    formats, 797–98
    functions, 796–97
    overview, 789
    Page area, 794–96
    PivotTable toolbar, 793
    rearranging fields, 794
pixels, 579
placeholders, PowerPoint
    anchoring, 867
    entering text in, 866
    positioning, 866–67
    slides, 852
planning meetings, 1037–39
PMT function (loan payments),
    738–39
PNG (Portable Network Graphics),
    1301–02
pointers, PowerPoint slide shows,
    935
points, units of measurement, 316

POP3 (Post Office Protocol version
    3), 1085
Portable Network Graphics (PNG),
    1301–02
portrait orientation
    page layout, 534
    worksheet print outs, 709
position, character formats, 310
Positioning toolbar, 1347
Post Office Protocol version 3
    (POP3), 1085
postage, printing on envelopes,
    561
postal bar codes, 566
.pot files, 865
pound sign (#), error values, 741
power outages, 69
PowerPoint, 849–76
    application window, 849–51
    audio and video. *See* audio and
        video, Power Point
    AutoContent Wizard, 857–59
    blank presentation, 859–61
    comments, 873–74
    custom templates, 865
    design templates, 861–63
    embedding Excel worksheet,
        174–76
    expanding and duplicating
        slides, 872–73
    formats. *See* formats,
        PowerPoint
    graphics. *See* graphics,
        PowerPoint
    Information Rights Management
        (IRM), 80–81
    macros, 225
    mapping to tasks, 8
    multiple documents, 74–75
    New command, 52
    new features, 13
    outlines, 871–72
    Outlining toolbar, 871
    presentation methods, 856–57,
        863–65
    presentations from existing
        presentations, 863
    Research task pane, 44
    saving presentations, 876
    slide shows. *See* slide shows,
        PowerPoint
    smart tags and, 868
    special effects. *See* special
        effects, PowerPoint presenta-
        tions
    spell checking, 874–76

    style checking, 875–76
    tables, 896–98
    text editing, 869
    text entry, 866–67
    text formatting, 867–68
    unable to link data, 164
    viewing presentations, 855
    views, 852–54
.ppt files, 876
presentation masters. *See* mas-
    ters, PowerPoint presentations
presentation templates, 864
presentations, PowerPoint
    creating from existing presenta-
        tions, 863
    creating from templates,
        861–63, 865
    creating with AutoContent Wiz-
        ard, 857–59
    methods for creating, 856–57,
        863–65
    saving, 876
    starting blank presentation,
        859–61
    types of, 858
    viewing options, 855
previewing Access reports, 1215
previewing Web pages, 15,
    1317–20
primary keys, Access tables, 1114,
    1127–28
primary tables, Access, 1177,
    1203
Print Area feature, Excel, 717–18
Print command, mail merge, 557
Print Layout view
    drawing tables, 355
    inserting comments, 459–61
    moving or resizing Word tables,
        353
    printing documents, 543
    tracking changes, 448
    viewing, editing, or deleting
        comments, 462–66
    Word, 249
Print Preview
    Access reports, 1215
    PowerPoint slides, 855
    Word, 249
    Word documents, 544
print view, InfoPath forms, 1411
printer-ready publications, Word,
    241
printers, duplex, 540
printing options, Access reports,
    1216

printing options, Excel, 708–18
  charts, 768
  defaults, 715
  gridlines, 716
  headers and footers, 710–14
  margins, 710
  page orientation, 709
  print area specification, 717–18
  range selection, 716
  repeating row or column head-
    ings, 718
printing options, InfoPath forms,
  1424
printing options, Outlook, 994–95
printing options, Power Point presentations, 936–37
printing options, Web pages,
  1319–20
printing options, Word documents,
  543–48
  highlighting text, 466
  macro for printing current selec-
    tion, 547–48
  options, 545
  pagination adjustments,
    546–47
  Print Layout view, 543
  Print Preview view, 544
printing outlines, 432
priorities, tasks, 1062
privacy
  distribution lists, 1054
  journal entries, 1072
  Outlook contacts, 1051
  Outlook tasks, 1062
Privacy Options, 476
procedure calls, 1448–50
profiles
  Outlook profiles, 1087–88
  speech recognition, 94
program statement, VBA, 1439–42
programming, VBA, 1438
Project Explorer. See Visual Basic
  Project Explorer
project management, Web sites,
  1262–65
projection screens, nonglare, 926
projectors, 926
proofing documents, 479–508
  grammar checking, customizing,
    496–97
  grammar checking existing text,
    493–95
  grammar checking while typing,
    490–92
  hyphenating automatically,
    501–02

  hyphenating manually, 503–05
  hyphenation methods, 500–501
  languages, detecting
    automatically, 507–08
  marking blocks of text, 505–08
  spell checking, customizing,
    485–90
  spell checking existing text,
    482–84
  spell checking while typing,
    479–82
  thesaurus, finding synonyms,
    497–99
  translations, 499–500
proofing Web page text, 1297–99
properties
  Access fields, 1122–26
  Access form controls, 1187,
    1189
  displaying in Screen Tips, 77
  documents, 76–79
  file properties in search criteria,
    77
  frames, Web pages, 1370–71
  FrontPage forms, 1366–67
  setting before applying, 357
  Table Properties dialog box, 401
  UserForms, 1481–83
  VBA, 77, 1436–38, 1440–41
  Web components, 1379
  Web page images, 1337–40
  Web pages, 1350–53
  WSS document libraries, 1247
Properties dialog box, 78–79,
  1322
protection. See security
Protect Workbook dialog box,
  701–02
.pst files, 1088–89
Publish As Web Page, 828–29, 940
publishing
  data access pages, 1197–98
  enhancements in FrontPage, 16
  reports, Web sites, 1270
  Web pages in Word, 593–94
  Web sites, 1273–77

Q

queries, Access, 1149–70. See
  also Web queries
  accessing from forms, 1176–78
  action queries, 1168–70
  calculated fields, 1163–65
  creating basic query with Simple
    Query Wizard, 1150–53
  crosstab queries, 1166–68

  maintenance queries, 1154
  modifying, 1154–57
  options for creating, 151–52
  running compared with viewing,
    1169
  select queries, 1160
  summarizing information from
    grouped records, 1160–63
  table relationships and, 1158
  top-value, 1158–59
Query, 799–800, 1101–02
quick flags, 15, 1007–08
Quick Launch toolbar
  adding buttons to, 40
  shortcut to Outlook on, 946
  starting applications from, 40
Quick Tag Selector, 16

R

RAM, 86
ranges of cells, 627–29
  Excel printing options, 716
  moving, 636
  selecting with keyboard, 628
  selecting with mouse, 627–28
RATE function (rate of return),
  Excel, 740–41
readability of text, 495
Reading Layout view, 13, 249,
  571–73
Reading pane
  new Outlook features, 14
  viewing e-mail messages in,
    1001–02, 1004
  viewing Outlook items without
    opening, 984–86
read-only mode, 475
Rearrange Commands dialog box,
  12, 220–21
receiving e-mail messages,
  1001–02
Recently Used File List, 63
recipient list, mail merge, 553
records
  database information stored in,
    1097
  deleting, 1136–37
  filtering by form, 1144–46
  filtering by selection, 1142–44
  other ways to sort and filter,
    1147
  queries, 1156
  sorting, 1141
record source, Access forms, 1172
recto page, 530
Redo command, 285, 634

Reduced Functionality Mode, 21
referential integrity, Access tables, 1132
Refresh XML Data command, 843–44
regions, currency symbols and, 655
regular expressions, 1294
rehearsals, PowerPoint slide shows, 926–27
Rehearse Timings command, 926–27
related tables, 1129
relational databases, 1098–99
relationships, Access tables
  Access forms, 1177
  creating/deleting, 1131–32
  defining before creating queries, 1152
  join types, 1158
  many-to-many relationships, 1133
  one-to-many relationships, 1130
  referential integrity, 1132
  viewing existing, 1129–31
relative cell references, Excel, 730–31
reminders, task due dates, 1062
Remote Web Site view, 1273–75
Repeat command (Ctrl+Y)
  Excel worksheets, 635
  Word, 265, 285
Repeat (F4), 285
repeating sections, InfoPath, 1405, 1421–22
repeating tables, InfoPath, 1405
replace. See find and replace
Report, database objects, 1103–04
report layout, Design view, 1216
Report Wizard, 1201–07
reports, Access, 1199–1216
  AutoReport, 1199
  columnar vs. tablular, 1200
  creating, 1199–1201
  editing, 1210–11
  field selection, 1201–02
  formats, 1205–06
  grouping information for, 1202–03
  inserting charts, 1200
  naming, 1207
  previewing, 1215
  printing, 1216
  Report Wizard, 1201–07
  sections, 1211–13
  sorting and grouping settings, 1213–15

sort order, 1204–05
summarizing information, 1204–05, 1207–09
reports, Excel scenario reports, 819–20
reports, Web sites
  enhancements in FrontPage, 16
  Hyperlinks reports, 1270–73
  list of, 1266–69
  publishing, 1270
  Site Summary report, 1265
Research task pane
  applying, 44–46
  functions of, 44
  Office 2003 new features, 11
resolution, Web page images, 1317–20, 1339
Reveal Formatting task pane, 338–40
Reviewing toolbar
  accepting/rejecting changes, 456–57
  comments, 461
  Reject Change/Delete Comment button, 464
  reviewing tracked changes, 452–54
  Track Changes tab, 450
  viewing change details, 455–56
Rich Text Format (.rtf), 573
right-drag, 40, 639
.rmi files, 905
rollover effects, hyperlinks, 1352
rows, Access tables, 1120
rows, Word tables
  adding, 346, 348–49
  adjusting height of, 352–53
  deleting, 350
rows, worksheets, 662–64
  adding to worksheets, 639
  adjusting height manually, 662–63
  adjusting with mouse, 663
  Height command, 663–64
  hiding, 664
  printing options, 718
  selecting with mouse, 627–28
rulers, Word, 248, 537–39
run time, VBA (Visual Basic for Applications), 1437
Running queries, 1169

S

Save As dialog box, 70–73, 255–56
saved formats
  advantages of, 329

applying, 330–33
assigning, 337
limitations of, 330
Save Embedded Files, 1253
Save My Settings Wizard, 235–37
Save Picture As option, 1253
saving documents. See documents, saving
saving Excel workbooks, 626
saving InfoPath forms, 1398, 1412–15, 1423
saving PowerPoint presentations, 876, 939–42
saving queries, 1157
saving Web pages, 576, 825, 1283
saving Web site files, 1254
saving workbooks, 626, 692
saving XML documents, 597, 600, 843
scale, character formats, 310
scanners
  adding artwork with, 621
  adding images to Web pages, 1300
Scenario Manager, 815–21
  creating scenario reports, 819–20
  creating scenarios, 816–18
  managing scenarios, 821
  viewing scenarios, 818–19
scenarios
  creating, 816–18
  defined, 816
  managing, 821
  reports, 819–20
  viewing, 818–19
scheduling
  appointments, 1027–31
  meetings, 1033–37
schema, XML, 595–96, 599, 838
Schema Library, 601
scientific notation, Excel numeric values, 612
ScreenTips
  animation schemes, 910
  displaying properties in, 77
  hyperlinks, 1262
  Word, 247
scroll bars, 281
scrolling text, 588
searches. See also find and replace
  browse commands, 297
  clips by keywords, 109
  file properties as search criteria, 77
  highlighted text, 467

searches, *continued*
  options for, 295–96
  records on Excel lists, 783–85
  regular expressions, 1294
  Search command, 293
  wildcards, 296–97
search folders, Outlook, 1019–20
  creating, 1020
  defaults, 1019
  information stored in, 948
  new features, 14
Search For text box, Research task pane, 45
Search Results task pane
  help topics in, 29
  search tools in, 33–34
  Troubleshoot Help topic, 27
section breaks
  columns, 372–73
  headers and footers, 530
  page layout, 522–23
  page numbers, 521, 531
sections, InfoPath, 1405, 1421–22
Secure Socket Layer (SSL), 1226
security
  e-mail, 14, 1005–06
  levels, 230–31
  macros, 229–32
  trusted sources, 230–31
  viruses, 229
  workbooks, 799–803
  worksheets, 699–701
Select Case decision structures, 1466–69
  determining document paper type with, 1467–68
  overview, 1466–67
select queries, 1160. *See also* queries, Access
selection
  F8 (text selection), 284
  mouse techniques, 284, 286
  shortcut keys for, 283
selection, Access
  field selection, 1201–02
  tables, 1142–44
selection, Excel
  cells, 608
  columns, 627–28, 630
  group selection, 684
  ranges of cells, 629, 716
selection, FrontPage Web pages, 1289
selection, Word
  table selection (Alt+5), 348

  text, 282–84, 286
  text with same formatting or style, 335–36
sending e-mail messages, 1014
Send/Receive
  e-mail, 1001
  groups, 1009–10
sentence grammar, 494
Sent Items folder, Outlook, 947
series, worksheets, 641–44
  AutoFill, 641–42
  Fill commands, 642–43
  Fill Series dialog box, 643–44
  keyboard shortcuts, 643
  overview, 641
Server Extensions, 1277
Service Options dialog box, Shared Workspace, 192
service packs, 23
Setup
  installing Office 2003 from CD, 17–19
  installing speech recognition, 84
  Outlook, 946
  revising, 19–21
Setup.exe, 17
shading, Excel cells, 660–61
shading, InfoPath tables, 1405
shading, Web pages, 1329–31
shading, Word
  applying, 366
  Borders And Shading dialog box, 366–69
  character formats, 311
  colors, 369
  overview, 361–63
  paragraph formats, 322
  patterns, 369
  Tables And Borders toolbar, 363–64
shadow effects, 880
shared attachments, Outlook, 14, 1018–19
shared borders, 1313–17
  command unavailable, 1314–15
  controlling settings, 1315–16
  defaults, 1313–14
  spell checking and, 1299–1300
  unavailable on Format menu, 1314–15
  Web sites, 1313
shared documents
  e-mail, 470–71
  networks, 469–70
  overview, 468–69
  protecting, 472–77

shared files and folders, 474
shared fonts, 477
shared InfoPath forms, 1414–15
shared workbooks
  accepting and rejecting revisions to, 696–98
  creating, 693–94
  monitoring, 695
Shared Workspace, 192
SharePoint team Web sites. *See also* **WSS (Windows Share-Point Services)**
  accessing, 179
  adding information components to, 1243–47
  components, 201–02
  creating, 1231–33
  features, 178
  form libraries, 1415
  importing contacts from Outlook, 1060
  modifying, 206–07
  opening, 188
  Web part pages on, 1286–88
Shift+Enter, creating new line, 259
Shockwave Flash files, 1300
shortcut menus
  Access commands, 1120
  customizing, 214
  managing workbooks, 683
  Office Clipboard, 162
  thesaurus, 499
shortcuts
  adding to desktop, 41
  customizing Shortcuts list, 1079–80
  keyboard. *See* keyboard shortcuts
  modifying graphic objects, 152
  opening Outlook folders, 952
Shortcuts list, Outlook, 1079–80
Show/Hide, 349, 526
side-by-side calendar folders, 14
side-by-side document views, 11, 75–76
Simple Mail Transfer Protocol (SMTP), 1085
Simple Query Wizard, 1150–53
size
  Access tables, 1125
  character formats, 309
  Web page images, 1337
size button, windows, 606
Slide Layout task pane, 860
slide masters, PowerPoint, 891
Slide Master View toolbar, 893

slide shows, PowerPoint, 923–42
 annotating slides in, 935–36
 CD presentations, 932–33
 customizing, 930–31
 dissemination methods, 942
 handouts, 937
 hiding slides, 931–32
 launching presentation, 933–35
 narration, 929–30
 overhead transparencies, 925
 overview, 923
 presentation methods, 924–25
 printing presentation, 936–37
 projecting 35 mm slides, 926
 publishing on Web, 938–42
 rehearsals, 926–27
 timing, 928–29
Slide Show view, PowerPoint, 853
Slide Sorter view, PowerPoint, 852
slides, PowerPoint
 adding graphics to, 898–99
 adding tables to, 896–97
 annotating, 935–36
 arranging, 872
 elements of, 851–52
 expanding and duplicating,
  872–73
 previewing, 855
 slide elements, 851–52
 slide summary, 873
 views, 852–53
smart documents, 11, 47
smart tags
 Access, 15, 1127
 automatic text formatting,
  867–68
 e-mail messages, 1004
 enabling, 277–78
 functions of, 276–77
 Outlook, 15
 PowerPoint, 13, 868
 recognizers, 868
 removing, 279
 turning off automatic conversion
  of, 280
 working with, 278–79
 worksheets, 640
**SMTP (Simple Mail Transfer
  Protocol), 1085**
soft page breaks, 547
**solutions (form templates),
  InfoPath, 1394**
Solver, 808–15
 editing forecasts, 813–14
 Guess button, 811
 handling multiple solutions, 815

 running, 810–13
 setting up worksheets for,
  808–10
sorting
 queries, 1156, 1158–60
 Sort command, 778
sorting, Access
 forms, 1192
 reports, 1204–05, 1213–15
 tables, 1141, 1147
sorting, Excel lists
 customizing sort order, 781–83
 more than one column, 779–81
 one column lists, 778–79
sorting, Outlook
 items, 979–83
 tasks, 1067
sorting, Word text, 384–87
sound clips. *See also* **audio and
  video, Power Point**
 adding to Web pages, 585–87,
  1300
 formats, 587, 905
 Power Point, 905–07
source code, HTML, 1382–90
 creating source code file,
  1384–85
 customizing source code editor,
  1389
 Design view and, 1383–84
 editing techniques, 1385–88
 making HTML conform to XML
  rules, 1388
 overview, 1382
source code editor
 creating source code file,
  1384–85
 customizing, 1389
 editing techniques, 1385–88
 making HTML conform to XML
  rules, 1388
spacing
 character formats, 310, 315
 paragraph formats, 320
 Web page images, 1338
special characters, 262, 656
special effects
 mathematical equations, 139–
  42
 WordArt, 133–36
**special effects, PowerPoint presen-
  tations, 909–21**
 actions, assigning to objects,
  920–21
 animating diagrams and charts,
  914

 animation schemes, 910–11
 custom animation, 911–14
 hyperlinks, 918–19
 motion paths, 914–16
 overview, 909
 transitions, 917–18
speech recognition, 83–96
 applying, 86–89
 customizing, 94–96
 dictation mode, 89–93
 installing, 84
 overview, 83–84
 punctuation characters, dictating, 90–91
 training, 84–85
 voice command mode, 93–94
Speech Training Wizard, 84
spell checking
 Access forms, 1190–91
 with AutoCorrect, 276
 customizing, 485–90
 existing text, 482–84
 InfoPath forms, 1411, 1420
 PowerPoint presentations,
  874–75
 Web pages, 1297–99
 while typing, 479–82
 worksheets, 644
spelling errors, in indexes, 442
Spike, 291–92
split boxes
 not visible, 251
 splitting worksheets into panes,
  719–20
 Word, 248
spreadsheet, interactive, 830–32
SQL (structured query language)
 extracting external data with
  SQL queries, 800
 form templates based on, 1402
SRC attribute, 1253
SSL (Secure Sockets Layer), 1226
Standard toolbar, Excel
 AutoSum, 735
 Chart Wizard, 755
 Help button, 607
 Sort buttons, 779
 Undo button, 633–34
 Zoom control, 707, 754
Standard toolbar, Outlook
 Follow Up button, 1007
 Forward button, 1014
 list of buttons and functions,
  1013
 New button, 1014
 Send/Receive, 1001

Standard toolbar, Word, 248
Insert Cells button, 349
Insert Columns button, 348
Insert Rows button, 348–49
Insert Table button, 346
Show/Hide button, 349
Spelling and Grammar, 483
Tables And Borders button, 355
Start menu, 39
statement syntax, VBA program statements, 1440
static copying and moving data, 155–58
Clipboard, 158–62
overview, 153
process, 155–57
static pictures, InfoPath, 1408
static Web pages, 824–25
statistical functions, worksheets, 689
status bar
Excel, 606–07
TRK indicator, 449
Word, 246–47
StdDev function, Excel worksheets, 689
Stop Recording toolbar, 227
Stripes dialog box, Format Menu, 401
structured query language (SQL)
extracting external data with SQL queries, 800
form templates based on, 1402
style checking, PowerPoint presentations, 875–76
Style For Following Paragraph option, 400
Style Gallery, 342–43
style sheets, XSLT, 596
styles, Excel, 668–72
applying existing to worksheets, 671
creating for worksheets, 668–70
merging from other workbooks, 671–72
Style command, 669
Style dialog box, 669
styles, FrontPage, 1324–25
styles, VBA, 1463–65
styles, Word
advantages of, 327–28
aliases, 400
applying, 330–33
built-in vs. user-defined, 333, 389–92

character styles, 393
compared with saved formats, 329–30
copying, 406–08
customizing by example text, 393
customizing with Modify Style dialog box, 394–99
customizing with New Style dialog box, 404–06
deleting, 402–03
displaying names of, 392
Format Menu of Modify Style dialog box, 400–402
formatting headers and footers, 527
formatting page numbers, 527
languages and, 506
list styles, 383–84
outline levels, 424
paragraph styles, 393, 404, 1323
shortcut keys, 337–38
Style For Following Paragraph option, 400
table styles, 357–58
templates, 406–08, 409, 410
types of, 328–29
Styles And Formatting task pane, 332–33, 335–36
subdatasheets, Access tables, 1139–41
subforms, Access forms, 1177
subroutines, 1429
subscripts, 315, 318
subsites, 1228
Subtotals command, 785–88
compared with PivotTables, 786
evaluating lists with, 785–86
functions of, 787
Outline view, 788
subtraction (-), 732
SUM function, Excel, 689, 735
summary queries, 1160–63
superscripts, 315, 318
surveys, WSS
adding to SharePoint team Web site, 1243–47
creating, 1246
customizing, 204–05
information managed by, 183
overview, 178
participating in, 198–201
symbol fonts, 261, 318
symbols
AutoCorrect, 273
inserting, 260–61
in Outline view, 421

synonyms, 497–99, 1297
syntax
Excel functions, 734
VBA program statements, 1440
system requirements, speech recognition, 86
system tray, Clipboard icon in, 158

T

Table menu, 359–60
table of contents
creating, 443
customizing, 444
field code switches, 445
modifying appearance of, 443–44
Table Of Contents command, 32
Table Properties dialog box, 401
table relationships, 1158
table styles, 329
3D Effects, 396
modifying, 396, 406
Table view, Outlook, 977–79, 982
tables, Access, 1113–47
accessing from forms, 1176–78
adding fields, 1119–20
creating, 1113–16
data entry, 1134–36
Datasheet view, 1134, 1137–39
deleting records, 1136–37
Design view, 1118–19
field properties, 1122–26
fields, 1120–21
primary keys, 1127–28
record filters, 1141–47
referential integrity, 1132
relationships, 1101–02, 1129–33
subdatasheets, 1139–41
XML documents in, 1116–18
tables, FrontPage, 1308–13
adding to Web pages, 1308–09
compared with Word tables, 1310
creating and editing, 1310–11
layout tables and cells, 1311–13
positioning elements in Web pages, 1346–49
tables, InfoPath, 1405, 1422
tables, PowerPoint, 896–98
tables, VBA, 1470–72
tables, Word, 345–61
adding blocks of cells, 349
adding content, 347

adding rows, columns, or cells, 348–49

alignment in cells, 354–55

borders and shading, 362

charts created from, 138

creating, 346

deleting rows, columns, or cells, 350

drawing, 355–57

moving and copying rows, columns, or cells, 353

negative indents, 361

nesting, 347

not linked to charts, 138

overview, 242

resizing cells, 350–53

sorting, 386–87

styles, 357–58

Table menu tasks, 359–60

text arrangement, 345

Tables And Borders toolbar, 355, 362, 363–64

Tablet PC, 618

tabs

changing color of worksheet tabs, 681

paragraph formats, 321

PowerPoint, 883–85

worksheets, 680

Tabs dialog box, Format Menu, 401

tabular layout, Access, 1174, 1200

tags

Quick Tag Selector, 16

smart tags, 13, 15

XML documents, 594–95, 599

target cells, 808

targets, hyperlinks, 1306

Task form, Outlook, 1062

task panes, 42–47

compared with toolbars, 212

displaying, 43

Getting Started task pane, 44

navigating among recently used, 44

overview, 42

PowerPoint, 850

Research task pane, 44–47

smart documents, 47

Word, 244–45

Task Timeline view, 1065

tasks, mapping Office applications to, 7–8

Tasks folder, Outlook, 1060–68

appearance options, 1067–68

assigning to contacts, 1056

creating assigned task, 1063–66

defining tasks, 1061–63

information stored in, 947

overview, 1060–61

recurring tasks, 1063

sort orders, 1067

Task form, 1062

Task Timeline view, 1066

working with, 1066–68

Tasks view, Web site projects, 1262–65

templates

creating new Office documents, 48, 55–56

dynamic templates, 15

file extensions, 50

online, 11

overview, 48

storing, 50–51

templates, Access databases, 1106

templates, Excel, 672–75

applying existing, 672

creating, 673–74

modifying, 674–75

templates, FrontPage

creating own, 1283–84

finding and downloading, 1224, 1283

forms, 1367

frames pages, 1369

overview, 49

Web pages created with, 1280–81

Web sites based on, 1223–28

templates, InfoPath, 1394

templates, Outlook mail merge, 551, 559

templates, PowerPoint presentations, 861–63, 865

templates, Word

attaching to documents, 415–16

basing on existing document, 415

copying style templates to documents, 406–08

creating, 414–15

creating style templates, 407–08

customizing, 411–13

global templates or add-ins, 416

items copied to new documents, 409

items stored within, 409–10

locations for, 415

style types, 410

text. *See also* documents

Add Text command, 152

adding in Word, 259–60

adding to Office diagrams, 132

adding to Word tables, 347

arranging with Word tables, 345

bookmarks, 300–301

columns, 371–72

combining with text boxes and graphics, 514–16

copying unformatted data, 156

deleting, 282

effects, 314

hiding, 315

inserting comments, 459–61

lists. *See* lists, Word

marking blocks of, 505–08

moving and copying with Clipboard, 289–91

moving and copying with mouse, 287–89

removing blocks of, 291–92

replacing, 299

reusing, 266–69

selecting, 282–84, 286

selecting with same formatting or style, 335–36

styles, 336

templates, 409

transferring multiple blocks of, 291–92

translating, 499

WordArt effects, 133–36

wrapping breaks, 517

wrapping line breaks, 259

wrapping styles, 121

text, Access

find and replace, 1136–37

forms, 1187–88

text, Excel

font and color, 656–58

text values, 613–14

text, PowerPoint

applying formatting, 878

bulleted lists, 881–83

copying, 881

editing, 869

entering, 866–67

fonts, 880–81

formatting, 867–68

indents and Tab settings, 883–85

methods for managing, 878–80

numbered lists, 881–83

text, PowerPoint, *continued*
  special effects, 899
  text alignment and line spacing,
    885
text, UserForms, 1491
text, VBA, 1454–56
text, Web pages
  adding to Web pages, 1291–93
  color formats, 1334–35
  find and replace, 1293–96
text and content layouts, Power
  Point, 903, 906
Text Boundaries options, 376
text boxes, 510–14
  creating and placing, 511–12
  functions of, 510
  height and width of, 512
  InfoPath forms, 1406–07
  linking, 513
  moving and copying, 512–13
  positioning elements with, 1349
  removing, 514
  text and graphics in page layout,
    514–16
  wrapping styles, 510
text orientation
  Excel, 651
  Word, 534–36
  Word tables, 354
text selection (F8), 284
TextBox control, 1487–91
themes
  automatic formatting, 342
  bullets, 380
  creating or customizing, 1355
  options, 1356
  Web pages, 1353–56
  Web pages, Word, 592–93
thesaurus, 11, 497–99
thumbnail images, 1303
Thumbnails view, 118
time
  Excel, 614–16
  PowerPoint slides, 852
  Word, 263–64
timelines, journal timelines, 1073
timing, PowerPoint slide shows,
  926–29
title masters, PowerPoint, 891
titles
  Excel, 760–61
  PowerPoint, 852, 885
toolbar buttons
  adding/removing, 214–15,
    219–20

  modifying, 216–17
  overview, 213
  positioning, 215
toolbars
  compared with task panes, 212
  customizing, 12, 210–12
  data access pages, 1195
  full-screen mode, 253
  managing, 212
  navigation toolbar, 1259
  Rearrange Commands dialog
    box, 220–21
  templates, 410
toolbars, Access, 1179–83
toolbars, Excel, 606
toolbars, Outlook, 953–54
toolbars, PowerPoint, 850
toolbars, VBA, 1433–34
toolbox controls, UserForms, 1477
ToolTips, 124
top-value queries, 1158–59
tracking changes, Excel work-
  books, 696–98
tracking changes, Word docu-
  ments, 447–56
  accepting/rejecting changes,
    456–57
  batch processing of, 457
  enabling, 448
  filters, 450
  marking modes, 449–50
  overview, 447
  reviewing tracked changes,
    452–54
  shortcut key, 449
  toggling between change mark-
    ing modes, 454–55
  viewing change details, 455–56
transforms
  Schema Library, 601
  XML documents, 596, 1117
transition effects, Web pages,
  1356–57
transitions, PowerPoint
  presentations, 917–18
translations, 499–500
  new Word features, 13
transparency controls, Web page
  images, 1343
TRK indicator, 449
Troubleshoot Help topic, 27
TrueType fonts, 314, 477
trusted sources, 230–31
Typing Replaces Selection option,
  287

U

Underline button, Formatting
  toolbar, 317
underlining
  character formats, 310
  not displayed, 317
  in PowerPoint, 879
  shortcut key for, 318
Undo (Ctrl+Z)
  Access actions, 1121
  Access forms, 1190
  Excel worksheets, 633–34
  formats, 285, 307
  Outlook items, 968
  reversing style changes, 399
undoing/redoing editing actions,
  Web pages, 1291
Undo options, macros, 229
Unformatted Text, pasting, 155–57
Unicode fonts, 261
Uniform Resource Name (URN),
  598
unit of measurement
  Web pages, 579
  Word, 316
update queries, 1170
URN (Uniform Resource Name),
  598
usage reports, FrontPage, 1232
user interface, 1477–78. *See also*
  application interface
UserForms, 1477–86
  building a custom dialog box,
    1478–81
  CommandButton, 1481
  event procedures, 1484–86
  Image button, 1480
  Label button, 1479–80
  setting properties, 1481–83
  TextBox control, 1487–91
  toolbox controls, 1477
  unloading, 1491
  user interface design, 1477–78
users profiles, speech recognition,
  94
utilities, Office 2003 suite, 3

V

validation. *See* **data validation**
value axis, Excel charts, 750
variable cells, Excel, 808
variables, VBA
  declaring, 1447–48
  making reservations (dim
    statements), 1447–48

for output, 1452–54
for processing text, 1454–56
storing input, 1448–51
VBA (Visual Basic for Applications), 1427–38
adding descriptive statements to macros, 1429
auto list feature in Code window, 1442
conditional expressions, 1461–62
constants, 1442–47
creating macros, 301
document properties, 77
editing macros, 224
exiting, 1438
For...Each loops, 1472–75
formulas, 1456–59
For...Next loops, 1469–72
functions, 1448
If...Then decision structures, 1462–66
inserting macros, 1428–29
logical operators, 1465–66
Menu bar, 1432–33
methods, 1441
Microsoft Visual Basic Help, 1441–42
Object Browser, 1441
object variables for processing text, 1454–56
objects, 1440
program statement, 1439–42
programming tools, 1429, 1431–32
Project Explorer, 1434–36
properties, 1440–41
Properties window, 1436–38
Select Case decision structures, 1466–69
toolbars, 1433–34
UserForms. See UserForms
variables, 1447–48
variables for output, 1452–54
variables for storing input, 1448–51
Venn diagrams, PowerPoint, 914
Versions command, Word, 257–58
verso page, 530
vertical alignment, Excel, 650
Vertical Head style, 670
vertical ruler, 537–39
vertical scroll bar, 251
PowerPoint, 851
worksheets, 608
Vertical Spacing, Web page images, 1338

video clips
adding to Web pages, 1301, 1305
PowerPoint, 903–04
Web page formats, 1344–45
video, PowerPoint. See audio and video, Power Point
view options
Access databases, 1110
Excel, 705–08
FrontPage, 1236–37
InfoPath forms, 1410–11
Outlook, 961–62, 973–77
PowerPoint, 852–54
Word, 249–51
View selection buttons, Word, 248
viruses
e-mail messages, 1003
Privacy Options, 476
security, 229
Visual Basic development environment. See VBA (Visual Basic for Applications)
Visual Basic Editor. See VBA (Visual Basic for Applications
Visual Basic Project Explorer, 1434–36
VML Graphics Office Drawing option, 1302
voice command mode, speech recognition, 93–94
volume adjustment, PowerPoint audio, 906

W

watermarks
adding, 517–18
overview, 517
removing or modifying, 518
.wav files, 905
Web, publishing Outlook calendar to, 1044
Web browsers
accessing SharePoint document libraries, 183–87
accessing Web pages, 1221
compatibility, 1320
data access pages, 1193
displaying Web pages in, 824
format compatibility, 577
interactive Web pages, 830–32
resolution options, 1318
viewing PowerPoint presentations, 855, 938–39
Web Collections, media clips, 112
Web components
adding to Web pages, 1377–78

functions of, 1374
obtaining, 1378
properties, 1379
types of, 1374–77
Web data, 837
Web discussion toolbar, 195–98
Web Distributed Authoring and Versioning (WebDAV), 1222, 1273
Web forms, 589–90
Web Layout view
creating Web pages, 575
drawing tables, 355
inserting comments, 459–61
moving or resizing Word tables, 353
tracking changes, 448
viewing, editing, or deleting comments, 462–66
Word and, 249
Web pages
background sounds, 588
customizing free-form or home pages, 203–04
defined, 569, 824
free-form, 202
HTML format, 576, 1221
importing into Web sites, 1252
newspaper-style columns, 371
Outlook Today, 997
page banners, 1260
previewing, 15
saving documents as, 73–74
saving PowerPoint presentation as, 939–42
themes, 342
Word and, 241
Web pages, Excel
design, 824
publishing, 825–30
running, 830
working with interactive, 830–32
Web pages, FrontPage, 1279–1320
advanced controls, 1378–82
basing on existing Web pages, 1282
character formats. See character formats, Web pages
CSS styles, 1358–61
deleting, 1291
dynamic templates, 1284–86
editing, 1289–91
find and replace text, 1293–96
finding and replacing HTML elements, 1389–90
formatting active page, 1350–53

Web pages, FrontPage, *continued*
formatting elements in, 1349–50
frames for displaying multiple pages, 1367–74
horizontal dividing lines, 1305
hyperlinks, 1306–08
image insertion, 1300–1302
interactive forms, 1363–67
moving and copying, 1289–90
opening existing page, 1288–89
page creation, 1279–83
paragraph formats. *See* paragraph formats, Web pages
photo galleries, 1304–05
positioning elements in, 1346–49
previewing, 1317–20
printing, 1319–20
proofing text, 1297–99
selecting, 1289
shared borders, 1313–17
source code. *See* source code, HTML
tables, 1308–13
template creation, 1283–84
templates for, 1280–81
text content, adding, 1291–93
themes, 1353–56
thumbnail images, 1303
transition effects, 1356–57
undoing/redoing editing actions, 1291
video clips, 1305
Web components, 1374–78
Web part pages, 1286–88
Web pages, Word, 573-94
background colors or patterns, 591–92
backing up, 576
creating, 573–74
editing, 574–75
formats, 591
frames, 590–91
horizontal dividing lines, 583–85
HTML formats, 576
hyperlinks, 580–83
movies and sounds, 585–87
options, 577–79
page elements, 580
publishing, 593–94
saving, 576
scrolling text, 588
themes, 592–93
Web forms, 589–90

Web part pages
creating, 202–03
creating on SharePoint team Web sites, 1286–88
new FrontPage features, 16
Web publishing, Excel, 823-47
importing data with Web queries, 833–35
options, 827
overview, 823
page design, 824
publishing Web pages, 825–30
revising Web queries, 835–37
running Web pages, 830
static vs. interactive Web pages, 824–25
Web queries, 832
working with interactive Web pages, 830–32
Web publishing, PowerPoint, 938-42
overview, 938
previewing presentation in browser, 938–39
saving presentation as Web page, 939–42
Web queries
importing data, 833–35
overview, 832
revising, 835–37
Web servers, 1221
Web services, 1402
Web sites, 1239-77
author's, 35
deleting, 1229
editing, 1231–32
FrontPage vs. Windows Explorer for file management, 1240
hyperlinks reports, 1270–73
Hyperlinks view, 1260–62
importing files and folders, 1250–51
importing Web pages, 1252
naming, 1228
navigation tools, 1233–35
Navigation view, 1254–60
Office Online, 33–35
online or offline, 1222–23
opening, 1229–31
opening documents from, 58
project management, 1262–65
publishing, 1273–77
reports, 1265–70
saving documents to, 71
SharePoint. *See* SharePoint team Web sites
subsites, 1228

synchronizing local and remote, 1273
templates, 1223–27
views, 1236–37
working with files, 1239–41, 1247–50
working with folders, 1239–43
working with imported files, 1254
Web Site task pane, 1224
Web toolbar
hyperlinks, 625
navigating with, 583
WebDAV (Web Distributed Authoring and Versioning), 1222, 1273
well-formed documents, XML, 596
what-if questions. *See* Scenario Manager
Width command, worksheet columns, 663–64
wildcards, 296–97
Window Font color, 368
Windows Clipboard, 158
Windows Explorer
compared with FrontPage for Web site file management, 1240
creating empty Office document in a folder, 52
launching PowerPoint presentation from, 933
opening documents from, 57
working with Web site files, 1247–48
Windows SharePoint Services. *See* **WSS (Windows SharePoint Services)**
windows, sizing buttons, 606
wizards
adding to Excel, 725
downloading from Office Online, 55
file extensions, 50
FrontPage, 49
icons for, 48
Word, 241-58
AutoShapes, 127
borders and shading. *See* borders, Word
charts, creating from Word tables, 138
columns. *See* columns, Word documents
Compare Side By Side mode, 75–76
converting file formats, 256–57

converting styles with If...Then decision structures, 1463–65
copying macros to Word's normal template, 1457
display options, 251–54
documents. *See* documents
Draw menu, 146–47
editing. *See* editing options, Word
Full Screen option, 253
Information Rights Management (IRM), 80–81
inline graphic objects in, 144
interface elements, 248
letter writing options, 567
linking Excel spreadsheet to Word report, 168–70
lists. *See* lists, Word
macros, 225
mailings. *See* mailings, Word
mapping to tasks, 7
multiple documents, 74–75
New command, 52
New Document task pane, 53
new features, 13
online documents, 569–73
page layout. *See* page layout, Word
printing documents. *See* printing options, Word documents
printing labels, 1201
processing text with TextBox control, 1487–91
proofing documents. *See* proofing documents
Research task pane, 44
ScreenTips, 247
setting up interface, 248
shortcut keys, 222–23
smart documents, 47
specialized documents, 241–42
standard file formats, 573
status bar, 246–47
storing document versions, 257–58
tables. *See* tables, Word
tasks performed with, 244–45
view options, 249–51
Web pages. *See* Web pages, Word
Word Letter Wizard, 1056
workgroups. *See* workgroup documents
XML documents. *See* XML documents

Word Letter Wizard, 1056

WordArt, 133–36
adding artwork to worksheets, 621
adding effects to Web pages, 1301
Gallery, 134
inserting, 133
toolbar, 135–36
words, applying character formatting to, 308
workbooks, Excel, 679–703
accepting/rejecting revisions to shared workbooks, 696–98
adding worksheets, 682–83
changing worksheet tab color, 681
consolidating worksheets with identical formats, 689–92
creating based on existing, 673
creating shared workbooks, 693–94
defined, 607–08
deleting worksheets from, 681–82
linking information between workbooks, 688–89
merging styles, 671–72
monitoring shared workbooks, 695
moving and copying worksheets in, 683–85
naming worksheets in, 681
password protection, 702–03
protecting workbook structure, 701–02
protecting worksheets, 699–701
referencing cells in other worksheets, 685–87
saving, 626
saving as Web pages, 827
saving before loading scenarios, 818
saving in workspace file, 692
saving in XML format, 838
switching between worksheets, 680
working with multiple, 687
workgroup documents, 447–77
accepting and rejecting changes, 456–57
comparing documents, 459
highlighting text, 466–68
ink annotations, 466
inserting comments, 459–61
merging documents, 458

protecting shared documents, 472–77
reviewing tracked changes, 452–54
sharing documents on a network, 469–70
sharing documents via e-mail, 470–71
sharing fonts, 477
toggling between change marking modes, 454–55
tracking changes, 447–52
viewing change details, 455–56
viewing, editing, and deleting comments, 462–64
worksheets
adding artwork to, 621–22
adding to workbooks, 682–83
appearance options, 722–23
cells, 607
changing tab color, 681
comments, 616–17
consolidating worksheets with identical formats, 689–92
creating charts from, 747
default, 680
deleting from workbooks, 681–82
entering numeric values, 611–13
freezing panes in, 719–20
Goal Seek, 805–06
Go To command, 610
group selection, 684
hyperlinks, 622–24
locking, 701
magnification, 706–07
moving and copying, 683–85
naming, 681
navigating, 608–11
protecting, 699–701
referencing cells in other worksheets, 685–87
rows and columns on, 607
saving as Web pages, 826
Solver, 808–10
splitting into panes, 719
statistical functions, 689
switching between, 680
workbooks, 607–08
worksheets, editing, 627–46
adding individual cells, 640
adding rows and columns, 639
clearing/deleting cells, 630–32
common errors list, 645–46

worksheets, editing, *continued*
Cut and Paste data, 635–37
dragging cells, 638
find and replace data, 632–33
overview techniques for, 627
Redo commands, 634
Repeat command, 635
selecting cells and ranges,
627–29
selecting rows and columns with
mouse, 630
series of labels, numbers, and
dates, 641–44
smart tags, 640
spell checking, 644
Undo commands, 633–34
workspace, 1040
workspace file, 692
wrapping styles
defined, 514
graphics, 515–16
line breaks, 259
text, 121
text boxes, 510
types of, 515–16
Web pages, 1292
Writing Pad window, 97–102
character formats, 99
handwriting recognition, 99–101
ink mode, 98–99
text mode, 101–02
Writing Style options, 496–97
**WSS (Windows SharePoint
Services), 177–207.** *See also*
SharePoint team Web sites
accessing document libraries
from applications, 187–88
accessing document libraries
from browsers, 183–87
accessing team Web site, 179
calendars, 1047–48
contacts list, 1058–60
customizing Web pages, 203–05

discussion boards, 193–95
document discussions, 195–98
FrontPage, 1222
hosting services, 1277
information exchange, 198–201
information pages, 182–83
main page task options, 179–81
meeting workspace, 1039–42
modifying team Web site,
206–07
new Outlook features, 14
Office 2003 new features, 12
overview, 12, 177–78
picture libraries, 189–90
publishing Excel list on, 802–03
saving documents to Web sites
and, 71
SharePoint site components,
creating, 201–03
sharing documents, 190–93
**WYSIWYG (What You See Is What
You Get), 1382**

making HTML conform to XML
rules, 1388
new Word features, 13
overview, 594–96
saving, 597
transforms, 601
Word and, 242
.xml filename extension, 594, 838
XML lists
customizing, 844–46
defined, 839
importing data, 841–43
import options, 844
Refresh XML Data command,
843
saving workbooks containing,
844
XML lists, 839
XML map. *See* **XML lists**
XML schema, 1118
XML schema (XSD), 1118
XML Step by Step (Young), 596
XML Step by Step (Young), 838
XSD (XML schema), 1118
**XSLT (Extensible Stylesheet
Language Transformations),
596**

X

x-axis, Excel charts, 750
.xls files, 838
XML (Extensible Markup Language)
exporting Access data to,
1116–18
InfoPath forms, 1393
new Access support features,
15
new Excel support features, 13
online documents, 569
XML data, in Excel, 838–43
customizing XML list, 844–46
importing, working with, and
exporting, 839–43
overview, 838
XML documents, 594–601
creating, 596
customizing, 597–601
importing/exporting, 1116–18

Y

y-axis, Excel charts, 750
Young, Michael J., 35

Z

z-axis, 3-D charts, 750
zoom
Access fields, 1136
Excel charts, 754
scaling characters and graphics,
252
worksheets, 706–07

About the Author

Michael J. Young is a computer technology writer who has authored books and articles for computer users and programmers since 1986. He has written more than two dozen computer books, including the best-selling *Microsoft Office XP Inside Out* and *Running Microsoft Office* series (with Michael Halvorson) as well as *XML Step by Step*, all from Microsoft Press. His user-level books have focused on Microsoft Office applications. His programmer books have covered MS-DOS, Windows, C, C++, Visual Basic, Java, XML, animation, game, and graphics programming. His book XML Step by Step won the top award, "Distinguished Technical Communication," in the 2000–2001 International Technical Publications Competition of the Society for Technical Communication.

Michael graduated from Stanford University, where he attended the campus in Vienna, Austria, during his junior year and completed the Honors Program in philosophy. He later studied computer science at College of Marin and San Francisco State University. Currently, he lives and works in Taos, New Mexico, situated at 7000 feet on a desert mesa nestled in the Sangre de Cristo Mountains.

You can contact Michael and find out more about what he does through his Web site at *http://www.mjyOnline.com.*

The manuscript for this book was prepared using Microsoft Word 2002. Pages were composed by Microsoft Press Using Adobe FrameMaker 7.0 for Windows, with text in Minion and display type in ITC Franklin Gothic. Composed pages were delivered to the printer as electronic prepress files.

Cover Designer: Todd Daman Studios
Interior Graphic Designer: James D. Kramer
Principal Compositors: Carl Diltz, Katherine Erickson, Ellie Fountain
Interior Electronic Artist: Joel Panchot
Proofreading Program Manager: Sandi Resnick

nSight, Inc.
Principal Compositors: Brenda Silva, Mary Beth McDaniel, Joanna Zito
Project Manager: Julie Nahil
Technical Editors: Don Lesser, Mannie White
Copyeditors: Joe Gustaitis, Nancy Pepper
Principal Proofreaders: Rob Saley, Lissa LeClerc
Indexer: Jack Lewis

Get a **Free**
e-mail newsletter, updates,
special offers, links to related books,
and more when you

register online!

Register your Microsoft Press® title on our Web site and you'll get a FREE subscription to our e-mail newsletter, *Microsoft Press Book Connections*. You'll find out about newly released and upcoming books and learning tools, online events, software downloads, special offers and coupons for Microsoft Press customers, and information about major Microsoft® product releases. You can also read useful additional information about all the titles we publish, such as detailed book descriptions, tables of contents and indexes, sample chapters, links to related books and book series, author biographies, and reviews by other customers.

Registration is easy. Just visit this Web page and fill in your information:

http://www.microsoft.com/mspress/register

Microsoft®

- -